THE INTERACTIVE CASEBOOK SERIES™

CONTRACTS

A Contemporary Approach

SECOND EDITION

By

Christina L. Kunz
PROFESSOR OF LAW
WILLIAM MITCHELL COLLEGE OF LAW

Carol L. Chomsky
PROFESSOR OF LAW
UNIVERSITY OF MINNESOTA LAW SCHOOL

WEST®

Mat # 41309438

Interactive Casebook Series is a trademark registered in the U.S. Patent and Trademark Office.

© 2010 Thomson Reuters
© 2013 LEG, Inc. d/b/a West Academic Publishing
    610 Opperman Drive
    St. Paul, MN 55123
    1-800-313-9378

Printed in the United States of America

ISBN: 978-0-314-28307-8

For Hassan – C.L.K.

For Steve, Aaron, and Emma – C.L.C.

Acknowledgments and Illustration Credits

First and foremost, we thank our husbands, our families, and our friends, who lived through and worked around our writing schedules through two editions, fellow travelers on our book odyssey. We are grateful for their good spirits, their patience, and their support. Special mention to friend Mark Broms, who traveled far to offer needed support to one of us at a crucial time.

We are grateful to Louis Higgins and to West Academic Publishing for giving us the opportunity to join in pioneering this new teaching format in textbooks. The features of the Interactive Casebook Series—the chance to incorporate case histories, diagrams, questions, and commentary at just the right place in the text—challenged us to think through each set of cases and explanations and make our teaching strategies accessible for both instructors and students. We have found that the format and content enlivens the reading experience for students and leads them to learn more actively. And the process of writing in this format has reshaped our concept of a casebook and has sparked new ideas about how to teach more effectively.

We thank our fellow teachers who offered comments on the first edition of the book that helped us improve the text. We especially thank our friend and colleague Lisa Schiltz from the University of St. Thomas School of Law, who went above and beyond, meeting us weekly through her first time teaching from the book to share with us her reactions, questions, comments, suggestions, and teaching ideas. We learned a great deal from those lengthy and engaging conversations.

Our students played invaluable roles in the development and editing of this book, making suggestions about our manuscript editions and providing feedback to make the final product better. We thank them for their insights and suggestions.

Our research assistants helped to breathe life into this textbook, finding new cases and case histories, providing student perspectives on the materials, and locating countless "needles in the haystack" of contract law. We thank Peter Rademacher, Jessica Zaiken, Heather Labat, and Jeffrey Pittman from William Mitchell College of Law and Molly Lehman and Eleanor Frisch from the University of Minnesota Law School.

On the administrative side, our work has been well supported by resources at both schools; our thanks to Dean Eric Janus at William Mitchell College of Law and to Dean David Wippman at the University of Minnesota Law School. We also owe a debt of gratitude to our administrative assistants, Meg Daniel and Morgan Gooch.

The logistics of creating a book of this type are challenging, and we thank Red Line Editorial for their dedication to producing the polished final product you have in your hands.

As has been our habit in our collaboration through two editions of our Sales book and now two editions of this book, we spent countless hours at coffee shops, talking, editing, writing, and buying many snacks, lunches, and cups of coffee. We would like to thank our current favorite haunt, Overflow Espresso.

Finally a toast to a friendship that has withstood, even thrived on, our innumerable and lengthy discussions arguing (but always coming to consensus on) the finer points of contract doctrine, the placement of commas and parentheticals, font sizes, and the wording of nearly everything!

C.L.K. & C.L.C.
April 2013

Case opinions appear with the permission of West Academic Publishing. Below are the attributions and credits for the photographs and images, by page number:

17	Photograph of E. Allan Farnsworth appears courtesy of Columbia Law School
113	Photograph of Samuel Williston appears courtesy of Historical & Special Collections, Harvard Law School Library http://law.harvard.edu/library/special/index.html (original dimensions 19.5 x 24.3 cm; unknown photographer).
128	Picture of Sir Edward Coke appears courtesy of National Portrait Gallery, London.
188	Picture of Lord Mansfield is photograph of a portrait of Lord Mansfield by Jean Baptiste van Loo in the National Portrait Gallery, London; copyright expired.
214	Photograph of Judge Spottswood W. Robinson, III, appears courtesy of the United States Court of Appeals for the District of Columbia Circuit.

239   The two photographs accompanying *Lucy v. Zehmer* appear with the generous permission of Professor Franklin Snyder at Texas Wesleyan University School of Law. The receipt appears in the record of the case.

246   Photograph of the barque appears at http://en.wikipedia.org/wiki/Barque (public domain).

261   Photograph of John Cheever appears at http://en.wikipedia.org/wiki/John_Cheever (Library of Congress, public domain).

266   Photograph of Maya Angelou appears on http://commons.wikimedia.org/wiki/File:Maya_angelou.jpg (public domain).

290-91 Advertisements from the Great Minneapolis Surplus Store appear courtesy of the Minnesota Historical Society.

301   Carbolic Smoke Ball advertisement is in the public domain and appears at http://en.wikipedia.org/wiki/Carlill_v_Carbolic_Smoke_Ball_Company.

382   Photograph of Justice Sonia Sotomayor appears at http://en.wikipedia.org/wiki/Sonia_Sotomayor (public domain).

396   Photograph of the "Consent To Be Photographed" sandwich board appears courtesy of the photographer, Christina L. Kunz.

437   Photograph of the Pickles' house appears with the permission of Professor Franklin Snyder at Texas Wesleyan University School of Law.

520-21 Photographs of the Walker-Thomas Furniture Store appear with the permission of Professor Franklin Snyder at Texas Wesleyan University School of Law.

681   Photograph of Elizabeth Arden appears at http://en.wikipedia.org/wiki/Elizabeth_Arden (public domain).

695   Photograph of Judge Henry Friendly is in the Bettmann Archive and appears courtesy of Corbis Images.

732   Photograph of Justice Roger Traynor appears courtesy of the photographer, Jean Moulin.

801   Photograph of Justice Benjamin Cardozo is in the Library of Congress (public domain).

810   Photograph of Judge Richard Posner appears courtesy of Judge Posner's office at the Seventh Circuit Court of Appeals.

977   Pictures of the music hall appear at http://en.wikipedia.org/wiki/Royal_Surrey_Gardens (public domain).

987   Photograph of King Edward VII appears at http://blog.londoncon nection.com (public domain).

991   Photograph of the flat in *Krell v. Henry* appears courtesy of the photographer, Jessica Zaiken.

1000   Map appears at http://thinklikeafox.wordpress.com/2012/02/06/egypt-and-syria/ (public domain).

1001   Photographs of the canal are in the public domain (taken toward the end of the 1800s) and appear on many websites. Photograph of Nasser (1956) appears at https://www.cia.gov/library/center-for-the-study-of-intelligence/csi-publications/csi-studies/studies/vol51no2/the-art-of-strategic-counterintelligence.html (public domain).

1002   Photograph of the canal appears at http://en.wikipedia.org/wiki/Suez_Canal (public domain).

1089   Picture of the steam engine appears at http://www.construction lawtoday.com/2009/06/consequential-damages-in-construction-contracts-and-architects-agreements-part-3-why-treat-conse quential-and-direct-damages-differently/ (public domain).

1090   Photograph of the mill in *Hadley* is courtesy of Michael Thorpe, Gloucester City Council, which has granted permission for its use in all educational or nonprofit contexts; it appears at http://lawpro fessors.typepad.com/contractsprof_blog/2005/06/hadleys_mill.html

1092   Photograph of Vanessa Redgrave was taken by Elena Torre and appears courtesy of a Creative Commons License; it appears at http://commons.wikimedia.org/wiki/File:Vanessa_Redgrave_by_Elena_Torre.jpg.

1102   Photograph of the Houston Astrodome (1965) appears at http://www.historicamerica.net/baseballhouston.html and other websites (public domain).

1103   Photograph of the ground-breaking (1962) appears at http://blog.chron.com/bayoucityhistory/2012/01/astrodome-groundbreak ing-started-with-a-bang/ and other websites (public domain).

1128   Photograph of Shirley MacLaine (1955) appears at http://en.wikipedia.org/wiki/Shirley_MacLaine (public domain).

1164   Photograph of Justice Shirley Abrahamson appears with the permission of the Director of State Courts, Wisconsin Supreme Court.

Summary Table of Contents

Detailed Table of Contents

Table of Cases

The principal cases are in bold type. Cases cited or discussed in the text are in roman type. References are to pages. Cases cited in principal cases and within other quoted materials are not included.

Table of Restatement, UCC, CISG, and UNIDROIT Provisions

Restatement (First) of Contracts

Restatement (Second) of Contracts

Chapter 2. Formation of Contracts—Parties and Capacity

Chapter 3. Formation of Contracts—Mutual Assent
Topic 3. Making of Offers

Topic 4. Duration of the Offeree's Power of Acceptance

CISG (United Nations Convention on Contracts for the International Sale of Goods)

UNIDROIT Principles of International Commercial Contracts

CHAPTER 1

Introduction

Table of Contents

§ 1. Overview

You no doubt have a general notion, and many mental images, of contracts and contract formation. A buyer and a seller of a product rise from a table and shake hands after hours of negotiation; a home buyer and seller sign a series of documents to "close" a home sale; a car owner leaves her car with the dealer to have maintenance work done on the vehicle; a man purchases a suit at a department store and leaves the suit for alterations; a tenant and a landlord agree to the terms of a lease; a child and a parent agree that excellent grades in school will result in an increase in allowance. Indeed, you have likely entered into many such arrangements in your own life. What makes all of these "contracts"—or are they all contracts?

In common language, "contract" may refer to a document representing an agreement (though as we will see, a contract does not have to be in writing), to an agreement-in-fact between or among people (whether or not that agreement is legally enforceable), to a legally binding obligation arising from an agreement-in-fact, or (going a bit farther afield!) to an arrangement with a paid assassin or the agreement between bridge partners regarding how many tricks they will take in a hand. We will most often use "contract" to mean "a promise or a set of promises for the breach of which the law gives a remedy"[2]*—that is, a legally binding obligation arising from a promise. This book focuses on determining under what circumstances the law will recognize the existence of and enforce such an obligation, and on the consequences—the remedies available—once a contract is recognized to exist.

Contract law governs promises, agreements, and exchanges and is one of the basic building blocks of law in the United States. Many of the transactions you encounter in your own daily life are grounded in contract, and the principles of contract law pervade many other areas, including commercial, consumer, family, property, and corporate law.

This book proceeds through a consideration of the following sequence of issues:

What kind of promises will the law enforce?	How do parties demonstrate assent to a contract?	What defenses to enforcement exist?	Is a writing required for enforcement? If so, what kind?	How is the content of a contract ascertained?	What are parties' rights and duties after breach?

	What situations lead to excusing contract performance?	What remedies are available for breach of contract?	What contractual rights and duties do non-parties to a contract have?

The issues identified in the diagram matter for purposes of contract drafting and planning, as well as for litigating contract claims. In the litigation context, some of the issues relate to elements a plaintiff must establish to enforce a promise; others are defenses that may be raised by the party resisting enforcement of the promise. Seen through that litigation lens, the issues addressed in the contracts course may be portrayed this way:

---

* Restatement (Second) of Contracts § 1. See page 6 for a description of the Restatement and its authority as a source of doctrinal rules.

Plaintiff's arguments to establish a contract claim:	Defendant's arguments to defeat a contract claim:
A contract was created (Chs. 2 & 4) or the facts show there is another rationale for enforcing the promise (Ch. 3). If someone other than plaintiff formed the contract with defendant, plaintiff is entitled to enforce the contract (Ch. 10).	One or more defenses bar contract enforcement (Chs. 5 and 10).
	The contract should have been represented in a writing and was not (Ch. 6).
The terms of the contract (Ch. 7) have been breached by the other party (Ch. 8), causing injury to plaintiff.	Circumstances justify excusing a breach (Ch. 8).
Plaintiff's injury should be compensated or alleviated by damages or some other relief (Ch. 9).	

One of the challenges of studying contract law is that determining the rights and liabilities of parties to an alleged contract often requires a sequential analysis of the entire contract relationship between them. As reflected in the charts above, one cannot determine whether a remedy exists for an alleged breach without considering whether the parties manifested assent, whether any defenses might be plausibly claimed to exist, whether any writing required for enforcement exists, what terms the parties agreed to, whether and how seriously one or both parties breached, and what remedies might be available and appropriate. As a result, although you will learn the concepts that govern the analysis of each step as you progress through the course, only at the end will you be able to fully answer the question: "Do the circumstances presented create enforceable contractual obligations, and who will be responsible for what?" Each building block is important, but none can stand on its own. Consequently, you will have to live with a degree of uncertainty and incompleteness until the whole picture emerges later in the course.

In the midst of this uncertainty and incompleteness, however, you will find certain consistencies in analysis that mark contract doctrine, no matter which issues are being considered. Courts, commentators, lawyers, and contracting parties will return, again and again, to underlying principles and assumptions that are part of the foundations of contract law, or of United States law in general. You should seek out, take note of, and critique those principles and how they operate to support (or challenge) outcomes of disputes. Examples of those principles include

- freedom of contract: parties should decide for themselves what responsibilities to undertake, with only the smallest of restrictions, and should not ask the court to choose for them;
- predictability and security: parties operate more effectively when they can comfortably predict and order their lives according to the legal implications of their actions;
- commercial reasonableness: rules should reflect the way parties actually conduct business;
- fairness: parties should be protected from being misled, unreasonably pressured, or otherwise led into contracts that do not represent their true choices or that shock the conscience.

Sometimes several principles will be implicated and will be in harmony with one another; sometimes they will be in conflict.

One of the reasons for the conflict among competing principles, and one of the challenges posed by the study of contract law, is the fact that, as Lawrence Friedman has noted, "Contract law is abstraction—what is left in the law relating to agreements when all particularities of person and subject-matter are removed."* Contract law purports to provide general principles to govern agreements, without acknowledging that rules may operate differently depending upon the nature of the parties (individual consumers or small businesses or large corporations), the nature of the transaction (small purchase or large commercial transaction), the relationship among the parties (one-time transaction or repeat players), and the economic landscape (free market or regulated, lightly or heavily).

Keeping in mind both the abstract rules and their impact on the particular will help you both understand and critique the rules you will be studying. Your understanding and use of contract doctrine will be deeper and more sophisticated if you seek out and pay attention to such broader principles and inquire whether the general rules adequately address the particular. To do that, when you consider each case or rule presented, you should ask yourself: Why was this outcome reached or rule adopted? What assumptions about human behavior lie behind that choice? What values are reflected in it? Whose interests are being protected, whether purposefully or not, and how well? What impact will the rule likely have on subsequent contract formation and performance? Is there a rule you think would be better than the one adopted? Why would it be better? Such questions

---

* Lawrence Friedman, *Contract Law in America* 20 (1965).

will help you to learn the rules of contract law better, while also expanding your understanding of the purposes and effect of legal rules in general.

§ 2. Sources of Contract Law and Authority

Where does the "law" of contracts come from? A variety of sources are cited by judges and commentators and used in this textbook. What follows is a brief introduction to those sources, their scope and authority. Understanding the nature of these sources now will help you make better sense of the reading and analyze more effectively.

§ 2.1. Judicial Opinions

Contract law in the United States is, in its origins, foundations, and implementation, a creature of the common law. That means the legal rules are primarily derived from and stated in judicial opinions (though, as we will discuss below, statutory law plays an increasingly large role). Contract law is also almost exclusively a matter of state, not federal, law. That means each set of state judges determines the common law contract rules for that jurisdiction. Judges generally rely on prior decisions by other judges—case precedents—in reaching their decisions, which helps to ensure uniformity in outcomes. But precedents from other jurisdictions are only persuasive, not binding. Thus, even though there is a degree of uniformity among the states, derived from common principles, there is also a significant amount of variation in the rules adopted by the various jurisdictions. One of the most difficult parts of studying contract law is dealing with these variations. Rules may be stated differently by different judges, and even

FYI

"Common law" countries, such as the United States, Canada, Australia, the United Kingdom, India, and Pakistan, draw on the British common law tradition. Many other countries, including most of Europe, Asia, Central and South America, and large portions of Africa, draw instead upon a "civil law" tradition descended from Roman law. In civil law jurisdictions, the primary law is statutory rather than judicial, and legislation is compiled into comprehensive codes that provide the rules for judicial decision-making. In such jurisdictions, judges decide cases primarily by interpreting and applying statutory provisions rather than by developing rules or being bound by case law arising from similar circumstances. Although located within a common law country, Louisiana and Puerto Rico retain civil law systems derived from their French and Spanish histories. The borderlines between common law and civil law adjudication have become more blurred as common law countries adopt more comprehensive statutes and civil law jurisdictions accumulate judicial opinions clarifying and applying the statutory law.

the same rule may be applied inconsistently by different judges. As you read the cases and commentary in this book, keep in mind that you are studying the way particular judges articulate the contract rules in question, which will resemble but may not be identical to the way the rule is articulated by another judge or in another jurisdiction. Sometimes there will be clear majority and minority articulations of the rules, sometimes not. The existence of variations makes it even more important to step back from the narrow rule at issue and consider the policies and principles that underlie the more specific contract doctrine.

§ 2.2. Restatements of the Law

In 1923, in part because of the uncertainties created by a system of common law rules based in so many jurisdictions, a group of prominent American judges, lawyers, and professors established the American Law Institute (ALI) for the purpose of bringing clarity and consistency to the common law. Over the years since its creation as a private nonprofit organization, the ALI has— among a variety of law reform projects—produced a series of subject-specific Restatements that seek to formulate clearly the principles and rules of the common law as reflected in judicial opinions and, sometimes, statutory enactments. Drafts of proposed provisions are prepared by a Reporter, an expert in the field appointed by the ALI Council, who works in consultation with knowledgeable advisors drawn from the ALI membership. After approval by the ALI Council, a draft is submitted to the full ALI membership for approval. The process of preparing a comprehensive Restatement and earning approval of the membership usually takes years and multiple redrafts.

Go Online!

For more information on the ALI, go to www.ali.org.

Although primarily intended to describe the law as it is, the lack of uniformity among jurisdictions means the Restatements inevitably must choose which of various rule articulations to propose for inclusion. Moreover, some Restatement provisions are promulgated to encourage courts to adopt what the drafters view to be more coherent or appropriate rules not yet widely embraced by courts, rather than simply to restate a rule that currently exists. Because the Restatements are the products of the ALI and its members, they are persuasive statements of the law, but they are not themselves law, unless and until a particular provision is adopted by a court or legislature.

As one of its first projects, the ALI produced the Restatement of Contracts, officially adopted by the ALI in 1932. The Restatement (Second) of Contracts was adopted by the ALI in 1979. Although the second Restatement provisions are a more accurate reflection of the law in many jurisdictions today, some courts continue to use the earlier version, and it is also often instructive to consider both versions to see how the law, or perception of the law, has changed over time.

The Restatements are comprised of "black letter" statements of law, "Comments" that explain more about the provisions, "Illustrations" (often drawn from case law), and "Notes" written by the leading scholars selected as the reporters of the Restatement adoption process. If your instructor has selected for your use a supplement containing Restatement provisions, you might scan the table of contents and some of those provisions to get a better sense of what the Restatement looks like and what it covers. You can find the entire table of contents and all the provisions of the first and second Restatements in online legal research resources as well. This casebook includes excerpts of selected Restatement sections at relevant points in the text and a table of the included Restatement provisions, but you may also find it helpful to look at those provisions in a supplement or in the full Restatement to see the surrounding context created by the comments, illustrations, notes and other related provisions.

§ 2.3. Statutory Law

Although this book is focused primarily on common law, a substantial number of contract cases are instead governed by statutory provisions. Statutory law always supersedes common law rules on the same subject matter because legislative enactments have greater authority than judicial decisions.

The statute most referenced in these materials is the Uniform Commercial Code (the UCC). The UCC purports to be what its name suggests—a uniform statute for all commercial matters, encompassing the activities of individuals and consumers as well as merchants and other commercial entities. The UCC was jointly promulgated by the American Law Institute (already mentioned for its role with respect to the Restatements) and the National Conference of Commissioners on Uniform State Laws (NCCUSL), now known as the Uniform Law Commission (ULC). Like other uniform laws, the UCC is a proposal to the states, but does not become effective as law in a state until adopted by the state's legislature. The UCC is comprised of "Articles," each addressing a different aspect of commercial transactions. This text will introduce you to selected portions of Article 1, which

contains general provisions and definitions, and Article 2, which establishes
rules of law for contracts for the sale
of goods. Other Articles govern leases
of goods (2A); bank transactions (3,
4 and 4A); letters of credit (5); documents of title (7); investment securities (8); and secured transactions (9).
Some UCC provisions covered in this
textbook supplement the common
law, but other provisions differ from
(and supersede) the common law, providing a comparative focus on how the
rules governing different kinds of contracts differ, and whether they should.

The UCC has been adopted in
whole or in part in all 50 states, as well
as in the District of Columbia, Puerto
Rico, and the U.S. Virgin Islands.
States are free to adopt variations on
uniform laws when enacting them,
and many have done so with respect
to particular provisions of the UCC,
though this book includes only the
uniform version.

What's That?

Since its founding as a private
nonprofit organization in 1892, NC-
CUSL/ULC has worked to consider
when uniformity among state laws
would be desirable and practical
and to draft, adopt, and advocate for
uniform codes to address those areas
of law. Each state names a group of
commissioners to represent its voice
in the adoption process. Internal
drafting committes often spend years
drafting proposed laws, with the
help of outside observers and advisors. When a proposed uniform law
is presented at the NCCUSL/ULC
annual meeting, each state has one
vote, and a majority of states attending (and no less than 20) must approve a proposal before it is officially
adopted as a Uniform or Model Act.
There are presently more than 100
uniform and model acts promulgated by NCCUSL, ranging widely in
subject matter. For more information, see www.uniformlaws.org.

When major revisions of or amendments to a uniform law are adopted, the
version in effect in some states may differ from the uniform version for a considerable period of time, as the states consider whether to make the proposed changes.
Article 1 was revised in 2001 and that version has been adopted by 43 states as
December 2012. This book focuses
on provisions drawn from revised
Article 1, though court opinions may
refer to the unrevised version. Not
every attempt at revision of a uniform
law is successful. In 2003, ALI and
NCCUSL adopted major changes to
Articles 2 and 2A of the UCC, but the
revisions were not received favorably
by state legislatures and they were
withdrawn in 2011. References to
Article 2 in this book are to the
unamended (and still official) version.

Take Note!

To fully understand the scope
of Article 2 requires exploration
of the statutorily-defined meaning of "sale" and "goods" as well as
consideration of what law governs
transactions that involve both a sale
of goods and something else, for example a contract for services. Such
issues are addressed in Chapter 2,
page 68.

In addition to state statutes, there are federal statutes that govern a few aspects of contractual transactions. As federal law, they supersede competing provisions of state law and are included in this book when relevant to the discussion.

§ 2.4. International Commercial Law and the CISG

Increasingly, commercial transactions are being undertaken in a global context, so understanding the international law related to those transactions is critical. A full review of international commercial law is beyond the scope of these materials, but this book introduces you to two international sources of law increasingly important in the domestic context.

The Convention on Contracts for the International Sale of Goods (CISG) is a United Nations treaty enacted by the United States and 78 other nations, making the treaty relevant in many transactions between parties from more than one country. In particular, the treaty applies

Go Online!

The list of countries ratifying the CISG is available through the website of the United Nations Commission on International Trade Law at www.uncitral.org/uncitral/en/uncitral_texts/sale_goods/1980CISG_status.html. Pace University hosts an extensive website on the CISG at www.cisg.law.pace.edu.

- if both parties to a contract have their places of business in countries that have ratified the CISG;
- if one party's place of business is in a country that has ratified the CISG *and* that country's law (including the CISG) is determined to be the governing law of the contract;
- if the parties elect to have the CISG govern their contract even though neither of them is from a country that has ratified the CISG (but the mandatory rules of the applicable domestic law supersede any conflicting CISG rules); or
- if a tribunal decides to apply the CISG as an appropriate rule of decision under the applicable law.

When it applies, the CISG takes precedence over state law, including enacted UCC provisions. The CISG operates as a package of default rules, so the parties' agreement may exclude entirely the application of the CISG or may vary its provisions. As an introduction to the CISG, this textbook includes selected provisions but does not attempt to cover the entire Convention..

The Principles of International Commercial Contracts was adopted by the International Institute for the Unification of Private Law (UNIDROIT). Like the Restatement, the UNIDROIT principles represent an effort to state guiding rules of law for contracts. The principles are not binding law unless the parties to a contract agree that they should be. Because the principles play only a secondary role, this textbook cites directly to them only occasionally, but you may find the principles helpful for comparative purposes.

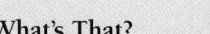
What's That?

UNIDROIT (pronounced "oo' nē dwah") is an independent inter-governmental organization whose purpose is to modernize and harmonize private law, in particular, commercial law, among the member States, including the United States. *See* www.unidroit.org.

The CISG and the UNIDROIT Principles were drafted with both common law and civil law rules in mind in order to effectively serve an international constituency. The drafters created hybrid rules when possible and, if not, sought a balance between favoring common law rules and civil law rules.

§ 3. Features of this Book

As you begin your law school studies, you will quickly see that learning law is about much more than just learning a set of legal rules. It is also about acquiring a set of skills associated with learning and practicing law. That skill set includes the ability to read judicial opinions (written in what may seem like a foreign language at first), figuring out what law is "made" by the case, and understanding how "black letter" statements of the law (such as Restatement provisions or rules derived from cases) would be applied in other circumstances. It includes, as well, the ability to think critically about the law as you learn it, to understand the connections between law and public policy, and to be creative in problem-solving using legal concepts and doctrines. In effect, you need to learn *how to learn the law* using traditional legal material, and *how to use the law* you learn, because you will spend much of your professional life learning and applying law on your own, based on the foundation begun in law school.

By offering specific and frequent guidance on how to approach and analyze the material as you read, this textbook will facilitate your acquisition of both the substantive law of contracts and the skill of learning and using legal concepts. You will find this guidance in several kinds of text boxes associated with the reading:

These are not "crutches" that tell you what to take away from the reading; rather, they are attempts to make the pedagogy more transparent by asking directed questions that will help you structure your thinking as you read and prepare for class. By considering the questions and comments in the text boxes, you will be better pre-

Reading the Law Critically

Offers questions to help frame your thinking as you read the material that follows the box so that you can be better prepared to discuss the specifics, as well as to think and talk about the policy implications.

Think About It!

Presents questions urging you to think about particular important issues raised, directly or indirectly, by the text, often providing additional information or commentary.

Food for Thought

Stretches your analysis after you have read associated material, often by raising additional questions or suggesting a broader context to consider.

pared to discuss the material in class, no matter what paths of analysis your teacher follows. And by paying attention to the questions themselves, you will learn something about how to structure your reading and analysis in all of your classes. Class discussion will, of course, push your understanding even further than your reading could, so the "reading the law critically" questions and other supplemental commentary are a starting point, not an end-point.

In addition to inviting you to interact with the text by including a variety of prompts to engage your thinking, this textbook also provides helpful supplemental information in text boxes appearing at the point in the text where you will need that information. They are of the following types:

Take Note!

Calls your attention to a particular aspect of a case or other material.

What's That?

Explains the meaning of terms that appear in the main text.

Who's That?

Provides biographical information about a person mentioned in the text.

It's Latin to Me!

The law is fond of Latin terms and phrases; when you encounter these in the text for the first time, this box will explain their meaning.

Behind the Scenes

Provides further background about material in the text, often by adding additional facts not included in the associated judicial opinion or by describing the aftermath of the case.

Make the Connection

Notes connections between concepts or discussions in the main text and (1) earlier or later material in this textbook or (2) other courses or law school subject matter.

FYI

Supplies additional information to augment the text.

Practice Pointer

Offers advice relevant to legal practice inspired by the actions (or inactions) of legal counsel in the cases or prompted by a particular contract clause.

See It

Points you to or includes visual information that is relevant to the material in the text.

For More Information

Points you to additional resources to consult for more information on a subject.

Go Online!

These boxes will direct you to relevant online resources that are worth consulting in relation to a matter being discussed.

In electronic form, this textbook also provides live online links to cited sources. You need not follow every such link (indeed, you would be spending far too much time on this course if you did so!), but the links are there when you need or want additional information.

Some final notes on form: In the trial court opinions and appellate decisions appearing in the book, courts may refer to parties as appellant and appellee, plaintiff and defendant, petitioner and respondent, or some combination of such terms. To help you make sense of the facts of each case, this book identifies in the captions the role that each party played in the trial court (plaintiff or defendant) and in the appeal (petitioner or appellant, respondent or appellee, depending on the terminology in that jurisdiction), even though the published case may not do so.

Most cases have been edited to omit less relevant material. Text omissions are noted with ellipses (. . .) but citations are usually omitted without such notation. Typographical errors have in some instances been corrected without specifying the original text. Some cases (especially older ones) have been "styled" (e.g., by adding paragraph breaks and indentations) to make the opinions more readable. Explanatory text added to cases appears within square brackets. The courts' footnotes retain their original numbers. Authors' footnotes are marked with asterisks.

Finally, one of the goals of this textbook is to cultivate your critical reading of documents that create, or purport to create, contracts. This textbook introduces you to common kinds of contract clauses and their customary variations. This orientation toward "transactional skills" helps to counter-balance the emphasis on litigation that flows from the use of litigated cases as the basic source material for this and other courses. In law practice, the volume of transactional practice equals—if not exceeds—the volume of litigation practice on contract-related issues, so it is important for the first-year contracts course to emphasize both.

CHAPTER 2

Consideration

What kind of promises will the law enforce?	How do parties demonstrate assent to a contract?	What defenses to enforcement exist?	Is a writing required for enforcement? If so, what kind?	How is the content of a contract ascertained?	What are parties' rights and duties after breach?

What situations lead to excusing contract performance?	What remedies are available for breach of contract?	What contractual rights and duties do non-parties to a contract have?

Table of Contents

§ 1. Introduction

Contracts are grounded in promises—assurances or declarations that one will do (or refrain from doing) some act. They are based on the notion that the parties themselves created obligations to each other, so proving the existence of a contract requires a showing that the parties took on those obligations—that they *assented* to the contract by effectively communicating their commitment. The element of assent is addressed in Chapter 4.

But should all promises be enforceable if assent exists? Professor Allan Farnsworth has suggested that "[n]o legal system has ever been reckless enough to make all promises enforceable. . . ."* Why would it be reckless to do so? What kinds of promises should not be enforceable in court, and why? Common sense suggests that gift promises are usually not enforceable, but why not? Is that the

---

*E. Allan Farnsworth, *Contracts* 11 (4th ed. 2004)

only category of unenforceable promises? What rule or standard can be used to reliably distinguish enforceable from unenforceable promises?

The cases in this chapter illustrate the courts' efforts to specify which kinds of promises will be enforced—to identify what, in addition to assent, will be required. That additional element—the "something else" that must accompany a promise—came to be called "consideration."

This fundamental requirement—that a promise must have consideration to be enforceable—is often confusing to legal neophytes. The requirement arose bit by bit from historical developments as the courts—first English, then American—decided which promises should be enforced, developing rationales for their decisions. The historical development was complicated by the concurrent jurisdictional battles between the common law courts and other available court systems (for example, courts of equity and church courts) and made more challenging by the structure of the English common law courts, which required that litigants fit their claims within emerging "forms of action" such as covenant, debt, and assumpsit, each of which had specific and unique requirements for specifying grounds for relief. The result was a changing and often inconsistent set of definitions of consideration, making study of the doctrine particularly demanding.

Who's That?

E. Allan Farnsworth was one of the country's most renowned legal scholars on the subject of contract law until his death in 2005. After serving as a lawyer in the U.S. Air Force, he began his academic career in 1954 as the youngest professor at Columbia Law School, where he taught for more than 50 years. In the 1970s, after publishing several commercial law casebooks, he was chosen by the American Law Institute to be the Reporter for development of the Restatement (Second) of Contracts (replacing Professor Robert Braucher, another leading contracts scholar who left the position when appointed to the Massachusetts Supreme Judicial Court). Farnsworth is the author of a multi-volume treatise on contract law (also published in a single-volume version) that is one of the most frequently referenced texts on contract doctrine. The last of his many publications was *Alleviating Mistakes: Reversal and Forgiveness for Flawed Perceptions*, published in 2004.

This book focuses only on the later stages of development of the concept, starting with nineteenth century American cases that already represented a distillation of centuries of development. Two different articulations of the test for finding consideration emerge. The cases that follow focus on the most-often-used definitions of consideration and the implications of those definitions for particular contracting circumstances.

Think About It!

As described by Professor Farnsworth, there are at least two ways to approach the task of framing a basis for enforcing promises. "One can begin with the assumption that promises are generally enforceable, and then create exceptions for promises considered undesirable to enforce. Or one can begin with the assumption that promises are generally unenforceable, and then create exceptions for promises thought desirable to enforce . . . . The common law courts chose this latter assumption." E. Allan Farnsworth, *Contracts* 11 (4th ed. 2004). Civil law systems usually start with the opposite assumption, that all promises are enforceable unless they fall into delineated categories. After struggling with the common law concept of "consideration," you may well wonder which choice is preferable!

§ 2. Consideration as Benefit or Detriment

Reading the Law Critically: *Hamer* and *Dougherty*

The material in this section introduces you to the definition of consideration in early cases. In each case, the court asks whether there is consideration for the promise that one of the parties seeks to enforce.

1. What promise is each plaintiff trying to enforce?

2. How does the court define consideration? If you find more than one definition, try to combine them into a single statement. If you fail to see an expressly articulated rule, try to find one arising out of the outcome of the case and the court's reasoning.

3. Why does the court find, or fail to find, consideration for the promise at issue?

4. Based on your reading of all three opinions, what's on your list of "everything I know about consideration"?

Hamer v. Sidway (I)

LOUISA W. HAMER, Plaintiff-Respondent

v.

FRANKLIN SIDWAY, as executor of William E. Story, deceased, Defendant-Appellant

Supreme Court, General Term

11 N.Y.S. 182 (Sup. Ct. 1890)

MARTIN, J.

The respondent seeks to uphold the recovery in this action primarily on the ground that in March, 1869, the defendant's testator promised his nephew, William E. Story (to whose rights the plaintiff claims to have succeeded), that if he would not drink, smoke, play cards for money, or play billiards until he was 21 years of age, he, the testator, would give him $5,000 on that day; and that that transaction constituted a valid and binding contract between the parties which can be enforced against the testator's estate. Thus at the threshold of this investigation we are presented with the broad question whether what occurred at that time amounted to a valid and binding contract.

Take Note!

In New York, the Supreme Court is a trial court, representing a divergence from the terminology used in most states. In 1890, when this case was decided, the Supreme Court "Special Term" sat as a trial court while its "General Term" sat (as here) as an intermediate appellate court, the predecessor to today's Appellate Division. The Court of Appeals (whose opinion in *Hamer* follows the Supreme Court opinion) is (and was in 1890) the highest appellate court.

The nature and character of this transaction will perhaps be better understood if we here group the evidence as to what was said and done by the parties. The testimony introduced by the plaintiff was to the effect that in March, 1869, when the testator and William E. Story were attending the golden wedding of the father of the testator, he said to William: "Willie, I am going to make you a proposition." William told him he would like to hear it. That the testator then said: "If you will not drink any liquor, will not smoke, will not play cards or billiards until you are 21, I will give you $5,000 that day. Of course, if you want to play for fun, that I don't consider playing cards." William said he would endeavor to carry it out; that he would do it.

This lawsuit is based on a promise made by W. E. Story to his nephew, William E. Story. So why is the litigation between Louisa Hamer and Franklin Sidway? Hamer's claim (more on that below) is brought against W. E. Story's estate. Because Story left a will, the matter is handled by the "executor"—the person named in the will to supervise distribution of the assets. If there had been no will, the court would have appointed an "administrator" to play the same role. The executor or administrator has a legal duty to contest arguable claims in order to preserve the estate's assets for the legitimate claimants and beneficiaries, which helps explain the number of suits of this kind you will encounter in the materials.

How did Louisa Hamer become the plaintiff in this case? In the Court of Appeals opinion that follows this one, the court says Louisa Hamer "acquired [her claim] through several mesne assignments from William E. Story, 2d.," suggesting William E. Story transferred his claim to Louisa, or to someone else who transferred the claim to her. Neither court mentions what appears in the trial record: Louisa Hamer was William's mother-in-law! Louisa's original complaint said that young William assigned the claim to her on the day of his uncle's funeral. But William had previously declared bankruptcy, making all his assets (including any claim on his uncle) the property of his creditors and therefore unassignable. Perhaps to avoid that result, Louisa filed an amended complaint stating that William assigned the claim to his wife before the bankruptcy, and his wife later assigned it to Louisa (her mother). The bankruptcy suggests that Uncle William was rightly concerned young William might fritter away the $5000 after he earned it. Douglas G. Baird, *Reconstructing Contracts: Hamer v. Sidway*, in *Contracts Stories* (2007). For more discussion of the back story, see "Behind the Scenes" following the second *Hamer* opinion.

The plaintiff also proved by the witness Maggie E. Judson that she was in the employ of William's father from 1864 for five or six years, and boarded in the family; that during that time the testator frequently visited there, and during those visits she frequently heard him, when in conversation with the family, make the statement that he had $5,000 in bank for his nephew, William E. Story; and that on two occasions he made the statement to her that he had $5,000 on deposit in the bank for his little nephew, William E. Story, when he became of age. This witness further testified that she never heard him mention any contract between himself and his nephew. This nephew was only a child then of eight or ten years of age. On cross-examination, the witness testified: "Just what he said to me was, 'I have five thousand dollars on deposit, at interest, for Willie when he comes of age.' He also said, at the same time, that when Willie came of age, if everything was favorable, he would start him in business, and help him; and he said he thought this five thousand dollars would be something for him to look forward to that would stimulate him to do right, and if he was steady and industrious this would be a good start, and if he was not, this would be enough for him to squander." The plaintiff also proved that the relations between the testator and his nephew were intimate.

Think About It!

The witness testified that "she never heard [the testator] mention any contract between himself and his nephew." This statement must have come in response to a question from one of the lawyers ("But did you ever hear him mention that he had a contract with Willie?"). Why would this have been asked? Why might the answer matter?

When William became 21 years of age he wrote the testator the following letter: "Dear Uncle: I am twenty-one years old to-day, and I am now my own boss, and I believe, according to agreement, that there is due me five thousand dollars. I have lived up to the contract to the letter in every sense of the word." The testator's reply to this letter, so far as material to the questions involved in this case, was as follows:

"Buffalo, February 26, 1875. W. E. Story, Jr.—Dear Nephew: Your letter of the 31st ult. came to hand all right, saying you had lived up to the promise made me several years ago. I have no doubt but what you have, for which you shall have $5,000, as I promised you. I had the money in the bank the day you were twenty-one years old that I intended for you, and you shall have the money certain. Now, Willie, I do not intend to interfere with this money in any way until I think you are capable of taking care of it, and the sooner that time comes the better it will please me. I would hate very much to have you start out in some adventure that you thought all right, and lose this money in one year. The first five thousand dollars I got together cost me a heap of hard work. . . . Willie, you are twenty-one, and you have many a thing to learn yet. This money you have earned much easier than I did, besides acquiring good habits at the same time, and you are quite welcome to the money. Hope you will make good use of it. I was ten long years getting this together after I was your age. Now, hoping this will be satisfactory, I stop. . . . P.S. You can consider this money on interest."

From this evidence, can it be properly said that there was a valid contract between the parties by which the testator became legally bound to pay William E. Story $5,000 when he became 21 years of age if he refrained until that time from indulging in the habits mentioned? The appellant claims not. His contention is that what occurred between the parties did not amount to and was not understood or intended by them as a legal and binding contract, but that it was simply a promise by the testator to make his nephew a gift of the sum of $5,000 when he became 21 years of age, if he should abstain from the evil and unnecessary habits referred to. The evidence, we think, shows that such was the nature and effect of that transaction.

The promise of the testator, as testified to by the plaintiff's witnesses, was that if his nephew would refrain from smoking, drinking, and gambling, during his minority, he would give him $5,000 on the day he became of age. It will be observed that this promise was not that he would pay him that amount for any service to be performed for the testator, but that he would give him that amount as a gratuity, as an incentive to his nephew to become a sober and worthy man, free from evil and useless habits. In its ordinary and familiar signification, the word "give" means to "transfer gratuitously," without any equivalent. Presumably the word was used in that sense by the testator. Unless the evidence shows that it was used in some other sense, its ordinary signification should be given it.

We find no sufficient evidence in this case to hold that the word "give" was used other than in its ordinary sense. The evidence of the witness Judson shows that when Willie was a child only eight or ten years of age the testator contemplated making him a gift of that sum when he became of age, and that he frequently mentioned his purpose in the family of his brother; and that he also contemplated starting him in business at that time, if everything was favorable. Thus the purpose of the testator would seem not to have been a new one arising at that time, but one which had existed for years, and which was known to the family. This witness also testified that this contemplated gift was not only a subject of frequent conversation between the testator and his brother's family, but that he conversed with her in relation to it upon at least two occasions, and still she never heard anything about any contract between the testator and William. This testimony tends to sustain the appellant's claim that the arrangement between the parties was in the nature of a promised gift by the testator.

But it may be said that the correspondence between the parties when William became of age tends to show that the arrangement was as claimed by the respondent. It is true that William, in his letter to the testator, refers to the arrangement between them as an agreement or contract, and states that he believes there is his due $5,000, but in the testator's reply to that letter he mentions the $5,000 only as a sum which he had promised to his nephew. In this letter there is nothing reflecting any light upon the original transaction which shows that the testator recognized any legal liability or binding contract upon which he regarded himself as indebted to his nephew. On the contrary, the testator's letter is inconsistent with that idea; for, after stating that he had the money in the bank that he intended for him, (William,) and after he again promised that he should have it, the testator states unqualifiedly that he does not intend to interfere with this money in any way until he thinks William capable of taking care of it. Thus the testator, instead of recognizing any legal liability to pay the money when William became 21 years of age, treated the matter just as he doubtless understood it, as a promise to make a gift at that time, and he then in effect refused to perfect the gift by delivery, but insisted upon retaining it under his own dominion and control until he should think William capable of taking care of it. When this letter was received by William, the evidence fails to show that he objected to it, or claimed that he had any right to the money until such time as the testator should see fit

FYI A gift becomes effective when the donor "perfects" it by delivering the gift to the donee.

to give it to him. This evidence is inconsistent with the existence of a valid contract, and consistent only with the appellant's theory that this transaction was a mere promise to make a gift, and that both parties so regarded it.

We think the transaction between the testator and William E. Story amounted to no more than a promise on the part of the testator that he would give William $5,000 when he became 21 years of age, if he should prove himself worthy of it by abstaining from certain useless, evil, and expensive habits. . . .

If, however, it could be held that the transaction between the testator and William E. Story was intended by the parties as a valid agreement by the testator to pay his nephew $5,000 to induce him to abstain from smoking, drinking, and gambling, until he was 21 years of age, still, it would be very difficult to discover any sufficient consideration to uphold such an agreement. There was doubtless a motive for this promise, but was there a consideration?

There are many motives which may induce an agreement which do not furnish sufficient consideration to uphold it. It may be that the testator was morally bound to keep his promise; but a gratuitous promise, not under seal, however strong may be the motives, or even the moral duty, on which it rests, will not be enforced by courts of justice. The doctrine that a moral obligation may become legally binding through an express promise, though formerly held in England and in the United States, has since been generally repudiated, except in Pennsylvania. That doctrine now forms no part of the jurisprudence of this state.

Only a valuable consideration will uphold an executory contract. The consideration must be something of value, something either beneficial to one party or disadvantageous to the other, in a pecuniary sense. How can it be said that William E. Story has performed any act which was in any pecuniary sense either beneficial to the testator or disadvantageous to himself by abstaining from habits which would have been not only expensive, but which were unnecessary and evil in their tendency? The only case cited by the respondent which tends to give the slightest countenance to the doctrine contended for is that of *Shadwell v. Shadwell*, 9 C. B. (N. S.) 169, but that case is clearly distinguishable from this. The decision in that case may well be sustained upon the ground that the plaintiff made a material change in his position, and incurred additional pecuniary liabilities. While in the case cited it might be said that the nephew changed his position by his marriage, and thus incurred additional pecuniary liabilities at the request of his uncle, such is not the case at bar. If the nephew in

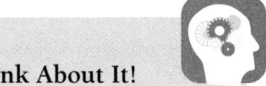

Think About It!

The court says a gratuitous promise will not ordinarily be enforced, but implies that a gratuitous promise "under seal" might be enforceable. A seal is a device that creates an impression on paper or melted wax, and is a way of formally authenticating and acknowledging a document. It was once common to have rules that made contracts under seal effective even when they lacked consideration, but such rules are rare now. As you think about the meaning and purpose of the requirement of consideration, consider why placing a seal on a contract document would have made a difference in enforceability. Have we lost something with the disappearance of those rules?

Take Note!

Shadwell v. Shadwell is an English case from 1860, which would not be binding precedent for this court, but might be considered persuasive. The Court of Appeals discusses *Shadwell* at greater length in the opinion that follows this one.

this case changed his position by abstaining from expensive habits which could in no way benefit him, it did not in any way add to his pecuniary liability, but could only have resulted to his pecuniary benefit. We doubt if there was any sufficient consideration to uphold an agreement between the testator and his nephew, even if the transaction between them were to be regarded as such. . . .

We are . . . of the opinion that there was no legal contract between the parties sufficient to uphold the recovery in this case, and that the judgment should be reversed. Judgment reversed, and a new trial granted, with costs to abide the event.

Think About It!

The *Hamer v. Sidway* case was appealed from the New York Supreme Court to the New York Court of Appeals, and the resulting case report is below. The Court of Appeals judgment prevails, of course, but what can you learn from reviewing both opinions? With which parts of the Supreme Court opinion does the Court of Appeals agree and disagree? What precisely did the Court of Appeals overrule? Are there aspects of the Supreme Court opinion that remain effective?

Hamer v. Sidway (II)

LOUISA W. HAMER, Plaintiff-Appellant

v.

FRANKLIN SIDWAY, as executor of William E. Story, deceased,
Defendant-Respondent

New York Court of Appeals
27 N.E. 256 (N.Y. 1891)

PARKER, J.

The question which provoked the most discussion by counsel on this appeal, and which lies at the foundation of plaintiff's asserted right of recovery, is whether by virtue of a contract defendant's testator, William E. Story, became indebted to his nephew, William E. Story, 2d, on his twenty-first birthday in the sum of $5,000. The trial court found as a fact that "on the 20th day of March, 1869, . . .

William E. Story agreed to and with William E. Story, 2d, that if he would refrain from drinking liquor, using tobacco, swearing, and playing cards or billiards for money until he should become twenty-one years of age, then he, the said William E. Story, would at that time pay him, the said William E. Story, 2d, the sum of $5,000 for such refraining, to which the said William E. Story, 2d, agreed," and that he "in all things fully performed his part of said agreement."

The defendant contends that the contract was without consideration to support it, and therefore invalid. He asserts that the promisee, by refraining from the use of liquor and tobacco, was not harmed, but benefited; that that which he did was best for him to do, independently of his uncle's promise, and insists that it follows that, unless the promisor was benefited, the contract was without consideration, a contention which, if well founded, would seem to leave open for controversy in many cases whether that which the promisee did or omitted to do was in fact of such benefit to him as to leave no consideration to support the enforcement of the promisor's agreement. Such a rule could not be tolerated, and is without foundation in the law.

The exchequer chamber in 1875 defined "consideration" as follows: "A valuable consideration, in the sense of the law, may consist either in some right, interest, profit, or benefit accruing to the one party, or some forbearance, detriment, loss, or responsibility given, suffered, or undertaken by the other." Courts "will not ask whether the thing which forms the consideration does in fact benefit the promisee or a third party, or is of any substantial value to anyone. It is enough that something is promised, done, forborne, or suffered by the party to whom the promise is made as consideration for the promise made to him." Anson, Cont. 63. "In general a waiver of any legal right at the request of another party is a sufficient consideration for a promise." Pars. Cont. "Any damage, or suspension, or forbearance of a right will be sufficient to sustain a promise." 2 Kent, Comm. (12th Ed.) *465.

What's That?

The Exchequer Chamber, established in 1822, was an English intermediate court of appeals hearing cases appealed from the three common law courts: the Court of King's Bench, the Court of Common Pleas, and the Court of Exchequer. Appeals from the Exchequer Chamber could be taken to the House of Lords. After 1875, the English courts were reorganized and the jurisdiction of the Exchequer Chamber was transferred to the newly-created Court of Appeals of England and Wales.

Pollock in his work on Contracts, (page 166,) after citing the definition given by the exchequer chamber, already quoted, says: "The second branch of this judicial description is really the most important one. 'Consideration' means not so much that one party is profiting as that the other abandons some legal right in the present, or limits his legal freedom of action in the future, as an inducement for the promise of the first."

Now, applying this rule to the facts before us, the promisee used tobacco, occasionally drank liquor, and he had a legal right to do so. That right he abandoned for a period of years upon the strength of the promise of the testator that for such forbearance he would give him $5,000. We need not speculate on the effort which may have been required to give up the use of those stimulants. It is sufficient that he restricted his lawful freedom of action within certain prescribed limits upon the faith of his uncle's agreement, and now, having fully performed the conditions imposed, it is of no moment whether such performance actually proved a benefit to the promisor, and the court will not inquire into it; but, were it a proper subject of inquiry, we see nothing in this record that would permit a determination that the uncle was not benefited in a legal sense.

Think About It!

The court says Willie had "a *legal* right" to use tobacco and drink liquor and restricted "his *lawful* freedom of action." Why does (or should) it matter if he had a legal right to engage in that activity?

In the last sentence in that paragraph, what does the court mean when it refers to whether the uncle was "benefited in a *legal* sense"? And why is the sentence phrased as it is, with a double negative ("we see *nothing* . . . that would permit a determination that the uncle was *not* benefited")?

Few cases have been found which may be said to be precisely in point, but such as have been, support the position we have taken. In *Shadwell v. Shadwell*, 9 C.B. (N.S.) 159, an uncle wrote to his nephew as follows: "My dear Lancey: I am so glad to hear of your intended marriage with Ellen Nicholl, and, as I promised to assist you at starting, I am happy to tell you that I will pay you 150 pounds yearly during my life and until your annual income derived from your profession of a chancery barrister shall amount to 600 guineas, of which your own admission will be the only evidence that I shall receive or require. Your affectionate uncle, CHARLES SHADWELL." It was held that the promise was binding, and made upon good consideration.

In *Lakota v. Newton*, (an unreported case in the superior court of Worcester, Mass.,) the complaint averred defendant's promise that "if you [meaning the plaintiff] will leave off drinking for a year I will give you $100," plaintiff's assent thereto, performance of the condition by him, and demanded judgment therefor. Defendant demurred, on the ground, among others, that the plaintiff's declaration did not allege a valid and sufficient consideration for the agreement of the defendant. The demurrer was overruled.

What's That?

A demurrer is a response to a complaint that says, in effect, "even if the facts you allege are true, I have no liability, because there is no law that provides for recovery under such circumstances." By overruling the demurrer, the court in the case cited held that there would be grounds for recovery if the alleged facts were proved to be true.

In *Talbott v. Stemmons*, 12 S. W. Rep. 297, (a Kentucky case, not yet officially reported), the step-grandmother of the plaintiff made with him the following agreement: "I do promise and bind myself to give my grandson Albert R. Talbott $500 at my death if he will never take another chew of tobacco or smoke another cigar during my life, from this date up to my death; and if he breaks this pledge he is to refund double the amount to his mother." The executor of Mrs. Stemmons demurred to the complaint on the ground that the agreement was not based on a sufficient consideration. The demurrer was sustained, and an appeal taken therefrom to the court of appeals, where the decision of the court below was reversed. In the opinion of the court it is said that "the right to use and enjoy the use of tobacco was a right that belonged to the plaintiff, and not forbidden by law. The abandonment of its use may have saved him money, or contributed to his health; nevertheless, the surrender of that right caused the promise, and, having the right to contract with reference to the subject matter, the abandonment of the use was a sufficient consideration to uphold the promise." Abstinence from the use of intoxicating liquors was held to furnish a good consideration for a promissory note in *Lindell v. Rokes*, 60 Mo. 249. The cases cited by the defendant on this question are not in point. . . .

The order appealed from should be reversed, and the judgment of the special term affirmed, with costs payable out of the estate. All concur.

———————————

Behind the Scenes

In *Reconstructing Contracts: Hamer v. Sidway*,* Professor Douglas Baird provides additional evidence about the circumstances of Uncle William's promise, and he questions the traditional understanding of the case. On the one hand, the trial record can be used to reinforce the conclusion that there was a bargain made between Uncle William and nephew Willie. After William made his promise, Willie negotiated to ensure he could play cards and billiards unless money were involved, and he took the promise very seriously, even refusing to take prescribed medicine with alcohol in it while away at college. On the other hand, there is also evidence—some of it appearing in the intermediate appellate opinion above—that shows William's promise was the culmination of a long-standing intention to help his nephew, and "the insistence that Willie cut out his bad habits was simply a string he tied to a promise." With these competing stories in mind, Baird argues that the Court of Appeals opinion was part of a battle over how to envision contract law—as a rigid set of rules that "forced lawyers to labor to reshape [the facts of a case] into the procrustean bed of a bargained-for exchange" or as a set of sensible principles arising from "the world as it was," where the appropriate question is "Should this promise be enforceable?" and not "Does this promise fit the previously articulated rule?" As presented in the two court opinions, the case provides important evidence about the development of the doctrine of consideration. Viewed through the lens of the complex family relationships revealed in the court record and discussed by Baird but not by the judges, the meaning of the case becomes less certain but also more intriguing.

---

* Appearing as a chapter in *Contracts Stories* (Douglas Baird ed. 2007).

Dougherty v. Salt

CHARLES N. DOUGHERTY, an Infant, by SUSAN M. TEVES, His Guardian ad Litem, Plaintiff-Respondent

v.

EMMA L. SALT, as Executrix of HELLENA M. DOUGHERTY, Deceased, Defendant-Appellant

Court of Appeals of New York
125 N.E. 94 (N.Y. 1919)

CARDOZO, J.

The plaintiff, a boy of eight years, received from his aunt, the defendant's testatrix, a promissory note for $3,000 payable at her death or before. Use was made of a printed form, which contains the words "value received." How the note came to be given, was explained by the boy's guardian, who was a witness for his ward. The aunt was visiting her nephew.

What's That?

"Testatrix" refers to a female "testator," one who specifies disposition of her assets in a will, rather than dying intestate, without a will. The "Executrix" in the case caption refers to a female "executor," one who carries out the will's provisions. The female forms of these words are now generally considered archaic. Note that the plaintiff is represented in this litigation by his "guardian ad litem," denoting an individual appointed by the court to appear on a child's behalf in a lawsuit.

"When she saw Charley coming in, she said 'Isn't he a nice boy?' I answered her, yes, that he is getting along very nice, and getting along nice in school, and I showed where he had progressed in school, having good reports, and so forth, and she told me that she was going to take care of that child, that she loved him very much. I said, 'I know you do, Tillie, but your taking care of the child will be done probably like your brother and sister done, take it out in talk.' She said: 'I don't intend to take it out in talk, I would like to take care of him now.' I said, 'Well, that is up to you.' She said, 'Why can't I make out a note to him?' I said, 'You can, if you wish to.' She said, 'Would that be right?' And I said, 'I do not know, but I guess it would; I do not know why it would not.' And she said, 'Well, will you make out a note for me?' I said, 'Yes, if you wish me to,' and she said, 'Well, I wish you would.'"

A blank was then produced, filled out, and signed. The aunt handed the note to her nephew with these words, "You have always done for me, and I have signed this note for you. Now, do not lose it. Some day it will be valuable."

The trial judge submitted to the jury the question whether there was any consideration for the promised payment. Afterwards, he set aside the verdict in favor of the plaintiff, and dismissed the complaint. The Appellate Division, by a divided court, reversed the judgment of dismissal, and reinstated the verdict on the ground that the note was sufficient evidence of consideration.

We reach a different conclusion. The inference of consideration to be drawn from the form of the note has been so overcome and rebutted as to leave no question for a jury. This is not a case where witnesses summoned by the defendant and friendly to the defendant's cause, supply the testimony in disproof of value (*Strickland v. Henry*, 175 N. Y. 372). This is a case where the testimony in disproof of value comes from the plaintiff's own witness, speaking at the plaintiff's instance. The transaction thus revealed admits of one interpretation, and one only. The note was the voluntary and unenforcible promise of an executory gift (*Harris v. Clark*, 3 N. Y. 93; *Holmes v. Roper*, 141 N. Y. 64, 66). This child of eight was not a creditor, nor dealt with as one. The aunt was not paying a debt. She was conferring a bounty (*Fink v. Cox*, 18 Johns. 145). The promise was neither offered nor accepted with any other purpose. "Nothing is consideration that is not regarded as such by both parties" (*Philpot v. Gruninger*, 14 Wall. 570, 577; *Fire Ins. Assn. v. Wickham*, 141 U. S. 564, 579; *Wisconsin & M. Ry. Co. v. Powers*, 191 U. S. 379, 386;

What's That?

A "promissory note" is a written promise to pay a stated sum of money, usually specifying a due date or payment schedule or indicating payment will be "on demand." Free "create your own promissory note" services are available online, where you can generate samples. The form used by Hellena Dougherty might have looked something like this:

PROMISSORY NOTE

For value received, _____ (the "Maker"), by this Promissory Note unconditionally promises to pay to _____ (the "Holder") the principal sum of _____, payable at or before the Maker's death.

This Promissory Note shall be governed by, and construed in accordance with, the laws of the State of New York, United States of America.

IN WITNESS WHEREOF, the Maker has duly executed this Promissory Note as of [insert date].

_____

(signed by Maker)

What's That?

In this context, "executory" means "not yet completed," so an executory gift is a gift promised but not yet delivered.

DeCicco v. Schweizer, 221 N. Y. 431, 438). A note so given is not made for "value received," however its maker may have labeled it. The formula of the printed blank becomes, in the light of the conceded facts, a mere erroneous conclusion, which cannot overcome the inconsistent conclusion of the law (*Blanshan v. Russell*, 32 App. Div. 103; affd., on opinion below, 161 N. Y. 629; *Kramer v. Kramer*, 181 N. Y. 477; *Bruyn v. Russell*, 52 Hun, 17). The plaintiff, through his own witness, has explained the genesis of the promise, and consideration has been disproved (Neg. Instr. Law, sec. 54; Consol. Laws, chap. 43). . . .

Hiscock, Ch. J., Chase, Collin, Hogan, Crane and Andrews, JJ., concur.

Judgment accordingly.

———————

Food for Thought:
Why is Consideration Required?

A court in New York applied the result in *Dougherty* in a later case, *In re Barker's Estate*, 287 N.Y.S. 841 (Surrogate's Court 1936), dealing with promissory notes given to two educational institutions "for value received." The court rejected claims based on the promissory notes and supported the result this way:

> Subscriptions or gifts to institutions of the character of the claimants in this case are worthy and commendable and make it possible for such institutions to attain their desired goal; however, there are recognized ways in which those gifts may be accomplished. If the gift is to be immediate, it must be completed and the money delivered. A promise to make a gift at some future date is not enforceable, for the reason that the person making the promise may, by reason of altered financial circumstances, change his mind and determine either that he cannot afford to make such a gift, or that he cannot afford to make a gift or subscription of the amount which he originally intended. And as this is purely a voluntary subscription upon his part, the law protects him and permits him to change his mind. Gifts and subscriptions of this kind may be legally carried out through the provisions of a will properly executed. This is a most wholesome way, because a will does not take effect until the death of the testator; and if he meets with adverse circumstances, he is at liberty to change his will to correspond.

Does this paragraph explain the result in *Dougherty* as well?

§ 3. Consideration as Bargain

This section presents the modern conceptualization of the doctrine of consideration as "bargain," illustrated both in cases and in the Restatement (Second) of Contracts.

Reading the Law Critically:
Baehr, *Meadors*, and *Meincke*

1. What definitions of consideration do the courts use? Do those definitions conform to the Restatement articulation?

2. How do these definitions compare to the definitions in *Hamer* and *Dougherty*?

3. Why does each court find, or fail to find, consideration? In *Meincke*, do you agree with the holding of the Court of Appeals (no consideration) or the Supreme Court (consideration existed)? Why?

4. Would applying the definitions in the Restatement and these cases have resulted in different outcomes in *Hamer* or *Dougherty*?

Restatement (Second) § 71. **Requirement of Exchange; Types of Exchange**

(1) To constitute consideration, a performance or a return promise must be bargained for.

(2) A performance or return promise is bargained for if it is sought by the promisor in exchange for his promise and is given by the promisee in exchange for that promise.

(3) The performance may consist of
   (a) an act other than a promise, or
   (b) a forbearance, or
   (c) the creation, modification, or destruction of a legal relation.

(4) The performance or return promise may be given to the promisor or to some other person. It may be given by the promisee or by some other person.

> Restatement (Second) § 81. **Consideration As Motive Or Inducing Cause**
>
> (1) The fact that what is bargained for does not of itself induce the making of a promise does not prevent it from being consideration for the promise.
> (2) The fact that a promise does not of itself induce a performance or return promise does not prevent the performance or return promise from being consideration for the promise.
>
> *Comments:*
>
> *a. "Bargained for."* Consideration requires that a performance or return promise be "bargained for" in exchange for a promise; this means that the promisor must manifest an intention to induce the performance or return promise and to be induced by it, and that the promisee must manifest an intention to induce the making of the promise and to be induced by it. See § 71 and Comment b. In most commercial bargains the consideration is the object of the promisor's desire and that desire is a material motive or cause inducing the making of the promise, and the reciprocal desire of the promisee for the making of the promise similarly induces the furnishing of the consideration.
>
> *b. Immateriality of motive or cause.* This Section makes explicit a limitation on the requirement that consideration be bargained for. Even in the typical commercial bargain, the promisor may have more than one motive, and the person furnishing the consideration need not inquire into the promisor's motives. Unless both parties know that the purported consideration is mere pretense, it is immaterial that the promisor's desire for the consideration is incidental to other objectives and even that the other party knows this to be so. Compare § 79 and Illustrations. Subsection (2) states a similar rule with respect to the motives of the promisee.

Baehr v. Penn-O-Tex Oil Corp.

E. J. BAEHR, Plaintiff-Appellant

v.

PENN-O-TEX OIL CORP., Defendant-Appellee

Supreme Court of Minnesota
104 N.W.2d 661 (Minn. 1960)

LOEVINGER, Justice.

This is an action for rents which defendant is claimed to owe plaintiff because of possession and contract.

Plaintiff leased certain gasoline filling stations to one Kemp, doing business as Webb Oil Company, under written leases. Kemp was purchasing the business known as Webb Oil Company and certain related property from defendant. On account of these transactions and purchases of petroleum products, Kemp was heavily indebted to defendant. Kemp became unable to meet payments due to defendant and on December 10, 1955, gave defendant an assignment of accounts receivable and to become receivable, including those involving the plaintiff's filling stations. Thereafter, during the period involved here, defendant collected rents paid by the operators of the filling stations, received other payments made to Webb Oil Company, paid some of its debts at Kemp's direction out of these sums, and installed its agent in the office to run the business.

Plaintiff was in Florida when he received a letter dated December 28, 1955, from Kemp, stating that defendant had all of Kemp's assets tied up. A short time after this, plaintiff called defendant's agent to ask about payment of the filling station rents. Plaintiff was told "that Mr. Kemp's affairs were in a very mixed up form but that he would get them straightened out and mail me (plaintiff) my checks for the rent." Hearing nothing further, plaintiff wrote a letter to defendant asking what he had to do to get his rent checks and adding: "Or will I have to give it to an attorney to sue." Defendant replied by letter stating it was attempting to assist Kemp in keeping the business going, "but in no way are operating or taken possession." The letter denied knowledge of or responsibility for any rent due plaintiff. A week or 10 days after receiving this letter, plaintiff again called defendant and asked for his rent. Defendant's agent then said to plaintiff, "they (the company) were interested and that they would see that I (plaintiff) got my rent, and would take care of it, and they would work it out with the head office. . . . . He said he would take it up with them and they would assure me my rent."

The rent was not paid, and in April or May 1956 plaintiff returned to Minneapolis from Florida. Soon after this plaintiff consulted a lawyer, and "shortly thereafter, as rapidly as the lawyer could get moving, a suit was started." On June 2, 1956, plaintiff sent defendant a letter advising that he was reentering and taking possession under the leases of the filling stations and because of failure to receive rent. On July 10, 1956, this suit was started for rents due on the filling stations for the period December 1, 1955, through June 2, 1956, upon the grounds that defendant was in possession of the stations and had contracted to pay the rent during this period.

The case was fully tried on all issues in the district court. At the conclusion of plaintiff's evidence, the court ruled that the evidence was conclusive that defendant neither took possession of the filling stations nor an assignment of Kemp's leases. Defendant then presented evidence on the issue of a contract to pay the rents, and this issue was submitted to the jury under proper instructions. The amount that would be due under such a contract was agreed upon; and the jury returned a verdict for plaintiff in that amount. Thereafter, the district court granted defendant's motion for judgment notwithstanding the verdict; and ordered a new trial in the event of reversal. Plaintiff appealed.

[The Supreme Court court agreed that the trial court properly rejected Baehr's claims based on assignment of the lease and possession of the service station.]

The issue whether there was a contract by defendant to pay plaintiff is more doubtful. Unfortunately, contract, like most of the basic terms constituting the intellectual tools of law, is conventionally defined in a circular fashion. By the most common definition, a contract is a promise or set of promises for the breach of which the law gives a remedy or the performance of which the law recognizes as a duty.[15] This amounts to saying that a contract is a legally enforceable promise. But a promise is legally enforceable only if it is a contract. Thus nothing less than the whole body of applicable precedents suffices to define the term "contract."

What's That?

An assignment of contract rights is a transfer to another (usually a non-party) of the right to receive contract performance from a party to the original contract, and may be accompanied by a "delegation" of duties, making a third party responsible for performing contract obligations. Recall that an assignment of rights played a part in *Hamer v. Sidway*: William E. Story assigned to Louisa Hamer his right to receive money from his uncle. In the current case, Baehr argued that Penn-O-Tex was responsible for the service station lease because Kemp had transferred the lease and all its obligations to Penn-O-Tex by both assigning rights (e.g., to collect money from service station customers) and delegating duties (e.g., to make lease payments to Baehr). The trial court ruled that no such transfer had taken place. Chapter 10 explores under what circumstances contract rights and duties may be assigned or delegated how such transfers of rights and obligations are made, and the effect such transfers have on the rights of the original contracting parties. You may find it helpful to consult the diagram in section 10.2 illustrating the claimed assignment and delegation in *Hamer* and *Baehr*.

Although the definition of contract does not help much in determining what expressions shall be held to impose legal obligations, it does direct attention to a promise as the starting point of inquiry. Both in popular and legal usage, a promise is an assurance, in whatever form of expression given, that a thing will or

---

[15] Restatement, Contracts, §1; 1 Williston, Contracts (3 ed.) § 1; see, 17 C.J.S., Contracts, § 1.

will not be done.[17] While we must take care to distinguish between statements meant to express merely present intention and those meant to give an assurance as to a future event, this involves no more than the common difficulty of seeking precise meaning in the usually imprecise, and often careless, expressions of ordinary colloquy.

If we accept plaintiff's version of the statements made by defendant's agent, as we are required to do by the verdict, there was an unequivocal assurance given that the rents would be paid. This cannot be anything but a promise.

However, the fact that a promise was given does not necessarily mean that a contract was made. It is clear that not every promise is legally enforceable. Much of the vast body of law in the field of contracts is concerned with determining which promises should be legally enforced. On the one hand, in a civilized community men must be able to assume that those with whom they deal will carry out their undertakings according to reasonable expectations. On the other hand, it is neither practical nor reasonable to expect full performance of every assurance given, whether it be thoughtless, casual and gratuitous, or deliberately and seriously made.

The test that has been developed by the common law for determining the enforceability of promises is the doctrine of consideration. This is a crude and not altogether successful attempt to generalize the conditions under which promises will be legally enforced.[19] Consideration requires that a contractual promise be the product of a bargain. However, in this usage, "bargain" does not mean an exchange of things of equivalent, or any, value. It means a negotiation resulting in the voluntary assumption of an obligation by one party upon condition of an act or forbearance by the other.[20] Consideration thus insures that the promise enforced as a contract is not accidental, casual, or gratuitous, but has been uttered intentionally as the result of some deliberation, manifested by reciprocal bargaining or negotiation. In this view, the requirement of consideration is no mere technicality, historical anachronism, or arbitrary formality. It is an attempt to be as reasonable as we can in deciding which promises constitute contracts. Although the doctrine has been criticized, no satisfactory substitute has been suggested. It is noteworthy that the civil law has a corresponding doctrine of "causa" which, to the eye of a common-law lawyer, is not much different than consideration.[22]

---

[17] Webster's New International Dictionary (2 ed.) (1947) p. 1980; Holmes, The Common Law, p. 299.

[19] See, Ballantine, Is the Doctrine of Consideration Senseless and Illogical?, 11 Mich.L.Rev. 423, Selected Readings on the Law of Contracts, p. 588.

[20] See, Ames, Two Theories of Consideration, 12 Harv.L.Rev. 515; id. 13 Harv.L.Rev. 29, Selected Readings on the Law of Contracts, p. 320.

[22] Lorenzen, Causa and Consideration in the Law of Contracts, 28 Yale L.J. 621, Selected Readings on the Law of Contracts, p. 565.

Consideration, as essential evidence of the parties' intent to create a legal obligation, must be something adopted and regarded by the parties as such.[23] Thus, the same thing may be consideration or not, as it is dealt with by the parties.[24] In substance, a contractual promise must be of the logical form: "If . . . (consideration is given) . . . then I promise that . . . ." Of course, the substance may be expressed in any form of words, but essentially this is the logical structure of those promises enforced by the law as contracts.[25]

[handwritten: delay in foreclosure]

Applying these principles to the present case, it appears that although defendant's agent made a promise to plaintiff, it was not in such circumstances that a contract was created. Plaintiff correctly states that an agreement of forbearance to sue may be sufficient consideration for a contract. Plaintiff further contends that his failure to institute suit immediately upon learning of Kemp's assignment to defendant permits an inference of an agreement to forbear from suit in consideration for defendant's assurance of payment of rents to plaintiff. This court has held that circumstantial evidence may support the inference of such an agreement to forbear. However, such an inference must rest upon something more than the mere failure to institute immediate suit. The difficulty with plaintiff's case is that there is no more than this.

[handwritten: what?!]

Plaintiff's conversation with defendant's agent was about the middle of February 1956 while plaintiff was in Florida. Plaintiff returned to Minneapolis, which was his residence as well as the jurisdiction where defendant was found, about the latter part of April or the first of May 1956. Soon after this he consulted a lawyer, and suit was started "as rapidly as the lawyer could get moving." There is nothing in the evidence to suggest that plaintiff deferred initiating legal action any longer than suited his own personal convenience. There is nothing in the evidence to suggest that defendant sought any forbearance by plaintiff or thought that it was securing such action; nor is there any evidence that plaintiff's delay from the middle of February until April or May in undertaking legal action was related to defendant's promises. There is no evidence that either of the parties took defendant's assurances seriously or acted upon them in any way. There was, therefore, no consideration, and the promises did not amount to a contract. Since the district court was correct in ordering judgment entered for the defendant, notwithstanding the verdict, on this ground, it is unnecessary to consider other points relating to enforceability of the alleged contract.

Affirmed.

————————————

[23] *Suske v. Straka*, 229 Minn. 408, 39 N.W.2d 745; *Nybladh v. Peoples State Bank*, 247 Minn. 88, 76 N.W.2d 492; 12 Am.Jur., Contracts, § 75; 17 C.J.S., Contracts, § 74.
[24] Holmes, The Common Law, p. 292.
[25] See, e.g., *Hartung v. Billmeier*, 243 Minn. 148, 66 N.W.2d 784.

United States v. Meadors

UNITED STATES OF AMERICA, Plaintiff-Appellee

v.

BETTY JO MEADORS, Defendant-Appellant

United States Court of Appeals for the Seventh Circuit
753 F.2d 590 (7th Cir. 1985)

Before CUDAHY, POSNER and COFFEY, Circuit Judges.

CUDAHY, Circuit Judge.

Appellant Meadors appeals an order of the district court granting the Small Business Administration (the "SBA") summary judgment in its action to collect from appellant as guarantor on a loan. The district court found that the Equal Credit Opportunity Act did not protect Meadors from liability; that she had waived certain protections by signing the guaranty; and that no independent consideration was necessary for her signature as a guarantor. On appeal she raises these defenses again, and also argues that, should she be liable, the district judge erred in calculating the interest due on the note. We reverse and remand.

I.

In January, 1977, M.J.D., Inc. ("MJD") applied to the Bargersville State Bank (the "Bank") for a loan to pay off debts and to provide for additional working capital for a lumber company MJD owned in Bargersville, Indiana. The Bank's board of directors approved the loan subject to a guaranty by the SBA. In April, 1977, the SBA approved the request for a 56% guaranty of the $281,000 loan, but required the principals Melton Meadors, Jay Judd and Harold Ducote and Ducote's wife Marie to sign a guaranty on SBA Form 148. In the January application, listed on page four as possible guarantors had been: "Melton E. Meadors—a single person, Jay A. Judd & Wife, Harold A. Ducote, Jr., & Wife." After considering the loan application and attached balance sheets, the SBA chose to have Meadors, Judd, Ducote and Ducote's wife sign the required guaranty.

On April 2, 1977, Melton Meadors and Betty, appellant here, were married. At the April 19 closing the three principals and their wives were all present. Although the SBA had provided places on its Form 148 for the signatures only of Meadors, Judd, Ducote, & Ducote's wife, and although no one from the SBA was present to request additional signatures, all six—the three principals and their wives—signed the guaranty form. Neither the SBA nor the Bank required Betty to sign any document as a prerequisite for disbursing loan proceeds. These facts are not disputed by either side.

MJD defaulted on its loan, and the Bank asked the SBA to take over the guaranteed portion of the loan. MJD turned over the collateral securing the loan to the SBA in July, 1980 and it was later sold. An action was subsequently instituted in district court to collect the deficiency from the guarantors, including Betty Meadors. Appellant raised several defenses, including lack of consideration and impairment of collateral. In November, 1983 appellee SBA filed a motion for summary judgment which was granted by the district court on February 2, 1984. It is from that grant of summary judgment that Betty Meadors appeals. . . .

There is apparently some confusion about whether Indiana law or federal law should govern in this case. In the district court appellant appealed to Indiana common law; the government has apparently relied on federal cases. Without raising the issue, the district court applied Indiana law.

Federal law governs questions involving the rights of the United States arising under nationwide federal programs. *United States v. Kimbell Foods, Inc.,* 440 U.S. 715, 726, 99 S.Ct. 1448, 1457, 59 L.Ed.2d 711 (1979). "In the absence of an applicable Act of Congress it is for the federal courts to fashion the governing rule of law according to their own standards." *Clearfield Trust Co. v. United States,* 318 U.S. 363, 367, 63 S.Ct. 573, 575, 87 L.Ed. 838 (1943). Nevertheless, federal courts may turn to state law in attempting to give content to the federal rule in question. *United States v. Kimbell Foods, Inc.,* 440 U.S. at 727, 99 S.Ct. at 1457. Thus, on certain issues, such as impairment of collateral and the right to notice, where "the state law on which private creditors base their daily commercial transactions is derived from a uniform statute [the U.C.C.]," and there is therefore no conflict with the federal interest in uniformity, appeal to state law is appropriate. *United States v. Kukowski,* 735 F.2d 1057, 1058 (8th Cir.1984). On those issues, then, we look to the Uniform Commercial Code, the Indiana statute based on it, and Indiana common law.

II.

Summary judgment is appropriate if "the pleadings, depositions, answers to

Take Note!

Contract law is almost invariably a matter of state law, whether under the common law, state-adopted UCC, or other state statutes, but an applicable federal statute will supersede state law. The circumstances in *Meadors* reflect one of the few instances where federal courts have authority to fashion common law principles of contract law, but, as you see, the court may nonetheless defer to state law, if that law sufficiently protects federal interests. As acknowledged by Judge Posner several years after he joined the *Meadors* opinion, the United States Supreme Court ruled six years before *Meadors* that federal courts should use the relevant state's law as the federal common law in disputes arising over loans guaranteed by the Small Business Administration, for the same reasons articulated by the court here. *See United States v. Stump Home Specialties Mfg., Inc.,* 905 F.2d 1117, 1119 (7th Cir. 1979).

interrogatories, and admissions on file, together with the affidavits, if any, show that there is no genuine issue as to any material fact and that the moving party is entitled to a judgment as a matter of law." Fed.R.Civ.Pro. 56(c). In the case before us the parties do not disagree about the facts, and our only role is to determine whether, on the facts as agreed, the district court was right as a matter of law.

[Discussion of the Equal Credit Opportunity Act and other issues omitted.]

III.

Betty Meadors argues, finally, that she received no consideration for her signature on the guaranty form. She reasons that the signature of a volunteer, who happens upon an agreement after the negotiations have been concluded and the terms set, and who signs as a guarantor although neither side has required her to sign, has not received consideration and therefore is not bound by the agreement.

Consideration has long and consistently been treated as an essential element of every contract. Yet there is little agreement about just what consideration is, and that fact makes it difficult to assess a defense of want of consideration in a novel setting. We venture that the setting in which it is raised here is very nearly unique, and the validity of the defense would seem to depend on which interpretation of the doctrine we adopt.

Every interpretation has serious faults. It used to be said that consideration was either a benefit to the promisor, or a detriment to the promisee. In other words, the one who made the promise receives consideration if he gets something, or if the one to whom he makes the promise gives something up. Either alternative will do. If I promise you a thousand dollars if you quit smoking, and you do quit, then even though there may be no benefit to me, I have received consideration: you have given something up. Similarly, I can promise you a thousand dollars if you teach my daughter to sing. If you do teach her—or if you promise to—then I have received consideration

Take Note!

The court says that either the *promise* to teach the daughter or the *actual teaching* of the daughter can count as consideration. The former situation—a promise serving as consideration—is the most common because so many contracts are formed by an exchange of promises. As you will see in Chapter 4, page 327, which of these (promise or performance) the promisor asks for or expects in order to create the commitment will affect the manner by which the promisee can accept the offer of a contract. But either one can constitute the consideration for the promise of the other party to perform.

even if all the practice sessions and even the final result are of no real benefit to me.

But reflection shows that benefit-detriment is neither necessary nor sufficient for consideration. I may promise to give you a thousand dollars if you quit smoking—I may even do it in writing—and you may give up smoking, and yet my promise may be unenforceable and may be the sort of thing that everyone would agree was without consideration. For you may have given up smoking without ever having learned of my promise. So the detriment in isolation is not sufficient for consideration. On the other hand, I might agree to pay you for something that was neither a benefit to me nor a detriment to you. I might promise to pay you for bringing a benefit on yourself. The reasoning in the classic case of *Hamer v. Sidway*, 124 N.Y. 538, 27 N.E. 256 (N.Y.App.1891), suggests that the courts will find consideration in such a case. An uncle had promised his nephew $5000 on his twenty-first birthday if the nephew would refrain from drinking, smoking, swearing and playing cards until that time. The nephew evidently fulfilled his part of the deal, but the uncle's executor resisted his claim against the estate. The court found the promise enforceable. . . .

Perhaps because of such difficulties, the benefit-detriment account of consideration was replaced by a "bargain" theory: there is consideration when each promise or performance has been bargained for, when each has been offered as inducement for the other:

> [I]t is the essence of a consideration, that, by the terms of the agreement, it is given and accepted as the motive or inducement of the promise. Conversely, the promise must be made and accepted as the conventional motive or inducement for furnishing the consideration. The root of the whole matter is the relation of reciprocal conventional inducement, each for the other, between consideration and promise.

O.W. Holmes, The Common Law 293-94 (1881)[2] The bargain-exchange account fits rather neatly into an economic analysis of common law, which sees in this version of the doctrine of consideration an attempt to select out for enforcement those contracts—namely bargained-for exchanges—that promote the increase of value in society.

The state has an independent interest in the enforcement of [bargain] promises. Exchange creates surplus, because each party presumably values what he gets more highly than what he gives. A modern free-enterprise system depends heavily on private planning and on credit transactions that involve exchanges over time. The extent to which private actors will be ready to engage in exchange,

---

[2] "Going back into the past, there was an indefinite number of cases which had imposed liability, in the name of consideration, where nothing like Holmes's 'reciprocal conventional inducement' was anywhere in sight." G. Gilmore, Death of Contract 63 (1974). Gilmore saw Holmes as trying to change the law, and succeeding. "There is never any point in arguing with a successful revolution. What Holmes told the young lawyers who flocked to his lectures in the spring of 1881 promptly became the truth—the indisputable truth—of the matter for his own and succeeding generations." *Id.* at 21.

and are able to make reliable plans, rests partly on the probability that bargain promises will be kept. Legal enforcement of such promises increases that probability. Eisenberg, *Principles of Consideration*, 67 Cornell L. Rev., 640, 643 (1982).[3] . . .

Of course, if any theory could persuade us that the cases that stand as counterexamples to it were wrongly decided, we might accept the theory in spite of the cases. But the tendency in the courts has been to favor the accumulated wisdom of the common law over the simplicity of any single-minded theory. Thus Eisenberg argues that consideration is a guise under which judges have tried to deal fairly with contract difficulties, and argues that it is time now to relegate the doctrine and its epicycles to the history books, and bring fairness out into the open in decision-making.

> In the past courts decided issues of fairness covertly, and expressed their decisions through the manipulation of rules and exceptions purportedly designed for other ends. . . . The agenda for the legal community is . . . to encourage the courts to perform such review openly.

67 Cornell L.Rev., at 640-41.

Although it is a beguiling thought to drop the mask and do justice openly, the present case seems to us to make manifest the emptiness of such an approach. Having dropped the guise of consideration, what is the fair outcome in a case in which a wife (apparently) gratuitously affixes her name to a guaranty intended for her husband? Where the rules of contract law clearly dictate one result or the other (and there is no fraud or unconscionability) then the fair outcome might be to enforce that result. But to find such rules we are driven back to the doctrine of consideration and its exceptions.[5]

Since the just solution does not leap out at us, therefore, let us begin by pressing the doctrine of consideration as far as it will go. Where there is no consideration, it has been the general rule that the contract is not enforceable. In this case, under the versions of the doctrine we are acquainted with, there has been no consideration. The government suffered no detriment: its undertaking would have been precisely the same (on the account we have before us) whether or not Mrs. Meadors had signed the guaranty. She gained no benefit, either; whatever

---

[3] This position is subject to two different sorts of criticism: (1) unilateral promises also increase surplus, Posner, *Gratuitous Promises in Economics and Law,* 6 J. of Legal Stud. 411, 412 (1977); and (2) if it is the promotion of exchanges in the market place that is sought, why extend enforcement to, for example, intrafamilial contracts or the contract between me and the fellow who sells me his car? C. Fried, *Contract as Promise* 36-37 (1981).

[5] It may seem that, in our effort to find a rule that gives the just result, we have given considerations of simplicity short shrift. Although we think that the best argument for a result different from the one we reach here would be based on the simplicity of a rule that automatically bound signers, the same argument could be made for any per se rule and does not seem to us to weigh heavily in the balance.

benefit passed to her and her husband because of the loan would have passed without her signature. ~~And no bargain was involved.~~ The SBA gave up nothing to induce Mrs. Meadors to sign; her signature induced no act or promise on the part of the SBA. Since there has been no consideration, the general rule would deny the government enforcement of the contract.

. . . .

If the promises of the principal and the surety are made simultaneously, they may be made for a single consideration; the loan of money by the creditor to the principal is a sufficient consideration for the promises of both principal and surety. Corbin on Contracts § 213.[6] That rule, on its face, suggests that because the signing was simultaneous the appellant here cannot raise the defense of lack of consideration. On a benefit-detriment theory, there is nothing more to be said about it.

We believe, however, that that outcome is wrong, and—although cases on this point are naturally rare—we are supported in our belief by the commentators and by the bargain-exchange interpretation of the doctrine of consideration. This is not the ordinary case of the guarantor signing simultaneously with the principal; this is more like the case mentioned earlier in which X promises to pay Y a thousand dollars if Y gives up smoking, and Y gives up smoking without ever learning of X's promise. Whether or not there has been benefit to one party or detriment to the other, there has been no bargain here, and the SBA made the loan apparently in ignorance of Mrs. Meadors' signature. If those are the facts, then we believe that . . . there has been no consideration at all.

. . . .

For Corbin, the lack of consideration is clear from the fact that the signature was not originally contemplated as part of the deal. Where the creditor does not even know of the signature—as we are assured by both parties is the case here— the lack of a bargain and consequent lack of consideration is even clearer:

> Even if the promisee takes some action subsequent to the promise (so that there is no problem of past consideration), and even if the promisor sought that action in exchange for his promise, ... that action is not bargained for unless it is given by the promisee in exchange for the promise. In other words, just as the promisor's purpose must be to induce an exchange, so the promisee's purpose must be to take advantage of the proposed exchange. *In practice, the principal effect of this requirement is to*

---

[6] Corbin distinguishes guaranties made subsequent to the principal agreement as requiring separate consideration. There are cases holding that even in such circumstances no separate consideration is necessary, but in each such case it is clear that the guaranty had been bargained for with the main agreement, or there is some other explanation for the apparent discrepancy.

deny enforcement of the promise if the promisee takes the action sought by the promisor without knowledge of the promise. As might be supposed, examples are infrequent.

E. Farnsworth, Contracts 64 (1982).[8] On the undisputed facts, this case is one of Farnsworth's infrequent examples.

. . . .

Indiana law does not raise any difficulties for the position we adopt. *See especially Davis v. B.C.L. Enterprises, Inc.,* 406 N.E.2d 1204, 1205 (Ind.App.1980) ("If the guaranty is made at the time of the contract to which it relates, *so as to constitute a part of the consideration of the contract,* it is sufficient.").

We hold, therefore, that summary judgment for plaintiff was not appropriate on this point. Although the parties have apparently agreed on the relevant facts, we feel that it would also be inappropriate for us to decide as a matter of law that the guaranty is unenforceable. The district court, relying on a different construction of the law, did not take evidence on the question. Construing the law as we have construed it, it must be resolved whether in fact Betty Meadors' signature was in any respect whatsoever required, anticipated, requested or relied upon (or, in fact, known of); because if it was not, it was wholly irrelevant to the transaction and does not create an enforceable obligation.

Reversed and remanded.

_____

---

[8] Eisenberg also suggests the rarity of such cases:

> The proposition that bargains involving the performance of a pre-existing contractual duty are often gratuitous is empirically far-fetched. Perhaps a few such cases could be found, but I have never run across one. In any event, if such cases really do arise, they neither need nor justify a special rule. As Comment a [to § 573 of the Restatement Second of Contracts] points out, "[i]f the performance was not in fact bargained for and given in exchange for the promise, the case is not within this section: in such cases there is no consideration . . . ." 67 Cornell L.Rev., at 644-45.

Meincke v. Northwest Bank & Trust Co. (I)

JANICE A. MEINCKE, Plaintiff-Appellant

v.

NORTHWEST BANK & TRUST CO. and SCRAMM ENTERPRISES, L.C.,
Defendants-Appellees

NORTHWEST BANK & TRUST CO., Cross-Claimant

v.

SCRAMM ENTERPRISES, L.C., Cross-Defendant

NORTHWEST BANK & TRUST CO., Third-Party Plaintiff,

v.

SANDRA R. MARTI AND C.A. MEINCKE PLUMBING, INC.,
Third-Party Defendant.

Court of Appeals of Iowa

2007 WL 4553476 (Iowa Ct. App. Dec. 28, 2007) (unpublished opinion)

SACKETT, C.J.

Plaintiff-appellant, Janice Meincke, appeals the trial court's ruling in favor of defendant-appellee, Northwest Bank & Trust Company (Northwest Bank). Plaintiff . . . contends the trial court erred by . . . finding the subordination agreement between the plaintiff and Northwest Bank was supported by consideration . . . . We reverse, finding no consideration to support the contract.

I. BACKGROUND

This case involves a family's financially troubled businesses and the debt the businesses incurred from an elderly family member and from two banks. C.A. Meincke Plumbing and Scramm Enterprises are owned by Sandra Marti and Craig Meincke. The plaintiff is Sandra's mother and is Craig's aunt. She is eighty-two years old. In July 2002, Sandra and Craig approached the plaintiff for a loan for the businesses. At the time, the plaintiff's husband was in the hospital and in very poor health. Sandra and Craig visited the hospital and made the request. The plaintiff and her husband initially refused to give the loan. After Sandra and Craig told them they would go bankrupt without the money, the plaintiff loaned Scramm Enterprises $90,000. The plaintiff's husband died two months after the loan was made. To secure the loan, Scramm gave the plaintiff a mortgage on the business's land and buildings. Scramm had already granted two mortgages on this property to secure loans from Rock Island Bank. Sandra and Craig had also mortgaged their personal homes to secure loans to the businesses.

James Legare was a loan officer at Rock Island Bank who worked with Craig and Sandra to obtain financing for the businesses. At some point, James Legare began working for Northwest Bank and eventually became vice president. He also helped the businesses obtain loans through this bank. In 2003, Scramm obtained loans from Northwest Bank and granted yet another mortgage on the property. The record shows a pattern of financial difficulty for the businesses. The businesses sought, and Northwest Bank approved, continual loan renewals and extensions, loans for paying suppliers, and loans to pay off other lenders. In 2003 and 2004 the businesses' payments on various loans were late over thirty times. In 2004, Sandra and Craig sought another loan from Northwest Bank. The loan was needed primarily to pay the balance owed to Rock Island Bank because these loans were due and Rock Island Bank refused to renew the loans. Northwest Bank agreed to provide these funds on the condition that Northwest Bank acquired the first lien on the mortgaged property.

What's That?

A mortgage is a document in which the owner of real property pledges its title to the property to another as security for money owed, often as part of the purchase price for the property. If the debt is not repaid, the mortgagee (the lender) can sell the property and use the proceeds to satisfy the loan. In this case, Janice Meinke loaned money to Scramm Enterprises; Scramm pledged title to its business property to Meincke so she would have something of value if Scramm did not repay. Multiple mortgages may be given on a single piece of property. If that occurs, the mortgagees' interests are satisfied in priority order; if the property is worth less than the total of the secured debts, holders of lower priority mortgages may not have their claims satisfied. Often—but not always—priority is controlled by the order in which the loans and security interests were established. The dispute in this case involved a change in the priority of the multiple mortgages that had been given on the Scramm property.

At this time, Rock Island Bank had first priority to the property, the plaintiff had second priority, and Northwest Bank had third priority. If Northwest Bank expended the funds owed to Rock Island Bank, the plaintiff would have first priority and Northwest Bank would have second priority. To protect its financial interest, Northwest Bank would not provide additional funding unless the plaintiff was willing to subordinate her priority position to Northwest Bank.

At trial, Sandra testified that she knew a subordination agreement was required but never discussed this or any financial matters of the businesses with the plaintiff. The plaintiff testified that Craig called her saying "I had to sign this paper to be second in line." A Northwest Bank employee drafted a subordination agreement and Craig went with the bank's vice president, James Legare, to the plaintiff's house to get her signature. Legare said hello to the plaintiff but no one discussed the agreement. Legare testified that he believed Craig had already explained the agreement to the plaintiff. The plaintiff signed the agreement. A notary was not present at the signing. Legare had the agreement notarized at a later time. The plaintiff was not present when it was notarized.

What's That?

Notarizing a signature means certifying it as belonging to the person named. A notary or notary public is a person authorized by the state to authenticate signatures. The presence of the person who signed is usually required by law.

After the subordination agreement was obtained, Northwest Bank made two loans to the businesses in March of 2004, issuing funds on behalf of the businesses in the amount of approximately $716,907. Of this amount, approximately $474,500 was paid for the Rock Island Bank loans. Approximately $242,000 was applied to refinance other Northwest Bank Loans. Sandra testified that this was a refinancing transaction and none of these funds were actually paid directly to the businesses. Jim Legare testified, and the banking documents show, that the transaction also provided another $4,000 in a line of credit to the businesses. It appears the businesses drew approximately $2,209 from this line of credit two days after the loan was made.

Approximately two months later, the plumbing business ceased operations because of financial problems. In 2005, Scramm and Northwest Bank entered into an agreement for non-judicial foreclosure. The mortgaged property was sold. Due to the subordination agreement, the proceeds from the sale were applied to the Northwest Bank loans first. The proceeds were insufficient to repay the total owed to Northwest Bank and consequently, the plaintiff received nothing toward the debt owed her. The plaintiff filed suit against Northwest Bank claiming, among other things, the subordination agreement was invalid and Northwest Bank intentionally interfered with the plaintiff's contract with Scramm Enterprises. At the close of the evidence at a bench trial, the plaintiff moved to amend her pleadings to conform to the evidence, seeking to add a claim of fraud. The trial court denied this motion and ruled in favor of the defendant on all counts. The plaintiff appeals the trial court's rulings.

II. STANDARD OF REVIEW

Claims based on a contract tried at law are reviewed for correction of errors at law. Iowa R.App. P. 6.4; *Equity Control Assocs., Ltd. v. Root*, 638 N.W.2d 664, 670 (Iowa 2001). The trial court's fact findings are binding upon us if they are supported by substantial evidence and we view the findings in a light most favorable to upholding the ruling. *Equity Control Assocs.*, 638 N.W.2d at 670. We reverse if there is an erroneous application of the law. *Id.*

III. CONSIDERATION

The plaintiff contends the trial court erred in finding the subordination agreement was supported by consideration. We must determine whether substantial evidence supports this finding. *Id.* A subordination agreement is generally governed by the rules of contract law. 68A Am.Jur.2d Secured Transactions § 741 (2007). "We presume a written, signed agreement is supported by consideration." *Kristerin Dev. Corp. v. Granson Inv.*, 394 N . W.2d 325, 331 (Iowa 1986); *see also* Iowa Code § 537A.2. "Either a benefit to a promisor or a detriment to a promisee constitutes consideration." *Doggett v. Heritage Concepts, Inc.*, 298 N.W.2d 310, 311 (Iowa 1980). There is consideration even if the benefit flows to a third party. *Clayman v. Bibler*, 210 Iowa 497, 500, 231 N.W. 334, 336 (1930); *Moench v. Hower*, 137 Iowa 621, 624, 115 N.W. 229, 230 (1908). We determine whether there is consideration from what is stated in the instrument or by what was contemplated by the parties at the time of the agreement. *Hubbard Milling Co. v. Citizens State Bank*, 385 N.W.2d 255, 259 (Iowa 1986); *Lane v. Richards*, 119 Iowa 24, 26-27, 91 N.W. 786, 787 (1902). The further extension of credit can serve as consideration in a subordination agreement. One treatise explains,

> An agreement subordinating a senior mortgage to a junior one is supported by consideration where the agreement is based on a conviction that further advances from the junior mortgagee would not be possible without the agreement, and that these future advances are necessary to carry on operations on the land to prevent the senior mortgage debt from being lost.

55 Am.Jur.2d Mortgages § 320 (2007) (citing *Stockmeyer v. Tobin*, 139 U.S. 176, 189, 11 S.Ct. 504, 509, 35 L.Ed. 123, 128 (1891)).

However, a party to a subordination agreement can use the failure of consideration or lack of consideration as a defense to invalidate the contract. Iowa Code § 537A.3; *Hubbard Milling Co.*, 385 N.W.2d at 259. In *Hubbard Milling*, the court invalidated a subordination agreement for failure of consideration. *Hubbard Milling Co.*, 385 N.W.2d at 259. The purported consideration stated in the agreement was a bank's promise to subordinate to another creditor in exchange for that creditor's promise to loan a farmer funds to purchase pig feed. *Id.* at 257, 259. The creditor never loaned the funds and no pig feed was purchased so the consideration failed. *Id.* at 259. The Eighth Circuit has also invalidated a subordination agreement on the ground that it lacked consideration. *In re Sepco*, 750

F.2d 51, 53 (8th Cir.1984). Consideration was lacking when the subordination clause was hidden, the creditor failed to explain the effect of the clause, and no benefit was provided to the subordinating creditor besides assurance it would get paid. *In re Sepco, Inc.,* 36 B.R. 279, 286 (Bkrtcy.S .D.1984).

The trial court found there was some consideration for the subordination agreement. It ruled that the plaintiff benefited by helping her relatives. The family businesses benefited because the refinancing provided by Northwest Bank allowed the businesses to continue operating at a lower monthly cost by reducing Scramm's monthly loan payments. The court also found Northwest Bank suffered a detriment through the agreement by loaning additional funds. The trial court explained, "[t]he fact that the Plaintiff's secured position on her mortgage was worsened as a result of the subordination agreement and the new loans in no way affects the outcome of the consideration issue."

Although the court properly analyzed the transaction to identify a potential benefit or detriment to serve as consideration, we find the court erred in failing to identify whether, in fact, this consideration was bargained for and contemplated by the parties at the time of the transaction. "Consideration requires the voluntary assumption of an obligation by one party *on the condition* of an act or forbearance by the other." *Summerhays v. Clark,* 509 N.W.2d 748, 751 (Iowa 1994) (emphasis added). If a detriment to a party is serving as the consideration, "it must appear that the disadvantage was suffered *at the request of* the promisor, express or implied." *Heggen v. Clover Leaf Coal & Mining Co.,* 217 Iowa 820, 824, 253 N.W. 140, 142 (1934) (emphasis added). These cases illustrate the requirement of reciprocal inducement or a bargained for exchange for a finding of consideration. Comments to the Restatement (Second) of Contracts explains:

> [T]he law is concerned with the external manifestation rather than the undisclosed mental state: it is enough that one party manifests an intention to induce the other's response and to be induced by it *and* that the other responds in accordance with the inducement. But it is not enough that the promise induces the conduct of the promisee *or* that the conduct of the promisee induces the making of the promise; both elements must be present, or there is no bargain. Moreover, a mere pretense of bargain does not suffice, as where there is a false recital of consideration or where the purported consideration is merely nominal.

Restatement (Second) of Contracts § 71, comment b, at 173 (1981) (emphasis added). Parties may have additional motives and other factors may induce a party's performance. Restatement (Second) of Contracts § 81, and comments a and b, at 206 (1981). However, both parties must manifest an intent to induce the other and be induced by the transaction for there to be bargained for consideration. Restatement (Second) of Contracts § 81, comment a, at 206 (1981).

It is the bargained for exchange requirement that is lacking in this transaction. There is no consideration stated in the instrument to identify what exchange was contemplated by the parties. The record shows no indication that the plaintiff subordinated her priority to induce Northwest Bank to make additional loans to the businesses. The plaintiff testified that she signed the agreement to get her money back. She stated that she really did not think of it as helping Craig and Sandra but conceded it may have benefited Craig and Sandra since they asked her to do it. It is clear that the plaintiff did not understand what was occurring in the transaction and did not contemplate a bargained exchange. In fact, the record shows that the plaintiff was unaware of any other loans or mortgages to the property. According to the plaintiff, she signed the paper to be "second in line." The testimony suggested that the plaintiff was not aware of her priority before she signed the subordination agreement. She simply believed she needed to sign the paper to obtain the funds owed to her from the sale of the business property. Of particular concern is the plaintiff's apparent lack of knowledge about the final loan made to the businesses by Northwest Bank. Although this final loan was supposed to be the inducement for the plaintiff's promise to subordinate, there is no evidence in the record that the plaintiff even knew that her signing the subordination agreement was a condition precedent to the businesses obtaining this funding. Under these circumstances, we find substantial evidence does not support a finding that this contract was supported by consideration. Rather, the subordination agreement is invalid due to a lack of consideration.

Given our resolution on this issue, we need not address the other claims of error. We reverse the trial court's ruling and hold as a matter of law, the subordination agreement is invalid due to a want of consideration.

REVERSED.

Meincke v. Northwest Bank & Trust Co. (II)

JANICE A. MEINCKE, Plaintiff-Appellant

v.

NORTHWEST BANK & TRUST CO., Defendant-Appellee

Supreme Court of Iowa

756 N.W.2d 223 (Iowa 2008)

WIGGINS, Justice.

Janice Meincke loaned her daughter and nephew $90,000. The loan was secured by a mortgage on property owned by the daughter and nephew's business.

A bank also held mortgages on the same property; however, Janice's mortgage had priority. For the daughter and nephew to obtain more financing, the bank required Janice to subordinate her mortgage to the bank's by signing a subordination agreement. Janice signed the agreement, but challenged its enforcement by arguing it lacked consideration. Janice appealed a district court judgment finding of consideration. Our court of appeals reversed the district court by finding substantial evidence did not support the judgment. However, upon further review, we find substantial evidence does support the judgment, and we affirm the judgment of the district court.

[Statement of facts is omitted.]

II. Issues

Janice originally appealed, claiming the district court erred: (1) in finding the subordination agreement was supported by consideration; (2) by failing to find the subordination agreement lacked proper acknowledgement; (3) by failing to find improper interference with an existing contract; and (4) by denying her motion to amend the petition to add a claim for fraud. The court of appeals found the first issue dispositive; therefore, it did not consider the others.

Northwest Bank petitioned for further review, which we granted. Because we find substantial evidence supported the district court's determination that the subordination agreement was supported by proper, bargained for consideration, we will address Janice's other claims on our further review.

III. Discussion

Claims based on a contract that are tried at law are reviewed for correction of errors at law. Iowa R.App. P. 6.4; *Harrington v. Univ. of N. Iowa*, 726 N.W.2d 363, 365 (Iowa 2007). The district court's findings of fact are binding on the court if they are supported by substantial evidence. Iowa R.App. P. 6.14(6)(a); *Fischer v. City of Sioux City*, 695 N.W.2d 31, 33 (Iowa 2005). We view the evidence in the light most favorable to the judgment when a party argues the trial court's ruling is not supported by substantial evidence. *Fischer*, 695 N.W.2d at 33. Evidence is substantial when reasonable minds accept the evidence as adequate to reach a conclusion. Id. "Evidence is not insubstantial merely because we may draw different conclusions from it; the ultimate question is whether it supports the finding actually made, not whether the evidence would support a different finding." *Raper v. State*, 688 N.W.2d 29, 36 (Iowa 2004) (citations omitted). However, appellate courts are not bound to a district court's conclusion of law or that court's application of legal conclusions. Id.

It is presumed that an agreement, which has been written and signed, is supported by consideration. *Kristerin Dev. Co. v. Granson Inv.,* 394 N.W.2d 325, 331 (Iowa 1986). A failure of consideration is a defense to enforcing the contract that must be proven by the party asserting the defense. *Hubbard Milling Co. v. Citizens State Bank,* 385 N.W.2d 255, 259 (Iowa 1986). We determine whether there is consideration from what is stated in the instrument or by what the parties contemplated at the time the instrument was executed. *Id.* A party can use want of consideration as a defense to a subordination agreement. *Id.*

Consideration can be either a legal benefit to the promisor, or a legal detriment to the promisee. *Magnusson Agency v. Pub. Entity Nat'l Company-Midwest,* 560 N.W.2d 20, 27 (Iowa 1997). The district court found the bank suffered a detriment by loaning the plumbing business additional funding. The detriment to the bank is adequate consideration for the subordination agreement. *See* 55 Am.Jur.2d Mortgages § 320, at 66 (2007) (stating the extension of future credit can serve as consideration for a subordination agreement). However, the question here is not whether this detriment was sufficient to constitute consideration; it is whether the benefit or the detriment was bargained for. *Magnusson,* 560 N.W.2d at 27. According to the Restatement (Second) of Contracts:

> (1) To constitute consideration, a performance or a return promise must be bargained for.
> (2) A performance or return promise is bargained for if it is sought by the promisor in exchange for his promise and is given by the promisee in exchange for that promise.

§ 71, at 172 (1981); *see also id.* § 72, at 177 (stating "[e]xcept as stated in §§ 73 and 74, any performance which is bargained for is consideration"). For consideration to be "bargained for," the consideration must "induce" the making of the promise. *Id.* § 71 cmt. *b,* at 173.

A sufficient legal detriment to the promisee exists if the promisee "promises or performs any act, regardless of how slight or inconvenient, which he is not obligated to promise or perform so long as he does so at the request of the promisor and in exchange for the promise." 3 Samuel Williston & Richard A. Lord, A Treatise on the Law of Contracts § 7:4, at 41 (4th ed. 1992). There is substantial evidence in the record the detriment suffered by the bank was bargained for.

Janice admitted that Craig and Sandra would receive a benefit if she signed the subordination agreement by stating the following:

Question: Okay. And Craig and Sandy received a benefit also because they asked you to do this and this would help their business, correct?
Janice: I suppose, yes.

"[I]t must appear that the disadvantage was suffered at the request of the promisor, *expressed or implied*." *Heggen v. Clover Leaf Coal & Mining Co.*, 217 Iowa 820, 824, 253 N.W. 140, 142 (1934) (citing *Handrahan v. O'Regan*, 45 Iowa 298, 300 (1876)) (emphasis added). Janice's statement implies she understood the bank would lend more money to Craig and Sandra if she signed the subordination agreement. By signing the subordination agreement, Janice impliedly requested Northwest Bank to refinance Craig and Sandra's loans, thus she requested the bank suffer a detriment.

Because there is substantial evidence the consideration was bargained for, we affirm the district court ruling on the consideration issue.

[Court's discussion of the remaining issues is omitted.]

IV. Disposition

Because we find substantial evidence to support the district court's judgment on the issues of consideration, [and the plaintiff's remaining claims], we vacate the decision of the court of appeals, and affirm the judgment of the district court.

Decision of Court of Appeals vacated; District Court judgment affirmed.

———

Problems: Is There Consideration?

Is there consideration for each of the promises described below? If so, what is the consideration? (Be sure to consider all the promises described in each problem.) Does it matter if you use the "benefit or detriment" or "bargain" theory?

2-1.   Anna promises to pay $25 to Ben in exchange for a book Ben owns. Ben promises to deliver the book.

2-2.   Same as Problem 2-1, but Ben thereafter fails to deliver the book to Anna. Is there consideration for Anna's promise?

2-3. Carla receives a gift from Deepak of a book worth $10. Subsequently, Carla promises to pay Deepak the value of the book.

2-4. Ellen promises to make a gift of $10 to Fernanda. In reliance on the promise, Fernanda buys a book from Glen and promises to pay Glen $10 for it.

2-5. Hannah desires to make a binding promise to give $1000 to her son Ivan. Being advised that a gratuitous promise is not binding, Hannah writes out and signs a false recital that Ivan has sold her a car for $1000 and a promise to pay that amount.

2-6. Julia desires to make a binding promise to give $1000 to her daughter Kate. Being advised that a gratuitous promise is not binding, Julia offers to buy from Kate for $1000 a book worth less than $1. Kate accepts the offer, knowing that the purchase of the book is mere pretense.

2-7. Luke offers to buy a book owned by Matt and to pay Matt $10 in exchange for it. Both parties know that such books regularly sell for $5 and that part of Luke's motive in making the offer is to make a gift to Matt.

2-8. Nadia promises to her good friend Otis to give him $1000 to help him pay his law school tuition. A month after Nadia delivers the money, Otis promises to repay it once he gets his first job.

2-9. Pablo says to Quinn, the owner of a garage, "I will pay you $100 if you will make my car run properly." Quinn does so.

2-10. Theresa and Rose sign a written agreement stating, "We will each buy 5 lottery tickets each week and are partners in any winnings we receive from the tickets, to be shared equally."

2-11. Sheila wishes to buy a home but, because she has an insufficient credit history, the bank is unwilling to approve a loan to her. Sheila's mother, Ula, promises Sheila that she will co-sign the loan so Sheila can make the purchase. Thereafter, Ula signs a note promising to pay the bank if Sheila defaults on the loan payments and the bank approves the loan. Sheila uses the loan funds to purchase the house.

2-12. In *Appeal of Clark,* 19 A. 332 (Conn. 1889), Sheldon Clark signed a $700 promissory note in favor of Charles B. Clark on August 29, 1887. Just over a month later, Sheldon wrote and signed his will, and 13 days later he died. The court reported the following facts:

> Sheldon Clark, who was unmarried and sick with the consumption of which disease he died, lived in the family of Charles B. Clark [no relation to him] a good part of the time, from about January 1, 1886, to the last of January, 1887, boarded there, and in a sort made his home there—not continuously, but at intervals. There was a price for board, which was paid.
>
> Charles and his wife, however, rendered services to Sheldon outside the regular contract for board—washed and mended his clothes, attended upon him when he was sick, cleaned his clothes and the bedding after a hemorrhage, took care of his cattle when he was not able to do so himself, and did the chores upon his place, etc.—matters not very great in themselves, and which seem never to have been the subject of any formal bargain between them. Sheldon appreciated their kindness and favors, and on several occasions said to Charles and to the wife of Charles that they should have their pay. In consequence of these statements by Sheldon, and in reliance upon them, Charles and his wife continued to render these services. Sheldon knew that Charles and his wife expected to be paid, and he fully intended to pay them. No price was ever fixed; it was left for Sheldon to pay such sum as in his judgment should be a full equivalent. . . .
>
> On the day the note was made Sheldon came to the house of Charles, and said to Mr. and Mrs. Clark that he wished them to draw a note for $700, which he desired them to have for what they had done for him. Mrs. Clark said: "Why, Sheldon, that is too much; that is more than we deserve." Sheldon said: "I want you to have that if I die, but if I get well I want the note back, and I will then pay you what is right." The note was then drawn, was examined and approved by Sheldon, and was duly signed by him, and delivered to Charles, in whose hands it has ever since remained.

Based on *Hamer, Dougherty, Baehr, Meadors,* and *Meincke,* was there consideration for the promissory note? If so, based on what particular facts? If not, why not? Was there any other enforceable promise made?

§ 4. Distinguishing Bargain from Conditional Gift

Recall that consideration is defined in Restatement (Second) § 71 as something "sought by the promisor in exchange for his promise and . . . given by the promisee in exchange for that promise." Because of the requirement of reciprocal inducement, we often find consideration by looking for what the promisor "asked for" and the promisee "gave" in exchange for the promise. Recall the statement in *Baehr* that a contractual promise appears in the logical form "If . . . (consideration is given) . . . then I promise that . . . ." But sometimes a promisor may ask the promisee to do something and yet not be proposing a bargain. The following cases consider such circumstances.

Reading the Law Critically:
Tomczak and *Pennsy Supply, Inc.*

1. Does the court conclude that the promise was a gift or that it was part of an enforceable bargain? How does the court distinguish between the two? Does the court get it right?

2. Are the two cases consistent with each other?

Tomczak v. Koochiching County Highway Dept.

MAUREEN TOMCZAK, Plaintiff-Appellant

v.

KOOCHICHING COUNTY HIGHWAY DEPT., Defendant-Respondent

Minnesota Court of Appeals
1999 WL 55501 (Minn. Ct. App. Feb. 9, 1999) (unpublished opinion)

PETERSON.

On appeal from entry of a partial summary judgment, Maureen and William Tomczak challenge dismissal of their contract claim . . . . We affirm.

FACTS

In April 1996, water levels were rising in a gravel pit near Maureen and William Tomczaks' home in Koochiching County. Although the pit was not owned or operated by the county, Maureen Tomczak brought the water level to the attention of a county commissioner, who told her to come to a county board meeting the following week.

At that meeting, many residents who lived near the gravel pit voiced their concerns. Initially, the board told them that the effects of the rising water in the pit were their responsibility as private landowners. Douglas Grindall, the county engineer, thought that pumping water from the pit to lower the water level by two feet might solve the problem. The board eventually authorized the highway department to furnish a pump at the county's expense. Maureen Tomczak stated that she and her husband would furnish a site for the pump and that they would keep it filled with fuel and oil.

According to Maureen Tomczak, Grindall told her that he would "pump [the pit] to two feet, to keep it safe, and then [she] had to sign a paper saying [she] wouldn't sue as long as they were pumping, I and Russell Christensen."

Grindall stated in his affidavit that the county was concerned about liability arising from pumping the pit. Therefore, before placing the pump, the county instructed him to obtain a release from the Tomczaks. He prepared the following typewritten document:

> In exchange for Koochiching County furnishing a pump to dewater the abandoned gravel pit near my property, we agreed to maintain the pump by fueling and checking the oil when necessary and waived all liability to the County for any action, damages, or injury that is caused by pumping the pit.

At the bottom of the document is a handwritten note stating:

> Please sign and have a neighbor witness. I'll pick up a copy tomorrow.
> [signed] Douglas Grindall
> County Engineer

After the Tomczaks signed this document, around-the-clock pumping began. The single pump, however, did not work as quickly as expected. A week later, the county installed a second, larger pump to supplement the pumping. The larger pump directed the water toward the west. When a neighbor to the west complained about flooding, the county directed both pumps toward the east, which caused flooding on another neighbor's property. The county then ran only the larger pump and limited pumping to working hours.

A week later, the county engineer advised the county board that the water level in the pit was dropping very slowly. The board authorized pumping to continue. Nevertheless, the water level once again rose due to heavy rains.

In early June, the county stopped pumping because the heavy volume of water had washed out a catch basin and another landowner complained that the pumping caused flooding on his property. In late June, the Tomczaks' house was flooded.

DECISION

1. Contract claim. Summary judgment is appropriate when there are no genuine issues of material fact and the moving party is entitled to judgment as a matter of law. *Wartnick v. Moss & Barnett*, 490 N.W.2d 108, 112 (Minn.1992). The court must view the evidence in the light most favorable to the party against whom summary judgment is granted. *Id.*

The Tomczaks argue that the district court erred by dismissing their contract claim. They contend that when they signed the document prepared by Grindall, they entered into a contract with the county. Under the contract, the Tomczaks contend, the county agreed to furnish a pump and they agreed to maintain the pump by fueling it and checking the oil. By withdrawing the pump, they argue, the county breached the contract. We disagree.

A contract requires valid consideration. *Franklin v. Carpenter*, 309 Minn. 419, 422, 244 N.W.2d 492, 495 (1976). Consideration is the exchange or price requested and received by the promisor for the promise. 1 Samuel Williston & Walter H.E. Jaeger, *A Treatise on the Law of Contracts* § 100, at 370 (3rd ed. 1957). A gratuitous conditional promise is unenforceable. *See e.g.,. Smith v. Force*, 31 Minn. 119, 119, 16 N.W. 704 704 (1883) (holding that arrangement between parties that defendant may take property in dispute and return it to plaintiff, if on plaintiff's writing to the post office department, the department did not claim the property as government property, was wholly without consideration and unenforceable against plaintiff's subsequent demand for return of property).

The difference between words that state a condition of a gratuitous promise and words that indicate a request for consideration has been explained as follows:

> In theory it seems possible that any event may be named in a promise as fixing the moment, on the happening of which a promisor (not as an exchange for the happening but as a mere coincidence in time) will perform a promise intended and understood to be gratuitous. The same thing, therefore, stated as the condition of a promise may or may not be consideration, according as a reasonable man would or would not understand that the performance of the condition was requested as the price or exchange for the promise. If a benevolent man says to

a tramp, "if you go around the corner to the clothing shop there, you may purchase an overcoat on my credit," no reasonable person would understand that the short walk was requested as the consideration for the promise, but that in the event of the tramp going to the shop the promisor would make him a gift. Yet the walk to the shop is in its nature capable of being consideration. It is a legal detriment to the tramp to take the walk, and the only reason why the walk is not consideration is because on a reasonable interpretation, it must be held that the walk was not requested as the price of the promise, but was merely a condition of a gratuitous promise.

It is often difficult to decide whether words of condition in a promise indicate a request for consideration or state a mere condition in a gratuitous promise. An aid, though not a conclusive test in determining which interpretation of the promise is more reasonable, is an inquiry whether the happening of the condition will be a benefit to the promisor. If so, it is a fair inference that the happening was requested as a consideration. On the other hand, if, as in the case of the tramp stated above, the happening of the condition will be not only of no benefit to the promisor but is obviously merely for the purpose of enabling the promisee to receive a gift, the happening of the event on which the promise is conditional, though brought about by the promisee in reliance on the promise, will not be interpreted as consideration.

Williston, *supra,* § 112, at 445-46. Minnesota has applied the benefit test to determine whether an act constituted consideration. *See, e.g., Skagerberg v. Blandin Paper Co.,* 197 Minn. 291, 300, 266 N.W. 872, 877 (1936) (employee's purchase of co-employee's house was not consideration going to, or in any way benefiting, employer to induce it to enter into contract nor did employee allege purchase benefited employer or injured employee).

Even if we assume that the county agreed that it would provide the pump until the water level in the pit was reduced by two feet, as Maureen Tomczak stated in her deposition, there is no contract because there is no consideration. Applying the benefit-to-promisor test, we conclude that the county's promise was a gratuitous conditional promise and that the Tomczaks' agreement to (1) operate the pump and (2) provide the county with a liability release was a condition of the promise. The county did no more than gratuitously promise to provide a pump. The Tomczaks' agreement to operate the pump was of no benefit to the county and was obviously merely for the purpose of enabling the Tomczaks to receive some benefit from the county's gratuitous promise. . . .

. . . .

Affirmed.

Pennsy Supply, Inc. v. American Ash Recycling Corp.

PENNSY SUPPLY, INC., Plaintiff-Appellant

v.

AMERICAN ASH RECYCLING CORP. OF PENNSYLVANIA, Defendant-Appellee

Superior Court of Pennsylvania
895 A.2d 595 (Pa. Super. Ct. 2006)

OPINION BY ORIE MELVIN, J.:

Appellant, Pennsy Supply, Inc. ("Pennsy"), appeals from the grant of preliminary objections in the nature of a demurrer in favor of Appellee, American Ash Recycling Corp. of Pennsylvania ("American Ash"). We reverse and remand for further proceedings.

The trial court summarized the allegations of the complaint as follows:

The instant case arises out of a construction project for Northern York High School (Project) owned by Northern York County School District (District) in York County, Pennsylvania. The District entered into a construction contract for the Project with a general contractor, Lobar, Inc. (Lobar). Lobar, in turn, subcontracted the paving of driveways and a parking lot to [Pennsy].

The contract between Lobar and the District included Project Specifications for paving work which required Lobar, through its subcontractor Pennsy, to use certain base aggregates. The Project Specifications permitted substitution of the aggregates with an alternate material known as Treated Ash Aggregate (TAA) or AggRite.

The Project Specifications included a "notice to bidders" of the availability of AggRite at no cost from [American Ash], a supplier of AggRite. The Project Specifications also included a letter to the Project architect from American Ash confirming the availability of a certain amount of free AggRite on a first come, first served basis.

Pennsy contacted American Ash and informed American Ash that it would require approximately 11,000 tons of AggRite for the Project. Pennsy subsequently picked up the AggRite from American Ash and used it for the paving work, in accordance with the Project Specifications.

Pennsy completed the paving work in December 2001. The pavement ultimately developed extensive cracking in February 2002. The District notified . . . Lobar [ ] as to the defects and Lobar in turn directed Pennsy to remedy the defective work. Pennsy performed the remedial work during summer 2003 at no cost to the District.

The scope and cost of the remedial work included the removal and appropriate disposal of the AggRite, which is classified as a hazardous waste material by the Pennsylvania Department of Environmental Protection. Pennsy requested American Ash to arrange for the removal and disposal of the AggRite; however, American Ash did not do so. Pennsy provided notice to American Ash of its intention to recover costs.

Trial Court Opinion, 5/27/05, at 1-3 (footnote omitted). Pennsy also alleged that the remedial work cost it $251,940.20 to perform and that it expended an additional $133,777.48 to dispose of the AggRite it removed.

On November 18, 2004, Pennsy filed a five-count complaint against American Ash alleging breach of contract (Count I); breach of implied warranty of merchantability (Count II); breach of express warranty of merchantability (Count III); breach of warranty of fitness for a particular purpose (Count IV); and promissory estoppel (Count V). American Ash filed demurrers to all five counts. Pennsy responded and also sought leave to amend should any demurrer be sustained. The trial court sustained the demurrers by order and opinion dated May 25, 2005 and dismissed the complaint. This appeal followed.

Pennsy raises three questions for our review:

(1) Whether the trial court erred in not accepting as true . . . [the] Complaint allegations that (a) [American Ash] promotes the use of its AggRite material, which is classified as hazardous waste, in order to avoid the high cost of disposing [of] the material itself; and (b) [American Ash] incurred a benefit from Pennsy's use of the material in the form of avoidance of the costs of said disposal sufficient to ground contract and warranty claims.

FYI

A "warranty" is a contract term guaranteeing some aspect of the transaction, often the quality of the goods, real estate, or services. A warranty may be express (explicitly articulated by a party to the contract) or implied (added to the express terms by operation of law). The breach of warranty claims in this case (express warranty, implied warranty of merchantability, implied warranty of fitness) are based on UCC Article 2 provisions that establish how promises related to goods are or may be made. In order for the UCC warranty claims to succeed, there must be a *contract* for the *sale of goods* between the parties, as the court discusses later in the opinion.

(2) Whether Pennsy's relief of [American Ash's] legal obligation to dispose of a material classified as hazardous waste, such that [American Ash] avoided the costs of disposal thereof at a hazardous waste site, is sufficient consideration to ground contract and warranty claims.

(3) Whether the trial court misconstrued the well-pled facts of the Complaint in dismissing Pennsy's promissory estoppel claim because Pennsy, according to the court, did not receive [American Ash's] product specifications until after the paving was completed, which was not pled and is not factual.

Appellant's Brief at 3.

"Preliminary objections in the nature of a demurrer test the legal sufficiency of the complaint." *Hospodar v. Schick*, 885 A.2d 986, 988 (Pa.Super.2005).

When reviewing the dismissal of a complaint based upon preliminary objections in the nature of a demurrer, we treat as true all well-pleaded material, factual averments and all inferences fairly deducible therefrom. Where the preliminary objections will result in the dismissal of the action, the objections may be sustained only in cases that are clear and free from doubt. To be clear and free from doubt that dismissal is appropriate, it must appear with certainty that the law would not permit recovery by the plaintiff upon the facts averred. Any doubt should be resolved by a refusal to sustain the objections. Moreover, we review the trial court's decision for an abuse of discretion or an error of law.

Id. In applying this standard to the instant appeal, we deem it easiest to order our discussion by count.

Count I raises a breach of contract claim. "A cause of action for breach of contract must be established by pleading (1) the existence of a contract, including its essential terms, (2) a breach of a duty imposed by the contract and (3) resultant damages." *Corestates Bank, N.A. v. Cutillo*, 723 A.2d 1053, 1058 (Pa. Super.1999). While not every term of a contract must be stated in complete detail, every element must be specifically pleaded. *Id.* at 1058. Clarity is particularly important where an oral contract is alleged. *Snaith v. Snaith*, 282 Pa.Super. 450, 422 A.2d 1379, 1382 (1980).

Instantly, the trial court determined that "any alleged agreement between the parties is unenforceable for lack of consideration." Trial Court Opinion, 5/27/05, at 5. The trial court also stated "the facts as pleaded do not support an inference that disposal costs were part of any bargaining process *or* that American Ash offered the AggRite with an intent to avoid disposal costs." *Id.* at 7 (emphasis added). Thus, we understand the trial court to have dismissed Count I for two reasons related to the necessary element of consideration: one, the allegations of the Complaint established that Pennsy had received a conditional gift from American Ash, *see id.* 6, 8, and, two, there were no allegations in the Complaint to show that American Ash's avoidance of disposal costs was part of any bargaining process between the parties. *See id.* at 7.

It is axiomatic that consideration is "an essential element of an enforceable contract." *Stelmack v. Glen Alden Coal Co.*, 339 Pa. 410, 414-415, 14 A.2d 127, 128 (1940). *See also Weavertown Transport Leasing, Inc. v. Moran*, 834 A.2d 1169, 1172 (Pa.Super.2003) (stating, "[a] contract is formed when the parties to it (1) reach a mutual understanding, (2) exchange consideration, and (3) delineate the terms of their bargain with sufficient clarity."). "Consideration consists of a benefit to the promisor or a detriment to the promisee." *Weavertown*, 834 A.2d at 1172 (citing *Stelmack*). "Consideration must actually be bargained for as the exchange for the promise." *Stelmack*, 339 Pa. at 414, 14 A.2d at 129.

> It is not enough, however, that the promisee has suffered a legal detriment at the request of the promisor. The detriment incurred must be the "quid pro quo", or the "price" of the promise, and the inducement for which it was made . . . . If the promisor merely intends to make a gift to the promisee upon the performance of a condition, the promise is gratuitous and the satisfaction of the condition is not consideration for a contract. The distinction between such a conditional gift and a contract is well illustrated in Williston on Contracts, Rev.Ed., Vol. 1, Section 112, where it is said: "If a benevolent man says to a tramp, 'If you go around the corner to the clothing shop there, you may purchase an overcoat on my credit,' no reasonable person would understand that the short walk was requested as the consideration for the promise, but that in the event of the tramp going to the shop the promisor would make him a gift."

Weavertown, 834 A.2d at 1172 (quoting *Stelmack*, 339 Pa. at 414, 14 A.2d at 128-29). Whether a contract is supported by consideration presents a question of law. *Davis & Warde, Inc. v. Tripodi*, 420 Pa.Super. 450, 616 A.2d 1384 (1992).

The classic formula for the difficult concept of consideration was stated by Justice Oliver Wendell Holmes, Jr. as "the promise must induce the detriment and the detriment must induce the promise." John Edward Murray, Jr., Murray on Contracts § 60 (3d. ed.1990), at 227 (citing *Wisconsin & Michigan Ry. v. Powers*, 191 U.S. 379, 24 S.Ct. 107, 48 L.Ed. 229 (1903)). As explained by Professor Murray:

> If the promisor made the promise for the purpose of inducing the detriment, the detriment induced the promise. If, however, the promisor made the promise with no particular interest in the detriment that the promisee had to suffer to take advantage of the promised gift or other

benefit, the detriment was incidental or conditional to the promisee's receipt of the benefit. Even though the promisee suffered a detriment induced by the promise, the purpose of the promisor was not to have the promisee suffer the detriment because she did not seek that detriment in exchange for her promise.

Id. § 60.C, at 230 (emphasis added). This concept is also well summarized in American Jurisprudence:

> As to the distinction between consideration and a condition, it is often difficult to determine whether words of condition in a promise indicate a request for consideration or state a mere condition in a gratuitous promise. An aid, though not a conclusive test, in determining which construction of the promise is more reasonable is an inquiry into *whether the occurrence of the condition would benefit the promisor. If so, it is a fair inference that the occurrence was requested as consideration.* On the other hand, if the occurrence of the condition is no benefit to the promisor but is merely to enable the promisee to receive a gift, the occurrence of the event on which the promise is conditional, though brought about by the promisee in reliance on the promise, is not properly construed as consideration.

17A Am. Jur.2d § 104 (2004 & 2005 Supp.) (emphasis added). *See also* **Restatement (Second) of Contracts** § 71 comment c (noting "the distinction between bargain and gift may be a fine one, depending on the motives manifested by the parties"); *Carlisle v. T & R Excavating, Inc.,* 123 Ohio App.3d 277, 704 N.E.2d 39 (1997) (discussing the difference between consideration and a conditional gift and finding no consideration where promisor who promised to do excavating work for preschool being built by ex-wife would receive no benefit from wife's reimbursement of his material costs).

Upon review, we disagree with the trial court that the allegations of the Complaint show only that American Ash made a conditional gift of the AggRite to Pennsy. In paragraphs 8 and 9 of the Complaint, Pennsy alleged:

> American Ash actively promotes the use of AggRite as a building material to be used in base course of paved structures, and provides the material free of charge, in an effort to have others dispose of the material and thereby avoid incurring the disposal costs itself . . . American Ash provided the AggRite to Pennsy for use on the Project, which saved American Ash thousands of dollars in disposal costs it otherwise would have incurred.

Compl. ¶¶ 8, 9. Accepting these allegations as true and using the Holmesian formula for consideration, it is a fair interpretation of the Complaint that American Ash's promise to supply AggRite free of charge induced Pennsy to assume the detriment of collecting and taking title to the material, and critically, that it was this very detriment, whether assumed by Pennsy or some other successful bidder to the paving subcontract, which induced American Ash to make the promise to provide free AggRite for the project. Paragraphs 8-9 of the Complaint simply belie the notion that American Ash offered AggRite as a conditional gift to the successful bidder on the paving subcontract for which American Ash desired and expected nothing in return.[4]

We turn now to whether consideration is lacking because Pennsy did not allege that American Ash's avoidance of disposal costs was part of any bargaining process between the parties. The Complaint does not allege that the parties discussed or even that Pennsy understood at the time it requested or accepted the AggRite that Pennsy's use of the AggRite would allow American Ash to avoid disposal costs.[5] However, we do not believe such is necessary.

"The bargain theory of consideration does not actually require that the parties bargain over the terms of the agreement . . . . According to Holmes, an influential advocate of the bargain theory, what is required [for consideration to exist] is that the promise and the consideration be in 'the relation of reciprocal conventional inducement, each for the other.'" E. Allen Farnsworth, Farnsworth on Contracts § 2.6 (1990) (citing O. Holmes, The Common Law 293-94 (1881)); *see also* Restatement (Second) of Contracts § 71 (defining "bargained for" in terms of the Holmesian formula). Here, as explained above, the Complaint alleges facts which, if proven, would show the promise induced the detriment and the detriment induced the promise. This would be consideration. Accordingly, we reverse the dismissal of Count I.

Counts II, III and IV alleged breach of warranty claims under Article 2 of the Uniform Commercial Code ("UCC"). The trial court dismissed these counts as a group upon concluding the facts alleged failed to show a contract for the "sale of goods" as required to trigger application of UCC Article 2. Trial Court Opinion,

---

[4] We understand the contract between Lobar and the District required Lobar to use certain specified base aggregates and permitted the substitution of AggRite for those aggregates. Realistically, however, it is a fair inference from this Complaint that the successful bidder on the paving subcontract could not have used anything other than the free material authorized by Lobar's contract with the District.

[5] Pennsy's complaint, by placing the allegation in ¶ 8 that American Ash promotes AggRite and provides it free of charge, before the allegations in ¶¶ 9-10 related to formation of the oral contract, is arguably structured to suggest Pennsy did contemplate American Ash's avoidance of disposal costs. We note also that during oral argument on the preliminary objections, Pennsy's counsel represented "it was understood by everybody that this [i.e., avoidance of disposal costs] was what American Ash was getting in return for [providing the AggRite for free]." Transcript of Proceedings, Feb. 1, 2005, at 14-15.

5/27/05, at 8 (concluding, "the transaction as pleaded, by which American Ash gave Pennsy free AggRite, amounted to a conditional gift, not a contract of sale"). Again, we disagree that the allegations reveal a transaction that can only be characterized as a conditional gift. We turn now to whether the allegations otherwise trigger application of Article 2.

Article 2 applies to "transactions in goods." 13 Pa.C.S.A. § 2102. AggRite is obviously a good. *See* 13 Pa.C.S.A. § 2105 (defining "goods" as "all things (including specially manufactured goods) which are moveable at the time of identification to the contract."). Before the protections of the Article 2 warranties apply, "there must be a sale of goods." *Turney Media Fuel, Inc. v. Toll Bros., Inc.*, 725 A.2d 836, 840 (Pa.Super.1999). *See also Whitmer v. Bell Tele. Co. of Pennsylvania*, 361 Pa.Super. 282, 522 A.2d 584, 588 (1987) (stating, "[a] prerequisite to an action for breach of warranty [under Article 2] is that there must be a *sale*.") (quoting *Williams v. West Penn Power Co.*, 313 Pa.Super. 461, 460 A.2d 278, 281 (1983), *modified*, 502 Pa. 557, 467 A.2d 811 (1983)).

"A sale [under Article 2] consists in the passing of title from the seller to the buyer for a price." 13 Pa.C.S.A. § 2106 (parenthetical reference omitted).[6] Section 2-304, entitled "Price payable in money, goods, realty or otherwise," provides in subsection (a) that as a general rule "[t]he price can be made payable in money or otherwise." 13 Pa.C.S.A. § 2304. Pennsy argues that its acquisition of the AggRite whereby American Ash was relieved of disposal costs can constitute a price within the meaning of the "or otherwise" language in 13 Pa.C.S.A. § 2304. We agree. The few courts to have interpreted the "or otherwise" language of a UCC provision like ours have concluded that it includes any consideration sufficient to ground a contract. *See Mortimer B. Burnside & Co. v. Havener Securities Corp.*, 25 A.D.2d 373, 269 N.Y.S.2d 724 (1966) (citing UCC § 2-304 generally); *Wheeler v. Sunbelt Tool Co., Inc.*, 181 Ill.App.3d 1088, 130 Ill.Dec. 863, 537 N.E.2d 1332 (applying Illinois version of UCC), *appeal denied*, 127 Ill.2d 644, 136 Ill.Dec. 610, 545 N.E.2d 134 (1989); *see also* William D. Hawkland, 2 UNIFORM COMMERCIAL CODE SERIES § 2-304:3 (1998) (stating, "the entire thrust of section 2-304 seems to be toward making the scope of Article 2 as broad as possible, limited only by due concern for the laws governing the disposition of real property.") (footnote omitted); *see also Hoffman v. Misericordia Hosp.*, 439 Pa. 501, 507-08, 267 A.2d 867, 870-71 (1970) (noting our Supreme Court has implied warranty protections in non-sales transactions, such as leases and bailments, and reversing lower court decision to dismiss warranty counts on demurrer in action involving blood transfusion). While we recognize Article 2 does not always apply simply because a transfer of goods is not a gift, . . . we believe the present situation falls within the scope

---

[6] A true gift of a good is not a "sale" because, although title may pass between the parties to the transaction, there is no price.

of the warranty provisions as intended by the drafters. *See Hoffman,* 439 Pa. at 508, 267 A.2d at 870-71 (faulting lower court for failing to consider whether the warranty policies would be furthered by their implication). This is not a situation where garbage is left on the curb for anyone to retrieve. *Contra Grigsby v. Crown Cork & Seal Co.,* 574 F.Supp. 128 (D.Del.1983) (predicting Delaware Supreme Court would find a sale of goods under Delaware's version of UCC 2-304 but not extend Article 2 warranties in situation where defendant abandoned waste oil to plaintiff because defendant "did not warrant the merchantability or fitness of its waste . . . any more than an ordinary citizen warrants the merchantability or fitness of his or her garbage at the time of a garbage collection"). Here, as Pennsy alleged:

> American Ash actively promotes the use of AggRite as a building material to be used in base course of paved structures . . . .

> American Ash's technical data sheets [attached as Ex. H to the Complaint], describing AggRite, indicate that it can be used as a roadbed material meeting the requirements of PennDOT specifications.

> American Ash's literature [attached as Ex. H to the Complaint] also indicates that AggRite can be used as a replacement for type 2A aggregate base course material.

Compl. ¶¶ 8, 47-48. On these facts, we cannot say the law would clearly preclude recovery on Counts II, III and IV, and, accordingly, we reverse the grant of the demurrer to the extent dismissal of these counts was based on Pennsy's failure to allege a sale of goods.

. . . .

For all of the foregoing reasons, we reverse the trial court's order granting the demurrers and dismissing the Complaint and remand for further proceedings. Jurisdiction relinquished.

———————————

Scope of Article 2 and the CISG:
"Transaction in Goods"/"Sale of Goods"

Pennsy is the first case we have seen that addresses the question whether a particular controversy falls within the scope of UCC Article 2 and is therefore governed, at least in part, by its provisions. As discussed in the case, UCC § 2-102 establishes that Article 2 applies to "transactions in goods." Although a few of the statutory sections apply to transactions other than sales, the language of almost all of the provisions, including the warranty provisions, limits coverage to contracts for "sales" of "goods." Whether a dispute is governed by Article 2 therefore depends on whether the transaction involves a contract for "sale" (§ 2-106: "passing of title from the seller to the buyer for a price") and whether it involves "goods" (§ 2-105: "all things . . . which are moveable at the time of identification to the contract"). Sales are distinguished from transactions such as leases, gifts, and mortgages. Goods are distinguished from contract subjects such as real property and intangibles (e.g., good will or data).

Article 2 coverage matters only when Article 2 and the common law rules would yield different results in a case. In *Pennsy,* the scope of Article 2 was not relevant to determine whether there was consideration to support the promise made because Article 2 contains no definition of consideration. The scope of Article 2 *was* relevant, however, to determine whether the Article 2 warranty provisions applied, leading the court to determine whether there was a "sale" of goods through Pennsy's payment of a "price" in return for title to American Ash's goods (the Aggrite).

The most difficult questions about the scope of Article 2 are raised when a transaction involves both a sale of goods and some other kind of transaction. For example, does Article 2 govern a purchase of carpeting that involves a sale of goods but also installation of those goods? Does it govern the hiring of a mechanic to replace one's car brakes, which involves both providing labor and selling parts? In such cases, courts apply the "predominant purpose" test; they look at the mixed contracts and ask "whether their predominant factor, their thrust, their purpose, reasonably stated, is the rendition of service, with goods incidentally involved (e.g., contract with artist for painting) or is a transaction of sale, with labor incidentally involved (e.g., installation of a water heater in a bathroom)," *Bonebrake v. Cox,* 499 F.2d 951 (8th Cir. 1974). In determining the predominant purpose, courts consider a variety of factors, including the language of the contract (how does it talk about the parties' relationship and their performance responsibilities?), the primary reason the parties entered the contract, the relative costs of the goods and services, the nature of the provider's business (primarily a goods merchant or a service provider?), and any other circumstances relevant to determining the "predominant purpose" behind the contract. *See, e.g., Pass v. Shelby Aviation, Inc.,* 2000 WL 388775 (Tenn. Ct. App. Apr. 13, 2000).

Examples of cases finding primarily a contract for sale of goods and therefore Article 2 coverage include *Pittsley v. Houser,* 875 P.2d 232

(Idaho Ct. App. 1994) (sale and installation of carpet); *Neibarger v. Universal Cooperatives, Inc.*, 486 N.W.2d 612 (Mich. 1992) (sale of milking system); and *True North Composites, LLC v. Trinity Industries, Inc.*, 65 Fed. App. 266 (Fed. Cir. 2003) (contract for custom design and manufacture of railcars). Examples of cases finding primarily a sale of services and therefore no Article 2 coverage include *Pass v. Shelby Aviation, Inc.*, 2000 WL 388775 (Tenn. Ct. App.) (contract to repair and service airplane); *Higgins v. Lauritzen*, 530 N.W.2d 171 (Mich. Ct. App. 1995) (contract for installation of a water system); *Care Display, Inc. v. Didde-Glaser, Inc.*, 589 P.2d 599 (Kan. 1979) (contract for custom design and construction of themed booths for trade fair); and *Heuerman v. B&M Construction, Inc.*, 833 N.E.2d 382 (Ill. Ct. App. 2005) (contract with trucking company to deliver gravel).

While UCC Article 2 applies to all sales of goods, whether the parties are individuals or merchants and no matter what kinds of goods are involved in the transaction, the United Nations Convention on Contracts for the International Sale of Goods (CISG) applies only to merchants and does not apply to sales of goods bought for personal, family, or household use, unless the seller did not know and had no reason to know the goods were intended for such restricted purposes. *See* CISG Article 2. The CISG has its own version of the predominant purpose test; it does not apply to "contracts in which the preponderant part of the obligations of the party who furnishes the goods consists in the supply of labour or other services" or when the party supplying goods has manufactured them from materials provided by the buyer, thereby acting more as an assembler than as a seller of the goods. CISG Article 3.

Problems: Distinguishing Bargain from Gift

2-13. Kathleen Irving entered a contract with Connie Beale, an interior designer. Under the contract, Beale was to present ideas for new furniture, re-upholstery, window coverings, wall coverings, fabrics, and floor covers for Irving's project. The contract specified that Beale was responsible for "developing an ambience, choosing a color scheme, and suggesting architectural changes" to make the project successful. After receiving Beale's design suggestions, Irving was to identify approved items. Beale would then order the furnishings at the wholesale price available to professional decorators. Beale was to bill Irving for each item, for the wholesale price plus a 20% mark-up. Beale's work on the project was to be compensated only through the 20% mark-up.

When a dispute arose, Irving filed suit, claiming a breach of several UCC Article 2 provisions. Beale moves to strike the Article 2 claims, arguing that the contract does not fall within the scope of Article 2. How should the court rule?

2-14. In *Weavertown Transport Leasing, Inc. v. Moran,* 834 A.2d 1169 (Pa. Super. 2003), the court recited the following facts:

> In July of 2000, Daniel Moran (Moran), a certified public accountant, accepted employment as controller for Appellee-Plaintiff Weavertown Transport Leasing, Inc. (Weavertown or Company). That summer, the Pittsburgh Steelers National Football League franchise (Steelers) prepared to relocate from Three Rivers Stadium to its new home, Heinz Field. Moran, a long-time season ticket-holder to Steelers' home games at Three Rivers Stadium, was offered four season tickets to Heinz Field comparable to his seats at Three Rivers Stadium as well as the opportunity to secure additional seats. Moran paid $11,000 for thirty-year licenses to the four seats that corresponded to his former seats. He also agreed to purchase seven-year licenses to four Club-Level seats, which cost $3,840. The purchase agreements precluded Moran from selling or transferring his licenses to another party for at least one year after purchase, but allowed for transfer thereafter.

> While these transactions took place, Moran began employment as Weavertown's controller. Soon after his arrival, he learned through Weavertown's President, Dawn Fuchs-Heiser, that the Company sought full ownership of season tickets to Heinz Field to entertain its clients. These tickets would augment the Company's season tickets to see the Pittsburgh Penguins (National Hockey League) at Mellon Arena and the Pittsburgh Pirates (Major League Baseball) at PNC Park. In prior years, the Company had purchased tickets to many Steelers home games on a per-game basis from another holder of season tickets.

Assume the following additional hypothetical facts:

Moran approached Fuchs-Heiser and said, "I know you want a place to entertain clients, and I have eight season tickets, half on the club level. If you'll pay the fees, you can use the club-level seats." Fuchs-Heiser was delighted and gave to Moran company checks made out to the Steelers for $3840 (the license fee) and $5804 (the cost of the seats for 2001/2002). Moran forwarded the checks to the Steelers. The company used the seats through the 2001/2002 season.

On May 11, 2001, before the Steelers began their first season at Heinz Field, Moran resigned his position with Weavertown, but he did not interfere with Weavertown's use of the seats throughout that season. After the 2001/2002 NFL playoffs, in the spring of 2002, Fuchs-Heiser asked Moran to transfer the seat licenses to Weavertown, since a year had passed after purchase. Moran refused, claiming he made no promise and, even if he did, there was no consideration for it. He also offered to repay Weavertown 6/7 of the license fee.

Is Moran right? Was there consideration for Moran's alleged promise to transfer the seat licenses?

2-15. In *Stelmack v. Glen Alden Coal Co.*, 14 A.2d 127 (Pa. 1940), Stelmack purchased a plot of land on which there was a building containing stores and residential apartments. The deed was made subject to certain reservations and conditions respecting the mineral rights in the land held by Glen Alden Coal Company, which appeared in prior conveyances in the chain of title of the property and were required to be continued with each subsequent sale of the property. Under the clauses in the deed, the owner of the mineral rights (Glen Alden) was not liable for any injury or damage to the surface of the property or to the buildings on the property that might be caused by mining or removal of coal and minerals. According to the deed, it was expressly understood that the value and price of the property was reduced to reflect the possibility that damage could be caused by the mining operations, without compensation to the owner of the property.

Five years after the purchase, Stelmack was informed by Glen Alden that mining was about to begin under the property, and that the operations would cause a "subsidence of the soil" (that is, the soil would sink as the result of mining and the building would likely be damaged). Glen Alden and Stelmack agreed that, if Stelmack would permit company employees to enter the land and prop up the building to minimize damage to the structure, the company would make all repairs necessary to restore the property to its original condition.

Stelmack permitted ties and supports to be erected around the building, which were something of an eyesore and allegedly resulted in loss of rents. Mining continued for five years, with Glen Alden making repairs to the property from time to time. Continued subsidence of the soil occurred, however, and Stelmack determined that additional work would be required, at a considerable cost, to restore the land and building to its previous condition. Glen Alden refused to do the additional work or provide funds to Stelmack to have the work done.

Stelmack seeks to enforce Glen Alden's promise to restore the building to its original condition. Is that promise enforceable (that is, was there consideration for Glen Alden's promise to repair the building)? If consideration were found, would the resulting contract fall within the scope of Article 2 of the UCC?

§ 5. What "Counts" as Consideration

Reading the Law Critically:
Appeal of Clark, Batsakis, Schnell, and Questar

The following cases add nuance to the definition of consideration by exploring what will "count" as consideration.

1. As you read each case, identify (a) the promise that the court is asked to enforce, (b) the consideration that is alleged, (c) whether or not the court finds consideration existed, and (d) the rationale for that conclusion.

2. What propositions can you derive from the cases to enhance your understanding of consideration? Are those propositions consistent with the
Restatement (Second) definition of consideration and with the definitions used in the cases in earlier sections?

3. Are all of these cases consistent with one another?

Appeal of Clark

APPEAL OF CLARK

Supreme Court of Errors of Connecticut
19 A. 332 (Conn. 1889)

[The facts of this case appear in Problem 2-12 on page 56. Recall that Sheldon
Clark executed a promissory note for $700 in favor of Charles Clark. The note
said it was "for value received." After reciting the facts, including a description
of the services rendered to Sheldon by Charles and his wife, the opinion of Chief
Justice Andrews continued:]

We think the note was made on sufficient consideration. Prof. John William
Smith, in his Lectures on the Law of Contracts, in answer to the question, "What
does the law recognize as a consideration capable of supporting a simple contract?" gives this short practical rule: "Any benefit accruing to him who makes the
promise, or any loss, trouble, or disadvantage undergone by or charge imposed
upon him to whom the promise is made, is a sufficient consideration in the eye
of the law to sustain the promise." And he adds: "Accordingly, in the absence of
fraud, mere inadequacy of consideration is no ground for avoiding a contract."
Smith, Cont. 141, 148. Judge Storrs, in *Clark v. Sigourney*, 17 Conn. 517, says:
"Any act done by the promisee at the request of the promisor, by which the former
sustains any loss, trouble, or inconvenience, constitutes a sufficient consideration
for a promise, although the latter obtains no advantage therefrom; and in respect
to the extent of such loss, trouble, or inconvenience it is immaterial that it is of
the most trifling description, provided it be not utterly worthless in fact and in
law." See, also, *Barnum v. Barnum*, 8 Conn. 469. "A valuable consideration, in
the sense of the law, may consist either in some right, interest, profit, or benefit
accruing to the one party, or some forbearance, detriment, loss, or responsibility
given, suffered, or undertaken by the other." *Currie v. Misa*, L. R. 10 Exch. 162.
"If the parties, being in a situation and having the ability to do so, have exercised
their own independent judgment as to the value of the subject-matter, courts of
equity should not and will not interfere with such valuation." Pom. Eq. Jur. §
926. "In the absence of . . . fraud, . . . inadequacy of consideration is not sufficient
to avoid a contract, even in equity." *Bedel v. Loomis*, 11 N. H. 19. Chancellor

Kent, in *Osgood v. Franklin*, 2 Johns. Ch. 1, says: "There is no case where mere inadequacy of price, independent of other circumstances, has been held sufficient to set aside a sale made between parties standing on equal ground, and dealing with each other without any imposition or oppression." "Inadequacy of consideration is not, then, of itself, a distinct principle of relief in equity. The common law knows no such principle. The consideration, be it more or less, supports the contract." 1 Story, Eq. Jur. § 245. See, also, *Warner v. Daniels*, 1 Woodb. & M. 110; *Train v. Gold*, 5 Pick. 380; *Boothe v. Fitzpatrick*, 36 Vt. 681.

The case of *Worth v. Case*, 42 N. Y. 362, is a case very similar in many respects to the one now in hand. It was brought against the defendant as the executor of Theron B. Worth, on a note for $10,000. The plaintiff and Theron were sister and brother. The plaintiff resided in Corning, not keeping house, but living in a furnished room. Theron lived in Southold. He visited the plaintiff at her residence several times. At a visit in January, 1864, he was very ill there. She gave up her room and bed to him, and he spent his entire time in them. She nursed him, bathed him, and rubbed his limbs every morning during his sickness. She also brought his meals to him from the hotel, and rendered other attention to him while he was sick. He paid the bill at the hotel, but paid her nothing for her service. Several times during his stay he spoke to her about paying her, and said he would pay her well. On the day he left her house, January 30, 1864, he handed her a sealed envelope indorsed: "Mary C. Worth. This is not to be unsealed while I live, and to be returned to me at any time I may wish it. T. B. WORTH." The plaintiff was not informed and did not know what the envelope contained until she opened it after her brother's death, in 1867, and found in it the note on which the suit was brought. Theron left a will by which he gave to the plaintiff the sum of $1,000. The plaintiff had a verdict for the amount of the note; in sustaining which the court of appeals said: The note was given for services rendered, and, if the note speaks truly, he then considered those attentions worth $10,000. "He chose for these services to execute the note. We have no pecuniary standard by which we can weigh or measure their value to him. He estimated them then, and continued to do so, at $10,000; and those who stand in his shoes have no right to repudiate the contract which he made." *Dean v. Carruth*, 108 Mass. 242, is another case of like kind. The case of *Wolford v. Powers*, 85 Ind. 294, was brought on a promissory note executed in consideration of a father's naming a child after the promisor, and in pursuance of the promisor's agreement that if the child were so named he would provide for its education and support. It was held that this was a valid consideration. In delivering the opinion the court said: "When a party contracts for the performance of an act which will afford him pleasure, gratify his ambition, please his fancy, or express his appreciation of a service another has done him, his estimate of value should be left undisturbed, unless there is evidence of fraud. There is in such a case absolutely no rule by which the courts can be guided, if once they depart from the value fixed by the promisor. If they attempt to fix some standard, it must necessarily be an arbitrary one, and ascertained only by mere conjecture. If, in the class of cases mentioned, there is any legal consideration for a promise, it must be sufficient for the one made; for, if this is not so, then the result is that the court substitutes its own judgment for that of the promisor, and in doing this makes a new contract. When the purpose of the party is to secure a pecuniary or property benefit, there is much more ground for judicial interference than in a case like this, where the controlling purpose is not gain, but the gratification of a desire or fancy. Even in the former class of cases, courts never do interfere upon the sole ground of inadequacy of consideration, and certainly should not in the class to which the one at bar belongs. No person in the world, other than the promisor, can estimate the value of an act which arouses his gratitude, gratifies his ambition, or pleases his fancy. If there be any consideration at all, it must be allotted the value the parties have placed upon it; or a conjectural estimate made arbitrarily, and without the semblance of a guide, must be substituted by the courts." *Earl v. Peck*, 64 N. Y., 596, was a case brought on a note for $10,000 executed by the defendant's testator. The plaintiff had been in the service of the deceased for some six or seven years as his housekeeper, and he was indebted to her for her services. The note was made only about two hours before his death. No contract had been made as to the rate of compensation for the services, but the deceased had said he would pay her well, and the evidence tended to show that the amount of compensation was to be left to him. The court said: "Mere inadequacy of consideration, except as a circumstance bearing upon the question of fraud, . . . is not a defense to a note. It is not necessary that the consideration of a note shall be equal in pecuniary value to the obligation incurred." See, also, *Cowee v. Cornell*, 75 N. Y. 91.

The services rendered by Charles Clark and his wife to Sheldon Clark, and for which this note is the promise to pay, if they should be drawn out on a book in the form of an account, with times and dates, and the thing done, and prices, might not amount to $700. But to Sheldon Clark, alone in the world, unmarried, without family or near kindred to make a home for him, sick of a wasting disease, who can measure their value so well as he? He put his own estimate upon them, deliberately and without "speck of imposition." If he chose to pay for the services rendered a much larger sum than they were apparently worth, he had the right to do so. The note was not a gratuity or a testamentary gift. There is no standard whereby courts can limit the measure of value in such a case; and the note is not wanting, even partially, in consideration, because the value of the consideration is less than the obligation. The superior court is advised to render judgment for the appellant to recover of the estate of Sheldon Clark the amount of the note.

The other judges concurred.

Batsakis v. Demotsis

GEORGE BATSAKIS, Plaintiff-Appellant

v.

EUGENIA DEMOTSIS, Defendant-Appellee

Court of Civil Appeals of Texas

226 S.W.2d 673 (Tex. Civ. App. 1949)

McGILL, Justice.

This is an appeal from a judgment of the 57th Judicial District Court of Bexar County. Appellant was plaintiff and appellee was defendant in the trial court. The parties will be so designated.

Plaintiff sued defendant to recover $2,000 with interest at the rate of 8% per annum from April 2, 1942, alleged to be due on the following instrument, being a translation from the original, which is written in the Greek language:

"Peiraeus
April 2, 1942
"Mr. George Batsakis
Konstantinou Diadohou #7
Peiraeus
"Mr. Batsakis:

"I state by my present (letter) that I received today from you the amount of two thousand dollars ($2,000.00) of United States of America money, which I borrowed from you for the support of my family during these difficult days and because it is impossible for me to transfer dollars of my own from America.

"The above amount I accept with the expressed promise that I will return to you again in American dollars either at the end of the present war or even before in the event that you might be able to find a way to collect them (dollars) from my representative in America to whom I shall write and give him an order relative to this. You understand until the final execution (payment) to the above amount an eight per cent interest will be added and paid together with the principal.

"I thank you and I remain yours with respects.

"The recipient,
(Signed) Eugenia The. Demotsis."

Trial to the court without the intervention of a jury resulted in a judgment in favor of plaintiff for $750.00 principal, and interest at the rate of 8% per annum from April 2, 1942 to the date of judgment, totaling $1163.83, with interest thereon at the rate of 8% per annum until paid. Plaintiff has perfected his appeal.

. . . .

The answer . . . consisted of a general denial contained in paragraph I thereof, and of paragraph IV, which is as follows:

> "IV. That under the circumstances alleged in Paragraph II of this answer, the consideration upon which said written instrument sued upon by plaintiff herein is founded, is wanting and has failed to the extent of $1975.00, and defendant pleads specially under the verification hereinafter made the want and failure of consideration stated, and now tenders, as defendant has heretofore tendered to plaintiff, $25.00 as the value of the loan of money received by defendant from plaintiff, together with interest thereon.

> "Further, in connection with this plea of want and failure of consideration defendant alleges that she at no time received from plaintiff himself or from anyone for plaintiff any money or thing of value other than, as hereinbefore alleged, the original loan of 500,000 drachmae. That at the time of the loan by plaintiff to defendant of said 500,000 drachmae the value of 500,000 drachmae in the Kingdom of Greece in dollars of money of the United States of America, was $25.00, and also at said time the value of 500,000 drachmae of Greek money in the United States of America in dollars was $25.00 of money of the United States of America. The plea of want and failure of consideration is verified by defendant as follows."

The allegations in paragraph II [of the answer] which were stricken, referred to in paragraph IV, were that the instrument sued on was signed and delivered in the Kingdom of Greece on or about April 2, 1942, at which time both plaintiff and defendant were residents of and residing in the Kingdom of Greece, and

> "*Plaintiff* (emphasis ours) avers that on or about April 2, 1942 she [defendant Demotsis] owned money and property and had credit in the United States of America, but was then and there in the Kingdom of Greece in straitened financial circumstances due to the conditions produced by World War II and could not make use of her money and property and credit existing in the United States of America. That in the circumstances the plaintiff agreed to and did lend to defendant the sum of 500,000 drachmae, which at that time, on or about April 2, 1942, had the value of $25.00 in money of the United States of America. That the

said plaintiff, knowing defendant's financial distress and desire to return to the United States of America, exacted of her the written instrument plaintiff sues upon, which was a promise by her to pay to him the sum of $2,000.00 of United States of America money."

Plaintiff specially excepted to paragraph IV because the allegations thereof were insufficient to allege either want of consideration or failure of consideration, in that it affirmatively appears there from that defendant received what was agreed to be delivered to her, and that plaintiff breached no agreement. The court overruled this exception, and such action is assigned as error. Error is also assigned because of the court's failure to enter judgment for the whole unpaid balance of the principal of the instrument with interest as therein provided.

Defendant testified that she did receive 500,000 drachmas from plaintiff. It is not clear whether she received all the 500,000 drachmas or only a portion of them before she signed the instrument in question. Her testimony clearly shows that the understanding of the parties was that plaintiff would give her the 500,000 drachmas if she would sign the instrument. She testified:

"Q. . . . . who suggested the figure of $2,000.00?

A. That was how he asked me from the beginning. He said he will give me five hundred thousand drachmas provided I signed that I would pay him $2,000.00 American money."

Behind the Scenes

Why would Demotsis make the contract described in the case, in effect receiving $25 but promising to repay $2000? Why was the contract written as it was? Although we do not know details of the particular transaction, we do know the broader context for the agreement. The contract was entered about one year after the German invasion of Greece during World War II. The occupation of Greece was especially harsh, resulting in plummeting employment, skyrocketing inflation, extreme food shortages, and a thriving black market. There were thousands of deaths due to starvation. *See* Mark Mazzower, *Inside Hitler's Greece: The Experience of Occupation 1941-44* (1993). Do these facts affect your understanding of the contract, the validity of the holding, or the meaning of the case?

The transaction amounted to a sale by plaintiff of the 500,000 drachmas in consideration of the execution of the instrument sued on, by defendant. It is not contended that the drachmas had no value. Indeed, the judgment indicates that the trial court placed a value of $750.00 on them or on the other consideration which plaintiff gave defendant for the instrument if he believed plaintiff's testimony. Therefore the plea of want of consideration was unavailing. A plea of want of consideration amounts to a contention that the instrument never became a valid obligation in the first place. *National Bank of Commerce v. Williams*, 125 Tex. 619, 84 S.W.2d 691.

Mere inadequacy of consideration will not void a contract. 10 Tex.Jur., Contracts, Sec. 89, p. 150; *Chastain v. Texas Christian Missionary Society*, Tex.Civ. App., 78 S.W.2d 728, loc. cit. 731(3), Wr. Ref.

Nor was the plea of failure of consideration availing. Defendant got exactly what she contracted for according to her own testimony. The court should have rendered judgment in favor of plaintiff against defendant for the principal sum of $2,000.00 evidenced by the instrument sued on, with interest as therein provided. We construe the provision relating to interest as providing for interest at the rate of 8% per annum. The judgment is reformed so as to award appellant a recovery against appellee of $2,000.00 with interest thereon at the rate of 8% per annum from April 2, 1942. Such judgment will bear interest at the rate of 8% per annum until paid on $2,000.00 thereof and on the balance interest at the rate of 6% per annum. As so reformed, the judgment is affirmed.

Food for Thought

Recall the *Meadors* court's suggestion (page 43) to "drop the mask and do justice openly." How would you follow that admonition if seeking relief for Demotsis in light of the principles articulated here and in *Appeal of Clark?*

Reformed and affirmed.

———————————

Schnell v. Nell

ZACHARIAS SCHNELL, Defendant-Appellant

v.

J.B. NELL, Plaintiff-Appellee

Supreme Court of Indiana
17 Ind. 29, 1861 WL 2779 (1861)

PERKINS, J.

Action by *J. B. Nell* against *Zacharias Schnell,* upon the following instrument:

"This agreement, entered into this 13th day of *February,* 1856, between *Zach. Schnell,* of *Indianapolis, Marion* county, State of *Indiana,* as party of the first part, and *J. B. Nell*, of the same place, *Wendelin Lorenz*, of *Stilesville*, *Hendricks* county, State of *Indiana*, and *Donata Lorenz*, of *Frickinger, Grand Duchy of Baden, Germany*, as parties of the second part, witnesseth: The said *Zacharias Schnell* agrees as follows:

whereas his wife, *Theresa Schnell*, now deceased, has made a last will and testament, in which, among other provisions, it was ordained that every one of the above named second parties, should receive the sum of $200;

and whereas the said provisions of the will must remain a nullity, for the reason that no property, real or personal, was in the possession of the said *Theresa Schnell*, deceased, in her own name, at the time of her death, and all property held by *Zacharias* and *Theresa Schnell* jointly, therefore reverts to her husband;

and whereas the said *Theresa Schnell* has also been a dutiful and loving wife to the said *Zach. Schnell*, and has materially aided him in the acquisition of all property, real and personal, now possessed by him;

for, and in consideration of all this, and the love and respect he bears to his wife; and, furthermore, in consideration of one cent, received by him of the second parties,

he, the said *Zach. Schnell*, agrees to pay the above named sums of money to the parties of the second part, to wit: $200 to the said *J. B. Nell*; $200 to the said *Wendelin Lorenz*; and $200 to the said *Donata Lorenz*, in the following installments, viz., $200 in one year from the date of these presents; $200 in two years, and $200 in three years; to be divided between the parties in equal portions of $66⅔ each year, or as they may agree, till each one has received his full sum of $200.

And the said parties of the second part, for, and in consideration of this, agree to pay the above named sum of money [one cent], and to deliver up to said *Schnell*, and abstain from collecting any real or supposed claims upon him or his estate, arising from the said last will and testament of the said *Theresa Schnell*, deceased.

In witness whereof, the said parties have, on this 13th day of *February,* 1856, set hereunto their hands and seals.

ZACHARIAS SCHNELL, [SEAL]
J.B. NELL [SEAL]
WEN. LORENZ. [SEAL]"

The complaint contained no averment of a consideration for the instrument, outside of those expressed in it; and did not aver that the one cent agreed to be paid, had been paid or tendered.

A demurrer to the complaint was overruled.

The defendant answered, that the instrument sued on was given for no consideration whatever.

He further answered, that it was given for no consideration, because his said wife, *Theresa,* at the time she made the will mentioned, and at the time of her death, owned, neither separately, nor jointly with her husband, or any one else (except so far as the law gave her an interest in her husband's property), any property, real or personal, &c. . . .

The Court sustained a demurrer to these answers, evidently on the ground that they were regarded as contradicting the instrument sued on, which particularly set out the considerations upon which it was executed. . . .

The case turned below, and must turn here, upon the question whether the instrument sued on does express a consideration sufficient to give it legal obligation, as against *Zacharias Schnell.* * It specifies three distinct considerations for his promise to pay $600:

1. A promise, on the part of the plaintiffs, to pay him one cent.

2. The love and affection he bore his deceased wife, and the fact that she had done her part, as his wife, in the acquisition of property.

3. The fact that she had expressed her desire, in the form of an inoperative will, that the persons named therein should have the sums of money specified.

The consideration of one cent will not support the promise of *Schnell.* It is true, that as a general proposition, inadequacy of consideration will not vitiate an agreement. *Baker v. Roberts,* 14 Ind. 552. But this doctrine does not apply to a mere exchange of sums of money, of coin, whose value is exactly fixed, but to the exchange of something of, in itself, indeterminate value, for money, or, perhaps, for some other thing of indeterminate value. In this case, had the one cent mentioned, been some particular one cent, a family piece, or ancient, remarkable coin, possessing an indeterminate value, extrinsic from its simple money value, a differ-

---

* [Authors' Note: As discussed earlier in this chapter, consideration was traditionally *not* required if a promise was made in a document under seal. That rule appears to have applied in Indiana around the time of the *Schnell* decision (*see Gregory v. Logan,* 1844 WL 2909 (May 1844)), so it is curious that the court did not rely upon it and therefore enforce the promise made without looking for consideration.]

ent view might be taken. As it is, the mere promise to pay six hundred dollars for one cent, even had the portion of that cent due from the plaintiff been tendered, is an unconscionable contract, void, at first blush, upon its face, if it be regarded as an earnest one. *Hardesty v. Smith*, 3 Ind. 39. The consideration of one cent is, plainly, in this case, merely nominal, and intended to be so.

Think About It!

The court says the proposition that "inadequacy of consideration will not vitiate an agreement" does not apply to "a mere exchange of sums of money, of coin whose value is exactly fixed." Can this statement and the result in *Schnell* be reconciled with *Batsakis*? What does the court mean when it says, "The consideration of one cent is . . . merely nominal . . . ."?

As the will and testament of *Schnell's* wife imposed no legal obligation upon him to discharge her bequests out of his property, and as she had none of her own, his promise to discharge them was not legally binding upon him, on that ground. A moral consideration, only, will not support a promise. Ind. Dig., p. 13. And for the same reason, a valid consideration for his promise can not be found in the fact of a compromise of a disputed claim; for where such claim is legally groundless, a promise upon a compromise of it, or of a suit upon it, is not legally binding. *Spahr v. Hollingshead*, 8 Blackf. 415. There was no mistake of law or fact in this case, as the agreement admits the will inoperative and void. The promise was simply one to make a gift.

The past services of his wife, and the love and affection he had borne her, are objectionable as legal considerations for *Schnell's* promise, on two grounds:

1. They are past considerations. Ind. Dig., p. 13.

2. The fact that *Schnell* loved his wife, and that she had been industrious, constituted no consideration for his promise to pay *J. B. Nell*, and the *Lorenzes,* a sum of money. Whether, if his wife, in her lifetime, had made a bargain with *Schnell,* that, in consideration of his promising to pay, after her death, to the persons named, a sum of money, she would be industrious, and worthy of his affection, such a promise would have been valid and consistent with public policy, we need not decide. Nor is the fact that *Schnell* now venerates the memory of his deceased wife, a legal consideration for a promise to pay any third person money.

The instrument sued on, interpreted in the light of the facts alleged in the second paragraph of the answer, will not support an action. The demurrer to the answer should have been overruled. See *Stevenson v. Druley,* 4 Ind. 519.

The judgment is reversed, with costs. Cause remanded &c.

Questar Builders, Inc. v. CB Flooring, LLC

QUESTAR BUILDERS, INC., Defendant-Appellant

v.

CB FLOORING, LLC., Plaintiff-Appellee

Maryland Court of Appeals
978 A.2d 651 (Md. App. 2009)

HARRELL, J.

Questar Builders, Inc. ("Questar") is a general contractor hired to construct a luxury midrise apartment and townhome complex known as Greenwich Place at Town Center ("Greenwich Place") in Owings Mills, Maryland. After receiving bids from three flooring subcontractors, Questar selected CB Flooring, LLC ("CB Flooring") to install carpeting at Greenwich Place for a total price of $1,120,000. Another bidder, Creative Touch Interiors ("CTI") submitted a proposal to complete the project for a total price of $1,240,000;[1] however, Questar rejected that bid in favor of CB Flooring's lower bid. On 29 September 2005, Questar and CB Flooring entered an agreement (the "Subcontract"), pursuant to which CB Flooring agreed to "[f]urnish all labor, materials, equipment and services necessary for and incidental to the execution and completion of all carpet and resilient flooring" for the project's 120 garage townhomes and 212 apartments, as well as its common areas and storage rooms, in exchange for $1,120,000. The Subcontract provided that the agreement was to remain effective "through [ ] DURATION OF THE PROJECT."

The focal point of this litigation concerns Paragraphs 12 and 14 of the Subcontract. Paragraph 12 provided in pertinent part:

Breach: Failure of Subcontractor to perform Work in accordance with each and every term and provision of this Subcontract shall be deemed to be a breach of this Subcontract. In the event of any breach, Contractor may avail itself of any or all of the following remedies: ... (d) to terminate this Subcontract by written notice and take over all or any work tools, equipment, materials and, which shall be effective upon receipt by Subcontractor, supplies of Subcontractor and complete the Work by whatever means Contractor deems appropriate, whereupon Subcontractor shall receive no further payments until the work is completed and shall be fully liable for any costs in excess of the

---

[1] Questar maintains in the present litigation that these prices do not reflect accurately the closeness of the bids of CB Flooring and CTI. According to the general contractor, CTI's bid of $1,240,000 included items not reflected in CB Flooring's bid or in the subcontract awarded to CB Flooring. Questar argues that CB Flooring's bid, when adjusted, was actually $3,000 higher than CTI's.

Subcontract sum [$1,120,000] resulting from Contractor's completing the Work (*if Subcontractor is not in breach then such termination shall be deemed termination for convenience pursuant to Paragraph 14 hereof*). . . .

(italics added). Paragraph 14 provided:

Termination for Convenience: If this Subcontract Agreement is terminated for convenience, Subcontractor shall be entitled, as its sole compensation, to be paid that portion of the total price provided in this Subcontract Agreement that is equal to the reasonable value of the authorized materials, equipment and incidentals furnished and delivered to the job site prior to the termination plus the reasonable value of properly authorized materials fabricated and properly stored ("Stored Materials") by Subcontractor prior to the termination, and of properly authorized special inventory items specifically purchased ("Special Inventory") by the Subcontractor for this project prior to the termination. The Subcontractor shall only be paid for Stored Materials and Special Inventory after the Subcontractor has delivered, at its expense, such Stored Materials and Special Inventory to a location specified by the Contractor and the Contractor has inspected and acknowledged in writing the acceptance of the Stored Materials and Special Inventory.

Three additional provisions of the Subcontract are also relevant to this matter. First, Paragraph 7 provided:

Changes: Contractor may, at any time, unilaterally or by agreement with Subcontractor, make changes in the Work. Any change order or agreement shall be in writing. Subcontractor shall perform the Work as changed without delay. Subcontractor shall be entitled to an equitable adjustment pursuant to Paragraph 13 hereof if the change involves an adjustment in the Subcontract sum . . . or the time of performance . . . .

Second, Paragraph 13 provided, in pertinent part:

Settlement of Disputes and Claims: (a) With respect to any dispute between Contractor and Subcontractor or any Claim by Subcontractor, Contractor shall make a good faith, unilateral determination as to the equitable adjustment, if any, to be allowed, and issue a decision which shall be followed by Subcontractor. Subcontractor shall continue to perform the Work without deficiency, interruption or delay, pending such determination. If Subcontractor's claim is allowed by Contractor or by arbitration as provided for in [Paragraph 16] hereof, Subcontractor shall be entitled to an equitable adjustment in the Subcontract sum . . . and/or the Subcontract time of performance . . . as its sole remedy. Notification of any such claim for equitable adjustment must be made in writing with complete supporting data within twenty (20) days of Subcontractor's knowledge of the claim.

Think About It!

Before continuing with the court's opinion, re-read carefully Paragraphs 12 and 14 of the contract, quoted in the opinion. How and under what circumstances may the Contractor (Questar) terminate the contract under each provision? What are the consequences of termination under Paragraph 12? Under Paragraph 14?

Finally, Paragraph 16 expressed the parties' mutual agreement to arbitrate all disputes concerning amounts less than $50,000, as well as Questar's right to elect arbitration for disputes concerning amounts greater than $50,000.

The complicated series of events from which this appellate "magic carpet ride" springs began even before the Subcontract was signed.* The architectural drawings that Questar supplied to CB Flooring, upon which CB Flooring based its bid, specified that Shaw Custom ("Shaw") "field" carpet was to be used in the corridors of Greenwich Place. The drawings did not indicate that "border" carpet would be installed in the corridors. Yet, the Subcontract, when drafted by Questar, plainly called for CB Flooring to install border carpet. The CB Flooring salesmen reviewing the draft Subcontract realized the discrepancy and sought to strike-out this proposed requirement; however, he failed to notice that his proposed change was not incorporated in the final draft.

In its executed form, the Subcontract required CB Flooring to install field and border carpets in the corridors of Greenwich Place and specified that the carpeting would be the same as the carpeting at Russett at Concord Park ("Concord Park"), a similar residential complex developed by Questar. The parties now agree that the corridors of Concord Park were furnished with Shaw field carpet and Bigelow Preview II ("Bigelow") border carpet.

Matters became more complicated after execution of the Subcontract when the interior design firm working on the Greenwich Place project changed the carpets to be installed in the clubhouse and corridors from Shaw and Bigelow carpets to Bentley Prince Street ("Prince Street") field carpet with Bentley New Stratford ("New Stratford") border carpet. In December 2005, the interior designer issued a set of plans, referred to as ID [Interior Decorator] Drawings (the "70% ID Draw-

---

* [Authors' Note: A charted timeline of the events apears on page 89. You may find it helpful to refer to the chart as you read through the court's statement of facts.]

ings"), specifying Prince Street as the new field carpet. The plans were only 70% complete and did not include any change with respect to the border carpeting; however, approximately one month later, the interior designer issued a complete set of plans (the "100% ID Drawings"), specifying New Stratford as the new border carpet.[8]

Before CB Flooring responded to either set of ID Drawings, however, Questar contacted CTI about installing carpeting at Greenwich Place, assertedly because it was "trying to keep CB Flooring honest" in the event that CB Flooring requested more money on account of the carpeting changes advanced by the interior designer. CTI submitted a new bid to Questar, proposing to install carpeting at Greenwich Place for $1,119,000; however, CTI's figures were based on the Shaw and Bigelow carpets used at the Concord Park project, not the Prince Street and New Stratford carpets specified by the ID Drawings. On 23 February 2006, CB Flooring, as anticipated, submitted a change order requesting an upward adjustment of $33,566 to the Subcontract price. Four days later, Questar sent an unexecuted subcontract to CTI, pursuant to which CTI would install carpeting at Greenwich Place in exchange for $1,120,000.

On 3 March, CB Flooring, citing a mathematical error, submitted a revised change order to Questar, changing its requested adjustment from $33,566 to $103,371 above the original Subcontract price. Shortly thereafter, Charles Bode, CB Flooring's Vice President, spoke by telephone with Donald Richards, Questar's Vice President and Production Manager, about the requested adjustment. Bode and Richards testified to quite different recollections of what transpired in that conversation. In any event, Bode asked Richards to call him back later in the week so that they could discuss the matter further, but Richards did not do so. Instead, in a letter dated 23 March 2006, Questar's Senior Vice President, Frank Maccherone, notified CB Flooring that Questar was terminating the Subcontract.

In the termination letter, Maccherone stated that the termination was for cause, charging that CB Flooring materially breached the Subcontract by refusing to perform; however, he iterated that, even in the absence of a breach by CB Flooring, Questar nevertheless enjoyed a right to terminate the Subcontract for convenience under Paragraph 14, entitling CB Flooring to no compensation. The letter also accused CB Flooring of acting in bad faith by using the interior designer's changes to seek an unwarranted increase in the Subcontract price.

After terminating its agreement with CB Flooring, Questar entered a subcontract with CTI on 5 April 2006, pursuant to which CTI agreed to install the carpeting at Greenwich Place in exchange for $1,120,000 ($1,000 more than its

---

[8] The differences are not necessarily in brand names only. Cost issues may arise with the design changes.

February 2006 bid price). This subcontract permitted CTI to install Bigelow border carpeting in the corridors, as opposed to the New Stratford border described by the ID Drawings. Questar apparently did not seek the interior designer's approval before deviating from the interior designer's plans.

Alleging that Questar terminated the Subcontract wrongfully, CB Flooring initiated a breach of contract action against the general contractor in the Circuit Court for Baltimore County in April 2006. Chiefly, CB Flooring contended that, although it requested an upward price adjustment due to the interior designer's change in carpeting, it did not refuse to perform its contractual obligation to install carpeting at Greenwich Place as asserted by Questar in the termination letter. CB Flooring denied that its request for an upward adjustment to the Subcontract price was made in bad faith. Additionally, the subcontractor claimed that the termination for convenience clause, cited by Questar as an alternative basis for terminating the Subcontract, did not apply under the circumstances because Questar acted in bad faith by invoking the clause after scheming to hire CTI in its place. To that end, CB Flooring asserted that Questar created an uneven playing field by allowing CTI to base its February 2006 bid on Shaw and Bigelow carpets, as opposed to the Prince Street and New Stratford carpets described by the ID Drawings. The subcontractor also complained that CTI's subcontract with Questar deviated unfairly from the ID Drawings by permitting CTI to install Bigelow border carpeting, as opposed to New Stratford border carpeting.

Questar countered that Bode informed Richards during their March telephone conversation that CB Flooring would not perform under the Subcontract unless Questar agreed to a price increase. Questar determined that the price increase was not warranted under the circumstances. The

Make the Connection

Questar is included here because of its discussion of the "termination for convenience" clause and illusory promises, but the case also raises questions about whether Questar and CB Flooring acted in good or bad faith in their dealings with each other. The existence and meaning of the requirement that parties act in "good faith" is discussed in Chapter 7, page 804, and the portions of the opinion dealing with that issue are included there.

general contractor also claimed that CB Flooring failed to attend weekly, on-site progress meetings as required by the Subcontract. Thus, so Questar's defense proceeded, it justifiably terminated the Subcontract for cause. Alternatively, Questar postulated that Paragraph 14 of the Subcontract gave it the right to terminate the agreement at its convenience. Questar claimed that this right was unlimited; however, it contended that, even if the court imposed some limitation on the exercise of the right, that limitation was satisfied because Questar lost confidence in CB Flooring's ability to perform its obligations in a satisfactory manner due to the subcontractor's absence from weekly on-site progress meetings and its delay in ordering carpeting.

See It!
Charting the Facts of the Case

When the facts of a case are complicated, as they are here, it may be helpful to construct a timeline that both summarizes the salient facts and lays them out in a fashion that allows easier recall when trying to understand the court's application of the law to those facts. Here is a timeline of the critical facts in *Questar*. Note that some events are listed without precise dates because the opinion does not specify exactly when those occurred, but they can nonetheless be placed on the timeline:

	CB and CTI submit bids on carpet installation project to Questar, using Shaw carpet, as specified in architectural drawings
9/29/05	Questar and CB enter subcontract for carpet installation for $1,120,000, specifying Shaw (field) and Bigelow (border) carpets
12/05	Interior designer issues plans changing carpet specifications to Prince Street and New Stratford carpets
	Questar contacts CTI about rebidding
	CTI submits bid for $1,119,000, using Shaw and Bigelow carpets
2/23/06	CB submits first change order based on change in carpet specifications, adding $33,566 to contract price
2/27/06	Questar sends unexecuted subcontract to CTI for $1,120,000
3/3/06	CB cites math error, submits second change order, adding $103,371 to subcontract price (instead of $33,566)
	Phone conversation between CB and Questar vice-presidents
3/23/06	Questar notifies CB of contract termination, allegedly for cause or under contract ¶ 14, and claiming bad faith by CB
4/5/06	Questar enters subcontract with CTI for $1,120,000 using Shaw and Bigelow carpets

[The evidence showed that the Prince Street and New Stratford carpets specified in the new interior design drawings were more expensive and had higher shipping costs than the Shaw carpet included in the original contract specifications, but the court concluded that, in view of the rest of its analysis, it did not have to determine whether those differences meant that CB Flooring was entitled to a price adjustment to the original contract.]

[Additonal facts are included in Chapter 7, page 828, in the court's examination of the obligation of good faith.]

. . . .

After closing arguments, the trial judge rendered her ruling orally from the bench. She observed that CB Flooring made a mistake in its summer 2005 bid, which translated to a mistaken belief as to its obligations under the Subcontract. She also recognized the possibility that CB Flooring might not have been entitled to its requested price increase, given the subcontractor's own error and the conflicting evidence adduced by both parties on the pricing of the carpets.

Penultimately, the trial judge found that CB Flooring did not breach the Subcontract.[12] She "d[id] not believe that [Richards] told [ ] Bode in their conversation that the defendant was ordering the subcontractor to proceed as directed by the [Sub]contract." The trial judge recognized that the Subcontract required CB Flooring to attend weekly on-site progress meetings, but concluded that CB Flooring's

Make the Connection

A "breach" of a contract occurs whenever the actual performance of a party does not match the promised performance. Chapter 8, page 902, addresses the question of when a breach qualifies as a "material" breach.

absence from those meetings did not constitute a material breach of the Subcontract. She noted that the subcontractor's Field Supervisor occasionally visited the Greenwich Place site and no one from Questar complained to him about the subcontractor's absence from the meetings. She rejected Questar's assertion that it directed CB Flooring representatives to attend the meetings. The trial judge also found that CB Flooring did not attempt to use the change order as leverage and did not jeopardize the timely performance of the Subcontract.

With respect to Questar's alternative defense that Paragraph 14 conveyed a right to terminate the Subcontract for convenience, the trial judge rejected Questar's contention that it enjoyed a right to terminate the Subcontract for any reason. She considered and rejected Questar's assertion that its subjective loss

---

[12] Specifically, she credited Bode's testimony that he did not communicate to Richards that CB Flooring would not perform under the Subcontract.

of faith in CB Flooring's ability to perform satisfactorily (or for the agreed upon price) satisfied whatever implied limitations there might be on the exercise of the termination for convenience clause, noting that Questar's "gut feeling" was not sufficient. She credited the testimony of CB Flooring's Senior Contract Administrator, who explained that the lead times for all of the custom carpets was six weeks or less. She also credited the testimony of CTI's salesperson, noting that the salesperson felt "uncomfortable" when Maccherone asked for confirmation that New Stratford and Bigelow carpets were of comparable price and quality.

The trial judge rejected much of the testimonies of Maccherone and Richards. Specifically, she observed:

> I don't think [Richards] made any effort to contact the plaintiff regarding any unhappiness about anything, including not having received a proposed change order sooner. I don't think that he communicated that he had lost confidence in the plaintiff in any way. I'm not even sure he had lost confidence in the plaintiff before perhaps being advised by Mr. Maccherone that that's what his attitude should be.

> . . . .

> It did not seem that Mr. Richards had communicated to the plaintiff that he was ordering them to proceed or that the defendant was contemplating terminating the contract or that he was demanding proof of what the plaintiff claimed was necessary in the change order.

> . . . .

> And although [Questar's counsel] has suggested that Mr. Maccherone was not scheming when he submitted the interior design drawings to CTI, it appears to the court otherwise.

> The suggestion that there was nothing sinister or unusual about Mr. Maccherone's communications with [CTI's salesperson] in January and February is rejected. There was—it was I think very unusual for a general contractor to behave as Mr. Maccherone did in this case.

> It was out of the ordinary to send the interior design drawings to a competitor of the subcontractor who had a written and signed contract with the general [contractor] and had never indicated any reluctance to perform that contract as agreed.

> If the defendant thought that it was commercially unreasonable or had been an inordinately long time to respond with proposed change orders,

that period in late January and February, I can't understand why the defendant never communicated that.

Accordingly, the trial judge concluded that Questar improperly terminated the Subcontract and awarded more than $243,000 in expectation damages to CB Flooring. Following the resolution of a series of post-judgment motions not pertinent here, Questar noted a timely appeal to the Court of Special Appeals. In its brief in that court, Questar presented the following questions:

What's That?

Expectation damages are a monetary equivalent of fulfilling the injured party's "expectation" as to contract performance. They provide compensation to place the injured party in the position it would have been— the expected result—if the contract had been performed as promised. Expectation damages are the norm when a breach of contract is proved, although alternative (and usually smaller) measures of damages exist. Chapter 9 considers how to compute the value of expectation and other forms of damages.

1. Whether a "termination for convenience" clause contained in a contract between private parties is enforceable under Maryland Law[?]

2. Whether the trial court erred by holding, as a matter of law, that the parties' "termination for convenience" clause was inapplicable and did not allow Questar to terminate the parties' Subcontract without cause[?]

Before argument in the intermediate appellate court, this Court, on its initiative, issued a writ of certiorari. *Questar Builders, Inc. v. CB Flooring LLC*, 406 Md. 744, 962 A.2d 370 (2008). For the reasons that follow, we hold that the "termination for convenience" clause in this case may be enforceable, subject to an implied obligation to exercise the right to terminate in good faith and in accordance with fair dealing. We also hold that, on the present record, it is not clear that the clause was inapplicable under the circumstances found by the trial court. Accordingly, we vacate the Circuit Court's judgment and remand the case to the Circuit Court to resolve the remaining, potentially relevant discrepancies in the parties' accounts of the events leading up to the termination of the Subcontract and to enter a judgment that is consistent with this Opinion.

Standard of Review

Under Maryland Rule 8–131(c),

When an action has been tried without a jury, the appellate court will review the case on both the law and the evidence. It will not set aside the judgment of the trial court on the evidence unless clearly erroneous, and will give due regard to the opportunity of the trial court to judge the credibility of the witnesses.

"'The deference shown to the trial court's factual findings under the clearly erroneous standard does not, of course, apply to legal conclusions.'" *Karsenty v. Schoukroun,* 406 Md. 469, 502, 959 A.2d 1147, 1166 (2008) (quoting *Griffin v. Bierman,* 403 Md. 186, 195, 941 A.2d 475, 480 (2008)). We review the lower court's legal conclusions for legal error under a non-differential standard. *Nesbit v. Gov't Employees Ins. Co.,* 382 Md. 65, 72, 854 A.2d 879, 883 (2004). "The interpretation of a contract . . . is a question of law." *Sy-Lene of Wash., Inc. v. Starwood Urban Retail II, L.L.C.,* 376 Md. 157, 163, 829 A.2d 540, 544 (2003).

Analysis

I.

Courts and commentators generally agree that the concept referred to here as contract "termination for convenience" developed during (and in the years following) the American Civil War as a tool for the U.S. government to avoid costly military procurements that were rendered unnecessary by changing war-time technology or by the cessation of conflict. *Krygoski Constr. Co. v. United States,* 94 F.3d 1537, 1540 (Fed.Cir.1996); *Torncello v. United States,* 231 Ct.Cl. 20, 681 F.2d 756, 763–64 (1982); John Cibnic, Jr. et al, Administration Of Government Contracts 1049 (4th ed. 2006); Maj. Bruce D. Page, Jr., When Reliance is Detrimental: Economic, Moral, and Policy Arguments for Expectation Damages in Contracts Terminated for the Convenience of the Government, 61 A.F. L. REV. 1, 2 (2008). For example, because commanders did not know how long their men would be stationed in a particular area, in 1863 the U.S. Army promulgated a rule requiring that all of its contracts with subsistence stores include a provision allowing the Commissary–General to terminate the contract at his discretion. *See generally United States v. Speed,* 75 U.S. (8 Wall.) 77, 82 (1868) (describing such contracts).

In *United States v. Corliss Steam–Engine Co.,* 91 U.S. 321 (1874), a case often cited as the legal cornerstone of the federal government's right to terminate a contract for convenience, the Secretary of the Navy terminated the Navy's contract with a ship builder, asserting that the Navy no longer needed the requested ships due to the end of the Civil War. . . . [Corliss sued the government], seeking the full value of the contract. *Corliss,* 91 U.S. at 322. In affirming the Court of Claims's decree denying Corliss's claim, the Supreme Court . . . emphasized the need for the government to have broad discretion with respect to terminating its war-time contracts:

Contracts for the armament and equipment of vessels of war may, and generally do, require numerous modifications in the progress of the work, where that work requires years for its completion. With improvements constantly made in shipbuilding and steam-machinery and in arms, some parts originally contracted for may have to be abandoned, and other parts substituted; and it would be of serious detriment to the public service if the power of the head of the Navy Department did not extend to providing for all such possible contingencies by modification or suspension of the contracts, and settlement with the contractors.

Id. at 323.

Justified by *Corliss,* the federal government expanded its reliance on broad powers to terminate many of its contracts during and after World War I. . . . In 1917, Congress passed the Urgent Deficiency Appropriation Act, authorizing the President "to modify, suspend, cancel, or requisition any existing or future contract for the building, production, or purchase of ships or material" ordered for the war effort. Pub.L. No. 65–23, 40 Stat. 182. The act directed the President to provide "just compensation" to companies whose war-time contracts were cancelled. *Id.* . . .

Although most terminations of government contracts following the Armistice of 1918 were pursuant to statutes such as the Urgent Deficiency Appropriations Act, some agencies terminated their unneeded contracts under broadly worded, express contractual provisions. *See* Page, *When Reliance is Detrimental,* at 6. . . .

. . . .

The "direct predecessor of the modern termination for convenience clause" developed during the military build-up to World War II. *Torncello,* 681 F.2d at 765. Mandatory in all fixed-price supply contracts, the clause provided, in pertinent part:

Termination for the convenience of the Government. (a) The Government may, at any time, terminate this contract, in whole or in part by a notice in writing from the Contracting Officer to the Contractor that the contract is terminated under this Article.

Id. (quoting 10 C.F.R. § 81.324 (Cum. Supp. 1938–43)). While this clause introduced the word "convenience," the consensus remained that the government's right to terminate a contract was justified by the exigencies and uncertainties of armed conflict. *See G.L. Christian & Assocs. v. United States,* 160 Ct.Cl. 1, 15, 312 F.2d 418 (1963) (noting that "[r]egularly since World War I, it has been a major government principle, in times of stress or increased military procurement, to provide for the cancellation of defense contracts when they are no longer needed"); *Torncello*, 681 F.2d at 765 (noting that war-time contractors during World War II "risked losing the benefits of full performance but only for the exigencies of war").

During the 1960s, however, the federal government's use of similar termination for convenience clauses expanded beyond contracts needed to wage large-scale military operations; such provisions gained widespread use in civilian and peace-time military contracts. *Torncello*, 681 F.2d at 765. Indeed, by 1967, the Federal Procurement Regulation made termination for convenience clauses mandatory in most fixed price supply contracts and construction contracts. *See* Cibnic, Administration Of Government Contracts, at 1050. At present, the federal government includes these clauses in a myriad of supply, construction, and research and development contracts. *See* 48 C.F.R. § 49.502 (2009). In its modern form, the clause ordinarily provides that the government may terminate "if the Contracting Officer determines that a termination is in the Government's interest." *See Krygoski Constr. Co.*, 94 F.3d at 1544; *Custom Printing Co. v. United States*, 51 Fed.Cl. 729, 733 (Fed.Cl.2002); *see also* 48 C.F.R. 52.249–1 to –5 (2009); *accord* 48 C.F.R. 52.212(l) (2009) (providing for clause in contracts for "commercial items" that allows government to terminate "for its sole convenience").

As noted by Professor Cibnic, the result of the federal government's expanded use of termination for convenience clauses is "that broad rights developed for war contracts have come to be applied to all types of contracts, civilian as well as military, in times of both peace and war." Cibnic, Administration Of Government Contracts, at 1050. Yet, as a general rule, contracts involving the U.S. government are interpreted (at least in theory) like any contract between private parties. *See Lynch v. United States*, 292 U.S. 571, 579, 54 S.Ct. 840, 78 L.Ed. 1434 (1934) ("When the United States enters into contract relations, its rights and duties therein are governed generally by the law applicable to contracts between private individuals.") . . . . Accordingly, federal courts have had difficulty reconciling contract provisions allowing the federal government to terminate at its convenience (in circumstances more mundane than the exigencies of war) with the common law rule that a valid contract must be supported by consideration and may not be illusory. *See, e.g., Krygoski Constr. Co.*, 94 F.3d at 1541; *Torncello*, 81 F.2d 756. Balancing these two concepts, federal courts, therefore, sought to protect the government's right to terminate a contract for convenience by implying limitations on its use. By our reckoning, there are two competing analytical frameworks that evolved to limit the government's right so as not to render a contract illusory.

The first standard is the "changed circumstances" test articulated by a plurality of the U.S. Court of Claims in *Torncello v. United States*, 231 Ct.Cl. 20, 681 F.2d 756 (1982). . . .

. . . .

[In *Torncello*, the Court of Claims concluded that "some change in circumstances must occur before the government may exercise" the contractual right to terminate for convenience and, thus, the government may not rely on the provision simply "to exculpate itself from liability for breach."]

The second analytical paradigm is the "bad faith/abuse of discretion" test. Under this test, "[w]hen tainted by bad faith or abuse of discretion, a termination for convenience causes a contract breach." *Krygoski Constr. Co.*, 94 F.3d at 1541. This test predates *Torncello's* "changed circumstances" test; however, since *Torncello*, the federal courts, for the most part, have returned to reviewing convenience terminations only for "bad faith/abuse of discretion." *See T & M Distribs., Inc. v. United States*, 185 F.3d 1279, 1284 n. 4 (Fed.Cir.1999); *Krygoski Constr. Co.*, 94 F.3d at 1544; *Custom Printing Co.*, 51 Fed.Cl. at 734. The deference accorded the government under the "bad faith/abuse of discretion" standard peaked in *Colonial Metals Co. v. United States*, 204 Ct.Cl. 320, 494 F.2d 1355 (1974). There, the court held that the Navy did not act in bad faith when it terminated its contract with a copper supplier in order to obtain a better price elsewhere, even though the contracting officer knew of the better price at the time the parties entered the contract. *Colonial Metals Co.*, 494 F.2d at 1357. Noting that a termination for convenience clause is "not designed to perpetuate error, but to permit its rectification," the court concluded that bad faith or abuse of discretion would not lie unless a plaintiff proves "malice or conspiracy against the plaintiff." *Id.* at 1361.

More recent decisions, however, declare that *Colonial Metals Co.* was decided wrongly, recognizing that the government cannot terminate a contract for convenience simply to get a "better bargain from another source," thus adding some teeth to the "bad faith/abuse of discretion" standard. *See Krygoski*, 94 F.3d at 1541. Nevertheless, in a breach of contract action against the federal government, the party challenging the government's exercise of its right to terminate for convenience must show " 'well-nigh irrefragable proof' that the Government acted in bad faith," in light of the strong presumption recognized in the federal cases that the government acts in good faith. *Custom Printing Co.*, 51 Fed.Cl. at 734 (citations omitted); *see also Krygoski Constr. Co.*, 94 F.3d at 1541.

As the present case evidences, termination for convenience clauses are included sometimes in contracts between private parties. Such clauses are popular in construction contracts. *See* David A. Senter, *Role of the Subcontractor, in* Fundamentals of Construction Law 133 (Carina Y. Enhada, et al. eds., American Bar Association 2001). They also are found frequently in contracts "in the high-tech industry, where [they have] been used to reduce the risk of rapidly changing markets." Hugh Alexander & James R. Walsh, *At Your Convenience: Courts Are*

Generally Enforcing Termination For Convenience Clauses in the Private Sector that Are Well Drafted and Prudently Invoked, 21 Los Angeles Lawyer 42, 44 (1998). While the history of the clause's development in the context of federal procurement is helpful to our consideration of the present case in that it illuminates the clause's purpose as a risk-allocating tool, the case-law supporting such a broad right in federal contracts obviously is of limited value when interpreting a contract between private parties. Simply stated, for political reasons, the federal government stands in a position entirely uncomparable to that of a private person. . . .

Accordingly, we decline to recognize for private parties the near *carte-blanche* power to terminate that courts have given the federal government under convenience termination clauses.[22] Instead, we shall interpret and apply Paragraphs 12 and 14 of the Subcontract according to the common law of contract as interpreted by this Court, which does not require "well-nigh irrefragable proof" of wrongdoing to establish bad faith.

Under Maryland law of contract, illusory contracts are unenforceable. *Cheek v. United Healthcare of the Mid–Atlantic, Inc.,* 378 Md. 139, 148, 835 A.2d 656, 662 (2003). "An 'illusory promise' appears to be a promise, but it does not actually bind or obligate the promisor to do anything. An illusory promise is composed of 'words in a promissory form that promise nothing.'" Id. (quoting Corbin On Contracts § 5.28 (2003)). A promise, therefore, is illusory if "'the promisor retains an unlimited right to decide later the nature or extent of his performance.'" Id. (quoting 1 Williston, Contracts, § 4:24 (4th ed. 1990)). An unlimited right to determine how to perform, or whether to perform at all, negates the promise to perform. Id.

This notwithstanding, courts generally "prefer a construction [of a contract] which will make the contract effective rather than one which will make it illusory or unenforceable." *Kelley Constr. Co. v. Wash. Suburban Sanitary Comm'n,* 247 Md. 241, 247, 230 A.2d 672, 676 (1967). To that end,

> If there is a restriction, express or implied, on the promisor's ability to perform, the promise is not illusory. The tendency of the law is to avoid the finding that no contract arose due to an illusory promise when it appears that the parties intended a contract. Through the process of interpretation, in the absence of express restrictions, courts find implied promises to prevent a party's promise from being performable merely at the whim of the promisor. . . . The nature of the promise to be implied will vary with the kind of transaction and the particular context surrounding the individual transaction.

2 Corbin On Contracts § 5:28 (1995).

---

[22] Nothing in this Opinion should be construed as commentary on how we would interpret a termination for convenience clause in a contract involving the State of Maryland. . . .

Furthermore, Maryland contract law generally implies an obligation to act in good faith and deal fairly with the other party or parties to a contract. Clancy v. King, 405 Md. 541, 565, 954 A.2d 1092, 1106 (2008). That implied obligation governs the manner in which a party may exercise the discretion accorded to it by the terms of the agreement. *Julian v. Christopher*, 320 Md. 1, 9, 575 A.2d 735, 739 (1990). Thus, a party with discretion is limited to exercising that discretion in good faith and in accordance with fair dealing. Clancy, 405 Md. at 569, 954 A.2d at 1108; Julian, 320 Md. at 9, 575 A.2d at 739.

Make the Connection

Note the statement that courts generally prefer an interpretation that makes a contract enforceable (one of many "canons of construction" that help guide contract interpretation) and the idea that courts may imply the existence of a promise to avoid unenforceability. Both of these subjects are treated in Chapter 7, at page 705 and page 803. The court also discusses the implied obligation to act in good faith and deal fairly with the other party to the contract, treated at greater length in Chapter 7, at page 804.

In this case, the Subcontract did not have a true termination for convenience "clause." The right to terminate for convenience, however, may be extrapolated by reading together Paragraphs 12 and 14. To that end, Paragraph 12 detailed Questar's rights in the event of a breach of the Subcontract by CB Flooring. Among other things, Paragraph 12 allowed Questar to terminate the Subcontract; however the paragraph also provided that, if Questar terminated the Subcontract, but CB Flooring was not in breach, the termination should "be deemed termination for convenience pursuant to Paragraph 14," which limited CB Flooring's compensation to the reasonable value of materials and incidentals already provided (and, as happened here, disallowed recovery entirely if performance did not commence). Thus, a fair reading of Paragraphs 12 and 14 makes clear that Questar was permitted to terminate the Subcontract, absent a default by CB Flooring.

Yet, Questar's contention that it was entitled to terminate the Subcontract for any reason whatsoever goes too far and is inconsistent with the terms of the Subcontract. To be sure, a right to terminate in the absence of the other party's breach does not equate necessarily with the right to terminate based on a whim. We shall not read into the Subcontract such unfettered power, where the instrument itself provided that the agreement was to "remain effective through [the] DURATION OF THE PROJECT." *Cf. Towson Univ. v. Conte*, 384 Md. 68, 80, 862 A.2d 941, 947 (2004) (noting that "by specifying the length or term of employment," an employment agreement is not "at will"). In that regard, we presume that the parties meant what their contract expressed. *Nat'l Union Fire Ins. Co. v. David A. Bramble, Inc.*, 388 Md. 195, 208, 879 A.2d 101, 109 (2005). Moreover, if the Subcontract was terminable at will, the express term specifying the agreement's duration would be meaningless because the duration of an "at will" arrangement is, by definition, indefinite. *See DIRECTV, Inc. v. Mattingly*, 376 Md. 302, 320, 829 A.2d 626, 637 (2003) (reiterating cardinal principle of contract interpretation that courts will not disregard provisions of a contract unless there is no other sound way to interpret the contract); *see also* Steven J. Burton & Eric G. Anderson, Contractual Good Faith: Formation, Performance, Breach, Enforcement § 7.3.2.1 (Little, Brown & Co. 1995) (noting that a clause permitting termination "at will" is a "mechanism for ending an agreement of indefinite duration"). Therefore, we decline to accept Questar's invitation to declare that the right to terminate for convenience here was a right to terminate the Subcontract for any reason whatsoever, including a bad reason or no reason. Furthermore, the history of convenience termination clauses as a risk-allocating tool suggests that Questar's right was not exercisable arbitrarily.

Thus, where the right to terminate established by Paragraphs 12 and 14 left off, the implied obligation of good faith and fair dealing picks-up, thereby limiting the manner in which Questar was permitted to exercise its discretion. We agree with Corbin on Contracts, which provides further clarification on contract provisions that vest one party with broad discretion to determine whether and to what extent it will perform under the contract:

> Looked at woodenly, it might appear that performance is dependant upon the party's own whim, but courts are not mindless wooden sticks. Judges are cognizant of the utility of such contracts and of the understanding of reasonable parties to such contracts. It is well understood that the party whose duty is subject to [ ] a condition will use reasonable efforts to help bring about the condition to its own liability. Since this is the reasonable understanding, it is an implicit term of the contract. Similarly, even if there is not an implied obligation to use reasonable efforts, an implied obligation to determine whether such a condition exists in good faith, supplies the consideration.

2 Corbin On Contracts § 6.14.

This Court's opinion in *Stamatiades v. Merit Music Service, Inc.*, 210 Md. 597, 124 A.2d 829 (1956), is illustrative. There, Stamatiades, a restaurant owner, entered a contract with Music Services, pursuant to which Music Service agreed to install and operate "coin-operated amusement devices" in the restaurant and Stamatiades agreed not to enter a similar arrangement with any of Music Service's competitors during the contract's duration. *Stamatiades*, 210 Md. at 602, 124 A.2d at 831. In pertinent part, the contract provided:

> c. Should there be any necessity in the sole discretion of [Music Service] for the equipment to be replaced or for the number of machines to be

decreased, [Stamatiades] agrees to permit [Music Service] to change or decrease the number of machines, but at no time shall [Music Service] increase the number or machines without [Stamatiades's] consent.

Id. at 602–03, 124 A.2d at 832. When Stamatiades disconnected Music Service's machines and had another company install similar machines in the restaurant, Music Service sued to enforce the contract. *Id.* at 603, 124 A.2d at 832.

In affirming the order of the Circuit Court for Baltimore City enjoining Stamatiades from contracting with Music Service's competitor, we rejected Stamatiades's assertion that the contract with Music Service was illusory. We observed:

> The agreement in the instant case permits Music Service, in case of any necessity, in its sole discretion, to change or reduce the number of machines. This does not mean that Music Service can evade its obligations to furnish machines and to maintain them in satisfactory operating condition simply by declaring a "necessity" which does not exist.
>
> . . . .
>
> The contract speaks of "necessity" for making a change in machines or for reducing their number. This does not mean that Music Service would be at liberty to withdraw any or all of its machines as a matter of its mere wish or caprice, and it is, therefore, not the equivalent of a contract cancellable at will....

Id. at 614–15, 124 A.2d at 838.

While the instant case concerns termination for convenience, not necessity, the right to terminate here similarly was not exercisable at the "mere wish or caprice" of Questar. *See* id. at 615, 124 A.2d at 838. As stated, our understanding of the right to terminate a contract for convenience is that it is a risk-allocating tool. Thus, Questar was permitted to terminate only if, in its discretion, it determined that continuing with the Subcontract would subject it potentially to a meaningful financial loss or some other difficulty in completing the project successfully. Questar's right to terminate the Subcontract for convenience, however, did not permit it to evade either its obligation to make a good faith (albeit unilateral) determination as to whether CB Flooring was entitled to an equitable adjustment to the Subcontract price under Paragraph 13(a) or its obligation to arbitrate disputes with CB Flooring under Paragraph 16. Likewise, Questar was required to act reasonably in ensuring that the Subcontract did not become inconvenient, and it certainly was not permitted to create an inconvenience in order to terminate the Subcontract.

Questar relies on *Niagara Mohawk Power Corp. v. Graver Tank & Manufacturing Co.*, 470 F.Supp. 1308 (N.D.N.Y.1979), for the proposition that a termination for convenience clause amounts to a right to terminate for any or no reason. To refute the obvious challenge that a right to terminate for any reason would render the Subcontract illusory (a disfavored interpretation in Maryland contract law), Questar maintains that other consideration was provided under the Subcontract, thereby rendering the Subcontract enforceable. We reject both premises asserted by the general contractor, addressing them in turn. First, Niagara Mohawk Power Corp. is distinguishable because it did not involve contract provisions like Paragraphs 12 and 14. Instead, although the district court characterized the clause at issue there as a "termination for convenience clause," the clause expressly authorized the terminating party to exercise its right to terminate "at any time for any reason." Niagara Mohawk Power Corp., 470 F. Supp. at 1313. But here, as observed, a fair reading of Paragraphs 12 and 14 establishes that Questar enjoyed the right to terminate in the absence of breach by CB Flooring, a far cry from authorizing the general contractor to terminate the Subcontract for any reason whatsoever.

Questar's second point is that other consideration supported its assertedly unfettered right to terminate the Subcontract. As this Court explicated, "an unlimited option to cancel does not invalidate a contract where it [otherwise] can be shown that it does not wholly defeat consideration." *Stamatiades*, 210 Md. at 613, 124 A.2d at 837. "[S]uch a power to terminate does not invalidate the contract . . . , so long as the party reserving the power to terminate is irrevocably bound for any appreciable time or has materially changed any of his relations or otherwise rendered some performance capable of operating as a consideration." *Acme Markets, Inc. v. Dawson Enters., Inc.*, 253 Md. 76, 87, 251 A.2d 839, 846 (1969); *see also Foster–Porter Enters., Inc. v. De Mare*, 198 Md. 20, 31, 81 A.2d 325, 331 (1951) (noting that a contract terminable at will upon 30 days written notice is "a contract terminable not wholly at will, but only upon 30 days written notice, which is a contract for at least 30 days").

Questar maintains that it was bound irrevocably by the Subcontract in at least one way—it was required to pay CB Flooring the reasonable value of CB Flooring's partial performance, if any, under Paragraph 14. This argument, however, shall not prevail. Because there was no appreciable period of time provided by the Subcontract, before which Questar was prohibited from exercising its right to terminate, interpreting the Subcontract to allow Questar to terminate it for any reason whatsoever would mean that Questar had absolute control over whether it paid any compensation to CB Flooring. Thus, under Questar's interpretation, it simply could have terminated the Subcontract before CB Flooring began performing (as apparently it did). Were that the case, the Subcontract would be illusory under this Court's opinion in *Cheek v. United Healthcare of the Mid–Atlantic, Inc.*, 378 Md. 139, 835 A.2d 656 (2003).[23]

There, we held that an arbitration clause authorizing one party to "alter, amend, modify, or revoke the [arbitration p]olicy at its sole and absolute discretion at any time with or without notice" rendered the agreement to arbitrate illusory.

---

[23] *See also Torncello*, 681 F.2d at 769 ("It is hornbook law . . . that a route of complete escape vitiates any other consideration furnished and is incompatible with the existence of a contract.").

Cheek, 378 Md. at 142–43, 835 A.2d at 658. In other words, if we accepted and applied Niagara Mohawk Power Corp., as Questar argues we should, the Subcontract would be illusory.[24]

As explained earlier, such an interpretation of a contract is not the preferred one and, here, it would disregard the plain and unambiguous language of the Subcontract, which contemplated that the agreement would remain effective for the duration of completion of the Greenwich Place project.

Accordingly, we hold that termination for convenience rights, like that provided for in Paragraphs 12 and 14 of this Subcontract, may be enforceable, subject to the implied limitation that they be exercised in good faith and in accordance with fair dealing. Thus, we agree with the Circuit Court to the extent that it concluded that Questar's right to terminate the Subcontract for convenience was not unlimited. Although there are few reported opinions discussing what, if any, limitations there are on the exercise of a termination for convenience right by a private party, those recognize generally that the right must be exercised in good faith. *See, e.g., Harris Corp. v. Giesting & Assocs., Inc.,* 297 F.3d 1270, 1272–73 (11th Cir.2002) ("Termination for convenience clauses may not be used to shield the terminating party from liability for bad faith or fraud."); *EDO Corp. v. Beech Aircraft Corp.,* 911 F.2d 1447, 1453 n. 6 (10th Cir.1990) ("We concur in the district court's determination that Beech's exercise of its right to terminate [for convenience] must have been exercised in good faith.").

Furthermore, with specific regard to construction contracts, one commentator observed:

> Sometimes an owner is given the right in a contract to terminate for "convenience." In other words, *if it is economically unfeasible to continue the project, the owner may be allowed to terminate* and to compensate the general contractor (and its subcontractors) for work performed and any losses incurred up to the date of termination.... Although "convenience" implies a very broad spectrum of circumstances, such a termination must be done in good faith, or the owner may have broader liability than the contract provisions contemplate.

David A. Senter, *Role of the Subcontractor,* in Fundamentals of Construction Law 133 (italics added).

There undeniably is utility in including a broad termination right in contracts in the context of rapidly changing industries and in contracts for large, long-term build-out projects. Such a right to terminate for convenience may serve as an

---

[24] Another key difference between this case and *Niagara Mohawk Power Corp.* is that the contract in the latter required 2 days notice to terminate. 470 F.Supp. at 1314. We decline to speculate whether a contract reserving the right to terminate for any reason, upon two days notice, would be enforceable under *Cheek.*

effective tool, protecting one party from the risk of loss in markets where there is a substantial risk due to changing technology or where loss, if it occurs, could result in a financial Waterloo, as in the construction industry. At the same time, the right to terminate for convenience, as we interpret it, provides adequate consideration for the other party to the contract, protecting that party's expectations in a binding enforceable agreement and prohibiting the terminating party from yanking out arbitrarily the carpet from underneath the agreement.

II.

We now turn to whether the trial judge correctly found that Questar was not permitted to terminate the Subcontract for its convenience under the circumstances of this case. [The court concluded that the trial judge did not make "an express or implied finding on the the ultimate fact of whether the general contractor acted in bad faith by terminating the Subcontract" and remanded the matter for the judge to do so. The remainder of the opinion, discussing the application of the good faith obligation of the parties, is included in Chapter 7.]

Judgment of the circuit court for Baltimore County vacated; case remanded for further proceedings consistent with this opinion; costs to abide the result.

Practice Pointer: Termination Clauses

A termination clause in a contract gives one or both parties the right to put an end to future performance obligations under the contract. After termination, the parties retain some rights based on already-completed performance, such as the right to payment for goods transferred or services performed but not yet paid for, warranties on goods already transferred, and remedies for the other party's past breach, but the contract's performance phase is ended.

Termination pursuant to a contract clause is not the same as "canceling" a contract after a material breach by the other party, which does not depend on the existence of a contractual clause, but which may have the same outcome (that is, liability for breach and the cessation of future performance). Courts and parties may use these terms (termination and cancellation) interchangeably, however, so it is important to identify clearly which right is being invoked, whatever wording is used.

Termination clauses come in two varieties.

- A termination-for-convenience clause, as you saw in *Questar*, gives one or both parties the right to end the performance obligations for any reason (or for no reason). These clauses are common in contracts of indefinite or long duration, such as long-term service contracts or distributorship arrangements between a manufacturer and distributor of goods. Such clauses also appear in contracts of set duration when one or both parties want the discretionary right to end the contract early without having to specify a reason. As you saw in *Questar*, termination-for-convenience clauses pose a special drafting challenge because of the danger that the contract promises will be considered illusory. If contracting parties appear to have reached an agreement of economic substance, however, courts may try to uphold the agreement by looking for any real commitment, no matter how small, to support a finding that consideration exists. For example, if the termination clause cannot be exercised until a brief period of time has passed or the party terminating must give at least some notice before termination occurs, a court may find the contract obligations are not entirely illusory. As you have seen, the obligation to act in good faith in exercising the termination clause can serve the same function.

- A termination-for-cause clause gives one or both parties the right to end performance obligations for specified reasons that may or may not constitute breaches of the contract, though they may be events that lead a party to be insecure about the likelihood of continued performance. Termination-for-cause clauses are especially common in loan documents, where the creditor may have the right to "call the loan" (accelerate payment and put an end to the extension of credit) upon events that make the creditor concerned that the debtor is becoming less credit-worthy.

Problems: Is There Consideration?

2-16. An agreement signed by Drew, Ebony, Farley, Garret, and Hakeem provided that (1) Drew and Ebony would serve as directors of a new company, Interchange, Inc., and have the right to manage the company "for a period of ten years or until their sooner resignation," and (2) Farley, Garret, and Hakeem would establish Interchange, Inc., install Drew and Ebony as directors, and enter a management agreement with them. After four years, Farley, Garret, and Hakeem (also directors of the company) ousted Drew and Ebony as directors and terminated the management contract. Drew and Ebony filed suit against the other three directors to compel them to continue the management contract. Defendants claim lack of consideration. What should the result be?

2-17. On March 10, Melissa Harvey was hired by National Golf Corporation (NGC) to work in the pro shop at the Bliss Hills Golf Course, a club managed by NGC, and was told she should report for work on March 22. On March 19, NGC gave Plaintiff a number of documents to review, including the Worker Handbook. Page 20 of the handbook discussed arbitration and states:

> I agree that any claim of unlawful harassment or discrimination or claims of wrongful discharge, arising out of my employment with AGC, including public policy claims, contract claims and claims involving any applicable Federal, State, or Local statute, ordinance or regulation relating to the termination of my employment, employment discrimination, harassment or retaliation, will be resolved exclusively by final and binding arbitration and not by court action. I acknowledge that I am knowingly and voluntarily waiving my right to pursue such claims in court and instead will pursue them through arbitration. This arbitration shall be the exclusive means of resolving any dispute(s) listed in this agreement and no other action will be brought in any court or administrative forum.

Page 23 of the handbook included the following acknowledgment form, which Harvey signed:

Acknowledgment

My signature below indicates that I have read this NGC Worker Agreement and handbook and promise and agree to abide by its terms and conditions. I further understand that the Company reserves the right to amend, supplement, rescind or revise any policy, practice, or benefit described in this handbook—other than employment at-will provisions— as it deems appropriate.

I acknowledge that my employment is at-will, which means that either the Company or I have the absolute right to end the employment relationship at any time with or without notice or reason. I further acknowledge that I have read and agree to be bound by the arbitration policy set forth on page 20 of this handbook.

Harvey worked for NGC until September 15. On November 1, she filed a complaint in court against NGC and her immediate supervisor alleging sexual discrimination and hostile work environment, sexual harassment, retaliation, and retaliatory discharge. NGC moved to compel binding arbitration pursuant to the acknowledgment form Harvey signed. Harvey argues that her agreement to arbitration is unenforceable because it lacks consideration. Is Harvey right?

2-18. When Lee Hunter died, State Bank held a promissory note for $3700 signed by Lee and also held 50 shares of capital stock of the Hunter Company, owned by Lee, as collateral for the payment of the promissory note. The company was insolvent at the time of Lee's death (its debts exceeded its assets), and his death made the promissory note unenforceable, so there was no value to these two "assets." Lee's widow, Zennetta, asked the bank to return to her both the stock certificate and promissory note. The bank told her it would surrender both documents if she gave the bank her own promissory note in the amount of $3700. When Zennetta failed to pay the amount due under her note, the bank sued. She claimed lack of consideration. What should the result be?

2-19. FireFighting Company and the U.S. Forest Service signed a document entitled "Pacific Northwest Engine Tender Agreement" that listed fire equipment the Company would make available if called upon by the Forestry Service during the two years during which the Agreement would be in effect. The Agreement contained the following clauses:

   (a) This Agreement does not preclude the Government from using an agency or other resources;
   (b) This Agreement does not guarantee there will be a need for equipment offered nor does it guarantee orders will be placed against the awarded agreements;
   (c) Because of the equipment needs of the government and availability of contractor's equipment during an emergency cannot be determined in advance, it is mutually agreed that, upon request of the government, the contractor shall furnish the equipment offered herein to the extent the contractor is willing and able at the time of order.

   Although several fires occurred during the two-year term of the Agreement, Forestry Service did not call upon FireFighting Company to provide any equipment or perform any other service during that time. Company sues, claiming breach of contract. Can FireFighting Company maintain a suit against the Forestry Service for failure to use its services during the term of the Agreement?

An agreement to settle a dispute, whether before or after a lawsuit is filed, usually consists of a promise by one party to waive further rights to pursue a claim in exchange for the transfer of certain rights or assets. For example, a patient alleging malpractice against a doctor may agree to give up the right to file or pursue a medical malpractice suit in exchange for a sum of money paid by the doctor's insurer. For such settlement agreements to be binding—that is, to foreclose a subsequent claim and to enforce a promise to pay an amount to settle the asserted claim—each promise must be supported by consideration. In particular, the promise to waive the claim must constitute consideration for the promised transfer.

Reading the Law Critically: *Dyer*

The *Dyer* case looks at whether and under what circumstances relinquishment of a claim can be consideration for a promise.

1. How do the principles discussed in *Appeal of Clark, Batsakis, Schnell,* and *Questar* apply to settlement of disputed claims?

2. As noted in *Dyer,* courts disagree on whether resolving a disputed but ultimately invalid claim can be consideration for a promise. Which do you think is the better rule to adopt? Why?

Dyer v. National By-Products, Inc.

DALE WARREN DYER, Plaintiff-Appellant

v.

NATIONAL BY-PRODUCTS, INC., Defendant-Appellee

Supreme Court of Iowa
380 N.W.2d 732 (Iowa 1986)

SCHULTZ, Justice.

The determinative issue in this appeal is whether good faith forbearance to litigate a claim, which proves to be invalid and unfounded, is sufficient consideration to uphold a contract of settlement. The district court determined, as a matter of law, that consideration for the alleged settlement was lacking because the forborne claim was not a viable cause of action. We reverse and remand.

On October 29, 1981, Dale Dyer, an employee of National By-Products, lost his right foot in a job-related accident. Thereafter, the employer placed Dyer on a leave of absence at full pay from the date of his injury until August 16, 1982. At that time he returned to work as a foreman, the job he held prior to his injury. On March 11, 1983, the employer indefinitely laid off Dyer.

Dyer then filed the present lawsuit against his employer claiming that his discharge was a breach of an oral contract. He alleged that he in good faith believed that he had a valid claim against his employer for his personal injury. Further, Dyer claimed that his forbearance from litigating his claim was made in exchange for a promise from his employer that he would have lifetime employment. The employer specifically denied that it had offered a lifetime job to Dyer after his injury.

Following extensive discovery procedures, the employer filed a motion for summary judgment claiming there was no genuine factual issue and that it was entitled to judgment as a matter of law. The motion was resisted by Dyer. The district court sustained the employer's motion on the basis that: (1) no reciprocal promise to work for the employer for life was present, and (2) there was no forbearance of any viable cause of action, apparently on the ground that workers' compensation provided Dyer's sole remedy.

On appeal, Dyer claims that consideration for the alleged contract of lifetime employment was his forbearance from pursuing an action against his employer. Accordingly, he restricts his claim of error to the second reason advanced by the district court for granting summary judgment. Summary judgment is only proper when there is no genuine issue of any material fact. Iowa R.Civ.P. 237(c). Dyer generally contends that an unresolved issue of material fact remains as to whether he reasonably and in good faith forbore from asserting a claim against his employer and his coemployees in exchange for the employer's alleged promise to employ him for life. Specifically, he asserts that the trial court erred because: (1) the court did not consider the reasonableness and good faith of his belief in the validity of the claim he forbore from asserting, and (2) the court considered the legal merits of the claim itself which Dyer forbore from asserting.

FYI

All states in the United States have adopted some form of workers' compensation system, as have many other industrialized nations. It mandates that injured workers' claims against their employers be paid under the workers' compensation rules and processes, and it preempts the employees' rights to tort recovery for such injuries. The amounts distributed are often less than what might be recovered in a tort lawsuit, but employees are more certain to get some kind of recovery than might be true based solely on the ability to bring and win tort claims.

The employer, on the other hand, maintains that workers' compensation benefits are Dyer's sole remedy for his injury and that his claim for damages is unfounded. It then urges that forbearance from asserting an unfounded claim cannot serve as consideration for a contract. For the purpose of this discussion, we shall assume that Dyer's tort action is clearly invalid and he had no basis for a tort suit against either his employer or his fellow employees. We recognize that the fact issue, as to whether Dyer in good faith believed that he had a cause of action based in tort against the employer, remains unresolved. The determinative issue before the district court and now on appeal is whether the lack of consideration for the alleged promise of lifetime employment has been established as a matter of law.

Preliminarily, we observe that the law favors the adjustment and settlement of controversies without resorting to court action. *Olson v. Wilson & Co.*, 244 Iowa 895, 899, 58 N.W.2d 381, 384 (1953). Compromise is favored by law. *White v.*

Flood, 258 Iowa 402, 409, 138 N.W.2d 863, 867 (1965). Compromise of a doubtful right asserted in good faith is sufficient consideration for a promise. *Id.*

The more difficult problem is whether the settlement of an unfounded claim asserted in good faith is consideration for a contract of settlement. Professor Corbin presents a view favorable to Dyer's argument when he states:

Think About It!

What is the difference between a "doubtful" and an "unfounded" claim? Why does the law draw this distinction? How do the rules governing them differ, as reflected in the discussion in *Dyer*? Do those differing rules make sense?

> [F]orbearance to press a claim, or a promise of such forbearance, may be a sufficient consideration even though the claim is wholly ill-founded. It may be ill-founded because the facts are not what he supposes them to be, or because the existing facts do not have the legal operation that he supposes them to have. In either case, his forbearance may be a sufficient consideration, although under certain circumstances it is not. The fact that the claim is ill-founded is not in itself enough to prevent forbearance from being a sufficient consideration for a promise.

1 *Corbin on Contracts* § 140, at 595 (1963). Further, in the same section, it is noted that:

> The most generally prevailing, and probably the most satisfactory view is that *forbearance is sufficient if there is any reasonable ground for the claimant's belief that it is just to try to enforce his claim. He must be asserting his claim "in good faith";* but this does not mean he must believe that his suit can be won. It means that he must not be making his claim or threatening suit for purposes of vexation, or in order to realize on its "nuisance value."

Id. § 140, at 602 (emphasis added). Indeed, we find support for the Corbin view in language contained in our cases. *See White v. Flood,* 258 Iowa at 409, 138 N.W.2d at 867 ("[C]ompromise of a doubtful right asserted in good faith is sufficient consideration for a promise."); *In re Estate of Dayton,* 246 Iowa 1209, 1216, 71 N.W.2d 429, 433 (1955) ("The good faith assertion of an unfounded claim furnishes ample consideration for a settlement."); *Messer v. Washington National Insurance Co.,* 233 Iowa 1372, 1380, 11 N.W.2d 727, 731 (1943) ("[I]f the parties act in good faith, even when they know all the facts and there is promise without legal liability on which to base it, the courts hesitate to disturb the agreements of the parties...."); *Lockie v. Baker,* 206 Iowa 21, 24, 218 N.W. 483, 484 (1928) (Claim settled, though perhaps not valid, must have been presented and demanded in good faith.); *First National Bank v. Browne,* 199 Iowa 981, 984, 203 N.W. 277, 278 (1925)

(Settlement of a disputed or doubtful claim in good faith is sufficient consideration for a compromise, even though judicial investigation might show claim to be unfounded.).

The Restatement (Second) of Contracts section 74 (1979), supports the Corbin view and states:

Settlement of Claims

(1) Forbearance to assert or the surrender of a claim or defense which proves to be invalid is not consideration unless

(a) the claim or defense is in fact doubtful because of uncertainty as to the facts or the law, or

(b) *the forbearing or surrendering party believes that the claim or defense may be fairly determined to be valid.*

Comment:

b. Requirement of good faith. The policy favoring compromise of disputed claims is clearest, perhaps, where a claim is surrendered at a time when it is uncertain whether it is valid or not. Even though the invalidity later becomes clear, *the bargain is to be judged as it appeared to the parties at the time;* if the claim was then doubtful, no inquiry is necessary as to their good faith. Even though the invalidity should have been clear at the time, the settlement of an honest dispute is upheld. But a mere assertion or denial of liability does not make a claim doubtful, and *the fact that invalidity is obvious may indicate that it was known.* In such cases Subsection (1)(b) requires a showing of *good faith.*

(Emphasis added.) *See also* 15 Am.Jur.2d *Compromise and Settlement* § 16, at 787 (1976); 15A C.J.S. *Compromise and Settlement* § 11(b), at 206 (1967), quoted in *Messer v. Washington National Insurance Co.,* 233 Iowa at 1380, 11 N.W.2d at 731.

However, not all jurisdictions adhere to this view. Some courts require that the claim forborne must have some merit in fact or at law before it can provide consideration and these jurisdictions reject those claims that are obviously invalid. *See Bullard v. Curry-Cloonan,* 367 A.2d 127, 131 (D.C.App.1976) ("[A]s a general principle, the forbearance of a cause of action advanced in good faith, which is neither absurd in fact nor obviously unfounded in law, constitutes good and valuable consideration."); *Frasier v. Carter,* 92 Idaho 79, 437 P.2d 32, 34 (1968) (The forbearance of a claim which is not utterly groundless is sufficient consideration to support a contract.); *Charles v. Hill* 260 N.W.2d 571, 575 (Minn.1977) ("[A] wholly baseless or utterly unfounded claim is not consideration for a contract."); *Agristor Credit Corporation v. Unruh,* 571 P.2d

1220, 1224 (Okla.1977) (In order to constitute consideration for a contract, "claim forborne must be reasonably doubtful in law or fact."); *see generally* 15A C.J.S. *Compromise and Settlement* § 10, at 201 (There are many decisions holding that a claim which is entirely baseless does not afford consideration for a compromise.).

In fact, we find language in our own case law that supports the view which is favorable to the employer in this case. *See Vande Stouwe v. Bankers' Life Co.*, 218 Iowa 1182, 1190, 254 N.W. 790, 794 (1934) ("A claim that is entirely baseless and without foundation in law or equity will not support a compromise."); *Peterson v. Breitag*, 88 Iowa 418, 422-23, 55 N.W. 86, 88 (1893) ("It is well settled that there must at least be some appearance of a valid claim to support a settlement to avoid litigation."); *Tucker v. Ronk*, 43 Iowa 80, 82 (1876) (The settlement of an illegal and unfounded claim, upon which no proceedings have been instituted, is without consideration.); *Sullivan v. Collins*, 18 Iowa 228, 229 (1865) (A compromise of a claim is not a sufficient consideration to sustain a note, when such claim is not sustainable in law or in equity, or, at least doubtful in some respect.). Additionally, Professor Williston notes that:

> While there is a great divergence of opinion respecting the kind of forbearance which will constitute consideration, the *weight of authority holds that although forbearance from suit on a clearly invalid claim is insufficient consideration for a promise,* forbearance from suit on a claim of doubtful validity is sufficient consideration for a promise if there is a sincere belief in the validity of the claim.

1 *Williston on Contracts* § 135, at 581 (3rd ed. 1957) (emphasis added).

We believe, however, that the better reasoned approach is that expressed in the Restatement (Second) of Contracts section 74. Even the above statement from *Williston*, although it may have been the state of the law in 1957, is a questionable assessment of the current law. In fact, most of the cases cited in the cumulative supplement to *Williston* follow the "good faith and reasonable" language. 1 *Williston on Contracts* § 135B (3rd ed. 1957 & Supp.1985). Additionally, Restatement (Second) of Contracts section 74 is cited in that supplement. *Id.* As noted before, as a matter of policy the law favors compromise and such policy would be defeated if a party could second guess his settlement and litigate the validity of the compromise. The requirement that the forbearing party assert the claim in good faith sufficiently protects the policy of law that favors the settlement of controversies. Our holdings which are to the contrary to this view are overruled.

In the present case, the invalidity of Dyer's claim against the employer does not foreclose him, as a matter of law, from asserting that his forbearance was consideration for the alleged contract of settlement. However, the issue of Dyer's good faith must still be examined. In so doing, the issue of the validity of Dyer's claim should not be entirely overlooked:

Although the courts will not inquire into the validity of a claim which was compromised in good faith, there must generally be reasonable grounds for a belief in order for the court to be convinced that the belief was honestly entertained by the person who asserted it. Sufficient consideration requires more than the bald assertion by a claimant who has a claim, and to the extent that the validity or invalidity of a claim has a bearing upon whether there were reasonable grounds for believing in its possible validity, evidence of the validity or invalidity of a claim may be relevant to the issue of good faith.

15A Am.Jur.2d *Compromise and Settlement* § 17, at 790. We conclude that the evidence of the invalidity of the claim is relevant to show a lack of honest belief in the validity of the claim asserted or forborne.

Under the present state of the record, there remains a material [question] as to whether Dyer's forbearance to assert his claim was in good faith. Summary judgment should not have been rendered against him. Accordingly, the case is reversed and remanded for further proceedings consistent with this opinion.

Reversed and remanded.

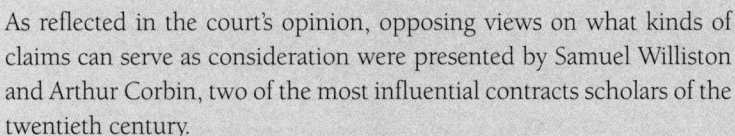

Who's That?

As reflected in the court's opinion, opposing views on what kinds of claims can serve as consideration were presented by Samuel Williston and Arthur Corbin, two of the most influential contracts scholars of the twentieth century.

Samuel Williston* (1861-1963) taught at Harvard Law School from 1890 to 1938. Among other accomplishments, he drafted several uniform laws that became the basis for the Uniform Commercial Code, published a five-volume treatise on contract law that remains authoritative (though now edited by others), was one of the original members of the American Law Institute, and was primary draftsman of the first Restatement

* Picture appears courtesy of Historical & Special Collections, Harvard Law School Library.

of Contracts. Williston is known as a "formalist," emphasizing the application of general principles of law sometimes seen as divorced from normative and policy considerations.

 Arthur Corbin (1874-1967) taught at Yale Law School from 1903 until his retirement in 1943. He helped to introduce the case method of teaching at Yale and was the author of many books and articles on the subject of contracts. He published his own eight-volume treatise on contracts in 1950 (like Williston's, it is still authoritative though edited by others), was adviser to the Reporters of both the first and second Restatement of Contracts, and his scholarship was influential in the creation of the Uniform Commercial Code. Corbin is known as a "realist," concerned that the law reflect the changing social and economic context.

How are the assumptions and philosophies of these two scholars reflected in *Dyer*? You should watch for references to both Corbin and Williston in the cases you read to help you understand and evaluate the arguments made, as well as to place those arguments in historical and theoretical context.

Problem 2-20: Settlement Agreements and Consideration

Recall the facts in *Schnell v. Nell*, page 80. Assume that instead of signing the agreement that appears in that opinion, Nell filed a claim against the estate of Theresa Schnell, seeking recovery of the $200 promised her in Theresa's will. Thereafter, Zacharias Schnell and Nell entered the following agreement:

> Zacharias Schnell and J.B. Nell agree as follows: Nell will withdraw her claim against the estate of Theresa Schnell and waive any further right to pursue such claim. In exchange, Zacharias Schnell agrees to pay $150 to Nell.

Schnell then refuses to pay any sum to Nell. Nell files suit to compel performance of the above agreement. Schnell claims lack of consideration. How should the court rule?

§ 6. Contract Modification and the Pre-Existing Duty Rule

Under the traditional common law rule, the requirement that a promise have consideration to be enforceable applies not only to the formation of a contract, but also to its modification, because the agreement to modify is itself a contract that must satisfy the rules on contract formation. If the duties of both parties to the contract change, there is no problem finding consideration because each party's promise to undertake new responsibilities is supported by the promise of the other party to perform new duties. For example, in a contract to build a structure, the builder may agree to add another interior wall to the original plans while the owner agrees to pay an additional amount for the work.

Often, however, the parties to a contract agree to a change in the responsibilities of only one party to a contract, perhaps because performance has become unexpectedly burdensome to one of the parties. For example, a natural disaster makes lumber and therefore the costs for a construction contractor considerably more expensive and the parties agree the increased cost to the builder will be shared on a specified basis with the homeowner, who originally agreed to a fixed price for the construction project. Or a debtor may face unexpected hardship and the creditor might agree to accept less than the full amount as satisfaction of the debt in order to consider the matter closed, perhaps out of sympathy for the debtor's situation. Under such circumstances, the requirement that consideration exist for the modification may be problematic. The duty promised under the original contract—the structure promised by the builder, or the amount of the debt, in the examples—is already owed to the other party. It is, in legal terms, a "pre-existing duty" and so, under traditional common law principles, it cannot serve as consideration for a new promise to pay more or receive less than originally required under the contract.

The pre-existing duty rule has been subject to substantial criticism since at least the early part of the nineteenth century in the United States and in England, where the rule originated.* Although the effect of the rule has been moderated by manipulation, by some common law reforms, and by some statutory enactments, the rule itself remains law in most jurisdictions.** The cases and statutory

---

* For example, the Minnesota Supreme Court long ago described the rule as "one of the relics of antique law which should have been discarded long ago. It is evidence of the former capacity of lawyers and judges to make the requirement of consideration an overworked shibboleth rather than a logical and just standard of actionability." *Rye v. Phillips*, 282 N.W. 459, 460 (Minn. 1938). Almost 40 years earlier, the Washington Supreme Court noted that, "[f]or many years, . . . courts have been dissatisfied with this rule, and have refused to extend the doctrine, but have sought to restrict the operation of the rule whenever it was possible. It is certainly not in accordance with ethics, and ought not to be in accord with the rules of law . . . ." *Brown v. Kern*, 57 P. 798, 799 (Wash. 1899).

** *See* Kevin M. Teeven, *Development of Reform of the Preexisting Duty Rule and its Persistent Survival*, 47 Ala. L. Rev. 387 (1996).

material in this section will introduce you to the application of the rule and its exceptions, the criticisms of the rule, and some of the reforms that have limited its influence.

Reading the Law Critically: *Angel* and *Birdsall*

1. What kind of modification is made to the original contract and why did the parties agree to it? What challenges does the pre-existing duty rule present to enforceability?

2. What justifications or rationale are or may be given for the pre-existing duty rule? What arguments are or may be made against its operation?

3. Does the court find that consideration existed, despite application of the pre-existing duty rule, or does the court create an exception to the rule?

4. What mechanisms or strategies do the courts describe to "get around" the pre-existing duty rule (that is, to avoid applying the rule while not changing it)?

Angel v. Murray

ALFRED L. ANGEL, Plaintiff-Appellee

v.

JOHN E. MURRAY, JR., Director of Finance of the City of Newport,
and JAMES L. MAHER, Defendants-Appellants

Supreme Court of Rhode Island
322 A.2d 630 (R.I. 1974)

ROBERTS, Chief Justice.

This is a civil action brought by Alfred L. Angel and others against John E. Murray, Jr., Director of Finance of the City of Newport, the city of Newport, and James L. Maher, alleging that Maher had illegally been paid the sum of $20,000 by the Director of Finance and praying that the defendant Maher be ordered to repay the city such sum. The case was heard by a justice of the Superior Court, sitting without a jury, who entered a judgment ordering Maher to repay the sum of $20,000 to the city of Newport. Maher is now before this court prosecuting an appeal.

The record discloses that Maher has provided the city of Newport with a refuse-collection service under a series of five-year contracts beginning in 1946.

On March 12, 1964, Maher and the city entered into another such contract for a period of five years commencing on July 1, 1964, and terminating on June 30, 1969. The contract provided, among other things, that Maher would receive $137,000 per year in return for collecting and removing all combustible and non-combustible waste materials generated within the city.

In June of 1967 Maher requested an additional $10,000 per year from the city council because there had been a substantial increase in the cost of collection due to an unexpected and unanticipated increase of 400 new dwelling units. Maher's testimony, which is uncontradicted, indicates the 1964 contract had been predicated on the fact that since 1946 there had been an average increase of 20 to 25 new dwelling units per year. After a public meeting of the city council where Maher explained in detail the reasons for his request and was questioned by members of the city council, the city council agreed to pay him an additional $10,000 for the year ending on June 30, 1968. Maher made a similar request again in June of 1968 for the same reasons, and the city council again agreed to pay an additional $10,000 for the year ending on June 30, 1969.

The trial justice found that each such $10,000 payment was made in violation of law. His decision, as we understand it, is premised on two independent grounds. First, he found that the additional payments were unlawful because they had not been recommended in writing to the city council by the city manager. Second, he found that Maher was not entitled to extra compensation because the original contract already required him to collect all refuse generated within the city and, therefore, included the 400 additional units. The trial justice further found that these 400 additional units were within the contemplation of the parties when they entered into the contract. It appears that he based this portion of the decision upon the rule that Maher had a preexisting duty to collect the refuse generated by the 400 additional units, and thus there was no consideration for the two additional payments.

[Discussion of the city council's power to modify the 1964 contract omitted.]

II.

Having found that the city council had the power to modify the 1964 contract without the written recommendation of the city manager, we are still confronted with the question of whether the additional payments were illegal because they were not supported by consideration.

A.

As previously stated, the city council made two $10,000 payments. The first was made in June of 1967 for the year beginning on July 1, 1967, and ending on

1st payment didn't need consideration because had already collected

June 30, 1968. Thus, by the time this action was commenced in October of 1968, the modification was completely executed. That is, the money had been paid by the city council, and Maher had collected all of the refuse. Since consideration is only a test of the enforceability of executory promises, the presence or absence of consideration for the first payment is unimportant because the city council's agreement to make the first payment was fully executed at the time of the commencement of this action. See *Salvas v. Jussaume*, 50 R.I. 75, 145 A. 97 (1929); *Young Foundation Corp. v. A. E. Ottaviano, Inc.*, 29 Misc.2d 302, 216 N.Y.S.2d 448, aff'd 15 A.D.2d 517, 222 N.Y.S.2d 685 (1961); . . . . However, since both payments were made under similar circumstances, our decision regarding the second payment (Part B, infra) is fully applicable to the first payment.

B.

It is generally held that a modification of a contract is itself a contract, which is unenforceable unless supported by consideration. See Simpson, supra, § 93. In *Rose v. Daniels*, 8 R.I. 381 (1866), this court held that an agreement by a debtor with a creditor to discharge a debt for a sum of money less than the amount due is unenforceable because it was not supported by consideration.

Rose is a perfect example of the preexisting duty rule. Under this rule an agreement modifying a contract is not supported by consideration if one of the parties to the agreement does or promises to do something that he is legally obligated to do or refrains or promises to refrain from doing something he is not legally privileged to do. See Calamari & Perillo, Contracts § 60 (1970); 1A Corbin, Contracts §§ 171-72 (1963); 1 Williston, supra, § 130; Annot., 12 A.L.R.2d 78 (1950). In *Rose* there was no consideration for the new agreement because the debtor was already legally obligated to repay the full amount of the debt.

Although the preexisting duty rule is followed by most jurisdictions, a small minority of jurisdictions, Massachusetts, for example, find that there is consideration for a promise to perform what one is already legally obligated to do because the new promise is given in place of an action for damages to secure performance. See *Swartz v. Lieberman*, 323 Mass. 109, 80 N.E.2d 5 (1948); *Munroe v. Perkins*, 26 Mass. (9 Pick.) 298 (1830). Swartz is premised on the theory that a promisor's forbearance of the power to breach his original agreement and be sued in an action for damages is consideration for a subsequent agreement by the promisee to pay extra compensation. This rule, however, has been widely criticized as an anomaly. See Calamari & Perillo, supra, § 61; Annot., 12 A.L.R.2d 78, 85-90 (1950).

The primary purpose of the preexisting duty rule is to prevent what has been referred to as the "hold-up game." See 1A Corbin, supra, § 171. A classic example of the "hold-up game" is found in *Alaska Packers' Ass'n v. Domenico*, 117 F. 99 (9th Cir. 1902). There 21 seamen entered into a written contract with Domenico to sail from San Francisco to Pyramid Harbor, Alaska. They were to work as sailors and fishermen out of Pyramid Harbor during the fishing season of 1900. The contract specified that each man would be paid $50 plus two cents for each red salmon he caught. Subsequent to their arrival at Pyramid Harbor, the men stopped work and demanded an additional $50. They threatened to return to San Francisco if Domenico did not agree to their demand. Since it was impossible for Domenico to find other men, he agreed to pay the men an additional $50. After they returned to San Francisco, Domenico refused to pay the men an additional $50. The court found that the subsequent agreement to pay the men an additional $50 was not supported by consideration because the men had a preexisting duty to work on the ship under the original contract, and thus the subsequent agreement was unenforceable.

Behind the Scenes

For a look at the history of the Alaska Packers' Association and the salmon industry, go to www.youtube.com/watch?v=qN55l8ejhdU. Recent research has suggested that the story told in *Alaska Packers' Ass'n* is more complicated, and there may well be reason to think the plaintiff seamen had a legitimate claim that the defendant was breaching its responsibilities under the contract to provide adequate nets for fishing. *See* Debora L. Threedy, *A Fish Story: Alaska Packers' Association v. Domenico*, 2000 Utah L. Rev. 185. If that were so, how would that change the analysis?

Another example of the "hold-up game" is found in the area of construction contracts. Frequently, a contractor will refuse to complete work under an unprofitable contract unless he is awarded additional compensation. The courts have generally held that a subsequent agreement to award additional compensation is unenforceable if the contractor is only performing work which would have been required of him under the original contract. See, e.g., *Lingenfelder v. Wainwright Brewing Co.*, 103 Mo. 578, 15 S.W. 844 (1891), which is a leading case in this area. See also cases collected in Annot., **25 A.L.R. 1450 (1923)**, supplemented by Annot., **55 A.L.R. 1333 (1928)**, and Annot., **138 A.L.R. 136 (1942)**; cf. *Ford & Denning v. Shepard Co.*, 36 R.I. 497, 90 A. 805 (1914).

These examples clearly illustrate that the courts will not enforce an agreement that has been procured by coercion or duress and will hold the parties to their original contract regardless of whether it is profitable or unprofitable. However, the courts have been reluctant to apply the preexisting duty rule when a party to a contract encounters unanticipated difficulties and the other party, not influenced by coercion or duress, voluntarily agrees to pay additional compensation for work already required to be performed under the contract. For example, the courts have found that the original contract was rescinded, *Linz v. Schuck*, 106 Md. 220, 67 A. 286 (1907); abandoned, *Connelly v. Devoe*, 37 Conn. 570 (1871), or waived, *Michaud v. McGregor*, 61 Minn. 198, 63 N.W. 479 (1895).

Although the preexisting duty rule has served a useful purpose insofar as it deters parties from using coercion and duress to obtain additional compensation, it has been widely criticized as a general rule of law. With regard to the preexisting duty rule, one legal scholar has stated: "There has been a growing doubt as to the soundness of this doctrine as a matter of social policy. . . . In certain classes of cases, this doubt has influenced courts to refuse to apply the rule, or to ignore it, in their actual decisions. Like other legal rules, this rule is in process of growth and change, the process being more active here than in most instances. The result of this is that a court should no longer accept this rule as fully established. It should never use it as the major premise of a decision, at least without giving careful thought to the circumstances of the particular case, to the moral deserts of the parties, and to the social feelings and interests that are involved. It is certain that the rule, stated in general and all-inclusive terms, is no longer so well-settled that a court must apply it though the heavens fall." 1A Corbin, supra, § 171; see also Calamari & Perillo, supra, § 61.

Think About It!

The opinion says courts have avoided applying the preexisting duty rule by finding the original contract was rescinded, abandoned, or waived. According to *Black's Law Dictionary*, to *rescind* is "to abrogate or cancel (a contract) unilaterally or by agreement"; *abandonment* is "the relinquishment of a right or interest with the intention of never reclaiming it'"; and *waiver* is "[t]he voluntary relinquishment or abandonment—express or implied— of a legal right or advantage . . . . The party alleged to have waived a right must have had both knowledge of the existing right and the intention of forgoing it." How would these theories operate to avoid the need to invoke the preexisting duty rule? Would such theories have worked in *Angel*? Why or why not?

The modern trend appears to recognize the necessity that courts should enforce agreements modifying contracts when unexpected or unanticipated difficulties arise during the course of the performance of a contract, even though there is no consideration for the modification, as long as the parties agree voluntarily.

Under the Uniform Commercial Code, § 2-209(1), which has been adopted by 49 states, "(a)n agreement modifying a contract (for the sale of goods) needs no consideration to be binding." See G.L.1956 (1969 Reenactment) § 6A-2-209(1). Although at first blush this section appears to validate modifications obtained by coercion and duress, the comments to this section indicate that a modification under this section must meet the test of good faith imposed by the Code, and a modification obtained by extortion without a legitimate commercial reason is unenforceable.

The modern trend away from a rigid application of the preexisting duty rule is reflected by § 89D(a) of the American Law Institute's Restatement Second of the Law of Contracts, which provides: "A promise modifying a duty under a contract not fully performed on either side is binding (a) if the modification is fair and equitable in view of circumstances not anticipated by the parties when the contract was made . . . ."

FYI

Draft § 89(D)(a) became § 89 in the Restatement (Second). The complete text of § 89 follows this opinion.

We believe that § 89D(a) is the proper rule of law and find it applicable to the facts of this case. It not only prohibits modifications obtained by coercion, duress, or extortion but also fulfills society's expectation that agreements entered into voluntarily will be enforced by the courts. See generally **Horwitz, The Historical Foundations of Modern Contract Law, 87 Harv.L.Rev. 917 (1974)**. Section 89D(a), of course, does not compel a modification of an unprofitable or unfair contract; it only enforces a modification if the parties voluntarily agree and if (1) the promise modifying the original contract was made before the contract was fully performed on either side, (2) the underlying circumstances which prompted the modification were unanticipated by the parties, and (3) the modification is fair and equitable.

The evidence, which is uncontradicted, reveals that in June of 1968 Maher requested the city council to pay him an additional $10,000 for the year beginning on July 1, 1968, and ending on June 30, 1969. This request was made at a public meeting of the city council, where Maher explained in detail his reasons for making the request. Thereafter, the city council voted to authorize the Mayor to sign an amendment to the 1964 contract which provided that Maher would receive an additional $10,000 per year for the duration of the contract. Under such circumstances we have no doubt that the city voluntarily agreed to modify the 1964 contract.

Having determined the voluntariness of this agreement, we turn our attention to the three criteria delineated above. First, the modification was made in June of 1968 at a time when the five-year contract which was made in 1964 had not been fully performed by either party. Second, although the 1964 contract provided that Maher collect all refuse generated within the city, it appears this contract was premised on Maher's past experience that the number of refuse-generating units would increase at a rate of 20 to 25 per year. Furthermore, the evidence is uncontradicted that the 1967-1968 increase of 400 units "went beyond any previous expectation." Clearly, the circumstances which prompted the city council to modify the 1964 contract were unanticipated.[4] Third, although the evidence does not indicate what proportion of the total this increase comprised, the evidence does indicate that it was a "substantial" increase. In light of this, we cannot say that the council's agreement to pay Maher the $10,000 increase was not fair and equitable in the circumstances.

The judgment appealed from is reversed, and the cause is remanded to the Superior Court for entry of judgment for the defendants.

Practice Pointer: Indemnification and Duty-to-Defend Clauses

The clause noted in the *Angel* court's footnote 4 is a "hold harmless" (indemnification) and duty-to-defend clause that shifts many risks from the city to the contractor.

An indemnification clause reallocates the risk of specified losses from the indemnified party (indemnitee) to the indemnifying party (indemnitor). If the indemnitee suffers the specified kind of loss, the indemnitor must reimburse the indemnitee for that loss. The clause may grant broad indemnification of, e.g., "all losses arising from the contract or its performance," or it may limit indemnification to a narrower scope, such as "any losses arising from the indemnitor's failure

---

[4] The trial justice found that sec. 2(a) of the 1964 contract precluded Maher from recovering extra compensation for the 400 additional units. Section 2(a) provided: "*The Contractor, having made his proposal after his own examinations and estimates, shall take all responsibility for, and bear, any losses resulting to him in carrying out the contract*; and shall assume the defence of, and hold the City, its agents and employees harmless from all suits and claims arising from the use of any invention, patent, or patent rights, material, labor or implement, by or from any act, omission or neglect of, the Contractor, his agents or employees, in carrying out the contract." (Emphasis added). The trial justice, quoting the italicized portion of sec. 2(a), found that this section required that any losses incurred in the performance of the contract were Maher's responsibility. In our opinion, however, the trial justice overlooked the thrust of sec. 2(a) when read in its entirety.

It is clearly a contractual provision requiring the contractor to hold the city harmless and to defend it in any litigation arising out of the performance of his obligations under the contract, whether a result of affirmative action or some omission or neglect on the part of Maher or his agents or employees. We are persuaded that the portion of sec. 2(a) specifically referred to by the court refers to losses resulting to Maher from some action or omission on the part of his own agents or employees. It cannot be disputed, however, that any losses that resulted from an increase in the cost of collecting from the increased number of units generating refuse in no way resulted from any action on the part of either Maher or his employees. Rather, whatever losses he did entail by reason of the requirement of such extra collection resulted from actions completely beyond his control and thus unanticipated.

to provide non-infringing software." The clause may limit the extent of indemnification by specifying a maximum dollar amount or limiting recovery in some other fashion, e.g., by capping liability at an amount equal to the indemnitee's payments to date to indemnitor or indemnitee's insurance deficiency.

A duty-to-defend clause requires one party to defend against claims brought against another party if the claims are within the scope of the clause. The clause may cover a broad or narrow range of claims, covering, for instance, "only claims filed in court," "any copyright infringement claim," or perhaps "any and all claims brought against the defended party that relate to this contract." Clauses vary as to the type and timing of notice given to the defending party; whether the defended party has a say in the choice of lawyers, the litigation strategy, and any settlement agreement; the nature of the cooperation the defended party owes the defending party; and whether the defended party must share some of the costs.

Birdsall v. Saucier

VIRGINIA BIRDSALL, *et al.*, Plaintiffs

v.

FERNANDO SAUCIER, *et al.*, Defendants

Connecticut Superior Court
1992 WL 37731 (Conn. Super. Ct. Feb. 24, 1992) (unpublished opinion)

BLUE, Judge.

One of the peculiarities of the common law is that a creditor may accept anything in satisfaction of a liquidated debt except a lesser sum of money. Almost four centuries ago, Sir Edward Coke opined that a creditor might take "a horse, hawk, or robe" if he chose and that would be accord and satisfaction. *Pinnell's Case,* 77 Eng.Rep. 237 (C.P.

What's That?

A "liquidated debt" is a debt whose amount has been determined by agreement of the parties or by operation of law. If the amount owed on a debt is not established, it is said to be unliquidated.

1602). The only thing that he may not take is ninety cents on the dollar. The present case involves a modern debtor who did not have a horse, hawk, or robe but did settle a debt with the assignment of a promissory note of a third party. The court holds that this assignment, which was satisfactory to the creditor at the time (much to her present chagrin), was sufficient consideration to satisfy the debt.

Virginia Birdsall is a real estate broker who does business under the names of Birdsall Agency and Birdsall Realty in Middlebury. Roy Birdsall ("Birdsall") is a real estate broker in her employ. Fernando Saucier ("Saucier") is a real estate entrepenuer who at the time of the events in question was the president and sole shareholder of B & S Realty of Bristol, Inc. ("B & S"). The only substantial asset of B & S, a now-dissolved corporation, was a large office and restaurant building in Bristol. The Birdsalls are the plaintiffs in this action; Saucier and B & S are the defendants. . . . From the evidence submitted at the hearing, the court finds the following facts.

[Birdsall agreed to help Saucier find a buyer for his building. He and Saucier agreed that, if Birdsall was able to find a buyer at an acceptable price, Saucier would pay Birdsall a commission of ten percent of the gross sales price. Birdsall found a pair of buyers, Mark Silverstein and Aryeh Shander, who agreed to purchase the building for $1,150,000, a price Saucier was willing to accept. Ten percent of that price, or $115,000, would be payable to Birdsall on the closing date, August 15. As the closing date approached, however, Saucier was experiencing cash flow problems, so he asked Birdsall to consider an alternative payment method. Instead of receiving $115,000 cash, Birdsall would receive $29,500 cash at the real estate closing and additional payments over five years, funded by the money that Silverstein and Shander would pay Saucier under a promissory note executed as part of the purchase agreement, which Saucier would assign to Birdsall. The additional payments would amount to 10% annual interest on a debt of $73,000, paid for five years, and then a lump sum of $73,000.]

. . . The court finds that Birdsall—and, by inference, his employer, Virginia Birdsall (who did not testify)—was satisfied with what he received. Perhaps the reason for this lies in simple mathematics. Had the note from Silverstein and Shander been fully paid, Birdsall would have received $22,500 in interest payments plus $73,000 in principal (admittedly after a delay of five and a half years). These payments when added to the $29,500 check that Birdsall received at the closing, would have equaled $125,000, or $10,000 more than he was originally entitled to receive. Of course, Birdsall was also aware from his previous meeting with Saucier that, if he had not been willing to take part of his compensation in "paper," the closing would not have gone through and his practical ability to collect the fee he was legally owed might well have been seriously impaired. It is a fair inference from these facts that there was a meeting of the minds between Birdsall and Saucier that the $29,500 in cash and the assignment of the $73,000 note were to constitute full satisfaction of any claim for commission against Saucier that Birdsall might have.

In any event, the building was sold, and Birdsall had his check and his "paper." [In an earlier part of the opinion, the court noted that, at or shortly after the closing, Birdsall gave Saucier a receipt, which acknowledged payment of $29,500 and assignment of the $73,000 note and concluded with the words "Commission paid in full."] Birdsall proceeded to contentedly collect his interest payments from Silverstein and Shander for three years. Then, Birdsall's bargain melted into the air. The last interest payment paid was that of January 1, 1989 (apparently paid sometime in December 1988). On April 1, 1989, Birdsall's mailbox was as bare as Mother Hubbard's cupboard. So, for that matter, was Saucier's. (Saucier was owed a substantially greater amount on his second mortgage.) Demands to Silverstein and Shander from all quarters proved fruitless. Nothing was paid thereafter.

. . . .

. . . On March 22, 1991, the Birdsalls commenced the present action.

The first count [of the complaint] seeks recovery of $73,000 as the allegedly unpaid balance of the plaintiffs' commission for their services under the open listing agreement of May 1, 1985. The second count alleges that Saucier is liable for the unpaid debts of B & S (which dissolved shortly after the 1985 closing) and that one of these debts is the $73,000 owed to the plaintiffs. . . . Because the first two counts involve the same underlying debt, they can be conveniently discussed together. As an affirmative defense to the first two counts, the defendants have pleaded accord and satisfaction. The court finds that defense to be established.

"An accord is a contract between creditor and debtor for the settlement of a claim by some performance other than that which is due. Satisfaction takes place when the accord is executed." *W.H. McCune, Inc. v. Revzon,* **151 Conn. 107, 109, 193 A.2d 601 (1963).** An accord, however, is an agreement, and an agreement will not be considered binding by the courts unless it is supported by consideration. *Id.* At an early date in English history it was held that a creditor could not take five pounds in satisfaction of a fifteen pound debt because he received no consideration for the other ten pounds. *Cumber v. Wane,* 93 Eng.Rep. 613 (1718); *Pinnell's Case, supra.* From the day this rule was announced, however, it has been recognized that dictates of fairness and considerations of business require that the rule be subject to certain exceptions. One well known exception is that an accord may be made "'[w]hen there is a good faith dispute about the existence of a debt or about the amount that is owed.'" *Blake v.*

> **Make the Connection**
>
> Recall the *Dyer* case, page 108, in which the court discussed the validity of settlement agreements entered into in good faith. An "accord," described here, is one kind of settlement agreement.

Blake, 211 Conn. 485, 491, 560 A.2d 396 (1989) (quoting *Fire Door Corp. v. C.F. Wooding Co.,* 202 Conn. 277, 281, 520 A.2d 1028 (1987)). That exception is not applicable here. There are, however, other well-established exceptions that are highly relevant to the instant case.

It was, in the first place, recognized in *Pinnell's Case* itself that, while a lesser sum cannot be satisfaction for a greater sum, "the gift of a horse, hawk, or robe . . . in satisfaction is good." 77 Eng.Rep. at 237. From that day to this, it has not been doubted that,

[handwritten: can payback with property]

> A liquidated money demand may, with the consent of the parties, be discharged by the delivery of property in payment thereof or by delivery of part money and part property; if the latter is received by the creditor in full discharge of the indebtedness, there is a good accord and satisfaction. The relative value of the property is immaterial as affecting the validity of the accord and satisfaction.

1 Am.Jur.2d *Accord and Satisfaction* Sect. 40 (1962).

This exception has long been acknowledged in Connecticut. In *Warren v. Skinner,* 20 Conn. 559 (1850), which recognized both the ancient English rule and its traditional exceptions,[1] it was stated that an agreement in satisfaction of a debt will be recognized when it "rests on a new and adequate consideration; as where the debtor pays a part of the debt . . . in a collateral article, agreed to be received in full payment." 20 Conn. at 561. . . .

Of course, not every debtor has a stock of cloth or pictures handy to pay off his debts. Commercially sensible arrangements are acceptable as well. In particular, it is well established that "[t]he acceptance, by a creditor, of the note of a third person, in satisfaction of an existing debt, is an extinguishment of such original indebtedness, and constitutes a good accord and satisfaction thereof, whether the note be for the full amount of the debt, or for a lesser sum." 1 C.J.S. *Accord and Satisfaction* Sect. 32 (1985). *See Barnett v. Rosen,* 235 Mass. 244, 126 N.E. 386, 388 (1920); *Dickinson v. Fletcher,* 181 Or. 316, 182 P.2d 371, 377 (1947); *In re Zeigler,* 83 S.C. 78, 64 S.E. 513, 514 (1909); *Welby v. Drake,* 171 Eng.Rep. 1315, 1316 (1825).

---

[1] *Warren v. Skinner* cites a number of English cases and apparently recognized English law on the subject to be controlling. That body of law makes it clear that even trivial objects may be good consideration for an accord and satisfaction. A piece of paper or a stick of sealing wax will do. *Sibree v. Tripp,* 153 Eng.Rep. 745, 752 (1846). So will a horse or a canary. *Couldery v. Bartrum,* 19 Ch.D. 394, 399 (1880). In a long-ago era, when it was accepted procedure for parties to buy time by the use of sham pleas, it was accepted procedure for a defendant to plead that he had given the plaintiff a beaver hat. *See Young v. Rudd,* 87 Eng.Rep. 535 (1696). "No one for a moment supposed that a beaver hat was really given and accepted; but everyone knew that the law was that if it was really given and accepted it was a good satisfaction." *Foakes v. Beer,* 9 App.Cas. 605, 618 (H.L.1884).

This latter exception has been recognized in Connecticut for over a hundred years. In *Argall v. Cook,* 43 Conn. 160, 166 (1875), it was held that a note endorsed by a third person may be taken in accord and satisfaction of a debt even when the note is for a lesser amount. The Supreme Court explained that, "The additional security which [the creditor] received by the indorsement was a sufficient legal consideration for the discharge." *Id.*

. . . .

The real question here is a factual one: did the parties—i.e., Birdsall and Saucier—agree that the settlement agreement *itself* constituted satisfaction of the original cause of action or did they instead agree that the *performance* of the agreement was to be the satisfaction. *See Air-Care N.O. Nelson Co. v. Patchet,* 5 Conn.App. 203, 205, 497 A.2d 771 (1985). This depends entirely "upon the intention of the parties." *Halloran v. Fischer,* 126 Conn. 44, 46, 9 A.2d 290 (1939). While there is "a strong presumption that the plaintiff would not, claiming a substantially undisputed amount to be due her, accept a mere promise to pay a much smaller sum in discharge of the larger amount," *id.,* that presumption is not applicable here, and to the extent that it is applicable, it is overcome by the facts. Here, Birdsall did not "accept a mere promise to pay a much smaller sum in discharge of the larger amount." As explained above, the note that he accepted, had it been fully paid, would have given him a *larger* sum at the end. In any event, there is no credible evidence that either party intended that the original debt of Saucier to Birdsall was to continue after the assignment of the note. There is, in contrast, credible evidence that both parties intended that the original debt was to be extinguished by the assignment. Were the facts otherwise, Birdsall—an experienced real estate broker—would not have given Saucier a written receipt stating "commission paid in full." It bears repeating that Birdsall was willing to do this because he wanted to save the deal and knew that a bird in the hand was worth two in the bush.

Birdsall was satisfied with the monetary payment of $29,500 and the note assigned to him by Saucier. He took money from Silverstein and Shander for three years without complaint. The debt that B & S owed to Birdsall was extinguished, and both parties intended it to be so. By any measure, the assignment of the note constituted a new and valid consideration. When Birdsall signed his receipt "commission paid in full," there was accord and satisfaction. Because of this he cannot now recover against the defendants no matter how bad his bargain has turned out to be.

Judgment shall enter for the defendants. *Birdsall loses, won't get paid*

Who's That?

Early in the *Birdsall* case, the opinion mentions Sir Edward Coke's opinion in *Pinnell's Case*, which established the pre-existing duty rule. Although that rule has been strongly criticized, Sir Edward Coke* (1552-1634) remains one of the most influential jurists in English history. Coke was a forceful champion of the supremacy of the common law, defending it against the prerogative power of the crown and the encroachments of ecclesiastical jurisdiction. He participated in many of the most notable cases of the day, either as attorney or as judge, including authoring the opinion in *Bonham's Case*, which played a role in challenges to the Stamp Act and writs of assistance in the period leading to the American Revolution and may have formed the basis for the rule in *Marbury v. Madison* that legislation may be declared unconstitutional in judicial review.

After serving as Member of Parliament, Solicitor General, and Attorney General of England and Wales, Coke became Chief Justice of the Court of Common Pleas in 1606. In 1613, Coke was elevated to Lord Chief Justice of the King's Bench. Although technically a promotion, the elevation may have been intended to moderate his attacks on the royal prerogative, placing him in the role of protector of the King's interests rather than of the people's rights. It failed to produce the desired result, however. In 1616, Coke—alone among the justices of the King's Bench—refused the request of the King to postpone proceedings in the *Case of Commendam*. When the justices were summoned by King James before the Privy Council, Coke refused to obey the King's command to stay the proceedings to permit time for the King to advise the court, but "would do that should be fit for a judge to do." As a result, Coke was removed as Lord Chief Judge in November 1616. In 1620, he was re-elected to Parliament, where he became leader of the opposition and, in 1628, drafted and helped enact the Petition of Right, one of the central English constitutional documents supporting civil liberties.

Coke's enduring influence is grounded in his writings, particularly his thirteen volumes of case reports and his four-volume treatise, *Institutes of the Lawes of England*, all of which continue to be important sources on the substance and development of early common law.

---

* Portrait appears courtesy of the National Portrait Gallery of England.

Reading the Law Critically:

Contract Modification in the Restatement, UCC and CISG

These sections from the Restatement (Second) of Contracts, the CISG, and selected statutory provisions address the issue of contract modification. What exceptions and reforms to the pre-existing duty rule are reflected in the Restatement and each of the other provisions? What advantages and disadvantages do you see in the rules chosen in each instance? How would these provisions affect the outcomes in *Angel* and *Birdsall*?

Restatement (Second) § 73. **Performance Of Legal Duty**

Performance of a legal duty owed to a promisor which is neither doubtful nor the subject of honest dispute is not consideration; but a similar performance is consideration if it differs from what was required by the duty in a way which reflects more than a pretense of bargain.

Restatement (Second) § 89. **Modification of Executory Contract**

A promise modifying a duty under a contract not fully performed on either side* is binding
(a) if the modification is fair and equitable in view of circumstances not anticipated by the parties when the contract was made; or
(b) to the extent provided by statute; or
(c) to the extent that justice requires enforcement in view of material change of position in reliance on the promise.

Illustrations:
1.   By a written contract A agrees to excavate a cellar for B for a stated price. Solid rock is unexpectedly encountered and A so notifies B. A and B then orally agree that A will remove the rock at a unit price which is reasonable but nine times that used in computing the original price, and A completes the job. B is bound to pay the increased amount.

---

* [Authors' Note: Restatement (Second) § 89 says it applies to an "executory contract," that is, one "not fully performed on either side." The only explanation for the restriction to executory contracts is the statement that the section "relates primarily to adjustments in on-going transactions. . . . [S]uch adjustments are ancillary to exchanges and have some of the same presumptive utility." Should the rule permitting modification of the duties of only one party be applied when duties remain unperformed by only one party to the contract?]

[handwritten margin notes: "Birdsall case" and "Angel case unanticipated difficulties"]

2. A contracts with B to supply for $300 a laundry chute for a building B has contracted to build for the Government for $150,000. Later A discovers that he made an error as to the type of material to be used and should have bid $1,200. A offers to supply the chute for $1,000, eliminating overhead and profit. After ascertaining that other suppliers would charge more, B agrees. The new agreement is binding.

3. A is employed by B as a designer of coats at $90 a week for a year beginning November 1 under a written contract executed September 1. A is offered $115 a week by another employer and so informs B. A and B then agree that A will be paid $100 a week and in October execute a new written contract to that effect, simultaneously tearing up the prior contract. The new contract is binding.

4. A contracts to manufacture and sell to B 2,000 steel roofs for corn cribs at $60. Before A begins manufacture a threat of a nationwide steel strike raises the cost of steel about $10 per roof, and A and B agree orally to increase the price to $70 per roof. A thereafter manufactures and delivers 1,700 of the roofs, and B pays for 1,500 of them at the increased price without protest, increasing the selling price of the corn cribs by $10. The new agreement is binding.

5. A contracts to manufacture and sell to B 100,000 castings for lawn mowers at 50 cents each. After partial delivery and after B has contracted to sell a substantial number of lawn mowers at a fixed price, A notifies B that increased metal costs require that the price be increased to 75 cents. Substitute castings are available at 55 cents, but only after several months delay. B protests but is forced to agree to the new price to keep its plant in operation. The modification is not binding.

***

UCC § 2-209. Modification, Rescission and Waiver

(1) An agreement modifying a contract within this Article needs no consideration to be binding.

(2) A signed agreement which excludes modification or rescission except by a signed writing cannot be otherwise modified or rescinded, but except as between merchants such a requirement on a form supplied by the merchant must be separately signed by the other party.

. . . .

(4) Although an attempt at modification or rescission does not satisfy the requirements of subsection (2) . . . it can operate as a waiver.

(5) A party who has made a waiver affecting an executory portion of the contract may retract the waiver by reasonable notification received by the other party that strict performance will be required of any term waived, unless the retraction would be unjust in view of a material change of position in reliance on the waiver.

Comments

1.   This section seeks to protect and make effective all necessary and desirable modifications of sales contracts without regard to the technicalities which at present hamper such adjustments.

2.   Subsection (1) provides that an agreement modifying a sales contract needs no consideration to be binding.

However, modifications made thereunder must meet the test of good faith imposed by this Act. The effective use of bad faith to escape performance on the original contract terms is barred, and the extortion of a "modification" without legitimate commercial reason is ineffective as a violation of the duty of good faith. Nor can a mere technical consideration support a modification made in bad faith.

The test of "good faith" between merchants or as against merchants includes "observance of reasonable commercial standards of fair dealing in the trade" (Section 2-103), and may in some situations require an objectively demonstrable reason for seeking a modification. But such matters as a market shift which makes performance come to involve a loss may provide such a reason even though there is no such unforeseen difficulty as would make out a legal excuse from performance under Sections 2-615 and 2-616.

———————

CISG Art. 29 (in Part III. Sale of Goods, Ch. 1 General Provisions)

(1) A contract may be modified or terminated by the mere agreement of the parties.

(2) A contract in writing which contains a provision requiring any modification or termination by agreement to be in writing may not be otherwise modified or terminated by agreement. However, a party may be precluded by his conduct from asserting such a provision to the extent that the other party has relied on that conduct.

UCC § 2-209 says that a "failed" modification may nonetheless operate as a "waiver," a concept mentioned by the *Angel* court on page 120. Unlike a valid modification, which is binding upon both parties' assent, a waiver results from the actions or communications of one party, and—as reflected in § 2-209(5) and also in case law—it may be retracted by that party, unless there has been material and reasonable reliance by the other party.

Problems: Contract Modification

In the following scenarios, what theory or theories offer support for the enforceability of the indicated promise?

2-21. Margery is hired by Narissa on January 1 to work for two years, for $1200 a month, with a termination date at the end of December of the second year. In October of the first year, Margery is offered a job by Oscar for $1500 a month. Margery and Narissa agree to tear up their existing contract and enter a new agreement for Margery to work for $1350 a month for the remainder of the original contract term. Is Narissa's promise to pay Margery an additional $150 a month enforceable? Consider the arguments suggested in *Angel* and highlighted in the Think About It! box on page 120.

2-22. Joseph Jockey was hired by the owner of the horse Winning Winnie to ride her in an important race. Ted is the owner of Winnie's sire (father) and dam (mother). In advance of the race, Ted promised Joseph that if he rode Winnie to victory, Ted would pay Joseph $5000, knowing that his own horses would be more valuable if Winnie takes first place. Is Ted's promise to Joseph enforceable? Should it matter that Joseph's original obligation is to Winnie's owner, not to Ted?.

2-23. Saybrook sold his farm to Pamela in January 2012 for $100,000. Under the terms of the sale, Pamela paid $40,000 at the time of the closing and agreed to pay Saybrook ½% interest a month on the remaining $60,000 (for an annual rate of 6%), due each month on the 15th, and then to make a final $60,000 payment on January 15, 2014. Under the terms of the sale, if Pamela did not make the scheduled payments, Saybrook could reclaim the land and sell it to make up the deficiency in payments.

Pamela made the interest payments each month through November 2013. On December 1, 2013, Pamela notified Saybrook that she could not make the final $60,000 payment on time because of financial difficulties she had been facing as the result of the market downturn. On December 10, Saybrook and Pamela agreed that Pamela would make the regular interest payment on December 15, would pay $20,000 on January 14, 2014, and would make a final payment of $42,000 on January 15, 2015, which would be the final payment of $40,000 on the original purchase price plus 5% interest on the $40,000 balance for the year. If Pamela does not pay as specified in the December 10, 2013 agreement, can Saybrook enforce the 2012 agreement or only the 2013 agreement?

2-24. On May 28, Husband and Wife signed a separation agreement. Husband agreed to convey all his right and interest in the couple's jointly owned property, including the house where they had lived together until the separation; to permit his wife absolute custody of their child; and to pay $100 per month in child support. The contract also provided that "the husband agrees to sign any and all papers necessary to effectuate the transfer of said property to the wife. The proceeds therefrom shall unconditionally and irrevocably go to the wife." Wife agreed to settle all her claims to alimony and support and waived any other claims she might have against Husband.

On the same night the agreement was signed, Wife received a phone call from her attorney requesting that she appear at his office the next day for a further conference. While there, she signed an "Addenda to the Agreement" of the previous day. The agreement specified that, "in exchange for consideration of one dollar," she agreed to give Husband $22,000 out of the proceeds when she sold the family home and that Husband would vacate the premises of that residence "as of today, May 29, and remove all his personal belongings therefrom."

Several months later, Wife sold the residence but did not pay any money to Husband. Husband sued to enforce her promise to pay $22,000. Wife claims lack of consideration. Can Husband enforce her promise?

If the agreement of Husband and Wife had been solely about transfer and sale of items of personal property (so the contract would fall under UCC Article 2), would the result be different?

2-25. In August 2005, Terry Teacher entered into a contract with the University to work from September 1, 2005, to August 31, 2006, as "Program Leader, Home Economics" at a specified salary. Teacher's duties under this position included planning, developing and executing educational programs in home economics. On November 1, her supervisor requested that she undertake the additional duties of acting leader for the 4-H Youth Development Program because the previous 4-H Program Leader did not return from his leave as expected in early October. Teacher and the University executed a formal, written addendum to Teacher's contract through August 31, 2006. The addendum changed Teacher's title from "Program Leader, Home Economics" to "Program Leader, Home Economics and Acting Program Leader, 4-H/Youth Development." The addendum said the change in title would be effective November 15, confirmed that Teacher's salary would stay the same, and expressed the University's thanks for Teacher's cooperation in "accepting this new assignment." Is Teacher's promise to perform the additional duties as 4-H Program leader enforceable?

§ 7. Stretching the Limits of Consideration Doctrine

Admittedly, it is usually much easier to determine whether consideration exists than would appear from the cases in this chapter. The difference between gift and contract is in most instances a bright line, and in most contract disputes it is easy to identify the consideration for each party's promises. But there *are* difficult cases, as is illustrated in this chapter, and it is those difficult cases that both explore the boundaries of the doctrine and offer opportunities to practice the subtle skill of legal argumentation.

Reading the Law Critically: *Lawrence*

The following case is a prime example of circumstances that test the limits of the doctrine of consideration and perhaps even challenge the worth of the concept as a dividing line between enforceable and unenforceable promises. Consider the arguments made by both the majority and the dissent. Who has the better position?

Lawrence v. Ingham County Health Dept.
Family Planning/Pre-Natal Clinic

ETHEL LAWRENCE, Individually and as Next Friend of JESSICA LAWRENCE, a Minor, and DOUGLAS J. LAWRENCE, Plaintiffs-Appellants

v.

INGHAM COUNTY HEALTH DEPARTMENT FAMILY PLANNING/PRE-NATAL CLINIC, Defendant-Appellee, and
A. BRECK, M.D., WILLIAM C. CARLEY, M.D., L. SANBORN, M.D., D. HOLDEN, M.D., A. CROW, M.D., EDWARD W. SPARROW HOSPITAL, ST. LAWRENCE HOSPITAL, ROBERT POSEY, M.D., and J.C. LESHOCK, M.D., Jointly and Severally, Defendants

Michigan Court of Appeals
408 N.W.2d 461 (Mich. Ct. App. 1987)

KELLY, Presiding Judge.

Plaintiffs appeal as of right from an order of summary disposition granted under MCR 2.116(C)(8) in favor of defendant Ingham County Health Department Family Planning/Pre-Natal Clinic. We affirm.

Plaintiffs filed this three-count complaint following the birth of their daughter, Jessica Lawrence. According to the allegations in the complaint, which are taken as true for purposes of deciding and reviewing a motion under MCR 2.116(C)(8), plaintiff Ethel Lawrence first visited defendant clinic on December 13, 1979, for a pregnancy test. She reported her last menstrual period as October 19, 1979, and tested positive for pregnancy. Plaintiff then continued routine prenatal treatment with the clinic. On August 19, 1980, she appeared at defendant St. Lawrence Hospital in labor, where she underwent an emergency Caesarean section. Jessica Lawrence suffered fetal distress and prenatal asphyxia, which plaintiffs theorized could have been prevented by applying standard procedures for postmature fetuses. Following the delivery, Jessica was resuscitated and transferred to defendant Edward W. Sparrow Hospital. She sustained permanent, serious brain damage.

Plaintiffs' original complaint alleged various acts of negligence on the part of the individual physicians, the clinic and the two hospitals. Defendant clinic was granted summary disposition as to the negligence claims on the ground of governmental immunity. See *Ross v. Consumers Power Co. (On Rehearing)*, 420 Mich. 567, 363 N.W.2d 641 (1984). Plaintiffs do not appeal from that ruling.

Plaintiffs' third amended complaint included two counts of breach of contract. In paragraphs 4 and 5 of Count II of their third amended complaint, plaintiffs allege breach of an enforceable agreement between plaintiffs Ethel and Douglas Lawrence and the clinic and clinic physicians:

"4. That thereafter, Defendant Ingham County Health Department Family Planning/Prenatal Clinic agreed to accept Plaintiff Ethel Lutman Lawrence as a patient and Plaintiff Ethel Lutman Lawrence agreed to follow the directions of the physicians and other medical personnel at the Defendant Clinic for the benefit of her unborn child.

> **FYI**
>
> In *Ross v. Consumers Power Co.*, cited by the Court of Appeals, the Michigan Supreme Court ruled that government agencies, both state and local, are immune from tort liability when engaged in the exercise or discharge of a governmental function, and are similarly immune from liability for actions of their employees carrying out such governmental functions. The court further concluded that a governmental function is any activity that is expressly or impliedly mandated or authorized by constitution, statute, or other law. The lower court in *Lawrence* considered the actions of the county health clinic to fall within those limits, so the clinic was immune from liability in tort for its actions and those of its doctors.

"5. That an implied contract in law was created as a result of the Defendant Clinic's offer to provide medical services to Plaintiff Ethel Lutman Lawrence within the then-existing and applicable standard of care and Plaintiff Ethel Lutman Lawrence's acceptance of said offer by agreeing to follow the directions of the Defendant Clinic's physicians and other medical personnel for the benefit of her unborn child."

. . . .

The lower court found that plaintiffs failed to state a cause of action for breach of contract and granted summary disposition in favor of defendant clinic. Summary disposition on this ground tests the legal basis of the complaint, not whether it can be factually supported, and is proper only when the claim is so clearly unenforceable as a matter of law that no factual development can possibly justify a right to recover. *Bradford v. Michigan,* 153 Mich.App. 756, 761, 396 N.W.2d 522 (1986). The trial court concluded that plaintiffs failed to plead facts that would support a finding of adequate consideration and that plaintiffs' contract claim must therefore fail.

Plaintiffs argue that the consideration provided by plaintiff Ethel Lawrence was her agreement not to have an abortion and her agreement to follow the directions of the clinic medical staff. Plaintiffs contend that, by entering into these agreements, Ethel Lawrence refrained from doing that which she was legally privileged to do and thereby rendered valuable consideration in return for defendant clinic's promise to provide adequate prenatal care. Since plaintiffs have not alleged in their complaint that Ethel Lawrence agreed not to have an abortion in return for the promise of medical care, we will not consider this argument further.[2]

The contract described by plaintiffs involves an exchange of promises: Ethel Lawrence's promise to follow directions in exchange for the clinic's promise to provide appropriate prenatal care. In order for Ethel Lawrence's promise to rise to the level of consideration sufficient to support a contract implied in fact, however, that promise must be of some value to defendant clinic. We think this means the promise must be enforceable. Although we recognize that mutuality of obligation is not always a necessary element to every contract, we are persuaded that, in the context of this case, lack of mutuality of obligation translates into lack of consideration:

> "Inasmuch as a promise by one person is merely one of the kinds of consideration that will support a promise by another, mutuality of obligation is not an essential element in every contract. Therefore, to say the least, language which is susceptible of the interpretation that consideration and mutuality of obligation are two distinct elements lacks precision in that, while consideration is essential, mutuality of obligation is not, *unless the want of mutuality would leave one party without a valid or available consideration for his promise.*" 17 Am.Jur.2d, Contracts, § 11, pp. 347-348. (Emphasis added.)

Plaintiff Ethel Lawrence's agreement to follow the advice of the clinic's medical staff regarding prenatal health care is not a legally enforceable promise. Contrary to the position of plaintiffs below, we are not persuaded that defendant clinic has or had a cause of action for breach of contract against plaintiff for failure on her part to follow its medical advice. Plaintiff Ethel Lawrence was given advice on health care conducive to the well-being of her unborn baby. We hold that her acceptance of that advice cannot be deemed consideration for a contract. . . .

We do not evaluate the adequacy of the consideration allegedly rendered in this case since that would be a question for the factfinder rather than for us in determining the adequacy of plaintiff's pleadings. We simply conclude that plaintiffs' claim of consideration is so clearly unenforceable as a matter of law that no factual development can possibly justify their right to recover on the theory of defendant's breach of an implied contract in fact.

---

[2] We note, however, that our analysis would be the same on sufficient consideration even if we did address this argument. We are saved from examining the public policy implications of such an anomolous agreement by plaintiffs' complaint.

Affirmed.

KNOBLOCK, J., concurred.

SAWYER, Judge (dissenting).

I dissent.

Defendant health clinic made a promise to Ethel Lawrence that if she would come to the clinic and promise thereafter to follow its staff's directions, it would provide her and her unborn child with appropriate prenatal care. Despite these promises, which defendants must admit as true for purposes of the summary disposition motion, the majority concludes that Ethel's promise to follow the clinic's directions had no value to the clinic and, therefore, "is not a legally enforceable promise."

It is not the office of the courts to scrutinize the adequacy of consideration. *Harwood v. Randolph Harwood, Inc.*, 124 Mich.App. 137, 142, 333 N.W.2d 609 (1983). In fact, even the majority concedes in its final paragraph that "the adequacy of the consideration . . . [is] a question for the factfinder . . . ." How, then, can the majority now say that Ethel's promise is lacking in value? As I will explain more fully below, I am unable to sign my name to an opinion which on the one hand states that it will let the factfinder worry about the adequacy of consideration and, then, on the other hand holds that plaintiff Ethel Lawrence's consideration "is so clearly unenforceable as a matter of law." . . .

Summary disposition under MCR 2.116(C)(8) tests the legal basis of the complaint, not whether it can be factually supported, and is proper only when the claim is so clearly unenforceable as a matter of law that no factual development can possibly justify a right to recover. *Bradford v. Michigan*, 153 Mich.App. 756, 761, 396 N.W.2d 522 (1986).

Regarding Count II of the complaint, plaintiffs allege that there was an implied contract which defendant health clinic breached. The trial court concluded that there could be no contract as there was no consideration on plaintiffs' behalf:

Looking at the complaint in the light most favorable to the Plaintiff even if Plaintiff were able to sustain her proofs that she had not gotten an abortion and she had followed the directives [of the Health Department's physicians] when she was not obligated by law to do so, the Court does not believe that under any stretch of the imagination could that be considered as adequate or any form of consideration. I think to take that as consideration would expand the definition of the contract beyond all recognition.

The majority seems to follow this view, with which I disagree.

The concept of consideration was discussed in Calamari and Perillo, Contracts (2d ed.), § 4-1, pp. 133-134:

> Since the doctrine of consideration is an historical phenomenon and therefore in some of its aspects affected by fortuitous circumstances, an encompassing definition is perhaps impossible. Nonetheless, an attempt should be made. A learned judge [Cardozo, C.J., in *Allegheny College v. Nat'l Chautauqua Co. Bank*, 246 N.Y. 369, 159 N.E. 173 (1927)] has identified the three elements which must concur before a promise is supported by consideration.
>
> (a) The promisee must suffer legal detriment; that is, do or promise to do what he is not legally obligated to do; or refrain from doing or promise to refrain from doing what he is legally privileged to do.
>
> (b) The detriment must induce the promise. In other words the promisor must have made the promise because he wished to exchange it at least in part for the detriment to be suffered by the promisee.
>
> (c) The promise must induce the detriment. This means in effect, as we have already seen, that the promisee must know of the offer and intend to accept. [Footnotes omitted.]

In this case, plaintiffs argue that the consideration given by Ethel Lawrence was her agreement not to have an abortion and her agreement to follow the directions of the attending physicians.[2] Either of these agreements, if in fact they were made, would constitute a form of consideration. Her agreement not to have an abortion constitutes an agreement to refrain from doing that which she was legally privileged to do.[3] Her agreement to follow the advice of the physicians constitutes an agreement to do that which she was not legally obligated to do. Assuming that a factual development is made to show that Ms. Lawrence's agreements were made to induce defendant health clinic's agreement to provide services and, conversely, that defendant health clinic required Ms. Lawrence to make those agreements

---

[2] I recognize that, as pointed out by the majority, plaintiffs did not allege in their complaint that Ethel Lawrence agreed to refrain from undergoing an abortion as part of her agreement. However, plaintiffs did so argue in the trial court. Since plaintiffs could easily have added such an allegation to their complaint by way of amendment, and since amendments to complaints should be freely given, MCR 2.118(A)(2), *Ben P. Fyke & Sons v. Gunter Co.*, 390 Mich. 649, 213 N.W.2d 134 (1973), I believe we can properly consider that argument as part of plaintiffs' claim of consideration. However, I would reach the same result if I considered only plaintiffs' claim of consideration arising from the agreement to follow the physicians' advice.

[3] See *Roe v. Wade*, 410 U.S. 113, 93 S.Ct. 705, 35 L.Ed.2d 147 (1973).

in order to receive the health services, then a contract would exist between the parties.

The flaw in the majority's reasoning is evident from the following statement:

> Plaintiff Ethel Lawrence's agreement to follow the advice of the clinic's medical staff regarding prenatal health care is not a legally enforceable promise.

The majority, however, offers no authority for this conclusion. I am aware of no rule of law, be it statutory, regulatory or common law, which would operate to prevent a person from contractually obligating himself to following the advice of a physician. Since a person is free to do so, upon contractually binding oneself to following a physician's advice, that person exposes himself to a breach of contract action for a subsequent failure to follow the advice. The majority apparently confuses the unusualness of plaintiffs' theory in application with its viability in the abstract. That is, while I would be surprised to learn that it is common practice for patients to contractually agree to be bound by their physicians' advice, I do not believe such contracts are unenforceable as a matter of law.[4]

The same principle applies to plaintiffs' argument concerning the agreement not to have an abortion. While I am aware of no institution which demands such a promise, I can easily imagine that a private health clinic, run by a charitable or religious organization, might well offer free prenatal care as an inducement to prevent women from having an abortion.[5] While such an arrangement would undoubtedly prove difficult for a court to attempt to enforce or to provide a remedy for a breach of such an arrangement, I am unwilling to conclude at this time that such agreements are legally unenforceable.

Once the conclusion is reached that a person may legally bind himself to follow a physician's advice, or to forego an action he is legally privileged to take, it becomes a factual question whether he has made such an agreement. It is improper to resolve that factual question in the context of a motion brought pursuant to MCR 2.116(C)(8) or in an appeal from an order granted under that subrule.

The majority's and the trial court's alternative conclusion, that the consideration, if any, was inadequate is more easily disposed of. It is not ordinarily the role of the courts to question the adequacy of the consideration supporting the

---

[4] In fact, I can imagine situations in which a physician would wish to contractually bind his patient to take certain actions. For example, a physician may offer services for free or at a reduced fee in order to develop a new technique wherein the patient's obeyance is essential to the physician's perfection and evaluation of the technique. While admittedly an uncommon occurrence, it does point to the flaw in the majority's broad-sweeping principle.

[5] The question of a governmental agency demanding such a promise from a woman in exchange for services opens a Pandora's Box which, fortunately, we have not yet been called upon to open.

contract. Any consideration, no matter how economically insignificant, is sufficient to support a contract. See *Harwood, supra,* 124 Mich.App. at 142, 333 N.W.2d 609.[6]

To summarize, I would hold that a person may contractually obligate himself to follow the directions of a physician, or to forego an action he is legally privileged to perform. Where such an obligation is given in exchange for the promise of another to perform services, that obligation serves as consideration and a contract is established.

I would stress, however, the fact that this case comes to us by way of a motion for summary disposition for failure to state a claim. I express no opinion as to whether plaintiffs will be able to prove at trial, or even be able to survive a motion for summary disposition for no genuine issue of material fact, that Ms. Lawrence made her agreements in exchange for defendant health department's agreement to provide the health services. If the agreement of one did not induce the agreement of the other, then there is no contract. Similarly, we have not been called upon to consider whether defendant health department has provided consideration. Its only agreement appears to have been to provide health services. If, for example, it was under a preexisting legal duty to provide Ms. Lawrence with the health services, then its agreement to do so cannot constitute consideration. *Lowery v. Dep't of Corrections,* 146 Mich.App. 342, 359, 380 N.W.2d 99 (1985).

While I recognize that plaintiffs' claim is, at best, novel and, at worst, tenuous, I do not believe that should provide the basis for summarily dismissing the complaint. Plaintiffs' theory is novel and, I suspect, it will prove difficult for them to establish the existence of the alleged promises and that the promise of each party induced the promise of the other. That is, I am not at all convinced that defendant health department required Ethel Lawrence to make the promises she allegedly did in order to receive medical attention. However, the point which seems to elude the majority and the trial court is that plaintiffs have not yet been called upon to convince anyone, be it this Court, the trial court, or a jury, that their claim can be borne out by the facts. To date, plaintiffs have only been called upon to state a claim. In my opinion, they have done so.

Judge Kelly once opined that "[a]s in most *trials,* somebody wins and somebody loses."[9] However, the majority today would have plaintiffs lose before they have even had their day in court. To me, that is unconscionable.

I would reverse.

---

[6] However, the adequacy of consideration may be relevant in certain instances, such as to determine the existence of fraud. *Harwood, supra,* 124 Mich.App. at 142, 333 N.W.2d 609.

[9] *Kovacs v. Chesapeake & O. R. Co.,* 134 Mich.App. 514, 542, 351 N.W.2d 581 (1984) (emphasis added).

Food for Thought:

Contractual Liability in Doctor-Patient Relationships

In contrast to recent claims that medical malpractice claims against doctors have spun out of control, for many years it was difficult for plaintiffs to succeed in medical malpractice suits against doctors, in part because other doctors were reportedly reluctant to testify against their colleagues to establish negligence. In the face of those difficulties, some plaintiffs turned to contract law as an alternative to tort suits, often with just as little success. As articulated in *Sullivan v. O'Connor,* 296 N.E.2d 183 (Mass. 1973):

It is not hard to see why the courts should be unenthusiastic or skeptical about the contract theory. Considering the uncertainties of medical science and the variations in the physical and psychological conditions of individual patients, doctors can seldom in good faith promise specific results. Therefore it is unlikely that physicians of even average integrity will in fact make such promises. Statements of opinion by the physician with some optimistic coloring are a different thing, and may indeed have therapeutic value. But patients may transform such statements into firm promises in their own minds, especially when they have been disappointed in the event, and testify in that sense to sympathetic juries. If actions for breach of promise can be readily maintained, doctors, so it is said, will be frightened into practicing "defensive medicine." On the other hand, if these actions were outlawed, leaving only the possibility of suits for malpractice, there is fear that the public might be exposed to the enticements of charlatans, and confidence in the profession might ultimately be shaken. See Miller, *The Contractual Liability of Physicians and Surgeons,* 1953 Wash.L.Q. 413, 416-423. The law has taken the middle of the road position of allowing actions based on alleged contract, but insisting on clear proof.

Reflecting concerns about protecting patients, as well as continuing reluctance to see the doctor-patient relationship as contractual in nature, courts have also consistently denied enforcement to agreements by which some doctors have sought limitations on their liability, including a patient's release of a physician from liability for negligence, a limitation of the patient to a specified damage amount, and an acceptance of binding arbitration by the patient. See Maxwell J. Mehlman, *The Patient-Physician Relationship in an Era of Scarce Resources: Is There a Duty to Treat?* 25 Conn. L. Rev. 349 (1993).

Do you think the policies and concerns articulated here had an effect on the outcome in *Lawrence*?

§ 8. Review Exercise: Consideration

One of the challenges of law school, especially for first year students, is to figure out a way to organize the reams of material—cases, Restatement provisions, statutes, commentary, and insights from discussions in and outside the classroom.   The topic of consideration is a good place to practice the skill of synthesizing, because there seem to be so many details to keep track of. This exercise is designed to help you review and organize the material in this chapter, and by extension will give you guidance in how to approach the same task for other topics in this and other classes.

Because cases play such a central role in the materials, it may seem that organizing what you have learned would mean creating a list of the cases you have read and what they stand for.   While that may be a good first step, your goal should be to create a topical summary of the rules and policies, with the cases used to illustrate and define those rules and policies.   In effect, you are aiming to take the individual "trees" from your day-to-day coursework and build from them a "forest" that lets you see how all the trees fit together. Perhaps a better metaphor is creating a garden, since you will have a variety of "plants" (e.g., cases, statutes, Restatement provisions, policies, commentary), you will need pathways through the garden, and sometimes need to remove or rearrange the "plants" you have. Keep in mind, as well, that your ultimate goal is a summary that will help you structure your thinking when called upon to analyze a new set of facts.

There is no single "right" way to move from the detail level of day-to-day coursework to an organized topical summary. It is a good idea to start with the table of contents and syllabus of your course, because that will show you the organizational scheme used by your instructor and by your textbook authors. There are a variety of published review tools available that may help you see the "bigger picture" as you review, but you should be cautious about relying too much on sources that are not connected to your particular course.

There is also no single "right" way to record your summary. Some students prefer a textual outline, while others prefer the more graphical representation of a flowchart. These preferences are based on personal learning styles; both formats have their merits. You should choose the format that best meshes with your style of learning.

Looking at the table of contents in this chapter, you are reminded that the materials covered two different (but related) definitions of consideration, and subsequent sections provided details about what counts and does not count as consideration. There is also a section that deals with consideration as it relates to contract modification. One way to approach organizing your understanding about consideration is to write down each piece of information or knowledge you learned that you think is significant (e.g., what rules emerged from the cases, what rules emerged from the Restatement and UCC provisions, what policies support those rules, what factual applications of the rules do you know, what questions need to be asked to apply the rules, what uncertainties exist) in the order you learned them and then rearrange them into a structure (perhaps an outline) that shows the topical relationship among the pieces (what elements are components of each rule, what order makes sense in applying the rules). Case law should appear as examples of factual applications of the rules, not as the organizing skeleton of your review materials.

Below is the beginning of an outline on the topic of consideration, drawn from the table of contents to Chapter 2 but making some initial judgments about reordering the points in a sensible fashion. (The synthesis of some topics in this course will flow more directly and naturally from the chapter organization than is true with respect to Chapter 2. Because the concept of consideration was introduced in a kind of widening circle of detail and understanding, a sequential ordering, proceeding chapter-section by chapter-section, would be less helpful here.)

Some questions are embedded in the outline below to help you think about "organizing principles" that you might use to order the detail inside each topic. Review the materials in this chapter, along with your case briefs and other notes, and fill in the rest of the outline. As you do so, make a note of any questions you have so that you can seek clarification, whether from your classmates or from your instructor. Once you have an outline that seems to be complete, try answering some hypothetical questions about consideration to see if your framework works for you as an analytical tool.

Consideration

1. What are the functions/purposes served by requiring consideration?
2. How is consideration defined?

    What are the two definitions? How do they relate to one another? What examples can be used (from the cases, from elsewhere) to demonstrate how the definitions work? How do you tell whether something is consideration or a conditional gift? Where do nominal consideration and illusory promises fit?
3. Special applications of the consideration rule:

    a. Settlements and doubtful claims

    What makes a claim doubtful? When does giving up a claim for relief count as consideration?

    b. Modifications

    (1) Traditional common law rule (pre-existing duty rule)

    How does consideration doctrine affect enforcement of modifications? What policies are served by denying enforcement without consideration? What conceptual or practical ways exist for creating an enforceable modification within the traditional common law rule?

    (2) Newer common law rule (see Restatement)

    (3) UCC variation

    (4) Other variations

CHAPTER 3

Alternatives to Consideration

What kind of promises will the law enforce?	How do parties demonstrate assent to a contract?	What defenses to enforcement exist?	Is a writing required for enforcement? If so, what kind?	How is the content of a contract ascertained?	What are parties' rights and duties after breach?

What situations lead to excusing contract performance?	What remedies are available for breach of contract?	What contractual rights and duties do non-parties to a contract have?

Table of Contents

§ 1. Introduction

Chapter 2 explored the requirement that, in order to be enforceable under traditional contract principles, a promise must have "consideration." This chapter covers two doctrines—promissory estoppel and promissory restitution (promise for benefit already received)—that allow promises without consideration to be enforced, and a third doctrine—non-promissory restitution—that provides for compensation under contract-like circumstances even if no promise at all was made. These "alternatives to consideration" arose historically and rhetorically as exceptions to the requirement that consideration exist for contract formation, though they have since developed into separate sources of "contract-like" liability. Because a court may choose a more limited remedy when any of these doctrines are the basis of a claim, it is almost always preferable to find a "true" contract— one with consideration as well as assent—rather than to rely on the doctrines described in this chapter. Sometimes a true contract cannot plausibly be argued, however; one of these alternatives may be all that is available. In other circumstances, the facts may profitably be analyzed under more than one doctrine, with liability dependent on which narrative is most persuasive.

An Introduction to Contract Remedies

Because determination of appropriate remedies for breach of contract occurs only if the existence, terms, and breach of a contract are first established, this book addresses remedies issues near the end, in Chapter 9. But many cases refer to remedies as they discuss issues of formation, interpretation, and liability for breach. To help you better understand those references, this note offers a brief primer on the kinds of remedies available to injured parties, including alternative ways to measure money damages to compensate for breach.

Once a judgment is made that a party is liable for injury caused by breach of a contract, a court may award an equitable remedy (specific performance, which means ordering the breaching party to perform as promised, or ordering the party to take or refrain from taking other actions) or may award damages (a dollar amount meant to compensate for the injury caused). Specific performance may seem like the most sensible relief, as it ought to result in the other party receiving the promised performance, but damage remedies are generally favored over equitable relief, for reasons noted later in this chapter.

If a damages remedy is warranted, those damages may be calculated in several different ways:

- A court may enforce the promise made, resulting in the award of "**expectation damages**," the amount necessary to fulfill the expectation created by the promise. This may also be described as putting the promisee in the position she would have been in if the promise had been performed.
- A court may instead award "**reliance damages**," the amount necessary to compensate the promisee for expenses or costs incurred in reliance on the existence of the promise. This may also be described as putting the promisee in the position she would be in today if the promise had not been made.
- If benefits have been conferred on one party, a court may require that party to "disgorge" the benefit by paying the other party the value of those benefits ("**restitution damages**").

The damage remedies (expectation, reliance, and restitution) intersect with but are not identical with the theories of liability (breach of contract, promissory estoppel, promissory restitution, and restitution). As you will see, promissory estoppel as a theory of liability is based in reliance, but courts may (and often do) award full expectation damages rather than limiting the award to reliance damages. Similarly, a court that finds a party liable on the basis of promissory restitution may enforce the promise as made or reduce the award, perhaps to an amount reflecting restitution damages. In restitution cases, there is no promise to enforce, so the courts must necessarily choose restitution damages.

As you will see more fully in Chapter 9, courts have some flexibility even in breach of contract actions to award the damages that are most appropriate under the circumstances to compensate the injured party. While expectation damages are most common, courts may choose measures based on reliance or restitution, if warranted.

Because of the overlap in terminology, it is important that you recognize and watch for the distinction between the basis of liability (contract, promissory estoppel, or restitution) and the determination of damages remedy (expectation, reliance, or restitution).

§ 2. Promissory Estoppel

Chapter 2 distinguished between consideration (where an action or forbearance is bargained for) and conditional gift (where an action is undertaken in order to receive a promised gift). In some circumstances, the action undertaken in response to a gift promise is minor (e.g., providing an email address to be used to receive a coupon by return email). In other instances, the action of the promisee is more substantial and may involve expenses incurred to obtain the promised gift or in the course of actions undertaken in reliance on the promise that the gift will be delivered. Under traditional concepts, none of those actions would "count" as consideration because they were not bargained-for, so no contract would be formed, but courts were sometimes convinced that an unbargained-for gift promise should be enforced anyway.

Kirksey v. Kirksey, 8 Ala. 131 (1845) is an early case presenting just such a dilemma. The defendant in *Kirksey* (Isaac Kirksey) wrote the following letter to his sister-in-law, whose husband (defendant's brother Henry) had just died:

Dear sister Antillico—Much to my mortification, I heard, that brother Henry was dead, and one of his children. I know that your situation is one of grief, and difficulty. You had a bad chance before, but a great deal worse now. I should like to come and see you, but cannot with convenience at present. . . . I do not know whether you have a preference on the place you live on, or not. If you had, I would advise you to obtain your preference, and sell the land and quit the country, as I understand it is very unhealthy, and I know society is very bad. If you will come down and see me, I will let you have a place to raise your family, and I have more open land than I can tend; and on the account of your situation, and that of your family, I feel like I want you and the children to do well.

Plaintiff moved with her family to the residence offered by the defendant, but after two years defendant ordered her to leave. Judge Ormond, reversing a jury verdict for plaintiff and writing for the court, stated: "The inclination of my mind, is, that the loss and inconvenience, which the plaintiff sustained in breaking up, and moving to the defendant's, a distance of sixty miles, is a sufficient consideration to support the promise, to furnish her with a house, and land to cultivate, until she could raise her family. My brothers, however, think that the promise on the part of the defendant, was a mere gratuity, and that an action will not lie for its breach." The court concluded, in other words, that defendant did not offer a place to live in exchange for the move but merely made a promise to give a gift of a place to live, conditioned on plaintiff's moving to that residence. Therefore the move was only a condition—an act necessary to receive the promised gift—and not consideration for the promise.

In contrast to his colleagues on the bench, Judge Ormond believed that the promise *should* be enforced because the move entailed loss and inconvenience to plaintiff. He would have called the loss and inconvenience "consideration," but he was overruled by the other members of the panel. The disagreement among the judges might signal a lack of consensus on the meaning of consideration at that time, with some judges favoring a narrow interpretation and others (Judge Ormond in particular) favoring a broader understanding that would include more than bargained-for acts. A modern court would agree with the *Kirksey* majority that Antillico's actions undertaken in reliance on and in order to take advantage of her brother-in-law's promise would not constitute consideration, but, as we will see below, courts have since found alternative ways to compensate promisees in Antillico's position.

Behind the Scenes

Recent scholarship about the *Kirksey* case reveals that Isaac Kirksey may have promised Antillico a place to live partly to help his widowed sister-in-law and her children, but at least equally so that she could claim the land for him pursuant to a federal land preemption statute. He had already claimed preemption rights of his own on other land, so he could not claim the additional land for himself, but he could reach the same result if Antillico acted as his proxy. She may thus have given up her own preemption (or "preference") rights on the land where she resided in order to help her brother-in-law.

After Antillico moved, however, a new federal statute made it possible for Antillico to claim title for the land for herself if she was in physical possession of it. Probably as a result, Isaac moved his own son onto the land—once the son was old enough to take advantage of the federal statute to claim the land for himself and, indirectly, for his father—and told Antillico to leave. Procuring Antillico's help to circumvent the pre-emption statute would have been considered fraudulent and so was not discussed at trial, although the local men who served on the jury may well have understood the situation. For the details of this story, *see* William R. Casto and Val D. Ricks, *"Dear Sister Antillico . . .": The Story of Kirksey v. Kirksey*, 94 Georgetown L.J. 321 (2006).

Under the likely "real" facts described here, would the promise have been enforceable under traditional contract principles?

More than fifty years after *Kirksey,* in *Ricketts v. Scothorn,* 77 N.W. 365 (Neb. 1898), the Nebraska Supreme Court faced a slightly different dilemma. Katie Scothorn's grandfather, "desiring to put her in a position of independence," gave her a promissory note for $2000. According to the testimony, he asked for nothing in return, though he hoped she would give up the job she then held: "'I have fixed out something that you have not got to work any more.' He says, 'none of my grandchildren work, and you don't have to.'" She immediately quit her job, although she returned to work as a bookkeeper a little more than a year later, with her grandfather's approval. While nothing was required of Katie Scothorn to receive the gift (unlike the situation in *Kirksey,* where Antillico had to move with her family in order to receive the gift of a place to live), she suffered some "loss and inconvenience" in reliance on the promise of $2000 when she went without employment for upwards of a year.

When Katie sued her grandfather's estate for payment of the promissory note, the executor defended by claiming there was no consideration for the promise embodied in the note. The court reviewed a number of earlier cases involving charitable donations in which courts found that an expenditure of money or assumption of liability by the charity "on the faith of the promise" constituted "a valuable and sufficient consideration," sounding much like Judge Ormond in *Kirksey.* The court did not think those actions were "consideration," and said "the true reason" for finding liability, in the earlier cases and in *Ricketts,* was the existence of an "equitable estoppel." That is, the executor, standing in the shoes of the grandfather, was "estopped" (prevented) from raising the defense of no consideration because the grandfather's actions had induced Katie to change her position, and it would be unjust to permit the estate to benefit. The *Ricketts* court relied on equitable estoppel, based on the existence of "acts, admissions, or conduct" inducing a change of position, but implicitly extended the concept to embrace what later became known as "*promissory* estoppel," preventing (estopping) a litigant from claiming no consideration when a *promise* (rather than conduct) induced reliance. "Having intentionally induced the plaintiff to alter her position for the worse on the faith of the note being paid when due, it would be grossly inequitable to permit the maker, or his executor, to resist payment on the ground that the promise was given without consideration."

In *Ricketts* and other early cases, promissory estoppel was invoked only as a response to the defense that consideration did not exist, preventing the other party from raising that defense, but the doctrine quickly evolved to become an independent source of promissory liability. It was written into the Restatement of Contracts in 1932 as section 90. It appeared with some changes in the Restatement (Second) of Contracts, again as section 90 (the retention of the same section number reflecting the considerable importance of the provision). "Section 90 has been described as the *Restatement*'s 'most notable and influential rule' [quoting E. Allan Farnsworth, *Contracts*] and as 'perhaps the most radical and expansive development of this century in the law of promissory liability.'* The section has had a profound influence on the law of contracts because it ratifies cases enforcing a promise in the absence of bargained-for consideration. By giving its imprimatur to those cases, the *Restatement* has encouraged courts to expand contractual liability beyond the traditional doctrinal limits of consideration." Edward Yorio & Steve Thel, *The Promissory Basis of Section 90*, 101 Yale L.J. 111 (1991).

Reading the Law Critically:
Promissory Estoppel in the Restatements

While many state courts have adopted or referred favorably to the Restatement (Second) articulation of promissory estoppel in § 90, others continue to rely on the formulation in the first Restatement, so you should be familiar with both versions. The Reporter's Note accompanying Restatement (Second) § 90 says, "The principal change from former § 90 is the recognition of the possibility of partial enforcement." What other differences do you see between the two versions? How significant do you think those differences are?

---

* Charles L. Knapp, *Reliance in the Revised* Restatement: *The Proliferation of Promissory Estoppel*, 81 Colum. L. Rev. 52, 53 (1981).

Restatement § 90. **Promise Reasonably Inducing Definite and Substantial Action**

A promise which the promisor should reasonably expect to induce action or forbearance of a definite and substantial character on the part of the promisee and which does induce such action or forbearance is binding if injustice can be avoided only by enforcement of the promise.

———————

Restatement (Second) § 90. **Promise Reasonably Inducing Action or Forbearance**

(1) A promise which the promisor should reasonably expect to induce action or forbearance on the part of the promisee or a third person and which does induce such action or forbearance is binding if injustice can be avoided only by enforcement of the promise. The remedy granted for breach may be limited as justice requires.

(2) A charitable subscription or a marriage settlement is binding under Subsection (1) without proof that the promise induced action or forbearance.

Food for Thought: Unpublished Opinions

Like *Tomczak* and *Birdsall* in Chapter 2 (pages 57 and 123), the next case, *Conrad* is designated as "unpublished" by the deciding courts. An unpublished decision is publicly available (in electronic form or from the court), but generally does not appear in the hard-copy case reporters, and citation to it may be limited by state statute or rule. The Minnesota court rule, for example, says that "unpublished opinions . . . are not precedential" and that counsel must give all other counsel in a case at least 48 hours notice before using an unpublished opinion in any pretrial conference, hearing, or trial. Minn. Stat. § 480A.08. Nebraska's Rule 2(E)(4) specifies that unpublished opinions "may be cited only when such case is related, by identity between the parties or the causes of action, to the case then before the court."

In 2000, a surprising three-quarters of the opinions of the federal courts of appeals were being issued unpublished* The prevalence of such opinions led courts and commentators to consider two distinct questions. First, should (or must) courts treat their unpublished opinions as binding precedent? Second, should parties be allowed to cite unpublished opinions in their briefs?

In Anastasoff v. United States, 223 F.3d 898 (8th Cir. 2000), a panel of the Eighth Circuit held that the Circuit's rule declaring unpublished opinions *not* precedential was an unconstitutional infringement of the Article III powers of the federal courts. That decision was later vacated by the court sitting en banc** because the underlying dispute had become moot, *see* id., 235 F.3d 1054, and no other court has agreed with the panel ruling. Other judges have argued that judicial decisions do not inherently create precedent. *See* Alex Kozinski & Stephen Reinhardt, *Please Don't Cite This! Why We Don't Allow Citation to Unpublished Opinions,* Cal. Lawyer, June 2000.

In 2006, after considerable discussion, the Federal Rules of Appellate Procedure were amended to bar federal courts from prohibiting or restricting the citation of unpublished opinions issued on or after January 1, 2007. The rule does not address whether unpublished opinions are or must be treated as precedential, and the federal courts may (and some do) restrict citation to unpublished opinions issued before the designated date.

Why do you think a court would choose not to publish some of its opinions? Why might the *Conrad*, *Tomczak*, and *Birdsall* courts have chosen not to publish those opinions? What are the implications of that choice? Should courts restrict citation to unpublished opinions? For an exploration of the arguments for and against citing unpublished opinions, *see* Patrick J. Schiltz, *Much Ado About Little: Explaining the Sturm und Drang over the Citation of Unpublished Opinions,* 62 Wash. & Lee L. Rev. 1429 (2005). Professor (now United States District Court Judge) Schiltz was Reporter for the Advisory Committee on the Federal Rules of Appellate Procedure during the discussion leading to adoption of the amended rule on the citation of unpublished opinions

---

* *See* Administrative Office of the United States Courts, 1998 Judicial Business of the United States Courts Table S-3 (1999).
** When a court sits "en banc," all active judges of the court—not just a smaller panel of judges—participate in the hearing or decision. Courts other than the highest court in the jurisdiction usually sit en banc only when hearing a matter the court deems particularly important or one that has produced a split in decisions by multiple panels of the court.

Whether precedential or not, unpublished opinions sometimes provide helpful explications of legal rules and interesting factual circumstances, which is why you will find several included in this textbook.

Reading the Law Critically:

Conrad, Hayes, *and Maryland National Bank*

Although many courts cite § 90 of the first or second Restatement with approval, some courts—even those that purport to rely on the Restatement—adopt variations of the standard. As you read the cases that follow, be alert to the details of the promissory estoppel standard adopted by each court and consider the similarities and differences between them. In addition, consider the following questions:

1. Why isn't the plaintiff able to establish the existence of consideration for the promise made?

2. If the promissory estoppel claim fails, which aspect of the test presents difficulty for the claimant, and why?

3. If the promissory estoppel claim succeeds, what particular facts support the outcome? How does the court measure the damages awarded?

4. How are the various promissory estoppel standards consistent with one another? How do they differ, and do you think those differences would lead to different outcomes on the same facts?

5. What policies do the courts identify that support the application of promissory estoppel? What policies do they identify that suggest limits on use of the doctrine?

Conrad v. Fields

MARJORIE CONRAD, Plaintiff-Respondent

v.

WALTER R. FIELDS, Defendant-Appellant

pay for law school

Court of Appeals of Minnesota
2007 WL 2106302 (Minn. Ct. App. July 24, 2007) (unpublished opinion)

Considered and decided by **PETERSON**, Presiding Judge; **SHUMAKER**, Judge; and **ROSS**, Judge.

PETERSON, Judge.

This appeal is from a judgment and an order denying posttrial motions. The judgment awarded respondent damages in the amount of the cost of her law-school tuition and books based on a determination that the elements of promissory estoppel were proved with respect to appellant's promise to pay for the tuition and books. We affirm the judgment and grant in part and deny in part respondent's motion to strike appellant's brief and appendix.

FACTS

Appellant Walter R. Fields and respondent Marjorie Conrad met and became friends when they were neighbors in an apartment complex in the early 1990's. Appellant started his own business and became a financially successful business-man. Appellant built a $1.2 million house in the Kenwood neighborhood in Minneapolis and leased a Bentley automobile for more than $50,000 a year. Appellant is a philanthropic individual who has sometimes paid education costs for others.

In the fall of 2000, appellant suggested that respondent attend law school, and he offered to pay for her education. Respondent, who had recently paid off an $11,000 medical bill and still owed about $5,000 for undergraduate student loans, did not feel capable of paying for law school on her own. Appellant promised that he would pay tuition and other expenses associated with law school as they became due. [Respondent] quit her job at Qwest, where she had been earning $45,000 per year, to attend law school. Appellant admitted at trial that before respondent enrolled in law school, he agreed to pay her tuition.

Respondent testified that she enrolled in law school in the summer of 2001 as a result of appellant's "inducement and assurance to pay for [her] education." Appellant made two tuition payments, each in the amount of $1,949.75, in August and October 2001, but he stopped payment on the check for the second payment. At some point, appellant told respondent that his assets had been frozen due to

Reasonable
reliance

an Internal Revenue Service audit and that payment of her education expenses would be delayed until he got the matter straightened out. In May 2004, appellant and respondent exchanged e-mail messages about respondent's difficulties in managing the debts that she had incurred for law school. In response to one of respondent's messages, appellant wrote, "to be clear and in writing, when you graduate law school and pas[s] your bar exam, I will pay your tuition." Later, appellant told respondent that he would not pay her expenses, and he threatened to get a restraining order against her if she continued attempting to communicate with him.

Respondent brought suit against appellant, alleging that in reliance on appellant's promise to pay her education expenses, she gave up the opportunity to earn income through full-time employment and enrolled in law school. The case was tried to the court, which awarded respondent damages in the amount of $87,314.63 under the doctrine of promissory estoppel. The district court denied appellant's motion for a new trial or amended findings. This appeal followed.

DECISION

The district court's "[f]indings of fact, whether based on oral or documentary evidence, shall not be set aside unless clearly erroneous, and due regard shall be given to the opportunity of the trial court to judge the credibility of the witnesses." Minn. R. Civ. P. 52.01. In applying this rule, "we view the record in the light most favorable to the judgment of the district court." *Rogers v. Moore,* 603 N.W.2d 650, 656 (Minn.1999). If there is reasonable evidence to support the district court's findings of fact, this court will not disturb those findings. *Fletcher v. St. Paul Pioneer Press,* 589 N.W.2d 96, 101 (Minn.1999). While the district court's findings of fact are reviewed under the deferential "clearly erroneous" standard, this court reviews questions of law de novo. *AFSCME, Council No. 14 v. City of St. Paul,* 533 N.W.2d 623, 626 (Minn.App.1995).

"Promissory estoppel implies a contract in law where no contract exists in fact." *Deli v. Univ. of Minn.,* 578 N.W.2d 779, 781 (Minn.App.1998), *review denied* (Minn. July 16, 1998). "A promise which the promisor should reasonably expect to induce action or forbearance on the part of the promisee or a third person and which does induce such action or forbearance is binding if injustice can be avoided only by enforcement of the promise." Restatement (Second) of Contracts § 90(1) (1981).

The elements of a promissory estoppel claim are (1) a clear and definite promise, (2) the promisor intended to induce reliance by the promisee, and the promisee relied to the promisee's detriment, and (3) the promise must be enforced to prevent injustice. *Cohen v. Cowles Media Co.,* 479 N.W.2d 387, 391

(Minn.1992). Judicial determinations of injustice involve a number of considerations, "including the reasonableness of a promisee's reliance." *Faimon v. Winona State Univ.*, 540 N.W.2d, 879, 883 (Minn.App.1995), *review denied* (Minn. Feb. 9, 1996).

"Granting equitable relief is within the sound discretion of the trial court. Only a clear abuse of that discretion will result in reversal." *Nadeau v. County of Ramsey*, 277 N.W.2d 520, 524 (Minn.1979). But

> [t]he court considers the injustice factor as a matter of law, looking to the reasonableness of the promisee's reliance and weighing public policies (in favor of both enforcing bargains and preventing unjust enrichment). When the facts are taken as true, it is a question of law as to whether they rise to the level of promissory estoppel.

Greuling v. Wells Fargo Home Mortgage, Inc., 690 N.W.2d 757, 761 (Minn. App.2005) (citation omitted).

I.

Appellant argues that respondent did not plead or prove the elements of promissory estoppel. . . .

Paragraph 12 of respondent's complaint states, "That as a direct and approximate result of the negligent conduct and breach of contract conduct of [appellant], [respondent] has been damaged . . . ." But the complaint also states:

> 4. That in 2000, based on the assurance and inducement of [appellant] to pay for [respondent's] legal education, [respondent] made the decision to enroll in law school at Hamline University School of Law (Hamline) in St. Paul, Minnesota which she did in 2001.
>
> 5. That but for the inducement and assurance of [appellant] to pay for [respondent's] legal education, [respondent] would not have enrolled in law school. [Appellant] was aware of this fact.

Paragraphs four and five of the complaint are sufficient to put appellant on notice of the promissory-estoppel claim.

At a pretrial deposition, respondent testified that negligence and breach of contract were the only two causes of action that she was pleading. Because promissory estoppel is described as a contract implied at law, respondent's deposition testimony can be interpreted to include a promissory-estoppel claim.

In its legal analysis, the district court stated:

> The Court finds credible [respondent's] testimony that [appellant] encouraged her to go to law school, knowing that she would not be able to pay for it on her own. He knew that she was short on money, having helped her pay for food and other necessities. He knew that she was working at Qwest and would need to quit her job to go to law school. He offered to pay for the cost of her going to law school, knowing that she had debts from her undergraduate tuition. He made a payment on her law school tuition after she enrolled. [Respondent] knew that [appellant] was a wealthy philanthropist, and that he had offered to pay for the education of strangers he had met in chance encounters. She knew that he had the wealth to pay for her law school education. She knew that [] he was established in society, older than she, not married, without children, an owner of a successful company, an owner of an expensive home, and a lessor of an expensive car. Moreover, [appellant] was a friend who had performed many kindnesses for her already, and she trusted him. [Appellant's] promise in fact induced [respondent] to quit her job at Qwest and enroll in law school, which she had not otherwise planned to do....
>
> . . . [T]he circumstances support a finding that it would be unjust not to enforce the promise. Upon reliance on [appellant's] promise, [respondent] quit her job. She attended law school despite a serious health condition that might otherwise have deterred her from going.

These findings are sufficient to show that respondent proved the elements of promissory estoppel.

Appellant argues that because he advised respondent shortly after she enrolled in law school that he would not be paying her law-school expenses as they came due, respondent could not have reasonably relied on his promise to pay her expenses to her detriment after he repudiated the promise. Appellant contends that the only injustice that resulted from his promise involved the original $5,000 in expenses that respondent incurred to enter law school. But appellant's statement that he would not pay the expenses as they came due did not make respondent's reliance unreasonable because appellant also told respondent that his financial problems were temporary and that he would pay her tuition when she graduated and passed the bar exam. This statement made it reasonable for respondent to continue to rely on appellant's promise that he would pay her expenses. . . .

IV.

In actions based on promissory estoppel, "[r]elief may be limited to damages measured by the promisee's reliance." *Dallum v. Farmers Union Cent. Exchange, Inc.*, **462 N.W.2d 608, 613 (Minn. App. 1990)**, *review denied* (Minn. Jan. 14, 1991). "In other words, relief may be limited to the party's out-of-pocket expenses made in reliance on the promise."*Id.*

Appellant objects to respondent seeking damages for lost income and living expenses, including housing. But the district court awarded respondent damages only for the cost of tuition and books. Appellant argues that respondent sought double recovery for the cost of tuition and the amount of her student loans. But an exhibit prepared by respondent and admitted into evidence shows that tuition totaled $86,462.21 and books cost $2,802.17. The district court awarded respondent $87,314.63 (tuition plus books minus payment made by appellant).

Appellant argues that respondent was obligated to mitigate her damages and she could have avoided all of her damages by dropping out of law school immediately after appellant refused to pay her tuition as it was incurred. But as we explained when addressing the reasonableness of respondent's reliance, appellant told respondent that his financial difficulties were temporary and that he would pay her expenses after graduation. Under these circumstances, respondent was not aware until after she graduated that she would suffer damages, and by the time she graduated, she had already paid for her tuition and books and had no opportunity to mitigate damages.

Make the Connection

As discussed at greater length in Chapter 9, page 1123, on remedies, mitigation is an important limitation on damage awards. An aggrieved party may recover only those damages caused by the breach and may not recover damages that she could have prevented by taking reasonable steps.

V.

Appellant argues that because respondent received a valuable law degree, she did not suffer any real detriment by relying on his promise. But receiving a law degree was the expected and intended consequence of appellant's promise, and the essence of appellant's promise was that respondent would receive the law degree without the debt associated with attending law school. Although respondent benefited from attending law school, the debt that she incurred in reliance on appellant's promise is a detriment to her. . . .

even w/ law degree
debt is detriment

Affirmed; motion granted in part.

History of Equity

When the *Conrad* court says, "Granting equitable relief is within the sound discretion of the trial court," it is referring to the equitable roots of promissory estoppel. As is clear in *Conrad* as well as in the Restatement, promissory estoppel is premised on determining the reasonableness of the behavior of promisor and promisee and on preventing injustice. Such concerns (reasonableness, fairness, justice) are classic equitable concerns. Understanding their historical roots may help clarify the relationship between the doctrine of consideration and the alternative paths to enforcement discussed in Chapter 3.

In the 14th century, the English common law courts operated on a rigid system of "writs" that narrowly limited available forms of action, so that many kinds of claims—including claims based on oral promises—could not successfully be pursued there. Writs for new kinds of claims were rarely created, so many claimants had no recourse. Contract defenses based on fraud, failure of performance, and prior satisfaction of the claimed debt were often precluded in common law courts. Procedures in common law courts were also restrictive. Parties to lawsuits could not offer evidence in their cases, witnesses could not be summoned unless they owned property, and discovery of documentary evidence could not be ordered.

Individuals with grievances who could not seek or obtain relief before the common law courts sometimes petitioned the King or the King's Council for redress, and such petitions were often referred to the chancellor, the King's chief councilor, who dispensed justice in individual cases. Over time, the petitions and responses became more regularized, and the Chancery Court and later other lesser equity courts emerged, handling what became known as equitable claims for relief. Until the middle of the 16th century, most chancellors were religious figures, generally bishops or cardinals. Because of the religious background of the chancellor, moral conduct and good conscience played a large role in the Chancery Court's reasoning, often leading to sensible and practical results not available under the more rigid restrictions on legal relief. Some contracts-related causes of action and defenses unavailable in common law courts *were* available in chancery.

Court procedures also varied considerably between the two systems. Because equity courts acted "in personam" (with respect to the individual rather than to his property), they had the ability to demand the appearance of the parties and other witnesses. Because decisions were made by the chancellor or, later, by judges, the equity courts permitted parties to testify rather than relying on the "self-informing" common law jury to decide cases based on the jurors' own knowledge. Although some equity court process was problematic (the absence of cross-examination and juries, for example), procedural advances over the common law courts nonetheless made the equity courts attractive to litigants.

To forestall political criticism that chancery was competing with the common law courts, the judges of the Chancery Court said they were "following the law"—supplementing the common law and responding to shortcomings, not replacing it. Equitable relief was "extraordinary" and granted only if legal relief was not available. Even today, when most jurisdictions have merged the courts of law and equity, the ghosts of the Chancery Court and its history still persist in some respects. Even though the same judge makes decisions in law and equity, an equitable claim or remedy usually is available only if the claimant has no adequate remedy at law and will suffer irreparable harm unless equitable relief is given. Equitable issues are still decided by the judge, not by a jury. Equity continues to focus on fashioning a result that is fair and morally sound. Equitable relief will be denied to a party "with unclean hands," and specific performance (an equitable remedy) may be denied if the contract has lop-sided consideration or is entered into in unfair circumstances. The standards and rules of equity generally reserve more discretion to the court than do comparable rules "at law."

As you consider the alternatives to consideration discussed in Chapter 3, think about the role of equitable factors in the elements of each claim.

See John H. Langbein, Renée Lettow Lerner & Bruce P. Smith, *History of the Common Law: The Development of Anglo-American Legal Institutions* (2009); Dan B. Dobbs, *Law of Remedies: Damages—Equity—Restitution* §§ 2.2-2.4 (2d ed. 1993).

Hayes v. Plantations Steel Co.

EDWARD J. HAYES , Plaintiff-Appellee

v.

PLANTATIONS STEEL COMPANY, Defendant-Appellant

Supreme Court of Rhode Island

438 A.2d 1091 (R.I. 1982)

SHEA, Justice

The defendant employer, Plantations Steel Company (Plantations), appeals from a Superior Court judgment for the plaintiff employee, Edward J. Hayes (Hayes). The trial justice, sitting without a jury, found that Plantations was obligated to Hayes on the basis of an implied-in-fact contract to pay him a yearly pension of $5,000. The award covered three years in which payment had not been made. The trial justice ruled, also, that Hayes had made a sufficient showing of detrimental reliance upon Plantations's promise to pay to give rise to its obligation based on the theory of promissory estoppel. . . .

What's That?

A contract "implied-in-fact" is one in which the required factual elements are inferred from the circumstances rather than explicitly stated by the parties to the transaction.

We reverse the findings of the trial justice regarding Plantations's contractual obligation to pay Hayes a pension. . . .

Plantations is a closely held Rhode Island corporation engaged in the manufacture of steel reinforcing rods for use in concrete construction. The company was founded by Hugo R. Mainelli, Sr., and Alexander A. DiMartino. A dispute between their two families in 1976 and 1977 left the DiMartinos in full control of the corporation. Hayes was an employee of the corporation from 1947 until his retirement in 1972 at age of sixty-five. He began with Plantations as an "estimator and draftsman" and ended his career as general manager, a position of considerable responsibility. Starting in January 1973 and continuing until January 1976, Hayes received the annual sum of $5,000 from Plantations. Hayes instituted this action in December 1977, after the then company management refused to make any further payments.

Hayes testified that in January 1972 he announced his intention to retire the following July, after twenty-five years of continuous service. He decided to retire because he had worked continuously for fifty-one years. He stated, however, that he would not have retired had he not expected to receive a pension. After he stopped working for Plantations, he sought no other employment.

Approximately one week before his actual retirement Hayes spoke with Hugo R. Mainelli, Jr., who was then an officer and a stockholder of Plantations. This conversation was the first and only one concerning payments of a pension to Hayes during retirement. Mainelli said that the company "would take care" of him. There was no mention of a sum of money or a percentage of salary that Hayes would receive. There was no formal authorization for payments by Plantations's shareholders and/or board of directors. Indeed, there was never any formal provision for a pension plan for any employee other than for unionized employees, who benefit from an arrangement through their union. The plaintiff was not a union member.

Mr. Mainelli, Jr., testified that his father, Hugo R. Mainelli, Sr., had authorized the first payment "as a token of appreciation for the many years of (Hayes's) service." Furthermore, "it was implied that that check would continue on an annual basis." Mainelli also testified that it was his "personal intention" that the payments would continue for "as long as I was around."

Mainelli testified that after Hayes's retirement, [Hayes] would visit the premises each year to say hello and renew old acquaintances. During the course of his visits, Hayes would thank Mainelli for the previous check and ask how long it would continue so that he could plan an orderly retirement.

The payments were discontinued after 1976. At that time a succession of several poor business years plus the stockholders' dispute, resulting in the takeover by the DiMartino family, contributed to the decision to stop the payments.

The trial justice ruled that Plantations owed Hayes his annual sum of $5,000 for the years 1977 through 1979. The ruling implied that barring bankruptcy or the cessation of business for any other reason, Hayes had a right to expect continued annual payments.

The trial justice found that Hugo Mainelli, Jr.'s statement that Hayes would be taken care of after his retirement was a promise. Although no sum of money was mentioned in 1972, the four annual payments of $5,000 established that otherwise unspecified term of the contract. The trial justice also found that Hayes supplied consideration for the promise by voluntarily retiring, because he was under no obligation to do so. From the words and conduct of the parties and from the surrounding circumstances, the trial justice concluded that there existed an implied contract obligating the company to pay a pension to Hayes for life. The trial justice made a further finding that even if Hayes had not truly bargained for a pension by voluntarily retiring, he had nevertheless incurred the detriment of foregoing other employment in reliance upon the company's promise. He specifically held that Hayes's retirement was in response to the promise and held also that Hayes refrained from seeking other employment in further reliance thereon.

The findings of fact of a trial justice sitting without a jury are entitled to great weight when reviewed by this court. His findings will not be disturbed unless it can be shown that they are clearly wrong or that the trial justice misconceived or overlooked material evidence. Lisi v. Marra, R.I., 424 A.2d 1052 (1981); Raheb v. Lemenski, 115 R.I. 576, 350 A.2d 397 (1976). After careful review of the record, however, we conclude that the trial justice's findings and conclusions must be reversed.

Assuming for the purpose of this discussion that Plantations in legal effect made a promise to Hayes, we must ask whether Hayes did supply the required consideration that would make the promise binding? And, if Hayes did not supply consideration, was his alleged reliance sufficiently induced by the promise to estop defendant from denying its obligation to him? We answer both questions in the negative.

We turn first to the problem of consideration. The facts at bar do not present the case of an express contract. As the trial justice stated, the existence of a contract in this case must be determined from all the circumstances of the parties' conduct and words. Although words were expressed initially in the remark that Hayes "would be taken care of," any contract in this case would be more in the nature of an implied contract. Certainly the statement of Hugo Mainelli, Jr., standing alone is not an expression of a direct and definite promise to pay Hayes a pension. Though we are analyzing an implied contract, nevertheless we must address the question of consideration.

Think About It!

Recall that, at the beginning of Chapter 2, (page 16), we defined a promise as an assurance or declaration that one will do or refrain from doing some act. Was Mainelli's statement a promise? Did the trial court find it was? Did the appellate court?

Contracts implied in fact require the element of consideration to support them as is required in express contracts. The only difference between the two is the manner in which the parties manifest their assent. J. Koury Steel Erectors, Inc. v. San-Vel Concrete Corp., R.I., 387 A.2d 694 (1978); Bailey v. West, 105 R.I. 61, 249 A.2d 414 (1969). In this jurisdiction, consideration consists either in some right, interest, or benefit accruing to one party or some forbearance, detriment, or responsibility given, suffered, or undertaken by the other. See Dockery v. Greenfield, 86 R.I. 464, 136 A.2d 682 (1957); Darcey v. Darcey, 29 R.I. 384, 71 A. 595 (1909). Valid consideration furthermore must be bargained for. It must induce the return act or promise. To be valid, therefore, the purported consideration must not have been delivered before a promise is executed, that is, given without reference to the promise Plowman v. Indian Refining Co., 20 F.Supp. 1 (E.D.Ill.1937). Consideration is therefore a test of the enforceability of executory promises, Angel v. Murray, 113 R.I. 482, 322 A.2d 630 (1974), and has no legal effect when rendered in the past and apart from an alleged exchange in the present. Zanturjian v. Boornazian, 25 R.I. 151, 55 A. 199 (1903).

In the case before us, Plantations's promise to pay Hayes a pension is quite clearly not supported by any consideration supplied by Hayes. Hayes had announced his intent to retire well in advance of any promise, and therefore the intention to retire was arrived at without regard to any promise by Plantations. Although Hayes may have had in mind the receipt of a pension when he first informed Plantations, his expectation was not based on any statement made to him or on any conduct of the company officer relative to him in January 1972. In deciding to retire, Hayes acted on his own initiative. Hayes's long years of dedicated service also is legally insufficient because his service too was rendered without being induced by Plantations's promise. See Plowman v. Indian Refining Co., supra.

Clearly then this is not a case in which Plantations's promise was meant to induce Hayes to refrain from retiring when he could have chosen to do so in return for further service. 1 Williston on Contracts, §130B (3d ed., Jaeger 1957). Nor was the promise made to encourage long service from the start of his employment. Weesner v. Electric Power Board of Chattanooga, 48 Tenn.App. 178, 344 S.W.2d 766 (1961). Instead, the testimony establishes that Plantations's promise was intended "as a token of appreciation for (Hayes's) many years of service." As such it was in the nature of a gratuity paid to Hayes for as long as the company chose. In Spickelmier Industries, Inc. v. Passander, 172 Ind.App. 49, 359 N.E.2d 563 (1977), an employer's promise to an employee to pay him a year-end bonus was unenforceable because it was made after the employee had performed his contractual responsibilities for that year.

. . . .

Hayes argues in the alternative that even if Plantations's promise was not the product of an exchange, its duty is grounded properly in the theory of promissory estoppel. This court adopted the theory of promissory estoppel in East Providence Credit Union v. Geremia, 103 R.I. 597, 601, 239 A.2d 725, 727 (1968) (quoting 1 Restatement Contracts §90 at 110 (1932)) stating:

> "A promise which the promisor should reasonably expect to induce action or forbearance of a definite and substantial character on the part of the promisee and which does induce such action or forbearance is binding if injustice can be avoided only by enforcement of its promise."

In East Providence Credit Union this court said that the doctrine of promissory estoppel is invoked "as a substitute for a consideration, rendering a gratuitous promise enforceable as a contract." Id. To restate the matter differently, "the acts of reliance by the promisee to his detriment (provide) a substitute for consideration." Id.

Hayes urges that in the absence of a bargained-for promise the facts require application of the doctrine of promissory estoppel. He stresses that he retired voluntarily while expecting to receive a pension. He would not have otherwise retired. Nor did he seek other employment.

We disagree with this contention largely for the reasons already stated. One of the essential elements of the doctrine of promissory estoppel is that the promise must induce the promisee's action or forbearance. The particular act in this regard is plaintiff's decision whether or not to retire. As we stated earlier, the record indicates that he made the decision on his own initiative. In other words, the conversation between Hayes and Mainelli which occurred a week before Hayes left his employment cannot be said to have induced his decision to leave. He had reached that decision long before.

An example taken from the Restatement provides a meaningful contrast:

"2. A promises B to pay him an annuity during B's life. B thereupon resigns profitable employment, as A expected that he might. B receives the annuity for some years, in the meantime becoming disqualified from again obtaining good employment. A's promise is binding." (Emphasis added.) 1 **Restatement Contracts §90 at 111 (1932).**

In **Feinberg v. Pfeiffer Co., 322 S.W.2d 163 (Mo.App.1959)**, the plaintiff-employee had worked for her employer for nearly forty years. The defendant corporation's board of directors resolved, in view of her long years of service, to obligate itself to pay "retirement privileges" to her. The resolution did not require the plaintiff to retire. Instead, the decision whether and when to retire remained entirely her own. The board then informed her of its resolution. The plaintiff worked for eighteen months more before retiring. She sued the corporation when it reduced her monthly checks seven years later. The court held that a pension contract existed between the parties. Although continued employment was not a consideration to her receipt of retirement benefits, the court found sufficient reliance on the part of the plaintiff to support her claim. The court based its decision upon the above Restatement example, that is, the defendant informed the plaintiff of its plan, and the plaintiff in reliance thereon, retired. Feinberg presents factors that also appear in the case at bar. There, the plaintiff had worked many years and desired to retire; she would not have left had she not been able to rely on a pension; and once retired, she sought no other employment.

However, the important distinction between Feinberg and the case before us is that in Feinberg the employer's decision definitely shaped the thinking of the plaintiff. In this case the promise did not. It is not reasonable to infer from the facts that Hugo R. Mainelli, Jr., expected retirement to result from his conversation with Hayes. Hayes had given notice of his intention seven months previously. Here there was thus no inducement to retire which would satisfy the demands of § 90 of the Restatement. Nor can it be said that Hayes's refraining from other employment was "action or forbearance of a definite and substantial character." The underlying assumption of Hayes's initial decision to retire was that upon leaving the defendant's employ, he would no longer work. It is impossible to say that he changed his position any more so because of what Mainelli had told him in light of his own initial decision. These circumstances do not lead to a conclusion that injustice can be avoided only by enforcement of Plantations's promise. Hayes received $20,000 over the course of four years. He inquired each year about whether he could expect a check for the following year. Obviously, there was no absolute certainty on his part that the pension would continue. Furthermore, in the face of his uncertainty, the mere fact that payment for several years did occur is insufficient by itself to meet the requirements of reliance under the doctrine of promissory estoppel.

For the foregoing reasons, the defendant's appeal is sustained and the judgment of the Superior Court is reversed. The papers of the case are remanded to the Superior Court.

Maryland Nat'l Bank v. United Jewish Appeal Fed'n of Greater Wash.

MARYLAND NATIONAL BANK et al., Defendant-Appellant

v.

UNITED JEWISH APPEAL FEDERATION OF GREATER WASHINGTON, INC.,
Plaintiff-Appellee

Court of Appeals of Maryland
407 A.2d 1130 (Md. Ct. App. 1979)

ORTH, Judge.

The issue in this case is whether a pledge to a charitable institution survives the death of the pledgor and is an enforceable obligation of his estate.

I

Milton Polinger pledged $200,000 to the United Jewish Appeal Federation of Greater Washington, Inc. (UJA) for the year 1975. He died on 20 December 1976.

His last will and testament was admitted to probate in the Orphans' Court for Montgomery County and letters were issued to Melvin R. Oksner and Maryland National Bank as personal representatives. At the time of Polinger's death $133,500 was unpaid on his pledge. The personal representatives disallowed the claim for the balance of the pledge. UJA filed a petition praying that the claim be allowed and moved for summary judgment. The personal representatives answered and filed a cross-motion for summary judgment. The court granted UJA's motion for summary judgment, denied the personal representatives' motion for summary judgment, allowed UJA's claim against the estate in the amount of

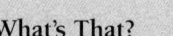 

What's That?

In Maryland, the "Orphans' Court" is the name for the court that handles wills and estates, often called probate or surrogate's court in other jurisdictions. The name derives from the old City of London's Court for Widows and Orphans, which Lord Baltimore brought to the colony of Maryland. In 1777, the Maryland General Assembly formally established an Orphans' Court and Register of Wills in each county and the City of Baltimore, a structure that continues to operate today.

$133,500, and assessed the costs against the personal representatives. The personal representatives noted an appeal to the Court of Special Appeals and petitioned this Court to issue a writ of certiorari to that court before decision by it. We did so.

II

The facts before the court were undisputed in material part. They showed the nature of UJA and its relationship with its beneficiaries. UJA, chartered in the District of Columbia, is a public non-profit corporation. In general, its objective is to solicit, collect and receive funds and property for the support of certain religious, charitable, philanthropic, scientific and educational organizations and institutions, and it enjoys tax exempt status federally and in Maryland, Virginia and the District of Columbia. Based on monies received and pledged, it makes allocations to tax exempt organizations. No formal commitment agreement is executed with respect to the allocations, but UJA undertakes to pay pursuant to the allocation and the beneficiary organizations "go ahead to act as though they are going to have the money and they spend it." In other words, UJA makes allocations to various beneficiary organizations based upon pledges made to it, and the beneficiary organizations incur liabilities based on the allocations. Historically 95% of the pledges are collected over a three year period, and allowance for the 5% which may be uncollected is made in determining the amount of the allocations. So, according to Meyer Brissman, Executive Vice-President Emeritus of UJA: "We always pay [the allocated amount]. I don't know of any case where we haven't paid." Pledges to "emergency funds" are not paid on the basis of an allocation by UJA. All monies actually collected on those pledges are paid to the emergency funds.

The facts before the court showed the circumstances surrounding the pledge of Polinger with which we are here concerned. It was evidenced by a card signed by Polinger under date of 9 November 1974. It recited:

> In consideration of the obligation incurred based upon this pledge, I hereby promise to pay to the United Jewish Appeal the amount indicated on this card.

The am⁓ ⁓" was $100,000 for "UJA including
l⁓ ⁓Israel Emergency Fund."

⁓of 1974. The mission was in no
sens⁓ ⁓in Israel, and the members of
the n⁓ ⁓rime Minister, and with other
gover⁓ ⁓e country faced. It was to be
involve⁓ ⁓Certain community leaders,
includi⁓ ⁓been active in the affairs of
UJA and⁓ ⁓o it.

"Pre-s⁓ ⁓ed who can be expected
to make lar⁓ ⁓stantially increase their
pledges of p⁓ ⁓nceived plan to obtain
large contribu⁓ ⁓which, according to
Brissman,

> [t]here is n⁓ ⁓s the interchange and people
> knowing eve⁓ ⁓⁓om, and if this one is thinking of a need
> of being so g⁓ ⁓to be willing to do something unusual, the others
> thought it was similarly important for them to demonstrate it.

The idea is that "if somebody thought it was important enough to give more than he gave before, [others would think] that they ought to give more, and they [give] more money. . . . [W]e get together and discuss reactions to what they have seen, what the needs are, and people sometimes make a speech before they decide what they are going to say about the money, and it is a free-flowing thing, and nobody knows in advance what anybody is going to say, but some of the people are talked to one by one privately to condition them to make some kind of a special response to influence the group. The whole purpose of fund raising is to get an example."

Polinger was selected to be an example on the Israel mission. He had pledged $65,000 for 1973. He had "participated willingly" in such a meeting in connection with the 1974 fund raising campaign and had pledged $150,000. He was one of those it was "felt was ready to do something unusual. . . ." He was pre-solicited by three or four individuals and went up to two hundred thousand dollars for 1975. It was agreed that his pledge would be made in a "caucus" at the King David Hotel in Jerusalem. The caucus was held and Polinger "came into the caucus," as Brissman said, "so we could announce all the gifts and influence other people of different levels." Polinger was to be a "pacesetter."

There were about thirty men at the caucus. About four of them had pledged an amount as large as $200,000 before Polinger made his announcement. Brissman thought that "there was an emotional impact that develops when a man has seen things that influence him to believe that there is something desperate and earth-shaking going on and he could do something about it beneficially, and he responds." When Polinger said he would give $200,000, he indicated that he wanted everybody to give as much as they could. He thought he was giving the greatest amount that he possibly could find himself able to so do. Of course, Polinger was only one of many people who spoke and made a pledge. Whether anyone in fact increased his pledge because of Polinger was never discussed at the meeting, and Brissman was unable to say whether anyone was influenced by Polinger's pledge.

> It is just a dynamics of an involvement where after two weeks of being together night and day in a setting of that kind after a major war, meeting with individuals who lived through three or four such wars, that everybody is strung out and you are like a family, and in the process of interchange, speeches are made, and maybe somebody [who] made a gift of $5,000.00 influenced people just as much as the man who gave $200,000.00 because of what the money meant in their view of this person's ability to give.

> It is just not the biggest number, but it is the concept of response to a need that these people are reacting to. And I don't know that you verbalize it in that way necessarily, but it does come out that one influences another in the interchange, because you are going around a room and everybody is talking about how they were moved by what they were into. So there is no question one influences another.

Brissman was asked "whether aside from the specific group of people who were present in Israel with Mr. Polinger, are there any other people here in the Washington area or anywhere else that you are aware of who made pledges, gifts, or increased gifts as a result of Mr. Polinger's gift?" He could not say. He could only give the procedure followed:

> I solicited personally hundreds of people, some face to face, some by telephone, some by appointment with two or three people talking to an individual. And frequently I, personally, and I know of others who do likewise, start to tell

people what kind of response we are getting when we get to the question of what is a standard for giving, or what you ought to consider as your share, and in the process I have used Milton Polinger as an example talking to individuals. They know who Milton is. And I would tell them what Milton had done in 1973 and in 1974 in trying to get them to respond in some way to move further ahead in their extension as far as they can, because we are talking of stretching. If you can give so much, can you give a little but more type of thing, and I frequently would use Milton as an illustration.

There is no question in my mind when I do it I know others do it, and I have seen at the time that we are talking about people reporting on the mission to others who were not there, soliciting gifts at meetings or in individual confrontations, telling what happened at the mission, and they would go down line by line everybody who made gifts, they had a list in front of them as a tool.

So it was used. There is no question about it. I cannot tell you this one increased his gift only because of that one's response, but it is part of a package. That is how you raise money.

III

We find that the law of Maryland with regard to the enforcement of pledges or subscriptions to charitable organizations is the rule thus expressed in the **Restatement of Contracts § 90 (1932)**:

> A promise which the promisor should reasonably expect to induce action or forbearance of a definite and substantial character on the part of the promisee and which does induce such action or forbearance is binding if injustice can be avoided only by enforcement of the promise.

We reach this conclusion through opinions of this Court in four cases, *Gittings v. Mayhew*, 6 Md. 113 (1854); *Erdman v. Trustees Eutaw M. P. Ch.*, 129 Md. 595, 99 A. 793 (1917); *Sterling v. Cushwa & Sons*, 170 Md. 226, 183 A. 593 (1936); and *American University v. Collings*, 190 Md. 688, 59 A.2d 333 (1948).

Gittings concerned the building of an Atheneum. The subscription contract authorized the calling of payment of installments by the subscribers when a certain amount had been pledged. The amount was reached, installments were called for and paid, contracts to erect the building were made and the Antheneum was completed. It was in these circumstances that the Court said:

> In whatever uncertainty the law concerning voluntary subscriptions
> of this character may be at this time, in consequence of the numerous

decisions pronounced upon the subject, it appears to be settled, that where advances have been made, or expenses or liabilities incurred by others, in consequence of such subscriptions, before notice of withdrawal, this should, on general principles, be deemed sufficient to make them obligatory, provided the advances were authorized by a fair and reasonable dependence on the subscriptions. . . . The doctrine is not only reasonable and just, but consistent with the analogies of the law. (6 Md. at 131-132.)

This statement of the law appeared to be obiter dictum in Gittings, but if it were, it became the law in Erdman.

What's That?

"Obiter dictum" is Latin for "something said in passing" and refers to a judicial comment made in an opinion that that is unnecessary to the decision in the case and therefore not precedential, though it may be considered persuasive. The reference is often shortened to simply "dictum."

Erdman dealt with a suit on a promissory note whereby there was a promise to pay the Eutaw Methodist Protestant Church the sum of $500 four years after date with interest. The consideration for the note was a subscription contract made with the trustees of the church for the purpose of paying off a building debt, which had been incurred for the erection of a new church building. It had been entered on the books of the church, the trustees had subsequently borrowed $2,000 on that subscription and other subscriptions to pay off the indebtedness for the erection of the church building. The Court held that in such circumstances the subscription contract was a valid and binding one and constituted a sufficient consideration to support the note, Id. 129 Md. at 602, 99 A. 793, observing that "[t]he policy of the law, to sustain subscription contracts of the character of the one here in question, is clearly stated by this court, and by other appellate courts, in a number of cases," Id. at 600, 99 A. at 795. The only Maryland case cited was Gittings. The holding in Gittings was said to be "that as the party had authorized others by the subscription to enter into engagements for the accomplishment of the enterprise, the law requires that he should save them harmless to the extent of his subscription." Erdman, 129 Md. at 601, 99 A. at 795. One case in another appellate court was discussed, *Trustees v. Garvey*, 53 Ill. 401 (1870) and two cited as to like effect, *McClure v. Wilson*, 43 Ill. 356 (1867) and *United Presbyterian Church v. Baird*, 60 Iowa 237, 14 N.W. 303 (1882). In **Garvey** the court noted that "[a]s a matter of public policy, courts have been desirous of sustaining the legal obligation of subscriptions of this character, and in some cases . . . have found a sufficient consideration in the mutuality of the promises, where no fraud or deception has been practiced." Id. at 403. "But," the court continued, "while we might be unwilling to go to that extent, and might hold that a subscription could be withdrawn before money had been expended or liability incurred, or work performed on the strength of the subscriptions, and in furtherance of the enterprise," the church trustees had, on the faith of the subscriptions, borrowed money, relying on the subscription as a means of payment and incurred a specific liability. Id. Thus, it seems that Erdman made law of the dictum in Gittings, but that law was that charitable subscriptions to be enforceable require reliance on the subscriptions by the charity which would lead to direct loss to the organization or its officers if the subscriptions were not enforced.

. . . .

In summary, the rule announced in Gittings, referred to in Collings and applied in Erdman and Sterling, is in substance the rule set out in **§ 90 of the Restatement of Contracts (1932)**. It is the settled law of this State.

IV

UJA would have us "view traditional contract law requirements of consideration liberally" in order to maintain what it believes to be a judicial policy of favoring charities. We deeply appreciate the fact that private philanthropy serves a highly important function in our society. This was well expressed by the Court some hundred and twenty-five years ago in observing that the maintenance of charitable institutions was "certainly of the highest merit":

> Whether projected for literary, scientific or charitable purposes, they address themselves to the favorable consideration of those whose success in life may have enabled them, in this way, to minister to the wants of others, and at the same time promote their own interests, by elevating the character of the community with whose prosperity their fortunes may be identified. (**Gittings, 6 Md. at 131.**)

But we are not persuaded that we should, by judicial fiat, adopt a policy of favoring charities at the expense of the law of contracts which has been long established in this state. We do not think that this law should be disregarded or modified so as to bestow a preferred status upon charitable organizations and institutions. It may be that there are cases in which judgments according to the law do not appear to subserve the purposes of justice, but this, ordinarily, the courts may not remedy. "It is safer that a private right should fail, or a wrong go unredressed, than that settled principles should be disregarded in order to meet the equity of a particular case." Gittings at 134. If change is to be made it should be by legislative enactment, as in the matter of the tax status of charitable organizations.

In advocating its position, UJA points to this statement in Gittings:

In some cases the courts, in furtherance of what they deemed a recognized public policy, have felt themselves warranted in relaxing, to some extent, the rigor of the common law, and have held the subscribers liable, when, perhaps, upon strict principles, there was not a legal consideration for the contract. (Id. at 131.)

That this was no more than an observation and not an adoption of the principle was made manifest by the further comments of the Court:

Indeed, considering the number of these [charitable] institutions, erected and maintained by private munificence alone, the cases are very rare in which subscribers have refused compliance with their engagements. Instances may occur in which parties, feeling themselves released in consequence of a failure of expectations reasonably entertained at the time of making the subscription, might avail themselves of legal defences, without justly forfeiting the good opinion of those who embarked with them in the enterprise. The propriety, however, of employing such means of resisting payment the parties must determine for themselves. Upon that portion of the present case, therefore, so much contested at the bar, we decline expressing any opinion. (Id.)

. . . .

Restatement (Second) of Contracts (Tent. Draft No. 2, 1965) proposes changes in § 90. It would read:

A promise which the promisor should reasonably expect to induce action or forbearance on the part of the promisee or a third person and which does induce such action or forbearance is binding if injustice can be avoided only by enforcement of the promise. The remedy granted for breach may be limited as justice requires.

This deletes from the existing section the qualification "of a definite and substantial character" with regard to the inducement of action or forbearance and has the inducement of forbearance apply to "a third person" as well as the promisee. It also adds the discretionary limitation as to the remedy. Comment c to the proposed Section concerns "[c]haritable subscriptions, marriage settlements, and other gifts." It begins:

One of the functions of the doctrine of consideration is to deny enforcement to a promise to make a gift. Such a promise is ordinarily enforced by virtue of the promisee's reliance only if his conduct is foreseeable and reasonable and involves a definite and substantial change of position which would not have occurred if the promise had not been made.

This reflects the previous section and the Maryland rule. The comment then notes that "[i]n some cases, however, other policies reinforce the promisee's claim." It states:

> American courts have traditionally favored charitable subscriptions and marriage settlements, and have found consideration in many cases where the element of exchange was doubtful or nonexistent. Where recovery is rested on reliance in such cases, a probability of reliance is likely to be enough, and no effort is made to sort out mixed motives or to consider whether partial enforcement would be appropriate.

Illustration 7 is of a charitable subscription:

> A orally promises to pay B, a university, $100,000 in five annual installments for the purposes of its fund-raising campaign then in progress. The promise is confirmed in writing by A's agent, and two annual installments are paid before A dies. The continuance of the fund-raising campaign by B is sufficient reliance to make the promise binding on A and his estate.

Section 90 of the tentative draft No. 2 of the Restatement (Second) of Contracts, 1965, has not been adopted by the American Law Institute, and we are not persuaded to follow it.

Take Note!

As you can see, the draft of Section 90 for the second Restatement suggested in its comments that "a probability of reliance is likely . . . enough" to support enforcement of a charitable pledge; that approach led to Restatement (Second) of Contracts § 90(2), which removes the requirement that actual reliance be shown. Despite the adoption of the provision by the American Law Institute, most courts—like the Maryland Court of Appeals here—have not been persuaded to follow that rule. When applying promissory estoppel to charitable subscriptions, courts continue to require the recipients to show actual reliance (though they sometimes seem to do so with "strained reasoning," as noted in the *Maryland National Bank* opinion).

"Cases throughout the country clearly reflect a conflict between the desired goal of enforcing charitable subscriptions and the realities of contract law. The result has been strained reasoning which has been the subject of considerable criticism." *Salsbury v. Northwestern Bell Telephone Company*, **221 N.W.2d 609, 611-612 (Iowa, 1974)**. When charitable subscriptions, even though clearly gratuitous promises, have been held either contracts or offers to contract, the "decisions are based on such a great variety of reasoning as to show the lack of any really sufficient consideration." Williston on Contracts, § 116 (3d ed. 1957) (footnotes omitted). "Very likely, conceptions of public policy have shaped, more or less subconsciously, the rulings thus made. Judges have been affected by the thought that 'defenses of [the] character [of lack of consideration are] breaches of faith towards the public, and especially towards those engaged in the same enterprise, and an unwarrantable disappointment of the reasonable expectations of those interested.'" *Allegheny College v. National Chautauqua County Bank*, 246 N.Y. 369, 159 N.E. 173, 175 (1927). Therefore, "[c]ourts have . . . purported to find consideration on various tenuous theories. . . . [The] wide variation in reasoning indicates the difficulty of enforcing a charitable subscription on grounds of consideration. Yet, the courts have generally striven to find grounds for enforcement, indicating the depth of feeling in this country that private philanthropy serves a highly important function in our society." J. Calamari & J. Perillo, The Law of Contracts, § 6-5 (1977) (footnotes omitted). Some courts have forthrightly discarded the facade of consideration and admittedly held a charitable subscription enforceable only in respect of what they conceive to be the public policy. See, for example, *Salsbury v. Northwestern Bell Telephone Company, supra;* **More Game Birds in America,** *Inc. v. Boettger,* 125 N.J.L. 97, 14 A.2d 778, 780-781 (1940).

We are not convinced that such departure from the settled law of contracts is in the public interest. A charitable subscription must be a contract to be enforceable, unless we characterize it as some other type of agreement, unknown to established contract law, for which a valid consideration is not essential. . . . We abide by that principle in determining the validity of the charitable subscriptions.

V

When the facts concerning the charitable subscription of Polinger are viewed in light of the Maryland law, it is manifest that his promise was not legally enforceable. There was no consideration as required by contract law. The incidents on which Gittings indicated a charitable pledge was enforceable, and on which Erdman and Sterling held the subscriptions in those cases were enforceable are not present here. The consideration recited by the pledge card was "the obligation incurred based upon this pledge. . . ." But there was no legal obligation incurred in the circumstances. Polinger's pledge was not made in consideration of the pledges of others, and there was no evidence that others in fact made pledges in consideration of Polinger's pledge. No release was given or binding agreement made by the UJA on the strength of Polinger's pledge. The pledge was not for a specific enterprise; it was to the UJA generally and to the Israel Emergency Fund. With respect to the former, no allocation by UJA to its beneficiary organization was threatened or thwarted by the failure to collect the Polinger pledge in its entirety, and, with respect to the latter, UJA practice was to pay over to the Fund only what it actually collected, not what was pledged. UJA borrowed no money on the faith and credit of the pledge. The pledge prompted no "action or forbearance of a definite and substantial character" on the part of UJA. No action was taken by UJA on the strength of the pledge that could reasonably be termed "definite and substantial" from which it should be held harmless. There was no change shown in the position of UJA made in reliance on the subscription which resulted in an economic loss, and, in fact, there was no such loss demonstrated. UJA was able to fulfill all of its allocations. Polinger's pledge was utilized as a means to obtain substantial pledges from others. But this was a technique employed to raise money. It did not supply a legal consideration to Polinger's pledge. On the facts of this case, it does not appear that injustice can be avoided only by enforcement of the promise.

To summarize, there was no specific goal prompting the pledge such as existed in Gittings, Erdman and Sterling with a mutual awareness of future reliance on the subscription. UJA did not enter into binding contracts, incur expenses or suffer liabilities in reliance on the pledge. UJA's function was to serve as a conduit or clearinghouse to collect gifts of money from many sources and to funnel them into various charitable organizations. It did, of course, plan for the future, in that it estimated the rate of cash flow based on the pledges it received and told its beneficiaries to expect certain amounts. In so doing, however, it expressly did not incur liabilities in reliance on specific pledges. It seems that none of the organizations to which it allocated money would have legal rights against UJA in the event of failure to pay the allocation, and, in any event, UJA, cognizant of the past history of collections, made due allowance for the fact that a certain percentage of the pledges would not be paid.

We hold that Polinger's pledge to UJA was a gratuitous promise. It had no legal consideration, and under the law of this State was unenforceable. The Orphans' Court for Montgomery County erred in allowing the claim for the unpaid balance of the subscription, and its order of 5 January 1979 is vacated with direction to enter an order disallowing the claim filed by UJA. . . .

Food for Thought:
The Future of Promissory Estoppel

Promissory estoppel was initially formulated to permit enforcement of promises in a limited set of circumstances where bargain would likely be absent, primarily promises within families and promises to donate to charities. It has since been extended to apply in a wide variety of commercial contexts, though some question whether such an extension is appropriate. At the very least, invoking promissory estoppel in a commercial context requires answering the question whether it would be reasonable, under the circumstances, for a party to rely on a promise that could have been, but was not, made as part of a "bargain" (that is, made without consideration).

Promissory estoppel continues to be the focus of a substantial amount of scholarly attention, with authors addressing the nature of the doctrine (e.g., Is it about reliance or is it about promising?), the appropriate extent of application for the doctrine (e.g., Should it be used to enforce a promise that otherwise would have to be in writing, as it is used to enforce a promise that would otherwise require consideration? Should it be used to compensate for pre-contractual reliance, an issue considered in Chapter 4, page 343), the appropriate damage award (Do or should courts limit damages to less than full contract damages?), and the extent to which courts actually enforce promises on the basis of promissory estoppel.

While questions clearly remain regarding its present application and future scope as a rationale for enforcing promises, promissory estoppel remains one of the most important and dynamic doctrines in the field of contract enforcement.

For discussion of these and other issues related to promissory estoppel, *see, e.g.* Marco Jimenez, *The Many Faces of Promissory Estoppel: An Empirical Analysis Under the Restatement (Second) of Contracts*, 57 UCLA Law Rev. 669 (2010); Juliet P. Kostritsky, *The Rise and Fall of Promissory Estoppel or Is Promissory Estoppel Really as Unsuccessful as Scholars Say It Is: A New Look at the Data*, 37 Wake Forest L. Rev. 531 (2002); Robert A. Hillman, *Questioning the "New Consensus" on Promissory Estoppel: An Empirical and Theoretical Study*, 98 Colum. L. Rev. 580 (1998); Charles L. Knapp, *Rescuing Reliance: The Perils of Promissory Estoppel*, 49 Hastings L.J. 1191 (1998); Jay M. Feinman,

The Last Promissory Estoppel Article, 61 Fordham L. Rev. 303 (1992); Edward Yorio & Steve Thel, *The Promissory Basis of Section 90,* 101 Yale L. J. 111 (1991); Daniel A. Farber & John H. Matheson, *Beyond Promissory Estoppel: Contract Law and the "Invisible Handshake,"* 52 U. Chi. L. Rev. 903 (1985).

§ 3. Promise for Benefit Already Received ("Promissory Restitution")

So far you have seen that promises may be enforced because they have consideration (they were "bargained for" or were made in order to induce action or forbearance by the promisee) or because, despite the absence of consideration, the promise induced reliance by the promisee in circumstances found to justify enforcement of the promise. What if the promise was made not to induce action by the promisee, but to reward or compensate the promisee for actions already taken or expenses already incurred? By definition, benefits already conferred by the promisee cannot constitute consideration. Although courts sometimes use the expression "past consideration," that is an oxymoron, to *be* consideration, the benefit *must* be in the future. Yet courts concluded that some promises of this kind were worthy of enforcement. The problem was finding a consistent articulable rationale for doing so.

Reading the Law Critically: *Mills, Drake,* and *Webb*

1. Why does each court enforce, or fail to enforce, the promise made?

2. On what authority does each court rely in reaching its result?

3. What role does moral obligation play in each court's analysis? Why isn't moral obligation enough to make a promise enforceable? What else is necessary to warrant enforcement?

Mills v. Wyman

nursed sick son does father pay? (handwritten margin note)

DANIEL MILLS, Plaintiff-Appellant

v.

SETH WYMAN, Defendant-Appellee

Supreme Judicial Court of Massachusetts
20 Mass. 207 (1825)

This was an action of *assumpsit* brought to recover a compensation for the board, nursing, &c., of Levi Wyman, son of the defendant, from the 5th to the 20th of February, 1821. The plaintiff then lived at Hartford, in Connecticut; the defendant, at Shrewsbury, in this county. Levi Wyman, at the time when the services were rendered, was about 25 years of age, and had long ceased to be a member of his father's family. He was on his return from a voyage at sea, and being suddenly taken sick at Hartford, and being poor and in distress, was relieved by the plaintiff in the manner and to the extent above stated. On the 24th of February, after all the expenses had been incurred, the defendant wrote a letter to the plaintiff, promising to pay him such expenses. There was no consideration for this promise, except what grew out of the relation which subsisted between Levi Wyman and the defendant, and Howe J., before whom the cause was tried in the Court of Common Pleas, thinking this not sufficient to support the action, directed a nonsuit. To this direction the plaintiff filed exceptions.

What's That?

"Assumpsit" is one of the old English and American forms of action or writs, used to bring suit for recovery of damages for non-performance of a promise or contract. In England, assumpsit was abolished in the 19th century along with other common law forms of action. In the United States, assumpsit became obsolete in the federal courts with adoption of the Federal Rules of Civil Procedure in 1938. Most but not all states have also ceased to use the old forms of action, replacing them with claims for breach of contract.

PARKER C. J.

General rules of law established for the protection and security of honest and fair-minded men, who may inconsiderately make promises without any equivalent, will sometimes screen men of a different character from engagements which they are bound in *foro conscientiæ* to perform. This is a defect inherent in all human systems of legislation. The rule that a mere verbal promise, without any consideration, cannot be enforced by action, is universal in its application, and cannot be departed from to suit particular cases in which a refusal to perform such a promise may be disgraceful.

The promise declared on in this case appears to have been made without any legal consideration. The kindness and services towards the sick son of the defendant were not bestowed at his request. The son was in no respect under the care of the defendant. He was twenty-five years old, and had long left his father's family. On his return from a foreign country, he fell sick among strangers, and the plaintiff acted the part of the good Samaritan, giving *didn't die* him shelter and comfort until he died. The defendant, his father, on being informed of this event, influenced by a transient feeling of gratitude, promises in writing to pay the plaintiff for the expenses he had incurred. But he has determined to break this promise, and is willing to have his case appear on record as a strong example of particular injustice sometimes necessarily resulting from the operation of general rules.

It is said a moral obligation is a sufficient consideration to support an express promise; and some authorities lay down the rule thus broadly; but upon examination of the cases we are satisfied that the universality of the rule cannot be supported, and that there must have been some preëxisting obligation, which has become inoperative by positive law, to form a basis for an effective promise. The cases of debts barred by the statute of limitations, of debts incurred by infants, of debts of bankrupts, are generally put for illustration of the rule. Express promises founded on such preëxisting equitable obligations may be enforced; there is a good consideration for them; they merely remove an impediment created by law to the recovery of debts honestly due, but which public policy protects the debtors from being compelled to pay. In all these

moral obligation requires some preexisting obligation

Take Note

In this case and the next, notice that a statement of facts precedes the court's opinion, and the judge in each case launches into a discourse on the legal rule without any attempt to summarize the facts. That pattern was especially common in the early years of state and federal court reports, when private individuals were the publishers of court opinions, adding their own summaries of the facts and the arguments of counsel. Although not part of the court's opinion, the reporter's statement of facts is often critical to understanding early cases, but, as we will see, it is not always correct.

The first official court reporter was named in Massachusetts in 1804. *Mills v. Wyman* was published by Octavius Pickering, the official reporter in that state from 1822 to 1839; for that reason, the original citation to the opinion was 3 Pick. 207.

For more information about the history of court reporting in the United States, *see* Erwin C. Surrency, *Law Reports in the United States,* 25 Am. J. Leg. History 48 (1981); Thomas Young, *A Look at American Law Reporting in the 19th Century,* 68 Law Libr. J. 294 (1975).

cases there was originally a *quid pro quo;* and according to the principles of natural justice the party receiving ought to pay; but the legislature has said he shall not be coerced; then comes the promise to pay the debt that is barred, the promise of the man to pay the debt of the infant, of the discharged bankrupt to restore to his creditor what by the law he had lost. In all these cases there is a moral obligation founded upon an antecedent valuable consideration. These promises therefore have a sound legal basis. They are not promises to pay something for nothing; not naked pacts; but the voluntary revival or creation of obligation which before existed in natural law, but which had been dispensed with, not for the benefit of the party obliged solely, but principally for the public convenience.

[handwritten margin note: reviving past unpaid obligations]

Think About It!

Why should a gratuitous promise to pay an old unenforceable debt be itself enforceable, but not a promise to pay for other past benefits, even though the promisor wants to offer payment?

If moral obligation, in its fullest sense, is a good substratum for an express promise, it is not easy to perceive why it is not equally good to support an implied promise. What a man ought to do, generally he ought to be made to do, whether he promise or refuse. But the law of society has left most of such obligations to the *interior* forum, as the tribunal of conscience has been aptly called. Is there not a moral obligation upon every son who has become affluent by means of the education and advantages bestowed upon him by his father, to relieve that father from pecuniary embarrassment, to promote his comfort and happiness, and even to share with him his riches, if thereby he will be made happy? And yet such a son may, with impunity, leave such a father in any degree of penury above that which will expose the community in which he dwells, to the danger of being obliged to preserve him from absolute want. Is not a wealthy father under strong moral obligation to advance the interest of an obedient, well disposed son, to furnish him with the means of acquiring and maintaining a becoming rank in life, to rescue him from the horrors of debt incurred by misfortune? Yet the law will uphold him in any degree of parsimony, short of that which would reduce his son to the necessity of seeking public charity. *[handwritten: extreme unwillingness to spend money]*

Without doubt there are great interests of society which justify withholding the coercive arm of the law from these duties of imperfect obligation, as they are called; imperfect, not because they are less binding upon the conscience than those which are called perfect, but because the wisdom of the social law does not impose sanctions upon them.

A deliberate promise, in writing, made freely and without any mistake, one which may lead the party to whom it is made into contracts and expenses, cannot be broken without a violation of moral duty. But if there was nothing paid or promised for it, the law, perhaps wisely, leaves the execution of it to the conscience of him who makes it. It is only when the party making the promise gains something, or he to whom it is made loses something, that the law gives the promise validity. And in the case of the promise of the adult to pay the debt of the infant, of the debtor discharged by the statute of limitations or bankruptcy, the principle is preserved by looking back to the origin of the transaction, where an equivalent is to be found. An exact equivalent is not required by the law; for there being a consideration, the parties are left to estimate its value: though here the courts of equity will step in to relieve from gross inadequacy between the consideration and the promise.

These principles are deduced from the general current of decided cases upon the subject, as well as from the known maxims of the common law. The general position, that moral obligation is a sufficient consideration for an express promise, is to be limited in its application, to cases where at some time or other a good or valuable consideration has existed. [citations omitted]

A legal obligation is always a sufficient consideration to support either an express or an implied promise; such as an infant's debt for necessaries, or a father's promise to pay for the support and education of his minor children. But when the child shall have attained to manhood, and shall have become his own agent in the world's business, the debts he incurs, whatever may be their nature, create no obligation upon the father; and it seems to follow, that his promise founded upon such a debt has no legally binding force.

>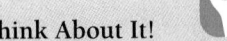
>
> ### Think About It!
>
> "Necessaries" are things that are indispensable to living, for example, food, shelter, and clothing, at least at subsistence levels. Why would a father's promise to pay for his minor child's necessaries or education have "a sufficient consideration" but his promise to pay for his adult child's debts would not?

. . . .

. . . [T]here seems to be no case in which it was nakedly decided, that a promise to pay the debt of a son of full age, not living with his father, though the debt were incurred by sickness which ended in the death of the son, without a previous request by the father proved or presumed, could be enforced by action.

. . . .

For the foregoing reasons we are all of opinion that the nonsuit directed by the Court of Common Pleas was right, and that judgment be entered thereon for costs for the defendant.

Behind the Scenes

As discovered by Professor Geoffrey Watson (*see* Geoffrey Watson, *In the Tribunal of Conscience: Mills v. Wyman Reconsidered*, 71 Tul. L. Rev. 1749 (1997)), the letter written by Seth Wyman to Daniel Mills, never quoted by the court or the reporter who wrote the statement of facts, read as follows:

> Dear Sir
>
> I received a line from you relating to my Son Levi's sickness and requesting me to come up and see him, but as the going is very bad I cannot come up at the present, but I wish you to take all possible care of him and if you cannot have him at your house I wish you to remove him to some convenient place and if he cannot satisfy you for it I will.
>
> I want that you should write me again immediately how he does and greatly oblige your most obedient servant
>
> Seth Wyman Feb. 24th 1821

By the time the letter arrived, Levi was apparently leaving or had already left Mills' establishment. (Despite Justice Parker's statement that Mills cared for Levi until the latter's death, Levi survived his illness and moved to Springfield, Massachusetts.) Mills wrote back to Wyman, informing him of Levi's departure and seeking payment of a bill of $16 for lodging and $6 for the doctor's fee, but heard nothing back from Wyman and filed suit in 1824.

As also reported by Professor Watson, "while Levi outlived the Supreme Judicial Court's pronouncement of his death, he did not outgrow his habit of getting into trouble." In 1829, a legal guardian was appointed for Levi, "'who spends and wastes his estate by excessive drinking and idleness.'"

What effect do these facts have on your evaluation of the correctness of the *Mills* opinion?

Drake v. Bell

JOSEPHINE C. DRAKE, Plaintiff

v.

EDWARD C. BELL, Defendant

Supreme Court, Kings County, New York

55 N.Y.S. 945 (Sup. Ct. 1899)

The plaintiff made a contract with a mechanic [Russell] to repair her vacant house for $210. By his own mistake he went into the vacant house of the defendant next door and repaired it instead. He discovered his mistake after the work was done. He then informed the defendant. The work was done without the defendant's knowledge. It was all of an irremovable character like plastering and painting. The defendant looked over the work, and disclaimed responsibility, but finally had the contractor reduce his bill to $194 and orally promised to pay him that sum. The work was of that value. The defendant's house which had stood vacant for lack of repair was benefited by such work to at least the value thereof, and by reason thereof was immediately let and became salable. The contractor filed a mechanic's lien against the house and the defendant as owner for the said work after the said promise, and assigned his claim against the defendant and his lien to the plaintiff. This is an action to foreclose the lien, etc.

What's That?

A "mechanic's lien" is a legal interest in property that is given to a person who has improved or repaired the property, providing security to the service provider. The right to file a mechanic's lien is granted by statute.

Take Note!

The defendant (Bell) made a promise to the contractor (Russell) to pay for the services mistakenly rendered on Bell's house. So why is Drake, Bell's neighbor (and the person who actually made a contract with Russell to repair *her* house) the plaintiff in the lawsuit? Note the second to last sentence in the case description above: contractor Russell "assigned his claim against the defendant" to Drake. That means Russell transferred to Drake any rights he had to payment. Why would he do that? A note after the case may explain his actions.

GAYNOR, J.

The defendant was under no legal obligation to pay for the work. Nor is there any question of acceptance as of a chattel, for there was nothing capable of being rejected or taken away. Did, then, his promise bind him? Lord Mansfield with his keen perception, broad mind, and aversion to alleged rules of law resting on misunderstood or inadvertent remarks of judges, instead of on foundations of reason and justice, said in Hawkes v. Saunders, Cowp. 289, that:

> "Where a man is under a moral obligation, which no court of law or equity can enforce, and promises, the honesty and rectitude of the thing is a consideration."

Buller, J., said in the same case:

> "If such a question were stripped of all authority it would be resolved by inquiring whether law were a rule of justice, or whether it was something that acts in direct contradiction to justice, conscience and equity."

If the rule so plainly stated by Lord Mansfield, that a moral obligation was of itself sufficient consideration for a subsequent promise, had been followed, the sole question in each case would be whether there was a moral obligation to support the promise. That would resolve the present case for the plaintiff. But it has not been always followed. I have examined the cases on the subject in England and here from the beginning. They are irreconcilable, and it would be no use to cite and review them.

But notwithstanding much stray remark by judges may be cited to the contrary, it seems to me that a prom-

What's That?

"Chattel" is movable personal property.

Who's That?

William Murray, 1st Earl of Mansfield, was Lord Chief Justice of England and Wales from 1756 to 1788, after a political career that included election to Parliament and service as Solicitor General and Attorney General. As Lord Chief Justice, Mansfield reformed court procedures and led efforts to modernize the commercial law of England. "The law relating to shipping, commercial transactions, and insurance was practically remade by Mansfield." Frederick Edwin Smith Birkenhead, *Fourteen English Judges* 186 (1926). Mansfield is perhaps best known as the author of Somerset's Case, 20 State Tr. 1 (1772), in which he condemned the practice of slavery in words that reverberated in English and later American law, though the case itself ruled more narrowly that a master could not by force remove a slave from the country. *See Oxford Dictionary of National Biography*.

ise to pay for antecedent value received by the promisor from the promisee binds, although there was never any obligation to pay which could be enforced. Why not? Such a case is not one of mere moral obligation resting on no consideration received, if there can be any such abstract moral obligation. The case is one of moral obligation created by a past valuable consideration derived from another. For instance, a promise after coming of age to pay a debt incurred during infancy, and which cannot be enforced, or by a woman after coming discovert to pay a like debt incurred while covert, is binding. . . . Goulding v. Davidson, 26 N. Y. 604.

What's That?

The court refers to a promise by a woman to pay a debt incurred "while covert." In the 19th century and earlier, a married woman was considered under coverture, meaning she was unable to enter contracts without the consent of her husband and could not be independently liable for a debt incurred. The court here refers to a woman who, perhaps through divorce or the death of her husband, ceases to be under coverture and thereafter affirms a debt incurred while she was still married.

On the other hand, a subsequent promise by a father to pay for the care of his adult son while sick among strangers, or of a son to pay for like care of his father, is not binding. Mills v. Wyman, 3 Pick. 207 . . . . The distinction is that in the former class of cases there was past valuable consideration to the promisor, while in the latter not. The promise in the one class is not a naked pact, for it is not to pay something for nothing; while in the other class just that is the case.

[handwritten note: was something valuable done before?]

. . . [O]nly a subsequent promise which revives an obligation formerly enforceable either at law or in equity, but which has grown extinct, is binding. "But a mere moral or conscientious obligation, unconnected with any prior legal or equitable claim, is not enough," is the rule reduced from the said note in a number of cases (as in Ehle v. Judson, 24 Wend. 97). And yet the same opinions say that the moral obligation "to pay a debt contracted during infancy or coverture, and the like," is sufficient to support a subsequent promise; as though in such cases the moral obligation rested on a prior legal or equitable claim, which it does not. Such is true though of a promise to pay a debt barred by the statute of limitations or by a discharge in bankruptcy, which all of the cases hold to be binding.

The actual decisions most worthy of attention (not feeling bound by mere general remarks of judges and their citation) make two classes. In one of them the promise is held binding because based on a former obligation enforceable at law or in equity, which obligation it revives; in the other because the promisor though never under any such obligation nevertheless received an antecedent valuable consideration. Hence the rule seems to be that a subsequent promise founded on a former enforceable obligation, or on value previously had from the promisee, is binding.

. . . .

Chancellor Kent does not confine the validity of such promises to cases of past legal obligation, but extends it to cases of the existence of a prior consideration. He says it is an unsettled point whether a moral obligation is of itself "a sufficient consideration for a promise, except in those cases in which a prior legal obligation or consideration had once existed." 2 Kent, Comm. 465.

I do not pretend that this question is free from doubt, but to use the words of Chief Justice Marshall, "I do not think that law ought to be separated from justice where it is at most doubtful" (Hoffman v. Porter, 2 Brock. 159, Fed. Cas. No. 6,577), and that has no doubt influenced me some in reaching a conclusion.

Judgment for the plaintiff.

Behind the Scenes

When *Drake v. Bell* was appealed, a few additional facts were revealed. First, during the negotiations between the carpenter (Russell) and the defendant homeowner (Bell), Bell promised that, if the plaintiff homeowner (Drake) would pay Russell the agreed sum of $194, he (Bell) would pay her that amount. Second, the appellate court noted the trial court's finding "that some of the said repairs consisted of windows and some articles which were not made part of the freehold, and could have been taken away by the said Russell, but by the defendant's said promise the said Russell was induced to leave everything there, and he did so." What effect should these facts have had on the trial court's analysis?

Webb v. McGowin

JOE WEBB, Plaintiff-Appellant

v.

N. FLOYD and JOSEPH F. McGOWIN,
as executors of the estate of J. Greeley McGowin, deceased,
Defendants-Appellees

Court of Appeals of Alabama
168 So. 196 (Ala. Ct. App. 1935)

BRICKEN, Presiding Judge.

This action is in assumpsit. The complaint as originally filed was amended. The demurrers to the complaint as amended were sustained, and because of this adverse ruling by the court the plaintiff took a non-suit, and the assignment of errors on this appeal are predicated upon said action or ruling of the court.

A fair statement of the case presenting the questions for decision is set out in appellant's brief, which we adopt.

"On the 3d day of August, 1925, appellant while in the employ of the W.T. Smith Lumber Company, a corporation, and acting within the scope of his employment, was engaged in clearing the upper floor of mill No. 2 of the company. While so engaged he was in the act of dropping a pine block from the upper floor of the mill to the ground below; this being the usual and ordinary way of clearing the floor, and it being the duty of the plaintiff in the course of his employment to so drop it. The block weighed about 75 pounds.

"As appellant was in the act of dropping the block to the ground below, he was on the edge of the upper floor of the mill. As he started to turn the block loose so that it would drop to the ground, he saw J. Greeley McGowin, testator of the defendants, on the ground below and directly under where the block would have fallen had appellant turned it loose. Had he turned it loose it would have struck McGowin with such force as to have caused him serious bodily harm or death. Appellant could have remained safely on the upper floor of the mill by turning the block loose and allowing it to drop, but had he done this the block would have fallen on McGowin and caused him serious injuries or death. The only safe and reasonable way to prevent this was for appellant to hold to the block and divert its direction in falling from the place where McGowin was standing and the only safe way to divert it so as to prevent its coming into contact with McGowin was for appellant to fall with it to the ground below. Appellant did this, and by holding to the block and falling with it to the ground below, he diverted the course of its fall in such way that McGowin was not injured. In thus preventing the injuries to McGowin appellant himself received serious bodily injuries, resulting in his right leg being broken, the heel of his right foot torn off and his right arm broken. He was badly crippled for life and rendered unable to do physical or mental labor.

"On September 1, 1925, in consideration of appellant having prevented him from sustaining death or serious bodily harm and in consideration of the injuries appellant had received, McGowin agreed with him to care for and maintain him for the remainder of appellant's life at the rate of $15 every two weeks from the time he sustained his injuries to and during the remainder of appellant's life; it being agreed that McGowin would pay this sum to appellant for his maintenance. Under the agreement McGowin paid or caused to be paid to appellant the sum so agreed on up until McGowin's death on January 1, 1934. After his death the payments were continued to and including January 27, 1934, at which time they were discontinued. Thereupon plaintiff brought suit to recover the unpaid installments accruing up to the time of the bringing of the suit.

"The material averments of the different counts of the original complaint and the amended complaint are predicated upon the foregoing statement of facts."

In other words, the complaint as amended averred in substance: (1) That on August 3, 1925, appellant saved J. Greeley McGowin, appellee's testator, from death or grievous bodily harm; (2) that in doing so appellant sustained bodily injury crippling him for life; (3) that in consideration of the services rendered and the injuries received by appellant, McGowin agreed to care for him the remainder of appellant's life, the amount to be paid being $15 every two weeks; (4) that McGowin complied with this agreement until he died on January 1, 1934, and the payments were kept up to January 27, 1934, after which they were discontinued.

The action was for the unpaid installments accruing after January 27, 1934, to the time of the suit.

The principal grounds of demurrer to the original and amended complaint are: (1) It states no cause of action; (2) its averments show the contract was without consideration; (3) it fails to allege that McGowin had, at or before the services were rendered, agreed to pay appellant for them; (4) the contract declared on is void under the statute of frauds.

The averments of the complaint show that appellant saved McGowin from death or grievous bodily harm. This was a material benefit to him of infinitely more value than any financial aid he could have received. Receiving this benefit, McGowin became morally bound to compensate appellant for the services rendered. Recognizing his moral obligation, he expressly agreed to pay appellant as alleged in the complaint and complied with this agreement up to the time of his death; a period of more than 8 years.

Had McGowin been accidentally poisoned and a physician, without his knowledge or request, had administered an antidote, thus saving his life, a subsequent promise by McGowin to pay the physician would have been valid. Likewise, McGowin's agreement as disclosed by the complaint to compensate appellant for saving him from death or grievous bodily injury is valid and enforceable.

Think About It!

Is the rule for which the court cites *Pittsburg Vitrified Paving* consistent with your understanding of the meaning of "consideration"? If not, how do you explain the statement?

Where the promisee cares for, improves, and preserves the property of the promisor, though done without his request, it is sufficient consideration for the promisor's subsequent agreement to pay for the service, because of the material benefit received. **Pittsburg Vitrified Paving & Building Brick Co. v. Cerebus Oil Co., 79 Kan. 603, 100 P. 631; Edson v. Poppe, 24 S.D. 466, 124 N.W. 441,26 L.R.A. (N.S.) 534; Drake v. Bell, 26 Misc. 237, 55 N.Y.S. 945.**

In **Boothe v. Fitzpatrick, 36 Vt. 681,** the court held that a promise by defendant to pay for the past keeping of a bull which had escaped from defendant's premises and been cared for by plaintiff was valid, although there was no previous request, because the subsequent promise obviated that objection; it being equivalent to a previous request. On the same principle, had the promisee saved the promisor's life or his body from grievous harm, his subsequent promise to pay for the services rendered would have been valid. Such service would have been far more material than caring for his bull. Any holding that saving a man from death or grievous bodily harm is not a material benefit sufficient to uphold a subsequent promise to pay for the service, necessarily rests on the assumption that saving life and preservation of the body from harm have only a sentimental value. The converse of this is true. Life and preservation of the body have material, pecuniary values, measurable in dollars and cents. Because of this, physicians practice their profession charging for services rendered in saving life and curing the body of its ills, and surgeons perform operations. The same is true as to the law of negligence, authorizing the assessment of damages in personal injury cases based upon the extent of the injuries, earnings, and life expectancies of those injured.

In the business of life insurance, the value of a man's life is measured in dollars and cents according to his expectancy, the soundness of his body, and his ability to pay premiums. The same is true as to health and accident insurance.

It follows that if, as alleged in the complaint, appellant saved J. Greeley McGowin from death or grievous bodily harm, and McGowin subsequently agreed to pay him for the service rendered, it became a valid and enforceable contract.

It is well settled that a moral obligation is a sufficient consideration to support a subsequent promise to pay where the promisor has received a material benefit, although there was no original duty or liability resting on the promisor. Lycoming County v. Union County, 15 Pa. 166, 53 Am.Dec. 575, 579, 580; Ferguson v. Harris, 39 S.C. 323, 17 S.E. 782, 39 Am.St.Rep. 731, 734; Muir v. Kane, 55 Wash. 131, 104 P. 153, 26 L.R.A. (N.S.) 519, 19 Ann.Cas. 1180; State ex rel. Bayer v. Funk, 105 Or. 134, 199 P. 592,209 P. 113, 25 A.L.R. 625, 634; Hawkes v. Saunders, 1 Cowp. 290; In re Sutch's Estate, 201 Pa. 305, 50 A. 943; Edson v. Poppe, 24 S.D. 466, 124 N.W. 441,26 L.R.A. (N.S.) 534; Park Falls State Bank v. Fordyce, 206 Wis. 628, 238 N.W. 516, 79 A.L.R. 1339; Baker v. Gregory, 28 Ala. 544, 65 Am.Dec. 366. In the case of State ex rel. Bayer v. Funk, supra, the court held that a moral obligation is a sufficient consideration to support an executory promise where the promisor has received an actual pecuniary or material benefit for which he subsequently expressly promised to pay.

The case at bar is clearly distinguishable from that class of cases where the consideration is a mere moral obligation or conscientious duty unconnected with receipt by promisor of benefits of a material or pecuniary nature. Park Falls State Bank v. Fordyce, supra. Here the promisor received a material benefit constituting a valid consideration for his promise.

Some authorities hold that, for a moral obligation to support a subsequent promise to pay, there must have existed a prior legal or equitable obligation, which for some reason had become unenforceable, but for which the promisor was still morally bound. This rule, however, is subject to qualification in those cases where the promisor, having received a material benefit from the promisee, is morally bound to compensate him for the services rendered and in consideration of this obligation promises to pay. In such cases the subsequent promise to pay is an affirmance or ratification of the services rendered carrying with it the presumption that a previous request for the service was made. McMorris v. Herndon, 2 Bailey

Think About It!

The *Webb* case pre-dates the adoption of a workers' compensation scheme in Alabama, so Webb retained the right to bring a lawsuit. Based on that fact, what additional argument for enforcement might have been made?

(S.C.) 56, 21 Am.Dec. 515; **Chadwick v. Knox, 31 N.H. 226, 64 Am.Dec. 329;** Kenan v. Holloway, 16 Ala. 53, 50 Am.Dec. 162; Ross v. Pearson, 21 Ala. 473.

Under the decisions above cited, McGowin's express promise to pay appellant for the services rendered was an affirmance or ratification of what appellant had done raising the presumption that the services had been rendered at McGowin's request.

The averments of the complaint show that in saving McGowin from death or grievous bodily harm, appellant was crippled for life. This was part of the consideration of the contract declared on. McGowin was benefited. Appellant was injured. Benefit to the promisor or injury to the promisee is a sufficient legal consideration for the promisor's agreement to pay. Fisher v. Bartlett, 8 Greenl. (Me.) 122, 22 Am.Dec. 225; State ex rel. Bayer v. Funk, supra.

Under the averments of the complaint the services rendered by appellant were not gratuitous. The agreement of McGowin to pay and the acceptance of payment by appellant conclusively shows the contrary. . . .

Think About It!

What does the court mean by saying the services were "not gratuitous"? Does that conclusion seem correct on the facts? Why should it matter if the services were gratuitous?

From what has been said, we are of the opinion that the court below erred in the ruling complained of; that is to say, in sustaining the demurrer, and for this error the case is reversed and remanded.

Reversed and remanded.   *yes, he should get pension*

SAMFORD, Judge (concurring).

The questions involved in this case are not free from doubt, and perhaps the strict letter of the rule, as stated by judges, though not always in accord, would bar a recovery by plaintiff, but following the principle announced by **Chief Justice Marshall in Hoffman v. Porter, Fed.Cas. No. 6,577, 2 Brock. 156, 159,** where he says, "I do not think that law ought to be separated from justice, where it is at most doubtful," I concur in the conclusions reached by the court.

Consistent with decisions described in *Mills* and *Drake,* the first and second Restatement of Contracts each contain a provision allowing for enforcement of promises to pay antecedent debts (that is, debts incurred in the past) that would be enforceable but for the effect of the statute of limitations. Another provision allowed enforcement of a promise to perform all or part of an antecedent but voidable contract that was not voided before the new promise was made. For example, minors (individuals under the age of the majority) generally can incur only "voidable" duties, so they may disavow contracts entered before they turn that age. The Restatement provisions make enforceable the promise of an adult to pay debts incurred under a voidable contract created when under the age of the majority.

Make the Connection

The rights and liabilities of minors entering contracts are addressed in Chapter 5, page 563.

Both the first and second Restatements also contain provisions making enforceable an express promise to pay all or part of an indebtedness discharged or dischargeable in bankruptcy, but federal bankruptcy law has added additional criteria that must be satisfied before such a promise will be considered binding. For example, the agreement must be made before the debt was discharged and must be filed with the court, the debtor may rescind the agreement as late as 60 days after it is so filed, and the debtor's attorney (or the court if the debtor is not represented by an attorney) must inform the debtor of the consequences of making the agreement and determine that the agreement is in the best interests of the debtor and will not cause the debtor undue hardship. *See* 11 U.S.C. §523(c).

Think About It!

Does the existence of the protections in the bankruptcy law suggest that the "promise for material benefit received" rule has gone too far? Are similar protections warranted in circumstances other than promises to pay debts discharged in bankruptcy? Do the bankruptcy law developments support or undercut the traditional rule that consideration is required to enforce a promise?

Although by 1930 there were a significant number of cases like *Drake v. Bell* that had also found a right to recover based on "moral obligation" arising from a promise to pay for past benefits, the drafters of the first Restatement did not include any provisions reflecting those developments. Additional cases continued to accumulate, however, and the concept was added to the Restatement (Second).

Reading the Law Critically:
Restatement (Second) Provisions and Illustrations

As reflected in *Drake* and *Webb*, court decisions whether to enforce a promise made in recognition of a past benefit invoked judgments whether the past benefit created a "moral obligation" that helped support the subsequent promise. The drafters of Restatement

(Second) § 86 rejected moral obligation as the justification for enforcement and sought to establish an alternative rationale by reference to the concepts underlying restitutionary recovery. "Making restitution" in this context means returning to the "status quo ante" (the prior state of affairs) by restoring to another the value of something lost, stolen, or given away. As you will see in the next section, the courts have limited the circumstances in which restitution will be ordered solely on the basis of a benefit received, no promise having been made. Section 86 tries to articulate when adding a promise to the benefit received should be enough to warrant ordering the restitution promised. Because the Restatement analysis joins "promise" to "restitution" as the basis for relief, the doctrine described in the cases and § 86 is sometimes called "promissory restitution."

Because § 86 says a promise for benefit received should be enforced "to the extent necessary to prevent injustice"—a standard as malleable and uncertain as one grounded in "moral obligation"—we have included extended portions of the comments and illustrations accompanying § 86 to help define how liability for such promises might be understood. As you read through the explanations and illustrations, consider why each promise is or is not enforced, and whether you agree with the outcomes. What general principles can you identify to help you decide subsequent cases? Do you recognize some of the illustrations from the cases you have read? You will have an opportunity to apply these principles to problems at the end of the chapter.

Restatement (Second) § 86. **Promise for Benefit Received**

(1) A promise made in recognition of a benefit previously received by the promisor from the promisee is binding to the extent necessary to prevent injustice.

(2) A promise is not binding under Subsection (1)
   a) if the promisee conferred the benefit as a gift or for other reasons the promisor has not been unjustly enriched; or
   b) to the extent that its value is disproportionate to the benefit.

Comment a: "Past consideration"; "moral obligation." . . . The mere fact of promise has been thought to create a moral obligation, but it is clear that not all promises are enforced. Nor are moral obligations based solely on gratitude or sentiment sufficient of themselves to support a subsequent promise.

Illustrations:

1. A gives emergency care to B's adult son while the son is sick and without funds far from home. B subsequently promises to reimburse A for his expenses. The promise is not binding under this Section.

2. A lends money to B, who later dies. B's widow promises to pay the debt. The promise is not binding under this Section.

3. A has immoral relations with B, a woman not his wife, to her injury. A's subsequent promise to reimburse B for her loss is not binding under this Section.

Comments:

b.   *Rationale.* Although in general a person who has been unjustly enriched at the expense of another is required to make restitution, restitution is denied in many cases in order to protect persons who have had benefits thrust upon them. . . . In other cases restitution is denied by virtue of rules designed to guard against false claims, stale claims, claims already litigated, and the like. In many such cases a subsequent promise to make restitution removes the reason for the denial of relief, and the policy against unjust enrichment then prevails. . . . Facts such as the definite and substantial character of the benefit received, formality in the making of the promise, part performance of the promise, reliance on the promise or the probability of such reliance may be relevant to show that no imposition results from enforcement.

c.   *Promise to correct a mistake.* One who makes a mistake in the conferring of a benefit is commonly entitled to restitution regardless of any promise. But restitution is often denied to avoid prejudice to the recipient of the benefit. Thus restitution of the value of services or of improvements to land or chattels may require a payment which the recipient cannot afford. . . . Where a subsequent promise shows that the usual protection is not needed in the particular case, restitution is granted to the extent promised.

Illustrations:

4. A is employed by B to repair a vacant house. By mistake A repairs the house next door, which belongs to C. A subsequent promise by C to pay A the value of the repairs is binding.

5. A pays B a debt and gets a signed receipt. Later B obtains a default judgment against A for the amount of the debt, and A pays again. B's subsequent promise to refund the second payment if A has a receipt is binding.

Comment d. Emergency services and necessaries. The law of restitution in the absence of promise severely limits recovery for necessaries furnished to a person under disability and for emergency services. . . . A subsequent promise in such a case may remove doubt as to the reality of the benefit and as to its value, and may negate any danger of imposition or false claim. A positive showing that payment was expected is not then required; an intention to make a gift must be shown to defeat restitution.

Illustrations:

6. A finds B's escaped bull and feeds and cares for it. B's subsequent promise to pay reasonable compensation to A is binding.

7. A saves B's life in an emergency and is totally and permanently disabled in so doing. One month later B promises to pay A $15 every two weeks for the rest of A's life, and B makes the payments for 8 years until he dies. The promise is binding.

Comment e. Benefit conferred as a gift. In the absence of mistake or the like, there is no element of unjust enrichment in the receipt of a gift, and the rule of this Section has no application to a promise to pay for a past gift. . . . But marginal cases arise in which both parties understand that what is in form a gift is intended to be reimbursed indirectly, or in which a subsequent promise to pay is expressly contemplated. . . . Enforcement of the subsequent promise is proper in some such cases.

Illustrations:

8. A submits to B at B's request a plan for advertising products manufactured by B, expecting payment only if the plan is adopted. Because of a change in B's selling arrangements, B rejects the plan without giving it fair consideration. B's subsequent promise to reimburse A's expenses in preparing the plan is binding.

9. A contributes capital to B, an insurance company, on the understanding that B is not liable to reimburse A but that A will be reimbursed through salary and commissions. Later A withdraws from the company and B promises to pay him ten percent of premiums received until he is reimbursed. The promise is binding.

Comment f. Benefit conferred pursuant to contract. By virtue of the policy of enforcing bargains, the enrichment of one party as a result of an unequal exchange is not regarded as unjust, and this Section has no application to a promise to pay or perform more or to accept less than is called for by a pre-existing bargain between the same parties. . . . Similarly, if a third person receives a benefit as a result of the performance of a bargain, this Section does not make binding the subsequent promise of the third person to pay extra compensation to the performing party. But a promise to pay in substitution for the return performance called for by the bargain may be binding under this Section.

Illustration 10. A digs a well on B's land in performance of a bargain with B's tenant C. C is unable to pay as agreed, and B promises to pay A the reasonable value of the well. The promise is binding.

Comment g. Obligation unenforceable under the Statute of Frauds. . . .[T]he problem seldom arises. . . . Where the question does arise, the new promise is binding if the policy of the Statute is satisfied.

Illustration 11. By statute an agreement authorizing a real estate broker to sell land for compensation is void unless the agreement or a memorandum thereof is in writing. A, a real estate broker, procures a purchaser for B's land without any written agreement. In the written sale agreement, signed by B, B promises to pay A $200, the usual commission, "for services rendered." The promise is binding.

Comments:

h. *Obligation unenforceable because usurious.* If a promise is unenforceable because it is usurious, an agreement in renewal or substitution for it that provides for a payment including the usurious interest is also unenforceable, even though the interest from the date of renewal or substitution is not usurious. However, a promise to pay the original debt with interest that is not usurious in substitution for the usurious interest is enforceable.

i. *Partial enforcement.* . . . A promise which is excessive may sometimes be enforced to the extent of the value of the benefit, and the remedy may be thought of as quasi-contractual rather than contractual. In other cases a promise of disproportionate value may tend to show unfair pressure or other conduct by the promisee such that justice does not require any enforcement of the promise.

Illustrations:

12. A, a married woman of sixty, has rendered household services without compensation over a period of years for B, a man of eighty living alone and having no close relatives. B has a net worth of three million dollars and has often assured A that she will be well paid for her services, whose reasonable value is not in excess of $6,000. B executes and delivers to A a written promise to pay A $25,000 "to be taken from my estate." The promise is binding.

13. The facts being otherwise as stated in Illustration 12, B's promise is made orally and is to leave A his entire estate. A cannot recover more than the reasonable value of her services.

Food for Thought

Promissory restitution is used relatively infrequently in reported cases, perhaps because there are few circumstances of this kind worth litigating and the results are relatively uncertain. The materials you have considered in this section are therefore most valuable not as a guide to important decisional rules, but instead as a study of how courts adapt legal principles to reach just results when precedent is not adequate to that task. They may also serve as a kind of cautionary tale about parties' inability to predict enforceability under some circumstances and their need to plan more effectively to reach desired results.

Some states have addressed the problem of promises after-the-fact through statutory rules rather than (or in addition to) through common law change. New York, for example, has enacted the following provision:

> A promise in writing and signed by the promisor or by his agent shall not be denied effect as a valid contractual obligation on the ground that consideration for the promise is past or executed, if the consideration is expressed in the writing and is proved to have been given or performed and would be a valid consideration but for the time when it was given or performed.

N.Y. Gen. Oblig. Law §5-1105 (McKinney 2001). Would you recommend adoption of the New York rule in a jurisdiction still relying on the common law rule? What are the advantages and disadvantages of this statutory approach?

§ 4. Liability for Restitution

All the kinds of liability considered so far—contract, promissory estoppel, and promissory restitution—have been based on the existence of a promise. This section considers liability when there is no promise to enforce. The basis of liability here is "restitution," the claim that the defendant obtained a benefit from the plaintiff and should be required to make restitution to the plaintiff (that is, restore the benefit to its rightful owner, the plaintiff). It shares with promissory restitution the existence of a benefit conferred but is missing the other central component—a promise to compensate made after-the-fact. Unlike the other doctrines at the core of contract law, restitution as a source of liability is *not* grounded in the idea of enforcing a voluntary obligation undertaken by a party, either through making a contract or through making some other kind of promise.

Why is restitution included at all in a course focused on the enforcement of promises? While it is articulated as a separate ground for liability, restitution has historical roots in contract law, and many restitution cases arise out of failed contractual relationships. Restitution operates at the borders of contract doctrine, and understanding the nature of restitutionary liability can help define the outer limits of contract law as well. This section touches only on the aspects of the law of restitution that intersect most closely with contract theory.

Legal responsibility for restitution begins with the notion that "[a] person who is unjustly enriched at the expense of another is subject to liability in restitution." Restatement (Third) of Restitution & Unjust Enrichment § 1 (2011). "Unjust enrichment" is not precisely defined; the Reporter's comment a. refers to the "inherent flexibility of the concept" and the fact that the concept "will not, by itself, yield a reliable indication of the nature and scope of the liability imposed." To determine the limits of restitutionary relief, the critical question to be answered is: When *is* it unjust to retain a benefit conferred by another? The cases that follow—and the other 70 sections of the Restatement (Third) of Restitution—are designed to help answer that question.

Note first that restitution or unjust enrichment is *not* an appropriate ground for relief if an enforceable contract exists. Entering an enforceable contract represents a choice to define the parties' relationship according to the terms of that contract. Any adjustment to the contractual relationship arising from nonperformance should be made by bringing an action to enforce the contract, not by seeking restitution on the basis of unjust enrichment. *See* **Restatement (Third) of Restitution and Unjust Enrichment § 2(z)**. (Restitution may be applicable as a *measure* of the compensation owed by the breaching party, however.)

But what if an agreement-in-fact of the parties turns out to be unenforceable for some reason—because, for example, one party lacks capacity, or the parties made a mutual mistake of fact about basic assumptions underlying the contract, or the contract has to be in writing to be enforceable, or the terms are too unclear for a party to enforce them? If one party or both of the parties has already performed some of the agreement's obligations, neither party can successfully claim breach of contract to be compensated for the work already performed, but restitution is available as a basis for relief to allow them each to be restored to the "status quo ante" by obtaining back the benefits conferred on the other. There was good reason for the benefits to be conferred at the time, as part of contract performance, and probably no good reason for them to be retained when the contract failed. *See* **Restatement (Third) of Restitution and Unjust Enrichment §§ 31-34.** You will see the application of this rationale for restitution reappear repeatedly in this course in materials dealing with defenses against contract enforceability and excuses from contract performance (in **Chapters 5** and **8**). When contracts are avoided or become unenforceable for such reasons, restitution is available as a ground for liability to assist the parties to reach a just allocation of the burdens that result.

If no contract exists, however, but an individual confers a benefit on another without being asked, when, if ever, should that individual be compensated, when no promise to pay was ever made? The rest of this section explores some answers to this question.

Take Note!

The courts use a sometimes confusing array of different terms to discuss restitution, including quasi-contract, quantum meruit, and implied-in-law contract, as well as restitution and unjust enrichment. Although they are often used interchangeably, there may be subtle differences among them, and they may be used differently (and inconsistently) by different courts.

The term "implied-in-law contract" indicates that there was no actual (in fact) agreement of the parties; instead, the law imposes a contract-like liability as a matter of law. "Quasi-contract" is similar. "Quasi" means "seemingly," "almost but not quite," or "having some resemblance." "Quasi-contract" thus carries with it the flavor of liability that is "almost but not quite" a contract; it is *not* based in agreement of the parties. As you read the cases below, ask yourself why the courts might have called this form of liability "quasi-contract" or "implied-in-law contract." What about the doctrine makes the relationship of the parties "seem" like a contract in some ways?

Quantum meruit is a Latin phrase meaning, literally, "as much as he has deserved." The term is sometimes used to describe a restitutionary measure of relief (the party gets not what was promised, since nothing was promised, but instead what he deserves based on the benefit conferred). It is also sometimes used to describe the basis for liability. Similarly, *quantum valebant* (literally, "as much as they were worth"), is used both to describe liability for goods delivered to another and to describe the measure of restitutionary relief for such delivery.

As you read the cases below, note the terminology used by each court.

Reading the Law Critically: *Nursing Care Services, Mitchell,* and *Bloomgarden*

1. What kind of benefit was conferred in each set of circumstances? What motivated the plaintiff to act and thereby confer the benefit? What was the relationship of the parties when the benefit was conferred? What role, if any, do all those facts play in the court's judgment and opinion?

2. What persuades the court to conclude that restitution is or is not warranted (that is, what makes retention of the benefit just or unjust)?

3. For each case, what rules does the court articulate or follow regarding the availability of restitution? You will find statements of when restitution is appropriate as well as exceptions or limitations to recovery, and even exceptions to the exceptions.

4. Recall that restitutionary damages measure the value to the recipient of the benefit that was conferred but should now be disgorged. If the case results in a finding of liability, how might the court measure that value?

Nursing Care Services, Inc. v. Dobos

NURSING CARE SERVICES, INC., Plaintiff-Appellant

v.

MARY DOBOS, Defendant-Appellee

District Court of Appeal of Florida
380 So. 2d 516 (Fla. Dist. Ct. App. 1980)

HURLEY, Judge.

Plaintiff, Nursing Care Services, Inc., appeals from that part of a final judgment which disallowed compensation for certain nursing care services. Our review of the record reveals substantial uncontradicted testimony supporting plaintiff's theory of recovery and thus we remand for entry of an amended final judgment.

Mary Dobos, the defendant, was admitted to Boca Raton Community Hospital with an abdominal aneurysm. Her condition was sufficiently serious to cause her doctor to order around-the-clock nursing care. The hospital implemented this order by calling upon the plaintiff which provides individualized nursing services.

Mrs. Dobos received nursing care which in retrospect can be divided into three periods: (1) two weeks of in-hospital care; (2) forty-eight hour post-release care; and (3) two weeks of at-home care. The second period of care (the forty-eight hour post-release care) was removed as an issue at trial when Mrs. Dobos conceded that she or her daughter authorized that period of care. The total bill for all three periods came to $3,723.90; neither the reasonableness of the fee, the competency of the nurses, nor the necessity for the services was contested at trial.

The gist of the defense was that Mrs. Dobos never signed a written contract nor orally agreed to be liable for the nursing services. Testifying about the in-hospital care, she said, "Dr. Rosen did all the work. I don't know what he done (sic), and he says, I needed a nurse." It is undisputed that Mrs. Dobos was mentally alert during her at-home recuperation period. Asked if she ever tried to fire the nurses or dispense with their care, she replied, "I didn't. I didn't know who I thought, maybe if they insist, the doctors insist so much, I thought the Medicare would take care of it, or whatever. I don't know."

After a non-jury trial, the court granted judgment for the plaintiff in the sum of $248.00, the cost of the forty-eight hour post-release care. It declined to allow compensation for the first and third periods of care, saying,

> ". . . [T]here certainly was a service rendered, but based on the total surrounding circumstances, I don't think there is sufficient

communications and dealings with Mrs. Dobos to make sure that she knew that she would be responsible for those services rendered. . . ."

We concur in the trial court's determination that the plaintiff failed to prove an express contract or a contract implied in fact. It is our view, however, that the uncontradicted testimony provided by plaintiff and defendant alike, clearly established a contract implied in law which entitles the plaintiff to recover.

Contracts implied in law, or as they are more commonly called "quasi contracts", are obligations imposed by law on grounds of justice and equity. Their purpose is to prevent unjust enrichment. Unlike express contracts or contracts implied in fact, quasi contracts do not rest upon the assent of the contracting parties. See generally, 28 Fla.Jur., Restitution and Implied Contracts.

One of the most common areas in which recovery on a contract implied in law is allowed is that of work performed or services rendered. The rationale is that the defendant would be unjustly enriched at the expense of the plaintiff if she were allowed to escape payment for services rendered or work performed. There is, however, an important limitation. Ordinarily liability is imposed to pay for services rendered by another only when the person for whose benefit they were rendered requested the services or knowingly and voluntarily accepted their benefits. **Yeats v. Moody, 128 Fla. 658, 175 So. 719 (1937); Strano v. Carr & Carr, Inc., 97 Fla. 150, 119 So. 864 (1929); Taylor v. Thompson, 359 So.2d 14 (Fla. 1st DCA 1978); and Tobin & Tobin Insurance Agency, Inc. v. Zeskind, 315 So.2d 518 (Fla. 3d DCA 1975).**

The law's concern that needless services not be foisted upon the unsuspecting has led to the formulation of the "officious intermeddler doctrine." It holds that where a person performs labor for another without the latter's request or implied consent, however beneficial such labor may be, he cannot recover therefor. **Tipper v. Great Lakes Chemical Company, 281 So.2d 10 (Fla.1973).** A notable exception to this rule, however, is that of emergency aid:

> A person who has supplied things or services to another, although acting without the other's knowledge or consent, is entitled to restitution therefor from the other if he acted unofficiously and with intent to charge therefore, and the things or services were necessary to prevent the other from suffering serious bodily harm or pain, and the person supplying them had no reason to know that the other would not consent to receiving them, if mentally competent, and it was impossible for the other to give consent or, because of extreme youth or mental impairment, the other's consent would have been immaterial. **66 Am.Jur.2d, Restitution and Implied Contract, §23.**

In the case at bar it is unclear whether Mrs. Dobos, during the period of in-hospital care, understood or intended that compensation be paid. Her condition was grave. She had been placed in the hospital's intensive care unit and thereafter had tubes and other medical equipment attached to her body which necessitated special attention. She was alone, unable to cope and without family assistance. It is worthy of note that at no point during the litigation was there any question as to the propriety of the professional judgment that the patient required special nursing care. To the contrary, the record demonstrates that the in-hospital nursing care was essential to Mrs. Dobos' health and safety. Given these circumstances it would be unconscionable to deny the plaintiff recovery for services which fall squarely within the emergency aid exception. Tipper v. Great Lakes Chemical Company, supra.

The third period of care is less difficult. It is unquestioned that during the at-home recuperation, Mrs. Dobos was fully aware of her circumstances and readily accepted the benefits conferred. Given such facts, we believe the rule set down in **Symon v. J. Rolfe Davis, Inc., 245 So.2d 278, 279 (Fla. 4th DCA 1971)** must govern:

> It is well settled that where services are rendered by one person for another which are knowingly and voluntarily accepted, the law presumes that such services are given and received in expectation of being paid for, and will imply a promise to pay what they are reasonably worth.

A patient's unannounced misconception that the cost of accepted services will be paid by an insurer or Medicare does not absolve her of responsibility to bear the cost of the services.

As a postscript we note that Mrs. Dobos' home recuperation was interrupted by her readmission to the hospital with an apparent heart attack. In this age of burgeoning malpractice actions it is not idle conjecture to ponder what her legal position might have been had the plaintiff unilaterally terminated its services at a time of vital need. To its credit, it did not and therefore it is entitled to just compensation. Accordingly, we remand the cause to the trial court with instructions to enter an amended final judgment for the plaintiff in the sum of $3,723.90 plus interest and court costs.

It is so ordered.

ANSTEAD and LETTS, JJ., concur.

Mitchell v. Moore

THOMAS MITCHELL, Plaintiff-Appellee

v.

WILLIAM MOORE, III, Defendant-Appellant

Superior Court of Pennsylvania
729 A.2d 1200 (Pa. Super. Ct. 1999)

CIRILLO, President Judge Emeritus:

William Moore, III (Moore), appeals from the order entered in the Court of Common Pleas of Chester County denying his post-trial motions and entering judgment on a jury verdict of $130,000.00 awarded to Appellee, Thomas Mitchell (Mitchell). We affirm in part and reverse in part.

Thomas Mitchell and William Moore first met in 1980; the two men quickly developed a romantic relationship. Moore resided in Elverson, Pennsylvania and Mitchell in South Carolina. In the spring of 1981, Mitchell accepted Moore's invitation to spend his "off season"[1] at Moore's Chester County farm. By 1985, Mitchell had permanently moved to Elverson, where he resided at Moore's farm without paying rent, worked a full-time job with a company located in Lancaster, Pennsylvania, and assisted Moore in maintaining his house and farm. Among other things, Mitchell took care of the farm animals, which included aiding in the breeding of sheep and birds. In 1990, Mitchell enrolled at Penn State University for graduate studies. As a result of his academic schedule, he was unable to run the sheep and bird businesses or maintain the farm. Soon thereafter, the parties' relationship soured; Mitchell moved out of Moore's residence in June of 1994.

In 1995, Mitchell brought an action against Moore sounding in fraud, *quantum meruit,* and implied contract. Specifically, Mitchell sought compensation, in the form of restitution, for the services he rendered to Moore throughout the thirteen years the two men lived together on the farm. In his complaint, Mitchell alleged that Moore had: promised him compensation for his services rendered to maintain and operate his farm; agreed to compensate him for his help in running an antique cooperative (co-op) that Mitchell [Moore?] had purchased; promised him future compensation and the devise of property in a will and codicil; and failed to compensate him for monetary contributions he had made towards Moore's purchase of real estate on Amelia Island, Florida.

In response to Mitchell's action, Moore filed preliminary objections seeking a demurrer. The court granted the objections in part and denied the objections in part, striking Mitchell's claim of fraud for lack of specificity, *see* **Pa.R.C.P. 1019(b)**, but granting Mitchell leave to file an amended complaint. Mitchell filed an amend-

---

[1] Mitchell was a tobacco broker in South Carolina. He did not work during the winter months.

ed complaint, now including only counts for *quantum meruit* /unjust enrichment[2] and implied contract. Moore filed a counterclaim seeking $139,300.00 representing reasonable rent for the 139 months Mitchell lived on his farm rent-free and as compensation for various utility and telephone bills, taxes, car payments, and other miscellaneous expenses paid by Moore on Mitchell's behalf.

After a jury trial, a verdict was rendered in favor of Mitchell on the basis of unjust enrichment and against Moore on the counterclaim. Moore filed post-trial motions seeking, among other remedies, a judgment in his favor; these motions were denied by the trial court. Moore filed a timely appeal, raising the following issues for our consideration:

> (1) Whether the verdict was against the weight of the evidence in that:
>
>> (a) appellee-plaintiff failed to produce evidence of an express contract;
>>
>> (b) appellee failed to prove an implied contract;
>>
>> (c) the nature of the relationship rebutted the presumption of a promise to pay and therefore, appellee failed to prove unjust enrichment; and
>>
>> (d) appellee failed to prove that appellant wrongfully secured or passively received benefits that would be unconscionable for him to retain?

. . .

> (5) Whether appellant is entitled to remittitur in that the verdict is not supported by the evidence?
>
> (6) Whether appellant is entitled to a new trial on his counterclaim as the verdict was against the weight of the evidence?

In reviewing a denial of judgment notwithstanding the verdict, an appellate court must decide whether there was sufficient evidence to sustain the verdict; our scope of review is very narrow: all evidence and all reasonable inferences drawn therefrom must be considered in the light most favorable to the verdict winner. *Johnson v. Hyundai Motor America*, 698 A.2d

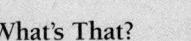

What's That?

If a court is convinced that a jury awarded higher damages than is supported by the evidence, the court may grant a "remittitur," which orders a new trial unless the plaintiff agrees to accept a specified lower amount that is supported by the evidence. A court may instead grant an "additur" if the jury award is below the minimum supported by the evidence, ordering a new trial unless the defendant agrees to the higher amount.

---

[2] A cause of action in quasi-contract for *quantum meruit,* a form of restitution, is made out where one person has been unjustly enriched at the expense of another. *Feingold v. Pucello*, 439 Pa.Super. 509, 654 A.2d 1093, 1095 (1995) (Beck, J., concurring) (citation omitted). Therefore, a claim of *quantum meruit* raises the issue of whether a party has been unjustly enriched, and in order to prove such claim a party must successfully prove the elements of unjust enrichment discussed *infra.*

631 (Pa.Super.1997). Judgment notwithstanding the verdict can be entered only if the movant is entitled to judgment as a matter of law or if evidence is such that no two reasonable minds could disagree that the outcome should have been rendered in favor of the movant. *Jara v. Rexworks, Inc.*, 718 A.2d 788 (Pa. Super.1998) (citations omitted). We will reverse a trial court's grant or denial of a judgment notwithstanding the verdict only when we find an abuse of discretion or an error of law that controlled the outcome of the case. *Id.*, *citing Jones v. Constantino*, 429 Pa.Super. 73, 631 A.2d 1289 (1993).

Mitchell's claim for restitution for services rendered lies not upon an express contract or written agreement, but, rather, upon the equitable theory of unjust enrichment. Further, we may not make a finding of unjust enrichment, as has the trial court, where a written or express contract between parties exists. *See* **First Wisconsin Trust Co. v. Strausser**, 439 Pa.Super. 192, 653 A.2d 688 (1995). We, therefore, confine our review to whether the court properly found Mitchell entitled to compensation under the legal theory of unjust enrichment.

"Unjust enrichment" is essentially an equitable doctrine. *Styer v. Hugo*, 422 Pa.Super. 262, 619 A.2d 347 (1993), *aff'd*, 535 Pa. 610, 637 A.2d 276 (1994). Where unjust enrichment is found, the law implies a contract, which requires the defendant to pay to the plaintiff the value of the benefit conferred. *Schenck v. K.E. David, Ltd.*, 446 Pa.Super. 94, 666 A.2d 327 (1995). The elements necessary to prove unjust enrichment are:

> (1) benefits conferred on defendant by plaintiff; (2) appreciation of such benefits by defendant; and (3) acceptance and retention of such benefits under such circumstances that it would be inequitable for defendant to retain the benefit without payment of value. (citations omitted). The application of the doctrine depends on the particular factual circumstances of the case at issue. **In determining if the doctrine applies, our focus is not on the intention of the parties, but rather on whether the defendant has been unjustly enriched.**

Id., 666 A.2d at 328. *Accord Torchia v. Torchia*, 346 Pa.Super. 229, 499 A.2d 581, 582 (1985) ("[t]o sustain a claim of unjust enrichment, a claimant must show that the party against whom recovery is sought either 'wrongfully secured or passively received a benefit that it would be unconscionable for her to retain.'") (citation omitted).

In its opinion, the trial court clearly determines that a benefit was conferred upon Moore as a result of the extensive labor and services Mitchell provided him on his farm and in his home. The critical question, with regard to whether as a result of this benefit Moore was unjustly enriched, was answered in the positive by the court as follows:

Assuming the jury established that a benefit had been conferred by Plaintiff [Mitchell] and received by Defendant [Moore], they only had to determine that Defendant's acceptance of these benefits and failure to compensate Plaintiff resulted in an unconscionable bargain. The jury was aware that Defendant [sic] moved hundreds of miles away from his job, house, friends and family to a different region of the country where he took on a new job and did work on Defendant's [Moore's] farm. It is not unreasonable to suggest that the jury believed Plaintiff [Mitchell] in that he made that life-altering change based on something besides his desire to develop his relationship with Defendant [Moore]. Given this potential scenario, it is likely that the jury could have found that the lack of compensation Plaintiff [Mitchell] received amounted to an unconscionable bargain and therefore, Defendant's [Moore's] unjust enrichment.

"It has been said, an intention to pay for work done will be assumed, except in the case of parent and child. Where, however, it is apparent that the parties, though not so related by blood, in reality bore like connection to each other, the implication does not arise." *Brown v. McCurdy*, 278 Pa. 19, 22, 122 A. 169, 170 (1923). While it has been held that the presumption of gratuitous services does not automatically arise in a daughter-in-law/mother-in-law context, where a claimant has become "part of the family" the contrary is true. *Id.*

Both parties concur that when Mitchell moved into Moore's home on a full-time basis, Moore paid many of Mitchell's bills, including car payments, VISA and Sears card charges, and phone bills. Moreover, Moore claims that Mitchell became part of his own family; Mitchell, himself, admits to having celebrated all the major holidays with Moore's immediate family and received gifts from them on special occasions.

In *Brown, supra*, the law and facts centered around the issue of whether a presumption of payment, based upon an express contract to pay for services rendered by a daughter-in-law to her mother-in-law, had been successfully established based upon the evidence at trial. The court demanded strict proof of an express contract in order to overcome any presumption that the services were gratuitous. Although the instant case is not based upon either an express contract or written agreement, we find the principles espoused in *Brown* equally applicable, namely, in order to prove that the defendant in the present case had been **unjustly** enriched by plaintiff's actions and services, there must be some convincing evidence establishing that plaintiff's services were not gratuitous.

We first note that Mitchell had complete access to a large farm house where he lived rent-free and virtually unencumbered by any utility expenses. The nature and amount of benefits that plaintiff received from living at Moore's farm rebuts any presumption that the benefit conferred upon Moore was unjust. In fact, the advantages plaintiff obtained were compensation enough for all the work he offered to do on the farm; further, Mitchell derived an obvious personal benefit by living with the defendant, his partner for thirteen years, at his farm.[3]

Think About It!

On what basis does the court here decide that Mitchell's actions were gratuitous? What facts, if proved, might lead to the opposite result? Courts have suggested that relevant factors include the extent of services provided, the nature of the relationship between the provider and the recipient of the services, and whether the provider ever sought compensation or appeared to be acting out of a sense of moral obligation.

Having found no evidence which would imply that Moore's services were anything but gratuitous, we cannot agree with the trial court that a theory of unjust enrichment has been proved. While defendant indisputably bequeathed plaintiff his farm (found within the provisions of two wills that were later supplanted by a codicil), the gift was exactly that, an intention to reward the plaintiff through a testamentary provision. . . .

Such bequest is not equivalent to a finding that the defendant intended to compensate the plaintiff for his services and that upon failure to remit such monies the defendant became unjustly enriched. *See Meehan v. Cheltenham Township*, 410 Pa. 446, 450, 189 A.2d 593, 596 (1963) ("[t]he mere fact that one party benefits from the act of another is not of itself sufficient to justify restitution."); *see also Torchia, supra* (to sustain a claim of unjust enrichment, the claimant must show that the party against whom recovery is sought either wrongfully secured or passively received a benefit that it would be unconscionable for the party to retain).

Furthermore, the defendant testified that the plaintiff himself suggested that he move in with the defendant because he could not afford to rent an apartment on his own at the time. He, as well as the defendant, thought such potential living arrangement would give the two men more time to foster their relationship. In fact, upon learning of plaintiff's potential job opportunity in nearby Lancaster, Pennsylvania, the defendant anticipated that the two parties would be able to grow closer in a permanent "live-in" situation—another indication that there existed no expectation of payment for plaintiff's voluntary work on the defendant's farm. Moreover, plaintiff testified that he never asked the defendant for compensation

---

[3] Plaintiff's own testimony at trial stated that he moved in with the defendant based upon the belief that he would be "provided for" by the defendant; to this end, plaintiff asserts that the defendant drew up a will "mak[ing] sure that [he] was protected for all the things that [he] had done for him in the past." He claims that he relied upon such financial security, thinking that it would be "a forever and forever situation." Such testimony seems to advance a theory of promissory estoppel, not unjust enrichment. Plaintiff, however, did not allege such a theory in his complaint; we, therefore, will not consider such a claim.

for his services and that the defendant never told him he would pay him for his help around the house and the farm.[5]

To solidify the fact that the plaintiff's actions were gratuitous services rendered during a "close, personal" relationship, the plaintiff testified at trial that after he moved in and began to help around the farm, the defendant told him he "did a great job, that he appreciated what I [plaintiff] did, and it was for—it made the house much better looking, it kept it stable, and that **we were building a future together and some day it would all be worth it for me [plaintiff]**." While Mitchell would characterize the nature of the parties' relationship as a type of business venture between partners, the evidence at trial indicates a very different aspect of their lives. As Mitchell, himself, testified, he had a "romantic or sexual aspect to his relationship with Dr. Moore." Furthermore, the parties conducted themselves around the home like parties in a loving relationship; they shared household chores, cooked dinners for each other, bestowed gifts upon one another, attended events together, and shared holidays and special occasions with Moore's family. Most potent, however, is the following language used in a letter written by Mitchell to Moore sometime in 1993, "The time I have given you breaking my back with the house and grounds were just that, **a gift to our relationship**." Moore testified that Mitchell was "his lover and we were living together as partners, and I felt like anything I could do for him, you know, gave me pleasure." To find restitution (compensation) proper for services performed in such a relationship, we would curtail the freedom associated in forming new personal bonds based upon the important facet of mutual dependence.

After a review of the record in this case, including the pivotal testimony of both Mitchell and Moore, we cannot find that the defendant benefited unjustly from plaintiff's services. While we do not attempt to characterize the services rendered in all unmarried couple's relationships as gratuitous, we do believe that such a presumption exists and that in order to recover restitution for services rendered, the presumption must be rebutted by clear and convincing evidence. The basis of this presumption rests on the fact that services provided by plaintiff to the defendant are not of the type for which one would normally expect to be paid, nor did they confer upon the defendant a benefit that is unconscionable for him to retain without making restitution to the plaintiff. *See Feingold, supra* (Beck, J., concurring).

The circumstances of this case do not require the law to imply a contract in order to avoid an injustice. *See Feingold*, **654 A.2d at 1095** (Beck, J., concurring) ("unlike true contracts, quasi-contracts are not based on the apparent intention of the parties to undertake the performances in question, nor are they promises. They are obligations created by law for reasons of justice."), *citing Schott v.*

---

[5] At trial, Moore characterized Mitchell's work on his farm during the period where he was living there only part-time as "voluntary," stating that "he [Mitchell] said he just couldn't sit around and sun bathe all day, he had to do something."

Westinghouse Elec. Corp, 436 Pa. 279, 290-93, 259 A.2d 443, 449 (1969). Accordingly, we reverse the trial court's verdict in favor of plaintiff; the verdict should have been rendered in defendant's favor. **Jara, supra.** We affirm the court's denial of defendant's counterclaim on the same basis. The various benefits plaintiff received over the parties' thirteen year relationship were also gratuitous in nature; the plaintiff did not "wrongfully secure a benefit that is unconscionable for him to retain." *Torchia, supra.*

Order reversed in part and affirmed in part.[6] Jurisdiction relinquished.

Bloomgarden v. Coyer

HENRY S. BLOOMGARDEN, Plaintiff-Appellant

v.

CHARLES B. COYER et al., Defendants-Appellees

United States Court of Appeals, District of Columbia Circuit

479 F.2d 201 (D.C. Cir. 1973)

SPOTTSWOOD W. ROBINSON, III, Circuit Judge:

Who's That?

Spottswood W. Robinson, III (1916-1998) was a Richmond, Virginia, civil rights lawyer who, as a private attorney and under the auspices of the NAACP Legal Defense and Educational Fund, litigated many significant civil rights cases, including one of the cases that led to the United States Supreme Court's 1954 decision in *Brown v. Board of Education.* He challenged discrimination in interstate transportation when he represented Irene Morgan who, more than a decade before Rosa Parks, refused to move to the "colored" seats at the back of an interstate bus, taking her case all the way to the U.S. Supreme Court. He worked on cases challenging racial restrictions in property transactions and in the use of public parks, in addition to his work challenging racial inequality in public schools. He was a faculty member at Howard University Law School from his graduation in 1939 until he joined the NAACP in 1948 and, in 1960, he returned to Howard as the law school dean. Judge Robinson "credited the law school with instilling the notion of social responsibil-

---

[6] Having determined that we must reverse the jury's verdict in favor of plaintiff, we need not address the remaining issues raised in appellant's brief based upon trial court error.

ity. 'One of the things that was drilled into my head was . . . "This legal education that you're getting is not just for you, it was for everybody. So when you leave here, you want to put it to good use.""'*

Spottswood Robinson was the first African-American to serve on the United States District Court for the District of Columbia (1963-1966) and on the United States Court of Appeals for the District of Columbia Circuit (1966-1992). He was the author of 411 opinions on the Court of Appeals, "each one both a beginning and an end to the issues discussed . . ., a one-stop dissertation on the law in a particular area— past, present, and future . . . . I am told [reported Patricia Wald, who succeeded Judge Robinson as Chief Judge of the D.C. Circuit] many law students found his opinions more than adequate substitute for a bar review cram course." **

This appeal follows appellant Bloomgarden's unsuccessful effort in the District Court to recover a $1 million finder's fee. The fee was sought for services leading to the inauguration of an enterprise to extensively develop certain property on the Georgetown waterfront in Washington. The principals in the enterprise are appellees Coyer and Guy, individual real estate developers, and appellee Georgetown-Inland Corporation (Georgetown-Inland), one of five companies organized, with Coyer and Guy as two of the stockholders in each, to effectuate the project. At the center of the controversy is Bloomgarden's assertion that it was he who brought the organizers together in this mutually beneficial venture and who, by the same token, should be rewarded for that contribution.

It is fully conceded that Bloomgarden introduced Coyer and Guy to those with whom they were later to join forces. There was, however, no express agreement, written or oral, pertaining to the part Bloomgarden played or calling for compensation therefor from any of the appellees. Bloomgarden's quest for a finder's fee proceeded on the theory that he was entitled to remuneration by virtue of a contract which should either be factually implied from prevalent custom and usage or recognized as a legal consequence of the transaction when viewed in light of the surrounding circumstances.

After the close of the pleadings and some amount of discovery, Bloomgarden moved for partial summary judgment on the issue of liability and appellees for summary judgment on the entire case. The District Court denied Bloomgarden's motion and granted appellees', in each instance on two separate grounds. The court held that because Bloomgarden did not hold the license required of real estate and business-chance brokers in the District of Columbia he was precluded

---

* *Spottswood Robinson, U.S. Appeals Judge, Dies in Virginia at 82,* Jet, (Nov. 2, 1998).
** Patricia M. Wald, *In Memoriam, Spottswood W. Robinson, III,* 15 Harv. Black Letter L.J. 3 (1999).

from charging for what he did. The court further held that Bloomgarden had no enforceable claim for recompense because it appeared without dispute that at the time he introduced the parties he did not expect to be personally compensated for so doing. Without reaching the first ground relied on by the District Court, we affirm for reasons underlying the second.

I

Bloomgarden's suit traces its origin to a series of events commencing in the fall of 1969 and extending into the spring of 1970. Throughout this period he was serving as president of Socio-Dynamics Industries, Inc. (SDI), a consulting and research firm in the field of urban and environmental affairs. Nearly half of SDI's capital stock was owned by David Carley, president of Public Facilities Associates, Inc. (PFA), which was engaged in the development of public and private housing and the redevelopment of urban areas. Carley had requested Bloomgarden to remain alert to any potentially fruitful investment opportunities for PFA in the Washington area.

At the time, Coyer and Guy held contracts or options on several parcels of real estate on the Georgetown waterfront. Bloomgarden met Coyer in the summer of 1969 while arranging to lease office space in a building in which Coyer had an interest. At one of their meetings, Coyer revealed to Bloomgarden the details of a plan for the assembly and development of a sizeable segment of the waterfront into a multipurpose business complex. Coyer explained that he and Guy lacked the financial resources needed to carry the project through, and Bloomgarden offered to put him in touch with Carley.

Bloomgarden promptly apprised Carley of Coyer's project and set up a meeting between them and others for January 26, 1970. Ideas were then exchanged but no suggestion was made by Bloomgarden to Carley or Coyer that he expected to be paid for bringing them together. By Bloomgarden's arrangement the group attended another meeting, on February 19 in Chicago, with representatives of subsidiaries of Inland Steel Company (Inland Steel). Again the plan was discussed and again Bloomgarden gave no indication that he anticipated a fee for introducing Coyer and Guy to Carley and his Inland associates. On the contrary, during a ride to the airport on the day after the Chicago meeting, Guy inquired of Bloomgarden as to what he hoped to get out of the project, and Bloomgarden responded merely that possibly SDI, his company, might garner some work in implementing the plan.[8] Aside from furnishing three of the principals—Coyer, Guy and Carley—with information about the others, Bloomgarden had no further role in the transaction.

An agreement in principle was reached between Coyer, Guy and the Inland Steel group in early April, 1970. This was formalized by a contract in June and a shareholders' agreement executed in August. Five corporations, among them Georgetown-Inland, were organized to handle the project. It was not until the end of March, 1970, however, that Bloomgarden asserted any monetary claim on behalf of SDI for bringing about the initial contact, and it was not until May that he asked for compensation for himself.[11] After each of these demands was rejected, Bloomgarden, on September 14, wrote to Coyer, again claiming a fee for sparking the business opportunity culminating in the Georgetown project. That likewise failing, Bloomgarden commenced his suit on October 1.

II

The District Court's judgment rested, as we have said, on two bases. The court ruled that since Bloomgarden was not licensed as a real estate or business-chance broker by the District of Columbia, he could not recover pay for his contribution to the Georgetown venture. The court also held that, as a matter of law, Bloomgarden was not entitled to relief because at the time he assisted appellees he had no expecta-

Make the Connection

What should the effect be if, indeed, the plaintiff did not have a license required to lawfully perform the activities for which he sought compensation? Should it matter whether the licensing scheme is set up to regulate those engaged in that kind of business or for some other purpose, e.g., to raise revenue for the jurisdiction? The effect of illegality and other public policy concerns are addressed in Chapter 5, page 596.

---

[8] The conversation, as portrayed by Bloomgarden on deposition, was:

> Q. You had discussed the [SDI] role in this project in February with Mr. Coyer, had you not?
>
> A. Yes, I had in the cab coming from the Palmer House to the airport . . . . Bill Guy said to me at some point and not in any context–I don't even know what we were discussing–he surprised me with the question, "Hank, if this project goes through, what do you expect out of it?" And I really wasn't prepared for the question because I had not thought it through in detail and I really didn't know in detail what I expected out of it. I expected something out of it and something substantial. I said, "Well, for one thing we have some capability in the environmental field and Chuck Coyer mentioned a possibility of a closed energy system here," and I said "We might be involved in that kind of thing." That was about the whole conversation. We did not at that point discuss a finder's fee or anything else.

[11] The change from a company to a personal claim resulted from SDI's ultimate decision not to participate in the Georgetown waterfront project. On October 30, 1969, Carley had entered into a five-year employment contract with Inland Steel, effective January 22, 1970, by which Carley bound himself to full-time service for one of Inland Steel's divisions and agreed that he would not become financially interested in any business which was competitive with his new employer. After the Georgetown project was agreed upon, Bloomgarden requested SDI to take part, but Carley, because of his employment relationship, felt that SDI should avoid any business undertaking involving Inland Steel or ISDC. SDI's board of directors sustained Carley's decision.

tion of personal reward for his efforts. Since our analysis leads us to a conclusion similar to the District Court's second reason, it is unnecessary here to consider the applicability of the licensing statute to Bloomgarden's activities.

Bloomgarden, we reiterate, sought a finder's fee on a twofold basis. He said that an agreement to pay such a fee, though not express, might be implied from the circumstances in which he brought the parties together, particularly in view of an alleged custom to reward those who discover advantageous business opportunities for others. Bloomgarden also said that in the context in which he introduced the parties, they came under a legal obligation–a quasi-contract–to compensate him for his services whether or not the elements of an enforceable contract were present. On this appeal Bloomgarden adds the contention that the District Court's disposition of his action by summary judgment was improper because there were important issues of fact, and because appellees had not demonstrated the validity of the legal position which the court accepted.

In reviewing the propriety of a summary judgment, it is our responsibility to determine whether there was any issue of fact pertinent to the ruling and, if not, whether the substantive law was correctly applied. The summary judgment procedure is properly and wholesomely invoked when it eliminates a useless trial but, of course, not when it would cut a litigant off from his right to have a jury resolve a factual issue bearing significantly on the outcome of the litigation. The party moving for summary judgment bears the burden of demonstrating the absence of a genuine issue as to any material fact, and even where his opponent comes forth with nothing, summary judgment must be denied if the facts supporting the motion do not establish the nonexistence of such an issue. Likewise, summary judgment must be denied where the movant fails to show his entitlement to a favorable determination as a matter of law. Thus, to be upheld, the summary judgment under review must withstand scrutiny on both its factual and legal foundations.

In the case at bar, the District Court, relying on Bloomgarden's own deposition, as was its prerogative in evaluating the summary-judgment motions made by the parties, concluded that Bloomgarden did not contemplate personal remuneration for his services, and that in consequence he lacked an indispensable prerequisite to recovery on either an implied-in-fact contract or a quasi-contract. Like the District Court, we are unable to perceive any factual basis upon which it could be asserted that, at the time he introduced the parties, Bloomgarden looked forward to any finder's fee for himself, as distinguished from a fee and future business for his company. His silence on the matter at the January meeting in Washington and again at the February meeting in Chicago, followed by his statements on the day after the Chicago meeting and later in his deposition, indicated unequivocally that at most the gain he then anticipated was work and compensation for SDI, of which he was president. Bloomgarden summed it up when in his deposition he said:

> It was always my intention that [SDI] should benefit, not myself personally, from putting Inland and Coyer together. [SDI] should have the credit; that [SDI] should get work assignments and that a finder's fee should be paid to [SDI]. It wasn't until I was told that I could not bring suit in the name of [SDI] and was urged to see if I wanted to sue Coyer as an individual that I began to recognize that I was in a very, very difficult spot.

In addition, the pleadings and depositions reveal that it was not until after Bloomgarden had done his service for the parties that they were put on notice that he had in mind a finder's fee, either for his company or for himself. Both Coyer and Guy avowed in their depositions that they thought Bloomgarden was acting either for SDI or Carley when in January he made the introductions. Their understanding in that regard was buttressed in February by Bloomgarden during the ride to the Chicago airport when, asked pointedly as to his expectations, he omitted reference to individual recompense and replied simply that he had in view the possibility that his company would receive work assignments flowing from the Georgetown project if it materialized. Moreover, Bloomgarden admitted in his deposition that not until the end of March—long after completion of the services for which remuneration was demanded—did he suggest compensation for SDI, his company, and not until May did he indicate that he anticipated personal compensation.

Against these damaging incidents and admissions—the underpinnings of appellees' motion for summary judgment—Bloomgarden advanced nothing more than the bare conclusory allegations of his complaint. We are mindful that on a motion for summary judgment the inferences to be drawn from the factual material before the court must be viewed in the light most favorable to the party opposing the motion. But we also recognize that in order to raise a material issue of fact precluding the grant of a properly supported motion for summary judgment, more is necessary that mere assertions in the pleadings. Our careful examination of the record leads us to concur with the District Court that appellees bore their burden as to the nonexistence of any genuine factual issue, and that Bloomgarden offered nothing substantial to bar their request for summary judgment. It remains for us to determine whether the principles of substantive law governing recovery on contracts implied in fact and quasi-contracts were correctly applied.

III

Despite the marked dissimilarity of contracts implied in fact to quasi-contracts, their separate characteristics have been blurred by courts and commentators over the years. For any satisfactory understanding of Bloomgarden's twofold legal approach, it is important to keep the two concepts clear and distinct.[30] An implied-in-fact contract is a true contract, containing all necessary elements of a binding agreement; it differs from other contracts only in that it has not been committed to writing or stated orally in express terms, but rather is inferred from the conduct of the parties in the milieu in which they dealt. A quasi-contract, on the other hand, is not a contract at all, but a duty thrust under certain conditions upon one party to requite another in order to avoid the former's unjust enrichment. The principles governing the two remedies differ, though in particular cases they may dictate the same result.

It is well settled that, in order to establish an implied-in-fact contract to pay for services, the party seeking payment must show (1) that the services were carried out under such circumstances as to give the recipient reason to understand (a) that they were performed for him and not for some other person, and (b) that they were not rendered gratuitously, but with the expectation of compensation from the recipient; and (2) that the services were beneficial to the recipient.

Particularly where commission-type fees are sought in business-opportunity transactions, such a contract will not be implied unless the recipient knows or has reasonable grounds to believe that the beneficial acts were performed in anticipation of remuneration therefor. The reasons underlying these requirements are evident. Activities beneficial to a party frequently proceed on behalf of another. Often they are engaged in without thought of remuneration. Not uncommonly, and irrespective of motivation, they are not really helpful to the recipient. An agreement to pay for services defies implication where the recipient not unreasonably fails to realize that the services were rendered for him in contemplation of *quid pro quo* for value conferred. And the point in time at which the elements essential to implication must concur is the time at which the services are rendered.[35]

We may assume on the record before us that Bloomgarden's introductions were valuable to appellees, or that at least there was a genuine issue as to whether they were. Yet, for Bloomgarden to recover on the basis of a contract implied in fact, he would have to show additionally that he looked forward to personal payment for his services, and that the circumstances under which he introduced Coyer and Guy to Carley were such as would reasonably have put them on notice that he had that in mind. From aught that appears from the record, Bloomgarden could not have met these standards at a trial.

---

[30] For a discussion of the distinction between quasi-contracts and contracts implied in fact, see 1 Williston, Contracts § 3A (3d ed. 1957).

[35] That is because an implied-in-fact contract to compensate for services arises, if at all, at the time the services are rendered, and only if the then-existing circumstances enable implication of a contract does it come into being. These precepts are elemental, and so much is implicit in the decisions holding that services performed without expectation of remuneration or simply in expectation of a nonmonetary business advantage do not warrant implication of a contract to pay. In all of these cases there was at some point a change of heart, and an effort in the suit to recover cash compensation not contemplated when the acts were performed.

. . . .

. . . . The record establishes without controversy that Bloomgarden introduced appellees on the chance that a coalition to develop the Georgetown waterfront would eventually produce business for SDI, his company, and that appellees reasonably understood that his activities were directed solely to that end. The record further establishes that even if Bloomgarden then entertained the notion of charging a finder's fee, appellees were not alerted to that possibility until long after his activities had ended. On these uncontradicted bases we find ample legal support for the District Court's conclusion that Bloomgarden failed to show an implied-in-fact contract supporting his claim.

IV

We turn finally to examine the sufficiency of Bloomgarden's quasi-contract theory as a basis for recovery of the finder's fee which he sought. At the outset, we again call attention to the need for conceptual clarity. The quasi-contract, as we have said, is not really a contract, but a legal obligation closely akin to a duty to make restitution. There is, of course, no need to resort to it when the evidence sustains the existence of a true contract, either express or implied in fact. For the purpose of preventing unjust enrichment, however, a quasi-contract—an obligation to pay money to another—will be recognized in appropriate circumstances, even though no intention of the parties to bind themselves contractually can be discerned.[52] And where, as here, the essential facts are not in dispute, the question whether a quasi-contract should be erected is one of law, and as such is a proper subject for summary disposition.

Generally, in order to recover on a quasi-contractual claim, the plaintiff must show that the defendant was unjustly enriched at the plaintiff's expense, and that the circumstances were such that in good conscience the defendant should make restitution. Because quasi-contractual obligations rest upon equitable considerations, they do not arise when it would not be unfair for the recipient to keep the benefit without having to pay for it. Thus, to make out his case, it is not enough for the plaintiff to prove merely that he has conferred an advantage upon the defendant, but he must demonstrate that retention of the benefit without compensating the one who conferred it is unjustified. What must be resolved here is whether Bloomgarden made such a showing or evinced his capability of possibly doing so at trial.

---

[52] . . . Relief by quasi-contract is really an equitable remedy which the common law labeled a contract in order to fit it into the procedural mold of assumpsit long before equitable doctrines became fully developed. *Fayette Tobacco Warehouse Co. v. Lexington Tobacco Bd. of Trade, supra,* 229 S.W.2d at 644.

By their very nature, the equitable principles of quasi-contracts are more difficult to apply where the court must determine whether services rendered by one person to another are to go unrewarded than where it must make that determination with respect to money or property unjustly retained. But since there is no general responsibility in quasi-contract law to pay for services *irrespective* of the circumstances in which they are carried out, a number

Think About It!

Why would the equitable principles of quasi-contracts be more difficult to apply in the case of services rendered than in the case of money or property retained, as the court suggests?

of factual criteria have been utilized by courts to ascertain whether in a given case the defendant has undeservedly profited by the plaintiff's efforts. Thus, in situations involving personal services, it has been variously stated that a duty to pay will not be recognized where it is clear that the benefit was conferred gratuitously or officiously, or that the question of payment was left to the unfettered discretion of the recipient. Nor is compensation mandated where the services were rendered simply in order to gain a business advantage.[60] And the courts have reached the same conclusion where the plaintiff did not contemplate a personal fee, or the defendant could not reasonably have supposed that he did.[62] As one court has pointed out: ". . . chagrin, disappointment, vexation, or supposed ingratitude cannot be used as a subsequent basis for a claim for compensation where none was originally intended or expected."[63] Nor, we add, can an uncommunicated expectation of remuneration serve the plaintiff's purpose where the defendant had no cause to believe that such was the fact.

Thus we come full circle to the identical considerations which were dispositive of Bloomgarden's claim for recovery on an implied-in-fact contract. There simply was no basis on which a jury could rationally find that when he brought the parties together[66] he entertained any thought of a finder's fee for himself, or that those with whom he dealt held the payment of such a fee in prospect. These circumstances defeat Bloomgarden's quasi-contract claim as well. On what emerges clearly and undisputably from the record, we find that the District Court

---

[60] Dunn v. Phoenix Village, Inc. 213 F.Supp. at 956; *Gould v. American Waterworks Serv. Co.*, 52 N.J. 226, 245 A.2d 14, 16-17 (1968), cert. denied, 394 U.S. 943, 89 S.Ct. 1274, 22 L.Ed.2d 477 (1969); *Anderson v. Distler*, 173 Misc. 261, 17 N.Y.S.2d 674, 679 (Sup. Ct.1940). Each of these cases involved an attempt to recover compensation for activities which the plaintiff engaged in for the purpose of securing future business with the defendant or others. . . . See **Restatement of Restitution** §§ 40-41 (1937).

[62] *Bellanca Corp. v. Bellanca, supra* note 61, 169 A.2d at 623. Recovery for the value of services which have inured to another's benefit is not generally allowed unless they were received with reason to know that compensation was expected for them. 13 S. Williston, Contracts § 1575 (3d ed. 1970).

[63] Anderson v. Distler, *supra* note 60, 17 N.Y.S.2d at 679.

[66] As in the instance of an implied-in-fact contract, the circumstances allegedly creating a quasi-contractual obligation to pay for services must have existed when the services were performed. No unfairness results from a denial of compensation to the claimant who had no expectation of personal remuneration at the time of performance. On the contrary, it would be unjust to impose a liability for payment on the party who accepts the services without any warning, from the surrounding circumstances or otherwise, that they were rendered for a price.

was fully warranted in holding that, as a matter of law, Bloomgarden was not entitled to recover on either a contract implied-in-fact or a quasi-contract, and its action in so doing is accordingly.

Affirmed.

Think About It!

The Bloomgarden court refers to the notion of "officiousness." Recall that in *Nursing Care Services*, on page 206, the court said the "officious intermeddler doctrine" bars recovery for services performed for another without request or consent, but then noted at least one exception to that rule, for emergency aid. Restatement (Third) of Restitution & Unjust Enrichment § 2(3) makes the point more broadly, saying there is "no liability in restitution for an unrequested benefit voluntarily conferred, unless the circumstances of the transaction justify the claimant's intervention in the absence of contract." Comment d to the section notes that those who cannot recover are variously labeled "officious," "intermeddler," or "volunteer." To say someone conferred a benefit "officiously" is thus more a conclusion than an argument: if there was no good reason to confer the benefit, the action is labeled officious interference in the affairs of others. *Nursing Care Services* establishes that emergency aid is not officious. What other interventions would be considered justified and therefore not officious? At least one court has suggested that an action is not officious if done "under the compulsion of a moral obligation, . . . a duty that . . . springs from the common sense of justice and fairness shared by all honorable persons" that is "perhaps best epitomized by the obligation family members commonly feel to support each other." *Estate of Cleveland*, 837 S.W.2d 68, 71 (Tenn. Ct. App. 1992). Would the actions of Mitchell in *Moore v. Mitchell* be considered officious under that standard? Perhaps not—but acts undertaken because of a sense of moral obligation might run up against the other limitation described in these cases, that restitution is not available for benefits conferred gratuitously!

Reading the Law Critically:
Restatement of Restitution & Unjust Enrichment

The Restatement of Restitution was adopted in 1937 and remained in effect until 2011. An effort to write a second Restatement of Restitution was suspended in 1985 after two drafts were circulated, though the drafts were sometimes cited for their persuasive value. The Restatement (Third) of Restitution & Unjust Enrichment was finally adopted in 2011. While the draft of the Restatement (Second) attempted to articulate a set of precise and detailed rules, similar to those identified in the cases in this section, the provisions of Restatement (Third) largely rely on general statements of liability, with the comments and illustrations offering additional guidance. Which approach—specifying rules for decision or leaving determination to the discretion of the decision-maker—do you think is the preferable approach? Why?

Restatement (Third) of Restitution & Unjust Enrichment § 20. **Protection of Another's Life or Health**

(1) A person who performs, supplies, or obtains professional services required for the protection of another's life or health is entitled to restitution from the other as necessary to prevent unjust enrichment, if the circumstances justify the decision to intervene without request.

(2) Unjust enrichment under this section is measured by a reasonable charge for the services in question.

Restatement (Third) of Restitution & Unjust Enrichment § 21. **Protection of Another's Property**

(1) A person who takes effective action to protect another's property from threatened harm is entitled to restitution from the other as necessary to prevent unjust enrichment, if the circumstances justify the decision to intervene without request. Unrequested intervention is justified only when it is reasonable to assume the owner would wish the action performed.

(2) Unjust enrichment under this section is measured by the loss avoided or by a reasonable charge for the services provided, whichever is less.

Restatement (Third) of Restitution & Unjust Enrichment § 22. **Performance of Another's Duty**

(1) A person who performs another's duty to a third person or to the public is entitled to restitution from the other as necessary to prevent unjust enrichment, if the circumstances justify the decision to intervene without request.

(2) Unrequested intervention may be justified in the following circumstances:

    (a) the claimant may be justified in paying another's money debt if there is no prejudice to the obligor in substituting a liability in restitution for the original obligation;

    (b) the claimant may be justified in performing another's duty to furnish necessaries to a third person, to avoid imminent harm to the interests of the third person; and

    (c) the claimant may be justified in performing another's duty to the public, if performance is urgently required for the protection of public health, safety, or general welfare.

(3) There is no unjust enrichment and no claim in restitution by the rule of this section except insofar as the claimant's intervention has relieved the defendant of an otherwise enforceable obligation.

Restatement (Third) of Restitution & Unjust Enrichment § 28. **Unmarried Cohabitants**

(1) If two persons have formerly lived together in a relationship resembling marriage, and if one of them owns a specific asset to which the other has made substantial, uncompensated contributions in the form of property or services, the person making such contributions has a claim in restitution against the owner as necessary to prevent unjust enrichment upon the dissolution of the relationship.

(2) The rule of subsection (1) may be displaced, modified, or supplemented by local domestic relations law.

Problems: Promissory Estoppel, Restitution, and Promissory Restitution

The following problems will give you an opportunity to craft arguments for why an individual who received a benefit should or should not be required to pay for it, whether or not that person made a promise to pay. As you have seen, there are often no clear answers to that question because the standards governing promissory estoppel, restitution, and promissory restitution invite the court to make judgments about what is fair and just. As an advocate, your task is to persuade the court, using the facts to explain why it would be unfair under the circumstances not to compensate the person who conferred the benefit or incurred expenses in reliance. Reference to other similar cases may be helpful, but you cannot escape the need to consider the moral dimension. It is not enough, of course, to claim "moral obligation," which by itself is not a justification for recovery.

It is often also unclear whether and when a promise was made, so it is often worth arguing both points—that a promise was made and should be enforced under the principles of promissory estoppel or promissory restitution and that, if no promise was made, restitution should be ordered to avoid unjust enrichment. The factors to be considered and the arguments to be made are similar, especially with respect to restitution and promissory restitution, though the claim will be strengthened by the existence of a promise.

3-1. Recall the case of *Hayes v. Plantations Steel Co.* (page 164). Just before Hayes retired from his job but after he had announced his intention to leave, his employer promised him the company "would take care of him" and then paid him a yearly pension of $5000 for four years before discontinuing the practice. Hayes was denied recovery as a matter of contract (no consideration) or promissory estoppel (no reliance). Should he have recovered under a theory of promissory restitution? Restitution?

3-2. Nadia Nussbaum's upstairs neighbor, Alexander, was found dead in his apartment due to natural causes. Knowing that he was Jewish (as was she) and apparently had no surviving relatives, Nadia arranged and paid $5000 for a traditional Jewish burial, which her rabbi said would be a "mitzvah." (A mitzvah refers to a Jewish religious obligation, derived from the commandments in the Torah, the first 5 books of the Bible; the word is sometimes used to refer generally to any good deed. As noted in the Jewish Virtual Library, the duty of burial, although primarily an obligation of the heirs, ultimately rests with the whole community. See www.jewishvirtuallibrary. org/jsource/judaica/ejud_0002_0004_0_03747.html.)

Shortly after the funeral was held, the neighbor's long-lost brother, Samuel, appeared. He had not seen his brother for 37 years. Samuel called on Nadia to express his gratitude for what she had done for Alexander. Should Nadia be able to recover the funeral expenses under the theory of restitution? If Samuel made a promise to reimburse Nadia and then did not, should she be able to recover under a theory of promissory restitution?

3-3.   While leasing commercial property from Leslie Landlord, Trudy Tenant hired Construction Contractor to perform renovations on the property. Under the lease, Tenant was responsible for such renovations. Tenant did not pay and Contractor will not be able to recover from her. Should Contractor be able to recover payment from Landlord under the theory of restitution? If Landlord made a promise to reimburse Contractor and then did not, should Contractor be able to recover under a theory of promissory restitution?

3-4.   ADS Unlimited (ADS), an advertising agency located in Minneapolis, talks with the regional manager of Staples, Inc., about the possibility of being hired on retainer by the New York-based company, which is looking to expand its national marketing. The regional manager encourages ADS to prepare an advertising plan for submission at the quarterly Board meeting in New York "to show your stuff" and assures ADS that it will have the "inside track" to receive the advertising account. ADS submits its plan, but the Board follows its usual practice of considering only local (to New York) agencies, so the retainer is offered to another firm. That firm makes use of the work submitted by ADS as it develops its own plan, which is then used on behalf of Staples. Should ADS be able to recover the fair value of its plan from Staples?

3-5.   Howard Lane has filed claims against the estate of his deceased companion, Lori Masters. Howard and Lori had lived together for several years and, according to Howard, they considered their relationship to be like a marriage, "except for the vows."

Lori owned 10 acres of land, titled in her name and purchased with her own funds. During the several years preceding Lori's death, Howard used equipment from his own construction business to improve the property Lori owned, primarily by grading and landscaping, and by putting in a road. He also paid taxes, insurance, and legal bills for Lori's property, drawing from a joint checking account that contained money Howard had inherited from his family along with rental income from additional property Lori owned.

After Lori was diagnosed with terminal cancer, Howard paid Lori's medical bills, since Lori had no insurance, and Howard provided personal care and services until Lori's death.

Howard says Lori had promised Howard to give him the ten-acre parcel of land, but she died without executing a will.

Howard has filed claims against Lori's estate for

A. $21,000 to compensate him for personal care given to Lori during her illness ($50 per day for taking care of Lori at home and transporting her to the hospital and other appointments);

B. 21,169 in medical bills he paid;

C. $70,000 for improvements Howard made to Lori's 10-acre parcel; and

D. An amount to cover the taxes, insurance, and legal bills for Lori's property that had been paid from the joint checking account during the three years preceding Lori's death.

Should Howard be able to recover these amounts from Lori's estate? You should consider each of the 4 claims separately.

3-6. Glenda owns a summer home in Minneapolis and a winter home in South Carolina. During July, high winds rip through the South Carolina neighborhood, and a large tree falls on the house, causing considerable damage. Glenda's neighbor, Tony, who works after-hours as a handyman, does preliminary work on the house, tacking plywood over a hole in the wall and a tarp over the roof, protecting the interior from the rains that followed the winds. Tony's home was also damaged in the storms, and he hires Professional Renovators to repair both of their homes. When Glenda sees the news about the storm, she contacts Discount Builders to inspect the damage; they agree she will pay for two hours of their time for the inspection trip, but that amount will be deducted from the final bill if she uses them to make the repairs. Discount Builders reports to Glenda that repair work is already underway and bills her $70 for the trip to the house.

A. Should Professional Renovators be able to recover from Glenda for the work done on her home? Should it make a difference if Glenda was phoned by Professional Renovators after the work was completed and she said she'd "make good" on the repairs?

B. Should Tony be able to recover from Glenda for his time working on her house? For anything he pays to Professional Renovators for the work the company did on her house? Should it make a difference if Glenda thanked Tony for everything he'd done and said "don't worry, I'll pay you back for everything"?

3-7. Cyclops Steel is a steel manufacturer and the owner of a dormant steel-forging facility in Aliquippa, Pennsylvania. (Forging is a manufacturing process that turns raw metal alloy into strong complex shapes for industrial use.) Ronald Crouse expressed an interest in purchasing the dormant facility, and the two parties agreed to go forward with the purchase, contingent on Crouse obtaining financing within six months.

Crouse learned that, to satisfy his investors that he had a workable business plan, he needed a commitment of future business for the facility, which he intended to operate under the name Aliquippa Forge. He discussed his needs with Cyclops, and on January 12, 2011, Cyclops issued a letter to Crouse that included the following:

> Cyclops is willing to commit to have Ronald Crouse (doing business as Aliquippa Forge) forge an average of 300,000 to 400,000 pounds of steel product per month, provided price and delivery are competitive and quality meets our requirements. Please be aware that we cannot and do not guarantee a uniform flow in quantity or type of forging work. We look forward to working with you in developing a mutually beneficial business relationship and to sending you our first lot of material in the near future.

On January 31, 2011, Crouse and Cyclops executed the agreement of sale for the facility. Aliquippa Forge started operations in February 2011, and in March 2011, Cyclops ordered 291,969 pounds of conversion work from the Forge. Cyclops made no complaints about the quality of the work performed, but made no further orders to Aliquippa. In December 2012, Aliquippa Forge ceased doing business based on financial difficulties, including an insufficient flow of business.

Does Aliquippa have any viable claims against Cyclops based on the circumstances described? If so, under what theories of recovery?

3-8.   Edward Oswald is the owner of an antebellum plantation-style house, "Chateau Haut Brian," currently vacant. He entered an agreement with Charles Buchanan for the sale of the property for the price of $430,000. As part of that agreement, Oswald agreed to allow Buchanan to make alterations to the property in advance of payment and closing on the purchase of the house.

Buchanan thereafter entered a contract with Orleans Onyx for installation of marble-like onyx tile and fixtures into two of the bathrooms in the house. The interior designer working with Buchanan told him the fixtures were not compatible with the style of the house, "but he insisted, and we gave him what he wanted." The contract between Buchanan and Orleans Onyx provided for a 30% down payment of the contract price of $30,000, with the remainder due upon completion of the work. The down payment was made, but the final $20,000 check Buchanan wrote was dishonored for insufficient funds. Buchanan did not complete the purchase of the house and discharged his debt to Orleans Onyx in bankruptcy proceedings.

Oswald was unable to sell the house after Buchanan's default and moved into the house himself. Orleans Onyx seeks recovery from Buchanan for the $20,000 owed for the work done on the bathrooms. Oswald has refused, describing the bathroom décor as "too flashy and gaudy," though acknowledging that the work was well-done and the bathrooms are fully operational. Should Orleans Onyx be able to recover from Oswald for the work done on the Chateau? If so, how much?

3-9.   General Liquors is a wholesale distributor of alcohol products. For more than 35 years, General had operated as a terminable-at-will distributor for Draco Distillers and other manufacturers. In April 2011, when two of its major suppliers withdrew their product lines from General, General faced a critical choice: It could sell the business to one of its competitors or it could continue in business with scaled-back operations. Not sure of the best course, it entered negotiations with National Wine and Spirits to sell the business, receiving an offer of $2.5 million on July 15. At the same time, having determined that it could remain in business if it retained both its remaining major suppliers, it approached Draco to seek assurances about its commitment to General. After listening to General's concerns and hearing about the possible sale, Draco told General that it had no intention of taking its line to another distributor. On July 25, with the offer from National about to expire, General contacted Draco again and was again told that it was staying General. Concluding that it could not continue without Draco, General approached National again, but National reduced its offer to $2 million, which General felt forced to accept.

Does General have any viable claims against Draco based on the circumstances described? If so, under what theories of recovery?

CHAPTER 4

Manifestation of Mutual Assent

What kind of promises will the law enforce?	How do parties demonstrate assent to a contract?	What defenses to enforcement exist?	Is a writing required for enforcement? If so, what kind?	How is the content of a contract ascertained?	What are parties' rights and duties after breach?

What situations lead to excusing contract performance?	What remedies are available for breach of contract?	What contractual rights and duties do non-parties to a contract have?

Table of Contents

§ 1. Introduction

As seen in Chapter 2, proving the existence of a contract requires the plaintiff to demonstrate that there was consideration for the promise that the plaintiff seeks to enforce. It also requires the plaintiff to demonstrate that the parties mutually manifested assent to the contract, and it is to this element of contract formation that we now turn our attention.

"Assent" means a party's agreement to the proposed deal, which must be articulated with sufficient clarity and specification to qualify as assent. A party's "manifestation" of assent is language or conduct that is directed toward the other party, who hears or sees or otherwise knows about the manifestation. The law focuses on the parties' *external* demonstrations of assent—the *communication* of each party's assent to the other party. "Manifestation of mutual assent" means that each of the parties has manifested assent to the proposed terms.

Make the Connection

By its nature, assent must be voluntary and not based on mistaken or misrepresented information. This chapter focuses on the mechanics of manifesting assent, assuming no underlying concern with the nature of the agreement process. Chapter 5 examines "the dark side of mutual assent"—defenses to contract formation based on allegations that fraud, duress, undue influence, mistake, or misrepresentation undercut the existence of true assent.

Note that *mutual* assent is not an element of promissory estoppel or promissory restitution (see Chapter 3), because these doctrines focus on the commitment of only the party who made the promise, even though the recipient of the promise could be seen as "agreeing" to receive the benefit.

The requirement of manifestation of mutual assent protects each party's freedom of contract. Each party should have the opportunity to know and understand the terms of the proposed contract before deciding whether to agree, and to have its choice—to commit to the contract or not—be respected. The law should make it neither too easy nor too hard for parties to form contracts and should strive to implement the intention of the parties, as well as that intention can be discerned.

Manifestation of mutual assent may occur simultaneously, with the parties together manifesting agreement to a single statement of terms, or it may be the result of sequential ("offer" and "acceptance") communications. Either way, two overarching issues require resolution in order to determine whether agreement was reached: (1) Are a party's communications to be judged by a subjective standard (what the person was thinking at the time) or an objective standard (what a reasonable person would think that the communication meant)? (2) How clear, detailed and certain must the terms be before they can be enforced as a contract? This chapter turns first to these two concerns and subsequently considers the details of the process of offer and acceptance.

§ 2. Should Mutual Assent Be Judged Objectively or Subjectively?

Because contract law is grounded in the notion of enforcing parties' voluntarily created rights and obligations, it involves a search for the intent of the parties. That intent must be found in the communications between the parties to an alleged contract. But sometimes there are multiple meanings—what a party was thinking at the time of the communication (her subjective meaning), what the other party understood (his subjective meaning), and what a reasonable person observing the communication would have understood (an objective meaning).

Reading the Law Critically: *Lucy*

1. What rule does this case use to determine the intent of the parties to an alleged contract? You will need to condense the court's multiple articulations into a single statement of the rule.

2. Does the rule focus on objective meaning, subjective meaning, or some combination? What difference does that choice make in the court's reasoning and holding?

3. What variation(s) in the facts would have led to a different outcome?

4. How does the objective test affect what evidence is presented to prove mutual assent? Would the subjective test be harder or easier to satisfy? What are the advantages and disadvantages of the subjective and objective tests?

Lucy v. Zehmer

W. O. LUCY and J. C. LUCY, Complainants-Appellants

v.

A. H. ZEHMER and IDA S. ZEHMER, Defendants-Appellees

Supreme Court of Appeals of Virginia
84 S.E.2d 516 (Va. Ct. App. 1954)

BUCHANAN, J., delivered the opinion of the court.

This suit was instituted by W. O. Lucy and J. C. Lucy, complainants, against A. H. Zehmer and Ida S. Zehmer, his wife, defendants, to have specific performance of a contract by which it was alleged the Zehmers had sold to W. O. Lucy a tract of land owned by A. H. Zehmer in Dinwiddie county containing 471.6 acres, more or less, known as the Ferguson farm, for $50,000. J. C. Lucy, the other complainant, is a brother of W. O. Lucy, to whom W. O. Lucy transferred a half interest in his alleged purchase.

The instrument sought to be enforced was written by A. H. Zehmer on December 20, 1952, in these words: "We hereby agree to sell to W. O. Lucy the Ferguson Farm complete for $50,000.00, title satisfactory to buyer," and signed by the defendants, A. H. Zehmer and Ida S. Zehmer.

The answer of A. H. Zehmer admitted that at the time mentioned W. O. Lucy offered him $50,000 cash for the farm, but that he, Zehmer, considered that the offer was made in jest; that so thinking, and both he and Lucy having had several drinks, he wrote out "the memorandum" quoted above and induced his wife to sign it; that he did not deliver the memorandum to Lucy, but that Lucy picked it up, read it, put it in his pocket, attempted to offer Zehmer $5 to bind the bargain, which Zehmer refused to accept, and realizing for the first time that Lucy was serious, Zehmer assured him that he had no intention of selling the farm and that the whole matter was a joke. Lucy left the premises insisting that he had purchased the farm.

What's That?

The plaintiffs in this suit asked for "specific performance" of the purchase contract, seeking an order compelling the defendants to do what was promised—deliver a deed for the property. For reasons suggested earlier (see the note on the history of equity in Chapter 3, page 162), money damages are the preferred remedy for a breach of contract. Sometimes, though, damages are inadequate to remedy a breach, especially where a piece of real estate or some other unique item is the subject of the dispute. In those instances, a court will consider whether to award the disputed item itself ("specific performance") rather than damages for the value of that item. Chapter 9, page 1183, covers the policies supporting and limiting the remedy of specific performance.

Depositions were taken and the decree appealed from was entered holding that the complainants had failed to establish their right to specific performance, and dismissing their bill. The assignment of error is to this action of the court.

W. O. Lucy, a lumberman and farmer, thus testified in substance: He had known Zehmer for fifteen or twenty years and had been familiar with the Ferguson farm for ten years. Seven or eight years ago he had offered Zehmer $20,000 for the farm which Zehmer had accepted, but the agreement was verbal and Zehmer backed out. On the night of December 20, 1952, around eight o'clock, he took an employee to McKenney, where Zehmer lived and operated a restaurant, filling station and motor court. While there he decided to see Zehmer and again try to buy the Ferguson farm. He entered the restaurant and talked to Mrs. Zehmer until Zehmer came in. He asked Zehmer if he had sold the Ferguson farm. Zehmer replied that he had not. Lucy said, "I bet you wouldn't take $50,000.00 for that place." Zehmer replied, "Yes, I would too; you wouldn't give fifty." Lucy said he would and told Zehmer to write up an agreement to that effect. Zehmer took a restaurant check and wrote on the back of it, "I do hereby agree to sell to W. O. Lucy the Ferguson Farm for $50,000 complete." Lucy told him he had better change it to "We" because Mrs. Zehmer would have to sign it too. Zehmer then tore up what he had written, wrote the agreement quoted above and asked Mrs. Zehmer, who was at the other end of the counter ten or twelve feet away, to sign it. Mrs. Zehmer said she would for $50,000 and signed it. Zehmer brought it back and gave it to Lucy, who offered him $5 which Zehmer refused, saying, "You don't need to give me any money, you got the agreement there signed by both of us."

The discussion leading to the signing of the agreement, said Lucy, lasted thirty or forty minutes, during which Zehmer seemed to doubt that Lucy could raise $50,000. Lucy suggested the provision for having the title examined and Zehmer made the suggestion that he would sell it "complete, everything there," and stated that all he had on the farm was three heifers.

Lucy took a partly filled bottle of whiskey into the restaurant with him for the purpose of giving Zehmer a drink if he wanted it. Zehmer did, and he and Lucy

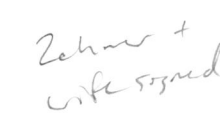

See It!

Here are pictures of the restaurant, its sign, and the handwritten agreement:

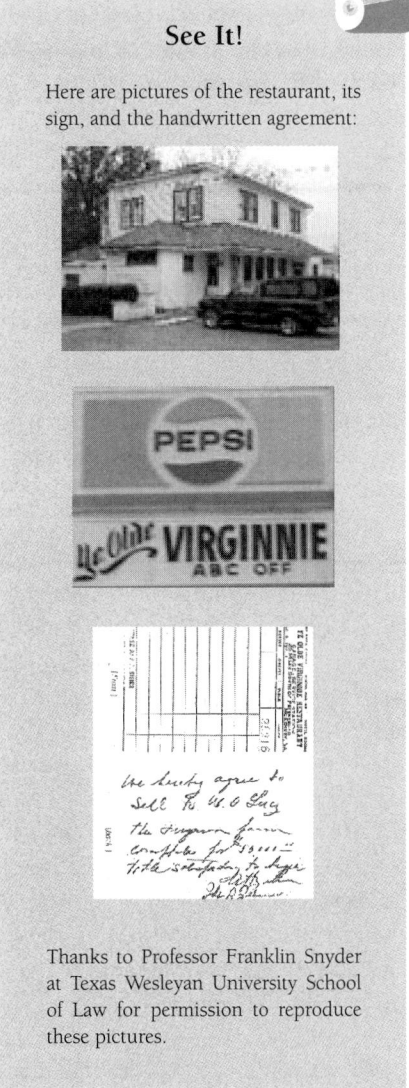

Thanks to Professor Franklin Snyder at Texas Wesleyan University School of Law for permission to reproduce these pictures.

had one or two drinks together. Lucy said that while he felt the drinks he took he was not intoxicated, and from the way Zehmer handled the transaction he did not think he was either.

December 20 was on Saturday. Next day Lucy telephoned to J. C. Lucy and arranged with the latter to take a half interest in the purchase and pay half of the consideration. On Monday he engaged an attorney to examine the title. The attorney reported favorably on December 31 and on January 2 Lucy wrote Zehmer stating that the title was satisfactory, that he was ready to pay the purchase price in cash and asking when Zehmer would be ready to close the deal. Zehmer replied by letter, mailed on January 13, asserting that he had never agreed or intended to sell.

didn't want to sell

Mr. and Mrs. Zehmer were called by the complainants as adverse witnesses. Zehmer testified in substance as follows:

He bought this farm more than ten years ago for $11,000. He had had twenty-five offers, more or less, to buy it, including several from Lucy, who had never offered any specific sum of money. He had given them all the same answer, that he was not interested in selling it. On this Saturday night before Christmas it looked like everybody and his brother came by there to have a drink. He took a good many drinks during the afternoon and had a pint of his own. When he entered the restaurant around eight-thirty Lucy was there and he could see that he was "pretty high." He said to Lucy, "Boy, you got some good liquor, drinking, ain't you?" Lucy then offered him a drink. "I was already high as a Georgia pine, and didn't have any more better sense than to pour another great big slug out and gulp it down, and he took one too."

After they had talked a while Lucy asked whether he still had the Ferguson farm. He replied that he had not sold it and Lucy said, "I bet you wouldn't take $50,000.00 for it." Zehmer asked him if he would give $50,000 and Lucy said yes. Zehmer replied, "You haven't got $50,000 in cash." Lucy said he did and Zehmer replied that he did not believe it. They argued "pro and con for a long time," mainly about "whether he had $50,000 in cash that he could put up right then and buy that farm."

do you even have $50,000?

Finally, said Zehmer, Lucy told him if he didn't believe he had $50,000, "you sign that piece of paper here and say you will take $50,000.00 for the farm. " He, Zehmer, "just grabbed the back off of a guest check there" and wrote on the back of it. At that point in his testimony Zehmer asked to see what he had written to "see if I recognize my own handwriting." He examined the paper and exclaimed, "Great balls of fire, I got 'Firgerson' for Ferguson. I have got satisfactory spelled wrong. I don't recognize that writing if I would see it, wouldn't know it was mine."

written while pretty drunk?

After Zehmer had, as he described it, "scribbled this thing off," Lucy said, "Get your wife to sign it." Zehmer walked over to where she was and she at first refused to sign but did so after he told her that he "was just needling him [Lucy], and didn't mean a thing in the world, that I was not selling the farm." Zehmer then "took it back over there . . . and I was still looking at the dern thing. I had the drink right there by my hand, and I reached over to get a drink, and he said, 'Let me see it.' He reached and picked it up, and when I looked back again he had it in his pocket and he dropped a five dollar bill over there, and he said, 'Here is five dollars payment on it.' . . . I said, 'Hell no, that is beer and liquor talking. I am not going to sell you the farm. I have told you that too many times before.'"

Mrs. Zehmer testified that when Lucy came into the restaurant he looked as if he had had a drink. When Zehmer came in he took a drink out of a bottle that Lucy handed him. She went back to help the waitress who was getting things ready for next day. Lucy and Zehmer were talking but she did not pay too much attention to what they were saying. She heard Lucy ask Zehmer if he had sold the Ferguson farm, and Zehmer replied that he had not and did not want to sell it. Lucy said, "I bet you wouldn't take $50,000 cash for that farm," and Zehmer replied, "You haven't got $50,000 cash." Lucy said, "I can get it." Zehmer said he might form a company and get it, "but you haven't got $50,000.00 cash to pay me tonight." Lucy asked him if he would put it in writing that he would sell him this farm. Zehmer then wrote on the back of a pad, "I agree to sell the Ferguson Place to W. O. Lucy for $50,000.00 cash." Lucy said, "All right, get your wife to sign it." Zehmer came back to where she was standing and said, "You want to put your name to this?" She said "No," but he said in an undertone, "It is nothing but a joke," and she signed it.

She said that only one paper was written and it said: "I hereby agree to sell," but the "I" had been changed to "We". However, she said she read what she signed and was then asked, "When you read 'We hereby agree to sell to W. O. Lucy,' what did you interpret that to mean, that particular phrase?" She said she thought that was a cash sale that night; but she also said that when she read that part about "title satisfactory to buyer" she understood that if the title was good Lucy would pay $50,000 but if the title was bad he would have a right to reject it, and that that was her understanding at the time she signed her name.

On examination by her own counsel she said that her husband laid this piece of paper down after it was signed; that Lucy said to let him see it, took it, folded it and put it in his wallet, then said to Zehmer, "Let me give you $5.00," but Zehmer said, "No, this is liquor talking. I don't want to sell the farm, I have told you that I want my son to have it. This is all a joke." Lucy then said at least twice, "Zehmer, you have sold your farm," wheeled around and started for the door. He paused at the door and said, "I will bring you $50,000.00 tomorrow. . . . No, tomorrow is Sunday. I will bring it to you Monday." She said you could tell definitely that he was drinking and she said to her husband, "You should have taken him home," but he said, "Well, I am just about as bad off as he is."

The waitress referred to by Mrs. Zehmer testified that when Lucy first came in "he was mouthy." When Zehmer came in they were laughing and joking and she thought they took a drink or two. She was sweeping and cleaning up for next day. She said she heard Lucy tell Zehmer, "I will give you so much for the farm," and Zehmer said, "You haven't got that much." Lucy answered, "Oh, yes, I will give you that much." Then "they jotted down something on paper . . . and Mr. Lucy reached over and took it, said let me see it." He looked at it, put it in his pocket and in about a minute he left. She was asked whether she saw Lucy offer Zehmer any money and replied, "He had five dollars laying up there, they didn't take it." She said Zehmer told Lucy he didn't want his money "because he didn't have enough money to pay for his property, and wasn't going to sell his farm." Both of them appeared to be drinking right much, she said.

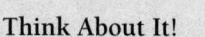
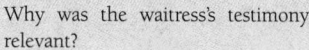

Think About It!

Why was the waitress's testimony relevant?

She repeated on cross-examination that she was busy and paying no attention to what was going on. She was some distance away and did not see either of them sign the paper. She was asked whether she saw Zehmer put the agreement down on the table in front of Lucy, and her answer was this: "Time he got through writing whatever it was on the paper, Mr. Lucy reached over and said, 'Let's see it.' He took it and put it in his pocket," before showing it to Mrs. Zehmer. Her version was that Lucy kept raising his offer until it got to $50,000.

The defendants insist that the evidence was ample to support their contention that the writing sought to be enforced was prepared as a bluff or dare to force Lucy to admit that he did not have $50,000; that the whole matter was a joke; that the writing was not delivered to Lucy and no binding contract was ever made between the parties.

It is an unusual, if not bizarre, defense. When made to the writing admittedly prepared by one of the defendants and signed by both, clear evidence is required to sustain it.

In his testimony Zehmer claimed that he "was high as a Georgia pine," and that the transaction "was just a bunch of two doggoned drunks bluffing to see who could talk the biggest and say the most." That claim is inconsistent with his attempt to testify in great detail as to what was said and what was done. It is contradicted by other evidence as to the condition of both parties, and rendered of no weight by the testimony of his wife that when Lucy left the restaurant she suggested that Zehmer drive him home. The record is convincing that Zehmer

wasn't that drunk

was not intoxicated to the extent of being unable to comprehend the nature and consequences of the instrument he executed, and hence that instrument is not to be invalidated on that ground. 17 C.J.S., Contracts, § 133 b., p. 483; *Taliaferro v. Emery,* 124 Va. 674, 98 S.E. 627. It was in fact conceded by defendants' counsel in oral argument that under the evidence Zehmer was not too drunk to make a valid contract.

Make the Connection

Note the standard the court uses in ruling that Zehmer was not intoxicated to assent to the contract. You will see this standard reappear in the material on mental incapacity to enter contracts in Chapter 5, page 595.

The evidence is convincing also that Zehmer wrote two agreements, the first one beginning "I hereby agree to sell." Zehmer first said he could not remember about that, then that "I don't think I wrote but one out. " Mrs. Zehmer said that what he wrote was "I hereby agree," but that the "I" was changed to "We" after that night. The agreement that was written and signed is in the record and indicates no such change. Neither are the mistakes in spelling that Zehmer sought to point out readily apparent.

spelling mistakes not here

The appearance of the contract, the fact that it was under discussion for forty minutes or more before it was signed; Lucy's objection to the first draft because it was written in the singular, and he wanted Mrs. Zehmer to sign it also; the rewriting to meet that objection and the signing by Mrs. Zehmer; the discussion of what was to be included in the sale, the provision for the examination of the title, the completeness of the instrument that was executed, the taking possession of it by Lucy with no request or suggestion by either of the defendants that he give it back, are facts which furnish persuasive evidence that the execution of the contract was a serious business transaction rather than a casual, jesting matter as defendants now contend.

On Sunday, the day after the instrument was signed on Saturday night, there was a social gathering in a home in the town of McKenney at which there were general comments that the sale had been made. Mrs. Zehmer testified that on that occasion as she passed by a group of people, including Lucy, who were talking about the transaction, $50,000 was mentioned, whereupon she stepped up and said, "Well, with the high-price whiskey you were drinking last night you should have paid more. That was cheap." Lucy testified that at that time Zehmer told him that he did not want to "stick" him or hold him to the agreement because he, Lucy, was too tight and didn't know what he was doing, to which Lucy replied that he was not too tight; that he had been stuck before and was going through with it. Zehmer's version was that he said to Lucy: "I am not trying to claim it wasn't a deal on account of the fact the price was too low. If I had wanted to sell $50,000.00 would be a good price, in fact I think you would get stuck at $50,000.00." A

"you can back out" I know you don't have $

disinterested witness testified that what Zehmer said to Lucy was that "he was going to let him up off the deal, because he thought he was too tight, didn't know what he was doing. Lucy said something to the effect that 'I have been stuck before and I will go through with it.'"

If it be assumed, contrary to what we think the evidence shows, that Zehmer was jesting about selling his farm to Lucy and that the transaction was intended by him to be a joke, nevertheless the evidence shows that Lucy did not so understand it but considered it to be a serious business

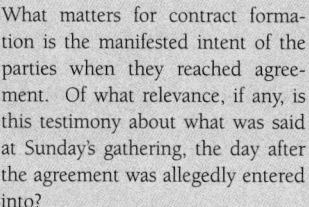

Think About It!

What matters for contract formation is the manifested intent of the parties when they reached agreement. Of what relevance, if any, is this testimony about what was said at Sunday's gathering, the day after the agreement was allegedly entered into?

transaction and the contract to be binding on the Zehmers as well as on himself. The very next day he arranged with his brother to put up half the money and take a half interest in the land. The day after that he employed an attorney to examine the title. The next night, Tuesday, he was back at Zehmer's place and there Zehmer told him for the first time, Lucy said, that he wasn't going to sell and he told Zehmer, "You know you sold that place fair and square." After receiving the report from his attorney that the title was good he wrote to Zehmer that he was ready to close the deal.

Not only did Lucy actually believe, but the evidence shows he was warranted in believing, that the contract represented a serious business transaction and a good faith sale and purchase of the farm.

In the field of contracts, as generally elsewhere, "We must look to the outward expression of a person as manifesting his intention rather than to his secret and unexpressed intention. 'The law imputes to a person an intention corresponding to the reasonable meaning of his words and acts.'" *First Nat. Bank v. Roanoke Oil Co.*, 169 Va. 99, 114, 192 S.E. 764, 770.

At no time prior to the execution of the contract had Zehmer indicated to Lucy by word or act that he was not in earnest about selling the farm. They had argued about it and discussed its terms, as Zehmer admitted, for a long time. Lucy testified that if there was any jesting it was about paying $50,000 that night. The contract and the evidence show that he was not expected to pay the money that night. Zehmer said that after the writing was signed he laid it down on the counter in front of Lucy. Lucy said Zehmer handed it to him. In any event there had been what appeared to be a good faith offer and a good faith acceptance, followed by the execution and apparent delivery of a written contract. Both said that Lucy put the writing in his pocket and then offered Zehmer $5 to seal the bargain. Not until then, even under the defendants' evidence, was anything said or done to indicate that the matter was a joke. Both of the Zehmers testified that when Zehmer asked his wife to sign he whispered that it was a joke so Lucy wouldn't hear and that it was not intended that he should hear.

Food for Thought

Under the objective test, the so-called "reasonable person" may be in one of the following positions: apart from the parties without any particular knowledge of the particular circumstances, or in the shoes of the sender or the recipient of a particular communication, knowing what that person reasonably should have known.

The mental assent of the parties is not requisite for the formation of a contract. If the words or other acts of one of the parties have but one reasonable meaning, his undisclosed intention is immaterial except when an unreasonable meaning which he attaches to his manifestations is known to the other party. **Restatement of the Law of Contracts, Vol. I, § 71, p. 74.**

". . . The law, therefore, judges of an agreement between two persons exclusively from those expressions of their intentions which are communicated between them. . . ." Clark on Contracts, 4 ed., § 3, p. 4.

An agreement or mutual assent is of course essential to a valid contract but the law imputes to a person an intention corresponding to the reasonable meaning of his words and acts. If his words and acts, judged by a reasonable standard, manifest an intention to agree, it is immaterial what may be the real but unexpressed state of his mind. **17 C.J.S., Contracts, § 32, p. 361** . . . .

So a person cannot set up that he was merely jesting when his conduct and words would warrant a reasonable person in believing that he intended a real agreement, **17 C.J.S., Contracts, § 47, p. 390** . . . .

Whether the writing signed by the defendants and now sought to be enforced by the complainants was the result of a serious offer by Lucy and a serious acceptance by the defendants, or was a serious offer by Lucy and an acceptance in secret jest by the defendants, in either event it constituted a binding contract of sale between the parties.

. . . .

Reversed and remanded.

Food for Thought: Two Ships Named "Peerless" and the Absence of Objective Meaning

What happens when the parties to a contract have different understandings of a crucial term of the agreement? Does the objective test furnish adequate means of judging the parties' manifestation of mutual assent? Is a contract formed?

Consider the well-known case of Raffles v. Wichelhaus, 159 Eng. Rep. 375 (Exch. 1864), in which the parties agreed in writing that the seller would send a load of cotton from Bombay to the buyers in Liverpool by way of a sailing ship, the Peerless—a "barque." (The photo shows the kind of barque that was the most common type of deep-water carrier in the mid-1800s. For more information, see http://en.wikipedia.org/wiki/Barque.)

Because sailing speed and route depended on wind speed and direction, the parties did not specify a shipping date or an arrival date—a practice which was in keeping with the usual practice of that era. There were, in fact, two ships named "Peerless" sailing from Bombay, but each party claimed to be aware of only one. The buyers said they had meant the ship that left Bombay in October; the sellers delivered cotton from the ship that left in December. Different arrival dates could affect the price the cotton would fetch upon resale in the English market; indeed, the cotton market was particularly volatile in the latter half of 1862 because of an imminent cotton famine. When the cotton arrived on the December "Peerless," the buyers refused to take delivery; the buyers would have suffered a loss on the resale (although it appears they would have lost more if the cotton had indeed arrived on the October ship, which they claim to have intended). The seller sued for breach; the buyers defended by claiming they meant (and therefore contracted for) the cotton on the October "Peerless." The seller demurred to this defense, essentially saying, "So what? My claim is good even if we each meant different ships. The contract was for cotton from a ship named Peerless, and that's what I delivered."

The case is sometimes described as examining the parties' actual (subjective) intent and finding that no contract existed because there was no "meeting of the minds." That understanding is challenged by Professor Brian Simpson, who has shown that the court made only a procedural ruling against the seller's demurrer, holding that the buyers' defense *could* make a difference, so the jury should be allowed to hear evidence as to the parties' intent on this latent ambiguity. The court never stated a substantive rule or hinted as to the likely outcome at trial. *See* A.W. Brian Simpson, *Contracts for Cotton to Arrive: The Case of the Two Ships Peerless*, 11 Cardozo L. Rev. 287 (1989), the source of the additional historical context described above.

Different subjective intent on a key term—the timing and therefore identity and value of the goods being purchased—could be seen as defeating contract formation, but the same result can also be supported under the objective theory if one concludes that both meanings were equally reasonable, with no way for a court to decide which was a "better" understanding that should have been the understanding of both parties. Consider the following variations, to explore the operation of the objective standard. Is a contract formed in each scenario? If so, on what terms? In each instance, the parties manifested assent to the same thing (shipment of cotton on the vessel "Peerless"), but at least one party misunderstood which vessel was meant by the other:

- Seller assented to the agreement knowing that two ships named "Peerless" were sailing from Bombay by the end of the year. Meanwhile, buyer knew only of the October sailing vessel. Would it matter if seller knew that buyer meant the October sailing vessel?
- Seller assented to the agreement knowing that two ships named "Peerless" were sailing from Bombay by the end of the year, and also knowing that buyer meant the October sailing vessel. Meanwhile, buyer assented to the agreement knowing of the two ships named "Peerless" sailing soon from Bombay, and also knowing that the seller meant the December sailing vessel.

§ 3. Assent to Indefinite or Incomplete Agreements

The realities of the agreement process (e.g., business constraints, time limitations, lack of complete knowledge) may lead to a "final agreement" that is incomplete in one or more ways. The cases in this section explore the degree of uncertainty that the courts will tolerate. Reluctance to enforce an indefinite agreement

Make the Connection

If a contract is formed despite the existence of uncertainties, the contested or missing terms of the contract will need to be ascertained by the rules governing interpretation of the contract. See Chapter 7, page 693.

arises from courts' concern the parties did not, in fact, reach agreement at all in light of the incompleteness, or that the agreement they reached leaves the court unable to determine how to enforce it.

The vast bulk of litigated cases arise from one or more of the following issues, which crop up with regularity:

- *Uncertain commitment to the deal*: A preliminary agreement, such as a "letter of intent" or a "memorandum of understanding," may reflect the parties' commitment to a deal that they will further define later. But sometimes the preliminary agreement reflects that one or both parties intend only to set up a framework for further negotiations, perhaps to enhance the chances of obtaining financing or to discourage competitors. How can a court distinguish between these two intents?
- *Vague terms*: The parties want to do business, but they have a difficult time bridging the gap between their views on one or more terms. Sometimes the parties try to solve that problem by drafting a clause that is intentionally vague. Sometimes the vagueness is unintentional, the result of inattention or sloppy drafting. How much vagueness will a court tolerate before it invalidates the parties' assent to the contract or determines that the vagueness signals that they have not truly reached agreement?
- *Missing terms*: The parties might (or might not) agree to a set of basic terms or some other preliminary agreement, but they never are able to come to agreement on additional terms of the contract or the terms are missing because of the parties' haste or because the parties did not foresee an issue arising. How much can the court fill in? Which terms must the parties agree to, in order to have the needed quantum of mutual assent? When is a contract not formed, for lack of assent to the core of the transaction?
- *Terms left for future resolution*: The parties need to agree on every aspect of their relationship. Some terms may be assigned to one party to resolve, or they can be left for future determination by both parties. Some terms can be filled in by default rules ("gapfillers"); others can be filled in by a court based on the context of the parties' transaction. But

other terms are so important and so undefinable that the lack of assent to them means that a contract was not formed. Where is the line to be drawn?

These issues illustrate the sometimes indistinct boundary between assent and non-assent. As the cases demonstrate, the standard for making the required judgment is difficult to articulate with precision.

Reading the Law Critically: *Quake Construction*

1. Which of the issues raised in the introductory note to this section (uncertain commitment, vague terms, missing terms, terms left for future resolution) does this case involve?

2. What factors does the court identify as relevant to determining whether the parties entered into a binding agreement?

3. What was the procedural posture of the trial court's ruling? How does that affect the standard of review on appeal?

4. Why is the case remanded to the trial court? What will happen on remand?

5. What important point(s) does the concurring opinion add?

Quake Construction v. American Airlines

QUAKE CONSTRUCTION, INC., Plaintiff-Appellee

v.

AMERICAN AIRLINES, INC., and JONES BROS. CONSTRUCTION CORP., Defendants-Appellants

Supreme Court of Illinois
565 N.E.2d 990 (Ill. 1990)

Justice CALVO delivered the opinion of the court:

Plaintiff, Quake Construction, Inc. (Quake), filed a . . . complaint against defendants, American Airlines, Inc. (American), and Jones Brothers Construction Corporation (Jones). In count I, plaintiff sought damages for breach of contract. . . . Upon defendants' motion, the circuit court of Cook County dismissed the complaint with prejudice . . . . On appeal, the Appellate Court reversed the dismissal . . . and remanded the cause to the circuit court. . . . We granted defendants' petition for leave to appeal . . . .

Quake alleged in its complaint the following facts. In February 1985, American hired Jones to prepare bid specifications, accept bids, and award contracts for construction of the expansion of American's facilities at O'Hare International Airport. Quake received an invitation to bid on the employee facilities and automotive maintenance shop project (hereinafter referred to as the project), and in April 1985 submitted its bid to Jones. Jones orally notified Quake that Quake had been awarded the contract for the project. Jones then asked Quake to provide the license numbers of the subcontractors Quake intended to use on the project. Quake notified Jones that the subcontractors would not allow Quake to use their license numbers until Quake submitted a signed subcontract agreement to them. Jones informed Quake that Quake would shortly receive a written contract for the project prepared by Jones. To induce Quake to enter into agreements with its subcontractors and to induce the subcontractors to provide Quake and Jones with their license numbers, Jones sent Quake the following letter of intent dated April 18, 1985:

"We have elected to award the contract for the subject project to your firm as we discussed on April 15, 1985. A contract agreement outlining the detailed terms and conditions is being prepared and will be available for your signature shortly.

Your scope of work as the general contractor includes the complete installation of expanded lunchroom, restroom and locker facilities for American Airlines employees as well as an expansion of American Airlines existing Automotive Maintenance Shop. The project is located on the lower level of 'K' Concourse. A sixty (60) calendar day period shall be allowed for the construction of the locker room, lunchroom and restroom area beginning the week of April 22, 1985. The entire project shall be complete by August 15, 1985.

> **See It!**
>
> The "K" Concourse is in Terminal 3 at O'Hare. For a map, see www. ohare.com/PDF/PassengerInformation/D32011terminal3.pdf.

Subject to negotiated modifications for exterior hollow metal doors and interior ceramic floor tile material as discussed, this notice of award authorizes the work set forth in the following documents at a lump sum price of $1,060,568.00.

a) Jones Brothers Invitation to Bid dated March 19, 1985.

b) Specifications as listed in the Invitation to Bid.

c) Drawings as listed in the Invitation to Bid.

d) Bid Addendum # 1 dated March 29, 1985.

Quake Construction Inc. shall provide evidence of liability insurance in the amount of $5,000,000 umbrella coverage and 100% performance and payment bond to Jones Brothers Construction Corporation before commencement of the work. The contract shall include MBE, WBE and EEO goals as established by your bid proposal. Accomplishment of the City of Chicago's residency goals as cited in the Invitation to Bid is also required. As agreed, certificates of commitment from those MBE firms designated on your proposal modification submitted April 13, 1985, shall be provided to Jones Brothers Construction Corporation.

Jones Brothers Construction Corporation reserves the right to cancel this letter of intent if the parties cannot agree on a fully executed subcontract agreement."

Make the Connection

As discussed later in Chapter 8, page 917, "cancellation" is a word usually used to identify a party's right, by law, to stop performing a contract because of the other party's total breach. Even though the agreement here reserves to Jones Brothers the right to "cancel" the letter of intent, the effect of the clause is to create a right to "terminate" the agreement upon occurrence of an event (the failure to execute a written contract). Recall the discussion of termination clauses in Chapter 2, page 103.

Jones and Quake thereafter discussed and orally agreed to certain changes in the written form contract. Handwritten delineations were made to the form contract by Jones and Quake to reflect these changes. Jones advised Quake it would prepare and send the written contract to Quake for Quake's signature. No such formal written contract, however, was entered into by the parties.

At a preconstruction meeting on April 25, 1985, Jones told Quake, Quake's subcontractors, and governmental officials present that Quake was the general contractor for the project. On that same date, immediately after the meeting, American informed Quake that Quake's involvement with the project was terminated. Jones confirmed Quake's termination by a letter dated April 25, 1985. The damages Quake allegedly suffered included the money it spent in procuring the contract and preparing to perform under the contract, and its loss of anticipated profit from the contract.

The main issue is whether the letter of intent from Jones to Quake is an enforceable contract such that a cause of action may be brought by Quake. This court has previously set forth the principles of law concerning the enforceability of letters of intent:

"The fact that parties contemplate that a formal agreement will eventually be executed does not necessarily render prior agreements mere negotiations, where it is clear that the ultimate contract will be substantially based upon the same terms as the previous document. . . . If the parties . . . intended that the . . . document be contractually binding, that intention would not be defeated by the mere recitation in the writing that a more formal agreement was yet to be drawn. However, parties may specifically provide that negotiations are not binding until a formal agreement is in fact executed. . . . If the parties construe the execution of a formal agreement as a condition precedent, then no contract arises unless and until that formal agreement is executed."

Chicago Investment Corp. v. Dolins (1985), 107 Ill.2d 120, 126-27, 89 Ill.Dec. 869, 481 N.E.2d 712. . . . Thus, although letters of intent may be enforceable, such letters are not necessarily enforceable unless the parties intend them to be contractually binding. . . .

. . . . If the language of an alleged contract is ambiguous regarding the parties' intent, the interpretation of the language is a question of fact which a circuit court cannot properly determine on a motion to dismiss. . . .

(handwritten margin note, left:) practice shift to court if already going to court to ford

(handwritten margin note, bottom left:) if language too ambiguous court can't make choice

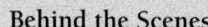

Behind the Scenes

This is admittedly an odd termination, occurring so soon after Quake's bid was selected and immediately after Jones confirmed Quake as the contractor. Research turned up no explanation for this termination, but Chicago newspapers discussed the pressures to include minority and local contractors, bribery convictions of an alderman and a board member on the Chicago Transit Authority, and pressure to optimize the project budget and accompanying bonding.* How might such facts help explain the timing of the termination?

(handwritten margin note, right:) why cancelled?

What's That?

A "condition precedent" is an event that must occur in order for a contract to be formed or in order for a performance duty to arise within a contract. Conditions precedent to contract formation are rarer than conditions precedent to contract performance, but the former nonetheless arise in situations such as the case quoted here. Chapters 7 and 8 cover express and implied conditions, respectively.

---

* Dean Baquet & Douglas Frantz, *Politically Linked Georgia Firm Key to O'Hare Contracts,* Feb. 24, 1985, at 1; Editorial, *Getting It Right at O'Hare,* Chi. Trib., April 18, 1986, at 18; John Gorman, *Ex-Ald. Humes Admits Taking Series of Bribes,* Chi. Trib., May 2, 1989, at 3; Joel Kaplan & James Strong, *Medley's Conviction Casts Cloud over O'Hare Pact,* Chi. Trib., Aug. 31, 1989, at 22.

In determining whether the parties intended to reduce their agreement to writing, the following factors may be considered: whether the type of agreement involved is one usually put into writing, whether the agreement contains many or few details, whether the agreement involves a large or small amount of money, whether the agreement requires a formal writing for the full expression of the covenants, and whether the negotiations indicated that a formal written document was contemplated at the completion of the negotiations. (*Ceres*, 114 Ill.2d at 144, 102 Ill.Dec. 379, 500 N.E.2d 1 . . . .) Other factors which may be considered are: "where in the negotiating process that process is abandoned, the reasons it is abandoned, the extent of the assurances previously given by the party which now disclaims any contract, and the other party's reliance upon the anticipated completed transaction." *A/S Apothekernes Laboratorium for Specialpraeparater v. I.M.C. Chemical Group, Inc.* (N.D.Ill.1988), 678 F.Supp. 193, 196, *aff'd* (7th Cir.1989), 873 F.2d 155.

. . . .

The circuit court in the case at bar dismissed Quake's complaint, relying principally on the following sentence in the letter: "Jones Brothers Construction Corporation reserves the right to cancel this letter of intent if the parties cannot agree on a fully executed subcontract agreement" (hereinafter referred to as the cancellation clause). The parties agreed during oral arguments that the subcontract agreement referred to in the cancellation clause concerned an agreement between Jones and Quake. Jones was the general contractor for the entire expansion project. Jones hired Quake as a subcontractor to handle only the work on the employee facilities and automotive shop. Quake, in turn, hired subcontractors to perform this work. The circuit court determined, based on the cancellation clause, that the parties agreed not to be bound until they entered into a formal written contract. Consequently, the circuit court held that the letter was not an enforceable contract and accordingly dismissed the complaint.

The appellate court, however, found the letter ambiguous. . . .

. . . .

We agree with the appellate court majority's analysis and its conclusion that the letter was ambiguous. Consequently, we affirm the decision of the appellate court. The letter of intent included detailed terms of the parties' agreement. The letter stated that Jones awarded the contract for the project to Quake. The letter stated further "this notice of award authorizes the work." Moreover, the letter indicated the work was to commence approximately 4 to 11 days after the letter was written. This short period of time reveals the parties' intent to be bound by the letter so the work could begin on schedule. We also agree with the appellate court that the cancellation clause exhibited the parties' intent to be bound by the letter because no need would exist to provide for the cancellation of the letter unless the letter had some binding effect. The cancellation clause also implied the parties' intention to be bound by the letter at least until they entered into the formal contract. We agree with the appellate court that all of these factors evinced the parties' intent to be bound by the letter.

On the other hand, the letter referred several times to the execution of a formal contract by the parties, thus indicating the parties' intent not to be bound by the letter. The cancellation clause could be interpreted to mean that the parties did not intend to be bound until they entered into a formal agreement. Therefore, the appellate court correctly concluded that the letter was ambiguous regarding the parties' intent to be bound by it.

Defendants contend the letter of intent did not contain all of the terms necessary for the formation of a construction contract. Defendants assert construction contracts typically include terms regarding payment, damages and termination. Defendants argue the detail in the contract is usually extensive if the value and complexity of the construction project are great. Defendants also note the letter stated the contract would include the detailed terms and conditions of the parties' agreement. The letter indicated *the contract* would include the MBE, WBE and EEO (Minority Business Enterprise, Women's Business Enterprise, and Equal Employment Opportunity, respectively) goals established by Quake's bid proposal. Defendants point out the letter stated certain terms of the agreement still had to be negotiated. Without the formal contract, defendants assert, the parties could not have continued toward the completion of the project because the letter excluded many terms of the agreement which would have been included in the contract. Defendants thus argue the absence in the letter of all the terms of the agreement reveals the parties' intent not to be bound by the letter.

The appellate court stated the number and extent of the terms in the letter can indicate the parties' intent to be bound by the letter. The final contract only need be *substantially based* on the terms in the letter as long as the parties intended the letter to be binding. (*Chicago*, 107 Ill.2d at 126-27, 89 Ill.Dec. 869, 481 N.E.2d 712.) Many of the details regarding the project were included in the letter. The letter adopted by reference the contents of certain documents which included even further details concerning the project. We agree Jones accepted the MBE, WBE and EEO goals established by Quake. The letter merely indicated that those goals would be reiterated in the contract. We acknowledge that the absence of certain terms in the letter indicates the parties' intent not to be bound by the letter. This only confirms our holding that the letter is ambiguous as to the parties' intent.

. . . .

Defendants contend even if the letter contained all of the essential terms of a contract, the cancellation clause negated any inference that the parties intended to be bound by the letter. The clause, according to defendants, clearly established the parties' intent not to be so bound. Defendants argue the letter only sets forth the provisions which would be included in the contract if one is ever executed. Defendants point out both the circuit court and the appellate court dissent found the cancellation clause unambiguously declared the parties' intent not to be bound until the parties entered into a formal contract.

We do not find defendants' argument persuasive. The appellate court stated that, in addition to the detailed terms of the parties' agreement, the letter also contained a sentence in which Jones said it awarded the contract for the project to Quake. Moreover, the letter stated "this notice of award *authorizes* the work." (Emphasis added.) Furthermore, the appellate court pointed out, the letter was dated April 18, while at the same time the letter indicated that Quake was to begin work the week of April 22 and complete the work by August 15. We agree with the appellate court's conclusion that a "reasonable inference from these facts is that the parties intended that work on the Project would begin prior to execution of a formal contract and would be governed by the terms of the 'Letter of Intent.'" (181 Ill.App.3d at 914, 130 Ill.Dec. 534, 537 N.E.2d 863.) All of these factors indicate the negotiations were more than merely preliminary and the parties intended the letter to be binding. The factors muddle whatever otherwise "clear" intent may be derived from the cancellation clause.

Defendants acknowledge the letter was dated April 18 and it stated the work would commence the week of April 22. Defendants point out that the letter also indicated Jones would submit a formal contract to Quake "shortly." Defendants argue a contract could conceivably have been written and signed within that period of time. Defendants conclude the appellate court's assumption regarding the date of the letter and the commencement of the work was invalid. While defendants' interpretation of these facts is plausible, we believe it only lends credence to our conclusion the letter is ambiguous concerning the parties' intent. Thus, the trier of fact should decide which interpretation is valid.

. . . .

Defendants further contend that the cancellation clause is not ambiguous. Defendants assert parties may agree, in a letter of intent, to the course of, and discontinuance of, their negotiations. Defendants argue the letter of intent in the case at bar merely reflects the parties' agreement regarding the course of their negotiations.

We, like the appellate court, find the cancellation clause itself ambiguous as to the parties' intent. We do not agree with defendants' assertion that the cancellation clause so clearly indicates the parties' intent not to be bound by the letter that the clause negates other evidence in the letter of the parties' intent to be bound. The clause can be construed as a condition precedent to the formation of a contract. The clause, however, also states that Jones can "cancel" the letter. As the appellate court noted, if the parties did not intend to be bound by the letter, they had no need to provide for its cancellation. We also agree with the appellate court that the cancellation clause "implies that the parties could be bound by the 'Letter of Intent' in the absence of a fully executed subcontract agreement." (181 Ill.App.3d at 914, 130 Ill.Dec. 534, 537 N.E.2d 863.) Thus, the ambiguity within the cancellation clause itself enhances the other ambiguities in the letter.

. . . .

Defendants allege that the appellate court's decision puts the continued viability of letters of intent at risk. Defendants contend if we uphold the appellate court's decision finding the cancellation clause ambiguous, negotiating parties will have difficulty finding limiting language which a court would unquestionably consider unambiguous. We disagree. Courts have found letters of intent unambiguous in several cases referred to in this opinion. (See *Interway*, 85 Ill.App.3d 1094, 41 Ill.Dec. 117, 407 N.E.2d 615 . . . .) Furthermore, contract cases each turn on their own particular set of facts. . . . Thus, the existence or absence of particular language or words will not ensure that a letter of intent is unambiguous. Our decision here follows the settled law in Illinois concerning letters of intent: The intent of the parties is controlling.

Neither we nor the appellate court have decided whether in fact a contract exists, that is, whether the parties intended to be bound by the letter. We merely hold that the parties' intent, based on the letter alone, is ambiguous. Therefore, upon remand, the circuit court must allow the parties to present other evidence of their intent. The trier of fact should then determine, based on the evidence and the letter, whether the parties intended to be bound by the letter.

. . . .

For the foregoing reasons, we affirm the decision of the appellate court.

Affirmed.

Justice STAMOS, specially concurring:

Because dismissal is unwarranted unless clearly no set of facts can be proved under the pleadings that will entitle a plaintiff to recover, I agree with the majority that the circuit court should not have dismissed [count I of] Quake's complaint. . . .

Instead of weighing as heavily for as against a construction contract, in my judgment the cancellation clause powerfully militates against any finding of such contract. . . .

The cancellation clause refers expressly to cancelling the *letter*, not to cancelling the construction contract that the letter anticipates. A construction contract certainly would bind the parties to that contract's terms, but upon acceptance by Quake the letter here would much more plausibly be viewed as, at most, only binding the parties to efforts at achieving a construction contract on the terms outlined. See, *e.g.*, *Evans, Inc. v. Tiffany & Co.* (N.D.Ill.1976), 416 F.Supp. 224 (obligation to negotiate derived from unclear letter of intent); see also *Precontractual Liability*, 87 Colum.L.Rev. at 250-69 (discussing letters of intent classified as "agreements with open terms" and "agreements to negotiate"); Knapp, *Enforcing the Contract to Bargain*, 44 N.Y.U.L.Rev. 673 (1969) (discussing need for recognizing good-faith bargaining duty as intermediate stage between ultimate contract and none); *cf.* Shell, *Substituting Ethical Standards for Common Law Rules in Commercial Cases: An Emerging Statutory Trend*, 82 Nw. U. L. Rev. 1198, 1199 & n.7 (1988) (noting case law on duty of good-faith negotiation pursuant to letters of intent).

. . . .

Hence, the letter itself, as distinguished from the anticipated construction contract, may be regarded as a contract in its own right: a contract to engage in negotiations. If so, it was this contract, not the anticipated construction contract, that might be cancelled by Jones pursuant to the cancellation clause. Indeed, the notion of cancelling a construction contract not yet entered into lacks meaning.

. . . .

. . . Yet, one might ask in reply: If the letter required only an effort to achieve a construction contract, and if failure of the effort would necessarily prevent any such contract from arising to bind the parties, how could the issue of cancelling a mere letter ever take on enough significance to explain inclusion of the cancellation clause? . . .

. . . .

. . . [S]everal hypotheses suggest themselves for explaining the present letter of intent's cancellation clause:

> Because the letter can be regarded as creating an obligation on Jones to attempt to achieve a construction contract, existence of the clause might be explained as a device by which Jones could put an end to its obligation to negotiate.

The fact that this letter, like many others, was intended to induce action by third parties furnishes another possible explanation for including the cancellation clause: It would give Jones a way to put an end to any further inducement based on Jones' once-expressed intention.

A third possible explanation lies in the possibility that, as a result of the parties' subsequent conduct (such as commencement of construction work by Quake), an uncancelled letter of intent might become a link in a chain leading to a finding of contract.

Still another possible explanation lies in the fact that, commercially if not legally, letters of intent have a certain weight as trustworthy indicators of business decisions; accordingly, an issuer might wish to cancel a letter once a decision had changed, in order not to mislead those who might otherwise rely on it.

Any or all of these possibilities would adequately explain the clause, without any need whatever to conclude that the clause betokens an intent to be bound to a construction contract thought to be embodied in the letter. See also *Precontractual Liability*, 87 Colum.L.Rev. at 257-58 (discussing other possible rationales for clause).

If letters of intent are to be used, their drafters would be well advised to avoid ambiguity on the point of whether the issuers are bound. As ever, obscurantist language can produce desired practical effects in the short term, but can well lead eventually to litigation and undesired contractual obligations. Extreme examples exist. (See, *e.g.*, Note, *The $10.53 Billion Question—When Are the Parties Bound?: Pennzoil and the Use of Agreements in Principle in Mergers and Acquisitions*, 40 Vand.L.Rev. 1367 (1987).) Some counsel and clients may opt for ambiguity on grounds of expediency and may account for the probability of resultant litigation costs in the clients' overall business decisionmaking, but many others could benefit from more precision. In turn, counsel for recipients of such letters should remain alert to the likelihood that the instruments lack contractual force.

. . . .

The *Pennzoil* Case

The "extreme example" of "undesired contractual obligations" cited by Justice Stamos in the final paragraph of the opinion is the case of *Texaco, Inc. v. Pennzoil Co.*, 729 S.W.2d 768 (Tex. Ct. App. 1987), *cert. denied*, 485 U.S. 994 (1988). The multi-billion dollar verdict in *Pennzoil* turned on a question of fact: whether Pennzoil's "agreement in principle" to merge with Getty Oil was a contract, despite the absence of an executed final writing. After the "agreement in principle" was made, Texaco tried to acquire Getty Oil for a higher price, and Pennzoil sued Texaco for tortious interference with Pennzoil's contract rights. (Of course, there could be no tortious interference with contract rights if no contract had been formed between Pennzoil and Getty.) Texaco paid Pennzoil $7.3 billion in compensatory damages and $1 billion in punitive damages—the largest civil judgment in history to that date. Much has been written on the dispute and the resulting rounds of litigation. For a small taste of the commentary, *see* T. Petzinger, *Oil & Honor: The Texaco-Pennzoil Wars* (1987); **Stephen M. Bundy**, *Commentary on "Understanding Pennzoil v. Texaco": Rational Bargaining and Agency Problems*, **75 Va. L. Rev.** 335 (1989); **David A. Lax**, *Commentary on 'Understanding Pennzoil v. Texaco': Market Expectations of Bargaining Inefficiency and Potential Roles for External Parties in Disputes between Publicly Traded Companies*, **75 Va. L. Rev.** 367 (1989); **Robert H. Mnookin**, *Rational Bargaining and Market Efficiency: Understanding Pennzoil v. Texaco*, **75 Va. L. Rev.** 295 (1989).

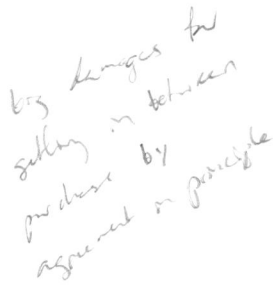

Reading the Law Critically: *Academy Chicago Publishers*

1. Which of the issues raised in the introductory note to this section (uncertain commitment, vague terms, missing terms, terms left for future resolution) does this case involve?

2. What terms were "missing" from the agreement? Which were filled in by the trial court? What changes did the intermediate appellate court make in the resulting agreement? Why?

3. What guidance does this opinion furnish regarding whether an agreement is too indefinite to be a valid contract and whether a court should fill in terms? Do you agree with the court's ruling? Why or why not?

Academy Chicago Publishers v. Cheever

ACADEMY CHICAGO PUBLISHERS, Plaintiff-Appellant

v.

MARY W. CHEEVER, Defendant-Appellee

Supreme Court of Illinois
578 N.E.2d 981 (Ill. 1991)

Justice **HEIPLE** delivered the opinion of the court:

What's That?

A party brings a suit for "declaratory judgment" in order to ask a court to determine the parties' rights and duties in advance of a breach or other action resulting in possible liability.

This is a suit for declaratory judgment. It arose out of an agreement between the widow of the widely published author, John Cheever, and Academy Chicago Publishers. Contact between the parties began in 1987 when the publisher approached Mrs. Cheever about the possibility of publishing a collection of Mr. Cheever's short stories which, though previously published, had never been collected into a single anthology. In August of that year, a publishing agreement was signed which provided, in pertinent part:

> "Agreement made this 15th day of August 1987, between Academy Chicago Publishers or any affiliated entity or imprint (hereinafter referred to as the Publisher) and Mary W. Cheever and Franklin H. Dennis of the USA (hereinafter referred to as Author).
>
> Whereas the parties are desirous of publishing and having published a certain work or works, tentatively titled *The Uncollected Stories of John Cheever* (hereinafter referred to as the Work):
>
> . . . .
>
> 2. The Author will deliver to the Publisher on a mutually agreeable date one copy of the manuscript of the Work as finally arranged by the editor and satisfactory to the Publisher in form and content.
>
> . . . .
>
> 5. Within a reasonable time and a mutually agreeable date after delivery of the final revised manuscript, the Publisher will publish the Work at its

own expense, in such style and manner and at such price as it deems best, and will keep the Work in print as long as it deems it expedient; but it will not be responsible for delays caused by circumstances beyond its control."

Academy and its editor, Franklin Dennis, assumed the task of locating and procuring the uncollected stories and delivering them to Mrs. Cheever. Mrs. Cheever and Mr. Dennis received partial advances for manuscript preparation. By the end of 1987, Academy had located and delivered more than 60 uncollected stories to Mrs. Cheever. Shortly thereafter, Mrs. Cheever informed Academy in writing that she objected to the publication of the book and attempted to return her advance.

Academy filed suit in the circuit court of Cook County in February 1988, seeking a declaratory judgment: (1) granting Academy the exclusive right to publish the tentatively titled, "The Uncollected Stories of John Cheever"; (2) designating Franklin Dennis as the book's editor; and (3) obligating Mrs. Cheever to deliver the manuscript from which the work was to be published.

> **Who's That?**
>
> John Cheever (1912-1982) is recognized as one of the most important fiction writers of the twentieth century. He was awarded the Pulitzer Prize for Fiction, the National Book Critics Circle Award, and the National Medal for Literature. For more information about his works and his role in American literature, see www.todayinliterature.com/biography/john.cheever.asp.

The trial court entered an order declaring, *inter alia:* (1) that the publishing agreement executed by the parties was valid and enforceable; (2) that Mrs. Cheever was entitled to select the short stories to be included in the manuscript for publication; (3) that Mrs. Cheever would comply with her obligations of good faith and fair dealing if she delivered a manuscript including at least 10 to 15 stories totaling at least 140 pages; (4) Academy controlled the design and format of the work to be published, but control must be exercised in cooperation with Mrs. Cheever.

Academy appealed the trial court's order, challenging particularly the declaration regarding the minimum story and page numbers for Mrs. Cheever's compliance with the publishing agreement, and the declaration that Academy must consult with defendant on all matters of publication of the manuscript.

just page #'s

no to mrs. Cheev

The appellate court affirmed the decision of the trial court with respect to the validity and enforceability of the publishing agreement and the minimum story and page number requirements for Mrs. Cheever's compliance with same. The appellate court reversed the trial court's declaration regarding control of publication, stating that the trial court erred in considering extrinsic evidence to interpret the agreement regarding control of the publication, given the explicit language of the agreement granting exclusive control to Academy. **(200 Ill.App.3d 677, 146 Ill.Dec. 386, 558 N.E.2d 349.)**

Make the Connection

Chapter 7 (page 693) includes coverage of when extrinsic evidence is admissible to interpret explicit language of a written agreement.

The parties raise several issues on appeal; this matter, however, is one of contract and we confine our discussion to the issue of the validity and enforceability of the publishing agreement.

While the trial court and the appellate court agreed that the publishing agreement constitutes a valid and enforceable contract, we cannot concur. The principles of contract state that in order for a valid contract to be formed, an "offer must be so definite as to its material terms or require such definite terms in the acceptance that the promises and performances to be rendered by each party are reasonably certain." (1 Williston, Contracts §§ 38 through 48 (3d ed. 1957); 1 Corbin, Contracts §§ 95 through 100 (1963).) Although the parties may have had and manifested the intent to make a contract, if the content of their agreement is unduly uncertain and indefinite no contract is formed. 1 Williston § 37; 1 Corbin § 95.

too much preliminary stuff to make a contract real

The pertinent language of this agreement lacks the definite and certain essential terms required for the formation of an enforceable contract. (*Midland Hotel Corp. v. Reuben H. Donnelley Corp.* (1987), 118 Ill.2d 306, 113 Ill.Dec. 252, 515 N.E.2d 61.) A contract "is sufficiently definite and certain to be enforceable if the court is enabled from the terms and provisions thereof, under proper rules of construction and applicable principles of equity, to ascertain what the parties have agreed to do. (*Morey v. Hoffman* (1957), 12 Ill.2d 125, 145 N.E.2d 644.) The provisions of the subject publishing agreement do not provide the court with a means of determining the intent of the parties.

nothing about pages

Trial testimony reveals that a major source of controversy between the parties is the length and content of the proposed book. The agreement sheds no light on the minimum or maximum number of stories or pages necessary for publication of the collection, nor is there any implicit language from which we can glean the intentions of the parties with respect to this essential contract term. The publishing agreement is similarly silent with respect to who will decide which stories will be included in the collection. Other omissions, ambiguities, unresolved essential

no debts either (handwritten)

terms and illusory terms are: No date certain for delivery of the manuscript. No definition of the criteria which would render the manuscript satisfactory to the publisher either as to form or content. No date certain as to when publication will occur. No certainty as to style or manner in which the book will be published nor is there any indication as to the price at which such book will be sold, or the length of time publication shall continue, all of which terms are left to the sole discretion of the publisher.

Think About It!

Why do you think the parties structured the agreement as they did? What advantages did the flexible terms provide? How might parties retain this flexibility while also having a valid contract? How much *can* be left to the sole discretion of one party?

A contract may be enforced even though some contract terms may be missing or left to be agreed upon, but if the essential terms are so uncertain that there is no basis for deciding whether the agreement has been kept or broken, there is no contract. (*Champaign National Bank v. Landers Seed Co.* (1988), 165 Ill.App.3d 1090, 116 Ill.Dec. 742, 519 N.E.2d 957; Restatement (Second) of Contracts § 33 (1981).) Without setting forth adequate terms for compliance, the publishing agreement provides no basis for determining when breach has occurred, and, therefore, is not a valid and enforceable contract.

An enforceable contract must include a meeting of the minds or mutual assent as to the terms of the contract. (*Midland Hotel*, 118 Ill.2d at 313, 113 Ill. Dec. 252, 515 N.E.2d 61.) It is not compelling that the parties share a subjective understanding as to the terms of the contract; the parties' conduct may indicate an agreement to the terms of same. (*Steinberg v. Chicago Medical School* (1977), 69 Ill.2d 320, 13 Ill.Dec. 699, 371 N.E.2d 634.) In the instant case, however, no mutual assent has been illustrated. The parties did not and do not share a common understanding of the essential terms of the publishing agreement.

In rendering its judgment, the trial court supplied minimum terms for Mrs. Cheever's compliance, including story and page numbers. It is not uncommon for a court to supply a missing material term, as the reasonable conclusion often is that the parties intended that the term be supplied by implication. However, where the subject matter of the contract has not been decided upon and there is no standard available for reasonable implication, courts ordinarily refuse to supply the missing term. (1 Williston § 42; 1 Corbin § 100.) No suitable standard was available for the trial court to apply. It is our opinion that the trial court incorrectly supplied minimum compliance terms to the publishing agreement, as the agreement did not consti-

supply missing term? (handwritten)

Think About It!

Might the *Quake Construction* lawsuit (page 249) on remand suffer the same fate as the *Cheever* lawsuit?

tute a valid and enforceable contract to begin with. As noted above, the publishing agreement contains major unresolved uncertainties. It is not the role of the court to rewrite the contract and spell out essential elements not included therein.

In light of our decision that there was no valid and enforceable contract between the parties, we need not address other issues raised on appeal. For the foregoing reasons, the decisions of the trial and appellate courts in this declaratory judgment action are reversed.

Reversed.

Justices **CLARK** and **FREEMAN** took no part in the consideration or decision of this opinion.

Behind the Scenes

The Cheever litigation took four years and raged across four courtrooms and twelve state and federal courts in New York and Illinois. As described by the lawyers who represented Mrs. Cheever: "The fight was unusually fierce, even by today's litigation standards. Academy referred to the Cheever family as 'venal people' and 'a traveling freak show,' while Academy's own executives were likened in the news media to grave robbers and rapists. After Academy's loss of its last appeal, what remained was a nationwide injunction issued by the federal court in New York, barring Academy from publishing an anthology of 68 previously uncollected Cheever stories, which Academy had hoped would be a blockbuster book, but which *The Washington Post* characterized as 'a literary scavenger job.'"* The case's biggest irony was that the Cheever family won a complete victory but conceded in 1988 that it would have to compile a book similar to the one that Academy Chicago Publishers originally envisioned in order to recover the family's legal costs.**

---

* *See* SmithDehn LLP, Overview: *Cheever v. Academy Chicago Publishers,* www.smithdornanshea.com/RealTime.cgi?case_id=cheever_v_academy&merge=cases|description. (site unavailable at time of this book's second edition).
** *See* David Streitfeld, *Cheevers, Publisher End Fight,* Washington Post, Jan. 25, 1992, *available at* www.smithdornanshea.com/RealTime.cgi?case_id=cheever_v_academy&category=MEDIA+COVERAGE&doc_id=19920125-cheevers_publish&merge=cases|document. For more information, see John Blades, *Cheever's Chaff: Cheever v. Academy Chicago Publishers,* Chicago Tribune, Feb. 27, 1989, *available at* www.smithdornanshea.com/RealTime.cgi?case_id=cheever_v_academy&category=MEDIA+COVERAGE&doc_id=19890227-cheevers_chaff&merge=cases|document; James Warren, *Contract Dispute: Publishers Tell Judge He Doesn't Get It, But Authors Say He Does,* Chicago Tribune, Sept. 1, 1991, *available at* www.smithdornanshea.com/RealTime.cgi?case_id=cheever_v_academy&category=MEDIA+COVERAGE&doc_id=19910901-contract_dispute&merge=cases|document.

Jordan and Anita Miller, the principals in Academy Chicago Publishers, maintained throughout the litigation and afterwards that their agreement with Mary Cheever reflected the level of specificity and flexibility needed and generally recognized as reasonable in the publishing world, and that their small publishing house was being bullied by those with more resources. See Anita Miller, *Uncollecting Cheever: The Family of John Cheever vs. Academy Chicago Publishers* (1998). Richard Dooling, in his review of Miller's book in the New York Times, said the circumstances seemed "more like the tale of a small publisher that carelessly drafted an important contract (without consulting a lawyer) and the family of a renowned author who foolishly signed it (without consulting a lawyer). Then both parties called in lawyers and fought for four years to best each other in a species of combat that differs from violence only insofar as there is usually no bloodshed in litigation. Perhaps both sides now appreciate Voltaire's observation: "I was never ruined but twice, once when I lost a lawsuit and once when I won one." Richard Dooling, "*The 5:48 is Cancelled*," at www. nytimes.com/books/98/12/27/reviews/981227.27doolint.html. Academy Chicago Publishers survived the ordeal and continues to publish new titles, including John Cheever, *Fall River and Other Uncollected Stories*, published in 2009 when the stories reverted to the public domain. See www.academychicago.com/newsite/.

Reading the Law Critically: *B. Lewis Productions, Inc.*

1. Which of the issues raised in the introductory note (insufficient commitment, vague terms, missing terms, terms left for future resolution) does this case involve?

2. Does the court lean toward or against enforcing contracts, as a matter of policy? What facts serve to persuade the court to enforce the contract?

3. How does the court deal with each of the identified gaps in the parties' agreement?

4. The court finds that the contracting parties owe each other a duty of good faith and fair dealing in their performance of the contract. What role does that finding play in establishing the validity of the contract?

B. Lewis Productions v. Angelou

B. LEWIS PRODUCTIONS, INC., Plaintiff

v.

MAYA ANGELOU and HALLMARK CARDS, INC., Defendants

United States District Court, Southern District of New York
2005 WL 1138474 (S.D.N.Y. May 12, 2005)

MUKASEY, J.

Plaintiff B. Lewis Productions, Inc. (BLP) sues defendant Maya Angelou for breach of contract and breach of the duty of good faith and fair dealing. BLP also sues defendant Hallmark Cards, Inc. for tortious interference with BLP's alleged contract with Angelou. . . . Jurisdiction is based on diversity of citizenship. Defendants Angelou and Hallmark move for summary judgment. For the reasons set forth below, both motions are denied.

I.

Who's That?

Dr. Maya Angelou has been recognized as a leading and influential poet and memoirist. She holds 36 honorary degrees and two Grammy Awards for Best Spoken Word Album. In 1999 she received a Lifetime Achievement Award for Literature and was named one of the top 100 best writers of the 20th century by Writer's Digest. She was chosen by President Bill Clinton to recite her poem "On the Pulse of the Morning" during his 1993 inauguration. For further information, see Dr. Angelou's official website, www.mayaangelou.com.

. . . .

Butch Lewis is the president and sole owner of plaintiff corporation B. Lewis Productions, Inc. BLP's business consists primarily of promoting boxing and other sports and entertainment events. Defendant Maya Angelou, a resident of North Carolina, is a renowned poet. Defendant Hallmark Cards, Incorporated, a Missouri corporation, manufactures greeting cards and related products. In this action, BLP claims that Angelou breached an agreement in which she granted BLP the exclusive right to exploit her original literary works for publication in greeting cards and similar products. . . .

Lewis and Angelou became acquainted in early 1994 when, at Lewis's request, Angelou visited Mike Tyson at an Indiana prison. . . . At that meeting, Angelou and Lewis discussed how she might reach a broader base of readers by publishing her works in greeting cards. . . . Several months after this initial meeting, Lewis met with Angelou at her North Carolina home to discuss a potential collaboration between Angelou and BLP to market Angelou's works to greeting card companies. . . . In November 1994, Lewis and Angelou signed a "letter agreement" that established what the letter called a "Joint Venture" to publish Angelou's writings in greeting cards and other media forms. The letter agreement, dated November 22, 1994 and signed by both parties, reads as follows:

> This letter agreement made between B. LEWIS PRODUCTIONS, INC. (BLP) with offices at 250 West 57th Street, New York, N.Y. 10019 and MAYA ANGELOU (ANGELOU) whose address is 2720 Reynolda Road, Suite # 1, Winston-Salem, NC 27106, sets forth the understandings of the parties with reference to the following:
>
> 1. The parties will enter into a Joint Venture (Venture), wherein ANGELOU will exclusively contribute original literary works (Property) to the Venture and BLP will seek to exploit the rights for publishing of said Property in all media forms including, but not limited to greeting cards, stationery and calendars, etc.
>
> 2. BLP will contribute all the capital necessary to fund the operation of the Venture.
>
> 3. ANGELOU will contribute, on an exclusive basis, original literary works to the Venture after consultations with and mutual agreement of Butch Lewis, who will be the managing partner of the Venture.
>
> 4. The Venture shall own the copyrights to all of ANGELOU's contributions to the Venture.
>
> > (a) If any of the subject copyrights do not produce any income for a consecutive five (5) year period as a result of the exploitation referred to [in] paragraph 1 herein then the ownership of these copyrights shall revert to Angelou exclusively.
>
> 5. The name of the Venture shall be mutually agreed upon.
>
> 6. Gross Revenue shall be distributed and applied in the following order:
>
> > (a) Return of BLP's capital contribution.
> >
> > (b) Reimbursement of any and all expenses of the Venture.
> >
> > (c) Balance (net profits) to be shared equally between BLP and ANGELOU.
> >
> > (d) ANGELOU shall have the right at any time, upon reasonable notice, to inspect all records including but not limited to the financial records of the Venture.
>
> This Agreement shall be binding upon the parties until a more formal detailed agreement is signed.

(Inwald Aff., Ex. F)

In late 1994, BLP began to market Angelou's work to Hallmark and several other greeting card companies. Lewis began to negotiate a license agreement with Hallmark on Angelou's behalf. When Hallmark asked Lewis for confirmation that he was indeed authorized to act on Angelou's behalf, on June 19, 1996, Lewis sent Hallmark a letter signed by Angelou that stated:

> This will confirm that BUTCH LEWIS PRODUCTIONS, INC. (BLP) has the exclusive right to represent DR. MAYA ANGELOU for the exploitation of her work product in the area of greeting cards, stationery, calendars, etc. as per the contract executed by BLP and Dr. Angelou dated November 22, 1994 which is still in full force and effect.

. . . . BLP declined to send Hallmark the November 22, 1994 agreement itself because Lewis wanted to keep its terms confidential. . . .

In March 1997, after extended negotiations, Hallmark sent BLP a license agreement for the use of Angelou's future exclusive works which would have paid her and BLP 9% of gross revenues from sales of licensed products, with a $50,000 advance payment and a guaranteed minimum $100,000 in royalties. . . . Angelou's greeting cards would be administered through Hallmark's Ethnic Business Center. . . .

Who's That?

Ronald "Butch" Lewis was a boxing promoter who passed away in 2011. A former car salesman, Lewis grew up in Philadelphia, was always fascinated by boxing, and became a close friend and associate of Joe Frazier and Muhammad Ali. In 1988, Lewis negotiated one of the largest guaranteed paydays, $13.5 million, in boxing history for Michael Spinks' fight against Mike Tyson. Lewis made his foray into the entertainment world in 1991, producing cable and feature films through his Butch Lewis Productions. He later started a partnership with Universal's Island Def Jam Music Group to create a record label, Voicez.

Also in March 1997, Lewis and Angelou encountered one another at an event in Las Vegas, where Angelou saw Lewis, who is black, punctuate a conversation with white people by grabbing his crotch. . . . After she witnessed Lewis's behavior, Angelou "burned up his ears.". . . She claims that she told him that the "venture" between them was off, and that she no longer wanted to work with him. . . . Lewis denies that Angelou made any such comment at the time.

However, when Lewis forwarded the Hallmark license agreement to Angelou, she did not sign it, and later told her literary agent Helen Brann to "start putting a little cold water on the prospect of this deal with Hallmark.". . . After meeting with Lewis and his associate Joy Farrell, Brann sent a letter to Lewis on May 5, 1997, informing him "that it is not going to work out now for Dr. Maya Angelou to make any deal with Hallmark Cards."

In her letter, Brann cited Angelou's commitment to Random House as the publisher of all of Angelou's "major work" as a reason for not proceeding with Hallmark. Brann noted that "[n]either Dr. Angelou nor I like to say never, and I suppose that sometime in the future we might all figure out a way, in cooperation with Random House and Hallmark and us, to launch some kind of greeting card program, but this year is definitely not the year to contemplate such a move.". . .

Lewis claims that at a later meeting in 1997, Angelou told him that she would sign the licensing agreement with Hallmark "after the New Year," and that in February 1998, she told him she was planning to sign the agreement "as soon as she [got] everything off her table." (Lewis Dep. at 144-50) However Angelou did not sign the Hallmark licensing agreement. . . . Additionally, because Hallmark did not hear from Lewis after it sent him the licensing agreement in 1997, Hallmark executives eventually concluded that the collaboration between BLP and Angelou was "dead.". . .

Hallmark wrote Angelou's agent Brann in March 1998 to inquire whether Angelou was still interested in pursuing a program of greeting cards, stating that its "discussions with Mr. Lewis ended in early 1997 when he could not deliver a program.". . . Brann responded that Angelou was not interested in entering into an agreement with Hallmark at that time. . . . However, in June 1999, Angelou's close friend Amelia Parker, who was acquainted with an executive at Hallmark, convinced Angelou to have lunch with Hallmark executives at the company's St. Louis headquarters when Angelou was in town for an unrelated speaking engagement. . . . Angelou was encouraged by this meeting and decided to try to arrange a licensing deal with Hallmark. . . .

Simultaneously, Angelou sought to assure that her ties to Lewis were severed. On June 16, 1999 Angelou's North Carolina counsel sent a letter to BLP stating that "any business relationship that you may have had or contemplated pursuant to a letter dated November 22, 1994 from you to Dr. Angelou, has been terminated.". . . Lewis claims that he never received this letter, and that as far as he was concerned, the November 1994 letter agreement was still in force in 1999. . . . According to Lewis, he contacted Angelou in 1999 about the Hallmark licensing agreement and she put him off again. . . . Lewis learned that Hallmark and Angelou had reached an agreement without his assistance when he saw a press release about the deal in November 2000. . . .

On June 28, 2000, after more than a year of negotiations and discussions, Hallmark and Angelou signed a licensing agreement which featured a sliding royalty scale based on net revenues, guaranteed Angelou a minimum payment of $2 million, and gave her a $1 million advance. This agreement allowed Hallmark to use Angelou's previously published work as well as future works she would create for the project; additionally, the marketing of Angelou's products would not be restricted to ethnic consumers.

II.

. . . .

In her motion for summary judgment, Angelou claims that as a matter of law, no bilateral contract existed between her and BLP because the Agreement was vague, indefinite, and lacking in essential terms. . . . The court finds that there is at least an issue of fact as to whether the Agreement was sufficiently definite to constitute a contract, with the result that it gave rise to good-faith obligations of performance by both BLP and Angelou.

A. Definiteness and Essential Terms

"In order for an agreement to be enforced, it must be sufficiently 'definite and explicit so [that the parties'] intention may be ascertained to a reasonable degree of certainty.'" *Best Brands Beverage, Inc. v. Falstaff Brewing Corp.*, 842 F.2d 578, 587 (2d Cir.1987) (quoting *Candid*

>
> **Take Note!**
> The parties' duty to perform in good faith arises only once a contract is formed. See Chapter 7, page 804.

Prods., Inc. v. Int'l Skating Union, 530 F. Supp. 1330, 1333 (S.D.N.Y.1982)) (alteration in original); . . . *see also* 1 Corbin on Contracts § 4.1 ("A court cannot enforce a contract unless it can determine what it is. It is not enough that the parties think that they have made a contract. They must have expressed their intentions in a manner that is capable of being understood. It is not even enough that they have actually agreed, if their expressions, when interpreted in the light of accompanying factors and circumstances, are not such that the court can determine what the terms of the agreement are.").

Moreover, an agreement cannot be enforced if it lacks essential terms, and if the court is unable to supply such missing terms in a reasonable fashion that is consistent with the parties' intent. *Best Brands*, 842 F.2d at 588; *Helms v. Prikopa*, 51 N.C.App. 50, 55, 275 S.E.2d 516, 519 (1981) . . . .

A court may not "rewrite the contract and impose liabilities not bargained for." *A/S Atlantica v. Moran Towing & Transp. Co.*, 498 F.2d 158, 161 (2d

Cir.1974) (internal quotation marks omitted); *Woods v. Nationwide Mut, Ins. Co.,* 295 N.C. 500, 506, 246 S.E.2d 773, 777 (1978). However, . . . courts are reluctant to strike down contracts for indefiniteness. *See* Lee v. Joseph E. Seagram & Sons, Inc., 552 F.2d 447, 453 (2d Cir.1977); Gonzalez v. Don King Prods., 17 F.Supp.2d 313, 314-15 (S.D.N.Y.1998) (holding that refusing to enforce a contract as indefinite and meaningless " 'is at best a last resort" '). . . ; *Goodyear v. Goodyear,* 257 N.C. 374, 379, 126 S.E.2d 113, 117 (1962) ("Where ... the parties have attempted to put in writing an agreement fixing the rights and duties owing to each other, courts will not deny relief because of vagueness and uncertainty in the language used, if the intent of the parties can be ascertained."). Courts are cautioned not to turn the requirements of definiteness and essential terms into a fetish, because

> at some point virtually every agreement can be said to have a degree of indefiniteness, and if the doctrine is applied with a heavy hand it may defeat the reasonable expectations of the parties in entering into a contract. While there must be a manifestation of mutual assent to essential terms, parties also should be held to their promises and courts should not be pedantic or meticulous in interpreting contract expressions.

Cobble Hill Nursing Home, Inc. v. Henry & Warren Corp., 74 N.Y.2d 475, 483, 548 N.Y.S.2d 920, 923 (1989) (internal quotation marks omitted).

A term is essential if "it seriously affects the rights and obligations of the parties and there is a significant evidentiary dispute as to its content." *Ginsberg Machine Co. v. J. & H. Label Processing Corp.,* 341 F.2d 825, 828 (2d Cir.1965). Terms that may be considered essential in any agreement include the price to be paid, the work to be done, and the time of performance. *See* 1 Williston on Contracts § 4.18; *Schenk v. Red Sage,* No. 91 Cv. 7868, 1994 U.S. Dist. LEXIS 399, at *35 (S.D.N.Y. Jan. 20, 1994). When a court encounters indefinite terms, but finds that the parties did intend to form a contract, as the court found in its first decision in this case, the court then must attempt to "attach a sufficiently definite meaning to [the] bargain." 1 Williston § 4.18. A court should be especially willing to do so if the plaintiff has fully or partly performed under the agreement "since the performance may either remove the uncertainty or militate in favor of recovery even if the uncertainty continues."*Id.* (citing Restatement (Second) of Contracts § 34)) . . . .

Of course, the court may not make a contract for the parties, *see* 1 Corbin § 4.1. However, because the parties in this case did intend a contract, the court is obligated to fill any gaps their Agreement contains, if it reasonably is able to do so. Voiding an agreement for lack of essential terms "is a step that courts should take only in rare and extreme circumstances." *Shann v. Dunk,* 84 F.3d 73, 81 (2d Cir.1996).

Make the Connection

The *Cheever* court mentions the parties' lack of common understanding as to "essential terms" and states that a court's role is not to furnish essential terms (pages 263-264). However, the courts have had a difficult time determining which terms are essential and which are not. *B. Lewis Productions* says that "an agreement cannot be enforced if it lacks essential terms" (page 270) and gives an unsatisfying definition of an essential term as a term that "seriously affects the rights and obligations of the parties" (page 271). Note how the *B. Lewis Productions* court handles the missing essential terms of price, duration, and subject matter. The issue of essential terms also arises in the statute of frauds; Restatement (Second) § 131 (page 647) requires the signed writing to "state with reasonable certainty the essential terms of the unperformed promises in the contract." As you read the remainder of this textbook, keep an eye out for other issues that refer to essential terms.

Angelou claims that the Agreement in this case is unenforceable because it lacks multiple essential terms. She notes that the Agreement does not specify or describe: what "original literary works" she would be contributing to the project; whether these literary works would be new or chosen from her previously published works; the quantity of works Angelou was to produce; when she was to contribute these works; the duration of the Agreement; or the extent of BLP's substantive or financial obligations under the Agreement. . . . Further, Angelou argues that the Agreement's designation of BLP's right to exploit Angelou's work in "all media forms" is overbroad and does not express the parties' intent, because this provision would have affected Angelou's agreement with her literary publisher Random House. . . . As explained below, these allegedly indefinite or missing terms are capable of reasonable interpretation.

1. Price

The general rule is that price is "an essential ingredient" of every contract, and that a compensation clause is enforceable only if payment can be determined from the agreement without any "further expression by the parties." *Van Diepen v. Baeza*, No. 96 Cv. 8731, 1998 U.S. Dist. LEXIS 5763, at *21-*22 (S.D.N.Y. Feb. 26, 1998) (internal quotation marks omitted); *see also, e.g., N.C. Coastal Motor Line, Inc. v. Everette Truck Line, Inc.*, 77 N .C. App. 149, 151, 334 S.E.2d 499, 501 (1985). Angelou notes that the Agreement does not state how much capital, if any, BLP was obligated to contribute to the project, and argues that this constitutes a failure to specify the essential term of price. . . . The Agreement does state, however, that BLP will contribute "all the capital necessary." The Agreement further specifies how gross revenue generated by the "Venture" was to be distributed: BLP's capital is returned, any of the Venture's expenses are reimbursed, and any net profits are shared equally between BLP and Angelou. . . . There is at least a material question of fact as to whether this payment and distribution scheme was sufficiently definite. BLP was obligated under the Agreement to contribute "all" capital—an arrangement with a meaning that arguably is capable of enforcement. Moreover, the capital necessary to a "Venture" of the sort at issue here would be modest, if indeed any capital expenditures would have been necessary. Even expense items were likely to be limited to funds required to produce greeting card mock-ups, postage, and perhaps some travel.

    . . . .

BLP's part performance too shows that the parties had a meeting of the minds on the financial aspects of the Agreement. *See* **Restatement (Second) of Contracts § 34**; 1 Corbin § 4.1. BLP paid all initial expenses as Lewis began to negotiate licensing deals with various greeting card companies, and Angelou raised no objection during that time.

The price terms of the Agreement are capable of reasonable interpretation, and therefore arguably are sufficiently definite for enforcement.

2. *Duration*

Angelou claims also that the Agreement's lack of a duration term renders it too vague for enforcement. . . . Indeed, in his deposition, Lewis admitted that "[t]here was no time set" on the Agreement. . . . .

Under both New York and North Carolina law, a duration clause is not necessary in a contract for services. If such a contract makes no provision for duration, the contract is presumed to be terminable at will. *See* ***Bishop v. Wood***, 426 U.S. 341, 346 (1976) (citing ***Still v. Lance***, 279 N.C. 254, 182 S.E.2d 403 (1971)) . . . . If the Agreement between Angelou and BLP is viewed not as a joint venture but as a simple bilateral contract, BLP was contracting for Angelou's services as a writer and Angelou was contracting for BLP's services as a marketer of her work; under this view, the Agreement is a contract for services that need not contain a provision for duration, and may be terminated at will.[5]

3. *Subject Matter*

Angelou argues that the Agreement insufficiently defined the works she would supply to the project and the form in which her works would be exploited. The Agreement provides that Angelou will "exclusively contribute original literary works (Property) to the Venture and BLP will seek to exploit the rights for pub-

---

[5] Again, because Angelou has not moved for summary judgment on the issue of termination . . . , the court expresses no opinion on the issue of whether the Agreement here was terminated, and if it was, what repercussions such termination would have on BLP's claim against Angelou.

lishing of said Property in all media forms including, but not limited to greeting cards, stationery and calendars, etc.". . . . The Agreement adds that Angelou will contribute, "on an exclusive basis, original literary works to the Venture after consultations with and mutual agreement of Butch Lewis, who will be the managing partner of the Venture.". . . .

BLP claims that the Agreement's subject matter was sufficiently definite because the Agreement stated that the details of the work would be mutually agreed upon, and could not be finalized until a licensing agreement with a specific greeting card company had been reached. . . . Angelou claims that this admission confirms her argument that the Agreement was merely an "agreement to agree," and not a binding Agreement in and of itself. However, this court has already held that the Agreement was more than simply an "agreement to agree"—the parties intended a binding contract here. *BLP Prods.*, 2003 U.S. Dist. LEXIS 12655, at *28. The parties understood that they were agreeing to work together to publish Angelou's writings in greeting cards, and potentially in related media forms such as calendars and stationery. The details of the arrangement would become final as individual projects were undertaken. . . . When the Agreement was signed, there was a meeting of the minds as to its subject matter, and given the expressed intent of the parties, the court reasonably would be able to supply missing details, if necessary. Any omitted details are not material.

Again, BLP partially performed under the Agreement when it procured from Hallmark at least a draft that proposed the licensing of Angelou's writings for use in greeting cards and related products. Although Angelou did not enter into this deal, neither did she question the propriety of BLP's discussions with Hallmark, or suggest that her obligations under the Agreement were too indefinite to validate those discussions. BLP's part performance thus helps to resolve uncertainty about the Agreement's subject matter--if there was any such uncertainty to begin with. *See* 1 Corbin § 4.1 ("[T]he argument that a particular agreement is too indefinite to constitute a contract frequently is an afterthought excuse for attacking an agreement that failed for reasons other than the indefiniteness."). Although defined in broad strokes, the Agreement's subject matter was not so indefinite as to constitute "rare and extreme" circumstances justifying invalidation of a binding contract intended by both parties. *Shann, 84 F.3d at 81.*

B. Duty of Good Faith and Fair Dealing

The above discussion of missing essential terms intersects with the issue of whether the parties here owed one another an obligation of good faith and fair dealing. New York and North Carolina courts have held that every contract contains an implied covenant of good faith and fair dealing, in which each party agrees not to injure the rights of the other to receive benefits under that agreement. *Dalton v. Educ. Testing Serv.*, 87 N.Y.2d 384, 396, 639 N.Y.S.2d 977, 984 (1995); *Bicycle Transit Auth., Inc. v. Bell*, 314 N.C. 219, 228-29, 333 S.E.2d 299, 305 (1985). In this case, BLP argues that each party's duty of good faith and fair dealing served to supply any missing terms relating to their respective obligations under the Agreement, and that Angelou breached her implied covenant of good faith when she failed to contribute any works to the project. . . . Angelou counters that this claim duplicates BLP's breach of contract claim, and that the duty of good faith and fair dealing may not be used to force her into obligations she never intended to assume. . . .

Think About It!

Why does the court wait to cover issues of good faith until after the court has ruled that the parties' agreement "was not so indefinite as to . . . justify[] invalidation"? How are the missing terms described above different from the missing terms described below?

1. *Duty of Good Faith and Missing Terms*

Then-Judge Cardozo's opinion in *Wood v. Lucy, Lady Duff-Gordon*, 222 N.Y. 88, 118 N.E. 214 (1917), underpins the analysis here. In that case, the defendant Lady Duff Gordon, a self-styled "creator of fashions," agreed with the plaintiff Otis Wood that he would have the exclusive right, subject to her approval, to sell her designs, to license others to market them, and to place her endorsement on the designs of others. As Cardozo phrased it, "[s]he employed the plaintiff to turn this vogue into money." *Id.* **at 90.** Under the agreement, Lady Duff Gordon was to receive one half of "all profits and revenues" derived from contracts made by the defendant involving her work. *Id.* **at 90.** The defendant sued Lady Duff Gordon, claiming that she had placed her endorsement on various products without his knowledge and kept the profits for herself. Lady Duff Gordon claimed in response that the original agreement between herself and Wood was unenforceable and illusory because it failed to specify Wood's obligation to sell and market her designs.

The facts here strongly resemble those in Cardozo's classic. As in that case, we have here an artistic defendant, a 50-50 arrangement to market her creations, and an alleged behind-the-back breach, with Ms. Angelou cast as a Lady Duff Gordon for the modern age.

In *Wood*, the Court held that although the contract between the parties did not spell out each party's obligations,

> [t]he law has outgrown its primitive stage of formalism when the precise word was the sovereign talisman, and every slip was fatal. It takes a broader view to-day. A promise may be lacking, and yet the whole writing may be instinct with an obligation, imperfectly expressed. If that is so, there is a contract.

Id. at 91 (internal quotation marks omitted). The Court found the implication of a binding promise between the parties from numerous aspects of the agreement. Lady Duff Gordon gave Wood the "exclusive" right to market her creations; she must have expected him to perform, because her business would have ceased to exist without him. Additionally, Lady Duff Gordon's sole compensation was to be one-half of the profits: Therefore unless Wood made reasonable efforts under the agreement, she could recover nothing under its terms, defeating the "business efficacy" that both parties must have desired when they made the agreement. *Id.* The contract between Wood and Lady Duff Gordon was upheld, and generated a body of law in which the duty of good faith upheld binding agreements with scant details. *See Curtis Props. Corp. v. Greif Cos.,* 212 A.D.2d 259, 265-66, 628 N.Y.S.2d 628, 632 (1st Dep't 1995); *Ultra Innovations, Inc. v. Food Lion, Inc.,* 130 N.C.App. 315, 317-18, 502 S.E.2d 685, 687 (1998); 2 Corbin § 5.27 ("The finding of implied promises is more common today than in the era before the *Wood* case. Courts recognize that if the parties intend a contract, rather than a nullity, implying promises to avoid the finding of illusoriness or indefiniteness protects the reasonable expectation of the parties engendered by the agreement.").

Angelou claims that the Agreement is unenforceable because it fails to define either party's obligations. She argues that the Agreement does not specify a quantity of work to be supplied by her, nor does it state what effort BLP was required to expend in furtherance of the Agreement. . . . According to Angelou, the Agreement was so vague that she could have complied with its terms and never provided any work to the project; similarly, BLP could have complied simply by making a few telephone inquiries. . . . Perhaps, but consider what might have occurred if Angelou had accepted some version of the proposal that Hallmark made to BLP. If Angelou had failed thereafter to contribute some works, but had published other works on her own that could have been used in greeting cards, BLP might have sued for damages stemming from Angelou's nonperformance. . . .

As was the case in *Wood*, it appears that the parties here intended to form a binding contract. Deficiencies or gaps in the Agreement regarding the parties' obligations may be filled by the obligation of good faith that each incurred upon signing it. As in *Wood*, the profit-sharing arrangement between the parties here meant that Angelou and BLP had nothing to gain from the Agreement if either failed to perform or gave minimal effort. Therefore we must assume that each party arguably had an obligation to make "reasonable efforts" in furtherance of the Agreement in order to vindicate the "business efficacy" that both parties must have contemplated when they entered the Agreement. *Wood, 222 N.Y. at 90, 92.*

. . . .

In this case, the evidence shows that Lewis and Angelou agreed on the terms of the contract and on the meaning of those terms. Angelou and BLP never argued over the substance of the Agreement, and as Lewis marketed the Angelou project to greeting card companies, Angelou never protested. To the contrary, she signed a confirmation of the Agreement on June 19, 1996, which was sent to Hallmark. . . . Angelou did eventually refuse to deal with BLP, but this decision was not motivated by any contractual dispute. Angelou testified that she did not like the mock-ups of the greeting cards that BLP presented to her . . . , that she was disgusted by Lewis's behavior at the event in Las Vegas . . . , and that she felt it was morally wrong to compromise her relationship with Random House by publishing her work elsewhere . . . . None of these reservations had anything to do with the terms of the contract Angelou signed with BLP. Angelou articulated no concerns about the nature or scope of the Agreement, and did not complain that she had been ensnared into contractual obligations she had unknowingly assumed. Angelou's plight . . . parallels that of Lady Duff Gordon, who signed a binding agreement that she later came to regret.

The repeated use of the language of exclusivity in the dealings between Angelou and BLP is further evidence that each party had a good faith obligation to perform under the Agreement. The Agreement twice uses the word "exclusive" in describing Angelou's contributions to the "Venture"—"Angelou will exclusively contribute original literary works," and "Angelou will contribute, on an exclusive basis, original literary works"—and in the letter sent by Angelou and BLP to Hallmark on June 19, 1996, Angelou stated that BLP had the "exclusive right" to represent her "for the exploitation of her work product in the area of greeting cards, stationery, calendars, etc." . . . [T]he Agreement and the June 19, 1996 confirmation letter both show that the parties intended to work with one another on the greeting card project, and Angelou promised that she would provide her work for use in greeting cards exclusively to BLP. This language is further evidence that the parties assumed that each would act in good faith to further the Agreement. As in *Wood*, "[w]e are not to suppose that one party was to be placed at the mercy of the other," 222 N.Y. at 91; rather, Angelou committed to work only with BLP to accomplish her contractual goal, and trusted that BLP would fulfill his obligations under the Agreement.

As discussed above, and bearing in mind that the court must construe all evidence in the light most favorable to the nonmoving party, the Agreement at least arguably contains most if not all required essential terms for enforcement. Any remaining vagueness or

Behind the Scenes

Maya Angelou's Hallmark collection was introduced in 2002, while this case was still in progress. Before trial of the contracts claim, Angelou and Lewis settled for $1 million plus royalties. Shortly after settlement, Lewis again filed suit against Angelou for fraud in negotiating the settlement and failure to pay a percentage on Hallmark's royalty advance payments to Angelou. The court granted summary judgment to Angelou on both counts. Angelou remained liable to Lewis under the original contract settlement.

uncertainty regarding the parties' obligations may be found immaterial, because the parties' reciprocal duty of good faith under the Agreement ensured that they would make reasonable efforts to perform.

[The court denied Angelou's summary judgment motion against an enforceable bilateral contract and also denied Hallmark's motion for summary judgment to dismiss BLP's tortious interference claim.]

For the reasons set forth above, both motions for summary judgment are denied.

———————

Think About It:
The Impact of Jurisprudential Philosophy

On what philosophical and policy grounds do the courts in *Cheever* and *B. Lewis Productions* differ? Consider their views on the realities of the contract formation process and the role of law in responding to them. Which court makes it easier to form a contract, and which one makes it more difficult to form a contract? How do these approaches affect future contracting parties? Which approach do you think is more appropriate?

Consider, too, the evidence that each opinion takes into account. In each case, does the court limit the extrinsic evidence to be considered for guidance on the meaning of the contract or look beyond the document to the broader context? (In Chapter 7, page 724, we look further at the differences between the plain-meaning and context-based approaches to interpretation.)

Food for Thought:
Indefinite or Incomplete Agreements

Toward the end of the *Cheever* case, the court said, "A contract may be enforced even though some contract terms may be missing or left to be agreed upon, but if the essential terms are so uncertain that there is no basis for deciding whether the agreement has been kept or broken, there is no contract." The court in *B. Lewis Productions* included a similar rule ("Where . . . the parties have attempted to put in writing an agreement fixing the rights and duties owing to each other, courts will not deny relief because of vagueness and uncertainty in the language used, if the intent of the parties can be ascertained."). Yet another rule appears in UCC § 2-204(3):

> Even though one or more terms are left open a contract for sale does not fail for indefiniteness if the parties intended to make a contract and there is a reasonably certain basis for a remedy.

This rule in UCC Article 2 works in part because many missing terms can be filled in by the "UCC gapfiller" provisions—default provisions that are meant to apply if the parties haven't expressly or impliedly agreed to a particular term—once a contract has been formed. These provisions can fill in the price, location of tender of the goods, timing of tender and payment, means of payment, whether performance will be in one or more installments, and many other items.

Many courts have applied UCC § 2-204(3) "by analogy" to contracts outside of the scope of UCC Article 2, allowing a contract to stand, even though some of its terms are missing (and even though those courts do not also apply the UCC gapfillers by analogy to fill in the terms). But many other courts have rejected this flexible approach, striking down agreements as void for indefiniteness and retaining the more traditional, and more restrictive, common law approach. George S. Geis, *An Embedded Options Theory of Indefinite Contracts*, 90 Minn. L. Rev. 1664, 1666-67 (2000).

Why do parties continue to write indefinite and incomplete agreements, in the face of a robust invalidating doctrine? One commentator has theorized that deliberately incomplete contracts that rely on self-enforcement (between the parties, without the court system) are more efficient than legally enforceable contracts. In a data pool of cases in which courts refused to enforce agreements because of indefiniteness, the intentionally incomplete agreements were generally "simple in form, clear in commitment, and structured to create opportunities for parties to reciprocate in ways that expand the contractual surplus." Other agreements, notably agreements to agree, were often structured to allow one or both parties to watch the other party in action, thereby "providing an opportunity . . . to observe the other's character over time" and to screen out business partners who weren't reciprocally fair.

Even without a valid contract, this opportunity was valuable. Robert E. Scott, *A Theory of Self-Enforcing Indefinite Agreements*, 103 Colum L. Rev. 1641, 1643 (2003). Thus, even with a marginally valid or even invalid contract, the parties might be satisfied with the end result of their negotiations. Legal validity is not always the goal. But one or both parties may end up ambushed and disadvantaged by the invalidity.

What competing policies underlie the varying attitudes displayed by the courts dealing with incomplete agreements? What is the right balance to be struck? Do you think the cases in this section show success in doing that?

Problem 4-1: Indefinite and Incomplete Agreements

Perry Kitt is a heart surgeon, founder and president of the Kitt Heart Institute. He serves as its president, medical director, and board member.

In Aug. 1972, just six months after the Institute was founded, Brandt Vimler became the assistant to the director (Kitt), with a starting salary of $20,000. Because Kitt appreciated Vimler's work, Vimler's salary tripled within 5 years, and he became the Institute's executive vice president and chief administrative officer. At the time of his "resignation" in Nov. 1982, Vimler was earning $84,000 per year.

On Nov. 15, 1982, Kitt asked for Vimler's resignation. He claimed Vimler had lost support among some important board members. In consideration of the resignation, he offered "a very generous and fair separation agreement that reflects the contributions that you have made to this organization and to me over this 10-year period." Vimler was reluctant to resign and doubted Kitt's ability to be fair under the circumstances. That same day, he voiced his doubts to Kitt's attorney, Michael Sipe (who was also attorney for the Institute, as well as a member of the board of trustees and its secretary). In response, Sipe proposed the appointment of a committee of the board to recommend a severance package. Sipe reasoned that many members of the board were business people familiar with personnel practices involving senior executives, their compensation packages, and severance agreements. Appointment of the committee would both relieve Kitt of the burden of determining what was fair and ensure that the package offered Vimler was equitable. When Vimler met with Sipe the next day, Sipe related Kitt's approval of the plan to have a committee appointed and Kitt's intention to personally ask the board chairman to appoint such a committee.

Vimler next met with Sipe and Kitt on the morning of Nov. 17, 1982. Angered that Vimler's resignation had not been forthcoming, Kitt now threatened to fire him by 5 p.m. that day if he did not resign by 4 p.m. When Vimler phoned Sipe in late afternoon to report his decision to resign, Sipe reassured him that he had no cause to worry about the separation agreement, "because we'll have a committee and they'll work out something we're sure will be fair and equitable." About 5:30 p.m. Vimler hand-delivered this letter of resignation to Kitt:

> Based on our recent discussions, I am offering my resignation at this time in reliance on your assurance that a separation agreement, to be subsequently worked out, will be equitable, fair, and commensurate with my 10½ years of tireless and devoted service to the building of the Kitt Heart Institute.

In response to the letter, Kitt expressed his regret that "it had to come to this." Vimler had done a good job, Kitt recalled, and had been loyal and supportive. Then Kitt reiterated Sipe's assurances that Vimler need not worry about severance pay. Kitt had already spoken to the board chairman and arranged for the appointment of a committee to formulate a recommendation for a separation agreement. (Vimler's resignation enabled Kitt to avoid the bitter debate that might have ensued with Vimler's supporters on the board over the sudden firing of an outstanding employee.)

Shortly thereafter, Kitt called Vimler to address another troubling issue. The Institute-sponsored International Cardiovascular Congress was three months away. This biennial program was Kitt's major educational and public relations showcase, attracting speakers and guests from around the world. Vimler had been concerned about abandoning his preparations for the event. Now Kitt seemed to share Vimler's concerns. Expressing his doubt that the Congress could succeed without Vimler's efforts, Kitt asked him to continue working on it. Kitt wrote a draft letter accepting Vimler's resignation and asked to meet with Vimler that night to read it to him in person. When the two met at the Institute, Kitt read aloud his letter:

With the deepest regret, I accept your resignation. Because you have exhibited tireless energy and devotion over the past 10½ years, I would like to make a request. You have directed and nurtured the International Cardiovascular Congress since its inception, and I would appreciate it very much if you would continue to coordinate the upcoming program for us and bring it to a successful completion. You can rest assured that I will develop an equitable and fair separation agreement for you.

Vimler accepted Kitt's offer of continued employment with the Institute at his present salary from Nov. 18, 1982, through Mar. 6, 1983. Vimler proceeded with his work on the Congress.

On Nov. 22, 1982, the board chairman appointed a committee to recommend an equitable financial arrangement for Vimler's severance. On Dec. 14, 1982, the committee met, developed its recommendation for a separation agreement, and communicated that recommendation to Kitt. Basing its recommendation on the Vimler's employment of ten years, the committee proposed that

Mr. Vimler be given one year's salary as separation pay. Mr. Vimler should be allowed to keep the leased automobile with covering insurance, his credit card and telephone during 1983.

Kitt received the Committee's report immediately but did not communicate it to Vimler. Vimler concluded his work on the Congress on Mar. 6, 1983. On Mar. 30, 1983, Kitt wrote Vimler to announce "the final terms of your separation agreement" with the Institute. He prefaced his offer by noting that "your service and contribution to the Institute were compromised severely many months prior to our Nov. termination meeting." He proposed that the Institute would pay "your full salary for four months" from Mar. 6, as well as the cost of Vimler's "automobile lease, health and insurance program" for the same period. Kitt acknowledged at trial that the specifics of the letter proposal were his "own idea." (The parties never agreed that Kitt or the Institute would be bound by the committee's recommendation.)

Vimler's letter of Apr. 11, 1983, strongly protested Kitt's negative characterization of his services to the Institute, rejected the terms of Kitt's severance proposal, and indicated his willingness to accept the committee's recommendation as "a fair-minded settlement proposal."

letter proposal were his "own idea." (The parties never agreed that Kitt or the Institute would be bound by the committee's recommendation.)

Vimler's letter of Apr. 11, 1983, strongly protested Kitt's negative characterization of his services to the Institute, rejected the terms of Kitt's severance proposal, and indicated his willingness to accept the committee's recommendation as "a fair-minded settlement proposal."

In summer 1983, the Institute paid Vimler four months of full salary as severance pay. Vimler sued Kitt and the Institute for breach of contract, claiming eight months of salary as his damages. Is the parties' agreement too uncertain, vague, or incomplete for the court to enforce?

§ 4. Sequential Assent by Offer and Acceptance

Although parties may manifest their assent to an agreement by together adopting a joint statement of terms, they may instead reach agreement through a series of back-and-forth communications. The courts have developed a set of rules or standards to evaluate whether such communications result in assent to an agreement. The rules establish an expected pattern of communications, beginning with an "offer" by one party (the "offeror") that manifests her assent to specified contractual terms. The offer gives the recipient (the "offeree") the power to "accept" the offer and to thereby create a contract by manifesting assent to the same terms. That assent occurs when the offeree communicates, through words or conduct, "I agree to that."

As reflected in the chart below, the complex web of communications between the parties may involve other "moves" that may or may not lead to mutual assent. An offer may be terminated before it is accepted; the left-hand column of the chart lists four events that result in termination—revocation, rejection, lapse, and death. Alternatively, the offeree may respond to the offer with a "counter-offer" of its own, thereby re-starting the quest for an acceptance. Yet another scenario occurs when preliminary discussions never progress to the point where either party makes an offer.

Section 4.1 of this chapter covers the blue-highlighted area of the chart below—whether a communication constitutes an offer. Section 4.2 (page 320) covers the left-hand column, considering whether the offeree's power to accept has been terminated by some event before the offer is accepted. Section 4.3 (page 350) covers the right-hand column, considering whether a responsive communication constitutes an acceptance or a counter-offer.

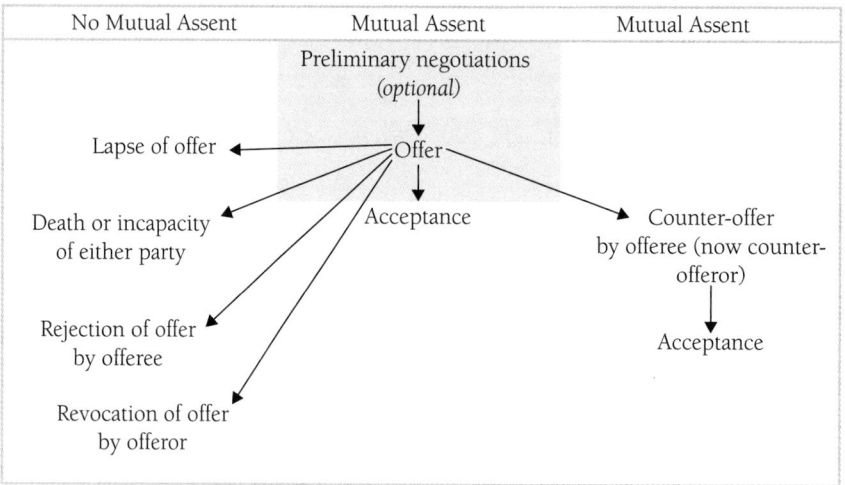

§ 4.1. Defining "Offer"

The first step in finding mutual assent by offer and acceptance is to determine whether either party has made an offer. In this section, we consider statements defining an offer, as well as factual examples that show the courts' judgments about which communications do and do not result in offers.

Everything about a communication—what it says and how it says it—is relevant to determining whether it constitutes an offer. Like all contract communications, a purported offer is judged by its objective meaning. Here, the objective test asks whether a reasonable person in the position of the offeree would understand the communication as an offer.

In marginal cases, courts are often reluctant to rule that an offer was made, because the result might be significant liability that the purported offeror did not mean to undertake. If the purported offer involves too much uncertainty or a shaky commitment, the other party should not yet have a power of acceptance that could be used to force the reluctant party into a contract.

Although one may wish for a crisp definitive statement of what constitutes an offer, the rules defining what is and is not an offer can, at best, be seen as collections of factors to be considered in determining whether there is an offer. Commentators have explained an offer in the following ways:

- An offer is an expression by one party of assent to certain definite terms, provided that the other party involved in the bargaining transaction will likewise express assent to the same terms.

- What is an offer? It can be defined as a manifestation to another of assent to enter into a contract if the other manifests assent in return by some action, often a promise but sometimes a performance. . . . An offer is not effective until it reaches the offeree.
- An offer, with minor exceptions . . ., is a promise to do or refrain from doing some specified thing in the future conditioned on the other party's acceptance.[*]

Other explanations of offers appear in codified rules:

Reading the Law Critically: Offers under the Restatement (Second), CISG, UNIDROIT

1. How are Restatement (Second) §§ 24, 26, and 33 related to each other?

2. In Restatement (Second) § 33(3), under what circumstances does the existence of open or uncertain terms show that an offer or an acceptance was not intended?

3. The UNIDROIT rule is a narrower version of the CISG rule. How do the CISG and UNIDROIT rules compare with the Restatement rules?

Restatement (Second) of Contracts § 24. **Offer Defined**

An offer is the manifestation of willingness to enter into a bargain, so made as to justify another person in understanding that his assent to that bargain is invited and will conclude it.

Restatement (Second) of Contracts § 26. **Preliminary Negotiations**

A manifestation of willingness to enter into a bargain is not an offer if the person to whom it is addressed knows or has reason to know that the person making it does not intend to conclude a bargain until he has made a further manifestation of assent.

Restatement (Second) of Contracts § 33. **Certainty**

(1) Even though a manifestation of intention is intended to be understood as an offer, it cannot be accepted so as to form a contract unless the terms of the contract are reasonably certain

---

[*] 1 Arthur L. Corbin, *Corbin on Contracts* 28 (2d ed. 1993); E. Allan Farnsworth, *Contracts* §§ 3.3, 3.10 (4th ed. 2004); Joseph M. Perillo, *Calamari and Perillo on Contracts* § 2.5 (6th ed. 2009).

(2) The terms of a contract are reasonably certain if they provide a basis for determining the existence of a breach and for giving an appropriate remedy.

(3) The fact that one or more terms of a proposed bargain are left open or uncertain may show that a manifestation of intention is not intended to be understood as an offer or as an acceptance.

———

CISG Art. 14. (in Part II. Formation of the Contract)

A proposal for concluding a contract addressed to one or more specific persons constitutes an offer if it is sufficiently definite and indicates the intention of the offeror to be bound in case of acceptance. A proposal is sufficiently definite if it indicates the goods and expressly or implicitly fixes or makes provision for determining the quantity and the price.

———

UNIDROIT Art. 2.1.2. Definition of Offer

A proposal for concluding a contract constitutes an offer if it is sufficiently definite and indicates the intention of the offeror to be bound in case of acceptance.

Problems: Was an Offer Made?

In each of the situations below, has either party made an offer?

4-2. A sent a letter to B that said, "Dear Sir: We are authorized to offer Michigan fine salt, in full car-load lots of 80-95 barrels, delivered at your city, at 85¢ per barrel, to be shipped per your specified railroad co. Shall be pleased to receive your order."

4-3. A wrote to B asking, "Will you sell me your [specified] property for $6000?" B wrote back, "Because of improvements, it would not be possible for me to sell it unless I was to receive $16,000 cash." A wrote back, "I accept your offer of $16,000 cash."

4-4. A wrote B, "I am writing several people, including yourself, who have previously expressed an interest in the property. Our price is $7,500. I will be interested in hearing from you further if you have any interest in this property, for as I said before, I am advising those who have asked for an opportunity to consider it."

While applying the general definitions of "offer" already described, courts have developed particularized rules and guidelines to determine whether advertisements, rewards, requests for bids, and price quotations constitute offers. The next three subsections cover these specialized settings.

§ 4.1.1. Advertisements and Rewards

As with most offer-and-acceptance questions, whether an advertisement or promise of a reward constitutes an offer depends on a close analysis of the facts. Advertisements are generally understood *not* to be offers, for one or more of the following reasons:

- The ad might not be understood as manifesting the advertiser's intent to be bound.
- The ad might not specify any quantity and so could be for any quantity between one and infinity.
- The reasonable recipient might know or have reason to know that the advertiser does not mean to give every recipient of the ad a chance to form a contract but means to have only an unspecified number of recipients form a contract.
- The ad might omit essential terms or leave them uncertain. Price may or may not be essential, depending on the situation.

Some of the same issues arise as to public promises of rewards. The two cases in this section wrestle with when an offer can arise from an advertisement or a public promise of a reward.

Reading the Law Critically: *Lefkowitz*

1. The court considers two advertisements in this case. Was each one an offer? If not, why not? If so, what did each ad require for acceptance?

2. What rule defining offers can you extract from this case?

3. What role did the objective test play in this case?

4. Why wasn't the "house rule" effective? What could the store have done to make it effective?

5. In light of the result and analysis in *Lefkowitz*, look at some newspaper or internet advertisements. Which ones might be considered offers? Which would not?

Lefkowitz v. Great Minneapolis Surplus Store

store didn't sell furs as advertised

MORRIS LEFKOWITZ, Plaintiff-Respondent

v.

GREAT MINNEAPOLIS SURPLUS STORE, INC., Defendant-Appellant

Supreme Court of Minnesota

86 N.W.2d 689 (Minn. 1957)

MURPHY, Justice.

This is an appeal from an order of the Municipal Court of Minneapolis denying the motion of the defendant for amended findings of fact, or, in the alternative, for a new trial. The order for judgment awarded the plaintiff the sum of $138.50 as damages for breach of contract.

This case grows out of the alleged refusal of the defendant to sell to the plaintiff a certain fur piece which it had offered for sale in a newspaper advertisement. It appears from the record that on April 6, 1956, the defendant published the following advertisement in a Minneapolis newspaper:

> "Saturday 9 A.M. Sharp 3 Brand New Fur Coats Worth to $100.00
> First Come First Served $1 Each"

On April 13, the defendant again published an advertisement in the same newspaper as follows:

> "Saturday 9 A.M. 2 Brand New Pastel Mink 3-Skin Scarfs Selling for $89.50
> Out they go Saturday. Each . . . $1.00
> 1 Black Lapin Stole [. . .] Beautiful, worth $139.50 . . . $1.00
> First Come First Served"

The record supports the findings of the court that on each of the Saturdays following the publication of the above-described ads the plaintiff was the first to present himself at the appropriate counter in the defendant's store and on each occasion demanded the coat and the stole so advertised and indicated his readiness to pay the sale price of $1. On both occasions, the defendant refused to sell the merchandise to the plaintiff, stating on the first occasion that by a "house rule" the offer was intended for women only and sales would not be made to men, and on the second visit that plaintiff knew defendant's house rules.

The trial court properly disallowed plaintiff's claim for the value of the fur coats since the value of these articles was speculative and uncertain. The only evidence of value was the advertisement itself to the effect that the coats were "Worth to $100.00," how much less being speculative especially in view of the price for which they were offered for sale. With reference to the offer of the defendant on April 13, 1956, to sell the "1 Black Lapin Stole . . . worth $139.50 . . ." the trial court held that the value of this article was established and granted judgment in favor of the plaintiff for that amount less the $1 quoted purchase price.

Think About It!

As reflected in the court's disallowance of the plaintiff's first claim, damages will not be awarded if the amount is speculative or cannot be proven with reasonable certainty. See Chapter 9 (page 1043). Could the plaintiff have proven certain-enough damages in *Leftowitz*?

The defendant contends that a newspaper advertisement offering items of merchandise for sale at a named price is a "unilateral offer" which may be withdrawn without notice. He relies upon authorities which hold that, where an advertiser publishes in a newspaper that he has a certain quantity or quality of goods which he wants to dispose of at certain prices and on certain terms, such advertisements are not offers which become contracts as soon as any person to whose notice they may come signifies his acceptance by notifying the other that he will take a certain quantity of them. Such advertisements have been construed as an invitation for an offer of sale on the terms stated, which offer, when received, may be accepted or rejected and which therefore does not become a contract of sale until accepted by the seller; and until a contract has been so made, the seller may modify or revoke such prices or terms. **Montgomery Ward & Co. v. Johnson, 209 Mass. 89, 95 N.E. 290; . . . Craft v. Elder & Johnson Co., 38 N.E.2d 416, 34 . . . .**

Think About It!

How does the court later address the defendant's arguments in this paragraph? What does the defendant mean by "unilateral offer" here?

. . . . On the facts before us we are concerned with whether the advertisement constituted an offer, and, if so, whether the plaintiff's conduct constituted an acceptance.

There are numerous authorities which hold that a particular advertisement in a newspaper or circular letter relating to a sale of articles may be construed by the court as constituting an offer, acceptance of which would complete a contract. **J. E. Pinkham Lumber Co. v. C. W. Griffin & Co., 212 Ala. 341, 102 So. 689** . . . .

The test of whether a binding obligation may originate in advertisements addressed to the general public is 'whether the facts show that some performance was promised in positive terms in return for something requested.' 1 Williston, Contracts (Rev. ed.) § 27.

See It

The following advertisements, courtesy of the Minnesota Historical Society, were the subject of the *Lefkowitz* case. In the first advertisement, the three fur coats appear under "Saturday." In the second advertisement, the two mink scarves and the black lapin stole appear in the middle circle, under "Dollar." Elsewhere in both ads, "6 Cocker Spaniel puppies" are free "to the first boys or girls accompanied by their parents."

The authorities above cited emphasize that, where the offer is clear, definite, and explicit, and leaves nothing open for negotiation, it constitutes an offer, acceptance of which will complete the contract. The most recent case on the subject is **Johnson v. Capital City Ford Co., La.App., 85 So.2d 75,** in which the court pointed out that a newspaper advertisement relating to the purchase and sale of automobiles may constitute an offer, acceptance of which will consummate a contract and create an obligation in the offeror to perform according to the terms of the published offer.

Could it be reasonably understood

Whether in any individual instance a newspaper advertisement is an offer rather than an invitation to make an offer depends on the legal intention of the parties and the surrounding circumstances. Annotation, 157 A.L.R. 744, 751 . . . . . We are of the view on the facts before us that the offer by the defendant of the sale of the Lapin fur was clear, definite, and explicit, and left nothing open for negotiation. The plaintiff[,] having successful[ly] managed to be the first one to appear at the seller's place of business to be served, as requested by the advertisement, and having offered the stated purchase price of the article, . . . was entitled to performance on the part of the defendant. We think the trial court was correct in holding that there was in the conduct of the parties a sufficient mutuality of obligation to constitute a contract of sale.

and was clear, buyer did as required

Think About It!

What do you think the court means when it refers to the "legal intention" of the parties? What evidence would be relevant to prove that intention?

This case and others state that an offer must be "clear, definite, and explicit, and [leave] nothing open for negotiation." That doesn't mean the offeror would refuse to negotiate. And the parties' manifested assent need cover only the "essential terms" of the contract. A court can fill in some missing terms, just as the court did in *B. Lewis Productions*. Thus, a communication may be an offer even if it leaves something open for negotiation.

The defendant contends that the offer was modified by a 'house rule' to the effect that only women were qualified to receive the bargains advertised. The advertisement contained no such restriction. This objection may be disposed of briefly by stating that, while an advertiser has the right at any time before acceptance to modify his offer, he does not have the right, after accep-

can't change conditions after acceptance

tance, to impose new or arbitrary conditions not contained in the published offer. Payne v. Lautz Bros. & Co., City Ct., 166 N.Y.S. 844, 848 . . . .

Affirmed.

———————————

Make the Connection

Notice that the buyer accepted the offer here by engaging in the conduct specified in the offer. An offer to be accepted by performance is called an "offer for a unilateral contract." If instead the offer had called for acceptance by a return promise, then it would be an "offer for a bilateral contract." The bilateral aspect of the contract is the offeror's expectation that the offer will be accepted by a reciprocal promise rather than by a reciprocal performance. This distinction is covered more thoroughly later in this chapter (page 327).

Reading the Law Critically: *Leonard*

1. The court discusses both advertisement and reward cases. How does the law treat these two categories of communications differently and similarly, in defining what is an offer?

2. What additional rules defining offers does this case add to your understanding?

3. What role does the objective test play in this case?

Leonard v. PepsiCo

JOHN D.R. LEONARD, Plaintiff

v.

PEPSICO, INC., Defendant

Southern District of New York
88 F. Supp. 2d 116 (S.D.N.Y. 1999),
aff'd on same grounds, 210 F.3d 88 (2d Cir. 2000)

[handwritten margin note: pepsi promotion for "jet" together — was tv commercial an offer?]

KIMBA M. WOOD, District Judge.

Plaintiff brought this action seeking, among other things, specific performance of an alleged offer of a Harrier Jet, featured in a television advertisement for defendant's "Pepsi Stuff" promotion. Defendant has moved for summary judgment pursuant to **Federal Rule of Civil Procedure 56.** For the reasons stated below, defendant's motion is granted.

[handwritten margin note: summary judgment granted]

I. Background

This case arises out of a promotional campaign conducted by defendant, the producer and distributor of the soft drinks Pepsi and Diet Pepsi. The promotion, entitled "Pepsi Stuff," encouraged consumers to collect "Pepsi Points" from specially marked packages of Pepsi or Diet Pepsi and redeem these points for merchandise featuring the Pepsi logo. Before introducing the promotion nationally, defendant conducted a test of the promotion in the Pacific Northwest from October 1995 to March 1996. A Pepsi Stuff catalog was distributed to consumers in the test market, including Washington State. Plaintiff is a resident of Seattle, Washington. While living in Seattle, plaintiff saw the Pepsi Stuff commercial that he contends constituted an offer of a Harrier Jet.

[handwritten margin note: Pepsi points for Pepsi stuff]

A. The Alleged Offer

Because whether the television commercial constituted an offer is the central question in this case, the Court will describe the commercial in detail. The commercial opens upon an idyllic, suburban morning, where the chirping of birds in sun-dappled trees welcomes a paperboy on his morn-

Go Online!

You can view the original commercial and a modified version on You-Tube.

ing route. As the newspaper hits the stoop of a conventional two-story house, the tattoo of a military drum introduces the subtitle, "MONDAY 7:58 AM." The stirring strains of a martial air mark the appearance of a well-coiffed teenager preparing to leave for school, dressed in a shirt emblazoned with the Pepsi logo, a red-white-and-blue ball. While the teenager confidently preens, the military drumroll again sounds as the subtitle "T-SHIRT 75 PEPSI POINTS" scrolls across the screen. Bursting from his room, the teenager strides down the hallway wearing a leather jacket. The drumroll sounds again, as the subtitle "LEATHER JACKET 1450 PEPSI POINTS" appears. The teenager opens the door of his house and, unfazed by the glare of the early morning sunshine, puts on a pair of sunglasses. The drumroll then accompanies the subtitle "SHADES 175 PEPSI POINTS." A voiceover then intones, "Introducing the new Pepsi Stuff catalog," as the camera focuses on the cover of the catalog.[2]

The scene then shifts to three young boys sitting in front of a high school building. The boy in the middle is intent on his Pepsi Stuff Catalog, while the boys on either side are each drinking Pepsi. The three boys gaze in awe at an object rushing overhead, as the military march builds to a crescendo. The Harrier Jet is not yet visible, but the observer senses the presence of a mighty plane as the extreme winds generated by its flight create a paper maelstrom in a classroom devoted to an otherwise dull physics lesson. Finally, the Harrier Jet swings into view and lands by the side of the school building, next to a bicycle rack. Several students run for cover, and the velocity of the wind strips one hapless faculty member down to his underwear. While the faculty member is being deprived of his dignity, the voiceover announces: "Now the more Pepsi you drink, the more great stuff you're gonna get."

The teenager opens the cockpit of the fighter and can be seen, helmetless, holding a Pepsi. "[L]ooking very pleased with himself," (Pl. Mem. at 3,) the teenager exclaims, "Sure beats the bus," and chortles. The military drumroll sounds a final time, as the following words appear: "HARRIER FIGHTER 7,000,000 PEPSI POINTS." A few seconds later, the following appears in more stylized script:

---

[2] At this point, the following message appears at the bottom of the screen: "Offer not available in all areas. See details on specially marked packages."

"Drink Pepsi—Get Stuff." With that message, the music and the commercial end with a triumphant flourish.

Inspired by this commercial, plaintiff set out to obtain a Harrier Jet. Plaintiff explains that he is "typical of the 'Pepsi Generation'" . . . he is young, has an adventurous spirit, and the notion of obtaining a Harrier Jet appealed to him enormously." Plaintiff consulted the Pepsi Stuff Catalog. The Catalog features youths dressed in Pepsi Stuff regalia or enjoying Pepsi Stuff accessories, such as "Blue Shades" ("As if you need another reason to look forward to sunny days."), "Pepsi Tees" ("Live in 'em. Laugh in 'em. Get in 'em."), "Bag of Balls" ("Three balls. One bag. No rules."), and "Pepsi Phone Card" ("Call your mom!"). The Catalog specifies the number of Pepsi Points required to obtain promotional merchandise. The Catalog includes an Order Form which lists, on one side, fifty-three items of Pepsi Stuff merchandise redeemable for Pepsi Points. Conspicuously absent from the Order Form is any entry or description of a Harrier Jet. The amount of Pepsi Points required to obtain the listed merchandise ranges from 15 (for a "Jacket Tattoo" ("Sew 'em on your jacket, not your arm.")) to 3300 (for a "Fila Mountain Bike" ("Rugged. All-terrain. Exclusively for Pepsi.")). It should be noted that plaintiff objects to the implication that because an item was not shown in the Catalog, it was unavailable.

The rear foldout pages of the Catalog contain directions for redeeming Pepsi Points for merchandise. These directions note that merchandise may be ordered "only" with the original Order Form. The Catalog notes that in the event that a consumer lacks enough Pepsi Points to obtain a desired item, additional Pepsi Points may be purchased for ten cents each; however, at least fifteen original Pepsi Points must accompany each order.

Although plaintiff initially set out to collect 7,000,000 Pepsi Points by consuming Pepsi products, it soon became clear to him that he "would not be able to buy (let alone drink) enough Pepsi to collect the necessary Pepsi Points fast enough." Reevaluating his strategy, plaintiff "focused for the first time on the packaging materials in the Pepsi Stuff promotion," and realized that buying Pepsi Points would be a more promising option. Through acquaintances, plaintiff ultimately raised about $700,000.

B. Plaintiff's Efforts to Redeem the Alleged Offer

On or about March 27, 1996, plaintiff submitted an Order Form, fifteen original Pepsi Points, and a check for $700,008.50. Plaintiff appears to have been represented by counsel at the time he mailed his check; the check is drawn on an account of plaintiff's first set of attorneys. At the bottom of the Order Form, plaintiff wrote in "1 Harrier Jet" in the "Item" column and "7,000,000" in the "Total Points" column. In a letter accompanying his submission, plaintiff stated that the check was to purchase additional Pepsi Points "expressly for obtaining a new Harrier jet as advertised in your Pepsi Stuff commercial."

On or about May 7, 1996, defendant's fulfillment house rejected plaintiff's submission and returned the check, explaining that:

> The item that you have requested is not part of the Pepsi Stuff collection. It is not included in the catalogue or on the order form, and only catalogue merchandise can be redeemed under this program.

> The Harrier jet in the Pepsi commercial is fanciful and is simply included to create a humorous and entertaining ad. We apologize for any misunderstanding or confusion that you may have experienced and are enclosing some free product coupons for your use.

Plaintiff's previous counsel responded on or about May 14, 1996, as follows:

> Your letter of May 7, 1996 is totally unacceptable. We have reviewed the video tape of the Pepsi Stuff commercial . . . and it clearly offers the new Harrier jet for 7,000,000 Pepsi Points. Our client followed your rules explicitly . . . .

> This is a formal demand that you honor your commitment and make immediate arrangements to transfer the new Harrier jet to our client. If we do not receive transfer instructions within ten (10) business days of the date of this letter you will leave us no choice but to file an appropriate action against Pepsi . . . .

This letter was apparently sent onward to the advertising company responsible for the actual commercial, BBDO New York ("BBDO"). In a letter dated May 30, 1996, BBDO Vice President Raymond E. McGovern, Jr., explained to plaintiff that:

> I find it hard to believe that you are of the opinion that the Pepsi Stuff commercial ("Commercial") really offers a new Harrier Jet. The use of the Jet was clearly a joke that was meant to make the Commercial more humorous and entertaining. In my opinion, no reasonable person would agree with your analysis of the Commercial.

On or about June 17, 1996, plaintiff mailed a similar demand letter to defendant.

Litigation of this case initially involved two lawsuits, the first a declaratory judgment action brought by PepsiCo in this district . . . , and the second an action brought by Leonard in Florida state court . . . . PepsiCo brought suit in this Court . . . seeking a declaratory judgment stating that it had no obligation to furnish plaintiff with a Harrier Jet. . . . . In response . . ., Leonard brought suit in Florida state court . . . , although this case had nothing to do with Florida. That suit was removed to the Southern District of Florida. . . [and then] transferred to this Court . . . .

. . . . PepsiCo moved for summary judgment pursuant to **Federal Rule of Civil Procedure 56**. The present motion . . . follows three years of jurisdictional and procedural wrangling.

II. Discussion

A. The Legal Framework

1. Standard for Summary Judgment

On a motion for summary judgment, a court "cannot try issues of fact; it can only determine whether there are issues to be tried." **Donahue v. Windsor Locks Bd. of Fire Comm'rs, 834 F.2d 54, 58 (2d Cir.1987)** . . . . The party seeking summary judgment "bears the initial responsibility of informing the district court of the basis for its motion," which includes identifying the materials in the record that "it believes demonstrate the absence of a genuine issue of material fact." **Celotex Corp., 477 U.S. at 323, 106 S.Ct. 2548**.

. . . . Although a court considering a motion for summary judgment must view all evidence in the light most favorable to the non-moving party, and must draw all reasonable inferences in that party's favor, see **Consarc Corp. v. Marine Midland Bank, N.A., 996 F.2d 568, 572 (2d Cir.1993)**, the nonmoving party "must do more than simply show that there is some metaphysical doubt as to the material facts." **Matsushita Elec. Indus. Co. v. Zenith Radio Corp., 475 U.S. 574, 586 (1986)**. If, based on the submissions to the court, no rational fact-finder could find in the non-movant's favor, there is no genuine issue of material fact, and summary judgment is appropriate. See **Anderson, 477 U.S. at 250**.

. . . . "Summary judgment is proper when the 'words and actions that allegedly formed a contract [are] so clear themselves that reasonable people could not differ over their meaning.'" **Krumme v. Westpoint Stevens, Inc., 143 F.3d 71, 83 (2d Cir.1998)** . . . ; see also **Wards Co. v. Stamford Ridgeway Assocs., 761 F.2d 117, 120 (2d Cir.1985)** (summary judgment is appropriate in contract case where interpretation urged by non-moving party is not "fairly reasonable"). . . .

2. Choice of Law

. . . . Because this action was transferred from Florida, the choice of law rules of Florida, the transferor state, apply. See **Ferens v. John Deere Co., 494 U.S.**

516, 523-33, 110 S.Ct. 1274, 108 L.Ed.2d 443 (1990). Under Florida law, the choice of law in a contract case is determined by the place "where the last act necessary to complete the contract is done." **Jemco, Inc. v. United Parcel Serv., Inc., 400 So.2d 499, 500-01 (Fla.Dist.Ct.App.1981)** . . . .

The parties disagree as to whether the contract could have been completed by plaintiff's filling out the Order Form to request a Harrier Jet, or by defendant's acceptance of the Order Form. If the commercial constituted an offer, then the last act necessary to complete the contract would be plaintiff's acceptance, in the state of Washington. If the commercial constituted a solicitation to receive offers, then the last act necessary to complete the contract would be defendant's acceptance of plaintiff's Order Form, in the state of New York. The choice of law question cannot, therefore, be resolved until after the Court determines whether the commercial was an offer or not. The Court agrees with both parties that resolution of this issue requires consideration of principles of contract law that are not limited to the law of any one state. Most of the cases cited by the parties are not from New York courts. As plaintiff suggests, the questions presented by this case implicate questions of contract law "deeply ingrained in the common law of England and the States of the Union."

B. Defendant's Advertisement Was Not an Offer

1. Advertisements as Offers

The general rule is that an advertisement does not constitute an offer. The Restatement (Second) of Contracts explains that:

> Advertisements of goods by display, sign, handbill, newspaper, radio or television are not ordinarily intended or understood as offers to sell. The same is true of catalogues, price lists and circulars, even though the terms of suggested bargains may be stated in some detail. It is of course possible to make an offer by an advertisement directed to the general public (see § 29), but there must ordinarily be some language of commitment or some invitation to take action without further communication.

Restatement (Second) of Contracts § 26 cmt. b (1979). Similarly, a leading treatise notes that:

> It is quite possible to make a definite and operative offer to buy or sell goods by advertisement, in a newspaper, by a handbill, a catalog or circular or on a placard in a store window. It is not customary to do this, however; and the presumption is the other way. ... Such advertisements are understood to be mere requests to consider and examine and negotiate; and no one can reasonably regard them as otherwise unless

the circumstances are exceptional and the words used are very plain and clear.

1 Arthur Linton Corbin & Joseph M. Perillo, Corbin on Contracts § 2.4, at 116-17 (rev. ed.1993) . . . . New York courts adhere to this general principle. See **Lovett v. Frederick Loeser & Co., 124 Misc. 81, 207 N.Y.S. 753, 755 (N.Y.Mun. Ct.1924)** (noting that an "advertisement is nothing but an invitation to enter into negotiations, and is not an offer which may be turned into a contract by a person who signifies his intention to purchase some of the articles mentioned in the advertisement") . . . .

An advertisement is not transformed into an enforceable offer merely by a potential offeree's expression of willingness to accept the offer through, among other means, completion of an order form. . . . See . . . **Alligood v. Procter & Gamble, 72 Ohio App.3d 309, 594 N.E.2d 668 (1991)** (finding that no offer was made in promotional campaign for baby diapers, in which consumers were to redeem teddy bear proof-of-purchase symbols for catalog merchandise); **Chang v. First Colonial Savings Bank, 242 Va. 388, 410 S.E.2d 928 (1991)** (newspaper advertisement for bank settled the terms of the offer once bank accepted plaintiffs' deposit, notwithstanding bank's subsequent effort to amend the terms of the offer). Under these principles, plaintiff's letter of March 27, 1996, with the Order Form and the appropriate number of Pepsi Points, constituted the offer. There would be no enforceable contract until defendant accepted the Order Form and cashed the check.

The exception to the rule that advertisements do not create any power of acceptance in potential offerees is where the advertisement is "clear, definite, and explicit, and leaves nothing open for negotiation"; in that circumstance, "it constitutes an offer, acceptance of which will complete the contract." **Lefkowitz v. Great Minneapolis Surplus Store, 251 Minn. 188, 86 N.W.2d 689, 691 (1957).** . . .

The present case is distinguishable from Lefkowitz. First, the commercial cannot be regarded in itself as sufficiently definite, because it specifically reserved the details of the offer to a separate writing, the Catalog.[6] The commercial itself made no mention of the steps a potential offeree would be required to take to accept the alleged offer of a Harrier Jet. The advertisement in Lefkowitz, in contrast, "identified the person who could accept." Corbin, supra, § 2.4, at 119. See generally **United States v. Braunstein, 75 F.Supp. 137, 139 (S.D.N.Y.1947)** ("Greater precision of expression may be required, and less help from the court given, when the parties are merely at the threshold of a contract."); Farnsworth, supra, at 239 ("The fact that a proposal is very detailed suggests that it is an

---

[6] It also communicated additional words of reservation: "Offer not available in all areas. See details on specially marked packages."

offer, while omission of many terms suggests that it is not."). Second, even if the Catalog had included a Harrier Jet among the items that could be obtained by redemption of Pepsi Points, the advertisement of a Harrier Jet by both television commercial and catalog would still not constitute an offer. . . . the absence of any words of limitation such as "first come, first served," renders the alleged offer sufficiently indefinite that no contract could be formed. . . . "A customer would not usually have reason to believe that the shopkeeper intended exposure to the risk of a multitude of acceptances resulting in a number of contracts exceeding the shopkeeper's inventory." Farnsworth, supra, at 242. There was no such danger in Lefkowitz, owing to the limitation "first come, first served."

The Court finds, in sum, that the Harrier Jet commercial was merely an advertisement. The Court now turns to the line of cases upon which plaintiff rests much of his argument.

2. Rewards as Offers

defenses best defense

In opposing the present motion, plaintiff largely relies on a different species of unilateral offer, involving public offers of a reward for performance of a specified act. Because these cases generally involve public declarations regarding the efficacy or trustworthiness of specific products, one court has aptly characterized these authorities as "prove me wrong" cases. See **Rosenthal v. Al Packer Ford, 36 Md.App. 349, 374 A.2d 377, 380 (1977)**. The most venerable of these precedents is the case of Carlill v. Carbolic Smoke Ball Co., [1893] **1 Q.B. 256 [, 1892 WL 9612]** (Court of Appeal, 1892), a quote from which heads plaintiff's memorandum of law: "[I]f a person chooses to make extravagant promises . . . he probably does so because it pays him to make them, and, if he has made them, the extravagance of the promises is no reason in law why he should not be bound by them." Carbolic Smoke Ball, 1 Q.B. at 268 (Bowen, L.J.).

Carbolic Smoke Ball

Long a staple of law school curricula, Carbolic Smoke Ball owes its fame not merely to "the comic and slightly mysterious object involved," A.W. Brian Simpson. Quackery and Contract Law: Carlill v. Carbolic Smoke Ball Company (1893), in Leading Cases in the Common Law 259, 281 (1995), but also to its role in developing the law of unilateral offers. The case arose during the London influenza epidemic of the 1890s. Among other advertisements of the time, for Clarke's World Famous Blood Mixture, Towle's Pennyroyal and Steel Pills for Females, Sequah's Prairie Flower, and Epp's Glycerine Jube-Jubes . . . appeared solicitations for the Carbolic Smoke Ball. The specific advertisement that Mrs. Carlill saw, and relied upon, read as follows:

very specific

100£ reward will be paid by the Carbolic Smoke Ball Company to any person who contracts the increasing epidemic influenza, colds, or any diseases caused by taking cold, after having used the ball three times daily for two weeks according to the printed directions supplied with each ball. 1000£ is deposited with the Alliance Bank, Regent Street, [showing] our sincerity in the matter.

During the last epidemic of influenza many thousand carbolic smoke balls were sold as preventives against this disease, and in no ascertained case was the disease contracted by those using the carbolic smoke ball.

Carbolic Smoke Ball, 1 Q.B. at 256-57. "On the faith of this advertisement,". . . Mrs. Carlill purchased the smoke ball and used it as directed, but contracted influenza nevertheless.[8] The lower court held that she was entitled to recover the promised reward.

Affirming the lower court's decision, Lord Justice Lindley began by noting that the advertisement was an express promise to pay £100 in the event that a consumer of the Carbolic Smoke Ball was stricken with influenza. . . . The advertisement was construed as offering a reward because it sought to induce performance, unlike an invitation to negotiate, which seeks a reciprocal promise. . . . "[A]dvertisements offering rewards . . . are offers to anybody who performs the conditions named in the advertisement, and anybody who does perform the condition accepts the offer.". . .[9] Because Mrs. Carlill had complied with the terms of the offer, yet contracted influenza, she was entitled to £100.

Like Carbolic Smoke Ball, the decisions relied upon by plaintiff involve offers of reward. In **Barnes v. Treece, 15 Wash.App. 437, 549 P.2d 1152 (1976),** for example, the vice-president of a punchboard distributor, in the course of hearings before the Washington State Gambling Commission, asserted that, "'I'll put a hundred thousand dollars to anyone to find a crooked board. If they find it, I'll pay it.'" **Id. at 1154.** Plaintiff, a former bartender, heard of the offer and located two

[8] Although the Court of Appeals's opinion is silent as to exactly what a carbolic smoke ball was, the historical record reveals it to have been a compressible hollow ball, about the size of an apple or orange, with a small opening covered by some porous material such as silk or gauze. The ball was partially filled with carbolic acid in powder form. When the ball was squeezed, the powder would be forced through the opening as a small cloud of smoke. . . . At the time, carbolic acid was considered fatal if consumed in more than small amounts. . . .

[9] Carbolic Smoke Ball includes a classic formulation of this principle: "If I advertise to the world that my dog is lost, and that anybody who brings the dog to a particular place will be paid some money, are all the police or other persons whose business it is to find lost dogs to be expected to sit down and write a note saying that they have accepted my proposal?" Carbolic Smoke Ball, 1 Q.B. at 270 (Bowen, L.J.).

crooked punchboards. Defendant, after reiterating that the offer was serious, providing plaintiff with a receipt for the punchboard on company stationery, and assuring plaintiff that the reward was being held in escrow, nevertheless repudiated the offer. . . . The court ruled that the offer was valid and that plaintiff was entitled to his reward. . . . The plaintiff in this case also cites cases involving prizes for skill (or luck) in the game of golf. See **Las Vegas Hacienda v. Gibson, 77 Nev. 25, 359 P.2d 85 (1961)** (awarding $5,000 to plaintiff, who successfully shot a hole-in-one); see also **Grove v. Charbonneau Buick-Pontiac, Inc., 240 N.W.2d 853 (N.D.1976)** (awarding automobile to plaintiff, who successfully shot a hole-in-one).

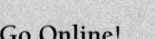

Go Online!

Many law graduates instantly recognize the *Carbolic Smoke Ball* case, a famous English case based on an odd and ineffective "patent medicine" from the late 1800s, and often included in law school casebooks. To see an enlarged picture of the advertisement for the smoke ball, locate the "carbolic smoke ball" entry in wikipedia.

Other "reward" cases underscore the distinction between typical advertisements, in which the alleged offer is merely an invitation to negotiate for purchase of commercial goods, and promises of reward, in which the alleged offer is intended to induce a potential offeree to perform a specific action, often for non-commercial reasons. In **Newman v. Schiff, 778 F.2d 460 (8th Cir.1985)**, for example, the Fifth Circuit held that a tax protestor's assertion that, "If anybody calls this show . . . and cites any section of the code that says an individual is required to file a tax return, I'll pay them $100,000," would have been an enforceable offer had the plaintiff called the television show to claim the reward while the tax protestor was appearing. . . . The court noted that, like Carbolic Smoke Ball, the case "concerns a special type of offer: an offer for a reward.". . . **James v. Turilli, 473 S.W.2d 757 (Mo.Ct.App.1971)**, arose from a boast by defendant that the "notorious Missouri desperado" Jesse James had not been killed in 1882, as portrayed in song and legend, but had lived under the alias "J. Frank Dalton" at the "Jesse James Museum" operated by none other than defendant. Defendant offered $10,000 "to anyone who could prove me wrong.". . . The widow of the outlaw's son demonstrated, at trial, that the outlaw had in fact been killed in 1882. On appeal, the court held that defendant should be liable to pay the amount offered. . . .

Make the Connection

On page 320, this chapter discusses occurrences that terminate an offeree's power to accept an offer. One such occurrence is the lapse of the offer after a stated or reasonable time. In the cited case of *Newman v. Schiff*, the court seems to have concluded that an offer made during a TV show lapsed at the end of the show.

In the present case, the Harrier Jet commercial did not direct that anyone who appeared at Pepsi headquarters with 7,000,000 Pepsi Points on the Fourth of July would receive a Harrier Jet. Instead, the commercial urged consumers to accumulate Pepsi Points and to refer to the Catalog to determine how they could redeem their Pepsi Points. The commercial sought a reciprocal promise, expressed through acceptance of, and compliance with, the terms of the Order Form. As noted previously, the Catalog contains no mention of the Harrier Jet. Plaintiff states that he "noted that the Harrier Jet was not among the items described in the catalog, but this did not affect [his] understanding of the offer." It should have.[10]

. . . . Because the alleged offer in this case was, at most, an advertisement to receive offers rather than an offer of reward, plaintiff cannot show that there was an offer made in the circumstances of this case.

C. An Objective, Reasonable Person Would Not Have Considered the Commercial an Offer

Plaintiff's understanding of the commercial as an offer must also be rejected because the Court finds that no objective person could reasonably have concluded that the commercial actually offered consumers a Harrier Jet.

1. Objective Reasonable Person Standard

In evaluating the commercial, the Court must not consider defendant's subjective intent in making the commercial, or plaintiff's subjective view of what the commercial offered, but what an objective, reasonable person would have understood the commercial to convey. See . . . **Mesaros, 845 F.2d at 1581** ("A basic rule of contracts holds that whether an offer has been made depends on the objective reasonableness of the alleged offeree's belief that the advertisement or solicitation was intended as an offer.") . . . .

If it is clear that an offer was not serious, then no offer has been made:

What kind of act creates a power of acceptance and is therefore an offer? It must be an expression of will or intention. It must be an act that leads the offeree reasonably to conclude that a power to create a contract is conferred. This applies to the content of the power as well as to the fact of its existence. It is on this ground that we must exclude invitations to deal or acts of mere preliminary negotiation, and acts evidently done in jest or without intent to create legal relations.

---

[10] In his affidavit, plaintiff places great emphasis on a press release written by defendant, which characterizes the Harrier Jet as "the ultimate Pepsi Stuff award." Plaintiff simply ignores the remainder of the release, which makes no mention of the Harrier Jet even as it sets forth in detail the number of points needed to redeem other merchandise.

Corbin on Contracts, § 1.11 at 30 . . . . An obvious joke, of course, would not give rise to a contract. . . . On the other hand, if there is no indication that the offer is "evidently in jest," and that an objective, reasonable person would find that the offer was serious, then there may be a valid offer. See . . . **Lucy v. Zehmer, 196 Va. 493, 84 S.E.2d 516, 518, 520 (1954)** (ordering specific performance of a contract to purchase a farm despite defendant's protestation that the transaction was done in jest as "'just a bunch of two doggoned drunks bluffing'").

. . . .

3. Whether the Commercial Was "Evidently Done In Jest"

Plaintiff's insistence that the commercial appears to be a serious offer requires the Court to explain why the commercial is funny. Explaining why a joke is funny is a daunting task; as the essayist E.B. White has remarked, "Humor can be dissected, as a frog can, but the thing dies in the process . . . ."[11] The commercial is the embodiment of what defendant appropriately characterizes as "zany humor."

First, the commercial suggests, as commercials often do, that use of the advertised product will transform what, for most youth, can be a fairly routine and ordinary experience. The military tattoo and stirring martial music, as well as the use of subtitles in a Courier font that scroll terse messages across the screen, such as "MONDAY 7:58 AM," evoke military and espionage thrillers. The implication of the commercial is that Pepsi Stuff merchandise will inject drama and moment into hitherto unexceptional lives. The commercial in this case thus makes the exaggerated claims similar to those of many television advertisements: that by consuming the featured clothing, car, beer, or potato chips, one will become attractive, stylish, desirable, and admired by all. A reasonable viewer would understand such advertisements as mere puffery, not as statements of fact, see, e.g., **Hubbard v. General Motors Corp., 95 Civ. 4362(AGS), 1996 WL 274018, at *6 (S.D.N.Y. May 22, 1996)** (advertisement describing automobile as "Like a Rock," was mere puffery, not a warranty of quality) . . . and refrain from interpreting the promises of the commercial as being literally true.

Second, the callow youth featured in the commercial is a highly improbable pilot, one who could barely be trusted with the keys to his parents' car, much less the prize aircraft of the United States Marine Corps. Rather

What's That?

"Puffing" or "puffery" is a statement that the recipient has reason to know is intended to promote a product and is not intended to accurately state a fact or reliably state a promise. In the context in the cited case, the issue is whether the manufacturer's statement was indeed a warranty about the car's quality or was instead "puffery" and therefore not actionable by the eventual buyer.

---

[11] Quoted in Gerald R. Ford, *Humor and the Presidency* 23 (1987).

than checking the fuel gauges on his aircraft, the teenager spends his precious preflight minutes preening. The youth's concern for his coiffure appears to extend to his flying without a helmet. Finally, the teenager's comment that flying a Harrier Jet to school "sure beats the bus" evinces an improbably insouciant attitude toward the relative difficulty and danger of piloting a fighter plane in a residential area, as opposed to taking public transportation.

Third, the notion of traveling to school in a Harrier Jet is an exaggerated adolescent fantasy. In this commercial, the fantasy is underscored by how the teenager's schoolmates gape in admiration, ignoring their physics lesson. The force of the wind generated by the Harrier Jet blows off one teacher's clothes, literally defrocking an authority figure. As if to emphasize the fantastic quality of having a Harrier Jet arrive at school, the Jet lands next to a plebeian bike rack. This fantasy is, of course, extremely unrealistic. No school would provide landing space for a student's fighter jet, or condone the disruption the jet's use would cause.

Fourth, the primary mission of a Harrier Jet, according to the United States Marine Corps, is to "attack and destroy surface targets under day and night visual conditions." United States Marine Corps, Factfile: AV-8B Harrier II (last modified Dec. 5, 1995) <http://www.hqmc.usmc.mil/factfile.nsf>. Manufactured by McDonnell Douglas, the Harrier Jet played a significant role in the air offensive of Operation Desert Storm in 1991. . . . The jet is designed to carry a considerable armament load, including Sidewinder and Maverick missiles. See id. As one news report has noted, "Fully loaded, the Harrier can float like a butterfly and sting like a bee—albeit a roaring 14-ton butterfly and a bee with 9,200 pounds of bombs and missiles." Jerry Allegood, Marines Rely on Harrier Jet, Despite Critics, News & Observer (Raleigh), Nov. 4, 1990, at C1. In light of the Harrier Jet's well-documented function in attacking and destroying surface and air targets, armed reconnaissance and air interdiction, and offensive and defensive anti-aircraft warfare, depiction of such a jet as a way to get to school in the morning is clearly not serious even if, as plaintiff contends, the jet is capable of being acquired "in a form that eliminates [its] potential for military use."

> **FYI**
> According to www.snopes.com, in September 1997 the Pentagon declared that Harrier Jets cannot be sold in flyable condition, so the plaintiff could not have bought a flyable plane.

Fifth, the number of Pepsi Points the commercial mentions as required to "purchase" the jet is 7,000,000. To amass that number of points, one would have to drink 7,000,000 Pepsis (or roughly 190 Pepsis a day for the next hundred years—an unlikely possibility), or one would have to purchase approximately $700,000 worth of Pepsi Points. The cost of a Harrier Jet is roughly $23 million dollars, a fact of which

306 ———— **CHAPTER 4** *Manifestation of Mutual Assent* ————

plaintiff was aware when he set out to gather the amount he believed necessary to accept the alleged offer. Even if an objective, reasonable person were not aware of this fact, he would conclude that purchasing a fighter plane for $700,000 is a deal too good to be true.[13]

Plaintiff argues that a reasonable, objective person would have understood the commercial to make a serious offer of a Harrier Jet because there was "absolutely no distinction in the manner" in which the items in the commercial were presented. Plaintiff also relies upon a press release highlighting the promotional campaign, issued by defendant, in which "[n]o mention is made by [defendant] of humor, or anything of the sort." These arguments suggest merely that the humor of the promotional campaign was tongue in cheek. Humor is not limited to what Justice Cardozo called "[t]he rough and boisterous joke . . . [that] evokes its own guffaws." **Murphy v. Steeplechase Amusement Co., 250 N.Y. 479, 483, 166 N.E. 173, 174 (1929)**. In light of the obvious absurdity of the commercial, the Court rejects plaintiff's argument that the commercial was not clearly in jest. . . .

III. Conclusion

In sum, there are three reasons why plaintiff's demand cannot prevail as a matter of law. First, the commercial was merely an advertisement, not a[n] . . . offer. Second, the tongue-in-cheek attitude of the commercial would not cause a reasonable person to conclude that a soft drink company would be giving away fighter planes as part of a promotion. [Third reason pertaining to statute of frauds is omitted.]

For the reasons stated above, the Court grants defendant's motion for summary judgment. . . .

Think About It: Reconsidering the Presumption about Advertisements

In *Leonard v. Pepsico,* Judge Wood begins her reasoning with a paragraph of weighty authorities saying that "[t]he general rule is that an advertisement does not constitute an offer." She then quotes a Restatement comment that says advertisements are not "ordinarily" intended as offers to sell and that there "ordinarily" must be language of commitment to make an advertisement an offer. Are these statements more

---

[13] In contrast, the advertisers of the Carbolic Smoke Ball emphasized their earnestness, stating in the advertisement that "£1,000 is deposited with the Alliance Bank, [showing] our sincerity in the matter.". . .

accurately characterized as *rules* (always true in application) or *guidelines* (usually true, but some fact situations might not proceed according to the guidelines)?

Professor Jay Feinman argues that the "general rule" that an advertisement does not constitute an offer is inaccurate—that plenty of cases, including *Lefkowitz*, hold that a particular advertisement *is* an offer. Like all alleged offers, he says, advertisements should be judged on the circumstances—the certainty of the terms, the level of commitment, the means by which the accepting persons are selected from the members of the public receiving the advertisement, etc. Professor Feinman posits that advertisements-are-not-offers statements should be replaced by either (1) a presumption in favor of advertisements being offers or (2) no statement either way so that advertisements are examined in the same light as other alleged offers without any leaning one way or the other. **Jay Feinman,** *Is an Advertisement an Offer? Why It Is, and Why It Matters,* **58 Hastings L.J. 61 (2006).**

According to Professor Melvin Eisenberg:

> *Lefkowitz* is open to several interpretations. It might be said that the advertisement was special because it involved foreseeable reliance—but so, really, does any other advertisement whose primary purpose is to induce customer response. Alternatively, it might be said that the advertisement in *Lefkowitz* was distinguishable from other advertisements on the ground that it stated the quantity available and the first-come-first-served method of allocating the quantity. However, it is implied in every advertisement that (only) a reasonable quantity is available and that the quantity will be allocated first come first served.

Melvin Aron Eisenberg, *Expression Rules in Contract Law and Problems of Offer and Acceptance,* **82 Cal. L. Rev. 1127, 1171 (1994).**

Considering *Lefkowitz, Leonard,* and the commentaries by Eisenberg and Feinman, how do you think advertisements should be treated in determining whether an offer exists?

Look again at any advertisements you reviewed in response to Question 5 on page 287. Is your analysis of whether those advertisements are offers the same in light of *Leonard* and these commentaries?

Problem 4-5: When Is an Advertisement an Offer?

On November 25 and 29, 1941, the following advertisement appeared in a newspaper circulated among municipal bond dealers:

Notice to Bondholders
Okeechobee County, Florida Road
and Bridge Refunding Bonds

Notice Is Hereby Given, by the Board of County Commissioners of Okeechobee County, Florida, as follows:
. . .

For the convenience of bondholders who may wish to surrender their bonds, the Board of County Commissioners of Okeechobee County has arranged to provide funds for the purchase of the above described bonds at par and interest to December 1, 1941. Holders may send their bonds to The Manufacturers Trust Company for surrender pursuant to such terms.

Done, Ordered and Adopted at a meeting of County Commissioners of Okeechobee County on the 24th day of November, 1941. C. F. Walker, Chairman.

A holder of the bonds saw the ad and followed the instructions, sending the bonds by messenger on December 10. Was the advertisement an offer?

§ 4.1.2. Price Quotations

Reading the Law Critically: *Nordyne, Inc.*

As you will see in this case, which communication operates as an offer can affect whether or when a contract was formed and therefore which terms become part of a contract. To understand the complicated back-and-forth between the parties and the implications with respect to the terms, you will find it helpful to construct a timeline identifying the date, sender, and contents of each communication.

1. The case involves a sale of goods, so Article 2 of the state's UCC applies to the transaction. Why does the court nonetheless apply common law principles to identify the offer?

2. What more do you learn about offers from the court's definitions and from its application of the definitions to these circumstances?

3. The court identified a particular communication as the offer. Do you agree with the court's choice? Are there other communications that the court might have chosen?

Nordyne v. International Controls & Measurements Corp.

NORDYNE, INC., Plaintiff-Appellant

v.

INTERNATIONAL CONTROLS & MEASUREMENTS CORP.,
Defendant-Appellee

United States Court of Appeals, Eighth Circuit
262 F.3d 843 (8th Cir. 2001)

RICHARD S. ARNOLD, Circuit Judge.

Nordyne, Inc., appeals from the District Court's order granting the motion of International Controls & Measurements Corporation (ICM) to dismiss Nordyne's breach-of-warranty action for improper venue. Nordyne, as buyer, and ICM, as seller, had been doing business for approximately ten years when the current dispute arose. Nordyne argues that the District Court erred in holding that a forum-selection clause on the reverse side of ICM's invoices was enforceable. We affirm.

I.

Nordyne, a Delaware corporation with its principal place of business in St. Louis, Missouri, manufactures heating, ventilation, and air conditioning equipment. ICM, a New York corporation, manufactures electronic defrost control boards for use in such equipment. Before the dispute underlying this law suit, Nordyne had purchased control boards from ICM for approximately ten years. In shipping products to Nordyne, ICM would forward a Customer Service Invoice with the following printed immediately below the heading: "CUSTOMER'S ORDER IS ACCEPTED ON THE EXPRESS CONDITION THAT THE TERMS AND CONDITIONS SET FORTH ON THE FACE AND REVERSE SIDE OF THIS INVOICE ... SHALL APPLY AND THEY SHALL CONSTITUTE THE COMPLETE AGREEMENT BETWEEN THE PARTIES."

One of the Terms and Conditions of Sale printed on the reverse side of the Customer Service Invoice was a forum-selection provision: "In any action or proceeding brought pursuant to this agreement venue shall be laid in Onondaga, New York." Another term provided that ICM warranted its products for one year from the date of shipment. On several occasions, Nordyne availed itself of this one-year warranty.

In 1997, ICM began marketing a new version of the control panel Nordyne had been purchasing. ICM sent the first quotation for this product to Nordyne on May 13, 1997. Upon Nordyne's determination that one of the new features was not necessary for its purposes, ICM modified the control panel, and on July 29, 1997, tendered a new quotation for the unit as modified. This quotation was for Nordyne's estimated annual usage of 40,000 units at $9.87 per unit. The quotation provided that it was valid until December 31, 1997, that "[b]lanket orders must be fully released within one year," that standard commercial packaging would apply, that shipment would be "net 30 days; FOB Syracuse, NY," and that all orders were non-cancelable and non-returnable.

Printed on the bottom of the quotation was the following: "*CONDITIONS ON REVERSE ARE PART OF THIS QUOTATION.*" These conditions included the following: "This quote is subject to the Seller's standard terms and conditions contained on the order acknowledgment." The conditions also included the statement, "All orders are subject to acceptance by the Seller at its home office in Cicero, New York."

Nordyne asked to see manufactured samples of the new control panel. On September 12, 1997, ICM sent five such samples to Nordyne with a letter from ICM's home office stating, "Full blown manufacturing of this device is awaiting your sign off of these check samples as approved for production. Please review the samples and 'sign off' this document and send it back by return fax so that we may fulfill your production requirements in a timely manner." On September 15, Nordyne signed the production approval.

> **FYI**
>
> The clause saying blanket orders "must be fully released within one year" means that the buyer must order the entire amount during the year, but that buyer can determine the quantities to be delivered on particular dates. The usual process for such "release" is for the buyer to send a purchase order to the seller asking for a specified quantity to be delivered on a specified date. Note that a purchase order, although often an offer, can instead be an acceptance or a release order against an existing contract.
>
> "FOB Syracuse" is a term specifying the delivery term, using a standard business shorthand. It means that the seller ships the goods from Syracuse, presumably to the buyer's location in St. Louis, and the buyer is responsible for the shipment cost and bears the risk if the goods are lost or damaged after the goods leave Syracuse.

Two days later Nordyne issued a purchase order for 20,000 units at the quoted price, and under the shipping, payment, and packaging terms set forth in the quotation of July 29. The purchase order form stated, "Please enter our order for the above, subject to terms and conditions printed on reverse side . . . . Please acknowledge by signing and returning the attached acknowledgment form giving date of shipment." On the reverse side of the purchase order appeared Terms and

Conditions, including the following: "Buyer shall not be bound by this order until Buyer receives the acknowledgment copy of this order executed by Seller, and acceptance of the order constitutes an acceptance of all of the conditions stated herein." None of the conditions related to choice of forum in case of a dispute. The acknowledgment form, which ICM signed on September 22, stated, "This order is acknowledged and accepted subject to the expressed terms and conditions thereon. Any exceptions are noted under vendor remarks at left." ICM did not insert any exceptions into the provided space.

ICM made its first shipment on September 30, 1997. Between that date and mid-August 1998, ICM shipped Nordyne's entire order of 46,151 units at the rate of approximately one shipment per week. With each shipment, ICM included the Customer Service Invoice described above, as had been the practice between the parties. Nordyne paid in full for all the units it ordered.

Thereafter, Nordyne began experiencing difficulties with the ICM control panel and filed a breach-of-warranty action in the District Court. ICM moved to dismiss the complaint for improper venue, invoking the forum-selection clause on the reverse side of its Customer Service Invoices.

II.

The District Court agreed with ICM that the forum-selection clause was part of the contract between the parties. Applying Missouri law, the Court held that the July 1997 price quotation was an offer because it was the result of negotiations between the parties and it was sufficiently complete and detailed. It stated price per unit, estimated quantity, and a description of the product. It also stated the date the quote would expire, the packaging to be used, and terms regarding delivery and payment. The Court held that the "order acknowledgment" referred to in this quotation was ICM's invoice, which as noted above, begins with the statement, "CUSTOMER'S ORDER IS ACCEPTED . . . ." Nordyne accepted the offer by signing the production approval on September 15, 1997. Thus, the terms and conditions, including the forum-selection clause, on the reverse side of ICM's invoices were incorporated by reference in ICM's offer, and Nordyne accepted these terms when it accepted ICM's quotation.

On appeal, Nordyne argues that the District Court erred as a matter of law in holding that the contract between the parties included the forum-selection clause. It argues that the July 1997 quotation did not amount to an offer because (1) it was not for immediate acceptance, but was subject to ICM's approval at its home office, and to ICM's providing acceptable samples, and (2) it did not specify quantity and did not include a delivery schedule. Nordyne proposes that its September 1997 purchase order was the offer, which ICM accepted by signing and returning Nordyne's acknowledgment form. Nordyne argues that the terms and conditions on ICM's invoices were not part of the contract because the first invoice arrived after the contract had been made. These terms and conditions were thus simply proposals for modifying an existing contract and not binding on Nordyne without its express consent.

III.

In this diversity case, we review *de novo* the District Court's application of state law, predicting how the highest court in Missouri would resolve the issues. See *Salve Regina College v. Russell*, 499 U.S. 225, 231, 111 S.Ct. 1217, 113 L.Ed.2d 190 (1991). The transaction between Nordyne and ICM for the sale of goods is governed by Article 2 of the Uniform Commercial Code (UCC), as adopted by Missouri, **Mo.Rev.Stat. § 400.1-201 et seq.** A determination of the terms of the contract between ICM and Nordyne must begin with identification of the offer and acceptance. Because the UCC does not define "offer," Missouri looks to its common law and to the Restatement of Contracts for the definition. See *Brown Machine, Division of John Brown, Inc. v. Hercules, Inc.,* 770 S.W.2d 416, 419 (Mo.App.1989).

Under Missouri case law, an "offer is made when the offer leads the offeree to reasonably believe that an offer has been made." *Id.* The **Restatement (Second) of Contracts § 24** defines offer as "the manifestation of willingness to enter into a bargain, so made as to justify another person in understanding that his assent to that bargain is invited and will conclude it." The general rule is that a price quotation, such as one appearing in a catalogue or on a flyer, is not an offer, but is rather a suggestion to induce offers by others. *Brown,* 770 S.W.2d at 419. However, a price quotation, "if detailed enough, can amount to an offer creating the power of acceptance; to do so it must reasonably appear from the price quote that assent to the quote is all that is needed to ripen the offer into a contract." *Id.*; see also *The Boese-Hilburn Co. v. Dean Machinery Co.,* 616 S.W.2d 520, 524 (Mo.App.1981). Factors relevant in determining whether a price quotation is an offer include the extent of prior inquiry, the completeness of the terms of the suggested bargain, and the number of persons to whom the price quotation is communicated. **Restatement (Second) of Contracts § 26**, comment *c.*

> **FYI**
>
> Comment c to **Restatement (Second) § 26** also states, "A 'quotation' of price is usually a statement of price per unit of quantity; it may omit the quantity to be sold, time and place of delivery, terms of payment, and other terms. It is sometimes associated with a price list or circular, but the word 'quote' is commonly understood as inviting an offer rather than as making one, even when directed to a particular customer. But just as the word 'offer' does not necessarily mean that an offer is intended, so the word 'quote' may be used in an offer."

Here all factors weigh in ICM's favor. ICM and Nordyne had been communicating for several months regarding the contract at issue before the July 29, 1997, quotation was sent, this quotation was sent only to Nordyne, and the quotation included quantity, price, and time in which to accept, as well as packaging, shipping, and payment terms. We note that the quotation was for a product specifically designed for Nordyne. We find Nordyne's argument that the quotation was not an offer because it did not contain a delivery schedule to be without merit. The quotation included sufficient terms to constitute an offer under Missouri law.

The fact that ICM's home office issued the letter of September 12, 1997, asking for Nordyne's production approval, i.e., Nordyne's acceptance of ICM's offer, undermines Nordyne's argument that the quotation was not an offer because it required ICM's home office approval. This approval in fact occurred, and thereafter Nordyne approved the beginning of production.

We also reject Nordyne's argument that the quotation could not be the offer because the quantity was not definite. The quoted price-per-unit was based on Nordyne's own estimated annual usage of 40,000 units. Once Nordyne signed the production approval, we believe it was bound to purchase approximately this many units, just as ICM was bound to provide them at the quoted price. In fact, each party lived up to its side of the bargain in these respects. Nordyne ordered and paid for 46,151 units; ICM shipped the units ordered and charged Nordyne $9.87 apiece. Each purchase order issued by Nordyne, including the first one for 20,000 units, was not a new offer, but rather part performance of the contract between the parties. This contract included the terms and conditions under which the parties had been dealing for approximately ten years. The forum-selection provision had been part of the parties' course of dealing and incorporated by reference into the present contract. Lastly, we perceive no unfairness in enforcing one term of the terms and conditions on ICM's invoices, when Nordyne itself had been taking advantage of another such term—namely, the one-year warranty. Thus the District Court correctly granted ICM's motion to dismiss on the basis of improper venue.

Accordingly, we affirm.

Think About It!

The court bases some of its reasoning on the parties' "course of dealing"—the patterns of dealings that they have established in their past contracts. Chapter 7, page 702, elaborates on this concept. What such patterns are noted in the statement of facts?

When Nordyne contracts with a new customer, the parties have no course of dealing. How might that affect the contract formation process?

If you were ICM's attorney, how would you edit the company's standard-term documents mentioned in this opinion?

Problem 4-6: When Is a Price Quotation an Offer?

A wrote B, "Please advise us the lowest price you can give us on our order for ten car loads of Mason green jars, complete, with caps, packed one dozen in a case, either delivered here, or f.o.b. cars your place, as you prefer. State terms and cash discount." B replied, "We quote you Mason fruit jars, complete, in one-dozen boxes, delivered in East St. Louis, Ill.: Pints $4.50, quarts $5.00, half gallons $6.50, per gross, for immediate acceptance, and shipment not later than May 15, 1895; sixty days' acceptance, cash in ten days." Was this an offer?

§ 4.1.3. The Bidding Process: RFPs, RFBs, and RFQs

The business process of bidding typically involves a flurry of forms, documents, and other communications among the parties interested in a particular project. To apply the general rules about assent to those communications, it is important to have a working understanding of how the bidding process works.

When a company wishes to contract for goods or services, it may initiate a "procurement process" by publishing or sending to one or more vendors or service providers (sellers) one of the following requests, referred to collectively as RFx:

- Request for Information (RFI)
- Request for Proposal (RFP)
- Request for Quotation (RFQ)
- Request for Bid (RFB)

In the construction industry, the bidding process can occur between the owner of a project and a contractor/vendor, or it can occur between a contractor and a subcontractor/vendor. These two bidding transactions are almost always business-to-business (B2B), and they raise the same legal concerns.

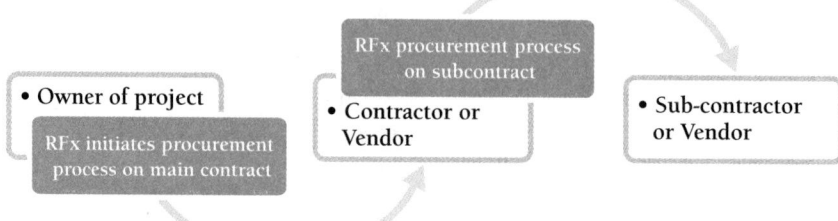

In many businesses, standardized software can facilitate an "eProcurement" process (called eRFx), which allows the bid process to be integrated into supply chain management with upstream and downstream businesses. The legal issue to be addressed is whether an RFx is an offer or merely an aspect of preliminary negotiations. In order to resolve this, you need to know more about the two main systems of procurement:

- "Direct procurement" (which uses the RFI, RFP, and RFQ)
- "Competitive procurement" (which uses the RFB and is also referred to as open procurement or open tender)

Direct Procurement

Direct procurement is used almost exclusively among non-governmental entities. It divides the procurement process into three distinct steps, initiated by three distinct documents, but a process need not use all three.

- The **RFI** (Request for Information) is a screening and information-gathering device. A buyer either publishes the RFI or sends a limited number to preselected providers. The request states the goals and invites the providers to describe their capabilities and skills as related to these goals. The document is designed to facilitate comparative analysis of the suppliers and provide information to the requesting party on which next steps can be based.
- The **RFP** (Request for Proposal) is sent to candidates who match the buyer's needs and who may have been identified from responses to an RFI. Generally, the RFP presents a specific set of requirements and goals (more specific than those in an RFI) and allows each candidate to suggest a solution based on its own creativity, skills, and resources.
- The **RFQ** (Request for Quotations) states a non-negotiable desired service or product, the parameters and requirements of the product, and the rules for submitting qualified bids. It is used in two distinct settings. One setting is as part of a procurement process initiated with an RFI or RFP, followed by an RFQ. Alternatively, the second use is as a stand-alone document asking for bids (not preceded by an RFI or RFP) without first getting advance information on the potential bidders or soliciting the expertise of the potential bidders in assembling the plans and specifications.

Competitive Procurement

Competitive procurement is an open but highly regulated bidding process that is standard for government contracts, especially public works contracts. In competitive procurement the government body or other project owner defines the project and then issues a single document:

- The **RFB** (Request for Bid) states a non-negotiable desired service or product, the parameters and requirements of the product, and the rules for submitting qualified bids. Suppliers/providers are invited to submit bids, and departures from stated specifications generally disqualify the bid.

Much of the case law involving RFBs involves procedural issues related to bids on public works. (For example: When does a statute require that the lowest qualified bid be accepted? When does the actual acceptance occur? Did particular bidders comply with the specified requirements?).

Which Documents Are Offers?

The RFI is unlikely to be an offer because it is mainly a request for providers to describe their skills and capabilities as related to a particular project. There is no discussion of terms such as price, dates, etc. which would suggest a definite expression of an offer.

The RFP narrows down these candidates by requesting information as to how a contractor would complete a project based on their proposed plan. Again, there is no expression of an intent to enter into a binding contract, so it is unlikely to be an offer.

The RFQ and RFB are likely to be requests for offers. They set out detailed parameters that contractors subsequently use in their bids. Those bids—now sufficiently definite as to terms and expressing commitment by the contractors—are likely to be offers.

For More Information

Here are some links to websites discussing RFI, RFQ, and RFP:

www.techsoup.org/learningcenter/ techplan/page5507.cfm

www.simplexity.net/articles/RFI_ RFP.html

http://it.toolbox.com/blogs/ original-thinking/outstanding- rfp-and-rfi-whats-the-difference- 24312

For instance, in *Quake Construction* **(page 249)**, the bidding process was by "direct procurement." American Airlines (AA), selected Jones as its agent to run the bidding process for AA. The stated facts aren't clear as to how Jones selected Quake to be one of the bidders (perhaps by RFI and/or RFP, but maybe not). If an RFI and/or RFP had been used, neither one would have been an offer, because they were merely asking for ideas and information; they didn't manifest any intent to be bound upon the contractor's assent, nor did they contain reasonably certain terms.

Jones' "invitation to bid" to Quake was an RFQ, and Quake's bid was the offer.

The RFQ wasn't an offer because it lacked Quake's price term and because neither Quake nor the other bidders could create a contract merely by saying "yes."

Note that Quake's bid/offer wasn't accepted by Jones on behalf of AA. Instead, as is sometimes the case, the parties then entered into negotiations about the subcontractors and other topics, which they agreed to memorialize into a final written agreement, which never happened.

Final Note

Although there is a high degree of consistency of usage of these terms within the business community, government entities sometimes use them interchangeably, incorrectly, or in meaningless combinations (e.g., "Request for Bid Proposal"). Court decisions seem not to take notice of the differences in the terms and sometimes do not focus enough on the function and content of the documents. When analyzing a client's situation or case law, it is thus essential to consider the language used, the parties' reasonable expectations, and the surrounding circumstances, in order to fully understand whether an offer has occurred in the bidding process.

Problems: Was an Offer Made?

Analyze each of the fact situations below to determine whether any of the parties made an offer. (As you learned in Chapter 3, there might be a viable claim for promissory estoppel or unjust enrichment, even if there is no offer or the offer is not accepted, but you should not include that analysis in this problem set.) Be precise about which language and circumstances support finding an offer or no offer.

4-7. The following set of communications was exchanged between Owner and Customer:

- Owner placed an ad in the newspaper asking payment in cash for 40 acres of land, "vicinity: Greenwood, Colorado."
- Customer sent letter expressing interest, asking for more details.
- Owner sent Customer a flyer describing the property, giving the location, and stating the price.
- Customer replied by letter stating he was not sure he found the property, asking for its legal description, and suggesting a certain bank as escrow agent.
- Owner wrote back stating that "it sounds like you found the correct lot," that Customer's bank is acceptable as an escrow agent, and that Customer "must decide fast if you are really interested in purchasing the land because I expect to have a buyer in the next week or so." Two days later, Owner sold the land to a third party.

[handwritten margin note: No time frame. was decision he asked for, but implied rejection.]

[handwritten margin note: this is offer on part of customer]

- Not knowing that Owner already sold the property, Customer replied to Owner's letter, saying that he was accepting Owner's offer to sell the property and was proceeding to deposit the purchase price immediately with the escrow agent.

When Customer discovered that Owner sold the land to a third party, he brought an action against Owner for breach of contract. Did Owner make an offer to sell the property? If so, in which communication? *[handwritten: No!]* Did Customer make an offer to buy the property? If so, in which communication? Why are the other communications not offers?

[handwritten: Only in last letter when offer had been rejected.]

When Customer discovered that Owner sold the land to a third party, he brought an action against Owner for breach of contract. Did Owner make an offer to sell the property? If so, in which communication? Did Customer make an offer to buy the property? If so, in which communication? Why are the other communications not offers?

4-8. Ace Manufacturing Company (AMC) sends an RFI for an overhaul of the electrical system for its main production line to 20 electrical contractors, 18 of which respond in writing with the requested information. AMC then issues an RFP for the same project to those 18 contractors, 15 of which respond with proposed solutions and an approximate price. AMC then issues to the 15 responding contractors an RFQ based on a combination of several of the proposed solutions above. Ten of those contractors respond with bids detailing the proposed charges for each item in the RFQ, as well as any subcontractors who would be participating in the work. The company selects one contractor and opens negotiations with that party. After two weeks of wrangling over terms, the parties sign a five-page agreement.

4-9. United States Mint sent advertising materials to selected persons, including previous buyers of coins and coin collectors, describing commemorative coins to be issued and sold pursuant to orders received with payment. The materials gave the price of the coins, promised a discount to persons placing an order before a certain date, said that delivery would take place 6 to 8 weeks after the issuance date of the coins, reserved to the U.S. Mint the "right to limit quantities shipped, subject to availability" and encouraged potential purchasers to forward early payment because the "Mint may

following language: "VERY IMPORTANT–PLEASE READ: Please accept my order for the coins I have indicated. I understand that all sales are final and not subject to refund. Verification of my order will be made by the U.S. Mint. . . . If my order is received by [date], I will be entitled to purchase the coins at the . . . discount price shown. I have read, understand and agree to the above. Demand exceeded the Mint's expectations for $5 gold coins, and the supplies were exhausted quickly. Within a few months of the deadline, the $5 coins had doubled in value. The buyers in the dispute at issue placed several orders for the coins by the specified date, paying for some with checks and others by credit card. They received the coins paid for with checks, but did not receive any of the coins paid for by credit card. Investigation revealed that the third party vendor handling the credit card transactions had mistakenly rejected the buyers' otherwise valid credit card. The buyers sued the U.S. government for damages for breach of contract. Were the Mint's advertising materials an offer or a mere invitation to offers?

4-10. J. Cheney Mason, a prominent criminal defense lawyer (*see* en.wikipedia.org/wiki/Cheney_Mason), represented a defendant who had been accused of murdering several people in Orlando in 1997. In support of his alibi—that he was in Atlanta at the time of the killings—the defendant introduced into evidence an Atlanta hotel surveillance camera tape showing that he was in that hotel a few hours after the murder took place in Orlando. A few months after the defendant was convicted, Mason appeared on the TV show "Dateline," where he asserted that it would be impossible for anyone to have travelled from Orlando to the Atlanta hotel in the time allotted. In particular, he said that the trip from the Atlanta airport to the hotel could not be done in the required time—28 minutes. Mason went on to say, "I challenge anybody to show me, I'll pay them a million dollars if they can do it." The Dateline reporter asked for clarification about the time allotted, and Mason responded, "Twenty-eight minutes. Can't happen. Didn't happen." A law student in Texas accomplished just that, made a video of the trip, and demanded $1,000,000 from the defense attorney, who claimed that the so-called offer was a joke and therefore could not be accepted to form a contract. See **www.courthousenews. com/2009/06/19/MAsonDateline.pdf** (complaint). Should the law student receive the reward?

§ 4.2. Termination of the Power of Acceptance

When an offer is made, the offeree gains the "power of acceptance"—the right to complete the process of mutual assent by saying "yes" to the offeror as long as acceptance occurs before the offer terminates. The offer, and the offeree's power to accept the offer, can terminate in any of the following ways:

- The offeree may do nothing, so the offer may end (lapse) thru passage of time.
- The offeree may "reject" the offer, either by manifesting an intent not to accept it or by making a counter-offer, which implicitly rejects the offer.
- The offeror or offeree may die or become incapacitated.
- The offeror may "revoke" (withdraw) the offer, unless it is not revocable at that time.

This section amplifies each of these means of terminating the offeree's power of acceptance.

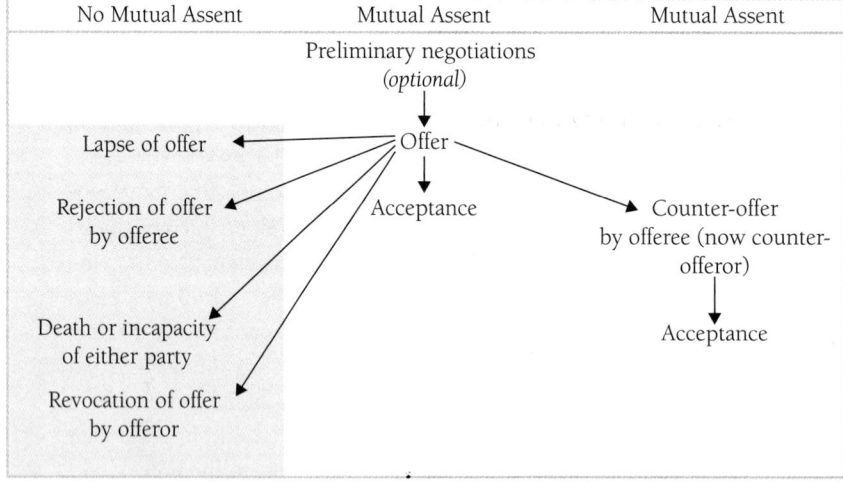

On a related topic, note that an offer may specify a condition that must be satisfied in order for the offer to be valid—that is, the offeree has no power of acceptance until the condition arises. For example, the owner of a race horse might promise to sell the horse to the offeree-buyer if the horse wins a specified race. If the horse does not win, the condition is not satisfied (and can never be satisfied), so the offer's power of acceptance never arises. Alternatively, an offer might specify that it is valid only as long as a particular condition exists; when the condition ceases to exist, so does the offeree's power of acceptance (if the offeree has not yet accepted the offer). For instance, a person who wishes to buy a particular piece of real estate might promise to buy the property as long as 30-year fixed mortgage interest rates remain below 4%. If interest rates reach 4%, then the buyer's offer (and the seller's power of acceptance) expires, because the condition ceased to exist. In Chapter 7, **page 836**, we will cover express conditions _within_ contracts.

§ 4.2.1. Lapse of Offer

Under the common law and the Restatement (Second), the offeree's power of acceptance is terminated by the "lapse" of the offer at the time specified in the offer (or if none, after a reasonable time). The international rules concur, but also take the vagaries of international communication into effect by allowing the offeror to decide whether to treat a late acceptance as effective:

Restatement (Second) § 41. Lapse of Time

(1) An offeree's power of acceptance is terminated at the time specified in the offer, or, if no time is specified, at the end of a reasonable time.

(2) What is a reasonable time is a question of fact, depending on all the circumstances existing when the offer and attempted acceptance are made.

(3) Unless otherwise indicated by the language or the circumstances, and subject to the rule stated in § 49, an offer sent by mail is seasonably accepted if an acceptance is mailed at any time before midnight on the day on which the offer is received

---

CISG Art. 18. (in Part II. Formation of the Contract)

(1) . . . .

(2) An acceptance of an offer becomes effective at the moment the indication of assent reaches the offeror. An acceptance is not effective if the indication of assent does not reach the offeror within the time he has fixed or, if no time is fixed, within a reasonable time, due account being taken of the circumstances of the transaction, including the rapidity of the means of communication employed by the offeror. An oral offer must be accepted immediately unless the circumstances indicate otherwise.

[Handwritten margin notes:]

Terminated time
1) specified time
2) reasonable time
when?
1) when was offer
2) when was acc.
(made)
✳ mail by midnight.

Acceptance: effective at moment
1. Effective offeror
receives outside of
2) not if fixed-time
✳ 30ral accept imm.

CISG Art. 21. (in Part II. Formation of the Contract)

(1) A late acceptance is nevertheless effective as an acceptance if without delay the offeror orally so informs the offeree or dispatches a notice to that effect.

(2) If a letter or other writing containing a late acceptance shows that it has been sent in such circumstances that if its transmission had been normal it would have reached the offeror in due time, the late acceptance is effective as an acceptance unless, without delay, the offeror orally informs the offeree that he considers his offer as having lapsed or dispatches a notice to that effect.

———————

UNIDROIT Art. 2.1.7. Time of Acceptance

1. Time fixed
2. Reasonable time
3. Oral immed.

An offer must be accepted within the time the offeror has fixed or, if no time is fixed, within a reasonable time having regard to the circumstances, including the rapidity of the means of communication employed by the offeror. An oral offer must be accepted immediately unless the circumstances indicate otherwise.

UNIDROIT Art. 2.1.8. Acceptance within a Fixed Period of Time

When offer is dispatched!

A period of time for acceptance fixed by the offeror begins to run from the time that the offer is dispatched. A time indicated in the offer is deemed to be the time of dispatch unless the circumstances indicate otherwise.

UNIDROIT Art. 2.1.9. Late Acceptance; Delay in Transmission

(1) A late acceptance is nevertheless effective as an acceptance if without undue delay the offeror so informs the offeree or gives notice to that effect.

(2) If a communication containing a late acceptance shows that it has been sent in such circumstances that if its transmission had been normal it would have reached the offeror in due time, the late acceptance is effective as an acceptance unless, without undue delay, the offeror informs the offeree that it considers the offer as having lapsed.

late acc eff
if - offeree informs ✓
late acc. w/ bad trans eff
unless - of informs ✗

In an upcoming case, ***Houston Dairy, Inc. v. John Hancock Mutual Life Ins. Co.*** **(page 372)**, the offer of a loan was specifically limited to an acceptance within seven days. The debtor attempted to accept eighteen days later, by which time the original offer had lapsed, so the attempted acceptance was instead a counter-offer. The remaining portion of the case focuses on whether the creditor had accepted the counter-offer before the debtor revoked it. If the creditor had not specifically limited the original offer to seven days, the court would have had to decide whether the debtor accepted the original offer within a "reasonable time" or whether the offer lapsed before the attempted acceptance.

§ 4.2.2. Rejection by the Offeree

An offeree's power of acceptance can also be terminated by the offeree's rejection of the offer. "A manifestation of intention by the offeree is a rejection if it gives the offeror reason to believe that it is the offeree's intention not to accept the offer."[*] Rejection can be express or implied (by conduct), and it also may occur by virtue of a counter-offer. But not all rejections terminate the power of acceptance. Can you articulate the exceptions in the rules below?

Restatement (Second) § 38. Rejection

(1) An offeree's power of acceptance is terminated by his rejection of the offer, unless the offeror has manifested a contrary intention.

(2) A manifestation of intention not to accept an offer is a rejection unless the offeree manifests an intention to take it under further advisement.

Restatement (Second) § 39. Counter-Offers

(1) . . . .

(2) An offeree's power of acceptance is terminated by his making of a counter-offer, unless the offeror has manifested a contrary intention or unless the counter-offer manifests a contrary intention of the offeree.

[handwritten margin notes: "1) offeror has contrary intention"; "2) offeree intends w/ further advisement"; "contrary intentions"]

The chart below provides examples of what is and is not rejection of an offer:

	Offer Rejected	Offer Not Rejected
Express rejection?	A offers to buy B's car for a specified price, and B responds, "I will not sell my car."	A offers to buy B's car for a specified price, and B responds, "I wasn't planning to sell my car, but let me think about it."

[handwritten margin note: "§38 (2) offeree further advisement"]

---

[*] E. Allan Farnsworth, *Contracts* § 3.20 (4th ed. 2004).

OR *ONR*

Implied rejection?	A offers to buy B's car for a specified price, and B subsequently <u>sells</u> the car to C.	A offers to buy B's car for a specified price, and B then <u>shows</u> the car to another potential buyer.
Counter-offer and rejection?	A offers to sell his car to B for $15,000, and B responds, "I will give you $12,000 for your car." *(only)*	A offers to sell a textbook to B for $100 and B responds, "I'll <u>think about that</u>, but I am willing to offer you $80." A offers to sell his bike to B for $125, and B responds, "<u>Would you take $100?</u>"

Of course, not every responsive utterance is clear on this issue. The issue is whether the statement is reasonably understood as manifesting rejection.

§ 4.2.3. Death or Incapacity of the Offeror or Offeree

An offeree's power of acceptance is terminated upon the death or incapacity of either the offeror or the offeree. Note that this is a rule about <u>termination of an offer, not termination of a contract</u>. If a contract is formed, death or incapacity excuses performance of that contract only if the disability or death affects an individual necessary for performance. (*See* **Chapter 8, pages 978 and 998**.) In some instances, a <u>critical question therefore</u> will be whether an offer was accepted (and the contract therefore formed) before the death or incapacity that would otherwise terminate the power of acceptance.

Problem 4-11: Death of the Offeror

Consider the following facts suggested by the case of *Earle v. Angell*, 32 N.E. 164 (1892):

> An elderly woman promises her nephew $500 if he will attend her funeral. Her <u>nephew promises that he will come</u> if he is notified in time. He does attend her funeral, and submits a claim to the estate for $500.

If the aunt dies before the contract is created, the offer terminates upon her death. If the contract is created before she dies, however, then the contract survives her death, and the estate must pay. Whether the nephew is entitled to collect $500 therefore depends on whether he accepted her offer before his power of acceptance was terminated. Does the estate have to pay the nephew? *Yes.*

[handwritten margin note: bilateral promise]

[handwritten margin note: She didn't die before he made the promise]

§ 4.2.4. Revocation by the Offeror

The fourth means by which the offeree's power of acceptance can be terminated is by the offeror revoking the offer. Like a rejection, revocation can be express or implied in fact.

Restatement (Second) § 42. Revocation by Communication from Offeror Received by Offeree

An offeree's power of acceptance is terminated when the offeree receives from the offeror a manifestation of an intention not to enter into the proposed contract.

Restatement (Second) § 43. Indirect Communication of Revocation

An offeree's power of acceptance is terminated when the offeror takes definite action inconsistent with an intention to enter into the proposed contract and the offeree acquires reliable information to that effect.

> *Illustration 1.* A offers a parcel of land to B at a stated price, and gives B a week in which to consider the proposal. Within the week, A contracts to sell the parcel to C, and B is informed of that fact by a tenant of the premises. B nevertheless sends a formal acceptance which is received by A within the week. There is no contract between A and B.

Restatement (Second) § 46. Revocation of General Offer

Where an offer is made by advertisement in a newspaper or other general notification to the public or to a number of persons whose identity is unknown to the offeror, the offeree's power of acceptance is terminated when a notice of termination is given publicly by advertisement or other general notification equal to that given to the offer and no better means of notification is reasonably available.

As with other communications related to assent, factual questions may arise regarding the application of these rules, such as whether particular language is "manifestation of an intention" not to enter into the transaction (under § 42), whether "no better means of notification is reasonably available" (under § 46), whether action by the offeror is "definite action" that is "inconsistent" with an intention not to enter into the transaction (under § 43), and whether the offeree has acquired "reliable" information about the offeror's action (also under § 43).

Problems: Terminating the Power of Acceptance

4-12. A popular cabaret singer makes an offer to perform on June 10th for $3500 in a performance hall owned by the offeree in Seattle. While the offeree is exploring how much income he could make selling tickets and related merchandise for her performance, he hears from his booking agent that the cabaret singer has just scheduled a month-long tour in Australia for June. The offeree quickly mails an acceptance to the singer. Is there acceptance? Would there be acceptance if the offeree instead hears that the singer has scheduled concerts on June 8th in Miami and June 11th in New Orleans?

4-13. AMC issues an RFQ for a project. Supplier B responds with a bid (expiring in a month) that includes a very competitive price, but a slightly different timeline than in the RFQ, because Supplier B has competing obligations for part of the proposed timeline in the RFQ. A week later, AMC opens the eight bids received. AMC is intrigued with the expertise of Supplier B and the price of B's bid. The AMC bid supervisor immediately calls Supplier B and says, "I need to check your timeline with my project manager, because it may be problematic. If you can do the work a month after our RFQ timeline, but in 2/3 of the time specified in the RFQ, we can close the deal now." After investigating the job further for three days, Supplier B tells AMC that it can't do the job so quickly. Then AMC tries to accept Supplier B's earlier bid, still within the one-month period specified in the offer. Supplier B argues that that bid is no longer available for consideration. Who's right? (Select two answers.)

    a. Supplier B is correct, because its initial bid has been impliedly rejected by AMC's counter-offer.

    b. Supplier B is correct, because its initial bid lapsed upon AMC's counter-offer.

    c. Supplier B is correct, because AMC revoked Supplier B's offer by AMC's counter-offer.

    d. AMC is correct, because B's bid was not rejected.

    e. AMC is correct, because Supplier B's initial bid had not yet lapsed.

4-14. Betta has a ski equipment store at a popular ski area. Her supplier sends her a catalog with the upcoming season's "hot sellers for cold days; shipment within ten days." She fills out the order sheet inside the catalog, ordering 12 boot-warmer appliances (which plug into a cigarette lighter outlet in a car

[handwritten: solicitation for offer]

and blow warm air into cold boots), and sends it to the supplier. Eight days later, Betta gets a handwritten postcard from the seller, saying that the boot-warmers are in stock and are available for a new 10% discount, if Betta orders at least 15. Betta reconsiders her order of 12 and phones in an order for 16 instead. Two days later, Betta receives a box in the mail with 12 boot-warmers. A day later, she receives a box with 16 boot-warmers. When was a contract formed and on what terms?

[handwritten: 2 contracts]

[handwritten: 1) unilateral 2) bilateral offer accepted by shipment at 12]

[handwritten: counter-offer rejection of first 12]

§ 4.2.4.1. Limitations on the Power to Revoke: Unilateral Contracts

The traditional common law rule is that the offeror may revoke the offer at any time before acceptance. However, that rule generates some unfairness, as illustrated by two well known hypotheticals:

- *The Brooklyn Bridge Hypothetical*: A says to B, "If you walk across the Brooklyn Bridge, I will give you $500." B eagerly starts across the bridge and is within a few feet of the end when A yells, "I revoke!"
- *The Flagpole Hypothetical*: A says to B, "If you climb this flagpole, I will give you $500." B eagerly starts to climb the flagpole and is within a few feet of the top when A yells, "I revoke!"

Courts and commentators have fashioned two rules to limit the unfairness, but—to understand those rules—you first need to understand the difference between unilateral and bilateral contracts.

[handwritten: 2 rules to limit unfairness of revocation]

Parties typically form contracts in order to exchange performances that will occur in the future (e.g., the seller will deliver goods, the buyer will pay for the goods), so they form the contract by exchanging *promises* to engage in those performances (e.g., the seller *promises* to deliver goods, the buyer *promises* to pay for the goods). Each party seeks the commitment of the other to a future performance in order to "seal the deal" rather than looking for immediate performance to signal agreement. A contract formed by such a mutual exchange of *promises* is often called a "bilateral contract," because both parties have made *promises*. The offer to enter such a contract is an "offer for a bilateral contract" because it seeks the commitment of the other party through a promise that constitutes acceptance. The offeree's promise may be made explicitly in words or implicitly by conduct (perhaps by the beginning of the requested performance). Regardless of the means of promising, the acceptance is the offeree's commitment to the performance that is sought by the offeror.

[handwritten: 1. bilateral contract = mutual exchange of promises]

Sometimes, however, an offeror may demand that the offeree accept not by promising to commit to the contract, but instead by actually performing the specified acts. If acceptance is to be made only by performance, then no contract is formed (and the *offeror* is therefore not bound) until the offeree completes the performance. The *offeree* is not bound until the moment he completes performance (if it even makes sense to talk about binding someone to performance already accomplished). Such arrangements are called "unilateral contracts" because only one party makes a promise. The offer to enter such a contract is called an "offer for a unilateral contract." Note that in a unilateral contract, *both* parties eventually *perform*. It is unilateral because only one party *promises* to perform; the other party assents by performing, but does not promise in advance to do so. Once a contract is formed, it doesn't matter whether it is unilateral or bilateral.

Offers for rewards are a prime example of offers for unilateral contracts. In *Carbolic Smoke Ball* (see *Leonard v. PepsiCo*, **page 300**), the company did not want purchasers of the product to promise to use it and catch influenza. Rather, the company promised that if a purchaser actually bought the smoke ball, used it as directed, and then caught the flu, the company would then pay. A business that offers a bonus to employees who remain with the business until a particular date but does not ask them to promise to remain is making an offer for a unilateral contract; the business will pay if they do stay, but the employees are free to leave at any time. In *Hamer v. Sidway* (**page 19**), the uncle made an offer for a unilateral contract if he did not seek his nephew's promise to refrain from smoking, drinking, and playing cards, but promised to pay if the nephew actually refrained.

Think About It!

Consider the newspaper advertisement in *Lefkowitz*, (**page 288**), in which the store specified that to buy the furs at the bargain price the offeree had to be the first person in line at the store by 9 a.m. on the next Saturday morning. Was that an offer for a unilateral or bilateral contract?

Why does it matter whether a contract is bilateral or unilateral? For both kinds of contracts, the critical issue is determining when the contract was formed. If an offeror makes an offer for a bilateral contract, then, at the moment the promises are exchanged, the contract is created and both parties are bound. If an offeror makes an offer for a unilateral contract, however, the offeree cannot create a contract by promising because the offeror did not ask for and will not accept a promise as the manner of acceptance. Under traditional analysis, that means the offeror is not bound and can withdraw her promise at any time until the offeree has fully performed, because only by full performance can the offeree create the contract. *offerer not bound until performance fulfilled.*

That result—that the offeror has the option to withdraw the offer, even if the offeree has performed much though not yet all of what was asked—is deeply problematical. Consider again the examples of unilateral contracts above. If employees are promised a bonus if they stay in their jobs until a particular date and in reliance on the promise they do remain, despite other opportunities, it is troubling if the employer can announce just before that date that the offer is withdrawn. If young Willie refrains from smoking, drinking, and gambling starting the day uncle William makes his promise, it is troubling if William can withdraw that promise the day before Willie's 21st birthday. Yet the definition of a unilateral contract leads to that result, and a claim of promissory estoppel might not be viable because it may not be reasonable for the promisee to rely on a promise that can be withdrawn at any time during the promisee's performance.

Courts and commentators have fashioned two rules that limit the effect of this dilemma. Under the first rule, an offer is understood as being an offer for a bilateral (rather than unilateral) contract, seeking a return promise, unless the offer makes it very clear that a unilateral contract is desired. Clarity may come from explicit language in the offer ("I do not want your promise; only performance will do") or it may come from the circumstances (an offer for a reward), but because clarity is required, the circumstances must be unusual, so that only a unilateral contract makes sense. Thus if an offer is silent, vague, or ambiguous with respect to whether performance alone is permitted as a means of acceptance, the offer will be understood as proposing a bilateral contract. The offeree may accept by means of an express return promise, or the offeree may accept by means of an implied promise—by performing or beginning performance—accepting the offer's terms and promising that performance will be completed. Once the offeree begins performance, both parties are bound. This rule also appears in the Restatement (Second):

Restatement (Second) § 32. **Invitation of Promise or Performance**

In case of doubt an offer is interpreted as inviting the offeree to accept either by promising to perform what the offer requests or by rendering the performance, as the offeree chooses.

Restatement (Second) § 62. **Effect of Performance by Offeree Where Offer Invites Either Performance or Promise**

(1) Where an offer invites an offeree to choose between acceptance by promise and acceptance by performance, the tender or beginning of the invited performance or a tender of a beginning of it is an acceptance by performance.

(2) Such an acceptance operates as a promise to render complete performance.

[Handwritten margin notes: "Promissory estoppel not reasonable for unilateral intention." "limits 1. express return promise 2. implied promise → by performance starting, both parties are bound." "Invites 1. promise to perform 2. performing → both acceptance starting = complete performance."]

Note that, under the Restatement (Second) rules, the offeror can

- Limit the offeree to acceptance by promise (an offer for bilateral contract);
- Limit the offeree to acceptance by performance (an offer for unilateral contract, so § 45 applies (see below));
- Expressly say in the offer that the offeree may choose (so § 62 applies); or
- Leave the offer silent as to the method of acceptance (so § 32 lets the offeree choose, and § 62 applies as well).

The second rule responding to the danger of revocation after performance has begun applies to the true unilateral contract situation (in which the offeree can accept only by performance). The Restatement (Second) of Contracts contains this provision:

Restatement (Second) § 45. Option Contract Created by Part Performance or Tender

(1) Where an offer invites an offeree to accept by rendering a performance and does not invite a promissory acceptance, an option contract is created when the offeree tenders or begins the invited performance or tenders a beginning of it.

(2) The offeror's duty of performance under any option contract so created is conditional on completion or tender of the invited performance in accordance with the terms of the offer.

Restatement (Second) § 45 in effect makes an offer for a unilateral contract temporarily irrevocable once the offeree begins performance. Under this provision, the offeree is not bound to begin or continue performing, but once the offeree begins performance (by tendering part of the consideration requested), the offeror must allow the offeree a reasonable time to finish performing. If the offeree completes the performance, there is a binding contract, so the offeror has a duty to fulfill the promise in the offer. If the offeree does not complete performance, the offeror has no duty to perform.

In determining whether an offer for a bilateral contract has been accepted by the beginning of performance or whether an offer for a unilateral contract has been made temporarily irrevocable by the beginning of performance under Restatement (Second) § 45, it is important to distinguish between mere preparation for performance and the beginning of actual performance. Only performance, not preparation for performance, satisfies these two rules, though the line between the two is sometimes hard to draw. Consider the following situations:

(1) An organization offers a reward for the best essay on a particular topic, and a potential essayist begins reading about the subject matter.

(2) A homeowner offers a painter $1000 to paint her house, and the painter purchases paint for the job.

(3) A property owner offers to sell a piece of property. The offeree spends time and money contacting others to join him in the purchase as well as flying across the country to visit the property.

Think About It!

In response to offers for both bilateral and unilateral contracts, the beginning of performance is significant. For offers for bilateral contracts, it constitutes acceptance of the offer. For offers for unilateral contracts, it invokes the protections in Restatement (Second) § 45. Given similar facts, would you expect courts to be more likely to find that the offeree began performance in a <u>bilateral</u> or in a unilateral contract situation?

Are these actions part of the performance requested by the offeror, or are they merely steps taken by the offeree to prepare herself to perform?

The terms "unilateral" and "bilateral" contract are now used in only some jurisdictions (and are not used in the Restatement (Second)), but the conceptual issue—whether acceptance is to be by promise or performance—continues to matter. However, the rules described above have decreased the number of cases in which the distinction is significant, because most offers are construed to be for bilateral contracts and because true unilateral contract offers often cannot be revoked once performance has begun.

§ 4.2.4.2. Other Limitations on Revocability

As we have seen, the general rule is that an offer is revocable by the offeror until accepted. The previous section reviewed one exception: offers for unilateral contracts. This section identifies and discusses additional exceptions, followed by a case that illustrates application of the exceptions and raises questions about additional exceptions that might be considered.

Offers may be at least temporarily irrevocable under the following circumstances:

Option Contract: Any offer (including those governed by UCC Article 2) can be made irrevocable if the offeree pays the offeror to keep the offer open, usually for a specified period of time, thereby creating an enforceable contract for an option on the underlying deal. Note that neither party is yet bound to the contract based on the offer; they are bound only to the option contract that gives the offeree a period of time in which to consider accepting the offer for the underlying transaction without fear the offer might be withdrawn. If no time is specified in the option contract terms, a court may determine that the option is available for a "reasonable time" (or, in proper circumstances, may decide the parties did not mean to commit to an option contract because no time period is specified). Recall that Restatement (Second) § 45 says an option contract is also created if the offeree begins performance in response to an offer for a unilateral contract; the option exists for a reasonable time to allow the offeree to complete performance.

Because the value of the option—the value of the right to take time to decide on the offer—is hard to quantify, courts often allow what may look like nominal consideration ($1 or $5 or even a promise to pay that amount without delivering it) to be sufficient consideration to create a contract. Restatement (Second) § 87(1) reflects similar flexibility:

Restatement (Second) § 87. **Option Contract**

(1) An offer is binding as an option contract if it
    (a) is in writing and signed by the offeror, recites a purported consideration for the making of the offer, and proposes an exchange on fair terms within a reasonable time; or
    (b) is made irrevocable by statute.

. . . .

"Firm Offers": If the transaction is governed by Article 2 because the predominant purpose involves a sale of goods, UCC § 2-205 applies. Under this section, a signed offer by a merchant promising it will be held open is enforceable, even without consideration, for the amount of time expressed (or for a reasonable time, if no time is given), up to three months. Note that if the offer is in a form supplied by the offeree, the offeror must "sign" (usually, initial) the assurance of irrevocability.

UCC § 2-205. **Firm Offers**

An offer by a merchant to buy or sell goods in a signed writing which by its terms give assurance that it will be held open is not revocable, for lack of consideration, during the time stated or if no time is stated for a reasonable time, but in no event may such period of irrevocability exceed three months; but any such term of assurance on a form supplied by the offeree must be separately signed by the offeror.

Some states have statutes that more broadly implement the same concept as UCC § 2-205—that a signed writing promising that an offer will be held open needs no consideration to be enforceable.*

In an option contract, because the offeror is bound by contract to keep the offer open as agreed, the offer is not governed by the usual rules on termination of the power of acceptance. It cannot be revoked or terminated by rejection or counter-offer. It lapses according to the terms of the option contract. Whether death or incapacity

Think About It!

Should firm offers (under UCC § 2-205 or comparable state statutes) be governed by the rules articulated in this paragraph?

affects the option depends on the rules regarding excuses from contract performance (*see* **Chapter 8, page 974**) rather than on the rules for termination of the power of acceptance. The exercise of an option is not governed by the mailbox rule and so is effective only when it reaches the offeror, unless the option contrat specifies otherwise.

In the absence of an option contract or a statutory firm offer, are there are other circumstances that might reasonably lead a court to limit revocation of an offer? In particular, if an offeree relies on the existence of an offer, perhaps spending resources to explore whether to accept the offer or in preparation for performing or taking other actions in reliance, should such reliance prevent the offeror from withdrawing the offer? For example, if a property owner offers to sell a piece of property and the offeree spends time and money contacting others to join him in the purchase and flies across the country to see the property, should those expenditures (if reasonably expected by the offeror) be grounds for requiring the offeror to keep the offer open to allow acceptance after those actions are taken?

The traditional answer to those questions is a clear "no"; if an offeree wants to ensure that the offer will remain open, she will have to seek the offeror's agreement to an option contract or to a firm offer under a relevant statutory provision. But, as illustrated in the case that follows, there may be special circumstances that lead courts to consider further restricting an offeror's power to revoke.

Reading the Law Critically: *Pavel Enterprises*

1. What was the precise sequence of communications between the general contractor and subcontractor that led to the dispute between them over whether a contract was agreed to by them?

---

* *See, e.g.,* N.Y. Gen. Oblig. L. § 5-1109 (McKinney 2001).

2. The court suggests at least four theories that could serve as the basis for finding a binding obligation between a general contractor and a subcontractor in similar bidding situations. What are those theories and what facts are necessary to support finding a contract on each theory? Why did they not operate to create a contract here?

3. Of the limitations on revocability reviewed in this section, which are discussed by the court in *Pavel*? Were any additional limitations discussed? Was the offeror's power to revoke limited by the application of any of those rules? Why or why not?

4. How does the bidding process pose additional challenges for the traditional rules on acceptance and irrevocability?

Pavel Enterprises v. A.S. Johnson Co.

PAVEL ENTERPRISES, INC., Plaintiff-Appellant

v.

A.S. JOHNSON COMPANY, Defendant-Respondent

Court of Appeals of Maryland
674 A.2d 521 (Md. Ct. App. 1996)

KARWACKI, Judge.

In this case we are invited to adapt the "modern" contractual theory of detrimental reliance,[1] or promissory estoppel, to the relationship between general contractors and their subcontractors. Although the theory of detrimental reliance is available to general contractors, it is not applicable to the facts of this case. For that reason, and because there was no traditional bilateral contract formed, we shall affirm the trial court.

I

The National Institutes of Health [hereinafter, "NIH"], solicited bids for a renovation project on Building 30 of its Bethesda, Maryland campus. The proposed work entailed some demolition work, but the major component of the job was mechanical, including heating, ventilation and air conditioning ["HVAC"].

---

[1] We prefer to use the phrase detrimental reliance, rather than the traditional nomenclature of "promissory estoppel," because we believe it more clearly expresses the concept intended. . . . *See* **Note**, *The "Firm Offer" Problem in Construction Bids and the Need for Promissory Estoppel*, **10 Wm & Mary L. Rev. 212, 214 n.17 (1968)** [hereinafter, *"The Firm Offer Problem"*].

Pavel Enterprises Incorporated [hereinafter, "PEI"], a general contractor from Vienna, Virginia and appellant in this action, prepared a bid for the NIH work. In preparing its bid, PEI solicited sub-bids from various mechanical subcontractors. The A.S. Johnson Company [hereinafter, "Johnson"], a mechanical subcontractor located in Clinton, Maryland and the appellee here, responded with a written scope of work proposal on July 27, 1993.[2] On the morning of August 5, 1993, the day NIH opened the general contractors' bids, Johnson verbally submitted a quote of $898,000 for the HVAC component.[3] Neither party disputes that PEI used Johnson's sub-bid in computing its own bid. PEI submitted a bid of $1,585,000 for the entire project.

General contractors' bids were opened on the afternoon of August 5, 1993. PEI's bid was the *second* lowest bid. The government subsequently disqualified the apparent low bidder,[4] however, and in mid-August, NIH notified PEI that its bid would be accepted.

With the knowledge that PEI was the lowest responsive bidder, Thomas F. Pavel, president of PEI, visited the offices of A.S. Johnson on August 26, 1993, and met with James Kick, Johnson's chief estimator, to discuss Johnson's proposed role in the work. Pavel testified at trial to the purpose of the meeting:

> "I met with Mr. Kick. And the reason for me going to their office was to look at their offices, to see their facility, to basically sit down and talk with them, as I had not done, and my company had not performed business with them on a direct relationship, but we had heard of their reputation. I wanted to go out and see where their facility was, see where they were located, and basically just sit down and talk to them. Because if we were going to use them on a project, I wanted to know who I was dealing with."

Pavel also asked if Johnson would object to PEI subcontracting directly with Powers for electric controls, rather than the arrangement originally envisioned in which Powers would be Johnson's subcontractor.[5] Johnson did not object.

Following that meeting, PEI sent a fax to all of the mechanical subcontractors from whom it had received sub-bids on the NIH job. The text of that fax is reproduced:

---

[2] The scope of work proposal listed all work that Johnson proposed to perform, but omitted the price term. This is a standard practice in the construction industry. The subcontractor's bid price is then filled in immediately before the general contractor submits the general bid to the letting party.

[3] PEI alleged at trial that Johnson's bid, as well as the bids of the other potential mechanical subcontractors contained a fixed cost of $355,000 for a sub-sub-contract to "Landis and Gear Powers" [hereinafter, "Powers"]. Powers was the sole source supplier of the electric controls for the project.

[4] The project at NIH was part of a set-aside program for small business. The apparent low bidder, J.J. Kirlin, Inc. was disqualified because it was not a small business.

[5] Pavel testified at trial that restructuring the arrangement in this manner would reduce the amount PEI needed to bond and thus reduce the price of the bond.

Pavel Enterprises, Inc.

TO: PROSPECTIVE MECHANICAL SUBCONTRACTORS
FROM: ESTIMATING DEPARTMENT
REFERENCE: NIH, BLDG 30 RENOVATION

We herewith respectfully request that you review your bid on the above referenced project that was bid on 8/05/93. PEI has been notified that we will be awarded the project as J.J. Kirlin, Inc. [the original low bidder] has been found to be nonresponsive on the solicitation. We anticipate award on or around the first of September and therefor request that you supply the following information.

1. Please break out your cost for the "POWERS" supplied control work as we will be subcontracting directly to "POWERS".

2. Please resubmit your quote deleting the above referenced item.

We ask this in an effort to allow all prospective bidders to compete on an even playing field.

Should you have any questions, please call us immediately as time is of the essence.

On August 30, 1993, PEI informed NIH that Johnson was to be the mechanical subcontractor on the job. On September 1, 1993, PEI mailed and faxed a letter to Johnson formally accepting Johnson's bid. That letter read:

Pavel Enterprises, Inc.

September 1, 1993

Mr. James H. Kick, Estimating Mngr.
A.S. Johnson Company
8042 Old Alexandria Ferry Road
Clinton, Maryland 20735
Re: NIH Bldg 30 HVAC Modifications
RC: IFB # 263-93-B (CM)-0422
Subject: Letter of Intent to award SUBJECT: Subcontract

Dear Mr. Kick;

We herewith respectfully inform your office of our intent to award a subcontract for the above referenced project per your quote received on 8/05/93 in the amount of $898,000.00. This subcontract will be forwarded upon receipt of our contract from the NIH, which we expect any day. A preconstruction meeting is currently scheduled at the NIH on 9/08/93 at 10 AM which we have been requested that your firm attend.

As discussed with you, a meeting was held between NIH and PEI wherein PEI confirmed our bid to the government, and designated your firm as our HVAC Mechanical subcontractor. This action was taken after several telephonic and face to face discussions with you regarding the above referenced bid submitted by your firm.

We look forward to working with your firm on this contract and hope that this will lead to a long and mutually beneficial relationship.

Sincerely,
/s/ Thomas F. Pavel,
President

Upon receipt of PEI's fax of September 1, James Kick called and informed PEI that Johnson's bid contained an error, and as a result the price was too low. According to Kick, Johnson had discovered the mistake earlier, but because Johnson believed that PEI had not been awarded the contract, they did not feel compelled to correct the error. Kick sought to withdraw Johnson's bid, both over the telephone and by a letter dated September 2, 1993:

A.S. Johnson Co.

September 2, 1993
PEI Construction
780 West Maples Avenue, Suite 101
Vienna, Virginia 22180
Attention: Thomas Pavel,
ATTENTION: President
Reference: NIH Building 30 HVAC Modifications

Dear Mr. Pavel,
We respectfully inform you of our intention to withdraw our proposal for the above referenced project due to an error in our bid.

As discussed in our telephone conversation and face to face meeting, the management of A.S. Johnson Company was reviewing this proposal, upon which we were to confirm our pricing to you.

Please contact Mr. Harry Kick, General Manager at [telephone number deleted] for any questions you may have.

Very truly yours,
/s/ James H. Kick

Estimating Manager

PEI responded to both the September 1 phone call, and the September 2 letter, expressing its refusal to permit Johnson to withdraw.

On September 28, 1993, NIH formally awarded the construction contract to PEI. PEI found a substitute subcontractor to do the mechanical work, but at a cost of $930,000.[6] PEI brought suit against Johnson in the Circuit Court for Prince George's County to recover the $32,000 difference between Johnson's bid and the cost of the substitute mechanical subcontractor.

The case was heard by the trial court without the aid of a jury. The trial court made several findings of fact, which we summarize:

1. PEI relied upon Johnson's sub-bid in making its bid for the entire project;
2. The fact that PEI was not the low bidder, but was awarded the project only after the apparent low bidder was disqualified, takes this case out of the ordinary;
3. Prior to NIH awarding PEI the contract on September 28, Johnson, on September 2, withdrew its bid; and
4. PEI's letter to all potential mechanical subcontractors, dated August 26, 1993, indicates that there was no definite agreement between PEI and Johnson, *and* that PEI was not relying upon Johnson's bid.

The trial court analyzed the case under both a traditional contract theory and under a detrimental reliance theory. PEI was unable to satisfy the trial judge that under either theory that a contractual relationship had been formed.

PEI appealed to the Court of Special Appeals, raising both traditional offer and acceptance theory, and "promissory estoppel." Before our intermediate appellate court considered the case, we issued a writ of certiorari on our own motion.

II

The relationships involved in construction contracts have long posed a unique problem in the law of contracts. A brief overview of the mechanics of the construction bid process, as well as our legal system's attempts to regulate the process, is in order.

A. Construction Bidding

Our description of the bid process in *Maryland Supreme Corp. v. Blake Co., 279 Md. 531, 369 A.2d 1017 (1977)* is still accurate:

---

[6] The record indicates that the substitute mechanical subcontractor used "Powers" as a sub-subcontractor and did not "break out" the "Powers" component to be directly subcontracted by PEI.

"In such a building project there are basically three parties involved: the letting party, who calls for bids on its job; the general contractor, who makes a bid on the whole project; and the subcontractors, who bid only on that portion of the whole job which involves the field of its specialty. The usual procedure is that when a project is announced, a subcontractor, on his own initiative or at the general contractor's request, prepares an estimate and submits a bid to one or more of the general contractors interested in the project. The general contractor evaluates the bids made by the subcontractors in each field and uses them to compute its total bid to the letting party. After receiving bids from general contractors, the letting party ordinarily awards the contract to the lowest reputable bidder."

Id. at 533-34, 369 A.2d at 1020-21 (citing *The Firm Offer Problem*)

B. The Construction Bidding Cases—An Historical Overview

The problem the construction bidding process poses is the determination of the precise points on the timeline that the various parties become bound to each other. The early landmark case was *James Baird Co. v. Gimbel Bros., Inc.*, 64 F.2d 344 (2d Cir.1933). The plaintiff, James Baird Co., ["Baird"] was a general contractor from Washington, D.C., bidding to construct a government building in Harrisburg, Pennsylvania. Gimbel Bros., Inc., ["Gimbel"], the famous New York department store, sent its bid to supply linoleum to a number of bidding general contractors on December 24, and Baird received Gimbel's bid on December 28. Gimbel realized its bid was based on an incorrect computation and notified Baird of its withdrawal on December 28. The letting authority awarded Baird the job on December 30. Baird formally accepted the Gimbel bid on January 2. When Gimbel refused to perform, Baird sued for the additional cost of a substitute linoleum supplier. The Second Circuit Court of Appeals held that Gimbel's initial bid was an offer to contract and, under traditional contract law, remained open only until accepted or withdrawn. Because the offer was withdrawn before it was accepted there was no contract. Judge Learned Hand, speaking for the court, also rejected two alternative theories of the case: unilateral contract and promissory estoppel. He held that Gimbel's bid was not an offer of a unilateral contract that Baird could accept by performing, *i.e.,* submitting the bid as part of the general bid; and second, he held that the theory of promissory estoppel was limited to cases involving charitable pledges.

Judge Hand's opinion was widely criticized, *see* Note, *Contracts—Promissory Estoppel,* 20 Va.L.Rev. 214 (1933) [hereinafter, "*Promissory Estoppel*"]; Note, *Contracts—Revocation of Offer Before Acceptance—Promissory Estoppel,* 28 Ill. L. Rev. 419 (1934), but also widely influential. The effect of the *James Baird* line of cases, however, is an "obvious injustice without relief of any description." *Promissory Estoppel,* at 215. The general contractor is bound to the price submitted to the letting party, but the subcontractors are not bound, and are free to withdraw.[8] As one commentator described it, "If the subcontractor revokes his bid before it is accepted by the general, any loss which results is a deduction from the general's profit and conceivably may transform overnight a profitable contract into a losing deal." **Franklin M. Schultz,** *The Firm Offer Puzzle: A Study of Business Practice in the Construction Industry,* 19 U. Chi. L. Rev. 237, 239 (1952).

The unfairness of this regime to the general contractor was addressed in *Drennan v. Star Paving,* 333 P.2d 757, 51 Cal.2d 409 (1958). Like *James Baird,* the *Drennan* case arose in the context of a bid mistake. Justice Traynor, writing for the Supreme Court of California, relied upon § 90 of the *Restatement (First) of Contracts:*

> "A promise which the promisor should reasonably expect to induce action or forbearance of a definite and substantial character on the part of the promisee and which does induce such action or forbearance is binding if injustice can be avoided only by enforcement of the promise."

Restatement (First) of Contracts § 90 (1932). Justice Traynor reasoned that the subcontractor's bid contained an implied subsidiary promise not to revoke the bid. As the court stated:

> "When plaintiff [, a General Contractor,] used defendant's offer in computing his own bid, he bound himself to perform in reliance on defendant's terms. Though defendant did not bargain for the use of its bid neither did defendant make it idly, indifferent to whether it would be used or not. On the contrary it is reasonable to suppose that defendant submitted its bid to obtain the subcontract. It was bound to realize the substantial possibility that its bid would be the lowest, and that it would be included by plaintiff in his bid. It was to its own interest that the contractor be awarded the general contract; the lower the subcontract bid, the lower the general contractor's bid was likely to be and the greater its chance of acceptance and hence the greater defendant's chance of getting the paving subcontract. Defendant had reason not only to expect

---

[8] Note that under the *Baird* line of cases, the general contractor, while bound by his offer to the letting party, is not bound to any specific subcontractor, and is free to "bid shop" prior to awarding the subcontract. **Michael L. Closen & Donald G. Weiland,** *The Construction Industry Bidding Cases: Application of Traditional Contract, Promissory Estoppel, and Other Theories to the Relations Between General Contractors and Subcontractors,* 13 J. Marshall L. Rev. 565, 583 (1980). At least one commentator argues that although potentially unfair, this system creates a necessary symmetry between general and subcontractors, in that neither party is bound. Note, *Construction Contracts— The Problem of Offer and Acceptance in the General Contractor-Subcontractor Relationship,* 37 U. Cinn. L. Rev. 798 (1980) [hereinafter, " *The Problem of Offer and Acceptance* "].

plaintiff to rely on its bid but to want him to. Clearly defendant had a stake in plaintiff's reliance on its bid. Given this interest and the fact that plaintiff is bound by his own bid, it is only fair that plaintiff should have at least an opportunity to accept defendant's bid after the general contract has been awarded to him."

Drennan, **51 Cal.2d at 415, 333 P.2d at 760.** The *Drennan* court however did not use "promissory estoppel" as a substitute for the entire contract, as is the doctrine's usual function. Instead, the *Drennan* court, applying the principle of § 90, interpreted the subcontractor's bid to be irrevocable. Justice Traynor's analysis used promissory estoppel as consideration for an implied promise to keep the bid open for a reasonable time. Recovery was then predicated on traditional bilateral contract, with the sub-bid as the offer and promissory estoppel serving to replace acceptance.

The *Drennan* decision has been very influential. Many states have adopted the reasoning used by Justice Traynor. *See,* e.g., *Debron Corp. v. National Homes Constr. Corp.,* 493 F.2d 352 (8th Cir.1974) (applying Missouri law); *Reynolds v. Texarkana Constr. Co.,* 237 Ark. 583, 374 S.W.2d 818 (1964); *Mead Assocs. Inc. v. Antonsen,* 677 P.2d 434 (Colo.1984); *Illinois Valley Asphalt v. J.F. Edwards Constr. Co.,* 45 Ill.Dec. 876, 413 N.E.2d 209, 90 Ill.App.3d 768 (Ill. Ct.App.1980); *Lichtefeld-Massaro, Inc. v. R.J. Manteuffel Co.,* 806 S.W.2d 42 (Ky.App.1991); *Constructors Supply Co. v. Bostrom Sheet Metal Works, Inc.,* 291 Minn. 113, 190 N.W.2d 71 (1971); *E.A. Coronis Assocs. v. M. Gordon Constr. Co.,* 90 N.J. Super 69, 216 A.2d 246 (1966).

Despite the popularity of the *Drennan* reasoning, the case has subsequently come under some criticism. The criticism centers on the lack of symmetry of detrimental reliance in the bid process, in that subcontractors are bound to the general, but the general is not bound to the subcontractors. The result is that the general is free to bid shop,[13] bid chop,[14] and to encourage bid peddling,[15] to the detriment of the subcontractors. One commentator described the problems that these practices create:

"Bid shopping and peddling have long been recognized as unethical by construction trade organizations. These 'unethical,' but common

---

[13] Bid shopping is the use of the lowest subcontractor's bid as a tool in negotiating lower bids from other subcontractors post-award.

[14] "The general contractor, having been awarded the prime contract, may pressure the subcontractor whose bid was used for a particular portion of the work in computing the overall bid on the prime contract to reduce the amount of the bid." Closen & Weiland, at 566 n.6.

[15] An unscrupulous subcontractor can save estimating costs, and still get the job by not entering a bid or by entering an uncompetitive bid. After bid opening, this unscrupulous subcontractor, knowing the price of the low sub-bid, can then offer to perform the work for less money, precisely because the honest subcontractor has already paid for the estimate and included that cost in the original bid. This practice is called bid peddling.

practices have several detrimental results. First, as bid shopping becomes common within a particular trade, the subcontractors will pad their initial bids in order to make further reductions during post-award negotiations. This artificial inflation of subcontractor's offers makes the bid process less effective. Second, subcontractors who are forced into post-award negotiations with the general often must reduce their sub-bids in order to avoid losing the award. Thus, they will be faced with a Hobson's choice between doing the job at a loss or doing a less than adequate job. Third, bid shopping and peddling tend to increase the risk of loss of the time and money used in preparing a bid. This occurs because generals and subcontractors who engage in these practices use, without expense, the bid estimates prepared by others. Fourth, it is often impossible for a general to obtain bids far enough in advance to have sufficient time to properly prepare his own bid because of the practice, common among many subcontractors, of holding sub-bids until the last possible moment in order to avoid pre-award bid shopping by the general. Fifth, many subcontractors refuse to submit bids for jobs on which they expect bid shopping. As a result, competition is reduced, and, consequently, construction prices are increased. Sixth, any price reductions gained through the use of post-award bid shopping by the general will be of no benefit to the awarding authority, to whom these price reductions would normally accrue as a result of open competition before the award of the prime contract. Free competition in an open market is therefore perverted because of the use of post-award bid shopping."

Bid Shopping, at 394-96 (citations omitted). *See also Flag Pole,* at 818 (bid mistake cases generally portray general contractor as victim, but market reality is that subs are usually in weaker negotiating position); Jay M. Feinman, *Promissory Estoppel and Judicial Method,* 97 Harv. L. Rev. 678, 707-08 (1984). These problems have caused at least one court to reject promissory estoppel in the contractor-subcontractor relationship. *Home Elec. Co. v. Underdown Heating & Air Conditioning Co.,* 86 N.C.App. 540, 358 S.E.2d 539 (1987). *See also* Note, *Construction Contracts—The Problem of Offer and Acceptance in the General Contractor-Subcontractor Relationship,* 37 U. Cinn. L. Rev. 798 (1980). But other courts, while aware of the limitations of promissory estoppel, have adopted it nonetheless. *See, e.g., Alaska Bussell Elec. Co. v. Vern Hickel Constr. Co.,* 688 P.2d 576 (Alaska 1984).

The doctrine of detrimental reliance has evolved in the time since *Drennan* was decided in 1958. The American Law Institute, responding to *Drennan,* sought to make detrimental reliance more readily applicable to the construction bidding scenario by adding § 87. This new section was intended to make subcontractors' bids binding:

"§ 87. Option Contract

. . . .

(2) An offer which the offeror should reasonably expect to induce action or forbearance of a substantial character on the part of the offeree before acceptance and which does induce such action or forbearance is binding as an option contract to the extent necessary to avoid injustice."

Restatement (Second) of Contracts § 87 (1979). Despite the drafter's intention that § 87 of the *Restatement (Second) of Contracts* (1979) should replace *Restatement (First) of Contracts* § 90 (1932)
in the construction bidding cases, few courts have availed themselves of the opportunity. *But see, Arango Constr. Co. v. Success Roofing, Inc.*, 46 Wash. App. 314, 321-22, 730 P.2d 720, 725 (1986). . . .

Section 90(1) of the *Restatement (Second) Contracts* (1979) defines the doctrine of detrimental reliance as follows:

> "A promise which the promisor should reasonably expect to induce action or forbearance on the part of the promisee or a third person and which does induce such action or forbearance is binding if injustice can be avoided only by enforcement of the promise. The remedy granted for breach may be limited as justice requires."

> **FYI**
>
> The language of § 87(2) is not limited to the circumstances of construction bidding cases. If applied as written, to all offers, it would make significant changes to the law of offer and acceptance. As the *Pavel* court notes, however, few courts have adopted § 87(2), but many courts follow *Drennan* in applying § 90 to construction bidding, and some courts have considered claims that § 90 should apply broadly to create liability for pre-contractual reliance in non-bidding cases. Extending promissory estoppel in that fashion could make an offeror potentially liable for any foreseeable expenses by an offeree considering whether to accept. However, aside from claims brought by potential franchisees induced by franchisors to incur expenses to prove themselves worthy contract partners, few such claims have succeeded. For further discussion, see E. Allan Farnsworth, *Contracts* §3.26 & nn. 39-41 (4th ed. 2004).

Courts and commentators have also suggested other solutions intended to bind the parties without the use of detrimental reliance theory. The most prevalent suggestion[19] is the use of the firm offer provision of the Uniform Commercial Code. Maryland Code (1992 Repl. Vol.), § 2-205 of the Commercial Law Article. That statute provides:

---

[19] *See Bid Shopping and Peddling* at 399-401; *Firm Offer Problem* at 215; Closen & Weiland, at 604 n.133.

"An offer by a merchant to buy or sell goods in a signed writing which by its terms gives assurance that it will be held open is not revocable, for lack of consideration, during the time stated or if no time is stated for a reasonable time, but in no event may such period of irrevocability exceed three months; but any such term of assurance on a form supplied by the offeree must be separately signed by the offeror."

Make the Connection

As the court later notes in footnote 22, UCC § 2-205 governs only contracts for the sale of goods (or in which the sale of goods predominates), so it could apply to a construction services bid only by analogy—a prospect that seems unlikely, considering the other means of irrevocability already available in contract law. Of course, the court could craft a similar rule by common law. At the end of this chapter, on page 421, we will discuss the common law process of applying a UCC rule "by analogy" to a situation outside of the rule's scope.

In this manner, subcontractor's bids, made in writing and giving some assurance of an intent that the offer be held open, can be found to be irrevocable.

The Supreme Judicial Court of Massachusetts has suggested three other traditional theories that might prove the existence of a contractual relationship between a general contractor and a sub: conditional bilateral contract analysis; unilateral contract analysis; and unrevoked offer analysis. *Loranger Constr. Corp. v. E.F. Hauserman Co.*, 384 N.E.2d 176, 376 Mass. 757 (1978). If the general contractor could prove that there was an exchange of promises binding the parties to each other, and that exchange of promises was made before bid opening, that would constitute a valid bilateral promise conditional upon the general being awarded the job. *Loranger*, 384 N.E.2d at 180, 376 Mass. at 762. This directly contrasts with Judge Hand's analysis in *James Baird*, that a general's use of a sub-bid constitutes acceptance conditional upon the award of the contract to the general. *James Baird*, 64 F.2d at 345-46.

Alternatively, if the subcontractor intended its sub-bid as an offer to a unilateral contract, use of the sub-bid in the general's bid constitutes part performance, which renders the initial offer irrevocable under the *Restatement (Second) of Contracts* § 45 (1979). *Loranger*, 384 N.E.2d at 180, 376 Mass. at 762. This resurrects a second theory dismissed by Judge Learned Hand in *James Baird*.

Finally, the *Loranger* court pointed out that a jury might choose to disbelieve that a subcontractor had withdrawn the winning bid, meaning that acceptance came before withdrawal, and a traditional bilateral contract was formed. *Loranger*, 384 N.E.2d at 180, 376 Mass. at 762-63.

Another alternative solution to the construction bidding problem is no longer seriously considered—revitalizing the common law seal. William Noel

Keyes, *Consideration Reconsidered—The Problem of the Withdrawn Bid*, 10 Stan.L.Rev. 441, 470 (1958). Because a sealed option contract remains firm without consideration this alternative was proposed as a solution to the construction bidding problem.[21]

It is here that the state of the law rests.

III

. . . .

The trial court held, and we agree, that Johnson's sub-bid was an offer to contract and that it was sufficiently clear and definite. We must then determine if PEI made a timely and valid acceptance of that offer and thus created a traditional bilateral contract, or in the absence of a valid acceptance, if PEI's detrimental reliance served to bind Johnson to its sub-bid. We examine each of these alternatives, beginning with traditional contract theory.[22]

A. Traditional Bilateral Contract

The trial judge found that there was not a traditional contract binding Johnson to PEI. A review of the record and the trial judge's findings make it clear that this was a close question. On appeal however, our job is to assure that the trial judge's findings were not clearly erroneous. **Maryland Rule 8-131(c)**. This is an easier task.

The trial judge rejected PEI's claim of bilateral contract for two separate reasons: 1) that there was no meeting of the minds; and 2) that the offer was withdrawn prior to acceptance. Both need not be proper bases for decision; if either of these two theories is not clearly erroneous, we must affirm.

There is substantial evidence in the record to support the judge's conclusion that there was no meeting of the minds. PEI's letter of August 26, to all potential

---

[21] Of course, general contractors could require their subcontractors to provide their bids under seal. The fact that they do not is testament to the lack of appeal this proposal holds.

[22] Because they were not raised, either below or in this Court, we need not address the several methods in which a court might interpret a subcontractor's bid as a firm, and thus irrevocable, offer. Nevertheless, for the benefit of bench and bar, we review those theories as applied to this case. First, PEI could have purchased an option, thus supplying consideration for making the offer irrevocable. This did not happen. Second, Johnson could have submitted its bid as a sealed offer. Md.Code (1995 Repl. Vol.), **§ 5-102 of the Courts & Judicial Proceedings Article**. An offer under seal supplants the need for consideration to make an offer firm. This did not occur in the instant case. The third method of Johnson's offer becoming irrevocable is by operation of Md.Code (1992 Repl.Vol.), **§ 2-205 of the Commercial Law Article**. We note that Johnson's sub-bid was made in the form of a signed writing, but without further evidence we are unable to determine if the offer "by its terms gives assurance that it will be held open" and if the sub-bid is for "goods" as that term is defined by Md.Code (1994 Repl. Vol.), **§ 2-105(1) of the Commercial Law Article** . . . .

mechanical subcontractors, reproduced *supra,* indicates, as the trial judge found, that PEI and Johnson "did not have a definite, certain meeting of the minds on a certain price for a certain quantity of goods . . . ." Because this reason is itself sufficient to sustain the trial judge's finding that no contract was formed, we affirm.

Alternatively, we hold, that the evidence permitted the trial judge to find that Johnson revoked its offer prior to PEI's final acceptance. We review the relevant chronology. Johnson made its offer, in the form of a sub-bid, on August 5. On September 1, PEI accepted. Johnson withdrew its offer by letter dated September 2. On September 28, NIH awarded the contract to PEI. Thus, PEI's apparent acceptance came one day *prior* to Johnson's withdrawal.

The trial court found, however, "that before there was ever a final agreement reached with the contract awarding authorities, that Johnson made it clear to [PEI] that they were not going to continue to rely on their earlier submitted bid." Implicit in this finding is the judge's understanding of the contract. Johnson's sub-bid constituted an offer of a contingent contract. PEI accepted that offer subject to the condition precedent of PEI's receipt of the award of the contract from NIH. Prior to the occurrence of the condition precedent, Johnson was free to withdraw. *See* 2 *Williston on Contracts* § 6:14 (4th ed.). On September 2, Johnson exercised that right to revoke.[23] The trial judge's finding that withdrawal proceeded valid final acceptance is therefore logical and supported by substantial evidence in the record. It was not clearly erroneous, so we shall affirm.

B. Detrimental Reliance

PEI's alternative theory of the case is that PEI's detrimental reliance binds Johnson to its bid. . . .

. . . .

. . . [W]e now clarify that Maryland courts are to apply the test of the *Restatement (Second) of Contracts* § 90(1) (1979), which we have recast as a four-part test:

1. a clear and definite promise;
2. where the promisor has a reasonable expectation that the offer will induce action or forbearance on the part of the promisee;

---

[23] We have also considered the possibility that Johnson's offer was not to enter into a contingent contract. This is unlikely because there is no incentive for a general contractor to accept a non-contingent contract prior to contract award but it would bind the general to purchase the subcontractor's services even if the general did not receive the award. Moreover, PEI's September 1 letter clearly "accepted" Johnson's offer subject to the award from NIH. If Johnson's bid was for a non-contingent contract, PEI's response substantially varied the offer and was therefore a counter-offer, not an acceptance. *Post v. Gillespie,* 219 Md. 378, 385-86, 149 A.2d 391, 395-96 (1959); 2 *Williston on Contracts* § 6:13 (4th ed.).

3. which does induce actual and reasonable action or forbearance by the promisee; and
4. causes a detriment which can only be avoided by the enforcement of the promise.

. . . .

In a construction bidding case, where the general contractor seeks to bind the subcontractor to the sub-bid offered, the general must first prove that the subcontractor's sub-bid constituted an offer to perform a job at a given price. We do not express a judgment about how precise a bid must be to constitute an offer, or to what degree a general contractor may request to change the offered scope before an acceptance becomes a counter-offer. That fact-specific judgment is best reached on a case-by-case basis. In the instant case, the trial judge found that the sub-bid was sufficiently clear and definite to constitute an offer, and his finding was not clearly erroneous.

Second, the general must prove that the subcontractor reasonably expected that the general contractor would rely upon the offer. The subcontractor's expectation that the general contractor will rely upon the sub-bid may dissipate through time.

In this case, the trial court correctly inquired into Johnson's belief that the bid remained open, and that consequently PEI was not relying on the Johnson bid. The judge found that due to the time lapse between bid opening and award, "it would be unreasonable for offers to continue." This is supported by the substantial evidence. James Kick testified that although he knew of his bid mistake, he did not bother to notify PEI because J.J. Kirlin, Inc., and not PEI, was the apparent low bidder. The trial court's finding that Johnson's reasonable expectation had dissipated in the span of a month is not clearly erroneous.

As to the third element, a general contractor must prove that he actually and reasonably relied on the subcontractor's sub-bid. We decline to provide a checklist of potential methods of proving this reliance, but we will make several observations. First, a showing by the subcontractor, that the general contractor engaged in "bid shopping," or actively encouraged "bid chopping," or "bid peddling" is strong evidence that the general did *not* rely on the sub-bid. Second, prompt notice by the general contractor to the subcontractor that the general intends to use the sub on the job, is weighty evidence that the general *did* rely on the bid.[31] Third, if a sub-bid is so low that a reasonably prudent general contractor would not rely upon it, the trier of fact may infer that the general contractor did not in fact rely upon the erroneous bid.

---

[31] Prompt notice and acceptance also significantly dispels the possibility of bid shopping, bid chopping, and bid peddling.

In this case, the trial judge did not make a specific finding that PEI failed to prove its reasonable reliance upon Johnson's sub-bid. We must assume, however, that it was his conclusion based on his statement that "the parties did not have a definite, certain meeting of the minds on a certain price for a certain quantity of goods and wanted to renegotiate . . . ." The August 26, 1993, fax from PEI to all prospective mechanical subcontractors, is evidence supporting this conclusion. Although the finding that PEI did not rely on Johnson's bid was indisputably a close call, it was not clearly erroneous.

Finally, as to the fourth prima facie element, the trial court, and not a jury, must determine that binding the subcontractor is necessary to prevent injustice. This element is to be enforced as required by common law equity courts—the general contractor must have "clean hands." This requirement includes, as did the previous element, that the general did not engage in bid shopping, chopping or peddling, but also requires the further determination that justice compels the result. The fourth factor was not specifically mentioned by the trial judge, but we may infer that he did not find this case to merit an equitable remedy.

Because there was sufficient evidence in the record to support the trial judge's conclusion that PEI had not proven its case for detrimental reliance, we must, and hereby do, affirm the trial court's ruling.

IV

In conclusion, we emphasize that there are different ways to prove that a contractual relationship exists between a general contractor and its subcontractors. Traditional bilateral contract theory is one. Detrimental reliance can be another. However, under the evidence in this case, the trial judge was not clearly erroneous in deciding that recovery by the general contractor was not justified under either theory.

Judgment affirmed, with costs.

———————————

Practice Pointer: Bid Bonds

A party receiving bids (the project owner or the general contractor) can protect itself by requiring a "bid bond" from each bidding contractor, thereby guaranteeing itself compensation if a contractor withdraws. A bid bond is obtained by paying a fee to a bonding company and entering into a contract that requires the bonding company to pay an agreed sum to the beneficiary (the owner or the general contractor, depending upon whether the contractor or the subcontractor purchases the bond) if the bid is not honored. (*See* Chapter 10 for more on such "intended beneficiaries.") The agreed sum may be a percentage of the bid or the amount by which a substitute contract exceeds the withdrawn bid. Usually the party buying the bid bond tries to pass on the cost of the bid bond in its bid, but in a highly competitive bidding situation, that may not be possible. If the bonding company has to pay, it may or may not have the contractual right to recover its costs from the party that purchased the bond, over and above the fee already paid.

Food for Thought: Making Bids Irrevocable

So far, the courts have been unable to fashion a solution to the bid-revocability problem that evenly balances the power between the contractor and the subcontractor. Abuses and unfairness accompany each solution. Is the current state of the law as good as it gets, or can it be improved upon? Where do you think that the arc of the law on this issue will or should proceed in the coming decades? Although sophisticated parties can protect themselves in some ways, less sophisticated and less powerful parties are more likely to suffer losses under some of the current rules. Which fact situations trigger this vulnerability, and what changes in the law would ameliorate this problem?

Problems: Irrevocable Offers

If multiple rules could apply, give all possible results.

4-15. Company A sends an email to Company B inquiring about the price of 300 electrical engines, model 45JR2. On October 1, Company B replies by email, "Our price for 300 engines, model 45JR2, is $5200. We guarantee that price until October 14, during which time the 300 engines can be shipped within two days of ordering. We await your order. Samuel Seller, Sales Agent, Company B." Assume that the price quote is an offer. Five days later, Company B emails Company A an email withdrawing the offer. Two days later, Company A emails Company B a purchase order for the 300 engines for $5200. Company B refuses to acknowledge the order or ship the engines. Did the offer still exist when the offeree tried to accept?

4-16. A makes an oral offer to B to settle a contract dispute, saying that it can be accepted only by B paying A $752 in cash no later than July 1. On July 1, B goes to A's apartment in order to pay the money to A. B knocks on the door, A opens the door just a crack (with the chain still on the door) to see who it is, and B fans a stack of bills in A's face. A then says "but I revoke the offer." Did the offer still exist when the offeree tried to accept? Does the result change if A yells "I revoke" through the door before he opens it?

4-17. In letters received by a prospective buyer and its broker, Seller offers, in writing, to sell real estate to the buyer and to pay a percentage of the sales price as a commission to Broker, if within six days Broker is successful in getting the buyer to accept the offer. On the fourth day, Seller mails Broker a writing revoking the offer. On the morning of the sixth day, Broker obtains the prospective buyer's acceptance of the offer. That afternoon, Broker receives Seller's revocation. Broker notifies Seller of Buyer's acceptance that evening by letter by messenger. Broker claims breach of the contract and sues Seller for the commission. Did the offer still exist when the offeree tried to accept?

§ 4.3. Defining Acceptance

Recall the chart that appeared at the beginning of § 4 of this chapter:

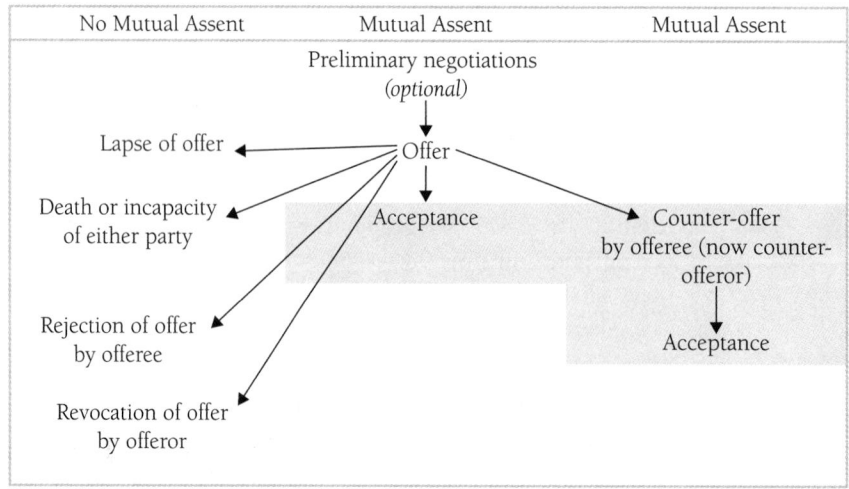

After an offer has been made, the offeree gains the "power of acceptance" and thus may accept or reject the offer, make a counter-offer, or let the offer lapse. This section examines acceptances and counter-offers.

Like an offer, an acceptance should be definite and certain, manifest the assenting party's willingness to be bound to the terms, and be communicated to the other party. Determining whether the offeree's response is an acceptance and therefore completes the mutual assent process involves several additional issues, discussed in the sections that follow:

Make the Connection

In § 3 of Chapter 4 (recall *Quake Construction, Cheever, B. Lewis Productions*), you learned that a valid mutual assent occurs when the parties manifest definite commitment to reasonably certain terms (at least as to the essential terms). The same is true when assent is manifested consecutively in an offer and an acceptance. Both the offeror and the offeree must manifest a definite commitment to reasonably certain terms.

- When is a purported acceptance a counter-offer, not an acceptance?
- Must the would-be acceptance be a "mirror image" of the offer?
- What is the acceptable "manner" of acceptance—a promise or performance?
- When is an acceptance effective—upon dispatch or upon receipt?
- In what situations should the offeree notify the offeror of acceptance?
- When can acceptance be by conduct or inaction?

§ 4.3.1. Distinguishing between Acceptance and Counter-Offer

In the chart on the previous page, note that the major branchpoint is whether the offeree responds to the offer with a counter-offer or an acceptance. Sometimes it isn't easy to tell (as in the next case). The following rules provide some guidance:

Restatement (Second) § 50.   Acceptance of Offer Defined . . .

(1) Acceptance of an offer is a manifestation of assent to the terms thereof made by the offeree in a manner invited or required by the offer.

. . . .

Restatement (Second) § 39. Counter-offers

(1) A counter-offer is an offer made by an offeree to his offeror relating to the same matter as the original offer and proposing a substituted bargain differing from that proposed by the original offer.

---

(2) An offeree's power of acceptance is terminated by his making of a counter-offer, unless the offeror has manifested a contrary intention or unless the counter-offer manifests a contrary intention of the offeree.

———————

CISG Art. 19 **(in Part II. Formation of the Contract);** UNIDROIT Art. 2.1.11. **Mode of Acceptance**

(1) A reply to an offer which purports to be an acceptance but contains additions, limitations or other modifications is a rejection of the offer and constitutes a counter-offer.

. . . .

The task is to distinguish between the offeree's "manifestation of assent" (§ 50) and "proposing a substituted bargain" (§ 39). An offeree can communicate some dissatisfaction with the offer but still manifest an acceptance, albeit a "grumbling" one. However, if the "grumble" goes so far as to make it doubtful that the offeree is expressing assent, then the offeree has not accepted but may have made a counter-offer.

[handwritten margin note: Grumbling acceptance is still probably acceptance]

Reading the Law Critically: *Ardente*

1. Which communication is an offer? Why are the preceding communications not offers? Why is the response to the offer not an acceptance?

2. What distinguishes a "conditional acceptance" from an acceptance with a request or suggestion? Why is a "conditional acceptance" not an operative acceptance? Is the court's approach in this case consistent with the Restatement (Second) sections preceding this case?

3. How does the procedural posture of the summary judgment appeal affect the substantive ruling about which action is an offer? If the appeal had not been from a summary judgment, what would the outcome have been? How would you have ruled?

Ardente v. Horan

ERNEST P. ARDENTE, Plaintiff-Appellant

v.

WILLIAM A. HORAN and KATHERINE L. HORAN, Defendants-Respondents

Supreme Court of Rhode Island

366 A.2d 162 (R.I. 1976) (unpublished opinion)

DORIS, Justice.

Ernest P. Ardente, the plaintiff, brought this civil action in Superior Court to specifically enforce an agreement between himself and William A. and Katherine L. Horan, the defendants, to sell certain real property. The defendants filed an answer together with a motion for summary judgment pursuant to **Super.R.Civ.P. 56**. Following the submission of affidavits by both the plaintiff and the defendants and a hearing on the motion, judgment was entered by a Superior Court justice for the defendants. The plaintiff now appeals.

In August 1975, certain residential property in the city of Newport was offered for sale by defendants. The plaintiff made a bid of $250,000 for the property which was communicated to defendants by their attorney. After defendants' attorney advised plaintiff that the bid was acceptable to defendants, he prepared a purchase and sale agreement at the direction of defendants and forwarded it to plaintiff's attorney for plaintiff's signature. After investigating certain title conditions, plaintiff executed the agreement. Thereafter plaintiff's attorney returned the document to defendants along with a check in the amount of $20,000 and a letter dated September 8, 1975, which read in relevant part as follows:

"My clients are concerned that the following items remain with the real estate: a) dining room set and tapestry wall covering in dining room; b) fireplace fixtures throughout; c) the sun parlor furniture. I would appreciate your confirming that these items are a part of the transaction, as they would be difficult to replace."

The defendants refused to agree to sell the enumerated items and did not sign the purchase and sale agreement.

> **FYI**
>
> In this case as in others we have seen, a party to a transaction—the "principal"—may be bound to a contract entered into by an "agent" acting on behalf of the principal if the situation follows the rules governing agency law. The agent is not personally liable on the contract. An employee of a corporation may be acting on behalf of the corporation (which is a legal person). Here, both buyer and sellers are represented by their attorneys, who are their "agents."

They directed their attorney to return the agreement and the deposit check to plaintiff and subsequently refused to sell the property to plaintiff. This action for specific performance followed.

In Superior Court, defendants moved for summary judgment on the ground that the facts were not in dispute and no contract had been formed as a matter of law. The trial justice ruled that the letter quoted above constituted a conditional acceptance of defendants' offer to sell the property and consequently must be construed as a counteroffer. Since defendants never accepted the counteroffer, it followed that no contract was formed, and summary judgment was granted.

Counteroffer

. . . .

The plaintiff's . . . contention is that the trial justice incorrectly applied the principles of contract law in deciding that the facts did not disclose a valid acceptance of defendants' offer. . . . [W]e cannot agree.

The trial justice proceeded on the theory that the delivery of the purchase and sale agreement to plaintiff constituted an offer by defendants to sell the property. Because we must view the evidence in the light most favorable to the party against whom summary judgment was entered, in this case plaintiff, we assume as the trial justice did that the delivery of the agreement was in fact an offer.[3]

The question we must answer next is whether there was an acceptance of that offer. The general rule is that where, as here, there is an offer to form a bilateral contract, the offeree must communicate his acceptance to the offeror before any contractual obligation can come into being. A mere mental intent to accept the offer, no matter how carefully formed, is not sufficient. The acceptance must be transmitted to the offeror in some overt manner. **Bullock v. Harwick, 158 Fla. 834, 30 So.2d 539 (1947).** . . .

Make the Connection

As we learned in *Lucy v. Zehmer*, the objective test is applied from the vantage point of a reasonable person in the position of the party receiving a communication—here, the offeror.

A review of the record shows that the only expression of acceptance which was communicated to defendants was the delivery of the executed purchase and sale agreement accompanied by the letter of September 8. Therefore it is solely on the basis of the language used in these two documents that we must determine whether there was a valid acceptance. Whatever plaintiff's

_____

[3] The conclusion that the delivery of the agreement was an offer is not unassailable in view of the fact that defendants did not sign the agreement before sending it to plaintiff, and the fact that plaintiff told defendants' attorney after the agreement was received that he would have to investigate certain conditions of title before signing the agreement. If it was not an offer, plaintiff's execution of the agreement could itself be no more than an offer, which defendants never accepted.

maybe sale agreement wasn't offer - no signed

- court has to accept person's opinion - in light most favorable

unexpressed intention may have been in sending the documents is irrelevant. We must be concerned only with the language actually used, not the language plaintiff thought he was using or intended to use.

There is no doubt that the execution and delivery of the purchase and sale agreement by plaintiff, without more, would have operated as an acceptance. The terms of the accompanying letter, however, apparently conditioned the acceptance upon the inclusion of various items of personalty. In assessing the effect of the terms of that letter we must keep in mind certain generally accepted rules. To be effective, an acceptance must be definite and unequivocal. "An offeror is entitled to know in clear terms whether the offeree accepts his proposal. It is not enough that the words of a reply justify a probable inference of assent." 1 Restatement Contracts § 58, comment a (1932). The acceptance may not impose additional conditions on the offer, nor may it add limitations. "An acceptance which is equivocal or upon condition or with a limitation is a counteroffer and requires acceptance by the original offeror before a contractual relationship can exist." John Hancock Mut. Life Ins. Co. v. Dietlin, 97 R.I. 515, 518, 199 A.2d 311, 313 (1964). . . .

However, an acceptance may be valid despite conditional language if the acceptance is clearly independent of the condition. Many cases have so held. Williston states the rule as follows:

> Frequently an offeree, while making a positive acceptance of the offer, also makes a request or suggestion that some addition or modification be made. So long as it is clear that the meaning of the acceptance is positively and unequivocally to accept the offer whether such request is granted or not, a contract is formed.

1 Williston, Contracts § 79 at 261-62 (3d ed. 1957). Corbin is in agreement with the above view. 1 Corbin, supra, § 84 at 363-65. Thus our task is to decide whether plaintiff's letter is more reasonably interpreted as a qualified acceptance or as an absolute acceptance together with a mere inquiry concerning a collateral matter.

In making our decision we recognize that, as one text states, "The question whether a communication by an offeree is a conditional acceptance or counter-offer is not always easy to answer. It must be determined by the same common-sense process of interpretation that must be applied in so many other cases." 1 Corbin, supra § 82 at 353. In our opinion the language used in plaintiff's letter of September 8 is not consistent with an absolute acceptance accompanied by a request for a gratuitous benefit. We interpret the letter to impose a condition on plaintiff's acceptance of defendants' offer. The letter does not unequivocally state that even without the enumerated items plaintiff is willing to complete the contract. In fact, the letter seeks "confirmation" that the listed items "are a part of the transaction". Thus, far from being an independent, collateral request, the sale of the items in question is explicitly referred to as a part of the real estate transaction. . . .

Accordingly, we hold that since the plaintiff's letter of acceptance dated September 8 was conditional, it operated as a rejection of the defendants' offer and no contractual obligation was created. . . .

————————

Problems: Acceptance or Counter-Offer?

4-18. A businessperson offers to buy out her partner's share of their business. Her partner writes back that she "accepts" and "proposes" that they "set December 15 as the closing date for the purchase." *acceptance*

4-19. Eight contractors make bids (offers) to build a school. The school district opens the bids, selects the winning bid, and sends a letter to that contractor "accepting your bid," stating some terms that were not in the RFQ or the bid, and saying that the final written agreement containing the bid terms and these new terms "is ready for your signature."

4-20. A professor receives his annual reappointment letter from the university and signs it "under protest that the salary does not reflect guarantees under present and past personnel policies." *acceptance, grumbling*

§ 4.3.2. The Mirror Image Rule

Under the common law, an acceptance must be a "mirror image" of the offer, matching the terms of the offer. A typical articulation of the rule says that "acceptance [of an offer] must be 'positive, unconditional, unequivocal and unambiguous, and must not change, add to, or qualify the terms of the offer.'"* *See also* **CISG Art. 19(1)**, appearing in the previous section. The mirror image rule supports the offeror's role as the "master of the offer": The offeror has made an offer proposing a contract on the offeror's terms, not on the offeree's terms.

The rule was originally applied strictly, so that any variance from the offer

————————

* *Wagner v. Rainier Mfg. Co.*, 371 P.2d 74, 77 (Or. 1962).

was enough to prevent the purported acceptance from being effective. Consider the following ruling from an 1867 case: A brewer sent a letter to a malt grower 100 miles away, inquiring about buying malt for the summer brewing season. The grower replied by letter: "The malt I have for sale is at Weedsport. I will sell you ten thousand bushels of the malt . . . at $1. 54 . . . per bushel, *delivered* on the boat at Weedsport." The brewer wrote back, "I will take your malt, ten thousand bushels, *deliverable* on boat at Weedsport, at 154 cents . . . ." The court considered the brewer's response to be "a manifest variance from the terms of the offer" and therefore a counter-offer. "The words ["deliverable" and "delivered"] do not mean the same thing; they require, or may require, something to be done quite different as one or the other should be exacted", the court stated. *

A few jurisdictions continue to apply the rule strictly. In Illinois, for example, "the acceptance must conform exactly to the offer. . . . [A]ny changes to an offer, even minor changes, constitute a counteroffer rather than an acceptance."** If strictly applied, however, the mirror image rule prevents contract formation based on a small difference between the offer and purported acceptance, even when the parties reasonably thought they had formed a contract.

However, the vast majority of jurisdictions now apply the mirror image rule leniently, allowing minor differences between offer and acceptance. For example, a teacher resigned from his position, specifying his last day of work as June 20 and his resignation effective August 31. The school district accepted the teacher's resignation, effective June 20. The teacher then attempted to rescind the resignation, claiming that, because of the difference in effective dates, there had been no acceptance of his offer to resign. The court held that the district had accepted the teacher's offer to resign, finding that the difference in effective date was an immaterial variation because it did not affect the teacher's work or pay.***

In another case, a seller offered to sell real estate to two buyers, who attempted to accept the offer with various additions and conditions. Seller protested that the changes prevented buyers' purported acceptance from being effective. When the buyers sued for damages for breach of contract, seller demurred. The court sided with the seller, reasoning that buyers attempted to add a "material and important" condition that title be acceptable to buyers' attorney. The court recognized that "immaterial differences in the phrasing of the offer and acceptance" should not defeat contract formation. It said that a court should "try to give to each writing a reasonable interpretation under which substantial justice may be reached according to the intent of the parties. But . . . there must be substantial agreement between offer and acceptance in all material particular in order that

---

* See *Myers v. Smith*, 48 Barb. 614 (N.Y. Sup. Ct. 1867)
** *Finnin v. Bob Lindsay, Inc.*, 852 N.E.2d 446, 448-49 (Ill. Ct. App. 2006) (quoting *Whitelaw v. Brady*, 121 N.E.2d 785 (Ill. 1954)).
*** See *Travis v. Tacoma Pub. Sch. Dist.*, 85 P.3d 959 (Wash. Ct. App. 2004).

such mutuality may appear. There must be no lack of identity between offer and acceptance, . . . and the parties must appear to have assented to the same thing in the same sense . . . ."* These articulations are all grounded in the same inquiry: determining when the purported acceptance has deviated enough from the offer that the offeree should not be understood to have exercised his or her power of acceptance and instead to have made a counter-offer. (Note again the application of the objective test.)

UCC Article 2 expressly rejects the mirror image rule and substitutes a complex rule in § 2-207. We will cover that rule at the end of Chapter 4 (page 399). The next case is decided under the common law rule.

Reading the Law Critically:
Rhode Island Dept. of Transportation

1. How does this court articulate its version of the mirror image rule?

2. Which aspects of the acceptance do not "mirror" the offer here? Why does the court allow those variations from the offer?

3. Do you agree with the court's solution? Does this holding make a crisp enough line between variations that prevent an acceptance and those that do not?

State of Rhode Island Dept. of Transp. v. Providence & Worcester R.R.

STATE OF RHODE ISLAND DEPARTMENT OF TRANSPORTATION, Plaintiff

v.

PROVIDENCE AND WORCESTER RAILROAD CO. and PROMET CORP.,
Defendants

Supreme Court of Rhode Island
674 A.2d 1239 (R.I. 1996)

LEDERBERG, Justice.

This case arose following the sale of a parcel of land by the defendant, Providence and Worcester Railroad Co. (P&W or the railway company), to the code-fendant, Promet Corp. (Promet). The conveyance was declared "null and void" by an amended judgment of the Superior Court that ordered P&W to convey

---

* *Richardson v. Greensboro Warehouse & Storage Co.,* 26 S.E.2d 897, 898 (N.C. 1943).

the parcel to the plaintiff, the State of Rhode Island Department of Transportation (state), for the purchase price of $100,000. The state was ordered to pay prejudgment interest on the purchase price, and P&W was required to reimburse Promet for interest on the purchase price and for property taxes that Promet paid while it was in possession of the parcel. The state appealed from the requirement that it pay interest on the purchase price; P&W appealed from the Superior Court's findings that the state was entitled to purchase the property and that P&W had to reimburse Promet for property taxes and for interest on the purchase price. Promet filed a brief in support of the amended Superior Court judgment. For the reasons recited below, we sustain in part and reverse in part the judgment of the Superior Court.

Facts and Procedural History

In 1985, P&W owned a 6.97-acre parcel of waterfront property in East Providence, Rhode Island. Railroad tracks were situated on the property, but the property was, and remains, otherwise unimproved. The railroad tracks at one time ran from the former Union Station in Providence through a tunnel under the East Side of Providence, and over a bridge spanning the Seekonk River. At that point the tracks reached the subject property where they split to form a Y, one of whose arms directed rail traffic north toward Pawtucket, and the other traveled south toward Providence on what is known as the Bristol secondary track. The railroad company had acquired this property in 1982 from the Consolidated Rail Corporation (Conrail) as part of P&W's purchase of all Conrail's Rhode Island freight operations.

The property, however, was acquired by P&W subject to an order of the Special Court under the Regional Rail Reorganization Act of 1973, 45 U.S.C. §§ 719(b) and 745(d). That order required P&W to "guarantee rail service [on the property] for four years from the date" of conveyance on May 1, 1982, and stipulated that P&W could "not seek to abandon or discontinue rail service . . . for such four-year period." . . .

On December 12, 1985, P&W entered into a purchase and sale agreement with Promet for the sale of the subject property at the price of $100,000. Although the tracks were still suitable for rail use, the property was not being used for rail purposes, or any other uses at the time of the transaction. The terms of the purchase and sale agreement expressly made the agreement "subject to a 30 day option in the State of Rhode Island to purchase the premises," as required by G.L.1956 § 39-6.1-9, which provided:

> "All rail properties within the state offered for sale by any railway corporation after April 9, 1976 shall be offered for sale to the state in the first instance at the lowest price at which the railway corporation is

willing to sell. The railway corporation shall notify the state in writing if it desires to offer for sale any rail properties. The state shall have a period of not more than thirty (30) days from receipt of the notification to accept the offer."

On November 20, 1985, Joseph Arruda (Arruda), assistant director for planning for the State Department of Transportation, wrote to P&W's agent, Joseph DiStefano (DiStefano). In that letter, Arruda referred to an October 22, 1985 meeting he had attended with DiStefano and principals of Promet at which "it was mentioned that Promet Property and P&W were discussing the sale of abandoned railroad properties." Arruda claimed that "the state must be given first option to acquire" the property and stated that "[i]f, in fact, P&W is pursuing the sale of any railroad property in this area, we would sincerely appreciate being notified at the earliest possible date." On December 12, 1985, DiStefano wrote to Arruda, stating:

"Dear Mr. Arruda:

"You are hereby notified, pursuant to **Section 39-6.1-9 of the Rhode Island General Laws**, that this company proposes to sell a certain parcel of land situated at East Providence, Rhode Island . . . for $100,000 with a closing to be held on January 17, 1986 . . . .

"Pursuant to statute, the State of Rhode Island has a period of thirty (30) days from the date of this notification within which to accept this offer to sell under the same terms and conditions as outlined in the enclosed Real Estate Sales Agreement.

"If the State's rights are not exercised within such period, we shall deem ourselves free to sell the property to Promet Corp. in accordance with the terms of the enclosed Real Estate Sales Agreement.

"This notice is sent to you although this company is of the opinion that the property in question is not covered by the provisions of **Section 39-6.1-9**."

On January 7, 1986, Herbert DeSimone (DeSimone), director of transportation for the state, accepted the offer in writing. In his letter to DiStefano, DeSimone wrote, "Of course, you understand that certain wording in the Real Estate Sales Agreement relating to 'buyer' and obligations concerning the removal of track would be inappropriate to the purpose of the State's purchase." The closing between P&W and Promet had been originally scheduled for January 17, 1986, but the parties rescheduled several times, finally agreeing to April 14, 1986, at 10 a.m. The reason for rescheduling the closing date was to allow the state and Promet's engineers to determine whether the property could accommodate Promet's development plans while preserving the state's rail options. Such a plan proved to be impossible.

Can rail still work? no

On April 11, 1986, the state was denied a temporary restraining order to enjoin the conveyance to Promet, after the Superior Court justice determined that the state had protected its rights and that P&W would be proceeding at its own risk.

Some minutes before 10 a.m. on April 14, 1986, Arruda appeared on behalf of the state at DiStefano's office and tendered a check for $100,000. Arruda was informed that P&W had already delivered the deed to the property to Promet earlier that morning. The closing between P&W and Promet had taken place at a location and time (8:30 a.m. instead of 10 a.m.) different from those originally scheduled, and P&W had taken no affirmative steps to inform the state of these changes.

state showed up, too late!

The state filed its amended complaint on December 9, 1986, naming both P&W and Promet as defendants, praying that the deed to Promet be declared null and void. . . . At trial, P&W and Promet argued that the subject property was not "rail property" subject to the statute because it was not being used for rail purposes at the time of the conveyance. The railroad company and Promet further argued that the state had waived any rights it possessed under the statute by having failed to tender payment for the property within the thirty days prescribed in § 39-6.1-9.

In his decision issued from the bench, the trial justice found that the property in question is "rail property" within the meaning of § 39-6.1-9, that it was dedicated for railroad use, and that it was available for rail purposes. The trial justice found "some of the testimony given by defendant's witness disingenuous when he made the comment that there was no function in 1986 for rail property uses, when that was exactly the same condition when the Special Court order was entered into in 1982, which specifically says that no abandonment or discontinu[ation] of rail use service should take place for a four-year period after the conveyance." The trial justice further found that the state had validly accepted P&W's offer within the thirty-day period and that the state was not required to tender payment at that time. Rather, the trial justice determined that the state had a "reasonable time" in which to pay for the property, and he indicated that such reasonable time coincided with the various closing dates scheduled by P&W and Promet.

yes, state was correct

Take Note!

As is usual in real estate sales, the purchase agreement is the contract, and the "closing" is the moment of performance, when the seller transfers the property and the buyer pays for the property.

The trial justice issued an amended judgment on March 17, 1994. In that judgment, the trial justice declared the deed from P&W null and void and ordered that the property be transferred to the state. In addition, the trial justice ordered P&W to repay to Promet the purchase price of $100,000 plus interest and to reimburse Promet for real estate taxes that Promet had paid on the property, plus interest on that amount. Finally, the amended judgment required the state to pay P&W the $100,000 purchase price plus interest.

. . . .

Did the State's January 7, 1986 Letter
Constitute a Valid Acceptance of P&W's Offer?

The trial justice found that on December 12, 1985, P&W extended an option to the state to purchase the subject property and that the January 7, 1986 letter from DeSimone to DiStefano was "a valid exercise of the **Section 39-6.1-9** option." The finding of a trial justice sitting without a jury in respect to the formation of a contract is entitled to great weight, and this Court will not disturb such a finding unless the trial justice "misconceived material evidence or was otherwise clearly wrong." ***Smith v. Boyd*, 553 A.2d 131, 134 (R.I.1989).** On appeal, P&W asserted that no contract for the sale of the subject parcel existed because the state's January 7, 1986 letter did not constitute a valid acceptance of P&W's December 12, 1985 offer. In support of its assertion, P&W argued that the January 7 letter in fact proposed additional terms to the agreement. The letter from DeSimone to DiStefano provided in pertinent part:

Take Note!

Although the issue of assent most often arises in the course of a determination of whether a contract exists, sometimes assent is important because of statutory provisions invoking common law concepts related to assent. Here, the statute required that the state "accept" P&W's offer within 30 days, leading to the court's treatment of that question.

"Pursuant to **Rhode Island General Law, Section 39-6.1-9,** I am writing to you on behalf of the State of Rhode Island to exercise its right to accept the offer to purchase 6.9 acres of land . . . .

Of course, you understand that certain wording in the Real Estate Sales Agreement [referring to the agreement between P&W and Promet] relating to 'buyer' and obligations concerning the removal of track would be inappropriate to the purpose of the State's purchase.

"Please contact Mr. Joseph F. Arruda of this department to arrange for a meeting to revise the existing offer to conform the State's acceptance."

P&W argued that "[a]s a matter of law, [the state's] letter was nothing more than an invitation to meet and attempt to reach agreement on the terms of the sale." We disagree.

This Court has held that a valid acceptance "must be definite and unequivocal," *Ardente v. Horan,* 117 R.I. 254, 259, 366 A.2d 162, 165 (1976), and that an "acceptance which is equivocal or upon condition or with a limitation is a counteroffer and requires acceptance by the original offeror before a contractual relationship can exist." *John Hancock Mutual Life Insurance Co. v. Dietlin,* 97 R.I. 515, 518, 199 A.2d 311, 313 (1964). It is not equivocation, however, "if the offeree merely puts into words that which was already reasonably implied in the terms of the offer." 1 *Corbin on Contracts,* § 3.32 at 478-79 (rev. ed.1993). It is further the case that "an acceptance must receive a reasonable construction" and that "the mere addition of a collateral or immaterial matters [sic] will not prevent the formation of a contract." *Raydon Exploration, Inc. v. Ladd,* 902 F.2d 1496, 1500 (10th Cir.1990). *See also Hoyt R. Matise Co. v. Zurn,* 754 F.2d 560, 566 (5th Cir.1985) ("[t]o transmogrify a purported acceptance into a counteroffer, it must be shown that the acceptance differs in some material respect from the offer").

The state's letter of acceptance points out that the name of the buyer in the original agreement would have to be changed. In our opinion, this statement simply reflected the obvious necessity to replace "the state" for "Promet" as the named buyer in the deed. Moreover, the letter's reference to P&W's obligation to Promet to remove tracks from the property as "inappropriate to the purpose of the State's purchase" did not *add* any terms or conditions to the contract but, instead, constituted a clear benefit to P&W. In pointing out that the "wording" that obligated P&W to remove tracks would be "inappropriate" in an agreement between P&W and the state, the state, in fact, relieved P&W from the obligation and expense it otherwise would have incurred in selling the property to Promet. When an offeree, in its acceptance of an offer, absolves the offeror of a material obligation, the "rules of contract construction and the 'rules of common sense' " preclude construing that absolution as an additional term that invalidates the acceptance. *Textron, Inc. v. Aetna Casualty and Surety Co.,* 638 A.2d 537, 541 (R.I.1994); *cf. New Castle County v. Hartford Accident and Indemnity Co.,* 970 F.2d 1267, 1270 (3rd Cir.1992), *cert. denied,* 507 U.S. 1030, 113 S.Ct. 1846, 123 L.Ed.2d 470 (1993) ("the question is not whether there is an ambiguity in the metaphysical sense, but whether the language has only one reasonable meaning when construed, not in a hypertechnical fashion, but in an ordinary, common sense manner"). Moreover, DeSimone explicitly and unequivocally stated, "I am writing to you on behalf of the State of Rhode Island to exercise its right *to accept* the offer to purchase 6.9 acres of land," and requested the meeting with Arruda in order "to revise the existing offer to conform the *State's acceptance.*" (Emphases added.)

Therefore, we concur, with the trial justice who found that the state validly accepted the option extended to it by P&W.

. . . .

In conclusion, therefore, we sustain the state's appeal, and we deny and dismiss the appeal of P&W. We affirm the amended judgment of the Superior Court except that we vacate the requirement that the state pay interest to P&W on the purchase price of the property. The papers in this case may be returned to the Superior Court with direction to enter judgment consistent with this opinion.

FLANDERS, J., did not participate.

————————

From the preceding rules and cases, you can see that the offeree's response to the offer can be understood as being somewhere on the progression below, from acceptance to counter-offer, depending upon the facts and the court's rigor in applying the mirror-image rule:

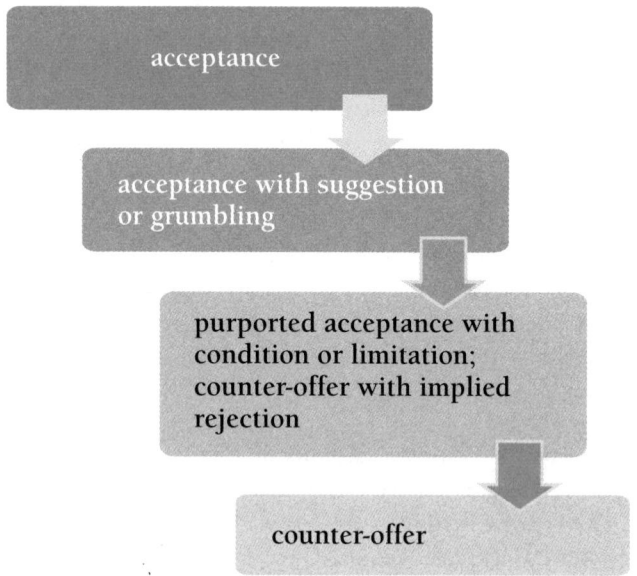

Problem 4-21: Applying the Mirror Image Rule

Fantasy Vacation Corp. (FVC) is in the business of selling fantasy vacation packages to buyers who will pay $7500 for a week of movie-making, including appearances with a "genuine" movie star. FVC sends Susan Starlet, the designated "star," a proposed 14-paragraph contract, specifying the dates and location of her appearance for an FVC vacation package, her duty to be "on call" from after breakfast until dinner each day, her acting roles and scenes, her release of publicity and filming rights, her duty to provide media appearances "as appropriate" during the specified days, FVC's duty to provide scripts and a director, FVC's duty to pay Starlet a $10,000 fee and up to $1000 for her expenses, and FVC's duty to provide Starlet with two first-class round-trip air tickets, hair and makeup services, wardrobe for the filming, hotel expenses, and a hotel suite with "two bathrooms if available." FVC's cover letter asks Starlet to sign the agreement as soon as possible and return it to FVC.

She signs the agreement and returns it, after making the following handwritten changes on the document: she inserts the word "one" in the sentence about media interviews, she adds "two bedrooms" to the hotel suite description, and she adds the words "to be supplied by Neiman Marcus department store" to the paragraph on wardrobe. Has she accepted FVC's offer? (If you think these facts are unrealistic, look at *Hollywood Fantasy Camp v. Gabor*, **151 F.3d 203** (5th Cir. 1998), but do your own analysis first and note that the facts here are slightly different and the court's conclusion is arguable).

§ 4.3.3. Permitted Manner of Acceptance

Because the offeror is master of the offer, the offer may specify the exclusive manner of acceptance, so that no other manner of acceptance is effective. For example, the offeror may say "in order to accept this offer, you must sign this contract document and return it to me." If the offeree instead telephones the offeror and says "I accept" there is no contract, because the acceptance did not conform to the offer's specification of the sole manner of acceptance. (The offeree has not accepted, but she has indicated her commitment to the offered terms. Her telephone call constitutes a counter-offer on those terms, which the original offeror may now accept if he chooses, and his reaction to the phone call may communicate that assent.)

Most often, however, an offeror does not exercise the power to define a required manner of acceptance. If the offer is silent as to the manner of acceptance, or if it includes only a preference or suggestion (not a demand) for a particular manner of acceptance, then the offeree is free to accept in any reasonable manner that is not precluded by the offer. This rule is memorialized in the Restatement (Second) and UCC Article 2.

Reading the Law Critically:
Manner of Acceptance in the Restatement (Second) and UCC

1. Restatement (Second) § 30(2) and UCC § 2-206(1)(a) contain almost identical statements of a general rule about manner of acceptance. What do § 30(1) and UCC § 2-206(1)(b) add to those general rules?

2. Recall the discussion of Restatement (Second) §§ 32 and 62 (page 329), which address whether offers are understood as inviting acceptance by promise or acceptance by performance. What is the relationship between those sections and Restatement (Second) § 30?

Restatement (Second) § 30. Form of Acceptance Invited

(1) An offer may invite or require acceptance to be made by an affirmative answer in words, or by performing or refraining from performing a specified act, or may empower the offeree to make a selection of terms in his acceptance.

(2) Unless otherwise indicated by the language or the circumstances, an offer invites acceptance in any manner and by any medium reasonable in the circumstances.

———————

UCC § 2-206. Offer and Acceptance in Formation of Contract

(1) Unless otherwise unambiguously indicated by the language or circumstances

　(a) an offer to make a contract shall be construed as inviting acceptance in any manner and by any medium reasonable in the circumstances;

　(b) an order or other offer to buy goods for prompt or current shipment shall be construed as inviting acceptance either by a prompt promise to ship or by the prompt or current shipment of conforming or nonconforming goods . . . .

(2) . . . .

[handwritten margin note: very specific rule — ship ___]

§ 4.3.4. Time of Effectiveness of Acceptance

Because assent requires knowledge by each party of the manifested intention of the other party, the default assumption in determining offer and acceptance is that a communication must be delivered to the other party to be effective. When the parties are in face-to-face conversation, that assumption causes no difficulties because the communication is sent and received at the same time. If the parties are at a distance, however, questions may arise about when a communication should be considered effective.

Because by definition an acceptance must be responding to an offer, the default assumption applies to offers; a communication becomes an offer only upon delivery to the offeree. The same is true of revocations. Because the offeree reasonably believes an offer may be accepted until notified otherwise, a revocation is effective only upon delivery to the offeree.

Acceptances pose a greater challenge. Acceptance marks agreement by both parties. At the moment the offeree dispatches her acceptance, there is a manifestation of agreement by both parties, but the offeree does not yet know that. If the acceptance is not effective until received by the offeror, however, the offeree remains at risk that the offer could be withdrawn before the acceptance and may hesitate to rely on the existence of a contract until she knows the offeror received it. But she will not know when the acceptance arrives without a responsive confirmation, producing continuing uncertainty as well as the necessity of an additional communication beyond an offer and an acceptance.

In England, this dilemma was addressed in 1818 by adoption of the "mailbox rule" in *Adams v. Lindsell*, **106 Eng. Rep. 250** (K.B. 1818). Courts in the United States soon followed suit. Here is the Restatement (Second) version of the mailbox rule:

Restatement (Second) § 63. **Time When Acceptance Takes Effect**

Unless the offer provides otherwise,
   (a) an acceptance made in a manner and by a medium invited by an offer is operative and completes the manifestation of mutual assent as soon as put out of the offeree's possession, without regard to whether it ever reaches the offeror . . . .
   (b) . . . .

Restatement (Second) § 66. **Acceptance Must Be Properly Dispatched**

An acceptance sent by mail or otherwise from a distance is not operative when dispatched, unless it is properly addressed and such other precautions taken as are ordinarily observed to insure safe transmission of similar messages.*

[handwritten: May ve invited this kind of acceptance]

---

* For instance, a letter sent via the U.S. Postal Service should be correctly addressed have the correct amount of postage. By email, the recipient's email address should be typed correctly.

[handwritten margin notes: mailbox rule problems which are courts?]

The mailbox rule solves one set of problems but potentially creates others. First, the offeror is bound to a contract before receiving the acceptance, even if the acceptance is never received. Second, having the acceptance be effective upon dispatch is problematic if the offeree sends an acceptance (effective upon dispatch) and also a rejection or counter-offer (effective only when received). What if those communications cross in transit? Suppose that an offeree dispatches an acceptance (considered to be effective when sent) but then the market shifts in a direction unfavorable to the offeree, so the offeree sends a rejection through faster means? Should first-in-time prevail (e.g., acceptance is effective because sent before the other communication arrived), even though the offeror receives conflicting information (e.g., both an acceptance and a counter-offer, or an acceptance and a rejection)?

[handwritten margin note: when arrives]

Perhaps because of these difficulties, the CISG and UNIDROIT do not follow the mailbox rule; they each say that an acceptance is effective when "the indication of assent reaches the offeror." CISG Art. 18(2); UNIDROIT Art. 2.1.6(2). Even where the mailbox rule prevails, as it does in common law jurisdictions, adjustments to it are made to ensure that the offeree cannot use the rule to gain an unfair advantage. Thus an acceptance is not effective upon dispatch if the offeree also sends a rejection or counteroffer; the offeror is entitled to rely on whichever communication (rejection, counteroffer, or acceptance) arrives first. Such adjustments strike a balance by permitting offerees to assume the existence of a contract once they send an acceptance, while protecting the offeror from confusion and preventing the offeree from speculating on the market or otherwise "gaming" the rules. And the offeror can protect herself by specifying in the offer that the acceptance must be received to be effective, thereby opting out of the effects of the mailbox rule.

[handwritten margin note: if sending accept & counter, first to arrive wins]

Today, with immediate communications available by telephone, email, and fax, concerns about when an acceptance becomes effective may arise less often, but it was a challenging issue when most communications were carried out by letters sent by post or messenger, and it remains an issue when mail or other methods of non-instantaneous communication are used. Even seemingly instantaneous forms of communication may raise questions about when those communications are to be considered "sent" and "received," since they still spend time in transit and may not be viewed by the intended recipient immediately upon arrival at a destination. In the 47 states adopting the Uniform Electronic Transactions Act (UETA), the following section helps to settle these kinds of questions by defining when an electronic record is sent or received:

[handwritten margin note: not as big an issue with instant communication]

UETA § 15. Time . . . of Sending and Receipt

(a) Unless otherwise agreed between the sender and the recipient, an electronic record is sent when it:

> (1) is addressed properly or otherwise directed properly to an informa-
>   tion processing system that the recipient has designated or uses for
>   the purpose of receiving electronic records or information of the
>   type sent and from which the recipient is able to retrieve the elec-
>   tronic record;
>
> (2) is in a form capable of being processed by that system; and
>
> (3) enters an information processing system outside the control of the
>   sender or of a person that sent the electronic record on behalf of
>   the sender or enters a region of the information processing system
>   designated or used by the recipient which is under the control of the
>   recipient.
>
> (b) Unless otherwise agreed between a sender and the recipient, an elec-
>   tronic record is received when:
>
> > (1) it enters a processing system that the recipient has designated or
> >   uses for the purpose of receiving electronic records or information
> >   of the type sent and from which the recipient is able to retrieve the
> >   electronic record; and
> >
> > (2) it is in a form capable of being processed by that system.
>
> . . . .
>
> (e) An electronic record is received under subsection (b) even if no indi-
>   vidual is aware of its receipt.
>
> . . . .

[margin handwriting: in inbox but not read = received]

Note that the mailbox rule (that an acceptance is effective when sent) assumes an oral or written communication of some kind. If an acceptance may be or must be made by performance or other conduct, is the acceptance effective when the conduct occurs or at some later time? Does the offeree have to take any additional steps after engaging in the conduct that will signify acceptance? The general rule is that the acceptance is valid at the time of the conduct, but if the conduct would not reliably come to the offeror's attention within a reasonable time, the offeree must take reasonable steps to notify the offeror of acceptance. No such notification is required if the offer waives it or if the offeror actually learns of the acceptance within a reasonable time, even if that was not likely at the time of the acceptance.

[margin handwriting: conduct = acceptance but make sure they know]

If the offeree fails to give the required notice, the offeror will be able to choose whether or not to recognize the existence of a contract, though the way in which the legal rules reach that result varies:

- In some jurisdictions, the acceptance is considered ineffective, so no contract is formed, but if the offeror eventually learns of the conduct signifying acceptance, the offeror may create a contract by treating the attempted acceptance as an offer and giving his own assent.

- In other jurisdictions, a contract is formed when the offeree performs the acts constituting acceptance, but the offeror may consider his contractual duties as "discharged" (nullified) because of the offeree's failure to notify the offeror of acceptance.
- UCC Article 2 allows the offeror to choose whether to treat the offer as lapsed because notice of acceptance was not given.

If no contract is formed, restitutionary relief may be necessary to prevent the offeror from being unjustly enriched by any performance given by the offeree.

Consider the following example: Ben mails to a screen-printing shop a written purchase order for 50,000 specialty T-shirts for an upcoming marathon. Ben's order requests that, if the shop agrees to print the shirts, it start production immediately, to be sure the shirts will be ready in time for the event. The shop accepts Ben's offer when it starts to produce the T-shirts, but it still must give notice to Ben with reasonable promptness. If it fails to do so, the consequence depends on whether UCC Article 2 governs the contract. If the sale is considered a sale of goods (T-shirts) under Article 2, Ben could treat his offer as lapsed or could recognize the contract despite the absence of timely notice. If the contract was instead considered to be a service contract (for silk-screening), then either no contract would be formed or a contract would be formed but Ben could consider his duty under the contract to be discharged. Either way, Ben would be free to recognize a contract or give assent to the shop's offer (made by conduct and communication to Ben) by accepting the T-shirts or making a new promise to pay.

Problems: Time of Effectiveness of Acceptance

4-22. When is or should the following acceptances be effective?

a. An acceptance sent via UPS or Federal Express
b. An acceptance expressed by clicking "I agree" on a website
c. An acceptance sent via text message
d. An acceptance sent by letter, which never arrives
e. An acceptance sent by letter, which never arrives, in response to an offer saying "I must hear from you within 10 days"
f. An acceptance sent by email, which bounces back as "undeliverable"
g. An acceptance sent by email from an email address widely known for sending spam, so it gets caught in the offeror's spam filter and never shows up in the offeror's email inbox

4-23. Which party does the mailbox rule favor? If an offeror wants the acceptance to be effective when he receives it, rather than when it was sent, how might he do that?

4-24.   Shep owns a coffee shop in a quaint back alley of a commercial district. One morning, he arrives to find that his shop has been vandalized—smashed front plate-glass window, painted graffiti on the shop's sign, and missing coffee machines and bags of coffee beans. He posts a dozen photocopies of the following announcement In the neighborhood:

Help Stop Vandalism!

Shep's Coffee Shop was broken into and vandalized on the night of December 10. Shep will pay $300 to the first person providing him with information identifying the perpetrators. Contact Shep at 651-234-5678 with any information. Thanks!

Sherry works down the street from the coffee shop and sees one of the postings. She takes a picture of the graffiti on her cell phone and begins asking around to see if someone can identify the graffiti style or maker. She also begins to do some research on break-ins in the area. Will it be necessary for her to take reasonable steps to notify Shep of her acceptance, after she completes performance?

a.   No, because the acceptance will make notification unnecessary.

b.   No, because no notice of acceptance is necessary for an offer that can be accepted only by performance.

c.   No, because Shep's posting did not require notification of acceptance.

d.   No, because Shep will find out about the acceptance within a reasonable time after acceptance.

e.   Yes, notification will be necessary.

Would your answer be different if the reward had been for anyone providing information directly to the police?

§ 4.3.5. Assent by Conduct or Inaction

If invited or reasonable under the cicumstances, a party's assent may be manifested by conduct rather than by express words. But conduct is inherently ambiguous as a source of meaning, so judging whether particular conduct actually represents assent, and to what terms, presents challenges and requires reflection on the context of the conduct. For example, you say to your friend, "If you will take care of my apartment while I'm on vacation in Prague, I promise to bring you a T-shirt from one of the underground jazz clubs there." You produce your apartment key and your friend silently takes it from your hand. Has he promised to care for your apartment while you are away, accepting your offer? What if he simply nodded his head in response, or shook your hand and wished you a good trip? Does it matter if the key was given immediately after your statement or a week later? If he did assent by one or more of these actions, to what terms has he assented?

When we consider whether conduct shows assent, we at least know that the individual voluntarily undertook the particular action, though it is often challenging to determine if the action is meant to or is reasonably understood to manifest assent. Can *inaction*—the failure to speak in response to an offer—ever be understood as showing agreement? What if you left a voice-mail for your friend, offering a Prague T-shirt in return for apartment care and saying, "If I don't hear back from you by tomorrow, I'll assume you agree and will leave my key in your mailbox when I leave town." Can the friend's inaction or silence constitute acceptance? Although we usually demand affirmative communication of assent through speech or conduct, silence or inaction can constitute assent in a few limited circumstances described and illustrated in the materials that follow.

Reading the Law Critically: *Houston Dairy*

1. Identify the parties' communications and conduct that are relevant to analyzing whether assent occurred. What was the legal effect (or non-effect) of each one? Why?

2. How would you advise each party to act differently to protect its interests better in the future?

Houston Dairy v. John Hancock Mutual Life Ins. Co.

HOUSTON DAIRY, INC., Plaintiff-Appellant

v.

JOHN HANCOCK MUTUAL LIFE INSURANCE CO.,
Defendant-Appellee

didn't accept loan, want money back

United States Court of Appeals, Fifth Circuit

643 F.2d 1185 (5th Cir. 1981)

AINSWORTH, Circuit Judge:

This is an appeal from a Mississippi diversity action in which appellant Houston Dairy, Inc. attempted to recover $16,000 sent to appellee John Hancock

Mutual Life Insurance Company as a "Good Faith Deposit" on a loan application which Houston Dairy claims never became binding. At the conclusion of the nonjury trial, the district court ruled that there was a binding contract between the parties and that the $16,000 deposit represented valid, liquidated damages forfeited by Houston Dairy when it breached the contract. We reverse.

found no contract

I. Facts

John Hancock mailed a commitment letter to Houston Dairy on December 30, 1977 in which it agreed to lend Houston Dairy $800,000 at 9¼% provided that within seven days Houston Dairy would return the commitment letter with a written acceptance and enclose either a letter of credit or a cashier's check in the amount of $16,000. The commitment letter stated the $16,000 was a "Good Faith Deposit" and was the appropriate measure of liquidated damages to be awarded John Hancock should Houston Dairy default. Dr. Dyer, president and principal shareholder of Houston Dairy, did not execute the letter until eighteen days later, on January 17, 1978. Along with the letter, Houston Dairy mailed a $16,000 cashier's check.

What's That?

"Liquidated damages" are damages whose amount is specified by the parties as part of the original contract. **Chapter 9** covers when a court may refuse to enforce a liquidated damages clause.

Upon receiving the returned commitment letter on January 23, an agent for John Hancock mailed the cashier's check to the John Hancock Depository and Service Center in Champaign, Illinois, for deposit and sent the loan-closing attorney, Harvey Henderson, the necessary information to close the loan. Meanwhile, Dr. Dyer delivered a copy of the commitment letter to Houston Dairy's attorney and asked him to call Henderson to ascertain his fee for closing the loan. On January 28, the two attorneys talked and agreed to the method they would use to close the loan and the manner in which the fee would be charged. However, on January 30, Houston Dairy was able to obtain a 9% loan from a state bank. Houston Dairy then requested a refund of its $16,000 deposit, which was refused by John Hancock.

In the district court, Houston Dairy contended that the return of the commitment letter constituted a counter offer since the seven-day time period for acceptance had expired, that John Hancock never communicated its acceptance of the counter offer, thus allowing Houston Dairy to revoke the counter offer, which it did on January 31. Therefore, the argument proceeds, no contract was ever formed and Houston Dairy was entitled to a refund of $16,000.

never accepted counteroffer

The district court disagreed, finding that John Hancock had both waived the seven-day limitation and validly accepted a counter offer. Accordingly, the court held that the parties had entered into a binding contract and awarded John Hancock the $16,000 deposit as valid, liquidated damages for breach of the loan agreement.

II. Was there a contract?

. . . [A]n offeror is free to limit acceptance to a fixed time period . . . . Once the time period has expired, a belated attempt to accept would be ineffective. However, such an untimely attempt to accept normally constitutes a counter offer.
. . .

It is . . . clear in the instant case that upon expiration of the seven-day time period, John Hancock's offer terminated. Thus the action taken by Houston Dairy in signing and returning the commitment letter subsequent to the termination of the offer constituted a counter offer which John Hancock could accept within a reasonable time.

In Mississippi, the courts have long recognized that for acceptance to have effect, it must be communicated to the proposer of the offer. See **Pioneer Box Co. v. Price Veneer & Lumber Co., 132 Miss. 189, 96 So. 103, 105 (1923)**. John Hancock contends it did accept Houston Dairy's counter offer and that the acceptance was communicated to Houston Dairy.

According to John Hancock, depositing Houston Dairy's check was itself sufficient to operate as communication of its acceptance of the counter offer. John Hancock argues that its silence plus retention of Houston Dairy's money constituted acceptance and notification. Indeed, Mississippi has specifically recognized the validity of acceptance by silence within the guidelines laid down in **Restatement § 72.*** See **Old Equity Life Insurance Co. v. Jones, 217 So.2d 648, 651 (Miss.1969)**; **Ammons v. Wilson & Co., 176 Miss. 645, 170 So. 227, 228 (1936)**.

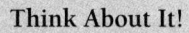

Think About It!

What dangers are presented by John Hancock's argument? Why not find acceptance here?

However, the present facts do not fit within these guidelines. Houston Dairy neither had previous dealings nor had otherwise been led to understand that John Hancock's silence and temporary retention of its deposit would operate as acceptance. In addition, Houston Dairy had no knowledge that its check had

---

* [Authors' Note: The Restatement (Second) version of this rule appears after this case.]

been deposited in John Hancock's depository. Since Houston Dairy sent a cashier's check, it could not have known the check had even been deposited unless notified by John Hancock or its bank. No such notice arrived from John Hancock and none is required from the bank.

The Mississippi Supreme Court held in **L. A. Becker v. Clardy, 96 Miss. 301, 51 So. 211 (1910)** that the mere depositing of a check was insufficient to constitute acceptance of an offer. There, an offeror sent a $100 downpayment along with its order for merchandise to the offeree. As was its policy, the offeree immediately deposited the check in its account, which was later paid in due course by the bank upon which the check was drawn. However, the offeree subsequently mailed a letter to the offeror rejecting the offer and enclosed a check for $100. The court held that upon receipt of the order and downpayment, the offeree was "entitled to a reasonable time in which to examine and determine whether it would accept or reject [the order] . . . . Depositing the check for collection, therefore, did not constitute acceptance of the order." **Id., 51 So. at 213.**[3]

John Hancock also contends that Houston Dairy was notified of its acceptance in the conversation between the attorneys for both parties on January 28. However, a review of the testimony concerning that conversation shows no communication of acceptance. Indeed, John Hancock's closing attorney testified that at the time of his conversation with Houston Dairy's attorney, he had not received the executed commitment letter and had no knowledge a counter offer had even been made. His conversation only concerned the method to be used to close the loan and the distribution of the fee to be charged, not acceptance of the counter offer. Houston Dairy cannot be deemed to have knowledge of John Hancock's acceptance simply by requesting and receiving information on the procedures for closing a loan should an agreement be reached.

III. Conclusion

In summary, Houston Dairy could not accept John Hancock's offer once the time period had lapsed. Thus, when Houston Dairy executed and returned the commitment letter several days late, it was proposing a counter offer which John Hancock could either accept or reject. Since the actions and policies of John Hancock were unknown to Houston Dairy, mere silence was not operative as an acceptance of the counter offer, no communication of acceptance having been

---

[3] John Hancock attempts to distinguish L.A. Becker by stating that the offeree in L.A. Becker did not have a policy of immediately returning checks on offers it did not wish to accept, as was John Hancock's policy here. With this argument, John Hancock suggests that since the $16,000 deposit was not returned immediately in accord with its policy, then Houston Dairy had notice the counter offer had been accepted. This argument is valid only if Houston Dairy first had knowledge of John Hancock's policy. Upon a review of the record, we have found no previous dealings or statements that would indicate knowledge by Houston Dairy of John Hancock's policy concerning offers it would not accept.

[handwritten: Dairy wins]

received. Houston Dairy therefore was entitled to revoke its counter offer, which it did on January 31. Accordingly, we reverse the judgment of the district court and render in favor of Houston Dairy for the amount of its deposit, $16,000.*

Reading the Law Critically: Acceptance by Conduct or Inaction in the Restatement (Second)

1. Why is it justifiable to treat silence or inaction as manifesting assent in the circumstances identified?

2. How does this Restatement provision relate to liability for restitution?

Restatement (Second) § 69. **Acceptance by Silence or Exercise of Dominion**

(1) Where an offeree fails to reply to an offer, his silence and inaction operate as an acceptance in the following cases only:

[handwritten: If I don't hear from you ...]

(a) Where an offeree takes the benefit of offered services with reasonable opportunity to reject them and reason to know that they were offered with the expectation of compensation.

(b) Where the offeror has stated or given the offeree reason to understand that assent may be manifested by silence or inaction, and the offeree in remaining silent and inactive intends to accept the offer.

(c) Where because of previous dealings or otherwise, it is reasonable that the offeree should notify the offeror if he does not intend to accept.

[handwritten: exercising dominion. with mine in my laptop - give it back - or require money]

(2) An offeree who does any act inconsistent with the offeror's ownership of offered property is bound in accordance with the offered terms unless they are manifestly unreasonable. But if the act is wrongful as against the offeror it is an acceptance only if ratified by him.**

---

*[Authors' Note: The court here orders John Hancock to refund Houston Dairy's payment of $16,000 because no contract was formed and there was no justification for John Hancock to retain the money. There is no general rule of law requiring return of such "down payments" on contract performance. If, as here, no contract is found to exist, the right to a refund depends on restitutionary principles. If a contract exists but performance ends for some reason, the right to a refund will depend on the terms of the contract or, in their absence, on restitutionary concepts.]

** Subsection (2) may require additional explanation to be understood. The first sentence creates a contract by the offeree's conduct of exercising dominion over the offeror's property, but the second sentence allows the offeror to choose between contract formation and the tort of conversion, if applicable. Thus, an offeror who does not want to be bound to a contract with the offeree can instead seek conversation remedies in tort for the offeree's use of or damage to the property.

Unsolicited Merchandise and Buying Clubs

More than likely, you have received in the mail some goods you did not order (mailing labels, greeting cards, DVDs), accompanied by a request for payment or contribution. Under Restatement (Second) § 69, is a contract formed if the recipient of such a mailing keeps and uses the goods? Gives them away? Discards them? Puts them on a shelf and forgets about them?

Because of the uncertainty about the answers to such questions and as a result of abuses by marketers attempting to foist unwanted merchandise on consumers, state and federal regulators have sought to police some of the abuses. According to the Postal Reorganization Act of 1970, 39 U.S.C. § 3009, a person who receives "unordered merchandise" *by way of the U.S. Postal Service* usually may treat it as a gift. The Federal Trade Commission (FTC) explains the rule on its website:

> Q. Am I obligated to return or pay for merchandise I never ordered?
>
> A. No. If you receive merchandise that you didn't order, you have a legal right to keep it as a free gift.
>
> Q. Must I notify the seller if I keep unordered merchandise without paying for it?
>
> A. You have no legal obligation to notify the seller. However, it is a good idea to write a letter to the company stating that you didn't order the item and, therefore, you have a legal right to keep it for free. This may discourage the seller from sending you bills or dunning notices, or it may help clear up an honest error. Send your letter by certified mail. Keep the return receipt and a copy of the letter for your records. You may need it later.
>
> . . . .
>
> Q. Is there any merchandise that may be sent legally without my consent?
>
> A. Yes. You may receive samples that are clearly marked free, and merchandise from charitable organizations asking for contributions. You may keep such shipments as free gifts.
>
> Q. Is there any way to protect myself from shippers of unordered merchandise?
>
> A. When you participate in sweepstakes or order goods advertised as "free," "trial," or "unusually low priced," be cautious. Read all the fine print to determine if you are joining a "club," with regular purchasing or notification obligations. Keep a copy of the advertisement or catalog that led you to place the order, too. This may make it easier to contact the company if a problem arises.

Federal Trade Commission, Consumer Information, Unordered Merchandise, www.consumer.ftc.gov/articles/0181-unordered-merchandise.

State statutes also address abuses resulting from the mailing of unsolicited goods, sometimes giving the recipient a defense against any action for the price or return of the goods. *See, e.g.,* Wisc. Stat. § 241.28 (2013) (unsolicited goods are gifts); *see also* state statutes listed in Joseph M. Perillo, *Calamari and Perillo on Contracts* § 2.19, at 77 n.13 (6th ed. 2009)

Perhaps in response to such regulation, marketers have sought to show customer assent through use of "negative option" features—asking individuals to agree to a trial delivery, website terms of use, or a membership agreement. The seller then can claim that the customer has assented receiving one or more shipments of goods and therefore must pay for any goods not returned, until the customer cancels the contract.

For this reason, the FTC recommends that consumers be cautious about entering into "buying clubs or plans," in which the consumer signs up for a club and then "shops" until she cancels her membership in the club:

> There are three common types of buying clubs: one tells you when a product is coming; one doesn't tell you when a product is coming; and one charges you for membership automatically.

> ### Plans That Tell You Products Are Coming

> These plans are a form of "opt out" shopping. You have to say no if you don't want to buy what the plan is sending. If you don't reject the item, you get the product automatically.

> The companies that operate this way need to follow some specific rules, spelled out in the FTC's Prenotification Negative Option Rule: they must have clear, prominent information in any promotional materials you use to enroll. A company must tell you:

> - how many announcements and rejection forms you may get each year, and how often
> - that you will have at least 10 days to reject a product before the company ships it to you

- if there's a minimum number of purchases required
- that you can cancel your membership any time after you've made the minimum number of purchases

Two important things to remember:

- **You get at least 10 days to decide.** If you don't want the product, you must mail back the rejection form either by the *return date* (when the company must receive it) or by the *mailing date* (the date the form has to be mailed by). The company will tell you which date it uses. If you don't get at least 10 days before the product is shipped, you can return it for a full credit, and the club has to pay the return postage.
- **The company has four weeks to ship.** If you sign up for a special offer like "5 Books for $1," the company has to ship your order within four weeks of receiving it or offer you an equivalent alternative. If you don't want the alternative introductory merchandise, you can cancel your membership, as long as you return the goods.

I Want To Cancel

Some plans require that you spend a certain amount of money on products at the club's regular prices before you can cancel your membership. They should tell you that from the beginning. If they don't, and you want to cancel your membership:

- **Send your request in writing.** The company has to cancel your membership promptly.
- **Return the first item that you received after the company had your written notice.** Consider any more unordered merchandise a gift. To avoid bills and collection notices, it's best to tell the company you're no longer a member each time you get unordered merchandise, and to send a copy of your cancellation letter.

Plans That Don't Tell You Products Are Coming

These plans are often called continuity plans. There's no heads up before the merchandise is sent. You get the products or services automatically until you cancel your "membership."

Some continuity plans have an "approval period" or "free trial" so you can try something out. If you keep the product or don't cancel the service before the free trial ends, you become a plan member. Other plans bill you for items—for example, flowers, books, movies, or software—when you get them. If you use your credit card when you enroll, the company may charge your card each time they send something.

Plans That Charge Membership Fees

In a third type of buying club, the monthly membership charge is automatic. Your fee gives you the ability to get what the plan describes as discounts.

Some people have told the FTC that they didn't know they were enrolled in this type of plan until they noticed charges on their debit or credit card statements. They *thought* they were paying a $1.99 shipping fee for a free trial. Actually, they were agreeing to be enrolled in a plan that would continue to charge them, regardless of the purchases they made. . . .

www.consumer.ftc.gov/articles/0068-how-buying-plans-work. If the company does not properly disclose the negative option or does not honor your cancellation, that may constitute a deceptive business practice, which is within the FTC's enforcement powers. *See* 16 C.F.R. pt. 310 (2013). Many states' attorneys general have similar enforcement powers under "little FTC Acts."

Reading the Law Critically:
Specht and *Douglas*

1. What conduct or inaction allegedly manifested assent?

2. What terms were allegedly assented to by that conduct or inaction?

3. Meaningful assent may be said to consist of reasonable notification that a contract is being offered, a reasonable opportunity to review the terms, notification that particular conduct would be understood as manifesting assent, and performance of the designated conduct. Which of these aspects of assent were missing in *Specht* and *Douglas*? How should the defendants change their communications to ensure that the next set of offerees will be held to have agreed to the offered terms?

Specht v. Netscape

CHRISTOPHER SPECHT, JOHN GIBSON, MICHAEL FAGAN, SEAN KELLY,
MARK GRUBER, and SHERRY WEINDORF, individually and on behalf of all
others similarly situated, Plaintiffs-Appellees

v.

NETSCAPE COMMUNICATIONS CORPORATION and AMERICA ONLINE,
INC., Defendants-Appellants

United States Court of Appeals, Second Circuit
306 F.3d 17 (2d Cir. 2002)

SOTOMAYOR, Circuit Judge.

This is an appeal from a judgment of the Southern District of New York
denying a motion by defendants-appellants Netscape Communications Corporation and its corporate parent, America Online, Inc. (collectively, "defendants"
or "Netscape"), to compel arbitration and to stay court proceedings. In order
to resolve the central question of arbitrability presented here, we must address
issues of contract formation in cyberspace. Principally, we are asked to determine
whether plaintiffs-appellees ("plaintiffs"), by acting upon defendants' invitation
to download free software made available on defendants' webpage, agreed to be
bound by the software's license terms (which included the arbitration clause at
issue), even though plaintiffs could not have learned of the existence of those terms
unless, prior to executing the download, they had scrolled down the webpage to
a screen located below the download button. We agree with the district court that
a reasonably prudent Internet user in circumstances such as these would not have
known or learned of the existence of the license terms before responding to defendants' invitation to download the free software, and that defendants therefore did
not provide reasonable notice of the license terms. In consequence, plaintiffs' bare
act of downloading the software did not unambiguously manifest assent to the
arbitration provision contained in the license terms.

. . . .

We therefore affirm the district court's denial of defendants' motion to compel
arbitration and to stay court proceedings.

Background
I. Facts

In three related putative class actions, plaintiffs alleged that, unknown to
them, their use of SmartDownload transmitted to defendants private information
about plaintiffs' downloading of files from the Internet, thereby effecting an elec-

*illegal activity
my way
- surveillance*

tronic surveillance of their online activities in violation of two federal statutes, the Electronic Communications Privacy Act, 18 U.S.C. §§ 2510 et seq., and the Computer Fraud and Abuse Act, 18 U.S.C. § 1030.

Who's That?

Former Court of Appeals Judge, now U.S. Supreme Court Justice, Sonia Sotomayor was born on June 25, 1954, in the Bronx borough of New York City, where she was raised in a household of modest income. After graduating summa cum laude from Princeton University, Justice Sotomayor entered Yale Law School, where she was an editor on the Yale Law Journal. Justice Sotomayor practiced law at Pavia & Harcourt, specializing in intellectual property litigation, international law, and arbitration. She was one of the founding members of the New York City Campaign Finance Board. In 1997, President Clinton appointed Justice Sotomayor to the Second Circuit Court of Appeals. In 2009, President Obama nominated her to replace retiring Justice Souter. She became the third woman and first Hispanic Justice on the United States Supreme Court. http://judgepedia. org/index.php/Sonia_Sotomayor; www.biography.com/people/sonia-sotomayor-453906.

browser

Specifically, plaintiffs alleged that when they first used Netscape's Communicator—a software program that permits Internet browsing—the program created and stored on each of their computer hard drives a small text file known as a "cookie" that functioned "as a kind of electronic identification tag for future communications" between their computers and Netscape. Plaintiffs further alleged that when they installed SmartDownload— a separate software "plug-in"[2] that served to enhance Communicator's browsing capabilities—SmartDownload created and stored on their computer hard drives another string of characters, known as a "Key," which similarly functioned as an identification tag in future communications with Netscape. According to the complaints in this case, each time a computer user employed Communicator to download a file from the Internet, SmartDownload "assume[d] from Communicator the task of downloading" the file and transmitted to Netscape the address of the file being downloaded together with the cookie created by Communicator and the Key created by SmartDownload. These processes, plaintiffs claim, constituted unlawful "eavesdropping" on users of Netscape's software products as well as on Internet websites from which users employing SmartDownload downloaded files.

---

[2] Netscape's website defines "plug-ins" as "software programs that extend the capabilities of the Netscape Browser in a specific way—giving you, for example, the ability to play audio samples or view video movies from within your browser." (http://wp.netscape.com/plugins/) SmartDownload purportedly made it easier for users of browser programs like Communicator to download files from the Internet without losing their progress when they paused to engage in some other task, or if their Internet connection was severed. *See Specht,* 150 F.Supp.2d at 587.

In the time period relevant to this litigation, Netscape offered on its website various software programs, including Communicator and SmartDownload, which visitors to the site were invited to obtain free of charge. It is undisputed that five of the six named plaintiffs—Michael Fagan, John Gibson, Mark Gruber, Sean Kelly, and Sherry Weindorf—downloaded Communicator from the Netscape website. These plaintiffs acknowledge that when they proceeded to initiate installation[3] of Communicator, they were automatically shown a scrollable text of that program's license agreement and were not permitted to complete the installation until they had clicked on a "Yes" button to indicate that they accepted all the license terms.[4] If a user attempted to install Communicator without clicking "Yes," the installation would be aborted. All five named user plaintiffs expressly agreed to Communicator's license terms by clicking "Yes." The Communicator license agreement that these plaintiffs saw made no mention of SmartDownload or other plug-in programs, and stated that "[t]hese terms apply to Netscape Communicator and Netscape Navigator"[6] and that "all disputes relating to this Agreement (excepting any dispute relating to intellectual property rights)" are subject to "binding arbitration in Santa Clara County, California."

Although Communicator could be obtained independently of SmartDownload, all the named user plaintiffs . . . downloaded and installed Communicator in connection with downloading SmartDownload. Each of these plaintiffs allegedly arrived at a Netscape webpage[8] captioned "SmartDownload Communicator" that urged them to "Download With Confidence Using SmartDownload!" At or near the bottom of the screen facing plaintiffs was the prompt "Start Download" and a tinted button labeled "Download." By clicking on the button, plaintiffs initiated the download of SmartDownload. Once that process was complete, SmartDownload, as its first plug-in task, permitted plaintiffs to proceed with downloading and

---

[3] There is a difference between downloading and installing a software program. When a user downloads a program from the Internet to his or her computer, the program file is stored on the user's hard drive but typically is not operable until the user installs or executes it, usually by double-clicking on the file and causing the program to run.

[4] This kind of online software license agreement has come to be known as "clickwrap" (by analogy to "shrinkwrap," used in the licensing of tangible forms of software sold in packages) because it "presents the user with a message on his or her computer screen, requiring that the user manifest his or her assent to the terms of the license agreement by clicking on an icon. The product cannot be obtained or used unless and until the icon is clicked." *Specht, 150 F.Supp.2d at 593-94* (footnote omitted). . . . [C]licking on a webpage's clickwrap button after receiving notice of the existence of license terms has been held by some courts to manifest an Internet user's assent to terms governing the use of downloadable intangible software, *see, e.g., Hotmail Corp. v. Van$ Money Pie Inc.*, 47 U.S.P.Q.2d 1020, 1025 (N.D.Cal.1998).

[6] While Navigator was Netscape's "stand-alone" Internet browser program during the period in question, Communicator was a "software suite" that comprised Navigator and other software products. All . . . user plaintiffs stated in affidavits that they had obtained upgraded versions of Communicator. . . .

[8] For purposes of this opinion, the term "webpage" or "page" is used to designate a document that resides, usually with other webpages, on a single Internet website and that contains information that is viewed on a computer monitor by scrolling through the document. To view a webpage in its entirety, a user typically must scroll through multiple screens.

installing Communicator, an operation that was accompanied by the clickwrap display of Communicator's license terms described above.

The signal difference between downloading Communicator and downloading SmartDownload was that no clickwrap presentation accompanied the latter operation. Instead, once plaintiffs Gibson, Gruber, Kelly, and Weindorf had clicked on the "Download" button located at or near the bottom of their screen, and the downloading of SmartDownload was complete, these plaintiffs encountered no further information about the plug-in program or the existence of license terms governing its use.[9] The sole reference to SmartDownload's license terms on the "SmartDownload Communicator" webpage was located in text that would have become visible to plaintiffs only if they had scrolled down to the next screen.

Had plaintiffs scrolled down instead of acting on defendants' invitation to click on the "Download" button, they would have encountered the following invitation: "Please review and agree to the terms of the *Netscape SmartDownload software license agreement* before downloading and using the software." Plaintiffs Gibson, Gruber, Kelly, and Weindorf averred in their affidavits that they never saw this reference to the SmartDownload license agreement when they clicked on the "Download" button. They also testified during depositions that they saw no reference to license terms when they clicked to download SmartDownload, although under questioning by defendants' counsel, some plaintiffs added that they could not "remember" or be "sure" whether the screen shots of the SmartDownload page attached to their affidavits reflected precisely what they had seen on their computer screens when they downloaded SmartDownload.

In sum, plaintiffs Gibson, Gruber, Kelly, and Weindorf allege that the process of obtaining SmartDownload contrasted sharply with that of obtaining Communicator. Having selected SmartDownload, they were required neither to express unambiguous assent to that program's license agreement nor even to view the license terms or become aware of their existence before proceeding with the invited download of the free plug-in program. Moreover, once these plaintiffs had initiated the download, the existence of SmartDownload's license terms was not mentioned while the software was running or at any later point in plaintiffs' experience of the product.

Even for a user who, unlike plaintiffs, did happen to scroll down past the download button, SmartDownload's license terms would not have been immediately displayed in the manner of Communicator's clickwrapped terms. Instead, if such a user had seen the notice of SmartDownload's terms and then clicked on the underlined invitation to review and agree to the terms, a hypertext link would

---

[9] Plaintiff Kelly, a relatively sophisticated Internet user, testified that when he clicked to download SmartDownload, he did not think that he was downloading a software program at all, but rather that SmartDownload "was merely a piece of download technology." He later became aware that Smart-Download was residing as software on his hard drive when he attempted to download electronic files from the Internet.

have taken the user to a separate webpage entitled "License & Support Agreements." The first paragraph on this page read, in pertinent part:

> The use of each Netscape software product is governed by a license agreement. You must read and agree to the license agreement terms BEFORE acquiring a product. Please click on the appropriate link below to review the current license agreement for the product of interest to you before acquisition. For products available for download, you must read and agree to the license agreement terms BEFORE you install the software. If you do not agree to the license terms, do not download, install or use the software.

Below this paragraph appeared a list of license agreements, the first of which was "*License Agreement for Netscape Navigator and Netscape Communicator Product Family* (Netscape Navigator, Netscape Communicator and Netscape SmartDownload)." If the user clicked on that link, he or she would be taken to yet another webpage that contained the full text of a license agreement that was identical in every respect to the Communicator license agreement except that it stated that its "terms apply to Netscape Communicator, Netscape Navigator, and Netscape SmartDownload." The license agreement granted the user a nonexclusive license to use and reproduce the software, subject to certain terms:

> BY CLICKING THE ACCEPTANCE BUTTON OR INSTALLING OR USING NETSCAPE COMMUNICATOR, NETSCAPE NAVIGATOR, OR NETSCAPE SMARTDOWNLOAD SOFTWARE (THE "PRODUCT"), THE INDIVIDUAL OR ENTITY LICENSING THE PRODUCT ("LICENSEE") IS CONSENTING TO BE BOUND BY AND IS BECOMING A PARTY TO THIS AGREEMENT. IF LICENSEE DOES NOT AGREE TO ALL OF THE TERMS OF THIS AGREEMENT, THE BUTTON INDICATING NON-ACCEPTANCE MUST BE SELECTED, AND LICENSEE MUST NOT INSTALL OR USE THE SOFTWARE.

Among the license terms was a provision requiring virtually all disputes relating to the agreement to be submitted to arbitration:

> Unless otherwise agreed in writing, all disputes relating to this Agreement (excepting any dispute relating to intellectual property rights) shall be subject to final and binding arbitration in Santa Clara County, California, under the auspices of JAMS/EndDispute, with the losing party paying all costs of arbitration.

> . . . . [Omitted here are claims by two additional plaintiffs with slightly different facts concerning the download process and setting.]

II. Proceedings Below

In the district court, defendants moved to compel arbitration and to stay court proceedings pursuant to the Federal Arbitration Act ("FAA"), 9 U.S.C. § 4, arguing that the disputes reflected in the complaints, like any other dispute relating to the SmartDownload license agreement, are subject to the arbitration clause contained in that agreement. Finding that Netscape's webpage, unlike typical examples of clickwrap, neither adequately alerted users to the existence of SmartDownload's license terms nor required users unambiguously to manifest assent to those terms as a condition of downloading the product, the court held that the user plaintiffs had not entered into the SmartDownload license agreement. *Specht*, 150 F.Supp.2d at 595-96.

. . . .

Discussion
I. Standard of Review and Applicable Law

A district court's denial of a motion to compel arbitration is reviewed *de novo*. *Collins & Aikman Prods. Co. v. Bldg. Sys., Inc.*, 58 F.3d 16, 19 (2d Cir.1995). The determination of whether parties have contractually bound themselves to arbitrate a dispute—a determination involving interpretation of state law—is a legal conclusion also subject to *de novo* review. *Chelsea Square Textiles, Inc. v. Bombay Dyeing & Mfg. Co., Ltd.*, 189 F.3d 289, 295 (2d Cir.1999); *see also Shann v. Dunk*, 84 F.3d 73, 77 (2d Cir.1996) ("The central issue—whether, based on the factual findings, a binding contract existed—is a question of law that we review *de novo*."). The findings upon which that conclusion is based, however, are factual and thus may not be overturned unless clearly erroneous. *Chelsea Square Textiles*, 189 F.3d at 295.

. . . .

III. Whether the User Plaintiffs Had Reasonable Notice of and
Manifested Assent to the SmartDownload License Agreement

Whether governed by the common law or by Article 2 of the Uniform Commercial Code ("UCC"), a transaction, in order to be a contract, requires a manifestation of agreement between the parties. *See Windsor Mills, Inc. v. Collins & Aikman Corp.*, 25 Cal.App.3d 987, 991, 101 Cal.Rptr. 347, 350 (1972) ("[C]onsent to, or acceptance of, the arbitration provision [is] necessary to create an agreement to arbitrate."); *see also* Cal. Com.Code § 2204(1) ("A contract for sale of goods may be made in any manner sufficient to show agreement, including conduct by both parties which recognizes the existence of such a contract.").[13] Mutual manifestation of assent, whether by written or spoken word or by conduct, is the touchstone of contract. *Binder v. Aetna Life Ins. Co.*, 75 Cal. App.4th 832, 848, 89 Cal.Rptr.2d 540, 551 (1999); *cf.* Restatement (Second) of Contracts § 19(2) (1981) ("The conduct of a party is not effective as a manifestation of his assent unless he intends to engage in the conduct and knows or has reason to know that the other party may infer from his conduct that he assents."). Although an onlooker observing the disputed transactions in this case would have seen each of the user plaintiffs click on the SmartDownload "Download" button, *see Cedars Sinai Med. Ctr. v. Mid-West Nat'l Life Ins. Co.*, 118 F.Supp.2d 1002, 1008 (C.D.Cal.2000) ("In California, a party's intent to contract is judged objectively, by the party's outward manifestation of consent."), a consumer's clicking on a download button does not communicate assent to contractual terms if the offer did not make clear to the consumer that clicking on the download button would signify assent to those terms, *see Windsor Mills*, 25 Cal.App.3d at 992, 101 Cal.Rptr. at 351 ("[W]hen the offeree does not know that a proposal has been made to him this objective standard does not apply."). California's common law is clear that "an offeree, regardless of apparent manifestation of his consent, is not bound by inconspicuous contractual provisions of which he is unaware, contained in a document whose contractual nature is not obvious." *Id.* . . .

> **FYI** Since this case was decided, a majority of courts have applied UCC Art. 2 to most software contracts, albeit with some dissension.

Arbitration agreements are no exception to the requirement of manifestation of assent. "This principle of knowing consent applies with particular force to provisions for arbitration." *Windsor Mills*, 101 Cal.Rptr. at 351. Clarity and conspicuousness of arbitration terms are important in securing informed assent. "If a party wishes to bind in writing another to an agreement to arbitrate future disputes, such purpose should be accomplished in a way that each party to the arrangement will fully and clearly comprehend that the agreement to arbitrate exists and binds the parties thereto." *Commercial Factors Corp. v. Kurtzman Bros.*, 131 Cal.App.2d 133, 134-35, 280 P.2d 146, 147-48 (1955) (internal

---

[13] The district court concluded that the SmartDownload transactions here should be governed by "California law as it relates to the sale of goods, including the Uniform Commercial Code in effect in California." *Specht*, 150 F.Supp.2d at 591. It is not obvious, however, that UCC Article 2 ("sales of goods") applies to the licensing of software that is downloadable from the Internet. . . . Some courts have also applied Article 2, occasionally with misgivings, to sales of off-the-shelf software in tangible, packaged formats. *See, e.g., ProCD*, 86 F.3d at 1450 . . . .

Downloadable software, however, is scarcely a "tangible" good . . . .

We need not decide today whether UCC Article 2 applies to Internet transactions in downloadable products. The district court's analysis and the parties' arguments on appeal show that, for present purposes, there is no essential difference between UCC Article 2 and the common law of contracts. We therefore apply the common law, with exceptions as noted.

quotation marks omitted). Thus, California contract law measures assent by an objective standard that takes into account both what the offeree said, wrote, or did and the transactional context in which the offeree verbalized or acted.

A. The Reasonably Prudent Offeree of Downloadable Software

Defendants argue that plaintiffs must be held to a standard of reasonable prudence and that, because notice of the existence of SmartDownload license terms was on the next scrollable screen, plaintiffs were on "inquiry notice" of those terms.[14] We disagree with the proposition that a reasonably prudent offeree in plaintiffs' position would necessarily have known or learned of the existence of the SmartDownload license agreement prior to acting, so that plaintiffs may be held to have assented to that agreement with constructive notice of its terms. *See* Cal. Civ.Code § 1589 ("A voluntary acceptance of the benefit of a transaction is equivalent to a consent to all the obligations arising from it, so far as the facts are known, or ought to be known, to the person accepting."). It is true that "[a] party cannot avoid the terms of a contract on the ground that he or she failed to read it before signing." *Marin Storage & Trucking*, 89 Cal.App.4th at 1049, 107 Cal. Rptr.2d at 651. But courts are quick to add: "An exception to this general rule exists when the writing does not appear to be a contract and the terms are not called to the attention of the recipient. In such a case, no contract is formed with respect to the undisclosed term." *Id.; cf. Cory v. Golden State Bank*, 95 Cal.App.3d 360, 364, 157 Cal.Rptr. 538, 541 (1979) ("[T]he provision in question is effectively hidden from the view of money order purchasers until after the transactions are completed. . . . Under these circumstances, it must be concluded that the Bank's money order purchasers are not chargeable with either actual or constructive notice of the service charge provision, and therefore cannot be deemed to have consented to the provision as part of their transaction with the Bank.").

Most of the cases cited by defendants in support of their inquiry-notice argument are drawn from the world of paper contracting. *See, e.g., Taussig v. Bode & Haslett*, 134 Cal. 260, 66

Take Note!

The rule cited here to *Marin Storage* is colloquially known as the "duty to read" rule, even though it is not a duty but instead a principle of estoppel. It prevents a person who assented to an agreement from later denying assent merely because she did not read the terms, as long as she had a reasonable opportunity to read the terms. The *Specht* court notes one exception to this rule, and other exceptions are discussed in Chapter 5, page 518. In the next paragraph, the court lists cases' holdings on the recipient's opportunity to read the terms and how much notice is necessary to alert the recipient to the existence of the terms.

---

[14] "Inquiry notice" is "actual notice of circumstances sufficient to put a prudent man upon inquiry." *Cal. State Auto. Ass'n Inter-Ins. Bureau v. Barrett Garages, Inc.*, 257 Cal.App.2d 71, 64 Cal.Rptr. 699, 703 (Cal.Ct.App.1967) (internal quotation marks omitted).

P. 259 (1901) (where party had opportunity to read leakage disclaimer printed on warehouse receipt, he had duty to do so); *In re First Capital Life Ins. Co.*, 34 Cal.App.4th 1283, 1288, 40 Cal.Rptr.2d 816, 820 (1995) (purchase of insurance policy after opportunity to read and understand policy terms creates binding agreement); *King v. Larsen Realty, Inc.*, 121 Cal.App.3d 349, 356, 175 Cal. Rptr. 226, 231 (1981) (where realtors' board manual specifying that party was required to arbitrate was "readily available," party was "on notice" that he was agreeing to mandatory arbitration); *Cal. State Auto. Ass'n Inter-Ins. Bureau v. Barrett Garages, Inc.*, 257 Cal.App.2d 71, 76, 64 Cal.Rptr. 699, 703 (1967) (recipient of airport parking claim check was bound by terms printed on claim check, because a "ordinarily prudent" person would have been alerted to the terms); *Larrus v. First Nat'l Bank*, 122 Cal.App.2d 884, 888, 266 P.2d 143, 147 (1954) ("clearly printed" statement on bank card stating that depositor agreed to bank's regulations provided sufficient notice to create agreement, where party had opportunity to view statement and to ask for full text of regulations, but did not do so); *see also Hux v. Butler*, 339 F.2d 696, 700 (6th Cir.1964) (constructive notice found where "slightest inquiry" would have disclosed relevant facts to offeree); *Walker v. Carnival Cruise Lines*, 63 F.Supp.2d 1083, 1089 (N.D.Cal.1999) (under California and federal law, "conspicuous notice" directing the attention of parties to existence of contract terms renders terms binding) (quotation marks omitted); *Shacket v. Roger Smith Aircraft Sales, Inc.*, 651 F.Supp. 675, 691 (N.D.Ill.1986) (constructive notice found where "minimal investigation" would have revealed facts to offeree).

[handwritten margin note: terms need to be discoverable for "ordinarily prudent" person]

As the foregoing cases suggest, receipt of a physical document containing contract terms or notice thereof is frequently deemed, in the world of paper transactions, a sufficient circumstance to place the offeree on inquiry notice of those terms. "Every person who has actual notice of circumstances sufficient to put a prudent man upon inquiry as to a particular fact, has constructive notice of the fact itself in all cases in which, by prosecuting such inquiry, he might have learned such fact." Cal. Civ.Code § 19. These principles apply equally to the emergent world of online product delivery, pop-up screens, hyperlinked pages, clickwrap licensing, scrollable documents, and urgent admonitions to "Download Now!". What plaintiffs saw when they were being invited by defendants to download this fast, free plug-in called SmartDownload was a screen containing praise for the product and, at the very bottom of the screen, a "Download" button. Defendants argue that under the principles set forth in the cases cited above, a "fair and prudent person using ordinary care" would have been on inquiry notice of SmartDownload's license terms. *Shacket*, 651 F.Supp. at 690.

[handwritten margin note: applies online too]

We are not persuaded that a reasonably prudent offeree in these circumstances would have known of the existence of license terms. Plaintiffs were responding to an offer that did not carry an immediately visible notice of the existence of license terms or require unambiguous manifestation of assent to those terms. Thus, plaintiffs' "apparent manifestation of . . . consent" was to terms "contained in a document whose contractual nature [was] not obvious." *Windsor Mills*, 25 Cal. App.3d at 992, 101 Cal.Rptr. at 351. Moreover, the fact that, given the position of the scroll bar on their computer screens, plaintiffs may have been aware that an unexplored portion of the Netscape webpage remained below the download button does not mean that they reasonably should have concluded that this portion contained a notice of license terms. In their deposition testimony, plaintiffs variously stated that they used the scroll bar "[o]nly if there is something that I feel I need to see that is on—that is off the page," or that the elevated position of the scroll bar suggested the presence of "mere[ ] formalities, standard lower banner links" or "that the page is bigger than what I can see." Plaintiffs testified, and defendants did not refute, that plaintiffs were in fact unaware that defendants intended to attach license terms to the use of SmartDownload.

We conclude that in circumstances such as these, where consumers are urged to download free software at the immediate click of a button, a reference to the existence of license terms on a submerged screen is not sufficient to place consumers on inquiry or constructive notice of those terms.[15] The SmartDownload webpage screen was "printed in such a manner that it tended to conceal the fact that it was an express acceptance of [Netscape's] rules and regulations." *Larrus*, 266 P.2d at 147. Internet users may have, as defendants put it, "as much time as they need[ ]" to scroll through multiple screens on a webpage, but there is no reason to assume that viewers will scroll down to subsequent screens simply because screens are there. When products are "free" and users are invited to download them in the absence of reasonably conspicuous notice that they are about to bind themselves to contract terms, the transactional circumstances cannot be fully analogized to those in the paper world of arm's-length bargaining. . . .

. . . .

C. Online Transactions

Cases in which courts have found contracts arising from Internet use do not assist defendants, because in those circumstances there was much clearer notice than in the present case that a user's act would manifest assent to contract terms. *See, e.g., Hotmail Corp. v. Van$ Money Pie Inc.*, 47 U.S.P.Q.2d 1020, 1025 (N.D.Cal.1998) (granting preliminary injunction based in part on breach of "Terms of Service" agreement, to which defendants had assented); *America Online, Inc. v. Booker*, 781 So.2d 423, 425 (Fla.Dist.Ct.App.2001) (upholding forum selection clause in "freely negotiated agreement" contained in online

---

[15] We do not address the district court's alternative holding that notice was further vitiated by the fact that the reference to SmartDownload's license terms, even if scrolled to, was couched in precatory terms ("a mild request") rather than mandatory ones. *Specht*, 150 F.Supp.2d at 596.

terms of service); *Caspi v. Microsoft Network, L.L.C.*, 323 N.J.Super. 118, 732 A.2d 528, 530, 532-33 (N.J.Super.Ct.App.Div.1999) (upholding forum selection clause where subscribers to online software were required to review license terms in scrollable window and to click "I Agree" or "I Don't Agree"); *Barnett v. Network Solutions, Inc.*, 38 S.W.3d 200, 203-04 (Tex.App.2001) (upholding forum selection clause in online contract for registering Internet domain names that required users to scroll through terms before accepting or rejecting them); *cf. Pollstar v. Gigmania, Ltd.*, 170 F.Supp.2d 974, 981-82 (E.D.Cal.2000) (expressing concern that notice of license terms had appeared in small, gray text on a gray background on a linked webpage, but concluding that it was too early in the case to order dismissal).[17]

After reviewing the California common law and other relevant legal authority, we conclude that under the circumstances here, plaintiffs' downloading of SmartDownload did not constitute acceptance of defendants' license terms. Reasonably conspicuous notice of the existence of contract terms and unambiguous manifestation of assent to those terms by consumers are essential if electronic bargaining is to have integrity and credibility. We hold that a reasonably prudent offeree in plaintiffs' position would not have known or learned, prior to acting on the invitation to download, of the reference to SmartDownload's license terms hidden below the "Download" button on the next screen. We affirm the district court's conclusion that the user plaintiffs, including Fagan, are not bound by the arbitration clause contained in those terms.

[additional issues omitted]

Conclusion

For the foregoing reasons, we affirm the district court's denial of defendants' motion to compel arbitration and to stay court proceedings.

---

[17] Although the parties here do not refer to it, California's consumer fraud statute, Cal. Bus. & Prof. Code § 17538, is one of the few state statutes to regulate online transactions in goods or services. The statute provides that in disclosing information regarding return and refund policies and other vital consumer information, online vendors must legibly display the information either:

(i) [on] the first screen displayed when the vendor's electronic site is accessed, (ii) on the screen on which goods or services are first offered, (iii) on the screen on which a buyer may place the order for goods or services, (iv) on the screen on which the buyer may enter payment information, such as a credit card account number, or (v) for nonbrowser-based technologies, in a manner that gives the user a reasonable opportunity to review that information.

Id. § 17538(d)(2)(A). The statute's clear purpose is to ensure that consumers engaging in online transactions have relevant information before they can be bound. Although consumer fraud as such is not alleged in the present action, and § 17538 protects only California residents, we note that the statute is consistent with the principle of conspicuous notice of the existence of contract terms that is also found in California's common law of contracts.

. . . .

Douglas v. Talk America

JOE DOUGLAS, on behalf of himself and on behalf of all others similarly situated, Petitioner

v.

UNITED STATES DISTRICT COURT FOR THE
CENTRAL DISTRICT OF CALIFORNIA, Respondent,
TALK AMERICA INC., a Pennsylvania corporation, Real Party in Interest

United States Court of Appeals, Ninth Circuit
495 F.3d 1062 (9th Cir. 2007)

PER CURIAM:

We consider whether a service provider may change the terms of its service contract by merely posting a revised contract on its website.

Facts

Joe Douglas contracted for long distance telephone service with America Online. Talk America subsequently acquired this business from AOL and continued to provide telephone service to AOL's former customers. Talk America then added four provisions to the service contract: (1) additional service charges; (2) a class action waiver; (3) an arbitration clause; and (4) a choice-of-law provision pointing to New York law. Talk America posted the revised contract on its website but, according to Douglas, it never notified him that the contract had changed. Unaware of the new terms, Douglas continued using Talk America's services for four years.

FYI

A mandamus action is one in which the petitioner seeks to compel a government body or official or an inferior court to do something that the respondent is legally required to do. If the court agrees that the conduct being sought by the petitioner is legally required, the court issues a writ of mandamus to compel the conduct. In this case, Douglas sought a writ of mandamus to compel the district court to decide the class action lawsuit, rather than enforcing the arbitration clause.

After becoming aware of the additional charges, Douglas filed a class action lawsuit in district court, charging Talk America with violations of the Federal Communications Act, breach of contract and violations of various California consumer protection statutes. Talk America moved to compel arbitration based on the modified contract and the district court granted the motion. Because the Federal Arbitration Act, 9 U.S.C. § 16, does not authorize interlocutory appeals of a district court order compelling arbitration, Douglas petitioned for a writ of mandamus.

Analysis

Because a writ of mandamus is an extraordinary remedy, we have developed five factors that cabin our power to grant the writ:

1. The party seeking the writ has no other adequate means, such as a direct appeal, to attain the relief he or she desires.
2. The petitioner will be damaged or prejudiced in a way not correctable on appeal.
3. The district court's order is clearly erroneous as a matter of law.
4. The district court's order is an oft-repeated error, or manifests a persistent disregard of the federal rules.
5. The district court's order raises new and important problems, or issues of law of first impression.

Bauman v. U.S. Dist. Court, 557 F.2d 650, 654-55 (9th Cir. 1977). The third factor is a necessary condition for granting a writ of mandamus. *Executive Software N. Am., Inc. v. U.S. Dist. Court*, 24 F.3d 1545, 1551 (9th Cir. 1994). But "all five factors need not be satisfied at once." *Valenzuela-Gonzalez v. U.S. Dist. Court*, 915 F.2d 1276, 1279 (9th Cir. 1990). If the district court clearly erred, we determine whether the four additional factors "in the mandamus calculus point in favor of granting the writ." *Executive Software*, 24 F.3d at 1551.

Douglas alleges that Talk America changed his service contract without notifying him. He could only have become aware of the new terms if he had visited Talk America's website and examined the contract for possible changes. The district court seems to have assumed Douglas had visited the website when it noted that the contract was available on "the web site on which Plaintiff paid his bills." However, Douglas claims that he authorized AOL to charge his credit card automatically and Talk America continued this practice, so he had no occasion to visit Talk America's website to pay his bills. Even if Douglas had visited the website, he would have had no reason to look at the contract posted there. Parties to a contract have no obligation to check the terms on a periodic basis to learn whether they have been changed by the other side.[1] Indeed, a party can't unilaterally change the terms of a contract; it must obtain the other party's consent before doing so. *Union Pac. R.R. v. Chi., Milwaukee, St. Paul & Pac. R.R.*, 549 F.2d 114, 118 (9th Cir. 1976). This is because a revised contract is merely an offer and does not bind the parties until it is accepted. *Matanuska Val Farmers Cooperating Ass'n v. Monaghan*, 188 F.2d 906, 909 (9th Cir. 1951). And gener-

---

[1] Nor would a party know *when* to check the website for possible changes to the contract terms without being notified that the contract has been changed and how. Douglas would have had to check the contract every day for possible changes. Without notice, an examination would be fairly cumbersome, as Douglas would have had to compare every word of the posted contract with his existing contract in order to detect whether it had changed.

ally "an offeree cannot actually assent to an offer unless he knows of its existence." 1 Samuel Williston & Richard A. Lord, A Treatise on the Law of Contracts § 4:13, at 365 (4th ed. 1990); *see also Trimble v. N.Y. Life Ins. Co.*, 255 N.Y.S. 292, 297 (App. Div. 1932) ("An offer may not be accepted until it is made and brought to the attention of the one accepting."). Even if Douglas's continued use of Talk America's service could be considered assent, such assent can only be inferred after he received proper notice of the proposed changes. Douglas claims that no such notice was given.

Crawford v. Talk America, Inc., No. 05-CV-0180-DRH, 2005 WL 2465909, at *4 (S.D.Ill. Oct. 6, 2005), and *Bischoff v. DirecTV, Inc.*, 180 F. Supp. 2d 1097, 1103-06 (C.D. Cal. 2002), on which the district court relied, are not to the contrary. The customers in these cases received notice of the modified contract by mail. The service provider in *Bischoff* mailed the contract to the customer, 180 F.Supp.2d at 1101, and the service provider in *Crawford* gave notice to the customer that she could see the contract terms online or call the service provider to learn of the terms. 2005 WL 2465909, at *3 n.3. Furthermore, *Crawford* and *Bischoff* involved new customers who necessarily would be on notice that they were required to assent to contract terms as a predicate for using the service. . . .

The district court thus erred in holding that Douglas was bound by the terms of the revised contract when he was not notified of the changes. The error reflects fundamental misapplications of contract law and goes to the heart of petitioner's claim. It would alone be sufficient to satisfy the third *Bauman* factor, but the district court also committed two additional errors. [The court discusses errors concerning unconscionability, concludes that the third *Bauman* factor is met, and then analyzes the remaining *Bauman* factors. It finds that the first and second *Bauman* factors favor mandamus relief.]

The fifth *Bauman* factor also favors mandamus relief. The district court's order enforcing new contractual terms when a customer is only given notice of the terms by having the contract posted on the internet "raises new and important problems" and addresses "issues of law of first impression." *Bauman*, 557 F.2d at 655. This is the first time any federal court of appeals has considered whether to enforce a modified contract with a customer where the customer claims that the only notice of the changed terms consisted of posting the revised contract on the provider's website. This issue is also of some significance, as it potentially affects the relationship of numerous service providers with millions of customers, and thus deserves immediate resolution.

Because four of the five *Bauman* factors favor mandamus relief, and only one factor (the fourth) militates against it, we conclude that the balance of factors favors issuing the writ. The district court's order compelling arbitration is vacated.

Petition granted.

Food for Thought: Creating and Modifying Online Agreements

As an increasing number of websites and software-installation protocols ask for user assent to terms of service, courts have needed to apply traditional rules of mutual assent to electronic settings, while attempting to keep the rules of contract formation operating in a media-neutral fashion. The easier cases involve affirmative actions of assent by the user, often in a "click-wrap" setting where the user electronically clicks a button or box that is labeled as indicating assent; a variation might require the user to type in a word or phrase of assent. The more challenging cases involve implied assent by conduct: the user engages in actions like the plaintiffs' downloads in *Specht* or the mere use of a website. In these cases, the issue is often whether the user had reason to know that that the terms existed, and had a chance to read them, before engaging in the conduct that purportedly assented to the terms. The same issue may arise in non-electronic settings, as where a credit card company notifies card holders of a contract change and that continued use of the card after a specified date will constitute assent to the new terms; this result is allowed by federal regulation.

Sometimes, though, vendors seek to have terms added by simply "posting" them, rather than by seeking affirmative contractual assent. In some non-contractual circumstances, "posting" will be sufficient to establish additional rights. For instance, a copyright owner gains certain rights by labeling the copyrighted work as specified by statute, an owner of real estate may gain additional rights under state law to exclude trespassers by posting "No Trespassing" signs around the perimeter of the property, and a user of a website may invoke privacy protection specified in a website's posted privacy policy (whether or not the policy is part of a contract with the user). In both *Specht* and *Douglas*, the vendors claimed that their posted terms were enforceable as contracts, but both courts rejected that argument.

In recent years, some vendors have attempted to use a hybrid of assent and notice. A vendor might include a contract provision saying "terms are subject to change at any time" and then periodically post changes to the contract on the company's website. In a small number of jurisdictions, courts have held that this term causes the contract to be "illusory"—lacking in consideration, because one party claims the right to change the terms and therefore is not committed to the supposed contract. In the majority of jurisdictions, though, the original contract is valid, and the issue becomes whether the later modification is effective. Issues like those in *Douglas* often arise.

[handwritten margin note: posting changes on website not enough]

A vendor who seeks to change its standard-form terms for hundreds, thousands, or even millions of customers may be able to do so easily if each visit to the website is a new contract (for instance, if each purchase from the vendor is a separate transaction) or if website subscribers can be shown the proposed modification on their next online visit before the modification needs to take effect. However, if the customers have an ongoing relationship with the vendor, with new transactions occurring even if the customers do not visit the website (as with the phone customer in *Douglas*), modifying the contract becomes a logistical nightmare if the vendor needs to obtain the assent of every customer (an "opt-in" system). As an alternative, some vendors have notified customers of an upcoming change in contract terms and have given them a specified number of days to expressly "opt out" of the modification or the contract, after which the remaining customers will be presumed to assent to the modified contract. In the bricks-and-mortar world, you will recall, silence is seldom valid assent (see *Houston Dairy*, page 372, and Restatement (Second) § 69, page 376). Should, or why should, the result be different in electronic settings? Considering your own online activity, have you encountered a change of terms of this sort? How did you handle the notice? Can you identify circumstances in which silence should, or should not, be considered to manifest assent?

Problems: Assent through Conduct or Inaction

4-25. Chris is walking along a wide public walkway on a city waterfront when she sees the signboard in the picture.

In all caps, it reads as follows:

Consent to be Photographed

In consideration for your admittance, and entering the premises and by your presence in this area, you consent to be photographed, filmed, interviewed and/or otherwise recorded. Your entry constitutes your consent to such photography, filming and/or recording and to any use, in any and all media, throughout the universe in perpetuity, or your appearance, voice, image and name for any purpose whatsoever in connection with the television production noted above.

You understand that the photography, filming and/or recording will be done in reliance on this consent given by you by entering this Area.

If you do not agree, please do not enter this area.

Chris doesn't want to make a three-block detour off and back onto the waterfront walkway so she continues walking past the signboard and sees the film crew.

Two months later, in Caesar's Palace in Las Vegas, she sees a similar signboard as she enters the pool area inside the hotel, where a film crew is working. She's wondering whether she assented to both sets of terms.

4-26. On the door of a restaurant is a sign that says that anyone entering the restaurant agrees to arbitrate any disputes concerning the restaurant. *See* the actual sign at **www.motherjones.com/mojo/2008/01/eat-burger-waive-right-sue**. Is it effective?

What if a patron walked into the restaurant wearing a T-shirt that read, "I do not assent to arbitration"? Professor Ian Ayres of Yale proposed to sell a "liabilitT shirt" saying, "Any disclaimer of liability notwithstanding, management, by serving me, accepts legal responsibility for any losses to my person or property that would result from my use of this establishment.©" Will either T-shirt have its intended effect for the wearer? *See* **www.whynot.net/merchandise/history.php**.

4-27. As reported by the ContractsProf Blog, the *New York Times* on June 22, 2011, reported that passengers of livery car services have been pulled out of the cars and searched by police, based on "the Taxi/Livery Robbery Inspection Program," which permits drivers to join the program to allow police to "inspect their car at any time in order to ensure the driver's safety." Drivers indicate their participation in the program by affixing a decal to their rear and side windows. When passengers asked why they were being instructed to step out of the back seat of their livery car or cab and be searched, the police informed them that they had consented to be searched when they got into a car displaying decals indicating that the driver was part of the Inspection Program. http://lawprofessors.typepad.com/contractsprof_blog/2011/06/new-york-city-police-on-consent.html. Did the passengers assent to the search by getting into the livery cars? (Ignore the constitutional issues under the Fourth Amendment on search and seizure.)

4-28. At the bottom of many website home pages is a small-font link to another page listing terms of use like any of the following:

> *Advanta Terms of Service*: "Please carefully read these terms and conditions. Your access to this Web site and any of its pages constitutes your agreement to be bound by the following terms and conditions. If you do not agree to the following terms and conditions, do not access this Web site or any of its pages."

> *AOL.com Terms of Use*: "YOUR AFFIRMATIVE ACT OF USING AOL.COM SIGNIFIES THAT YOU AGREE TO THE FOLLOWING TERMS OF USE, YOU CONSENT TO THE INFORMATION PRACTICES DISCLOSED IN THE AOL NETWORK PRIVACY POLICY, AND YOU CONSENT TO RECEIVE REQUIRED NOTICES AND TO TRANSACT WITH US ELECTRONICALLY. IF YOU DO NOT AGREE, DO NOT USE AOL.COM."

> *Google Terms of Service*: "By using our services, you are agreeing to these terms. Please read them carefully . . . ."

Do users automatically assent to these terms, merely by going onto the website?

Go to Google and keep track of how many "clicks" it takes you to find the Terms of Service. What impact, if any, does that have on your analysis of the user's assent?

A "South Park" episode addresses a similar issue, with website terms of use. *See* http://outsourcehouse.co.za/southpark-and-itunes-i-agreed-by-accident/#.UOS36-CWSo, or search YouTube for "south park i agreed by accident."

Similar situations appeared twice in the Dilbert comic strip. See www.dilbert.com and search for the comic strips on Jan. 14 and June 7, 1997.

4-29. Do your answers to the above questions and the preceding cases suggest any unifying factors or policies? Is there any strength to the argument that "everyone does it"?

§ 4.4. UCC Article 2 Abandons the Mirror Image Rule

As noted on page 358, UCC Article 2 expressly rejects the common law mirror image rule, which requires that an acceptance vary little if at all from the offer. This section tackles the alternative rule in Article 2.

When the mirror image rule was crafted, it was reasonable to think that a contract would be created through one party's assent to the other party's most recent articulation of terms, perhaps after a series of communications that produced an agreeable package of provisions. As time went on, changes in business practice challenged that assumption. During the 1800s and 1900s, standard-form terms and forms gradually became more common as commercial printing services, photocopy machines, and fax machines became more available to a wider range of businesses. This greater availability of printing and reproduction technologies encouraged parties to draft longer and longer versions of their desired terms, which were increasingly likely to diverge from the other party's standard (printed) terms. Because of the mirror image rule, under traditional contract law the exchange of such divergent documents would likely prevent contract formation. This problem was especially prevalent with respect to the documents exchanged to form contracts for sale of goods, so the drafters of UCC Article 2 crafted a new rule to handle the situation.

Before looking at the Article 2 solution, consider the implications of traditional common law doctrine, which still operates in contracts for services and other contracts not involving sales of goods. Party A makes an offer, using its standard form. Party B responds with its own standard form, differing in a few or many ways from the offer. Whether applied strictly or leniently, the mirror image rule likely means Party B's purported acceptance is, instead, a counter-offer. That counter-offer impliedly rejects the offer. Typically, the parties have not read each other's standard terms and often do not further discuss the terms but instead begin performance. Because no contract was created by the exchange of documents, performance by Party A has the legal consequence of acting as an acceptance of Party B's counter-offer. It is also possible that, after Party B has sent its counter-offer, additional documents are exchanged between the parties, none of them creating a contract because each one contains different terms than the previous document. When performance begins, that performance may act as acceptance of the most recent counter-offer. This "last shot rule" runs contrary to the parties' expectations that a contract was created by their exchange of documents and that those documents, not the last-sent document, determined the contract terms.

In sale of goods transactions, the buyer often makes the offer with a purchase order, and the seller attempts to accept the purchase order with an acknowledgment form. Each of these forms contains standard terms favoring the drafting party and therefore differing from the other's form, so under the common law the seller's acknowledgment would become an inadvertent counter-offer, rather than an acceptance. If the seller then ships goods and the buyer receives and keeps the goods, the buyer's performance would effectively accept the seller's counteroffer and its terms.

The unfairness of the "last shot rule" and the resulting asymmetry between business expectations and the legal result was at odds with the philosophy of the nascent Uniform Commercial Code and the existing "law merchant"—that the law should follow good business practices and lead to legal results consistent with the beliefs of reasonable persons. Accordingly, the drafting committee working on UCC Article 2 abandoned the mirror image rule and formulated a replacement rule in § 2-207. The problem addressed in § 2-207 is often dubbed "the battle of the forms," but as you will see in the statutory language, the section's coverage is not limited to form-based communications.

Section 2-207 allows contracts to be formed even though there may be significant variations between offer and acceptance. As a result, § 2-207 also must determine what terms are in the resulting contract. As you will see as you read the text of § 2-207 and work your way through the materials that follow, this UCC provision has had mixed successes and failures, but it was a visionary attempt to reduce the anomalies resulting from applying the mirror image rule to situations involving standard forms.

UCC § 2-207. **Additional Terms in Acceptance . . .** *

(1) A definite and seasonable expression of acceptance . . . operates as an acceptance even though it states terms additional to or different from

---

* The omitted text covers confirmations with additional or different terms. Our focus is instead on acceptances with terms additional to or different from the offer.

> those offered . . . , unless acceptance is expressly made conditional on assent to the additional or different terms.
>
> (2) The additional terms are to be construed as proposals for addition to the contract. Between merchants such terms become part of the contract unless:
>
>   (a) the offer expressly limits acceptance to the terms of the offer;
>
>   (b) they materially alter it; or
>
>   (c) notification of objection to them has already been given or is given within a reasonable time after notice of them is received.
>
> (3) Conduct by both parties which recognizes the existence of a contract is sufficient to establish a contract for sale although the writings of the parties do not otherwise establish a contract. In such case the terms of the particular contract consist of those terms on which the writings of the parties agree, together with any supplementary terms incorporated under any other provisions of this Act.

[handwritten margin note: additions are okay for merchants — as long as not too different]

§ 4.4.1. Understanding § 2-207(1): Acceptance by Language

Section 2-207(1) says a communication may be an acceptance "even though" it does not mirror the offer, but only if the communication is a "definite and seasonable expression of acceptance." What is needed to satisfy that standard?

- There is no requirement of a writing, so an acceptance can be oral.
- "Seasonable" means that the purported acceptance is made within the time specified by the offer or, if none is specified, within a reasonable time after the offer, judging reasonableness based on all of the circumstances.
- A "definite . . . expression of acceptance" means that the language must show a willingness to commit to the contract by accepting the offer. For instance, if a buyer sends an order to a seller, and the seller responds with a postcard saying, "We have received your order and will give it our prompt and careful attention," the seller's response is not a "definite . . . expression of acceptance," but, instead, merely notification of receipt of the offer. For more guidance on this requirement, consult case law on what constitutes sufficient commitment to demonstrate assent.

In some jurisdictions, courts have described "definite and seasonable expression of acceptance" as a purported acceptance that does not "diverge[] *significantly* as to a *dickered* term."*

---

* *See, e.g., U.S. Industries, Inc. v. Semco Manufacturing, Inc.,* 562 F.2d 1061, 1067 (8ᵗʰ Cir. 1977).

A dickered term is a term on which the parties have negotiated or that does not appear in standard-form language. For instance, the item number, color, delivery date, quantity, and price are nearly always dickered terms because they are specific to the transaction and not part of the standard-form language. Warranties, payment terms, remedy provisions and the like may ordinarily be in standard-form language but may become dickered terms if the parties discuss them explicitly and directly.

- For example, in *Koehring Co. v. Glowacki,** the seller sent a letter to multiple potential purchasers listing machinery for sale "as is, where is." The buyer offered to buy for $16,500 "FOB, our truck, your plant, loaded" (a term that would have required seller to move the machinery onto the truck, at a cost of $1200 to $2100). Seller sent a telegram saying the bid was "accepted" but reiterating the "as is, where is" term. The court held that seller's response was a counter-offer because there was an "absence of agreement between the parties as to whether the sales price included loading risks and costs."

- In contrast, in *Southern Idaho Pipe & Steel Co. v. Cal-Cut Pipe & Supply, Inc.,*** the buyer struck out seller's delivery date for the pipe being purchased, inserted a date two months later, then signed and returned the form with a $20,000 check, which seller deposited. The court found an acceptance because the buyer's change did not "diverge[] so radically from the terms of the offer," as the seller "failed to establish the urgency" of the earlier date and appeared to acquiesce easily to the new date.

Section 2-207 (1) says further that, even if the purported acceptance is a "definite and seasonable expression of acceptance," it does not "operate as an acceptance" if it is "*expressly made conditional* on *assent* to additional or different terms." An *express condition* is usually flagged by phrases such as "provided that," "subject to," "conditional on," "but only if," or "except that the accepting party must also . . . ," each of which shows explicitly that the responding party does not mean to accept without its *own* terms being included.

- A majority of courts follow the statutory language precisely by also requiring that the express condition be explicitly conditioned on the offeror's "assent" to the additional or different terms.*** Under that majority approach, the following phrases in

---

* 253 N.W.2d 64, 68 (Wisc. 1977).

** 567 P.2d 1246 (Idaho 1977), *cert. denied*, 434 U.S. 1056 (1978).

*** *See e.g. Dorton v. Collins & Aikman Corp.*, 453 F.2d 1161, 1168 (6th Cir. 1972) A minority of courts hold that a counteroffer results when a condition is attached to the new terms in the purported acceptance (for instance, "I accept, subject to the terms below."). The condition need not be attached to *the offeree's assent to* the new terms in the purported acceptance. *See, e.g., Construction Aggregates Corp. v. Hewitt-Robins, Inc.*, 404 F.2d 505 (7th Cir. 1968) (minority approach).

response to an offer made the purported acceptance "expressly conditional on assent" to the additional or different terms, resulting in a counter-offer rather than an acceptance:

- Buyer's purchase order was made *subject to acceptance* of the 'Additional Terms and Conditions' on the reverse side."*
- Seller's invoice said, "Seller's willingness to sell to you is *conditioned on your acceptance* of these terms of sale."**

To generate a counter-offer rather than an acceptance under the majority approach, the express condition must connect the offeree's assent to the new terms in the purported acceptance. For example:

- A buyer responded to a seller's offer with a purchase order that said: "Acceptance of this order shall be deemed to constitute an agreement upon the part of the seller to the conditions named hereon and supersedes all previous agreements." The court held that the purchase order was not expressly conditional because "the language used does not clearly reveal that [Buyer] was 'unwilling to proceed with the transaction unless . . . assured of [Seller's] assent to additional or different terms.'"***
- An offer stated that "I agree to contract only if your acceptance contains all of my terms, and I hereby object to any additional terms." The acceptance included the offer's terms and added terms of its own. The acceptance was not expressly conditional on assent to those additional terms and so operated as an acceptance.****

Thus, we can paraphrase § 2-207(1) as follows: *A purported acceptance that does not diverge significantly from the offer (as to the dickered terms) is an acceptance (of an offer), even though it does not mirror the offer, unless it states that assent to the offer is conditional on the offeror's assent to the new terms in the purported acceptance.* That's quite a change from the mirror-image rule in the common law.

If subsection (1) results in an acceptance, then we move to subsection (2), to figure out how to handle the additional or different terms in the acceptance. If instead subsection (1) did *not* result in an acceptance, then we move to subsection (3), to see if the parties' conduct generated a contract. Thus, no fact situation will ever use all three subsections, but every fact situation will use subsection (1), and then *either* (2) *or* (3).

---

* *See Rich Products Corp. v. Kemutec, Inc.*, 66 F. Supp. 2d 937 (E.D. Wisc. 1999) (emphasis supplied).

** *See Textile Unlimited, Inc. v. A..BMH & Co.*, 240 F.3d 781, 788 (9th Cir. 2001) (emphasis supplied).

*** *See Idaho Power Co. v. Westinghouse Elec. Corp.*, 596 F.2d 924 (9th Cir. 1979).

**** *See Lockheed Electronics Co. v. Keronix, Inc.*, 170 Cal. Rptr. 591 (1981).

§ 4.4.2. Understanding § 2-207(2): Terms of a Contract Formed under Subsection (1)

If a contract is formed under § 2-207(1) even though the terms in the offer and acceptance do not match, what terms are in the resulting contract? Section 2-207(2), which addresses this question, is repeated below, with two official comments.

UCC § 2-207(2). **Additional Terms in Acceptance . . .**

The additional terms are to be construed as proposals for addition to the contract. Between merchants such terms become part of the contract unless:
(a) the offer expressly limits acceptance to the terms of the offer;
(b) they materially alter it; or
(c) notification of objection to them has already been given or is given within a reasonable time after notice of them is received.

Comments:

4. Examples of typical clauses which would normally "materially alter" the contract and so result in surprise or hardship if incorporated without express awareness by the other party are: a clause negating such standard warranties as that of merchantability or fitness for a particular purpose in circumstances in which either warranty normally attaches; a clause requiring a guaranty of 90% or 100% deliveries in a case such as a contract by cannery, where the usage of the trade allows greater quantity leeways; a clause reserving to the seller the power to cancel upon the buyer's failure to meet any invoice when due; a clause requiring that complaints be made in a time materially shorter than customary or reasonable.

5. Examples of clauses which involve no element of unreasonable surprise and which therefore are to be incorporated in the contract unless notice of objection is seasonably given are: a clause setting forth and perhaps enlarging slightly upon the seller's exemption due to supervening causes beyond his control, similar to those covered by the provision of this Article on merchant's excuse by failure of presupposed conditions or a clause fixing in advance any reasonable formula of proration under such circumstances; a clause fixing a reasonable time for complaints within customary limits, or in the case of a purchase for sub-sale, providing for inspection by the sub-purchaser; a clause providing for interest on overdue invoices or fixing the seller's standard credit terms where they are within the range of trade practice and do not limit any credit bargained for; a clause limiting the right of rejection for defects which fall within the customary trade tolerances for acceptance "with adjustment" or otherwise limiting remedy in a reasonable manner (see Sections 2-718 and 2-719).

Although it is not immediately obvious, the "additional terms" in the first sentence of subsection (2), "such terms" in the second sentence, "they" in (2)(b), and "them" in (2)(c) all refer back to any additional terms in the acceptance in subsection (1). Subsection (1) also mentions "different terms," so we need to differentiate additional terms from different terms:

- If the offer is silent on a particular topic, then any term on that topic in the acceptance is an _"additional term"_ because the term is "additional to" the offer.
- If the offer contains a term on a particular topic, then any term on that topic in the acceptance is a _"different term"_ because the term is "different from" the offer.

In subsection (2), the first sentence contains a rule that, by implication, applies when the contract _is not_ "between merchants," because the rule in the second sentence (including (a), (b), and (c)) applies when the contract is "between merchants." For our purposes, you should assume that any business entity is a "merchant."

If the contract is not "between merchants," then any additional terms in the acceptance under subsection (1) are "proposals for addition to the contract"—offers to modify the contract. As with other offers, the offeree (here, the original offeror in subsection (1)) can decide whether to accept or reject the offers to modify or can just let the offers lapse (which is what usually happens).

If the contract is "between merchants," then the additional terms in the acceptance under subsection (1) "become part of the contract unless" (a) or (b) or (c) applies:

- Subpart (a) refers to offers that contain a "my way or the highway" clause—a clause that expressly says something like "my terms and only my terms govern this proposed contract."
- Subpart (b) excludes any additional terms that materially alter "it"— the contract formed under (1). Comments 4 and 5 seem to define "material alteration" as terms that would lead to unreasonable surprise or hardship. They furnish examples of additional terms that meet this test, as well as those that don't.
- Subpart (c) is in passive voice, so it omits the actor of the verbs. Rewritten, subpart (c) reads: "The offeror has already notified the offeree that he or she objects to the additional terms (in the acceptance) or does so within a reasonable time after receiving the acceptance."

Thus, between merchants, any additional term in the acceptance under subsection (1) becomes part of the contract unless the offer contains a my-way-or-the-highway clause, the additional term materially alters the contract (causes unreasonable surprise or hardship), or the offeror has already notified the offeree that it objects to the additional term or does so within a reasonable time of receiving the offer.

Subsection (2) furnishes rules on how to deal with *additional* terms in the acceptance, but it does not furnish any rules on how to handle *different* terms in the acceptance, so the courts have had to fashion rules on what to do with different terms:

- The majority approach for contracts between merchants is a "knock-out rule"—the different terms cancel each other out, leaving the gaps to be filled in by supplementary provisions under the UCC.
- The minority approach for contracts between merchants is the "first shot rule"—the offeror, as the "master of the offer," prevails, and the different term in the acceptance is dropped.

For exchanges not "between merchants," the courts have not fashioned an answer, perhaps because the situation rarely arises.

§ 4.4.3. Understanding § 2-207(3): Contract Formation Recognized by Conduct

> **UCC § 2-207(3).** **Additional Terms in Acceptance . . .**
>
> Conduct by both parties which recognizes the existence of a contract is sufficient to establish a contract for sale although the writings of the parties do not otherwise establish a contract. **In such** case the terms of the particular contract consist of those terms on which the writings of the parties agree, together with any supplementary terms incorporated under any other provisions of this Act.

If there is no acceptance by language (express acceptance) under subsection (1) and if "the writings of the parties do not otherwise establish a contract," there might still be an implied-in-fact contract if there is "[c]onduct by both parties which recognizes the existence of a contract" under subsection (3). For instance, if the buyer's purported acceptance is expressly conditional on seller's assent to buyer's additional terms, no contract arises under subsection (1) unless the seller then expressly assents to buyer's counter-offer to create a contract. Similarly, no contract arises when the parties' dickered terms diverge significantly. If the seller then ships the goods to buyer, who receives them and keeps them, *both* parties' conduct "recognizes the existence of a contract" and is therefore "sufficient to establish a contract for sale." If, instead, the buyer refuses to take the goods from the seller's delivery driver, the actions of only one party, *but not both*, recognizes a contract, so there is no contract under § 2-207(3).

If, indeed, both parties' conduct recognizes the existence of a contract, then the terms of that contract are decided according to the second sentence of subsection (3). Assemble all of the parties' writings concerning this transaction (even though the writings themselves didn't establish a contract), and determine "those terms on which the writings of the parties agree." This rule is known colloquially as the "knock-out rule," because the other terms in the parties' writings are "knocked out."* Any missing terms are filled in with "supplementary terms incorporated under any other provisions of this Act." As you will learn in the next case, *C. Itoh*, and in Chapter 7, these supplementary terms include

- "Course of performance" (the parties' patterns of dealings in *this* contract)
- "Course of dealing" (the parties' patterns of dealings in their *past* contracts)
- "Usage of trade" (customs in the vocation, trade, geographic area, etc.)
- Default provisions (also known as "gap-fillers"; these rules in UCC Art. 2 fill in missing terms not filled in by course of performance, course of dealing, or usage of trade)

§ 4.4.4. Integrating Your Understanding of § 2-207

Drawing from the preceding discussion, the following flowchart sketches the flow of analysis under § 2-207. You may want to construct a more detailed flowchart that adds in all of the preceding content about § 2-207. In case of doubt, consult the statute's exact wording. Remember that this section applies only if the purported acceptance includes additional

See It!

Test your understanding of § 2-207 by comparing it with the YouTube video entitled "This Form Is Your Form," by "profblaw." Is the video accurate?

or different terms. If not, do not apply § 2-207, and focus instead on § 2-204 (page 279) or § 2-206 (page 366), as well as common law principles.

---

* This is a different knock-out rule then the majority rule governing different terms, as discussed in the previous section.

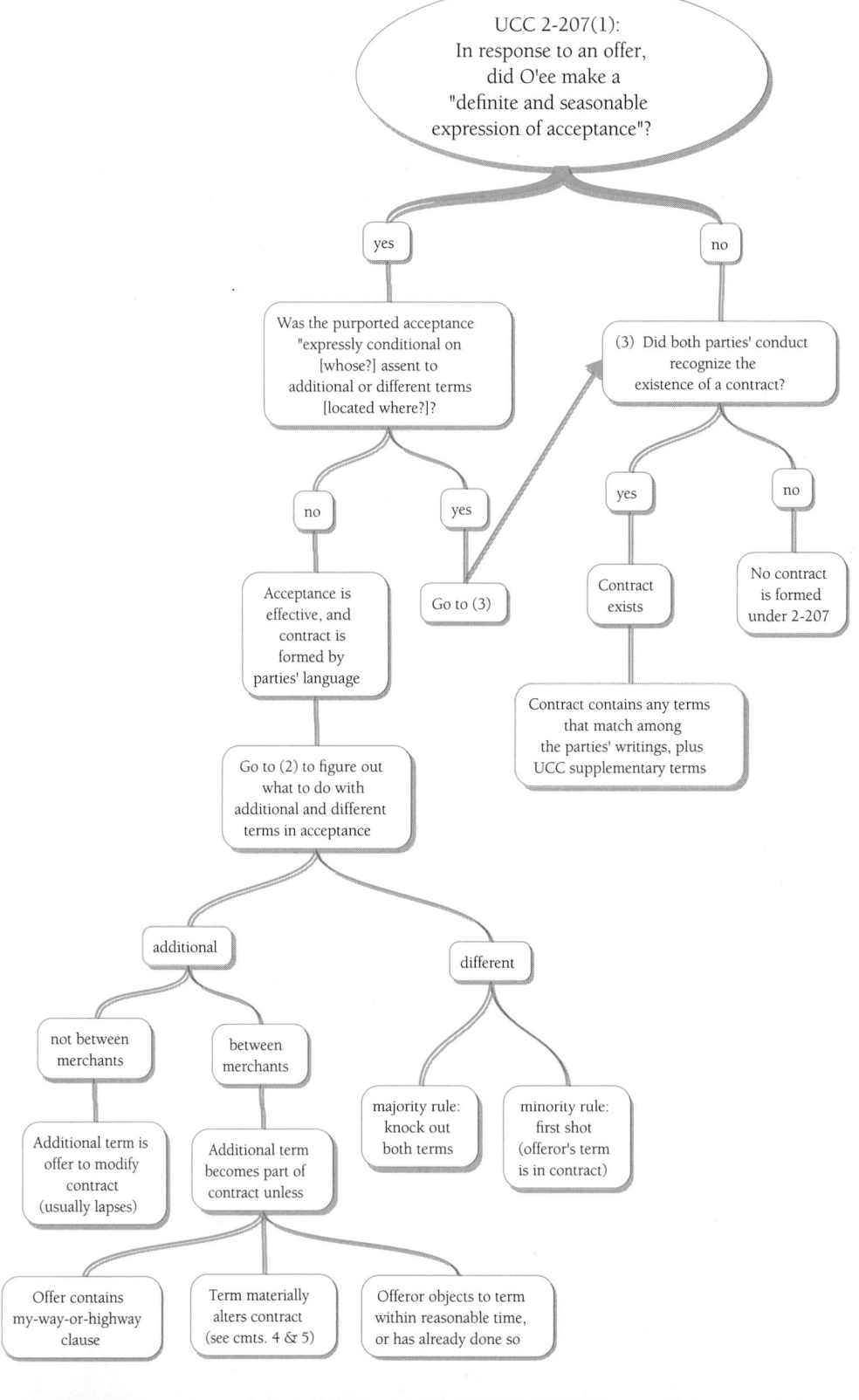

Reading the Law Critically:

Egan Machinery Co. **and** *C. Itoh & Co.*

1. How does the court apply § 2-207 to resolve the issue of contract formation? Does it do so correctly, according to the preceding flowchart and your understanding of the provision?

2. How does the court apply § 2-207 to determine the terms of the parties' contract? Does it do so correctly?

3. What policies support the court's result?

4. How does the court's ruling and reasoning supplement the flowchart?

5. If § 2-207 had not applied to the transaction, when and how would the parties' assent be found? What result would have occurred under the mirror image rule?

Egan Machinery Co. v. Mobil Chemical Co.

EGAN MACHINERY CO. and
AMERICAN MUTUAL INSURANCE CO., Plaintiffs

v.

MOBIL CHEMICAL CO., Defendant

United States District Court, D. Connecticut
660 F. Supp. 35 (D. Conn. 1986)

EGINTON, District Judge.

After review and absent objection the opinion of the Magistrate is hereby ADOPTED, RATIFIED, and AFFIRMED.

THOMAS P. SMITH, United States Magistrate.

In a classic UCC § 2–207 battle of the forms the warring parties use their boilerplate armies in an attempt to control the high ground by making their assent conditional on their right to set the conditions of the contract. In fashioning a peace between the combatants the court first looks to whether the exchanged forms created a contract. If a contract has been formed in this way, the court next determines which additional or different terms control by reference to § 2–207(2). *Daitom, Inc. v. Pennwalt Corporation,* 741 F.2d 1569 (10th Cir.1984). In deciding defendant's renewed motion for summary judgment, the court here considers the significance of two boilerplate contract clauses. The first is plaintiff's assertion that "this offer is accepted on the condition that our Standard Conditions of Sale, which are attached hereto and made a part hereof, are accepted by you." The second is defendant's clause stating: "Important—this order expressly limits acceptance to terms stated herein, and any additional or different terms proposed by seller are rejected unless expressly agreed to in writing." For the reasons set out below, the court concludes that a contract was created by the exchange of forms and that the additional term at issue here— an indemnity provision—did not become part of the contract. Accordingly, summary judgment should enter for the defendant.

The facts pertinent to the instant motion are easily recounted. In response to the defendant's Request for Bid on a two-sided eighty inch precoater, the plaintiff submitted two Quotations, one on April 5, 1973, and one on April 27, 1973. These Quotations describe in detail the components of the precoater, the precoater's operation, and those material[s] to be supplied by the plaintiff and the defendant. Aside from price, conditions of sale are not included in the Quotations.

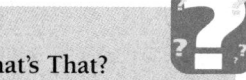

What's That?

The *Egan Machinery Co.* case is a decision by a federal district court judge, ratifying a written opinion by a United States magistrate judge, a position created by statute. Federal magistrate judges have jurisdiction to hear non-dispositive matters in civil cases before the federal district court and to hear preliminary criminal proceedings (e.g., arraignments). They also consider administrative appeals (e.g., Social Security Act determinations), issue Reports and Recommendations to the presiding federal district court judge, and conduct full trials if the parties waive their right to a hearing before a federal district court ("Article III") judge. The magistrate judges are selected by the chief judge of the district court for eight-year terms. As reflected here, a report and recommendation from a magistrate judge is presented to the federal district court to whom the case is assigned; it may be accepted by that judge as is or modified.

On May 2, 1973, the defendant submitted a Requisition/Purchase order ("Order") for the precoater described in the plaintiff's quotations. The Requisition/Purchase Order contained the following language:

> Please enter our order for the following, subject to conditions set forth in this order and on the reverse side hereof. Important—this order expressly limits acceptance to terms stated herein, and any additional or different terms proposed by the seller are rejected unless expressly agreed to in writing.

The conditions listed in the Order did not include an indemnification provision.

In response to the defendant's Order, the plaintiff submitted an Order Acknowledgment ("Acknowledgment") on May 8, 1973. This Acknowledgment provided that

> This order is accepted on the condition that our Standard Conditions of Sale, which are attached hereto and made a part hereof, are accepted by you, notwithstanding any modifying or additive conditions contained on your purchase order. Receipt of this acknowledgment by you without prompt written objection thereto shall constitute an acceptance of these terms and conditions.

Paragraph 12 of the plaintiff's Standard Conditions of Sale, the provision at issue here, provides that

> The purchaser shall use and shall require its employees to use all safety devices and guards and maintain the same in proper working order. Purchaser shall use and require its employees to use safe operating procedures in operating the equipment. If purchaser fails to observe the obligations contained in this paragraph, purchaser agrees to indemnify and save Egan harmless from any liability or obligation incurred by Egan to persons injured directly or indirectly in connection with the operation of the equipment. Purchaser further agrees to notify Egan promptly and in any event within 30 days, of any accident or malfunction involving Egan's equipment which results in personal injury or damage to property and to cooperate fully with Egan in investigating and determining the causes of such accident or malfunction. In the event the purchaser fails to give such notice to Egan, purchaser agrees to indemnify and save Egan harmless from any claims arising from such accident or malfunction.

Make the Connection

This is an indemnification clause that shifts the cost of third parties' losses resulting from poor training and supervision from the manufacturer to the purchaser. Recall that *Angel v. Murray* (page 116) also involved an indemnification clause.

In October 1977 one of the defendant's employees was injured while operating the precoater purchased from the plaintiff. The employee filed suit against the plaintiff and its insurer, Amico. This action culminated in a stipulated judgment by which Amico, as the plaintiff's insurer, paid the Mobil employee $75,000. The instant action then followed the stipulated judgment.

The defendant filed its initial motion for summary judgment on June 20, 1984. On November 24, 1985, this court denied that motion without prejudice and alerted counsel to *Daitom, Inc. v. Pennwalt Corporation, 741 F.2d 1569 (10th Cir. 1984)*, a case cited by neither party but which the court considered sound and persuasive on the issues raised by the defendant's motion. Heeding the court's suggestion, both parties on the pending renewed motion for summary judgment have looked to *Daitom* for a useful analytical framework and for substantive law. As a result, the issues to be resolved are narrow.

Before reaching those issues, however, a few points need be briefly mentioned. The first is that Connecticut's version of UCC § 2–207, Conn. Gen. Stat. § 42a–2–207, applies here. But because the Connecticut Supreme Court has not addressed the issues presented by the defendant's motion, this court, sitting in diversity, must make an estimate of what that court would do if faced with the same issues. *Brastex Corp. v. Allen International, Inc., 702 F.2d 326, 330 (2d Cir.1983)*. Next, it is well settled that to prevail on a motion for summary judgment the moving party must demonstrate the absence of any genuine issue of material fact and that it is entitled to judgment as a matter of law. *Heyman v. Commerce and Industry Ins. Co., 524 F.2d 1317, 1320 (2d Cir.1975)*. Summary judgment may be employed in disputes involving the interpretation of unambiguous contracts. *Wards Co., Inc. v. Stamford Ridgeway Associates, 761 F.2d 117, 120 (2d Cir.1985)*.

The arguments of the parties can also be sketched briefly. In opposing the motion, the plaintiff argues that no contract was formed by the exchange of documents because its conditional acceptance clause meets the specificity requirement of § 2–207(1)'s exception provision. Continuing, the plaintiff argues that a contract was formed instead by the conduct of the parties and that according to the UCC's gap fillers of custom and usage it became a genuine issue of material fact as to whether the indemnity provision became a term of the contract, thus making summary judgment inappropriate.

In contrast, the defendant argues that a contract was formed by the exchange of documents because the plaintiff failed to explicitly declare its unwillingness to proceed with the contract unless its conditions, including the indemnity provision, were accepted. Moreover, the defendant contends the indemnity provision did not become part of the contract because it was an additional term that the defendant rejected by not expressly assenting to it.

Turning first to the claimed conditional acceptance language of the plaintiff's Order Acknowledgment,[1] it is clear, following the lead of *Daitom,* and predicting

———

[1]The defendant's Requisition/Purchase order became the offer in this exchange of documents partly because it was the first exchanged form with conditions, *Reaction Molding Technologies v. General Electric Co.*, 585 F.Supp. 1097, 1106–07 (E.D. Pa. 1984) (citing J. White & R. Summers, Uniform Commercial Code at 27), and partly because the plaintiff's Order/Acknowledgment form characterizes itself as an acceptance with the phrase "this order is accepted."

that the Connecticut Supreme Court would do the same, that the clause is not sufficiently explicit to declare the plaintiff's intention to abort the contract unless it were sure of the defendant's assent to additional or different terms because the clause does not come out and state just that. *Daitom, supra,* 741 F.2d at 1577. Courts have required that clauses such as the one here be strictly construed. *Reaction Molding Technologies v. General Electric Co.,* 588 F.Supp. 1280, 1288 (E.D.Pa.1984). The conditional acceptance clause will convert an acceptance into a counteroffer only where the offeree clearly reveals its unwillingness to proceed with the transaction unless it is assured of the offeror's assent to additional or different terms. *Dorton v. Collins & Aikman Corp.,* 453 F.2d 1161, 1168 (6th Cir.1972). This the plaintiff's clause did not do.

The plaintiff's clause here falls short of creating a conditional acceptance partly because it fails to declare in clear terms the plaintiff's unwillingness to go forward unless its additional [or] different terms are assented to by the defendant. Instead, the clause speaks in generalities, using limiting rather than conditional language. *Reaction Molding, supra,* 588 F.Supp. at 1258, presuming the defendant's acceptance of its Standard Conditions at Sale unless the defendant responded with prompt written objection. This is not enough. The focus of § 2–207(1) is on explicit, not implicit, statements of intent. *See Dorton, supra,* 453 F.2d at 1168.

Moreover, the single case upon which the plaintiff relies is distinguishable. In *Uniroyal, Inc. v. Chambers Gasket and Manufacturing,* 177 Ind.App. 508, 380 N.E.2d 571 (1978), the seller's disputed clause used the word "conditional" and required the buyer to notify the seller in writing within seven days if it does not accept the conditions of sale. Such specific references are lacking in the clause at issue here.

The plaintiff's failure to explicitly declare its unwillingness to proceed with the contract unless its conditions were accepted compels the conclusion that a contract was formed by the exchanged forms on the consistent terms but leaves unresolved the issue of whether the indemnity provision became a term of the contract. In resolving this issue it should be noted first that the indemnity provision must be considered an additional term not only because there is no conflicting term but because the plaintiff has so acknowledged it. With this established, the question narrows, under the *Daitom* analysis, to whether the defendant's offer, under § 2–207(2), expressly limits acceptance to the terms of the offer. This it clearly did with the statement, "important—this order expressly limits acceptance to terms stated herein, and any additional or different terms proposed by the seller are rejected unless expressly agreed to in writing." Nearly identical language was found equal to the task of limitation in *Lockheed Electronics Co., Inc. v. Keronix, Inc.,* 114 Cal App.3d 304, 170 Cal.Rptr. 591, 30 U.C.C.Rep. 827 (1981), and, similarly, it is sufficient for the defendant's purposes here. As a result, the indemnity provision proposed by the plaintiff did not become part of the contract.

As the indemnity provision at issue here did not become a term of the contract, the defendant's motion should be granted.

The parties are entitled to seek timely review.

C. Itoh & Co. v. The Jordan International Co.

C. ITOH & CO. (AMERICA) INC., Plaintiff-Appellee

v.

THE JORDAN INTERNATIONAL CO., Defendant-Appellant

United States Court of Appeals, Seventh Circuit
552 F.2d 1228 (7ᵗʰ Cir. 1977)

SPRECHER, Circuit Judge.

The sole issue on this appeal is whether the district court properly denied a stay of the proceedings pending arbitration under Section 3 of the Federal Arbitration Act, 9 U.S.C. § 3.

I

C. Itoh & Co. (America) Inc. ("Itoh") submitted a purchase order dated August 15, 1974 for a certain quantity of steel coils to the Jordan International Company ("Jordan"). In response, Jordan sent its acknowledgment form dated August 19, 1974. On the face of Jordan's form, the following statement appears:

> Seller's acceptance is, however, expressly conditional on Buyer's assent to the additional or different terms and conditions set forth below and printed on the reverse side. If these terms and conditions are not acceptable, Buyer should notify seller at once.

One of the terms on the reverse side of Jordan's form was a broad provision for arbitration.[1] Itoh neither expressly assented nor objected to the additional arbitration term in Jordan's form until the instant litigation.

Itoh also entered into a contract to sell the steel coils that it purchased from Jordan to Riverview Steel Corporation, Inc. ("Riverview"). The contract between

---

[1] The arbitration clause provides:

Any controversy arising under or in connection with the contract shall be submitted to arbitration in New York City in accordance with the rules then obtaining of the American Arbitration Association. Judgment on any award may be entered in any court having jurisdiction. The parties hereto submit to the jurisdiction of the Federal and State courts in New York City, and notice of process in connection with arbitral or judicial proceedings may be served upon the parties by registered or certified mail, with the same effect as if personally served.

Itoh and Riverview contained an arbitration term which provided in pertinent part:

> Any and all controversies arising out of or relating to this contract, or any modification, breach or cancellation thereof, except as to quality, shall be settled by arbitration. . . .

After the steel had been delivered by Jordan and paid for by Itoh, Riverview advised Itoh that the steel coils were defective and did not conform to the standards set forth in the agreement between Itoh and Riverview; for these reasons, Riverview refused to pay Itoh for the steel. Consequently, Itoh brought the instant suit against Riverview and Jordan. Itoh alleged that Riverview had wrongfully refused to pay for the steel; as affirmative defenses, Riverview claimed that the steel was defective and that tender was improper since delivery was late. Itoh alleged that Jordan had sold Itoh defective steel and had made a late delivery of that steel.

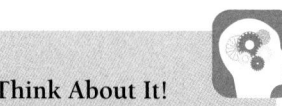

Think About It!

The parties' forms contained two arbitration clauses. Which one was at issue in this case?

Jordan then filed a motion in the district court requesting a stay of the proceedings pending arbitration under Section 3 of the Federal Arbitration Act, 9 U.S.C. § 3. The district court concluded that, as between Itoh and Riverview, the issue of whether the steel coils were defective was not referable to arbitration because of the "quality" exclusion in the arbitration provision of the contract between Itoh and Riverview. Since arbitration would not necessarily resolve all the issues raised by the parties, the district court, apparently assuming arguendo that there existed an agreement in writing between Jordan and Itoh to arbitrate their dispute, denied the stay pending arbitration. In the district court's opinion, sound judicial administration required that the entire litigation be resolved in a single forum; since some of the issues [(]those relating to quality[)] between Itoh and Riverview were not referable to arbitration, this goal could only be accomplished in the judicial forum.

It is from this denial of a stay pending arbitration that Jordan appeals.

. . . .

III

Having concluded that the district court had no discretion under Section 3 of the Federal Arbitration Act, 9 U.S.C. § 3, to deny Jordan's timely application for a stay of the action pending arbitration if there existed an agreement in writing for such arbitration between Jordan and Itoh, the remaining issue is whether there existed such an agreement.

. . . .

IV

[The court quotes UCC § 2-207.] Under Section 2-207 it is necessary to first determine whether a contract has been formed under Section 2-207(1) as a result of the exchange of forms between Jordan and Itoh.

At common law, "an acceptance . . . which contained terms additional to . . . those of the offer . . . constituted a rejection of the offer . . . and thus became a counter-offer." Dorton, supra, at 1166. Thus, the mere presence of the additional arbitration term in Jordan's acknowledgment form would, at common law, have prevented the exchange of documents between Jordan and Itoh from creating a contract, and Jordan's form would have automatically become a counter-offer.

Section 2-207(1) was intended to alter this inflexible common law approach to offer and acceptance:

> This section of the Code recognizes that in current commercial transactions, the terms of the offer and those of the acceptance will seldom be identical. Rather, under the current "battle of the forms," each party typically has a printed form drafted by his attorney and containing as many terms as could be envisioned to favor that party in his sales transactions. Whereas under common law the disparity between the fine-print terms in the parties' forms would have prevented the consummation of a contract when these forms are exchanged, Section 2-207 recognizes that in many, but not all, cases the parties do not impart such significance to the terms on the printed forms. . . . Thus, under Subsection (1), a contract . . . [may be] recognized notwithstanding the fact that an acceptance . . . contains terms additional to . . . those of the offer . . . .

Id. at 1166. See also Comment 2 to Section 2-207; Air Products & Chemicals, supra; John Thallon, supra. And it is now well-settled that the mere presence of an additional term, such as a provision for arbitration, in one of the parties' forms will not prevent the formation of a contract under Section 2-207(1). See, e.g., Dorton, supra; Valmont Industries, supra; Just Born, supra; John Thallon, supra; In re Barclay Knitwear Co., supra; In re Tunis Manufacturing Corp., supra; Mystic Mills, supra; Air Products & Chemicals, supra.

However, while Section 2-207(1) constitutes a sharp departure from the common law "mirror image" rule, there remain situations where the inclusion of an additional term in one of the forms exchanged by the parties will prevent the consummation of a contract under that section. Section 2-207(1) contains a proviso which operates to prevent an exchange of forms from creating a contract where "acceptance is expressly made conditional on assent to the additional . . . terms." In the instant case, Jordan's acknowledgment form contained the following statement:

> Seller's acceptance is . . . expressly conditional on Buyer's assent to the additional or different terms and conditions set forth below and printed on the reverse side. If these terms and conditions are not acceptable, Buyer should notify Seller at once.

The arbitration provision at issue on this appeal is printed on the reverse side of Jordan's acknowledgment, and there is no dispute that Itoh never expressly assented to the challenged arbitration term.

The Court of Appeals for the Sixth Circuit has held that the proviso must be construed narrowly:

> Although . . . [seller's] use of the words "subject to" suggests that the acceptances were conditional to some extent, we do not believe the acceptances were "expressly made conditional on [the buyer's] assent to the additional or different terms," as specifically required under the Subsection 2-207(1) proviso. In order to fall within this proviso, it is not enough that an acceptance is expressly conditional on additional or different terms; rather, an acceptance must be expressly conditional on the offeror's *assent to* those terms (emphasis in original).

Dorton, supra, at 1168. In Construction Aggregates Corp. v. Hewitt-Robins, Inc., 404 F.2d 505 (7th Cir. 1968), this court found that an acceptance came within the ambit of the Section 2-207(1) proviso even though the language employed in the acceptance did not precisely track that of the proviso. Under either Construction Aggregates or Dorton, however, it is clear that the statement contained in Jordan's acknowledgment form comes within the Section 2-207(1) proviso.

Hence, the exchange of forms between Jordan and Itoh did not result in the formation of a contract under Section 2-207(1), and Jordan's form became a counteroffer. "[T]he consequence of a clause conditioning acceptance on assent to the additional or different terms is that as of the exchanged writings, there is no contract. Either party may at this point in their dealings walk away from the transaction." Duesenberg & King, supra, § 3.06(3) at 73. However, neither Jordan nor Itoh elected to follow that course; instead, both parties proceeded to performance Jordan by delivering and Itoh by paying for the steel coils.

At common law, the "terms of the counter-offer were said to have been accepted by the original offeror when he proceeded to perform under the contract without objecting to the counter-offer." Dorton, supra, at 1166. Thus, under pre-Code law, Itoh's performance (i.e., payment for the steel coils) probably constituted acceptance of the Jordan counter-offer, including its provision for arbitration. However, a different approach is required under the Code.

Section 2-207(3) of the Code first provides that "[c]onduct by both parties which recognizes the existence of a contract is sufficient to establish a contract for sale although the writings of the parties do not otherwise establish a contract." As the court noted in Dorton, supra, at 1166:

> [W]hen no contract is recognized under Subsection 2-207(1) . . . the entire transaction aborts at this point. If, however, the subsequent conduct of the parties particularly, performance by both parties under what they apparently believe to be a contract recognizes the existence of a contract, under Subsection 2-207(3) such conduct by both parties is sufficient to establish a contract, notwithstanding the fact that no contract would have been recognized on the basis of their writings alone.

Thus, "[s]ince . . . [Itoh's] purchase order and . . . [Jordan's] counter-offer did not in themselves create a contract, Section 2-207(3) would operate to create one because the subsequent performance by both parties constituted 'conduct by both parties which recognizes the existence of a contract.'" Construction Aggregates, supra, at 509.

What are the terms of a contract created by conduct under Section 2-207(3) rather than by an exchange of forms under Section 2-207(1)?[7] As noted above, at common law the terms of the contract between Jordan and Itoh would be the terms of the Jordan counter-offer. However, the Code has effectuated a radical departure from the common law rule. The second sentence of Section 2-207(3) provides that where, as here, a contract has been consummated by the conduct of the parties, "the terms of the particular contract consist of those terms on which the writings of the parties agree, together with any supplementary terms incorporated under any other provisions of this Act." Since it is clear that the Jordan and Itoh forms do not "agree" on arbitration, the only question which remains under the Code is whether arbitration may be considered a supplementary term incorporated under some other provision of the Code.

We have been unable to find any case authority shedding light on the question of what constitutes "supplementary terms" within the meaning of Section 2-207(3) and the Official Comments to Section 2-207 provide no guidance in

---

[7] If a contract had been formed by the exchange of forms between Jordan and Itoh, it would have been necessary to look to Section 2-207(2) to ascertain the terms of that contract.

this regard. We are persuaded, however, that the disputed additional terms (i. e., those terms on which the writings of the parties do not agree) which are necessarily excluded from a Subsection (3) contract by the language, "terms on which the writings of the parties agree," cannot be brought back into the contract under the guise of "supplementary terms." This conclusion has substantial support among the commentators who have addressed themselves to the issue. As two noted authorities on Article Two of the Code have stated:

> It will usually happen that an offeree-seller who returns an acknowledgment form will also concurrently or shortly thereafter ship the goods. If the responsive document (sent by the seller) contains a printed assent clause, and the goods are shipped and accepted, Subsection (3) of Section 2-207 comes into play. . . . [T]he terms on which the exchanged communications do not agree drop out of the transaction, and reference to the Code is made to supply necessary terms. . . . Rather than choosing the terms of one party over those of the other . . . it compels supplying missing terms by reference to the Code. . . .

Duesenberg & King, supra, § 3.06(4) at 73-74. Similarly, Professors White and Summers have concluded that "contract formation under subsection (3) gives neither party the relevant terms of his document, but fills out the contract with the standardized provisions of Article Two." White & Summers, supra, at 29.[10]

Accordingly, we find that the "supplementary terms" contemplated by Section 2-207(3) are limited to those supplied by the standardized "gap-filler" provisions of Article Two. See, e. g., Section 2-308(a) ("Unless otherwise agreed . . . the place for delivery of goods is the seller's place of business or if he has none his residence"); Section 2-309(1) ("The time for shipment or delivery or any other action under a contract if not . . . agreed upon shall be a reasonable time"); Section 2-310(a) ("Unless otherwise agreed . . . payment is due at the time and place at which the buyer is to receive the goods even though the place of shipment is the place of delivery"). Since provision for arbitration is not a necessary or missing term which would be supplied by one of the

> **FYI**
>
> Contrary to what the court says here, the "supplementary terms" contemplated by § 2-207(3) are not limited to Article 2's gapfiller provisions. Additional supplementary terms include any established patterns of performance in the parties' previous contracts ("course of dealing") and trade customs ("usage of trade"), both of which are discussed in Chapter 7. There are no such supplementary terms on the arbitration issue, so the court's narrow statement did not result in an erroneous holding.

---

[10] See also Collins, Arbitration and the Uniform Commercial Code, 41 N.Y.U.L.Rev. 736, 744-45 n.33 (1966) ("While not entirely clear as to meaning, § 2-207(3) seems to provide that the terms of the contract formed by such conduct will exclude any item that is in dispute").

Code's "gap-filler" provisions unless agreed upon by the contracting parties, there is no arbitration term in the Section 2-207(3) contract which was created by the conduct of Jordan and Itoh in proceeding to perform even though no contract had been established by their exchange of writings.

We are convinced that this conclusion does not result in any unfair prejudice to a seller who elects to insert in his standard sales acknowledgement form the statement that acceptance is expressly conditional on buyer's assent to additional terms contained therein. Such a seller obtains a substantial benefit under Section 2-207(1) through the inclusion of an "expressly conditional" clause. If he decides after the exchange of forms that the particular transaction is not in his best interest, Subsection (1) permits him to walk away from the transaction without incurring any liability so long as the buyer has not in the interim expressly assented to the additional terms. Moreover, whether or not a seller will be disadvantaged under Subsection (3) as a consequence of inserting an "expressly conditional" clause in his standard form is within his control. If the seller in fact does not intend to close a particular deal unless the additional terms are assented to, he can protect himself by not delivering the goods until such assent is forthcoming. If the seller does intend to close a deal irrespective of whether or not the buyer assents to the additional terms, he can hardly complain when the contract formed under Subsection (3) as a result of the parties' conduct is held not to include those terms. Although a seller who employs such an "expressly conditional" clause in his acknowledgement form would undoubtedly appreciate the dual advantage of not being bound to a contract under Subsection (1) if he elects not to perform and of having his additional terms imposed on the buyer under Subsection (3) in the event that performance is in his best interest, we do not believe such a result is contemplated by Section 2-207. Rather, while a seller may take advantage of an "expressly conditional" clause under Subsection (1) when he elects not to perform, he must accept the potential risk under Subsection (3) of not getting his additional terms when he elects to proceed with performance without first obtaining buyer's assent to those terms. Since the seller injected ambiguity into the transaction by inserting the "expressly conditional" clause in his form, he, and not the buyer, should bear the consequence of that ambiguity under Subsection (3).

. . . . As noted above, there is no written arbitration provision included in the contract created under Section 2-207(3) when Jordan and Itoh proceeded to performance.

Accordingly, for the reasons stated in this opinion, the decision of the district court is affirmed.

Food for Thought:
Which UCC Sections Should Be Applied by Analogy?

Some UCC sections can be "applied by analogy"—that is, a court can choose to apply the UCC rule to fact situations outside of the scope of the statute, thereby broadening the scope of the rule by common law extension. The UCC sections applied by analogy are usually those that deal with general contract principles, rather than those dealing with matters more specific to contracts for sale of goods. For example, UCC § 2-204 (on contract formation generally; see page 279) has been popular with courts deciding common law contract cases.

However, some sections are rarely if ever applied by analogy because the UCC rule is tailored to a sale of goods, or because the UCC rule is inconsistent with the common law rule(s) and the court sees no reason to change, or because a common law rule serves a similar purpose so there is no pressure to extend the UCC rule by analogy. UCC § 2-207 is rarely if ever applied by analogy because it is inconsistent with the common law versions of the mirror image rule, and the courts are not motivated to expand the reach of the complex rules in § 2-207.

As you study additional UCC sections in the remainder of the book, you should ask how likely it is that the court will apply each section by analogy.

Problems: Contracts and Their Terms under UCC § 2-207

4-30. Which one of the following (if included in an offer) most likely "expressly limits acceptance to the terms of the offer," per § 2-207(2)(a)?

    a. "The terms of this offer are subject to the assent of the offeree."

    b. "This offer's terms can be accepted only by a written assent delivered to Offeror."

    c. "Only these terms, and no others, will be included in the contract."

4-31. Gerry runs an office furniture store that sells bookcases, file cabinets, desks, shelving, office chairs, and other office paraphernalia. Vera looks at the store's online catalog, sees four items that she needs for her business, and mails Gerry a purchase order (P.O.) for those items. On Vera's P.O. is the following preprinted term: "The terms of this purchase order supersede seller's catalog terms. If a contract is formed, only the terms of this purchase order prevail. All goods guaranteed of sufficient quality to remain serviceable for 1 year after sale." Vera's form does not have any term about remedies.

Gerry receives the purchase order and sends back an acknowledgment form, promising shipment at the end of the week, but he does not read Vera's term quoted above. The pre-printed terms in Gerry's acknowledgment form state: "Seller expressly disclaims all warranties or guarantees on the quality of the goods sold. Buyer's remedies for any breach are limited to a refund of the amount paid for items sold." (In UCC Article 2, the default remedy for breach is *not* limited to a refund of the purchase price.)

a.   Do the parties have a contract? If so, how was it created (under which part of § 2-207)?

b.   Assuming a contract was created, is the refund limitation on Gerry's form part of the contract?

c.   Assuming a contract was created, is there a guarantee that the goods will remain serviceable for a year?

4-32. Same facts as above, except that when Gerry receives the P.O., he sends back an acknowledgment form that says, "This acknowledgment supersedes all previous documents. Any contract formed with any buyer can be created only on the terms in this acknowledgment. Acceptance of any purchase order is conditional on the following terms: Seller expressly disclaims all warranties and guarantees on the quality of the goods sold. Buyer's remedies for any breach are limited to a refund of the amount paid for items sold." Gerry delivers the four items. Vera accepts delivery and pays for them.

a.   Do the parties have a contract? If so, how was it created (under which part of § 2-207)?

b.   Assuming a contract was created, is the refund limitation on Gerry's form part of the contract?

c.   Assuming a contract was created, does the contract contain a guarantee that the goods will remain serviceable for a year?

4-33.   Celine is planning to move her small business to a new location in the next month. On October 8, she phones a box supplier to find out the price for 200 corrugated cardboard boxes (100 small, 50 medium, and 50 large). The supplier's employee quotes a price of $420 (subject to availability), says they could deliver the boxes for an additional $50, and says that the company buys back boxes that still are in good condition after a move, for something less than the purchase price. The employee warns Celine that boxes often are in short supply at the end of the month, and strongly suggests that she choose a moving date in the first three weeks of the month. On October 10, Celine sends a "Purchase Order" to the box supplier on her company's letterhead that states:

> Please deliver 200 boxes to the loading dock behind 424 N. Ambrose St. on October 21 between 8 am and 4 pm. Assortment: 100 small, 50 medium, and 50 large. Price: $470.

On October 13, the box supplier replies back by email, saying that the boxes will be delivered on October 22 but otherwise per the specifications in Celine's Purchase Order.

a.   Did either party make an offer in any of the phone calls or correspondences? If so, was that offer accepted by the other party? If a contract was formed, what were its terms?

b.   Same facts, but assume that the box supplier, on Oct. 13, agrees to Celine's Oct. 21 delivery date but also includes the following language: "However, you must agree to make an advance payment of 20% of the purchase price, delivered to our business within three days." Does this alter any of your answers to the preceding version of the problem?

c.   Same facts, but assume that the parties did not create a contract during their negotiations.   Celine's company does not respond to the October 13 email. On October 21, the box company delivers the boxes according to the specifications of the purchase order. Celine takes the boxes inside and calls the box supplier to say that she already got her needed boxes elsewhere. Is there a contract, and if so, with what terms?

Think About It!

According to two leading commentators, "The law as to terms must be sophisticated enough to nullify the efforts of fine-print lawyers, it must be sufficiently reliance-oriented to protect the legitimate expectations of the parties, and it must be fair and evenhanded." James J. White & Robert S. Summers, *Uniform Commercial Code* § 1-2 (1972). Based on what you have learned about how § 2-207 operates in determining what terms are in a contract, how well does the section fulfill those objectives?

How might offerors and offerees "game" § 2-207 by drafting their offers and purported acceptances to their advantage? Can either party ever completely "win the game"?

Reading the Law Critically: CISG, UNIDROIT, and UCC § 2-207

The CISG rules governing the battle of forms use some of the same language as UCC § 2-207, but in a different analytical framework. UNIDROIT tracks much of the CISG language, but also adds new provisions.

1. What are the major differences among UCC § 2-207, CISG Art. 19, and the UNIDROIT rules?

2. Do the CISG or UNIDROIT rules do a better job of fulfilling the objectives set out by White and Summers in the preceeding "Think About It" box?

CISG Art. 19 (in Part II. Formation of the Contract)

(1) A reply to an offer which purports to be an acceptance but contains additions, limitations or other modifications is a rejection of the offer and constitutes a counter-offer.

(2) However, a reply to an offer which purports to be an acceptance but contains additional or different terms which do not materially alter the terms of the offer constitutes an acceptance, unless the offeror, without undue delay, objects orally to the discrepancy or dispatches a notice to that effect. If he does not so object, the terms of the contract are the terms of the offer with the modifications contained in the acceptance.

(3) Additional or different terms relating, among other things, to the price, payment, quality and quantity of the goods, place and time of delivery, extent of one party's liability to the other or the settlement of disputes are considered to alter the terms of the offer materially.

———————

UNIDROIT Art. 2.1.11. **Modified Acceptance**

(1) A reply to an offer which purports to be an acceptance but contains additions, limitations or other modifications is a rejection of the offer and constitutes a counter-offer.

(2) However, a reply to an offer which purports to be an acceptance but contains additional or different terms which do not materially alter the terms of the offer constitutes an acceptance, unless the offeror, without undue delay, objects to the discrepancy. If the offeror does not object, the terms of the contract are the terms of the offer with the modifications contained in the acceptance.

UNIDROIT Art. 2.1.20. **Surprising Terms**

(1) No term contained in standard terms which is of such a character that the other party could not reasonably have expected it, is effective unless it has been expressly accepted by that party.

(2) In determining whether a term is of such a character regard shall be had to its content, language and presentation.

UNIDROIT Art. 2.1.22. **Battle of Forms**

Where both parties use standard terms and reach agreement except on those terms, a contract is concluded on the basis of the agreed terms and of any standard terms which are common in substance unless one party clearly indicates in advance, or later and without undue delay informs the other party, that it does not intend to be bound by such a contract.

§ 5. Review Exercise: Manifestation of Mutual Assent

The end of Chapter 2 contained a review exercise that discussed how you could organize the material in that chapter into a cohesive topic-based summary that would help you to structure your thinking when called upon to analyze a new set of facts—whether it be an exam question or the facts posed by a client. Consider rereading the tips in that review exercise as you respond to this exercise, which suggests a similar process to draw together your understanding of mutual assent.

The table of contents in this chapter shows three major topics: judging assent objectively or subjectively, assent to indefinite or incomplete agreements, and mutual assent by offer and acceptance, with the last of those topics having multiple sub-topics. Below is the skeleton of an outline on the topic of mutual assent, drawn from the table of contents to Chapter 4. Some questions are embedded in the text to help you think about organizing principles that you might use to order the detail inside each topic. Review the materials in this chapter, along with your case briefs and other notes, and fill in the rest of the outline. As you do so, make a note of any questions you have so that you can seek clarification, whether from your classmates or from your instructor. Once you have an outline that seems to be complete, try answering some hypothetical questions about assent to see if your framework works for you as an analytical tool.

1. How is mutual assent judged (subjectively or objectively)?
2. Assent to indefinite or incomplete agreements

   What kinds of indefiniteness or incompleteness may exist during contract formation? What rules of law and policies address those issues? How much indefiniteness or incompleteness is allowed in enforceable contracts?
3. Mutual assent by offer and acceptance

   a. Offer

      What is the definition of offer? How do you know when a communication is an offer? What are the consequences of finding an offer was made? What issues arise in identifying an offer? What rules of law address those issues? What policies are important in applying the rules on offer?

   b. Termination of power of acceptance

      What events cause termination of the offeree's power of acceptance? What rules of law govern the determination whether an offer terminated? What policies are important in the creation and application of those rules?

   c. Acceptance

      What is the definition of an acceptance? How do you know when a communication is an acceptance? What are the consequences of finding an acceptance was made? When is an acceptance effective? How is the Article 2 rule different from the common law rule?

CHAPTER 5

Defenses to Contract Enforcement

| What kind of promises will the law enforce? | How do parties demonstrate assent to a contract? | What defenses to enforcement exist? | Is a writing required for enforcement? If so, what kind? | How is the content of a contract ascertained? | What are parties' rights and duties after breach? |

| What situations lead to excusing contract performance? | What remedies are available for breach of contract? | What contractual rights and duties do non-parties to a contract have? |

§ 1. Introduction

As discussed in Chapters 2 and 4, a contract is created if a promise is supported by consideration and the parties mutually assent to the exchange. Despite the apparent existence of a contract, however, one or both parties may have a defense to enforcement of the contract based on defects in the bargaining process, incapacity of one of the parties, or public policy constraints.

The first set of defenses, discussed in section 2, involve circumstances in which one or both parties' assent was illusory or fundamentally flawed, perhaps because of inaccurate or misleading information or because the assent occurred in a setting marred by exceptional pressure or unfair circumstances. Although it may appear that there was agreement from both parties, additional facts demonstrate that there was no true assent. These defenses are based on the same policies that underlie manifestation of mutual assent (see Chapter 4)—freedom of contract and the need for clarity and predictability in contractual terms. They also police against parties' use of unacceptable conduct during the contract formation process. The following defenses fall into this category:

- Mistake
- Misrepresentation
- Duress
- Undue influence
- Unconscionability

A second set of defenses, discussed in section 3, involve agreements by a party who lacked the capacity to contract by being too young or cognitively disabled to engage in the assent process. The following defenses fall into this category:

- Infancy (a party is below the age of majority and therefore a minor)
- Mental illness or defect
- Intoxication

The final defense, discussed in section 4, involves agreements in which the parties' mutual assent was unimpaired, but the substance of the agreement violates societal norms. In such instances, the contract may be unenforceable on the grounds of public policy.

The boundary lines among these defenses are not crisp, and overlap is possible in some fact situations, so a party challenging a contract often raises multiple defenses. For instance, a party who is misled or mistaken as to a crucial fact in a contract may raise defenses of misrepresentation and mistake. Similarly, a party whose free will has been impaired during contract formation may raise both duress and undue influence.

If a contract violates public policy (the defense discussed in section 4), it is considered void (or void ab initio, "from its inception"), and enforcement of the agreement can be challenged by either party as well as by third parties in appropriate circumstances. Under all of the other defenses (aside from public policy), a contract is voidable, so the party protected by the defense has the power to affirm or avoid the agreement, which is otherwise valid and enforceable.

If a contract is declared void (by a court or by a party with power to avoid the agreement), it is as if the contract never existed, and the parties should generally be placed back into their "status quo ante," the situation existing before the contract was formed. A court can use the remedy of restitution to effectuate that goal, requiring each party to disgorge the benefits (or the value of the benefits) already received. For example, if the contract in *Wood v. Boynton*, page 433, had been declared void, a court would have required Wood to return the $1 paid to her and Boynton to return the jewel.

If a contract or a contract clause is determined to be unconscionable, the court has additional remedies available: It has equitable discretion to void the entire contract, to void the unconscionable clause, or to limit application of the offending clause to eliminate the unconscionability. As noted in the discussion of mistake (page 442), if the parties make a clerical ("scrivener's") error, the court may "reform" the written agreement by correcting the error.

The UNIDROIT Principles include defenses for fraud, threat, and "gross disparity" (economic duress and unconscionability). The CISG does not address defenses to contract formation. Therefore, in contracts for sale of goods governed by the CISG, the law otherwise applicable to the transaction (the law chosen by the parties or by default choice-of-law principles) will govern defenses.

§ 2. Defenses Related to Defects in Mutual Assent

When parties manifest assent to an agreement, both parties should be acting voluntarily and without being misled about the key aspects of the transaction. In other words, both parties have a right not to be tricked or forced into a contract ("freedom from contract") and to have the resulting contract be the agreement intended by them. If either party is unduly pressured to assent or is fundamentally misled as to the nature of the contract, the policies underlying the requirement of mutual assent are not met, even though the parties' assent may appear to be valid under the standards and rules discussed in Chapter 4. These policies underlie the defenses of mistake, misrepresentation, duress, undue influence, and unconscionability.

§ 2.1. Mistake

The **Restatement (Second) § 151** defines a mistake as "a belief that is not in accord with the facts." A fact is a past or present state of things—something that actually exists or an event or circumstance that has occurred. *Facts* differ from *promises* (commitments to do or not do something in the future), *predictions* (expectations about a future occurrence or state of things), and *opinions* (personal views, attitudes, or professional appraisals about present circumstances or the future, or beliefs or judgments based on grounds insufficient to produce complete certainty).

To illustrate these distinctions, recall the case at the beginning of Chapter 4, *Lucy v. Zehmer* **(page 237)** (the land purchase contract negotiated in a bar). By changing the facts slightly, we can identify the kinds of mistake that could have occurred:

- *Mistake of opinion*: If Lucy had mistakenly thought that the farm was worth 50% more than the agreed-upon price
- *Mistake of prediction*: If Lucy had mistakenly thought that Zehmer's farm could produce bumper crops of soybeans, if the farm were properly run
- *Mistake of fact*: If Lucy (or both Lucy and Zehmer) had mistakenly believed that Zehmer's land contained valuable mineral deposits
- *Mistake of law*: If Lucy (or both Lucy and Zehmer) had mistakenly believed that Zehmer's land was eligible for agricultural subsidies for growing sunflowers

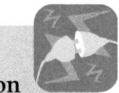

Make the Connection

The distinctions between fact, opinion, and prediction are discussed again in § 2.2 (page 460), which covers the closely related defense of misrepresentation.

The defense of mistake applies to assertions of fact, but not to promises, predictions or opinions. Traditionally mistakes of law were denied coverage, but some recent cases have treated the existing law as part of the facts existing at the time of agreement and have allowed the defense.

If *both* parties were mistaken about a fact at the time of contract formation, the disadvantaged party can attempt to avoid the contract by using the defense of *mutual* mistake. If instead only *one* party was mistaken about a fact at contract formation, the mistaken party may be able to use the defense of *unilateral* mistake.*

Problems: Distinguishing Mistake of Fact, Law, Opinion, and Prediction

Below are statements by a party who has entered into a contract and now seeks to be excused from the contract on the basis of mistake. For each statement, indicate whether the mistake relates to fact, law, opinion, or prediction. If you think it might fit in more than one category, is there additional information that would help you decide between those possibilities?

5-1. "I bought this drought-resistant seed from the co-op because I thought it would rain only 40 inches this year, but instead it rained 92 inches." *prediction*

5-2. "I bought this ring for $1,000 because the antiques store clerk told me he thought it was a diamond ring. Now I find that it's instead a cubic zirconia, which is worth only 25% of a diamond." *opinion*

5-3. "I purchased an easement from Kato to cross his lakefront land because he said I could boat on that lake, but now I find that the Department of Natural Resources does not allow boating there." *law*

5-4. "The seller and I thought that the house satisfied the building code. That's why she priced it at $250,000, and that's why I agreed to buy it for $250,000. Now I find that it met the building code of 15 years ago, but not today's building code." *fact, but possible opinion if "I think it"*

5-5. "I posted this boat for sale on a website, meaning to sell it for $5,000, but I left out a zero and now a buyer has accepted my $500 offer." *fact* *scriveners error*

---

* Note that these kinds of mistakes are being raised as a defense to contract formation. If instead a contract is formed but it contains ambiguous contract language, then the issue is one of contract interpretation, which is discussed in Chapter 7 (page 693).

§ 2.1.1. Mutual Mistake

Reading the Law Critically: *Wood*

1. What was the alleged mistake in the sales transaction?

2. What justifications were offered, or might be offered, for denying relief to the plaintiff in this case?

3. According to the opinion, what kind of mistake *would* have been grounds for declaring the contract void?

4. Do you agree with the result in this case? Why or why not? If not, what rule would you offer to support a different result?

Wood v. Boynton

WOOD, Plaintiff-Appellant

v.

SAMUEL B. BOYNTON and Another, Defendants-Respondents

Supreme Court of Wisconsin

25 N.W. 42 (Wisc. 1885)

TAYLOR, J.

This action was brought in the circuit court for Milwaukee County to recover the possession of an uncut diamond of the alleged value of $1,000. The case was tried in the circuit court, and after hearing all the evidence in the case, the learned circuit judge directed the jury to find a verdict for the defendants. The plaintiff excepted to such instruction, and, after a verdict was rendered for the defendants, moved for a new trial upon the minutes of the judge. The motion was denied, and the plaintiff duly excepted, and after judgment was entered in favor of the defendants, appealed to this court. The defendants are partners in the jewelry business. On the trial it appeared that on and before the twenty-eighth of December, 1883, the plaintiff was the owner of and in the possession of a small stone of the nature and value of which she was ignorant; that on that day she sold it to one of the defendants for the sum of one dollar. Afterwards it was ascertained that the stone was a rough diamond, and of the value of about $700. After hearing this fact the plaintiff tendered the defendants the one dollar, and ten cents as interest, and demanded a return of the stone to her. The defendants refused to deliver it, and therefore she commenced this action.

The plaintiff testified to the circumstances attending the sale of the stone to Mr. Samuel B. Boynton, as follows: "The first time Boynton saw that stone he was talking about buying the topaz, or whatever it is, in September or October. I went into the store to get a little pin mended, and I had it in a small box,—the pin,— a small ear-ring; . . . this stone, and a broken sleeve-button were in the box. Mr. Boynton turned to give me a check for my pin. I thought I would ask him what the stone was, and I took it out of the box and asked him to please tell me what that was. He took it in his hand and seemed some time looking at it. I told him I had been told it was a topaz, and he said it might be. He says, 'I would buy this; would you sell it?' I told him I did not know but what I would. What would it be worth? And he said he did not know; he would give me a dollar and keep it as a specimen, and I told him I would not sell it; and it was certainly pretty to look at. He asked me where I found it, and I told him in Eagle. He asked about how far out, and I said right in the village, and I went out. Afterwards, and about the twenty-eighth of December, I needed money pretty badly, and thought every dollar would help, and I took it back to Mr. Boynton and told him I had brought back the topaz, and he says, 'Well, yes; what did I offer you for it?' and I says, 'One dollar;' and he stepped to the change drawer and gave me the dollar, and I went out." In another part of her testimony she says: "Before I sold the stone I had no knowledge whatever that it was a diamond. I told him that I had been advised that it was probably a topaz, and he said probably it was. The stone was about the size of a canary bird's egg, nearly the shape of an egg,—worn pointed at one end; it was nearly straw color,—a little darker." She also testified that before this action was commenced she tendered the defendants $1.10, and demanded the return of the stone, which they refused. This is substantially all the evidence of what took place at and before the sale to the defendants, as testified to by the plaintiff herself. She produced no other witness on that point.

Go Online!

Various websites calculate the value of a dollar in a particular year, albeit with different measuring algorithms, so results can vary considerably. Find out the current worth of the $1 paid by Samuel Boynton. For the diamond's history, go to www.eaglebusinessassn.org and follow the "Eagle Diamond" link in the "History" section.

The evidence on the part of the defendant is not very different from the version given by the plaintiff, and certainly is not more favorable to the plaintiff. Mr. Samuel B. Boynton, the defendant to whom the stone was sold, testified that at the time he bought this stone, he had never seen an uncut diamond; had seen cut diamonds, but they are quite different from the uncut ones; "he had no idea this was a diamond, and it never entered his brain at the time." Considerable evidence was given as to what took place after the sale and purchase, but that evidence has very little if any bearing upon the main point in the case.

This evidence clearly shows that the plaintiff sold the stone in question to the defendants, and delivered it to them in December, 1883, for a consideration of one dollar. By such sale the title to the stone passed by the sale and delivery to the defendants. How has that title been divested and again vested in the plaintiff? The contention of the learned counsel for the appellant is that the title became vested in the plaintiff by the tender to the Boyntons of the purchase money with interest, and a demand of a return of the stone to her. Unless such tender and demand revested the title in the appellant, she cannot maintain her action. The only question in the case is whether there

Think About It!

In *Lucy v. Zehmer* (page 237), the court found relevant the evidence of what took place after the sale. Why, in contrast, does this court find the evidence of what took place after the sale to have "very little . . . bearing upon the main point in the case"?

was anything in the sale which entitled the vendor (the appellant) to rescind the sale and so revest the title in her. The only reasons we know of for rescinding a sale and revesting the title in the vendor so that he may maintain an action at law for the recovery of the possession against his vendee are (1) that the vendee was guilty of some fraud in procuring a sale to be made to him; (2) that there was a mistake made by the vendor in delivering an article which was not the article sold,—a mistake in fact as to the identity of the thing sold with the thing delivered upon the sale. This last is not in reality a rescission of the sale made, as the thing delivered was not the thing sold, and no title ever passed to the vendee by such delivery.

In this case, upon the plaintiff's own evidence, there can be no just ground for alleging that she was induced to make the sale she did by any fraud or unfair dealings on the part of Mr. Boynton. Both were entirely ignorant at the time of the character of the stone and of its intrinsic value. Mr. Boynton was not an expert in uncut diamonds, and had made no examination of the stone, except to take it in his hand and look at it before he made the offer of one dollar, which was refused at the time, and afterwards accepted without any comment or further examination made by Mr. Boynton. The appellant had the stone in her possession for a long time, and it appears from her own statement that she had made some inquiry as to its nature and qualities. If she chose to sell it without further investigation as to its intrinsic value to a person who was guilty of no fraud or unfairness which induced her to sell it for a small sum, she cannot repudiate the sale because it is afterwards ascertained that she made a bad bargain. *Kennedy v. Panama, etc., Mail Co.,* L. R. 2 Q. B. 580. There is no pretense of any mistake as to the identity of the thing sold. It was produced by the plaintiff and exhibited to the vendee before the sale was made, and the thing sold was delivered to the vendee when the purchase price was paid. *Kennedy v. Panama, etc., Mail Co., supra.,* 587 . . . . Suppose the appellant had produced the stone, and said she had been told it was a diamond, and she believed it was, but had no knowledge herself as to its character or value, and Mr. Boynton had given her $500 for it, could he have rescinded the sale if it had turned out to be a topaz or any other stone of very small value? Could Mr. Boynton have rescinded the sale on the ground of mistake? Clearly not, nor could he rescind it on the ground that there had been a breach of warranty, because there was no warranty, nor could he rescind it on the ground of fraud, unless he could show that she falsely declared that she had been told it was a diamond, or, if she had been so told, still she knew it was not a diamond. See *Street* v. *Blay, supra.*

It is urged, with a good deal of earnestness, on the part of the counsel for the appellant that, because it has turned out that the stone was immensely more valuable than the parties at the time of the sale supposed it was, such fact alone is a ground for the rescission of the sale, and that fact was evidence of fraud on the part of the vendee. Whether inadequacy of price is to be received as evidence of fraud, even in a suit in equity to avoid a sale, depends upon the facts known to the parties at the time the sale is made. When this sale was made the value of the thing sold was open to the investigation of both parties, neither knowing its intrinsic value, and, so far as the evidence in this case shows, both supposed that the price paid was adequate. How can fraud be predicated upon such a sale, even though after investigation showed that the intrinsic value of the thing sold was hundreds of times greater than the price paid? It certainly shows no such fraud as would authorize the vendor to rescind the contract and bring an action at law to recover the possession of the thing sold. Whether that fact would have any influence in an action in equity to avoid the sale we need not consider. See *Stettheimer* v. *Killip,* 75 N. Y. 287; *Etting v. Bank of U.S.,* 11 Wheat. 59.

We can find nothing in the evidence from which it could be justly inferred that Mr. Boynton, at the time he offered the plaintiff one dollar for the stone, had any knowledge of the real value of the stone, or that he entertained even a belief that the stone was a diamond. It cannot, therefore, be said that there was a suppression of knowledge on the part of the defendant as to the value of the stone which a court of equity might seize upon to avoid the sale. The following cases show that, in the absence of fraud or warranty, the value of the property sold, as compared with the price paid, is no ground for a rescission of a sale. *Wheat* v. *Cross,* 31 Md. 99; *Lambert* v. *Heath,* 15 Mees. & W. 487; *Bryant* v. *Pember,* 45 Vt. 487; *Kuelkamp* v. *Hidding,* 31 Wis. 503-511. However unfortunate the plaintiff may have been in selling this valuable stone for a mere nominal sum, she has failed entirely to make out a case either of fraud or mistake in the sale such as will entitle her to a rescission of such sale so as to recover the property sold in an action at law.

The judgment of the circuit court is affirmed.

———————————

Reading the Law Critically: *Lenawee*

1. What was the parties' mistake in the sales transaction(s)? What determines whether that mistake has legal significance?

2. *Lenawee* discusses at some length, and then declines to follow, the much earlier case of *Sherwood v. Walker* (a favorite in contracts casebooks). Some jurisdictions still retain their own versions of the *Sherwood* rule, however. What is the standard articulated in *Sherwood,* and how does it differ from the rule adopted in *Lenawee*? Which is the better rule? Why?

3. What role does the contract itself play in determining the result?

See It!

The *Lenawee* property transfers and lawsuits are diagrammed below:

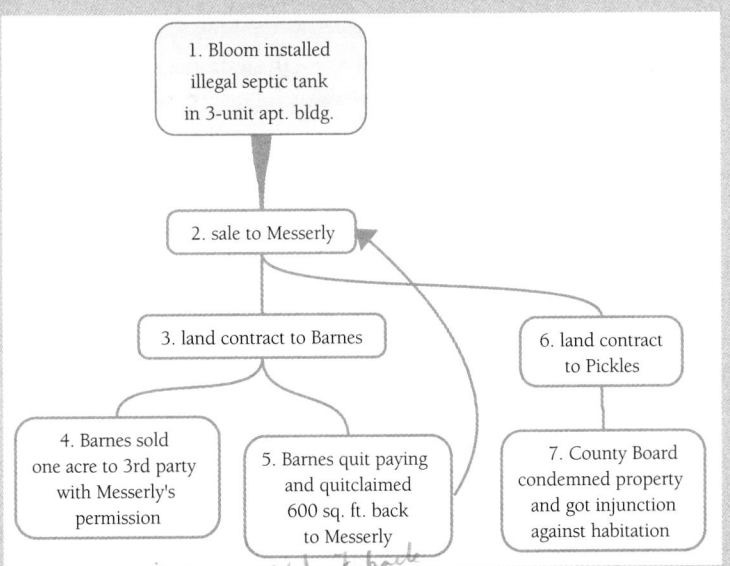

To the right is a picture of the property. Thanks to Professor Franklin Snyder at Texas Wesleyan University School of Law for permission to reproduce this picture.

Lenawee County Board of Health v. Messerly

LENAWEE COUNTY BOARD OF HEALTH, Plaintiff

v.

WILLIAM H. MESSERLY and MARTHA B. MESSERLY, Defendants and Cross-Plaintiffs/Appellants*

Supreme Court of Michigan

331 N.W.2d 203 (Mich. 1982)

RYAN, Justice.

In March of 1977, Carl and Nancy Pickles, appellees, purchased from appellants, William and Martha Messerly, a 600-square-foot tract of land upon which is located a three-unit apartment building. Shortly after the transaction was closed, the Lenawee County Board of Health condemned the property and obtained a permanent injunction which prohibits human habitation on the premises until the defective sewage system is brought into conformance with the Lenawee County sanitation code.

We are required to determine whether appellees should prevail in their attempt to avoid this land contract on the basis of mutual mistake and failure of consideration. We conclude that the parties did entertain a mutual misapprehension of fact, but that the circumstances of this case do not warrant rescission.

I.

The facts of the case are not seriously in dispute. In 1971, the Messerlys acquired approximately one acre plus 600 square feet of land. A three-unit apartment building was situated upon the 600-square-foot portion. The trial court found that, prior to this transfer, the Messerlys' predecessor in title, Mr. Bloom, had installed a septic tank on the property without a permit and in violation of the applicable health code. The Messerlys used the building as an income investment property until 1973 when they sold it, upon land contract, to James Barnes who likewise used it primarily as an income-producing investment.[1]

---

* In this appeal, the Messerlys are the appellants and the Board of Health is no longer a party, but the Barneses (unlisted in the Supreme Court caption here) are. In the intermediate appellate court, the case title is *Board of Health v. Messerlys v. Pickles v. Barnes*. The Pickleses are both defendants (sued by the Board of Health) and cross-defendants (sued by the Messerlys). The Messerlys are defendants (sued by the Board of Health) and cross-plaintiffs (suing the Pickleses). James E. and Joan L. Barnes are also defendants (sued by the Pickleses).

[1] James Barnes was married shortly after he purchased the property. Mr. and Mrs. Barnes lived in one of the apartments on the property for three months and, after they moved, Mrs. Barnes continued to aid in the management of the property.

Mr. and Mrs. Barnes, with the permission of the Messerlys, sold approximately one acre of the property in 1976, and the remaining 600 square feet and building were offered for sale soon thereafter when Mr. and Mrs. Barnes defaulted on their land contract. Mr. and Mrs. Pickles evidenced an interest in the property, but were dissatisfied with the terms of the Barnes-Messerly land contract. Consequently, to accommodate the Pickleses' preference to enter into a land contract directly with the Messerlys, Mr. and Mrs. Barnes executed a quit-claim deed which conveyed their interest in the property back to the Messerlys. After inspecting the property, Mr. and Mrs. Pickles executed a new land contract with the Messerlys on March 21, 1977. It provided for a purchase price of $25,500. A clause was added to the end of the land contract form which provides:

> "17. Purchaser has examined this property and agrees to accept same in its present condition. There are no other or additional written or oral understandings."

Five or six days later, when the Pickleses went to introduce themselves to the tenants, they discovered raw sewage seeping out of the ground. Tests conducted by a sanitation expert indicated the inadequacy of the sewage system. The Lenawee County Board of Health subsequently condemned the property and initiated this lawsuit in the Lenawee Circuit Court against the Messerlys as land contract vendors, and the Pickleses, as vendees, to obtain a permanent injunction proscribing human habitation of the premises until the property was brought into conformance with the Lenawee County sanitation code. The injunction was granted, and the Lenawee County Board of Health was permitted to withdraw from the lawsuit by stipulation of the parties.

When no payments were made on the land contract, the Messerlys filed a cross-complaint against the Pickleses seeking foreclosure, sale of the property, and a deficiency judgment. Mr. and Mrs. Pickles then counterclaimed for rescission against the Messerlys, and filed a third-party complaint against the Barneses, which incorporated, by reference, the allegations of the counterclaim against the Messerlys. In count one, Mr. and Mrs. Pickles alleged failure of consideration. Count two charged Mr. and Mrs. Barnes with willful concealment and misrepresentation as a result of their failure to disclose the condition of the sanitation system. Additionally, Mr. and Mrs. Pickles sought to hold the Messerlys liable in equity for the Barneses' alleged misrepresentation. The Pickleses prayed that the land contract be rescinded.

After a bench trial, the court concluded that the Pickleses had no cause of action against either the Messerlys or the Barneses as there was no fraud or misrepresentation. This ruling was predicated on the trial judge's conclusion that none of the parties knew of Mr. Bloom's earlier transgression or of the resultant problem with the septic system until it was discovered by the Pickleses, and that the sanitation problem was not caused by any of the parties. The trial court held that the property was purchased "as is", after inspection and, accordingly, its "negative . . . value cannot be blamed upon an innocent seller". Foreclosure was ordered against the Pickleses, together with a judgment against them in the amount of $25,943.09.[3]

Mr. and Mrs. Pickles appealed from the adverse judgment. The Court of Appeals unanimously affirmed the trial court's ruling with respect to Mr. and Mrs. Barnes but, in a two-to-one decision, reversed the finding of no cause of action on the Pickleses' claims against the Messerlys. **Lenawee County Board of Health v. Messerly, 98 Mich.App. 478, 295 N.W.2d 903 (1980)**. It concluded that the mutual mistake[5] between the Messerlys and the Pickleses went to a basic, as opposed to a collateral, element of the contract,[6] and that the parties intended to transfer income-producing rental property but, in actuality, the vendees paid $25,500 for an asset without value.[7]

We granted the Messerlys' application for leave to appeal. 411 Mich. 900 (1981).[8]

II

We must decide initially whether there was a mistaken belief entertained by one or both parties to the contract in dispute and, if so, the resultant legal significance.

---

[3] The parties stipulated that this amount was due on the land contract, assuming that the contract was valid and enforceable.

[5] Mr. and Mrs. Pickles did not allege mutual mistake as a ground for rescission in their pleadings. However, the trial court characterized their failure of consideration argument as mutual mistake resulting in failure of consideration. . . . Since the mutual mistake issue was dispositive in the Court of Appeals, we find its consideration necessary to a proper determination of this case.

[6] Mr. and Mrs. Pickles did not appeal the trial court's finding that there was no fraud or misrepresentation by the Messerlys or Mr. and Mrs. Barnes. Likewise, the propriety of that ruling is not before this Court today.

[7] The trial court found that the only way that the property could be put to residential use would be to pump and haul the sewage, a method which is economically unfeasible, as the cost of such a disposal system amounts to double the income generated by the property. There was speculation by the trial court that the adjoining land might be utilized to make the property suitable for residential use, but, in the absence of testimony directed at that point, the court refused to draw any conclusions. The trial court and the Court of Appeals both found that the property was valueless, or had a negative value.

[8] The Court of Appeals decision to affirm the trial court's finding of no cause of action against Mr. and Mrs. Barnes has not been appealed to this Court and, accordingly, the propriety of that ruling is not before us today.

A contractual mistake "is a belief that is not in accord with the facts". 1 Restatement Contracts, 2d, § 151, p 383. The erroneous belief of one or both of the parties must relate to a fact in existence at the time the contract is executed. Richardson Lumber Co. v. Hoey, 219 Mich. 643, 189 N.W. 923 (1922); Sherwood v. Walker, 66 Mich. 568, 580, 33 N.W. 919 (1887) (Sherwood, J., dissenting). That is to say, the belief which is found to be in error may not be, in substance, a prediction as to a future occurrence or non-occurrence. Henry v. Thomas, 241 Ga. 360, 245 S.E.2d 646 (1978); Hailpern v. Dryden, 154 Colo. 231, 389 P.2d 590 (1964). But see Denton v. Utley, 350 Mich. 332, 86 N.W.2d 537 (1957).

>
>
> ### Make the Connection
>
> The mistake defense applies only if the parties had an erroneous belief about facts in existence at the time of contract formation. If the erroneous belief relates not to facts at the time of formation but instead to predictions about what will or will not come to pass during the term of the contract, then the appropriate claim is not "mistake" but the "excuse" of impracticability based on the assertion that the party's performance has become impossible or extremely difficult because of the unexpected turn of events. The excuse defense is covered in Chapter 8, (page 974).

The Court of Appeals concluded, after a de novo review of the record, that the parties were mistaken as to the income-producing capacity of the property in question. 98 Mich.App. 487-488, 295 N.W.2d 903. We agree. The vendors and the vendees each believed that the property transferred could be utilized as income-generating rental property. All of the parties subsequently learned that, in fact, the property was unsuitable for any residential use.

Appellants assert that there was no mistake in the contractual sense because the defect in the sewage system did not arise until after the contract was executed. The appellees respond that the Messerlys are confusing the date of the inception of the defect with the date upon which the defect was discovered.

This is essentially a factual dispute which the trial court failed to resolve directly. Nevertheless, we are empowered to draw factual inferences from the facts found by the trial court. GCR 1963, 865.1(6).

An examination of the record reveals that the septic system was defective prior to the date on which the land contract was executed. The Messerlys' grantor installed a nonconforming septic system without a permit prior to the transfer of the property to the Messerlys in 1971. Moreover, virtually undisputed testimony indicates that, assuming ideal soil conditions, 2,500 square feet of property is necessary to support a sewage system adequate to serve a three-family dwelling.

Likewise, 750 square feet is mandated for a one-family home. Thus, the division of the parcel and sale of one acre of the property by Mr. and Mrs. Barnes in 1976 made it impossible to remedy the already illegal septic system within the confines of the 600-square-foot parcel.[10]

Appellants do not dispute these underlying facts which give rise to an inference contrary to their contentions.

Having determined that when these parties entered into the land contract they were laboring under a mutual mistake of fact, we now direct our attention to a determination of the legal significance of that finding.

A contract may be rescinded because of a mutual misapprehension of the parties, but this remedy is granted only in the sound discretion of the court. **Harris v. Axline, 323 Mich. 585, 36 N.W.2d 154 (1949).** Appellants argue that the parties' mistake relates only to the quality or value of the real estate transferred, and that such mistakes are collateral to the agreement and do not justify rescission, citing **A & M Land Development Co. v. Miller, 354 Mich. 681, 94 N.W.2d 197 (1959).**

In that case, the plaintiff was the purchaser of 91 lots of real property. It sought partial rescission of the land contract when it was frustrated in its attempts to develop 42 of the lots because it could not obtain permits from the county health department to install septic tanks on these lots. This Court refused to allow rescission because the mistake, whether mutual or unilateral, related only to the value of the property.

"There was here no mistake as to the form or substance of the contract between the parties, or the description of the property constituting the subject matter. The situation involved is not at all analogous to that presented in **Scott v Grow, 301 Mich 226; 3 NW2d 254; 141 ALR 819 (1942).** There the plaintiff sought relief by way of reformation of a deed on the ground that the instrument of conveyance had not been drawn in accordance with the intention and agreement of

> ### What's That?
>
> If the parties inaccurately memorialized their agreement in a writing or an electronic record (as in *Scott v. Grow*, where the parties made a clerical mistake), either party may ask the court to correct ("reform") the writing or record to eliminate the clerical mistake.

---

[10] It is crucial to distinguish between the date on which a belief relating to a particular fact or set of facts becomes erroneous due to a change in the fact, and the date on which the mistaken nature of the belief is discovered. By definition, a mistake cannot be discovered until after the contract is executed. If the parties were aware, prior to the execution of a contract, that they were in error concerning a particular fact, there would be no misapprehension in signing the contract. Thus stated, it becomes obvious that the date on which a mistaken fact manifests itself is irrelevant to the determination whether or not there was a mistake.

the parties. It was held that the bill of complaint stated a case for the granting of equitable relief by way of reformation. In the case at bar plaintiff received the property for which it contracted. The fact that it may be of less value than the purchaser expected at the time of the transaction is not a sufficient basis for the granting of equitable relief, neither fraud nor reliance on misrepresentation of material facts having been established."

354 Mich. 693-694, 94 N.W.2d 197.

Appellees contend, on the other hand, that in this case the parties were mistaken as to the very nature of the character of the consideration and claim that the pervasive and essential quality of this mistake renders rescission appropriate. They cite in support of that view Sherwood v. Walker, 66 Mich. 568, 33 N.W. 919 (1887), the famous "barren cow" case. In that case, the parties agreed to the sale and purchase of a cow which was thought to be barren, but which was, in reality, with calf. When the seller discovered the fertile condition of his cow, he refused to deliver her. In permitting rescission, the Court stated:

> "It seems to me, however, in the case made by this record, that the mistake or misapprehension of the parties went to the whole substance of the agreement. If the cow was a breeder, she was worth at least $750; if barren, she was worth not over $80. The parties would not have made the contract of sale except upon the understanding and belief that she was incapable of breeding, and of no use as a cow. It is true she is now the identical animal that they thought her to be when the contract was made; there is no mistake as to the identity of the creature. Yet the mistake was not of the mere quality of the animal, but went to the very nature of the thing. A barren cow is substantially a different creature than a breeding one. There is as much difference between them for all purposes of use as there is between an ox and a cow that is capable of breeding and giving milk. If the mutual mistake had simply related to the fact whether she was with calf or not for one season, then it might have been a good sale; but the mistake affected the character of the animal for all time, and for her present and ultimate use. She was not in fact the animal, or the kind of animal, the defendants intended to sell or the plaintiff to buy. She was not a barren cow, and, if this fact had been known, there would have been no contract. The mistake affected the substance of the whole consideration, and it must be considered that there was no contract to sell or sale of the cow as she actually was. The thing sold and bought had in fact no existence. She was sold as a beef creature would be sold; she is in fact a breeding cow, and a valuable one.

"The court should have instructed the jury that if they found that the cow was sold, or contracted to be sold, upon the understanding of both parties that she was barren, and useless for the purpose of breeding, and that in fact she was not barren, but capable of breeding, then the defendants had a right to rescind, and to refuse to deliver, and the verdict should be in their favor." 66 Mich. 577-578, 33 N.W. 919.

Behind the Scenes

The cow in *Sherwood*, Rose of Aberlone, was famously (or infamously) memorialized in a 350-line poem written by a law professor. See www.law.berkeley.edu/faculty/rubinfeldd/LS145/roseofaberlone. htm The dissenting opinion and some commentators doubt that Sherwood shared Walker's assessment that Rose was infertile and think he bought her believing that "she would breed." 33 N.W. at 925. If the mistake lay only with the seller, then it was unilateral, not mutual (see page 447).

After winning the lawsuit, Walker sold Rose to Sherwood (again) for a higher price. Both parties were prosperous businessmen. Sherwood was an established banker who later became Michigan's first commissioner of banking, while Walker ran a liquor business that produced the widely distributed Hiram Walker's whiskey (later known as Canadian Club), which was sold in 1926 for $14 million. *See* Norman Otto Stockmeyer, *To Err is Human, to Moo, Bovine: The Rose of Aberlone Story*, 24 Thomas M. Cooley L. Rev. 491 (2007).

As the parties suggest, the foregoing precedent arguably distinguishes mistakes affecting the essence of the consideration from those which go to its quality or value, affording relief on a per se basis for the former but not the latter. See, e.g., Lenawee County Board of Health v. Messerly, 98 Mich.App. 478, 492, 295 N.W.2d 903 (1980) (Mackenzie, J., concurring in part).

However, the distinctions which may be drawn from Sherwood and A & M Land Development Co. do not provide a satisfactory analysis of the nature of a mistake sufficient to invalidate a contract. Often, a mistake relates to an underlying factual assumption which, when discovered, directly affects value, but simultaneously and materially affects the essence of the contractual consideration. It is disingenuous to label such a mistake collateral. McKay v. Coleman, 85 Mich. 60, 48 N.W. 203 (1891). Corbin, Contracts (One Vol. ed.), § 605, p. 551.

not just value

Appellant and appellee both mistakenly believed that the property which was the subject of their land contract would generate income as rental property. The fact that it could not be used for human habitation deprived the property of its income-earning potential and rendered it less valuable. However, this mistake, while directly and dramatically affecting the property's value, cannot accurately be characterized as collateral because it also affects the very essence of the consideration. "The thing sold and bought [income generating rental property] had in fact no existence". Sherwood v. Walker, 66 Mich. 568, 33 N.W. 919.

not what they bought

We find that the inexact and confusing distinction between contractual mistakes running to value and those touching the substance of the consideration serves only as an impediment to a clear and helpful analysis for the equitable resolution of cases in which mistake is alleged and proven. Accordingly, the holdings of **A & M Land Development Co.** and Sherwood with respect to the material or collateral nature of a mistake are limited to the facts of those cases.

Instead, we think the better-reasoned approach is a case-by-case analysis whereby rescission is indicated when the mistaken belief relates to a basic assumption of the parties upon which the contract is made, and which materially affects the agreed performances of the parties. **Denton v. Utley, 350 Mich. 332, 86 N.W.2d 537 (1957); Farhat v. Rassey, 295 Mich. 349, 294 N.W. 707 (1940); Richardson Lumber Co. v. Hoey, 219 Mich. 643, 189 N.W. 923 (1922).** 1 Restatement Contracts, 2d, § 152, p. 385-386.[11] Rescission is not available, however, to relieve a party who has assumed the risk of loss in connection with the mistake. **Denton v. Utley, 350 Mich. 344-345, 86 N.W.2d 537; Farhat v. Rassey, 295 Mich. 352, 294 N.W. 707;** Corbin, Contracts (One Vol. ed.), § 605, p. 552; 1 Restatement Contracts, 2d, §§ 152, 154, pp. 385-386, 402-406.[12]

> **FYI**
>
> Although the *Lenawee* court limited *Sherwood* to its facts, the same court (albeit with different justices on the bench) discussed *Sherwood* at length, ignored *Lenawee* completely, and announced that *Sherwood* was still a valuable case on the issue of mutual mistake. *Ford Motor Co. v. Woodhaven*, 716 N.W.2d 247 (Mich. 2006), *discussed* in Norman Otto Stockmeyer, *To Err Is Human, To Moo Bovine: The Rose of Aberlone Story*, 24 Thomas M. Cooley L. Rev. 491 (2007).

All of the parties to this contract erroneously assumed that the property transferred by the vendors to the vendees was suitable for human habitation and could be utilized to generate rental income. The fundamental nature of these assumptions is indicated by the fact that their invalidity changed the character of the property transferred, thereby frustrating, indeed precluding, Mr. and Mrs. Pickles' intended use of the real estate. Although the Pickleses are disadvantaged

---

[11] . . . . Section 152 [of the Restatement (Second)] delineates the legal significance of a mistake.

"§ 152. When Mistake of Both Parties Makes a Contract Voidable

"(1) Where a mistake of both parties at the time a contract was made as to a basic assumption on which the contract was made has a material effect on the agreed exchange of performances, the contract is voidable by the adversely affected party unless he bears the risk of the mistake under the rule stated in § 154.

"(2) In determining whether the mistake has a material effect on the agreed exchange of performances, account is taken of any relief by way of reformation, restitution, or otherwise."

[12] "§ 154. When a Party Bears the Risk of a Mistake

"A party bears the risk of a mistake when

"(a) the risk is allocated to him by agreement of the parties, or

"(b) he is aware, at the time the contract is made, that he has only limited knowledge with respect to the facts to which the mistake relates but treats his limited knowledge as sufficient, or

"(c) the risk is allocated to him by the court on the ground that it is reasonable in the circumstances to do so."

by enforcement of the contract, performance is advantageous to the Messerlys, as the property at issue is less valuable absent its income-earning potential. Nothing short of rescission can remedy the mistake. Thus, the parties' mistake as to a basic assumption materially affects the agreed performances of the parties.

Despite the significance of the mistake made by the parties, we reverse the Court of Appeals because we conclude that equity does not justify the remedy sought by Mr. and Mrs. Pickles.

Rescission is an equitable remedy which is granted only in the sound discretion of the court. Harris v. Axline, 323 Mich. 585, 36 N.W.2d 154 (1949); Hathaway v. Hudson, 256 Mich. 694, 239 N.W. 859 (1932). A court need not grant rescission in every case in which the mutual mistake relates to a basic assumption and materially affects the agreed performance of the parties.

In cases of mistake by two equally innocent parties, we are required, in the exercise of our equitable powers, to determine which blameless party should assume the loss resulting from the misapprehension they shared.[13] Normally that can only be done by drawing upon our "own notions of what is reasonable and just under all the surrounding circumstances".[14]

Equity suggests that, in this case, the risk should be allocated to the purchasers. We are guided to that conclusion, in part, by the standards announced in § 154 of the Restatement of Contracts 2d, for determining when a party bears the risk of mistake. See fn 12. Section 154(a) suggests that the court should look first to whether the parties have agreed to the allocation of the risk between themselves. While there is no express assumption in the contract by either party of the risk of the property becoming uninhabitable, there was indeed some agreed allocation of the risk to the vendees by the incorporation of an "as is" clause into the contract which, we repeat, provided:

> "Purchaser has examined this property and agrees to accept same in its present condition. There are no other or additional written or oral understandings."

That is a persuasive indication that the parties considered that, as between them, such risk as related to the "present condition" of the property should lie with the purchaser. If the "as is" clause is to have any meaning at all, it must be interpreted to refer to those defects which were unknown at the time that the

---

[13] This risk-of-loss analysis is absent in both A & M Land Development Co. and Sherwood, and this omission helps to explain, in part, the disparate treatment in the two cases. Had such an inquiry been undertaken in Sherwood, we believe that the result might have been different. Moreover, a determination as to which party assumed the risk in A & M Land Development Co. would have alleviated the need to characterize the mistake as collateral so as to justify the result denying rescission. Despite the absence of any inquiry as to the assumption of risk in those two leading cases, we find that there exists sufficient precedent to warrant such an analysis in future cases of mistake.

[14] Hathaway v. Hudson, 256 Mich. 702, 239 N.W. 859, quoting 9 C.J., p. 1161.

contract was executed.[15] Thus, the parties themselves assigned the risk of loss to Mr. and Mrs. Pickles.

We conclude that Mr. and Mrs. Pickles are not entitled to the equitable remedy of rescission and, accordingly, reverse the decision of the Court of Appeals.

WILLIAMS, C.J., and COLEMAN, FITZGERALD, KAVANAGH and LEVIN, JJ., concur.

RILEY, J., not participating.

Think About It!

Do you agree that the specified contract clause allocated the risk of the mistake made by the parties to the sale? How should the case have been decided if the contract had not included the "as is" clause?

Pickles lose
- horrible purchase

---

§ 2.1.2. Unilateral Mistake

As already noted, whether mutual or unilateral mistake applies depends on whether both or only one party was mistaken about the relevant fact. Distinguishing between mutual and unilateral mistake is challenging,* but one can at least say that bidding mistakes are treated as unilateral mistakes in the caselaw. A bidding error occurs when a party makes a one-sided technical error (typographical, mathematical, or other) that results in an offer that is "incorrect" (from the perspective of the offeror), and the offeree accepts that offer. One could say that both parties were mistaken about the correctness of the bid, but the usual conclusion is that only one party made the mistake, the other party being indifferent to the particulars. In electronic commerce, such errors occur with surprising regularity not only in bids, but also in advertisements, raising unilateral mistake issues.

offered for wrong amount

Reading the Law Critically: Comparing Mutual and Unilateral Mistake under the Restatement (Second)

You have already seen the Restatement (Second) provisions on mutual mistake (in footnotes 11 and 12 in *Lenawee*). They are reprinted here, along with the provision on unilateral mistake.

1.   Compare the two defenses under the Restatement (Second). How does § 153 differ from § 152? What role does § 154 play?

---

[15] An "as is" clause waives those implied warranties which accompany the sale of a new home, Tibbitts v. Openshaw, 18 Utah 2d 442, 425 P.2d 160 (1967), or the sale of goods. M.C.L. § 440.2316(3) (a); M.S.A. § 19.2316(3)(a). Since implied warranties protect against latent defects, an "as is" clause will impose upon the purchaser the assumption of the risk of latent defects, such as an inadequate sanitation system, even when there are no implied warranties.

* See Eric Rasmussen & Ian Ayres, *Mutual and Unilateral Mistake in Contract Law*, 22 J. Legal Studies 309 (2000).

2. Which defense is more difficult to prove? Does that make sense?

3. If the court in *Wood v. Boynton* (page 433) had applied Restatement (Second) §§ 152 and 154, would the decision have been the same? Why or why not?

Restatement (Second) § 152. **When Mistake of Both Parties Makes a Contract Voidable**

(1) Where a mistake of both parties at the time a contract was made as to a basic assumption on which the contract was made has a material effect on the agreed exchange of performance, the contract is voidable by the adversely affected party unless he bears the risk of the mistake under the rule in § 154.

(2) In determining whether the mistake has a material effect on the agreed exchange of performances, account is taken of any relief by way of reformation, restitution, or otherwise.

Restatement (Second) § 153. **When Mistake of One Party Makes a Contract Voidable**

Where a mistake of one party at the time a contract was made as to a basic assumption on which he made the contract has a material effect on the agreed exchange of performances that is adverse to him, the contract is voidable by him if he does not bear the risk of the mistake under the rule stated in § 154, and

    (a) the effect of the mistake is such that enforcement of the contract would be unconscionable, or

    (b) the other party had reason to know of the mistake or his fault caused the mistake.

Restatement (Second) § 154. **When a Party Bears the Risk of a Mistake**

A party bears the risk of a mistake when

    (a) the risk is allocated to him by agreement of the parties, or

    (b) he is aware, at the time the contract is made, that he has only limited knowledge with respect to the facts to which the mistake relates but treats his limited knowledge as sufficient, or

    (c) the risk is allocated to him by the court on the ground that it is reasonable in the circumstances to do so.

Reading the Law Critically: *Wil-Fred's, Inc.*

1. What was the mistake made in *Wil-Fred's*? Why was this a unilateral and not a mutual mistake?

2. What standard does the court adopt for determining when a unilateral mistake will support rescission of a contract? Is it harder or easier to get relief for a unilateral than for a mutual mistake? Why?

3. Compare the unilateral mistake defense in the common law (in *Wil-Fred's*) and Restatement (Second) § 153. Are they substantively different or merely worded differently?

Wil-fred's Inc. v. Metropolitan Sanitary District

WIL-FRED'S INC., Plaintiff-Appellee

v.

THE METROPOLITAN SANITARY DISTRICT OF GREATER CHICAGO, Defendant-Appellant

Appellate Court of Illinois, First District, Second Division
372 N.E.2d 946 (Ill. App. Ct. 1978)

PERLIN, Justice.

Make the Connection

Recall that the *Pavel* case, in Chapter 4 (page 334), discussed issues surrounding revocability or irrevocability of contractor bids to owners. This case illustrates some related difficulties that may arise regarding subcontractors' bids to contractors. Note that, in *Wil-Fred's*, the bidder's $100,000 certified check alleviated the need for a bid bond. Also recall the discussion in § 4.1.4 about "The Bidding Process: RFPs, RFBs, and RFQs." The Sanitary District's advertisement here was an RFB.

In response to an advertisement published by the Metropolitan Sanitary District of Greater Chicago (hereinafter Sanitary District) inviting bids for rehabilitation work at one of its water reclamation plants, Wil-Fred's Inc. submitted a sealed bid and, as a security deposit to insure its performance, a $100,000 certified check. After the bids were opened, Wil-Fred's, the low bidder, attempted to withdraw. The Sanitary District rejected the request and stated that the contract would be awarded to Wil-Fred's in due course. Prior to this award, Wil-Fred's filed a complaint for preliminary injunction and rescission. After hearing testimony and the arguments of counsel, the trial court granted rescission and ordered the Sanitary District to return the $100,000 bid deposit to Wil-Fred's. The Sanitary District seeks to reverse this judgment order.

The Sanitary District's advertisement was published on November 26, 1975, and it announced that bids on contract 75-113-2D for the rehabilitation of sand drying beds at the District's West-Southwest plant in Stickney, Illinois, would be accepted up to January 6, 1976. This announcement specified that the work to be performed required the contractor to remove 67,500 linear feet of clay pipe and 53,200 cubic yards of gravel from the beds and to replace these items with plastic pipe and fresh filter material. Although plastic pipes were called for, the specifications declared that "all pipes . . . must be able . . . to withstand standard construction equipment."

The advertisement further stated that "[t]he cost estimate of the work under Contract 75-113-2D, as determined by the Engineering Department of the . . . Sanitary District . . . is $1,257,000.00."

A proposal form furnished to Wil-Fred's provided:

> "The undersigned hereby certifies that he has examined the contract documents . . . and has examined the site of the work, ... The undersigned has also examined the Advertisement, the 'bidding requirements,' has made the examinations and investigation therein required . . . .
>
> The undersigned hereby accepts the invitation of the Sanitary District to submit a proposal on said work with the understanding that this proposal will not be cancelled or withdrawn.
>
> It is understood that in the event the undersigned is awarded a contract for the work herein mentioned, and shall fail or refuse to execute the same and furnish the specified bond within thirteen (13) days after receiving notice of the award of said contract, then the sum of One Hundred Thousand Dollars ($100,000.00), deposited herewith, shall be retained by the Sanitary District as liquidated damages and not as a penalty, it being understood that said sum is the fair measure of the amount of damages that said Sanitary District will sustain in such event." (Emphasis added.)

On December 22, 1975, the Sanitary District issued an addendum that changed the type of sand filter material which was to be supplied by the contractor. During the bidding period the District's engineering department discovered that the material originally specified in the advertisement was available only out of state and consequently was extremely expensive. This addendum changed the filter material to a less expensive type that could be obtained locally.

On January 6, 1976, Wil-Fred's submitted the low bid of $882,600 which was accompanied by the $100,000 bid deposit and the aforementioned proposal form signed on behalf of the company by Wil-Fred's vice president. Eight other companies submitted bids on January 6. The next lowest bid was $1,118,375, and it was made by Greco Contractors, Inc.

On January 8, 1976, Wil-Fred's sent the Sanitary District a telegram which stated that it was withdrawing its bid and requested return of its bid deposit. This telegram was confirmed by a subsequent letter mailed the same day.

On January 12, 1976, Wil-Fred's, at the request of the Sanitary District, sent a letter setting forth the circumstances that caused the company to withdraw its bid. The letter stated that upon learning the amount by which it was the low bidder, Wil-Fred's asked its excavating subcontractor, Ciaglo Excavating Company, to review its figures; that excavation was the only subcontracted trade in Wil-Fred's bid; that the following day Ciaglo informed Wil-Fred's that there had been a substantial error in its bid, and therefore it would have to withdraw its quotation since performing the work at the stated price would force the subcontractor into bankruptcy; that Wil-Fred's then checked with other excavation contractors and confirmed that Ciaglo's bid was in error; that Wil-Fred's had used Ciaglo as an excavating subcontractor on many other projects in the past, and Ciaglo had always honored its previous quotations; that Ciaglo had always performed its work in a skillful fashion; that because of these facts Wil-Fred's acted reasonably in utilizing Ciaglo's quoted price in formulating its own bid; and that with the withdrawal of Ciaglo's quotation Wil-Fred's could not perform the work for $882,600.

On February 2, 1976, Wil-Fred's received a letter from Thomas W. Moore, the Sanitary District's purchasing agent. Moore's letter stated that in his opinion the reasons cited in Wil-Fred's letter of January 12 did not justify withdrawal of the bid. For this reason Moore said that he would recommend to the Sanitary District's general superintendent that the contract be awarded to Wil-Fred's at the original bid price.

At a February 20 meeting between representatives of the Sanitary District and Wil-Fred's, the company was informed that the District's board of trustees had rejected its withdrawal request, and that it would be awarded the contract. In response to this information, Wil-Fred's filed its complaint for preliminary injunction and rescission on February 26, 1976. The complaint alleged that the company would be irreparably injured if required to perform the contract at such an unconscionably low price or if forced to forfeit the $100,000 bid deposit. The hearing on this complaint commenced on March 10, 1976.

At the hearing William Luxion, president of Wil-Fred's, testified that the company had been in business for 18 years; that Wil-Fred's did 13 to 14 million dollars worth of business in 1975; that 95% of the company's work was done on a competitive bid basis; that Wil-Fred's never had withdrawn a competitive bid in the past; and that he personally examined the company's bid prior to its submission. Luxion further stated that he told Wil-Fred's chief estimator to review the company's quotation immediately after he was notified on January 6 that Wil-Fred's bid was more than $235,000 below the next lowest bid. At this time he also requested that Ciaglo Company review its figures.

Make the Connection

As indicated in the note on the history of equity in Chapter 3 (page 162), an equitable remedy like an injunction is "extraordinary" relief and is available only if the claimant proves that it has no adequate remedy at law and that "irreparable injury" will result if relief is not given. The standards for awarding equitable relief are covered in more depth in Chapter 9 (page 1182).

The reexamination by the chief estimator revealed that there was no material error in the portion of the bid covering work to be done by Wil-Fred's. However, the president of Ciaglo contacted Luxion on January 8 and stated that his bid was too low on account of an error and that, because of this, he was withdrawing his quotation. Upon receiving this information, Luxion sent the Sanitary District the telegram and letter in which he informed the District of this error, withdrew Wil-Fred's bid and requested a return of the company's bid deposit.

Lastly, Luxion testified that a loss of the $100,000 security deposit would result in the company's loss of bonding capacity in the amount of two to three million dollars; that Wil-Fred's decided not to attempt to force Ciaglo to honor its subcontract because the company felt that Ciaglo was not financially capable of sustaining a $150,000 loss; and that he was aware of the Sanitary District's cost estimate before Wil-Fred's submitted its bid. However, Luxion stated that he took the addendum changing the filter material into account when calculating the price of the bid and concluded that this alteration would result in a cost savings of over $200,000.

Dennis Ciaglo, president of Ciaglo Excavating, Inc., also testified on behalf of Wil-Fred's and stated that prior to January 6, 1976, his company submitted a quote of $205,000 for the removal of the existing material in the sand beds, for digging trenches for the new pipe and for spreading the new filter materials. Ciaglo further stated that a representative of Wil-Fred's called him on January 6 and asked him to review his price quotation. During his examination the witness discovered that he underestimated his projected costs by $150,000. Ciaglo said that this error was caused by his assumption that heavy equipment could be driven into the beds to spread the granular fill. Although he was aware that plastic pipes were to be used in the beds, Ciaglo still presumed that heavy equipment could be employed because the specifications called for the utilization of standard construction equipment. Ciaglo first learned that the plastic pipes would not support heavy equipment when, as part of his review of the price quote, he contacted the pipe manufacturer.

Ciaglo testified additionally that his company probably would have to file for bankruptcy if forced to take a $150,000 loss; that Ciaglo Excavating Co. had never before withdrawn a price quotation given to Wil-Fred's or any other company; and that in his opinion the change in the filter material called for by the second addendum would cause a $300,000 reduction in "the cost of the material for the bids . . . ."

Ciaglo had good record (handwritten margin note)

Only one witness testified for the Sanitary District. Leslie Dombai, a registered structural engineer for the District, stated that the Sanitary District's cost estimate was based directly upon the expense of the material specified in the advertisement, and he confirmed that the filter material was changed because the type initially called for was expensive and was not available locally. However, Dombai claimed that this substitution increased the District's original cost estimate by $40,000.

By bidding on the Sanitary District's rehabilitation project, Wil-Fred's made a binding commitment. Its bid was in the nature of an option to the District based upon valuable consideration: the assurance that the award would be made to the lowest bidder. The option was both an offer to do the work and a unilateral agreement to enter into a contract to do so. When the offer was accepted, a bilateral contract arose which was mutually binding on Wil-Fred's and the Sanitary District. (People ex rel. Department of Public Works and Buildings v. South East National Bank of Chicago (1st Dist. 1971), 131 Ill.App.2d 238, 240, 266 N.E.2d 778, 779-80; 11 Williston on Contracts § 1441 (3rd ed. Jaeger 1968).) When Wil-Fred's attempted to withdraw its bid, it became subject to the condition incorporated in the proposal form furnished by the Sanitary Dis-

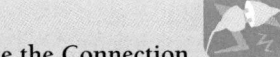

Make the Connection

The reference here to an "option" indicates the court's conclusion that the bid was an offer, made irrevocable because it was supported by consideration (the Sanitary District's promise to award the contract to the lowest bidder). See Chapter 4 (page 332). It is unclear what the court's reference to a "unilateral agreement" means. Do you agree with the conclusion that there was consideration for Wil-Fred's implicit promise to keep the offer open until the Sanitary District made its decision?

Consequences as laid out in bid submission form (handwritten margin note)

trict. Under this condition, the company's bid deposit was forfeited when it refused to execute the contract within the specified time period.

The principal issue, therefore, is whether Wil-Fred's can obtain rescission of its contract with the Sanitary District because of its unilateral mistake. Wil-Fred's argues that the mistake was material to the contract; that this error was directly caused by the Sanitary District's misleading specifications; that the Sanitary District did not alter its position in reliance upon the erroneous bid because the company promptly notified the District of the mistake; and that under these circumstances it would be unconscionable to enforce the contract or to allow the Sanitary District to retain the security deposit.

Take Note!

This paragraph articulates one rationale for affording relief based on unilateral mistake: because the mistake was "so palpable" that the other party is "put on notice" about the mistake. Similarly, courts sometimes say a party cannot snap up a deal that is "too good to be true."

. . . [U]nilateral mistake may afford ground for rescission where there is a material mistake and such mistake is so palpable that the party not in error will be put on notice of its existence. 13 Williston on Contracts § 1578 (3rd ed. Jaeger 1970).

In Illinois the conditions generally required for rescission are: that the mistake relate to a material feature of the contract; that it occurred notwithstanding the exercise of reasonable care; that it is of such grave consequence that enforcement of the contract would be unconscionable; and that the other party can be placed in statu[s] quo. (Department of Public Works and Buildings v. South East National Bank.) Evidence of these conditions must be clear and positive. Winkelman v. Erwin (1929), 333 Ill. 636, 640, 165 N.E. 205, 207.

If Ciaglo's misestimation was established by competent evidence, it is apparent that the error was material. This determination is based on the fact that the $150,000 mistake represents approximately 17% of Wil-Fred's bid. See Department of Public Works and Buildings v. South East National Bank.

. . . .

Think About It!

Jurisdictions are split on whether to require a showing that the mistake occurred "notwithstanding the exercise of reasonable care." The alternative approach appears in Restatement (Second) § 157, which provides:

A mistaken party's fault in failing to know or discover the facts before making the contract does not bar him from avoidance or reformation under [the mistake defenses], unless his fault amounts to a failure to act in good faith and in accordance with reasonable standards of fair dealing.

Which standard is preferable? Would *Wil-Fred's* have been decided differently if the Illinois court had adopted the Restatement standard?

Il requirements

Def. 605 enough

. . . . It is manifest from the trial court's judgment order that the trier of fact decided that Ciaglo's mistake related to a material feature of the rehabilitation contract and that this condition was supported by clear and positive evidence. After carefully examining the record, we are in agreement with this finding.

Dennis Ciaglo testified that he gave Wil-Fred's a price quotation of $205,000 for his work allotment, and he indicated that the amount of this bid was based directly upon his incorrect assumption that heavy trucks could be driven into the sand drying beds and onto the plastic pipes. This testimony is corroborated by the subcontractor's price estimate sheet which was introduced into evidence by the Sanitary District.

It is true, nevertheless, that plaintiff's witnesses failed to describe the correct spreading method, and that Ciaglo made only a conclusionary statement to the effect that employment of the proper procedure would have increased his original quotation by $150,000. However, the District did not cross-examine the subcontractor concerning this matter, and it failed to produce any evidence, testimonial or otherwise, that contravened his statement. Consequently, Ciaglo's conclusion stands uncontradicted.

Furthermore, it is our opinion that the accuracy of the estimated error is supported by the fact that Ciaglo had eight years experience in the excavating business and by the fact that he confirmed this figure by checking with other contractors who had submitted bids on the same portion of the project. Under these particular circumstances we feel that Wil-Fred's produced sufficient evidence to sustain its claim of a $150,000 error.

In addition to satisfying the first condition for rescission, Wil-Fred's has decidedly fulfilled two of the three remaining requirements. The consequences of Ciaglo's error were grave. Since the subcontractor was not capable of sustaining a $150,000 loss, Wil-Fred's stood to lose the same amount if it performed the contract for $882,600. Wil-Fred's will forfeit $100,000 if the contract is enforced. A loss of $100,000 will decrease the plaintiff's bonding capacity by two to three million dollars. It is evident, therefore, that either deprivation will constitute substantial hardship. The Sanitary District was not damaged seriously by the withdrawal of the bid. When the subcontractor's mistake was discovered 48 hours after the bid opening, Wil-Fred's promptly notified the District by telegram and declared its intention to withdraw. The rehabilitation contract had not been awarded at this time. Accordingly, the District suffered no change in position since it was able, with no great loss other than the windfall resulting from Ciaglo's error, to award the contract to the next lowest bidder . . . .

The central question, therefore, is whether the error occurred despite the use of reasonable care. The Sanitary District asserts that the mistake itself evidences Wil-Fred's failure to use ordinary care in the preparation of its bid and argues that rescission is not warranted under such circumstances.

We cannot agree with this contention. Wil-Fred's unquestionably exercised due care when it selected Ciaglo Excavating Company as its subcontractor. Ciaglo Excavating Company had been in business for five years; its president had eight years experience in the excavating field; the company had worked for Wil-Fred's on 12 previous occasions; it had never failed to honor a prior quotation; and it had always performed its assignments in a highly skilled manner. Also, Dennis Ciaglo testified that prior to submitting his bid to Wil-Fred's, he inspected the jobsite and carefully examined the specifications with plaintiff's estimators. Taking into account the experience and preparations of the subcontractor, the prior business dealings between the two companies and the high quality of Ciaglo Excavating Company's past performance, we conclude that Wil-Fred's was justified in relying on the subcontractor's quotation in formulating its own bid.

> **Think About It!**
>
> Why should Wil-Fred's be able to use the unilateral mistake defense, when the mistake was actually made by Ciaglo and when Wil-Fred's apparently could have attempted to hold Ciaglo to its bid?

Similarly, we feel that Wil-Fred's exercised reasonable care in the preparation of its portion of the total bid. The plaintiff made two separate reviews of its price quotation. The first was conducted prior to the bid's submission, and it took into account the addendum that substituted a cheaper filter material for the type originally called for by the specifications.[3] The second examination was made immediately after Wil-Fred's president learned that his company's bid was the lowest quotation. It revealed that plaintiff had not erred in estimating expenses for its part of the rehabilitation project.

The question of due care is a factual question to be determined by the trial court, and such determination will not be disturbed unless it is against the manifest weight of the evidence. (**Santucci Construction Co. v. County of Cook (1st Dist. 1974), 21 Ill.App.3d 527, 532, 315 N.E.2d 565, 569.**) For the aforemen-

---

[3] We believe that the change in filter material explains why the Sanitary District's cost estimate was $374,000 higher than Wil-Fred's quotation. Plaintiff's witnesses testified that the substitution of cheaper material would result in a cost savings of $200,000 to $300,000. Additionally, the Sanitary District's engineer stated that the District's estimate was based directly upon the cost of the material specified in the advertisement, and he admitted that the initial type of filter material was very expensive because it was not available locally. In view of this testimony we must conclude that the large discrepancy would not necessarily have alerted Wil-Fred's president to the fact that there was a substantial error in his company's bid.

tioned reasons we feel that the record supports the trial court's finding of due care on the part of Wil-Fred's.

The Sanitary District asserts that even if due care was exercised by Wil-Fred's, Illinois courts have granted relief only in cases where the bid has contained a clerical or mathematical error. Defendant argues that the trial court's grant of rescission should not be upheld because Ciaglo's mistake was not a factual error but an error in business judgment.

Regarding the District's argument, it is the opinion of this court that Ciaglo's error amounts to a mixed mistake of judgment and fact. Ciaglo's belief that the plastic pipes would support heavy trucks was judgmental in nature and in this narrow sense his mistake was one of business judgment. However, his belief was predicated on a misunderstanding of the actual facts occasioned, at least in part, by his reliance on the Sanitary District's misleading specifications which stated that all pipes had to be able to withstand standard construction equipment.

Generally, relief is refused for errors in judgment and allowed for clerical or mathematical mistakes. (Annot. 59 A.L.R. 827; 80 A.L.R. 586; 52 A.L.R.2d 792.) Nonetheless, we believe, in fairness to the individual bidder, that the facts surrounding the error, not the label, i.e., "mistake of fact" or "mistake of judgment," should determine whether relief is granted. White v. Berrenda Mesa Water District of Kern County (1970), 7 Cal.App.3d 894, 907, 87 Cal.Rptr. 338, 347-348.

The testimonial evidence reveals that Wil-Fred's acted in good faith and that Ciaglo's error occurred notwithstanding the exercise of reasonable care. Furthermore, it was established that Wil-Fred's quotation was $235,775 lower than the next lowest bid. It is apparent that such a sizable discrepancy should have placed the Sanitary District on notice that plaintiff's bid contained a material error. (See Santucci.) Accordingly equity will not allow the District to take advantage of Wil-Fred's low offer.

Think About It!

Why does the law refuse relief for errors in judgment, but allow it for mistakes of fact and for clerical and mathematical mistakes? Why doesn't the court characterize the mistake in judgment as one involving opinion or prediction?

We are aware of the importance of maintaining the competitive bidding system which is used in the letting of municipal construction contracts. Consequently we do not mean to imply by affirming the trial court's order that a bidder who has submitted the lowest quotation on a municipal contract may cavalierly disregard the contract's irrevocability clause and seek rescission. Allowing such action would be unfair to the other bidders and would result in the destruction of the system's integrity. However, we are certain that the courts of this state are capable of preventing such a result by refusing to grant rescission where, unlike the present circumstances, the facts do not justify relieving the lowest bidder from his bid. See John J. Calnan Co. v. Talsma Builders, Inc. (1977), 67 Ill.2d 213, 10 Ill.Dec. 242, 367 N.E.2d 695, in which our supreme court, although not dealing with a municipal construction contract, recently denied rescission of a plumbing subcontract where the subcontractor failed to include the cost of the entire water supply system in its bid, a concededly material feature of the subcontract. The supreme court held that the subcontractor had not exercised reasonable care by failing to utilize its own bid preparation review system and by not discovering its error until four months after acceptance of its bid. The court also found that the general contractor could not be placed in statu[s] quo since work had begun and the general contractor had no options; it either had to account for the error ($31,000) or had to negotiate another subcontract, at a greater cost with lack of continuity in work.

> **Think About It!**
>
> Earlier in the opinion, the *Wil-Fred's* court set out a rule from Williston and a rule from Illinois precedent regarding when rescission is available. Which rule does the court use to reach its conclusion here?

. . . . For the above stated reasons, the trial court's order granting rescission and the return of Wil-Fred's security deposit is affirmed.

Wilfred wins

Affirmed.

STAMOS, P. J., and PUSATERI, J., concur.

Problems: The Mistake Defense

Could the defense of mutual or unilateral mistake apply to give relief in the following fact situations? If the result is uncertain, develop the arguments on both sides. If you would seek to discover additional facts, specify those facts.

5-6. Branch Bank was the executor of the estate of Olga Mestrovic. At the time of her death, Olga owned a residence as well as a large number of paintings and sculptures created by her husband, Sergei, a noted artist who died twenty years earlier. Olga's will provided that all works of art she owned at the time of her death should be sold and the proceeds be divided among the members of the Mestrovic family.

The Bank, in its capacity as executor of the estate, entered into a purchase agreement to sell Olga's house to Wilkin, who was familiar with Sergei's artwork and was elighted to be purchasing a house where Sergei had produced some of his art. When Wilkin was given a key to walk through the home, much of the furniture was still in place and rooms were filled with boxes of unmoved goods, making it difficult for Wilkin to thoroughly explore the residence. He mailed the Bank an inquiry about any remaining artwork, but received no reply. The purchase agreement included provisions for sale to Wilkin of specified personal property on the premises, including the stove, refrigerator, dishwasher, drapes, curtains, and sconces, but neither party made any mention of any artwork prior to or at the closing.

After the closing, Wilkin complained that the house required substantial cleaning. The Bank proposed two options: the Bank could hire a rubbish removal service to clean the property, or Wilkin could clean the premises and keep any items of personal property he wanted. Wilkin opted to clean the property himself. During the clean-up, he found eight drawings and a sculpture by Sergei. Wilkin claimed ownership, citing the agreement with the Bank—that he could keep any personal property found while cleaning up the property. The Bank argued that it had a fiduciary duty to the Mestrovics' heirs, so it had no right to enter into an agreement to transfer the artwork to Wilkin and had not done so. Should the Bank be able to rescind the "clean up and keep" agreement based on mistake?

5-7. On Sunday, Central Airlines advertised in eight metropolitan newspapers that it would be featuring special "cheapo fares" on its website during the following week. At 8 a.m. on Monday, Central Airlines posted fifteen "cheapo fares" on its website, including a Dallas-Denver fare mistakenly listed at $5, rather than $125. At 8:45 a.m., Central discovered the error and immediately corrected it. By then, 18 customers had bought Dallas-Denver tickets for $5 on Central's website, paying with credit cards. Can Central Airlines rescind the contracts with those customers based on mistake? Would your answer be different if Central's website displayed the following message just before the customer checked the "I agree" box in the purchasing process?

"If an item's price is posted incorrectly, we will, at our discretion, either contact you for instructions or cancel your order, notifying you of such cancellation."

§ 2.2. Misrepresentation

Recall that the purchasers in *Wood* and *Lenawee* claimed (unsuccessfully) not only that they were mistaken about the nature of what they bought, but also that they were misled about the purchase by the sellers. Such claims of misrepresentation are based on allegations that one of the parties, at the time of contract formation, made a material or fraudulent "assertion of fact" that was not in accord with the facts. An assertion of fact (a past or present fact) must be distinguished from a promise (a commitment to do or not do something in the future), a prediction (an opinion about the future), and an opinion (a guess or hypothesis).

A party can mislead another by affirmatively stating a mistruth, by taking affirmative steps to hide the truth, or by remaining silent and knowingly permitting the other party to misunderstand. Each of these may be thought of as a misrepresentation. While affirmatively stating a false fact is universally considered a misrepresentation, not all jurisdictions recognize concealment and nondisclosure. The following graphic suggests the relative strength of the three forms of misrepresentation, as well as the likelihood of each being recognized as actionable:

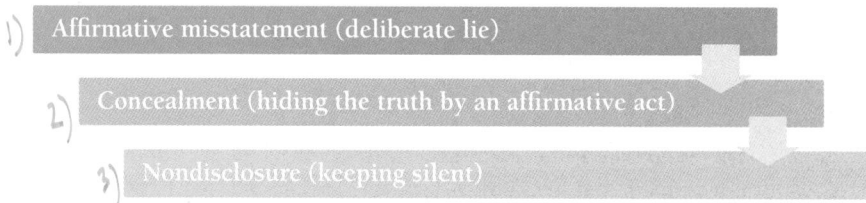

Affirmative misstatement (deliberate lie)

Concealment (hiding the truth by an affirmative act)

Nondisclosure (keeping silent)

Examples of misrepresentation through acts of concealment include a seller of real estate paneling over a leaky wall or preventing a potential buyer from viewing a room with cracks in the walls. Misrepresentation through concealment also can occur if a party makes a statement that reveals some facts but fails to disclose other related facts that would be necessary for the statement to be accurate.

Because parties entering a contract generally must protect their own interests without depending on the other party to reveal every known relevant fact, nondisclosure only rarely makes a contract voidable based on misrepresentation. Circumstances that have led some jurisdictions to find misrepresentation through nondisclosure include the following:

1. A relation of trust and confidence exists between the parties, entitling one of them to a disclosure of the fact in question, but the other party fails to so disclose;
2. A party makes a statement that is true at the time, but the party later acquires knowledge that makes the earlier assertion false, and that party doesn't disclose the subsequent knowledge; or
3. A party knows the other is acting under a mistaken impression, and it would be a violation of good faith and fair dealing to remain silent.

The last thread is challenging to apply because most often parties have no responsibility to disclose their knowledge to each other.

Whether a misrepresentation is made through affirmative statement or concealment or nondisclosure of a fact, the fact itself usually must be "fraudulent" or important enough ("material") to the transaction to warrant relief, and an affirmative statement must be one on which it is reasonable for the other party to rely. In addition, an affirmative misstatement must not amount to "puffing" or "puffery"— advertising hyperbole and exaggerated statements meant to grab attention and inflate a potential buyer's estimation of a particular item being considered for purchase. Whether a statement is puffing depends on the reasonable understanding of the statement in context— is it an assertion on which it is reasonable for the recipient to rely?—and it is often devilishly hard to discern how courts and juries will rule on this issue. Puffing is more likely when the statement is general rather than specific, hedged rather than unqualified, oral rather than written, informal rather than formal, and phrased as opinion rather than fact.

> **Make the Connection**
>
> Recall that "puffing" or "puffery" is a statement that a reasonable recipient should know is meant to promote a product and is not necessarily an accurate statement of fact. "Puffing" or "puffery" is discussed in the "What's That?" box in Chapter 4 (page 304).

The UNIDROIT principles recognize fraudulent misrepresentation, including non-disclosure:

UNIDROIT Art. 3.8. **Fraud**

A party may avoid the contract when it has been led to conclude the contract by the other party's fraudulent representation, including language or practices, or fraudulent non-disclosure of circumstances which, according to reasonable commercial standards of fair dealing, the latter party should have disclosed.

---

*really good
fraud checklist*

Reading the Law Critically: *Barrer* and *Kannavos*

There are significant variations among jurisdictions in how the three types of misrepresentation are defined and when each of them applies. As you read the *Barrer* and *Kannavos* cases, consider the following issues and what effect these concerns have on the outcome in each case:

1. What are the elements of misrepresentation applied by each court? In *Barrer*, the court begins with common law elements, then uses the Restatement (Second) to supplement those elements. In *Kannavos*, you can deduce the elements from the master's factual conclusions at the top of page 480, but the court "tweaks" these elements in its subsequent opinion.

2. Was each representation one of fact or was it a statement of prediction, opinion, or law?

3. Was each misrepresentation an affirmative statement, an effort to conceal the truth, or a nondisclosure? If a nondisclosure, what makes it actionable as a misrepresentation? What guidelines does the court give about when a nondisclosure constitutes a misrepresentation?

4. Did the party making the misrepresentation know he was being untruthful? Did he intend to mislead? What "state of mind" was required for the claim to succeed?

5. What effect did the misrepresentation have on the decision of the other party whether to enter the contract? What effect was required for the claim to be successful?

6. Was the party who relied on the representation justified in doing so? What standard does the court use in deciding whether reliance was justified?

7. Was there any special relationship between the parties to the contract that made reliance more justifiable? Did that relationship affect any other element of the misrepresentation claim? Why should such a relationship matter in the analysis? What other kinds of relationships should receive similar treatment?

Barrer v. Women's National Bank

LESTER A. BARRER, Plaintiff-Appellant

v.

WOMEN'S NATIONAL BANK, Defendant-Respondent

United States Court of Appeals, District of Columbia Circuit
761 F.2d 752 (D.C. Cir. 1985)

HARRY T. EDWARDS, Circuit Judge.

The appellant, Lester A. Barrer, brought this action against Women's National Bank ("the Bank" or "WNB") for damages he allegedly sustained as the result of the Bank's eleventh hour decision to rescind a loan agreement. WNB defended and moved for summary judgment on the ground that Barrer had made innocent material misrepresentations in his loan application that justified the Bank's avoidance of the contract. The magistrate found that Barrer had made five material representations to the Bank that were not in accord with the facts and, on that basis, granted WNB's motion for summary judgment. We find that the magistrate failed to apply the correct legal test for determining when an innocent material misrepresentation permits the rescission of a contract, and that there are material issues of fact that make summary judgment inappropriate. Accordingly, we reverse and remand for further proceedings consistent with this opinion.

I. BACKGROUND

A. *Factual Background*

On June 24, 1981, Lester Barrer's personal home was sold at a tax sale by the Internal Revenue Service ("IRS") because of his inability to pay certain employment taxes. The taxes were owed by Barrer's closely-held corporation, Today News Service, Inc., and had been asserted against him personally as a 100 percent penalty pursuant to 26 U.S.C. § 6672 (1982). At the tax sale, Barrer's home was purchased by Edward L. Curtis, Jr., for $16,326, subject to the underlying mortgage. The Internal Revenue Code provides for the redemption of real property within 120 days of a tax sale upon payment to the purchaser of the purchase price plus interest. Barrer accordingly was advised by the IRS that he could redeem his home by delivering $17,400, in cash or its equivalent, to the IRS or to Curtis on or before October 22, 1981.

On October 20, 1981, Barrer went to WNB to discuss a personal loan for the redemption amount. Apparently, on the previous day, Barrer had approached one other bank about the possibility of a loan; however, he had been advised by the President of that bank that it would not be possible to process an application for a loan in the amount sought by Barrer in such a short period of time. Barrer indicated in his deposition statement that he waited until the last minute to seek a bank loan because he had been involved in serious negotiations over the sale of his business and had expected to close on the sale before October 20, 1981, and that he had intended to use the proceeds from that sale to redeem his house.

At WNB, Barrer spoke with Emily Womack, the President of the Bank, with whom he had a professional acquaintance. Barrer's corporation published the *Women Today Newsletter,* a periodical to which the Bank subscribed and which, according to Barrer's deposition statement, had published an article on the Bank. Barrer's corporation also maintained an account with the Bank. Womack gave Barrer a loan application form, which he completed and returned to her the next day, October 21, along with certain supporting documents, including those concerning the tax sale and his efforts to sell the business.

Barrer evidently explained to Womack that he had experienced severe financial difficulties since his wife and long-time professional collaborator died of cancer in 1978. At his deposition, Barrer testified that he told Womack that, for a period after his wife died, he lost his motivation to work and that the business they had jointly owned and managed suffered serious economic reverses as a consequence. Those reverses led to Today News Service, Inc.'s inability to pay its employment taxes and ultimately to the tax sale of Barrer's home. Womack sympathized with Barrer's plight and expressed to one of her bank officers the hope that they could help him.

On October 21, Barrer and Womack reviewed his loan application line by line. With reference to his home mortgage, Barrer told her that his house was worth approximately $130,000 and that Columbia First Federal Savings and Loan Association ("Columbia") held a $65,000 mortgage on it. When asked whether his mortgage payments were up-to-date, Barrer recalls replying that he "thought" he was two months behind. By contrast, Womack testified that Barrer said he was current. In fact, Barrer was six months behind. Barrer explained that he thought his obligation to pay his mortgage ceased at the time of the tax sale and that he did not realize that he was responsible for more than the two months' mortgage payments that had been due before the sale.

Because Barrer's mortgage payments were in arrears, Columbia had begun foreclosure proceedings—also a fact that Barrer did not disclose to Womack. In his deposition statement, Barrer accounted for this failure by stating that on October 21, 1981, he did not know that Columbia had initiated foreclosure proceedings.

On the liability side of the loan application, Barrer revealed that he had borrowed $40,000 from friends and relatives. Barrer testified that he explained to Womack that he had borrowed this sum to ease the financial difficulties he had encountered since his wife's death.

Barrer also disclosed the $38,000 tax liability which was the cause of the tax sale. He did not indicate, however, a contingent liability for an additional $11,000 in employment taxes owed by his corporation which had not, at that time, been asserted against him personally under 26 U.S.C. § 6672. Barrer seems to argue both that this $11,000 was included in the $38,000 figure, and that because the $11,000 tax liability had not been assessed against him personally it was not a contingent liability that he was obligated to reveal.

Nor did Barrer list as a contingent liability a $5,300 debt owed by his wife's estate to IBM. The Bank argues that this debt should have been revealed because Barrer had demonstrated, by requesting the probate court to charge the obligation to him, that he thought himself responsible for the debt. Barrer contends that because the probate court ultimately ruled that the obligation belonged to the estate, his failure to list the amount on the loan application was not a misrepresentation.

Finally, Barrer did not indicate on the loan application that he had approximately $1,500 in unsatisfied judgments pending against him. However, he answered in the affirmative to a specific question on the application form which inquired whether he was "a defendant in any suits or legal actions." Barrer also stated at his deposition that he told Womack that he owed small amounts arising out of these lawsuits. He said that he explained to her that these debts involved disputes over medical bills and that he expected his major medical insurance to cover most of them.

After Barrer and Womack finished discussing the content of the completed loan application form and Barrer's financial situation, Womack indicated that, in order for the Bank to grant the loan, the IRS would have to agree to subordinate its claim with respect to Barrer's house to that of WNB. On October 22, 1981, the last redemption day, Barrer obtained the subordination agreement from the IRS and delivered it to the Bank. Barrer then executed a collateral note for $17,400, payable in 90 days at 15 percent interest, which gave the Bank the right to a security interest in his house. The Bank's Vice President, Emma Carrera, gave Barrer a cashier's check, payable to him, for the loan amount. Prior to granting the loan, neither Womack nor Carrera obtained a credit report on Barrer and neither officer phoned Columbia about the status of his mortgage.

That afternoon, Barrer delivered the endorsed check to the IRS in accordance with the required redemption procedure and returned home, believing that his home had been saved.

In the meantime, the tax sale purchaser, Curtis, phoned WNB and spoke with Carrera. According to her deposition, their conversation was as follows:

He stated that he had some information that he thought would be of interest to me on the loan that the bank had made to Mr. Barrer. I told him at that time that I could not discuss any loan with him in regards to who it was or what it was for. He said he didn't want me to do any discussing, but he just wanted to tell me some facts.

He then told me he was the purchaser of the property at the tax sale. He couldn't believe that a bank would make a loan to a man who was in the credit position that he was in; that there were liens and judgments and so forth against him and at that time, I signalled for my secretary to bring me the file on Mr. Barrer.

I quickly looked through the file and found there wasn't a credit report in the file. At that time I told her to pull a credit report on him, which she did, and brought it to me within just a couple of minutes.

In the meantime, Mr. Curtis was continuing to talk. He had mentioned something about some kind of code that says that a person who buys a property at a tax sale cannot interfere with the owner's right to redeem, but that he didn't feel he was doing that just by informing the bank of Mr. Barrer's situation.

[handwritten: knew he overstepped]

He put me on a conference call with a gentleman who identified himself as an official of the mortgage company [Columbia] that held the mortgage on Mr. Barrer's property. He [Mr. Ford] asked me at that time who, in his organization, had given us a credit report.

. . . I . . . answer[ed] him . . . that it was my understanding that all of the savings and loan associations required a written request for credit rating [sic] on any of the mortgages that they held and it had always been, to my knowledge, their policies not to give a reference by phone.

[Mr. Ford] said at that point he thought it was important that we know that Mr. Barrer's mortgage was six months in arrears and they were prepared to go to foreclosure on the property. He excused himself and Mr. Curtis stayed on the line.

[Mr. Curtis] said that he had knowledge that IRS had not made an agreement with Mr. Barrer to repay the balance of the taxes; that they were ready to go back to another tax sale as soon as this $17,400 was paid.

Based on the information furnished by Curtis, Ford, and the credit report, the Bank decided to stop payment on the cashier's check. The Bank's counsel called Barrer later that day to inform him that the check would not be honored. When Curtis, to whom the IRS had turned over the check, presented it for payment the Bank refused to cash it. Barrer, therefore, did not effect the redemption of his home within the statutory period and Curtis became the owner.

B. *Procedural History*

Barrer filed suit against the Bank in District Court to recover damages to compensate him for the loss of $94,000 equity in his home—the difference between the market value of the house and the balance due on the mortgage—that he allegedly suffered as a result of the Bank's rescission of the loan agreement. Barrer also claimed punitive damages for the embarrassment he endured and the rent he has been required to pay Curtis in order to remain in his home.

The case was referred to a magistrate for pretrial proceedings. On the Bank's motion for summary judgment, the magistrate found that Barrer did not disclose the following five material facts to the Bank: (1) that he was six months delinquent in mortgage payments, (2) that Columbia had begun foreclosure procedures, (3) that Barrer had at least an $11,000 contingent liability to the IRS in addition to his $38,000 actual liability, (4) that he had a contingent liability to IBM of approximately $5,000, and (5) that he had approximately $1,500 in unsatisfied judgments pending against him. The magistrate purported to rely on the law of innocent material misrepresentation to hold that these disclosure omissions justified WNB's rescission of the loan contract. On that basis, he granted summary judgment in favor of the Bank. This appeal followed.

II. ANALYSIS

A. *Standards for Summary Judgment*

A motion for summary judgment may be granted only where the record makes clear "that there is no genuine issue as to any material fact and that the moving party is entitled to a judgment as a matter of law."[19] The burden of demonstrating the absence of any genuine issue of material fact is on the movant. In assessing a motion for summary judgment, the court must view all inferences to be drawn from the evidence in the light most favorable to the party opposing the motion. All doubts as to the existence of a material dispute must be resolved against summary judgment. If conflict appears as to a material fact, summary judgment is not proper, "unless the evidence on one or the other hand is too incredible to be accepted by reasonable minds or is without legal probative force even if true."

---

[19] Fed.R.Civ.P. 56(c) . . . .

As we demonstrate below, the magistrate failed both to apply the correct legal test for determining whether an "innocent" misrepresentation justifies the rescission of a contract and to recognize that with regard to each of the five alleged misrepresentations there exist legally probative, material issues of fact in dispute. Thus, the award of summary judgment in favor of the Bank was erroneous and must be reversed.

B. *Elements of Innocent Material Misrepresentation*

It is well established that misrepresentation of material facts may be the basis for the rescission of a contract, even where the misrepresentations are made innocently, without knowledge of their falsity and without fraudulent intent.[25] The rationale supporting this rule, which has its origins in equity,[26] is that, as between two innocent parties, the party making the representation should bear the loss. Stated another way, the rule is based on the view that "one who has made a false statement ought not to benefit at the expense of another who has been prejudiced by relying on the statement."[28] This rule may be employed "actively," as in a suit at equity or law for rescission and restitution, or "passively," as a defense to a suit for breach of contract.

In some jurisdictions, including the District of Columbia, recipients of innocent material misrepresentations may, under certain circumstances, choose between the mutually exclusive options of rescission of the contract accompanied by restoration of the parties to the *status quo ante,* and a cause of action for damages in tort. . . . *Dresser v. Sunderland Apartment Tenants Ass'n,* 465 A.2d 835, 840 (D.C.1983); *Kent Homes, Inc. v. Frankel,* 128 A.2d 444, 445 (D.C.1957); . . . Restatement (Second), *supra* note 25, at 425. . . . [U]nder certain circumstances, tort liability for honest material misrepresentation may lie: *Isen v. Calvert Corp.,* 379 F.2d 126 (D.C.Cir.1967); *Darnell v. Darnell,* 200 F.2d 747 (D.C.Cir.1952); *Stein v. Treger,* 182 F.2d 696 (D.C.Cir.1950). *See generally* Hill, *Damages for Innocent Misrepresentation,* 73 Colum.L.Rev. 677, 747 (1973) (concluding that the jurisdictions that recognize tort liability for innocent misrepresentations remain a minority).

Take Note!

As the court notes, a misrepresentation that induced contract formation can, in some fact situations, be a tort that results in damages, and it can be a contract defense that results in rescission of the contract. The recipient of the misrepresentation cannot "have it both ways" and therefore must elect between the tort and contract remedies.

---

[25] *See, e.g., Lockwood v. Christakos,* 181 F.2d 805, 807 (D.C.Cir.1950); . . . E. Farnsworth, Contracts § 4.12, At 242 (1982); Restatement (Second) of Contracts § 164 and comment b (1981) . . . .

[26] James & Gray, Misrepresentation—Part II, 37 Md.L.Rev. 488, 534 (1978).

[28] James & Gray, *supra* note 26, at 535.

. . . [F]our conditions must be met before a contract may be avoided for innocent misrepresentation. The recipient of the alleged misrepresentation must demonstrate that the maker made an assertion: (1) that was not in accord with the facts, (2) that was material, and (3) that was relied upon (4) justifiably by the recipient in manifesting his assent to the agreement.[30] District of Columbia law adds a fifth condition, *i.e.,* that the recipient relied to his detriment.[31]

Unfortunately, the applicable precedent does not elaborate on the meaning of these conditions. In trying to give them content, we have found that the *Restatement (Second) of Contracts . . .* provides helpful guidance concerning the first four conditions.

1. *Misrepresentation*

Section 159 of the *Restatement (Second)* defines a misrepresentation as "an assertion that is not in accord with the facts." Comment c explains that an "assertion must relate to something that is a fact at the time the assertion is made in order to be a misrepresentation. Such facts include past events as well as present circumstances but do not include future events." Comment d observes that a person's state of mind is a fact and that an assertion of one's opinion constitutes a misrepresentation if the state of mind is other than as asserted.

According to section 161, the only non-disclosures that may be considered assertions of fact for purposes of misrepresentation analysis[34] are non-disclosures of facts known to the maker where the maker knows that disclosure: (a) is necessary to prevent a previous assertion from being a misrepresentation or from being fraudulent or material, (b) would correct a mistake of the other party as to a basic assumption on which that party is making the contract, if non-disclosure amounts to a failure to act in good faith and in accordance with reasonable standards of fair dealing, or (c) would correct a mistake of the other party as to the contents or effect of a writing. The section also provides that where the other person is entitled to know the non-disclosed facts because a relation of trust and confidence exists between the parties, non-disclosure is equivalent to an assertion of facts.

2. *Materiality*

In section 162, comment c, the *Restatement (Second)* explains that a misrepresentation is material "if it would be likely to induce a reasonable person to manifest his assent." The court in *Cousineau v. Walker* elaborated on the material-

---

[30] *See, e.g., Lockwood,* 181 F.2d at 807; *Cousineau,* 613 P.2d at 612; *Notte,* 97 Wis.2d at 222, 293 N.W.2d at 538; E. Farnsworth, *supra* note 25, § 4.10, at 236; Restatement (Second), *supra* note 25, § 164(1) and comment a.

[31] *Lockwood,* 181 F.2d at 807; *see also* E. Farnsworth, *supra* note 25, § 4.13, at 245-46.

[34] The *Restatement (Second)* distinguishes between nondisclosures, § 161 and comment a, and actions that are equivalent to assertions (concealment), § 160.

ity requirement, noting that it is a mixed question of law and fact that asks whether the assertion is one to which a reasonable person might be expected to attach importance in making a choice of action.[35] A material fact is one that could reasonably be expected to influence a person's judgment or conduct concerning a transaction.[36]

Take Note!

This court's definition of materiality is not the only one used. Other courts have defined a misrepresentation as material if it affects the purpose of the contract, if it substantially adds to the supposed value of the contract for the other party, or if the party would not have assented to the contract without it.

The justification for the materiality requirement is that it is believed to encourage stability in contract relations. It prevents parties who become disappointed at the outcome of their bargain from seizing upon any insignificant discrepancy to void the contract.

3. Reliance

Section 167 requires that the misrepresentation be causally related to the recipient's decision to agree to the contract—that it have been an inducement to agree. Inducement, as comment a explains, is shown through actual reliance. Comment a goes on to state that this reliance need not, however, be the sole or predominant factor influencing the recipient's decision. Comment b indicates that circumstantial evidence is often important in determining whether there was actual reliance.

4. *Justifiability of Reliance*

Section 172 of the *Restatement (Second)* provides that a recipient's fault in not knowing or discovering the facts before making the contract does not make his reliance unjustified unless it amounts to a failure to act in good faith and in accordance with reasonable standards of fair dealing.

While section 169 suggests that reliance on an assertion of opinion often is not justified, section 168(2) and the accompanying comment d make clear that in some situations the recipient may reasonably understand a statement of opinion to be more than an assertion as to the maker's state of mind. Where circumstances justify it, a statement of opinion may also be reasonably understood as carrying with it an assertion that the maker knows facts sufficient to justify him in forming it.[40]

---

[35] 613 P.2d at 613.

[36] *Id.; see also Homelite v. Trywilk Realty Co.,* 272 F.2d 688, 691 (4th Cir. 1959).

[40] *See, e.g., Johnson v. Healy,* 176 Conn. 97, 101, 405 A.2d 54, 57 (1978) (finding that assertion by builder that there was "nothing wrong" with the house could reasonably have been understood by the buyer to be an assertion that the builder had sufficient factual information to justify his opinion and finding that, in context, this assertion could reasonably have induced reliance) . . . .

5. *Detriment*

Because the *Restatement (Second)* does not require a showing of detriment for rescission, it does not define it. We think that, in the innocent material misrepresentation context, a recipient is appropriately considered to have relied to his detriment where he receives something that is less valuable or different in some significant respect from that which he reasonably expected.[42]

C. *Application of Legal Standards*

Application of the foregoing principles to the facts of this case requires that the case be remanded for trial. The magistrate tested Barrer's alleged misrepresentations against only two of the five elements necessary for rescission—he asked only if the representations were in accord with the facts and if they were material. In making this inquiry, the magistrate failed to consider the legal distinctions between assertions of fact and nondisclosure and between assertions of fact and statements of opinion. He neglected to investigate whether the Bank actually relied on the representations in deciding to make the loan; whether that reliance, if it existed, was justifiable; and whether the Bank relied to its detriment. Furthermore, the magistrate incorrectly concluded that there were no legally probative, material issues of fact in dispute.

trial court ignored 3 elements

1. *Elements the Magistrate Failed to Consider*

Initially, assuming for a moment that Barrer actually "misrepresented" certain facts, the materiality of the representations is hardly obvious. After deciding which representations meet the legal definition of misrepresentation, the trial court must determine with regard to each individual misrepresentation whether it was "likely to induce a reasonable [bank] to manifest [its] assent"[43] to the loan agreement. If no single misrepresentation is found to be material, the court may consider, after ascertaining the assertions upon which WNB justifiably relied, whether those assertions are material when taken together.

Think About It!

If a nondisclosure is the basis for a claim of misrepresentation, what does it mean to say that the other party "relied" on that misrepresentation? How can someone rely on silence?

All five alleged "misrepresentations" also raise serious factual questions as to whether the Bank actually and justifiably relied on them. Womack's expressed sympathy for Barrer combined with the fact that the loan was issued in a very short time, without either a credit check, which was obtainable in minutes, or an inquiry

---

[42] *See, e.g.,* E. Farnsworth, *supra* note 25, § 4.13, at 245-46; McCleary, *Damage as Requisite to Rescission for Misrepresentation: II,* 36 Mich.L.Rev. 227, 227-44 (1937).

[43] Restatement (Second), *supra* note 25, § 162 comment c.

into the status of Barrer's mortgage, and the fact that the loan was withdrawn only when the Bank was placed in an embarrassing position by the tax sale purchaser—all these circumstances could suggest that the Bank was not very interested in the particulars of Barrer's financial condition. Indeed, it was clear from the loan application that Barrer did admit that he was experiencing financial difficulties, yet WNB chose to make no further inquiry into the details of these problems. These facts could be construed to show that Womack's sympathy for Barrer's predicament was the real inducement for the loan. If the trial court finds that the Bank actually relied on Barrer's alleged "misrepresentations," it nonetheless must proceed to decide whether that reliance was justified.

The trial court must also determine whether the Bank's reliance on Barrer's alleged "misrepresentations" caused it any detriment. Did WNB receive as its benefit of the bargain something less valuable or significantly different from what it reasonably expected? In addition, the trial court should consider whether the subordination agreement, in combination with the right to a security interest in Barrer's house granted by the collateral note, fully satisfied the Bank's expectations.

The magistrate also made individual errors with respect to the five representations. These errors are outlined below.

2. Delinquency in Mortgage Payments

Barrer and Womack disagree over whether he told her that he "thought" he was two months behind in his mortgage payments or whether he said that he was current. Because this case is before us on appeal from the magistrate's grant of summary judgment for the Bank, we must accept Barrer's statement of the facts. The Bank argues that even if Barrer's version is accepted, a misrepresentation still occurred because Barrer was actually six months behind. The Bank's position is not necessarily correct.

Barrer's statement that he "thought" he was in arrears by two months initially raises the factual question whether he made *any* misrepresentation. On the surface, the fact asserted by Barrer was his state of mind—what he thought. No finding was made below that Barrer's state of mind was other than what he declared. On remand, before it may determine that this statement constituted a misrepresentation, the court must find either that Barrer misstated his thoughts, in accordance with the rule laid out in section 159, comment d of the *Restatement (Second)*, or that Barrer's statement could reasonably have been understood as carrying with it an assertion that Barrer knew sufficient facts that justified him in forming his opinion, in accordance with section 168(2).

When evaluating the materiality of this particular representation, the court should keep in mind the concession made by WNB's counsel at oral argument—

that by itself this representation might not be sufficient to justify summary judgment.

3. Failure to Disclose Mortgage Foreclosure Proceedings

Although the Bank evidently did not ask Barrer directly whether his mortgage was being foreclosed upon, it contends that he had an obligation to volunteer that information and that his failure to do so is tantamount to a misrepresentation. Barrer argues that he had no duty to reveal the existence of the foreclosure proceedings because he did not know about them. The Bank maintains that he must have known, because before Barrer applied for the loan his teen-age daughter signed for a certified letter from Columbia notifying him of the foreclosure.

The magistrate erred in finding on summary judgment that this non-disclosure is equivalent to a misrepresentation. The *Restatement (Second)* provides that a non-disclosure may be considered an assertion of fact for purposes of misrepresentation analysis only if the non-disclosed fact is *known*[46] to the maker and if certain other conditions are met. Because there exists a material issue of fact as to whether Barrer knew that Columbia had begun to foreclose, summary judgment was inappropriate.

4. $11,000 Contingent Liability

The magistrate also erred in finding on summary judgment that Barrer's alleged failure to list as a personal contingent liability an $11,000 tax debt owed to the IRS by his corporation constituted a misrepresentation. First, summary judgment is precluded by the existence of a factual dispute over whether this $11,000 was included in the $38,000 tax liability that Barrer did list. Barrer seems to contend that at least some of this amount was included in the $38,000 figure; the Bank seems to dispute this contention. Second, there is a mixed question of law and fact as to whether the IRS had, at the time of the loan application, taken any action to assert the $11,000 tax debt owed by Today News Service, Inc., against Barrer personally and, if not, whether the corporation's liability may be considered Barrer's contingent liability. If the $11,000 tax debt could not at that time have been considered Barrer's liability, his failure to list such a debt was not a misrepresentation.[48]

---

[46] We do not consider the presumption of knowledge of the truth about one's own business or property that this court has employed in actions for damages caused by material misrepresentations, *see Isen*, 379 F.2d at 129-30; *Darnell*, 200 F.2d at 748, to be pertinent to *non-disclosures*. Where non-disclosure is alleged to constitute a misrepresentation, actual knowledge of the non-disclosed fact must be demonstrated.

[48] According to the *Restatement (Second)*, a misrepresentation includes past and present events, but not future ones. *See* § 159 comment c.

5. $5,300 Debt Owed to IBM

The magistrate found that Barrer's failure to reveal as a personal liability a $5,300 debt owed to IBM for equipment purchased by his wife was a misrepresentation. We disagree as a matter of law. Although Barrer asked the probate court handling his wife's estate to charge him with the debt, the court refused, ruling that the debt was hers alone. Contrary to the Bank's protestations, it makes no difference to the determination whether a misrepresentation occurred that Barrer asked the probate court to charge him with the debt before, and the court refused after, Barrer submitted the loan application. A misrepresentation is "an assertion that is not in accord with the facts."[49] The fact is that a court decided that this debt *never* legally belonged to Barrer. Barrer's thoughts or wishes on the matter are irrelevant. He made no legal misrepresentation to the Bank on this subject.

6. $1,500 in Judgments

Finally, the magistrate determined that Barrer's failure to list $1,500 in judgments that were outstanding against him constituted a misrepresentation. This issue should not have been resolved on summary judgment. Barrer disclosed on the loan application that he was a defendant in some lawsuits. Furthermore, in his deposition he stated that he had informed Womack that he owed some small judgments arising out of these suits and that he expected his health insurance to cover most of them. Accepting Barrer's version of the facts, as we must in reviewing a grant of summary judgment, he revealed both his defendant status and the existence of judgments against him. It is true that he did not list them on the application form. Because, however, Barrer contends that he adequately disclosed these debts in connection with the question concerning lawsuits and in his discussion with Womack, there exists a dispute over whether he actually revealed these debts; consequently the magistrate should not have resolved this issue on summary judgment. On remand, two factual questions must be decided. First, what information concerning these judgments did Barrer give to Womack? Second, was that information sufficient to give the Bank notice of them?[52] If it was sufficient, then Barrer made no misrepresentation.

III. CONCLUSION

The magistrate both failed to utilize the correct legal test for determining when an innocent material misrepresentation permits the rescission of a contract

---

[49] Restatement (Second), *supra* note 25, § 159.

[52] We note that, as counsel for the Bank conceded at oral argument, Barrer was not represented by an attorney when he filled out the loan application or when he discussed it with Womack. In considering whether adequate notice was given, it should be kept in mind that a layman might not appreciate the distinction urged by the bank between being a defendant in an ongoing lawsuit and having a judgment entered against one. The substance of the information concerning the judgment debts should therefore be given greater weight than its form.

and to recognize that this case presents disputed material issues of fact that render summary judgment inappropriate. We reverse and remand for further proceedings consistent with this opinion.

[handwritten margin note: sum judge not good — must litigate]

Reading the Law Critically:
Misrepresentation under the Restatement (Second)

The Restatement (Second) sections below all appear in *Barrer* and appear again here as a convenient reference.

1. The *Barrer* court focused on whether the misrepresentation was material. Alternatively, the court could have looked at whether the misrepresentation was fraudulent. What kind of evidence would have been necessary in *Barrer* to establish that the misrepresentation was fraudulent under the Restatement (Second) definition?

2. Which kind of misrepresentation—fraudulent or material—do you suppose is proven more often? Why?

Restatement (Second) § 159. **Misrepresentation Defined**

A misrepresentation is an assertion that is not in accord with the facts.

Restatement (Second) § 161. **When Non-Disclosure is Equivalent to an Assertion**

A person's non-disclosure of a fact known to him is equivalent to an assertion that the fact does not exist in the following cases:

(a) where he knows that disclosure of the fact is necessary to prevent some previous assertion from being a misrepresentation or from being fraudulent or material.
(b) where he knows that disclosure of the fact would correct a mistake of the other party as to a basic assumption on which that party is making the contract and if non-disclosure of the fact amounts to a failure to act in good faith and in accordance with reasonable standards of fair dealing.
(c) where he knows that disclosure of the fact would correct a mistake of the other party as to the contents or effect of a writing, evidencing or embodying an agreement in whole or in part.
(d) where the other person is entitled to know the fact because of a relation or trust and confidence between them.

Restatement (Second) § 162. **When a Misrepresentation is Fraudulent or Material**

(1) A misrepresentation is fraudulent if the maker intends his assertion to induce a party to manifest his assent and the maker
  (a) knows or believes that the assertion is not in accord with the facts, or
  (b) does not have the confidence that he states or implies in the truth of the assertion, or
  (c) knows that he does not have the basis that he states or implies for the assertion.
(2) A misrepresentation is material if it would be likely to induce a reasonable person to manifest his assent, or if the maker knows that it would be likely to induce the recipient to do so

Restatement (Second) § 167. **When a Misrepresentation is an Inducing Cause**

A misrepresentation induces a party's manifestation of assent if it substantially contributes to his decision to manifest his assent.

Restatement (Second) § 168. **Reliance on Assertions of Opinion**

(1) An assertion is one of opinion if it expresses only a belief, without certainty, as to the existence of a fact or expresses only a judgment as to quality, value, authenticity, or similar matters..
(2) If it is reasonable to do so, the recipient of an assertion of a person's opinion as to facts not disclosed and not otherwise known to the recipient may properly interpret it as an assertion
  (a) that the facts known to that person are not incompatible with his opinion, or
  (b) that he knows facts sufficient to justify him in forming it.

Restatement (Second) § 169. **When Reliance on a Assertion of Opinion is Not Justified**

To the extent that an assertion is one of opinion only, the recipient is not justified in relying on it unless the recipient
  (a) stands in such a relation of trust and confidence to the person whose opinion is asserted that the recipient is reasonable in relying on it, or
  (b) reasonably believes that, as compared with himself, the person whose opinion is asserted has special skill, judgment or objectivity with respect to the subject matter, or
  (c) is for some other special reason particularly susceptible to a misrepresentation of the type involved.

> Restatement (Second) § 172. **When Fault Makes Reliance Unjustified**
>
> A recipient's fault in not knowing or discovering the facts before making the contract does not make his reliance unjustified unless it amounts to a failure to act in good faith and in accordance with reasonable standards of fair dealing.

recipient should also check some facts

Kannavos v. Annino

APOSTOLOS C. KANNAVOS and JOHN G. BELLAS, Plaintiffs-Respondents

v.

CARRIE L. ANNINO, JOSEPH SANTOSPIRITO and SAMUEL V. ANNINO, III, individually and as trustees of ANNINO REALTY TRUST, Defendants-Appellants

APOSTOLOS C. KANNAVOS and his wife, Plaintiffs

v.

CARRIE L. ANNINO, JOSEPH SANTOSPIRITO and SAMUEL V. ANNINO, III, individually and as trustees of ANNINO REALTY TRUST, Defendants

Supreme Judicial Court of Massachusetts

247 N.E.2d 708 (Mass. 1969)

CUTTER, Justice.

These bills in equity are brought by the vendees of real estate, fixtures, and personal property in Ingersoll Grove, Springfield, against the vendors, to rescind the purchases made in 1965. The amended bills alleged that the vendees bought in reliance on the vendors' fraudulent misrepresentations and concealment of material facts. Demurrers to the amended bills were overruled. The facts are stated on the basis of a confirmed master's report. By final decree rescission of the purchases was ordered. The vendors appealed.

rescind granted

What's That?

Under Massachusetts law, the "master's report" is a recommendation to a trial judge as to how a case should be decided. If acceptable to the trial judge, the master's report is "confirmed" and may then be appealed, as happened in this case. The quotations in the opinion's statement of facts appear to be from the master's report.

Kannavos and his wife acquired 11 Ingersoll Grove from the vendors (who are the trustees of Annino Realty Trust) on June 28, 1965. Kannavos and Bellas bought 71-73 and 79 Ingersoll Grove from the vendors on July 12, 1965. The situation as to each purchase is substantially the same.[2]

---

[2] The purchasers, for convenience, are referred to, for the most part, merely as the vendees, without regard to the circumstance that Kannavos had a different associate in each transaction.

Mrs. Annino (who at all pertinent times "was authorized to act and did act on behalf of . . . Annino Realty Trust") had bought the Ingersoll Grove properties in 1961 and 1962. At that time there was a single family house on each property. Each house was, under the Springfield zoning ordinance, in a Residence A district, where multi-family uses are prohibited. This zoning has remained in effect at all times since 1961. Despite the zoning provisions, Mrs. Annino converted each single family house into a multi-family apartment building. Each was furnished and rented as a multi-family dwelling. All the work of conversion was done "without obtaining any building permit," as each trustee of the realty trust knew. Each trustee also knew that the use of the buildings for multi-family purposes was in violation of the zoning ordinance.

In 1965 Kenneth F. Foote was retained as real estate broker "to try to sell the properties." He caused advertisements, of which the following is an example, to appear in Springfield newspapers: "Income gross $9,600 yr. in lg. single house, converted to 8 lovely, completely furn. (includ. TV and china) apts. 8 baths, ideal for couple to live free with excellent income. By apt. only. Foote Realty." Each advertisement clearly advertised, in some form of words, the particular property as being income property of multi-family use.

Kannavos, a self-employed hairdresser, about thirty-eight years old,[4] read one advertisement. He "wanted to acquire some income real estate." He got in touch with Foote, who showed him the 11 Ingersoll Grove property and gave him income and expense figures obtained from Mrs. Annino. Kannavos executed a purchase agreement to buy 11 Ingersoll Grove. The vendees had no lawyer representing them with respect to the negotiations, the agreement, or the final closing. An attorney representing a mortgagee, under a mortgage obtained by the vendees, drew and recorded the papers used at the closing, at which the vendors were also represented by an attorney "to check the adjustments."

"No statements were made by the . . . [vendors], by . . . Foote . . . (or by either attorney) at any time during the negotiations or closing, to the . . . [vendees] with respect to zoning or building permits. The . . . [vendees] made no inquiry of the" vendors, Foote, or the vendors' "attorney at any

Think About It!

Why does the court note the plaintiffs' jobs, educations, English proficiencies, immigrant backgrounds, and lack of real estate experience? How are these facts relevant to this decision?

---

[4] He had come to the United States in 1957 from Greece where he had received the equivalent of a high school education. He learned to speak, read, and write English after coming to the United States. Bellas, who was associated with Kannavos in the purchase of 71-73 and 79 Ingersoll Grove was about thirty years old. He was a produce manager in a chain grocery store, who came to the United States in 1955 and learned to read and write English at night school. He also had received the equivalent of a high school education in Greece. He had no previous experience in real estate before these events.

time before or during the closing with respect to zoning or building permits. All statements made by the" vendors, Foote, or the vendors' attorney to the vendees "were substantially true and the . . . [vendees] do not complain of any spoken misrepresentation."

Mrs. Annino and Foote both represented to the vendees "that the property . . . consisted of eight . . . furnished apartments which were being rented to the public for multi-family purposes. They knew that Kannavos' reason for buying the property was to rent the apartments to the public. . . . Kannavos had no prior experience with real estate. He was unaware of any zoning or building permit violation and would not have purchased the property if he had known of any such violation."

The sale of the other properties [71-73 and 79 Ingersoll Grove] occurred in substantially similar circumstances. Discussion of other property owned by the vendors stated shortly before Kannavos acquired 11 Ingersoll Grove. The vendees saw an advertisement of the houses at 71-73 and 79 Ingersoll Grove in July, 1965, and then went to see them. Mrs. Annino and Foote "represented to . . . Kannavos and Bellas, that the property [71-73 and 79 Ingersoll Grove] was rented as multi-dwelling property and that Bellas and Kannavos could continue to operate it as multi-dwelling property. The . . . [vendees] continued to operate the buildings as multi-dwelling property up to and including the date of the hearing. The operation showed a profit . . . ." The vendors represented to Bellas that "71-73 [and] 79 Ingersoll Grove would be a good investment for him as rental multi-family real estate."

"By . . . registered letters dated July 26, 1965 . . . the city . . . notified Bellas and Kannavos with respect to . . . 79 Ingersoll Grove that the property was being used for multi-family purposes in violation of the building code and zoning ordinance . . . that the wiring was illegal and should be corrected by a licensed electrician with a valid building permit . . . and that the plumbing was in violation of the building code and should be corrected by a licensed plumber with a valid building permit . . . . By three registered letters of July 26, 1965 with respect to . . . 71-73 Ingersoll Grove, Bellas and Kannavos were notified by the Building Commissioner . . . of the same violations of zoning, wiring, and plumbing."

The two groups of vendees "had no actual knowledge of the zoning or building code violations until . . . notified" by the city authorities. The vendees promptly through their attorney "notified the . . . [vendors] of the rescission of" each sale.

"Each property is worth substantially less if operated only as a single family dwelling instead of [as] a multi-family dwelling." The city has started civil proceedings "to abate the use of each property as [a] multi-family" dwelling.

From his subsidiary findings summarized above the master concluded, among other things, that the vendors made no actual spoken misrepresentations; that they "intentionally withheld" from the vendees that the operation of the buildings "was in violation of the zoning ordinance"; that the vendors "represented . . . that the buildings . . . were being used as multi-family dwellings and . . . in each case that the . . . [vendees] could continue" so to operate them; and that the vendees "would not have bought the real estate if . . . [they] had known of the violations of the zoning ordinance, or the building code." He also concluded that the vendees "relied upon representations of the . . . [vendors] and the appearances of the real estate in that it was being used for multi-family purposes" and that they "made no independent inquiry concerning any violation of the zoning ordinance or building code."[5]

never asked about zoning

From the master's subsidiary findings, we draw our own conclusions. See Samia v. Central Oil Co., 339 Mass. 101, 122, 158 N.E.2d 469; Corrigan v. O'Brien, 353 Mass. 341, 345-346, 231 N.E.2d 554. These sub-

> ### Think About It!
>
> Why did the master draw alternative conclusions (see footnote 5)?

sidiary findings are amplified in minor respects by the master's conclusions just summarized which expressly are based upon his subsidiary findings.

1. We assume that, if the vendors had been wholly silent and had made no references whatsoever to the use of the Ingersoll Grove houses, they could not have been found to have made any misrepresentation. See Swinton v. Whitinsville Sav. Bank, 311 Mass. 677, 678-679, 42 N.E.2d 808, 141 A.L.R. 965,[6] where this court affirmed an order sustaining a demurrer to a declaration in an action of tort brought by a purchaser of a house. The seller knew that the house was infested with termites and remained silent. This court (per Qua, J. at p. 678) said, "There is no allegation of any false statement or representation, or of the uttering of a half truth which may be tantamount to a falsehood. There is no intimation that the defendant by any means prevented the plaintiff from acquiring information as to the condition of the house. There is nothing to show any fiduciary relation between the parties, or that the plaintiff stood in a position of con-

---

[5] The master's ultimate conclusions were expressed in the alternative, viz. if the vendors' silence in "the circumstances constitute[s] an actionable misrepresentation and if" the vendees properly could rely on such misrepresentation, then the vendees are entitled to rescission; but, if the vendors' silence did "not constitute an actionable misrepresentation, or if" the vendees could not properly rely on the "misrepresentation by silence," then rescission could not be allowed.

[6] The Swinton case may not represent the law elsewhere. See Restatement 2d: Torts, § 551 (Tent. draft No. 11, April 15, 1965), p. 43; Prosser, Torts (3d ed.), § 101, p. 711. Cf. discussions of situations in landlord and tenant cases like Cutter v. Hamlen, 147 Mass. 471, 474, 18 N.E. 397, 1 L.R.A. 429; Stumpf v. Leland, 242 Mass. 168, 172-174, 136 N.E. 399; Cooper v. Boston Housing Authy., 342 Mass. 38, 40, 172 N.E.2d 117. For general consideration of silence as misrepresentation, see Restatement: Restitution, § 8; Williston, Contracts (2d ed.) § 1497.

fidence toward or dependence upon the defendant. So far as appears the parties made a business deal at arm's length. The charge is concealment and nothing more; and it is concealment in the simple sense of mere failure to reveal, with nothing to show any peculiar duty to speak." The court (p. 679) indicated that it was applying a long standing "rule of nonliability for bare nondisclosure" (emphasis supplied).

As in the Swinton case, the parties here were dealing at arm's length, the vendees were in no way prevented from acquiring information, and the vendors stood in no fiduciary relationship to the vendees. In two aspects, however, the present cases differ from the Swinton case: viz. (a) The vendees themselves could have found out about the zoning violations by inquiry through public records, whereas in the Swinton case the purchaser would have probably discovered the presence of termites only by retaining expert investigators; and (b) there was something more here than the "bare nondisclosure" of the seller in the Swinton case.

(a) We deal first with the affirmative actions by the vendors, their conduct, advertising, and statements. Was enough said and done by the vendors so that they were bound to disclose more to avoid deception of the vendees and reliance by them upon a half truth? In other words, did the statements made by the vendors in their advertising and otherwise take the cases out of the "rule of nonliability for bare nondisclosure" applied in the Swinton case?

Take Note!

As Professor Farnsworth observed, "Courts have had great difficulty in dealing with the extent to which candor, as opposed to honesty, is required." In a 1817 case, a buyer bought a large quantity of tobacco immediately after hearing that a shipping blockade had been ended by the signing of a treaty (ending the War of 1812 and the British blockade of New Orleans). The seller didn't hear about the treaty until later, when the news was made more public. When the price of tobacco subsequently increased by 30-50%, the seller sought to rescind the contract for fraud. The case eventually came before the U.S. Supreme Court, where Justice Marshall, in dictum, said that the buyer had no duty to disclose the treaty to the seller.* Subsequent cases have had difficulty in defining the extent to which a party is expected to share its own separately acquired information with the other party, if the first party knows that the other party is laboring under a misapprehension material to the contract, even though the first party didn't contribute to that misapprehension. The easier cases have involved houses infested with termites, where an increasing number of courts have held that failure to disclose this fact amounts to an assertion that the house is termite-free. However, the *Swinton* case discussed here held to the contrary. *The* gradual trend in the case law is to recognize liability for some types of non-disclosures. See footnote 6.

---

* See E. Allan Farnsworth, *Contracts* § 4.11 (4th ed. 2004) (discussing *Laidlaw v. Organ*, 15 U.S. 178, 195 (1817)).

Although there may be "no duty imposed upon one party to a transaction to speak for the information of the other . . . if he does speak with reference to a given point of information, voluntarily or at the other's request, he is bound to speak honestly and to divulge all the material facts bearing upon the point that lie within his knowledge. Fragmentary information may be as misleading . . . as active misrepresentation, and half-truths may be as actionable as whole lies . . . " See Harper & James, Torts, § 7.14. See also Restatement: Torts, § 529; Williston, Contracts (2d ed.) §§ 1497-1499. The existence of substantially this principle was assumed in the Swinton case, 311 Mass. 677, 678, 42 N.E.2d 808, 141 A.L.R. 965, in the first sentence of the passage from that case quoted above. Massachusetts decisions have applied this principle. See Kidney v. Stoddard, 7 Metc. 252, 254-255 (a father represented that his son was entitled to credit but failed to disclose that the son was a minor; statement treated as a fraudulent representation); Burns v. Dockray, 156 Mass. 135, 137, 30 N.E. 551 (assertion that title was good (see Lyman v. Romboli, 293 Mass. 373, 374, 199 N.E. 916) but omitting to refer to the possible insanity of one whose incompetence might cloud title); Van Houten v. Morse, 162 Mass. 414, 417-419, 38 N.E. 705, 26 L.R.A. 430 (partial disclosure by a woman to her fiance about a prior divorce. See also . . . Boston Five Cents Sav. Bank v. Brooks, 309 Mass. 52, 55-56, 34 N.E.2d 435, 437 ("Deception need not be direct . . . Declarations and conduct calculated to mislead . . . which . . . do mislead one . . . acting reasonably are enough to constitute fraud"). Cf. Wade v. Ford Motor Co., 341 Mass. 596, 597-598, 171 N.E.2d 282.

The master's report provides ample basis for treating the present cases as within the decisions just cited. The original advertisements in effect offered the houses as investment properties and referred to them as single houses converted to apartments. The investment aspect of the houses was emphasized by Foote's action in furnishing income and expense figures. There was an express assertion that 11 Ingersoll Grove was "being rented to the public for multi-family purposes" and that Kannavos and Bellas "could continue to operate . . . (the other properties) as multi-dwelling property." The master's conclusions indicate that this statement applied to all the properties.[7] The buildings were divided into apartments. The sales included refrigerators, stoves, and other furnishings appropriate for apartment use, as well as real estate. The vendors knew that the vendees were planning

> **Think About It!**
>
> What definition does the court use in holding that the disclosure here was "fraudulent"? In some jurisdictions, a misrepresentation must be either fraudulent or material, but need not be both. Restatement (Second) § 162 (page 476) defines both. Could the *Kannavos* court have alternatively held that the misrepresentation was material? What facts would have been pertinent to this determination?

---

[7] In any event some discussions with respect to all these properties in the same neighborhood were going on about the same time and the later transaction appears to have been commenced either before or about the time the earlier one was completed.

to continue to use the buildings for apartments, and yet the vendors still failed to disclose the zoning and building violations. We conclude that enough was done affirmatively to make the disclosure inadequate and partial, and, in the circumstances, intentionally deceptive and fraudulent.

(b) The second difference between these cases and the Swinton case is the character of the defect not disclosed.

In the Swinton case, the presence of predatory insects threatened the structure sold. In the absence of any seller's representations whatsoever, there was no duty to disclose this circumstance, even though doubtless it would have been difficult to discover. In the present cases, the defect in the premises related to a matter of public regulation, the zoning and building ordinances. Its applicability to these premises could have been discovered by these vendees or by the vendees' counsel if, acting with prudence, they had retained counsel, which they did not. The bank mortgagee's counsel presumably was looking only to the protection of the bank's security position. Nevertheless, where there is reliance on fraudulent representations or upon statements and action treated as fraudulent, our cases have not barred plaintiffs from recovery merely because they "did not use due diligence . . . [when they] could readily have ascertained from . . . records" what the true facts were. See Yorke v. Taylor, 332 Mass. 368, 373, 124 N.E.2d 912. There this court allowed rescission because of the negligent misrepresentation, innocent but false, of the current assessed value of the property being sold. Here the representations made by the advertising and the vendors' conduct and statements in effect were that the property was multi-family housing suitable for investment and that the housing could continue to be used for that purpose. Because the vendors did as much as they did do, they were bound to do more. Failing to do so, they were responsible for misrepresentation. We think the situation is comparable to that in Yorke v. Taylor, 332 Mass. 368, 374, 124 N.E.2d 912, even though there the misrepresentation was "not consciously false" and here it was by half truth.

We hold that the vendors' conduct entitled the vendees to rescind. See Yorke v. Taylor, 332 Mass. 368, 371-372, 374, 124 N.E.2d 912; Restatement: Contracts, §§ 472, 489; Restatement: Restitution, § 28; Williston, Contracts (2d ed.) §§ 1497-1500. There was, in our opinion, much more than "bare nondisclosure" as in the Swinton case. Cf. Spencer v. Gabriel, 328 Mass. 1, 2, 101 N.E.2d 369; Donahue v. Stephens, 342 Mass. 89, 92, 172 N.E.2d 101.

. . . .

. . . . The cases are remanded to the Superior Court for further proceedings consistent with this opinion.

So ordered.

Problems: The Misrepresentation Defense

As you saw in *Barrer* and *Kannavos*, liability for misrepresentation depends on (a) the nature of the misrepresentation, (b) the importance of the misrepresented fact and its effect on assent, (c) the state of mind of the person making the alleged misrepresentation, and (d) whether reliance on the misrepresentation was reasonable. Consider how those factors would affect the outcomes in the circumstances below. If you think there was a misrepresentation in fact, what was it? If the result of liability is uncertain, pinpoint the key points of contention and articulate the arguments each party would make. Also consider whether these circumstances could constitute "puffing," discussed on page 461.

5-8. Buyers entered into negotiations to purchase a resort facility. During the negotiations, sellers told buyers the resort was making "good money" and that the profits would enable buyers to easily make the future payments on the purchase contract. Before signing the purchase agreement, buyers asked several times to be shown the operations records for the resort, but the sellers delayed and made excuses. After the parties signed the purchase agreement, the buyers got access to the records, which showed that the resort had lost money in two of the last four years. Can the buyers rescind the purchase agreement on the grounds of misrepresentation? *yes, actively concealing no, should have pressed*

5-9. Bekko negotiated with Garfield to design a new home on a lake. Garfield told Bekko that he had designed a number of homes on that lake and that there should be no problem building within 50 feet of the shoreline. The parties then entered into a written contract to have the design work completed. After Garfield completed the preliminary design, Bekko submitted it to the city for approval and was informed that the home could not be built within 75 feet of the shoreline. The lot was not large enough for the design to be set back another 25 feet, so the entire project was scrapped. Garfield sued to get payment for the work done before the project was cancelled. Can Bekko rescind the contract based on misrepresentation?

5-10. An elderly woman purchased a home after the sellers told her the house was in good condition and was great for an "elderly lady living alone." The sellers did not tell her that a woman and her four children had been murdered in the house ten years earlier, something well known in the neighborhood. After she purchased the house, one of her new neighbors told her about the crime and also that the sellers had asked her not to mention anything about the murders if she ran into anyone viewing the house. Can the purchaser rescind the sales contract on the grounds of misrepresentation? Would the outcome be different if the sellers did not ask the neighbors "not to tell"?

5-11. Why was the misrepresentation or fraud defense unsuccessful in the two cases on mutual mistake—*Wood v. Boynton* (page 433) and *Lenawee County Board of Health v. Messerly* (page 438)?

§ 2.3. Duress and Undue Influence

The defenses of duress and undue influence apply when a party was forced or coerced into agreeing to enter a contract so that his apparent assent was not truly voluntary. The defense of duress is based on a claim that agreement was *compelled* by threats or other forms of pressure, while the defense of undue influence is based on claims that the other party obtained assent by *coercing* agreement through abuse of a relationship of trust and dependence.

§ 2.3.1. Duress

Although the duress defense originally required physical compulsion or an unlawful threat of death or bodily harm, it has been broadened so that a variety of threats may suffice—threats of criminal prosecution, sometimes even threats of civil process, threats to withhold goods, and other threats to a person's proprietary or business interests (also known as "economic duress"). Courts have granted the duress defense in a wide range of settings. For example:

- In *Astley v. Reynolds*, 93 Eng. Rep. 939 (K.B. 1732), the court held that duress occurred when a pawn shop retained a pawned plate in order to induce the true owner to pay excess interest.

- In *Rubenstein v. Rubenstein*, 120 A.2d 11 (N.J. 1956), the court held that "a compulsive yielding . . . , rather than the volitional act of a free mind . . ." resulted from threats of gangster violence and poisoning, which induced the conveyance of property.
- In *Wise v. Midtown Motors*, 42 N.W.2d 404 (Minn. 1950), the court stated that freedom of choice was eliminated when the threat of unfounded legal claims and loss of employment was used to compel settlement of an adverse claim.
- In *Kaplan v. Keith*, 377 N.E.2d 279 (Ill. App. Ct. 1978), the court found duress when the defendants refused to close the sale of real estate without the inclusion of a release clause, when plaintiffs had no other place to live and no time to find other accommodations.

However, the duress defense fails more often than it succeeds, indicating the courts' reluctance to interfere with freedom of contract or to disturb any imbalance existing between the parties.

- In *Radich v. Hutchins*, 95 U.S. 210 (1877), the court ruled that a threat of confiscation did not result from a publication of notice that cotton may not be exported from the State of Texas to Mexico, unless the merchant sold an equal amount to the Confederate government, without "some actual or threatened exercise of power possessed, or believed to be possessed . . . ."
- In *Cable v. Foley*, 47 N.W. 1135 (Minn. 1891), the court held that duress did not result from a threat to withhold payment due on an oral contract unless a written contract was signed by both parties, because there was adequate remedy to enforce the due payment.

In the two cases that follow, *Holler* shows the use of the classic duress defense, while *Totem Marine* discusses the use of the defense of economic duress.

Reading the Law Critically:
Holler and *Totem Marine Tug & Barge, Inc.*

1. What are the elements of the duress defense, as articulated in *Holler* and in *Totem Marine*? What commonalities do the definitions share? In what respects are they different?

2. What policies underlie the duress defense? What competing policies suggest caution in application of the defense?

3. What make *Holler* and *Totem Marine* appropriate cases for granting relief for duress?

Holler v. Holler

NATALIYA HOLLER, Plaintiff-Respondent

v.

WILLIAM HOLLER, Defendant-Appellant

Court of Appeals of South Carolina

612 S.E.2d 469 (S.C. Ct. App. 2005)

Anderson, J.

William Holler (Husband) appeals from the family court's determination that a premarital agreement signed by Nataliya[1] Holler (Wife) is not enforceable. We affirm.

Factual/Procedural Background

Wife is originally from Ukraine. She was educated in Ukraine and taught college students in that country. English is not Wife's first language. After seeing Husband's picture in "a feminine magazine," Wife wrote a letter to him in English and included her phone number. Thereafter, Husband and Wife talked on the phone for "[a]bout a year." Their conversations were in English. During this time, Husband visited Wife in Ukraine.

On September 5, 1997, Wife traveled to the United States to marry Husband. At the time of her arrival, Wife's English was "really poor." Husband disputed Wife's inability to speak English, claiming she spoke "[v]ery well." Upon completing an English course, Wife received a certificate from Central Piedmont College in May of 1998.

In October or early November 1997, Wife became pregnant with Husband's child. Wife's visa was scheduled to expire on December 4, 1997, and she would have to return to Ukraine unless she married Husband. Wife came to the United States without money and relied upon Husband to provide support.

Wife admitted that, while she was still in Ukraine, Husband told her about the premarital agreement. However, Wife believed she "needed to sign some papers under the law of South Carolina before we g[o]t married." Wife claimed: "[Husband] faxed me some documents for American Embassy, and one page was he told me that we need—when you get to United States we have to sign that agreement before we get married because this is under [the] law of South Carolina." Husband delivered the premarital agreement to Wife sometime before the

---

[1] Wife is referred to in the record as both Nataliya and Natasha.

marriage. Husband first stated he faxed it to her five or six months before she arrived in the United States. Husband maintained he handed her a copy to sign within a week after she arrived. Yet, Wife declared Husband gave her a copy of the premarital agreement only two weeks before she signed it.

Prior to signing the premarital agreement, Wife attempted to translate a portion of the agreement from English into Russian, but was unable to complete the translation. "Because it was too hard," Wife became frustrated with the translation and quit. Wife had eleven pages of translation before she determined the effort was futile. Wife professed the agreement "had specific language which [she did not] understand even in Russian." Wife never retained counsel because she had no money to pay someone to review the agreement.

Wife signed the agreement on November 25, 1997. The parties were married on December 1, 1997, merely three days before Wife's visa was set to expire.

Husband and Wife separated on February 13, 2000. Wife brought this action seeking a divorce, custody of the parties' child, child support, equitable distribution of marital property, and alimony. Husband answered and counterclaimed. Subsequently, he filed a motion to dismiss the claims for alimony and equitable distribution asserting the premarital agreement controlled. After a hearing, the family court denied the motion to dismiss. The court ruled the premarital agreement was invalid and unenforceable because it was signed under duress . . . .

. . . .

II. Premarital Agreement

Husband contends the trial court erred in finding the premarital agreement was invalid and unenforceable as a result of being unconscionable and signed under duress.

Premarital agreements, also called antenuptial or prenuptial agreements, are agreements between prospective spouses made in contemplation of marriage. *Black's Law Dictionary* defines a prenuptial agreement as "[a]n agreement made before marriage usu[ally] to resolve issues of support and property division if the marriage ends in divorce or by the death of a spouse." *Black's Law Dictionary* 1220 (8th ed. 2004). Antenuptial settlements are contracts or agreements entered into between a man and woman before marriage, but in contemplation and generally in consideration of marriage, whereby the property rights and interests of either the prospective husband or wife, or of both of them, are determined, or where property is secured to either or to both of them, or to their children. 41 C.J.S. *Husband and Wife* § 61 (1991).

marriage = consideration

The consideration for a premarital agreement is the marriage itself. Because such agreements are executory, they become effective only upon marriage. *See South Carolina Loan & Trust Co. v. Lawton*, 69 S.C. 345, 48 S.E. 282 (1904).
. . .

ENFORCED ELEMENTS?

. . . . An antenuptial contract is valid and will be upheld when, and only when, it is entered into freely, fairly, and in good faith by parties legally competent to contract. 41 C.J.S. *Husband and Wife* § 62 (1991). An antenuptial agreement must be free from duress, fraud, deceit, misrepresentation, or overreaching. *Id.* Further, the agreement must not be unconscionable. *Id.*

have to know if should be enforced

. . . . In determining whether a premarital agreement should be enforced, our supreme court professed:

(1) Was the agreement obtained through fraud, duress, or mistake, or through misrepresentation or nondisclosure of material facts? (2) Is the agreement unconscionable? (3) Have the facts and circumstances changed since the agreement was executed, so as to make its enforcement unfair and unreasonable?

Id. at 389, 585 S.E.2d at 504 (internal quotations omitted).

A. Duress

Husband avers the family court improperly concluded Wife signed the premarital agreement while under duress. We disagree.

DEF.

Duress is a condition of mind produced by improper external pressure or influence that practically destroys the free agency of a party and causes him to do an act or form a contract not of his own volition. *Cherry v. Shelby Mut. Plate Glass & Cas. Co.*, 191 S.C. 177, 4 S.E.2d 123 (1939); *Cox & Floyd Grading, Inc. v. Kajima Constr. Servs., Inc.*, 356 S.C. 512, 589 S.E.2d 789 (Ct. App.2003); *Willms Trucking Co. v. JW Constr. Co.*, 314 S.C. 170, 442 S.E.2d 197 (Ct.App.1994).

Corpus Juris Secundum defines duress:

"Duress" may be defined as subjecting a person to a pressure which overcomes his or her will and coerces him or her to comply with demands to which he or she would not yield if acting as a free agent. Some definitions of "duress" contain not only the element of pressure overcoming the victim's will but also the element that the pressure or compulsion consists of improper, wrongful, or unlawful conduct, acts, or threats.

> Further, "duress" has been defined as the condition of mind produced by the wrongful conduct of another rendering a person incompetent to contract with the exercise of his or her free will power, or as the condition of mind produced by an improper external pressure destroying free agency so as to cause the victim to act or contract without use of his or her own volition, or as unlawful constraint whereby a person is forced to do some act against his or her will.

17A C.J.S. *Contracts* § 175 (1999) (footnotes omitted).

The central question with respect to whether a contract was executed under duress is whether, considering all the surrounding circumstances, one party to the transaction was prevented from exercising his free will by threats or the wrongful conduct of another. 17A Am.Jur.2d *Contracts* § 218 (2004). Freedom of will is essential to the validity of an agreement. *Id.* A party claiming "duress" can prevail if he shows that he has been the victim of a wrongful or unlawful act or threat of a kind that deprives the victim of unfettered will, with the result that he was compelled to make a disproportionate exchange of values. *Id.*

In order to establish that a contract was procured through duress, three things must be proved: (1) coercion; (2) putting a person in such fear that he is bereft of the quality of mind essential to the making of a contract; and (3) that the contract was thereby obtained as a result of this state of mind. *In re Nightingale's Estate*, 182 S.C. 527, 189 S.E. 890 (1937). The fear which makes it impossible for a person to exercise his own free will is not so much to be tested by the means employed to accomplish the act, as by the state of mind produced by the means invoked. *Id.; Willms Trucking Co.*, 314 S.C. at 179, 442 S.E.2d at 202. If one of the parties to an agreement is in a position to dictate its terms to such an extent as to substitute his will for the will of the other party thereto, it is not a mutual, voluntary agreement, but becomes an agreement emanating entirely from his own mind. *In re Nightingale's Estate*, 182 S.C. at 547, 189 S.E. at 898; *Willms Trucking Co.*, 314 S.C. at 179, 442 S.E.2d at 202. If a party's manifestation of assent is induced by an improper threat by the other party that leaves the victim no reasonable alternative, the contract is voidable by the victim. *Willms Trucking Co.*, 314 S.C. at 179, 442 S.E.2d at 202. Whether or not duress exists in a particular case is a question of fact to be determined according to the circumstances of each case, such as the age, sex, and capacity of the party influenced. *Id.; see also Santee Portland Cement Corp. v. Mid-State Redi-Mix Concrete Co.*, 273 S.C. 784, 260 S.E.2d 178 (1979) (stating whether or not duress was present is a question ordinarily determined on a case by case basis).

Duress is viewed with a subjective test which looks at the individual characteristics of the person allegedly influenced, and duress does not occur if the victim

Alternative?

has a reasonable alternative to succumbing and fails to take advantage of it. *Blejski v. Blejski*, 325 S.C. 491, 480 S.E.2d 462 (Ct.App.1997) (citing Restatement (Second) of Contracts § 175 cmt. b & c (1981)). Duress is a defense to an otherwise valid contract. 17A Am.Jur.2d *Contracts* § 218. Duress renders a contract voidable at the option of the oppressed party. *Santee Portland Cement Corp.*, 273 S.C. at 784, 260 S.E.2d at 178.

Think About It!

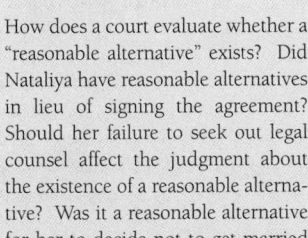

How does a court evaluate whether a "reasonable alternative" exists? Did Nataliya have reasonable alternatives in lieu of signing the agreement? Should her failure to seek out legal counsel affect the judgment about the existence of a reasonable alternative? Was it a reasonable alternative for her to decide not to get married or to return to Ukraine unmarried?

Assumptively concluding Wife was allowed the opportunity to view the premarital agreement three months in advance, the evidence in the record indicates: (1) Wife did not understand the contents of the agreement; (2) she did not freely enter into the agreement; (3) she attempted to translate the agreement into Russian in order to better comprehend the document; (4) she became frustrated as she was unable to complete a satisfactory translation; and (5) her notes indicate there are several words for which she could not find a translation, including "undivided," "equitable," and "pro rata." Consequently, Wife could not understand the agreement.

viewing agreement issues/holding.

Additionally, Husband was aware of the deadline with respect to Wife's visa. According to his own testimony, Husband made it perfectly clear to Wife that she must sign the agreement if she wanted to be married prior to the expiration of her visa. Wife was in the United States with no means to support herself. She relied solely and completely on Husband for support. Wife had no money of her own with which to retain and consult an attorney or a translator. Whether a party obtained independent legal advice is a significant consideration in evaluating whether an antenuptial agreement was voluntarily and understandingly made. *See* 41 C.J.S. *Husband and Wife* § 62 (1991). The family court found if Wife was not able to marry, then she would be forced to return to Ukraine. Because she was pregnant with Husband's child, she sought to insure his continued support and to remain in the United States.

why it's duress

Wife did not enter into the agreement freely and voluntarily. Ample evidence exists to support the family court's determination that Wife, given the circumstances she faced, signed the agreement under duress and without a clear understanding of what she was signing. The family court did not err in finding Wife signed the agreement under duress.

trial court was right

. . . .

Totem Marine Tug & Barge, Inc. v. Alyeska Pipeline Service Co.

TOTEM MARINE TUG & BARGE, INC., PACIFIC, INC., and RICHARD STAIR,
Plaintiffs-Appellants

v.

ALYESKA PIPELINE SERVICE COMPANY, et al., Defendants-Respondents

Supreme Court of Alaska
584 P.2d 15 (Alaska 1978)

BURKE, Justice.

This appeal arises from the superior court's granting of summary judgment in favor of defendants-appellees Alyeska Pipeline Services, et al., in a contract action brought by plaintiffs-appellants Totem Marine Tug & Barge, Inc., Pacific, Inc., and Richard Stair.

The following summary of events is derived from the materials submitted in the summary judgment proceedings below.

Totem is a closely held Alaska corporation which began operations in March of 1975. Richard Stair, at all times relevant to this case, was vice-president of Totem. In June of 1975, Totem entered into a contract with Alyeska under which Totem was to transport pipeline construction materials from Houston, Texas, to a designated port in southern Alaska, with the possibility of one or two cargo stops along the way. In order to carry out this contract, which was Totem's first, Totem chartered a barge (The "Marine Flasher") and an ocean-going tug (the "Kirt Chouest"). These charters and other initial operations costs were made possible by loans to Totem from Richard Stair individually and Pacific, Inc., a corporation of which Stair was principal stockholder and officer, as well as by guarantees by Stair and Pacific.

By the terms of the contract, Totem was to have completed performance by approximately August 15, 1975. From the start, however, there were numerous problems which impeded Totem's performance of the contract. For example, according to Totem, Alyeska represented that approximately 1,800 to 2,100 tons of regular uncoated pipe were to be loaded in Houston, and that perhaps another 6,000 or 7,000 tons of materials would be put on the barge at later stops along the west coast. Upon the arrival of the tug and barge in Houston, however, Totem found that about 6,700 to 7,200 tons of coated pipe, steel beams and valves, haphazardly and improperly piled, were in the yard to be loaded. This situation called for remodeling of the barge and extra cranes and stevedores, and resulted in the loading taking thirty days rather than the three days which Totem had anticipated it would take to load 2,000 tons. The lengthy loading period was also caused in part by Alyeska's delay in assuring Totem that it would pay for the additional expenses, bad weather and other administrative problems.

The difficulties continued after the tug and barge left Houston. It soon became apparent that the vessels were travelling more slowly than anticipated because of the extra load. In response to Alyeska's complaints and with its verbal consent, on August 13, 1975, Totem chartered a second tug, the "N. Joseph Guidry." When the "Guidry" reached the Panama Canal, however, Alyeska had not yet furnished the written amendment to the parties' contract. Afraid that Alyeska would not agree to cover the cost of the second tug, Stair notified the "Guidry" not to go through the Canal. After some discussions in which Alyeska complained of the delays and accused Totem of lying about the horsepower of the first tug, Alyeska executed the amendment on August 21, 1975.

By this time the "Guidry" had lost its preferred passage through the Canal and had to wait two or three additional days before it could go through. Upon finally meeting, the three vessels encountered the tail of a hurricane which lasted for about eight or nine days and which substantially impeded their progress.

The three vessels finally arrived in the vicinity of San Pedro, California, where Totem planned to change crews and refuel. On Alyeska's orders, however, the vessels instead pulled into port at Long Beach, California. At this point, Alyeska's agents commenced off-loading the barge, without Totem's consent, without the necessary load survey, and without a marine survey, the absence of which voided Totem's insurance. After much wrangling and some concessions by Alyeska, the freight was off-loaded. Thereafter, on or about September 14, 1975, Alyeska terminated the contract. Although there was talk by an Alyeska official of reinstating the contract, the termination was affirmed a few days later at a meeting at which Alyeska officials refused to give a reason for the termination.

Following termination of the contract, Totem submitted termination invoices to Alyeska and began pressing the latter for payment. The invoices came to something between $260,000 and $300,000. An official from Alyeska told Totem that they would look over the invoices but that they were not sure when payment would be made—perhaps in a day or perhaps in six to eight months. Totem was in urgent need of cash as the invoices represented debts which the company had incurred on 10-30 day payment schedules. Totem's creditors were demanding payment

Make the Connection

In Chapter 8 (page 917), you will learn that an aggrieved party can cancel a contract because of the other party's total breach. Cancellation differs from termination, which is a right granted by agreement. See Chapter 2 (page 103). If a party puts an end to a contract without a right to terminate or cancel the contract, that party breaches the contract by repudiating it. Did the contract in this case contain any termination clause? Did Alyeska terminate, or cancel, or repudiate the contract?

and, according to Stair, without immediate cash, Totem would go bankrupt. Totem then turned over the collection to its attorney, Roy Bell, directing him to advise Alyeska of Totem's financial straits. Thereafter, Bell met with Alyeska officials in Seattle, and after some negotiations, Totem received a settlement offer from Alyeska for $97,500. On November 6, 1975, Totem, through its president Stair, signed an agreement releasing Alyeska from all claims by Totem in exchange for $97,500.

On March 26, 1976, Totem, Richard Stair, and Pacific filed a complaint against Alyeska, which was subsequently amended. In the amended complaint, the plaintiffs sought to rescind the settlement and release on the ground of economic duress and to recover the balance allegedly due on the original contract. In addition, they alleged that Alyeska had wrongfully terminated the contract and sought miscellaneous other compensatory and punitive damages.

Before filing an answer, Alyeska moved for summary judgment against the plaintiffs on the ground that Totem had executed a binding release of all claims against Alyeska and that as a matter of law, Totem could not prevail on its claim of economic duress. In opposition, plaintiffs contended that the purported release was executed under duress in that Alyeska wrongfully terminated the contract; that Alyeska knew that Totem was faced with large debts and impending bankruptcy; that Alyeska withheld funds admittedly owed knowing the effect this would have on plaintiffs and that plaintiffs had no alternative but to involuntarily accept the $97,500 in order to avoid bankruptcy. Plaintiffs maintained that they had thus raised genuine issues of material fact such that trial was necessary, and that Alyeska was not entitled to judgment as a matter of law. Alyeska disputed the plaintiffs' assertions.

On November 30, 1976, the superior court granted the defendant's motion for summary judgment. This appeal followed.

. . . .

II

. . . [A] court's initial task in deciding motions for summary judgment is to determine whether there exist genuine issues of material fact. In order to decide whether such issues exist in this case, we must examine the doctrine allowing avoidance of a release on grounds of economic duress.

This court has not yet decided a case involving a claim of economic duress or what is also called business compulsion. At early common law, a contract could be avoided on the ground of duress only if a party could show that the agreement was entered into for fear of loss of life or limb, mayhem or imprisonment. 13

Williston on Contracts, § 1601 at 649 (3d ed. Jaeger 1970). The threat had to be such as to overcome the will of a person of ordinary firmness and courage. Id., § 1602 at 656. Subsequently, however, the concept has been broadened to include myriad forms of economic coercion which force a person to involuntarily enter into a particular transaction. The test has come to be whether the will of the person induced by the threat was overcome rather than that of a reasonably firm person. Id., § 1602 at 657.

Buisness Duress

At the outset it is helpful to acknowledge the various policy considerations which are involved in cases involving economic duress. Typically, those claiming such coercion are attempting to avoid the consequences of a modification of an original contract or of a settlement and release agreement. On the one hand, courts are reluctant to set aside agreements because of the notion of freedom of contract and because of the desirability of having private dispute resolutions be final. On the other hand, there is an increasing recognition of the law's role in correcting inequitable or unequal exchanges between parties of disproportionate bargaining power and a greater willingness to not enforce agreements which were entered into under coercive circumstances.

Make the Connection

Recall that the policy favoring finality for settlement agreements also played a major role in the *Dyer* case, Chapter 2 (page 108), in which an injured employee signed a release of his worthless claim against the employer, apparently not knowing that his claim was precluded by the workers' compensation system.

There are various statements of what constitutes economic duress, but as noted by one commentator, "The history of generalization in this field offers no great encouragement for those who seek to summarize results in any single formula." Dawson, Economic Duress—An Essay in Perspective, 45 Mich.L.Rev. 253, 289 (1947). Section 492(b) of the Restatement of Contracts defines duress as:

> any wrongful threat of one person by words or other conduct that induces another to enter into a transaction under the influence of such fear as precludes him from exercising free will and judgment, if the threat was intended or should reasonably have been expected to operate as an inducement.

DEF

Professor Williston states the basic elements of economic duress in the following manner:

> 1. The party alleging economic duress must show that he has been the victim of a wrongful or unlawful act or threat, and
> 2. Such act or threat must be one which deprives the victim of his unfettered will.

Econ. Duress Elements

13 Williston on Contracts, § 1617 at 704 (footnotes omitted).

Many courts state the test somewhat differently, eliminating use of the vague term "free will," but retaining the same basic idea. Under this standard, duress exists where: (1) one party involuntarily accepted the terms of another, (2) circumstances permitted no other alternative, and (3) such circumstances were the result of coercive acts of the other party. Undersea Engineering & Construction Co. v. International Telephone & Telegraph Corp., 429 F.2d 543, 550 (9th Cir. 1970); Urban Plumbing and Heating Co. v. United States, 408 F.2d 382, 389, 187 Ct.Cl. 15 (1969); W. R. Grimshaw Co. v. Nevil C. Withrow Co., 248 F.2d 896, 904 (8th Cir. 1957); Fruhauf Southwest Garment Co. v. United States, 111 F.Supp. 945, 951, 126 Ct.Cl. 51 (1953). The third element is further explained as follows:

> In order to substantiate the allegation of economic duress or business compulsion, the plaintiff must go beyond the mere showing of reluctance to accept and of financial embarrassment. There must be a showing of acts on the part of the defendant which produced these two factors. The assertion of duress must be proven by evidence that the duress resulted from defendant's wrongful and oppressive conduct and not by the plaintiff's necessities.

W. R. Grimshaw Co., supra, 111 F. Supp. at 904.

As the above indicates, one essential element of economic duress is that the plaintiff show that the other party, by wrongful acts or threats, intentionally caused him to involuntarily enter into a particular transaction. Courts have not attempted to define exactly what constitutes a wrongful or coercive act, as wrongfulness depends on the particular facts in each case. This requirement may be satisfied where the alleged wrongdoer's conduct is criminal or tortious but an act or threat may also be considered wrongful if it is wrongful in the moral sense. Restatement of Contracts, § 492, comment (g); Gerber v. First National Bank of Lincolnwood, 30 Ill.App.3d 776, 332 N.E.2d 615, 618 (1975); Fowler v. Mumford, 48 Del. 282, 9 Terry 282, 102 A.2d 535, 538 (Del.Supr.1954).

In many cases, a threat to breach a contract or to withhold payment of an admitted debt has constituted a wrongful act. Hartsville Oil Mill v. United States, 271 U.S. 43, 49, 46 S.Ct. 389, 391, 70 L.Ed. 822, 827 (1926); Austin Instrument, Inc. v. Loral Corp., 29 N.Y.2d 124, 324 N.Y.S.2d 22, 25, 272 N.E.2d 533, 535 (1971); Capps v. Georgia-Pacific Corporation, 253 Or. 248, 453 P.2d 935 (1969); See also 13 Williston, supra, § 1616A at 701. Implicit in such cases is the additional requirement that the threat to breach the contract or withhold payment be done in bad faith. See Louisville Title Insurance Co. v. Surety Title & Guaranty Co., 60 Cal.App.3d 781, 132 Cal.Rptr. 63, 76, 79 (1976); Restatement (Second) of Contracts, § 318 comment (e).

Economic duress does not exist, however, merely because a person has been the victim of a wrongful act; in addition, the victim must have no choice but to agree to the other party's terms or face serious financial hardship. Thus, in order to avoid a contract, a party must also show that he had no reasonable alternative to agreeing to the other party's terms, or, as it is often stated, that he had no adequate remedy if the threat were to be carried out. **First National Bank of Cincinnati v. Pepper, 454 F.2d 626, 632-33 (2d Cir. 1972); Austin Instrument, supra, 324 N.Y.S.2d at 25, 272 N.E.2d at 535;** Capps, supra; **Ross Systems v. Linden Dari-Delite, Inc., 35 N.J. 329, 173 A.2d 258, 261 (1961); Leeper v. Beltrami, 53 Cal.2d 195, 1 Cal.Rptr. 12, 19, 347 P.2d 12, 19 (1959); Tri-State Roofing Company of Uniontown v. Simon, 187 Pa.Super. 17, 142 A.2d 333, 335-36 (1958).** What constitutes a reasonable alternative is a question of fact, depending on the circumstances of each case. An available legal remedy, such as an action for breach of contract, may provide such an alternative. First National Bank of Cincinnati, supra; Austin Instrument, supra; Tri-State Roofing, supra. Where one party wrongfully threatens to withhold goods, services or money from another unless certain demands are met, the availability on the market of similar goods and services or of other sources of funds may also provide an alternative to succumbing to the coercing party's demands. Austin Instrument, supra; Tri-State Roofing, supra. Generally, it has been said that "[t]he adequacy of the remedy is to be tested by a practical standard which takes into consideration the exigencies of the situation in which the alleged victim finds himself." **Ross Systems, 173 A.2d at 262.** See also **First National Bank of Cincinnati, supra at 634**; Dalzell, Duress by Economic Pressure I, 20 N. Carolina L. Rev. 237, 240 (1942).

An available alternative or remedy may not be adequate where the delay involved in pursuing that remedy would cause immediate and irreparable loss to one's economic or business interest. For example, in Austin Instrument, supra, and **Gallagher Switchboard Corp. v. Heckler Electric Co., 36 Misc.2d 225, 232 N.Y.S.2d 590 (N.Y.Sup.Ct.1962)**, duress was found in the following circumstances: A subcontractor threatened to refuse further delivery under a contract unless the contractor agreed to modify the existing contract between the parties. The contractor was unable to obtain the necessary materials elsewhere without delay, and if it did not have the materials promptly, it would have been in default on its main contract with the government. In each case such default would have had grave economic consequences for the contractor and hence it agreed to the modifications. In both, the courts found that the alternatives to agreeing to the modi-

Make the Connection

Recall that in **Chapter 2 (page 116)**, *Angel v. Murray* discussed the public policy against contract modifications obtained by one party "holding the other party over a barrel." This policy underlies the pre-existing duty rule and the alternative rules considered by the *Angel* court. The duress defense is an alternative solution to respond to such circumstances.

fication were inadequate (i.e., suing for breach of contract or obtaining the materials elsewhere) and that modifications therefore were signed under duress and voidable.

Professor Dalzell, in **Duress by Economic Pressure II, 20 N. Carolina L. Rev. 340, 370 (1942)**, notes the following with regard to the adequacy of legal remedies where one party refuses to pay a contract claim:

> Nowadays, a wait of even a few weeks in collecting on a contract claim is sometimes serious or fatal for an enterprise at a crisis in its history. The business of a creditor in financial straits is at the mercy of an unscrupulous debtor, who need only suggest that if the creditor does not care to settle on the debtor's own hard terms, he can sue. This situation, in which promptness in payment is vastly more important than even approximate justice in the settlement terms, is too common in modern business relations to be ignored by society and the courts.

This view finds support in **Capps v. Georgia Pacific Corporation, 253 Or. 248, 453 P.2d 935 (1969)**. There, the plaintiff was owed $157,000 as a commission for finding a lessee for defendant's property but in exchange for $5,000, the plaintiff signed a release of his claim against defendant. The plaintiff sued for the balance of the commission, alleging that the release had been executed under duress. His complaint, however, was dismissed. On appeal, the court held that the plaintiff had stated a claim where he alleged that he had accepted the grossly inadequate sum because he was in danger of immediately losing his home by mortgage foreclosure and other property by foreclosure and repossession if he did not obtain immediate funds from the defendant. One basis for its holding was found in the following quote by a leading commentator in the area of economic duress:

> The most that can be claimed (regarding the law of economic duress) is that change has been broadly toward acceptance of a general conclusion that in the absence of specific countervailing factors of policy or administrative feasibility, restitution is required of any excessive gain that results, in a bargain transaction, from impaired bargaining power, whether the impairment consists of economic necessity, mental or physical disability, or a wide disparity in knowledge or experience.

Dawson, Economic Duress—An Essay in Perspective, 45 Mich. L. Rev. 253, 289 (1947).

We recognize that "freedom of contract" is a qualified and not an absolute right, and cannot be applied on a strict, doctrinal basis. An established principle

is that a court will not permit itself to be used as an instrument of inequity and injustice. . . . In determining whether certain contractual provisions should be enforced, the court must look realistically at the relative bargaining posi-
tions of the parties in the framework of contemporary business practices and commercial life. If we find those positions are such that one party has unscrupulously taken advantage of the economic necessities of the other, then in the interest of justice as a matter of public policy we would refuse to enforce the transaction. But the grounds for judicial interference must

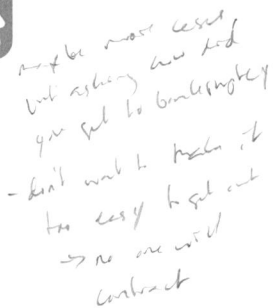

> ### Think About It!
>
> Is economic duress more or less likely to occur during an economic downturn? What special challenges would an economic downturn pose for a judge deciding a case involving the economic duress defense?

be clear. Whether the court should refuse to recognize and uphold that which the parties have agreed upon is a question of fact upon which evidence is required.

III

Turning to the instant case, we believe that Totem's allegations, if proved, would support a finding that it executed a release of its contract claims against Alyeska under economic duress. Totem has alleged that Alyeska deliberately with-
held payment of an acknowledged debt, knowing that Totem had no choice but to accept an inadequate sum in settlement of that debt; that Totem was faced with impending bankruptcy; that Totem was unable to meet its pressing debts other than by accepting the immediate cash payment offered by Alyeska; and that through necessity, Totem thus involuntarily accepted an inadequate settlement offer from Alyeska and executed a release of all claims under the contract. If the release was in fact executed under these circumstances,[5] we think that under the legal principles discussed above that this would constitute the type of wrongful conduct and lack of alternatives that would render the release voidable by Totem on the ground of economic duress. We would add that although Totem need not necessarily prove its allegation that Alyeska's termination of the contract was wrongful in order to sustain a claim of economic duress, the events leading to the termination would be probative as to whether Alyeska exerted any wrongful pressure on Totem and whether Alyeska wrongfully withheld payment from Totem.

. . . .

Our examination of the materials presented by Totem in opposition to Alyeska's motion for summary judgment leads us to conclude that Totem has made a

---

[5] By way of clarification, we would note that Totem would not have to prove that Alyeska admitted to owing the precise sum Totem claimed it was owed upon termination of the contract but only that Alyeska acknowledged that it owed Totem approximately that amount which Totem sought.

sufficient factual showing as to each of the elements of economic duress to withstand that motion. There is no doubt that Alyeska disputes many of the factual allegations made by Totem[7] and drawing all inferences in favor of Totem, we believe that genuine issues of material fact exist in this case such that trial is necessary. Admittedly, Totem's showing was somewhat weak in that, for example, it did not produce the testimony of Roy Bell, the attorney who represented Totem in the negotiations leading to the settlement and release. At trial, it will probably be necessary for Totem to produce this evidence if it is to prevail on its claim of duress. However, a party opposing a motion for summary judgment need not produce all of the evidence it may have at its disposal but need only show that issues of material fact exist. 10 C. Wright and A. Miller, **Federal Practice and Procedure: Civil, § 2727 at 546 (1973)**. Therefore, we hold that the superior court erred in granting summary judgment for appellees and remand the case to the superior court for trial in accordance with the legal principles set forth above.

Think About It!

How do you think the trial court will resolve the case on remand?

. . . .

Reading the Law Critically:
Duress under the Restatement (Second) and UNIDROIT

1. What are the differences between the duress defenses in Restatement §§ 174 and 175? Why are the legal consequences different?

2. How and why are threats of civil suit treated differently from threats of criminal prosecution?

3. How would the Restatement sections apply to the facts in *Holler* and *Totem Marine*?

4. Compare the standards for establishing duress under the Restatement (Second) to the UNIDROIT rule and to the rules derived from the cases in this Section.

---

[7] For example, Alyeska has denied that it ever admitted to owing any particular sum to Totem and has disputed the truthfulness of Totem's assertions of impending bankruptcy. Other factual issues which remain unresolved include whether or not Alyeska knew of Totem's financial situation after termination of the contract and whether Alyeska did in fact threaten by words or conduct to withhold payment unless Totem agreed to settle.

Restatement (Second) § 174. **When Duress by Physical Compulsion Prevents Formation of a Contract** *[handwritten: ...evidence is okay, too]*

If conduct that appears to be a manifestation of assent by a party who does not intend to engage in that conduct is physically compelled by duress, the conduct is not effective as a manifestation of assent.

[handwritten marginal note: Sum t head = void]

Restatement (Second) § 175. **When Duress by Threat Makes a Contract Voidable**

(1) If a party's manifestation of assent is induced by an improper threat [see § 176] by the other party that leaves the victim no reasonable alternative, the contract is voidable by the victim.
(2) If a party's manifestation of assent is induced by one who is not a party to the transaction, the contract is voidable by the victim unless the other party to the transaction in good faith and without reason to know of the duress either gives value or relies materially on the transaction.

[handwritten marginal notes: can choose 1. keep contract or not / threat by outside party / can't void if non-threatened party wants to keep it]

Restatement (Second) § 176. **When a Threat Is Improper**

(1) A threat is improper if
    (a) what is threatened is a crime or a tort, or the threat itself would be a crime or a tort if it resulted in obtaining property,
    (b) what is threatened is a criminal prosecution,
    (c) what is threatened is the use of civil process and the threat is made in bad faith, or
    (d) the threat is a breach of the duty of good faith and fair dealing under a contract with the recipient.
(2) A threat is improper if the resulting exchange is not on fair terms, and
    (a) the threatened act would harm the recipient and would not significantly benefit the party making the threat,
    (b) the effectiveness of the threat in inducing the manifestation of assent is significantly increased by prior unfair dealing by the party making the threat, or
    (c) what is threatened is otherwise a use of power for illegitimate ends.

UNIDROIT Art. 3.9. **Threat**

A party may avoid the contract when it has been led to conclude the contract by the other party's unjustified threat which, having regard to the circumstances, is so imminent and serious as to leave the first party no reasonable alternative. In particular, a threat is unjustified if the act or omission with which a party has been threatened is wrongful in itself, or it is wrongful to use it as a means to obtain the conclusion of the contract.

Food for Thought: Expansion of the Duress Defense?

How far should the defense of duress extend? Does economic duress fulfill the same purposes as the original defense of duress? What kinds of actions, or threats of actions, should result in making a contract unenforceable on that basis? In answering these questions, consider these three cases:

- In *U.S. v. Bethlehem Steel Corp.*, 315 U.S. 289 (1942), the government challenged 13 contracts for shipbuilding services during what is now known as World War I. Among other defenses, the government argued that the contracts were unconscionable, based on two elements: duress and Bethlehem Steel's profits grossly in excess of customary standards. The Court characterized duress as "feebleness on one side, overpowering strength on the other." Noting that this "as far as we know, is the first instance in which government has claimed to be a victim of duress . . . ," the Court distilled the government's duress arguments down to two propositions: "(1) The government's representatives involuntarily accepted Bethlehem's terms. (2) The circumstances permitted the government no other alternative." Neither proposition was borne out by the facts, which showed that the government's negotiators had a range of choices and were not forced to take Bethlehem's terms.

- In *Austin Instrument, Inc. v. Loral Corp.*, 29 N.Y.2d 124 (1971), the court ruled that a classic case of economic duress resulted when a general contractor and a subcontractor entered into an initial supply contract for 23 parts to enable the general contractor to meet its radar manufacturing commitments to the U.S. Navy. While the subcontractor was delivering the parts under the first contract, the general contractor entered into a second contract with the Navy and let bids on 40 additional parts. The subcontractor bid on all 40 parts, but the general contractor notified the subcontractor that it would only get the contracts on the parts for which it was the lowest bidder. The subcontractor refused to take a contract for anything less than all 40 parts and told the general contractor that it would cease deliveries under the first contract unless the general contractor awarded it the contract for all 40 parts and agreed to substantial price increases (retrospective and prospective) under the first contract. The subcontractor then ceased all deliveries. The general contractor "feverishly" contacted other manufacturers and found no one who could take the subcontractor's place in a timely fashion, so it agreed to the subcontractor's demands. The Navy contracts required staggered monthly deliveries, liquidated damages for the government, and a possible cancellation upon default. The court found that the general contractor had no choice but to accede to the subcontractor's demands and had no adequate legal remedy of suing for breach of contract rather than continuing performance.

• In *United States ex rel. Trane Co. v. Bond*, 586 A.2d 734 (Md. 1991), Lorna Bond sought to rescind her agreement to be surety on a payment bond guaranteeing work done by her husband's company for the United States government at Walter Reed Hospital. When her husband's company breached the contract and then declared bankruptcy, the government sued Lorna as surety on the payment bond. She asserted the defense of duress, "contending that she was not liable because Albert 'physically threatened her and abused her to coerce her to sign a number of documents, including the payment bond, and would not answer her regarding their content.' Lorna did not claim that Albert 'actually picked up her hand and forced her to sign the contract'; nor did she claim that the plaintiff 'knew of any coercive actions taken by defendant's husband.'" The question for the court was whether such actions, which stopped short of actual physical compulsion, would make the contract void or only voidable. If only voidable, the defense of duress would not be available against the other party to the contract, who was not responsible for and did not know about the duress. The court concluded that "a contract may be held void where, in addition to actual physical compulsion, a threat of imminent physical violence is exerted upon the victim of such magnitude as to cause a reasonable person, in the circumstances, to fear loss of life, or serious physical injury, or actual imprisonment for refusal to sign the document."

[handwritten margin note: imminent threat limits]

Problems: The Duress Defense

5-12. Husband and Wife lived together unmarried for four years when Wife became pregnant. She went to a clinic to terminate the pregnancy, but Husband called her and asked her not to have the abortion and to marry him. She agreed. Nine or ten days before the wedding, Husband gave Wife a premarital agreement to sign, saying it was just a formality but that he would call off the wedding if she did not sign. She took the agreement to an attorney, but the attorney informed her he did not have time to fully inspect the document before the wedding.

After consulting with Husband and his counsel, Wife agreed to sign the agreement only if the life insurance benefit was increased and the alimony amount in the agreement was adjusted upwards for each year of marriage. The agreement was modified and signed. At the time, Wife had a net worth of approximately $10,000, while Husband's net worth was approximately $8.5 million.

After 18 years of marriage, Husband filed for divorce and sought enforcement of the premarital agreement, which provided Wife with $2,900 alimony per month for four years and allow Husband to retain all the assets with which he entered the marriage and all assets they accumulated during the marriage. When he filed for divorce, Husband's net worth was $22.7 million. Wife sought to avoid the agreement on several grounds, one of which was duress. Should she succeed?

5-13. Recall *Batsakis v. Demotsis* from Chapter 2 (page 77). Could Batsakis have successfully claimed duress to avoid her promise to pay $2000 to Demotsis? *[handwritten: Yes; no good alternatives but no threat]*

5-14. Recall *Angel v. Murray* from Chapter 2 (page 116). Suppose that Maher says that his refuse collection business can't survive without being compensated for his increased costs in picking up refuse from 400 new dwelling units. The city initially resists his request, but Maher then stirs up public sentiment in his favor by publicizing his plight. Fearful of the political consequences, the city ultimately agrees to pay the additional compensation. Can the city later rescind the modification, based on duress? *[handwritten: political consequences aren't enough NO]*

[handwritten margin note: not much of threat; price or reasonable alt]

§ 2.3.2. Undue Influence

Undue influence is closely related but separate from the duress defense. It guards against a party's tactics that produce less than full assent by the other party—an individual who is vulnerable to domination by the first party.

Reading the Law Critically: *G.A.S.*

1. How is mental incapacity relevant to the subsequent issue of undue influence?

2. What test does the court use for the defense of undue influence? Compare that test to the standard in Restatement (Second) § 177(1) (below).

3. How do the facts meet or not meet the test for undue influence?

4. In light of this opinion, what advice would you have given the wife in this case, if you had been the attorney she consulted about getting a separation agreement?

5. How does the defense of undue influence differ from the defense of duress? In what respects are they similar? Does each defense use the objective standard, subjective standard, or both? Recall that the objective standard uses the perspective of the reasonable person, while the subjective standard uses the actual person's perspective. *See Lucy v. Zehmer* (page 237).

Restatement (Second) § 177. **When Undue Influence Makes a Contract Voidable**

(1) Undue influence is unfair persuasion of a party who is under the domination of the person exercising the persuasion or who by virtue of the relation between them is justified in assuming that that person will not act in a manner inconsistent with his welfare.

(2) If a party's manifestation of assent is induced by undue influence by the other party, the contract is voidable by the victim.

(3) . . . .

G.A.S. v. S.I.S.

G.A.S., Petitioner

v.

S.I.S., Respondent

Family Court of Delaware, New Castle County
407 A.2d 253 (Del. Fam. Ct. 1978)

JAMES, Judge:

Action by petitioner to rescind the separation agreement he and his former wife, respondent S.I.S., executed on February 20, 1975.

Petitioner and respondent were married on January 19, 1957, and four children were born of this marriage. Petitioner's mental health problems began in 1970 when he was hospitalized at the Delaware State Hospital for eight weeks. Similar illnesses occurred in 1972 and the early part of 1974, with petitioner suffering such symptoms as acceleration of the mind followed by paranoia and loss of a sense of reality. During the two to three day onset of the illness, petitioner generally becomes violent toward himself, but not other people. After commitment, and drug therapy, petitioner slowly comes down from this state of aggressiveness, begins to communicate with others and, according to psychiatric testimony, becomes extremely dependent. After release from the hospital, petitioner usually continues to take medication for thirty to ninety days. Petitioner has been diagnosed as suffering from schizophrenia, paranoid type, and manic-depression.

On December 23, 1974, petitioner suffered a reoccurrence of this illness and was committed again to the Delaware State Hospital by police after being called by respondent. At this time, petitioner was employed by Hercules as a design engineer at a yearly salary of approximately $21,000. Although petitioner claims there had been no marital discord prior to the December 23, 1974 mental breakdown, respondent testified that she consulted an attorney in March of 1974, during petitioner's previous reoccurrence of this illness, for the purpose of securing a legal separation. However, petitioner pleaded with her to stay with him and she agreed if he promised to take his medication. In any event, respondent filed for a divorce in Superior Court alleging the mental illness of petitioner as the sole ground for the action, and petitioner was personally served with the divorce summons on January 10, 1975, while still committed to the Delaware State Hospital.

Petitioner told respondent that he did not want the divorce and he was referred, by the hospital's patient advocate, to an attorney with whom he had a very brief consultation on January 16, 1975, the details of which are the subject of some dispute. However, all parties agree that petitioner was primarily concerned with returning to the marital home and reconciling with respondent. While there may have been some discussion as to what property petitioner owned, he did not discuss with the attorney any type of proposed written separation agreement between petitioner and respondent. Although the attorney indicated he was willing to take the case, petitioner never followed up on the initial visit.

The separation agreement which is the subject of the current dispute was prepared by respondent's attorney and signed by petitioner on February 20, 1975 at her attorney's office, at her request. Petitioner never spoke with respondent's attorney about the contents of the agreement, nor did petitioner read it in the office prior to signing the document. It is clear that petitioner was not independently represented by counsel when he executed this agreement, although at the time he was still committed to the Delaware State Hospital in the night hospital program, under which he left during working hours to attend his job and returned to the hospital at night for continuing treatment. Both petitioner's testimony and the hospital records indicate that he was working with only mild success during this period. He complained of being very stiff and unable to sit or concentrate for any length of time, often returning either to the hospital or to his grandmother's house after only a few hours on the job.

Throughout February 1975, petitioner continued on extensive medication, and the hospital records reveal that on the date he signed the separation agreement he was given Akineton, Berolla C and Esidorex, medications which adversely affected petitioner's reasoning powers.

During his hospitalization from December 23, 1974 and until his discharge on February 26, 1975, petitioner was dependent upon respondent for transportation, cigarettes, money to spend and permission to leave the hospital and to return home. Furthermore, she took over his paycheck and ran the family during the course of his illness. Since petitioner did not want respondent to proceed with the divorce action, he testified that he was extremely cooperative toward her during the time when the separation agreement was executed in hopes of reconciling the marriage.

The major factual dispute centers around petitioner's knowledge and comprehension of the terms and conditions of the agreement prior to its execution, and his participation, if any, in establishing its contents.

Respondent testified that the $750 per month child support figure was established by petitioner after negotiations between them. She also indicated that during the week prior to the signing of the agreement, she and petitioner sat at the kitchen table and went over a draft of the entire separation agreement. The secretary of the respondent's attorney testified that it was office procedure that a party to the agreement would be given an original copy; however, she could not recall whether petitioner, in fact, received one.

Petitioner admits having conversations with respondent, but claims the discussions dealt only with child support, the Bethany Beach property and the Heritage Park (marital) home. Specifically, he indicated that he wished the beach property and would give the marital home to respondent; but she insisted on the beach property and, after he agreed, she also insisted on occupying the marital home with the children until the youngest reached 19. He denies setting the $750 monthly child support figure, although he does remember that respondent originally asked for $1,100 out of his $1,300 net monthly income. He further claims he did not read the separation agreement before signing it and signed it as an act of good faith and a first step toward reconciliation. In fact, he insists that he never received a copy of the agreement until August of 1977 when he requested a copy from respondent's attorney.

Petitioner did meet with respondent's attorney at his office on March 31, 1975, when settlement was made on the sale of the Marshallton property, which had been previously inherited by petitioner. The net sale proceeds were first applied to pay off the marital debts and then the balance was divided equally between petitioner and respondent.

Petitioner was released from Delaware State Hospital on February 26, 1975, six days after the agreement was signed, and subsequently lived with his grandmother. Within a few months, he was laid off by Hercules and next secured employment at Franklin Mint, as an outside contractor, through August of 1975. He then worked for Beloit Corporation in Dowington, Pennsylvania until it was sold in April of 1977, and he was transferred to Wisconsin with the successor corporation where he continued until July of 1978 when he was terminated as a result of a reoccurrence of his illness in January of 1978. This most recent illness was precipitated by his father's sickness and resulted in petitioner's commitment to Delaware Division, with subsequent transfers to Delaware State Hospital and Rockford Center until the end of February 1978, when he was discharged to live with his father in Temperanceville, Virginia. Fortunately, petitioner's last employer agreed to continue paying him his $24,000 annual salary until December of 1978.

Following his discharge from the Delaware State Hospital on February 26, 1975, petitioner began sending respondent a mortgage payment of $155, plus child support of $750 for a total of $905 each month for approximately two and a half years, until August of 1977, when he unilaterally reduced the $750 child support payment by one-fourth upon learning that his child support obligation under Delaware law ceased when a child reached 18.

The Court must answer the following questions in order to resolve the issue of the validity of the February 20, 1975 separation agreement: first, whether petitioner had the legal capacity to contract on that date; second, assuming that he did, in fact, have capacity, whether the agreement should be rescinded as a result of either constructive fraud or undue influence on the part of respondent.

Only competent persons can make a contract, and where there is no capacity to understand or agree, there can be no contract. 17 Am.Jur.2d Contracts, § 16.
. . .

Although petitioner was still under commitment to Delaware State Hospital at the time of execution of the separation agreement, he had not been judicially adjudicated mentally incompetent, and therefore the agreement is not void but may be voidable. Industrial Trust Co. v. Miller, Del.Super., 170 A. 923 (1933); Poole v. Newark Trust Co., Del.Super. 8 A.2d 10 (1939).

The mental incapacity sufficient to permit the [rescission] of an agreement must render the afflicted individual incapable of understanding the nature and effect of the transaction. 13 Am.Jur.2d Cancellation of Instruments, § 13; Sutcliffe v. Heatley, 232 Mass. 231, 122 N.E. 317 (1919). The Court must determine whether his mental faculties have been impaired to such an extent that he is unable to properly, intelligently and fairly protect and preserve his property rights. Monroe v. Shrives, 29 Ohio App. 109, 162 N.E. 780 (1927).

At the time of the execution of the separation agreement not only was petitioner a diagnosed paranoid schizophrenic still receiving in-patient treatment, but he was also receiving significant amounts of "anti-psychotic" medication. The only psychiatrist to testify, Dr. S, treated petitioner in Feb-

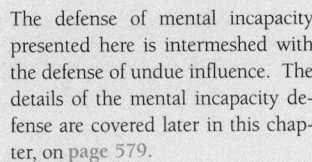

Make the Connection

The defense of mental incapacity presented here is intermeshed with the defense of undue influence. The details of the mental incapacity defense are covered later in this chapter, on page 579.

ruary of 1978, and based his testimony upon direct knowledge of petitioner and a review of the existing medical records. Dr. S's opinion, based upon reasonable medical certainty, was that when petitioner executed the separation agreement on February 20, 1975, he would not have been fully able to understand or comprehend what he was signing nor the implications thereof. At the time of the signing, petitioner was just emerging from an acute state (psychotic decompensation) through the use of medication. Most significantly, the drugs administered to petitioner tranquilize the nervous system and permit reality orientation; however, they also adversely affect reasoning ability. Dr. S concluded that petitioner may have thought he knew what he was doing when, in fact, he did not; petitioner would neither have fully understood a complicated document nor would his value judgment have been sufficient to comprehend the effect of the transaction.

. . . .

The facts of this case do not require this Court to make the extremely difficult decision as to whether petitioner was, in fact, incapable of comprehending and acting rationally in executing the separation agreement. For even if the mental weakness of the petitioner in this case did not rise to the level of contractual incapacity, such weakness is a circumstance that operates to make the separation agreement voidable when coupled with the evidence of lack of independent counsel, undue influence and unfairness in the transaction that is present in this case. 41 Am.Jur.2d Incompetent Persons, § 95 states as follows, at 633:

The elements of . . . undue influence and knowledge on the part of the person participating in a transaction that the other party thereto is afflicted mentally are material in many instances where the validity of a contract or deed executed on such a transaction is questioned. For example, even though the mental infirmity of a party to a contract, or the grantor in a conveyance, is not of such a degree as in itself to render the contract void or voidable, if the nature of the contract or the conveyance justifies the conclusion that the party has not exercised a deliberate judgment, but that he has been imposed upon, circumvented, or overcome by cunning, artifice, or undue influence and it appears that the other party was guilty of fraud or bad faith or imposed upon the infirm person by taking advantage of his infirmity to secure from him a contract or conveyance that he otherwise would not have executed the contract or conveyance may be set aside.

. . . .

It is undisputed that respondent had knowledge of petitioner's mental illness. Beyond the fact of the illness, she knew both the diagnosis and the normal course of petitioner's infirmity. Indeed, she had authorized his release from Delaware State Hospital so that he could execute the agreement. Whether or not she was aware of the particular medication that petitioner had taken on the date of the execution of the agreement, the Court finds that she knew he was undergoing extensive drug therapy. However, there appears to be no fraudulent intention on the part of respondent. Nevertheless, the peculiar susceptibility of petitioner due to his mental weakness, coupled with respondent's knowledge of this infirmity, imposes upon her a higher responsibility and requires that the transaction be viewed with suspicion. **25 Am.Jur.2d Duress and Undue Influence, § 37.** Such suspicion is particularly warranted where the weaker party has not been protected by the proper independent advice of competent counsel disassociated from the interest of respondent so as to be in a position to advise the petitioner impartially and confidentially as to the consequences to himself of the proposed agreement. See Post v. Hagan, 71 N.J.Eq. 234, 65 A. 1026 (1907); **Hickman v. Hickman,** N.J.Chanc., 121 A. 728 (1923); **Giacobbi v. Anselmi, 18 N.J.Super. 600, 87 A.2d 748 (1952).**

Close scrutiny of the circumstances surrounding the drafting and execution of the separation agreement, and a look at its contents, present almost textbook evidence of the elements establishing undue influence.

Undue influence is an excessive or inordinate influence considering the circumstances of the particular case. The degree of influence exerted, to be considered undue, must subjugate the free agency of the person influenced to the will of another. **Conner v. Brown, 39 Del. 529, 3 A.2d 64 (1938).**

> "The essentials of undue influence are a susceptible testator, opportunity to exert influence, a disposition so to do for an improper purpose, the actual exertion of such influence, and the result demonstrating its effect."

Id. at 71; **25 Am.Jur.2d Duress and Undue Influence, § 36.** The facts set forth above establish petitioner's susceptibility to influence. There can be no question that there was a confidential and fiduciary relationship between the parties in view of their long marriage and the respondent's running of the family during petitioner's periodic mental breakdowns. Furthermore, petitioner's testimony revealed that when he signed the agreement, he did so in hopes of reconciling the marriage and avoiding the divorce.

In view of petitioner's mental instability and strong desire to return to the marital home, it is clear that respondent was the dominant party in the relationship at the time of the signing of the agreement.

> "Confidential relations are presumed to exist between husband and wife. . . . Confidential and fiduciary relations have the same meaning in law; and as every fiduciary relation implies a condition of superiority of one of the parties over the other, equity raises a presumption against the validity of a transaction by which the superior obtains a possible benefit at the expense of the inferior, and casts upon him the burden of showing affirmatively his compliance with all equitable requisites."

Peyton v. William C. Peyton Corp., 2 Del.Ch. 321, 7 A.2d 737, 747, 123 A.L.R. 1482 (1939).

The presumption of undue influence is present where, as here, the dominant party obtains a contract. Therefore, she has the burden of proving fairness. Swain v. Moore, Del.Ch., 71 A.2d 264 (1950). The test in such a situation is whether the separation agreement is fair and equitable, having regard for petitioner's material interests. Brown v. Mercantile Trust & Deposit Co., Md., 40 A. 256 (1898). Respondent has failed to meet this burden. The agreement goes far beyond that which would have been ordered by this Court.

The initial support agreement was for $1,000 out of the $1,300 monthly net pay of petitioner. Following the divorce, the $750 monthly child support plus $155 monthly mortgage payment bring the total charges to about 70% of petitioner's salary, and the support payments, subject to annual cost of living increases, are not deductible by petitioner nor taxable to respondent. Additionally, petitioner's support obligation extends until each child reaches 21 rather than 18.

As to the property division controlled by the agreement, respondent immediately obtained sole ownership of the parties' beach property, which had approximately the same equity as the marital home. Petitioner's right to the marital home is subject to the respondent's right to live there until the youngest child reaches 19. Furthermore, petitioner's interest in the home is subject to forfeiture if he becomes totally disabled or incapacitated, which is stipulated to mean if petitioner's income decreases to at least 50% of the salary he earned at the time of the execution of the agreement. In view of petitioner's reoccurring mental illnesses, which adversely affected his employment, it is extremely likely that respondent's attorney would have the opportunity to exercise this forfeiture option.

Petitioner has the further obligation to maintain medical and hospital insurance on respondent and the children plus responsibility for the children's extraordinary ("more than $25 for any single visit or treatment of any specific condition") medical, dental or optical expenses.

By its terms, this agreement severely overreaches the obligation of the petitioner to either respondent to their children. Respondent in this situation clearly has received a benefit at the expense of the mentally ill petitioner. Her attorney drew up the agreement and she persuaded petitioner to accept its terms, or to sign it without in-depth knowledge of its import to him. The means of her control over him are not important, and it is irrelevant whether they consisted of importunities, overpersuasion, or moral coercion of any kind. **25 Am.Jur.2d Duress and Undue Influence, § 36.**

Make the Connection

The *G.A.S.* court says that the agreement is "cancelled" when it really means "rescinded." It also orders "the parties restored as closely as possible to their status quo at the time of execution"—the remedy of restitution, which includes both restitution damages and specific restitution of items conveyed between the parties. See the FYI box on "An Introduction to Contract Remedies" at the beginning of Chapter 3 (page 148).

A separation agreement procured by the undue influence of either of the parties is subject to being set aside. 41 Am.Jur.2d Husband and Wife, § 272; **Rendlen v. Rendlen, Mo., 367 S.W.2d 596 (1967).**

Applying the foregoing facts to the applicable law, the Court concludes that the separation agreement dated February 20, 1975 should be cancelled and declared a nullity and the parties restored as closely as possible to their status quo at the time of execution.

§ 2.4. Unconscionability

The unconscionability defense gives courts the means to police against contracts or clauses that "shock the conscience." Indeed, the word "unconscionability" is derived from the word "conscience." Determining exactly what shocks the conscience is not straightforward, however. In 1750, an English court said that an unconscionable contract was "such as no [person] in his senses and not under delusion would make on the one hand, and as no honest and fair [person] would accept on the other."* More than 200 years later, a New Jersey court noted the difficulty of defining unconscionability in more than abstract terms, but suggested that "there must be an inequality so strong, gross, and manifest that it must be impossible to state it to a [person] of common sense without producing an exclamation at the inequality of it."**

A leading commentator has observed that unconscionability often involves "substantive unfairness . . . mixed with an absence of bargaining ability that does not fall to the level of incapacity or with an abuse of the bargaining process that does not rise to the level of misrepresentation, duress, or undue influence."***

Make the Connection

The unconscionability defense relates solely to the contract as it was created. It does *not* police against unfair conduct during the performance of the contract. As discussed in Chapter 7 (page 804), the requirement of good faith sometimes performs that function.

By its nature, the unconscionability defense is raised by the contracting party with less knowledge, power, or bargaining strength in the transaction. It is an "extreme" defense, not often a winning one.

Reading the Law Critically: *Williams*

1. How does the court define unconscionability?

2. What role does the Uniform Commercial Code provision on unconscionability play in the court's decision?

3. The contract challenged by the plaintiff is an installment sales contract. The clause at issue reads:

    > The amount of each periodical installment payment to be made by [purchaser] to the Company under this present lease shall be inclusive of and not in addition to the amount of each installment payment to be made by [purchaser] under such prior leases, bills or accounts; and all payments now and hereafter made by [purchaser] shall be credited pro rata on all outstanding leases, bills and accounts due the Company by [purchaser] at the time each such payment is made.

---

* *Hume v. United States*, 132 U.S. 406 (1889) (quoting *Earl of Chesterfield v. Janssen*, 28 Eng. Rep. 82, 100 (Ch. 1750)).

** *Toker v. Westerman*, 274 A.2d 78, 80 (N.J. Dist. Ct. 1970).

*** 1 E. Allan Farnsworth, *Farnsworth on Contracts* § 4.27, at 492 (1990).

What is the meaning and effect of this clause? What effect does it have when the purchaser makes a payment? What effect does it have if she fails to pay the whole amount for a particular item? (Answer these questions before you read the opinion as well as afterwards.)

4. On remand from the decision here, what arguments would you make for and against unconscionability? Consider both the majority and dissenting opinions in crafting your arguments. Which set of arguments do you think is stronger?

5. If the contract is held unconscionable, what remedy should be granted?

Williams v. Walker-Thomas Furniture Co.

ORA LEE WILLIAMS, Defendant-Appellant

v.

WALKER-THOMAS FURNITURE COMPANY, Plaintiff-Appellee

WILLIAM THORNE et al., Defendants-Appellants

v.

WALKER-THOMAS FURNITURE COMPANY, Plaintiff-Appellee

United States Court of Appeals District of Columbia Circuit
350 F.2d 445 (D.C. Cir. 1965)

J. SKELLY WRIGHT, Circuit Judge:

Appellee, Walker-Thomas Furniture Company, operates a retail furniture store in the District of Columbia. During the period from 1957 to 1962 each appellant in these cases purchased a number of household items from Walker-Thomas, for which payment was to be made in installments. The terms of each purchase were contained in a printed form contract which set forth the value of the purchased item and purported to lease the item to appellant for a stipulated monthly rent payment. The contract then provided, in substance, that title would remain in Walker-Thomas until the total of all the monthly payments made equaled the stated value of the item, at which time appellants could take title. In the event of a default in the payment of any monthly installment, Walker-Thomas could repossess the item.

The contract further provided that "the amount of each periodical installment payment to be made by [purchaser] to the Company under this present lease shall be inclusive of and not in addition to the amount of each installment payment to be made by [purchaser] under such prior leases, bills or accounts; and all payments now and hereafter made by [purchaser] shall be credited pro rata on all outstanding leases, bills and accounts due the Company by [purchaser] at the time each such payment is made." The effect of this rather obscure provision was to keep a balance due on every item purchased until the balance due on all items, whenever purchased, was liquidated. As a result, the debt incurred at the time of purchase of each item was secured by the right to repossess all the items previously purchased by the same purchaser, and each new item purchased automatically became subject to a security interest arising out of the previous dealings.

On May 12, 1962, appellant Thorne purchased an item described as a Daveno, three tables, and two lamps, having total stated value of $391.10. Shortly thereafter, he defaulted on his monthly payments and appellee sought to replevy all the items purchased since the first transaction in 1958. Similarly, on April 17, 1962, appellant Williams bought a stereo set of stated value of $514.95.[1] She too defaulted shortly thereafter, and appellee sought to replevy all the items purchased since December, 1957. The Court of General Sessions granted judgment for appellee. The District of Columbia Court of Appeals affirmed, and we granted appellants' motion for leave to appeal to this court.

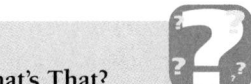

What's That?

Although the contracts in *Williams* and *Thorne* were written as leases, with the seller retaining title and a right of repossession upon buyer's payment default, the law construes such a contract as a sale with an accompanying "security interest." A security interest is, loosely, a creditor's right to seize the agreed-upon collateral if the debtor defaults on a payment obligation. The "cross-collateral clause" in the contract applied each of the buyer's payments pro rata to all contracts not yet paid off, rather than "first-in, first-out" (FIFO), so that all of buyer's purchases were collateral securing all of buyer's contracts, as long as buyer had not yet paid off all of the contracts before making additional purchases.

Appellants' principal contention, rejected by both the trial and the appellate courts below, is that these contracts, or at least some of them, are unconscionable and, hence, not enforceable. In its opinion in Williams v. Walker-Thomas Furniture Company, 198 A.2d 914, 916 (1964), the District of Columbia Court of Appeals explained its rejection of this contention as follows:

---

[1] At the time of this purchase her account showed a balance of $164 still owing from her prior purchases. The total of all the purchases made over the years in question came to $1,800. The total payments amounted to $1,400.

"Appellant's second argument presents a more serious question. The record reveals that prior to the last purchase appellant had reduced the balance in her account to $164. The last purchase, a stereo set, raised the balance due to $678. Significantly, at the time of this and the preceding purchases, appellee was aware of appellant's financial position. The reverse side of the stereo contract listed the name of appellant's social worker and her $218 monthly stipend from the government. Nevertheless, with full knowledge that appellant had to feed, clothe and support both herself and seven children on this amount, appellee sold her a $514 stereo set."

"We cannot condemn too strongly appellee's conduct. It raises serious questions of sharp practice and irresponsible business dealings. A review of the legislation in the District of Columbia affecting retail sales and the pertinent decisions of the highest court in this jurisdiction disclose, however, no ground upon which this court can declare the contracts in question contrary to public policy. We note that were the Maryland Retail Installment Sales Act, Art. 83 §§ 128-153, or its equivalent, in force in the District of Columbia, we could grant appellant appropriate relief. We think Congress should consider corrective legislation to protect the public from such exploitive contracts as were utilized in the case at bar."

We do not agree that the court lacked the power to refuse enforcement to contracts found to be unconscionable. In other jurisdictions, it has been held as a matter of common law that unconscionable contracts are not enforceable.[2] While no decision of this court so holding has been found, the notion that an unconscionable bargain should not be given full enforcement is by no means novel. In Scott v. United States, 79 U.S. (12 Wall.) 443, 445, 20 L.Ed. 438 (1870), the Supreme Court stated:

> ". . . If a contract be unreasonable and unconscionable, but not void for fraud, a court of law will give to the party who sues for its breach damages, not according to its letter, but only such as he is equitably entitled to. . . ."[3]

Since we have never adopted or rejected such a rule, the question here presented is actually one of first impression.

Congress has recently enacted the Uniform Commercial Code, which specifically provides that the court may refuse to enforce a contract which it finds to be

---

[2] Campbell Soup Co. v. Wentz, 3 Cir., 172 F.2d 80 (1948); Indianapolis Morris Plan Corporation v. Sparks, 132 Ind.App. 145, 172 N.E.2d 899 (1961); Henningsen v. Bloomfield Motors, Inc., 32 N.J. 358, 161 A.2d 69, 84-96, 75 A.L.R.2d 1 (1960). Cf. 1 Corbin, Contracts § 128 (1963).

[3] See Luing v. Peterson, 143 Minn. 6, 172 N.W. 692 (1919); Greer v. Tweed, N.Y.C.P., 13 Abb.Pr., N.S., 427 (1872); Schnell v. Nell, 17 Ind. 29 (1861); and see generally the discussion of the English authorities in Hume v. United States, 132 U.S. 406, 10 S.Ct. 134, 33 L.Ed. 393 (1889).

unconscionable at the time it was made. 28 D.C.Code § 2-302 (Supp. IV 1965). The enactment of this section, which occurred subsequent to the contracts here in suit, does not mean that the common law of the District of Columbia was otherwise at the time of enactment, nor does it preclude the court from adopting a similar rule in the exercise of its powers to develop the common law for the District of Columbia. In fact, in view of the absence of prior authority on the point, we consider the congressional adoption of § 2-302 persuasive authority for following the rationale of the cases from which the section is explicitly derived. Accordingly, we hold that where the element of unconscionability is present at the time a contract is made, the contract should not be enforced.

Unconscionability has generally been recognized to include an absence of meaningful choice on the part of one of the parties together with contract terms which are unreasonably favorable to the other party. Whether a meaningful choice is present in a particular case can only be determined by consideration of all the circumstances surrounding the transaction. In many cases the meaningfulness of the choice is negated by a gross inequality of bargaining power.[7] The manner in which the contract was entered is also relevant to this consideration. Did each party to the contract, considering his obvious education or lack of it, have a reasonable opportunity to understand the terms of the contract, or were the important terms hidden in a maze of fine print and minimized by deceptive sales practices? Ordinarily, one who signs an agreement without full knowledge of its terms might be held to assume the risk that he has entered a one-sided bargain.[8] But when a party of

> **FYI**
>
> Because Washington, D.C., is not a state, Congress plays a special role in its governance. In 1973, the Home Rule Act gave the District of Columbia an increased measure of self-governance, including the establishment of an elected legislature (the City Council). In 1965, however, Congress was still the source of legislation for the District of Columbia. Then and now, suits in the D.C. court system, if appealed, proceed to the D.C. Circuit of the U.S. Court of Appeals.

---

[7] See Henningsen v. Bloomfield Motors, Inc., supra Note 2, 161 A.2d at 86, and authorities there cited. Inquiry into the relative bargaining power of the two parties is not an inquiry wholly divorced from the general question of unconscionability, since a one-sided bargain is itself evidence of the inequality of the bargaining parties. This fact was vaguely recognized in the common law doctrine of intrinsic fraud, that is, fraud which can be presumed from the grossly unfair nature of the terms of the contract. See the oft-quoted statement of Lord Hardwicke in Earl of Chesterfield v. Janssen, 28 Eng. Rep. 82, 100 (1751):

> ". . . [Fraud] may be apparent from the intrinsic nature and subject of the bargain itself; such as no man in his senses and not under delusion would make . . ."

[8] See Restatement, Contracts § 70 (1932); Note, 63 Harv.L.Rev. 494 (1950). See also Daley v. People's Building, Loan & Savings Ass'n, 178 Mass. 13, 59 N.E. 452, 453 (1901), in which Mr. Justice Holmes, while sitting on the Supreme Judicial Court of Massachusetts, made this observation:

> ". . . Courts are less and less disposed to interfere with parties making such contracts as they choose, so long as they interfere with no one's welfare but their own. . . . It will be understood that we are speaking of parties standing in an equal position where neither has any oppressive advantage or power . . . ."

little bargaining power, and hence little real choice, signs a commercially unreasonable contract with little or no knowledge of its terms, it is hardly likely that his consent, or even an objective manifestation of his consent, was ever given to all the terms. In such a case the usual rule that the terms of the agreement are not to be questioned[9] should be abandoned and the court should consider whether the terms of the contract are so unfair that enforcement should be withheld.

In determining reasonableness or fairness, the primary concern must be with the terms of the contract considered in light of the circumstances existing when the contract was made. The test is not simple, nor can it be mechanically applied. The terms are to be considered "in the light of the general commercial background and the commercial needs of the particular trade or case."[11] Corbin suggests the test as being whether the terms are "so extreme as to appear unconscionable according to the mores and business practices of the time and place." 1 Corbin, op. cit. supra Note 2.[12] We think this formulation correctly states the test to be applied in those cases where no meaningful choice was exercised upon entering the contract.

Because the trial court and the appellate court did not feel that enforcement could be refused, no findings were made on the possible unconscio-

Take Note!

The fact that a party does not read a contract is not enough by itself to undermine assent. Parties to contracts often do not read them. Consider the many times you have signed a contract or clicked your agreement without reading the terms. Courts usually respond by concluding that a person who objectively manifests assent to an agreement has assented to all of the terms in it, regardless of whether he or she has read the agreement. These cases are colloquially called "duty to read" cases, although there is not actually a duty to read. Rather, the assenting party is barred from using its lack of actual knowledge of a term or terms to claim no assent. If an agreement is presented in a foreign language, however, a court may not impose a "duty to read" in this fashion. Why would courts view such circumstances as different and therefore not apply the rule?

Restatement (Second) § 211(3) contains the following controversial exception to the "duty to read:" "Where the other party has reason to believe that the party manifesting . . . assent would not do so if he knew that the writing contained a particular term, the term is not part of the agreement." This provision has generated intense opposition by companies that utilize standard-form agreements, has been adopted only a few jurisdictions, and has mainly been applied to insurance contracts.

---

[9] This rule has never been without exception. In cases involving merely the transfer of unequal amounts of the same commodity, the courts have held the bargain unenforceable for the reason that "in such a case, it is clear, that the law cannot indulge in the presumption of equivalence between the consideration and the promise." 1 Williston, Contracts § 115 (3d ed. 1957).

[11] Comment, Uniform Commercial Code § 2-307.

[12] See Henningsen v. Bloomfield Motors, Inc., supra Note 2; Mandel v. Liebman, 303 N.Y. 88, 100 N.E.2d 149 (1951). The traditional test as stated in Greer v. Tweed, supra Note 3, 13 Abb.Pr.,N.S., at 429, is "such as no man in his senses and not under delusion would make on the one hand, and as no honest or fair man would accept, on the other."

nability of the contracts in these cases. Since the record is not sufficient for our deciding the issue as a matter of law, the cases must be remanded to the trial court for further proceedings.

So ordered.

DANAHER, Circuit Judge (dissenting):

The District of Columbia Court of Appeals obviously was as unhappy about the situation here presented as any of us can possibly be. Its opinion in the Williams case, quoted in the majority text, concludes: "We think Congress should consider corrective legislation to protect the public from such exploitive contracts as were utilized in the case at bar."

My view is thus summed up by an able court which made no finding that there had actually been sharp practice. Rather the appellant seems to have known precisely where she stood.

There are many aspects of public policy here involved. What is a luxury to some may seem an outright necessity to others. Is public oversight to be required of the expenditures of relief funds? A washing machine, e.g., in the hands of a relief client might become a fruitful source of income. Many relief clients may well need credit, and certain business establishments will take long chances on the sale of items, expecting their pricing policies will afford a degree of protection commensurate with the risk. Perhaps a remedy when necessary will be found within the provisions of the "Loan Shark" law, D.C.Code §§ 26-601 et seq. (1961).

I mention such matters only to emphasize the desirability of a cautious approach to any such problem, particularly since the law for so long has allowed parties such great latitude in making their own contracts. I dare say there must annually be thousands upon thousands of installment credit transactions in this jurisdiction, and one can only speculate as to the effect the decision in these cases will have.[1]

I join the District of Columbia Court of Appeals in its disposition of the issues.

---

[1] However the provision ultimately may be applied or in what circumstances, D.C.Code § 28-2-301 (Supp. IV, 1965) did not become effective until January 1, 1965.

Behind the Scenes

Much has been written about the facts in *Walker-Thomas Furniture*. Williams had seven children and received $218 per month from public assistance from the welfare department. Her initial purchase from Walker-Thomas Furniture was in 1957, when she bought two pairs of draperies for $12.95 after signing the form presented by the store. The form was in closely spaced 4-point type and contained the language at issue in the case. Over the next five years, she purchased a wallet, an apron set, a pot holder set, several rugs, more draperies and curtains, two beds, a mattress, a chest, sheets, a fan, a typewriter, a toy gun and holster, four chairs, a bath mat set, a washing machine, and, finally, the $514 stereophonic record player on which she did not keep up the payments. Her purchases totaled about $1500, on which she had paid about $1056. She signed the same form each time, and most of the purchases were made when a store representative came to her house. The store (pictured below) knew she was on welfare; the name of her social worker was listed on the reverse side of the form for the stereo. One study of sales practices in the District of Columbia showed that sales representatives often approached customers and suggested new purchases just before they paid off their debts.

After Williams defaulted on her payments, the store filed an action for replevin of all of the items listed above, based on the contract's lease-to-own clause and the cross-collateral clause. The store's records showed that Williams still owed 25¢ for the first pair of draperies (out of $45.65), 3¢ on the second item (out of $13.21), $2.34 on the third item (out of $127.40), and so on. The other defendants, the Thornes, were in a similar position. They faced repossession of items purchased in eleven transactions over four years, on which they had paid $1422 and had $433.13 yet owing. After the

U.S. Marshal seized all of the items under the writ, the subsequent appraisal of their worth valued them at $209.

[handwritten margin notes: "house sell" near top left; "owed more than worth" near bottom left]

In the picture below, the sign in the right-hand window says, "Credit
. . . Buy Now, Pay Later!" For additional pictures, go to
www.aalscontracts.com/williams.html. Thanks to Professor Franklin Snyder at Texas Wesleyan

University School of Law for
permission to reproduce
these pictures.

In the decade before *Williams
v. Walker-Thomas Furniture*,
the same furniture store
had filed and successfully
executed as many as a thou-
sand writs of replevin to enforce contracts against its customers. Other
merchants serving poor neighborhoods were using similar practices,
saying that the harsh credit practices were necessary because the stores'
profits were slim as a result of their customers' default rates. The
attorneys representing Williams and Thorne asked for the assistance of
the Federal Trade Commission in curbing the abusive credit practices,
but the FTC declined to help. A year after the case, the Federal Trade
Commission conducted a study at the small claims court in which the
furniture store and other stores in the area filed their actions. The FTC
found 2,690 court judgments, most by default. This translated into
one judgment for every $2,200 in sales. The stores often sold with
the "expectation and hope" that the goods would eventually be repos-
sessed and resold. As one commentator put it, Walker-Thomas was "a
middle-class solution to a lower-class problem." For more background,
see Eben Colby, *What Did the Doctrine of Unconscionability Do to the
Walker-Thomas Furniture Company?*, 34 Conn. L. Rev. 625 (2002).
For the viewpoint of Williams's attorney from the Legal Assistance
Office of The Bar Association of the District of Columbia, *see* Pierre E.
Dostert, *Appellate Restatement of Unconscionability: Civil Legal Aid
Work*, 54 A.B.A.J. 1183 (1968), cited in Robert H. Skilton & Orrin L.
Helstad, *Protection of the Installment Buyer of Goods under the Uni-
form Commercial Code*, 65 Mich. L. Rev. 1465, 1476-777 (1967).

Predatory lending practices did not end with this case, at the
Walker-Thomas furniture store or elsewhere. Although legislation and court action have made the cross-collateralization
clause obsolete in consumer contracts, lenders have developed other aggressive models for offering credit to the poor.

For instance, banks and credit card issuers regularly engage in "fee harvesting" of their customers. National Consumer Law Center, Fee Harvesters: Low-Credit, High-Cost Cards Bleed Consumers (Nov. 2007) (available at www.consumerlaw.org).

Four years after Judge Wright wrote the opinion in *Walker-Thomas Furniture*, he wrote *The Courts Have Failed the Poor*, which appeared in The New York Times Magazine, p. 26 (March 9, 1969). "Though our most pressing social, moral and political imperative is to liberate the urban poor from their degradation," he wrote, "the courts continue to apply ancient legal doctrines which merely compound the plight of the poverty-stricken." He quoted former Attorney General Nicholas Katzenbach, who said, "'[L]aws and regulations are protections and guides, established for our benefit and for us to use,' but to the poor they are 'a hostile maze, established as harassment, at all costs to be avoided.'" Using examples from *Williams v. Walker-Thomas Furniture*, criminal law, service of process, default judgments, the holder-in-due-course rule, confession-of-judgment clauses, small claims courts, deficiency judgments, wage garnishment, landlord-tenant law, and welfare, he concluded that "[t]here is a law for the poor and a law for the rest of us." Quoting a Yale professor, he said, "'All too often, law is used as an excuse for maintaining an unjust status quo . . . . But no form of law is ever necessary or inevitable. Law is the servant of social policy, not a determinant of it. It is our policy that must change.' The courts can and must participate in bringing about that change by changing the law, at least in the areas where judges made the offending law in the first place."

§ 2.4.1. Codifications of the Unconscionability Defense

Unconscionability had its roots in the English chancellor's office (later the chancery court), which had exclusive jurisdiction over equitable remedies such as specific performance and injunctive relief. The chancellor could withhold equitable relief for a breach of contract if the consideration was greatly disproportionate ("inadequacy of consideration"), if the parties' rights or obligations were lop-sided ("lack of mutuality of obligation"), or if the contract was otherwise unfair, unjust, or unconscionable. Underlying these discretionary withholdings of relief was the belief that a court of equity ought not be a party to the enforcement of such contracts, even though courts of law were not bound by the same limitations. For perhaps as long as 500 years, these doctrines were applied *only* to requests for equitable relief, even after the merger of law and equity jurisdiction in many American courts. The first Restatement (promulgated in 1932) had no rule on unconscionability.

Whether intending to change the common law rules or not, some courts in the first half of the twentieth century began to apply unconscionability and lack of mutuality to breach-of-contract suits for damages, even though no equitable remedy was involved. Then, in the 1950s, UCC § 2-302 codified the doctrine of unconscionability for contracts for sale of goods, even when an equitable remedy was not sought. Since then, courts have also extended the defense more regularly to contracts not within UCC Article 2, whether by applying § 2-302 by analogy or by simply applying the common law defense of unconscionability. The drafters of the Restatement (Second) followed suit in 1979.

The equitable roots of the doctrine continue to influence its use. A court has equitable discretion whether or not to grant relief based on unconscionability, making the doctrine unpredictable and incapable of precise definition.

Unconscionability is most often successfully invoked by consumers (individuals contracting for their own personal, family, or household purposes, usually with a company or corporation). It has also been raised successfully by franchisees against franchisors and by employees against employers. Unconscionability claims by businesses rarely succeed.

For More Information

Dan B. Dobbs, *Law of Remedies* §§ 2.4, 12.8 (2d ed., Practitioner's Ed. 1993); 1 E. Allan Farnsworth, *Farnsworth on Contracts* §§ 4.27, 4.28 (1990).

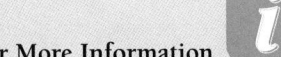

Reading the Law Critically: Unconscionability under the UCC, Restatement (Second), and UNIDROIT

1. Neither the UCC nor the Restatement (Second) defines unconscionability. What guidance do the UCC and Restatement comments provide as to the meaning?

2. Under these provisions, is unconscionability a question of law or fact? Does the judge decide what is unconscionable, or does the jury make the decision? Why?

3. Compare the UCC provision, the Restatement provision, and the UNIDROIT provision. How do they compare to the rule applied in *Williams*? Consider these codifications as you read the unconscionability cases that follow.

UCC § 2-302. **Unconscionable Contract or Clause.**

(1) If the court as a matter of law finds the contract or any clause of the contract to have been unconscionable at the time it was made the court may refuse to enforce the contract, or it may enforce the remainder of the contract without the unconscionable clause, or it may so limit the application of any unconscionable clause as to avoid any unconscionable result.

(2) When it is claimed or appears to the court that the contract or any clause thereof may be unconscionable the parties shall be afforded a reasonable opportunity to present evidence as to its commercial setting, purpose and effect to aid the court in making the determination.

Comment 1. . . . . The basic test is whether, in the light of the general commercial background and the commercial needs of the particular trade or case, the clauses involved are so one-sided as to be unconscionable under the circumstances existing at the time of the making of the contract. . . . The principle is one of the prevention of oppression and unfair surprise . . . and not of disturbance of allocation of risks because of superior bargaining power.

————————

Restatement (Second) § 208. **Unconscionable Contract or Term**

If a contract or term thereof is unconscionable at the time the contract is made a court may refuse to enforce the contract, or may enforce the remainder of the contract without the unconscionable term, or may so limit the application of any unconscionable term as to avoid any unconscionable result.

Comments:
c. Overall imbalance.   Inadequacy of consideration does not of itself invalidate a bargain, but gross disparity in the values exchanged may be an important factor in a determination that a contract is unconscionable . . . . Theoretically it is possible for a contract to be oppressive taken as a whole, even though there is no weakness in the bargaining process and no single term which is in itself unconscionable. Ordinarily, however, an unconscionable contract involves other factors as well as overall imbalance.

d. Weakness in the bargaining process.   A bargain is not unconscionable merely because the parties to it are unequal in bargaining position, nor even because the inequality results in an allocation of risks to the weaker party. But gross inequality of bargaining power, together with terms unreasonably favorable to the stronger party, may confirm indications that the transaction involved elements of deception or compulsion, or may show that the weaker party had no meaningful choice, no real alternative, or did not in fact assent or appear to assent to the unfair terms. Factors which may contribute to a finding of unconscionability in the bargaining process include the following: belief by the stronger party that there is no reasonable probability that the weaker party will fully perform the contract; knowledge of the stronger party that the weaker party will be unable to receive substantial benefits from the contract; knowledge of the stronger party that the weaker party is unable reasonably to protect his interests by reason of physical or mental infirmities, ignorance, illiteracy or inability to understand the language of the agreement, or similar factors.

———————

UNIDROIT Art. 3.10. **Gross Disparity**

(1) A party may avoid the contract or an individual term of it if, at the time of the conclusion of the contract, the contract or term unjustifiably gave the other party an excessive advantage. Regard is to be had, among other factors, to
   (a) the fact that the other party has taken unfair advantage of the first party's dependence, economic distress or urgent needs, or of its improvidence, ignorance, inexperience or lack of bargaining skill, and
   (b) the nature and purpose of the contract.
(2) Upon the request of the party entitled to avoidance, a court may adapt the contract or term in order to make it accord with reasonable commercial standards of fair dealing.
(3) A court may also adapt the contract or term upon the request of the party receiving notice of avoidance, provided that that party informs the other party of its request promptly after receiving such notice and before the other party has reasonably acted in reliance on it. . . .

§ 2.4.2. Substantive and Procedural Unconscionability

As unconscionability expanded beyond its limited role in equitable remedies, courts and commentators sought to define the concept with more particularity. They began to articulate unconscionability as including aspects of both substantive and procedural unconscionability, so that they could distinguish between problems with the content of the contract and concerns about the circumstances of contract formation. As cases developed additional guidelines for determining whether unconscionability should or should not be granted, jurisdictions began to diverge between stricter or more lenient requirements for finding unconscionability.

Reading the Law Critically: *Sitogum Holdings* and *American Software*

1. Which facts in each case are categorized as related to procedural unconscionability? Substantive unconscionability? Which facts in *Williams v. Walker-Thomas Furniture* fit into each category?

2. Do these cases require both procedural and substantive unconscionability to establish the defense? Does *Williams?* How do the courts use the two categories of unconscionability to decide whether to grant the defense?

3. What might explain the differences in approach and result between these two cases? Do they differ on policy or law, or do the differing outcomes result purely from differing facts?

4. Based on these cases, what specific advice would you offer a client to avoid having a contract be found to be unconscionable?

Sitogum Holdings, Inc. v. Ropes

SITOGUM HOLDINGS, INC., Plaintiff-Respondent

v.

PHYLLIS ELINE ROPES, Defendant-Appellant

v.

MARLENE VAN NOORD; TIMOTHY P. SULLIVAN; NEIL COLES; and JOHN DOE and JANE DOE (the yet unnamed officers and directors of the Plaintiff corporation), Third-party Defendants-Respondents

Superior Court of New Jersey
800 A.2d 915 (N.J. Super. Ct. 2002)

FISHER, P.J.Ch.

The common law doctrine of unconscionability has proved difficult to define and has been rarely invoked undoubtedly because, other than in exceptional cases, it has been largely viewed as grossly interfering with the freedom to contract. Notwithstanding this philosophical discomfort, the surrounding circumstances regarding defendant's desire to sell her property provided fertile ground for, and did in fact result in, a one-sided agreement which this court finds unconscionable.[1]

I.

Defendant Phyllis E. Ropes ("Mrs. Ropes") and her husband, John M. Ropes, Jr., were the owners of waterfront property in Brielle, New Jersey. This was their principal residence although they also owned a winter home in the Cayman Islands. It was in the Cayman Islands that John M. Ropes, Jr. died suddenly on January 3, 2000.

Grief-stricken, Mrs. Ropes, then 81 years old, took a number of rapid and inconsistent steps regarding the Brielle property. Apparently, not long before his death, it had been her and Mr. Ropes' desire to sell the property. With his death, Mrs. Ropes almost immediately executed two separate powers of attorney on the same day—January 13, 2000; one in favor of third-party defendant Marlene Van Noord and the other in favor of Linda Dowhan. On January 26, 2000 another power of attorney, prepared by plaintiff Sitogum Holdings, Inc. ("Sitogum"), was also executed by Mrs. Ropes in favor of Ms. Van Noord. The next day, Ms. Van Noord executed an option to purchase the Brielle property in favor of Sitogum.[2] This option contract, which Mrs. Ropes now claims is unconscionable, provided Sitogum—an entity which would not even be incorporated for another six days—with the right to purchase the Brielle property, within eight months, for $800,000. Sitogum agreed to pay $1000 per month for this option.

A February, 2000 appraisal suggested the Brielle property was worth between $1,500,000 and $1,750,000. Apparently recognizing the windfall about to come its way, Sitogum claims to have prepaid six of its monthly $1000 payments on or about February 28, 2000.

Apparently, at the same time, efforts were being made to market the property through Mrs. Ropes' other attorney-in-fact. Sitogum may have become aware of this since it recorded a "Memorandum of Option to Purchase Real Property" on or about April 11, 2000. On April 13, 2000, Mrs. Ropes executed a contract for the sale of the Brielle property to another party for $1,500,000. Upon learning of this, Sitogum, on April 28, 2000, exercised its option to purchase. Notwithstanding,

---

[1] The matter is before the court by way of defendant's motion for summary judgment. There do not appear to be any disputed questions of fact . . . . [T]he application of the doctrine of unconscionability in this case turns on its sufficiency as a matter of law. In reciting the facts relating to this contention, the court will also give plaintiff, as the opponent of the motion, all reasonable inferences to be drawn from the facts provided.

[2] According to Sitogum, on January 19, 2000—only 3 days after the execution of the power of attorney and 16 days after Mr. Ropes died—Ms. Van Noord received a telephone call from a Florida attorney expressing an interest in the Brielle property. No explanation has been provided by Sitogum as to how this Florida attorney came to learn of the property or Mrs. Ropes' desire to sell it.

Mrs. Ropes advised that she would not transfer the property to Sitogum. As a result, on May 19, 2000, Sitogum filed this suit to compel specific performance of the January 27, 2000 option agreement.[4] Mrs. Ropes now moves for summary judgment.

II.

Mrs. Ropes recognizes that the claim of her alleged capacity to contract or the voluntariness of the power of attorney elude resolution by way of summary judgment.[5] Other contentions also cannot be resolved on this motion.[6] The only issue which is ripe for summary judgment is Mrs. Ropes' claim that the option contract is unconscionable.

A.

The power of a court to relieve parties from unconscionable contracts has ancient roots.[7] In *Earl of Chesterfield v. Janssen*, [28 Eng. Rep. 82, 100 (1750),] plaintiff borrowed 5000 pounds in exchange for his agreement

Make the Connection

In its footnote 6, the court notes that late payment of some of the $1000 owed monthly under the option contract "does not necessarily relieve Mrs. Ropes of her obligations." Why should that be the case? As we will see in subsequent chapters, not every failure to perform contractual duties allows the other party to withhold performance. One would have to ask whether the required performance (payment of $1000 each month) is an express condition of Mrs. Ropes' promise to allow Sitogum to buy (see Chapter 7, page 836) and, if not, whether the failure to pay on time was a material or non-material breach of an implied condition (Chapter 8, page 887).

---

[4] On March 14, 2001, an order was entered which (1) permitted the sale of the property to this other contracting party for $1,500,000 . . . and (3) required that the net proceeds be placed in escrow pending final judgment or such other order of the court.

[5] That is, the motion invites the court to assume, for present purposes only, that Mrs. Ropes was of sound mind in January 2000, that she freely and voluntarily provided a power of attorney to Marlene Van Noord, that the power of attorney was given the day before the option contract was executed and that the power of attorney authorized Ms. Van Noord to sign the option contract.

[6] Besides the claim of unconscionability, the motion was based on two points. The first relies on the fact—apparently undisputed—that Sitogum was not incorporated at the time the option contract came into existence; as a result, Mrs. Ropes contends there could be no valid contract. However, a court of equity could conclude that the lack of certain ministerial steps to the creation of a corporation need not preclude the enforceability of a contract made by such a nascent entity. Second, Mrs. Ropes contends there was a default in the timely submission of the monthly $1000 payments required by the option contract and, thus, there was either no consideration for the attorney-in-fact's promise to sell or Sitogum otherwise breached the option contract. The parties dispute whether those payments were made. And, while the $6000 prepayment may have been mailed or received a few days late[, that] does not necessarily relieve Mrs. Ropes of her obligations under the option contract. There is nothing in the present record to suggest that time was of the essence for those $1000 payments. The option contract states only that "[t]ime is of essence *of this option.*" The emphasized portion might suggest that time was of the essence of the exercise of the option, not the $1000 payments.

[7] Roman law recognized the doctrine of "laesio ultra dimidum vel enormis" which permitted rescission upon a disproportionate exchange of promises. . . .

to pay 20,000 pounds upon the death of his then 70-year old grandmother. In referring to the agreement as "unconscientious," the Chancellor described the power to set it aside, which still has traces in the doctrine currently applied by modern courts:

> It may be apparent from the intrinsic nature and subject of the bargain itself; such as no man in his sense and not under a delusion would make on the one hand, and as no honest man would accept on the other; which are unequitable and unconscientious bargains, and of such even the common law take notice.

[2 *Ves. Sr.* 125, 155, 28 *Eng. Rep.* 82, 100 (1750).] The Supreme Court of the United States recognized this common law authority in the nineteenth century[8] and courts of equity have traditionally refused their assistance to parties who obtain such one-sided bargains.

Notwithstanding its venerable history, the application of the doctrine has always been viewed as controversial and it would appear, judging from the paucity of reported decisions, that its use has been infrequent. The reason for this is undoubtedly over a heightened concern that its uncertain parameters "increase[] the potential for unreasoned or arbitrary decisions based on personal value judgments." Hillman, "Debunking Some Myths about Unconscionability: A New Framework for U.C.C. Section 2-302," 67 *Cornell L. Rev.* 1, 15 (1981). Courts normally examine challenges to the validity of contracts by first recognizing the parties' freedom to contract and by applying the principle that the execution of a contract manifests an intent to be bound by all its terms. *See, e.g., Restatement of Contracts*, § 70 (1932). As a result, the principle that courts "should not rewrite contracts," is often intoned in such disputes. *See, e.g., Kampf v. Franklin Life Ins. Co.*, 33 N.J. 36, 43, 161 A.2d 717 (1960). . . . . Regardless, however, of the unease which its potential use produces, the doctrine of unconscionability has a place in our jurisprudence so that grossly unfair or one-sided contracts may be properly "policed." White & Summers, *Uniform Commercial Code* (4th ed., 1995) 206; *Wille v. Southwestern Bell Tel. Co.*, 219 Kan. 755, 549 P.2d 903 (1976).

     . . . .

B.

Besides existing at common law, the doctrine of unconscionability was included within the Uniform Commercial Code, becoming, as Professor Hawkland said, "undoubtedly the most controversial section in the entire Code." Hawkland, *A*

---

[8] *See, Eyre v. Potter*, 56 U.S. 42, 45, 15 How. 42, 14 L.Ed. 592 (1853) ("A disposition of property so revolting to common sense and natural affection ought to be looked upon with suspicion"); *Hume v. United States*, 132 U.S. 406, 411, 10 S.Ct. 134, 33 L.Ed. 393 (1889) (quoting *Earl of Chesterfield, supra* with approval).

Transactional Guide to the U.C.C., Vol. I, § 1.16 at p. 44 (1964). The Uniform Commercial Code ("the Code") handles the issue in two interesting ways. First, the Code "assigns the issue of unconscionability exclusively to the judge." White & Summers, *Uniform Commercial Code* (2d ed. 1980) 151. . . . Second, the Code provision contains no helpful definition or parameters . . . .

. . . .

. . . . Unquestionably the common law rule, the Code's controversial sec- tion 2-302 and the *Restatement* 's descriptions are general and abstract, but they also possess wisdom—the wisdom of understanding that the bright-line rule sought by the leading commentators is not only utterly elusive but also quite undesirable.[12] Instead, the erecting of parameters has been left to the courts to consider in light of their general experience with contract disputes and upon an understanding of the particular facts of each case. In short, the lawmakers undoubtedly anticipated that the skeletal unconscionability framework would be filled out through case-by-case determinations. While the risk of defining the doctrine through such a case-by-case approach is the possible loss of restraint and consistency, the advantage is a device inherently governed by the particular circumstances of each case measured against the experiences of past and present judges, the lifeblood of the common law.

C.

. . . .

For the most part, the unconscionability cases follow *Williams v. Walker-Thomas* and look for two factors: (1) unfairness in the formation of the contract, and (2) excessively disproportionate terms. Professor Leff labelled these two ele- ments as "procedural" and "substantive" unconscionability. Leff, *supra,* 115 U. Pa. L.Rev. at 487. The first factor—procedural unconscionability—can include a variety of inadequacies, such as age, literacy, lack of sophistication, hidden or unduly complex contract terms, bargaining tactics, and the particular setting existing during the contract formation process. *See, e.g., Gillman v. Chase Man- hattan Bank,* 73 N.Y.2d 1, 537 N.Y.S.2d 787, 534 N.E.2d 824 1988) . . . . The second factor—substantive unconscionability—simply suggests the exchange of obligations so one-sided as to shock the court's conscience. *See, e.g., State ex rel. Lefkowitz v. ITM, Inc.,* 52 Misc.2d 39, 275 N.Y.S.2d 303 (Sup.Ct.1966) (purchase price/market value ratio approximately 2½ times); *American Home Improvement, Inc. v. MacIver,* 105 N.H. 435, 201 A.2d 886 (1964) (2½ times);

---

[12] While critical of the phrasing of 2-302 and the Code's comments, Professors White and Summers also recognize that such criticism is unrealistic: "It is not possible to *define* unconscionability. It is not a *concept,* but a determination to be made in light of a variety of factors not unifiable into a formula." White & Summers, *supra,* at 151.

Toker v. Perl, 103 *N.J.Super.* 500, 247 A.2d 701 (Law Div.1968), *aff'd on other grounds,* 108 *N.J.Super.* 129, 260 A.2d 244 (App.Div.1970) (2½ times).

Most courts have looked for a sufficient showing of both factors in finding a contract unconscionable. *See, e.g., Williams v. Walker-Thomas, supra; Patterson v. Walker-Thomas Furniture,* 277 A.2d 111 (D.C.1971) . . . . Other courts have been satisfied merely by proof of substantive unconscionability, *i.e.,* an excessively disproportionate exchange of material promises. *See, e.g., Ahern v. Knecht,* 202 *Ill.App.*3d 709, 150 *Ill.Dec.* 660, 563 N.E.2d 787, 792 (1990) ("[g]ross excessiveness of price alone can make an agreement unconscionable"); *MacIver, supra,* 105 N.H. 435, 201 A.2d 886; *Frostifresh Corp. v. Reynoso,* 52 *Misc.*2d 26, 274 *N.Y.S.*2d 757 (Dist.Ct.1966), *rev'd as to damages only,* 54 *Misc.*2d 119, 281 *N.Y.S.*2d 964 (App.Div.1967); *Toker v. Perl, supra,* 103 *N.J.Super.* 500, 247 A.2d 701; *Toker v. Westerman,* 113 *N.J.Super.* 452, 274 A.2d 78 (Dist. Ct.1970).[13] Still other courts have determined that the two elements need not have equal effect but work together, creating a "sliding scale" of unconscionability.* *Funding Systems Leas. Corp. v. King Louie Intern.,* 597 S.W.2d 624, 634 (Mo.Ct.App.1979) ("if there exists gross procedural unconscionability then not much be needed by way of substantive unconscionability, and that the same 'sliding scale' be applied if there be great substantive unconscionability but little procedural unconscionability"); *Tacoma Boatbuilding, Inc. v. Delta Fishing Co.,* 28 UCC Rep. Serv. 26, 1980 WL 98403 n.20 (W.D. Wash.1980) ("The substantive/ procedural analysis is more of a sliding scale than a true dichotomy"); Spanogle, *supra,* 117 *U. Pa. L.Rev.* at 950 (if a "court considered the terms especially harsh, only a slight procedural abuse would be necessary") . . . .

D.

[The court examined New Jersey precedent and found it to be consistent with the "sliding scale" relation between substantive and procedural unconscionability.]

III.

Against this flexible standard, the court must canvass the factual record to determine whether the option contract was the product of both procedural and substantive unconscionability. . . .

---

* [Authors' Note: The *Sitogum* court mentions a "sliding scale" approach, which was subsequently adopted by some jurisdictions. It has since become the majority rule.]

[13] There do not appear to be any decisions where procedural unconscionability was present but not substantive unconscionability. This should not come as any surprise. No matter how the contract came about, it would be unlikely that a party would complain—or a court would listen—if the contract was otherwise fair or reasonable. It would be much like arguing about negligent conduct which failed to result in any damage.

A.

The concept of procedural unconscionability arises in this case in an unusual way. That is, Mrs. Ropes' situation does not fit the pattern seen in most of the cases cited above. She was not financially vulnerable nor does it appear she was either illiterate or of limited education. But, the events in question came immediately upon her husband's unexpected death and, thus, it is fair to say that Mrs. Ropes was vulnerable to an unfair transaction, albeit in a different sense from the consumer in *Williams v. Walker-Thomas* and most other such cases. Certainly, the law, and particularly courts of equity, have shown special solicitude to persons of Mrs. Ropes' age and situation.

Also, while it may have been her own voluntary way of approaching the sale of her Brielle property, Mrs. Ropes was not directly involved in the transaction because she had given a power of attorney to Ms. Van Noord. While it is recognized that the question of Mrs. Ropes' competency or vulnerability to influence cannot be resolved on this motion, the fact that more than one power of attorney was executed at the same time adds further procedural irregularities to the transaction. In addition, while Sitogum had the assistance of counsel (indeed, Sitogum appears to be made up of a consortium of attorneys), neither Mrs. Ropes nor Ms. Van Noord appeared to have received any sound advice from counsel. While counsel on the Cayman Islands assisted in the preparation and execution of certain documents, there admittedly was no advice rendered as to the appropriate steps to be taken in securing the highest and best price. And the rationale behind simultaneously appointing two different attorneys-in-fact, as occurred here, both with the power to sell the same property on Mrs. Ropes' behalf—with the potential for different contracts concerning the same property—has not been explained or justified.

After communications with a Florida attorney regarding the sale of the Brielle property, Ms. Van Noord received yet another form of a power of attorney and a proposed option contract. Ms. Van Noord claims to have brought these papers to Mrs. Ropes, who "appeared to be nervous but certainly seemed to know what she was doing and what she wanted to do." A few days later, according to Ms. Van Noord, she received a telephone call from Mrs. Ropes indicating that she wanted to sell the property. They both went to the office of a second Cayman Islands attorney. No explanation has been offered to explain why they did not return to the Cayman Islands attorney they saw a few days earlier. Mrs. Ropes signed yet another power of attorney, apparently in the form proposed by Sitogum's Florida attorney. For reasons, also not explained, Ms. Van Noord did not then sign the option contract but did so the next day. Ms. Van Noord then sent both the January 25 power of attorney and the January 26 option contract to the Florida attorney. In the same time frame, Mrs. Ropes' other attorney-in-fact reached an agreement with a different buyer.

So many questions arise from these events. Most notable is the curious fact that Mrs. Ropes did not sign the option contract, but only signed a power of attorney which authorized Ms. Van Noord to sign the option contract. Why would she first sign a power of attorney in favor of Ms. Van Noord on one day, in the presence of an attorney, allowing Ms. Van Noord to sign an option contract the next day, apparently outside the presence of an attorney, when, according to Ms. Van Noord, the option contract had already been seen and reviewed by Mrs. Ropes? Clearly, if Ms. Van Noord's version is accurate, the events in question must be found to be quite irregular. And, most incredibly, nearly all these events appeared to occur in the presence of attorneys apparently engaged to assist in Mrs. Ropes' efforts to sell the Brielle property. Accepting as true all the facts asserted by Sitogum in opposition to this motion, the court must conclude that the transactions in question, leading up to the creation of the option contract, were most unusual and made in the absence of the meaningful representation of counsel. Neither Mrs. Ropes nor those acting on her behalf obtained the type of zealous and careful advocacy required by aged persons or, for that matter, any other person in Mrs. Ropes' situation. While the present record does not yet suggest sufficient irregularity about the procedural events as to rise to the level of fraud, at best Mrs. Ropes' attorney-in-fact exhibited only some desultory interest in obtaining fair value for the property. The court is satisfied that a sufficient degree of procedural unconscionability is present to permit examination into the substantive fairness of the contract.

Think About It!

What defenses other than unconscionability were or might have been raised by Mrs. Ropes? What strategic decisions may have led to her choice of defenses?

B.

Most startling about this transaction is the size of the purchase price locked in by the option contract. As indicated, Ms. Van Noord entered into the option contract without having engaged professional assistance for determining the value of the Brielle property. As a result, the price set by the option contract was $800,000, a figure apparently discussed and considered by Mrs. Ropes' husband prior to his untimely death. However, as later revealed, the Brielle property's true value was approximately twice that amount. An appraisal rendered by Diane Turton Realtors, at the request of Mrs. Ropes' current counsel, opined that the value of the property ranged between $1,500,000 and $1,750,000 and, in fact, the property was ultimately sold for $1,500,000. The great disparity between the $800,000 at which Sitogum had gained the right to purchase the property for and the later appraisal and the ultimate sale of the property to others for nearly twice that much demonstrates the substantive unconscionability of the option contract.

In seeking to defeat the claim of substantive unconscionability, Sitogum observes that Ms. Van Noord believed Mrs. Ropes was more concerned about disposing of the property than the price. In her answers to interrogatories, Ms. Van Noord swore to the following facts:

> [Mrs. Ropes] was adamant that she wanted the "Brielle property off my back." [Ms. Van Noord] counseled [Mrs. Ropes] in the presence of everyone to not do anything rash, to be patient. [Mrs. Ropes] kept stating that she wanted the property off her back, regardless of the content of house—regardless of the price—just sell it. [Ms. Van Noord] accompanied [Mrs. Ropes] to at least three or four meetings with Mr. Broadbent [the first of the two Cayman Island attorneys mentioned earlier]. During each of those conversations, I remember that there was a desire by [Mrs. Ropes] to get rid of, to just sell the Brielle property in New Jersey.

If those facts are true—as the court presently assumes—it becomes apparent that Ms. Van Noord did not act consistently with that goal. Not only did she obligate Mrs. Ropes to sell for approximately half the property's value, but she failed to "get the property off" Mrs. Ropes' back. Instead, Ms. Van Noord entered into an option contract which had the potential of tying up the property for eight months, without any guarantee of it actually being sold. Within that eight month period, Sitogum could unilaterally determine whether it would purchase the property; if Sitogum chose to walk away, Mrs. Ropes would be left where she started. And, if Sitogum decided to purchase within the initial eight month period, the transaction need not actually occur for yet another 90 days. So, the result of the option contract was to require Mrs. Ropes to potentially wait for as long as 11 months to be "rid" of the property at an unreasonably low price. The contention that this option contract is not unconscionable because Mrs. Ropes allegedly did not care about the price (so long as it was at least $800,000) if the property could be gotten rid of quickly is proved fallacious in light of the terms of the option contract. And the option contract appears all the more unconscionable when it is observed that Mrs. Ropes received no consideration for tying up the property for potentially eight months (and possibly eleven months) if Sitogum ultimately decided to purchase because the option payments—which were either never sent, sent but not received, or received by Ms. Van Noord but lost, purloined, or at least never given to Mrs. Ropes—were to be deducted from the purchase price. On the other hand, if Sitogum determined not to exercise the option, then Mrs. Ropes would only have benefitted to the meagre tune of $1000 per month, and still would not have been rid of the property.

While the existing case law does not precisely define what exchange of promises might be classified as "substantively unconscionable," certainly a price

$700,000 less than what the property ultimately sold for meets this court's definition of unconscionability.

IV.

For the foregoing reasons, Mrs. Ropes' motion for summary judgment will be granted, declaring the option contract void *ab initio.* . . .

Relief for Substantive Unconscionability Alone?
The Refrigerator Cases

In Part II. C., the *Sitogum* court cites three well known cases involving a consumer purchase of a new refrigerator and/or freezer. At least two of them involve door-to-door sales (a sales setting that has since been regulated by the Federal Trade Commission to eliminate many of its common abuses):

- In *Frostifresh Corp. v. Reynoso,* 274 N.Y.S.2d 757 (Sup. Ct.), *rev'd on damages,* 281 N.Y.S.2d 964 (App. Div. 1967), seller negotiated the sale of a refrigerator/freezer unit orally in Spanish to buyers, who didn't think they could afford it. Seller told them it would be free because they would get commissions from sales to neighbors. The signed contract in English was never translated or explained to buyers. The contract price was $1,146 for a unit that cost seller $348. The trial court awarded seller damages of $316 (seller's cost minus buyers' payments to date). The appellate court reversed, to allow seller to "recover its net cost for the [unit], plus a reasonable profit, in addition to trucking and service charges necessarily incurred and reasonable finance charges."

- In *Toker v. Westerman,* 274 A.2d 78 (N.J. Union County Ct. 1970), buyer purchased a refrigerator/freezer unit from an appliance dealer for $899.98, plus sales tax, group life insurance, and time price differential, for a total cost of $1,230. At trial, seller testified that the unit was a "stripped unit" worth no more than $400. Buyer had paid $656 before the suit, and the court refused to enforce the remainder of the contract price.

- In *Toker v. Perl,* 247 A.2d 701 (N.J. Super. Ct. Law Div. 1968), seller arranged a home visit to sell a food plan to buyers. After 2½ hours, buyers claimed not to have room for the amount of food discussed. Seller replied that a freezer was included in the food plan. Around midnight, buyers signed three forms, which seller had stacked to make only the signature lines visible on a financing application and an installment contract to purchase a freezer. The freezer price was $800, plus sales tax of $24, creditor life insurance for $17, and a credit service charge (time price differential) of $252, for a total price of $1,093, but its maximum value was $300. The court refused to enforce the contract because it had been procured by fraud and unconscionability.

Courts rarely rely solely on substantive unconscionability, but these cases remain as examples of egregious pricing that could be enough to support a finding of unconscionabililty, perhaps even without the accompanying facts showing procedural unconscionability as well.

American Software, Inc. v. Ali

AMERICAN SOFTWARE, INC., Defendant-Appellant

v.

MELANE ALI, Plaintiff-Respondent

California Court of Appeal
54 Cal. Rptr. 2d 477 (Ct. App. 1996)

KING, Associate Justice.

The appellant, American Software, Inc., appeals from a decision of the trial court granting a former employee, respondent Melane Ali, unpaid commissions based upon software sales she generated while in American Software's employ but which were remitted by customers after she voluntarily severed her employment. The key issue in this appeal is whether a provision of Ali's employment contract which, generally speaking, terminates her right to receive commissions on payments received on her accounts 30 days after severance of her employment is unconscionable, and therefore, unenforceable. The trial court found that Ali was entitled to recover the disputed commissions because this contractual provision was unconscionable. We disagree and reverse.

Facts

Ali was an account executive for American Software from September 5, 1991, to March 2, 1994. The employment relationship commenced after Ali was approached by a professional recruiter on behalf of American Software and was terminated when Ali voluntarily resigned because she had a job offer from one of American Software's competitors. Ali was hired to sell and market licensing agreements for software products to large companies. These products are designed to the customer's specifications for the purpose of integrating the customer's accounting, manufacturing, sales and distribution processes.

In exchange for her services, American Software agreed to pay Ali a base monthly salary plus a draw. If products were sold during the month, any commissions paid were reduced by the amount of the draw. However, the draw portion of the salary was paid regardless of whether or not the salesperson earned commissions to cover the draw. Any negative amount would be carried over from month-to-month until such time as the commissions were large enough to cover the previous draws, or until such time as the employment relationship was severed. If the amount of draws exceeded commissions at the time of termination, American Software would suffer the loss. At the time of her resignation, Ali's annual guaranteed salary, exclusive of commissions, was $75,000. Her base monthly salary was $3,333 per month and her nonrefundable draw was $2,917.

The terms and conditions of Ali's employment were set out in a written contract which was prepared by American Software. Ali reviewed the contract, and had an attorney, who she described as a "buddy," review it prior to employment. Of pertinence to the instant controversy, the contract included the specific circumstances under which Ali was to receive commissions after termination of employment with American Software. The employment agreement first states that "[c]ommissions are considered earned when the payment is received by the Company." It goes on to provide: "In the event of termination, the right of all commissions which would normally be due and payable are forfeited 30 days following the date of termination in the case of voluntary termination and 90 days in the case of involuntary termination."

Based on her testimony at trial, there is no question that Ali was aware of this provision prior to her execution of the agreement and commencement of work at

> **What's That?**
>
> A "draw" is a form of compensation advanced by an employer to an employee, in anticipation of all or part of the employee's expected commission, to provide the employee with cash flow issues before the commission can actually be paid. There are two common types of draws:
>
> *Non-recoverable or guaranteed:* The employer may not recoup any amount advanced in excess of the commission actually earned by the employee.
>
> *Recoverable:* The employer may recoup any amount advanced in excess of commission actually earned, either by employee repayment or by carrying the balance of the draw to the next pay period.

advance on expected commissions

American Software. She testified she reviewed the two and one-half page contract for one-half hour and caused certain handwritten deletions and revisions to be made to it, most notably deleting a provision requiring her to reimburse American Software $5,000 for the recruiter's fee in the event that she terminated her employment within a year. Ali testified that she signed the employment contract even though she believed certain provisions were unenforceable in California.

After Ali left American Software's employment, she sought additional commissions in connection with transactions with IBM and Kaiser Foundation Health Plan. American Software received payment from both companies more than 30 days after Ali's resignation.

After Ali's claim for unpaid commissions was denied by the Labor Commissioner, she sought de novo review in the superior court. (Lab.Code, § 98.2.) The trial court awarded Ali approximately $30,000 in unpaid commissions after finding that the contract provision regarding post-employment commissions was unconscionable and thus, unenforceable. The trial court found the evidence "overwhelming that the forfeiture provision inures to the benefit of the party with superior bargaining power without any indication of a reason for tying such benefit to the timing of a payment, rather than to the service actually provided in completing the sale." American Software timely appealed.

Discussion

In 1979, our Legislature enacted Civil Code section 1670.5, which codified the established doctrine that a court can refuse to enforce an unconscionable provision in a contract. . . .

> **FYI**
>
> The court refers to § 1670.5 of California's Civil Code, which is worded identically to UCC § 2-302 (see page 524).

Most California cases analyze unconscionability as having two separate elements—procedural and substantive. (See, e.g., *Shaffer v. Superior Court* (1995) 33 Cal.App.4th 993, 1000, 39 Cal.Rptr.2d 506; *Vance v. Villa Park Mobilehome Estates* (1995) 36 Cal.App.4th 698, 709, 42 Cal.Rptr.2d 723.) Substantive unconscionability focuses on the actual terms of the agreement, while procedural unconscionability focuses on the manner in which the contract was negotiated and the circumstances of the parties. California courts generally require a showing of both procedural and substantive unconscionability at the time the contract was made. (See *A & M Produce Co. v. FMC Corp.* (1982) 135 Cal.App.3d 473, 487, 186 Cal.Rptr. 114.) Some courts have indicated that a sliding scale applies for example, a contract with extraordinarily oppressive substantive terms will require less in the way of procedural unconscionability. (*Ilkhchooyi v. Best* (1995) 37 Cal.App.4th 395, 410, 45 Cal.Rptr.2d 766 . . . .

Indicia of procedural unconscionability include "oppression, arising from inequality of bargaining power and the absence of real negotiation or a meaningful choice" and "surprise, resulting from hiding the disputed term in a prolix document." (*Vance v. Villa Park Mobilehome Estates, supra,* 36 Cal.App.4th at p. 709, 42 Cal.Rptr.2d 723.) Substantive unconscionability is indicated by contract terms so one-sided as to "*shock the conscience.*" (*California Grocers Assn. v. Bank of America* (1994) 22 Cal.App.4th 205, 214, 27 Cal.Rptr.2d 396, italics in original.) . . . . With a concept as nebulous as "unconscionability" it is important that courts not be thrust in the paternalistic role of intervening to change contractual terms that the parties have agreed to merely because the court believes the terms are unreasonable. The terms must shock the conscience.

The critical juncture for determining whether a contract is unconscionable is the moment when it is entered into by both parties—not whether it is unconscionable in light of subsequent events. (Civ.Code, § 1670.5.) Unconscionability is ultimately a question of law for the court. (*Ilkhchooyi v. Best, supra,* 37 Cal. App.4th at p. 411, 45 Cal.Rptr.2d 766 . . . .)

In assessing procedural unconscionability, the evidence indicates that Ali was aware of her obligations under the contract and that she voluntarily agreed to assume them. In her business as a salesperson it is reasonable to assume she had become familiar with contracts and their importance. In fact, in Ali's testimony, she indicated that as part of her responsibilities for American Software, she helped negotiate the terms of a contract with IBM representing over a million dollars in sales. The salient provisions of the employment contract are straightforward, and the terms used are easily comprehensible to the layman. She had the benefit of counsel.[3] Nor is this a situation in which one party to the contract is confronted by an absence of meaningful choice. The very fact that Ali had enough bargaining "clout" to successfully negotiate for more favorable terms on other provisions evidences the contrary. She admits that she was aware of the post-employment commissions clause, but did not attempt to negotiate for less onerous terms.[4] In short, this case is a far cry from those cases where fine print, complex terminology, and presentation of a contract on a take-it-or-leave-it basis constitutes the groundwork for a finding of unconscionability.

Nor do we find substantive unconscionability. Ali's arguments of substantive unconscionability rest largely on events that occurred several years after the contract was entered into–her loss of sizable commissions on sales she had solicited during her employment but where payment was delayed for various reasons so that it was not received within 30 days after her departure. However, as indicated

---

[3] Some courts have considered the presence and advice of counsel to constitute circumstantial, if not conclusive, evidence that a contract is not unconscionable. (See e.g., *Resource Management Co. v. Weston* Ranch (Utah 1985) 706 P.2d 1028, 1045; *Bernina Distributors, Inc. v. Bernina Sewing Mach.* (10th Cir.1981) 646 F.2d 434, 440.)

[4] A company representative testified at trial that a number of individuals have successfully negotiated for modification of this provision.

by the very wording of California's unconscionability statute, we must analyze the circumstances as they existed "at the time [the contract] was made" to determine if gross unfairness was apparent at that time. (Civ.Code, § 1670.5, subd. (a).)

When viewed in light of the circumstances as they existed on August 23, 1991, when the instant contract was executed, we cannot say the contract provision with respect to compensation after termination was so unfair or oppressive in its mutual obligations as to "shock the conscience." (*California Grocers Assn. v. Bank of America, supra,* 22 Cal.App.4th at p. 214, 27 Cal.Rptr.2d 396.) If the official notes accompanying Uniform Commercial Code section 2-302, upon which Civil Code section 1670.5 is based, is to be relied upon as a guide, the contract terms are to be evaluated "in the light of the general commercial background and the commercial needs of the particular trade or case, . . ." (Cal. U. Com.Code, § 2-302, comment 1). Corbin suggests that the test is whether the terms are "so extreme as to appear unconscionable according to the mores and business practices of the time and place." (1 Corbin, Contracts (1963) § 128, p. 551.)

Our survey of case law indicates that the contract provision challenged here is commonplace in employment contracts with sales representatives, such as Ali, who have ongoing responsibilities to "service" the account once the sale is made. (See, e.g., *Chretian v. Donald L. Bren Co.* (1984) 151 Cal.App.3d 385, 389, 198 Cal.Rptr. 523 . . . .) In briefing below, the rationale for deferring commissions until payment is actually received by the customer was explained by American Software: "[I]f the entire commission were to be deemed earned by merely obtaining buyers, the burden of servicing those buyers pending receipt of revenues would fall on American Software's other salespersons unfamiliar with the earlier transaction who would receive nothing for their efforts." In *Watson v. Wood Dimension, Inc.* (1989) 209 Cal.App.3d 1359, 1363-1365, 257 Cal.Rptr. 816, the court upheld an award of post-termination commissions for a reasonable period of time based on quantum meruit in the total absence of contractual provisions governing the situation. If a court can impose these terms on parties in the absence of an agreement, then it is difficult to see how such terms can be considered "unconscionable" when the parties agree to them.

Nor do we find that the terms of this contract represent "an overly harsh allocation of risks . . . which is not justified by the circumstances under which the contract was made." (*Carboni v. Arrospide, supra,* 2 Cal.App.4th at p. 83, 2 Cal.Rptr.2d 845.) The contract terms with regard to Ali's compensation involved certain risks to both parties to the bargain. The contract in the instant case placed a risk on Ali that she would lose commissions from her customers if payment was not received by American Software within 30 days after her resignation. American Software took the risk that at the time of Ali's termination, she would not have earned sufficient commissions to cover the substantial draws "credited" to her. This is part of the bargaining process–it does not necessarily make a contract unconscionable. The contract simply does not appear to be "overly harsh or one-sided, with no justification for it at the time of the agreement." (*Vance v. Villa Park Mobilehome Estates, supra,* 36 Cal.App.4th at p. 709, 42 Cal.Rptr.2d 723.)

. . . .

In the present case, there are no unclear or hidden terms in the employment agreement and no unusual terms that would shock the conscience, all leading to the conclusion that the contract accurately reflects the reasonable expectations of the parties. Overall, the evidence establishes that this employment contract was the result of an arm's-length negotiation between two sophisticated and experienced parties of comparable bargaining power and is fairly reflective of prevailing practices in employing commissioned sales representatives. Therefore, the contract fails to qualify as unconscionable.

The judgment is reversed. Costs are awarded to American Software, Inc.

PETERSON, P.J., and HANING, J., concur.

_____

§ 2.4.3. Unconscionability Issues in Arbitration Agreements

Partly in response to the delays and expense associated with litigation, businesses have more regularly included arbitration clauses and agreements in their contracts, especially in consumer transactions. Because arbitration is a private means of dispute resolution that often lacks the procedural and evidentiary safeguards of traditional litigation and because arbitration clauses appear often in standard-form agreements, arbitration agreements have frequently been challenged based on claims of unconscionability and violation of public policy. Indeed, the increasing use of arbitration clauses has fueled a surge in unconscionability claims. Professor Charles Knapp has noted a nearly tenfold increase in unconscionability cases between 1990 and 2008 after a previous slowdown, with unconscionability decisions involving arbitration clauses "account[ing] for the lion's share of the overall increase," rising "from 1 or 2 at most through 1996, up to an average of 38 from the years 2003 through 2007, and to 115 in 2008."* Arbitration clauses are

_____

* Charles L. Knapp, *Blowing the Whistle on Mandatory Arbitration: Unconscionability as a Signaling Device*, 46 San Diego L. Rev. 609, 621-25 (2009).

not the only provisions regularly scrutinized for unconscionability; choice-of-law, choice-of-forum, and class action waiver clauses have also faced many challenges.

For a number of years, the increasing number of unconscionability claims was mirrored by increased success in challenging arbitration clauses, particularly in California but also in 21 other states. That rise in successful challenges was at least stalled by several rulings by the United States Supreme Court on the impact on arbitration clauses of the Federal Arbitration Act (FAA), 9 U.S.C. § 1 *et seq.* The next case, *AT&T Mobility LLC v. Concepcion,* was the latest of those rulings, as of when we went to press.

>    ### Reading the Law Critically: *AT&T Mobility LLC*
>
> 1. On what basis did the California courts hold arbitration provisions like that found in the AT&T Mobility contract to be unconscionable?
>
> 2. What provision of the Federal Arbitration Act did AT&T invoke to counter the Concepcions' claim of unconscionability?
>
> 3. Why does the majority conclude that the unconscionability claim is barred by the FAA? Why does the dissent disagree?
>
> 4. After *Concepcion,* can an arbitration provision be found unconscionable? What facts or factors would help to support that outcome?

AT&T Mobility LLC v. Concepcion

AT & T MOBILITY LLC, Petitioner,

v.

Vincent CONCEPCION et ux.

Supreme Court of the United States
___ U.S. ___, 131 S. Ct. 1740 (2011)

Justice SCALIA delivered the opinion of the Court.

Section 2 of the Federal Arbitration Act (FAA) makes agreements to arbitrate "valid, irrevocable, and enforceable, save upon such grounds as exist at law or in equity for the revocation of any contract." 9 U.S.C. § 2. We consider whether the FAA prohibits States from conditioning the enforceability of certain arbitration agreements on the availability of classwide arbitration procedures.

I

In February 2002, Vincent and Liza Concepcion entered into an agreement for the sale and servicing of cellular telephones with AT & T Mobility [LLC] (AT & T). The contract provided for arbitration of all disputes between the parties, but required that claims be brought in the parties' "individual capacity, and not as a plaintiff or class member in any purported class or representative proceeding."[2] The agreement authorized AT & T to make unilateral amendments, which it did to the arbitration provision on several occasions. The version at issue in this case reflects revisions made in December 2006, which the parties agree are controlling.

The revised agreement provides that customers may initiate dispute proceedings by completing a one-page Notice of Dispute form available on AT & T's Web site. AT & T may then offer to settle the claim; if it does not, or if the dispute is not resolved within 30 days, the customer may invoke arbitration by filing a separate Demand for Arbitration, also available on AT & T's Web site. In the event the parties proceed to arbitration, the agreement specifies that AT & T must pay all costs for nonfrivolous claims; that arbitration must take place in the county in which the customer is billed; that, for claims of $10,000 or less, the customer may choose whether the arbitration proceeds in person, by telephone, or based only on submissions; that either party may bring a claim in small claims court in lieu of arbitration; and that the arbitrator may award any form of individual relief, including injunctions and presumably punitive damages. The agreement, moreover, denies AT & T any ability to seek reimbursement of its attorney's fees, and, in the event that a customer receives an arbitration award greater than AT & T's last written settlement offer, requires AT & T to pay a $7,500 minimum recovery and twice the amount of the claimant's attorney's fees.[3]

The Concepcions purchased AT & T service, which was advertised as including the provision of free phones; they were not charged for the phones, but they were charged $30.22 in sales tax based on the phones' retail value. In March 2006, the Concepcions filed a complaint against AT & T in the United States District Court for the Southern District of California. The complaint was later consolidated with a putative class action alleging, among other things, that AT & T had engaged in false advertising and fraud by charging sales tax on phones it advertised as free.

In March 2008, AT & T moved to compel arbitration under the terms of its contract with the Concepcions. The Concepcions opposed the motion, contend-

---

[2] That provision further states that "the arbitrator may not consolidate more than one person's claims, and may not otherwise preside over any form of a representative or class proceeding." App. to Pet. for Cert. 61a.

[3] The guaranteed minimum recovery was increased in 2009 to $10,000. Brief for Petitioner 7.

ing that the arbitration agreement was unconscionable and unlawfully exculpatory under California law because it disallowed classwide procedures. The District Court denied AT & T's motion. It described AT & T's arbitration agreement favorably, noting, for example, that the informal dispute-resolution process was "quick, easy to use" and likely to "promp[t] full or . . . even excess payment to the customer *without* the need to arbitrate or litigate"; that the $7,500 premium functioned as "a substantial inducement for the consumer to pursue the claim in arbitration" if a dispute was not resolved informally; and that consumers who were members of a class would likely be worse off. *Laster v. T–Mobile USA, Inc.*, 2008 WL 5216255, *11-*12 (S.D.Cal., Aug.11, 2008). Nevertheless, relying on the California Supreme Court's decision in *Discover Bank v. Superior Court*, 36 Cal.4th 148, 30 Cal.Rptr.3d 76, 113 P.3d 1100 (2005), the court found that the arbitration provision was unconscionable because AT & T had not shown that bilateral arbitration adequately substituted for the deterrent effects of class actions. **Laster, 2008 WL 5216255, *14.**

The Ninth Circuit affirmed, also finding the provision unconscionable under California law as announced in **Discover Bank. Laster v. AT & T Mobility LLC, 584 F.3d 849, 855 (2009).** It also held that the **Discover Bank** rule was not preempted by the FAA because that rule was simply "a refinement of the unconscionability analysis applicable to contracts generally in California." 584 F.3d at 857. In response to AT & T's argument that the Concepcions' interpretation of California law discriminated against arbitration, the Ninth Circuit rejected the contention that "class proceedings will reduce the efficiency and expeditiousness of arbitration" and noted that "*Discover Bank* placed arbitration agreements with class action waivers on the *exact same footing* as contracts that bar class action litigation outside the context of arbitration." *Id.* at 858 (quoting *Shroyer v. New Cingular Wireless Services, Inc.*, 498 F.3d 976, 990 (C.A.9 2007)).

We granted certiorari, 560 U.S. ——, 130 S.Ct. 3322 (2010).

II

The FAA was enacted in 1925 in response to widespread judicial hostility to arbitration agreements. See *Hall Street Associates, L.L.C. v. Mattel, Inc.*, 552 U.S. 576, 581 (2008). Section 2, the "primary substantive provision of the Act," *Moses H. Cone Memorial Hospital v. Mercury Constr. Corp.*, 460 U.S. 1, 24 (1983), provides, in relevant part, as follows:

> A written provision in any maritime transaction or a contract evidencing a transaction involving commerce to settle by arbitration a controversy thereafter arising out of such contract or transaction . . . shall be valid, irrevocable, and enforceable, save upon such grounds as exist at law or in equity for the revocation of any contract.

9 U.S.C. § 2. We have described this provision as reflecting both a "liberal federal policy favoring arbitration," *Moses H. Cone, supra*, at 24, and the "fundamental principle that arbitration is a matter of contract," *Rent-A-Center, West, Inc. v. Jackson*, 561 U.S. ——, ——, 130 S.Ct. 2772, 2776 (2010). In line with these principles, courts must place arbitration agreements on an equal footing with other contracts, *Buckeye Check Cashing, Inc. v. Cardegna*, 546 U.S. 440, 443 (2006), and enforce them according to their terms, *Volt Information Sciences, Inc. v. Board of Trustees of Leland Stanford Junior Univ.*, 489 U.S. 468, 478 (1989).

The final phrase of § 2, however, permits arbitration agreements to be declared unenforceable "upon such grounds as exist at law or in equity for the revocation of any contract." This saving clause permits agreements to arbitrate to be invalidated by "generally applicable contract defenses, such as fraud, duress, or unconscionability," but not by defenses that apply only to arbitration or that derive their meaning from the fact that an agreement to arbitrate is at issue. *Doctor's Associates, Inc. v. Casarotto*, 517 U.S. 681, 687 (1996); see also *Perry v. Thomas*, 482 U.S. 483, 492-493, n.9 (1987). The question in this case is whether § 2 preempts California's rule classifying most collective-arbitration waivers in consumer contracts as unconscionable. We refer to this rule as the *Discover Bank* rule.

Under California law, courts may refuse to enforce any contract found "to have been unconscionable at the time it was made," or may "limit the application of any unconscionable clause." Cal. Civ.Code Ann. § 1670.5(a) (West 1985). A finding of unconscionability requires "a 'procedural' and a 'substantive' element, the former focusing on 'oppression' or 'surprise' due to unequal bargaining power, the latter on 'overly harsh' or 'one-sided' results." *Armendariz v. Foundation Health Pyschcare Servs., Inc.*, 24 Cal.4th 83, 114, 99 Cal.Rptr.2d 745, 6 P.3d 669, 690 (2000); accord, *Discover Bank*, 36 Cal.4th, at 159-161, 30 Cal. Rptr.3d 76, 113 P.3d, at 1108.

In *Discover Bank*, the California Supreme Court applied this framework to class-action waivers in arbitration agreements and held as follows:

> [W]hen the waiver is found in a consumer contract of adhesion in a setting in which disputes between the contracting parties predictably involve small amounts of damages, and when it is alleged that the party with the superior bargaining power has carried out a scheme to deliberately cheat large numbers of consumers out of individually small sums of money, then . . . the waiver becomes in practice the exemption of the party "from responsibility for [its] own fraud, or willful injury to the person or property of another." Under these circumstances, such waivers are unconscionable under California law and should not be enforced.

Id. at 162, 30 Cal.Rptr.3d 76, 113 P.3d, at 1110 (quoting Cal. Civ.Code Ann. § 1668). California courts have frequently applied this rule to find arbitration agreements unconscionable. See, *e.g., Cohen v. DirecTV, Inc.*, 142 Cal.App.4th 1442, 1451-1453, 48 Cal.Rptr.3d 813, 819-821 (2006); *Klussman v. Cross Country Bank*, 134 Cal.App.4th 1283, 1297, 36 Cal.Rptr.3d 728, 738-739 (2005); *Aral v. EarthLink, Inc.*, 134 Cal.App.4th 544, 556-557, 36 Cal.Rptr.3d 229, 237-239 (2005).

III

A

The Concepcions argue that the *Discover Bank* rule, given its origins in California's unconscionability doctrine and California's policy against exculpation, is a ground that "exist[s] at law or in equity for the revocation of any contract" under FAA § 2. Moreover, they argue that even if we construe the *Discover Bank* rule as a prohibition on collective-action waivers rather than simply an application of unconscionability, the rule would still be applicable to all dispute-resolution contracts, since California prohibits waivers of class litigation as well. See *America Online, Inc. v. Superior Ct.*, 90 Cal.App.4th 1, 17-18, 108 Cal.Rptr.2d 699, 711-713 (2001).

When state law prohibits outright the arbitration of a particular type of claim, the analysis is straightforward: The conflicting rule is displaced by the FAA. *Preston v. Ferrer*, 552 U.S. 346, 353 (2008). But the inquiry becomes more complex when a doctrine normally thought to be generally applicable, such as duress or, as relevant here, unconscionability, is alleged to have been applied in a fashion that disfavors arbitration. In *Perry v. Thomas*, 482 U.S. 483 (1987), for example, we noted that the FAA's preemptive effect might extend even to grounds traditionally thought to exist "at law or in equity for the revocation of any contract." *Id.* at 492 n.9 (emphasis deleted). We said that a court may not "rely on the uniqueness of an agreement to arbitrate as a basis for a state-law holding that enforcement would be unconscionable, for this would enable the court to effect what . . . the state legislature cannot." *Id.* at 493 n.9.

An obvious illustration of this point would be a case finding unconscionable or unenforceable as against public policy consumer arbitration agreements that fail to provide for judicially monitored discovery. The rationalizations for such a holding are neither difficult to imagine nor different in kind from those articulated in *Discover Bank*. A court might reason that no consumer would knowingly waive his right to full discovery, as this would enable companies to hide their wrongdoing. Or the court might simply say that such agreements are exculpatory—restricting discovery would be of greater benefit to the company than the consumer, since the former is more likely to be sued than to sue. See *Discover Bank, supra,* at 161, 30 Cal.Rptr.3d 76, 113 P.3d at 1109 (arguing that class waivers are similarly one-sided). And, the reasoning would continue, because such a rule applies the general principle of unconscionability or public-policy disapproval of exculpatory agreements, it is applicable to "any" contract and thus preserved by § 2 of the FAA. In practice, of course, the rule would have a disproportionate impact on arbitration agreements; but it would presumably apply to contracts purporting to restrict discovery in litigation as well.

Other examples are easy to imagine. The same argument might apply to a rule classifying as unconscionable arbitration agreements that fail to abide by the Federal Rules of Evidence, or that disallow an ultimate disposition by a jury (perhaps termed "a panel of twelve lay arbitrators" to help avoid preemption). . . . California›s courts have been more likely to hold contracts to arbitrate unconscionable than other contracts. Broome, *An Unconscionable Applicable of the Unconscionability Doctrine: How the California Courts are Circumventing the Federal Arbitration Act,* 3 Hastings Bus. L.J. 39, 54, 66 (2006); Randall, *Judicial Attitudes Toward Arbitration and the Resurgence of Unconscionability,* 52 Buffalo L. Rev. 185, 186-187 (2004).

. . . .

B

The "principal purpose" of the FAA is to "ensur[e] that private arbitration agreements are enforced according to their terms." Volt, 489 U.S. at 478; see also *Stolt–Nielsen S.A. v. AnimalFeeds Int'l Corp.,* 559 U.S. ——, ——, 130 S.Ct. 1758, 1763 (2010). This purpose is readily apparent from the FAA's text. Section 2 makes arbitration agreements "valid, irrevocable, and enforceable" as written (subject, of course, to the saving clause); § 3 requires courts to stay litigation of arbitral claims pending arbitration of those claims "in accordance with the terms of the agreement"; and § 4 requires courts to compel arbitration "in accordance with the terms of the agreement" upon the motion of either party to the agreement (assuming that the "making of the arbitration agreement or the failure . . . to perform the same" is not at issue). In light of these provisions, we have held that parties may agree to limit the issues subject to arbitration, *Mitsubishi Motors Corp. v. Soler Chrysler–Plymouth, Inc.,* 473 U.S. 614, 628 (1985), to arbitrate according to specific rules, *Volt, supra,* at 479, and to limit *with whom* a party will arbitrate its disputes, *Stolt–Nielsen, supra,* at ——, 130 S.Ct. at 1773.

The point of affording parties discretion in designing arbitration processes is to allow for efficient, streamlined procedures tailored to the type of dispute. It can be specified, for example, that the decisionmaker be a specialist in the relevant field, or that proceedings be kept confidential to protect trade secrets. And the informality of arbitral proceedings is itself desirable, reducing the cost and increasing the speed of dispute resolution. *14 Penn Plaza LLC v. Pyett*, 556 U.S. 247, ——, 129 S.Ct. 1456, 1460 (2009); Mitsubishi Motors Corp., supra, at 628.

The dissent quotes *Dean Witter Reynolds Inc. v. Byrd*, 470 U.S. 213, 219 (1985), as "reject[ing] the suggestion that the overriding goal of the Arbitration Act was to promote the expeditious resolution of claims." *Post,* at 4 (opinion of Breyer, J.). That is greatly misleading. After saying (accurately enough) that "the overriding goal of the Arbitration Act was [not] to promote the expeditious resolution of claims," but to "ensure judicial enforcement of privately made agreements to arbitrate," 470 U.S. at 219, *Dean Witter* went on to explain: "This is not to say that Congress was blind to the potential benefit of the legislation for expedited resolution of disputes. Far from it . . . ." *Id.* at 220. It then quotes a House Report saying that "the costliness and delays of litigation . . . can be largely eliminated by agreements for arbitration." *Ibid.* (quoting H.R.Rep. No. 96, 68th Cong., 1st Sess., 2 (1924)). The concluding paragraph of this part of its discussion begins as follows:

> We therefore are not persuaded by the argument that the conflict between two goals of the Arbitration Act—enforcement of private agreements and encouragement of efficient and speedy dispute resolution—must be resolved in favor of the latter in order to realize the intent of the drafters.

470 U.S. at 221. In the present case, of course, those "two goals" do not conflict—and it is the dissent's view that would frustrate *both* of them.

Contrary to the dissent's view, our cases place it beyond dispute that the FAA was designed to promote arbitration. They have repeatedly described the Act as "embod[ying] [a] national policy favoring arbitration," *Buckeye Check Cashing,* 546 U.S. at 443, and "a liberal federal policy favoring arbitration agreements, notwithstanding any state substantive or procedural policies to the contrary," *Moses H. Cone,* 460 U.S. at 24; see also *Hall Street Assocs.,* 552 U.S. at 581. Thus, in *Preston v. Ferrer,* holding preempted a state-law rule requiring exhaustion of administrative remedies before arbitration, we said: "A prime objective of an agreement to arbitrate is to achieve 'streamlined proceedings and expeditious results,'" which objective would be "frustrated" by requiring a dispute to be heard by an agency first. 552 U.S. at 357–358. That rule, we said, would "at the least, hinder speedy resolution of the controversy." *Id.* at 358.[5]

California's *Discover Bank* rule similarly interferes with arbitration. Although the rule does not *require* classwide arbitration, it allows any party to a consumer contract to demand it *ex post*. The rule is limited to adhesion contracts, *Discover Bank*, 36 Cal.4th, at 162-163, 30 Cal.Rptr.3d 76, 113 P.3d, at 1110, but the times in which consumer contracts were anything other than adhesive are long past. *Carbajal v. H & R Block Tax Servs., Inc.*, 372 F.3d 903, 906 (7th Cir.2004). . . . The rule also requires that damages be predictably small, and that the consumer allege a scheme to cheat consumers. *Discover Bank, supra*, at 162-163, 30 Cal.Rptr.3d 76, 113 P.3d, at 1110. The former requirement, however, is toothless and malleable (the Ninth Circuit has held that damages of $4,000 are sufficiently small, see *Oestreicher v. Alienware Corp.*, 322 Fed. Appx. 489, 492 (2009) (unpublished)), and the latter has no limiting effect, as all that is required is an allegation. Consumers remain free to bring and resolve their disputes on a bilateral basis under *Discover Bank*, and some may well do so; but there is little incentive for lawyers to arbitrate on behalf of individuals when they may do so for a class and reap far higher fees in the process. And faced with inevitable class arbitration, companies would have less incentive to continue resolving potentially duplicative claims on an individual basis.

Although we have had little occasion to examine classwide arbitration, our decision in *Stolt–Nielsen* is instructive. In that case we held that an arbitration panel exceeded its power under § 10(a)(4) of the FAA by imposing class procedures based on policy judgments rather than the arbitration agreement itself or some background principle of contract law that would affect its interpretation. 559 U.S. at ——, 130 S.Ct. at 1773-1776. We then held that the agreement at issue, which was silent on the question of class procedures, could not be interpreted to allow them because the "changes brought about by the shift from bilateral arbitration to class-action arbitration" are "fundamental." *Id.* at ——, 130 S.Ct. at 1776. This is obvious as a structural matter: Classwide arbitration includes absent parties, necessitating additional and different procedures and involving higher stakes. Confidentiality becomes more difficult. And while it is theoretically

---

[5] Relying upon nothing more indicative of congressional understanding than statements of witnesses in committee hearings and a press release of Secretary of Commerce Herbert Hoover, the dissent suggests that Congress "thought that arbitration would be used primarily where merchants sought to resolve disputes of fact . . . [and] possessed roughly equivalent bargaining power." *Post*, at 6. Such a limitation appears nowhere in the text of the FAA and has been explicitly rejected by our cases. "Relationships between securities dealers and investors, for example, may involve unequal bargaining power, but we [have] nevertheless held . . . that agreements to arbitrate in that context are enforceable." *Gilmer v. Interstate/Johnson Lane Corp.*, 500 U.S. 20, 33 (1991); see also *id.* at 32–33 (allowing arbitration of claims arising under the Age Discrimination in Employment Act of 1967 despite allegations of unequal bargaining power between employers and employees). Of course the dissent's disquisition on legislative history fails to note that it contains nothing—not even the testimony of a stray witness in committee hearings—that contemplates the existence of class arbitration.

possible to select an arbitrator with some expertise relevant to the class-certification question, arbitrators are not generally knowledgeable in the often-dominant procedural aspects of certification, such as the protection of absent parties. The conclusion follows that class arbitration, to the extent it is manufactured by *Discover Bank* rather than consensual, is inconsistent with the FAA.

First, the switch from bilateral to class arbitration sacrifices the principal advantage of arbitration—its informality—and makes the process slower, more costly, and more likely to generate procedural morass than final judgment. "In bilateral arbitration, parties forgo the procedural rigor and appellate review of the courts in order to realize the benefits of private dispute resolution: lower costs, greater efficiency and speed, and the ability to choose expert adjudicators to resolve specialized disputes." 559 U.S. at ——, 130 S.Ct. at 1775. But before an arbitrator may decide the merits of a claim in classwide procedures, he must first decide, for example, whether the class itself may be certified, whether the named parties are sufficiently representative and typical, and how discovery for the class should be conducted. A cursory comparison of bilateral and class arbitration illustrates the difference. According to the American Arbitration Association (AAA), the average consumer arbitration between January and August 2007 resulted in a disposition on the merits in six months, four months if the arbitration was conducted by documents only. AAA, Analysis of the AAA's Consumer Arbitration Caseload, online at http:// www. adr. org/ si.asp?id=5027 (all Internet materials as visited Apr. 25, 2011, and available in Clerk of Court's case file). As of September 2009, the AAA had opened 283 class arbitrations. Of those, 121 remained active, and 162 had been settled, withdrawn, or dismissed. Not a single one, however, had resulted in a final award on the merits. Brief for AAA as *Amicus Curiae* in *Stolt–Nielsen,* O.T.2009, No. 08-1198, pp. 22-24. For those cases that were no longer active, the median time from filing to settlement, withdrawal, or dismissal—not judgment on the merits—was 583 days, and the mean was 630 days. *Id.* at 24.[7]

Second, class arbitration *requires* procedural formality. The AAA's rules governing class arbitrations mimic the Federal Rules of Civil Procedure for class litigation. Compare AAA, Supplementary Rules for Class Arbitrations (effective Oct. 8, 2003), online at http:// www. adr. org/ sp.asp? id=21936, with Fed. Rule Civ. Proc. 23. And while parties can alter those procedures by contract, an alternative is not obvious. If procedures are too informal, absent class members would not be bound by the arbitration. For a class-action money judgment to bind absentees in litigation, class representatives must at all times adequately represent absent class members, and absent members must be afforded notice, an opportunity to

---

[7] The dissent claims that class arbitration should be compared to class litigation, not bilateral arbitration. *Post,* at 6-7. Whether arbitrating a class is more desirable than litigating one, however, is not relevant. A State cannot defend a rule requiring arbitration-by-jury by saying that parties will still prefer it to trial-by-jury.

be heard, and a right to opt out of the class. *Phillips Petroleum Co. v. Shutts*, 472 U.S. 797, 811-812 (1985). At least this amount of process would presumably be required for absent parties to be bound by the results of arbitration.

We find it unlikely that in passing the FAA Congress meant to leave the disposition of these procedural requirements to an arbitrator. Indeed, class arbitration was not even envisioned by Congress when it passed the FAA in 1925; as the California Supreme Court admitted in *Discover Bank*, class arbitration is a "relatively recent development." 36 Cal.4th at 163, 30 Cal.Rptr.3d 76, 113 P.3d, at 1110. And it is at the very least odd to think that an arbitrator would be entrusted with ensuring that third parties' due process rights are satisfied.

Third, class arbitration greatly increases risks to defendants. Informal procedures do of course have a cost: The absence of multilayered review makes it more likely that errors will go uncorrected. Defendants are willing to accept the costs of these errors in arbitration, since their impact is limited to the size of individual disputes, and presumably outweighed by savings from avoiding the courts. But when damages allegedly owed to tens of thousands of potential claimants are aggregated and decided at once, the risk of an error will often become unacceptable. Faced with even a small chance of a devastating loss, defendants will be pressured into settling questionable claims. Other courts have noted the risk of "in terrorem" settlements that class actions entail, see, *e.g., Kohen v. Pacific Inv. Management Co. LLC*, 571 F.3d 672, 677-678 (C.A.7 2009), and class arbitration would be no different.

Arbitration is poorly suited to the higher stakes of class litigation. In litigation, a defendant may appeal a certification decision on an interlocutory basis and, if unsuccessful, may appeal from a final judgment as well. Questions of law are reviewed *de novo* and questions of fact for clear error. In contrast, 9 U.S.C. § 10 allows a court to vacate an arbitral award *only* where the award "was procured by corruption, fraud, or undue means"; "there was evident partiality or corruption in the arbitrators"; "the arbitrators were guilty of misconduct in refusing to postpone the hearing . . . or in refusing to hear evidence pertinent and material to the controversy[,] or of any other misbehavior by which the rights of any party have been prejudiced"; or if the "arbitrators exceeded their powers, or so imperfectly executed them that a mutual, final, and definite award . . . was not made." The AAA rules do authorize judicial review of certification decisions, but this review is unlikely to have much effect given these limitations; review under § 10 focuses on misconduct rather than mistake. And parties may not contractually expand the grounds or nature of judicial review. *Hall Street Assocs.*, 552 U.S. at 578. We find it hard to believe that defendants would bet the company with no effective means of review, and even harder to believe that Congress would have intended to allow state courts to force such a decision.[8]

. . . .

The dissent claims that class proceedings are necessary to prosecute small-dollar claims that might otherwise slip through the legal system. See *post,* at 9. But States cannot require a procedure that is inconsistent with the FAA, even if it is desirable for unrelated reasons. Moreover, the claim here was most unlikely to go unresolved. As noted earlier, the arbitration agreement provides that AT & T will pay claimants a minimum of $7,500 and twice their attorney's fees if they obtain an arbitration award greater than AT & T's last settlement offer. The District Court found this scheme sufficient to provide incentive for the individual prosecution of meritorious claims that are not immediately settled, and the Ninth Circuit admitted that aggrieved customers who filed claims would be "essentially guarantee[d]" to be made whole, 584 F.3d at 856, n.9. Indeed, the District Court concluded that the Concepcions were *better off* under their arbitration agreement with AT & T than they would have been as participants in a class action, which "could take months, if not years, and which may merely yield an opportunity to submit a claim for recovery of a small percentage of a few dollars." *Laster,* 2008 WL 5216255, at *12.

* * *

Because it "stands as an obstacle to the accomplishment and execution of the full purposes and objectives of Congress," *Hines v. Davidowitz,* 312 U.S. 52, 67 (1941), California's Discover Bank rule is preempted by the FAA. The judgment of the Ninth Circuit is reversed, and the case is remanded for further proceedings consistent with this opinion.

It is so ordered.

Justice THOMAS, concurring.

Section 2 of the Federal Arbitration Act (FAA) provides that an arbitration provision "shall be valid, irrevocable, and enforceable, save upon such grounds as exist at law or in equity for the revocation of any contract." 9 U.S.C. § 2. The

---

[8] The dissent cites three large arbitration awards (none of which stems from classwide arbitration) as evidence that parties are willing to submit large claims before an arbitrator. *Post,* at 7-8. Those examples might be in point if it could be established that the size of the arbitral dispute was predictable when the arbitration agreement was entered. Otherwise, all the cases prove is that arbitrators can give huge awards—which we have never doubted. The point is that in class-action arbitration huge awards (with limited judicial review) will be entirely predictable, thus rendering arbitration unattractive. It is not reasonably deniable that requiring consumer disputes to be arbitrated on a classwide basis will have a substantial deterrent effect on incentives to arbitrate.

question here is whether California's *Discover Bank* rule, see *Discover Bank v. Superior Ct.*, 36 Cal.4th 148, 30 Cal.Rptr.3d 76, 113 P.3d 1100 (2005), is a "groun[d] . . . for the revocation of any contract."

. . . .

. . . . As I would read it, the FAA requires that an agreement to arbitrate be enforced unless a party successfully challenges the formation of the arbitration agreement, such as by proving fraud or duress. 9 U.S.C. §§ 2, 4. Under this reading, I would reverse the Court of Appeals because a district court cannot follow both the FAA and the *Discover Bank* rule, which does not relate to defects in the making of an agreement.

. . . .

The FAA generally requires courts to enforce arbitration agreements as written. Section 2 provides that "[a] written provision in . . . a contract . . . to settle by arbitration a controversy thereafter arising out of such contract . . . shall be valid, irrevocable, and enforceable, save upon such grounds as exist at law or in equity for the revocation of any contract." Significantly, the statute does not parallel the words "valid, irrevocable, and enforceable" by referencing the grounds as exist for the "invalidation, revocation, or nonenforcement" of any contract. . . .

. . . .

. . . . When a party seeks to enforce an arbitration agreement in federal court, § 4 requires that "upon being satisfied that the making of the agreement for arbitration or the failure to comply therewith is not in issue," the court must order arbitration "in accordance with the terms of the agreement."

Reading §§ 2 and 4 harmoniously, the "grounds . . . for the revocation" preserved in § 2 would mean grounds related to the making of the agreement. This would require enforcement of an agreement to arbitrate unless a party successfully asserts a defense concerning the formation of the agreement to arbitrate, such as fraud, duress, or mutual mistake. See *Prima Paint Corp. v. Flood & Conklin Mfg. Co.*, 388 U.S. 395, 403-404 (1967) (interpreting § 4 to permit federal courts to adjudicate claims of "fraud in the inducement of the arbitration clause itself" because such claims "g[o] to the 'making' of the agreement to arbitrate"). Contract defenses unrelated to the making of the agreement—such as public policy—could not be the basis for declining to enforce an arbitration clause.

II

Under this reading, the question here would be whether California's *Discover Bank* rule relates to the making of an agreement. I think it does not.

. . . .

Accordingly, the *Discover Bank* rule is not a "groun[d] . . . for the revocation of any contract" as I would read § 2 of the FAA in light of § 4. Under this reading, the FAA dictates that the arbitration agreement here be enforced and the *Discover Bank* rule is pre-empted.

Justice BREYER, with whom Justice GINSBURG, Justice SOTOMAYOR, and Justice KAGAN join, dissenting.

The Federal Arbitration Act says that an arbitration agreement "shall be valid, irrevocable, and enforceable, *save upon such grounds as exist at law or in equity for the revocation of any contract.*" 9 U.S.C. § 2 (emphasis added). California law sets forth certain circumstances in which "class action waivers" in *any* contract are unenforceable. In my view, this rule of state law is consistent with the federal Act's language and primary objective. It does not "stan[d] as an obstacle" to the Act's "accomplishment and execution." *Hines v. Davidowitz*, 312 U.S. 52, 67 (1941). And the Court is wrong to hold that the federal Act pre-empts the rule of state law.

I

The California law in question consists of an authoritative state-court interpretation of two provisions of the California Civil Code. The first provision makes unlawful all contracts "which have for their object, directly or in-directly, to exempt anyone from responsibility for his own . . . violation of law." Cal. Civ.Code Ann. § 1668 (West 1985). The second provision authorizes courts to "limit the application of any unconscionable clause" in a contract so "as to avoid any unconscionable result." § 1670.5(a).

The specific rule of state law in question consists of the California Supreme Court›s application of these principles to hold that "some" (but not "all") "class action waivers" in consumer contracts are exculpatory and unconscionable under California "law." *Discover Bank v. Superior Ct.*, 36 Cal.4th 148, 160, 162, 30 Cal.Rptr.3d 76, 113 P.3d 1100, 1108, 1110 (2005). In particular, in *Discover Bank* the California Supreme Court stated that, when a class-action waiver

> is found in a consumer contract of adhesion in a setting in which disputes between the contracting parties predictably involve small amounts of damages, and when it is alleged that the party with the superior bargaining power has carried out a scheme to deliberately cheat large numbers of consumers out of individually small sums of money, then . . . the waiver becomes in practice the exemption of the party "from responsibility for [its] own fraud, or willful injury to the person or property of another."

Id. at 162-163, 30 Cal.Rptr.3d 76, 113 P.3d, at 1110. In such a circumstance, the "waivers are unconscionable under California law and should not be enforced." *Id.* at 163, 30 Cal.Rptr.3d 76, 113 P.3d, at 1110.

The *Discover Bank* rule does not create a "blanket policy in California against class action waivers in the consumer context." *Provencher v. Dell, Inc.,* 409 F.Supp.2d 1196, 1201 (C.D.Cal.2006). Instead, it represents the "application of a more general [unconscionability] principle." *Gentry v. Superior Ct.,* 42 Cal.4th 443, 457, 64 Cal.Rptr.3d 773, 165 P.3d 556, 564 (2007). Courts applying California law have enforced class-action waivers where they satisfy general unconscionability standards. See, *e.g., Walnut Producers of Cal. v. Diamond Foods, Inc.,* 187 Cal.App.4th 634, 647–650, 114 Cal.Rptr.3d 449, 459-462 (2010) . . . . And even when they fail, the parties remain free to devise other dispute mechanisms, including informal mechanisms, that, in context, will not prove unconscionable. See *Volt Information Sciences, Inc. v. Board of Trustees of Leland Stanford Junior Univ.,* 489 U.S. 468, 479 (1989).

II

A

The *Discover Bank* rule is consistent with the federal Act's language. It "applies equally to class action litigation waivers in contracts without arbitration agreements as it does to class arbitration waivers in contracts with such agreements." 36 Cal.4th, at 165-166, 30 Cal.Rptr.3d 76, 113 P.3d at 1112. Linguistically speaking, it falls directly within the scope of the Act's exception permitting courts to refuse to enforce arbitration agreements on grounds that exist "for the revocation of *any* contract." 9 U.S.C. § 2 (emphasis added). The majority agrees. *Ante,* at 9.

B

The *Discover Bank* rule is also consistent with the basic "purpose behind" the Act. *Dean Witter Reynolds Inc. v. Byrd,* 470 U.S. 213, 219 (1985). We have described that purpose as one of "ensur[ing] judicial enforcement" of arbitration agreements. . . . [P]rior to the federal Act, many courts expressed hostility to arbitration, for example by refusing to order specific performance of agreements to arbitrate. See S.Rep. No. 536, 68th Cong., 1st Sess., 2 (1924). The Act sought to eliminate that hostility by placing agreements to arbitrate "*upon the same footing as other contracts.*" *Scherk v. Alberto–Culver Co.,* 417 U.S. 506, 511 (1974) (quoting H.R.Rep. No. 96, at 2; emphasis added).

. . . .

Thus, insofar as we seek to implement Congress' intent, we should think more than twice before invalidating a state law that does just what § 2 requires, namely, puts agreements to arbitrate and agreements to litigate "upon the same footing."

III

The majority's contrary view (that *Discover Bank* stands as an "obstacle" to the accomplishment of the federal law's objective, *ante,* at 9–18) rests primarily upon its claims that the *Discover Bank* rule increases the complexity of arbitration procedures, thereby discouraging parties from entering into arbitration agreements, and to that extent discriminating in practice against arbitration. These claims are not well founded.

For one thing, a state rule of law that would sometimes set aside as unconscionable a contract term that forbids class arbitration is not (as the majority claims) like a rule that would require "ultimate disposition by a jury" or "judicially monitored discovery" or use of "the Federal Rules of Evidence." *Ante,* at 8, 9. Unlike the majority's examples, class arbitration is consistent with the use of arbitration. It is a form of arbitration that is well known in California and followed elsewhere. See, *e.g.,* . . . American Arbitration Association (AAA), Supplementary Rules for Class Arbitrations (2003), http://www.adr.org/sp.asp?id= 21936 (as visited Apr. 25, 2011, and available in Clerk of Court's case file) . . . . Indeed, the AAA has told us that it has found class arbitration to be "a fair, balanced, and efficient means of resolving class disputes." Brief for AAA as *Amicus Curiae* in *Stolt–Nielsen S.A. v. AnimalFeeds Int'l Corp.,* O.T.2009, No. 08–1198, p. 25 (hereinafter AAA *Amicus* Brief). And unlike the majority's examples, the *Discover Bank* rule imposes equivalent limitations on litigation; hence it cannot fairly be characterized as a targeted attack on arbitration.

Where does the majority get its contrary idea—that individual, rather than class, arbitration is a "fundamental attribut[e]" of arbitration? *Ante,* at 9. The majority does not explain. And it is unlikely to be able to trace its present view to the history of the arbitration statute itself.

When Congress enacted the Act, arbitration procedures had not yet been fully developed. Insofar as Congress considered detailed forms of arbitration at all, it may well have thought that arbitration would be used primarily where merchants sought to resolve disputes of fact, not law, under the customs of their industries, where the parties possessed roughly equivalent bargaining power. See *Mitsubishi Motors, supra, at 646* (Stevens, J., dissenting); Joint Hearings on S. 1005 and H.R. 646 before the Subcommittees of the Committees on the Judiciary, 68th Cong., 1st Sess., 15 (1924) . . . . This last mentioned feature of the history—roughly equivalent bargaining power—suggests, if anything, that California's statute is consistent with, and indeed may help to further, the objectives that Congress had in mind.

Regardless, if neither the history nor present practice suggests that class arbitration is fundamentally incompatible with arbitration itself, then on what basis can the majority hold California's law pre-empted?

For another thing, the majority's argument that the *Discover Bank* rule will discourage arbitration rests critically upon the wrong comparison. The majority compares the complexity of class arbitration with that of bilateral arbitration. See *ante,* at 14. . . . But . . . the *relevant* comparison is . . . between class arbitration and judicial class actions. After all, in respect to the relevant set of contracts, the *Discover Bank* rule similarly and equally sets aside clauses that forbid class procedures—whether arbitration procedures or ordinary judicial procedures are at issue.

Why would a typical defendant (say, a business) prefer a judicial class action to class arbitration? AAA statistics "suggest that class arbitration proceedings take more time than the average commercial arbitration, but may take *less time* than the average class action in court." AAA *Amicus* Brief 24 (emphasis added). Data from California courts confirm that class arbitrations can take considerably less time than in-court proceedings in which class certification is sought. . . . And a single class proceeding is surely more efficient than thousands of separate proceedings for identical claims. Thus, if speedy resolution of disputes were all that mattered, then the *Discover Bank* rule would reinforce, not obstruct, that objective of the Act.

The majority's related claim that the *Discover Bank* rule will discourage the use of arbitration because "[a]rbitration is poorly suited to . . . higher stakes" lacks empirical support. *Ante,* at 16. Indeed, the majority provides no convincing reason to believe that parties are unwilling to submit high-stake disputes to arbitration. And there are numerous counterexamples. Loftus, Rivals Resolve Dispute Over Drug, Wall Street Journal, Apr. 16, 2011, p. B2 (discussing $500 million settlement in dispute submitted to arbitration); Ziobro, Kraft Seeks Arbitration In Fight With Starbucks Over Distribution, Wall Street Journal, Nov. 30, 2010, p. B10 (describing initiation of an arbitration in which the payout "could be higher" than $1.5 billion); Markoff, Software Arbitration Ruling Gives I.B.M. $833 Million From Fujitsu, N.Y. Times, Nov. 30, 1988, p. A1 (describing both companies as "pleased with the ruling" resolving a licensing dispute).

Further, even though contract defenses, *e.g.,* duress and unconscionability, slow down the dispute resolution process, federal arbitration law normally leaves such matters to the States. *Rent-A-Center, West, Inc. v. Jackson*, 561 U.S. ——, ——, 130 S.Ct. 2772, 2775 (2010) . . . . California is free to define unconscionability as it sees fit, and its common law is of no federal concern so long as the State does not adopt a special rule that disfavors arbitration. . . .

Because California applies the same legal principles to address the unconscionability of class arbitration waivers as it does to address the unconscionability of any other contractual provision, the merits of class proceedings should not factor into our decision. . . .

Regardless, the majority highlights the disadvantages of class arbitrations, as it sees them. See *ante,* at 15-16 (referring to the "greatly increase[d] risks to defendants"; the "chance of a devastating loss" pressuring defendants "into settling questionable claims"). But class proceedings have countervailing advantages. In general agreements that forbid the consolidation of claims can lead small-dollar claimants to abandon their claims rather than to litigate. I suspect that it is true even here, for as the Court of Appeals recognized, AT & T can avoid the $7,500 payout (the payout that supposedly makes the Concepcions' arbitration worthwhile) simply by paying the claim's face value, such that "the maximum gain to a customer for the hassle of arbitrating a $30.22 dispute is still just $30.22." *Laster v. AT & T Mobility LLC*, 584 F.3d 849, 855, 856 (C.A.9 2009).

What rational lawyer would have signed on to represent the Concepcions in litigation for the possibility of fees stemming from a $30.22 claim? See, *e.g., Carnegie v. Household Int'l, Inc.*, 376 F.3d 656, 661 (C.A.7 2004) ("The *realistic* alternative to a class action is not 17 million individual suits, but zero individual suits, as only a lunatic or a fanatic sues for $30"). In California's perfectly rational view, nonclass arbitration over such sums will also sometimes have the effect of depriving claimants of their claims (say, for example, where claiming the $30.22 were to involve filling out many forms that require technical legal knowledge or waiting at great length while a call is placed on hold). *Discover Bank* sets forth circumstances in which the California courts believe that the terms of consumer contracts can be manipulated to insulate an agreement's author from liability for its own frauds by "deliberately cheat[ing] large numbers of consumers out of individually small sums of money." 36 Cal.4th at 162–163, 30 Cal.Rptr.3d 76, 113 P.3d, at 1110. Why is this kind of decision—weighing the pros and cons of all class proceedings alike—not California's to make?

. . . .

At the same time, we have repeatedly referred to the Act's basic objective as assuring that courts treat arbitration agreements "like all other contracts." *Buckeye Check Cashing, Inc. v. Cardegna*, 546 U.S. 440, 447 (2006). . . . And we have recognized that "[t]o immunize an arbitration agreement from judicial challenge" on grounds applicable to all other contracts "would be to elevate it over other forms of contract." *Prima Paint Corp. v. Flood & Conklin Mfg. Co.*,

388 U.S. 395, 404 n.12 (1967); see also *Marchant v. Mead-Morrison Mfg. Co.*, 252 N.Y. 284, 299, 169 N.E. 386, 391 (1929) (Cardozo, C.J.) ("Courts are not at liberty to shirk the process of [contractual] construction under the empire of a belief that arbitration is beneficent any more than they may shirk it if their belief happens to be the contrary"); Cohen & Dayton, 12 Va. L. Rev., at 276 (the Act "is no infringement upon the right of each State to decide for itself what contracts shall or shall not exist under its laws").

. . . .

IV

By using the words "save upon such grounds as exist at law or in equity for the revocation of any contract," Congress retained for the States an important role incident to agreements to arbitrate. 9 U.S.C. § 2. . . . See, *e.g., Medtronic, Inc. v. Lohr*, 518 U.S. 470, 485 (1996) ("[B]ecause the States are independent sovereigns in our federal system, we have long presumed that Congress does not cavalierly pre-empt state-law causes of action"). But federalism is as much a question of deeds as words. It often takes the form of a concrete decision by this Court that respects the legitimacy of a State's action in an individual case. Here, recognition of that federalist ideal, embodied in specific language in this particular statute, should lead us to uphold California's law, not to strike it down. We do not honor federalist principles in their breach.

Food for Thought

After this case, how should lawyers adjust their drafting practices as to arbitration clauses? What lessons can other states learn from this case, in terms of developing case law on unconscionability?

With respect, I dissent.

Problem 5-15: The Unconscionability Defense

Ms. Carla Sosa signed a document entitled "Physician-Patient Arbitration Agreement" shortly before undergoing knee surgery performed by Dr. Paulos, an orthopedic surgeon. At the time of signing, Ms. Sosa was undressed and in her surgical clothing. She was presented three documents by one of Dr. Paulos' staff less than one hour before surgery. No one discussed the documents with Ms. Sosa before she was scheduled for surgery, when she signed, after surgery, or at any subsequent hospital visits. Above the signature line was the following notice:

NOTICE: BY SIGNING THIS DOCUMENT, YOU ARE AGREEING TO NEUTRAL ARBITRATION IN THE EVENT OF ANY MALPRACTICE CLAIM YOU MAY BRING AGAINST DR. PAULOS AND WAIVING YOUR RIGHT TO A JURY TRIAL.

IF YOU HAVE QUESTIONS ABOUT THIS FORM, PLEASE DIRECT THEM TO HOSPITAL ADMINISTRATION.

The document's fine print (1) required any medical malpractice disputes to be submitted to arbitration; (2) required any arbitrator to be a board-certified orthopedic surgeon; and (3) awarded Dr. Paulos $150 per hour spent in arbitration in addition to payment of all other expenses, costs, arbitrator fees, and attorney fees in the event that Ms. Sosa was awarded less than one-half of the amount she sought. The document also provided that Ms. Sosa could revoke the agreement within ten days after her discharge from the hospital.

The surgery was an apparent success, and Ms. Sosa was released the next day. She was given a two-week prescription for hydrocodone to suppress the pain. The medication substantially reduced Ms. Sosa's pain and allowed her to sleep restfully, often throughout the day.

Ms. Sosa's first visit to the hospital, a week after the surgery, was to check for pain and examine the stitching. There were no problems, and Ms. Sosa was again released. However, on the second visit, three weeks after the surgery, Ms. Sosa complained that her pain had drastically increased after she was taken off of her hydrocodone prescription. Dr. Paulos x-rayed the incision, only to discover that he had dropped an orthopedic screw into Ms. Sosa's knee incision, which he failed to remove before closing the incision. The screw was causing inflammation and needed to be removed. Ms. Sosa had to undergo an additional surgery.

Ms. Sosa brought suit against Dr Paulos for medical malpractice, claiming damages for pain, further surgery, pain medication, recovery time, and lost wages. Dr. Paulos moved to stay the proceedings and compel arbitration, referencing the "Physician-Patient Arbitration Agreement."

Is the "Physician-Patient Arbitration Agreement" unconscionable? What factors point to and against procedural unconscionability? What factors point to and against substantive unconscionability? What arguments lean against unconscionability here? Would any of your answers change if the agreement allowed Ms. Sosa to revoke the agreement within thirty days of discharge? What impact, if any, does the ruling in *AT & T Mobility* have on this situation?

Food for Thought:
Unfair or Deceptive Acts or Practices (UDAP)

Conduct that triggers the defense of misrepresentation, unconscionability, or economic duress may also trigger an enforcement action based on an "unfair or deceptive act or practice" (UDAP). At the federal level, the Federal Trade Commission enforces the UDAP provision in § 5 of the Federal Trade Commission Act (FTCA), 15 U.S.C. § 45. Similar provisions appear in statutes in all fifty states; they are often called "little FTC Acts" and "consumer protection acts" (CPAs).*

A state consumer protection act typically authorizes the state attorney general (AG) to bring claims against a deceptive business on behalf of groups of consumers, by obtaining a "cease and desist order" or other injunctive relief, a declaratory judgment, or a settlement agreement with the business, to prevent further instances of that UDAP. States' AGs interact through the National Association of Attorneys General (NAAG), to coordinate their consumer protection efforts and share evidence of UDAPs that occur in multiple states. *See* www.naag.org.

A prominent feature of most state CPAs is express authorization for a consumer to act as a "private attorney general" by bringing a private enforcement action against a business's unfair or deceptive conduct affecting that consumer. The FTCA has no comparable provision.**

Here is a sampling of enforcement actions by state AGs:

- In 1998, AOL entered into a settlement agreement with 44 state attorneys general, promising (1) to make clear to customers that its 50-hour "free trial offer" must be used within a month and to give notice of when charges would accrue, (2) to disclose the cost of its "toll-free access number" that was actually being billed out at $6 per hour and to provide a pop-up screen that gives customers a chance to disconnect without charges, (3) to provide customers with 30 days' notice via mail or email before making any price changes or

---

* Jack E. Karns, *State Regulation of Deceptive Trade Practices Under "Little FTC Acts": Should Federal Standards Control?*, 94 Dick. L. Rev. 373 (1990).
** Howard J. Alperin & Roland F. Chase, Consumer Law: *Sales & Credit Regulation* § 133 (Westlaw, through Sept. 2012).

material changes to member agreements (material changes include changing fee structures, methods of access, and services available, among others).*

- In 2002, the New York attorney general, Eliot Spitzer, reached a settlement with Juno Online, an internet service provider. The New York AG claimed that Juno had posted a modified service agreement on its web site, effective immediately as to existing subscribers, permitting Juno to have unfettered access to subscribers' computers to create a "virtual supercomputer project," requiring subscribers to continuously operate their computers, and permitting Juno to download software onto subscribers' computers, replace their screensavers, and make subscribers liable for costs and expenses that might arise from the distributed computing network. The settlement invalidated the modifications to the agreement and required Juno to provide its subscribers with clear, conspicuous, and advance notice of all material changes to its service agreement. Juno promised to clearly state the effective date, to provide a comparison between the old and new terms, and to give subscribers at least 30 days in which to opt out before the new terms take effect.**

§ 3. Defenses Based on Lack of Capacity to Contract

Contract liability is grounded in the belief that there is social and economic value to enforcing the voluntary private choices of contracting parties. Some private choices to enter contracts are not enforceable because they were not truly voluntary because of misrepresentation or some form of coercion (see previous sections of this Chapter). This section discusses defenses based on a party's lack of *capacity* to contract, protecting individuals whose characteristics or status make them especially vulnerable to over-reaching or unable to muster the necessary mental state to truly assent.

Defenses to contract enforcement may also be based on lack of *authority* to contract. For example, an individual may purportedly enter into a contract as an agent on behalf of a principal but not have authority to do so. A corporation or government agency may purportedly enter into a contract but it may be outside the scope of the authorized power of the contracting party ("ultra vires"), resulting in a void or voidable contract. These topics are typically covered in courses on agency, business associations, or administrative law.

---

* www.atg.wa.gov/pressrelease.aspx?&id=4866; http://news.cnet.com/AOL-settles-case-with-44-states/2100-1023_3-211634.html

** www.oag.state.ny.us/media_center/2002/may/may07b_02.html

Restatement (Second) § 12. **Capacity to Contract**

(1) No one can be bound by contract who has not legal capacity to incur at least voidable contractual duties. Capacity to contract may be partial and its existence in respect of a particular transaction may depend upon the nature of the transaction or upon other circumstances.

(2) A natural person who manifests assent to a transaction has full legal capacity to incur contractual duties thereby unless he is
   (a) under guardianship, or
   (b) an infant, or
   (c) mentally ill or defective, or
   (d) intoxicated.

---

§ 3.1. Infancy

The infancy defense seeks to protect all minors—children up to the age of majority*—from the legal consequences of entering into contracts. Subject to some limitations discussed below, the infancy defense makes all contracts formed by minors voidable at the option of the minor, giving the minor (but not the other party) the opportunity to disaffirm–that is, to rescind–the obligation.

The infancy defense is governed by common law and state statutes that vary considerably among jurisdictions, more so than other defenses. This text relies upon the Restatement (Second) provisions as a useful model for discussion because they reflect principles commonly found in state law, although the Restatement provisions are not directly adopted in most jurisdictions.

Restatement (Second) § 14. **Infants**

Unless a statute provides otherwise, a natural person has the capacity to incur only voidable contractual duties until the beginning of the day before the person's eighteenth birthday.

Comments
a. Who are infants. The . . . rule that the critical moment is the beginning of the preceding day was established on the ground that the law disregards fractions of a day. . . . [I]n some [states], both men and women have full capacity upon marriage.

c. Restoration of consideration. An infant need not take any action to disaffirm his contracts until he comes of age. If sued upon the contract, he may defend on the ground of infancy without returning the consideration received. His disaffirmance revests in the other party the title to any

---

* The traditional common law age of majority was 21, but most states have lowered this age to 18, considerably reducing the number of instances in which the defense is available.

> property received by the infant under the contract. If the consideration received by the infant has been dissipated by him, the other party is without remedy unless the infant ratifies the contract after coming of age or is under some non-contractual obligation. . . .

As reflected in the Restatement provision, the infancy defense gives the minor a defense to the enforcement of any contractual obligation if that right is exercised during the period of minority or within a reasonable time after the individual achieves the age of majority. The minor must return whatever is left of the item received from the other party (or any remaining proceeds from the sale of the item to a third party) but is not responsible for any loss or damage or depreciation to the item (with a few exceptions), nor is the minor responsible for the price of any services received. The defense is available regardless of the sophistication of the child. The minor cannot waive the defense, nor can the contracting parties agree to a contrary rule.

The policy behind the infancy defense is to protect minors from their immaturity and to prevent their exploitation by adults. The danger is especially keen in teenagers, who overestimate their ability to handle the complexities of adult life and underestimate what they do not know and what could go wrong. Making contracts voidable until the age of majority is easier and arguably more workable than deciding each teenager's capacity on a case-by-case basis in a particular setting. The sharp line also puts adult contracting parties on notice that they proceed at risk that the minor will void the proposed contract. On the other hand, the availability of the defense means that even mature teens, and those who need contracting capability, may find it difficult to find contract partners, or they may need an adult co-signer or have to pay a higher price. And merchants who do business with minors do so at their own peril, even when those merchants deal in good faith. It is such drawbacks that have led to some limitations to the infancy defense, addressed in the case below.

These competing interests and policies may be part of the reason why there is so much variation in the state rules on contractual capacity for minors, as different jurisdictions have honored differing interests and policies. Another source of non-uniformity might be the "bright line" test of age, which tempts courts to carve out exceptions to accommodate the huge range of behaviors that older teenagers and young twenty-somethings exhibit.

Reading the Law Critically: *Webster Street Partnership*

1. The opinion treats contracts for "necessaries" differently than other contracts with respect to the infancy defense. What are "necessaries," in the view of this court? Under what circumstances are contracts for necessaries enforceable or not enforceable against minors? What policies justify those rules?

2. What is the role of the minor's "emancipation" in determining liability of the minor or of his parents?

3. The minors in *Webster Street Partnership* are permitted to void their contract. What relief is then available to each party to the contract? Is that relief based on expectation, reliance, or restitutionary principles?

Webster Street Partnership, Ltd. v. Sheridan

WEBSTER STREET PARTNERSHIP, LTD., Plaintiff, Appellant and Cross-Appellee

v.

MATTHEW SHERIDAN and PAT WILWERDING, Defendants, Appellees and Cross-Appellants

Supreme Court of Nebraska
368 N.W.2d 439 (Neb. 1985)

KRIVOSHA, Chief Justice.

Webster Street Partnership, Ltd. (Webster Street), appeals from an order of the district court for Douglas County, Nebraska, which modified an earlier judgment entered by the municipal court of the city of Omaha, Douglas County, Nebraska. The municipal court entered judgment in favor of Webster Street and against the appellees, Matthew Sheridan and Pat Wilwerding, in the amount of $630.94. On appeal the district court found that Webster Street was entitled to a judgment in the amount of $146.75 and that Sheridan and Wilwerding were entitled to a credit in the amount of $150. The district court therefore entered judgment in favor of Sheridan and Wilwerding and against Webster Street in the amount of $3.25. It is from this $3.25 judgment that appeal is taken to this court.

Webster Street is a partnership owning real estate in Omaha, Nebraska. On September 18, 1982, Webster Street, through one of its agents, Norman Sargent, entered into a written lease with Sheridan and Wilwerding for a second floor apartment at 3007 Webster Street. The lease provided that Sheridan and Wilwerding would pay to Webster Street by way of monthly rental the sum of $250 due on the first day of each month until August 15, 1983. The lease also required the payment of a security deposit in the amount of $150 and a payment of $20 per month for utilities during the months of December, January, February, and March. Liquidated damages in the amount of $5 per day for each day the rent was late were also provided for by the lease.

The evidence conclusively establishes that at the time the lease was executed both tenants were minors and, further, that Webster Street knew that fact. At the time the lease was entered into, Sheridan was 18 and did not become 19 until November 5, 1982.[*2] Wilwerding was 17 at the time the lease was executed and never gained his majority during any time relevant to this case.

The tenants paid the $150 security deposit, $100 rent for the remaining portion of September 1982, and $250 rent for October 1982. They did not pay the rent for the month of November 1982, and on November 5 Sargent advised Wilwerding that unless the rent was paid immediately, both boys would be required to vacate the premises. The tenants both testified that, being unable to pay the rent, they moved from the premises on November 12. In fact, a dispute exists as to when the two tenants relinquished possession of the premises, but in view of our decision that dispute is not of any relevance.

In a letter dated January 7, 1983, Webster Street's attorney made written demand upon the tenants for damages in the amount of $630.94. On January 12, 1983, the tenants' attorney denied any liability, refused to pay any portion of the amount demanded, stated that neither tenant was of legal age at the time the lease was executed, and demanded return of $150 security deposit.

Webster Street thereafter commenced suit against the tenants and sought judgment in the amount of $630.94, which was calculated as follows:

Rent due Nov.	$250.00
Rent due Dec.	250.00
Dec. utility allowance	20.00
Garage rental	40.00
Clean up and repair broken window, degrease kitchen stove, shampoo carpet, etc.	46.79
Advertising	24.15
Re-rental fee	150.00
	780.94
Less security deposit	- 150.00
	$630.94

---

* [Authors' Note: By this statement, we surmise that the age of majority in this jurisdiction at the time of this case was 19 years of age.]

To this petition the tenants filed an answer alleging that they were minors at the time they signed the lease, that the lease was therefore voidable, and that the rental property did not constitute a necessary for which they were otherwise liable. In addition, Sheridan cross-petitioned for the return of the security deposit, and Wilwerding filed a cross-petition seeking the return of all moneys paid to Webster Street. Following trial, the municipal court of the city of Omaha found in favor of Webster Street and against both tenants in the amount of $630.94.

The tenants appealed to the district court for Douglas County. The district court found that the tenants had vacated the premises on November 12, 1982, and therefore were only liable for the 12 days in which they actually occupied the apartment and did not pay rent. The district court also permitted Webster Street to recover $46.79 for cleanup and repairs. The tenants, however, were given credit for their $150 security deposit, resulting in an order that Webster Street was indebted to the tenants in the amount of $3.25.

Webster Street then perfected an appeal to this court . . . . Webster Street's position [appears to be] that the district court erred in failing to find that Sheridan had ratified the lease within a reasonable time after obtaining majority, and was therefore responsible for the lease, and that the minors had become emancipated and were therefore liable, even though Wilwerding had not reached majority. Webster Street is simply wrong in both matters.

As a general rule, an infant does not have the capacity to bind himself absolutely by contract. See, *Smith v. Wade*, 169 Neb. 710, 100 N.W.2d 770 (1960); 43 C.J.S. *Infants* § 166 (1978). The right of the infant to avoid his contract is one conferred by law for his protection against his own improvidence and the designs of others. See *Burnand v. Irigoyen*, 30 Cal.2d 861, 186 P.2d 417 (1947). The policy of the law is to discourage adults from contracting with an infant; they cannot complain if, as a consequence of violating that rule, they are unable to enforce their contract. As stated in *Curtice Co. v. Kent*, 89 Neb. 496, 500, 131 N.W. 944, 945 (1911): "The result seems hardly just to the [adult], but persons dealing with infants do so at their peril. The law is plain as to their disability to contract, and safety lies in refusing to transact business with them."

However, the privilege of infancy will not enable an infant to escape liability in all cases and under all circumstances. For example, it is well established that an infant is liable for the value of necessaries furnished him. 42 Am.Jur.2d *Infants* § 65 (1969). See, also, *Burnand v. Irigoyen, supra; Merrick v. Stephens*, 337 S.W.2d 713 (Mo.App.1960); *Englebert v. Troxell*, 40 Neb. 195, 58 N.W. 852 (1894). An infant's liability for necessaries is based not upon his actual contract to pay for them but upon a contract implied by law, or, in other words, a quasi-contract. 42 Am.Jur.2d, *supra*.

Just what are necessaries, however, has no exact definition. The term is flexible and varies according to the facts of each individual case. In *Cobbey v. Buchanan*, 48 Neb. 391, 397, 67 N.W. 176, 178 (1896), we said: "The meaning of the term 'necessaries' cannot be defined by a general rule applicable to all cases; the question is a mixed one of law and fact, to be determined in each case from the particular facts and circumstances in such case." A number of factors must be considered before a court can conclude whether a particular product or service is a necessary. As stated in *Schoenung v. Gallet*, 206 Wis. 52, 54, 238 N.W. 852, 853 (1931):

> "The term 'necessaries,' as used in the law relating to the liability of infants therefor, is a relative term, somewhat flexible, except when applied to such things as are obviously requisite for the maintenance of existence, and depends on the social position and situation in life of the infant, as well as upon his own fortune and that of his parents. The particular infant must have an actual need for the articles furnished; not for mere ornament or pleasure. The articles must be useful and suitable, but they are not necessaries merely because useful or beneficial. Concerning the general character of the things furnished, to be necessaries the articles must supply the infant's personal needs, either those of his body or those of his mind. However, the term 'necessaries' is not confined to merely such things as are required for a bare subsistence. There is no positive rule by means of which it may be determined what are or what are not necessaries, for what may be considered necessary for one infant may not be necessaries for another infant whose state is different as to rank, social position, fortune, health, or other circumstances, the question being one to be determined from the particular facts and circumstances of each case."

. . . . This appears to be the law as it is generally followed throughout the country.

In *Ballinger v. Craig*, 95 Ohio App. 545, 121 N.E.2d 66, (1953), the defendants were husband and wife and were 19 years of age at the time they purchased a house trailer. Both were employed. However, prior to the purchase of the trailer, the defendants were living with the parents of the husband.

Think About It!

Necessaries are often limited to food, shelter, and clothing of a reasonable kind, medical and dental services and medicines, and transportation to and from a workplace and places to shop for necessities. Why should (as the court says here) the "necessaries" be based on the needs of a reasonable person with the minor's "rank, social position, fortune, health, or other circumstances"? What policies argue for and against this flexible definition?

The Court of Appeals for the State of Ohio held that under the facts presented the trailer was not a necessary. The court stated:

> "To enable an infant to contract for articles as necessaries, he must have been in actual need of them, and obliged to procure them for himself. They are not necessaries as to him, however necessary they may be in their nature, if he was already supplied with sufficient articles of the kind, or if he had a parent or guardian who was able and willing to supply them. The burden of proof is on the plaintiff to show that the infant was destitute of the articles, and had no way of procuring them except by his own contract."

. . . . *Id.* at 547, 121 N.E.2d at 67. Under Ohio law the marriage of the parties did not result in their obtaining majority.

In 42 Am.Jur.2d *Infants* § 67 at 68-69 (1969), the author notes:

> Thus, articles are not necessaries for an infant if he has a parent or guardian who is able and willing to supply them, and an infant residing with and being supported by his parent according to his station in life is not absolutely liable for things which under other circumstances would be considered necessaries.

The undisputed testimony is that both tenants were living away from home, apparently with the understanding that they could return home at any time. Sheridan testified:

> Q. During the time that you were living at 3007 Webster, did you at any time, feel free to go home or anything like that?
> A. Well, I had a feeling I could, but I just wanted to see if I could make it on my own.
> Q. Had you been driven from your home?
> A. No.
> Q. You didn't have to go?
> A. No.
> Q. You went freely?
> A. Yes.
> Q. Then, after you moved out and went to 3417 for a week or so, you were again to return home, is that correct?
> A. Yes, sir.

It would therefore appear that in the present case neither Sheridan nor Wilwerding was in need of shelter but, rather, had chosen to voluntarily leave home, with the understanding that they could return whenever they desired. One may at first blush believe that such a rule is unfair. Yet, on further consideration, the wisdom of the rule is apparent. If, indeed, landlords may not contract with minors, except at their peril, they may refuse to do so. In that event, minors who voluntarily leave home but who are free to return will be compelled to return to their parents' home—a result which is desirable. We therefore find that both the municipal court and the district court erred in finding that the apartment, under the facts in this case, was a necessary.

Having therefore concluded that the apartment was not a necessary, the question of whether Sheridan and Wilwerding were emancipated is of no significance. The effect of emancipation is only relevant with regard to necessaries. If the minors were not emancipated, then their parents would be liable for necessaries provided to the minors. As we recently noted in *Accent Service Co., Inc. v. Ebsen,* 209 Neb. 94, 96, 306 N.W.2d 575, 576 (1981):

> "In general, even in the absence of statute, parents are under a legal as well as a moral obligation to support, maintain, and care for their children, the basis of such a duty resting not only upon the fact of the parent-child relationship, but also upon the interest of the state as parens patriae of children and of the community at large in preventing them from becoming a public burden. However, various voluntary acts of a child, such as marriage or enlistment in military service, have been held to terminate the parent's obligation of support, the issue generally being considered by the courts in terms of whether an emancipation of the child has been effectuated. In those cases involving the issue of whether a parent is obligated to support an unmarried minor child who has voluntarily left home without the consent of the parent, the courts, in actions to compel support from the parent, have uniformly held that such conduct on the part of the child terminated the support obligation. . . ."

Take Note!

Emancipation may be full or partial. Some minors are allowed by their parents to spend money earned in full-time employment but are not released from parental custody and control. For some courts, emancipation may have the effect stated in the case when the minor earns enough money to procure all necessaries without parental assistance.

If, on the other hand, it was determined that the minors were emancipated and the apartment was a necessary, then the minors would be liable. But where, as here, we determine that the apartment was not a necessary, then neither the parents nor the infants are liable and the question of emancipation is of no moment.

Because the rental of the apartment was not a necessary, the minors had the right to avoid the contract, either during their minority or within a reasonable time after reaching their majority. See *Smith v. Wade,* 169 Neb. 710, 100 N.W.2d 770 (1960). Disaffirmance by an infant completely puts an end to the contract's existence, both as to him and as to the adult with whom he contracted. *Curtice Co. v. Kent,* 89 Neb. 496, 131 N.W. 944 (1911). Because the parties then stand as if no contract had ever existed, the infant can recover payments made to the adult, and the adult is entitled to the return of whatever was received by the infant. *Id.*

Think About It!

What amounts to a "reasonable time" for the minor to disaffirm the contract after reaching the age of majority? Compare the circumstances in *Webster Street Partnership* to *In re The Score Board, Inc.,* 238 B.R. 585 (D.N.J. 1999). In that case, Kobe Bryant attempted to disaffirm an endorsement contract that he entered when he was 17 years old, just as he began his professional basketball career. The court found Bryant had affirmed the contract when he deposited a $10,000 check from the other party 3 days after his 18th birthday and thereafter consciously performed his contractual duties by signing autographs and making personal appearances.

The record shows that Pat Wilwerding clearly disaffirmed the contract during his minority. Moreover, the record supports the view that when the agent for Webster Street ordered the minors out for failure to pay rent and they vacated the premises, Sheridan likewise disaffirmed the contract. The record indicates that Sheridan reached majority on November 5. To suggest that a lapse of 7 days was not disaffirmance within a reasonable time would be foolish. Once disaffirmed, the contract became void; therefore, no contract existed between the parties, and the minors were entitled to recover all of the moneys which they paid and to be relieved of any further obligation under the contract. The judgment of the district court for Douglas County, Nebraska, is therefore reversed and the cause remanded with directions to vacate the judgment in favor of Webster Street and to enter a judgment in favor of Matthew Sheridan and Pat Wilwerding in the amount of $500, representing September rent in the amount of $100, October rent in the amount of $250, and the security deposit in the amount of $150.

Reversed and remanded with directions.

Reading the Law Critically: *Halbman*

1. Does the contract in *Halbman* involve purchase of a "necessary"? Why or why not?

2. The minor in *Halbman* is permitted to void his contract. What relief is then available to each party to the contract? What variations does the court describe in the rules on relief after disaffirmance?

3. Based on the court's discussion, what difference does it make if a minor misrepresents his or her age? Based on the policies underlying the infancy defense, what difference should it make?

4. Toward the end of *Webster Street Partnership*, page 571, the court says that "the adult is entitled to the return of whatever was received by the infant." What is the *Halbman* court's holding on that issue?

Halbman v. Lemke

JAMES HALBMAN, JR., Plaintiff-Respondent and Cross-Appellant

v.

MICHAEL LEMKE, Defendant-Appellant and Cross-Respondent-Petitioner

Supreme Court of Wisconsin

298 N.W. 2d 562 (Wis. 1980)

CALLOW, Justice.

FYI

In this opinion, a "necessity" seems to mean the same as a "necessary" in the preceding opinion. The latter term is more common.

On this review we must decide whether a minor who disaffirms a contract for the purchase of a vehicle which is not a necessity must make restitution to the vendor for damage sustained by the vehicle prior to the time the contract was disaffirmed. The court of appeals, 91 Wis.2d 847, 282 N.W.2d 638, affirmed the judgment in part, reversed in part, and remanded the cause to the circuit court . . . .

I.

This matter was before the trial court upon stipulated facts. On or about July 13, 1973, James Halbman, Jr. (Halbman), a minor, entered into an agreement with Michael Lemke (Lemke) whereby Lemke agreed to sell Halbman a 1968 Oldsmobile for the sum of $1,250. Lemke was the manager of L & M Standard

Station in Greenfield, Wisconsin, and Halbman was an employee at L & M. At the time the agreement was made Halbman paid Lemke $1,000 cash and took possession of the car. Arrangements were made for Halbman to pay $25 per week until the balance was paid, at which time title would be transferred. About five weeks after the purchase agreement, and after Halbman had paid a total of $1,100 of the purchase price, a connecting rod on the vehicle's engine broke. Lemke, while denying any obligation, offered to assist Halbman in installing a used engine in the vehicle if Halbman, at his expense, could secure one. Halbman declined the offer and in September took the vehicle to a garage where it was repaired at a cost of $637.40. Halbman did not pay the repair bill.

In October of 1973 Lemke endorsed the vehicle's title over to Halbman, although the full purchase price had not been paid by Halbman, in an effort to avoid any liability for the operation, maintenance, or use of the vehicle. On October 15, 1973, Halbman returned the title to Lemke by letter which disaffirmed the purchase contract and demanded the return of all money theretofore paid by Halbman. Lemke did not return the money paid by Halbman.

The repair bill remained unpaid, and the vehicle remained in the garage where the repairs had been made. In the spring of 1974, in satisfaction of a garageman's lien for the outstanding amount, the garage elected to remove the vehicle's engine and transmission and then towed the vehicle to the residence of James Halbman, Sr., the father of the plaintiff minor. Lemke

> **Take Note!**
>
> The seller's signing over title (that is, transferring the motor vehicle certificate of title) to the buyer might have had an impact on seller's tort liability, depending on the state's certificate-of-title law, but it did not affect the parties' contract rights.

was asked several times to remove the vehicle from the senior Halbman's home, but he declined to do so, claiming he was under no legal obligation to remove it. During the period when the vehicle was at the garage and then subsequently at the home of the plaintiff's father, it was subjected to vandalism, making it unsalvageable.

Halbman initiated this action seeking the return of the $1,100 he had paid toward the purchase of the vehicle, and Lemke counterclaimed for $150, the amount still owing on the contract. Based upon the uncontroverted facts, the trial court granted judgment in favor of Halbman, concluding that when a minor disaffirms a contract for the purchase of an item, he need only offer to return the property remaining in his hands without making restitution for any use or depreciation. In the order granting judgment, the trial court also allowed interest to the plaintiff dating from the disaffirmance of the contract. On postjudgment motions, the court amended its order for judgment to allow interest to the plaintiff from the date of the original order for judgment, July 26, 1978.

Lemke appealed to the court of appeals, and Halbman cross-appealed from the disallowance of prejudgment interest. The appellate court affirmed the trial court with respect to the question of restitution for depreciation, but reversed on the question of prejudgment interest, remanding the cause for reimposition of interest dating from the date of disaffirmance. The question of prejudgment interest is not before us on this review.

II.

The sole issue before us is whether a minor, having disaffirmed a contract for the purchase of an item which is not a necessity and having tendered the property back to the vendor, must make restitution to the vendor for damage to the property prior to the disaffirmance. Lemke argues that he should be entitled to recover for the damage to the vehicle up to the time of disaffirmance, which he claims equals the amount of the repair bill.

Neither party challenges the absolute right of a minor to disaffirm a contract for the purchase of items which are not necessities. That right, variously known as the doctrine of incapacity or the "infancy doctrine," is one of the oldest and most venerable of our common law traditions. See: Grauman, Marx & Cline Co. v. Krienitz, 142 Wis. 556, 560, 126 N.W. 50 (1910); 2 Williston, Contracts sec. 226 (3d ed. 1959); 42 Am.Jur.2d Infants sec. 84 (1969). Although the origins of the doctrine are somewhat obscure, it is generally recognized that its purpose is the protection of minors from foolishly squandering their wealth through improvident contracts with crafty adults who would take advantage of them in the marketplace. Kiefer v. Fred Howe Motors, Inc., 39 Wis.2d 20, 24, 158 N.W.2d 288 (1968). Thus it is settled law in this state that a contract of a minor for items which are not necessities is void or voidable at the minor's option. Id. at 23, 158 N.W.2d 288; Schoenung v. Gallet, 206 Wis. 52, 55, 238 N.W. 852 (1931); Grauman, Marx & Cline v. Krienitz, supra 142 Wis. at 560-61, 126 N.W. 50; Thormaehlen v. Kaeppel, 86 Wis. 378, 380, 56 N.W. 1089 (1893).

Once there has been a disaffirmance, however, as in this case between a minor vendee and an adult vendor, unresolved problems arise regarding the rights and responsibilities of the parties relative to the disposition of the consideration exchanged on the contract. As a general rule a minor who disaffirms a contract is entitled to recover all consideration he has conferred incident to the transaction. Schoenung v. Gallet, supra. In return the minor is expected to restore as much of the consideration as, at the time of disaffirmance, remains in the minor's possession. Thormaehlen v. Kaeppel, supra, 86 Wis. at 380, 56 N.W. 1089; Grauman, Marx & Cline v. Krienitz, supra 142 Wis. at 560-61, 126 N.W. 50. See also: Restatement of Restitution, sec. 62, comment b, (1937); Restatement (Second) of Contracts, sec. 18B, comment c, (Tent. Draft No. 1, 1964).

The minor's right to disaffirm is not contingent upon the return of the property, however, as disaffirmance is permitted even where such return cannot be made. Olson v. Veum, 197 Wis. 342, 345, 222 N.W. 233 (1928). See also: Nelson v. Browning, 391 S.W.2d 873, 875-76 (Mo.1965); Boudreaux v. State Farm Mutual Auto. Ins. Co., 385 So.2d 480, 483 (La.App.1980); Williston, supra, sec. 238, 39-41.

The return of property remaining in the hands of the minor is not the issue presented here. In this case we have a situation where the property cannot be returned to the vendor in its entirety because it has been damaged and therefore diminished in value, and the vendor seeks to recover the depreciation. Although this court has been cognizant of this issue on previous occasions, we have not heretofore resolved it. See: Schoenung v. Gallet, supra, 206 Wis. at 57-58, 238 N.W. 852; Wallace v. Newdale Furniture Co., 188 Wis. 205, 207-08, 205 N.W. 819 (1925).

The law regarding the rights and responsibilities of the parties relative to the consideration exchanged on a disaffirmed contract is characterized by confusion, inconsistency, and a general lack of uniformity as jurisdictions attempt to reach a fair application of the infancy doctrine in today's marketplace. See: Robert G. Edge, Voidability of Minors' Contracts: A Feudal Doctrine in a Modern Economy, 1 Ga.L.Rev. 205 (1967); Walter D. Navin, Jr., The Contracts of Minors Viewed from the Perspective of Fair Exchange, 50 N.C.L.Rev. 517 (1972); Note, Restitution in Minors' Contracts in California, 19 Hastings L.Rev. 1199 (1968); 52 Marq.L.Rev. 437 (1969). See also John D. McCamus, Restitution of Benefits Conferred Under Minors' Contracts, 28 U.N.B.L.J. 89 (1979); Annot., Infant's Liability for Use or Depreciation of Subject Matter, in Action to Recover Purchase Price Upon His Disaffirmance of Contract to Purchase Goods, 12 A.L.R.3d 1174 (1967). That both parties rely on this court's decision in Olson v. Veum, supra, is symptomatic of the problem.

In Olson a minor, with his brother, an adult, purchased farm implements and materials, paying by signing notes payable at a future date. Prior to the maturity of the first note, the brothers ceased their joint farming business, and the minor abandoned his interest in the material purchased by leaving it with his brother. The vendor initiated an action against the minor to recover on the note, and the minor (who had by then reached majority) disaffirmed. The trial court ordered judgment for the plaintiff on the note, finding there had been insufficient disaffirmance to sustain the plea of infancy. This court reversed, holding that the contract of a minor for the purchase of items which are not necessities may be disaffirmed even when the minor cannot make restitution. Lemke calls our attention to the following language in that decision:

> "To sustain the judgment below is to overlook the substantial distinction between a mere denial by an infant of contract liability where the other

party is seeking to enforce it and those cases where he who was the minor not only disaffirms such contract but seeks the aid of the court to restore to him that with which he has parted at the making of the contract. In the one case he is using his infancy merely as a shield, in the other also as a sword." 197 Wis. at 344, 222 N.W. 233.

From this Lemke infers that when a minor, as a plaintiff, seeks to disaffirm a contract and recover his consideration, different rules should apply than if the minor is defending against an action on the contract by the other party. This theory is not without some support among scholars. See: Calamari and Perillo, The Law of Contracts, sec. 126, 207-09 (Hornbook Series 1970), treating separately the obligations of the infant as a plaintiff and the infant as a defendant.

Additionally, Lemke advances the thesis in the dissenting opinion by court of appeals Judge Cannon, arguing that a disaffirming minor's obligation to make restitution turns upon his ability to do so. For this proposition, the following language in Olson v. Veum, supra, 197 Wis. at 345, 222 N.W. 233, is cited:

> "The authorities are clear that when it is shown, as it is here, that the infant cannot make restitution, then his absolute right to disaffirm is not to be questioned."

In this case Lemke argues that the Olson language excuses the minor only when restitution is not possible. Here Lemke holds Halbman's $1,100, and accordingly there is no question as to Halbman's ability to make restitution.

Halbman argues in response that, while the "sword-shield" dichotomy may apply where the minor has misrepresented his age to induce the contract, that did not occur here and he may avoid the contract without making restitution notwithstanding his ability to do so.

The principal problem is the use of the word "restitution" in Olson. A minor, as we have stated, is under an enforceable duty to return to the vendor, upon disaffirmance, as much of the consideration as remains in his possession. When the contract is disaffirmed, title to that part of the purchased property which is retained by the minor revests in the vendor; it no longer belongs to the minor. See, e. g., Restatement (Second) of Contracts, sec. 18B, comment c, (Tent. Draft No. 1, 1964). The rationale for the rule is plain: a minor who disaffirms a purchase and recovers his purchase price should not also be permitted to profit by retaining the property purchased. The infancy doctrine is designed to protect the minor, sometimes at the expense of an innocent vendor, but it is not to be used to bilk merchants out of property as well as proceeds of the sale. Consequently, it is clear that, when the minor no longer possesses the property which was the subject matter of the contract, the rule requiring the return of property does not apply.[1] The minor will not be required to give up what he does not have. We conclude that Olson does no more than set forth the foregoing rationale and that the word "restitution" as it is used in that opinion is limited to the return of the property to the vendor. We do not agree with Lemke and the court of appeals' dissent that Olson requires a minor to make restitution for loss or damage to the property if he is capable of doing so.

[margin handwritten note: just because can pay, doesn't mean should pay]

Here Lemke seeks restitution of the value of the depreciation by virtue of the damage to the vehicle prior to disaffirmance. Such a recovery would require Halbman to return more than that remaining in his possession. It seeks compensatory value for that which he cannot return. Where there is misrepresentation by a minor or willful destruction of property, the vendor may be able to recover damages in tort. See, e. g., Kiefer v. Fred Howe Motors, Inc., supra ; 42 Am.Jur.2d Infants sec. 105 (1969). But absent these factors, as in the present case, we believe that to require a disaffirming minor to make restitution for diminished value is, in effect, to bind the minor to a part of the obligation which by law he is privileged to avoid. See: Nelson v. Browning, supra at 875-76; Williston, supra, sec. 238, 39-41.

The cases upon which the petitioner relies for the proposition that a disaffirming minor must make restitution for loss and depreciation serve to illustrate some of the ways other jurisdictions have approached this problem of balancing the needs of minors against the rights of innocent merchants. In Barber v. Gross, 74 S.D. 254, 51 N.W.2d 696 (1952), the South Dakota Supreme Court held that a minor could disaffirm a contract as a defense to an action by the merchant to enforce the contract but that the minor was obligated by a South Dakota statute, upon sufficient proof of loss by the plaintiff, to make restitution for depreciation. Cain v. Coleman, 396 S.W.2d 251 (Tex.Civ.App.1965), involved a minor seeking to disaffirm a contract for the purchase of a used car where the dealer claimed the minor had misrepresented his age. In reversing summary judgment granted in

---

[1] Although we are not presented with the question here, we recognize there is considerable disagreement among the authorities on whether a minor who disposes of the property should be made to restore the vendor with something in its stead. The general rule appears to limit the minor's responsibility for restoration to specie only. Terrace Company v. Calhoun, 37 Ill.App.3d 757, 347 N.E.2d 315, 320 (1976); Adamowski v. Curtiss-Wright Flying Service, 300 Mass. 281, 15 N.E.2d 467 (1938); Quality Motors v. Hays, 216 Ark. 264, 225 S.W.2d 326, 328 (1949). But see: Boyce v. Doyle, 113 N.J.Super. 240, 273 A.2d 408 (1971), adopting a "status quo" theory which requires the minor to restore the precontract status quo, even if it means returning proceeds or other value; Fisher v. Taylor Motor Co., 249 N.C. 617, 107 S.E.2d 94 (1959), requiring the minor to restore only the property remaining in the hands of the minor, "'or account for so much of its value as may have been invested in other property which he has in hand or owns and controls.'" Id. at 97. Finally, some attention is given to the "New Hampshire Rule" or benefits theory which requires the disaffirming minor to pay for the contract to the extent he benefited from it. Hall v. Butterfield, 59 N.H. 354 (1879); Porter v. Wilson, 106 N.H. 270, 209 A.2d 730 (1965). See also: 19 Hastings L.J. 1199, 1205-08 (1968); 52 Marq.L.Rev. 437 (1969); Calamari and Perillo, The Law of Contracts, secs. 129, 215-16 (Hornbook Series 1970).

favor of the minor, the court recognized the minor's obligation to make restitution for the depreciation of the vehicle. The Texas court has also ruled, in a case where there was no issue of misrepresentation, that upon disaffirmance and tender by a minor the vendor is obligated to take the property "as is." **Rutherford v. Hughes, 228 S.W.2d 909, 912 (Tex.Civ.App.1950). Scalone v. Talley Motors, Inc., 158 N.Y.S.2d 615, 3 App.Div.2d 674 (1957), and Rose v. Sheehan Buick, Inc., 204 So.2d 903 (Fla.App.1967),** represent the proposition that a disaffirming minor must do equity in the form of restitution for loss or depreciation of the property returned. Because these cases would at some point force the minor to bear the cost of the very improvidence from which the infancy doctrine is supposed to protect him, we cannot follow them.

As we noted in Kiefer, modifications of the rules governing the capacity of infants to contract are best left to the legislature. Until such changes are forthcoming, however, we hold that, absent misrepresentation or tortious damage to the property, a minor who disaffirms a contract for the purchase of an item which is not a necessity may recover his purchase price without liability for use, depreciation, damage, or other diminution in value.

Recently the Illinois Court of Appeals came to the same conclusion. In **Weisbrook v. Clyde C. Netzley, Inc., 58 Ill.App.3d 862, 374 N.E.2d 1102 (1978),** a minor sought to disaffirm a contract for the purchase of a vehicle which developed engine trouble after its purchase. In the minor's action the dealer counterclaimed for restitution for use and depreciation. The court affirmed judgment for the minor and, with respect to the dealer's claim for restitution, stated:

> "In the present case, of course, the minor plaintiff never misrepresented his age and, in fact, informed defendant that he was 17 years old. Nor did plaintiff represent to defendant that his father was to be the owner or have any interest in the automobile. There is no evidence in the present case that plaintiff at the time of entering the contract with defendant intended anything more than to enjoy his new automobile. He borrowed the total purchase price and paid it to defendant carrying out the transaction fully at the time of taking delivery of the vehicle. Plaintiff sought to disaffirm the contract and the return of the purchase price only when defendant declined to make repairs to it. In these circumstances we believe the weight of authority would permit the minor plaintiff to disaffirm the voidable contract and that defendant-vendor would not be entitled to recoup any damages which he believes he suffered as a result thereof."

Id. at 1107. See also: **Johnson Motors, Inc. v. Coleman, 232 So.2d 716 (Miss.1970); Rutherford v. Hughes, supra; Fisher v. Taylor Motor Co., 249**

N.C. 617, 107 S.E.2d 94 (1959). We believe this result is consistent with the purpose of the infancy doctrine.

doesn't have to pay

The decision of the court of appeals is affirmed.

---

§ 3.2. Mental Illness or Defect

Although individuals suffering from mental illness or defect should be protected both from exploitation by others and from taking action that does not truly represent their voluntary choice because of their mental condition, the line dividing mental competency from incompetency is rarely a sharp one. The infancy defense can use a bright line standard based on age; no similar bright line is available for mental competency, except if the individual has already been placed under guardianship as the result of a formal ruling of incompetency. Contracts with mentally incompetent persons who have been adjudicated incompetent are generally void, but contracts with others who are (but not adjudicated to be) mentally incompetent are generally voidable at the option of the incompetent person (or someone acting on his behalf).

The policies underlying this defense tug in several, often competing, directions. Incompetent persons need protection, but so do the persons with whom they interact, especially if the incompetency is not obvious. As with minors, even incompetent individuals may have a need for contracting capability, especially if the incompetency is transitory rather than permanent, and the existence of the defense may make others wary of contracting with someone who is merely odd. The defense may be used by family and friends in an effort to control the affairs of the allegedly incompetent person, even though the incompetency is partial, transient, or not yet sufficiently advanced to meet the mental incompetency standard. Ambiguity in the definition or application of the standard of mental incompetency may invite some to use the defense to avoid choices that were merely unwise, not driven by mental illness or defect.

Issues of mental competency also arise in other areas of law, such as the competency of testators to make wills and trusts, the intent necessary to commit an intentional tort, and the ability the intent necessary or state of mind to be responsble for a criminal act. The mental competency standards in these areas of law have some similarity, but are not identical or interchangeable.

Sometimes the tests for mental competency seem arcane and even antiquated, because the law lags behind medicine's understanding of defective mental processing. Other tests may seem harsh or insensitive, mirroring society's reactions to mental illness.

Reading the Law Critically: *Fingerhut*

1. What are the two standards for judging mental incompetency in contract law? Which standard does plaintiff rely upon, and why? Which standard was used in *G.A.S.* (page 505)?

2. What facts support plaintiff's claim of mental incapacity? What facts support defendant's position? Why does the court reject the defense?

3. In light of plaintiff's failure to establish incapacity, why does the court consider the defendant's ratification argument? Why does the court rule in favor of that argument?

4. Of what significance is plaintiff's failure to testify? Why do you suppose plaintiff and his attorney made that choice?

Fingerhut v. Kralyn Enterprises, Inc.

STANLEY FINGERHUT, Plaintiff

v.

KRALYN ENTERPRISES, INC., Defendant

Supreme Court, New York County, New York
337 N.Y.S.2d 394 (Sup. Ct. 1971)

Vincent A. Lupiano, J.

The plaintiff, Stanley Fingerhut, sues the defendant, Kralyn Enterprises, Inc., to rescind a contract allegedly made when he was mentally incompetent, in that he was in the manic phase of the ailment, manic-depressive psychosis.

In the summer of 1968, he was the sole general partner in a private investment company called Mt. Vernon Associates. He was then 33 years old and unmarried. He was an investment advisor, having been a customer's man for a well-known brokerage house. His yearly earnings averaged more than $50,000 over a period of five years. In 1967 he formed the investment company with 16 limited partners, which increased its capital from $3,000,000 to over $5,000,000 within a period of two years. This large increase was greatly due to plaintiff's efforts who, himself, had invested $153,000.

He was a member of a golf club and prior to the transaction involved here, toured various country clubs, because he wanted to buy one. He investigated the Bel Aire Golf & Country Club. He obtained an appraisal of Bel Aire which valued the property on February 21, 1968, at $2,728,000 exclusive of the personal property, furnishings, etc. The personal property represented an investment of $275,819.70.

On September 22, 1968 plaintiff and his attorney, Richard J. Rubin, . . . drove to Bel Aire. They informed the Krassners, majority stockholders of the club, that plaintiff desired to purchase the golf club. The Krassners then sent for their lawyer, Seymour Rabinowitz. Negotiations took place between the parties and their lawyers and the price of $3,075,000 was agreed upon. Rubin, in the presence of plaintiff, wrote the binder in longhand. The parties executed it, in the presence of their respective lawyers. Plaintiff gave a check for $25,000 to the defendant.

On September 25, 1968, the parties met at the offices of plaintiff's lawyers to discuss the making of a formal contract and after six hours of strenuous negotiating a contract was made.

On September 26, 1968 that contract was executed and plaintiff paid a further sum of $200,000. Both sums were to be held in escrow by defendant's attorney, Rabinowitz. The balance of $2,850,000, was to be paid upon the closing of title scheduled on November 15, 1968, or sooner, at the option of the purchaser who also had the right to adjourn the closing to December 15, 1968.

The property was encumbered with three mortgages aggregating $1,950,000. At least $900,000 was needed to take title, plus adjustments and inventory, depending on whether preliminary negotiations relating to the extinguishment or extensions of the existing mortgages were successful. If not successful, the buyer was obligated to cover such mortgages with cash. In this area, the binder had provided for an all cash deal. However, the buyer, in the subsequent contract, was allowed to arrange his own financing, with provision that the seller would assist the buyer in obtaining extensions of the first and second mortgages; in such case, the seller would accept a purchase-money mortgage up to $400,000. Such co-operation was afforded, apparently, on the premise that plaintiff might not have available to him sufficient funds to acquire the property free of all the mortgages at the time of closing.

At the request of plaintiff's counsel, a liquidated damages clause, providing that in the event of buyer's default, seller was entitled to retain all sums paid in escrow, was eliminated. In the contract, the escrowee was authorized to use the escrow funds in making payment of $22,894.73 for the 1968-1969 school taxes, $1,422.89 for supplies and labor to maintain the golf course, and $100,000 on account of the third mortgage, which installment was coming due in December. Such payment reduced the mortgage to $194,000. Plaintiff, having consented to such payments amounting to $124,317.62, with credit to be given the buyer at the closing, the sum of $100,682.82 was left.

The deal was never consummated.

On November 8, 1968, plaintiff, through his attorney, sent a letter to the defendant which, amongst other matters, "elected to adjourn closing of title until December 15, 1968." On November 19, 1968, plaintiff's attorneys wrote defendant's attorneys as follows:

> Yesterday, November 18, 1968, we met with Stanley Fingerhut for the purpose of discussing with him the progress, if any, of his arranging financing for the above transaction.

Make the Connection

A liquidated damages clause in a contract specifies a dollar amount (or a formula for computing a dollar amount) of damages, rather than leaving damages to be determined by the court after breach. Here the liquidated damage amount was the cash previously paid into escrow, but the parties removed the clause from the final contract. Chapter 9 (page 1162) discusses limitations on the parties' right to specify liquidated and other forms of agreed damages.

> We were apprised for the first time that Mr. Fingerhut suffers from a manic depressive psychosis, a condition for which he has received medical treatment for the past years. We were advised, and competent medical authority will substantiate, that Mr. Fingerhut prior to September 22, 1968, and until recently, was in the manic stage of his illness and wholly incompetent and totally incapable of managing his own affairs during that time.

> Accordingly, we submit that the binder agreement between the parties, and the contract dated September 26, 1968, were made during a period when our client wholly lacked sufficient mental competence to contract on his behalf and would not have entered into the agreement but for the existence of the mental disorder.

> Based upon the foregoing, our client has instructed us to give you notice, and we do so, by this letter that he elects to rescind the binder of September 22, 1968, and the contract of September 26, 1968, and demands the return of the $225,000 given by him thereunder as a down payment. . . .

> We must request that you contact us in order that we may confer on this matter.

No agreement was reached and this action was commenced on December 16, 1968; a *lis pendens* in the sum of $124,317.62 was filed on the basis that such moneys were expended to increase defendant's equity in the property. Prior to the commencement of the action, on the date set for the closing, defendant tendered a deed and demanded payment of $2,850,000. The deed contained no recital that it was subject to any existing mortgages or encumbrances. After the plaintiff elected to rescind, the escrowee handed over the moneys to the defendant.

What's That?

Plaintiff filed a *lis pendens* notice on the real estate at issue. "Lis pendens" means "suit pending." The lis pendens notice of pending action is usually filed in the county where the real estate is located, so that the property owner and potential buyers are put on notice of a potential claim on the property. A person who files a false lis pendens notice may have to pay attorney fees.

The complaint asks for judgment that the contract be rescinded and declared null and void, and defendant be ordered to return the down payment of $225,000, and that a lien be impressed on the property for the sum of $124,317.62.

. . . .

. . . . [D]efendant sought to amend the pleadings to conform with the proof to the extent that plaintiff, after recovery from his alleged psychotic condition, proceeded to perform acts in reliance upon and in furtherance of the September 26, 1968 contract, and thereby ratified the contract and waived any right he might have had to rescind. While not originally pleaded, defendant urges that it was impossible to plead ratification in advance of trial, since sufficient facts relating to the proposed ratification were not uncovered or divulged until the trial developed. Decision thereon was reserved.

didn't rescind right away

The motion is granted in the exercise of discretion, and ratification will be considered.

It was stipulated that the defendant and its attorneys, during the crucial period involved herein, were unaware of the mental condition of the plaintiff; nor did they have any reason to believe that such condition existed; plaintiff's attorneys were also unaware of such condition, and similarly had no reason to believe such condition existed. Further, it is uncontradicted that the purchase price was fair and reasonable and there was no overreaching.

Think About It!

Why should it matter whether Kralyn Enterprises knew or had reason to know of Fingerhut's mental condition? Recall that, in the discussion of the defense of infancy, it did not matter whether the contracting party knew or had reason to know the other party was a minor. Why might the defenses differ in this respect?

no one knew he wasn't in right mind

The contract of a mental incompetent is voidable at the election of the incompetent (*Blinn v. Schwarz*, 177 N.Y. 252, 69 N.E. 542), and the burden of proving incompetence is upon the party alleging it.

This case, with its interesting facets, should be particularly examined in light of two recent cases: *Ortelere v. Teachers' Retirement Bd. of City of N. Y.*, 25 N.Y.2d 196, 303 N.Y.S.2d 362, 250 N.E.2d 460 (1969) and *Faber v. Sweet Style Mfg. Corp.*, 40 Misc. 2d 212, 242 N.Y.S.2d 763 (1963).

Before the advent of these cases, contractual mental capacity was measured by the so-called cognitive test (see *Aldrich v. Bailey*, 132 N.Y. 85, 30 N.E.2d 264). Similarly, in *Paine v. Aldrich*, 133 N.Y. 544, 546, 30 N.E. 725, 726, it was held that if rational judgment could be based on "[a] mental capacity at the time of the execution . . . that he could collect in his mind without prompting, all the elements of the transaction and retain them for a sufficient length of time to perceive their obvious relations to each other", such judgment would be enough to prevent avoidance of the transaction on the claim of mental incompetency.

The *Faber* case, followed by the *Ortelere* case, became landmark authorities, which legally recognized the ailment manic-depressive psychosis where the afflicted one is aware of what he is doing but cannot help himself against the compulsion which controls his actions and impairs rational judgment.

Judge Breitel, writing for the majority in *Ortelere, supra*, 25 N.Y.2d at 202, 303 N.Y.S.2d at 367, 250 N.E.2d at 464, said: "The well-established rule is that contracts of a mentally incompetent person who has not been adjudicated insane are voidable. . . . Traditionally, in this State and elsewhere, contractual mental capacity has been measured by what is largely a cognitive test [citing authorities]". In further discussion of the evolution of the law from the cognitive test based on traditional standards to a more enlightened psychiatric acceptance of the mental illness manic-depressive psychosis, Judge Breitel alluded to the standards of the past governing competency to contract which were formulated "when psychiatric knowledge was quite primitive . . . [and which] fail to account for one who by reason of mental illness is unable to control his conduct even though his cognitive ability seems unimpaired" ([25 N.Y.] at 203, 303 N.Y.S. at 368, 250 N.E.2d at 464). Thus, a motivational standard has found its place in the law by dint and force of what persuasive psychiatrists expounded.

With such progress and understanding, we have gone beyond the days when psychiatric knowledge was finding itself. And these cases, *Faber* and *Ortelere* (*supra*), representative of the problem at hand, plainly say that incompetency to contract may exist, despite the presence of cognition, when a contract is made under the compulsion of manic depressive psychosis.

In *Faber*, 40 Misc. 2d at 216, 242 N.Y.S.2d at 768, guidelines are given: "Whether under the latter test a manic will be held incompetent to enter into a particular contract will depend upon an evaluation of (1) testimony of the claimed incompetent, (2) testimony of psychiatrists, and (3) the behavior of the claimed incompetent as detailed in the testimony of others (Green, Judicial Tests of Mental Incompetency, 6 Mo. L. R. 141), including whether by usual business standards the transaction is normal or fair (Green, Proof of Mental Incompetency and the Unexpressed Major Premise, 53 Yale L.J. 271, 299–305)."

A caveat, however, in *Ortelere*, 25 N.Y.2d at 206, 303 N.Y.S.2d at 370, 250 N.E.2d at 466, is handed down by the Court of Appeals while placing its seal of approval on the motivational standard. "Of course, nothing less serious than medically classified psychosis should suffice or else few contracts would be invulnerable to some kind of psychological attack".

Make the Connection

Ortelere is a well known case that is more complex than this court's references to it. For additional background on *Ortelere*, see the "Food for Thought" box following this case, on page 593.

As this court views this problem, the evidence, for our purpose, must involve the personality of the plaintiff, the nature of the deal at stake, the circumstances and the manner in which the contract was entered into, the behavior of the plaintiff juxtaposed to the contract and in some aspects of his life going beyond the limited range of the making of the contract, the medical history and evaluations regarding plaintiff's alleged psychosis or lack thereof. Upon such considerations, the ultimate and salient determination will be made as to whether the plaintiff was a manic-depressive psychotic and, if so, was he in the manic phase of that illness when the binder and contract were executed.

Plaintiff's medical history dates back to October 14, 1964 when he was hospitalized at the Gracie Square Hospital for manic-depressive reaction, manic type. On October 21, 1964 he was transferred to Mt. Sinai Hospital, from which he was discharged on October 27, 1964. Mt. Sinai diagnosed his condition as "schizophrenic reaction with manic manifestation." On November 16, 1964 plaintiff was admitted for the second time to Gracie Square Hospital, diagnosed as "manic depressive reaction, manic," and discharged on December 2, 1964. There he received six electric shock treatments.

On September 5, 1965 plaintiff was again admitted to Gracie Square Hospital for "manic depressive reaction" and discharged on October 5, 1965.

During the period from November 14, 1964 to September 16, 1965 plaintiff was under the care of Dr. Leonard Cammer, a psychiatrist. Dr. Cammer diagnosed plaintiff's condition as manic-depressive psychosis, mixed type.

From March 31, 1966 until May, 1968 he was treated by Dr. Alexander Thomas, who made the following diagnosis: "(1) Manic depressive syndrome, (2) Psychoneurosis, character disorder. The symptoms were severe. Although he was at no time psychotic during my period of treatment of him."

. . . . In July Dr. [Richard S.] Dolins saw plaintiff 9 times; 11 times in August; 9 times in September; 3 times between October 1 and 15; 6 times in November; twice in December and, in 1969, on January 4, 7, 8 and on January 25, when he saw him for the last time. Dr. Dolins, plaintiff's witness, testified and diagnosed plaintiff's condition as manic-depressive psychosis, but qualified such finding in declaring that he did not find plaintiff psychotic until . . . about September 13, [lasting] until November 5, 1968 when he was no longer psychotic. . . .

Dr. Nathan Kline[, plaintiff's witness] . . . testified as one who has been and is still treating plaintiff from February 17, 1969. His evaluations were further based on previous reports of the doctors and the hospital records in evidence. He stated that the characteristic symptoms of manic-depressive psychosis are mood swings, which pass the bounds of normalcy, so that the individual, in one or more areas, is no longer responsible or capable of managing his life in a general fashion, particularly in areas in which he is not familiar. He further testified that the lay person might not recognize either the symptoms as being related to the illness, or that the individual was psychotic.

In his opinion, therefore, it is possible to be psychotic in certain areas and not psychotic at all in other areas, during the same time. When asked when plaintiff became psychotic, if at all in September, 1968, he responded, "I would, if you wanted to be strictly technical about it, if by psychosis you mean getting so far out of touch with reality that you are seriously injuring yourself, I would say that the time he gave a check for $25,000, which constituted this point of fact, direct evidence of his having passed over the border from normality to pathology." In answer to the question as to whether it was psychotic for this man to enter into this deal involving $3,075,000, the answer came: ". . . . For this particular man that act was psychotic. It may not have been for someone else and it may not have been for him under other circumstances."

Dr. Abrahamsen testified as defendant's expert psychiatrist. He examined plaintiff on April 6, 1971. He read plaintiff's medical history, was present in court when Dr. Dolins testified and read the stenographic record of the testimony of Dr. Kline. He states that plaintiff had some mood swings and many neurotic traits but found nothing psychotic about him. He found that plaintiff was not psychotic at all during the period from mid-September to November, 1968. He character- *[margin note: other doc says not psychotic]* ized plaintiff's personality makeup as a neurotic character disorder with reactive depression. He found it medically significant that plaintiff was not hospitalized in 1968, or given strong medication or shock treatment and that the frequency of treatment was not increased. He states that psychosis is a condition and that one cannot on the same day be psychotic as to some actions and not as to others. The lines are thusly drawn with respect to the crucial time involved. Plaintiff's experts *[margin note: conflict]* say plaintiff was psychotic. Defendant's expert says plaintiff was only neurotic. In *Faber* (40 Misc. 2d 212, 216–217, *supra*) the court uttered the following:

> Moreover, in the great majority of cases psychiatrists of equal qualification and experience will reach diametrically opposed conclusions on the same behavioral evidence. The courts have, therefore, tended to give less weight to expert testimony than to objective behavioral evidence (Halpern, Civil Insanity: The New York Treatment of the Issue of Mental Incapacity in Non-Criminal Cases, 44 Corn. L.Q. 76; Green, *op cit.*, 53 Yale L.J., p. 306).

In September, 1968 plaintiff sought to amend the agreement of limited partnership under which Mt. Vernon Associates had been established. He retained a prestigious law firm in this connection. On October 1, 1968 plaintiff sent a memorandum to his partners in Mr. Vernon Associates asking their consent to certain transactions including:

> 1. The purchase of Stanley Fingerhut of the Bel-Aire Country Club located in Westchester County. Mr. Fingerhut does not plan to be active in the day to day management of the club but will retain professional management to do so.

On October 7, 1968 plaintiff, with his attorney, and the Krassners and their attorney, met with one Bogert, an officer of the bank which held the first mortgage on Bel Aire. They discussed the refinancing of the club mortgage on behalf of the prospective purchaser. Plaintiff gave the bank his reference and authorized the bank to check it, and it received the following report:

> The subject [Stanley Fingerhut] is an ex-broker and partner in a major brokerage house. He is the founder and manager of Mt. Vernon Associates . . . . The fund has been very successful and is now worth over $3MM . . . . He is very well versed in the operation and is one of the most respected men in the hedge fund business. His personal net worth is in seven figures.

> The bank has extended loans to the fund to moderate 7 figures, secured by marketable securities. Mr. Roach and other members of Chemical's

management know Fingerhut personally and have a high opinion of him and of the company. Mr. Roach expressed the opinion that Fingerhut should have no trouble paying off an $864 M mortage over a number of years.

[handwritten: Bogert said he was normal]

Bogert testified that during his conference the words and actions of plaintiff impressed him as rational.

[handwritten: bizarre behavior]

Plaintiff sought to bolster the testimony of his medical experts by adducing bizarre conduct on his part. Within this province, Goldner, plaintiff's co-manager in Mt. Vernon Associates, testified that in about August, 1968, plaintiff began to act strangely with regard to security investments, that he gambled and lost large sums of money, contributed to the Black Panther movement, boasted about women, bought a large quantity of ducks for a party he was giving, and employed unqualified and unnecessary people for a period of a month to indulge a whim on his part. Mary Scully, plaintiff's secretary, testified about quarrels between Goldner and plaintiff concerning investment decisions and that plaintiff resorted to foul language, which had not been his custom. Other so-called "bizarre" conduct was alluded to and testified to.

Defendant, in contradiction, . . . presented witnesses to prove plaintiff's words and actions were rational. In this framework, Donald Klopfer, the Chairman of a large publishing house and a limited partner in Mt. Vernon Associates, having invested $200,000 after meeting the plaintiff in September, 1968, testified that plaintiff's words and actions impressed him as being rational.

[handwritten: but everyone thought he was fine]

Martin Mayer, an author, who in September, 1968, was writing a book to be called "New Breed on Wall Street," interviewed plaintiff in connection with that book on September 20, 1968 at the office of Mt. Vernon Associates. . . . Mr. Mayer concluded that plaintiff's words and actions impressed him as rational. . . .

In similar vein, Harry G. Herman, a former Surrogate of Westchester County who has known plaintiff and his parents for many years, testified. Both plaintiff and the witness were members of the same golf club and played golf together.

Robert L. Livingston, who became a limited partner in Mt. Vernon Associates on July 1, 1968 to the extent of investing $100,000, had spoken to plaintiff on the telephone several times and had met plaintiff for lunch in the latter part of October, 1968. He, too, stated that plaintiff's words and actions were rational.

Morris Thau, an old friend of plaintiff's and his father, on the basis of that friendship and business dealings since 1964, characterized plaintiff's conduct as rational. Thau had become a limited partner in Mt. Vernon Associates when it was organized and had invested $200,000.

The situation before us here is unlike that in the *Faber case, supra*. Plaintiff did not go on a buying spree. He invested in a $3 million hedge fund he had started in 1967 which, in a short period of time, grew to over $5 million. Plaintiff was known as a super-salesman. Dr. Dolins agreed that he was. Plaintiff had a penchant and ability for raising money. Differently, the frenetic conduct of the incompetent, in *Faber*, as affecting that transaction, was characterized by the court as being irrational and abnormal, highlighted by "The rapidity by which the incompetent moved" in the performance of those questionable acts. Without detailing such acts, it suffices to say that the incompetent's conduct, done without the benefit of legal representation, as is found here, was so greatly abnormal that the court was convinced, with the aid of medical testimony, that he had acted under the compulsion of a psychosis. In our circumstances, the plaintiff accepted, in major and important part, the advice of his lawyers. In *Faber*, the incompetent acted against the advice given by his lawyer, and the contract was signed in the absence of any lawyer. It should be further noted, that about two weeks following the signing of the contract, the incompetent, Faber, was sent to a mental institution. There is no parallelism in the essential aspects. On the contrary, the evidence at hand moves across a wider period of time with a more calculated and studied purpose, reflected from the concerned comparison of country and golf clubs, extending to November 19, 1968, when the plaintiff elected to rescind the contract he had made with the expert advice and collaboration of his lawyers, precautionary and deliberate acts intervening.

Plaintiff, unlike the *Ortelere case*, was able and did care for himself, attended to his business, had a substantial income and net worth of about $350,000. Also, *Ortelere* deals with a sick woman who was so completely unable to manage her affairs that her husband gave up his job and devoted himself to taking care of her. Moreover, the court there observed that the defendant was, or should have been, fully aware of her condition, which gave rise to the retirement option she selected. Here, the defendant and attorneys for both parties, were unaware of any alleged psychosis, and knowledge of a condition could not be imputed to any of them.

On the whole, whatever behavior has been ascribed to the plaintiff as being irrational or bizarre does not reach sufficient level to overcome the strength and character of plaintiff's conduct, which was testified to as rational. The net result of the credible evidence in this area, conjoining with the medical evaluation of the experts and other medical evidence, convinces the court that the plaintiff was not in the manic phase of the ailment, manic-depressive psychosis, during the period the binder and the agreement were entered into. Asked by the court for a definition of "psychotic", Dr. Kline replied: "Psychotic means there is a defect in thinking, in feeling, in behaving and memory in relationship to reality in general to such a degree that the individual is incapacitated or is incapable of adequately managing his affairs".

The credible evidence does not put the plaintiff within that definition. With cognition, and without stress of psychosis, his rational judgment was not impaired during the period the binder and agreement were made. And while there were some neurotic manifestations, the condition responsible for this behavior was insufficient to render him legally incompetent to make a contract.

It follows that plaintiff has failed to sustain his burden of proving that when he executed the binder and contract he "did so solely as a result of serious mental illness, namely, psychosis". (*Ortelere, supra,* 25 N.Y.2d at 206, 303 N.Y.S.2d at 370, 250 N.E.2d at 466.)

. . . .

Therefore, plaintiff in a competent mental state, had no valid excuse in refusing to perform an enforceable contract . . . .

. . . .

Moreover, the contract may be validated on the basis that even had the binder and agreement been tainted with psychosis, the contract was later ratified by the "conscious action" of the plaintiff after November 5, 1968, when Dr. Dolins says he was free of psychosis. Dr. Dolins, plaintiff's treating and testifying doctor, declared that on November 5, 1968, plaintiff was no longer psychotic. With such a concession, the letter dated November 8, 1968, from plaintiff's lawyers to defendant's lawyer, Seymour Rabinowitz, takes on cogent and significant evidentiary meaning. Therein it was stated that "the purchaser has elected to adjourn closing of title until December 15, 1968." The letter was more than a mere request for adjournment purpose. Other matters, in recognition of the contract, were taken up. A dispute over a billing for labor was made the subject of discussion and was resolved, by authorization, to remit to Rabinowitz's client, the seller, the amount of $1,422.89, constituting "payment for material and labor as per said correspondence". Acknowledgment of that remittance was requested by letter. The letter continues:

> Your[s] of October 29 is in error concerning the furnishing of material for membership application. Mr. Fingerhut presented to seller in writing his proposed rate schedule which was unacceptable to sellers. There were several conferences between the parties concerning this schedule, the last of which was attended not only by the parties but by their respective counsel. No agreement [or] solution was arrived at and it was decided that further negotiations would continue. We will not accept any expenses incurred in the solicitation by your clients of renewal applications and preparation of any material for same . . . . You have also failed to mention whether or not your clients are notifying

prospective members and existing members that a minimum food and beverage charge of $600 will be levied on the 1969 members. In light of our notice herein adjourning the closing, no comment need be made on the Thanksgiving Dinner reservations. Please be advised that we are continuing to interview prospective managers and have not as yet found someone whom we deem suitable for this position of great consequence.

The communication was written after November 5, 1968, when Dr. Dolins testified he saw plaintiff following the doctor's return from a vacation. Dr. Dolins was then satisfied that plaintiff was no longer psychotic. It was on that visit that plaintiff told the doctor he "could not raise the money" and he "was considering the adjournment of that closing from November 15 to December 15, so that he could raise the money". . . .

. . . .

On November 19, 1968, when they met again, Dr. Dolins testified, plaintiff told him he "wished he could get out of it".

The November 8 letter when read represents confirmation and indicates a purpose, on plaintiff's part, to proceed with the contract and effect the closing. For that important reason, the letter has been, in part, quoted. It bears heavily on defendant's defense that plaintiff, by acts of recognition and reliance, ratified the contract at a time he was competent to do so, if, indeed, he had not been at the time of its making.

He did not testify or raise his voice in any manner to protest that such a letter was sent without his permission or knowledge. At this point, comment on his refusal to take the stand is appropriate, since that question affects the matter being instantly considered, as well as other matters developed at the trial, which could have been the subject, or object, of his supporting or countervailing testimony. The plaintiff was in the courtroom for at least part of the trial, which extended beyond three weeks. He elected not to take the stand. He could have contradicted, corroborated or explained, if he chose, the evidence bearing upon his conduct and the motivation which prompted the making of the binder and contract. He could have even lent support to any phase which was favorable to his cause, but which had come under attack requiring bolstering.

He never reappeared at the trial. He was and is not a judicially declared incompetent. Dr. Kline testified that plaintiff is not presently psychotic and continues under his care and treatment. Yet, no opinion was sought for or advanced that because of illness, or for any cause, he was not available or unable to testify. Interestingly, at some juncture during the trial, while plaintiff was seated in the spectator part of the courtroom, the question of his age arose during the examination of a witness. Voluntarily, Mr. Fingerhut arose in and in open court, responded: "I will be 36 June 5th." That was the fullest extent of his "testimony," albeit unsworn.

Under these circumstances, the court will invoke the adverse inference rule applicable to one who is able to testify with knowledge upon certain matters in the record, but does not. Specifically, plaintiff has failed to testify concerning his participation in the making of the November 8, 1968 letter; whether he had any knowledge of it, or its purpose. In face of the evidence, it becomes an accepted fact that he did have knowledge of the letter and approved its purpose. Certainly, the testimony of Dr. Dolins, as to plaintiff's knowledge of the letter, recounted above, would in itself be corroboration of that finding.

Plaintiff cannot palliate this failure on the ground that the defendant expressed an interest to call the plaintiff on its side of the case, and did not. Firstly, plaintiff had the roles of party and witness, and the party who is naturally expected to call a witness should not be relieved of the possible unfavorable consequence of his own failure to do so[, p]articularly where the witness, such as the plaintiff, could be a hostile witness. (*Reehil v. Fraas*, 129 App. Div. 563, 566, *revd. on other grounds*, 197 N.Y. 64.) There is warrant, therefore, to apply the stamp of weakness with respect to much of the evidence that pervades the record in this particular vein (see *Perlman v. Shanck*, 192 App. Div. 179; *Milio v. Railway Motor Trucking Co.*, 257 App. Div. 640). As aptly stated in *Dowling v. Hastings* (211 N.Y. 199, 202) "where one party to an action knowing the truth of a matter in controversy and having the evidence in his possession, omits to speak, every inference warranted by the evidence will be indulged in against him."

The defendant has sustained the burden of proving ratification of the contract. The evidence clearly indicates that plaintiff, without mental disability, ratified the contract. Borrowing from *Faber*, 40 Misc. 2d at 217, 242 N.Y.S.2d at 768, there was "conscious action" on plaintiff's part which recognized the contract at a time when he was not psychotic. In adjourning the closing of title and conduct pertaining thereto, he demonstrated knowledge of the existence of the contract, with confirmation of it as a contractual obligation; and though he regretted its making, he, nevertheless, acted in furtherance of the contract.

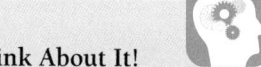

Think About It!

Sometimes the tests for mental competency seem arcane and even antiquated, because the law lags behind medicine's understanding of defective mental processing. Other tests may seem harsh or insensitive, mirroring society's reactions to mental illness.

What challenges do these tests and attitudes pose for attorneys who are seeking to be professional and compassionate about mental health issues?

While it may be unfortunate that the plaintiff "bit off more than he could chew", the relief he seeks must be denied.

The motion to dismiss the complaint is granted.

Think About It: *Ortelere* and the Challenges of Finding Mental Incapacity

The *Fingerhut* opinion relies on *Ortelere v. Teachers' Retirement Board of City of New York* (1969) as establishing legal recognition of manic-depressive psychosis (now more commonly called bipolar disorder). Although *Ortelere* did recognize that mental incapacity might arise in circumstances that do not satisfy the older "cognitive" standard, the facts of the case are more challenging than acknowledged in *Fingerhut*. *Ortelere* involved "the evidently unwise and fool-hardy selection of [retirement] benefits" by a 60-year-old upon her retirement after 40 years as a public school teacher. She had suffered a "nervous breakdown," took a leave of absence, and was diagnosed as having "involutional psychosis, melancholia type." Her husband left his job to care for his wife full-time. She died a little less than two months after making her election to have maximum benefits paid during her lifetime, leaving no survivor benefits for her husband of 38 years and their two grown children. Her husband was left with meager savings and no income; as her executor, he brought suit to set aside his wife's last-minute choice to take larger benefits during the short remainder of her life with no payments to her family after her death. *Ortelere*, 303 N.Y.S.2d at 364, 250 N.E.2d at 198.

Although the *Ortelere* court set aside her contractual choice based on some evidence of mental illness in her history, it is far from clear that Mrs. Ortelere was under a compulsion that was comparable to that experienced by those with bipolar disorders. The alternate view is that she was unwilling to acknowledge her physical ailments and preferred to ignore her likely impending death by choosing the benefit package she did. She might also have rationally opted to receive the larger immediate payout for the indeterminate duration of her life to help the family cash-flow when her husband quit work to take care of her.* One can sympathize with the court's desire to undo Mrs. Ortelere's contractual choice, even if one questions the correctness of the court's application of the legal doctrine.

The facts of *Ortelere* and *Fingerhut* illustrate the difficulty of determining when an individual crosses the line from bad decision-making and lack of will power** to compulsion based on mental illness. That is why the *Ortelere* court required "nothing less serious than medically classified psychosis" as grounds for challenging capacity, as noted by the *Fingerhut* court (page 585). But given ongoing developments in neuroscience and the changes over time in medical definitions of incompetency, relying on medical definitions does not answer all the difficult questions raised by claims of mental incompetency.

 Reading the Law Critically: Restatement (Second) § 15

The following Restatement (Second) section drew its "cognitive" test from criminal law standards.

1. What are the key differences between the alternative tests in (1)(a) (known as the "cognitive" test and drawn from criminal standards) and (1)(b) (known as the "motivational" or "affective" approach)? Why do the differences make sense (if they do)?

2. Does the rule in (2) apply to both (1)(a) and (b)?

3. How does the "cognitive" test in (1)(a) compare to the test applied in *G.A.S.* (page 505)?

4. How does the "motivational" test in (1)(b) compare to the test applied in *Fingerhut*?

---

* For the trial court opinion and transcript (including testimony of Mrs. Ortelere's husband, daughter, and psychiatrist) and additional background information on the case, see Richard Danzig & Geoffrey R. Watson, *The Capability Problem in Contract Law* 242-306 (2d ed. 2004).

** For humorous versions of the dilemma, see YouTube videos of Flip Wilson's routine "The Devil Made Me Do It" or recent ads showing a devil and angel perched on a buyer's shoulder urging him for or against the purchase.

Restatement (Second) § 15. **Mental Illness or Defect**

(1) A person incurs only voidable contractual duties by entering into a transaction if by reason of mental illness or defect
   (a) he is unable to understand in a reasonable manner the nature and consequences of the transaction, or
   (b) he is unable to act in a reasonable manner in relation to the transaction and the other party has reason to know of his condition.
(2) Where the contract is made on fair terms and the other party is without knowledge of the mental illness or defect, the power of avoidance under Subsection (1) terminates to the extent that the contract has been so performed in whole or in part or the circumstances have so changed that avoidance would be unjust. In such a case a court may grant relief as justice requires.

Comment b. The standard of competency. It is now recognized that there is a wide variety of types and degrees of mental incompetency. Among them are congenital deficiencies in intelligence, the mental deterioration of old age, the effects of brain damage caused by accident or organic disease, and mental illnesses evidenced by such symptoms as delusions, hallucinations, delirium, confusion and depression. Where no guardian has been appointed, there is full contractual capacity in any case unless the mental illness or defect has affected the particular transaction: a person may be able to understand almost nothing, or only simple or routine transactions, or he may be incompetent only with respect to a particular type of transaction. Even though understanding is complete, he may lack the ability to control his acts in the way that the normal individual can and does control them; in such cases the inability makes the contract voidable only if the other party has reason to know of his condition. Where a person has some understanding of a particular transaction which is affected by mental illness or defect, the controlling consideration is whether the transaction in its result is one which a reasonably competent person might have made.

§ 3.3. Intoxication

The defense of intoxication raises issues of capacity similar in some respects to those raised by the defense of mental illness (inability to understand the transaction or control one's actions) but the cause of the incapacity is different, resulting from voluntary behavior (drinking) or behavior caused by a condition akin to mental illness (alcoholism).

Reading the Law Critically: Restatement (Second) § 16

1. Compare Restatement (Second) § 16 (on the defense of intoxication) with § 15 (on the defense of mental illness or defect; see previous section). What similarities exist between these two defenses? How do they differ? What rationale would you offer for the differences?

2. Recall that the intoxication defense was discussed briefly in *Lucy v. Zehmer,* Chapter 4 (page 237). What would the result have been if § 16 had been applied to the facts of that case?

Restatement (Second) § 16. **Intoxicated Persons**

A person incurs only voidable contractual duties by entering into a transaction if the other party has reason to know that by reason of intoxication
(a) he is unable to understand in a reasonable manner the nature and consequences of the transaction, or
(b) he is unable to act in a reasonable manner in relation to the transaction.

§ 4. Violation of Public Policy

Many of the defenses discussed in this chapter could be characterized as based on public policy to protect party autonomy and prevent oppression. When a court refuses to enforce part or all of a contract expressly on the grounds of public policy, however, it is focused not on protecting the promisor, as is true in those other defenses, but on avoiding enforcement of contracts seen as being against the public interest.

It is easy to determine that a contract violates public policy if the legislature has enacted a statute saying so explicitly. In most states, statutes invalidate contracts involving the following activities, based on underlying public policy:

• Buying an individual's vote
• Engaging in certain kinds of restraint of trade
• Obstructing justice
• Lending at usurious interest rates
• Buying favorable treatment from a government worker or elected representative

In these situations, the defense of violation of public policy is not necessary.

In a second set of cases, no statute invalidates a contract, but a statute forbids or criminalizes the activity promised or engaged in by a party to the contract, such as

- Committing murder
- Selling alcohol to a minor
- Extorting money

In these situations, a court will look to the purpose of the statute and the legislative history for indications of the legislature's intentions regarding the validity of the underlying contract.

For instance, a statute may bar an individual from performing a particular job without a license but not declare the contract itself to be illegal or unenforceable. If the licensing statute was meant to certify critical skills or ensure moral fitness of the contracting party, there is more reason to deny enforcement than if the statute was meant as a measure to obtain revenue from the sale of licenses.* The more attenuated the connection between the agreement and the public policy, the more likely the contract will be enforceable.**

In yet a third set of cases, the legislature is silent about the legality of and public interests surrounding a particular activity, such as

- Wagering or gambling (in jurisdictions where this activity is not illegal)
- Committing a non-criminalized tort
- Breaching a fiduciary duty or breaching a contract
- Restricting a person from the right to marry (depending on the facts)

In these situations, the court must discern whether the contract involving that activity should be upheld or struck down, based on the court's assessment of public policy. The court derives public policy from "community common sense and common conscience . . . applied . . . to matters of public morals, public health, public safety, public welfare, and the like."*** These determinations are made by the judge, not the jury. Given the breadth of concerns that may be involved and the difficulty of obtaining clear guidance on public policy from sources other than legislation directly addressing the contractual concern, it is hardly surprising that courts are hesitant to establish new bases for denying enforcement. This final section of Chapter 5 focuses on this third set of cases—how a court decides whether public policy warrants refusing to enforce a contract, in the absence of legislative mandate or clear guidance.

If an illegal contract is unenforceable or void, a court most often leaves the parties as they are, refusing to order restitution or other compensation. This deters parties from engaging in similar contracts in the future, and it avoids having the

---

* *See* Joseph M. Perillo, *Calamari and Perillo on Contracts* § 22.3, at 737 (6th ed. 2009).

** *See* E. Allan Farnsworth, *Contracts* § 5.1 (4th ed. 2004).

*** *Naylor, Benzon & Co. v. Krainische Industrie Gesellschaft*, 1 K.B. 331 (1881) (McCardie, J.).

court be involved in the sometimes sordid details of the parties' transaction. As one court said, "The law will not aid a man who founds his cause of action upon his own illegal acts. The courts should leave such parties where they found them. . . . Straight shooters should always win, but when there are none, bad guys need not look to us for help."* Exceptions exist, however. A court may order restitution in favor of a party who would otherwise suffer a forfeiture disproportionate to the magnitude and significance of the public policy violation, for a party who was excusably ignorant of the facts or law related to a minor public policy matter, or for a party who is not equally in the wrong as the other party or who withdrew from the transaction before the improper purpose was achieved.**

The Restatement (Second) provision describing the public policy defense articulates many of the factors that courts consider when ruling on this defense:

Restatement (Second) § 178. **When a Term Is Unenforceable on Grounds of Public Policy**

(1) A promise or other term of an agreement is unenforceable on grounds of public policy if legislation provides that it is unenforceable or the interest in its enforcement is clearly outweighed in the circumstances by a public policy against the enforcement of such terms.

(2) In weighing the interest in the enforcement of a term, account is taken of
   (a) the parties' justified expectations,
   (b) any forfeiture that would result if enforcement were denied, and
   (c) any special public interest in the enforcement of a particular term.

(3) In weighing a public policy against enforcement of a term, account is taken of
   (a) the strength of that policy as manifested by legislation or judicial decisions,
   (b) the likelihood that a refusal to enforce the term will further that policy,
   (c) the seriousness of any misconduct involved and the extent to which it was deliberate, and
   (d) the directness of a connection between that misconduct and the term.

Reading the Law Critically: *Tunkl* and *Johnson*

1. In the two cases that follow, what concerns do the courts take into account in determining whether the contract violates the public interest? How do the courts balance the wide range of considerations?

---

* *Certa v. Wittman*, 370 A.2d 573, 577 (Md. 1977).
** *See* Restatement (Second) §§ 198, 199.

2. If you were the judge, how would you resolve each case? Should the contract be enforceable? Why or why not?

3. Is the court or the legislature the more appropriate body to make a decision about unenforceability based on public policy concerns? What effect should the answer to that question have on the court's decision?

Tunkl v. Regents of the University of California

OLGA TUNKL, as Executrix of the Estate of Hugo Tunkl, Deceased, Plaintiff-Appellant

v.

THE REGENTS OF THE UNIVERSITY OF CALIFORNIA, Defendant-Respondent

Supreme Court of California, In Bank
383 P.2d 441 (Cal. 1963)

TOBRINER, Justice.

This case concerns the validity of a release from liability for future negligence imposed as a condition for admission to a charitable research hospital. For the reasons we hereinafter specify, we have concluded that an agreement between a hospital and an entering patient affects the public interest and that, in consequence, the exculpatory provision included within it must be invalid under Civil Code section 1668.

Hugo Tunkl brought this action to recover damages for personal injuries alleged to have resulted from the negligence of two physicians in the employ of the University of California Los Angeles Medical Center, a hospital operated and maintained by the Regents of the University of California as a nonprofit charitable institution. Mr. Tunkl died after suit was brought, and his surviving wife, as executrix, was substituted as plaintiff.

> ### What's That?
>
> This case was decided "in bank" (often spelled "en banc"), meaning that all the active justices on the court participated, the usual practice in most state supreme courts as well as at the United States Supreme Court. Until adoption of a constitutional amendment in 1966, the California Supreme Court heard many cases in smaller panels and only some cases were designated to be heard in bank. As noted in Chapter 3 (page 155), courts sit "in bank" for only a limited set of cases.

The University of California at Los Angeles Medical Center admitted Tunkl as a patient on June 11, 1956. The Regents maintain the hospital for the primary purpose of aiding and developing a program of research and education in the field of medicine; patients are selected and admitted if the study and treatment of their condition would tend to achieve these purposes. Upon his entry to the hospital, Tunkl signed a document setting forth certain "Conditions of Admission." The crucial condition number six reads as follows: "RELEASE: The hospital is a non-profit, charitable institution. In consideration of the hospital and allied services to be rendered and the rates charged therefor, the patient or his legal representative agrees to and hereby releases The Regents of the University of California, and the hospital from any and all liability for the negligent or wrongful acts or omissions of its employees, if the hospital has used due care in selecting its employees."

Plaintiff stipulated that the hospital had selected its employees with due care. The trial court ordered that the issue of the validity of the exculpatory clause be first submitted to the jury and that, if the jury found that the provision did not bind plaintiff, a second jury try the issue of alleged malpractice. When, on the preliminary issue, the jury returned a verdict sustaining the validity of the executed release, the court entered judgment in favor of the Regents.[1] Plaintiff appeals from the judgment.

We shall first set out the basis for our prime ruling that the exculpatory provision of the hospital's contract fell under the proscription of Civil Code section 1668; we then dispose of two answering arguments of defendant.

We begin with the dictate of the relevant Civil Code section 1668. The section states: "All contracts which have for their object, directly or indirectly, to exempt anyone from responsibility for his own fraud, or willful injury to the person or property of another, or violation of law, whether willful or negligent, are against the policy of the law."

The course of section 1668, however, has been a troubled one. Although, as we shall explain, the decisions uniformly uphold its prohibitory impact in one circumstance, the courts' interpretations of it have been diverse. Some of the cases have applied the statute strictly, invalidating any contract for exemption from liability for negligence. The court in England v. Lyon Fireproof Storage Co. (1928) 94 Cal.App.562, 271 P. 532, categorically states, "The court correctly instructed the jury that 'The defendant cannot limit its liability against its own negligence

---

[1] Plaintiff at the time of signing the release was in great pain, under sedation, and probably unable to read. At trial plaintiff contended that the release was invalid, asserting that a release does not bind the releasor if at the time of its execution he suffered from so weak a mental condition that he was unable to comprehend the effect of his act . . . . The jury, however, found against plaintiff on this issue. Since the verdict of the jury established that plaintiff either knew or should have known the significance of the release, this appeal raises the sole question of whether the release can stand as a matter of law.

by contract, and any contract to that effect would be void.'"... The recent case of Mills v. Ruppert (1959) 167 Cal.App.2d 58, 62-63, 333 P.2d 818; however, apparently limits "[N]egligent . . . violation of law" exclusively to statutory law.[3] Other cases hold that the statute prohibits the exculpation of gross negligence only;[4] still another case states that the section forbids exemption from active as contrasted with passive negligence.[5]

In one respect, as we have said, the decisions are uniform. The cases have consistently held that the exculpatory provision may stand only if it does not involve "the public interest."[6] Interestingly enough, this theory found its first expression in a decision which did not expressly refer to section 1668. In Stephens v. Southern Pacific Co. (1895) 109 Cal. 86, 41 P. 783, 29 L.R.A. 751, a railroad company had leased land, which adjoined its depot, to a lessee who had constructed a warehouse upon it. The lessee covenanted that the railroad company would not be responsible for damage from fire "caused by any . . . means." (109 Cal. p. 87, 41 P. p. 783.) This exemption, under the court ruling applied to the lessee's damage resulting from the railroad company's carelessly burning dry grass and rubbish. Declaring the contract not "violative of sound public policy" (109 Cal. p. 89, 41 P. p. 784), the court pointed out ". . . As far as this transaction was concerned, the parties, when contracting, stood upon common ground, and dealt with each other as A. and B. might deal with each other with reference to any private business undertaking. . . ." (109 Cal. p. 88, 41 P. p. 784.) The court concluded "that the interests of the public in the contract are more sentimental than real" (109 Cal. p. 95, 41 P. p. 786; emphasis added) and that the exculpatory provision was therefore enforceable.

In applying this approach and in manifesting their reaction as to the effect of the exemptive clause upon the public interest, some later courts enforced, and others invalidated such provisions under section 1668. Thus in Nichols v. Hitchcock Motor Co. (1937) 22 Cal.App.2d 151, 159, 70 P.2d 654, 658, the court enforced an exculpatory clause on the ground that "the public neither had nor could have any interest whatsoever in the subject-matter of the contract,

---

[3] To the same effect: Werner v. Knoll (1948) 89 Cal.App.2d 474, 201 P.2d 45; 15 Cal.L.Rev. 46 (1926). This interpretation was criticized in Barkett v. Brucato (1953) 122 Cal.App.2d 264, 277, 264 P.2d 978, and 1 Witkin, Summary of California Law 228 (7th ed. 1960). The latter states: "Apart from the debatable interpretation of 'violation of law' as limited strictly to violation of statutes, the explanation appears to make an unsatisfactory distinction between (1) valid exemptions from liability for injury or death resulting from types of ordinary or gross negligence not expressed in statutes, and (2) invalid exemptions where the negligence consists of violation of one of the many hundreds of statutory provisions setting forth standards of care."

[4] See Butt v. Bertola (1952) 110 Cal.App.2d 128, 242 P.2d 32; Ryan Mercantile Co. v. Great Northern Ry. Co. (D.Mont.1960) 186 F.Supp. 660, 667-668. . . .

[5] Barkett v. Brucato (1953) 122 Cal.App.2d 264, 277, 264 P.2d 978.

[6] The view that the exculpatory contract is valid only if the public interest is not involved represents the majority holding in the United States. Only New Hampshire, in definite opposition to "public interest" test, categorically refuses to enforce exculpatory provisions. The cases are collected in an extensive annotation in 175 A.L.R. 8 (1948). . . .

considered either as a whole or as to the incidental covenant in question. The agreement between the parties concerned "their private affairs" only."[7]

In Barkett v. Brucato (1953) 122 Cal.App.2d 264, 276, 264 P.2d 978, 987, which involved a waiver clause in a private lease, Justice Peters summarizes the previous decisions in this language: "These cases hold that the matter is simply one of interpreting a contract; that both parties are free to contract; that the relationship of landlord and tenant does not affect the public interest; that such a provision affects only the private affairs of the parties. . . ." (Emphasis added.)

On the other hand, courts struck down exculpatory clauses as contrary to public policy in the case of a contract to transmit a telegraph message (Union Constr. Co. v. Western Union Tel. Co. (1912) 163 Cal. 298, 125 P. 242) and in the instance of a contract of bailment (England v. Lyon Fireproof Storage Co. (1928) 94 Cal.App. 562, 271 P. 532). In Hiroshima v. Bank of Italy (1926) 78 Cal.App. 362, 248 P. 947, the court invalidated an exemption provision in the form used by a payee in directing a bank to stop payment on a check. The court relied in part upon the fact that "the banking public, as well as the particular individual who may be concerned in the giving of any stop notice, is interested in seeing that the bank is held accountable for the ordinary and regular performance of its duties, and also in seeing that directions in relation to the disposition of funds deposited in the bank are not heedlessly, negligently, and carelessly disobeyed, and money paid out contrary to directions given." . . .

If, then, the exculpatory clause which affects the public interest cannot stand, we must ascertain those factors or characteristics which constitute the public interest. The social forces that have led to such characterization are volatile and dynamic. No definition of the concept of public interest can be contained within the four corners of a formula. The concept, always the subject of great debate, has ranged over the whole course of the common law; rather than attempt to prescribe its nature, we can only designate the situations in which it has been applied. We can determine whether the instant contract does or does not manifest the characteristics which have been held to stamp a contract as one affected with a public interest.

In placing particular contracts within or without the category of those affected with a public interest, the courts have revealed a rough outline of that type of transaction in which exculpatory provisions will be held invalid. Thus the attempted but invalid exemption involves a transaction which exhibits some or all of the following characteristics. It concerns a business of a type generally thought

---

[7] See also Hischemoeller v. Nat. Ice etc. Storage Co. (1956) 46 Cal.2d 318, 328, 294 P.2d 433 (contract upheld as an "ordinary business transaction between businessmen"); Mills v. Ruppert (1959) 167 Cal.App.2d 58, 62, 333 P.2d 818 (lease held not a matter of public interest); Inglis v. Garland (1936) 19 Cal.App.2d Supp. 767, 773, 64 P.2d 501 (same); cf. Northwestern Mutual Fire Ass'n v. Pacific Co. (1921) 187 Cal. 38, 41, 200 P. 934 (exculpatory clause in bailment upheld because of special business situation).

suitable for public regulation.[9] The party seeking exculpation is engaged in performing a service of great importance to the public,[10] which is often a matter of practical necessity for some members of the public.[11] The party holds himself out as willing to perform this service for any member of the public who seeks it, or at least for any member coming within certain established standards.[12] As a result of the essential nature of the service, in the economic setting of the transac-

---

[9] "Though the standard followed does not always clearly appear, a distinction seems to be made between those contracts which modify the responsibilities normally attaching to a relationship which has been regarded in other connections as a fit subject for special regulatory treatment and those which affect a relationship not generally subjected to particularlized control." (11 So.Cal.L.Rev. 296, 297 (1938)); see also Note 175 A.L.R. 8, 38-41 (1948).

In *Munn v. Illinois* (1877) 94 U.S. 133, the Supreme Court appropriated the common law concept of a business affected with a public interest to serve as the test of the constitutionality of state price fixing laws, a role it retained until *Nebbia v. New York* (1934) 291 U.S. 502, and *Olsen v. Nebraska* (1941) 313, U.S. 236. For discussion of the constitutional use and application of the "public interest" concept, see generally Hall, Concept of Public Business (1940); Hamilton, *Affectation with a Public Interest 39 Yale L.J. 1089 (1930)*.

[10] See *New York Cent. Railroad Co. v. Lockwood* (1873) 84 U.S. 357, 378-382; *Millers Mut. Fire Ins. Assn. v. Parker* (1951) 234 N.C. 20, 65 S.E.2d 341; *Hiroshima v. Bank of Italy* (1926) 78 Cal.App. 362, 377 248 P. 947; cf. *Lombard v. Louisiana* (1963) 373 U.S. (Douglass J., concurring) (holding that restaurants cannot discriminate on racial grounds, and noting that "places of public accommodation such as retail stores, restaurants, and the like render a 'service which has become a public interest' . . . in the manner of the innkeepers and common carriers of old."); *Charles Wolff Packing Co. v. Court of Industrial Relations* (1923) 262 U.S. 522 ("public interest" as test of constitutionality of price fixing); *German Alliance Ins. Co. v. Lewis* (1914) 233 U.S. 389 (same); Hamilton, *Affectation with a Public Interest* (1930) 39 Yale L.J. 1089 (same); Arterburn, *The Origin and First Test of Public Callings*, 75 U.Pa.L.Rev. 411, 428 (1927) ("public interest" as one test of whether business has duty to serve all comers). But see *Simmons v. Columbus Venetian Stevens Buildings, Inc.* (1958) 20 Ill.App.2d 1, 25-32, 155 N.E.2d 372, 384-387 (apartment leases, in which exculpatory clauses are generally permitted, are in aggregate as important to society as contracts with common carriers).

[11] See *Bisso v. Inland Waterways Corp.* (1955) 349 U.S. 85, 91; *New York Cent. Railroad Co. v. Lockwood, supra; Fairfax Gas & Supply Co. v. Hadary* (4th Cir. 1945) 151 F.2d 939; *Millers Mut. Fire Ins. Assn. v. Parker* (1951) 234 N.C. 20, 65 S.E.2d 341; *Irish & Swartz Stores v. First Nat. Bank of Eugene* (1960) 220 Ore. 362, 375, 349 P.2d 814, 821; 15 U.Pitt.L.Rev. 493, 499-500 (1954); Note 175 A.L.R. 8, 16-17 (1948); cf. *Charles Wolff Packing Co. v. Court of Industrial Relations* (1923) 262 U.S. 522 (constitutional law); *Munn v. Illinois* (1877) 94 U.S. 133 (same); Hall, Concept of Public Business 94 (1940) (same).

[12] See Burdick, *The Origin of the Peculiar Duties of Public Service Companies* (1911), 11 Colum.L.Rev. 514, 616, 743; *Lombard v. Louisiana, supra,* n.10. There is a close historical relationship between the duty of common carriers, public warehousemen, innkeepers, etc. to give reasonable service to all persons who apply, and refusal of courts to permit such businesses to obtain exemption from liability for negligence. See generally Arterburn, *supra*. n.10. This relationship has led occasional courts and writers to assert that exculpatory contracts are invalid only if the seller has a duty of public service. 28 Brooklyn L.Rev. 357, 359 (1962); see *Ciofalo v. Vic Tanney Gyms, Inc.* (1961) 10 N.Y.2d 294, 220 N.Y.S.2d 962, 177 N.E.2d 925. A seller under a duty to serve is generally denied exemption from liability for negligence; (however, the converse is not necessarily true) 44 Cal.L.Rev. 120 (1956); cf. *Charles Wolff Packing Co. v. Court of Industrial Relations* (1923) 262 U.S. 522, 538 (absence of duty to serve public does not necessarily exclude business from class of those constitutionally subject to state price regulation under test of *Munn v. Illinois); German Alliance Ins. Co. v. Lewis* (1914) 233 U.S. 389, 407 (same). A number of cases have denied enforcement to exculpatory provisions although the seller had no duty to serve. See, e.g., *Bisso v. Inland Waterways Corp.* (1955) 349 U.S. 85; *Millers Mut. Fire Ins. Assn. v. Parker* (1951) 234 N.C. 20, 65 S.E.2d 341; cases on exculpatory provisions in employment contracts collected in 35 Am.Jur., Master & Servant, § 136.

tion, the party invoking exculpation possesses a decisive advantage of bargaining strength against any member of the public who seeks his services.[13] In exercising a superior bargaining power the party confronts the public with a standardized adhesion contract of exculpation,[14] and makes no provision whereby a purchaser may pay additional reasonable fees and obtain protection against negligence.[15] Finally, as a result of the transaction, the person or property of the purchaser is placed under the control of the seller,[16] subject to the risk of carelessness by the seller or his agents.

While obviously no public policy opposes private, voluntary transactions in which one party, for a consideration, agrees to shoulder a risk which the law would otherwise have placed upon the other party, the above circumstances pose a different situation. In this situation the releasing party does not really acquiesce voluntarily in the contractual shifting of the risk, nor can we be reasonably certain that he receives an adequate consideration for the transfer. Since the service is one which each member of the public, presently or potentially, may find essential to him, he faces, despite his economic inability to do so, the prospect of a compulsory assumption of the risk of another's negligence. The public policy of this state has been, in substance, to posit the risk of negligence upon the actor; in instances in which this policy has been abandoned, it has generally been to allow or require that the risk shift to another party better or equally able to bear it, not to shift the risk to the weak bargainer.

---

[13] Prosser, Torts (2d ed. 1955) p. 306: "The courts have refused to uphold such agreements . . . where one party is at such obvious disadvantage in bargaining power that the effect of the contract is to put him at the mercy of the other's negligence." Note 175 A.L.R. 8, 18 (1948): "Validity is almost universally denied to contracts exempting from liability for its negligence the party which occupies a superior bargaining position." Accord: *Bisso v. Inland Waterways Corp.* (1955) 349 U.S. 85, 91; *Hiroshima v. Bank of Italy* (1926) 78 Cal.App. 362, 377, 248 P. 947; *Ciofalo v. Vic Tanney Gyms, Inc.* (1961) 13 App.Div.2d 702, 214 N.Y.S.2d 99; (Kleinfeld, J. dissenting); 6 Williston, Contracts (Rev. ed. 1938) § 1751C; Note, *The Significance of Comparative Bargaining Power in the Law of Exculpation* (1937) 37 Colum.L.Rev. 248; 20 Corn. L.Q. 352 (1935); 8 U.Fla.L.Rev. 109, 120-121 (1955); 15 U.Pitt.L.Rev. 493 (1954); 19 So.Cal.L.Rev. 441 (1946); see *New York Cent. Railroad Co. v. Lockwood* (1873) 17 Wall. 357, 84 U.S. 357, 378-382, 21 L.Ed. 627; *Fairfax Gas & Supply Co. v. Hadary* (4th Cir. 1945) 151 F.2d 939; *Northwestern Mut. Fire Assn. v. Pacific Co.* (1921) 187 Cal. 38, 43-44, 200 P. 934; *Inglis v. Garland* (1936) 19 Cal. App. 2d Supp. 767, 773, 64 P.2d 501; *Jackson v. First Nat. Bank of Lake Forest* (1953) 415 Ill. 453, 462-463, 114 N.E.2d 721, 726; *Simmons v. Columbus Venetian Stevens Buildings, Inc.* (1958) 20 Ill.App.2d 1, 26-32, 155 N.E.2d 372, 384-387; *Hall v. Sinclair Refining Co.* (1955) 242 N.C. 707, 89 S.E.2d 396; *Millers Mut. Fire Ins. Assn. v. Parker* (1951) 234 N.C. 20, 65 S.E.2d 341; *Irish & Swartz Stores v. First Nat. Bank of Eugene* (1960) 220 Ore. 362, 375, 349 P.2d 814, 821; 44 Cal.L.Rev. 120 (1956); 4 Mo.L.Rev. 55 (1939).

[14] See *Simmons v. Columbus Venetian Stevens Buildings, Inc.* (1958) 20 Ill.App.2d 1, 30-33, 155 N.E.2d 372, 386-387; *Irish & Swartz Stores v. First Nat. Bank of Eugene* (1960) 220 Ore. 362, 376, 349 P.2d 814, 821; Note 175 A.L.R. 8, 15-16, 112 (1948).

[15] See 6A Corbin, Contracts (1962) § 1472 at p. 595; Note 175 A.L.R. 8, 17-18 (1948).

[16] See *Franklin v. Southern Pac. Co.* (1928) 203 Cal. 680, 689-690, 265 P. 936, 59 A.L.R. 118; *Stephens v. Southern Pac. Co.* (1895) 109 Cal. 86, 90-91, 41 P. 783, 29 L.R.A. 751; *Irish & Swartz Stores v. First Nat. Bank of Eugene* (1960) 220 Ore. 362, 377, 349 P.2d 814, 822; 44 Cal.L.Rev. 120, 128 (1956); 20 Corn.L.Q. 352, 358 (1935).

In the light of the decisions, we think that the hospital-patient contract clearly falls within the category of agreements affecting the public interest. To meet that test, the agreement need only fulfill some of the characteristics above outlined; here, the relationship fulfills all of them. Thus the contract of exculpation involves an institution suitable for, and a subject of, public regulation. That the services of the hospital to those members of the public who are in special need of the particular skill of its staff and facilities constitute a practical and crucial necessity is hardly open to question.

The hospital, likewise, holds itself out as willing to perform its services for those members of the public who qualify for its research and training facilities. While it is true that the hospital is selective as to the patients it will accept, such selectivity does not negate its public aspect or the public interest in it. The hospital is selective only in the sense that it accepts from the public at large certain types of cases which qualify for the research and training in which it specializes. But the hospital does hold itself out to the public as an institution which performs such services for those members of the public who can qualify for them.[18]

In insisting that the patient accept the provision of waiver in the contract, the hospital certainly exercises a decisive advantage in bargaining. The would-be patient is in no position to reject the proffered agreement, to bargain with the hospital, or in lieu of agreement to find another hospital. The admission room of a hospital contains no bargaining table where, as in a private business transaction, the parties can debate the terms of their contract. As a result, we cannot but conclude that the instant agreement manifested the characteristics of the so-called adhesion contract. Finally, when the patient signed the contract, he completely placed himself in the control of the hospital; he subjected himself to the risk of its carelessness.

In brief, the patient here sought the services which the hospital offered to a selective portion of the public; the patient, as the price of admission and as a result of his inferior bargaining position, accepted a clause in a contract of adhesion waiving the hospital's negligence; the patient thereby subjected himself to control of the hospital and the possible infliction of the negligence which he had thus been compelled to waive. The hospital, under such circumstances, occupied a status different than a mere private party; its contract

Think About It!

Could the plaintiffs also have raised unconscionability as a defense? Would it have been an easier or more difficult defense to establish?

---

[18] See Wilmington General Hospital v. Manlove (Del.1961) 174 A.2d 135, holding that a private hospital which holds itself out as rendering emergency service cannot refuse to admit a patient in an emergency[,] and comment on the above case in 14 Stan.L.Rev. 910 (1962).

with the patient affected the public interest. We see no cogent current reason for according to the patron of the inn a greater protection than the patient of the hospital; we cannot hold the innkeeper's performance affords a greater public service than that of the hospital.

We turn to a consideration of the two arguments urged by defendant to save the exemptive clause. Defendant first contends that while the public interest may possibly invalidate the exculpatory provision as to the paying patient, it certainly cannot do so as to the charitable one. Defendant secondly argues that even if the hospital cannot obtain exemption as to its 'own' negligence it should be in a position to do so as to that of its employees. We have found neither proposition persuasive.

As to the first, we see no distinction in the hospital's duty of due care between the paying and nonpaying patient. (But see Rest., Contracts, § 575(1) (b).) The duty, emanating not merely from contract but also tort, imports no discrimination based upon economic status. (See Malloy v. Fong (1951) 37 Cal.2d 356, 366, 232 P.2d 241; Rest., Torts, §§ 323-324.) Rejecting a proposed differentiation between paying and nonpaying patients, we refused in Malloy to retain charitable immunity for charitable patients. Quoting Rutledge, J. in President & Directors of Georgetown College v. Hughes (1942) 76 U.S.App.D.C. 123, 130 F.2d 810, 827, we said: "Retention (of charitable immunity) for the nonpaying patient is the least defensible and most unfortunate of the distinction's refinements. He, least of all, is able to bear the burden. More than all others, he has no choice. * * * He should be the first to have reparation, not last and least among those who receive it." (37 Cal.2d p. 365, 232 P.2d p. 246.) To immunize the hospital from negligence as to the charitable patient because he does not pay would be as abhorrent to medical ethics as it is to legal principle.

Defendant's second attempted distinction, the differentiation between its own and vicarious liability, strikes a similar discordant note. In form defendant is a corporation. In everything it does, including the selection of its employees, it necessarily acts through agents. A legion of decisions involving contracts between common carriers and their customers, public utilities and their customers, bailees and bailors, and the like, have drawn no distinction between the corporation's 'own' liability and vicarious liability resulting from negligence of agents. We see no reason to initiate so far-reaching a distinction now. If, as defendant argues, a right of action against the negligent agent is in fact a sufficient remedy, then defendant by paying a judgment against it may be subrogated to the right of the patient against the negligent agent, and thus may exercise that remedy.

Think About It!

To what extent does tort law policy play a role in this decision?

In substance defendant here asks us to modify our decision in Malloy, which removed the charitable immunity; defendant urges that otherwise the funds of the research hospital may be deflected from the real objective of the extension of medical knowledge to the payment of claims for alleged negligence. Since a research hospital necessarily entails surgery and treatment in which fixed standards of care may not yet be evolved, defendant says the hospital should in this situation be excused from such care. But the answer lies in the fact that possible plaintiffs must prove negligence; the standards of care will themselves reflect the research nature of the treatment; the hospital will not become an insurer or guarantor of the patient's recovery. To exempt the hospital completely from any standard of due care is to grant it immunity by the side-door method of a contractual clause exacted of the patient. We cannot reconcile that technique with the teaching of Malloy.

We must note, finally, that the integrated and specialized society of today, structured upon mutual dependency, cannot rigidly narrow the concept of the public interest. From the observance of simple standards of due care in the driving of a car to the performance of the high standards of hospital practice, the individual citizen must be completely dependent upon the responsibility of others. The fabric of this pattern is so closely woven that the snarling of a single thread affects the whole. We cannot lightly accept a sought immunity from careless failure to provide the hospital service upon which many must depend. Even if the hospital's doors are open only to those in a specialized category, the hospital cannot claim isolated immunity in the interdependent community of our time. It, too, is part of the social fabric, and prearranged exculpation from its negligence must partly rend the pattern and necessarily affect the public interest.

The judgment is reversed.

Johnson v. Calvert

ANNA JOHNSON, Appellant

v.

MARK and CRISPINA CALVERT, Respondents

Supreme Court of California, In Bank
851 P.2d 776 (Cal. 1993)

PANELLI, Justice.

In this case we address several of the legal questions raised by recent advances in reproductive technology. When, pursuant to a surrogacy agreement, a zygote formed of the gametes of a husband and wife is implanted in the uterus of another woman, who carries the resulting fetus to term and gives birth to a child not genetically related to her, who is the child's "natural mother" under California law? Does a determination that the wife is the child's natural mother work a deprivation of the gestating woman's constitutional rights? And is such an agreement barred by any public policy of this state?

We conclude that the husband and wife are the child's natural parents, and that this result does not offend the state or federal Constitution or public policy.

FACTS

Mark and Crispina Calvert are a married couple who desired to have a child. Crispina was forced to undergo a hysterectomy in 1984. Her ovaries remained capable of producing eggs, however, and the couple eventually considered surrogacy. In 1989 Anna Johnson heard about Crispina's plight from a coworker and offered to serve as a surrogate for the Calverts.

On January 15, 1990, Mark, Crispina, and Anna signed a contract providing that an embryo created by the sperm of Mark and the egg of Crispina would be implanted in Anna and the child born would be taken into Mark and Crispina's home "as their child." Anna agreed she would relinquish "all parental rights" to the child in favor of Mark and Crispina. In return, Mark and Crispina would pay Anna $10,000 in a series of installments, the last to be paid six weeks after the child's birth. Mark and Crispina were also to pay for a $200,000 life insurance policy on Anna's life.[4]

The zygote was implanted on January 19, 1990. Less than a month later, an ultrasound test confirmed Anna was pregnant.

Unfortunately, relations deteriorated between the two sides. Mark learned that Anna had not disclosed she had suffered several stillbirths and miscarriages. Anna felt Mark and Crispina did not do enough to obtain the required insurance policy. She also felt abandoned during an onset of premature labor in June.

In July 1990, Anna sent Mark and Crispina a letter demanding the balance of the payments due her or else she would refuse to give up the child. The following month, Mark and Crispina responded with a lawsuit, seeking a declaration they were the legal parents of the unborn child. Anna filed her own action to be declared the mother of the child, and the two cases were eventually consolidated. The parties agreed to an independent guardian ad litem for the purposes of the suit.

---

[4] At the time of the agreement, Anna already had a daughter, Erica, born in 1987.

The child was born on September 19, 1990, and blood samples were obtained from both Anna and the child for analysis. The blood test results excluded Anna as the genetic mother. The parties agreed to a court order providing that the child would remain with Mark and Crispina on a temporary basis with visits by Anna.

At trial in October 1990, the parties stipulated that Mark and Crispina were the child's genetic parents. After hearing evidence and arguments, the trial court ruled that Mark and Crispina were the child's "genetic, biological and natural" father and mother, that Anna had no "parental" rights to the child, and that the surrogacy contract was legal and enforceable against Anna's claims. The court also terminated the order allowing visitation. Anna appealed from the trial court's judgment. The Court of Appeal for the Fourth District, Division Three, affirmed. We granted review.

DISCUSSION

Determining Maternity Under the Uniform Parentage Act

The Uniform Parentage Act (the Act) was part of a package of legislation introduced in 1975 . . . . The legislation's purpose was to eliminate the legal distinction between legitimate and illegitimate children. The Act followed in the wake of certain United States Supreme Court decisions mandating equal treatment of legitimate and illegitimate children. . . .

. . . .

[In the Act,] Civil Code sections 7001 and 7002 replace the distinction between legitimate and illegitimate children with the concept of the "parent and child relationship." The "parent and child relationship" means "the legal relationship existing between a child and his natural or adoptive parents incident to which the law confers or imposes rights, privileges, duties, and obligations. It includes the mother and child relationship and the father and child relationship." (Civ.Code, § 7001.) "The parent and child relationship extends equally to every child and to every parent, regardless of the marital status of the parents." (Civ. Code, § 7002.) The "parent and child relationship" is thus a legal relationship encompassing two kinds of parents, "natural" and "adoptive."

adopted as natural parent

Passage of the Act clearly was not motivated by the need to resolve surrogacy disputes, which were virtually unknown in 1975. Yet it facially applies to *any* parentage determination, including the rare case in which a child's maternity is in issue. We are invited to disregard the Act and decide this case according to other criteria, including constitutional precepts and our sense of the demands of public policy. We feel constrained, however, to decline the invitation. Not uncommonly, courts must construe statutes in factual settings not contemplated by the enacting

Act not for this situation

legislature. . . . [T]he Act offers a mechanism to resolve this dispute, albeit one not specifically tooled for it. We therefore proceed to analyze the parties' contentions within the Act's framework.

[The court concludes that Crispina and Anna can each offer evidence under the Act that she is the mother of the child, Anna by showing she gave birth and Crispina by showing the genetic relationship.]

Think About It!

Is the court correct in declining to disregard the Uniform Parentage Act in making its decision? Should new advances be regulated by legislation not drafted with those advances in mind, or should the court develop common law solutions until the legislature makes new law? How else could the court make this decision, if not on the basis of the Act?

. . . . Both women thus have adduced evidence of a mother and child relationship as contemplated by the Act. (Civ.Code, §§ 7003, subd. (1), 7004, subd. (a), 7015; Evid. Code, §§ 621, 892.) Yet for any child California law recognizes only one natural mother, despite advances in reproductive technology rendering a different outcome biologically possible.[8]

. . . .

intent

Because two women each have presented acceptable proof of maternity, we do not believe this case can be decided without enquiring into the parties' intentions as manifested in the surrogacy agreement. Mark and Crispina are a couple who desired to have a child of their own genetic stock but are physically unable to do so without the help of reproductive technology. They affirmatively intended the birth of the child, and took the steps necessary to effect in vitro fertilization. But for their acted-on intention, the child would not exist. Anna agreed to facilitate the procreation of Mark's and Crispina's child. The parties' aim was to bring Mark's and Crispina's child into the world, not for Mark and Crispina to donate a zygote to Anna. Crispina from the outset intended to be the child's mother. Although the gestative function Anna performed was necessary to bring about the child's birth, it is safe to say that Anna would not have been given the opportunity to gestate or deliver the child had she, prior to implantation of the zygote, manifested her own intent to be the child's mother. No reason appears why Anna's later change of heart should vitiate the determination that Crispina is the child's natural mother.

---

[8] We decline to accept the contention of amicus curiae the American Civil Liberties Union (ACLU) that we should find the child has two mothers. Even though rising divorce rates have made multiple parent arrangements common in our society, we see no compelling reason to recognize such a situation here. The Calverts are the genetic and intending parents of their son and have provided him, by all accounts, with a stable, intact, and nurturing home. To recognize parental rights in a third party with whom the Calvert family has had little contact since shortly after the child's birth would diminish Crispina's role as mother.

We conclude that although the Act recognizes both genetic consanguinity and giving birth as means of establishing a mother and child relationship, when the two means do not coincide in one woman, she who intended to procreate the child—that is, she who intended to bring about the birth of a child that she intended to raise as her own—is the natural mother under California law.[10]

Our conclusion finds support in the writings of several legal commentators. (See Hill, *What Does It Mean to Be a "Parent"? The Claims of Biology As the Basis for Parental Rights, supra,* 66 N.Y.U.L.Rev. 353; Shultz, *Reproductive Technology and Intent-Based Parenthood: An Opportunity for Gender Neutrality* (1990) Wis.L.Rev. 297 [Shultz]; Note, *Redefining Mother: A Legal Matrix for New Reproductive Technologies* (1986) 96 Yale L.J. 187, 197-202 [note].) . . .

>
>
> **Think About it**
>
> Another way to view this dispute is from the perspective of a "stakeholder diagram." On a blank piece of paper, draw a circle in the middle and place the child in the circle. Then draw two spokes from the circle, to the left and right. Place Mark and Crispina on the left spoke and Anna on the right spoke. Now ask yourself who else in society might have a stake or interest in this case or its precedential value. For instance, what about the child's grandparents? What about other couples considering a similar procedure? And so on. Arrange those parties on additional spokes around the circle, so that they align with the party whose interests match theirs.

. . . .

In deciding the issue of maternity under the Act we have felt free to take into account the parties' intentions, as expressed in the surrogacy contract, because in our view the agreement is not, on its face, inconsistent with public policy.

. . . .

---

[10] Thus, under our analysis, in a true "egg donation" situation, where a woman gestates and gives birth to a child formed from the egg of another woman with the intent to raise the child as her own, the birth mother is the natural mother under California law.

The dissent would decide *parentage* based on the best interests of the child. Such an approach raises the repugnant specter of governmental interference in matters implicating our most fundamental notions of privacy, and confuses concepts of parentage and custody. Logically, the determination of parentage must precede, and should not be dictated by, eventual custody decisions. The implicit assumption of the dissent is that a recognition of the genetic intending mother as the natural mother may sometimes harm the child. This assumption overlooks California's dependency laws, which are designed to protect *all* children irrespective of the manner of birth or conception. Moreover, the best interests standard poorly serves the child in the present situation: it fosters instability during litigation and, if applied to recognize the gestator as the natural mother, results in a split of custody between the natural father and the gestator, an outcome not likely to benefit the child. Further, it may be argued that, by voluntarily contracting away any rights to the child, the gestator has, in effect, conceded the best interests of the child are not with her.

Anna urges that surrogacy contracts violate several social policies. Relying on her contention that she is the child's legal, natural mother, she cites the public policy embodied in Penal Code section 273, prohibiting the payment for consent to adoption of a child. She argues further that the policies underlying the adoption laws of this state are violated by the surrogacy contract because it in effect constitutes a prebirth waiver of her parental rights.

We disagree. Gestational surrogacy differs in crucial respects from adoption and so is not subject to the adoption statutes. The parties voluntarily agreed to participate in in vitro fertilization and related medical procedures before the child was conceived; at the time when Anna entered into the contract, therefore, she was not vulnerable to financial inducements to part with her own expected offspring. As discussed above, Anna was not the genetic mother of the child. The payments to Anna under the contract were meant to compensate her for her services in gestating the fetus and undergoing labor, rather than for giving up "parental" rights to the child. Payments were due both during the pregnancy and after the child's birth. We are, accordingly, unpersuaded that the contract used in this case violates the public policies embodied in Penal Code section 273 and the adoption statutes. For the same reasons, we conclude these contracts do not implicate the policies underlying the statutes governing termination of parental rights. (See Welf. & Inst.Code, § 202.)

It has been suggested that gestational surrogacy may run afoul of prohibitions on involuntary servitude. . . . [A]lthough at one point the contract purports to give Mark and Crispina the sole right to determine whether to abort the pregnancy, at another point it acknowledges: "All parties understand that a pregnant woman has the absolute right to abort or not abort any fetus she is carrying. Any promise to the contrary is unenforceable." We therefore need not determine the validity of a surrogacy contract purporting to deprive the gestator of her freedom to terminate the pregnancy.

Finally, Anna and some commentators have expressed concern that surrogacy contracts tend to exploit or dehumanize women, especially women of lower economic status. Anna's objections center around the psychological harm she asserts may result from the gestator's relinquishing the child to whom she has given birth. Some have also cautioned that the practice of surrogacy may encourage society to view children as commodities, subject to trade at their parents' will.

We are all too aware that the proper forum for resolution of this issue is the Legislature, where empirical data, largely lacking from this record, can be studied and rules of general applicability developed. However, in light of our responsibility to decide this case, we have considered as best we can its possible consequences.

We are unpersuaded that gestational surrogacy arrangements are so likely to cause the untoward results Anna cites as to demand their invalidation on public policy grounds. Although common sense suggests that women of lesser means serve as surrogate mothers more often than do wealthy women, there has been no proof that surrogacy contracts exploit poor women to any greater degree than economic necessity in general exploits them by inducing them to accept lower-paid or otherwise undesirable employment. We are likewise unpersuaded by the claim that surrogacy will foster the attitude that children are mere commodities; no evidence is offered to support it. The limited data available seem to reflect an absence of significant adverse effects of surrogacy on all participants.

The argument that a woman cannot knowingly and intelligently agree to gestate and deliver a baby for intending parents carries overtones of the reasoning that for centuries prevented women from attaining equal economic rights and professional status under the law. To resurrect this view is both to foreclose a personal and economic choice on the part of the surrogate mother, and to deny intending parents what may be their only means of procreating a child of their own genetic stock. Certainly in the present case it cannot seriously be argued that Anna, a licensed vocational nurse who had done well in school and who had previously borne a child, lacked the intellectual wherewithal or life experience necessary to make an informed decision to enter into the surrogacy contract.

. . . .

. . . . It is not the role of the judiciary to inhibit the use of reproductive technology when the Legislature has not seen fit to do so; any such effort would raise serious questions in light of the fundamental nature of the rights of procreation and privacy. Rather, our task has been to resolve the dispute before us, interpreting the Act's use of the term "natural mother" (Civ.Code, § 7003, subd. (1)) when the biological functions essential to bringing a child into the world have been allocated between two women.

> **Think About It!**
>
> What role does the contract play in the court's application of the parentage statute? What role does it play in the dissenting opinion's application of the statute? What policy concerns lead to their different approaches? Which approach do you think is more appropriate? Why?

DISPOSITION

The judgment of the Court of Appeal is affirmed.

ARABIAN, Justice, concurring to opinion by PANELLI, Justice.

I concur in the decision to find under the Uniform Parentage Act that Crispina Calvert is the natural mother of the child she at all times intended to parent and raise as her own with her husband Mark, the child's natural father. That determination answers the question on which this court granted review, and in my view sufficiently resolves the controversy between the parties to warrant no further analysis. I therefore decline to subscribe to the dictum in which the majority find surrogacy contracts "not . . . inconsistent with public policy." (Maj. opn., *ante,* pp. 501-503 of 19 Cal.Rptr.2d, pp. 783-785 of 851 P.2d.)

Surrogacy contracts touch upon one of the most, if not *the* most, sensitive subjects of human endeavor. Not only does the birth of a new generation perpetuate our species, it allows every parent to contribute, both genetically and socially, to our collective understanding of what it means to be human. Every child also offers the opportunity of a unique lifetime relationship, potentially more satisfying and fulfilling than any other pursuit. (See *Adoption of Kelsey S.* (1992) 1 Cal.4th 816, 837, 4 Cal.Rptr.2d 615, 823 P.2d 1216.)

The multiplicity of considerations at issue in a surrogacy situation plainly transcend traditional principles of contract law and require careful, nonadversarial analysis. For this reason, I do not think it wise for this court to venture unnecessarily into terrain more appropriately cleared by the Legislature in the first instance. . . .

. . . . The implications of addressing the general soundness of surrogacy contracts are vast and profound. To date, the legislative process has failed to produce a satisfactory answer. This court should be chastened and not emboldened by that failure.

KENNARD, Justice, dissenting.

When a woman who wants to have a child provides her fertilized ovum to another woman who carries it through pregnancy and gives birth to a child, who is the child's legal mother? Unlike the majority, I do not agree that the determinative consideration should be the intent to have the child that originated with the woman who contributed the ovum. In my view, the woman who provided the fertilized ovum and the woman who gave birth to the child both have substantial claims to legal motherhood. Pregnancy entails a unique commitment, both psychological and emotional, to an unborn child. No less substantial, however, is the contribution of the woman from whose egg the child developed and without whose desire the child would not exist.

For each child, California law accords the legal rights and responsibilities of parenthood to only one "natural mother." When, as here, the female reproductive role is divided between two women, California law requires courts to make a decision as to which woman is the child's natural mother, but provides no standards by which to make that decision. The majority's resort to "intent" to break the "tie" between the genetic and gestational mothers is unsupported by statute, and, in the absence of appropriate protections in the law to guard against abuse of surrogacy arrangements, it is ill-advised. To determine who is the legal mother of a child born of a gestational surrogacy arrangement, I would apply the standard most protective of child welfare—the best interests of the child.

. . . .

II. THIS OPINION'S APPROACH

The determination of a question of parental rights to a child born of a surrogacy arrangement was before the New Jersey Supreme Court in *Matter of Baby M.* (1988) 109 N.J. 396, 537 A.2d 1227, a case that received worldwide attention. But in the surrogacy arrangement at issue there the woman who gave birth to the child, Marybeth Whitehead, had been impregnated by artificial insemination with the sperm of the intending father, William Stern. Whitehead thus provided the genetic material and carried the fetus to term. This case is different, because here those two aspects of the female role in reproduction were divided between two women. This process is known as "gestational" surrogacy, to distinguish it from the surrogacy arrangement involved in *Baby M.*

Behind the Scenes

The dissenting opinion refers to *In re Baby M*, a pivotal surrogacy case that was decided by the New Jersey Supreme Court in 1988. In that case, William and Elizabeth Stern entered into a surrogacy agreement with Mary Beth Whitehead. Elizabeth Stern was not infertile, but had multiple sclerosis and was concerned with the health risks a pregnancy would pose, based on a friend's experience. Mary Beth Whitehead was artificially inseminated with William Stern's sperm. She agreed to surrender all parental rights to Stern, and Stern promised to pay her $10,000. After the birth of the baby, Mary Beth Whitehead became severely depressed and threatened to commit suicide if the baby was taken from her. She fled the state with the baby and was eventually located in a search that was covered closely by the national press.

The Sterns sued for full custody, termination of all of Mary Beth Whitehead's parental rights, and enforcement of the surrogacy contract. The New Jersey Supreme Court relied heavily on laws governing the termination of parental rights and on the state's adoption laws in coming to its decision. The policy that parents should not be induced to surrender their rights for money was paramount in the ultimate holding, disfavoring the use of money in the adoption process. There was also substantial input from the court-appointed guardian ad litem, who presented findings about what kind of parenting situation would serve the best interests of the child. The court held that the surrogacy contract was void and remanded the case for determination of Mary Beth Whitehead's visitation rights.

When Baby M (Melissa Stern) turned 18, she terminated her birth mother's parental rights and initiated the process to allow Elizabeth Stern to adopt her. For more information about the *Baby M* case, *see* Carol Sanger, *Developing Markets in Baby-Making: In the Matter of Baby M, in Contracts Stories* 127 (Douglas G. Baird 2007).

In this opinion, I first discuss gestational surrogacy in light of the medical advances that have made it a reality. I next consider the wider social and philosophical implications of using gestational surrogacy to give birth to a child, and set out some of the suggested models for deciding the child's parentage in this situation. I then review a comprehensive model legislative scheme, not enacted in California, designed to accommodate the interests of all participants in surrogacy arrangements. I next turn to California's Uniform Parentage Act, and critique the majority's reliance on "intent" as the determinative factor under that act in deciding who is the "natural," and thus legal, mother of a child born of a gestational surrogacy arrangement. Finally, I explain why, in the absence of legislation designed to address the unique problems of gestational surrogacy, courts deciding who is the legal mother of a child born of gestational surrogacy should look to the best interests of that child.

III. GESTATIONAL SURROGACY

Recent advances in medical technology have dramatically expanded the means of human reproduction. . . .

The division of the female reproductive role in gestational surrogacy points up the three discrete aspects of motherhood: genetic, gestational and social. The woman who contributes the egg that becomes the fetus has played the genetic role of motherhood; the gestational aspect is provided by the woman who carries the fetus to term and gives birth to the child; and the woman who ultimately raises the child and assumes the responsibilities of parenthood is the child's social mother. (Shalev, Birth Power: The Case for Surrogacy, *supra,* at p. 115; see also Macklin, *Artificial Means of Reproduction and Our Understanding of the Family* (1991) 21 Hastings Center Rep. 5, 6.)

IV. POLICY CONSIDERATIONS

The ethical, moral and legal implications of using gestational surrogacy for human reproduction have engendered substantial debate. A review of the scholarly literature that addresses gestational surrogacy reveals little consensus on the desirability of surrogacy arrangements, particularly those involving paid surrogacy, or on how best to decide questions of the parentage of children born of such arrangements.

Surrogacy proponents generally contend that gestational surrogacy, like the other reproductive technologies that extend the ability to procreate to persons who might not otherwise be able to have children, enhances "individual freedom, fulfillment and responsibility." (Shultz, *Reproductive Technology, supra,* 1990 Wis.L.Rev. 297, 303.) Under this view, women capable of bearing children should be allowed to freely agree to be paid to do so by infertile couples desiring to form a family. (Shalev, Birth Power: The Case for Surrogacy, *supra,* at p. 145 [arguing for a "free market in reproduction" in which the "reproducing woman" operates as an "autonomous moral and economic agent"]; see also Posner, Economic Analysis of Law (3 ed. 1986) p. 139; Landes & Posner, *The Economics of the Baby Shortage* (1978) 7 J. Legal Stud. 323 [proposing a "market in babies"].) The "surrogate mother" is expected "to weigh the prospective investment in her birthing labor" before entering into the arrangement, and, if her "autonomous reproductive decision" is "voluntary," she should be held responsible for it so as "to fulfill the expectations of the other parties . . . ." (Shalev, Birth Power: The Case for Surrogacy, *supra,* at p. 96.)

. . . .

Surrogacy critics, however, maintain that the payment of money for the gestation and relinquishment of a child threatens the economic exploitation of poor women who may be induced to engage in commercial surrogacy arrangements out of financial need. (Capron & Radin, *Choosing Family Law Over Contract Law as a Paradigm for Surrogate Motherhood,* in Surrogate Motherhood, *supra,* p. 62.) Some fear the development of a "breeder" class of poor women who will be regularly employed to bear children for the economically advantaged. (See *Women and Children Used in Systems of Surrogacy: Position Statement of the Institute on Women and Technology,* in Surrogate Motherhood, *supra,* at p. 322; and Corea, *Junk Liberty,* testimony before Cal. Assem. Judiciary Com., April 5, 1988, in Surrogate Motherhood, *supra,* at pp. 325, 335.) Others suggest that women who enter into surrogacy arrangements may underestimate the psychological impact of relinquishing a child they have nurtured in their bodies for nine months. (See Macklin, *Artificial Means of Reproduction and Our Understanding of the Family, supra,* 21 Hastings Center Rep. 5, 10.)

Gestational surrogacy is also said to be "dehumanizing" (Capron & Radin, *Choosing Family Law Over Contract Law as a Paradigm for Surrogate Motherhood*, in Surrogate Motherhood, *supra*, at p. 62) and to "commodify" women and children by treating the female reproductive capacity and the children born of gestational surrogacy arrangements as products that can be bought and sold (Radin, *Market-Inalienability* (1987) 100 Harv.L.Rev. 1849, 1930-1932). The commodification of women and children, it is feared, will reinforce oppressive gender stereotypes and threaten the well-being of all children. (*Medical Technology, supra,* 103 Harv.L.Rev. 1519, 1550; Annas, *Fairy Tales Surrogate Mothers Tell*, in Surrogate Motherhood, *supra*, p. 50.) Some critics foresee promotion of an ever-expanding "business of surrogacy brokerage." (E.g., Goodwin, *Determination of Legal Parentage, supra,* 26 Fam.L.Q. at p. 283.)

Whether surrogacy contracts are viewed as personal service agreements or agreements for the sale of the child born as the result of the agreement, commentators critical of contractual surrogacy view these contracts as contrary to public policy and thus not enforceable. (Radin, *Market-Inalienability, supra,* 100 Harv.L.Rev. at p. 1924, fn. 261; Capron & Radin, *Choosing Family Law Over Contract Law as a Paradigm for Surrogate Motherhood, supra,* in Surrogate Motherhood, at pp. 62-63; see also Krimmel, *Can Surrogate Parenting Be Stopped? An Inspection of the Constitutional and Pragmatic Aspects of Outlawing Surrogate Mother Arrangements* (1992) 27 Val.U.L.Rev. 1, 4-5.)

Organizations representing diverse viewpoints share many of the concerns highlighted by the legal commentators. For example, the American Medical Association considers the conception of a child for relinquishment after birth to pose grave ethical problems. (Rep. of the Judicial Council, in Surrogate Motherhood, *supra*, at p. 304.) Likewise, the official position of the Catholic Church is that surrogacy arrangements are "'contrary to the unity of marriage and to the dignity of the procreation of the human person.'" (Magisterium of the Catholic Church, Instruction on Respect for Human Life in Its Origin and on the Dignity of Procreation: Replies to Certain Questions of the Day 25 (Feb. 22, 1987), cited in Radin, *Market-Inalienability, supra,* 100 Harv.L.Rev. 1849, 1928, fn. 271.)

The policy statement of the New York State Task Force on Life and the Law sums up the broad range of ethical problems that commercial surrogacy arrangements are viewed to present: "The gestation of children as a service for others in exchange for a fee is a radical departure from the way in which society understands and values pregnancy. It substitutes commercial values for the web of social, affective and moral meanings associated with human reproduction. . . . This transformation has profound implications for childbearing, for women, and for the relationship between parents and the children they bring into the world. . . . Surrogate parenting allows the genetic, gestational and social components of parenthood to be fragmented, creating unprecedented relationships among people bound together by contractual obligation rather than by the bonds of kinship and caring. . . . Surrogate parenting alters deep-rooted social and moral assumptions about the relationship between parents and children. . . . . [It] is premised on the ability and willingness of women to abdicate [their parental] responsibility without moral compunction or regret [and] makes the obligations that accompany parenthood alienable and negotiable." (New York State Task Force on Life and the Law, *Surrogate Parenting: Analysis and Recommendations for Public Policy* (May 1988) in Surrogate Motherhood, *supra,* at pp. 317-318.)

Proponents and critics of gestational surrogacy propose widely differing approaches for deciding who should be the legal mother of a child born of a gestational surrogacy arrangement. Surrogacy advocates propose to enforce pre-conception contracts in which gestational mothers have agreed to relinquish parental rights, and, thus, would make "bargained-for intentions determinative of legal parenthood." (Shultz, *Reproductive Technology, supra,* 1990 Wis.L.Rev. at p. 323.) Professor Robertson, for instance, contends that "The right to noncoital, collaborative reproduction also includes the right of the parties to agree how they should allocate their obligations and entitlements with respect to the child. Legal presumptions of paternity and maternity would be overridden by this agreement of the parties." (Robertson, *Procreative Liberty and the Control of Conception, Pregnancy, and Childbirth, supra,* 69 Va.L.Rev. 405, 436; . . . .)

Surrogacy critics, on the other hand, consider the unique female role in human reproduction as the determinative factor in questions of legal parentage. They reason that although males and females both contribute genetic material for the child, the act of gestating the fetus falls only on the female. . . . Under this approach, the laws governing adoption should govern the parental rights to a child born of gestational surrogacy. Upon the birth of the child, the gestational mother can decide whether or not to relinquish her parental rights in favor of the genetic mother. (*Ibid.*)

V. MODEL LEGISLATION

The debate over whom the law should recognize as the legal mother of a child born of a gestational surrogacy arrangement prompted the National Conference of Commissioners on Uniform State Laws to propose the Uniform Status of Children of Assisted Conception Act. (9B West's U. Laws Ann. (1992 Supp.) Uniform Status of Children of Assisted Conception Act (1988 Act) pp. 122-137 [hereafter also USCACA]). This model legislation addresses many of the concerns discussed above.

. . . .

is surrogacy approved?

In its key components, the proposed legislation provides that "a woman who gives birth to a child is the child's mother" (USCACA, § 2) unless a court has approved a surrogacy agreement before conception (USCACA, §§ 5, 6). In the absence of such court approval, any surrogacy agreement would be void. (USCACA, § 5, subd. (b).) If, however, the arrangement for gestational surrogacy has court approval, "the intended parents are the parents of the child." (USCACA, § 8, subd. (a)(1).)

court decides if contract okay

To obtain court approval, the parties to the surrogacy arrangement must file a petition. (USCACA, § 6, subd. (a).) The model legislation provides for the court to appoint a guardian ad litem for the intended child and legal counsel for the surrogate mother. (*Ibid.*) Before approving a surrogacy arrangement, the trial court must conduct a hearing and enter detailed findings, including the following: medical evidence shows the intended mother's inability to bear a child or that for her to do so poses an unreasonable risk to the unborn child or to the physical or mental health of the intended mother; all parties to the surrogacy agreement (including the surrogate's husband if she has one) meet the standards of fitness of adoptive parents; the agreement was voluntary and all parties understand its terms; the surrogate mother has undergone at least one successful pregnancy and medical evidence shows that another pregnancy will not endanger her physical or mental health or pose an unreasonable risk to the unborn child; and all parties have received professional mental health counseling pertaining to the effect of the surrogacy arrangement. (USCACA, § 6, subd. (b).) These provisions serve to minimize the potential for overreaching and to ensure that all parties to a surrogacy arrangement understand their respective roles and obligations.

Think About It!

Why do you suppose the dissent discusses the USCACA, even though California didn't adopt it? Only Virginia adopted the USCACA, which the Uniform Law Commission (ULC) withdrew in 2000, when the ULC amended the Uniform Parentage Act to include Art. 7 on "Child of Assisted Conception" and Art. 8 on "Gestational Agreement."*

. . . .

Because California Legislature has not enacted the Uniform Status of Children of Assisted Conception Act, its provisions were not followed in this case.

VI. THE UNIFORM PARENTAGE ACT

[Justice Kennard analyses the Uniform Parentage Act and determines that both mothers have shown statutory claims to the child, but that the UPA does not provide standard for breaking the "tie" and determining the natural mother in this situation.]

---

* http://uniformlaws.org/ActSummary.aspx?title=Parentage%20Act.

. . . .

VII. ANALYSIS OF THE MAJORITY'S "INTENT" TEST

Faced with the failure of current statutory law to adequately address the issue of who is a child's natural mother when two women qualify under the UPA, the majority breaks the "tie" by resort to a criterion not found in the UPA—the "intent" of the genetic mother to be the child's mother.

This case presents a difficult issue. The majority's resolution of that issue deserves serious consideration. Ultimately, however, I cannot agree that "intent" is the appropriate test for resolving this case.

The majority offers four arguments in support of its conclusion to rely on the intent of the genetic mother as the exclusive determinant for deciding who is the natural mother of a child born of gestational surrogacy. Careful examination, however, demonstrates that none of the arguments mandates the majority's conclusion.

[The majority's first argument is founded on "but-for" causation, which the concurrence finds illogical because—but for the genetic mother's and the gestational mother's actions—the child would not exist. The concurrence therefore would reject the premise that the genetic mother's intent should be the determinative factor in deciding surrogacy cases.]

[The majority's second argument is derived from a student note that argues that "[t]he mental concept of the child is a controlling factor of its creation, and the originators of that concept merit full credit as conceivers." The concurrence notes that this concept is based on intellectual property law and that a child should not be seen as property, so the concurrence would reject the argument.]

. . . [T]he majority offers as its third rationale the notion that bargained-for expectations support its conclusion regarding the dispositive significance of the genetic mother's intent. Specifically, the majority states that "'intentions that are voluntarily chosen, deliberate, express and bargained-for ought presumptively to determine legal parenthood.'" (Maj. opn., *ante,* at p. 501, of 19 Cal.Rptr.2d, p. 783 of 851 P.2d, quoting Schultz, *Reproductive Technology, supra,* 1990 Wis.L.Rev. at p. 323.)

It is commonplace that, in real or personal property transactions governed by contracts, "intentions that are voluntarily chosen, deliberate, express and bargained-for" ought presumptively to be enforced and, when one party seeks to escape performance, the court may order specific performance. (See, e.g., § 3384 et seq.; 11 Witkin, Summary of Cal. Law (9th ed. 1990), Equity, § 21,

p. 698.) But the courts will not compel performance of all contract obligations. For instance, even when a party to a contract for personal services (such as employment) has wilfully breached the contract, the courts will not order specific enforcement of an obligation to perform that personal service. (§ 3390; see 11 Witkin, Summary of Cal. Law, *supra,* Equity, § 59, p. 736.) The unsuitability of applying the notion that, because contract intentions are "voluntarily chosen, deliberate, express and bargained-for," their performance ought to be compelled by the courts is even more clear when the concept of specific performance is used to determine the course of the life of a child. Just as children are not the intellectual property of their parents, neither are they the personal property of anyone, and their delivery cannot be ordered as a contract remedy on the same terms that a court would, for example, order a breaching party to deliver a truckload of nuts and bolts.

Thus, three of the majority's four arguments in support of its exclusive reliance on the intent of the genetic mother as determinative in gestational surrogacy cases cannot withstand analysis. . . . .

To summarize, the woman who carried the fetus to term and brought a child into the world has, like the genetic mother, a substantial claim to be the natural mother of the child. The gestational mother has made an indispensable and unique biological contribution, and has also gone beyond biology in an intangible respect that, though difficult to label, cannot be denied. Accordingly, I cannot agree with the majority's devaluation of the role of the gestational mother.

I find the majority's reliance on "intent" unsatisfactory for yet another reason. By making intent determinative of parental rights to a child born of a gestational surrogacy arrangement, the majority would permit enforcement of a gestational surrogacy agreement without requiring any of the protections that would be afforded by the Uniform Status of Children of Assisted Conception Act. Under that act, the granting of parental rights to a couple that initiates a gestational surrogacy arrangement would be conditioned upon compliance with the legislation's other provisions. They include court oversight of the gestational surrogacy arrangement before conception, legal counsel for the woman who agrees to gestate the child, a showing of need for the surrogacy, medical and mental health evaluations, and a requirement that all parties meet the standards of fitness of adoptive parents. (USCACA, §§ 5, 6.)

In my view, protective requirements such as those set forth in the USCACA are necessary to minimize any possibility in gestational surrogacy arrangements for overreaching or abuse by a party with economic advantage. . . . The model act's carefully drafted provisions would assure that the surrogacy arrangement is a matter of medical necessity on the part of the intending parents, and not merely the product of a desire to avoid the inconveniences of pregnancy, together with the financial ability to do so. Also, by requiring both pre-conception psychological counseling for all parties and judicial approval, the model act would assure that parties enter into a surrogacy arrangement only if they are legally and psychologically capable of doing so and fully understand all the risks involved, and that the surrogacy arrangement would not be substantially detrimental to the interests of any individual. . . . In contrast, here the majority's grant of parental rights to the intending mother contains no provisions for the procedural protections suggested by the commissioners who drafted the model act. The majority opinion is a sweeping endorsement of unregulated gestational surrogacy.

The majority's final argument in support of using the intent of the genetic mother as the exclusive determinant of the outcome in gestational surrogacy cases is that preferring the intending mother serves the child's interests, which are "'[u]nlikely to run contrary to those of adults who choose to bring [the child] into being.'" (Maj. opn., *ante,* at p. 501, of 19 Cal.Rptr.2d, p. 783 of 851 P.2d, quoting Schultz, *Reproductive Technology, supra,* 1990 Wis.L.Rev. at p. 397.)

I agree with the majority that the best interests of the child is an important goal; indeed, as I shall explain, the best interests of the child, rather than the intent of the genetic mother, is the proper standard to apply in the absence of legislation. The problem with the majority's rule of intent is that application of this inflexible rule will not serve the child's best interests in every case.

I express no view on whether the best interests of the child in this case will be served by determining that the genetic mother is or is not the natural mother under California's Uniform Parentage Act. It may be that in this case the child's interests will be best served by recognizing Crispina as the natural mother. But this court is not just making a rule to resolve this case. Because the UPA does not adequately address the situation of gestational surrogacy, this court is of necessity making a rule that, unless new legislation is enacted, will govern all future cases of gestational surrogacy in California. And all future cases will not be alike. The genetic mother and her spouse may be, in most cases, considerably more affluent than the gestational mother. But "[t]he mere fact that a couple is willing to pay a good deal of money to obtain a child does not vouchsafe that they will be suitable parents . . . ." (Capron & Radin, *Choosing Family Law Over Contract Law as a Paradigm for Surrogate Motherhood,* in Surrogate Motherhood, *supra,* at pp. 65-66.) It requires little imagination to foresee cases in which the genetic mothers are, for example, unstable or substance abusers, or in which the genetic mothers' life circumstances change dramatically during the gestational mothers' pregnancies, while the gestational mothers, though of a less advantaged socioeconomic class, are stable, mature, capable and willing to provide a loving family environment in which the child will flourish. Under those circumstances, the majority's rigid reliance on the intent of the genetic mother will not serve the best interests of the child.

VIII. THE BEST INTERESTS OF THE CHILD

As I have discussed, in California the existing statutory law applicable to this case is the Uniform Parentage Act, which was never designed to govern the new reproductive technology of gestational surrogacy. Under the UPA, both the genetic mother and the gestational mother have an equal right to be the child's natural mother. But the UPA allows one natural mother for each child, and thus this court is required to make a choice. To break this "tie" between the genetic mother and the gestational mother, the majority uses the legal concept of intent. In so doing, the majority has articulated a rationale for using the concept of intent that is grounded in principles of tort, intellectual property and commercial contract law.

But, as I have pointed out, we are not deciding a case involving the commission of a tort, the ownership of intellectual property, or the delivery of goods under a commercial contract; we are deciding the fate of a child. In the absence of legislation that is designed to address the unique problems of gestational surrogacy, this court should look not to tort, property or contract law, but to family law, as the governing paradigm and source of a rule of decision.

The allocation of parental rights and responsibilities necessarily impacts the welfare of a minor child. And in issues of child welfare, the standard that courts frequently apply is the best interests of the child. . . . Indeed, it is highly significant that the UPA itself looks to a child's best interests in deciding another question of parental rights. (§ 7017, subd. (d)(2).) This "best interests" standard serves to assure that in the judicial resolution of disputes affecting a child's well-being, protection of the minor child is the foremost consideration. Consequently, I would apply "the best interests of the child" standard to determine who can best assume the social and legal responsibilities of motherhood for a child born of a gestational surrogacy arrangement.[4]

---

[4] In a footnote responding to this opinion, the majority confuses questions of custody, which I do not address, with the issue of maternal parentage, which I do address. (See maj. opn., *ante,* at p. 500, fn. 10 of 19 Cal.Rptr.2d, p. 782, fn. 10 of 851 P.2d.) The majority suggests that it is somehow inappropriate for a court to look to the child's best interests when deciding a question of parentage under the UPA; this is refuted by the express terms of the UPA itself, which, as noted above, requires the court to consider the child's best interests in deciding another question of parentage. (§ 7017, subd. (d)(2).)

The majority is also wrong when it suggests that the "best interests" approach for resolving the disputed issue of parentage, more than the majority's "intent" approach, raises the "specter of governmental interference" in fundamentally private matters. (Maj. opn., *ante,* at p. 500, fn. 10 of 19 Cal.Rptr.2d, p. 782, fn. 10 of 851 P.2d.) This court's grant of review to decide who is the natural mother of the child placed one branch of government squarely in the middle of this controversy—as did the parties' decisions to resort to the court system in the first place. Judicial resolution of family law matters, by its nature, necessarily involves some governmental interference in what would otherwise be private concerns.

On another point, the majority writes that the gestational mother could "voluntarily contract[] away any rights to the child," and that this would represent a "concession" as to the child's best interests. (Maj. opn., *ante,* at p. 500, fn. 10 of 19 Cal.Rptr.2d, p. 782, fn. 10 of 851 P.2d.) It is questionable whether the parentage of children is a proper subject of contract. But even assuming that a parent could contract away parental rights to a child—for instance, by selling the child into slavery—this would not logically amount to a binding "concession" that such a sale would be in the child's best interests.

The determination of a child's best interests does not depend on the parties' relative economic circumstances, which in a gestational surrogacy situation will usually favor the genetic mother and her spouse. (See *Matter of Baby M., supra,* 537 A.2d at p. 1249.) As this court has recognized, however, superior wealth does not necessarily equate with good parenting. (See *Burchard v. Garay* (1986) 42 Cal.3d 531, 540, 229 Cal.Rptr. 800, 724 P.2d 486.)

Factors that are pertinent to good parenting, and thus that are in a child's best interests, include the ability to nurture the child physically and psychologically (Cahill, *The Ethics of Surrogate Motherhood: Biology, Freedom, and Moral Obligation,* in Surrogate Motherhood, *supra,* at p. 160), and to provide ethical and intellectual guidance (see *In re Marriage of Carney* (1979) 24 Cal.3d 725, 739, 157 Cal. Rptr. 383, 598 P.2d 36). Also crucial to a child's best interests is the "well recognized right" of every child "to stability and continuity." (*Burchard v. Garay, supra,* 42 Cal.3d at p. 546, 229 Cal.Rptr. 800, 724 P.2d 486 (conc. opn. of Mosk, J.).) The intent of the genetic mother to procreate a child is certainly relevant to the question of the child's best interests; alone, however, it should not be dispositive.

Here, the child born of the gestational surrogacy arrangement between Anna Johnson and Mark and Crispina Calvert has lived continuously with Mark and Crispina since his birth in September 1990. The trial court awarded parental rights to Mark and Crispina, concluding that as a matter of law they were the child's "genetic, biological and natural" parents. In reaching that conclusion, the trial court did not treat Anna's statutory claim to be the child's legal mother as equal to Crispina's, nor did the trial court consider the child's best interests in deciding between those two equal statutory claims. Accordingly, I would remand the matter to the trial court to undertake that evaluation.

CONCLUSION

Recent advances in medical technology have made it possible for the human female reproductive role to be divided between two women, the genetic mother and the gestational mother. Such gestational surrogacy arrangements call for sensitivity to each of the adult participants. But the paramount concern must be the well-being of the child that gestational surrogacy has made possible.

. . . .

In this opinion, I do not purport to offer a perfect solution to the difficult questions posed by gestational surrogacy; perhaps there can be no perfect solution. But in the absence of legislation specifically designed to

Behind the Scenes

Anna Johnson appealed to the United States Supreme Court, which denied certiorari. Denials of certiorari have no precedential value for future cases.

address the complex issues of gestational surrogacy and to protect against potential abuses, I cannot join the majority's uncritical validation of gestational surrogacy.

I would reverse the judgment of the Court of Appeal, and remand the case to the trial court for a determination of disputed parentage on the basis of the best interests of the child.

Food for Thought:

Surrogacy Contracts in Flux

The law concerning surrogacy contracts is complex and largely unsettled. The contracts are criminalized in three states, while two others have held them to be completely unenforceable. Some states have adopted different rules for traditional and gestational surrogacy contracts. If a distinction exists, a gestational surrogacy, in which a surrogate mother more or less "rents" her womb for an implanted fertilized zygote, is more likely to be upheld than a traditional surrogacy, in which the surrogate provides the egg herself. In some situations, whether or not the intended parents are married or LGBT can have an effect on the enforceability of the contract. It is also possible that state adoption laws and laws regulating foster care may narrow the interpretation of an otherwise broadly worded surrogacy statute to exclude LGBT parents. Compensation for surrogacy arrangements is disfavored and could make an otherwise enforceable contract void, although courts may regard reimbursement of medical expenses and other pregnancy-related costs as being outside the realm of compensation. Darra L. Hofman, *"Mama's Baby, Daddy's Maybe:" A State-By-State Survey of Surrogacy Laws and Their Disparate Gender Impact*, 35 Wm. Mitchell L. Rev. 449 (2009) (including a detailed chart documenting various states' approaches to this issue).

Problems: Contract Defenses

In Problems 5-16 to 5-19, identify which defense(s) might be raised. Evaluate each defense. If more than one defense is available, determine which one has the greatest chance of succeeding and whether it will.

5-16. Aaron is a criminal defense attorney at a large firm in New York. Sarah is the vice dean of labor relations at a large university. As part of the dissolution of their marriage, Aaron and Sarah entered into settlement negotiations about division of their vehicles, miscellaneous personal property, real estate, financial accounts and instruments, and retirement accounts. They intended to divide their combined estate equally. Only Sarah was represented by counsel--an experienced divorce attorney with considerable negotiation expertise.

The final settlement document stated that the retirement accounts were to be divided equally. Aaron was to retain two vehicles; Sarah, three. Aaron was to retain the residences in New York and Paris; Sarah, the residence in Los Angeles, plus a $445,000 payment from Aaron. Both parties retained the retirement accounts held in their respective names. Aaron's investment fund of $5.4 million was used to pay Sarah a one-time payment of $2.7 million "in satisfaction for the Wife's support and marital property rights." They signed the settlement. The court approved the settlement and the divorce.

For three years Aaron continued to invest in the mutual fund. Then, the parties learned that Aaron's investment fund was part of a Ponzi scheme (check Wikipedia if you need a definition), so its assets ended up being used to pay off other investors in order to keep the scheme going. The $2.7 million paid to Sarah had actually come from an investment made by a newer victim to the scheme. By good fortune, Sarah did not need to relinquish the funds to the bankruptcy trustee, due to statutes of limitations and bankruptcy law. Aaron, however, had a balance of zero in his investment fund. If Aaron brings suit to adjust the divorce settlement, which defense(s) should he raise, and will he succeed?

5-17. Brian, an accomplished politician, sought to enlist the services of Grant to run his next election campaign. Brian and Grant engaged in hard negotiations, during which Brian threatened to ruin Grant's reputation by disclosing some little known facts if he did not agree to a term of employment through the election and to pay liquidated damages if he left early. Grant begrudgingly agreed, so long as Brian would pay Grant cash bonuses of $2,000 a month, for nine months. At the time of the agreement, campaign regulations did not allow for such compensation, due to the challenges it posed to recordkeeping. However, the two agreed and began the campaign.

After four months, campaign regulations changed to allow for monthly cash bonuses. However, two months later, Brian got fed up with Grant's poor performance and stopped payment of the monthly bonuses. If Grant brings suit to collect the remainder of the amount due, which defense(s) should he raise, and will he succeed?

5-18. Richard decided to move to Providence, New Jersey. He found a listing for a lease-to-buy home in a nice part of town and arranged to meet with the homeowner's agent, John. At their first meeting at the house, Richard asked John if the house had been inspected, to which John replied yes. (House inspections are not required of sellers in this jurisdiction.)

In the next visit, Richard met the homeowner, Jody. Richard asked Jody if the house had been inspected for termites. Jody said yes but that she was unsure of what that inspection included. John interjected that the house had no termite issues. John had been selling homes for over a decade and was familiar with the neighborhood where Richard wanted to buy. No neighborhood houses had termite issues at that time. Additionally, John was familiar with how to look for termite infestations that had caused severe damage, and he had not seen any such damage in Jody's home.

When the parties met to sign a lease-to-buy agreement, Richard again asked if Jody was sure that house was free of termites. Jody looked to John who nodded affirmatively. Jody responded that the house was free of termites, and Richard signed the agreement.

For six months, Richard worked on remodeling the home. When he began working in the basement, he discovered a load-bearing beam that had a small pile of dust below it. Richard called in an inspector who confirmed that the beam was infested with termites. The inspector said that the termites had likely been there from before the sale and had caused substantial damage to the inside of the beam. The inspector didn't find any further termite infestation.

Richard ceased making lease payments, moved out of the house, and three months later informed Jody that he wanted his six months of payments returned. Jody refused, because the lease-to-buy agreement provided that Richard forfeited any lease payments and title to the home if he fell two months behind his payment schedule. If Richard brings suit to have the lease payments returned, which defense(s) should he raise, and will he succeed?

5-19. Don and Patti owned a manufacturing company that specialized in high-end electronics. The company employed more than 200 workers who received compensation 5% below industry averages, because of the company's decreased business as a result of the economic downturn.

The company won negotiation rights for an output contract with an international distributor that had a strong market for the parts produced by the company. When Don and Patti announced the pending agreement, the employees unionized and obtained representation to renegotiate their compensation.

The union representative, Billy, was quite the negotiator. He threatened a strike if Don and Patti refused to increase employee compensation to 15% above industry standards. Billy knew that the company was negotiating a contract that could make the company much more profitable, and he used that point as leverage. But he was unaware of how precarious those negotiations were. If the company could not retain its employees, it would likely lose the contract to competitors. As a result, Don and Patti agreed to Billy's terms.

During subsequent price negotiations with the international distributor, Don's and Patti's hands were tied as a result of the new employee compensation rates, so they lost out on the output contract. After that, the company continued to limp along in difficult economic shape, but worse because it was paying its employees 20% more. After two months, the company reneged on the new pay rates and returned to the earlier pay rates. Infuriated, the employees brought suit through the union. Assume that labor law has no impact on your analysis here. Which defense(s) should the union raise, and will it succeed?

5-20. At age 64, Kai loses his wife after her long battle with cancer. A month later, he retires from his job. Exhausted and bereft, he sits around his house for several months. He gets some grief counseling, and, at the advice of his counselor, decides to do something he had wanted to do for a long time—take painting lessons. He goes to the local art center and pays $300 for a twelve-lesson beginner package in a group setting, so that he can see others progress. He enjoys the camaraderie of the group and the praise of his young instructor. At the beginning of the tenth lesson, his instructor tells him that he is "a natural" and could soon be painting well enough to exhibit and sell his paintings. She encourages him to buy the "master painter super-package" of 24 private weekly lessons for $2400. Flattered and enheartened, he does so, signing up for the same instructor. Toward the end of the 24 private lessons, she tells him that he will have enough high-quality paintings to exhibit if he signs up for another 12 private lessons for $1200. He does so, even though these lessons and his painting supplies are straining his household budget. He finishes his paintings for exhibit and pays the art center an additional $1000 for exhibit space for a week. He invites his friends and family, who are appalled at his lack of talent. No paintings sell. Several of his friends eventually take him aside to tell him the harsh truth—they think he got preyed upon because of his emotional vulnerability after his wife's death, and they urge him to get his money back. He is able to contest payment on the final $2200 in payments, which are on his credit card bill. The art center sues him for $2200. He consults you as his attorney. What kinds of evidence will you look for, in trying to determine whether he has a valid defense to the contract?

CHAPTER 6

Statute of Frauds

What kind of promises will the law enforce?	How do parties demonstrate assent to a contract?	What defenses to enforcement exist?	Is a writing required for enforcement? If so, what kind?	How is the content of a contract ascertained?	What are parties' rights and duties after breach?

		What situations lead to excusing contract performance?	What remedies are available for breach of contract?	What contractual rights and duties do non-parties to a contract have?

§ 1. Introduction

Even if a contract has been formed according to traditional contract principles, it will not be enforceable in court unless the contract satisfies the relevant "statute of frauds," a set of provisions that specify which contracts must be evidenced in some kind of writing. Modern statute of frauds provisions are descended from the English Act for Prevention of Frauds and Perjuries of 1677. A state's statute of frauds is likely to be embodied in more than one legislative enactment, addressing both general contracts and contracts related to specific subject matters. The UCC includes a statute of frauds for contracts for or predominated by the sale of goods, and this chapter explores that provision along with general principles pertinent to application of any statute of frauds.

The English statute of frauds, as its full name implies, was enacted to counter use of perjured testimony and other fraudulent practices by requiring that certain contracts could not be enforced "unless the agreement . . . or some memorandum or note thereof, shall be in writing, and signed by the party to be charged therewith, or some other person . . . by him lawfully authorized." By requiring some form of written acknowledgement of an agreement, the statute was designed to prevent oral testimony alone from serving as sufficient evidence of the existence of a contract. It was enacted at a time when parties were not permitted to testify, jurors could use their own knowledge of the facts in rendering decisions, and judges had few tools to control decisions that might be based on sympathy or prejudice rather than on fact. Having written evidence of the existence of a contract was seen as a way to provide some certainty that a contract existed, in order to counter such evidentiary limitations.

In the years since 1677, three rationales have been articulated for requiring a signed writing, paralleling reasons for requiring other kinds of legal formalities:

- **Evidentiary:** to ensure that a contract will be enforced only when there is reliable evidence of the contract's existence. Underlying the writing requirement is an assumption that written evidence is more reliable than oral testimony, whether because of shaky memories or the temptation to lie about past events. If an alleged agreement is ruled unenforceable based on the relatively simple determination that a sufficient writing does not exist, the court will never have to reach the often more thorny question of whether the parties assented to the agreement, based on more questionable evidence about the existence and content of the contract.

- **Cautionary:** to "give pause" to persons entering into contracts, so that they recognize the importance and content of the contractual relationship that they are about to establish. Underlying this rationale is the assumption that people will be more cautious when signing a document than when simply speaking or shaking hands on an oral deal.

- **Channeling:** to provide an effective marker to designate enforceable agreements so parties may more easily express their intentions regarding enforceability and courts can easily and dependably distinguish enforceable from unenforceable agreements. Underlying this rationale is the assumption that parties use the formality of a writing to signal their intent to be bound.

In circumstances presenting difficult questions about interpretation and application of the statute of frauds, it may be helpful to return to these three principles to determine whether and how the statute should be applied.

Whether the purposes of the original statute of frauds and its progeny are adequately and effectively served by modern use of the rule is a subject of some controversy. In a 1934 report, an English Law Revision Committee summarized the major criticisms of the statute, saying it was "a product of conditions which have long passed away," that the requirement of a writing is "out of accord with the way in which business is normally done" and "promotes more frauds than it prevents . . . ," and that the "operation [of the statute] is often lopsided and partial."* In 1954, Parliament repealed most of the British statute of frauds. Article 1.2 of the UNIDROIT Principles and Article 11 of the Convention on the International Sale of Goods (CISG) also dispense with a writing requirement. The CISG allows any country adopting the Convention to declare Article 11 inapplicable if any party has a place of business in that country, but the United States has not made such a declaration, despite the continuing existence of statutes of frauds in domestic law.

Restatement (Second) of Contracts § 131 comment c reflects concern about misuse of the statute of frauds, cautioning that the statutory purpose is *not* "to facilitate repudiation of firm oral agreements fairly made, to protect a promisor from temptation to perjure himself by false denial of the promise, or to reward a candid contract-breaker by denying enforcement." Despite such widely

---

* Report of the English Law Revision Committee on the Statute of Frauds and the Doctrine of Consideration (Sixth Interim Report, Cmd. 5449, 1937), reprinted in 15 Can. B. Rev. 585, 589 (1937).

expressed doubts, American jurisdictions retain statutes of frauds, and it remains important to understand their workings, as well as the varying attitudes that lead some courts to support and others to limit application of the rules.

Applying the statute of frauds requires answering a series of related questions:

1. Is the contract within the statute of frauds—that is,
    a. Does the statute of frauds require this category of contract to be evidenced in a writing?
    b. If so (if this category of contract must be evidenced by a writing), does the contract nevertheless fall within one of the exceptions to the statute of frauds that eliminate the requirement of a writing under particular circumstances?
2. If the contract is within the statute of frauds, what kind of writing is required to satisfy the statute, and does such a writing exist?

If the contract is within the statute of frauds but does not meet its requirements, the consequence is that the contract cannot be enforced in court. (Some statutes and courts say that the contract is "void," "invalid," or "not binding.") If the contract is *not* within the statute of frauds or if the requirements of the statute *are* met, then the court may proceed to consider the merits of the contract claim.

In flowchart form, the statute of frauds (S/F) inquiry might look like this:

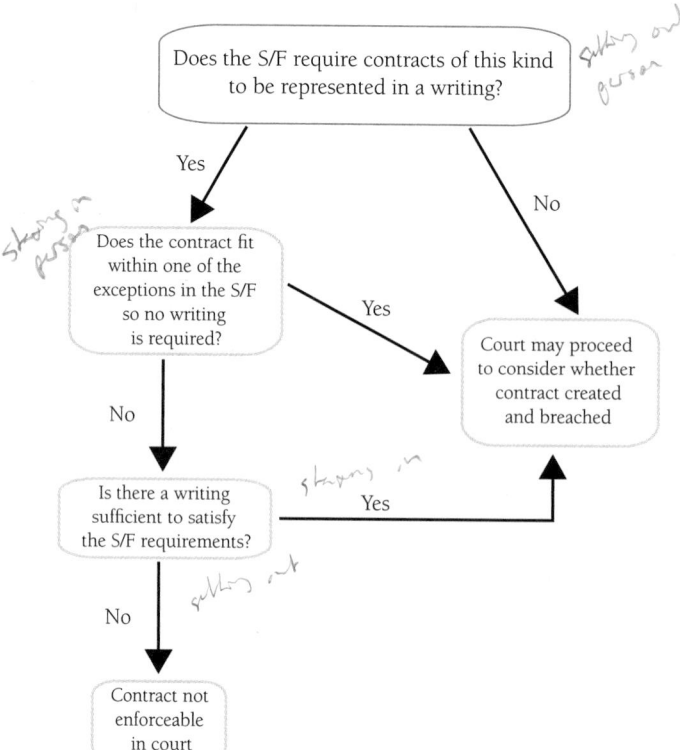

§ 2. Manner and Effect of Invoking the Statute of Frauds

If a plaintiff brings a breach-of-contract claim, the defendant—the "party against whom [contract] enforcement is sought" or the "party to be charged"—may move to dismiss the claim based on the statute of frauds, if the facts warrant such a motion. If the defendant is seeking to enforce a contract (perhaps in a counterclaim or based on a settlement agreement), then the plaintiff (in that instance being the "party against whom enforcement is sought" or the "party to be charged") may consider raising the statute of frauds to deny enforcement of that contract.

Under Federal Rule of Civil Procedure 8(c)(1), the party raising the statute of frauds must do so in or before the responsive pleading to the pleading raising the contract claim (so usually in the answer), and cannot raise it later. A court will not raise the statute of frauds *sua sponte* (on its own motion).

The burden is on the party raising the statute of frauds as a defense to contract enforcement to show that the alleged contract is of a kind that is within the statute of frauds (that is, it is of a kind that is required to have a writing). If that is established, the party seeking enforcement of the contract then has the burden of demonstrating that the contract fits within one of the exceptions to the statute or providing a writing that meets the requirements. If she fails—that is, the contract is found to be not within an exception the statute of frauds and the statute's requirements are not satisfied—then the contract enforcement claim will be dismissed, and the party seeking contract enforcement will have no opportunity to present evidence about the existence and breach of the contract. If the party seeking enforcement succeeds in establishing that no writing is required or that, the statute of frauds is satisfied, the court may proceed to consider the breach of contract claim, but that party must still prove the existence, terms, and breach of the contract in order to win her suit.

See It

To help you see and remember the burdens of proof described in this paragraph, you should return to the chart in the previous section and label each pair of arrows to show which party has the burden of proof at that step and whether that party must prove the answer to be Yes or No.

The statute of frauds is a powerful tool for limiting the expense and effort of defending a lawsuit because it can prevent the lawsuit from proceeding past very preliminary phases. If successful, the defense will prevent the court from considering the merits of the contract claim. Its very success—and the fact that otherwise-valid contracts may be entirely oral—leads some judges to narrowly interpret the statute in order to avoid barring meritorious contract claims. Others apply the statute expansively to ensure solid evidence that an agreement exists and encourage parties to record their agreements in written form.

Even if the alleged contract is within the statute of frauds and does not satisfy its requirements, the resulting bar on judicial enforcement does not prevent resolution of claims in arbitration, mediation, or settlement agreements. Nor does it bar the use of the contract for other purposes, even in court. For example, the existence of the contract may help establish a right to, or help defend against, a claim of restitution, or serve as evidence in a misrepresentation or fraud claim. UCC § 2-201 comment 4 says that

> [f]ailure to satisfy the requirements [of §2-201] does not render the contract void for all purposes, but merely prevents it from being judicially enforced in favor of a party to the contract. For example, a buyer who takes possession of goods[,] as provided in an oral contract which the seller has not meanwhile repudiated, is not a trespasser. Nor would the statute of frauds provisions of this section be a defense to a third person who wrongfully induces a party to refuse to perform an oral contract, even though the injured party cannot maintain an action for damages against the party so refusing to perform.

§ 3. Is the Contract within the Statute of Frauds?

As indicated in the introduction to this chapter, the question whether an alleged contract is within the scope of the statute of frauds is really two related questions: (1) Is the contract within the general category or class of contracts identified as requiring a writing and (2) if so, does it nevertheless fit within an exception within that category?

§ 3.1. Is the Contract within a Class of Contracts Covered by the Statute of Frauds?

For any contract within the scope of UCC Article 2 (generally contracts for sale of goods, see page 68), UCC § 2-201 requires a writing if the contract has a total price of $500 or more. If the price is not specified in dollars (e.g., a trade of goods for services), the value of what is received for the goods is used as the price for purposes of invoking the statute of frauds.

For contracts other than for sale of goods, the list of covered contracts in the Restatement (Second) of Contracts § 110 is typical of many general state statutes of frauds.*

Restatement (Second) § 110. Classes of Contracts Covered

(1) The following classes of contracts are subject to a statute, commonly called the Statute of Frauds, forbidding enforcement unless there is a written memorandum or an applicable exception:

    (a) a contract of an executor or administrator to answer for a duty of his decedent (the executor-administrator provision);

    (b) a contract to answer for the duty of another (the suretyship provision);

    (c) a contract made upon consideration of marriage (the marriage provision);

    (d) a contract for the sale of an interest in land (the land contract provision);

    (e) a contract that is not to be performed within one year from the making thereof (the one-year provision).

(2) . . . .

The *executor-administrator provision*, Restatement (Second) § 110(1)(a), refers to promises made by the executor or administrator of an estate to personally (that is, out of personal, not estate, funds) pay creditors sums owed by the decedent at the time of death. For example, if Edward, the executor of Deborah's estate, personally (not on behalf of the estate) guarantees to pay Charles 50% of the amount Deborah owed on a promissory note at the time of her death (perhaps in exchange for Charles's promise not to seek payment of the additional 50%), the promise would not be enforceable without a written memorandum that satisfies the requirements of the statute of frauds.

The *suretyship provision*, § 110(1)(b), is similar. If the promisor acts as a surety—guaranteeing personal payment of another's obligation if the primary obligor does not pay—the promise must be reflected in a written memorandum that satisfies the statute of frauds. For example, if Drew agrees to co-sign a loan agreement between Ethan and a bank, promising to pay the bank if Ethan defaults, Drew's promise is within the statute of frauds because Drew is promising to pay Ethan's obligation; Drew is promising "to answer for the duty of another." Similarly, if

---

* In addition to the categories listed in Restatement (Second) § 110, state statutes commonly require a writing for agreements to arbitrate contract disputes or to extend a statute of limitations; for ante-nuptial and real-estate broker commission agreements; for contracts to make a testamentary distribution, to make a will or not to revoke an existing will; and for contracts that cannot be performed within a lifetime. Such requirements often appear in subject-matter-specific statutes, not in the general statute of frauds, so it is advisable to look beyond the general statute to determine whether any particular agreement must have a writing.

Craig caused an accident and was therefore obligated to compensate Violet, the victim, for her injuries, Sam's promise to pay if Craig does not would be "answering for the duty of another" and would be within the statute of frauds. But if Sam promised to pay Violet to induce her not to sue Craig, Sam would be creating an obligation of his own, not acting as a surety, so an oral promise may be enforced.

The *marriage provision,* § 110(1)(c), has usually been narrowly interpreted so that it applies only to promises made to third parties, not to mutual promises to marry. As noted by the English Law Revision Committee when it critiqued the English statute of frauds in 1937 (see the footnote on page 633), "the construction was narrowed so as to cover only contracts to pay marriage portions and the like, no doubt because in practice a person accepting a proposal of marriage did not as a rule cold-bloodedly demand a 'note or memorandum' from the party whom she might later desire to 'charge' on the promise." With the proliferation of prenuptial agreements in recent years, many states have adopted statute of frauds provisions requiring that such agreements must be in writing and signed by both parties. A writing requirement is contained in the Uniform Premarital Agreement Act, adopted in 1983 by the National Conference of Commissioners on Uniform State Laws, which serves as a model for many state laws.

The *land contract provision,* § 110(1)(d), has usually been interpreted broadly to apply to transactions transferring any interest in land, including contracts involving mortgages, easements (rights of access), mineral rights, and options to purchase land. Although a lease is considered a transfer of a property right (the right to occupy the premises), most states require only longer-term leases (those lasting more than a year) to be in writing.

The most challenging of the categories to apply is the *one-year provision,* the § 110(1)(e) requirement of a writing for a contract "not to be performed within one year from the making thereof." The time is to be measured from the day after the contract is entered (not the date of the the contract or when performance begins). As reflected in § 110 comment a (quoted below), the one-year provision is commonly construed narrowly, thereby restricting the number of contracts requiring a writing:

> Under the prevailing interpretation, the enforceability of a contract under the one-year provision does not turn on the actual course of subsequent events, nor on the expectations of the parties as to the probabilities. Contracts of uncertain duration are simply excluded; *the provision covers only those contracts whose performance cannot possibly be completed within a year.* [Emphasis supplied.]

Using this narrow interpretation, the Supreme Court of Connecticut ruled that an oral contract for the "construction of twenty industrial buildings, a 280 room hotel and convention center, and housing for 592 graduate students and professors" was enforceable without a writing because the contract did not explicitly indicate the contract would not be fully performed within a year, even though the construction was expected to take well more than that amount of time.* Similarly, a contract to insure against a contingency that could *possibly* occur within a year (e.g., a life insurance contract payable upon death of the insured) would not be within the statute of frauds (no writing required). Nor would a contract to confer property to another upon death (of the promisor or another), because the death could occur within a year.

But not all courts agree with such a narrow interpretation, and some ask what is possible in fact, not just what is possible in theory. Thus one court found a writing required for a joint venture agreement to construct a condominium complex where there was no "reasonable possibility of performance within a year."** Another noted that "the possibility of performance which would take an agreement out of the statute of frauds must be such as could fairly and reasonably be said to have been within the contemplation of the parties." An "unforeseen or remote possibility" that the contract could be performed within a year "will not rescue the agreement from invalidity."***

Courts may also distinguish between the possibility that the contract performance could be *excused* within a year because of impossibility of performance (still within the statute, so a writing required) and the possibility that the contract would be *fully performed* or *terminated* within the year (not within the statute, so no writing required). The decisions sometimes turn on whether the events that put an end to contract performance are seen as fulfilling or instead frustrating the contract. Based on this distinction, a writing would be required for a two-year employment contract, even though performance would be excused upon the death of the employee, which could occur within a year, because performance of the two-year contract would be frustrated by an early death. But a writing would not be required for a contract for lifetime employment because the contract would be fully performed upon the individual's death.

Courts have disagreed about whether the existence of an early termination option for either party means the contract may be performed within a year, even if the original contemplated duration is longer. Courts are also divided on whether a contract for an indefinite period (e.g., an agreement to be a beer distributor as long as the other party continues to sell in the area, or an agreement by an agent to repurchase bonds any time the other party needs funds) falls within the one-year provision. Finally, courts have split on whether a contract is within the statute of

---

* *C.R. Klewin, Inc. v. Flagship Properties*, 600 A.2d 772, 773 (Conn. 1991).
** *Dean v. Myers*, 466 So. 2d 952 (Ala. 1985).
*** *Stanley v. A. Levy & J. Zentner Co.*, 112 P.2d 1047, 1052 (Nev. 1941).

frauds if the only thing not to be performed within a year is the payment of money owed for performance.

If a contract's terms are changed, and the contract *as modified* is in a category of contracts that must be in writing, the modified agreement will not be enforceable unless the statute of frauds is satisfied. Courts disagree about whether that requirement means that the *modification* must be written or, instead, that the *modified contract* must have a writing (a requirement that could be satisfied by a writing prepared before the modification was agreed to). Whether *renewal* of a contract requires a separate writing is a contested issue as well. Some courts have viewed the renewal as a new and different agreement that requires a separate writing. Other courts have concluded that a renewal merely makes the original agreement operative for an extended period of time, so a writing that satisfies the statute of frauds for the original agreement satisfies it for the renewal as well. The CISG does not require any contract, including a contract modification, a modified contract, or a renewal, to be in writing; a country ratifying the CISG may retain a writing requirement for contracts involving any party with a place of business in that jurisdiction, but the United States has not done so.*

Parties to a contract may create their own private statute-of-frauds requirement by including a "no oral modification" (NOM) clause specifying that all changes to the contract must be in writing.** However, if the parties engage in one or more oral modifications after executing the written contract, their conduct may be found to have waived the NOM clause. Even a non-waiver clause will not prevent this result because the parties may also be found to have waived the non-waiver clause through their later actions! A waiver may be express or implied by conduct, and the waiver may operate with respect to a particular change or it may have continuing effect. Some (but not all) courts require that the party claiming waiver must show reasonable reliance on the waiver. The CISG and UNIDROIT Principles also provide for enforcement of NOM clauses, except to the extent that either party has reasonably relied on an oral modification.***

As seen in the litany of decisions decribed here, courts have sometimes limited application of the statute of frauds "in ways not noted for their logic,"**** leading to difficulty in applying the rules with consistency, especially when the duration of a contract depends on contingencies. The outcome of a statute of frauds defense based on the one-year provision may depend on the particular court's judgment about the purposes served by the writing requirement, the effectiveness of the statute of frauds in effectuating those purposes, and the court's resulting conclusion about whether to apply the statute narrowly or expansively.

---

* CISG Arts. 29(1), 96.

** For contracts governed by UCC Article 2, the clause must be separately signed by a non-merchant if it is on a form supplied by a merchant. *See* UCC § 2-209(2).

***CISG Art. 29 (2); UNIDROIT Art. 2.1.18.

**** E. Allan Farnsworth, *Contracts* 373 (4th ed. 2004)

Likely adopted to serve evidentiary purposes (to avoid relying on hazy memories and to require better evidence for contracts of longer duration), the one-year provision has been criticized as being ill-contrived to serve those ends.

Problems: The One-Year Provision

Consider the following examples. Would the specified contracts likely (or definitely) be within the statute of frauds (so a writing would be required)?

6-1. Contract for 18 months of window-cleaning service

6-2. Contract for construction of an apartment complex, with construction expected to be completed in 18 months.

6-3. Contract for performance of a single concert, to be held on a specified date 13 months after the contract was entered.

6-4. Contract for 72 (or 260, or 2600) one-hour piano lessons, to be completed within 18 months.

6-5. Contract for 11 months of technology service, with service to begin 2 months after the contract is entered.

6-6. Contract to provide a life-time supply of Brand X car wax to the winner of a contest to submit "the best Brand X jingle."

In any of these cases, would it matter if the breach occurred the day after the contract was entered or, instead, the day before completion of contract performance? Would it matter whether the injured party filed a lawsuit immediately after breach or, instead, one day before expiration of the applicable statute of limitations?

§ 3.2. Does the Agreement Fall within an Exception to the Writing Requirement?

As discussed in an earlier section (page 632), the requirement of a writing is designed to accomplish evidentiary, cautionary, and channeling objectives: to provide courts with sufficient reliable evidence that a contract was formed; to ensure the contracting parties make thoughtful judgments in deciding to enter contracts; and to provide courts and parties with an easily applied line between enforceable and unenforceable contracts. The exceptions to the statute of frauds are grounded in the judgment that, under some circumstances, those purposes are served even without a writing.

§ 3.2.1. Contracts for the Sale of Goods

Reading the Law Critically: UCC Article 2 Exceptions

1. There are four exceptions identified in UCC § 2-201 (a confirmation between merchants, specially manufactured goods, admissions made by a party, and part performance). For each one, make a bullet list of the elements necessary to establish the exception. Some of the subsections contain multiple elements compressed into complex sentences; be sure to identify each separate requirement embedded in those provisions.

2. How should a party raise the statute of frauds defense so as not to risk invoking § 2-201(3)(b)?

3. Can performance by one party satisfy § 2-201(3)(c)?

4. Consider whether and how the purposes of the statute of frauds are accommodated by each exception (that is, why the exception should be recognized, given the purposes of the statute of frauds).

UCC § 2-201: Formal Requirements; Statute of Frauds

(1) . . . .

(2) Between merchants if within a reasonable time a writing in confirmation of the contract and sufficient against the sender is received and the party receiving it has reason to know its contents, it satisfies the requirements of subsection (1) against such party unless written notice of objection to its contents is given within 10 days after it is received.

(3) A contract which does not satisfy the requirements of subsection (1) but which is valid in other respects is enforceable

   (a) if the goods are to be specially manufactured for the buyer and are not suitable for sale to others in the ordinary course of the seller's business and the seller, before notice of repudiation is received and under circumstances which reasonably indicate that the goods are for the buyer, has made either a substantial beginning of their manufacture or commitments for their procurement; or

   (b) if the party against whom enforcement is sought admits in his pleading, testimony, or otherwise in court that a contract for sale was made, but the contract is not enforceable under this provision beyond the quantity of goods admitted; or

   (c) with respect to goods for which payment has been made and accepted or which have been received and accepted (Sec. 2-606).

What's That?

Under UCC § 2-606 (cited in § 2-201(3)(c)), "acceptance of goods" occurs only after the buyer has had a reasonable opportunity to inspect the goods to see if they conform to the contract. "Acceptance" may occur through express statements of the buyer, or because the buyer fails to effectively reject the goods, or because the buyer engages in acts that constitute an exercise of ownership over the goods.

§ 3.2.2. Part Performance Exception

The fact that a contractual promise has already been partially performed is a basis for enforcing some but not all classes of oral contracts. The "part performance exception" to the statute of frauds is grounded in equity and so is available only to obtain specific performance of a contract, not as a basis for obtaining damages for breach (though compelling specific information may include ordering payment of sums owed for part performance).

Make the Connection

The previous section reviewed UCC Article 2 exceptions to the requirement of a writing, applicable only to contracts for the sale of goods. This section and the next one discuss exceptions to the writing requirement applicable to other types of contracts. What parallels do you see between the UCC and non-UCC exceptions?

The most frequent application of this exception is to contracts for the sale of an interest in land. The party seeking enforcement must prove at least some acts in performance of the alleged contract (1) that demonstrate the injustice of failing to enforce the alleged contract and (2) that are, in the words of Judge Cardozo, "'unequivocally referable' to the agreement, performance which alone and without the aid of words of promise is unintelligible or at least extraordinary unless an incident of ownership."* The acts in performance thus serve an evidentiary function, establishing with a high degree of certainty the existence of the contract even in the absence of a signed written memorandum. Courts have usually considered only steps taken in performance of the contract

---

* *Burns v. McCormick*, 135 N.E. 273 (N.Y. 1922). Similarly, Corbin says that "the performance must be one that is in some degree evidential of the contract and not readily explainable on any other ground." 2 Arthur L. Corbin, *Corbin on Contracts* § 425 (1950). For a modern statement of a similar rule, *see, e.g., Owens v. M.E. Schepp Ltd. Partnership*, 182 P.3d 664, 668 (Ariz. 2008) ("So that this exception does not swallow the rule, the acts of part performance take an alleged contract outside the statute only if they cannot be explained in the absence of the contract.").

terms, such as taking possession of the land or making permanent improvements on it with the knowledge of the seller; paying all or part of the purchase price; payment of taxes on the land; and extensive services performed for the seller without other compensation.

The Restatement would broaden the exception for part performance of land transfer contracts to allow enforcement of any contract "if it is established that the party seeking enforcement, in reasonable reliance on the contract and on the continuing assent of the party against whom enforcement is sought, has so changed his position that injustice can be avoided only by specific enforcement." Restatement (Second) of Contracts § 129. At least one court has agreed with this approach, though it did not cite the Restatement provision. In Piazza v. Combs, 226 S.W.3d 211 (Mo. Ct. App. 2007), the plaintiff had spent considerable time and effort in anticipation of owning the property being sold, gathering information about the property's resources, developing business relationships and agreements with persons interested in acquiring those resources, and entering into agreements to resell portions of the property. Although these were acts "in preparation for, ancillary or collateral to, or in anticipation of" contract performance rather than actions in part performance of the land sales contract, the court concluded this to be the rare case in which "a party so changes his position in reliance upon a verbal contract . . . that to prevent the enforcement of the contract would amount to a deep-seated injustice." Id. at 224.

Most courts have refused to go as far as *Piazza* or Restatement (Second) § 129, expressing concern that modifying the standard in this fashion would undermine the statute of frauds for land sale contracts by weakening the evidentiary function of the part performance requirements. Such courts typically consider only acts of performance when deciding whether the party seeking enforcement has shown the existence of the contract sufficiently, though they will consider all acts of reliance to determine whether she has demonstrated a compelling need for intervention on equitable grounds.

The part performance exception has been applied to prenuptial contracts (contracts "in consideration of marriage") and to contracts to pay the debts of another. As with contracts for the transfer of interests in land, the party seeking enforcement must show part performance that is unequivocally referable to the existence of the alleged contract. See, e.g., Hall v. Hall, 222 Cal. App. 3d 578 (1990).

Courts have generally refused to apply the part performance exception to the one-year provision. Typical is the comment in *Coca-Cola Co. v. Babyback's International, Inc.*, 841 N.E.2d 557, 567 (Ind. 2006): "In

Think About It!

Why would the evidence of part performance be problematic with respect to the one-year provision, as *Coca-Cola Co.* suggests?

contrast to real estate contracts, where evidence of part performance is relatively clear, definite, and substantial, the nature of evidentiary facts potentially asserted to show part performance of an agreement not performable within one year would be vague, subjective, imprecise, and susceptible to fraudulent application."

§ 3.2.3. Equitable and Promissory Estoppel

Recall that a party may invoke equitable estoppel based on her reasonable reliance on the acts or representations of the other party inducing such reliance (see page 152 in Chapter 3). Thus, if a party to a contract represents that a writing is not needed or already was executed and the other party reasonably relies on that representation, the relying party may invoke equitable estoppel to prevent the party who made the representation from thereafter contradicting the representation by claiming that a writing *is* needed or was *not* executed. In effect, that party is barred from using the statute of frauds as a defense because of the other party's reasonable reliance on representations about the existence of a writing. Similarly, if a party had *promised* to put an agreement in writing or *promised* not to insist upon a writing for enforcement, the relying party may invoke promissory estoppel to prevent the promisor from reneging on that promise, effectively preventing her from raising the statute of frauds as a defense.

In the absence of any such promises to execute a writing or not to insist on having one, should an oral promise be enforceable based on promissory estoppel even though a writing is required by the statute of frauds? Courts are divided on that question. Such a use of promissory estoppel, it is argued, undermines the very purpose of requiring a writing; failing to enforce the statute of frauds based on the promisee's reliance rewards and thereby encourages reliance on oral promises and directly circumvents a rule designed to deter such reliance. Nonetheless, the trend appears to be in favor of recognizing the use of promissory estoppel, although—perhaps in recognition of those difficulties—courts often require that a party make an especially strong showing that the promise exists or show that she suffered substantial detriment, more than might be required to satisfy the Restatement (Second) § 90 standard. In response to such cases, the Restatement (Second) added new § 139, which uses the familiar language and syntax of § 90 (note the *italicized* language below) to craft a section applicable to statute-of-frauds situations:

Restatement (Second) § 139. **Enforcement by Virtue of Action in Reliance**

(1) *A promise which the promisor should reasonably expect to induce action or forbearance on the part of the promisee or a third person and which does induce the action or forbearance is* enforceable notwithstanding the

Statute of Frauds *if injustice can be avoided only by enforcement of the promise. The remedy granted for breach is to be limited as justice requires.*

(2) In determining whether injustice can be avoided only by enforcement of the promise, the following circumstances are significant:

    (a) the availability and adequacy of other remedies, particularly cancellation and restitution;

    (b) the definite and substantial character of the action or forbearance in relation to the remedy sought;

    (c) the extent to which the action or forbearance corroborates evidence of the making and terms of the promise, or the making and terms are otherwise established by clear and convincing evidence;

    (d) the reasonableness of the action or forbearance;

    (e) the extent to which the action or forbearance was foreseeable by the promisor.

Since the promulgation of § 139, more courts have been willing to entertain the promissory estoppel exception, but a minority of courts still hold that reliance should not be grounds for circumventing the statute of frauds, so the controversy continues. Because application of the promissory estoppel exception is uncertain, it is wise to use other exceptions to the statute of frauds before trying to invoke promissory estoppel.

Take Note!

In establishing when promissory estoppel should be available to make a promise enforceable "notwithstanding the Statute of Frauds," § 139(2) lists factors that may be considered in determining whether "injustice can be avoided only by enforcement." The list of factors— not included in the otherwise parallel § 90—reinforces the notion that "the requirement of consideration is more easily displaced than the requirement of a writing. . . . Each factor relates either to the extent to which reliance furnishes a compelling substantive basis for relief in addition to the expectations created by the promise or to the extent to which the circumstances satisfy the evidentiary purpose of the Statute and fulfill any cautionary, deterrent, and channeling functions it may serve." Restatement (Second) of Contracts § 139 comment b. While the Restatement drafters thus suggest that the factors are relevant to meeting a higher standard than is necessary under § 90, the list articulates factors that are useful to a court that must determine if injustice can be avoided only by enforcement of a promise, e.g, in § 87(2) (promissory restitution) and even in § 90 itself.

§ 4. Is there a Writing that Satisfies the Statute of Frauds?

§ 4.1. What Kind of Writing is Required?

If a contract is within the class of contracts identified as requiring the existence of a writing, if it does not fall within one of the exceptions, and if the statute of frauds is appropriately raised as an affirmative defense, the party seeking to enforce the contract in court must demonstrate that there is a writing that meets the requirements set out in the particular statute of frauds. Many of the state statutes require that the contract "or some note or memorandum thereof" be in writing and "subscribed" (signed) by the party to be charged. Some statutes also specify that the writing "express the consideration." These requirements are usually interpreted consistently with Restatement (Second) § 131:

Restatement (Second) § 131. **General Requisites of a Memorandum**

Unless additional requirements are prescribed by the particular statute, a contract within the Statute of Frauds is enforceable if it is evidenced by any writing, signed by or on behalf of the party to be charged, which
  (a) reasonably identifies the subject matter of the contract,
  (b) is sufficient to indicate that a contract with respect thereto has been made between the parties or offered by the signer to the other party, and
  (c) states with reasonable certainty the essential terms of the unperformed promises in the contract.

Comment g: Terms; accuracy. The degree of particularity with which the terms of the contract must be set out cannot be reduced to a formula. The writing must be the agreement or a memorandum "thereof"; a memorandum of a different agreement will not suffice. The "essential" terms of unperformed promises must be stated; "details or particulars" need not. What is essential depends on the agreement and its context and also on the subsequent conduct of the parties, including the dispute which arises and the remedy sought. Omission or erroneous statement of an agreed term makes no difference if the same term is supplied by implication or by rule of law. Erroneous statement of a term can sometimes be corrected by reformation. See § 155. Otherwise omission or misstatement of an essential term means that the memorandum is insufficient.

The requirement that there be a writing evidencing the contract is generally understood to mean:

- The writing does not have to be made as a memorandum of a contract; that is, the party need not have had the intent of writing down the contract, as long as the writing has the appropriate content. See Restatement (Second) § 133 (explaining in comment b that the memorandum "may consist of an entry in a diary or in the minutes of a meeting . . . or . . . communication of an informal letter to a third person").

Make the Connection

Note the similarity between the statute of frauds requirement that there be a writing that "states with reasonable certainty the essential terms" of the contract and the requirement that, for a contract to be enforceable, its terms must be sufficiently definite for the court to determine whether there has been a breach.(see Chapter 4, page 247)

- The writing does not have to be communicated to the other party to the contract. See Restatement (Second) § 133 cmt. b.

- The writing may be made "at any time before or after the formation of the contract." Restatement (Second) § 136.

- The writing need not exist at the time of trial; if the writing is lost or destroyed, "the contents of a memorandum [sufficient to satisfy the statute] may be shown by an unsigned copy or by oral evidence." Restatement (Second) § 137.

The requirement that the writing be "subscribed" or "signed" is further defined in the Restatement as well:

Restatement (Second) § 134. **Signature**

The signature to a memorandum may be any symbol made or adopted with an intention, actual or apparent, to authenticate the writing as that of the signer.

Comments:

a. Types of symbol. The traditional form of signature is of course the name of the signer, handwritten in ink. But initials, thumbprint or an arbitrary code sign may also be used; and the signature may be written in pencil, typed, printed, made with a rubber stamp, or impressed into the paper. Signed copies may be made with carbon paper or by photographic process.

b. Place of signature; "subscribed." . . . .[T]he signature need not appear on any particular part of the writing. Although it is usual to sign at the end of a document, a printed letterhead or billhead may be adopted as a signature. . . .

Reading the Law Critically:

Sufficiency of a Writing under UCC Article 2

Read UCC §§ 2-201 and 1-201 below. In what ways, if any, is the Restatement standard (see page 647, 648) harder to satisfy? In what ways, if any, is the UCC standard harder?

UCC § 2-201: **Formal Requirements; Statute of Frauds**

(1) Except as otherwise provided in this section a contract for the sale of goods for the price of $500 or more is not enforceable by way of action or defense unless there is some writing sufficient to indicate that a contract for sale has been made between the parties and signed by the party against whom enforcement is sought or by his authorized agent or broker. A writing is not insufficient because it omits or incorrectly states a term agreed upon but the contract is not enforceable under this paragraph beyond the quantity of goods shown in such writing.

. . . .

Comment 1: The required writing need not contain all the material terms of the contract and such material terms as are stated need not be precisely stated. All that is required is that the writing afford a basis for believing that the offered oral evidence rests on a real transaction. It may be written in lead pencil on a scratch pad. It need not indicate which party is the buyer and which the seller. The only term which must appear is the quantity term which need not be accurately stated but recovery is limited to the amount stated. The price, time and place of payment or delivery, the general quality of the goods, or any particular warranties may all be omitted. . . .

    Only three definite and invariable requirements as to the memorandum are made by this subsection. First, it must evidence a contract for the sale of goods; second, it must be "signed," a word which includes any authentication which identifies the party to be charged; and third, it must specify a quantity.

UCC § 1-201. **General Definitions**

. . . .

(37) "Signed" includes using any symbol executed or adopted with present intention to adopt or accept a writing. . . .

(43) "Writing" includes printing, typewriting, or any other intentional reduction to tangible form. "Written" has a corresponding meaning.

Comment 37: "Signed". . . . This provision also makes it clear that, as the term "signed" is used in the Uniform Commercial Code, a complete signature is not necessary. The symbol may be printed, stamped or written; it may be by initials or by thumbprint. It may be on any part of the document and in appropriate cases may be found in a billhead or letterhead. No catalog of possible situations can be complete and the court must use common sense and commercial experience in passing upon these matters. The question always is whether the symbol was executed or adopted by the party with present intention to adopt or accept the writing.

Reading the Law Critically: *Howard Construction Co.*

1. The parties disagreed about whether they ever reached an agreement for the sale of a particular kind of rock. Why does the court conclude that whether the contract was made is not a "material issue of fact"?

2. What particular language in UCC § 2-201 is the focus of the court's analysis? How does the court interpret that language?

3. Many sales of goods occur not through execution of a single contract document, but through the exchange of documents sent by buyer and seller to each other, identifying the goods to be sold along with quantity and price. In view of the court's analysis, what should a seller of goods put in a document it uses to respond to a purchase order, in order to ensure that the buyer will fail if the buyer raises a statute of frauds defense? What should a buyer of goods put in a purchase order it sends after receiving an offer to sell, in order to ensure that the seller will fail if the seller raises a statute of frauds defense?

Howard Construction Co. v. Jeff-Cole Quarries, Inc.

HOWARD CONSTRUCTION CO., Plaintiff-Appellant

v.

JEFF–COLE QUARRIES, INC., Defendant-Respondent

Missouri Court of Appeals

669 S.W.2d 221 (Mo. Ct. App. 1983)

NUGENT, Judge.

This case arose out of an action brought by Howard Construction Company (hereinafter "Howard Construction" or "Plaintiff") against Jeff-Cole Quarries, Inc. (hereinafter "Jeff-Cole" or "Defendant"), seeking damages on a breach of contract theory (Count I), or in the alternative, a promissory estoppel theory (Count II). The trial court granted summary judgment in favor of defendant on both Counts. Plaintiff contends on appeal that the trial court (1) erred in granting defendant's motion for summary judgment as to Count I . . . and (2) erred in finding that the statute of frauds barred Count I of plaintiff's complaint. We affirm the judgment.

Howard Construction was the successful bidder on a Missouri Highway Department project to construct a portion of Highway 54. Before Howard Construction was awarded the contract, it received from Jeff-Cole a typewritten document entitled "Proposal" [contained in an Appendix to the opinion] which referred to the Missouri Highway Project and listed descriptions, quantities and prices on types of rock needed for the project. The proposal contains six separate entries including a base type and asphaltic types of rock. It was dated November 21, 1972, and was signed by Harry Adrian, president of Jeff-Cole. The bid letting for the highway project took place in December, 1972, and Howard Construction was awarded the contract. Within a few weeks after the bid letting, the general superintendent of Howard Construction, Glenn Moore, met with Harry Adrian at defendant's office. The foregoing facts are not in dispute.

The parties do disagree, however, as to what occurred at that meeting. Plaintiff contends that Glenn Moore and Harry Adrian reached an oral agreement at the meeting and that Glenn Moore altered the typewritten prices on the proposal in his own handwriting to reflect the agreement that was reached. Plaintiff relies on Glenn Moore's deposition which reads as follows:

Q: Now, this particular document appears to have some figures written on it. Do you know anything about the various figures that are written in over the typing?

A: Yes, sir.

Q: What are those figures?

A: Those is [sic] after we got the job I went to Jeff-Cole's office and sat down with them. And those are the prices we came up with.

Q: All right, when you say you sat down with them, are you talking about Roger Adrian and Harry Adrian?

A: I'm talking about Harry Adrian.

. . . .

Q: Whose handwriting are those figures in if you know?

A: They are mine.

Q: You after discussion with Harry Adrian, changed—

A: We agreed on those prices that's [sic] written in.

Although defendant admits in its pleadings that discussions ensued between Jeff-Cole and Howard Construction, defendant denies that any agreement was ever reached in those discussions. Thus, the only disputed fact is whether the parties ever arrived at an agreement for the sale of asphaltic rock.

After the meeting between Mr. Moore and Mr. Adrian, at which the proposal was altered, Howard Construction, on January 12, 1973, mailed a purchase order to Jeff-Cole. It contained essentially the same items, quantities and prices listed on the altered proposal. The only other written document is a formal contract dated June 12, 1973, for the sale of base rock signed by agents of both parties. The subject matter of the contract, a base rock, is of the same description, quantity and price as the second entry on the altered proposal and the first entry on the purchase order.[3] The contract, however, does not refer to any of the other types of rock which the proposal and the purchase order listed.

On appeal, Howard Construction first claims that . . . the trial court's grant of summary judgment was . . . in error. Howard Construction contends that a genuine issue exists as to a material fact because the parties dispute whether or not they ever entered into an agreement for the sale of asphaltic rock.

. . . .

. . . Defendant argues that the dispute over whether an agreement was reached does not involve material facts because even if the court accepts as true plaintiff's assertion that an oral agreement was reached, the statute of frauds bars enforcement of that agreement.

---

[3] The contract was for the sale of: "ITEM NO. 304–01.02 TYPE 1 AGGR. FOR BASE APPROX. 99,600 TONS FOR A PRICE PER TON OF $1.55 WATER INCLUDED." The purchase order is reproduced in the appendix to this opinion.

If the contract for the sale of asphaltic rock is indeed unenforceable because of the statute of frauds, then the issue whether the oral contract was made is not a material issue of fact which would preclude the entry of summary judgment for Jeff-Cole. *Hammonds v. Calhoun Distributing Co.*, Inc., 584 S.W.2d 473, 475 (Tex.Civ.App.1979).

[The court quotes the text of § 2-201.] Subsection (1) sets forth the basic rules for satisfying the statute of frauds in a contract for the sale of goods for $500 or more. The Official Comment to the Uniform Commercial Code establishes "three definite and invariable requirements" as to the writing. First, the memorandum must evidence a contract for the sale of goods; second, it must be "signed," a word which includes any authentication which identifies the party to be charged; and third, the memorandum must specify a quantity.

Subsection (2) eliminates the signature requirement when both parties are merchants. If the merchant sending the confirmatory memorandum has met the requirements of the subsection and if the merchant receiving the writing does not give any notice of objection within ten days of its receipt, then the confirmatory writing need not be signed by the receiving merchant in order to satisfy the statute of frauds. Courts have, however, required that the writing be signed by the sender in order to be "sufficient against the sender." *E.g., Evans Implement Co. v. Thomas Industries, Inc.*, 117 Ga.App. 279, 160 S.E.2d 462, 463 (1968). The confirmatory memorandum must also state a quantity term and must be sufficient to indicate that a contract for sale has been made. Thus, in order for a writing to satisfy the requirements of subsection (2) it must meet the basic requirements of subsection (1) except that the confirmatory memorandum under subsection (2) need not be signed by the party to be charged; only the signature of the sender is required. *See Perdue Farms, Inc. v. Motts, Inc. of Mississippi*, 459 F.Supp. 7, 16 and nn. 15–16 (N.D.Miss.1978).

The primary requirement under both subsections (1) and (2) is that the writing evidence an agreement between the parties. Although the language of the two subsections differs in that subsection (1) requires "some writing sufficient to indicate that a contract for sale has been made" and subsection (2) requires "a writing in confirmation of the contract and sufficient against the sender," courts have found that the § 2-201(2) confirmatory memorandum must satisfy the "sufficient to indicate" requirement of § 2-201(1). *Harry Rubin & Sons, Inc. v. Consolidated Pipe Co. of America, Inc.*, 396 Pa. 506, 153 A.2d 472, 476 (1959). *See also* J. White & R. Summers, *Handbook of the Law Under the Uniform Commercial Code*, 62, 64 (2d ed. 1980).

The official comment to U.C.C. § 2-201 explains that "[a]ll that is required" for a writing to sufficiently indicate that a contract for sale has been made "is that the writing afford a basis for believing that the offered oral evidence rests on a real transaction." One writer has suggested that the spirit of the comments seems to be that "sufficient to indicate" is roughly equivalent to "more probably than not." J. White, *supra,* at 62. In other words, if it is more probable than not that the writing evidences a deal between the parties, then the writing should be found sufficient.

Case law on the "sufficient to indicate" requirement arises from interpretations of both § 2-201(1) and (2). Most courts have required that the writing indicate the consummation of a contract, not mere negotiations. *See, e.g., Oakley v. Little,* 49 N.C.App. 650, 272 S.E.2d 370, 372–73 (1980); *Rockland Industries, Inc. v. Frank Kasmir Associates,* 470 F.Supp. 1176, 1178–79 (N.D.Tex.1979). Thus, a writing which contained language indicating a tentative agreement has been found insufficient to indicate that a contract for sale had been made. *Arcuri v. Weiss,* 198 Pa.Super.Ct. 506, 184 A.2d 24, 26 (1962) (check inscribed with "tentative deposit on tentative purchase" held insufficient because it indicated no final commitment had been made). Writings which do not contain words indicating that a binding or completed transaction has occurred have been found insufficient. *E.g., Trilco Terminal v. Prebilt Corp.,* 167 N.J.Super. 449, 400 A.2d 1237, 1240–41 (N.J.Super.Ct.Law Div.1979) *aff'd. per curiam,* 174 N.J.Super. 24, 415 A.2d 356 (N.J.Super.Ct.App.Div.1980) (mere purchase orders which did not refer to previous agreement held insufficient). Some courts have required that the writings completely acknowledge the evidence of an agreement. *E.g., N. Dorman & Co., Inc. v. Noon Hour Food Products, Inc.,* 501 F.Supp. 294 (E.D.N.Y.1980). Even those courts giving a liberal interpretation to the requirement that the writing evidence an agreement have insisted that the terms of the writing at least must allow for the inference that an agreement had been reached between the parties. *See, e.g., Harry Rubin & Sons v. Consolidated Pipe Co. of America, Inc., supra,* 153 A.2d at 475–76; *Perdue Farms, Inc. v. Motts, Inc. of Mississippi, supra,* at 17 (where the words "confirmation of purchase" allow for inferences that writing confirmed some agreement previously made by the parties); *M.K. Metals, Inc. v. Container Recovery Corp.,* 645 F.2d 583, 591 (8th Cir.1981) (where the terms of the purchase order were so specifically and clearly geared to the desires of the party to be charged that the purchase order reflected a completed contract).

The Kansas Supreme Court, however, in *Southwest Engineering Co., Inc. v. Martin Tractor Co., Inc.,* 205 Kan. 684, 473 P.2d 18 (1970), held at 473 P.2d 26 that a mere price list afforded "a substantial basis for the belief that it rest[ed] on a real transaction." In that case, employees of the buyer and seller met and discussed the sale of a generator. The seller's employee listed the generator, various accessories, and their prices on a piece of paper on which he also handprinted his name and his company's name. The seller later refused to deliver the generator, and the buyer purchased a substitute for $27,541. The buyer sued for the difference in price, and the seller contended that the contract was unenforceable because of the statute of frauds, Kan. Stat. Ann. § 84.2-201 (1965). The Kansas Supreme Court held for the buyer and found that the writing met the statutory requirements.

The court's finding that the writing evidenced a contract has been severely criticized. See 84 Harv.L.Rev. 1737 (1971). That criticism stems from the fact that "[t]he memorandum before the court—on its face nothing more than a price list—was proof not of agreement, but, at most, only of negotiations." Id. at 1738. Finding such writing sufficient plants the seeds for allowing the statute of frauds to be satisfied by any evidence of mere negotiations.

While U.C.C. § 2-201 was indeed designed to eliminate much of the rigidity produced by prior interpretations of the statute of frauds, it retained some safeguards against fraudulent commercial practices. *Arcuri v. Weiss, supra*, 184 A.2d at 26. The requirement that the writing indicate that a contract for sale has been made is one of those safeguards. The words "as per our agreement," "in confirmation of," or "sold to buyer," would indicate that the parties had reached an agreement. Even the terms of the writing itself might be so specific and favorable to the party against whom the writing is offered that the court at least could draw the inference that an agreement had been reached. *See, e.g., M.K. Metals, Inc. v. Container Recovery Corp., supra,* at 591. Such writings would deter fraudulent assertions that a contract had been agreed upon where in fact only negotiations had taken place. The price list which the Kansas Supreme Court found sufficient to indicate that a contract had been made, however, contained no such words or terms. Thus, the decision in *Southwest Engineering* has been criticized as one that substantially weakens the protection offered by the statute of frauds, 84 Harv.L.Rev., supra, at 1739, and as a "case that may go too far." J. White, *supra,* at 62 n. 63.

In the case at bar, the writings are similar to the document in *Southwest Engineering.* We hold that they do not satisfy the requirements of U.C.C. § 2-201(1) or (2) because the writings, considered either separately or together, do not even allow for the inference that an agreement had been reached between the parties for the sale of asphaltic rock.

Although the typewritten proposal was signed by an agent of Jeff-Cole (prior to the handwritten alterations made thereon by plaintiff's agent) and states specific quantity terms, no words on the writing allow for the inference that any agreement was reached between the parties and therefore it does not by itself meet the primary requirement of either § 2-201(1) or (2).[6]

---

[6] The proposal could not suffice as a confirmatory memorandum under § 2-201(2) for the obvious reason that it was not delivered to Jeff-Cole.

Viewed in the light most favorable to the plaintiff, the unaltered proposal could be no more than an offer by Jeff-Cole.[7]

[The court concludes that the hand-written notations on the Proposal added by the plaintiff's agent did not constitute an acceptance under UCC § 2-207 because the changes in pricing were "significant divergences of material terms." The formal contract between Jeff-Cole and Howard also was not an acceptance for sale of asphaltic rock because it showed an agreement only as to sale of base rock.] Thus, the writings when taken together do not evidence a contract for the sale of asphaltic rock. At best, they evidence negotiations for the sale of asphaltic rock and a separate and completed contract for the sale of base rock.

Make the Connection

In footnote 7, the court discusses whether the price quotation in the proposal constituted an offer or instead an invitation to deal. The court's approach is consistent with the treatment in Chapter 4 (page 308), which covered when a price quotation may be understood as an offer.

Although Howard Construction concedes that the handwritten alterations on the proposal were made by Glenn Moore (Howard Construction's agent) *after* the proposal was signed by Jeff-Cole's agent, Howard Construction appears to argue that the proposal as altered reflects an agreement reached by the parties and thus satisfies § 2-201(1). Plaintiff argues that Glenn Moore's deposition, in which he asserted that he and Harry Adrian "agreed on those prices that's written in," tends to prove that an agreement was reached. While such evidence is indeed relevant to the issue of whether an agreement was reached between the parties (and would prevent the grant of summary judgment in favor of Jeff-Cole were it not for the bar of the statute of frauds), it is not relevant to the issue of whether the *writing itself* reflects an agreement. *R.S. Bennett & Co., Inc. v. Economy Mechanical Industries, Inc.*, 606 F.2d 182 (7th Cir.1979).

. . . .

Thus, the determination of whether the altered proposal satisfies the statute of frauds requirement that the writing at least allow for the inference that an

---

[7] A question remains as to whether the unaltered proposal even constituted an offer as opposed to a mere invitation to deal. Ordinarily, preliminary price quotations are not considered offers binding on the supplier. Thomas J. Sheehan Co. v. Crane Co., 418 F.2d 642, 645–46 (8th Cir.1969). Whether the proposal was an offer, and not merely a quotation of prices, depends upon the intentions of the offerer as manifested by the facts and circumstances of each particular case. Interstate Indus. v. Barclay Indus., 540 F.2d 868, 871 (7th Cir.1976); La Grange Metal Prod. v. Pettibone Mulliken Corp., 106 Ill.App.3d 1046, 62 Ill.Dec. 619, 624, 436 N.E.2d 645, 650 (1982). The *Sheehan* case does not control here because of the "specific terms" contained in the unaltered proposal. Moreover, Jeff-Cole refers to the unaltered proposal as an offer in its motion for summary judgment.

agreement was reached, must be made by looking solely to the writing itself. In so doing, we find that the proposal as altered by Glenn Moore's handprinted figures does not contain any terms which indicate that an agreement had been reached. The altered proposal is similar to the typewritten proposal in that neither contains terms from which the inference can be drawn that an agreement was reached between the parties. *Compare M.K. Metals, Inc. v. Container Corp., supra.* At best, the altered proposal may allow for the inference that the parties had negotiated.[8]

Howard Construction next contends that the purchase order sent by them to Jeff-Cole is a confirmatory memorandum which meets the requirements of § 2-201(2). The requirement under § 2-201(1) that the writing evidence an agreement applies with equal force to § 2-201(2). *Perdue Farms, Inc. v. Motts, Inc. of Mississippi, supra.* The purchase order thus fails to meet the requirements of § 2-201(2) for the same reason that the proposal (in its typewritten and altered form) failed to meet the requirements of § 2-201(1). It does not indicate that an agreement had been made. The purchase order, like the proposal, is void of any terms on its face which indicate or would allow us to infer that an agreement was ever reached between the parties. *See Trilco Terminal v. Prebilt Corp., supra; Harry Rubin & Sons v. Consolidated Pipe Co. of America, Inc., supra.* Nor does the fact that the terms of the purchase order correspond to the terms of the altered proposal create any basis on which we can make such an inference, either. *Compare M.K. Metals, Inc. v. Container Recovery Corp., supra* (where the terms of the purchase order allowed for inference of agreement even though no words indicating or referring to an agreement appeared in the writing). As we stated above, the altered proposal, at best, reflects nothing more than negotiations. It does not indicate that an agreement was ever reached between the parties for the sale of asphaltic rock.

None of the writings, whether analyzed separately or in conjunction with each other allows for the inference that an agreement was reached between Jeff-Cole and Howard Construction. The primary requirement under § 2-201(1) and (2) that the writing evidence a contract has thus not been satisfied. The statute of frauds therefore bars further evidence of the alleged agreement and bars enforcement of the same as a matter of law. *Womack v. Worthington, supra; Hammonds v. Calhoun Distributing Co., supra.* Because the alleged oral contract for the sale of asphaltic rock is unenforceable as a matter of law under the statute of frauds, we hold that the trial court's grant of summary judgment in favor of Jeff-Cole was proper.

Howard Construction's contention that the statute of frauds should not bar Count I of its complaint because the "defendant has performed in part," is without merit. U.C.C. § 2-201(3)(c) provides:

---

[8] As was explained above, the altered proposal might also constitute a counteroffer by Howard Construction but as no acceptance was ever given by Jeff-Cole to Howard Construction for the sale of asphaltic rock, the writings evidence only negotiations.

(3) A contract which does not satisfy the requirements of subsection (1) but which is valid in other respects is enforceable

. . . .

(c) with respect to goods for which payment has been made and accepted or which have been received and accepted....

The exception to the writing requirement in this subsection limits enforceability to the goods that the buyer has received and accepted or paid for. *Sedmak v. Charlie's Chevrolet, Inc.*, 622 S.W.2d 694 (Mo.App.1981).

base rock contract fulfilled

This subsection validates a divisible contract only for as much of the goods as have been delivered and paid for. *Sedmak v. Charlie's Chevrolet, Inc., supra.* Only the base rock—the subject matter of the formal contract—was delivered and paid for. No asphaltic rock—the subject matter of the alleged oral contract—was ever delivered or paid for. The delivery of the base rock can only be deemed complete performance of the parties' separate contract for the sale of base rock. Thus, the statute of frauds still bars enforcement of Howard Construction's alleged oral contract for the sale of asphaltic rock.

. . . .

Accordingly, we affirm the judgment of the trial court.

All concur.

APPENDIX EXHIBIT 1

JEFF-COLE QUARRIES, .INC.
GENERAL CONTRACTORS
HIGHWAY 54 SOUTH
JEFFERSON CITY, MISSOURI 65101

NOVEMBER 21, 1972

P R O P O S A L

RE: MISSOURI STATE HIGHWAY
PROJ. OP-F-54-3(37)
ROUTE 54. COLE COUNTY

ITEM NO.	DESCRIPTION	QUANTITY	UNIT	UNIT PRICE	TOTAL AMOUNT
301-20.00	MINERAL AGGR. AITUM. BASE	85,795.0	TONS 1.55	1.65	HAUL .52 1.70
304-01.02	✓TYPE 1 AGGR. FOR BASE	99,600.0	TONS 1.55	1.55	TAX 05 2.22
310-50.02	✓GRAVEL (n) OR STONE (B)	3,908.0	TONS 1.80	1.85	
390-90.00	✓TEMPORARY SURFACING	150.0	TONS 1.80	1.85	
403-70.00	1″ MIN'L AGGR. TYPE "B" ASPH.	13,000 35,996.0	TONS 2 331.00	2.45	2.40 2.65 / 2.65
403-80.00	½″ MIN'L AGGR. TYPE "C" ASPH.	5,000 20,13,117.0	TONS /	2.45	2.40

TOTAL FOR PROJECT.. _____

WE HAVE THREE (3) SITES AVAILABLE ON THE PROJECT. SITE __A__ IS BETWEEN STA. *plant ut.*
763+00 AND STA. 775+00, APPROX. 500 FT OFF RT. 54. SITE __B__ IS BETWEEN STA.
815+00 AND STA. 830+00, APPROX. 2000 FT. OFF RT. 54. SITE __C__ IS BETWEEN STA.
940+00 AND STA. 970+00, APPROX. 500 FT. OFF AT 54.

WE PREFER SITE _____ , HOWEVER, IT WILL BE OUR OPTION TO SELECT THE SITE AFTER
FINAL DETERMINATION OF THE ROCK QUALITY IS MADE. AN ASPHALT PLANT SITE WILL BE
AVAILABLE AT 3 LOCATIONS.

THE PRICE FOR TYPE 1 AGGR. FOR BASE ABOVE INCLUDES PUGGING. IF YOU PREFER
TO USE HIGHWAY DEPARTMENT BATCH WEIGHTS IN LIEU OF OUR SCALE WEIGHTS ON THE MINERAL
AGGR. BITUMINOUS BASE AND AGGR. FOR TYPES "B" & "C" ASPHALT MIX, ADD THE FOLOWING;

MINERAL AGGR. PITUM. BASE   15% 10%
MINERAL AGGR. TYPE "B"   15% 10%
MINERAL AGGR. TYPE "C"   15% 10%

RESPECTFULLY SUBMITTED,

Harry M. Adrian

HARRY M. ADRIAN, PRESIDENT
JEFF-COPE QUARRIES, INC.

APPENDIX EXHIBIT 2

APPENDIX—Continued

EXHIBIT 2

PURCHASE ORDER

N⁰ 322

Howard Construction Company

& AFFILIATED COMPANIES
1504 North Osage — Sedalia, Missouri

SOLD TO: Jeff ~~IKIII~~ Cole Quarries.
Highway 54 South
Jefferson City, Missouri

PROJECT: DP-7-54-3(37)
Route 54
Cole, County

lease Invoice   HOWARD ☒ CONSTRUCTION COMPANY.   Job #92

☐ BRIDGE
☐ QUARRIES

PRICES AS PER QUOTATION DATED: **1/2/73**

QUANTITY	ITEM	UNIT PRICE	TOTAL PRICE
99,600 Tons	Type 1 Aggregate for Base (Pugged)	1.55	154,380.00
3,908 Tons	Crushed Stone (B)	1.80	7,034.40
150 Tons	Temporary Surfacing	1.80	270.00
85,795 Tons	Mineral Aggregate (Bit. Base)	1.70	145,851.50
33,000 Tons	Crushed Rock for Type B & C Asphalt	2.65	87,450.00

Rock for Mineral Aggregate (Bit. Base) and
Type B & C Asphalt will be batch weights
from job mix approved by the M.S.H.D.

Net 15 Days   TOTAL

ALL MATERIAL TO MEET THE MINIMUM REQUIREMENTS OF THE SPECIFICATIONS FOR THE PROJECT SHOWN ABOVE.

By: *Jake Moore*
General Supt.

ACCEPTED BY:

Title:

(handwritten left margin) all base rock prices are same as scribbles

WEST KEY NUMBER SYSTEM

Problems: What Kind of Writing is Required?

Under each standard (the Restatement and the UCC):

6-7. True or False: The statute of frauds requires certain kinds of contracts to be <u>entirely</u> written. *no*

6-8. If the plaintiff sues, alleging breach of contract, and the defendant raises the statute of frauds defense, whose signature is necessary for enforcement of the contract? *D*

6-9. Does a printed copy of a word-processing document constitute a "writing"? *yes* *intentional reduction into tangible form*

6-10. Does the name in the "From" field of an email constitute a signature under the statute of frauds? *maybe, yes - you can control who it comes from*

6-11. Does a written signed offer satisfy the statute of frauds in a suit against the offeror? In a suit against the offeree? *nope, only contract*

Reading the Law Critically: *Sterling*

As already noted, Restatement (Second) § 131 requires that contracts within the statute of frauds be evidenced by a writing that "states with reasonable certainty the essential terms of the unperformed promises in the contract," and state statutes of frauds are generally understood as specifying the same requirements. But how much certainty is required? And should a court consider evidence from outside the writing itself to create sufficient certainty to satisfy the statute of frauds?

1. What does the court conclude about how much certainty is required, and what evidence may be used to establish it?

2. Do you agree with the rule the court adopts? With the way the court applies the rule to the facts of the case?

Sterling v. Taylor

ROCHELLE STERLING et al., Plaintiffs-Appellants

v.

LAWRENCE N. TAYLOR et al., Defendants-Respondents

Supreme Court of California

152 P.3d 420 (Cal. 2007)

CORRIGAN, J.

The statute of frauds provides that certain contracts "are invalid, unless they, or some note or memorandum thereof, are in writing and subscribed by the party to be charged. . . ." (Civ.Code, § 1624.) In this case, the Court of Appeal held that a memorandum regarding the sale of several apartment buildings was sufficient to satisfy the statute of frauds. Defendants contend the court improperly considered extrinsic evidence to resolve uncertainties in the terms identifying the seller, the property, and the price.

We reverse, but not because the court consulted extrinsic evidence. Extrinsic evidence has long been held admissible to clarify the terms of a memorandum for purposes of the statute of frauds. Statements to the contrary appear in some cases, but we disapprove them. A memorandum serves only an evidentiary function under the statute. If the writing includes the essential terms of the parties' agreement, there is no bar to the admission of relevant extrinsic evidence to explain or clarify those terms. The memorandum, viewed in light of the evidence, must be sufficient to demonstrate with reasonable certainty the terms to which the parties agreed to be bound. Here, plaintiffs attempt to enforce a price term that lacks the certainty required by the statute of frauds.

1. FACTUAL AND PROCEDURAL BACKGROUND

In January 2000, defendant Lawrence Taylor and plaintiff Donald Sterling discussed the sale of three apartment buildings in Santa Monica owned by the Santa Monica Collection partnership (SMC). Defendant was a general partner in SMC. Plaintiff and defendant, both experienced real estate investors, met on March 13, 2000 and discussed a series of transactions including the purchase of the SMC properties. At this meeting, plaintiff drafted a handwritten memorandum entitled "Contract for Sale of Real Property."

The memorandum encompasses the sale of five properties; only the [three] SMC properties are involved here. They are identified in the memorandum as "808 4th St.," "843 4th St.," and "1251 14th St.," with an aggregate price term of "approx. 10.468 x gross income[,] estimated income 1.600.000, *Price $16,750.00.*"

Although defendant had given plaintiff rent rolls showing the income from the properties, neither man brought these documents to the March 13 meeting. Plaintiff dated and initialed the memorandum as "Buyer," but the line he provided for "Seller" was left blank. Plaintiff contends the omission was inadvertent. Defendant, however, asserts he did not sign the document because he needed approval from a majority of SMC's limited partners.

On March 15, 2000, plaintiff wrote to defendant, referring to the properties by street address only, and stating "[t]his letter will confirm our contract of sale of the above buildings." The letter discussed deposits plaintiff had given to defendant, and noted "our agreement that the depreciation allocation and tax benefits will be given to me no later than April 1, 2000, since I now have equitable tittle [sic]." Price terms were not mentioned. Both parties signed the letter, defendant beneath the handwritten notation "Agreed, Accepted, & Approved."

Plaintiff claims the March 13 memorandum was attached to the March 15 letter, which defendant annotated and signed in his presence. Defendant insists nothing was attached to the March 15 letter, which he did not sign until March 30. According to defendant, his signature reflected only an accommodation to acknowledge the deposits he had received from plaintiff.

On April 4, 2000, defendant sent plaintiff three formal purchase agreements with escrow instructions, identifying the properties by their legal descriptions. SMC was named as the seller and the Sterling Family Trust as the buyer. The price terms totalled $16,750,000. Defendant signed the agreements as a general partner of SMC. Plaintiff refused to sign. Defendant claims plaintiff telephoned on April 28, saying the purchase price was unacceptable. Plaintiff asserts that after reviewing the rent rolls, he determined the actual rental income from the SMC buildings was $1,375,404, not $1,600,000 as estimated on the March 13 memorandum. Plaintiff claims he tried to have defendant correct the escrow instructions, but defendant did not return his calls. Plaintiff wanted to lower the price to $14,404,841, based on the actual rental income figure and the 10.468 multiplier noted in the memorandum.[2]

Plaintiff did not ask for the $16,750.00 purchase price stated in the memorandum. He admits that he "accidentally left off one zero" when he wrote down that figure. Defendant also acknowledges that the price recorded on the memorandum was meant to be $16,750,000.[3]

---

[2] The formula does not yield the plaintiff's modified price: $1,375,404 multiplied by 10.468 is $14,397,729. In a declaration filed in the trial court, plaintiff explained that he made two mistakes in arriving at the figure of $14,404,841, one in the rental income calculation and another in the multiplier he applied to that figure.

[3] Given the superscript notation employed by plaintiff when he wrote "$16,750.00" [the number appeared as $16,750.00 in the handwritten memorandum], it might be said that *three* zeros were omitted from the price. However, the characterization of the error is immaterial in light of the parties' agreement that the intended figure was $16,750,000.

Defendant returned plaintiff's uncashed deposit checks on May 23. The parties conducted further negotiations in December 2000 and January 2001. Defendant provided additional rent rolls, but no agreement was reached.

In March 2001 the trustees of the Sterling Family Trust sued Taylor, SMC, and related entities, alleging breach of a written contract to sell the properties for a total price of $14,404,841. The March 13 memorandum and the March 15 letter were attached to the complaint as the "Purchase Agreement." The complaint included causes of action for breach of the implied covenant of good faith and fair dealing, specific performance, declaratory relief, an accounting, intentional misrepresentation, and imposition of a constructive trust.

Defendants sought summary judgment, claiming that no contract was formed, the alleged contract violated the statute of frauds, and plaintiffs could not prove fraud. Defendants contended the memorandum and letter did not satisfy the statute because they established no agreement on price, failed to sufficiently identify either the contracting parties or the properties, and were not signed by Taylor and Christina Development. The trial court granted summary judgment. It ruled that the price term was too uncertain to be enforced and the writings did not comply with the statute of frauds. The court also concluded that the undisputed facts disclosed neither a fraudulent intent on defendant's part nor damages to plaintiff, thus foreclosing the misrepresentation claim.

The Court of Appeal reversed as to the contract causes of action, but remanded for entry of summary adjudication in defendants' favor on the fraud claim. The court held that Taylor's name and signature on the writings submitted by plaintiffs satisfied the statute of frauds. It also deemed the identification of the properties by street address sufficient, in light of extrinsic evidence specifying the city and state. Likewise, the court held that the price terms in the March 13 memorandum, while ambiguous, could be clarified by examining extrinsic evidence. It concluded that defendants' evidence raised a triable issue as to whether the parties had agreed on a formula for determining the purchase price. The court further ruled that the fraud claim failed because plaintiffs could not prove damages. Only the contract claims are at issue in this appeal.

II. DISCUSSION

Defendants contend the Court of Appeal improperly considered extrinsic evidence to establish essential contract terms. They insist the statute of frauds requires a memorandum that, standing alone, supplies all material elements of the contract. Plaintiffs, on the other hand, argue that extrinsic evidence is routinely admitted for the purpose of determining whether memoranda comply with the statute of frauds.[4]

Both sides of this debate find support in California case law, sometimes in the same opinion. Part A of our discussion explains that plaintiffs' view is correct. The statute of frauds does not preclude the admission of evidence in any form; it imposes a writing requirement, but not a comprehensive one. In part B, however, we conclude that defendants are nevertheless entitled to judgment. The Court of Appeal properly considered the parties' extrinsic evidence, but erroneously deemed it legally sufficient under the statute of frauds to establish the price sought by plaintiffs.

A. The Memorandum Requirement of the Statute of Frauds

The statute of frauds does not require a written contract; a "note or memorandum . . . subscribed by the party to be charged" is adequate. (Civ.Code, § 1624, subd. (a).)[5] In *Crowley v. Modern Faucet Mfg. Co.* (1955) 44 Cal.2d 321, 282 P.2d 33, we observed that "[a] written memorandum is not identical with a written contract [citation]; it is merely evidence of it and usually does not contain all of the terms." (Id. at p. 323, 282 P.2d 33; see also *Kerner v. Hughes Tool Co.* (1976) 56 Cal.App.3d 924, 934, 128 Cal.Rptr. 839; 1 Witkin, Summary of Cal. Law, *supra,* Contracts, § 350, p. 397.) Indeed, in most instances it is not even necessary that the parties intended the memorandum to serve a contractual purpose.[6] (Rest.2d Contracts, § 133; 1 Witkin, Summary of Cal. Law, *supra,* Contracts, § 352, p. 398; see *Moss v. Atkinson* (1872) 44 Cal. 3, 16–17.)

A memorandum satisfies the statute of frauds if it identifies the subject of the parties' agreement, shows that they made a contract, and states the essential contract terms with reasonable certainty. (Rest.2d Contracts, § 131; 1 Witkin, Summary of Cal. Law, *supra,* Contracts, § 353, p. 399.) "Only the essential terms must be stated, ' "details or particulars" need not [be]. What is essential depends on the

---

[4] Defendants' argument is supported by amicus curiae Professor Richard A. Lord, current editor of the fourth edition of Williston on Contracts. The Apartment Association of Greater Los Angeles has also contributed an amicus curiae brief, urging us in cursory fashion to reverse the Court of Appeal's decision in order to discourage "dishonest dealing and sharp real estate practice."

   Amicus curiae California Association of Realtors favors plaintiffs' position, arguing that ambiguities are not unusual in real estate transactions and resort to extrinsic evidence is required to prevent parties who have second thoughts from escaping their contractual obligations.

[5] Civil Code section 1624, subdivision (a) states: "The following contracts are invalid, unless they, or some note or memorandum thereof, are in writing and subscribed by the party to be charged or by the party's agent[.]" Subdivision (a)(3) of section 1624 includes agreements for the sale of real property. Our discussion does not apply to any other "statute of frauds" imposing a stricter writing requirement. (. . . See, e.g., Fam.Code, § 852 [transmutation agreements involving separate and community property]; Fam.Code, § 1611 [premarital agreements]; Civ.Code, § 1803.1 et seq. [retail installment contracts].) Nor does our discussion govern the more liberal statute of frauds provided in the California Uniform Commercial Code. (Cal. U. Com.Code, § 2201.)

agreement and its context and also on the subsequent conduct of the parties. . . .' (*Rest.2d Contracts*, § 131, com. g, p. 338.)" (*Seaman's Direct Buying Service, Inc. v. Standard Oil Co.* (1984) 36 Cal.3d 752, 762–763, 206 Cal.Rptr. 354, 686 P.2d 1158, overruled on another point in *Freeman & Mills, Inc. v. Belcher Oil Co.* (1995) 11 Cal.4th 85, 88, 44 Cal.Rptr.2d 420, 900 P.2d 669.)

This court recently observed that the writing requirement of the statute of frauds "'serves only to prevent the contract from being unenforceable' [citation]; it does not necessarily establish the terms of the parties' contract." (*Casa Herrera, Inc. v. Beydoun* (2004) 32 Cal.4th 336, 345, 9 Cal.Rptr.3d 97, 83 P.3d 497.) Unlike the parol evidence rule, which "determines the enforceable and incontrovertible terms of an integrated written agreement," the statute of frauds "merely serve[s] an evidentiary purpose." (*Ibid.*) As the drafters of the Second Restatement of Contracts explained: "The primary purpose of the Statute is evidentiary, to require reliable evidence of the existence and terms of the contract and to prevent enforcement through fraud or perjury of contracts never in fact made. The contents of the writing must be such as to make successful fraud unlikely, but the possibility need not be excluded that some other subject matter or person than those intended will also fall within the words of the writing. Where only an evidentiary purpose is served, *the requirement of a memorandum is read in the light of the dispute which arises and the admissions of the party to be charged*; there is no need for evidence on points not in dispute." (*Rest.2d Contracts*, § 131, com. c, p. 335, italics added; accord, *Seaman's Direct Buying Service, Inc. v. Standard Oil Co., supra,* 36 Cal.3d at pp. 764–765, 206 Cal.Rptr. 354, 686 P.2d 1158.)

Make the Connection

The question addressed in *Sterling* is whether and how to use extrinsic evidence in establishing that a writing is sufficient to satisfy the statute of frauds. As the court's reference suggests, whether extrinsic evidence may be used along with the writing to determine the terms of the contract is a different question, analyzed under the parol evidence rule, which is discussed in chapter 7, (page 749).

Thus, when ambiguous terms in a memorandum are disputed, extrinsic evidence is admissible to resolve the uncertainty. (*In re Marriage of Benson, supra,* 36 Cal.4th at p. 1108, 32 Cal.Rptr.3d 471, 116 P.3d 1152; *Seaman's Direct Buying Service, Inc. v. Standard Oil Co., supra,* 36 Cal.3d at p. 763, fn. 2, 206 Cal.Rptr. 354, 686 P.2d 1158; *Beverage v. Canton Placer Mining Co.* (1955) 43 Cal.2d 769, 774–775, 278 P.2d 694; *Searles v. Gonzalez* (1923) 191 Cal. 426, 431–433, 216 P. 1003.) Extrinsic evidence can also support reformation of a memorandum to correct a mistake. (*Rest.2d Contracts*, § 131, com. g, p. 338; *Calhoun v. Downs* (1931) 211 Cal. 766, 768–770, 297 P. 548; 1 Witkin, Summary of Cal. Law, *supra,* Contracts, §§ 355, 356, pp. 403–404.)

Because the memorandum itself must include the essential contractual terms, it is clear that extrinsic evidence cannot *supply* those required terms. (See, e.g., *Friedman v. Bergin* (1943) 22 Cal.2d 535, 537–539, 140 P.2d 1.) It can, however, be used to *explain* essential terms that were understood by the parties but would otherwise be unintelligible to others. Two early cases from this court demonstrate that a memorandum can satisfy the statute of frauds, even if its terms are too uncertain to be enforceable when considered by themselves.

In *Preble v. Abrahams* (1891) 88 Cal. 245, 26 P. 99, a written agreement for the sale of land described the property to be sold as " 'forty acres of the eighty-acre tract at Biggs.' " (*Id.* at p. 248, 26 P. 99.) The court observed: "An agreement not in writing for the sale and purchase of real estate is void. And the description of the property in the written agreement is so entirely uncertain as to render the instrument inoperative and void, unless we can go beyond the face of it to ascertain its meaning." (*Id.* at pp. 249–250, 26 P. 99.)

To give effect to the agreement, the *Preble* court relied on extrinsic evidence that another buyer had purchased one 40-acre tract and the defendant had agreed to purchase the remainder. (*Preble v. Abrahams*, supra, 88 Cal. at p. 250, 26 P. 99.) "We think the evidence makes the subject-matter sufficiently certain, and that is all that is necessary. Professor Pomeroy says: 'It is not strictly accurate to say that the subject-matter must be absolutely certain from the writing itself, or by reference to some other writing. The true rule is, that the situation of the parties and the surrounding circumstances, when the contract was made, can be shown by parol evidence, so that the court may be placed in the position of the parties themselves; and if *then* the subject-matter is identified, and the terms appear reasonably certain, it is enough.' (Pomeroy on Contracts, sec. 227, note.)" (*Preble v. Abrahams*, supra, 88 Cal. at pp. 250–251, 26 P. 99.)

In *Brewer v. Horst–Lachmund Co.* (1900) 127 Cal. 643, 60 P. 418, a contract was memorialized by two telegrams employing a form of shorthand notation so arcane that "[i]f there were nothing to look to but the telegrams, the court might find it difficult, if not impossible, to determine the nature of the contract, or that any contract was entered into between the parties." (*Id.* at p. 646, 60 P. 418.) The defendant contended the telegrams were an insufficient "note or memorandum" to satisfy the statute of frauds. (*Ibid.*) The *Brewer* court disagreed, stating: "[T]he court is permitted to interpret the memorandum (consisting of the two telegrams) by the light of all the circumstances under which it was made; and if, when the court is put into possession of all the knowledge which the parties to the transaction had at the time, it can be plainly seen from the memorandum who the parties to the contract were, what the subject of the contract was, and what were its terms, then the court should not hesitate to hold the memorandum sufficient. Oral evidence may be received to show in what sense figures or abbreviations were used; and their meaning may be explained as it was understood between the parties." (*Ibid.*)

. . . .

Despite this venerable authority, conflicting statements appear in other California cases: "The sufficiency of a writing to satisfy the statute of frauds cannot be established by evidence which is extrinsic to the writing itself. (Code Civ. Proc., § 1973.) " (*Franklin v. Hansen* (1963) 59 Cal.2d 570, 573–574, 30 Cal.Rptr. 530, 381 P.2d 386.) "The preeminent qualification of a memorandum under the statute of frauds is 'that it must contain the essential terms of the contract, expressed with such a degree of certainty that it may be understood without recourse to parol evidence to show the intention of the parties.' (5 Browne on Statute of Frauds, sec. 371.)" (*Zellner v. Wassman* (1920) 184 Cal. 80, 85–86, 193 P. 84; accord, e.g., *Seymour v. Oelrichs* (1910) 156 Cal. 782, 787, 106 P. 88.) "The whole object of the statute would be frustrated if any substantive portion of the agreement could be established by parol evidence." (*Craig v. Zelian* (1902) 137 Cal. 105, 106, 69 P. 853; accord, e.g., *Seymour v. Oelrichs, supra,* 156 Cal. at p. 787, 106 P. 88.)[10]

"Unless the writing, considered alone, expresses the essential terms with sufficient certainty to constitute an enforceable contract, it fails to meet the demands of the statute. [Citations.]" (*Burge v. Krug* (1958) 160 Cal.App.2d 201, 207, 325 P.2d 119; *Ellis v. Klaff* (1950) 96 Cal.App.2d 471, 477, 216 P.2d 15.) Defendants rely on these and similar cases to argue that the Court of Appeal improperly considered extrinsic evidence to determine the meaning of essential but imperfectly stated terms in the memorandum drafted by plaintiff Sterling.

To clarify the law on this point, we disapprove the statements in California cases barring consideration of extrinsic evidence to determine the sufficiency of a memorandum under the statute of frauds. The purposes of the statute are not served by such a rigid rule, which has never been a consistent feature of the common law. Corbin observes: "Judicial dicta abound to the effect that the writing must contain all of the 'essential terms and conditions' of the contract, and it is often said that these must be so clear as to be understood 'without any aid from parol testimony.' But the long course of judicial decision shows that 'essential

---

[10] *Craig* presents an interesting comparison with *Preble v. Abrahams, supra.* The description of the land to be conveyed in *Craig* ("'a strip of land in front of Golden Rule Store and Stent Market'") was as vague as the description in *Preble* ("'forty acres of the eighty-acre tract at Biggs'"). (*Craig v. Zelian, supra,* 137 Cal. at p. 106, 69 P. 853; *Preble v. Abrahams, supra,* 88 Cal. at p. 250, 26 P. 99.) But in *Preble* extrinsic evidence explained the description in the memorandum, whereas in *Craig* the only extrinsic aid to locating the property was a map that was not in evidence. (*Craig v. Zelian, supra,* 137 Cal. at p. 106, 69 P. 853.) On its facts, *Craig* is properly viewed as a case of insufficient extrinsic evidence, rather than one where the writing itself was necessarily deficient.

terms and conditions' is itself a term of considerable flexibility and that the courts do not in fact blind themselves by excluding parol testimony when it is a necessary aid to understanding." (4 Corbin on Contracts (rev. ed.1997) § 22.2, pp. 706–707, fns. omitted.)[12]

"Some confusion is attributable to a failure to keep clearly in mind the purpose of the statute and the informal character of the evidence that the actual words of the statute require; some is no doubt due to differences in the attitude of the judges as to the beneficence of the statute and the wisdom of its existence. Further, there are differences in the strictness of judicial requirements as to the contents of the memorandum. It is believed that sometimes these apparent differences can be explained by the degree of doubt existing in the court's mind as to the actual making and performance of the alleged contract. The better and the more disinterested is the oral testimony offered by the plaintiff, the more convincing the corroboration that is found in the surrounding circumstances, and the more limited the disputed issue because of admissions made by the defendant, the less that should be and is required of the written memorandum." (4 Corbin on Contracts, *supra,* § 22.2, p. 709, fn. omitted.)

Williston offers similar counsel: "In determining the requisites and meaning of a 'note or memorandum in writing,' courts often look to the origin and fundamental purpose of the Statute of Frauds. In fact, a failure to do so will often result in a futile preoccupation with the numerous and conflicting precepts and decisions involving the clauses providing for a note or memorandum, and a corresponding failure to see the forest for the trees.

"The Statute of Frauds was not enacted to afford persons a means of evading just obligations; nor was it intended to supply a cloak of immunity to hedging litigants lacking integrity; nor was it adopted to enable defendants to interpose the Statute as a bar to a contract fairly, and admittedly, made. In brief, the Statute 'was intended to guard against the perils of perjury and error in the spoken word.' Therefore, if after a consideration of the surrounding circumstances, the pertinent facts and all the evidence in a particular case, the court concludes that enforcement of the agreement will not subject the defendant to fraudulent claims, the purpose of the Statute will best be served by holding the note or memorandum sufficient even though it is ambiguous or incomplete." (10 Williston on Contracts (4th ed.1999) § 29:4, pp. 437–438, fns. omitted.)[12]

The governing principle is: "That is certain which can be made certain." (Civ. Code, § 3538; *Beverage v. Canton Placer Mining Co., supra,* 43 Cal.2d at p. 774, 278 P.2d 694; see also, e.g., *Preble v. Abrahams, supra,* 88 Cal. at p. 251,

---

[12] Williston, like this court in *Franklin v. Hansen* (see fn. 9, *ante*), has embraced conflicting views. In a later section, the treatise quotes *Ellis v. Klaff, supra,* 96 Cal.App.2d 471, 216 P.2d 15, for the proposition that " 'the writing, considered alone' " must " 'express[ ] the essential terms with sufficient certainty to constitute an enforceable contract.' " (10 Williston on Contracts, *supra,* § 29:8, p. 472.)

26 P. 99; *Alameda Belt Line v. City of Alameda* (2003) 113 Cal.App.4th 15, 21, 5 Cal.Rptr.3d 879.) We hold that if a memorandum includes the essential terms of the parties' agreement, but the meaning of those terms is unclear, the memorandum is sufficient under the statute of frauds if extrinsic evidence clarifies the terms with reasonable certainty and the evidence as a whole demonstrates that the parties intended to be bound. Conflicts in the extrinsic evidence are for the trier of fact to resolve, but whether the evidence meets the standard of reasonable certainty is a question of law for the court. (*Phillippe v. Shapell Industries* (1987) 43 Cal.3d 1247, 1258, 241 Cal.Rptr. 22, 743 P.2d 1279; *Niles v. Hancock* (1903) 140 Cal. 157, 163, 73 P. 840.)

We emphasize that a memorandum of the parties' agreement is *controlling* evidence under the statute of frauds. Thus, extrinsic evidence cannot be employed to prove an agreement at odds with the terms of the memorandum. This point was made in *Beazell v. Schrader* (1963) 59 Cal.2d 577, 30 Cal.Rptr. 534, 381 P.2d 390. There, the plaintiff sought to recover a 5 percent real estate broker's commission under an oral agreement. (*Id.* at p. 579, 30 Cal.Rptr. 534, 381 P.2d 390.) The escrow instructions, which specified a 1.25 percent commission, were the "memorandum" on which the plaintiff relied to comply with the statute. However, he contended the instructions incorrectly reflected the parties' actual agreement, as shown by extrinsic evidence. (*Id.* at p. 580, 30 Cal.Rptr. 534, 381 P.2d 390.) The *Beazell* court rejected this argument, holding that under the statute of frauds, "the parol agreement of which the writing is a memorandum must be one whose terms are consistent with the terms of the memorandum." (*Id.* at p. 582, 30 Cal.Rptr. 534, 381 P.2d 390.) Thus, in determining whether extrinsic evidence provides the certainty required by the statute, courts must bear in mind that the evidence cannot contradict the terms of the writing.

B. The Sufficiency of This Memorandum

As noted above, it is a question of law whether a memorandum, considered in light of the circumstances surrounding its making, complies with the statute of frauds. (*Phillippe v. Shapell Industries, supra,* 43 Cal.3d at p. 1258, 241 Cal.Rptr. 22, 743 P.2d 1279.) Accordingly, the issue is generally amenable to resolution by summary judgment. (Cf. *Kahn v. East Side Union High School Dist.* (2003) 31 Cal.4th 990, 1004, 4 Cal.Rptr.3d 103, 75 P.3d 30.) We independently review the record to determine whether a triable issue of fact might defeat the statute of frauds defense in this case. (*Id.* at p. 1003, 4 Cal.Rptr.3d 103, 75 P.3d 30.)

A memorandum of a contract for the sale of real property must identify the buyer, the seller, the price, and the property.[14] (*King v. Stanley* (1948) 32 Cal.2d 584, 589, 197 P.2d 321.) Defendants contend the memorandum drafted by plaintiff Sterling fails to adequately specify the seller, the property, or the price.[15]

The Court of Appeal correctly held that the seller and the properties were sufficiently identified. The parties themselves displayed no uncertainty as to those terms before their dispute over the price arose. It is a "cardinal rule of construction that when a contract is ambiguous or uncertain the practical construction placed upon it by the parties before any controversy arises as to its meaning affords one of the most reliable means of determining the intent of the parties." (*Bohman v. Berg* (1960) 54 Cal.2d 787, 795, 8 Cal.Rptr. 441, 356 P.2d 185.) The same rule governs the interpretation of a memorandum under the statute of frauds. (See Rest.2d Contracts, § 131, com. g, p. 338; *Seaman's Direct Buying Service, Inc. v. Standard Oil Co., supra,* 36 Cal.3d at pp. 762–763, 206 Cal.Rptr. 354, 686 P.2d 1158.)[16]

The memorandum referred to "Seller Larry Taylor, & Christina Development." Defendants argue that the omission of the actual owner of the properties, SMC, is fatal. However, they do not dispute Taylor's authorization to act as SMC's agent, or his actual performance of that role. A contract made in the name of an agent may be enforced against an undisclosed principal, and extrinsic evidence is admissible to identify the principal. (*Sunset Milling & Grain Co. v. Anderson* (1952) 39 Cal.2d 773, 778, 249 P.2d 24; 2 Witkin, Summary of Cal. Law, *supra,* Agency, §§ 158 & 159, pp. 202–203; see also *California Canneries Co. v. Scatena* (1897) 117 Cal. 447, 449–450, 49 P. 462.) If a term is stated in a memorandum with sufficient certainty to be enforced, it satisfies the statute of frauds. (*Seaman's Direct Buying Service, Inc. v. Standard Oil Co., supra,* 36 Cal.3d at p. 763, 206 Cal.Rptr. 354, 686 P.2d 1158.) Therefore, the reference to Taylor was adequate, regardless of the apparently mistaken inclusion of Christina Development. (See Rest.2d Contracts, § 131, com. f, p. 337.)

---

[14] The traditional formulation of essential terms also included the time and manner of payment, factors not at issue in this case. (*King v. Stanley, supra,* 32 Cal.2d at p. 589, 197 P.2d 321.) In *House of Prayer v. Evangelical Assn. for India* (2003) 113 Cal.App.4th 48, 53–54, 7 Cal.Rptr.3d 24, the court reasoned that because contracts for the sale of real property are enforceable without specification of a time of performance, that term is not essential under the statute of frauds.

[15] Defendants do not here challenge the sufficiency of Taylor's signature on the March 15 letter to meet the subscription requirement of the statute of frauds. Both the letter and the March 13 memorandum may be considered together to satisfy the statute. (*King v. Stanley, supra,* 32 Cal.2d at p. 588, 197 P.2d 321.) The parties' dispute concerns only the terms of the memorandum.

[16] This rule of construction undermines the contention in Professor Lord's amicus curiae brief that the multiple ambiguities in the memorandum before us, considered together in the abstract, render it insufficient under the statute of frauds. A skillful attorney can conjure ambiguities from nearly any document, but such hypothetical difficulties often disappear when the surrounding circumstances are considered.

Similarly, while the properties were identified in the memorandum only by street address, neither party displayed any confusion over their actual location. The purchase agreements Taylor prepared included full legal descriptions, and when Sterling received those agreements he did not object that he wanted to buy buildings on 4th and 14th Streets in Manhattan rather than Santa Monica. In any event, the better view has long been that extrinsic evidence may be consulted to locate property described in imprecise terms, even though a memorandum with a more complete description would be preferable. (*Beverage v. Canton Placer Mining Co., supra,* 43 Cal.2d at pp. 774–775, 278 P.2d 694, citing cases.)

As defendants forthrightly conceded in the trial court, "[t]he problem here is the price term." The Court of Appeal concluded that the lines in the memorandum stating "approx. 10.468 x gross income[,] estimated income 1.600.000, *Price $16,750.00* " were ambiguous, given the use of the modifier "approx." before the multiplier, the omitted zero in the price, and the uncertain meaning of "gross income." The court then considered Sterling's testimony that "approx." was meant to modify the total price, not the multiplier; that the missing zero was merely an error; and that "gross income" was used by the parties to refer to actual gross annual income. It decided that this evidence, if accepted by the trier of fact, could establish an agreement to determine the price based on a formula, which would be binding under *Carver v. Teitsworth* (1991) 1 Cal.App.4th 845, 852, 2 Cal. Rptr.2d 446. In *Carver,* a bid for either a specified price or $1,000 over any higher bid was deemed sufficiently certain. (*Id.* at pp. 849, 852–853, 2 Cal. Rptr.2d 446.)

In this court, plaintiffs also cite *Cal. Lettuce Growers v. Union Sugar Co.* (1955) 45 Cal.2d 474, 289 P.2d 785, to show that a price term may be calculated from a formula. There, a price formula was derived from industry custom and the parties' past practice. (*Id.* at pp. 482–483, 289 P.2d 785.) Plaintiffs contend the parties here negotiated a 10.468 multiplier to be applied to the actual gross rental income from the buildings in March 2000, as indicated by the fact that Taylor gave Sterling rent rolls before their March 13 meeting.

The Court of Appeal erred by deeming Sterling's testimony sufficient to establish his interpretation of the memorandum for purposes of the statute of frauds. Had Taylor testified that the parties meant to leave the price open to determination based on a rental income figure that was yet to be determined, this would be a different case. Then, the "admissions of the party to be charged" might have supported a reasonably certain price term derived from a negotiated formula. (Rest.2d Contracts, § 131, com. c, p. 335.) Here, however, Taylor insists the price was meant to be $16,750,000, and Sterling agrees that was the number he intended to write down, underlined, as the "Price."

$16,750,000 is clearly an approximate product of the formula specified in the memorandum, applied to the income figure stated there.[17] On the other hand, Sterling's asserted price of $14,404,841 cannot reasonably be considered an approximation of $16,750,000. It is instead an approximate product of the formula applied to an actual income figure not found in the memorandum. The writing does not include the term "actual gross income," nor does it state that the price term will vary depending on proof or later agreement regarding the actual rental income from the buildings. In effect, Sterling would employ only the first part of the price term ("approx. 10.468 x gross income") and ignore the last parts ("estimated income 1.600.000, *Price $16,750.00* "). He would hold Taylor to a price that is 10.468 times the actual rental income figure gleaned from the rent rolls, but only "approximately" so because of Sterling's computational errors. (See fn. 2, *ante*.)

Thus, two competing interpretations of the memorandum were before the court. Taylor's is consistent with the figures provided in the memorandum, requiring only the correction of the price by reference to undisputed extrinsic evidence. Sterling's price is not stated in the memorandum, and depends on extrinsic evidence in the form of his own testimony, disputed by Taylor, that the parties intended to apply the formula to actual gross rental income instead of the estimated income noted in the memorandum. Even if the trier of fact were to accept Sterling's version of the parties' negotiations, the price he seeks is not reflected in the memorandum; indeed, it is inconsistent with the price term that appears in the memorandum. Under these circumstances, we conclude the evidence is insufficient to establish Sterling's price term with the reasonable certainty required by the statute of frauds. (See *Beazell v. Schrader, supra*, 59 Cal.2d at p. 582, 30 Cal.Rptr. 534, 381 P.2d 390.)

The statute of frauds demands written evidence that reflects the parties' mutual understanding of the essential terms of their agreement, when viewed in light of the transaction at issue and the dispute before the court. The writing requirement is intended to permit the enforcement of agreements actually reached, but "to prevent enforcement through fraud or perjury of contracts never in fact made." (**Rest.2d Contracts**, § 131, com. c, p. 335.) The sufficiency of a memorandum to fulfill this purpose may depend on the quality of the extrinsic evidence offered to explain its terms. In *Preble v. Abrahams, supra*, 88 Cal. 245, 26 P. 99, the memorandum failed to describe the property to be sold with any certainty, but extrinsic evidence established that the parties could only have been referring to the portion of a tract that was not sold to another buyer. (*Id.* at p. 250, 26 P. 99.) Similarly, in *Brewer v. Horst–Lachmund Co., supra*, 127 Cal. 643, 60 P. 418, telegrams that were otherwise inscrutable demonstrated an ascertainable agreement when the court considered the circumstances of the transaction and the parties' understanding of the terms employed. (*Id.* at pp. 646–647, 60 P. 418.)

---

[17] The actual product of $1,600,000 multiplied by 10.468 is $16,748,800.

Here, unlike in the *Preble* and *Brewer* cases, the extrinsic evidence offered by plaintiffs is at odds with the writing, which states a specific price and does not indicate that the parties contemplated any change based on actual rental income. Therefore, the evidence is insufficient to show with reasonable certainty that the parties understood and agreed to the price alleged by plaintiffs. The price terms stated in the memorandum, considered together with the extrinsic evidence of the contemplated price, leave a degree of doubt that the statute of frauds does not tolerate. The trial court properly granted defendants summary judgment.

III. DISPOSITION

The judgment of the Court of Appeal is reversed with directions to affirm the trial court judgment in its entirety.

GEORGE, C.J., **BAXTER, CHIN,** and **MORENO,** JJ., concur.

Concurring and Dissenting Opinion by **KENNARD,** J.

I agree with the majority that extrinsic evidence is admissible to resolve the meaning of an ambiguity in a written memorandum required by the statute of frauds as evidence of an agreement, and that conflicts in the evidence are for the trier of fact to resolve. The majority, however, goes astray when it takes it upon itself to resolve an existing conflict in the evidence. In my view, the ambiguity in the language of the memorandum at issue should be resolved by the trier of fact.

. . . .

As the Court of Appeal observed, the language in the memorandum is ambiguous; that is, it can reasonably be read as each party proposes. (*Dore v. Arnold Worldwide, Inc.* (2006) 39 Cal.4th 384, 391, 46 Cal.Rptr.3d 668, 139 P.3d 56 ("An ambiguity arises when language is reasonably susceptible of more than one application to material facts").) To accept plaintiff's argument would give meaning to the language in the disputed statement of "10.468 x gross income [¶] estimated 1.600.000." To accept defendant's argument would give meaning to the term *"Price $16,750,000."* Which view should be accepted is a determination to be made by the trier of fact, based on its consideration of the extrinsic evidence presented. (See Maj. opn., *ante,* 55 Cal.Rptr.3d at 123, 152 P.3d at 425 ("when ambiguous terms in a memorandum are disputed, extrinsic evidence is admissible to resolve the uncertainty").) Either way, the trier of fact's resolution would result in a specific purchase price: one arrived at through application of a formula expressed in the memorandum, the other through acceptance of the figure $16,750,000 mentioned in the memorandum.

The majority, however, simply adopts defendant's view instead of leaving it to the trier of fact to resolve the conflict in the evidence. In accepting defendant's view, the majority rejects plaintiff's view as attempting to alter rather than explain the terms of the memorandum. (Maj. opn., *ante,* 55 Cal.Rptr. 3d at 129–30, 152 P.3d at 430–31.) I disagree.

. . . .

Unlike the majority, I would affirm the judgment of the Court of Appeal.

WERDEGAR, J., concurs.

_____

§ 4.2. Writing or Writings?

Under both the Restatement and UCC provisions, the statute of frauds is satisfied if a single writing exists that contains the required elements and is signed by the party to be charged. But what if multiple writings must be considered to find the required elements, and not all of them are signed by that party? May a court combine the documents together in evaluating whether the statute of frauds is satisfied? If so, what relationship must there be between the various writings? Courts have reached differing answers to these questions.

Reading the Law Critically: *Owen* and *Crabtree*

1. What does the court in each case say must be in the required writing to satisfy the statute of frauds? Which aspects are in the signed writing in the alleged contract at issue? Which are in the unsigned writing?

2. Does the court permit the signed and unsigned contract documents to be considered together to satisfy the statute of frauds? If not, why not? If so, what connection between the documents does the court require be demonstrated to allow the unsigned document to be used to satisfy the statute of frauds? Does the court permit the use of extrinsic evidence to connect the writings?

3. In what particulars are the "multiple writings" rules adopted by the two courts in agreement? In what ways are they different? How does Corbin's analysis compare to the *Owen* and *Crabtree* approaches? Does either court adopt Corbin's analysis?

Owen v. Hendricks

H. B. OWEN, Petitioner-Appellant

v.

RAY HENDRICKS, Respondent-Appellee

Supreme Court of Texas

433 S.W.2d 164 (Tex. 1968)

WALKER, Justice.

This suit was brought by H. B. Owen, petitioner, against Ray Hendricks, respondent, to recover a real estate dealer's commission. Respondent filed a motion for summary judgment, urging: (1) that the description of the land in the written memorandum he signed is not sufficient to satisfy the requirements of [a portion of the Texas statute of frauds] and (2) that the memorandum does not contain a promise or agreement to pay any particular commission. His motion was sustained by the trial court, and the Court of Civil Appeals affirmed. 426 S.W.2d 955. We think the first ground urged in the motion for summary judgment is sound, and the judgment of the Court of Civil Appeals is accordingly affirmed.

Petitioner says that the memorandum of the listing agreement is composed of two letters. The first letter, which was written and signed by petitioner, is as follows:

October 7, 1965
Mr. Ray Hendricks
Roscoe, Texas
Dear Mr. Hendricks:

I wrote you earlier pertaining to your 960 acres in Dallam County. Also, talked with you on the phone about the possibility of selling the place for you.

There is a party I wish to talk with about the place, but thought that perhaps you should be contacted before going ahead. If you will sell the place, would you advise me by return letter, stating price, terms and allotments. Did I understand that you were guaranteeing the water?

Will you do some trading on this place?

Have been thinking that I would get down to see you before now, but have been trying to get some ranch deals working.

Enclosed self-addressed, stamped envelope for your convenience.

Very truly yours,

/s/ H. B. Owen

The second letter, which was written and signed by respondent, is as follows:

October 11, 1965
H. B. Owen
Box 658
Canyon, Texas

Mr. Owen:

The 960 acres in Dallam County is for sale. The price is $225.00 per acre net to me. If you sell the place, you will need to add your commission on top of this.

I can take a large down payment at this time and would require as much down as possible.

The allotment status is 100% Milo.

I will not guarantee water, but the place has good water on two sides of it and I feel that water is a certainty.

I will not do any trading.

Sincerely,
/s/ Ray Hendricks

Section 28 of Article 6573a [of the Texas Civil Statutes] provides that no action shall be brought for the recovery of a commission for the sale or purchase of real estate unless the promise or agreement upon which the action is brought, or some memorandum thereof, shall be in writing and signed by the person to be charged or his lawfully authorized agent. To satisfy the requirements of this statute, the written memorandum must furnish within itself, or by reference to some other existing writing, the means or data by which the particular land may be identified. The sufficiency of the description is determined by the test that is used in cases arising under the Statute of Frauds and the Statute of Conveyances. See Tidwell v. Cheshier, 153 Tex. 194, 265 S.W.2d 568; Wilson v. Fisher, 144 Tex. 53, 188 S.W.2d 150.

Think About It!

Assuming the Texas statute of frauds parallels Restatement (Second) § 131, what is likely the basis for the court's statement that "the written memorandum must furnish . . . the means or data by which the particular land may be identified"?

Petitioner recognizes that the letter signed by respondent does not contain enough information to identify the land. He insists, however, that the two letters must be read together since one is responsive to the other and they obviously relate to the same transaction. Petitioner then says that the reference in the letter signed by him to "your 960 acres in Dallam County" brings the case within the rule of Pickett v. Bishop, 148 Tex. 207, 223 S.W.2d 222, where we stated that:

> . . . the use in the memorandum or contract of such words as 'my property', 'my land', or 'owned by me', is sufficient when it is shown by extrinsic evidence that the party to be charged and who has signed the contract or memorandum owns a tract and only one tract of land answering the description in the memorandum."

We assume for the purpose of this opinion that respondent owns only one tract of land and that the same consists of 960 acres and is located in Dallam County, Texas. It is further assumed that in view of such facts the letter written by petitioner contains an adequate description of the land. The problem then is to determine whether the two letters, one signed by respondent and the other not signed by him, may be taken together as constituting a memorandum of the agreement.

It is uniformly held that an unsigned paper may be incorporated by reference in the paper signed by the person sought to be charged. The language used is not important provided the document signed by the defendant plainly refers to another writing. An extension of this doctrine may be observed in some decisions, where it is said that several instruments may be read together when it appears from their terms that they necessarily relate to the same transaction. See Annotation, 85 A.L.R. 1184. According to Professor Williston, most of these cases were correctly decided on their facts, because the paper signed by the defendant did refer to the unsigned writing. See IV Williston on Contracts, 3rd ed. 1961, § 582, note 4.

The rule that several writings may be taken together provided there is internal evidence showing that they relate to the same transaction was recognized in Oliver v. Corzelius, Tex.Civ.App., 215 S.W.2d 231 (holding approved but judgment reversed, 148 Tex. 76, 220 S.W.2d 632), and Shook v. Parton, Tex. Civ.App., 211 S.W.2d 368 (no writ). Cf. Lindale Realty Co. v. Weary, Tex.Civ. App., 417 S.W.2d 436 (wr. ref. n.r.e.). According to the American Law Institute, the memorandum may consist of several writings when an examination of all the writings shows that the one executed by the defendant was signed with reference to the other writings. Restatement, Contracts, § 208. Professor Corbin favors a flexible approach and suggests that internal references may be dispensed with if, in the light of the surrounding circumstances, the court is convinced that no fraud is being perpetrated and that the several writings, taken together, evidence with reasonable certitude the terms of the contract. See II Corbin on Contracts, 1950 ed., § 512.

As pointed out by Professor Williston, however, it is difficult to justify the extension of the doctrine of incorporation to permit several writings to be read together simply because it appears that they relate to the same transaction. "There is no difficulty in making out a written memorandum that evidently relates to the same transaction, but the memorandum is not signed by the party to be charged" as required by the statute. The only permissible extension "of the doctrine requiring an express reference in the signed paper is where the signed paper at the time of the signature can be shown from its contents to be based on an adoption of a then existing unsigned paper." IV Williston on Contracts, 3rd ed. 1961, § 582.

We agree with Professor Williston. Any further extension of the doctrine of incorporation would permit the defendant to be bound, contrary to the terms of the statute, by a writing which he had not signed. An unsigned instrument which is not referred to in or adopted by the signed memorandum is as easily fabricated as false testimony. When the two letters in the present case are read together, it appears that the one written by respondent is in reply to the earlier letter written by petitioner. The two letters obviously relate to the same subject matter, but there is nothing in the letter signed by respondent that even remotely suggests the existence of another writing. Since the contents of such letter do not show that it is based on an adoption of the letter written by petitioner, we hold that the two letters cannot be taken together as constituting the signed memorandum required by Article 6573a.

The judgment of the Court of Civil Appeals is affirmed.

Crabtree v. Elizabeth Arden Sales Corp.

NATE CRABTREE, Plaintiff-Appellee

v.

ELIZABETH ARDEN SALES CORP., Defendant-Appellant

Court of Appeals of New York
110 N.E.2d 551 (N.Y. 1953)

FULD, Judge.

In September of 1947, Nate Crabtree entered into preliminary negotiations with Elizabeth Arden Sales Corporation, manufacturers and sellers of cosmetics, looking toward his employment as sales manager. Interviewed on September 26th, by Robert P. Johns, executive vice-president and general manager of the corporation, who had apprised him of the possible opening, Crabtree requested a three-year contract at $25,000 a year. Explaining that he would be giving up a secure well-paying job to take a position in an entirely new field of endeavor which he believed would take him some years to master he insisted upon an agreement for a definite term. And he repeated his desire for a contract for three years to Miss Elizabeth Arden, the corporation's president. When Miss Arden finally indicated that she was prepared to offer a two-year contract, based on an annual salary of $20,000 for the first six months, $25,000 for the second six months and $30,000 for the second year, plus expenses of $5,000 a year for each of those years, Crabtree replied that that offer was "interesting." Miss Arden thereupon had her personal secretary make this memorandum on a telephone order blank that happened to be at hand:

> "EMPLOYMENT AGREEMENT WITH NATE CRABTREE
> Date Sept. 26-1947 6: PM
> At 681-5th Ave
> * * *
>
> | Begin | 20000. |
> | 6 months | 25000. |
> | 6 months | 30000. |
>
> 5000.–per year
> Expense money
> [2 years to make good]
> Arrangement with
> Mr Crabtree
> By Miss Arden
> Present Miss Arden
> Mr John
> Mr Crabtree
> Miss OLeary"

A few days later, Crabtree phoned Mr. Johns and telegraphed Miss Arden; he accepted the "invitation to join the Arden organization", and Miss Arden wired back her "welcome". When he reported for work, a "pay-roll change" card was made up and initialed by Mr. Johns, and then forwarded to the payroll department. Reciting that it was prepared on September 30, 1947, and was to be effective as of October 22d, it specified the names of the parties, Crabtree's "Job Classification" and, in addition, contained the notation that "This employee is to be paid as follows:

First six months of employment	$20,000. per annum
Next six months of employment	25,000. per annum
After one year of employment	30,000. per annum

Approved by RPJ (initialed)

After six months of employment, Crabtree received the scheduled increase from $20,000 to $25,000, but the further specified increase at the end of the year was not paid. Both Mr. Johns and the comptroller of the corporation, Mr. Carstens, told Crabtree that they would attempt to straighten out the matter with Miss Arden, and, with that in mind, the comptroller prepared another "pay-roll change" card, to which his signature is appended, noting that there was to be a "Salary increase" from $25,000 to $30,000 a year, "per contractual arrangements with Miss Arden". The latter, however, refused to approve the increase and, after further fruitless discussion, plaintiff left defendant's employ and commenced this action for breach of contract.

At the ensuing trial, defendant denied the existence of any agreement to employ plaintiff for two years, and further contended that, even if one had been made, the statute of frauds barred its enforcement. The trial court found against defendant on both issues and awarded plaintiff damages of about $14,000, and the Appellate Division, two justices dissenting, affirmed. Since the contract relied upon was not to be performed within a year, the primary question for decision is whether there was a memorandum of its terms, subscribed by defendant, to satisfy the statute of frauds, Personal Property Law, § 31.

Each of the two payroll cards, the one initialed by defendant's general manager, the other signed by its comptroller, unquestionably constitutes a memorandum under the statute. That they were not prepared or signed with the intention of evidencing the contract, or that they came into existence

Who's That?

Elizabeth Arden (born Florence Nightingale Graham in 1884) was a Canadian-American businesswoman who as a young immigrant to the United States started her first salon on Fifth Avenue in New York in 1910 and over the next half-century built a world-wide cosmetics empire that made her one of the wealthiest women in the world. She was instrumental in introducing cosmetics to American women at a time when their use was mostly confined to celebrities. During World War II, she created a lipstick called Montezuma Red for women in the armed forces and, according to the Elizabeth Arden corporate website, she "once marched past her Red Door Salon on Fifth Avenue alongside 15,000 fellow suffragettes, all wearing red lipstick as a symbol of strength." See www.elizabetharden.com/Elizabeth-Arden-Biography/herstory,default,pg.html. In recognition of her contribution to the cosmetics industry, she was awarded the Légion d'Honneur by the French government in 1962. She died in 1966, apparently without having arranged her affairs to minimize estate taxes, resulting in the sale of many of the company's salons.

subsequent to its execution, is of no consequence, see **Marks v. Cowdin, 226 N.Y. 138, 145, 123 N.E. 139, 141**; **Spiegel v. Lowenstein, 162 App.Div. 443, 448-449, 147 N.Y.S. 655, 658**; see, also, **Restatement, Contracts, §§ 209, 210, 214**; it is enough, to meet the statute's demands, that they were signed with intent to authenticate the information contained therein and that such information does evidence the terms of the contract. See **Marks v. Cowdin, supra, 226 N.Y. 138, 123 N.E. 139**; **Bayles v. Strong, 185 N.Y. 582, 78 N.E. 1099**, affirming 104 App.Div. 153, 93 N.Y.S. 346; **Spiegel v. Lowenstein, supra, 162 App.Div. 443, 448, 147 N.Y.S. 655, 658**; see, also, 2 Corbin on Contracts (1951), pp. 732-733, 763-764; 2 Williston on Contracts (Rev. ed., 1936), pp. 1682-1683. Those two writings contain all of the essential terms of the contract: the parties to it, the position that plaintiff was to assume, the salary that he was to receive, except that relating to the duration of plaintiff's employment. Accordingly, we must consider whether that item, the length of the contract, may be supplied by reference to the earlier unsigned office memorandum, and, if so, whether its notation, "2 years to make good", sufficiently designates a period of employment.

The statute of frauds does not require the "memorandum . . . to be in one document. It may be pieced together out of separate writings, connected with one another either expressly or by the internal evidence of subject-matter and occasion.": **Marks v. Cowdin, supra, 226 N.Y. 138, 145, 123 N.E. 139, 141**, see, also, 2 Williston, op cit., p. 1671; **Restatement, Contracts, § 208**, subd. (a). Where each of the separate writings has been subscribed by the party to be charged, little if any difficulty is encountered. See, e. g., **Marks v. Cowdin, supra, 226 N.Y. 138, 144-145, 123 N.E. 139, 141**. Where, however, some writings have been signed and others have not, as in the case before us, there is basic disagreement as to what constitutes a sufficient connection permitting the unsigned papers to be considered as part of the statutory memorandum. The courts of some jurisdictions insist that there be a reference, of varying degrees of specificity, in the signed writing to that unsigned, and, if there is no such reference, they refuse to permit consideration of the latter in determining whether the memorandum satisfies the statute. See, e.g., **Osborn v. Phelps, 19 Conn. 63**; **Hewett Grain & Provision Co. v. Spear, 222 Mich. 608, 193 N.W. 291**. That conclusion is based upon a construction of the statute which requires that the connection between the writings and defendant's acknowledgment of the one not subscribed appear from examination of the papers alone, without the aid of parol evidence. The other position which has gained increasing support over the years is that a sufficient connection between the papers is established simply by a reference in them to the same subject matter or transaction. See, e. g., **Frost v. Alward, 176 Cal. 691, 169 P. 379**; **Lerned v. Wannemacher, 9 Allen, 412, 91 Mass. 412**. The statute is not pressed "to the extreme of a literal and rigid logic", **Marks v. Cowdin, supra, 226 N.Y. 138, 144, 123 N.E. 139, 141**, and oral testimony is admitted to show the connection between the documents and to establish the acquiescence, of the party to be charged, to the contents of the one unsigned. See Beckwith v. Talbot, 95 U.S. 289, 24 L.Ed. 496; Oliver v. Hunting, 44 Ch.D. 205, 208-209; see, also, 2 Corbin, op. cit., §§ 512-518; cf. Restatement, Contracts,§ 208, subd. (b), par. (iii).

The view last expressed impresses us as the more sound, and, indeed although several of our cases appear to have gone the other way, see, e. g., Newbery v. Wall, 65 N.Y. 484; Wilson v. Lewiston Mill Co., 150 N.Y. 314, 44 N.E. 959 this court has on a number of occasions approved the rule, and we now definitively adopt it, permitting the signed and unsigned writings to be read together, provided that they clearly refer to the same subject matter or transaction. See, e. g., Peabody v. Speyers, 56 N.Y. 230; Raubitscheck v. Blank, 80 N.Y. 478; Peck v. Vandemark, 99 N.Y. 29, 1 N.E. 41; Coe v. Tough, 116 N.Y. 273, 22 N.E. 550; Delware Mills v. Carpenter Bros., 235 N.Y. 537, 139 N.E. 725, affirming 200 App.Div. 324, 193 N.Y.S. 201.

The language of the statute—"Every agreement . . is void, unless . . . some note or memorandum thereof be in writing, and subscribed by the party to be charged", Personal Property Law, § 31—does not impose the requirement that the signed acknowledgment of the contract must appear from the writings alone, unaided by oral testimony. The danger of fraud and perjury, generally attendant upon the admission of parol evidence, is at a minimum in a case such as this. None of the terms of the contract are supplied by parol. All of them must be set out in the various writings presented to the court, and at least one writing, the one establishing a contractual relationship between the parties, must bear the signature of the party to be charged, while the unsigned document must on its face refer to the same transaction as that set forth in the one that was signed. Parol evidence to portray the circumstances surrounding the making of the memorandum serves only to connect the separate documents and to show that there was assent, by the party to be charged, to the contents of the one unsigned. If that testimony does not convincingly connect the papers, or does not show assent to the unsigned paper, it is within the province of the judge to conclude, as a matter of law, that the statute has not been satisfied. True, the possibility still remains that, by fraud or perjury, an agreement never in fact made may occasionally be enforced under the subject matter or transaction test. It is better to run that risk, though, than to deny enforcement to all agreements, merely because the signed document made no specific mention of the unsigned writing. As the United States Supreme Court declared, in sanctioning the admission of parol evidence to

Think About It!

The opinion says the judge may decide "as a matter of law" that the statute is not satisfied. The conclusion that the statute is not satisfied is based on a factual finding about the evidence of assent to the unsigned document, however. Why is a judge's ruling under such circumstances considered "a matter of law"?

establish the connection between the signed and unsigned writings. "There may be cases in which it would be a violation of reason and common sense to ignore a reference which derives its significance from such (parol) proof. If there is ground for any doubt in the matter, the general rule should be enforced. But where there is no ground for doubt, its enforcement would aid, instead of discouraging, fraud." Beckwith v. Talbot, supra, 95 U.S. 289, 292, 24 L.Ed. 496; see, also, Raubitschek v. Blank, supra, 80 N.Y. 478; Freeland v. Ritz, 154 Mass. 257, 259, 28 N.E. 226,12 L.R.A. 561; Gall v. Brashier, 10 Cir., 169 F.2d 704, 708-709, 12 A.L.R.2d 500; 2 Corbin, op. cit. § 512, and cases there cited.

Turning to the writings in the case before us—the unsigned office memo, the payroll change form initialed by the general manager Johns, and the paper signed by the comptroller Carstens—it is apparent, and most patently, that all three refer on their face to the same transaction. The parties, the position to be filled by plaintiff, the salary to be paid him, are all identically set forth; it is hardly possible that such detailed information could refer to another or a different agreement. Even more, the card signed by Carstens notes that it was prepared for the purpose of a "Salary increase per contractual arrangements with Miss Arden". That certainly constitutes a reference of sorts to a more comprehensive "arrangement," and parol is permissible to furnish the explanation.

The corroborative evidence of defendant's assent to the contents of the unsigned office memorandum is also convincing. Prepared by defendant's agent, Miss Arden's personal secretary, there is little likelihood that that paper was fraudulently manufactured or that defendant had not assented to its contents. Furthermore, the evidence as to the conduct of the parties at the time it was prepared persuasively demonstrates defendant's assent to its terms. Under such circumstances, the courts below were fully justified in finding that the three papers constituted the "memorandum" of their agreement within the meaning of the statute.

Nor can there be any doubt that the memorandum contains all of the essential terms of the contract. See N. E. D. Holding Co. v. McKinley, 246 N.Y. 40, 157 N.E. 923; Donald Friedman & Co. v. Newman, 255 N.Y. 340, 174 N.E. 703, 73 A.L.R. 95. Only one term, the length of the employment, is in dispute. The September 26th office memorandum contains the notation, "2 years to make good". What purpose, other than to denote the length of the contract term, such a notation could have, is hard to imagine. Without it, the employment would be at will, see Martin v. New York Life Ins. Co., 148 N.Y. 117, 121,42 N.E. 416, 417, and its inclusion may not be treated as meaningless or purposeless. Quite obviously, as the courts below decided, the phrase signifies that the parties agreed to a term, a certain and definite term, of two years, after which, if plaintiff did not "make good", he would be subject to discharge. And examination of other parts of the memorandum supports that construction. Throughout the writings, a scale of wages, increasing plaintiff's salary periodically, is set out; that type of arrangement is hardly consistent with the hypothesis that the employment was meant to be at will. The most that may be argued from defendant's standpoint is that "2 years to make good", is a cryptic and ambiguous statement. But, in such a case, parol evidence is admissible to explain its meaning. See Martocci v. Greater New York Brewery, 301 N.Y. 57, 63, 92 N.E.2d 887, 889; Marks v. Cowdin, supra, 226 N.Y.

What's That?

If employment is "at will," either party may terminate the employment at any time, even without any particular justification. A promise to employ someone for a specified period of time means the employment is *not* at will, so the employee could not be terminated without cause.

138, 143-144, 123 N.E. 139, 140, 141; 2 Williston, op. cit., § 576; 2 Corbin, op. cit., § 527. Having in mind the relations of the parties, the course of the negotiations and plaintiff's insistence upon security of employment, the purpose of the phrase or so the trier of the facts was warranted in finding was to grant plaintiff the tenure he desired.

The judgment should be affirmed, with costs.

LOUGHRAN, C. J., and LEWIS, CONWAY, DESMOND, DYE and FROESSEL, JJ., concur.

---

§ 4.3. The Statute of Frauds in Electronic Commerce

What happens when the parties' contract or correspondence or notes are in electronic form? Do those constitute "writings"? And how are they "signed"? Those were difficult questions until 1999 and 2000, when a pair of statutes resolved such issues under many circumstances. The Uniform Electronic Transactions Act (UETA) was promulgated in 1999 and was quickly adopted by 47 state legislatures. Meanwhile, Congress passed a similar statute at the federal level, called Electronic Signatures in Global and National Commerce Act (E-SIGN), codified at 15 U.S.C. §§ 7001-7031.

Both UETA and E-SIGN establish that electronic records and signatures can satisfy statutory provisions (including those in the UCC) that require an agreement be in writing or signed:

UETA § 7. **Legal Recognition of Electronic Records, Electronic Signatures, and Electronic Contracts.**

(a) A record or signature may not be denied legal effect or enforceability solely because it is in electronic form.

(b) A contract may not be denied legal effect or enforceability solely because an electronic record was used in its formation.

(c) If a law requires a record to be in writing, an electronic record satisfies the law.

(d) If a law requires a signature, an electronic signature satisfies the law.

UETA § 2(7), (8), (13). **Definitions.**

. . .

(7) "Electronic record" means a record created, generated, sent, communicated, received, or stored by electronic means.

(8) "Electronic signature" means an electronic sound, symbol, or process attached to or logically associated with a record and executed or adopted by a person with the intent to sign the record.

(13) "Record" means information that is inscribed on a tangible medium or that is stored in an electronic or other medium and is retrievable in perceivable form.

E-SIGN § 101(a), 15 U.S.C. § 7001(a). **General Rule of Validity.**

(a) In general. Notwithstanding any statute, regulation, or other rule of law . . . , with respect to any transaction in or affecting interstate or foreign commerce—

(1) a signature, contract, or other record relating to such transaction may not be denied legal effect, validity, or enforceability solely because it is in electronic form; and

(2) a contract relating to such transaction may not be denied legal effect, validity, or enforceability solely because an electronic signature or electronic record was used in its formation.

E-SIGN § 106(4), (5), (9), 15 U.S.C. § 7006(4), (5), (9). **Definitions.**

(4) Electronic record.—The term "electronic record" means a contract or other record created, generated, sent, communicated, received, or stored by electronic means.

(5) Electronic signature.—The term "electronic signature" means an electronic sound, symbol, or process, attached to or logically associated with a contract or other record and executed or adopted by a person with the intent to sign the record.

> (9) Record.—The term "record" means information that is inscribed on a tangible medium or that is stored in an electronic or other medium and is retrievable in perceivable form.

Note the connection between the definition of "electronic signature" in UETA and E-SIGN ("executed or adopted by a person with the intent to sign the record") and the definition of "signed" in the UCC ("executed or adopted with the present intention to adopt or accept a writing") and the Restatement ("made or adopted with an intention, actual or apparent, to authenticate the writing as that of the signer"). UETA and E-SIGN allow a party to use an electronic mechanism to sign; the electronic mechanism counts as a signature if it is used with an intent to adopt/ accept/authenticate the electronic record.

The provisions of UETA and E-SIGN are parallel (and often identical), but the scope of coverage of the two statutes is different. UETA applies to transactions between parties "each of which has agreed to conduct transactions by electronic means." **UETA § 5.** Under UETA, parties are not required to use electronic records or electronic signatures, but if they have agreed to do so (which may be implied from "the context and surrounding circumstances, including the parties' conduct", *id.*), electronic records and signatures satisfy provisions that require writings and signatures. E-SIGN, in contrast, applies to all interstate commerce transactions, whether or not the parties have agreed to the use of electronic means of contract formation.

Because the two acts cover much of the same subject matter, Congress could have used E-SIGN to pre-empt UETA but chose not to do so.* Thus, in most states, E-SIGN and UETA both apply, providing a wider scope for the rules covering electronic contracting practices than would be provided by either statute alone.

Although E-SIGN and UETA make clear that an electronic communication *may* serve as a writing, and an electronic signature *may* count as a signature for the statute of frauds, the critical question remains whether the purported signature satisfies the requirement that the sender was manifesting her intention to authenticate the document, as required by the definition of "signed." The requirement is satisfied by a sender who adds her name or a signature block to an email or acquiesces in the software program doing so for her (despite possible concerns

---

* E-SIGN contains a "savings clause" that exempts UETA from federal pre-emption, as long as the state legislature enacts the uniform version of UETA (or an equivalent statute) and that statute (if adopted after E-SIGN) refers to E-SIGN. **E-SIGN § 102.**

about the "quick and casual nature" of e-mails and the absence of the "cautionary and memorializing functions a traditional signed writing serves").* Whether information such as the automatic identifier of the sender accompanying an e-mail also serves that purpose depends on the particular factual circumstances.

While the intricacies of UETA and E-SIGN are beyond the scope of this textbook, it is worth noting that the effect of E-SIGN and UETA on the statute of frauds is to greatly expand the range of "writings" and "signatures" that satisfy the statute and greatly decrease the number of contracts that are unenforceable because of the statute of frauds.

Problems: Applying the Statute of Frauds

Questions 6-12 through 6-14 are based on the following facts:

> Therese runs a business that sells restaurant equipment. On December 1, a local customer calls to inquire whether Therese has 400 water glasses, catalog # 36CX, available on very short notice.
>
> The catalog price is $1.25 per glass. These glasses more commonly sell for $1.50 each, but Therese sells some items at a discount to build a customer base. Therese replies that she will have to check her inventory. When she locates the 400 glasses, Therese calls the customer back and leaves a message saying she does have 400 glasses, with delivery time of 2 days. The customer calls back and orally places an order for 400 glasses.

6-12. Does the statute of frauds require the existence of an appropriate writing for sale of the glasses to be enforceable?
   a.   No, because the contract can be performed within a year.
   b.   No, because the price of each glass is only $1.25.
   c.   Yes, because the contract specifies a quantity.
   d.   Yes, because the value of the goods is more than $500.
   e.   Yes, because the contract price is $500.

6-13. Assume that a writing is required for enforcement. When the customer calls in the order, Therese's order department records it on a Sales Confirmation form pre-printed with the company letterhead and mails a copy to the customer. Is the contract enforceable by the customer? By Therese?

─────────────

* *See* Singer v. Adamson, 2003 WL 23641985, *5 (**Mass. Land Ct. 2003**).

6-14. Assume that a writing is required for enforcement. Ignore the facts in Problem 6-13 and assume that all the phone calls described in the basic facts were emails. Therese delivers the glasses to the customer on December 3, but the customer refuses them, saying that no contract was formed. If Therese sues the customer for breach of contract, will the customer be successful in its motion to dismiss the lawsuit based on the statute of frauds?

    a.   No, because the emails met the requirements for a signed writing.

    b.   No, because the part performance exception was met.

    c.   No, because the customer admitted the contract's existence when it placed the order.

    d.   No, because of the promissory estoppel exception to the statute of frauds.

    e.   Yes, because the emails did not contain price, an essential term.

    f.   Yes, because the customer's email was an order, not a confirmation.

    g.   Yes, because Therese did not object to the customer's email within ten days after receipt.

6-15. Annie runs a business that produces leather briefcases and handbags for sale at retail outlets. While touring the local art fair, she is impressed with the work displayed in one of the booths and stops to talk with the owner, Barry. Barry works alone and is able to produce only a small number of items each year. Annie offers to hire Barry to design a new line of bags that her company would produce in quantity; Barry would earn a royalty on each bag sold, but would have to stop selling competing products on his own. Barry is interested, but says, to make it worth his while, he wants a two-year agreement and to be paid a guaranteed amount for each design in addition to the royalty fee. Annie says she'd like to see some new designs first, if she's going to commit to a longer term arrangement. She writes her name and contact information on one of Barry's invoice pads and says she'll be in touch.

A week later, Annie sends Barry a letter suggesting he produce a sample design that she can review and show to her production staff. He produces a design for a small handbag and sends it to Annie with a note that says, "Here's a sample of what I can do. I hope you're satisfied and we can move forward." Annie sends back a letter that says: "Thanks for sending us a sample of your work. Everyone here is impressed. We have to see if the numbers look good on production before we can commit." Several days later, she calls and says: "Everything looks great. We think we can swing $1000 for each design you submit and 5% royalty for each copy sold." Barry is pleased, and they agree orally to work together.

Barry begins work and sends six new designs to Annie at the rate of about one a month, each time with an invoice for $1000 annotated "per our agreement." In response, Annie sends back a "confirmation of receipt of your design" and a company check for $1000. The memo line on the check says "For bag design."

When Barry sends a seventh design, Annie returns it to Barry with a note that says "Thanks for the work you've done for us over the last several months. You've done everything we asked, but in the current market we're not able to continue production of new products." Barry protests that they had a two-year agreement and asks about the royalty payments due him. Annie says she's paid him everything he's owed, that they paid for designs they liked but had made no promises either to take further designs or to pay him any royalties on production. Barry is livid; among other things, he has stopped producing any bags of his own based on the agreement with Annie and has given up his preferred spot in several important art fairs, making it more difficult for him to market his bags once he begins to produce more of them on his own.

Barry sues Annie for breach of contract, alleging a two-year agreement for design work, including payment of 5% royalty on each item sold. Annie moves to dismiss based on the statute of frauds. Will she succeed in her motion?

CHAPTER 7

Content and Meaning of the Contract

What kind of promises will the law enforce?

How do parties demonstrate assent to a contract?

What defenses to enforcement exist?

Is a writing required for enforcement? If so, what kind?

How is the content of a contract ascertained?

What are parties' rights and duties after breach?

What situations lead to excusing contract performance?

What remedies are available for breach of contract?

What contractual rights and duties do non-parties to a contract have?

§ 1. Introduction

Once it is established that a contract exists, that no defense bars enforcement, and that the statute of frauds either is not applicable or is satisfied, the next step is to determine what performance is promised in the contract. That process requires not only looking at the words written or spoken in creating the contract, but also interpreting those words, and then considering whether terms or understandings not expressed in contract formation are nonetheless implicitly part of the contract. Chapter 4 addressed one issue relevant to determing content: the impact of UCC § 2-207 on ascertaining what terms are incorporated in a contract for sale of goods. This chapter addresses additional questions that often arise in establishing the content and meaning of a contract:

- Interpreting express contract terms (§ 2);
- Determining when extrinsic evidence may be used in contract interpretation (§ 3);
- Supplementing express terms with implied contract terms (§ 4);
- Understanding the implied covenant of good faith (§ 4.2); and
- Distinguishing between promises and conditions as contract terms (§ 5)

§ 2. Interpreting Express Contract Terms

There would be no need for contract interpretation if words and phrases had unique meanings, understood by all contracting parties. Of course, that is not the world in which we live. Words are often vague or ambiguous, and parties often have different understandings of the words they use in contract creation. Courts are therefore called upon to interpret or construe contract language. Contract interpretation is, at its core, a search for the meaning intended by the parties. But how is a court to determine that intent, especially when the parties now disagree on what their intent was? What rules should a court use to ascertain meaning?

What's That?

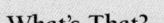

Courts and commentators sometimes distinguish between "interpreting" contract language (ascertaining the meaning intended by the parties) and "construing" it (using legal rules to choose a meaning and determining the legal effect of contract language). More often, the two terms are used interchangeably, and this textbook will do the same. It is nonetheless useful to understand the distinction between the two ways of ascertaining meaning and be able to articulate whether an advocate or court is proposing a meaning intended by the parties or one inferred by law.

Recall that in determining whether parties assented to a contract, courts consider the meaning a reasonable person would give to each communication and whether the recipient of the communication understood it that way. Remember, too, that if the parties have different understandings of a critical contract term (as in the case of the two ships "Peerless," discussed in Chapter 4, page 246), there may be no contract created. The courts treat contract interpretation in a similar fashion, determining a reasonable meaning by considering what each party claims to have meant by the contract language and whether either party knew or should have known of the meaning intended by the other party. Keep that perspective in mind as you consider each issue of interpretation in this chapter.

§ 2.1. A Case Study in Interpretation

The case of *Frigaliment v. B.N.S. International Sales* is the "first course," to whet your appetite and prepare you to consider the more "meaty" aspects of interpretation.

Reading the Law Critically: *Frigaliment*

1. Judge Friendly finds that "chicken" is ambiguous, but how does he reach that conclusion? Does he consider only the contract language itself, or does he look at other evidence to decide that question?

2. After deciding that the term is ambiguous, Judge Friendly considers additional evidence on the meaning of the word. What kinds of evidence does he consider? How does each party support its interpretation by reference to that evidence?

3. How would you rank the value of the kinds of evidence the parties use in trying to prove the meaning of "chicken"? What value does the court place on them?

4. Does the court decide what the contract meant by "chicken"? Note which party (buyer or seller) is the plaintiff in the litigation. Would the interpretive outcome have been different if the other contracting party had sued?

Frigaliment Importing Co. v. B.N.S. International Sales Corp.

FRIGALIMENT IMPORTING CO., Plaintiff

v.

B.N.S. INTERNATIONAL SALES CORP., Defendant

United States District Court

190 F. Supp. 116 (S.D.N.Y. 1960)

FRIENDLY, Circuit Judge.

Who's That?

Called by fellow federal judge Jon O. Newman "quite simply the pre-eminent appellate judge of his era," Judge Henry J. Friendly clerked for Justice Louis Brandeis after graduating from Harvard Law School with the highest numeric average earned in the 20th century. In private practice, he built a reputation as an expert in railroad reorganizations and then worked for Pan American World Airways, where he became vice president and general counsel. He served on the United States Court of Appeals from his appointment by President Eisenhower in 1959 until his death in 1986. Even in semi-retirement he worked on more than 125 opinions a year and took on the additional role of presiding judge of a special court that dealt with the bankruptcy and reorganization of many of the nation's railroads. He decided *Frigaliment* while sitting by designation as a district court judge in his first year on the bench. On the Court of Appeals, Friendly "became known for crafting lucid legal opinions on a wide range of legal issues—business, criminal matters, admiralty law, jurisdiction of the courts"* and was said to have "authored the definitive opinions for the nation in each area of the law that he had occasion to consider."** His working methods reflected his erudition. As described by former Friendly clerk and now United States Court of Appeals Judge Pierre Leval: "After reading the briefs and appendices in a case, [the judge] would begin writing, as quickly as he would if he were copying a text.

---

* Henry J. Friendly, Federal Judge in Court Of Appeals, is Dead at 82, New York Times, 3/12/86.
** Letter from United States Court of Appeals Judge Jon O. Newman, New York Times, 3/24/86.

> When he wanted a citation or quotation, he could simply pluck the exact volume he needed off the shelf. Judge Friendly had all of law in his head, with an extraordinary understanding of the interrelationships between all different doctrines." See http://www.law.harvard.edu/news/2012/11/28_judge-henry-friendly-event.html (November 2012 panel discussion on his legacy held at Harvard Law School); see also David M. Dorsen, Henry Friendly: Greatest Judge of His Era (2012).

The issue is, what is chicken? Plaintiff says "chicken" means a young chicken, suitable for broiling and frying. Defendant says "chicken" means any bird of that genus that meets contract specifications on weight and quality, including what it calls "stewing chicken" and plaintiff pejoratively terms "fowl". Dictionaries give both meanings, as well as some others not relevant here. To support its, plaintiff sends a number of volleys over the net; defendant essays to return them and adds a few serves of its own. Assuming that both parties were acting in good faith, the case nicely illustrates Holmes' remark "that the making of a contract depends not on the agreement of two minds in one intention, but on the agreement of two sets of external sign—not on the parties' having meant the same thing but on their having said the same thing." The Path of the Law, in Collected Legal Papers, p. 178. I have concluded that plaintiff has not sustained its burden of persuasion that the contract used "chicken" in the narrower sense.

The action is for breach of the warranty that goods sold shall correspond to the description, New York Personal Property Law, McKinney's Consol. Laws, c. 41, § 95. Two contracts are in suit. In the first, dated May 2, 1957, defendant, a New York sales corporation, confirmed the sale to plaintiff, a Swiss corporation, of

"US Fresh Frozen Chicken, Grade A, Government Inspected, Eviscerated 2½-3 lbs. and 1½-2 lbs. each all chicken individually wrapped in cryovac, packed in secured fiber cartons or wooden boxes, suitable for export

75,000 lbs. 2½-3 lbs........	@$33.00
25,000 lbs. 1½-2 lbs........	@$36.50
per 100 lbs. FAS New York	

scheduled May 10, 1957 pursuant to instructions from Penson & Co., New York."

The second contract, also dated May 2, 1957, was identical save that only 50,000 lbs. of the heavier "chicken" were called for, the price of the smaller birds was $37 per 100 lbs., and shipment was scheduled for May 30. The initial ship-ment under the first contract was short but the balance was shipped on May 17. When the initial shipment arrived in Switzerland, plaintiff found, on May 28, that the 2½-3 lbs. birds were not young chicken suitable for broiling and frying but stewing chicken or "fowl'; indeed, many of the cartons and bags plainly so indicated. Protests ensued. Nevertheless, shipment under the second contract was made on May 29, the 2½-3 lbs. birds again being stewing chicken. Defendant stopped the transportation of these at Rotterdam.

This action followed. Plaintiff says that, notwithstanding that its acceptance was in Switzerland, New York law controls under the principle of Rubin v. Irving Trust Co., 1953, 305 N.Y. 288, 305, 113 N.E.2d 424, 431; defendant does not dispute this, and relies on New York decisions. I shall follow the apparent agree-ment of the parties as to the applicable law.

Since the word "chicken" standing alone is ambiguous, I turn first to see whether the contract itself offers any aid to its interpretation. Plaintiff says the 1½-2 lbs. birds necessarily had to be young chicken since the older birds do not come in that size, hence the 2½-3 lbs. birds must likewise be young. This is unpersuasive—a contract for "apples" of two different sizes could be filled with different kinds of apples even though only one species came in both sizes. Defendant notes that the contract called not simply for chicken but for "US Fresh Frozen Chicken, Grade A, Government Inspected." It says the contract thereby incorporated by refer-ence the Department of Agriculture's regulations, which favor its interpreta-tion; I shall return to this after review-ing plaintiff's other contentions.

Go Online!

For an amusing display of the many kinds of chicken, see Julia Child presenting "the chicken sisters" on YouTube, www.youtube.com/ watch?v=h8prY-yHyoE and R.B.Craswell's musical rendition of the case at www.youtube.com/ watch?v=EL.wt-KXz8GA.

The first hinges on an exchange of cablegrams which preceded execution of the formal contracts. The negotiations leading up to the contracts were conducted in New York between defendant's secretary, Ernest R. Bauer, and a Mr. Stovicek, who was in New York for the Czechoslovak government at the World Trade Fair. A few days after meeting Bauer at the fair, Stovicek telephoned and inquired whether defendant would be interested in exporting poultry to Switzerland. Bauer then met with Stovicek, who showed him a cable from plaintiff dated April 26, 1957, announcing that they "are buyer" of 25,000 lbs. of chicken 2½-3 lbs. weight, Cryovac packed, grade A Government inspected, at a price up to 33¢ per pound, for shipment on May 10, to be confirmed by the following morning, and were interested in further offerings. After testing the market for price, Bauer accepted, and Stovicek sent a confirmation that evening. Plaintiff stresses that, although these and subsequent cables between plaintiff and defendant, which laid the basis for the additional quantities under the first and for all of the second contract, were predominantly in German, they used the English word "chicken"; it claims this was done because it understood "chicken" meant young chicken whereas the German word, "Huhn," included both "Brathuhn" (broilers) and "Suppenhuhn" (stewing chicken), and that defendant, whose officers were thoroughly conversant with German, should have realized this. Whatever force this argument might otherwise have is largely drained away by Bauer's testimony that he asked Stovicek what kind of chickens were wanted, received the answer "any kind of chickens," and then, in German, asked whether the cable meant "Huhn" and received an affirmative response. Plaintiff attacks this as contrary to what Bauer testified on his deposition in March, 1959, and also on the ground that Stovicek had no authority to interpret the meaning of the cable. The first contention would be persuasive if sustained by the record, since Bauer was free at the trial from the threat of contradiction by Stovicek as he was not at the time of the deposition; however, review of the deposition does not convince me of the claimed inconsistency. As to the second contention, it may well be that Stovicek lacked authority to commit plaintiff for prices or delivery dates other than those specified in the cable; but plaintiff cannot at the same time rely on its cable to Stovicek as its dictionary to the meaning of the contract and repudiate the interpretation given the dictionary by the man in whose hands it was put. See **Restatement of the Law of Agency, 2d, § 145**; 2 Mecham, Agency § 1781 (2d ed. 1914); **Park v. Moorman Mfg. co., 1952, 121 Utah 339, 241 P.2d 914, 919, 40 A.L.R.2d 273; Henderson v. Jimmerson, Tex.Civ.App.1950, 234 S.W.2d 710, 717-718.** Plaintiff's reliance on the fact that the contract forms contain the words "through the intermediary of:", with the blank not filled, as negating agency, is wholly unpersuasive; the purpose of this clause was to permit filling in the name of an intermediary to whom a commission would be payable, not to blot out what had been the fact.

Plaintiff's next contention is that there was a definite trade usage that "chicken" meant "young chicken." Defendant showed that it was only beginning in the poultry trade in 1957, thereby bringing itself within the principle that "when one of the parties is not a member of the trade or other circle, his acceptance of the standard must be made to appear" by proving either that he had actual knowledge of the usage or that the usage is "so generally known in the community that his actual individual knowledge of it may be inferred." 9 Wigmore, Evidence (3d ed. § 1940) 2464. Here there was no proof of actual knowledge of the alleged usage; indeed, it is quite plain that defendant's belief was to the contrary. In order to meet the alternative requirement, the law of New York demands a showing that "the usage is of so long continuance, so well established, so notorious, so universal and so reasonable in itself, as that the presumption is violent that the parties contracted with reference to it, and made it a part of their agreement." **Walls v. Bailey, 1872, 49 N.Y. 464, 472-473.**

Take Note!

Two years after *Frigaliment* was decided, in 1962, New York adopted Article 2 of the Uniform Commercial Code, including its (somewhat different) definition of trade usage. That definition appears in UCC § 1-303(c), which is reproduced along with the rest of § 1-303 on page 702. The opinion also refers to evidence that would be called "course of performance" under the UCC; see UCC § 1-303(a). UCC § 1-303(d) says that trade usage, course of performance, and course of dealing (see § 1-303(b)) are "relevant in ascertaining the meaning of the parties' agreement, may give particular meaning to specific terms of the agreement, and may supplement or qualify the terms of the agreement." The UCC provisions have had significant impact both in sale-of-goods and common law cases, leading decision-makers to interpret contractual language with such broader commercial context in mind.

Plaintiff endeavored to establish such a usage by the testimony of three witnesses and certain other evidence. Strasser, resident buyer in New York for a large chain of Swiss cooperatives, testified that "on chicken I would definitely understand a broiler." However, the force of this testimony was considerably weakened by the fact that in his own transactions the witness, a careful businessman, protected himself by using "broiler" when that was what he wanted and "fowl" when he wished older birds. Indeed, there are some indications, dating back to a remark of Lord Mansfield, Edie v. East India Co., 2 Burr. 1216, 1222 (1761), that no credit should be given "witnesses to usage, who could not adduce instances in verification." 7 Wigmore, Evidence (3d ed. 1940), § 1954; see **McDonald v. Acker, Merrall & Condit Co., 2d Dept.1920, 192 App.Div. 123, 126, 182 N.Y.S. 607**. While Wigmore thinks this goes too far, a witness' consistent failure to rely on the alleged usage deprives his opinion testimony of much of its effect. Niesielowski, an officer of one of the companies that had furnished the stewing chicken to defendant, testified that "chicken" meant "the male species of the poultry industry. That could be a broiler, a fryer or a roaster", but not a stewing chicken; however, he also testified that upon receiving defendant's inquiry for "chickens", he asked whether the desire was for "fowl or frying chickens" and, in fact, supplied fowl, although taking the precaution of asking defendant, a day or two after plaintiff's acceptance of the contracts in suit, to change its confirmation of its order from "chickens," as defendant had originally prepared it, to "stewing chickens." Dates, an employee of Urner-Barry Company, which publishes a daily market report on the poultry trade, gave it as his view that the trade meaning of "chicken" was "broilers and fryers." In addition to this opinion testimony, plaintiff relied on the fact that the Urner-Barry service, the Journal of Commerce, and Weinberg Bros. & Co. of Chicago, a large supplier of poultry, published quotations in a manner which, in one way or another, distinguish between "chicken," comprising broilers, fryers and certain other categories, and "fowl," which, Bauer acknowledged, included stewing chickens. This material would be impressive if there were nothing to the contrary. However, there was, as will now be seen.

Defendant's witness Weininger, who operates a chicken eviscerating plant in New Jersey, testified "Chicken is everything except a goose, a duck, and a turkey. Everything is a chicken, but then you have to say, you have to specify which category you want or that you are talking about." Its witness Fox said that in the trade "chicken" would encompass all the various classifications. Sadina, who conducts a food inspection service, testified that he would consider any bird coming within the classes of "chicken" in the Department of Agriculture's regulations to be a chicken. The specifications approved by the General Services Administration include fowl as well as broilers and fryers under the classification "chickens." Statistics of the Institute of American Poultry Industries use the phrases "Young chickens" and "Mature chickens," under the general heading "Total chickens." and the Department of Agriculture's daily and weekly price reports avoid use of the word "chicken" without specification.

Defendant advances several other points which it claims affirmatively support its construction. Primary among these is the regulation of the Department of Agriculture, 7 C.F.R. § 70.300-70.370, entitled, "Grading and Inspection of Poultry and Edible Products Thereof." and in particular 70.301 which recited:

> "*Chickens*. The following are the various classes of chickens:
> (a) Broiler or fryer . . .
> (b) Roaster . . .
> (c) Capon . . .
> (d) Stag ...
> (e) Hen or stewing chicken or fowl . . .
> (f) Cock or old rooster . . ."

Defendant argues, as previously noted, that the contract incorporated these regulations by reference. Plaintiff answers that the contract provision related simply to grade and Government inspection and did not incorporate the Government definition of "chicken," and also that the definition in the Regulations is ignored in the trade. However, the latter contention was contradicted by Weininger and Sadina; and there is force in defendant's argument that the contract made the regulations a dictionary, particularly since the reference to Government grading was already in plaintiff's initial cable to Stovicek.

Defendant makes a further argument based on the impossibility of its obtaining broilers and fryers at the 33¢ price offered by plaintiff for the 2½-3 lbs. birds. There is no substantial dispute that, in late April, 1957, the price for 2½-3 lbs. broilers was between 35 and 37¢ per pound, and that when defendant entered into the contracts, it was well aware of this and intended to fill them by supplying fowl in these weights. It claims that plaintiff must likewise have known the market since plaintiff had reserved shipping space on April 23, three days before plaintiff's cable to Stovicek, or, at least, that Stovicek was chargeable with such knowledge. It is scarcely an answer to say, as plaintiff does in its brief, that the 33¢ price offered by the 2½-3 lbs. "chickens" was closer to the prevailing 35¢ price for broilers than to the 30¢ at which defendant procured fowl. Plaintiff must have expected defendant to make some profit—certainly it could not have expected defendant deliberately to incur a loss.

Finally, defendant relies on conduct by the plaintiff after the first shipment had been received. On May 28 plaintiff sent two cables complaining that the larger birds in the first shipment constituted "fowl." Defendant answered with a cable refusing to recognize plaintiff's objection and announcing "We have today ready for shipment 50,000 lbs. chicken 2½-3 lbs. 25,000 lbs. broilers 1½-2 lbs.," these being the goods procured for shipment under the second contract, and asked immediate answer "whether we are to ship this merchandise to you and whether you will accept the merchandise." After several other cable exchanges, plaintiff replied on May 29 "Confirm again that merchandise is to be shipped since resold by us if not enough pursuant to contract chickens are shipped the missing quantity is to be shipped within ten days stop we resold to our customers pursuant to your contract chickens grade A you have to deliver us said merchandise we again state that we shall make you fully responsible for all resulting costs."[2] Defendant argues that if plaintiff was sincere in thinking it was entitled to young chickens, plaintiff would not have allowed the shipment under the second contract to go forward, since the distinction between broilers and chickens drawn in defendant's cablegram must have made it clear that the larger birds would not be broilers. However, plaintiff answers that the cables show plaintiff was insisting on delivery of young chickens and that defendant shipped old ones at its peril. Defendant's point would be highly relevant on another disputed issue—whether if liability were established, the measure of damages should be the difference in market value of broilers and stewing chicken in New York or the larger difference in Europe, but I cannot give it weight on the issue of interpretation. Defendant points out also that plaintiff proceeded to deliver some of the larger birds in Europe, describing them as "poulets"; defendant argues that it was only when plaintiff's customers complained about this that plaintiff developed the idea that "chicken" meant "young chicken." There is little force in this in view of plaintiff's immediate and consistent protests.

When all the evidence is reviewed, it is clear that defendant believed it could comply with the contracts by delivering stewing chicken in the 2½-3 lbs. size. Defendant's subjective intent would not be significant if this did not coincide with an objective meaning of "chicken." Here it did coincide with one of the dictionary meanings, with the definition in the Department of Agriculture Regulations to which the contract made at least oblique reference, with at least some usage in the trade, with the realities of the market, and with what plaintiff's spokesman had said. Plaintiff asserts it to be equally plain that plaintiff's own subjective intent was to obtain broilers and fryers; the only evidence against this is the material as to

---

[2] These cables were in German; "chicken", "broilers" and, on some occasions, "fowl," were in English.

market prices and this may not have been sufficiently brought home. In any event it is unnecessary to determine that issue. For plaintiff has the burden of showing that "chicken" was used in the narrower rather than in the broader sense, and this it has not sustained.

This opinion constitutes the Court's findings of fact and conclusions of law. Judgment shall be entered dismissing the complaint with costs. *no one really won*

P cost show
didn't smaller
this meant
was
D wins because sellers

Reading the Law Critically:
The UCC on Contract Interpretation

As noted earlier, UCC Article 2 was adopted in New York in 1962, several years after the litigation in *Frigaliment*.

1. What effect would the UCC provision below have had on the outcome in *Frigaliment*? What differences, if any, do you see between the UCC terms and the rules that Judge Friendly discussed in the case?

2. What are the similarities and differences among "course of dealing," "course of performance," and "usage of trade"?

3. Why should conflicts among sources of meaning be resolved as indicated by § 1-303 (e)?

A note of explanation: Section 1-303 below is from the 2001 revision of UCC Article 1, now adopted in a majority of states. It combines definitions that appeared in §§ 1-205 and 2-208 in earlier versions of Articles 1 and 2.

UCC § 1-303. **Course of Performance, Course of Dealing, and Usage of Trade.**

(a) A "course of performance" is a sequence of conduct between the parties to a particular transaction that exists if:
   (1) the agreement of the parties with respect to the transaction involves repeated occasions for performance by a party; and
   (2) the other party, with knowledge of the nature of the performance and opportunity for objection to it, accepts the performance or acquiesces in it without objection.
(b) A "course of dealing" is a sequence of conduct concerning previous transactions between the parties to a particular transaction that is fairly to be regarded as establishing a common basis of understanding for interpreting their expressions and other conduct.

(c) A "usage of trade" is any practice or method of dealing having such regularity of observance in a place, vocation, or trade as to justify an expectation that it will be observed with respect to the transaction in question. The existence and scope of such a usage must be proved as facts. If it is established that such a usage is embodied in a trade code or similar record, the interpretation of the record is a question of law.

(d) A course of performance or course of dealing between the parties or usage of trade in the vocation or trade in which they are engaged or of which they are or should be aware is relevant in ascertaining the meaning of the parties' agreement, may give particular meaning to specific terms of the agreement, and may supplement or qualify the terms of the agreement. A usage of trade applicable in the place in which part of the performance under the agreement is to occur may be so utilized as to that part of the performance.

(e) Except as otherwise provided in subsection (f), the express terms of an agreement and any applicable course of performance, course of dealing, or usage of trade must be construed whenever reasonable as consistent with each other. If such a construction is unreasonable:

   (1) express terms prevail over course of performance, course of dealing, and usage of trade;

   (2) course of performance prevails over course of dealing and usage of trade; and

   (3) course of dealing prevails over usage of trade.

(f) Subject to **Section 2-209** and **Section 2A-208**, a course of performance is relevant to show a waiver or modification of any term inconsistent with the course of performance.

(g) Evidence of a relevant usage of trade offered by one party is not admissible unless that party has given the other party notice that the court finds sufficient to prevent unfair surprise to the other party.

Comments:

1. The Uniform Commercial Code rejects both the "lay-dictionary" and the "conveyancer's" reading of a commercial agreement. Instead the meaning of the agreement of the parties is to be determined by the language used by them and by their action, read and interpreted in the light of commercial practices and other surrounding circumstances. The measure and background for interpretation are set by the commercial context, which may explain and supplement even the language of a formal or final writing.

2. "Course of dealing," as defined in subsection (b), is restricted, literally, to a sequence of conduct between the parties previous to the agreement. A sequence of conduct after or under the agreement, however, is a "course of performance." "Course of dealing" may enter the agreement either by explicit provisions of the agreement or by tacit recognition.

. . . .

4. A usage of trade under subsection (c) must have the "regularity of observance" specified. The ancient English tests for "custom" are abandoned in this connection. Therefore, it is not required that a usage of trade be "ancient or immemorial," "universal," or the like. Under the requirement of subsection (c) full recognition is thus available for new usages and for usages currently observed by the great majority of decent dealers, even though dissidents ready to cut corners do not agree. . . .

§ 2.2. Canons of Construction

As demonstrated in *Frigaliment*, the meaning of contract terms is often determined by considering the context in which the contract was created. Additional assistance comes from various articulated rules ("canons") of construction. Many of these rules are "semantic canons": rules based on assumptions about ordinary language usage, leading to presumptions about what the parties likely intended particular language to mean (but those presumptions will give way to contrary evidence regarding the parties' actual intent). Some are "substantive canons": rules that construe contract meaning in light of public policy concerns. Some rules combine public policy concerns with assumptions about the likely intent of the parties.

Reading the Law Critically: Canons of Construction

The chart below identifies a group of the most widely used canons, including the Latin phrases by which some of them are known, and provides examples of each canon's application.

1. As you read the rules below, make a list identifying which are semantic canons, which are policy-based, and which draw on both.

2. For semantic canons, what are the underlying assumptions about language usage, and do you agree with those assumptions?

3. For policy-based canons, what is the likely rationale behind the rule?

most on language

most of contracts litigation is over contract interpretation

Canon of construction	Example of application
Technical terms and words of art are given their technical meaning when used in a transaction within that technical field.	Whether Mylanta is a compound combination within the meaning and intentions of the contracting parties in a patent license agreement is interpreted according to the meaning attributed by experts in the field. *Moraine Prods., Inc. v. Parke, Davis & Co.*, 203 N.W.2d 917 (Mich. Ct. App. 1972).
A writing is interpreted as a whole, and all writings that are part of the same transaction are interpreted together.	An agreement for sale of real estate provides that the broker will be paid a commission "upon the signing of this agreement" by both buyer and seller. In the last paragraph, the seller added: "The commission being due and payable upon the transfer of the property." The property was never transferred because the buyer was unable to go forward with the sale. The commission was not owed, because the former statement must be read with the final clause, which shows the commission was owed not upon signing but upon transfer. *Mealey v. Kanealy*, 286 N.W. 500 (Iowa 1939).
An interpretation is preferred that gives force to every term and provision of the contract rather than one that creates an irreconcilable conflict between provisions.	A printed term in a charter contract says "vessel to have turn in loading." Handwritten below that is the phrase "vessel to be loaded promptly." One party argued that the second phrase took precedence over the first, so that the vessel did not have to wait its turn for loading when it arrived. The court concluded that, read together, the terms meant the vessel would wait its turn, but when it reached the front of the line it would be loaded expeditiously. *Harding v. Cargo of 4,698 Tons of New Rivers Steam Coal*, 147 F. 971 (D. Me. 1906).
Specific terms and exact terms are given greater weight than general language.	A specific clause shifting the cost of conforming to regulations enacted after the bid was submitted took precedence over a more general clause requiring that the contractor's work conform with all relevant regulations. *Hills Materials Co. v. Rice*, 982 F.2d 514 (Fed. Cir. 1992).
When the same word is used in different parts of the contract, it will be presumed to be used in the same sense throughout the contract.	The term "insured" in an insurance policy had the same meaning throughout the policy. *Holter v. Nat'l Union Fire Ins. Co.*, 459 P.2d 61 (Wash. Ct. App. 1969).

semantics

language

common one

chicken

Words derive meaning from the words with which they are associated in an agreement (in Latin, "noscitur a sociis").

Semantics

In insurance contract, "flood" meant inundation from natural water sources, not damage from a broken water main, because the contract referred to loss from "flood, surface water, waves, tidal water or tidal wave, overflow of streams or other bodies of water or spray from any of the foregoing, all whether driven by wind or not." *Popkin v. Sec. Mut. Ins. Co.,* 367 N.Y.S.2d 492 (App. Div. 1975).

General terms derive meaning from the specific terms that precede them (in Latin, "ejusdem generis").

Semantics

Insurance contract excluded coverage for the covered aircraft while "subject to bailment, lease, conditional sale, mortgage or other encumbrance . . . ." Court concluded that the list was intended to refer to encumbrances involving financial interest in the aircraft, so the aircraft was insured when a pilot flew the plane to show it to a possible buyer. *Smith v. Southeastern Pa. Transp. Auth.,* 707 A.2d 604 (Pa. Commw. Ct. 1998).

Separately negotiated or added terms are given greater weight than standardized terms or other terms not separately negotiated. As a result, terms handwritten on a form are given greater weight than standard terms.

Semantics/policy

Invoice from contractor contained a smaller typewritten amount and a larger handwritten number. Although normally the handwritten amount would control, testimony showed they were written to record a disputed amount claimed, not to record the amount agreed to. *Roylex, Inc. v. Avco Cmty. Developers, Inc.,* 559 S.W.2d 833 (Tex. Civ. App. 1977).

When some things are specified in detail in a contract, other things of the same character are excluded by implication (in Latin, "expressio unius est exclusio alterius"). *Semantics*

A franchise contract mentioned two specific locations but did not mention a third location, so the logical implication was that the third site was not approved. *S.M.R. Enters., Inc. v. S. Haircutters, Inc.,* 662 S.W.2d 944 (Tenn. Ct. App. 1983).

If a contractual provision is susceptible of two reasonable constructions, only one of which comports with law, the court should choose the interpretation that will make the provision legal.

policy + language

An ambiguous installment contract clause was interpreted to mean the company could not collect unearned interest, because the alternative construction would violate usury laws. *Ford Motor Credit Co. v. McDaniel,* 613 S.W.2d 513 (Tex. App. 1981).

A modifying phrase at the end of a list is understood as referring only to the last item in the list, unless there is reason to understand the phrase as applying to the rest of the items in the list (the "last antecedent rule"; in Latin, "reddondo singular sin-guilis"). *Semantics*

A guaranty agreement contains the following phrase: "All amounts due, debts, liabilities and payment obligations described in clauses (i) and (ii), above, are referred to herein as 'Indebtedness.'" Applying the canon, the court concludes that "described in clauses (i) and (ii)" applies only to the "payment obligations," not to "amounts due, debts, liabilities." *JRG Capital Investors I v. Doppelt,* 2012 WL 2529256 (S.D. Tex. June 28, 2012).

In interpreting contract language, courts should follow rules of grammar and pay attention to the usage of words such as "and" vs. "or", "may" vs. "shall" vs. "must", etc.

A contract was "cancellable by either party upon ninety (90) days written notice on or after January 1, 1977." The rule that modifying phrases refer to the last antecedent means the contract could be canceled, at the earliest, 90 days after 1/1/77, not 90 days after contract formation, but the clause was still too ambiguous for a ruling on summary judgment. *Stanbalt Realty Co. v. Commercial Credit Corp.,* 401 A.2d 1043 (Md. Ct. Spec. App. 1979).

A settlement agreement contained the phrase "claims asserted or which could have been asserted by one party against another, as well as *that party's agent, officer, director, employee, representative, attorney, or accountant.*" "[T]he article 'that,' when coupled with a noun, refers to the most recent appearance of that noun" so the italicized phrase modifies the party against whom a claim may be brought, not the party who might bring the claim. *McCollum v. Huffstutter,* 2002 WL 31247077 (Tenn. Ct. App. Oct. 8, 2002).

If a provision has two reasonable meanings, the court should prefer the meaning less favorable to the party drafting the contract language, unless the parties have equal bargaining power or the contract is otherwise the product of negotiation rather than imposed by one party on the other. (In Latin, "omnia praesumuntur contra proferentem.")

See, e.g., Joyner v. Adams, 361 S.E.2d 902 (N.C. Ct. App. 1987); *Terra Int'l, Inc. v. Mississippi Chem. Corp.,* 119 F.3d 688 (8th Cir. 1997).

policy - interpret against party that drafted

policy

Problems: Interpreting Express Terms

In each of the following problems, you should answer the interpretation question using only the contract document, dictionary definitions as appropriate, and any applicable canons of construction. Not all of the contract language will be relevant to the question you are asked to address, but you should read carefully through all the contract text in order to create the best arguments you can muster for the competing interpretations.

7-1. Guardian Casualty provides its customers with homeowners insurance that protects against "accidental direct physical loss." The policy contains a clause excluding coverage for "loss resulting directly or indirectly from: . . . discharge, release, escape, seepage, migration or dispersal of pollutants." The policy defines "pollutants" as "any solid, liquid, gaseous or thermal irritant or contaminant, including smoke, vapor, soot, fumes, acids, alkalis, chemicals, liquids, gases and waste. Waste includes materials to be recycled, reconditioned or reclaimed."

Customers of Guardian have filed claims, seeking recovery for losses resulting from (1) inadequate ventilation of exhaled carbon dioxide; (2) lead-based paint chips, flakes, and dust; and (3) the presence of bats and bat guano between the structure's siding and walls, making the building uninhabitable. Guardian has denied each claim, asserting that they are all covered by the pollutant exclusions clause.

For each claim, identify the arguments that Guardian and its customers would make, for and against coverage. How would you interpret the contract on the contested point if you were the judge?

7-2. In November 1998, the attorneys general of 46 states entered a settlement agreement with major manufacturers of cigarettes, including R.J. Reynolds, as part of litigation over medical expenses from tobacco-related diseases. The settlement agreement barred Reynolds and the other manufacturers from "using or causing to be used . . . any Cartoon in the advertising, promoting, packaging or labeling of tobacco products." The agreement defined "Cartoon" as

> Any drawing or other depiction of an object, person, animal, creature or other similar caricature that satisfies any of the following criteria:
> (1) The use of comically exaggerated features;

(2) The attribution of human characteristics to animals, plants or other objects, or the similar use of anthropormorphic technique; or
(3) The attribution of unnatural or extra-human abilities, such as imperviousness to pain or injury, X-ray vision, tunneling at very high speeds or transformation

While operating under the settlement agreement, Reynolds placed an advertisement in Rolling Stone magazine, promoting independent rock music and record labels in connection with its Camel cigarette brand. The advertisement included a page depicting an "odd pastoral scene." The images are each realistic photographs, but they are arranged in a surreal fashion. A woman drives a floating tractor that has enormous film reels for wheels and a telephoto camera lens protruding from the engine. A rooster rides on top, with a bird on his back. There is a radio with a propeller, flying through the air above an eagle carrying a picture frame through which a human hand protrudes. Old-style radios, televisions and speakers are perched on stems as if growing out of the ground. Above the images is the Camel logo and the heading "The Farm Free Range Music, Committed To Supporting and Promoting Independent Record Labels." You can view the Rolling Stone advertisement at: blog.legalzoom.com/wp-content/uploads/2011/07/seeit_02.jpg and other sites.

The attorneys general of several states claim that Reynolds violated the settlement agreement by promoting its cigarettes using cartoons. Reynolds claims that the advertisement does not contain cartoons as that term is used in the settlement agreement. Identify the arguments supporting each side's interpretation of the contract. How would you interpret the contract on the contested point if you were the judge?

7-3. Brook Chemicals, Inc. (BCI) is in the business of selling agricultural chemicals and products. As part of its ongoing business operations, BCI frequently purchases supplies from other companies on credit and, to safeguard their advances, the suppliers obtain security interests in BCI's property and inventory to the extent of the credit advanced. In 2001, BCI and Sylvan Supply entered such an arrangement. The agreement provided that Sylvan would have a security interest in all BCI inventory, notes and accounts receivable, machinery and equipment, now owned or hereafter acquired, including all replacements, substitutions and additions thereto.

In 2003, Brook and Sylvan entered a new agreement to finance additional purchases, using a preprinted standard "Business Security Agreement." In the field on the form for describing the collateral (that is, the property in which Sylvan would have a security interest), the parties inserted language, drafted by Sylvan, that described the security interest as being in

all BCI inventory, including but not limited to agricultural chemicals, fertilizers, and fertilizer materials sold to BCI by Sylvan whether now owned or hereafter acquired, including all replacements, substitutions and additions thereto, and the accounts, notes, and any other proceeds therefrom.

The 2003 agreement also contained a preprinted clause providing

as additional collateral all additions to and replacements of all such collateral and all accessories, accessions, parts and equipment now or hereafter affixed thereto or used in connection with and the proceeds from all such collateral.

In 2005, BCI entered a contract with State Bank, pursuant to which State Bank would provide BCI with a $4 million line of credit, secured by all of BCI's inventory, subject to any earlier-established security interests; that is, debts secured by earlier-established security interests in all or part of BCI's inventory (e.g., Sylvan's security interests) would be satisfied before debts secured under the contract with State Bank.

BCI's business suffered increasing financial challenges, and in 2010 the company filed for voluntary bankruptcy. In the bankruptcy proceedings, Sylvan claimed that under the 2003 financing agreement it held a security interest in all of BCI's inventory (and its proceeds); State Bank claimed that under that agreement Sylvan held a security interest in only inventory purchased from Sylvan.

Identify the arguments supporting each side's interpretation of the contract. How would you interpret the contract on the contested point if you were the judge?

7-4. Charlotte Stone was hired to work as a physician's assistant for the Clayton Health Care System. One of the benefits of Ms. Stone's job was participation in a group life-insurance policy administered by the Perpetual Life Insurance Company. The policy provides life-insurance coverage to "active full-time employees" of Clayton. Ms. Stone completed and signed the required enrollment forms.

According to Ms. Stone's employment contract, she was hired to work full-time (a 40-hour work week), and her effective date of employment was Monday, December 27, 2004. Ms. Stone's actual first day of work was Monday, January 3, 2005. Ms. Stone's coverage under the Perpetual policy was scheduled to start on Saturday, January 1, 2005.

Unfortunately, after Ms. Stone accepted the offer from Clayton, but before her first day of work, she was diagnosed with an aggressive form of cancer. Ms. Stone's health deteriorated rapidly, which limited her ability to work. Although she was paid her full-time salary, Ms. Stone never worked a full 40-hour week. Ms. Stone stopped working altogether in April 2005 and died in July 2005.

After Ms. Stone's death, her husband (Dennis Stone) submitted a claim for life-insurance benefits to Perpetual. Perpetual denied Mr. Stone's claim, stating that Ms. Stone had never been an "active full-time employee" of Clayton. Perpetual claims that, according to the terms of the insurance policy, Ms. Stone was required to work at least one 32-hour week in order to be eligible for coverage and she did not do so.

Mr. Stone disputes Perpetual's reading of the policy, claiming that Ms. Stone was an "active full-time employee" even if she never worked a 32-hour week.

Read the provisions of the contract between Clayton and Perpetual, reproduced below, and identify the arguments supporting each side's interpretation of the contract. How would you interpret the contract on the contested point if you were the judge? (Mr. Stone is an intended beneficiary of the contract between Clayton and Perpetual so he would be able to enforce that contract even though he was not a party to the contract itself. See Chapter 10, page 1255)

ELIGIBILITY FOR LIFE COVERAGES

Eligible Employees

Subject to the Conditions of Eligibility set forth below, and to all of the other conditions of the plan, all of your employees who are in an eligible class will be eligible if: (a) they are active full-time employees; or (b) qualified retirees.

Conditions of Eligibility:

Full-Time Requirement: We won't insure an employee unless he or she is an active full-time employee, or a qualified retiree.

Proof of Insurability Requirements: Part or all of an employee's insurance amounts may be subject to proof that he or she is insurable. The Schedule of Insurance explains if and when we require proof. An employee won't be covered for any amount that requires such proof until he or she gives the proof to us and we approve that proof in writing.

An employee whose active full-time service ends before he or she meets any proof of insurability requirements that apply to him or her will still have to meet those requirements if he or she is later re-employed by you.

The Waiting Period: Employees in an eligible class are eligible for life insurance under this plan after they complete the service waiting period established by the employer, if any.

WHEN EMPLOYEE COVERAGE STARTS

An employee must be actively at work, and working his or her regular number of hours, on the date his or her coverage is scheduled to start. And he or she must have met all of the conditions of eligibility which apply to him or her. If an employee is not actively at work on his or her scheduled effective date, we will postpone the start of his or her coverage until he or she returns to active full-time work.

Sometimes, a scheduled effective date is not a regularly scheduled work day. But an employee's coverage will start on that date if he or she was actively at work, and working his or her regular number of hours, on his or her last regularly scheduled work day.

Whether an employee must pay all or part of the cost of employee coverage, he or she must elect to enroll and agree to make the required payments within 31 days of his or her eligibility date. If he or she does this on or before the eligibility date, his or her coverage is scheduled to start on his or her eligibility date. If he or she does this within 31 days after his or her eligibility date, his or her coverage is scheduled to start on the date he or she signs his or her enrollment form.

However, if he or she elects to enroll and agrees to make the required payments more than 31 days after his or her eligibility date, his or her coverage won't start until he or she sends us proof that he or she is insurable. Once we've approved it, his or her coverage is scheduled to start on the effective date shown in the endorsement section of his or her application.

Any part of an employee's coverage which is subject to proof that he or she is insurable won't start unless he or she sends this proof to us, and we approve it in writing. Once we have approved it, that part of his or her coverage is scheduled to start on the effective date shown in the endorsement section of his or her application.

WHEN EMPLOYEE COVERAGE ENDS

When Employee Coverage Ends: Except as explained in the "When Active Service Ends" section of this plan, an employee's insurance will end on the first of the following dates:

- The date an employee's active full-time service ends for any reason. Such reasons include disability, death, retirement (except for qualified retirees), lay-off, leave of absence, and the end of employment.
- The date an employee stops being an eligible employee under this plan.
- The date the group plan ends, or is discontinued for a class of employees to which the employee belongs.
- The last day of the period for which required payments are made for the employee.

Also, an employee may have the right to continue certain group benefits for a limited time after his or her coverage would otherwise end. And an employee may have the right to replace certain group benefits with converted policies. The plan's benefit provisions explain these situations. Read the plan's provisions carefully.

When Active Service Ends: You may continue an employee's life insurance under this plan after his active service with you ends only as follows:

- If an employee's active service ends because he is disabled you may continue his insurance subject to all of the terms of this plan.
- If an employee's active service ends because he goes on a non-parental leave of absence or is laid off, you may continue his insurance, except for disability income insurance, if any, under this plan for the rest of the policy month in which the non-parental leave or layoff starts, plus *01* more full policy month(s). However, if the employee joins any armed force before this period ends, you may continue his insurance until the date he becomes a member of such armed force.

- If an employee's active full-time service ends because he goes on parental leave, you must continue the employee's group insurance for the duration of the parental leave, subject to all of the terms of the plan. You may require the employee to pay the full cost of the employee's coverage during such parental leave.
- If you continue an employee's benefits under this plan as set forth above, it must be based on a plan which prevents individual selection by you.
- And, any such continuation is subject to the payment of premiums, and to all of the other terms and conditions of this plan.
- The amount of an employee's insurance during any such continuation will be the amount in force on his last day of active service, subject to any reductions that would have otherwise applied if he had remained an active employee.

DEFINITIONS

Employee means a person who works for the employer at the employer's place of business, and whose income is reported for tax purposes using a W-2 form.

Full-time means the employee regularly works at least the number of hours in the normal work week set by the employer (but not less than 32 hours per week), at his employer's place of business.

Plan means the Perpetual group plan purchased by the employer.

Proof or Proof of Insurability means an application for insurance showing that a person is insurable.

Qualified Retiree means present retired physicians from the age 55 to 65 with at least 20 years of active continuous full-time service with the employer.

We, Us, Our and Perpetual mean The Perpetual Life Insurance Company of America.

———

Semantic canons, which make assumptions about what parties meant by the language they used, are generally applied only in conjunction with consideration of all evidence relevant to determining the parties' intent. Indeed, the canons are often articulated as providing a rule of interpretation unless evidence shows a contrary meaning was intended. But substantive canons implement policy considerations that may be independent of the parties' intent. Should a substantive canon be applied without regard to what the evidence shows the parties meant? The next case tries to answer that question, with respect to "omnia praesumuntur contra preferentem," the canon that favors the meaning less favorable to the party drafting the contract where the parties have unequal bargaining power.

Reading the Law Critically: *Klapp*

1. How does the court describe the roles of judge and jury in determining contractual meaning?

2. What relative roles do ambiguity, extrinsic evidence, and rules of construction play in the court's analysis of the contract language? What roles does the concurring judge believe they should play?

3. The majority and concurring opinions support the same outcome but for different reasons. On what do the opinions disagree? With which one do you agree?

Klapp v. United Insurance Group Agency

CRAIG A. KLAPP, Plaintiff-Appellant

v.

UNITED INSURANCE GROUP AGENCY, INC., Defendant-Appellee

Michigan Supreme Court

663 N.W.2d 447 (Mich. 2003)

MARKMAN, J.

We granted leave to appeal in this case to consider whether defendant breached the parties' written contract by refusing to pay plaintiff retirement renewal commissions on insurance policies that plaintiff sold on behalf of defendant while plaintiff was working for defendant. . . . Because we agree with the trial court that the language of this contract is ambiguous and, thus, that its interpretation raises a question of fact for the jury to determine in light of relevant extrinsic evidence, we reverse the judgment of the Court of Appeals and remand this case to the Court of Appeals for consideration of defendant's other appellate issue and plaintiff's cross-appeal.

I. FACTS AND PROCEDURAL HISTORY

[Plaintiff Craig Klapp worked for the defendant United Insurance Group Agency from 1990 to 1997. Klapp claimed that United Insurance failed to pay him commissions due when his former clients renewed their insurance policies, interpreting the contract to require such payments after an individual served as an insurance agent for seven years. United Insurance denied Klapp was owed commissions, interpreting the contract to require that an agent have worked for at least ten years and have reached the age of sixty-five in order to be eligible to receive renewal commissions.] The trial court denied defendant's motion for summary disposition, finding the contract to be ambiguous,[6] and the jury subsequently found in favor of plaintiff.[7] The Court of Appeals then reversed, concluding that the contract unambiguously requires that an agent must be at least sixty-five years old and have worked at least ten years for defendant in order to qualify for retirement renewal commissions. We granted plaintiff's application for leave to appeal.[9]

II. STANDARD OF REVIEW

We review de novo a trial court's ruling on a motion for summary disposition. *Stanton v. Battle Creek,* 466 Mich. 611, 614, 647 N.W.2d 508 (2002). Similarly, whether contract language is ambiguous is a question of law that we review de novo. *Farm Bureau Mut. Ins. Co. v. Nikkel,* 460 Mich. 558, 563, 596 N.W.2d 915 (1999). Finally, the proper interpretation of a contract is also a question of law that we review de novo. *Henderson v. State Farm Fire & Cas. Co.,* 460 Mich. 348, 353, 596 N.W.2d 190 (1999).

III. ANALYSIS

[The different interpretations offered by plaintiff and defendant were based on conflicting understandings of language that appeared in the Agent's Agreement and the Agent's Manual.]

When defendant moved for summary disposition, it argued that plaintiff was not entitled to renewal commissions because [he had not worked for the company for ten years.] Defendant further argued that, because the contract was unambiguous, extrinsic evidence may not be considered in interpreting the contract.

Plaintiff, on the other hand, argued that the contract was ambiguous [because of conflict between the Agent's Agreement and the Agent's Manual.] Plaintiff further argued that, because this contract was ambiguous, its interpretation was a question of fact that must be decided by the jury in light of relevant extrinsic

---

[6] Although the trial court stated, in a written opinion, "it is an issue for the trier of fact to determine whether or not the language of the contract and actions by the parties render an ambiguous or unambiguous contract," the court's final instructions to the jurors told them to consider both the contract and the relevant extrinsic evidence, and then decide what the contract meant. The court did not instruct the jurors to determine whether the contract was ambiguous.

[7] The jury awarded plaintiff $45,882 in renewal commissions for the period from August 1997 through the January 1999 trial, and one hundred percent of all future renewal commissions as they accrue.

[9] We directed the parties to include among the issues to be briefed: "Where, as in the present case, a contract is drafted entirely by one party, without any bilateral negotiations, is extrinsic evidence admissible to clarify ambiguity in the contract or is any ambiguity in the contract simply to be construed against the drafter (without considering any extrinsic evidence)?" 467 Mich. 867, 651 N.W.2d 918 (2002).

evidence. As already noted, the trial court agreed with plaintiff that the contract was ambiguous and, thus, must be interpreted by the jury in light of relevant extrinsic evidence.

A. THE CONTRACT LANGUAGE IS AMBIGUOUS

"An insurance contract is ambiguous when its provisions are capable of conflicting interpretations." *Nikkel, supra* at 566, 596 N.W.2d 915. Accordingly, if two provisions of the same contract irreconcilably conflict with each other, the language of the contract is ambiguous. Further, courts cannot simply ignore portions of a contract in order to avoid a finding of ambiguity or in order to declare an ambiguity. Instead, contracts must be "'construed so as to give effect to every word or phrase as far as practicable.'" *Hunter v. Pearl Assurance Co., Ltd,* 292 Mich. 543, 545, 291 N.W. 58 (1940), quoting *Mondou v. Lincoln Mut. Cas. Co.,* 283 Mich. 353, 358-359, 278 N.W. 94 (1938).

In our judgment, the . . . Agent's Agreement irreconcilably conflicts with the Agent's Manual's definition of retirement, which the Agent's Agreement incorporates. . . . Therefore, the language of the contract is ambiguous.

The Court of Appeals attempted to avoid a finding of ambiguity by [reading the definition of "retirement" in the Manual narrowly, to avoid conflict with the language in the Agreement]. Because there is no way to read the provisions of the contract in reasonable harmony, the language of the contract is ambiguous.

B. INTERPRETATION OF AMBIGUOUS CONTRACT

It is well settled that the meaning of an ambiguous contract is a question of fact that must be decided by the jury. *Hewett Grocery Co. v. Biddle Purchasing Co.,* 289 Mich. 225, 236, 286 N.W. 221 (1939). . . .

> **FYI**
>
> Although the court says it is "well settled" that the meaning of an ambiguous contract is a question for the jury, courts are not entirely consistent in establishing the boundary line between questions for the jury and questions for the court regarding matters of interpretation. *See* E. Allan Farnsworth, *Contracts* § 7.14 (4th ed. 2004).

Where a written contract is ambiguous, a factual question is presented as to the meaning of its provisions, requiring a factual determination as to the intent of the parties in entering the contract. Thus, the fact finder must interpret the contract's terms, in light of the apparent purpose of the contract as a whole, the rules of contract construction, and extrinsic evidence of intent and meaning. [11 Williston, Contracts (4th ed.), § 30:7, at. 87-91.]

. . . .

In interpreting a contract whose language is ambiguous, the jury should also consider that ambiguities are to be construed against the drafter of the contract. *Herweyer v. Clark Hwy. Services, Inc.*, 455 Mich. 14, 22, 564 N.W.2d 857 (1997). This is known as the rule of contra proferentem. However, this rule is only to be applied if all conventional means of contract interpretation, including the consideration of relevant extrinsic evidence, have left the jury unable to determine what the parties intended their contract to mean. Accordingly, if the extrinsic evidence indicates that the parties intended their contract to have a particular meaning, this is the meaning that should be given to the contract, regardless of whether this meaning is in accord with the drafter's or the non-drafter's view of the contract. In other words, if a contract is ambiguous regarding whether a term means "a" or "b," but relevant extrinsic evidence leads the jury to conclude that the parties intended the term to mean "b," then the term should be interpreted to mean "b," even though construing the document in the nondrafter's favor pursuant to an application of the rule of contra proferentem would produce an interpretation of the term as "a."

However, if the language of a contract is ambiguous, and the jury remains unable to determine what the parties intended after considering all relevant extrinsic evidence, the jury should only then find in favor of the nondrafter of the contract pursuant to the rule of contra proferentem. In other words, the rule of contra proferentem should be viewed essentially as a "tie-breaker," to be utilized only after all conventional means of contract interpretation, including the consideration of relevant extrinsic evidence, have been applied and found wanting.

This view of the rule of construing against the drafter of the contract is in accordance with [the Restatement (Second) of Contracts and with articulations of the rule in treatises by Corbin and Williston].

The rule of contra proferentem is a rule of last resort because, "The primary goal in the construction or interpretation of any contract is to honor the intent of the parties," *Rasheed v. Chrysler Corp.*, 445 Mich. 109, 127 n. 28, 517 N.W.2d 19 (1994), and the rule of contra proferentem does not aid in determining the parties' intent. . . . As stated in Corbin, *supra*, p. 306:

> The rule is not actually one of interpretation, because its application does not assist in determining the meaning that the two parties gave to the words, or even the meaning that a reasonable person would have assigned to the language used. It is chiefly a rule of policy, generally favoring the underdog. It directs the court to choose between two or more possible reasonable meanings on the basis of their legal operation, i.e., whether they favor the drafter or the other party.

. . . .

The concurring opinion asserts that, "when a contract is drafted entirely by one party, without any bilateral negotiations," the rule of contra proferentem "should be applied as the primary rule of construction, not as a last resort. . . ." *Post* at 1, 2. That is, when a contract whose language is ambiguous is drafted without bilateral negotiations, a jury should not be allowed to look at relevant extrinsic evidence in order to discern the parties' intent. Instead, the ambiguous language is simply to be construed against the drafter.

We respectfully disagree with the concurring opinion's reference to the rule of contra proferentem as a "rule of construction." In our judgment, the rule of contra proferentem is not a rule of construction, rather, as explained above, it is a rule of legal effect. While rules of construction are designed to help determine the parties' intent, the rule of contra proferentem is designed to resolve a dispute where the parties' intent cannot be determined.

Further, as the concurring opinion correctly states, "[t]he ultimate objective in interpreting an ambiguous contract is to ascertain the intent of the parties . . . ." Therefore, in our judgment, it is only obvious that a method of construing a contract that helps ascertain the intent of the parties should be preferred over one that does not. We agree with the concurring opinion that extrinsic evidence "'provides an incomplete guide with which to interpret contractual language.'" *Post* at 461. That is, extrinsic evidence is not the best way to determine what the parties intended. Rather, the language of the parties' contract is the best way to determine what the parties intended. However, where, as in cases such as this one, it is not possible to determine the parties' intent from the language of their contract, the *next* best way to determine the parties' intent is to use relevant extrinsic evidence. Such evidence at least affords a way by which to ascertain the parties' intent, unlike the rule of contra proferentem, which focuses solely on the status of the parties to a contract.

[The concurring opinion claims that earlier cases establish the precedent of using the rule of contra proferentem not as a tie-breaker, but as a primary rule of construction. The court disagrees with that interpretation of the cases, believing that the rule was used in those cases because there was "no relevant extrinsic evidence available" so contra proferentem was "the only tool available" to resolve the ambiguity.] In this case, plaintiff introduced as extrinsic evidence an older version of the Agent's Agreement and deposition testimony from defendant's executives showing that defendant's past practice had been to pay former agents the renewal commissions specified by . . . the vesting schedule, regardless of whether those agents had ten years of service with defendant or had reached age sixty-five.

. . . .

Defendant argues that the jury should not have considered this extrinsic evidence. However, as discussed above, the jury is to consider relevant extrinsic evidence when interpreting a contract whose language is ambiguous. How the drafting party has interpreted ambiguous contractual language in the past is certainly relevant in determining what the parties intended such language to mean. The meaning of a provision in a contract whose language is ambiguous "must be ascertained in the light of all of the relevant circumstances, . . . including, . . . the meanings accepted by the parties." *Davis v. Kramer Bros. Freight Lines, Inc.*, 361 Mich. 371, 375, 105 N.W.2d 29 (1960). "There is no doubt that evidence of practical interpretation by the parties is admissible as an aid in the determination of the meaning to be given legal effect." *Id.* at 375-376, 105 N.W.2d 29.

> Where parties by such a uniform course of conduct for a long time have given a contract a particular construction, that construction will be adopted by the courts.

> "The practical interpretation given to contracts by the parties to them, while engaged in their performance and before any controversy has arisen concerning them, is one of the best indications of their true intent." [*People ex rel Blair Attorney General v. Michigan Central R. Co.*, 145 Mich. 140, 166, 108 N.W. 772 (1906) (citation omitted) (portion of dissent by GRANT, J., assented to by the majority at 150, 108 N.W. 772).]

Think About It!

The court here speaks of adopting the "practical interpretation" given the contract by only one of the parties to the contract. Is this treatment consistent with the *Frigaliment* court's handling of such "practical construction" by a party? Did the actions here constitute a "course of dealing"?

Because the language of the contract here is ambiguous, and because defendant had, in the past, construed this contract to require the payment of retirement renewal commissions according to the vesting schedule, even if the agent was not at least sixty-five years old and had not served as an agent with defendant for at least ten years, the trial court did not err in instructing the jury to consider this evidence.

Although the trial court correctly instructed the jury that it could consider relevant extrinsic evidence and that any ambiguities should be construed against the drafter pursuant to the rule of contra proferentem, the trial court failed to inform the jury that it could only apply the rule of contra proferentem if it was unable to discern the parties' intent from the extrinsic evidence. However, in this case, this error was harmless. The jury did one of two things here. The jury either construed the language of the contract in favor of plaintiff pursuant to the rule of contra proferentem, or it construed the language of the contract in favor of plaintiff because the extrinsic evidence pointed to a construction of the contract in plaintiff's favor.[20]   Accordingly, regardless of which approach the jury used, it reached the (same) right result and, thus, failure to reverse is not inconsistent with substantial justice. MCR 2.613(A);   *Cox v. Flint Bd. of Hosp. Managers,* 467 Mich. 1, 8, 651 N.W.2d 356 (2002).

. . . .

. . . [W]e reverse the judgment of the Court of Appeals and remand this case to the Court of Appeals for consideration of defendant's other appellate issue and plaintiff's cross-appeal.

WEAVER, J. (*concurring*).

I concur in the decision to reverse the judgment of the Court of Appeals and remand the case to that Court for consideration of issues raised, but not addressed, below. I write separately because I disagree with the majority's holding that "the rule of contra proferentem is only to be applied if the intent of the parties cannot be discerned through the use of all conventional rules of interpretation, including an examination of relevant extrinsic evidence." Although I agree that this is the general rule, I would hold that when a contract is drafted entirely by one party, without any bilateral negotiations, the rule that a contract is to be strictly construed against its drafter should be applied as the primary rule of construction, not as a last resort, and extrinsic evidence is not admissible to clarify ambiguity in the contract.

. . . .

The ultimate objective in interpreting an ambiguous contract is to ascertain the intent of the parties so the agreement can be carried out according to that intent. *Loyal Order of Moose, Adrian Lodge 1034 v. Faulhaber,* 327 Mich. 244, 250, 41 N.W.2d 535 (1950);   *Stine v. Continental Cas. Co.,* 419 Mich. 89, 112, 349 N.W.2d 127 (1984). When there are bilateral negotiations between the parties, a court can assume that there is a relation between the contract terms that were agreed upon and the parties' expectations as revealed by extrinsic evidence. However, "unless extrinsic evidence can speak to the intent of *all* parties to a contract, it provides an incomplete guide with which to interpret contractual language." *SI Mgt. LP v. Wininger,* 707 A.2d 37, 43 (Del. 1998) (emphasis in original).

The Supreme Court of Delaware has held that where ambiguity arises in a contract drafted solely by one side and offered to others on a take-it-or-leave-it

---

[20] All the extrinsic evidence presented at trial favors plaintiff's construction of the contract. Defendant did not present any extrinsic evidence at trial that favors its construction.

basis, the rule of construing against the drafter is determinative. *SI Mgt, supra;* followed by *Intel Corp. v. VIA Technologies, Inc.,* 174 F.Supp. 2d 1038 (N.D.Cal., 2001). In *SI Mgt* the Delaware court analyzed its approach to interpreting insurance contracts. The Delaware courts had said that if an insurance contract is ambiguous, "'the principle of *contra proferentem* dictates that the contract must be construed against the drafter.'" *SI Management, supra* at 42 (citation omitted). The court found that the policy behind that principle of construing against the drafter is that the insurer was in complete control of creating and drafting the policy, while the insured had little say about those terms except to take them or leave them or to select from limited terms offered by the insurer. Because of that, the Delaware courts had consistently held that the insurer had an obligation to make the terms clear and should suffer the consequences of convoluted or confusing terms. In *SI Mgt* the Delaware Supreme Court expanded this principle to other contracts where there was not a bilaterally negotiated agreement, and one party had signed onto an agreement that it had no hand in drafting.

Take Note!

Although a Delaware case may appear to be just like any other persuasive precedent, Delaware rulings on business law matters have particular significance. As the state's website says, "The State of Delaware is a leading domicile for U.S. and international corporations. . . . More than 50% of all publicly-traded companies in the United States including 63% of the Fortune 500 have chosen Delaware as their legal home." http://corp.delaware.gov/aboutagency.shtml

There are sound public-policy reasons behind a black letter rule that when contractual provision are drafted entirely by one party, any ambiguity in the contract is to be construed against the drafter. First, the rule of contra proferentem provides a strong incentive for a party drafting a contract to use clear and unambiguous language. Second, the use of extrinsic evidence in circumstances involving ambiguity could be destabilizing to contractual relations and require more involved litigation by allowing parties to use assertions of oral understandings and examples of past behavior rather than relying on a written contract with the understanding that any ambiguity should be construed against its drafter.

[The concurrence discusses a series of cases in which "this Court has consistently applied the rule of construing against the drafter as its primary, indeed sole, aid to construction" and disagrees with the majority regarding how to understand those rulings. The majority finds the cases inapt because there was no extrinsic evidence to be considered in those cases; the concurrence notes that the cases simply do not establish the appropriate use of contra preferentem because they did not consider that issue, which is presented here as question of first impression. The concurrence also finds guidance in insurance contract cases in which the customer is presented with contracts "in a take-it-or-leave-fashion" and in which contra preferentem was applied "as the primary rule of construction."]

Here defendant was the entity in sole control of the process of creating and setting forth the terms of the contract. The parties did not engage in bilateral negotiation; the plaintiff's only choice in the terms of the contract was to take them or leave them. In such a situation, any ambiguity in the contract should have been construed against the drafter, without considering the extrinsic evidence.

In this case, the trial judge allowed the plaintiff to introduce a variety of extrinsic evidence, including references to the older version of the Agent's Agreement and deposition testimony by the defendant's executives. I would hold that the trial court erred in admitting the extrinsic evidence to resolve the contract's ambiguity. However, that error was harmless, because the same result was achieved as would have been if the contract had been construed against its drafter, defendant.

Accordingly, I concur with the decision to reverse the judgment of the Court of Appeals and remand the case to that Court for consideration of those issues raised, but not addressed, below.

_____

§ 3. Using Extrinsic Evidence to Understand a Contract

At its heart, contract interpretation seeks to determine the meaning intended by the parties when they chose the particular words used to express the contract terms. We have seen that contract interpretation begins with the words themselves, but the words were adopted in a broader context, including all the speech and conduct of the parties as well as the surrounding commercial and other circumstances. The evidence of that context is often called *extrinsic* evidence because it is outside the expressed contract terms.

One might think that the judge or jury would consider all relevant extrinsic evidence when construing the contract terms, but that is not always the case. You have already seen one example of a limitation on the use of extrinsic evidence. In *Klapp v. United Insurance Group Agency* (page 715), the majority and dissent disagreed about whether extrinsic evidence of intent should be considered to clarify ambiguous contract language if the ambiguity could be resolved by reference to the substantive canon of *omnia praesumuntur contra proferentem*, and both opinions cited authority for their competing arguments. In the materials that follow, you will see other examples of rules that operate to limit the admissibility of extrinsic evidence to determine contract meaning, and other instances of disagreement among the courts on the appropriateness and applicability of those rules.

§ 3.1. Determining Ambiguity

In *Frigaliment,* Judge Friendly declared that the critical word "chicken" was ambiguous and proceeded to consider additional evidence, including the parties' negotiations prior to entering the contract, to resolve the meaning of that word in the contract. But should a seemingly clear contract term be interpreted according to that "plain meaning" without reference to the prior negotiations? Should a judge make a finding that a term is ambiguous before the fact-finder (judge or jury) is allowed to consider all relevant evidence, including prior negotiations, to determine contract meaning? If so, what evidence should the judge consider in deciding whether the term is ambiguous? In particular, should the judge consider the parties' prior negotiations, even if the contract term, understood in the context of the surrounding circumstances, appears clear? The cases reflect a philosophical split regarding the answer to that question.

Reading the Law Critically:
C. & A. Construction and Pacific Gas & Electric Co.

1. According to each opinion (the majority and dissent in *C. & A. Construction Co.* and the decision in *Pacific Gas & Electric Co.*), what kinds of evidence should be considered to determine whether contract language is ambiguous? What rationales are offered for the different approaches? Which do you think is the best rule? Why?

2. According to the opinions, is the decision whether extrinsic evidence should be considered a question of law or a question of fact? Is the determination of the meaning of the contract a question of law or of fact?

3. Do you think there was ambiguity in the contract terms being construed? If so, was it patent or latent ambiguity? On what evidence do you base your conclusions?

C. & A. Construction Co. v. Benning Construction Co.

C. & A. CONSTRUCTION CO., Defendant-Appellant

v.

BENNING CONSTRUCTION CO., Plaintiff-Appellee

Supreme Court of Arkansas
509 S.W.2d 302 (Ark. 1974)

Payment to sub-contractors

HOLT, Justice.

The appellant and appellee are subcontractors who entered into an agreement involving the installation of sewer lines. Paragraph 7 of the agreement between these parties provided:

> It is further agreed that the 2nd subcontractor will receive $20,000 for supervision which will be added to the actual cost figure. It is further agreed that the difference between actual cost and bid price will be divided as follows: 33⅓% to 2nd subcontractor; 66⅔% to 1st subcontractor.

Appellee was paid $517,451.11 and appellee brought suit for an alleged payment deficit of $55,243.20 on the contract. The trial court, sitting as a jury, after hearing parol evidence, awarded appellee judgment for $40,349.11. Appellant questions only that part of the judgment which awarded $18,600 (in addition to $20,000 for supervision) for the salary and living expenses of appellee's president and sole stockholder during the time he was personally engaged in the supervision of the construction. Appellant contends that the extra award of $18,600 is double recovery in that it is contrary to the terms of the contract which designates a specific sum of $20,000 for supervision.

When contracting parties express their intention in a written instrument in clear and unambiguous language, it is our duty to construe the written agreement according to the plain meaning of the language employed. Miller v. Dyer, 243 Ark. 981, 423 S.W.2d 275 (1968). However, where the meaning of a written contract is ambiguous, parol evidence is admissible to explain the writing. Brown and Hackney v. Daubs, 139 Ark. 53, 213 S.W. 4 (1919). Ambiguities are both patent and latent. When, on its face, the reader can tell that something must be added to the written contract to determine the parties' intent, the ambiguity is patent; a latent ambiguity arises from undisclosed facts or uncertainties of the written instrument. Dorr v. School District No. 26 &c, 40 Ark. 237 (1882) . . . . However, the initial determination of the existence of an ambiguity rests with the court and if ambiguity exists, then parol evidence is admissible and the meaning of the term becomes a question for the factfinder. . . . Easton v. Washington County Insurance Co., 391 Pa. 28, 137 A.2d 332 (1957), cited in 4 Williston on Contracts, § 627 (3d Ed. 1961). . . .

In the case at bar, we cannot strain the plain, obvious, and unambiguous language of the contract. Appellee agreed to a definite amount for supervision. Had appellee's president and sole owner of the corporation desired that the sum of $20,000 represent a guaranteed profit, as he and his witnesses so understood from their verbal agreement during negotiations, the wording of the contract should have so indicated. Had appellee's president and owner intended, as he now contends was their verbal understanding, that his salary should be in addition to the $20,000 for supervision, the written contract could easily have so reflected. The lower court's award for salary ($15,500) is contrary to the plain and unambiguous terms of their written agreement and the judgment should be adjusted accordingly.

. . . .

. . .[I]n the case at bar, even though the verbal evidence and tentative drafts attending the negotiations be true, it cannot alter the terms of the clearly unambiguous written agreement as to his compensation for supervisory services. The contracting parties were knowledgeable and certainly capable of reducing their negotiations to unambiguous written terms. In such situations, we cannot interfere.

The court found that appellee was entitled to $3,100 for its owner's expenses during the time he actually was "on the job." The contract clearly provides for recovery of actual costs. In the circumstances, the court was justified in this award.

We deem it unnecessary to discuss appellant's other contentions.

The judgment is modified to exclude the salary allowance.

Affirmed as modified.

FOGLEMAN and BROWN, JJ., dissent.
FOGLEMAN, Justice.

The majority opinion is apparently based upon the premise that the existence of ambiguity must be determined by the court upon the basis of an examination of the contract. This is the case in determining whether there is a patent ambiguity. It is not in the case of a latent ambiguity. By definition, a latent ambiguity is one which does not appear upon the face of the instrument and cannot be detected by examination of the document. It arises from facts not disclosed in the instrument. Dorr v. School District No. 26, 40 Ark. 237. . . .

The term "latent ambiguity" is defined to mean an ambiguity which arises not upon the words of the instrument, as looked at in themselves, but upon those words when applied to the object or subject which they describe. It is one which does not appear on the face of the language used or the instrument being considered, or when the words apply equally to two or more different subjects or things, as where the language employed is clear and intelligible and suggests but a single meaning, but some extrinsic fact or evidence *aliunde*, creates a necessity for interpretation or a choice among two or more possible meanings.

. . . .

It's Latin to Me!

"Aliunde" means "from another source" or "from elsewhere."

In order for the court to determine whether a latent ambiguity exists, it is obviously necessary that it consider evidence of extraneous and collateral facts as to extrinsic circumstances. Logan v. Wiley, 357 Pa. 547, 55 A.2d 366 (1947). It is a well settled rule that extrinsic evidence is admissible to show that a latent ambiguity exists. Hall v. Equitable Life Assurance Society, 295 Mich. 404, 295 N.W. 204 . . . .

It is generally held that the question whether an ambiguity exists is one of law for the court. Steele v. McCargo, 260 F.2d 753 (8th Cir. 1958) . . . . In determining whether an ambiguity exists, a contract must be read in the light of what the parties intended as gathered from the language thereof in view of all surrounding circumstances. Arkansas Amusement Corp. v. Kempner, 57 F.2d 466 (8th Cir. 1932). . . . The words of a contract, which are not ambiguous in the abstract, may, when considered in relation to the circumstances surrounding the making of it, create an ambiguity requiring interpretation. Arkansas Amusement Co. v. Kempner, supra; . . . . In making the determination, courts may acquaint themselves with the persons and circumstances that are the subjects of the statements in the written agreement and place themselves in the position of the parties who made the contract, so as to view the circumstances as they did. Wood v. Kelsey, 90 Ark. 272, 119 S.W. 258.

There is another facet of the problem of admissibility of parol testimony to explain a contract very closely related to the question whether a latent ambiguity exists. Our cases clearly recognize that parol evidence is admissible to explain the meaning of the terms or words used when they have a technical meaning or, by custom and usage, are used in a sense other than in an ordinary meaning of the words. Paepcke-Leicht Lbr. Co. v. Talley, supra; Wilkes v. Stacy, 113 Ark. 556, 169 S.W. 796. In the case last cited, we quoted from Lawson on Contracts, Second Edition, § 390, p. 450, as follows:

> The customs of particular classes of men soon give to particular words different meanings from those which they may have among other classes, or in the community generally. Mercantile contracts are commonly framed in a language peculiar to merchants, and hardly understood outside their world. Agreements which are entered into every day in the year between members of different trades and professions are expressed in technical and uncommon terms. The intentions of the parties, though perfectly well known to themselves, would be defeated were the language

employed to be strictly construed according to its ordinary meaning in the world at large. Hence, while words in a contract relating to the ordinary transactions of life [are] to be construed according to their plain, ordinary, and popular meaning, yet if, in reference to the subject-matter of the contract, particular words and expressions have, by usage, acquired a meaning different from their plain, ordinary, and popular meaning, the parties using those words in such a contract must be taken to have used them in their peculiar sense. And so words, technical or ambiguous on their face, or foreign or peculiar to the sciences or the arts, or to particular trades, professions, occupations, or localities, may be explained, where they are employed in written instruments, by parol evidence of usage.

Obviously the trial court found that an ambiguity existed. The pertinent contract terms hang upon the meaning of the words "supervision" and "actual cost." The real issue is whether the salary and expenses of Benning while he was acting as superintendent of the Crossett job are a part of the "actual costs" as distinguished from the allowance of $20,000 for "supervision." Benning testified that the charge in question covered only the time he spent on the North Crossett job, and that appellee employed no superintendent on the job, although there were four working foremen. It is significant that appellant thought that evidence of the original negotiations was admissible, because its attorney introduced evidence thereof by cross-examination of Benning over appellee's attorney's objection that it should be considered for impeachment only.

There was evidence that the following circumstances existed at the time that contract being construed was entered into:

Sutton Construction Company had failed. A representative of appellant had prepared a contract relating to unfinished sewer jobs at Hope and McGehee. Benning agreed with the two persons then representing appellant that he would not charge any of his time to these two jobs, but that it would be charged for the North Crossett job, which apparently had not been commenced by Sutton. Benning told the interested parties how much salary he was drawing ($300 per week) and that he was drawing $50 per week as expenses, which he said was to be charged to the Hope and McGehee jobs. According to Benning, it was agreed that he was to get a guaranteed profit of $20,000 on the North Crossett job and one-third of any profit, and his salary to be charged to the job was not included in the $20,000 figure. The first estimate made by appellee included two $20,000 items, one for profit and the other for supervision. On most construction jobs the size of the North Crossett job there is a construction superintendent. The original contract required that a construction superintendent or foreman who had full authority to act for the contractor be employed at the site.

Carrie New testified that he was familiar with the custom in the construction business as to whether the managing executive of a company is entitled to charge his salary to the job in addition to a fixed fee for supervision. He stated that the practice is that when the contract is let on a cost-plus fixed fee basis, the fee is over and above all job costs, which include office overhead, executives' salaries, general contractor's labor, material and all subcontract costs. Normally, he said, a corporation would have an office staff and executive officers, and the duties of the latter may vary in that they double as superintendents, estimators, expeditors and purchasers. In a small organization, he said that one man may act as all these. He was present when the final draft of the contract was made and did not understand that the $20,000 figure therein was to be for Benning's salary and expenses, but did understand that was a fee to be paid over and above any profit or whether any profit was realized or not. John W. Cole, Jr., appellee's attorney at the drafting, was not familiar with usage in the construction field, but had the same understanding as New as to the $20,000. He recalled that there was discussion directed at the amount of Benning's personal salary and stated that it was agreed that the $20,000 payment would not be a substitute for it. A portion of the stated contract form of the American Institute of Architects for use when cost of work plus a fixed fee forms the basis of payment was introduced as an exhibit. It contained a clause under the heading of "Costs to be Reimbursed" providing for payment of salaries of the contractor's employees stationed at the field office in whatever capacity employed.

The contract in question was not abstracted but the paragraph in question is stated thus:

It is further agreed that 2nd Subcontractor will receive $20,000.00 for supervision which will be added to actual cost figure. It is further agreed that the difference between actual cost and bid price will be divided as follows: 33⅓% to 2nd Subcontractor; 66⅔% to 1st Subcontractor. (Plaintiff's Exhibit No. 2)

It must be noted that the payment of this $20,000 was to be made to appellee, a corporation, and not to Benning. Appellant's attorney emphasizes the fact that this language constituted a change of the same paragraph in the next preceding draft in that it was therein provided that "the 2nd Subcontractor will, nevertheless, receive the sum of $20,000 for his supervisory services."

I do not see how we can say the court erred in holding that the contract was ambiguous in view of the surrounding circumstances and collateral facts. If it was ambiguous, then we only have to determine whether there is any substantial evidence to support the judgment, since the judge also sat as the jury, and the question was for the jury. **Ft. Smith Appliance & Service Co. v. Smith, 218 Ark. 411, 236 S.W.2d 583** . . . .

Once it was shown that there was a latent ambiguity or that the words used by the parties were commonly accorded a meaning different from their ordinary meaning, oral evidence was admissible to explain them. . . . **Ellege v. Henderson, 142 Ark. 421, 218 S.W. 831.** Evidence of the way in which a particular term is understood commercially, or in a particular trade or business is admissible, as is evidence of custom and usage, including local popular and general use. . . . **Davis v. Martin Stave Co., 113 Ark. 325, 168 S.W. 553.** Testimony of the parties as to the meaning of the terms is also admissible. Ellege v. Henderson, supra. Parol evidence is also competent to explain the situation and relation of the parties and the surrounding circumstances at the time of the execution of the contract. **Clear Creek Oil & Gas Co. v. Bushmaier, 165 Ark. 303, 264 S.W. 830.**

The matter is treated in the Uniform Commercial Code. See Ark.Stat.Ann. § 85-1-205.* A usage of trade in the vocation or trade in which the parties are engaged or of which they should be aware gives particular meaning to and supplements or qualifies terms of an agreement. Ark.Stat.Ann. § 85-1-205(4). An applicable usage of trade in the place where any part of performance is to occur shall be taken into consideration as to that part of performance. A usage of trade is any practice or method of dealing having such regularity of observance in a place, vocation or trade as to justify an expectation that it will be observed with respect to the transaction in question. Ark.Stat.Ann. § 85-1-205(2), (5). The committee comments are particularly enlightening. In part, they are:

> This Act rejects both the "lay-dictionary" and the "conveyancer's" reading of a commercial agreement. Instead the meaning of the agreement of the parties is to be determined by the language used by them and by their action, read and interpreted in the light of commercial practices and other surrounding circumstances. The measure and background for interpretation are set by the commercial context, which may explain and supplement even the language of a formal or final writing.

> This Act deals with "usage of trade" as a factor in reaching the commercial meaning of the agreement which the parties have made. The language used is to be interpreted as meaning what it may fairly be expected to mean to parties involved in the particular commercial

---

* [Authors' Note: The UCC provision cited in the case now appears in § 1-303 in revised Article 1.].

transaction in a given locality or in a given vocation or trade. By adopting in this context the term "usage of trade" this Act expresses its intent to reject those cases which see evidence of "custom" as representing an effort to displace or negate "established rules of law".

A usage of trade under subsection (2) must have the "regularity of observance" specified. The ancient English tests for "custom" are abandoned in this connection. Therefore, it is not required that a usage of trade be "ancient or immemorial", "universal" or the like. Under the requirement of subsection (2) full recognition is thus available for new usages and for usages currently observed by the great majority of decent dealers, even though dissidents ready to cut corners do not agree.

See also, 17 Am.Jur.2d 643, Contracts, § 251.

In addition to the evidence set out above, there was other substantial evidence in appellee's favor. Benning testified he spent 95% of his time on the North Crossett sewer job. Carrie New said that Benning acted as construction superintendent on the North Crossett job and that he knew of no other person employed in that capacity.

It is true that there is also evidence from which a contrary result might have been reached, but this does not affect the substantiality of the evidence to support the conclusion reached by the court sitting as a jury. I would affirm the judgment.

I am authorized to state that Mr. Justice BROWN joins in this dissent.

Pacific Gas & Electric Co. v. G.W. Thomas Drayage & Rigging Co.

PACIFIC GAS & ELECTRIC CO., Plaintiff-Respondent

v.

G. W. THOMAS DRAYAGE & RIGGING CO., Defendant-Appellant

Supreme Court of California, In Bank
442 P.2d 641 (Cal. 1968)

TRAYNOR, Chief Justice.

Who's That?

Justice Roger Traynor served on the California Supreme Court from 1940-1970, the last six as chief justice. Upon his death in 1983, the *New York Times* noted that he "was often called one of the greatest judicial talents never to sit on the United States Supreme Court."* Born in 1900 in a small mining community in Utah, his humble beginnings reportedly led to "a lifelong disdain for display and pomposity, a beautiful simplicity and directness, an empathy  with common people of heterogeneous race and background, and an abiding humanity."**

After earning a law degree and a Ph.D. in political science at the University of California at Berkeley, he joined the Berkeley faculty, first in the political science department and the next year at the law school. He became a leading scholar on state and federal tax, serving as a consultant to both the U.S. Treasury Department and the California State Board of Equalization.

In his 30 years on the California Supreme Court, Traynor published some 900 opinions and more than two dozen law review articles. He is widely viewed as enormously influential in a broad variety of subject areas, from torts (leading the move to strict product liability and away from charitable and sovereign immunity) to conflicts (proposing analysis of the interests and public policies of the states affected rather than using the law of the site of the tort or contract) to criminal law (opening the door to discovery by defendants in criminal cases) to civil procedure (rejecting the mutuality requirement for collateral estoppel).

---

* Les Ledbetter, "Roger J. Traynor, California Justice," *New York Times*, 17 May 1983.
** California Associate Supreme Court Justice Mathew Tobriner, *Chief Justice Roger Traynor*, 83 Harv. L. Rev. 1769 (1970)

United States Court of Appeals Judge Henry Friendly (author of the *Frigaliment* opinion) said Traynor "illuminated and modernized every field of law that he touched, and, in the course of his long judicial service, he touched almost all."* Donald Barrett, senior attorney at the California Supreme Court, said Traynor "was always able to detect cant, hypocrisy, or pettifogging. He had an innate sense that told him when a seemingly irrefragable legal argument was leading to an impossible result, and was therefore necessarily flawed; a conclusion he often telegraphed with the terse observation, 'ain't law wonderful.'" **

Defendant appeals from a judgment for plaintiff in an action for damages for injury to property under an indemnity clause of a contract.

In 1960 defendant entered into a contract with plaintiff to furnish the labor and equipment necessary to remove and replace the upper metal cover of plaintiff's steam turbine. Defendant agreed to perform the work "at [its] own risk and expense" and to "indemnify" plaintiff "against all loss, damage, expense and liability resulting from . . . injury to property, arising out of or in any way connected with the performance of this contract." Defendant also agreed to procure not less than $50,000 insurance to cover liability for injury to property. Plaintiff was to be an additional named insured, but the policy was to contain a cross-liability clause extending the coverage to plaintiff's property.

During the work the cover fell and injured the exposed rotor of the turbine. Plaintiff brought this action to recover $25,144.51, the amount it subsequently spent on repairs. During the trial it dismissed a count based on negligence and thereafter secured judgment on the theory that the indemnity provision covered injury to all property regardless of ownership.

Defendant offered to prove by admissions of plaintiff's agents, by defendant's conduct under similar contracts entered into with plaintiff, and by other proof that in the indemnity clause the parties meant to cover injury to property of third

---

* *Henry Friendly, Ablest Judge of His Generation,* 71 Calif. L. Rev. 1039 (1983).
** Donald Barrett, *Master of Judicial Wisdom,* 71 Cal. L. Rev. 1060 (1983). In addition to the sources noted above, see Stewart Macaulay, *Justice Traynor and the Law of Contracts,* 13 Stan. L. Rev. 812 (1961) and John Poulos, *The Judicial Philosophy of Roger Traynor,* 46 Hastings L. J. 1643 (1995).

parties only and not to plaintiff's property. Although the trial court observed that the language used was "the classic language for a third party indemnity provision" and that "one could very easily conclude that . . . its whole intendment is to indemnify third parties," it nevertheless held that the "plain language" of the agreement also required defendant to indemnify plaintiff for injuries to plaintiff's property. Having determined that the contract had a plain meaning, the court refused to admit any extrinsic evidence that would contradict its interpretation.

When a court interprets a contract on this basis, it determines the meaning of the instrument in accordance with the ". . . extrinsic evidence of the judge's own linguistic education and experience." (3 Corbin on Contracts (1960 ed.) (1964 Supp. § 579, p. 225, fn. 56).) The exclusion of testimony that might contradict the linguistic background of the judge reflects a judicial belief in the possibility of perfect verbal expression. (9 Wigmore on Evidence (3d ed. 1940) § 2461, p. 187.) This belief is a remnant of a primitive faith in the inherent potency[2] and inherent meaning of words.[3]

The test of admissibility of extrinsic evidence to explain the meaning of a written instrument is not whether it appears to the court to be plain and unambiguous on its face, but whether the offered evidence is relevant to prove a meaning to which the language of the instrument is reasonably susceptible. (Continental Baking Co. v. Katz (1968) 68 A.C. 527, 536-537, 67 Cal.Rptr. 761, 439 P.2d 889; Parsons v. Bristol Development Co. (1965) 62 Cal.2d 861, 865, 44 Cal. Rptr. 767, 402 P.2d 839; Hulse v. Juillard Fancy Foods Co. (1964) 61 Cal.2d 571, 573, 39 Cal.Rptr. 529, 394 P.2d 65; [additional citations omitted].

A rule that would limit the determination of the meaning of a written instrument to its four-corners merely because it seems to the court to be clear and unambiguous, would either deny the relevance of the intention of the parties or presuppose a degree of verbal precision and stability our language has not attained.

---

[2] E.g., "The elaborate system of taboo and verbal prohibitions in primitive groups; the ancient Egyptian myth of Khern, the apotheosis of the word, and of Thoth, the Scribe of Truth, the Giver of Words and Script, the Master of Incantations; the avoidance of the name of God in Brahmanism, Judaism and Islam; totemistic and protective names in mediaeval Turkish and Finno-Ugrian languages; the misplaced verbal scruples of the 'Pre cieuses'; the Swedish peasant custom of curing sick cattle smitten by witchcraft, by making them swallow a page torn out of the psalter and put in dough. . . ." from Ullman, The Principles of Semantics (1963 ed.) 43. (See also Ogden and Richards, The Meaning of Meaning (rev. ed. 1956) pp. 24-47.)

[3] "Rerum enim vocabula immutabilia sunt, homines mutabilia," (Words are unchangeable, men changeable) from Dig. XXXIII, 10, 7, § 2, de sup. leg. as quoted in 9 Wigmore on Evidence, op. cit. supra, § 2461, p. 187.

Some courts have expressed the opinion that contractual obligations are created by the mere use of certain words, whether or not there was any intention to incur such obligations.[4] Under this view, contractual obligations flow, not from the intention of the parties but from the fact that they used certain magic words. Evidence of the parties' intention therefore becomes irrelevant.

In this state, however, the intention of the parties as expressed in the contract is the source of contractual rights and duties. A court must ascertain and give effect to this intention by determining what the parties meant by the words they used. Accordingly, the exclusion of relevant, extrinsic evidence to explain the meaning of a written instrument could be justified only if it were feasible to determine the meaning the parties gave to the words from the instrument alone.

If words had absolute and constant referents, it might be possible to discover contractual intention in the words themselves and in the manner in which they were arranged. Words, however, do not have absolute and constant referents. "A word is a symbol of thought but has no arbitrary and fixed meaning like a symbol of algebra or chemistry, ..." (**Pearson v. State Social Welfare Board** (1960) 54 Cal.2d 184, 195, 5 Cal.Rptr. 553, 559, 353 P.2d 33, 39.) The meaning of particular words or groups of words varies with the ". . . verbal context and surrounding circumstances and purposes in view of the linguistic education and experience of their users and their hearers or readers (not excluding judges). . . . . A word has no meaning apart from these factors; much less does it have an objective meaning, one true meaning." (**Corbin, The Interpretation of Words and the Parol Evidence Rule (1965) 50 Cornell L.Q. 161, 187.**) Accordingly, the meaning of a writing ". . . can only be found by interpretation in the light of all the circumstances that reveal the sense in which the writer used the words. The exclusion of parol evidence regarding such circumstances merely because the words do not appear ambiguous to the reader can easily lead to the attribution to a written instrument of a meaning that was never intended. (Citations omitted.)" (**Universal Sales Corp. v. Cal. Press Mfg. Co., supra, 20 Cal.2d 751, 776, 128 P.2d 665, 679** (concurring opinion); see also, e.g., **Garden State Plaza Corp. v. S. S. Kresge Co. (1963) 78 N.J.Super. 485, 189 A.2d 448, 454; Hurst v. W. J. Lake & Co. (1932) 141 Or. 306, 310, 16 P.2d 627, 629, 89 A.L.R. 1222**; 3 Corbin on Contracts (1960 ed.) § 579, pp. 412-431; Ogden and Richards, The Meaning of Meaning, op. cit. 15; Ullmann, The Principles of Semantics, supra, 61; McBaine, The Rule Against Disturbing Plain Meaning of Writings (1943) 31 Cal.L.Rev. 145.)

---

[4] "A contract has, strictly speaking, nothing to do with the personal, or individual, intent of the parties. A contract is an obligation attached by the mere force of law to certain acts of the parties, usually words, which ordinarily accompany and represent a known intent." **Hotchkiss v. National City Bank of New York (S.D.N.Y.1911) 200 F. 287, 293.** . . . .

Although extrinsic evidence is not admissible to add to, detract from, or vary the terms of a written contract, these terms must first be determined before it can be decided whether or not extrinsic evidence is being offered for a prohibited purpose. The fact that the terms of an instrument appear clear to a judge does not preclude the possibility that the parties chose the language of the instrument to express different terms. That possibility is not limited to contracts whose terms have acquired a particular meaning by trade usage,[6] but exists whenever the parties' understanding of the words used may have differed from the judge's understanding.

Accordingly, rational interpretation requires at least a preliminary consideration of all credible evidence offered to prove the intention of the parties.[7] (Civ.Code, § 1647; Code Civ.Proc. § 1860; see also 9 Wigmore on Evidence, op. cit. supra, § 2470, fn. 11, p. 227.) Such evidence includes testimony as to the "circumstances surrounding the making of the agreement . . . including the object, nature and subject matter of the writing . . ." so that the court can "place itself in the same situation in which the parties found themselves at the time of contracting." (**Universal Sales Corp. v. Cal. Press Mfg. Co.**, supra, 20 Cal.2d 751, 761, 128 P.2d 665, 671; **Lemm v. Stillwater Land & Cattle Co.**,

Take Note!

The statement made here— "extrinsic evidence is not admissible to add to, detract from, or vary the terms of a written contract"—is a version of the "parol evidence rule," which will be considered in the section that follows. As you will see, the question whether extrinsic evidence is admissible to establish ambiguity—the question dealt with in this section—is separate from, but intimately related to, the application of the parol evidence rule to decide whether extrinsic evidence is admissible to change or add to terms of a written contract.

[handwritten margin note:] plain meaning might not be actual meaning

---

[6] Extrinsic evidence of trade usage or custom has been admitted to show that the term "United Kingdom" in a motion picture distribution contract included Ireland (**Ermolieff v. R.K.O. Radio Pictures** (1942) 19 Cal.2d 543, 549-552, 122 P.2d 3); that the word "ton" in a lease meant a long ton or 2,240 pounds and not the statutory ton of 2,000 pounds (**Higgins v. Cal. Petroleum, etc., Co.** (1898) 120 Cal. 629, 630-632, 52 P. 1080); that the word "stubble" in a lease included not only stumps left in the ground but everything "left on the ground after the harvest time" (**Callahan v. Stanley** (1881) 57 Cal. 476, 477-479); that the term "north" in a contract dividing mining claims indicated a boundary line running along the "magnetic and not the true meridian" (**Jenny Lind Co. v. Bower & Co.** (1858) 11 Cal. 194, 197-199) and that a form contract for purchase and sale was actually an agency contract (**Body-Steffner Co. v. Flotill Products** (1944) 63 Cal.App.2d 555, 558-562, 147 P.2d 84). See also Code Civ.Proc. § 1861; Annot., 89 A.L.R. 1228; Note (1942) 30 Cal.L.Rev. 679.)

[7] When objection is made to any particular item of evidence offered to prove the intention of the parties, the trial court may not yet be in a position to determine whether in the light of all of the offered evidence, the item objected to will turn out to be admissible as tending to prove a meaning of which the language of the instrument is reasonably susceptible or inadmissible as tending to prove a meaning of which the language is not reasonably susceptible. In such case the court may admit the evidence conditionally by either reserving its ruling on the objection or by admitting the evidence subject to a motion to strike. (See Evid.Code, § 403.)

supra, 217 Cal. 474, 480-481, 19 P.2d 785.) If the court decides, after considering this evidence, that the language of a contract, in the light of all the circumstances, is "fairly susceptible of either one of the two interpretations contended for . . . ," extrinsic evidence relevant to prove either of such meanings is admissible.[8]

In the present case the court erroneously refused to consider extrinsic evidence offered to show that the indemnity clause in the contract was not intended to cover injuries to plaintiff's property. Although that evidence was not necessary to show that the indemnity clause was reasonably susceptible of the meaning contended for by defendant, it was nevertheless relevant and admissible on that issue. Moreover, since that clause was reasonably susceptible of that meaning, the offered evidence was also admissible to prove that the clause had that meaning, and did not cover injuries to plaintiff's property.[9] Accordingly, the judgment must be reversed.

---

[8] Extrinsic evidence has often been admitted in such cases on the stated ground that the contract was ambiguous (e.g., Universal Sales Corp. v. Cal. Press Mfg. Co., supra, 20 Cal.2d 751, 761, 128 P.2d 665). This statement of the rule is harmless if it is kept in mind that the ambiguity may be exposed by extrinsic evidence that reveals more than one possible meaning.

[9] The court's exclusion of extrinsic evidence in this case would be error even under a rule that excluded such evidence when the instrument appeared to the court to be clear and unambiguous on its face. The controversy centers on the meaning of the word "indemnify" and the phrase "all loss, damage, expense and liability." The trial court's recognition of the language as typical of a third party indemnity clause and the double sense in which the word "indemnify" is used in statutes and defined in dictionaries demonstrate the existence of an ambiguity. (Compare Civ.Code, § 2772, "Indemnity is a contract by which one engages to save another from a legal consequence of the conduct of one of the parties, or of some other person," with Civ.Code, § 2527, "Insurance is a contract whereby by one undertakes to indemnify another against loss, damage, or liability, arising from an unknown or contingent event." Black's Law Dictionary (4th ed. 1951) defines "indemnity" as "A collateral contract or assurance, by which one person engages to secure another against an anticipated loss or to prevent him from being damnified by the legal consequences of an act or forbearance on the part of one of the parties or of some third person." Stroud's Judicial Dictionary (2d ed. 1903) defines it as a "Contract . . . to indemnify against a liability. . . ." One of the definitions given to "indemnify" by Webster's Third New Internat. Dict. (1961 ed.) is "to exempt from incurred penalties or liabilities.")

Plaintiff's assertion that the use of the word "all" to modify "loss, damage, expense and liability" dictates an all inclusive interpretation is not persuasive. If the word "indemnify" encompasses only third-party claims, the word "all" simply refers to all such claims. The use of the words "loss," "damage," and "expense" in addition to the word "liability" is likewise inconclusive. These words do not imply an agreement to reimburse for injury to an indemnitee's property since they are commonly inserted in third-party indemnity clauses, to enable an indemnitee who settles a claim to recover from his indemnitor without proving his liability. (Carpenter Paper Co. v. Kellogg (1952) 114 Cal. App.2d 640, 651, 251 P.2d 40.Civ.Code, § 2778, provides: "1. Upon an indemnity against liability . . . the person indemnified is entitled to recover upon becoming liable; 2. Upon an indemnity against claims, or demands, or damages, or costs . . . the person indemnified is not entitled to recover without payment thereof; . . . .")

The provision that defendant perform the work "at his own risk and expense" and the provisions relating to insurance are equally inconclusive. By agreeing to work at its own risk defendant may have released plaintiff from liability for any injuries to defendant's property arising out of the contract's performance, but this provision did not necessarily make defendant an insurer against injuries to plaintiff's property. Defendant's agreement to procure liability insurance to cover damages to plaintiff's property does not indicate whether the insurance was to cover all injuries or only injuries caused by defendant's negligence.

Food for Thought

Pacific Gas & Electric Co. has been criticized by some judges and commentators as undercutting the finality of written contracts in unacceptable ways, a criticism that might also be made of the dissenting opinion in *C. & A. Construction Co.* See, for example, the comment by Judge Kozinski in *Trident Center v. Connecticut General Life Insurance Co.*, 847 F.2d 564 (9th Cir. 1988):

> Under *Pacific Gas*, it matters not how clearly a contract is written, nor how completely it is integrated, nor how carefully it is negotiated, nor how squarely it addresses the issue before the court: the contract cannot be rendered impervious to attack by parol evidence. If one side is willing to claim that the parties intended one thing but the agreement provides for another, the court must consider extrinsic evidence of possible ambiguity. If that evidence raises the specter of ambiguity where there was none before, the contract language is displaced and the intention of the parties must be divined from self-serving testimony offered by partisan witnesses whose recollection is hazy from passage of time and colored by their conflicting interests. . . . *Pacific Gas* casts a long shadow of uncertainty over all transactions negotiated and executed under the law of California. As this case illustrates, even when the transaction is very sizeable, even if it involves only sophisticated parties, even if it was negotiated with the aid of counsel, even if it results in contract language that is devoid of ambiguity, costly and protracted litigation cannot be avoided if one party has a strong enough motive for challenging the contract. While this rule creates much business for lawyers and an occasional windfall to some clients, it leads only to frustration and delay for most litigants and clogs already overburdened courts.

Id. at 569. California Supreme Court Justice Mosk expressed similar concerns in his dissent in *Delta Dynamics, Inc. v. Arioto*, 446 P.2d 785 (Cal. 1968), noting that "I had misgivings at the time, [but] I must confess to joining the majority [in *Pacific Gas* and in *Masterson v. Sine*, 436 P.2d 561 (Cal. 1968)]. Now, however, that the majority deem negotiations leading to execution of contracts admissible, the trend has become so unmistakably ominous that I must urge a halt."

Others have continued to offer support for context-based interpretation as articulated in *Pacific Gas*:

We recognize that *Pacific Gas* has its critics. . . . We too would recoil if *Pacific Gas* meant that mere complexity required a finding of ambiguity or that courts must listen to wholly unpersuasive extrinsic evidence to create ambiguity where words are clear beyond dispute. . . . [T]he court must first decide what the agreement says and, as a preliminary matter, must decide if it reasonably could be interpreted in different ways, given the language and the factual context surrounding the making of the agreement. Admittedly, the process is not without risk, but we believe the game is worth the candle. After all, the purpose is to produce the contract result the parties intended, not that which the judge intends. Some words are clear beyond dispute. Some may mean one thing to the judge but could have meant something else to the parties. It is the latter meaning that is important.

Taylor v. State Farm Mutual Automobile Insurance Co., 854 P.2d 1134, 1141 (Ariz. 1993).

In your view, which interpretation methodology is preferable?

§ 3.2. Stretching the Limits of Interpretation: Contracts and Commercial Context under the UCC

As reflected in *Frigaliment* and UCC § 1-303 (pages 695 and 702), the meaning of contract terms may be affected by course of performance, course of dealing, and usage of trade. The case below considers the impact on contract interpretation of considering such evidence. Although the case itself rules only on application of Article 2, its impact may extend to interpretation questions under the common law as well.

Reading the Law Critically:
Nanakuli Paving & Rock Co.

1. What is the contract term being interpreted? What meaning would you attribute to the term in the absence of extrinsic evidence? Does the term appear ambiguous?

2. What kind of evidence does the plaintiff seek to introduce to explain the contract? Is it the same or a different kind of evidence than offered in *C. & A. Construction Co.* and *Pacific Gas & Electric*? If different, how does that difference affect the analysis?

3. What rule can be derived from this case about the role of usage of trade (and course of dealing) in determining contract terms? What test does the court use for determining the admissibility and effect of the additional evidence offered?

4. Do you agree with the court's result and reasoning? Why or why not?

5. Recall the way UCC § 1-303(e) ranks the various sources of evidence about parties' intent (express terms, course of performance, course of dealing, usage of trade). What effect does *Nanakuli* have on that ranking?

6. What statement could Shell Oil have placed in the contract to avoid the outcome in the *Nanakuli* case?

Nanakuli Paving & Rock Co. v. Shell Oil Co.

NANAKULI PAVING AND ROCK CO., a Division of Grace Brothers, Ltd.,
Plaintiff-Appellant

v.

SHELL OIL CO., Defendant-Appellee

United States Court of Appeals, Ninth Circuit
664 F.2d 772 (9th Cir. 1981)

HOFFMAN, District Judge:

Appellant Nanakuli Paving and Rock Company (Nanakuli) initially filed this breach of contract action against appellee Shell Oil Company (Shell) in Hawaiian State Court in February, 1976. Nanakuli, the second largest asphaltic paving contractor in Hawaii, had bought all its asphalt requirements from 1963 to 1974 from Shell under two long-term supply contracts; its suit charged Shell with breach of the later 1969 contract. The jury returned a verdict of $220,800 for Nanakuli on its first claim, which is that Shell breached the 1969 contract in January, 1974, by failing to price protect Nanakuli on 7200 tons of asphalt at the time Shell raised the price for asphalt from $44 to $76. Nanakuli's theory is that price-protection, as a usage of the asphaltic paving trade in Hawaii, was incorporated into the 1969 agreement between the parties, as demonstrated by the routine use of price protection by suppliers to that trade, and reinforced by the way in which Shell actually performed the 1969 contract up until 1974. Price protection, appellant claims, required that Shell hold the price on the tonnage Nanakuli had already committed because Nanakuli had incorporated that price into bids put out to or contracts awarded by general contractors and government agencies. The District Judge set aside the verdict and granted Shell's motion for judgment n. o. v., which decision we vacate. We reinstate the jury verdict because we find that, viewing the evidence as a whole, there was substantial evidence to support a finding by reasonable jurors that Shell breached its contract by failing to provide protection for Nanakuli in 1974. . . .

Nanakuli [argues that] Shell's failure to offer price protection in 1974 was a breach of the 1969 contract [because] all material suppliers to the asphaltic paving trade in Hawaii followed the trade usage of price protection and thus it should be assumed, under the U.C.C., that the parties intended to incorporate price protection into their 1969 agreement. This is so, Nanakuli continues, even though the written contract provided for price to be "Shell's Posted Price at time of delivery," F.O.B. Honolulu. Its proof of a usage that was incorporated into the contract is reinforced by evidence of the commercial context, which under the U.C.C. should form the background for viewing a particular contract. The full agreement must be examined in light of the close, almost symbiotic relations between Shell and Nanakuli on the island of Oahu, whereby the expansion of Shell on the island was intimately connected to the business growth of Nanakuli. The U.C.C. looks to the actual performance of a contract as the best indication of what the parties intended those terms to mean. Nanakuli points out that Shell had price protected it on the two occasions of price increases under the 1969 contract other than the 1974 increase. In 1970 and 1971 Shell extended the old price for four and three months, respectively, after an announced increase. This was done, in the words of Shell's agent in Hawaii, in order to permit Nanakuli's to "chew up" tonnage already committed at Shell's old price.[4]

What's That?

F.O.B. means "Free on Board," an indication that the seller has the obligation to get the goods to the designated place (here, Honolulu) and, if that is not the final destination, the buyer has the responsibility to transport the goods the rest of the way.

. . . .

. . . [W]e hold that, although the express price terms of Shell's posted price of delivery may seem, at first glance, inconsistent with a trade usage of price protection at time of increases in price, a closer reading shows that the jury could have reasonably construed price protection as consistent with the express term. We

---

[4] Price protection was practiced in the asphaltic paving trade by either extending the old price for a period of time after a new one went into effect or charging the old price for a specified tonnage, which represented work committed at the old price. In addition, several months' advance notice was given of price increases.

reach this holding for several reasons. First, we are persuaded by a careful reading of the U.C.C., one of whose underlying purposes is to promote flexibility in the expansion of commercial practices and which rather drastically overhauls this particular area of the law. The Code would have us look beyond the printed pages of the contract to usages and the entire commercial context of the agreement in order to reach the "true understanding" of the parties. Second, decisions of other courts in similar situations have managed to reconcile such trade usages with seemingly contradictory express terms where the prior course of dealings between the parties, trade usages, and the actual performance of the contract by the parties showed a clear intent by the parties to incorporate those usages into the agreement or to give to the express term the particular meaning provided by those usages, even at times varying the apparent meaning of the express terms. Third, the delineation by thoughtful commentators of the degree of consistency demanded between express terms and usage is that a usage should be allowed to modify the apparent agreement, as seen in the written terms, as long as it does not totally negate it. We believe the usage here falls within the limits set forth by commentators and generally followed in the better reasoned decisions. The manner in which price protection was actually practiced in Hawaii was that it only came into play at times of price increases and only for work committed prior to those increases on non-escalating contracts. Thus, it formed an exception to, rather than a total negation of, the express price term of "Shell's Posted Price at time of delivery." Our decision is reinforced by the overwhelming nature of the evidence that price protection was routinely practiced by all suppliers in the small Oahu market of the asphaltic paving trade and therefore was known to Shell; that it was a realistic necessity to operate in that market and thus vital to Nanakuli's ability to get large government contracts and to Shell's continued business growth on Oahu; and that it therefore constituted an intended part of the agreement, as that term is broadly defined by the Code, between Shell and Nanakuli.

II. Trade Usage Before and After 1969

The key to price protection being so prevalent in 1969 that both parties would intend to incorporate it into their contract is found in one reality of the Oahu asphaltic paving market: the largest paving contracts were let by government agencies and none of the three levels of government—local, state, or federal—allowed escalation clauses for paving materials. If a paver bid at one price and another went into effect before the award was made, the paving company would lose a great deal of money, since it could not pass on increases to any government agency or to most general contractors. Extensive evidence was presented that, as a consequence, aggregate suppliers routinely price protected paving contractors in the 1960's and 1970's, as did the largest asphaltic supplier in Oahu, Chevron. Nanakuli presented documentary evidence of routine price protection by aggregate suppliers as well as two witnesses: . . . . Both testified that price protection to their knowledge had always been practiced . . . . Such protection consisted of advance notices of increases, coupled with charging the old price for work committed at that price or for enough time to order the tonnage committed. The smallness of the Oahu market led to complete trust among suppliers and pavers . . . .

. . . .

III. Shell's Course of Performance of the 1969 Contract

The Code considers actual performance of a contract as the most relevant evidence of how the parties interpreted the terms of that contract. In 1970 and 1971, the only points at which Shell raised prices between 1969 and 1974, it price protected Nanakuli by holding its old price for four and three months, respectively, after announcing a price increase. . . . Those actions were in accord with Shell's own policy, as professed by Bohner [Shell's Hawaiian representative], and that of other asphalt and aggregate suppliers: to give at least several months' advance notice of price increases. . . . By its actions, Bohner testified, Shell allowed Nanakuli time to make arrangements to buy up tonnage committed at the old price, that is, to "chew up" tonnage bid or contracted. Shell apparently offered this testimony to impress the jury with its subsequent good faith towards Nanakuli. In fact, it may also have reinforced the impression of the universality of price protection in the asphaltic paving trade on Oahu . . . .

IV. Shell-Nanakuli Relations, 1973-74

Two important factors form the backdrop for the 1974 failure by Shell to price protect Nanakuli: the Arab oil embargo and a complete change of command and policy in Shell's asphalt management. The jury was read a page or so from the World Book about the events and effect of the partial oil embargo, which shortened supplies and increased the price of petroleum, of which asphalt is a byproduct. The federal government imposed direct price controls on petroleum, but not on asphalt. Despite the international importance of those events, the jury may have viewed the second factor as of more direct significance to this case. The structural changes at Shell offered a possible explanation for why Shell in 1974 acted out of step with, not only the trade usage and commercially rea-

What's That?

The Arab oil embargo consisted of price increases, production cuts, and prohibitions on shipments of oil to the United States by members of the Organization of Petroleum Exporting Countries in response to military conflict in the Middle East and to financial and military support of Israel by the United States. Among other results was a quadrupling of the market price of oil. For more information on the Arab oil embargo, see http://en.wikipedia.org/wiki/Arab_Oil_Embargo and http://history.state.gov/milestones/1969-1976/OPEC.

sonable practices of all suppliers to the asphaltic paving trade on Oahu, but also with its previous agreement with, or at least treatment of, Nanakuli.

Bohner testified to a big organizational change at Shell in 1973 when asphalt sales were moved from the construction sales to the commercial sales department [and there were major changes in the "top echelon" of Shell's asphalt sales division]. When the philosophy toward asphalt pricing changed, apparently no one was left who was knowledgeable about the peculiarities of the Hawaiian market or about Shell's long-time relations with Nanakuli or its 1969 agreement, beyond the printed contract.

Shell had begun rethinking its asphalt pricing policies several years before. . . . This rethinking apparently led to a November 25, 1970, letter setting out "Shell's New Pricing Policy" at its Honolulu and Hilo terminals. The letter explained the elimination of price protection: "In other words, we will no longer guarantee asphalt prices for the duration of any particular construction projects or for the specific lengths of time. We will, of course, honor any existing prices which have been committed for specific projects for which we have firm contractual commitments.". . .

. . . .

We conclude that the decision to deny Nanakuli price protection was made by new Houston management without a full understanding of Shell's 1969 agreement with Nanakuli or any knowledge of its past pricing practices toward Nanakuli. If Shell did commit itself in 1969 to price protect Nanakuli, the Shell officials who made the decisions affecting Nanakuli in 1974 knew nothing about that commitment. Nor did they make any effective effort to find out. They acted instead solely in reliance on the 1969 contract's express price term, devoid of the commercial context that the Code says is necessary to an understanding of the meaning of the written word. Whatever the legal enforceability of Nanakuli's right, Nanakuli officials seem to have acted in good faith reliance on its right, as they understood it, to price protection and rightfully felt betrayed by Shell's failure to act with any understanding of its past practices toward Nanakuli.

V. Scope of Trade Usage

The validity of the jury verdict in this case depends on four legal questions. First, how broad was the trade to whose usages Shell was bound under its 1969 agreement with Nanakuli: did it extend to the Hawaiian asphaltic paving trade or was it limited merely to the purchase and sale of asphalt, which would only include evidence of

Make the Connection

As you read this portion of the opinion, recall the discussion of trade usage in *Frigaliment* (page 669), and the language of UCC § 1-303 and its comments (page 702).

practices by Shell and Chevron? [The second question is omitted.] Third, could the jury have construed an express contract term of Shell's posted price at delivery as reasonably consistent with a trade usage and Shell's course of performance of the 1969 contract of price protection, which consisted of charging the old price at times of price increases, either for a period of time or for specific tonnage committed at a fixed price in non-escalating contracts? [The fourth question is omitted].

We approach the first issue in this case mindful that an underlying purpose of the U.C.C. as enacted in Hawaii is to allow for liberal interpretation of commercial usages. The Code provides, "This chapter shall be liberally construed and applied to promote its underlying purposes and policies." Haw.Rev.Stat. § 490:1-102(1). Only three purposes are listed, one of which is "[t]o permit the continued expansion of commercial practices through custom, usage and agreement of the parties . . . ." Id. § 490:1-102(2)(b). . . .

. . . .

> Under pre-Code law, a trade usage was not operative against a party who *was not a member of the trade unless* he actually knew of it or *the other party could reasonably believe he knew of it.*

J. White & R. Summers, Uniform Commercial Code, § 12-6 at 371 (1972) (emphasis supplied) (citing 3 A. Corbin, Corbin on Contracts § 557 at 248 (1960)). See also **Restatement of Contracts § 247**, Comment b (1932); 5 S. Williston, Williston on Contracts § 661 at 113-18 (3d. ed. 1961). White and Summers add (emphasis supplied):

> This view has been carried forward by 1-205(3), ... [U]sage of the trade is only binding on *members of the trade* involved *or persons* who know or *should know about it.* Persons who should be aware of the trade usage doubtless *include those who regularly deal with members of the relevant trade,* and also members of a second trade that commonly deals with members of a relevant trade (for example, farmers should know something of seed selling). . . .

. . . .

> The ancient English tests for "custom" are abandoned in this connection. Therefore, it is not required that a usage of trade be "ancient or immemorial," "universal" or the like . . . . [F]ull recognition is thus available for new usages and for usages currently observed by the great

majority of decent dealers, even though dissidents ready to cut corners do not agree.

[UCC §1-205, Comment 5.] The Comment's demand that "not universality but only the described 'regularity of observance'" is required reinforces the provision only giving "effect to usages of which the parties 'are or should be aware' . . . ." Id., Comment 7. A "regularly observed" practice of protection, of which Shell "should have been aware," was enough to constitute a usage that Nanakuli had reason to believe was incorporated into the agreement.[28]

Nanakuli went beyond proof of a regular observance. It proved and offered to prove that price protection was probably a universal practice by suppliers to the asphaltic paving trade in 1969. It had been practiced by H.C. & D. since at least 1962, by P.C. & A. since well before 1960, and by Chevron routinely for years, with the last specific instance before the contract being March, 1969, as shown by documentary evidence. The only usage evidence missing was the behavior by Shell, the only other asphalt supplier in Hawaii, prior to 1969. That was because its only major customer was Nanakuli and the judge ruled prior course of dealings between Shell and Nanakuli inadmissible. Shell did not point in rebuttal to one instance of failure to price protect by any supplier to an asphalt paver in Hawaii before its own 1974 refusal to price protect Nanakuli. Thus, there clearly was enough proof for a jury to find that the practice of price protection in the asphaltic paving trade existed in Hawaii in 1969 and was regular enough in its observance to rise to the level of a usage that would be binding on Nanakuli and Shell.

. . . .

VII. Express Terms as Reasonably Consistent with Usage in Course of Performance

Perhaps one of the most fundamental departures of the Code from prior contract law is found in the parol evidence rule and the definition of an agreement between two parties. Under the U.C.C., an agreement goes beyond the written words on a piece of paper. "'Agreement' means the bargain of the parties in fact as found in their language or by implication from other circumstances including course of dealing or usage of trade or course of performance as provided in this chapter (**sections 490:1-205** and **490:2-208**)." Id. § 490:1-201(3). Express terms, then, do not constitute the entire agreement, which must be sought also in evidence of usages, dealings, and performance of the contract itself. The purpose

---

[28] White and Summers write that Code requirements for proving a usage are "far less stringent" than the old ones for custom. "A usage of trade need not be well known, let alone 'universal.'" It only needs to be regular enough that the parties expect it to be observed. White & Summers, supra § 3-3 at 87 (emphasis supplied). "Note particularly (in 1-205 (1) & (2)) that it is not necessary for both parties to be consciously aware of the trade usage. It is enough if the trade usage is such as to 'justify an expectation' of its observance." Id. at 84.

of evidence of usages, which are defined in the previous section, is to help to understand the entire agreement.

. . . .

A commercial agreement, then, is broader than the written paper and its meaning is to be determined not just by the language used by them in the written contract but "by their action, read and interpreted in the light of commercial practices and other surrounding circumstances. The measure and background for interpretation are set by the commercial context, which may explain and supplement even the language of a formal or final writing." Id., Comment 1. Performance, usages, and prior dealings are important enough to be admitted always, even for a final and complete agreement; only if they cannot be reasonably reconciled with the express terms of the contract are they not binding on the parties. "The express terms of an agreement and an applicable course of dealing or usage of trade shall be construed wherever reasonable as consistent with each other; but when such construction is unreasonable express terms control both course of dealing and usage of trade and course of dealing controls usage of trade." Id. § 490:1-205(4).

. . . .

Our study of the Code provisions and Comments, then, form the first basis of our holding that a trade usage to price protect pavers at times of price increases for work committed on nonescalating contracts could reasonably be construed as consistent with an express term of seller's posted price at delivery. Since the agreement of the parties is broader than the express terms and includes usages, which may even add terms to the agreement, and since the commercial background provided by those usages is vital to an understanding of the agreement, we follow the Code's mandate to proceed on the assumption that the parties have included those usages unless they cannot reasonably be construed as consistent with the express terms.

. . . .

. . . . Here the evidence was overwhelming that all suppliers to the asphaltic paving trade price protected customers under the same types of circumstances. Chevron's contract with H.B. was a similar long-term supply contract between a buyer and seller with very close relations, on a form supplied by the seller, covering sales of asphalt, and setting the price at seller's posted price, with no mention of price protection. . . .

[J. H. Levie, *Trade Usage and Custom Under the Common Law and the Uniform Commercial Code*, 40 N.Y.U.L.Rev. 1101, 1112 (1965) states:] "Astonishing as it will seem to most practicing attorneys, under the Code it will be possible in some cases to use custom to contradict the written agreement . . . . Therefore usage may be used to 'qualify' the agreement, which presumably means to 'cut down' express terms although not to negate them entirely." Here, the express price term was "Shell's Posted Price at time of delivery." A total negation of that term would be that the buyer was to set the price. It is a less than complete negation of the term that an unstated exception exists at times of price increases, at which times the old price is to be charged, for a certain period or for a specified tonnage, on work already committed at the lower price on nonescalating contracts. Such a usage forms a broad and important exception to the express term, but does not swallow it entirely. Therefore, we hold that, under these particular facts, a reasonable jury could have found that price protection was incorporated into the 1969 agreement between Nanakuli and Shell and that price protection was reasonably consistent with the express term of seller's posted price at delivery.

. . . .

Because the jury could have found for Nanakuli on its price protection claim . . . , we reverse the judgment of the District Court and reinstate the jury verdict for Nanakuli in the amount of $220,800, plus interest according to law.

. . . .

Food for Thought

Nanakuli has become a classic case of contextual interpretation of contract language, along with *Columbia Nitrogen v. Royster*, 451 F.2d 3 (4th Cir. 1971), which used evidence of usage of trade to conclude that the seemingly firm commitment in a long-term contract for purchase of phosphate was subject to cancellation based on market price changes. Authors have both celebrated *Nanakuli* and reviled it. In *Framing Contract Law: An Economic Perspective* (2006), Professor Victor Goldberg called *Nanakuli* and *Columbia Nitrogen* the "Terrible Twosome." Although he endorsed interpreting a contract in context, Goldberg believed that by "rewrit[ing] contracts that were plain on their face," the *Nanakuli* court opened the door to any anything-goes approach. "The danger of a *Nanakuli-Columbia Nitrogen* interpretive strategy is that parties will be frustrated in trying to devise the terms of their agreement, and they will have little confidence in their ability to predict the outcomes if their disputes do end up in litigation." *Id.* at 162. On the other hand, Professor Douglas Newell sees the *Nanakuli* case as affording "an opportunity to examine major changes from the classical contract law of Williston to the realism of Llewellyn incorporated into the Uniform Commercial Code." Douglas K. Newell, *Will Kindness Kill Contract?*, 24 Hofstra L. Rev. 455, 458 (1995).

For additional discussions of *Nanakuli*, *see* Harold Dubroff, *The Implied Covenant of Good Faith in Contract Interpretation and Gap-Filling: Reviling a Revered Relic*, 80 St. John's L. Rev. 559 (2006); Jack M. Graves, *Course of Performance as Evidence of Intent or Waiver: A Meaningful Preference for the Latter and Implications for Newly Broadened Use Under Revised U.C.C. Section 1-303*, 52 Drake L. Rev. 235 (2004); Larry A. DiMatteo, *Reason and Context: A Dual Track Theory of interpretation*, 109 Penn. St. L. Rev. 397 (2004).

What is your view of the *Nanakuli* case and its implications? Did the court interpret the contract or did it allow Nanakuli to add a term not contained in the contract itself? How far should a court go in using context to interpret contract terms?

§ 3.3. The Parol Evidence Rule

As we have seen, courts disagree about whether to allow parties to introduce evidence from their pre-contract negotiations to show ambiguity in the contract terms, or whether they must instead establish ambiguity only from the words of the contract and the general circumstances surrounding its adoption. This section addresses a different but related question: in the absence of ambiguity (however established), may either party use evidence of prior negotiations to *add to or alter* the terms of a written agreement? The answer appears in the "parol evidence rule," which (1) bars use of such evidence to alter a term that the parties considered final in the written contract and (2) bars use of such evidence to add a term to a contract the parties considered fully expressed in the written contract. The rule is deceptively simple to state, but notoriously hard to apply.

Take Note!

"Parol" means "oral," but the parol evidence rule controls the use of both oral and written evidence of the results of prior negotiations.

The policies underlying the parol evidence rule are sensible ideas. The rule presumes that written evidence is better than conflicting oral evidence on the same term. It presumes that a subsequent written agreement is better evidence than a conflicting earlier agreement on the same topic. It presumes that when parties produce a written contract document,* they usually intend it to take priority

---

* Recall from Chapter 6 (page 685) that UETA and ESIGN ensure that references to writing and to written documents encompass both physical writings and electronic records. References in this chapter to written contracts should be understood to have that broader meaning.

over what they said or did leading up to the adoption of the written contract. It affirms that certainty and stability of contracts is promoted if parties can depend upon written terms. And it presumes that, if the parties expressly say that their written agreement supersedes all of their previous agreements and dealings, all evidence from those prior dealings should be excluded, even to add additional terms consistent with those in the written document. At the same time, the rule acknowledges that words must always be understood in their commercial context and that courts may need additional evidence to explain ambiguous or incomplete terms.

The parol evidence rule is a rule of substantive (not procedural or evidentiary) law because it is at base a rule about which terms become part of a contract. Although it operates by controlling what evidence is admissible, the decision on admissibility is not based on evidentiary considerations of credibility or trustworthiness. Rather, the underlying question is whether the written expression of a contract should take precedence over terms discussed or agreed upon before the written expression was adopted.

The rule is generally considered a rule of law, to be applied by the court, not the jury; that is, the judge must apply the rule and decide that the evidence is admissible to prove a term of the contract before the evidence can be presented to the fact-finder.* Some factual questions may need to be answered in order to apply the rule (e.g., whether the parties intended their written contract to be a "final expression" that would supersede earlier agreements). Some courts submit such factual questions to a jury for decision, while other jurisdictions allow the jury to see only the evidence that has "run the gauntlet" of the parol evidence rule.

The parol evidence rule is challenging to understand and apply because the lines that the rule draws are often indistinct, and judges disagree about how to apply them. "'Few things,' wrote Professor Thayer, 'are darker than . . . [the parol evidence rule] or fuller of subtle difficulties'; and this condition of the law all members of the profession will concede. . . . [T]he so-called parol evidence rule is attended with confusion and obscurity which make it the most discouraging subject in the whole field of evidence."** Moreover, some courts are skeptical of the parol evidence rule, much as they are of the statute of frauds, because it operates to keep evidence—often credible evidence—from the jury and may prevent the fact-finder from considering apparently legitimate disputes about the substance of the agreement reached. As with the statute of frauds, courts therefore differ in how they apply the rule as a result of the variations in their commitment to the rule itself.

---

* The fact-finder could be the judge, not a jury, if the parties waive their rights to a jury trial (or if no jury trial is available on the matter, as with equitable claims). In that case, the judge rules first whether the extrinsic evidence can be considered to find the content of the contract; if the answer is "no", then the judge decides the content of the contract without reference to the excluded evidence. For ease of reference, this chapter uses "the jury" to mean the fact-finder.

** 9 John Henry Wigmore, *Evidence* § 2400, at 3 (Chadbourn rev. ed. 1981).

With some exceptions, the common law and UCC versions of the parol evidence rule are similar, though they use different terminology. The materials below draw on both sources.

§ 3.3.1. The Effect of the Parol Evidence Rule

The parol evidence rule is designed to implement the parties' intent as to the effect of a written memorialization of the contract terms. To do so, the rule organizes the inquiry about parties' intent by categorizing the kind of document the writing represents. As articulated in UCC § 2-202, the rule asks:

- First, did the parties intend the document to be a "final expression of the parties' agreement" (superseding any *conflicting* terms they may have agreed to before).

- Second, did the parties *also* intend the document to be a "complete and exclusive statement of the terms of the agreement" (superseding *all* terms they may have agreed to before, whether conflicting or not).

The common law asks the same questions, but what the UCC calls a "final expression" is instead called an "integrated agreement" (or "partially integrated agreement") and what the UCC calls a "complete and exclusive statement" is instead called a "completely integrated agreement." The following chart summarizes these categories and their meaning:

Intent of parties	UCC terminology	Common law terminology
Written terms supersede conflicting terms previously agreed to	"Final expression of the parties' agreement"	Integrated agreement; partially integrated agreement
Written terms supersede *all* terms previously agreed to, whether conflicting or additional	"Complete and exclusive statement of the terms of the agreement"	Completely integrated agreement

A final expression of the parties' agreement (an integrated or partially integrated agreement) supersedes all previous agreements (written or oral) and contemporaneous oral agreements *as to terms that are part of that final expression,* so it bars the use of such extrinsic evidence to *contradict* or *change* the terms written into the contract document but does *not* bar use of that evidence to *add* express terms.

A complete and exclusive statement of the parties' agreement (a completely integrated agreement) comprises *all* terms to which the parties agreed, so it completely supersedes all previous agreements (written or oral) and contemporaneous oral agreements and therefore bars use of such extrinsic evidence to *add* express terms or to *contradict* or *vary* the terms in the written contract document.

> Why the difference in treatment between oral agreements (barred if they occurred before or at the same time as the writing) and written agreements (barred only if they occurred before the writing)? Two or more writings adopted at the same time would generally be considered part of the same written memorialization of the contract terms and so would together constitute the written contract that would be protected by the parol evidence rule.

As should be clear from the descriptions above, the application of the parol evidence rule flows from analysis of two critical questions:

1. What kind of document is the written contract? Is it a final expression of the terms it contains (integrated)? Is it a complete and exclusive statement of the contract terms (completely integrated)?

2. Is the evidence offered *to add to* the written contract terms? To *change* the written terms?

Even if the parties meant their written contract to contain all the terms so far agreed upon (that is, the document is a "complete and exclusive statement" or "completely integrated agreement"), evidence of a prior agreement may be admissible if offered for reasons that fall outside the scope of (or within an "exception" to) the parol evidence rule, as explained in the next section.

§ 3.3.2. Scope of the Parol Evidence Rule: To What Evidence Does It Apply?

The parol evidence rule is designed to prevent parties from undercutting the finality of their written agreements by later attempting to incorporate into the contract written agreements made before, or oral agreements made before or at the same time as, the writing was adopted. The rule therefore does not affect evidence offered for another purpose (*not* to vary or supplement the terms in the written agreement) or evidence offered from another source (*not* from prior or contemporaneous agreements or negotiations). These limitations are sometimes identified as "exceptions" to the parol evidence rule, but they are better understood as instances outside the scope of the rule, since the rule addresses only the use of evidence of prior or contemporaneous agreements offered to add to or change terms in a written agreement. Thus, the parol evidence rule does not bar use of evidence to establish:

The meaning of an ambiguous term: Relevant evidence of all kinds (including prior agreements, course of performance, course of dealing, and usage of trade) is always admissible to explain ambiguity or clarify terms that cannot be interpreted without the assistance of that evidence. As we saw in § 3.1, courts differ on whether they will consider prior negotiations or agreements to *find* ambiguity, but once ambiguity is established, all courts will consider any relevant evidence (including evidence from prior or contemporaneous agreements) to resolve the ambiguity.

A course of performance, course of dealing, or usage of trade: Under the U.C.C., evidence of course of performance, course of dealing, and usage of trade is admissible to establish the existence of contract terms as well as to interpret contract language, even if the agreement is "complete and exclusive," because it is presumed—unless carefully negated by the parties' agreement—that the agreement was made in the commercial context represented by the course of dealing or usage of trade and that course of performance reflects the parties' intentions. The contract thus cannot be understood without that evidence. Terms that become part of a contract through proof of course of dealing or usage of trade are considered part of the original agreement, not "added" to the agreement from prior negotiations.

Practice Pointer: Is Course of Performance Evidence Always Admissible?

As reflected in the text, course of performance enjoys a favored position with respect to the parol evidence rule because of the number of ways in which it can escape the effect of the rule. Evidence of course of performance is admissible:

- To interpret the express terms of the agreement if there is ambiguity;
- To supplement or explain the writing, unless the parties carefully negate that possibility in the agreement; or
- To show modification of the agreement.

A skillful use of one or more of these arguments should prevent the parol evidence rule from blocking admission of evidence of course of performance.

Subsequent modifications of contract: The parol evidence rule has no effect on admissibility of the negotiations or agreements that occurred after the writing was executed. Nor does it affect evidence of course of performance because that always arises after contract formation. The function of the parol evidence rule is to ensure that the written final expression prevails over much of the evidence leading up to the moment of contract formation, not to set the contract in stone so that the parties cannot change it in the future.

Existence and contents of a collateral agreement: Evidence of an agreement that is separate from (or "collateral" to) the writing is allowed, because the parties did not intend it to be part of the integrated contract. What the court will consider to be a separate or collateral agreement is not always clear. The *Lee* case included in the next section addresses this issue.

Problems with contract formation: Evidence is admissible if offered to show fraud, duress, undue influence, mistake, illegality, lack of consideration, or other circumstances that would invalidate the formation of a contract. The parol evidence rule does not apply to such evidence because a writing that is considered the "final expression of the parties' agreement" does not take on its privileged status until the court is convinced that there was, in fact, an agreement. Similarly, evidence to show that the contract is created only if a particular condition is satisfied is admissible, because it relates to the question whether a contract was ever formed, not to determination of the terms of the contract.

Grounds for granting particular remedies (e.g., rescission, reformation, specific performance): Evidence offered to show circumstances that support the availability of particular remedies is not subject to the parol evidence rule because that evidence is not being used to vary the terms of the contract but instead to show equitable circumstances (e.g., fraud, mistake, unconscionability) that affect how to enforce the agreement reflected in the writing.

The operation and scope of the parol evidence rule is summarized in the following chart, which indicates the effect of the rule and which evidentiary questions are outside the scope of the rule:

Make the Connection

A condition may affect whether a contract exists at all, as described in the text here and in Chapter 4 (page 321), or it may be a term of the contract, affecting whether particular acts of contract performance will be required or excused (see § 5 of this chapter, page 836). For example, the parties may agree that a buyer will commit to a house purchase only if he is able to get financing at or below a particular interest rate (no contract formed unless the condition is satisfied) or they may commit to a house purchase but the buyer will be excused from performing if he cannot get such financing (contract formed but a contract term creates a condition that may excuse performance). The parol evidence rule does not prevent introduction of evidence of a condition affecting contract formation, but it may prevent introduction of extrinsic evidence that performance was understood as being conditional on particular events or actions.

	If document is not integrated	If document is a final expression (integrated)	If document is a complete and exclusive state-ment (completely integrated)
Evidence of prior agreement	May be used to establish contract terms	May be used to add terms but not to change terms in the written contract	May not be used to add or to change terms in the written contract
Evidence to interpret ambiguous contract term	Admissible; outside scope of parol evidence rule		
Evidence to show course of performance, usage of trade, or course of dealing	Admissible; outside scope of parol evidence rule		
Evidence from separate (collateral) agreement	Admissible; outside scope of parol evidence rule		
Evidence to show formation problems (e.g., duress)	Admissible; outside scope of parol evidence rule		
Evidence to show grounds for granting a particular remedy	Admissible; outside scope of parol evidence rule		
Evidence to show modification	Admissible; outside scope of parol evidence rule		

[handwritten margin note: outside rule]

As you read the cases applying the parol evidence rule, make note of the courts' statements about when the parol evidence rule does *not* apply and their application of these particular "exceptions."

§ 3.3.3 Collateral Agreements

As noted in the previous section, evidence of an agreement that is entirely separate from (or "collateral" to) the written agreement is allowed because the parties would not have intended to supersede one agreement when memorializing another separate agreement. But when is an agreement separate enough to be considered "collateral"? The next case explores that question.

Reading the Law Critically: *Lee*

1. Why does the court conclude that the additional agreement was collateral and is therefore admissible? What test does the court rely upon in reaching its conclusion?

2. Does the court conclude that the contract for sale of assets was a partial or a complete integration of the parties' agreement? Does it matter which it is, for application of the rule on collateral agreements?

Lee v. Joseph E. Seagram & Sons, Inc.

HAROLD S. LEE et al., Plaintiffs-Appellees

v.

JOSEPH E. SEAGRAM & SONS, INC., Defendant-Appellant

United States Court of Appeals
552 F.2d 447 (2d Cir. 1977)

GURFEIN, Circuit Judge:

This is an appeal by defendant Joseph E. Seagram & Sons, Inc. ("Seagram") from a judgment entered by the District Court, Hon. Charles H. Tenney, upon the verdict of a jury in the amount of $407,850 in favor of the plaintiffs on a claim asserting common law breach of an oral contract. The court also denied Seagram's motion under **Rule 50(b), Fed.R.Civ.P.**, for judgment notwithstanding the verdict. **Harold S. Lee, et al. v. Joseph E. Seagram and Sons, 413 F.Supp. 693 (S.D.N.Y.1976)**. It had earlier denied Seagram's motion for summary judgment. The plaintiffs are Harold S. Lee (now deceased) and his two sons, Lester and Eric ("the Lees"). Jurisdiction is based on diversity of citizenship. We affirm.

The jury could have found the following. The Lees owned a 50% interest in Capitol City Liquor Company, Inc. ("Capitol City"), a wholesale liquor distributorship located in Washington, D.C. The other 50% was owned by Harold's brother, Henry D. Lee, and his nephew, Arthur Lee. Seagram is a distiller of alcoholic beverages. Capitol City carried numerous Seagram brands and a large portion of its sales were generated by Seagram lines.

The Lees and the other owners of Capitol City wanted to sell their respective interests in the business and, in May 1970, Harold Lee, the father, discussed the possible sale of Capitol City with Jack Yogman ("Yogman"), then Executive Vice

President of Seagram (and now President), whom he had known for many years. Lee offered to sell Capitol City to Seagram but conditioned the offer on Seagram's agreement to relocate Harold and his sons, the 50% owners of Capitol City, in a new distributorship of their own in a different city.

About a month later, another officer of Seagram, John Barth, an assistant to Yogman, visited the Lees and their co-owners in Washington and began negotiations for the purchase of the assets of Capitol City by Seagram on behalf of a new distributor, one Carter, who would take it over after the purchase. The purchase of the assets of Capitol City was consummated on September 30, 1970 pursuant to a written agreement. The promise to relocate the father and sons thereafter was not reduced to writing.

Harold Lee had served the Seagram organization for thirty-six years in positions of responsibility before he acquired the half interest in the Capitol City distributorship. From 1958 to 1962, he was chief executive officer of Calvert Distillers Company, a wholly-owned subsidiary. During this long period he enjoyed the friendship and confidence of the principals of Seagram.

In 1958, Harold Lee had purchased from Seagram its holdings of Capitol City stock in order to introduce his sons into the liquor distribution business, and also to satisfy Seagram's desire to have a strong and friendly distributor for Seagram products in Washington, D.C. Harold Lee and Yogman had known each other for 13 years.

The plaintiffs claimed a breach of the oral agreement to relocate Harold Lee's sons, alleging that Seagram had had opportunities to procure another distributorship for the Lees but had refused to do so. The Lees brought this action on January 18, 1972, fifteen months after the sale of the Capitol City distributorship to Seagram. They contended that they had performed their obligation by agreeing to the sale by Capitol City of its assets to Seagram, but that Seagram had failed to perform its obligation under the separate oral contract between the Lees and Seagram. The agreement which the trial court permitted the jury to find was "an oral agreement with defendant which provided that if they agreed to sell their interest in Capitol City, defendant in return, within a reasonable time, would provide the plaintiffs a Seagram distributorship whose price would require roughly an amount equal to the capital obtained by the plaintiffs for the sale of their interest in Capitol City, and which distributorship would be in a location acceptable to plaintiffs." No specific exception was taken to this portion of the charge. By its verdict for the plaintiffs, we must assume as Seagram notes in its brief that this is the agreement which the jury found was made before the sale of Capitol City was agreed upon.[2]

Appellant urges several grounds for reversal. It contends that, as a matter of law, (1) plaintiffs' proof of the alleged oral agreement is barred by the parol evidence rule . . . .

I

Judge Tenney, in a careful analysis of the application of the parol evidence rule, decided that the rule did not bar proof of the oral agreement. We agree.

The District Court, in its denial of the defendant's motion for summary judgment, treated the issue as whether the written agreement for the sale of assets was an "integrated" agreement not only of all the mutual agreements concerning the sale of Capitol City assets, but also of all the mutual agreements of the parties. Finding the language of the sales agreement "somewhat ambiguous," the court decided that the determination of whether the parol evidence rule applies must await the taking of evidence on the issue of whether the sales agreement was intended to be a complete and accurate integration of all of the mutual promises of the parties.

Seagram did not avail itself of this invitation. It failed to call as witnesses any of the three persons who negotiated the sales agreement on behalf of Seagram regarding the intention of the parties to integrate all mutual promises or regarding the failure of the written agreement to contain an integration clause.

Appellant contends that, as a matter of law, the oral agreement was "part and parcel" of the subject-matter of the sales contract and that failure to include it in the written contract barred proof of its existence. **Mitchill v. Lath, 247 N.Y. 377, 380, 160 N.E. 646 (1928).** The position of appellant, fairly stated, is that the oral agreement was either an inducing cause for the sale or was a part of the consideration for the sale, and in either case, should have been contained in the written contract. In either case, it argues that the parol evidence rule bars its admission.

---

[2] The complaint alleged that Seagram agreed to "obtain" or "secure" or "provide" a "similar" distributorship within a reasonable time, and plaintiffs introduced some testimony to that effect. Although other testimony suggested that Seagram agreed merely to provide an opportunity for the Lees to negotiate with third parties, and Judge Tenney indicated in his denial of judgment n. o. v. that Seagram merely agreed "to notify plaintiffs as they learned of distributors who were considering the sale of their businesses," 413 F.Supp. at 698-99, the jury was permitted to find that the agreement was in the nature of a commitment to provide a distributorship. There was evidence to support such a finding, and the jury so found.

Appellees maintain, on the other hand, that the oral agreement was a collateral agreement and that, since it is not contradictory of any of the terms of the sales agreement, proof of it is not barred by the parol evidence rule. Because the case comes to us after a jury verdict we must assume that there actually was an oral contract, such as the court instructed the jury it could find. The question is whether the strong policy for avoiding fraudulent claims through application of the parol evidence rule nevertheless mandates reversal on the ground that the jury should not have been permitted to hear the evidence. See Fogelson v. Rackfay Constr. Co., 300 N.Y. 334 at 337-38, 90 N.E.2d 881 (1950).

The District Court stated the cardinal issue to be whether the parties "intended" the written agreement for the sale of assets to be the complete and accurate integration of all the mutual promises of the parties. If the written contract was not a complete integration, the court held, then the parol evidence rule has no application.* We assume that the District Court determined intention by objective standards. See 3 Corbin on Contracts §§ 573-574. The parol evidence rule is a rule of substantive law. Fogelson v. Rackfay Constr. Co., supra; Higgs v. De Maziroff, 263 N.Y. 473, 477, 189 N.E. 555 (1934); Smith v. Bear, 237 F.2d 79, 83 (2d Cir. 1956).

The law of New York is not rigid or categorical, but is in harmony with this approach. As Judge Fuld said in Fogelson:

> "Decision in each case must, of course, turn upon the type of transaction involved, the scope of the written contract and the content of the oral agreement asserted."

FYI

The appellant in *Lee* relies on *Mitchill v. Lath*, which, despite its age, continues to be a leading case addressing the definition of "collateral" agreements for purposes of the parol evidence rule. *Mitchill* involved a written contract for sale of farmland. The buyer claimed there was an oral agreement that the seller would remove an unsightly ice house seller had on a neighboring tract. The court concluded that the alleged agreement was not collateral to the sales agreement because it would "ordinarily be expected" to be embodied in the writing and was "so clearly connected with the principal transaction as to be part and parcel of it." The court also said that a collateral agreement "must in form be a collateral one" and "must not contradict express or implied provisions of the written contract." 160 N.E. at 647.

---

* [Authors' Note: In context, the district court statement that the parol evidence rule "has no application" if the contract was not a complete integration means that the parol evidence rule would not bar adding a term if the contract was not a complete integration. The parol evidence rule does, of course, apply to partial integrations.]

300 N.Y. at 338, 90 N.E.2d at 883. And the Court of Appeals wrote in Ball v. Grady, 267 N.Y. 470, 472, 196 N.E. 402, 403 (1935):

> "In the end, the court must find the limits of the integration as best
> it may by reading the writing in the light of surrounding circumstances."

Accord, Fogelson, supra, 300 N.Y. at 338, 90 N.E.2d 881. Thus, certain oral collateral agreements, even though made contemporaneously, are not within the prohibition of the parol evidence rule "because [if] they are separate, independent, and complete contracts, although relating to the same subject. . . . [t]hey are allowed to be proved by parol, because they were made by parol, and no part thereof committed to writing." Thomas v. Scutt, 127 N.Y. 133, 140-41, 27 N.E. 961, 963 (1891).

Although there is New York authority which in general terms supports defendant's thesis that an oral contract inducing a written one or varying the consideration may be barred, see, e.g., Fogelson v. Rackfay Constr. Co., supra, 300 N.Y. at 340, 90 N.E.2d 881, the overarching question is whether, in the context of the particular setting, the oral agreement was one which the parties would ordinarily be expected to embody in the writing. Ball v. Grady, supra, 267 N.Y. at 470, 196 N.E. 402; accord, Fogelson v. Rackfay Constr. Co., supra, 300 N.Y. at 338, 90 N.E.2d 881. See Restatement on Contracts § 240. For example, integration is most easily inferred in the case of real estate contracts for the sale of land, e. g., Mitchill v. Lath, supra, 247 N.Y. 377, 160 N.E. 646, or leases, Fogelson, supra; Plum Tree, Inc. v. N.K. Winston Corp., 351 F.Supp. 80, 83 (S.D.N.Y.1972). In more complex situations, in which customary business practice may be more varied, an oral agreement can be treated as separate and independent of the written agreement even though the written contract contains a strong integration clause. See Gem Corrugated Box Corp. v. National Kraft Container Corp., 427 F.2d 499, 503 (2d Cir. 1970).

Thus, as we see it, the issue is whether the oral promise to the plaintiffs, as individuals, would be an expectable term of the contract for the sale of assets by a corporation in which plaintiffs have only a 50% interest, considering as well the history of their relationship to Seagram.

Here, there are several reasons why it would not be expected that the oral agreement to give Harold Lee's sons another distributorship would be integrated into the sales contract. In the usual case, there is an identity of parties in both the claimed integrated instrument and in the oral agreement asserted. Here, although it would have been physically possible to insert a provision dealing with only the shareholders of a 50% interest, the transaction itself was a corporate sale of assets. Collateral agreements which survive the closing of a corporate deal, such as employment agreements for particular shareholders of the seller or consulting agreements, are often set forth in separate agreements. See Gem Corrugated Box Corp. v. National Kraft Container Corp., supra, 427 F.2d at 503 ("it is . . . plain that the parties ordinarily would not embody the stock purchase agreement in a writing concerned only with box materials purchase terms"). It was expectable that such an agreement as one to obtain a new distributorship for certain persons, some of whom were not even parties to the contract, would not necessarily be integrated into an instrument for the sale of corporate assets. As with an oral condition precedent to the legal effectiveness of an otherwise integrated written contract, which is not barred by the parol evidence rule if it is not directly contradictory of its terms, Hicks v. Bush, 10 N.Y.2d 488, 225 N.Y.S.2d 34, 180 N.E.2d 425 (1962); cf. 3 Corbin on Contracts § 589, "it is certainly not improbable that parties contracting in these circumstances would make the asserted oral agreement . . . ." 10 N.Y.2d at 493, 225 N.Y.S.2d at 39, 180 N.E.2d at 428.

Similarly, it is significant that there was a close relationship of confidence and friendship over many years between two old men, Harold Lee and Yogman, whose authority to bind Seagram has not been questioned. It would not be surprising that a handshake for the benefit of Harold's sons would have been thought sufficient. In point, as well, is the circumstance that the negotiations concerning the provisions of the sales agreement were not conducted by Yogman but by three other Seagram representatives, headed by John Barth. The two transactions may not have been integrated in their minds when the contract was drafted.[4]

Finally, the written agreement does not contain the customary integration clause, even though a good part of it (relating to warranties and negative covenants) is boilerplate. The omission may, of course, have been caused by mutual trust and confidence, but in any event, there is no such strong presumption of exclusion because of the existence of a detailed

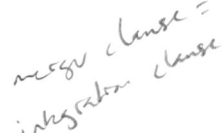

Make the Connection

An "integration clause" (also called a "merger clause") is a contract clause that declares the parties' intent to completely integrate the agreement. This kind of clause is discussed in the next two cases.

merger clause = integration clause

integration clause, as was relied upon by the Court of Appeals in Fogelson, supra, 300 N.Y. at 340, 90 N.E. 881.

Nor do we see any contradiction of the terms of the sales agreement. Mitchill v. Lath, supra, 247 N.Y. at 381, 160 N.E. 646; 3 Corbin on Contracts § 573,

---

[4] Barth in a confidential memorandum dated June 12, 1970 to Yogman and Edgar Bronfman stated that "he [Harold Lee] would very much like to have another distributorship in another area for his two sons." Apparently Barth, who was not present at Harold Lee's meeting with Yogman, assumed that this was a desire on the part of Lee rather than a promise made by Yogman for Seagram.

at 357. The written agreement dealt with the sale of corporate assets, the oral agreement with the relocation of the Lees. Thus, the oral agreement does not vary or contradict the money consideration recited in the contract as flowing to the selling corporation. That is the only consideration recited, and it is still the only consideration to the corporation.[5]

We affirm Judge Tenney's reception in evidence of the oral agreement and his denial of the motion under **Rule 50(b)** with respect to the parol evidence rule.

. . . .

Affirmed.

---

§ 3.3.4 Is the Written Contract Integrated, Either Partially or Completely?

As we have already seen, whether and how the parol evidence rule applies depends on determining whether the parties' agreement is in a writing that is a partial or a complete integration (merely a "final expression of their agreement with respect to such terms as are included therein" or also a "complete and exclusive statement"). How, and based on what evidence, does a court determine whether a writing is integrated, and if integrated, whether it is a partial or a complete integration? If the contract includes a "merger clause" (also known as an "integration clause") declaring the writing to be the final, or final and exclusive, agreement, what effect should such a clause have? The set of cases that follow address these issues and illustrate the application of the parol evidence rule in particular circumstances.

> **Reading the Law Critically:**
>
> *Middletown Concrete, UAW-GM Human Resource Center,*
>
> and *Sierra Diesel*
>
> 1. What evidence does one of the parties seek to introduce in each case? What term does that party seek to prove? Does the term contradict anything in the written contract document or should it be considered a "consistent additional term"?

---

[5] Cf. Mitchill v. Lath, 247 N.Y. 377, 380-81, 160 N.E. 646, 647 (1928)(to escape the parol evidence rule, the oral agreement "must not contradict express or implied provisions of the written contract"). The parties do not contend, and we would be unwilling to hold, that the oral agreement was not "in form a collateral one." Id.

2. What evidence does the court consider, and say should be considered, in deciding whether the contract document is partially or completely integrated?

3. Each of the contracts includes a merger clause. What is the language in that clause, and what effect does it have on the court's determination?

4. Does the court conclude that the contract document is merely a "final expression" ("partial integration") or also a "complete and exclusive statement" ("complete integration") or neither? Why does it reach the result it does? Do you agree with the court's conclusion?

Middletown Concrete Products, Inc. v. Black Clawson Co.

MIDDLETOWN CONCRETE PRODUCTS, INC., Plaintiff

v.

BLACK CLAWSON CO., and
HYDROTILE MACHINERY CO., Defendants

United States District Court
802 F. Supp. 1135 (D. Del. 1992)

MURRAY M. SCHWARTZ, Senior District Judge.

On October 11, 1990, Middletown Concrete Products, Inc. ("MCP") filed a complaint against Black Clawson Co. ("Black Clawson") and Hydrotile Machinery Company ("Hydrotile") over the sale of machinery for which the contract price exceeded $2,000,000. Before the Court now in this diversity action is MCP's motion for summary judgment on counts I and II and defendants' motion for summary judgment on all counts. The parties agree that the contract claims are governed by Iowa law and the tort claims are governed by Delaware law. This Court has jurisdiction under 28 U.S.C. § 1332.

For the reasons that follow, MCP's motion for summary judgment will be denied; Hydrotile's motion for summary judgment will also be denied.

I.

In 1988, Kenneth Kershaw ("Kershaw"), Joseph J. Corrado ("Corrado"), Stephen A. Cole ("Cole"), Frank Corrado, Leonard Iacono ("Iacono"), Arnold Boyer ("Boyer") and Verino Pettinaro, all of whom are Delaware contractors, formed and became shareholders in Middletown Concrete Products, Inc., a precast concrete manufacturing plant in Middletown Delaware. Each of the founders is an experienced businessman. Boyer invested approximately $500,000, and subsequent investments by Kershaw and Corrado have brought their investments in MCP to approximately $1.3 million each. MCP's primary product was to be concrete pipe.

In March of 1989, MCP entered into a series of contracts (the "Contracts") with Hydrotile, a wholly owned division of Black Clawson, under which defendants agreed to sell to MCP a machinery system to manufacture concrete pipe (the "System"). . . [including] the Multipak/Neptune machine (the "Neptune") . . . . On August 8, 1989, MCP entered into an additional contract with Hydrotile for the purchase of equipment for the production of elliptical concrete pipe.

Apparently, the parties' relationship began when David Mack ("Mack"), Hydrotile's regional sales manager, visited Corrado to discuss the generalities of the pipe manufacturing business as well as Hydrotile's products. . . .

At one of the [parties'] meetings in 1988, Mack gave Corrado a promotional brochure for the Neptune. Part of this brochure contained a list of rates at which the Neptune could produce various sizes of pipe.

        . . . .

In August of 1988, Hydrotile and MCP intensified negotiations for the purchase of a highly automated system. On August 11 and 12, 1988, Mack and [Daryl Haar, vice president and marketing manager for Hydrotile] met with MCP to go over Hydrotile's quote for the System. Although experienced businessmen, none of the shareholders of MCP had ever purchased pipe making machinery before. Among other things, Haar and Mack discussed proposed plant layouts. The parties also discussed pipe quality, production rates, and changeover time.

During this meeting Corrado and other shareholders of MCP shared with Haar concerns they wanted satisfied before purchasing the System from Hydrotile. At the time of the meeting MCP was concerned about the Neptune's performance as Neptune had not developed a track record and as another company was experiencing problems with the Neptune's predecessor, the Saturn. Accordingly, MCP requested that Hydrotile guarantee production rates. Indeed, MCP was "screaming" and "shouting" about the production guarantee's importance. MCP also requested that Hydrotile accept different payment terms than those proposed by Hydrotile, and agree to buy back the System if it did not perform satisfactorily. After initially dismissing MCP's requests as "out of the question," Haar agreed to discuss the requests with his superiors.

        . . . .

On August 24, 1988 [in a meeting between MCP and Hydrotile], Haar also told MCP that Hydrotile could not guarantee the production levels in the promotional brochure because actual production levels could depend on a number of factors. In response to this MCP told Haar to advise MCP of rates Hydrotile would guarantee. Specifically, Boyer told Haar and Fell that if they were unwilling to guarantee the rates in their promotion literature, they should pick a number they could live with. MCP never insisted that Hydrotile guarantee the rates reflected by its advertising.

During the August 24, 1988, meeting, Haar also stated that changeovers could be made in about an hour. Both Haar and Ronald Schriever, Hydrotile's National Sales Manager, made this representation on several occasions. Plaintiff urges that such representations were insupportable because Mack, during his deposition, testified that Hydrotile never attempted to change over any Neptune prior to marketing the machine. Also, plaintiffs note Hydrotile's theoretical production rates for the Neptune were calculated partially by extrapolating theoretical production rates of the Saturn. MCP actually experienced changeover times in excess of four to eight hours.

On August 30, 1988, Haar, Mack and [the president of Hydrotile] met with Corrado, Boyer and Iacono. The parties discussed production rates. Around the time of the meeting, Haar presented MCP with Hydrotile's definition of "Acceptable Performance" of the System. The definition was in the form of a letter (the "Acceptable Performance Letter") authored by Mr. Haar in response to MCP's demand on August 24. The production rate listed was less than that contained in Hydrotile's literature.

. . . .

Plaintiff maintains that although Hydrotile would not agree to make payment contingent upon the System achieving Acceptable Performance, Haar told MCP that such performance levels would be guaranteed by Hydrotile. Plaintiff further maintains that it informed Hydrotile representatives that it was relying on these guaranteed Acceptable Performance numbers in making its decision to purchase the System.[2]

On March 21, 1989, a meeting was held in Wilmington, Delaware, during which the final negotiations of the Contracts took place. Cole, Corrado and Kershaw were present on behalf of MCP. Haar and Mack attended on behalf of Hydrotile. Cole eventually signed the quotations brought by Haar and Mack.

Printed near the top of the first page of each contract was the following:

We [Hydrotile] hereby offer for a limited period of 30 days following the date hereof the items described below and/or in the specifications, if any

---

[2] The parties dispute whether the performance criteria set forth in the Acceptable Performance Letter became part of the Contracts. For the purposes of MCP's summary judgment motion, MCP is willing to assume, *arguendo*, that the criteria of the Acceptable Performance Letter are not part of the Contracts.

consisting of [ ] pages attached hereto. This offer is subject to the terms and conditions contained on this and the other side hereof and in said specifications, if any, and to no others whatsoever.

. . .

The System was delivered piecemeal beginning in October, 1989, and into January, 1990. By March 21, 1990, the System was installed and ready to manufacture pipe.

[In the subsequent months, MCP identified various performance problems with the installed machinery. Hydrotile acknowledged some of these, but did not repair or replace allegedly malfunctioning equipment to MCP's satisfaction.]

III.

Hydrotile first urges MCP's breach of contract and warranty causes of action fail as a matter of law because the contracts exclude the terms on which these claims are based. Count I alleges that Hydrotile breached its contract with MCP because the pipe-making equipment that it delivered pursuant to the Round Pipe Contract produces pipe at the rate of 34 pipes per hour rather than 54 pipes per hour that had allegedly been represented. Count II alleges that Hydrotile "expressly" warranted that it would repair or replace that equipment which did not meet the performance standards contained in the unsigned August 29, 1988, letter, and that Hydrotile breached this warranty. Count IV alleges that the Elliptical Pipe Contract required the equipment to make two elliptical pipes at a time and that this provision was breached. Hydrotile argues that because the written contracts each contain a written integration clause, and because it is undisputed the written contracts do not warrant or guarantee *any* particular production rate nor specify that the elliptical equipment could be used two at a time, settled principles governing parol evidence require judgment in Hydrotile's favor.

The parol evidence rule has been codified in Iowa's Uniform Commercial Code ("UCC"). **Iowa Code Annotated section 554.2202** states:

554.2202 Final written expression—parol or extrinsic evidence

Terms with respect to which the confirmatory memoranda of the partes agree or which are otherwise set forth in a writing intended by the parties as a final expression of their agreement with respect to such terms as are included therein may not be contradicted by evidence of any prior agreement or of a contemporaneous oral agreement but may be explained or supplemented

    a. by course of dealing or usage of trade (Section 554.1205) or by course of performance (Section 554.2208); and

    b. by evidence of consistent additional terms unless the court

finds the writing to have been intended also as a complete and
exclusive statement of the terms of the agreement.

Iowa Code Ann. § 554.2202 (West 1991).

In determining the applicability of the parol evidence rule, a court must first
determine whether there is an integrated agreement. *See Restatement (Second) of
Contracts* § 209(2) at 115 (1981). If a court concludes there is no integration,
the parol evidence rule does not apply and evidence of contradictory prior or
contemporaneous agreements may be introduced. "An integrated agreement is
a writing or writings constituting a final expression of one or more terms of an
agreement." *Id.* at § 209(1). Professor Farnsworth has noted, "[n]o particular form
is required for an integrated agreement, and the writing need not be signed by
either party." E. Allan Farnsworth, *Contracts* § 7.3, at 471 (2nd ed. 1990) (footnotes omitted) [hereinafter Farnsworth]. "Whether a writing has been adopted as
an integrated agreement is a question of fact to be determined in accordance with
all relevant evidence." *Restatement (Second) of Contracts* § 209 cmt. c.[6] Case
law explaining how courts actually determine the intent of the parties is scant.
Often courts simply assume a contract is integrated and move on to determine
whether that contract is merely final as to the terms it contains or is the complete
and exclusive final agreement of the parties.

Although nothing in the UCC indicates what a court is to consider, there are
certain general principles that should guide a court in determining whether the
parties intended a writing to be a final expression of their agreement. Professor
Farnsworth, for instance, has observed that "the intention of the parties is determined from all the circumstances, including their language and other conduct,
just as intention is determined for any other purpose." Farnsworth, § 7.3 at 472.
Although the writing itself is useful in determining intent, Professor Corbin cau-
tions, "No written document is sufficient, standing alone, to determine [if a writing
is an integration], . . . however long and detailed it may be, however formal, and
however many may be the seals and signatures and assertions." 3 Arthur Linton
Corbin, *Corbin on Contracts* § 573 at 360 (1960) [hereinafter *Corbin*]. The Court
of Appeals for the Ninth Circuit has emphasized: "In deciding whether a writing is
final the most important issue is the intent of the parties." *Sierra Diesel Injection
Service v. Burroughs Corp.*, 890 F.2d 108, 112 (9th Cir.1989) (interpreting
Nevada's codification of 2-202 which is substantially similar to Iowa's codification
of the same).

In this case defendants have identified three documents which they maintain
constitute the "contracts." The first writing, #149, involves the sale of an Hydro-
tile/Rekers Automatic Offbearing System and Cured Pipe Handling System. The

---

[6] Comment c to section 209 of the Second Restatement notes, "[o]rdinarily the issue whether there is
an integrated agreement is determined by the trial judge in the first instance as a question preliminary
to an interpretive ruling or to the application of the parol evidence rule." *Restatement (Second) of
Contracts* § 209 cmt. c (1981).

second writing, #148, involves the sale of kiln cars, a car moving system, and a hydraulic pumping unit. The third writing, #146, involves the sale of a Hydro-tile Multipak/Neptune Concrete Pipe Machine, form mounted cage positioner controls, equipment required to run round pipe, and equipment to produce 15" through 42" R-4 Forsheda 138 joint pipe. Defendants maintain the three writings constitute the complete and exclusive final expression of the parties' agreement. Plaintiff, on the other hand, disputes that the three writings were ever integrated in the first place. Plaintiff argues that when presented with documents #146, #148, and #149, it refused to sign them unless defendants agreed that the 1988 Acceptable Performance Letter was part of the contracts. Plaintiff further argues that only after it received assurances that the documents would be part of the contracts between the parties, did it sign the documents #146, #148, and #149.[7] Therefore, plaintiff urges neither party intended documents #146, #148, and #149 to be the final expression of their agreement; rather, the final agreement between the parties was meant to include documents #146, #148, #149, *and* the Acceptable Performance Letter.

The facts, however, ultimately belie plaintiff's position. First, plaintiff's principals are sophisticated businessmen who negotiated with defendants for several months. Second, the relative bargaining strengths of the parties were commensurate. Third, each of the writings is signed by an MCP representative and dated March 21, 1989. Fourth, on the reverse side of the contracts is a pre-printed limitation of warranties which reads:

> THE FOREGOING WARRANTY [that the equipment will be free from defects in material and workmanship under normal use and service for a period of 90 days from delivery] IS EXCLUSIVE AND IS IN LIEU OF ALL OTHER WARRANTIES (WHETHER WRITTEN, ORAL OR IMPLIED) INCLUDING THE WARRANTY OF MERCHANTABILITY IN OTHER RESPECTS THAN EXPRESSLY SET FORTH ABOVE AND WARRANTY OF FITNESS FOR A PARTICULAR PURPOSE.

Fifth, also on the reverse side of each writing is the following pre-printed merger clause:

> There are no rights, warranties or conditions, express or implied, statutory or otherwise, other than those herein contained. This agreement between Buyer and Seller can be modified or rescinded only by a writing signed by both parties. No waiver of any provision of this agreement shall be binding unless in writing signed by an authorized representative of the party against whom the waiver is asserted and unless expressly

---

[7] Defendants vehemently deny that they ever gave such assurances.

made generally applicable shall only apply to the specific case for which the waiver is given.

On the date the Contracts were signed, plaintiff sent Hydrotile a letter reading as follows:

> Please accept our order per your Sales contracts 146, 148, 149 this date. We reserve the right to have the sales contracts read and cause remedy to language before the close of day Thursday, March 23, 1989.

Practice Pointer

What the court calls above a "pre-printed merger clause" is actually a merger clause (first sentence), a no-oral-modification clause (second sentence), and a non-waiver clause (third sentence).

The letter was acknowledged through signature by Haar, a Hydrotile representative. Above Haar's signature is the caption: "Accepted." Therefore, the contracts consisted of the three documents plus any modifications made during the three-day period of March 21, 1989, to March 23, 1989.[9] Sixth, the entire set of documents were reviewed by plaintiffs' counsel.[10] Accordingly, the only reasonable inference to be drawn from the facts is that the parties intended the three writings and any modifications made between March 21 and March 23, 1989, to constitute the final expression of the parties as to those terms contained therein.

Having determined that writings #146, #148, and #149 are final expressions, the parol evidence rule has some application. The next question the Court must address is whether the writings constitute merely the final expression of the parties' agreement as to the terms contained in each writing, or the complete and exclusive final expression of the parties' agreement. As explained by Professor Murray:

> (1) if the parties intend their written expression of agreement to be merely *final*, the terms of that final agreement may not be *contradicted* by any prior [agreement] or contemporaneous oral agreement. (2) Such terms in a final writing may, however, be explained or supplemented by evidence of consistent additional terms or by evidence of course of dealing, usage of trade or course of performance. (3) If the parties intended their writing to be not merely *final* but also a *complete and exclusive* statement of the terms of their agreement, evidence of consistent additional terms

---

[9] Neither party has suggested that the Acceptable Performance Letter was made a part of the Contracts during the three day window.

[10] At oral argument the Court asked counsel for plaintiff if the acceptable performance letter could be made part of the contract. Counsel responded: "I assume our firm could. I assume that our client could . . . . Certainly it could have been stapled on; it could have been referred to therein or it could have been discussed separately, as some of the other modifications . . . were."

is excluded, but even with respect to such a complete and exclusive expression of agreement, evidence of trade usage, course of dealing, and course of performance is admissible. There is, therefore, no presumption that the writing is the complete and exclusive expression of the parties' agreement. Rather, the opposite is assumed, i.e., the writing will not be viewed as complete and exclusive unless the court finds that the parties intended it to be complete and exclusive.

John Edward Murray, Jr., *Murray on Contracts* § 84, at 394-95 (3d ed. 1990) (emphasis in original) (footnotes omitted).

. . . .

Defendants argue the presence of the three separate merger clauses in each of the three writings should, as a matter of law, determine that the writings were the complete and exclusive agreement between the parties. Defendants cite *Montgomery Properties Corp. v. Economy Forms Corp.,* 305 N.W.2d 470 (Iowa 1981), for the proposition that because each of the contracts contains an integration clause, the Court should conclude that the parties intended the written contract "as the final and complete expression of the agreement." In *Montgomery Properties,* the Supreme Court of Iowa held that in an integrated agreement involving a handcrafted integration clause in a contract between sophisticated parties of equal bargaining strength, the existence of the integration clause is controlling on the issue of whether the written contract is the whole integrated agreement, so as to exclude parol evidence on the issue. *Id.* at 476. In 1986, the Iowa Supreme Court made clear, however, that *Montgomery* was "expressly limited to 'handcrafted' contracts between parties of equal bargaining strength." *Wolfe v. Graether,* 389 N.W.2d 643, 654 (Iowa 1986). Because the case presently before the Court involves a pre-printed integration clause, *Montgomery* is not directly on point. Moreover, the fact that there are *three* separate integration clauses on each of the writings, #146, #148, and #149, each of which recites, "[t]his agreement contains the entire agreement between Buyer and Seller . . ." belies the conclusion that any one of the writings *alone* is the *entire* agreement between the parties. It is, therefore, concluded that the writings #146, #148 and #149 are merely final as to the terms each writing contains.

Think About It

Do you agree with the court's judgment that writings 146, 148, and 149 are final but not complete and exclusive? How would you argue that they should be understood instead as a complete and exclusive statement of the contract terms?

Accordingly, the terms contained in writings #146, #148 and #149 may not be contradicted by any prior or contemporaneous agreement, but may be supplemented or explained by consistent additional terms. *See* Iowa Code Ann. § 554.2202. In this case, the Acceptable Performance Letter, which guarantees production rates for the systems contained in writing #146, #148, and #149, would contradict the partially integrated agreements which exclude all warranties not contained in the writings. *See* J. White & R. Summers, *Uniform Commercial Code,* § 12-4 at 568 n. 2 (3d ed. 1988) ("If . . . the writing that includes a disclaimer is intended to be final, most courts hold that parol warranties are "contradictory" within 2-202 and hence inadmissible."). Therefore, the Court finds the parol evidence rule prohibits evidence of the Acceptable Performance Letter to establish the letter was part of the original contract between the two parties.

[The court went on to conclude that the contract as reflected in the specified documents was not modified to include the Acceptable Performance Letter, but that a genuine issue of material fact existed as to MCP's claim that a waiver occurred.]

VI.

For the reasons set forth above, both defendants' and plaintiff's respective motions for summary judgment will be denied.

UAW-GM Human Resource Center v. KSL Recreation Corp.

UAW-GM HUMAN RESOURCE CENTER, Plaintiff-Appellee

v.

KSL RECREATION CORP. and KSL HOTEL CORP., Defendants-Appellants

Court of Appeals of Michigan
579 N.W.2d 411 (Mich. Ct. App. 1998)

MARKMAN, Presiding Judge.

Defendants appeal as of right a trial court order granting summary disposition to plaintiff on its claims of breach of contract, conversion, and fraud. Defendants also appeal as of right the trial court's denial of their motion for summary disposition. We reverse and remand for determination of damages pursuant to the liquidated damages formula set forth in the contract.

Facts

In December 1993, plaintiff entered into a contract with Carol Management Corporation (CMC) for the use of its property, Doral Resort and Country Club, for a convention scheduled in October 1994. The "letter of agreement" included a merger clause that stated that such agreement constituted "a merger of all proposals, negotiations and representations with reference to the subject matter and provisions." The letter of agreement did not contain any provision requiring that

~ugu clauses ar other bodies/clis

What's That?

An "appeal as of right" is an appeal that a higher court is required to consider if a party chooses to file. In contrast, some appeals in both state and federal courts will be considered only if the higher court grants permission or leave to appeal. The categories of cases that result in appeals as of right or by leave are specified by statute or by court rule.

Doral Resort employees be union-represented. However, plaintiff contends in its appellate brief that it signed the letter of agreement in reliance on an "independent, collateral promise to provide [plaintiff] with a union-represented hotel." Plaintiff provided the affidavits of Herschel Nix, plaintiff's agent, and Barbara Roush, CMC's agent, who negotiated the contract. In his affidavit, Nix states that during the contract negotiation he and Roush discussed plaintiff's requirement that the hotel employees be union-represented and that Roush agreed to this requirement. In her affidavit, Roush states that "prior to and at the time" the contract at issue was negotiated she "was well aware" of plaintiff's requirement that the hotel employees be union-represented and that "that there is no doubt that I agreed on behalf of the Doral Resort to provide a union hotel." The letter of agreement also included a liquidated damages clause in the event plaintiff canceled the reservation "for any reason other than the following: Acts of God, Government Regulation, Disaster, Civil Disorders or other emergencies making it illegal to hold the meeting/convention."

no union now · want money back

Make the Connection

A liquidated damages clause is a contract term that specifies, by amount or formula, the damages that will be owed for a contract breach, rather than leaving determination of damages to a court enforcing the contract. The parties are free to agree to such a term, but courts do not always enforce them. The limitations on liquidated damages clauses are discussed in Chapter 9 (page 1162).

Later in December 1993, the hotel was sold to defendants, who subsequently replaced the resort's union employees with a nonunionized work force. In June 1994, when plaintiff learned that the hotel no longer had union employees, it canceled the contract and demanded a refund of its down payment. Defendants refused to refund the down payment, retaining it as a portion of the liquidated damages allegedly owed to them pursuant to the contract. Plaintiff filed suit for return of the down payment and asserted claims of breach of contract, conversion of the deposit, and fraud. Defendants filed a counterclaim and moved for summary disposition and enforcement of the liquidated damages clause. Plaintiff filed a cross-motion for summary disposition. The trial court granted plaintiff's motion for summary disposition regarding the breach of contract count on the basis of its determination that there was a separate agreement requiring that the hotel employees be union-represented. . . .

This Court reviews decisions on motions for summary disposition de novo to determine if the moving party was entitled to judgment as a matter of law. *Stehlik v. Johnson* (On Rehearing), 206 Mich.App. 83, 85, 520 N.W.2d 633 (1994). . . .

Merger Clause

Defendants claim that the trial court erred in granting plaintiff's motion for summary disposition and in denying defendants' motion for summary disposition. Regarding the breach of contract count, they specifically contend that parol evidence of a separate agreement providing that the hotel would have union employees at the time of the convention was inadmissible because the letter of agreement included an express merger clause.

We begin by reiterating the basic rules regarding contract interpretation. "The primary goal in the construction or interpretation of any contract is to honor the intent of the parties." *Rasheed v. Chrysler Corp.*, 445 Mich. 109, 127, n. 28, 517 N.W.2d 19 (1994).

> We must look for the intent of the parties in the words used in the instrument. This court does not have the right to make a different contract for the parties or to look to extrinsic testimony to determine their intent when the words used by them are clear and unambiguous and have a definite meaning." [*Sheldon-Seatz, Inc. v. Coles*, 319 Mich. 401, 406-407, 29 N.W.2d 832 (1947), quoting Michigan Chandelier Co. v. Morse, 297 Mich. 41, 49, 297 N.W. 64 (1941).]

In *Port Huron Ed. Ass'n v. Port Huron Area School Dist.*, 452 Mich. 309, 323, 550 N.W.2d 228 (1996), the Court stated:

> The initial question whether contract language is ambiguous is a question of law. If the contract language is clear and unambiguous, its meaning is a question of law. Where the contract language is unclear or susceptible to multiple meanings, interpretation becomes a question of fact. [Citations omitted.]

A contract is ambiguous if "its words may reasonably be understood in different ways." *Raska v. Farm Bureau Ins. Co.*, 412 Mich. 355, 362, 314 N.W.2d 440

(1982). Courts are not to create ambiguity where none exists. *Smith v. Physicians Health Plan, Inc.*, 444 Mich. 743, 759, 514 N.W.2d 150 (1994). "Contractual language is construed according to its plain and ordinary meaning, and technical or constrained constructions are to be avoided." *Dillon v. DeNooyer Chevrolet Geo*, 217 Mich.App. 163, 166, 550 N.W.2d 846 (1996). If the meaning of an agreement is ambiguous or unclear, the trier of fact is to determine the intent of the parties. *Chrysler Corp. v. Brencal Contractors, Inc.*, 146 Mich.App. 766, 775, 381 N.W.2d 814 (1985).

The parol evidence rule may be summarized as follows: "[p]arol evidence of contract negotiations, or of prior or contemporaneous agreements that contradict or vary the written contract, is not admissible to vary the terms of a contract which is clear and unambiguous." *Schmude Oil Co. v. Omar Operating Co.*, 184 Mich.App. 574, 580, 458 N.W.2d 659 (1990). This rule recognizes that in "[b]ack of nearly every written instrument lies a parol agreement, merged therein." *Lee State Bank v. McElheny*, 227 Mich. 322, 327, 198 N.W. 928 (1924). "The practical justification for the rule lies in the stability that it gives to written contracts; for otherwise either party might avoid his obligation by testifying that a contemporaneous oral agreement released him from the duties that he had simultaneously assumed in writing." 4 Williston, Contracts, § 631. In other words, the parol evidence rule addresses the fact that "disappointed parties will have a great incentive to describe circumstances in ways that escape the explicit terms of their contracts." Fried, *Contract as Promise* (Cambridge: Harvard University Press, 1981) at 60.

However, parol evidence of prior or contemporaneous agreements or negotiations is admissible on the threshold question whether a written contract is an integrated instrument that is a complete expression of the parties' agreement. In re *Skotzke Estate*, 216 Mich.App. 247, 251-252, 548 N.W.2d 695 (1996); *NAG Enterprises, Inc. v. All State Industries, Inc.*, 407 Mich. 407, 410-411, 285 N.W.2d 770 (1979). The *NAG* Court noted four exceptions to the parol evidence rule, stating that extrinsic evidence is admissible to show (1) that the writing was a sham, not intended to create legal relations, (2) that the contract has no efficacy or effect because of fraud, illegality, or mistake, (3) that the parties did not integrate their agreement or assent to it as the final embodiment of their understanding, or (4) that the agreement was only partially integrated because essential elements were not reduced to writing. *NAG, supra* at 410-411, 285 N.W.2d 770. See also 4 Williston, Contracts, § 631. Importantly, neither *NAG* nor *Skotzke* involved a contract with an explicit integration clause.

The first issue before us is whether parol evidence is admissible with regard to the threshold question of integration even when the written agreement includes an explicit merger or integration clause. In other words, the issue is whether *NAG* applies to allow parol evidence regarding this threshold issue when a contract includes an explicit merger clause. . . .

. . . [B]oth Corbin and Williston indicate that an explicit integration clause is con-clusive and that parol evidence is not admissible to determine whether a contract is integrated when a written contract contains such a clause. In the context of an explicit integration clause, Corbin recognizes exceptions to the barring of parol evidence only for fraud (or other grounds sufficient to set aside a contract) and for the rare situation when the written document is obviously incomplete "on its face" and, therefore, parol evidence is necessary "for the filling of gaps." *Id.* The conclusion that parol evidence is not admissible to show that a written agree-ment is not integrated when the agreement itself includes an integration clause is consistent with the general contract principles of honoring parties' agreements as expressed in their written contracts and not creating ambiguities where none exist.[4] See *Rasheed, supra* at 127, n. 28, 517 N.W.2d 19; *Sheldon-Seatz, supra* at 406-407, 29 N.W.2d 832; *Smith, supra* at 759, 514 N.W.2d 150. This conclusion accords respect to the rules that the parties themselves have set forth to resolve controversies arising under the contract. The parties are bound by the contract because they have chosen to be so bound.

they wrote it, so must follow

Further, and most fundamentally, if parol evidence were admissible with regard to the threshold issue whether the written agreement was integrated despite the existence of an integration clause, there would be little distinction between contracts that include an integration clause and those that do not. When the parties choose to include an integration clause, they clearly indicate that the written agreement is integrated; accordingly, there is no longer any "threshold issue" whether the agreement is integrated and, correspondingly, no need to resort to parol evidence to resolve this issue.[5] Thus *NAG*, which allows resort to

agreement made w/ different party, so can't expect them to know about side agreements — writing or all

---

[4] This is the only rule that treats the parties to the contract as consenting adults who are able to establish their own rules for the resolution of future controversies between themselves. The dissenting opinion fails to respect the parties' clearly expressed intent to be bound only by the terms of the letter of agreement. While the dissenting opinion attempts to minimize the import of the merger clause, the merger clause is an explicit term of the parties' contract and therefore an expression of their intent to which this Court is obligated to give meaning.

[5] The increased use of explicit integration clauses appears to be a response to the growing number of exceptions that have arisen in modern contract law to the traditional rule that courts will not look beyond the language of the contract itself in order to interpret the contract. Plaintiff now proposes to embark upon the same course by creating exceptions even to contracts that contain explicit integration clauses. We do not agree with plaintiff's contention during oral argument that there is no effective means by which parties to a contract can preclude courts from looking beyond the four corners of a contract in interpreting such contract. Were we to accept plaintiff's contention, as the dissenting opinion does, the likely response by members of the bar would be increasingly explicit merger clauses designed to compel the judiciary to respect the parties' decision to be bound only by the terms of the written agreement. Such "super-merger" clauses should not be necessary, but clear merger provisions of the sort contained in the instant contract are apparently insufficient to convince some that the parties mean what they say when they agree to a contract that includes an integration clause. Would it have made any difference if the parties had included language in the contract to the effect that the merger clause here "means what it says" or that the clause was "consciously" included in the agreement or that "it is not intended to be mere boilerplate"? What can parties to a contract do to ensure that they are held *only* to the terms explicitly agreed to in a written agreement?

parol evidence to resolve this "threshold issue," does not control when a contract includes a valid merger clause. . . .

This rule is especially compelling in cases such as the present one, where defendants, successor corporations, assumed performance of another corporation's obligations under a letter of agreement. Because defendants were not parties to the negotiations resulting in the letter of agreement, they would obviously be unaware of any oral representations made by CMC's agent to plaintiff's agent in the course of those negotiations. Defendants assumed CMC's obligations under the letter of agreement, which included an explicit merger clause. Defendants could not reasonably have been expected to discuss with every party to every contract with CMC whether any parol agreements existed that would place further burdens upon defendants in the context of a contract with an explicit merger clause. Under these circumstances, it would be fundamentally unfair to hold defendants to oral representations allegedly made by CMC's agent. Of the participants involved in this controversy, defendants are clearly the least blameworthy and the least able to protect themselves. Unlike plaintiff, which could have addressed its concerns by including appropriate language in the contract, and unlike CMC, which allegedly agreed to carry out obligations not included within the contract, defendants did nothing more than rely upon the express language of the instant contract, to wit, that the letter of agreement represented the full understanding between plaintiff and CMC. We believe that defendants acted reasonably in their reliance and that the contract should be interpreted in accordance with its express provisions.

. . . .

Fraud

. . . Parol evidence is generally admissible to demonstrate fraud. . . . [W]hen a contract contains a valid merger clause, the only fraud that could vitiate the contract is fraud that would invalidate the merger clause itself, i.e., fraud relating to the merger clause or fraud that invalidates the entire contract including the merger clause. 3 Corbin, Contracts, § 578.

. . . In its fraud count, plaintiff contends that Roush's representations that the hotel would have union employees and her failure to inform plaintiff of the impending sale of the hotel constituted fraud. . . . Here, the merger clause made it unreasonable for plaintiff's agent to rely on any representations not included in the letter of agreement. Any injury suffered by plaintiff appears to have resulted from its agent's failure to include a requirement that hotel employees be union-represented in the integrated letter of agreement rather than from reliance on any misrepresentations by Roush. Thus, the allegations in plaintiff's fraud count are not the type of fraud claims that could invalidate a contract with a valid merger clause.[9]

Plaintiff made no allegations of fraud that would invalidate the contract or the merger clause itself. Nix, plaintiff's agent, had over seven years' experience in negotiating contracts for such conventions as demonstrated by his own affidavit. There is no allegation that he was defrauded regarding the integration clause or defrauded into believing that the written contract included a provision requiring the hotel to use union-represented employees when it did not. In his affidavit, he states that in a 1991 letter of agreement with the same hotel, provisions were made for the hotel to provide bus transportation with union drivers. This evidence demonstrates that the plaintiff's agent knew how to include agreements regarding the union status of employees in a written contract, had done so in the past when negotiating with CMC, and yet apparently decided not to include any such agreement here. In light of the obvious importance of this issue to plaintiff, it is difficult to understand why an agreement regarding the union status of employees was not included in the same way in the instant agreement. Instead, the letter of agreement contained no such provision and included a clear integration clause.[11] The written agreement is detailed and complete on its face, see 3 Corbin, Contracts, § 578,[12] and its words are unambiguous, see Raska, supra at 362, 314 N.W.2d 440; Smith, supra at 759, 514 N.W.2d 150. There is no indication that the inte-

---

[9] Although not necessary to our analysis, we additionally note that plaintiff's allegations fail to meet the elements of fraud . . . . Here, plaintiff offered no documentary evidence to indicate that, at the time she allegedly represented that the hotel employees would be union-represented, Roush knew that defendants intended to eliminate the union work force, Roush knew that the possible sale of the hotel to defendants would be significant to the contract negotiations or that she had a duty to disclose the fact that negotiations for the sale of the hotel were under way. According to defendants' answer to the complaint, they purchased the hotel on or about December 30, 1993; thus, they purchased the hotel after the letter of agreement at issue was signed. Plaintiff's belated claim for innocent misrepresentation would have similarly failed because plaintiff failed to demonstrate that Roush had any duty to disclose the impending sale that would make a failure to disclose this information a representation that was false in fact.

[11] Although not necessary to our analysis, we note that the letter of agreement expressly set forth reasons justifying cancellation, i.e., "Acts of God, Government Regulation, Disaster, Civil Disorders or other emergencies making it illegal to hold the meeting/convention." These reasons did not include failure to maintain a union-represented staff. This cancellation clause would have been the logical place to provide for termination of the contract if the hotel employees did not continue to be union-represented.

[12] This exception applies when a contract with a merger clause fails to specify obvious elements of the deal struck. [Authors' Note: The exception the court refers to is "where an agreement is obviously incomplete 'on its face' and, therefore, parol evidence is necessary for the 'filling of gaps .'" 3 Corbin, Contracts § 578.] For example, under the letter of agreement at issue, if the hotel were to provide rooms without furniture or running water, this Court could fill the gaps in the letter of agreement by recognizing that such minimal amenities are essential to what constitutes a hotel room. But union-represented hotel employees are not essential to providing a hotel room. Rather, it is a particular desire of plaintiff, not common to all hotel patrons, that it use only hotels with union-represented employees. Unlike a failure to specify obvious elements of a contract, a party's failure to specify particular requests it may have will not make a contract with a merger clause "obviously incomplete on its face" such that parol evidence may be used "for the filling of gaps." . . .

gration clause itself is void for any reason. Accordingly, as a matter of law, parol evidence was not admissible here to contradict the explicit integration clause.[13]

Therefore, we hold that the trial court erred in granting plaintiff's motion for summary disposition and equally erred in denying defendants' motion for summary disposition.[14]

. . . .

Reversed and remanded for proceedings consistent with this opinion. We do not retain jurisdiction.

HOLBROOK, JR., J., (dissenting).

I respectfully dissent.

The event that precipitated this legal dispute was Carol Management's sale of the resort to defendants, without informing plaintiff during contract negotiations that the resort was for sale or that a sale was pending, and defendants' subsequent firing of the resort's union staff, less than one month after the contract with plaintiff was negotiated and signed. The contract—drafted by Carol Management— included a standardized integration or merger clause, but was silent regarding plaintiff's acknowledged requirement that the resort employ a union-represented staff. Attempts to pigeonhole these unusual facts into established black-letter rules

---

[13] Here, the merger clause, which was not void for fraud and not part of a contract that was incomplete on its face, dispositively answers the question whether the letter of agreement was integrated. Accordingly, here, there is no longer a threshold question whether the letter of agreement is integrated. The dissenting opinion cites Corbin, §§ 582 and 583 for the proposition that parol evidence is admissible to make the threshold determination whether a contract is completely integrated. However, Corbin, § 578 clearly states that a merger clause that is neither void itself nor part of a contract that is "obviously incomplete on its face" is conclusive. It is unclear whether there is anything that consenting parties can do in Michigan, pursuant to the theory of the dissenting opinion, to ensure that their future contract disputes will be resolved exclusively through resort to the language of their agreements.

[14] To construe the integration clause as precluding summary disposition for plaintiff, but not also as requiring summary disposition for defendants, is to accept the premise that the integration clause does not mean what it says. Contrary to plaintiff's contention during oral argument, we believe that the parties to a contract can agree to an integration clause that will effectively preclude courts from looking outside the contract to interpret the contract. The raison d'etre of an integration clause is to prohibit consideration of parol evidence by nullifying agreements not included in the written agreement. See 3 Corbin, Contracts, § 578. To consider parol evidence in interpreting a written contract that includes an integration clause is to accord the integration clause no meaning. An integration clause is not merely an additional "factor" to be weighed in light of the affidavits and other extrinsic evidence to determine the parties' understandings, nor is it merely one more piece of evidence to be used to determine whether there is a "genuine issue of material fact" to be evaluated at trial. Rather, an integration clause, if construed as precluding summary disposition for plaintiff, does so because it establishes an internal rule of construction for the contract explicitly agreed to by the parties to the contract. Specifically, an integration clause is an internal rule of construction that any previous or contemporaneous agreements are nullified. The parties' choice to include such an internal rule of construction precludes consideration of any prior or contemporaneous agreements and compels summary disposition here for defendants.

of contract law lead to harsh and unintended results. Hard cases do, indeed, make bad law.[1]

The contract's merger clause—"a merger of all proposals, negotiations and representations with reference to the subject matter and provisions"—appears plain and unambiguous. While it is often stated that courts may not create an ambiguity in a contract where none exists, and that parol evidence is generally not admissible to vary or contradict the terms of a written contract, Professor Corbin acknowledges that strict adherence to these rules can be problematic:

> The fact that the [parol evidence] rule has been stated in such a definite and dogmatic form as a rule of admissibility is unfortunate. It has an air of authority and certainty that has grown with much repetition. Without doubt, it has deterred counsel from making an adequate analysis and research and from offering parol testimony that was admissible for many purposes. Without doubt, also it has caused a court to refuse to hear testimony that ought to have been heard. The mystery of the written word is still such that a paper document may close the door to a showing that it was never assented to as a complete integration.

> No injustice is done by exclusion of the testimony if the written integration is in fact what the court assumes or decides that it is. . . .

> The trouble is that the court's assumption or decision as to the completeness and accuracy of the integration may be quite erroneous. *The writing cannot prove its own completeness and accuracy. Even though it contains an express statement to that effect, the assent of the parties thereto must still be proved. Proof of its completeness and accuracy, discharging all antecedent agreements, must be made in large part by the oral testimony of parties and other witnesses.* The very testimony that the "parol evidence rule" is supposed to exclude is frequently, if not always, necessary before the court can determine that the parties have agreed upon the writing as a complete and accurate statement of terms. The evidence that the rule seems to exclude must sometimes be heard and weighed before it can be excluded by the rule. This is one reason why the working of this rule has been so inconsistent and unsatisfactory. This is why so many exceptions and limitations to the supposed rule of evidence have been recognized by various courts.

> There is ample judicial authority showing that, in determining the issue of completeness of the integration in writing, evidence extrinsic to the writing itself is admissible. *The oral admissions of the plaintiff that the agreement included matters not contained in the writing may be proved to show that it was not assented*

---

[1] Paraphrasing Justice Holmes' statement, "Great cases, like hard cases, make bad law." *Northern Securities Co. v. United States*, 193 U.S. 197, 400-401, 24 S.Ct. 436, 468, 48 L.Ed. 679 (1904).

to as a complete integration, however complete it may look on its face. On this issue, parol testimony is certainly admissible to show the circumstances under which the agreement was made and the purposes for which the instrument was executed. [3 Corbin, Contracts, § 582, pp. 447-451 (emphasis added).]

And, in § 583 of his treatise, Professor Corbin continues:

No written document can prove its own execution or that it was ever assented to as a complete integration, supplanting and discharging what preceded it. . . . There are plenty of decisions that additional terms and provisions can be proved by parol evidence, thereby showing that the written document in court is not a complete integration. This is true, even though it is clear that the additional terms form a part of one contractual transaction along with the writing. [3 Corbin on Contracts, § 583, pp. 465-467.]

Accord Stimac v. Wissman, 342 Mich. 20, 26-27, 69 N.W.2d 151 (1955) (extrinsic evidence was admissible regarding a collateral independent promise so as to give full effect to the intent of the contracting parties); Restatement Contracts, 2d, § 216, comment e, p. 140 (observing that a merger "clause does not control the question of whether the writing was assented to as an integrated agreement").

The fact that plaintiff's representative read and signed the contract does not obviate the applicability of the principles outlined in Corbin, §§ 582 and 583. Indeed, Professor Corbin illustrates the principles of the section by analyzing the case of Int'l Milling Co. v. Hachmeister, Inc., 380 Pa. 407, 110 A.2d 186 (1955), in which the parties entered into a contract for the sale and purchase of flour. During negotiations, buyer insisted that each shipment of flour meet certain established specifications and that such a provision be included in the contract. Seller refused to put the provision in the contract, but agreed to write a confirmation letter to buyer tying in the required specifications. Buyer placed a written order, indicating that the flour must meet the required specifications. Seller sent to buyer a printed contract form, which contained none of the specifications, but did contain an express integration clause. Seller also sent a separate letter assuring delivery in accordance with the required specifications. Buyer signed the written contract form. When a subsequent shipment of flour failed to meet the specifications, buyer rejected it and canceled all other orders. The Pennsylvania Supreme Court held that extrinsic evidence of the parties' negotiations and antecedent agreements was admissible with regard to the issue whether buyer had assented to the printed contract form as a complete and accurate integration of the contract, *notwithstanding its express provision to the contrary.* Corbin, *supra* at 458.[2] Professor Corbin notes that the court's decision was fully supported by § 582, and explained at p. 459:

> It appears that in the instant case the buyer's evidence was very strong, so strong that it would be a travesty on justice to keep it from the jury. This is not because the express provision of integration was concealed from the buyer; he was familiar with the printed contract form and knew that the provision was in it and the specifications were not. The court rightly refuses to deprive him of the opportunity to prove that its statement was untrue. . . . Bear in mind, however, that throughout the chapter the author has warned against the acceptance of flimsy and implausible assertions by parties to what has turned out to be a losing contract.

Section 582 of Corbin, allowing admission of extrinsic evidence with regard to the threshold question whether in fact the parties mutually assented to the written document as a completely integrated contract, does not contradict, but rather dovetails with, § 578, on which the lead opinion relies. Indeed, in § 578, p. 402, Professor Corbin hinges a finding of conclusiveness of an express integration clause on whether the written document was "*mutually assented to.*" Further, in language excerpted out of the lead opinion's quotation of § 578, Professor Corbin observes:

> The fact that a written document contains one of these express provisions does not prove that the document itself was ever assented to or ever became operative as a contract. Neither does it exclude evidence that the document was not in fact assented to and therefore never became operative.
>
> . . . .
>
> . . . [P]aper and ink possess no magic power to cause statements of fact to be true when they are actually untrue. Written admissions are evidential; *but they are not conclusive.* [*Id.* at 405, 407 (emphasis added).]

Thus, examination of the written document alone is insufficient to determine its completeness; extrinsic evidence that is neither flimsy nor implausible is admissible to establish whether the writing was in fact intended by the parties as a completely integrated contract. See *Brady v. Central Excavators, Inc.*, 316 Mich.

---

[2] The presence of an integration clause cannot invest a writing with any greater sanctity than the writing merits where, as here, it assuredly does not fully express the essential elements of the parties' undertakings." *Hachmeister, supra* at 417, 110 A.2d 186.

594, 25 N.W.2d 630 (1947); *In re Frost*, 130 Mich.App. 556, 562, n. 1, 344 N.W.2d 331 (1983) (parol evidence admissible where it was clear from the face of the writing that the writing did not contain the complete agreement as assented to by the parties); *Franklin v. White*, 493 N.E.2d 161, 166 (Ind., 1986) ("An integration clause is only some evidence of the parties' intentions. The trial court should consider an integration clause along with all other relevant evidence on the question of integration."); *Sutton v. Stacey's Fuel Mart, Inc.*, 431 A.2d 1319, 1322, n. 3 (Me., 1981) (citing Restatement Contracts, 2d for the proposition that a "merger clause does not control the question of whether a writing was intended to be a completely integrated agreement"); **Restatement Contracts, 2d, § 209,** comment b, p. 115 ("Written contracts . . . may include an explicit declaration that there are no other agreements between the parties, but such a declaration may not be conclusive.").

"The cardinal rule in the interpretation of contracts is to ascertain the intention of the parties. To this rule all others are subordinate." **McIntosh v. Groomes,** 227 Mich. 215, 218, 198 N.W. 954 (1924). It is undisputed in this case that plaintiff's decision to hold its convention at the resort was predicated on the understanding of the representatives for both defendants' predecessor and plaintiff that the resort employed a unionized staff. Had plaintiff been made aware that the resort was for sale or that a sale was pending, I believe it is reasonable to assume that plaintiff's representative would have insisted that such a clause be incorporated into the agreement. Courts should not require that contracting parties include provisions in their agreement contemplating every conceivable, but highly improbable, manner of breach. In my opinion, the circumstances surrounding execution of the contract, as well as the material change in circumstance that occurred when the resort was sold and the union staff fired, establishes as a matter of law that plaintiff did not assent to a completely integrated agreement. Corbin's warning against the admission of "flimsy and implausible" evidence is not implicated here.

Accordingly, I would affirm the trial court's order granting summary disposition in favor of plaintiff pursuant to MCR 2.116(C)(10).

————————

Sierra Diesel Injection Service, Inc. v. Burroughs Corp.

SIERRA DIESEL INJECTION SERVICE, INC., Plaintiff

v.

BURROUGHS CORP., Defendant

United States District Court

656 F. Supp. 426 (D. Nev. 1987)

EDWARD C. REED, JR., Chief Judge.

On March 2, 1987, an evidentiary hearing was held before this Court on . . .

(a) Whether there was integration of the written agreements between the parties for the purchase and sale of certain computer equipment and related merchandise.

. . . .

[This is an issue] for the Court rather than the jury to decide.

In the fall of 1977, executives of plaintiff reached the conclusion that plaintiff needed an improved bookkeeping machine. Defendant's local office was located only a couple of blocks away from plaintiff's place of business. It was known that Burroughs was a substantial purveyor of bookkeeping equipment and so defendant was contacted. Salespersons of defendant called upon plaintiff to review its needs and recommended that instead of an improved bookkeeping machine a computer be acquired. Defendant's salespersons worked out a proposed computer setup which they represented to plaintiff's officials would meet plaintiff's needs for accounting for accounts receivable, accounts payable and inventory.

James Cathey, the president of plaintiff was in charge of acquisition of the new computer equipment for plaintiff. With the assistance of his daughter-in-law, Caroline Cathey, (who appears to have been in charge of plaintiff's accounting or bookkeeping department), Mr. Cathey negotiated the agreements for plaintiff with defendant's salespersons. Written contracts were prepared by defendant and delivered to plaintiff to provide for the purchase of the recommended computer equipment and related software. Mr. Cathey only scanned over the proposed agreements, except that he did actually read the portions which provided for the equipment to be purchased, the price, the parties involved and the delivery date. He was not familiar with computer terminology and in signing the agreements he was relying upon the representations of defendant's personnel as to what computer equipment and software should be purchased and what it was expected to accomplish. The contracts merely identified the items to be purchased according to defendant's assigned designations of certain names and numbers which to some extent contained a description in general terms of the particular items. A reasonable person in Mr. Cathey's position would not have had any way of knowing from the contracts themselves what he was purchasing or what the equipment would do. Mr. Cathey signed the agreements in behalf of plaintiff, or they were signed for him in his name with his authorization.

Each of the equipment agreements contained the following clause (the integration clause):

> "This Agreement constitutes the entire agreement, understanding and representations, express or implied, between the Customer and Burroughs with respect to the equipment and/or related services to be furnished and this Agreement supersedes all prior communications between the parties including all oral and written proposals."

The issue to be addressed in determining integration of a written agreement is whether the agreement is to be recognized as the sole agreement between the parties, barring any other prior or contemporaneous representations or agreements. The fundamental test of integration is whether the parties intended the writing as a final expression of their agreement to the terms included therein. While the wording of the integration clause in the agreement is some evidence of integration it is not conclusive.

Mr. Cathey was an experienced businessman with some knowledge of warranties, but was not particularly versed in contract law or computer science. He scanned and in part read the agreements, as noted above, but he did not understand that the integration clause meant that the representations of defendant's salespersons as to what the computer could accomplish might be nullified. On the other hand, what the computer would accomplish was an essential part of the agreement of the parties. The equipment and software were useless to plaintiff unless they would accomplish the specific needed tasks in question. They were just so much useless metal, plastic and paper if they would not do the job required for plaintiff's business. A reasonable buyer would have insisted that these representations as to what the computer would do be included in the agreement if he believed they would otherwise not be binding on the seller.

Provided he understood the possible legal effect of the integration clause in question, a reasonable businessman in Mr. Cathey's position would have insisted that the prior written and oral representations which had been made regarding the computer be included in the written agreement. The preponderance of the evidence is that Mr. Cathey did not understand that the integration clause would relieve defendant of the representations it had made as to what the computer would do.

From the standpoint of defendant, on the other hand, it wanted to sell the equipment and this necessitated making the representations which were made. Yet, defendant apparently may have believed or hoped that the integration clause would protect it from responsibility or liability for the representations of its salespersons, so long as they were not included in the agreement. Plaintiff, however, was relying upon defendant's expertise as to what the purchase of these items would accomplish. From the standpoint of plaintiff, there could be no agreement at all for the sale of the computer absent the accompanying representations.

Integration requires a mutual intent by both of the contracting parties that the written agreement contain all of the agreements of the parties and the further mutual intent that the written agreement is intended to be the sole agreement, barring reliance upon any other prior or contemporaneous representations or agreements. The preponderance of the evidence is that there was no such mutual intent of the parties in this case that the agreement be integrated.

Think About It!

When the court here uses the term "integration," does it mean partial or complete integration?

The contracts were not integrated. . . .

. . . .

Take Note!

If there is no effective merger clause in a contract, a court considering admissibility of evidence under the parol evidence rule may inquire not whether the writing is complete as to *all possible additional terms* but instead whether the writing is complete as to *the particular terms that a party alleges were part of the agreement.* Under the common law, the test used is whether the alleged terms would "naturally" have been included in the writing if the parties meant to include them at all. The UCC version of the parol evidence rule suggests a higher bar for excluding evidence of the alleged terms: § 2-202 comment 3 says that "[i]f the additional terms are such that, if agreed upon, they would *certainly* have been included in the document in the view of the court, then evidence of their alleged making must be kept from the trier of fact" (emphasis supplied). Note that both standards apply only to the question whether particular terms should be excluded, although, as noted, the courts often use language suggesting that finding the alleged term to be excluded (under either the "naturally" or "certainly" test) means the contract is completely integrated as to all terms.

Problems: Parol Evidence

7-5. As reflected in several of the cases, the existence of a "merger" or "integration" clause is an important factor to be considered in determining whether a contract is partially or completely integrated. The mere existence of a merger clause is not sufficient by itself to determine the outcome, but a well drafted clause can influence the court's conclusion.

Consider the language of each of the following clauses standing alone. Which ones appear to create "final agreements" or "complete and exclusive agreements"? Which are ambiguous? What changes would you make to improve the drafting of any of the clauses?

a. This Agreement supersedes all prior agreements and representations, written or oral, <u>concerning the subject matter herein.</u>

b. This writing is the final embodiment of the parties' contractual rights and obligations.

c. These documents contain the <u>exclusive</u> statement of the parties' contract terms.

d. This Contract represents the complete agreement of the parties and supersedes all prior agreements and representations.

e. This agreement contains the parties' entire agreement with respect to the specifications of the goods.

7-6. If a written agreement is final, complete, and exclusive, which item or items does it bar?

a. a collateral agreement
b. evidence to interpret a contract term
c. evidence of fraud or mistake

    d.   course of performance, course of dealing, usage of trade *no*

    e.   a subsequent agreement *no*

    f.   none of the above

    g.   all of the above   *about after contract formed*

7-7.   Evidence of a course of performance can be used, in spite of the parol evidence rule, for all of the following purposes except one. Which is that one?

    a.   To interpret a term.

    b.   To show a defect in the contract formation process. *— before, so no*

    c.   To show an agreement subsequent to the final writing.

    d.   To supplement the agreement.

    e.   To show modification.

7-8.   Which statement is not accurate with respect to a "collateral agreement"?

    a.   It is outside the application of the parol evidence rule. *true*

    b.   It is collateral in form, does not contradict the main agreement, and is the kind of agreement that the parties wouldn't ordinarily put in their writing. *true*

    c.   It would certainly have been put in the writing, had the parties agreed to it. *false*

    d.   It is unaffected by a merger clause.

if it should have been in agreement, isn't collateral — therefore parol applies

7-9.   Evidence of course of dealing

    a.   is excluded by a merger clause.

    b.   is controlled by a conflicting usage of trade.

    c.   is not admissible when the agreement is completely integrated.

    d.   is admissible to establish the meaning of an ambiguous term.

7-10.   True or False: If evidence is offered to prove terms from an oral agreement not later memorialized in writing, the parol evidence rule will bar that evidence.

7-11.   Penny's Painting Service gets a call from Bob, who wants most of the interior of his new house painted and who has heard that Penny is a very careful painter. Penny walks through the house, orally discussing the job with Bob. The next day, she gives him a bid on a pre-printed form that includes her business's name, address, phone number, fax number, and email, as well as blanks to be filled in for customer's name and phone number, address of painting job, which rooms are to be painted, which color and type of paint in each room, and additional services such as plaster repair. She has filled in the blanks with the pertinent information and has bid the job at $3100, including $600 in paint and $2500 in services. Bob likes the bid amount and the care with which Penny prepared it, so he accepts the bid by signing and dating the bid form on the customer's signature line at the bottom of the form, then sending it back to Penny. Would you characterize the agreement as partially integrated, completely integrated, or not integrated? Why?

7-12. Same facts as in previous question. Later that month, when Penny is in the middle of the job, Penny and Bob disagree over whether, during her pre-bid walk-through, she orally agreed to paint the closet interiors in each room. Penny says that she doesn't remember any such thing, but Bob is sure that Penny had orally agreed to that task. If their dispute ends up in small claims court, Bob's best two arguments in favor of introducing evidence of this oral conversation are that the oral conversation

    a.   is a collateral agreement.

    b.   interprets the written terms that list the rooms to be painted.

    c.   is a prior agreement.

    d.   is a contemporaneous oral agreement.

    e.   shows fraud on Penny's part.

    f.   is a consistent additional term that supplements the agreement.

7-13. Adam purchases an old painting from Betty pursuant to a written purchase agreement that lists the parties, the painting, the price, and the delivery date. After Adam discovers that the painting is a valuable original by a well-known local artist, worth more than twice the purchase price, Betty sues to get the painting back. She wants to testify that in a conversation before Adam bought the painting, they agreed that he would have it appraised after the purchase and if the value was more than 50% higher than the contract price, Betty would have the option of buying back the painting at 175% of the purchase price. Betty tried to exercise that option, but Adam refused, denying that such promises had been made. If Betty seeks to introduce evidence of the alleged oral agreement, will it be admissible?

7-14. Suppose that the written agreement in *Lee v. Seagram & Sons, Inc.* expressly promised that Seagram would find a replacement liquor distributorship for the seller's sons in a "suitable city." If the seller tried to introduce evidence about conversations the parties had regarding which cities might be appropriate, would that evidence be allowed by a court?

a. The evidence will not be allowed in a context jurisdiction, but it will be allowed in a four-corners jurisdiction.

b. The evidence will be allowed because it is a collateral agreement.

c. The evidence will be allowed in either a context jurisdiction or a four-corners jurisdiction.

d. The evidence will not be allowed in a four-corners jurisdiction, but it will be allowed in a context jurisdiction.

7-15. Ted has been admiring Terra's three-year-old mountain bike for a year, since he saw it on several bicycle trips sponsored by a local bicycling club. Terra is now ready to buy a new bike and wants to sell her old one to provide cash for the new purchase. While drinking Gatorade after a bike trip, Terra and Ted orally agree that Terra will sell her bike to Ted for $350, and that Ted can pick up the bike two weekends from now, in return for cash. They write out the following agreement on a notepad:

> March 27, 2009
> Terra will sell Ted her Bianca gray-blue mountain bike for $350 cash, to be picked up and paid for by Ted on April 10, 2009, at Terra's house. The sale includes the water bottle holster on the bike and the water bottle that fits it, the Kryptonite lock/cable/bracket attached to the bike, and the spiffy bell on the handlebar. It doesn't include Terra's helmet. We're done bargaining about this bike, so this really is our final agreement.

Both Ted and Terra sign the agreement. When Ted shows up at Terra's house on April 10th, he's disappointed to find that Terra is not including the lightweight Blackberry bike pump that's always been clipped onto the bike with a spring-loaded clamp. He claims that during their off-and-on negotiations over the bike, they had a conversation in which Terra said that the pump would be included. Terra disagrees. If they went to small claims court over the dispute, would the court admit Ted's evidence of this conversation?

§ 4. Implied Contract Terms and Provisions

In addition to interpreting the terms that are explicitly part of a contract, and adding any terms that may be proved through extrinsic evidence (taking into account the application of the parol evidence rule), a court may need to consider whether additional terms not supplied expressly by the parties are necessary to effectuate the purposes of the contract. Contracts often fail to explicitly address issues the parties later dispute, sometimes because the parties did not foresee the circumstances that have arisen or because, having foreseen the circumstances, they chose not to deal with it at the time the contract was created. Moreover, contracts would be far too long—and transaction costs far too high—if parties tried to include every possible term in their agreements.* Assuming the agreement is sufficiently definite and complete to be enforceable, a court will try to select terms to fill the gaps.

Sometimes a court will be able to select a term that effectuates the parties' intent and expectations at the time the contract was created, drawing on the broader purposes of the contract and the context in which it was created. It may be unclear whether such terms should be considered "implied in fact" (agreed to by the parties implicitly rather than explicitly) or "implied in law" (selected by the court to fill in the gap, consistent with but not representing the parties' choice). Course of performance, course of dealing, or usage of trade may also be the source of implied terms, representing the presumed intent of the parties.

Sometimes a court will fill a gap by using default provisions (off-the-rack solutions that are binding only if the parties did not agree to the contrary) or by reference to relevant public policies (such as preventing unjust enrichment, forfeiture, and overreaching) that form a backdrop to the articulated terms. Default provisions or "gap-fillers," drawn from case law or statutes, usually identify terms that reasonable parties would likely have agreed upon if they were acting fairly and sensibly. Examples of gap-fillers include:

- A real estate lease is month-by-month (rather than yearly or a fixed term) if no lease term is specified.
- In the absence of any provision on assignment of contract rights, most rights are assignable by the obligee unless the rights are personal to the obligee. (*See* Chapter 10, page 1208, for more on assignability.)

For sale-of-goods contracts:

- If nothing is said as to price, the contract price is a reasonable price (usually fair market value) at the time of delivery. (§ 2-305)
- Goods will be delivered in a single lot (not multiple lots) if no selection is made in the contract. (§ 2-307)

---

* Recall that, if too many terms are omitted, the resulting agreement may not be enforceable. *See* Chapter 4 (page 247).

- If no place of delivery is specified, goods will be delivered to the seller's place of business, or, if none exists, to seller's residence. But if the parties know at the time of contract formation that the goods are elsewhere, the place of delivery is where the goods are. (§ 2-308)
- The time for delivery, shipment, or other contractual actions is "a reasonable time" if no time is specified. (§ 2-309)
- The goods are covered by Article 2's implied warranties, unless the seller disclaims the warranties effectively. (§§ 2-314, 2-315)

Gap-fillers allow parties to concentrate on the important dickered terms and leave others to be filled in as default terms. Using default terms does not preclude disputes over the meaning of the contract, especially because a number of the gap-fillers depend upon determining what is "reasonable" under all the facts and circumstances, but it cuts down on transaction costs in contract drafting and on efforts to determine what the parties otherwise would have wanted to fill in the gaps.

Contracting parties are also bound by mandatory rules of law that specify fundamental expectations regarding contract performance or enforcement, and these, too, will be added as "implied" contract terms, whether or not the parties address those subjects in their contract. Mandatory rules might come from statutes, regulations, or court decisions. Examples include statutes of limitations, statutes of frauds, the parol evidence rule, regulations on unfair and deceptive trade and business practices, rulings on the (in)validity of certain clauses, and regulations governing the businesses of one or both of the parties (e.g., insurance or banking).

The subsections that follow address implied-in-fact terms and the meaning of particular default and mandatory provisions.

§ 4.1. Terms Implied from the Circumstances

Reading the Law Critically:
Fisher, First National Bank of Lawrence, and Wood

1. What terms do the courts supply in enforcing the contracts? Why were the terms left out by the parties? What arguments might be made against the conclusion that those terms were implied?

2. Do the courts supply terms based on the intent of the parties? If not, how do the courts determine the terms?

3. In each case, are the added terms implied "in fact" or implied "in law"?

4. What similarities/differences do you see in the approaches of the courts?

Fisher v. Congregation B'nai Yitzhok

HERMAN FISHER, Plaintiff-Appellee

v.

CONGREGATION B'NAI YITZHOK, Defendant-Appellant

Pennsylvania Superior Court
110 A.2d 881 (Pa. Super. 1955)

HIRT, Judge.

Plaintiff is an ordained rabbi of the orthodox Hebrew faith. He however does not officiate except on occasion as a professional rabbi-cantor in the liturgical service of a synagogue. The defendant is an incorporated Hebrew congregation with a synagogue in Philadelphia. Plaintiff, in response to defendant's advertisement in a Yiddish newspaper, appeared in Philadelphia for an audition before a committee representing the congregation. As a result, a written contract was entered into on June 26, 1950, under the terms of which plaintiff agreed to officiate as cantor at the synagogue of the defendant congregation "for the High Holiday Season of 1950", at six specified services during the month of September 1950. As full compensation for the above services the defendant agreed to pay plaintiff the sum of $1,200.

The purpose upon which the defendant congregation was incorporated is thus stated in its charter: "The worship of Almighty God according to the faith, discipline, forms and rites of the orthodox Jewish religion." And up to the time of the execution of the contract the defendant congregation conducted its religious services in accordance with the practices of the orthodox Hebrew faith. On behalf of the plaintiff there is evidence that under the law of the Torah and other binding authority of the Jewish law, men and women may not sit together at services in the synagogue. In the orthodox synagogue, where the practice is observed, the women sit apart from the men in a gallery, or they are separated from the men by means of a partition between the two groups.

The contract in this case is entirely silent as to the character of the defendant as an orthodox Hebrew congregation and the practices observed by it as to the seating at the services in the synagogue. At a general meeting of the congregation on July 12, 1950, on the eve of moving into a new synagogue, the practice of separate seating by the defendant formerly observed was modified and for the future the first four rows of seats during religious services were set aside exclusively for the men, and the next four rows for the women, and the remainder for mixed seating of both men and women.

When plaintiff was informed of the action of the defendant congregation in deviating from the traditional practice as to separate seating, he through his attorney notified the defendant that he, a rabbi of the orthodox faith, would be unable to officiate as cantor because "this would be a violation of his beliefs." Plaintiff persisted in the stand taken that he would not under any circumstances serve as cantor for defendant as long as men and women were not seated separately. And when defendant failed to rescind its action permitting men and women to sit together during services, plaintiff refused to officiate. It then was too late for him to secure other employment as cantor during the 1950 Holiday season except for one service which paid him $100, and he brought suit for the balance of the contract price.

. . . . Judge Smith did specifically find that defendant, at the time the contract was entered into, "Was conducting its services according to the Orthodox Hebrew Faith." Judge Smith accepted the testimony of three rabbis learned in Hebrew law, who appeared for plaintiff, to the effect: "That Orthodox Judaism required a definite and physical separation of the sexes in the synagogue." And he also considered it established by the testimony that an orthodox rabbi-cantor "could not conscientiously officiate in a 'trefah' synagogue, that is, one that violates Jewish law"; and it was specifically found that the old building which the congregation left, "had separation in accordance with Jewish orthodoxy." The ultimate finding was for the plaintiff in the sum of $1,100 plus interest. And the court entered judgment for the plaintiff on the finding. In this appeal it is contended that the defendant is entitled to judgment as a matter of law.

The finding for the plaintiff in this trial without a jury has the force and effect of a verdict of a jury and in support of the judgment entered by the lower court, the plaintiff is entitled to the benefit of the most favorable inferences from the evidence. Jann v. Linton's Lunch, 150 Pa.Super. 653, 29 A.2d 219. Findings of fact by a trial judge, sitting without a jury, which are supported by competent substantial evidence are conclusive on appeal. Scott-Smith Cadillac Co., Inc., v. Rajeski, 166 Pa.Super. 116, 70 A.2d 454.

Although the contract is silent as to the nature of the defendant congregation, there is no ambiguity in the writing on that score and certainly nothing was omitted from its terms by fraud, accident or mistake. The terms of the contract therefore could not be varied under the parol evidence rule. Bardwell v. Willis Co., 375 Pa. 503, 100 A.2d 102; Mathers v. Roxy Auto Co., 375 Pa. 640, 101 A.2d 680. Another principle controls the interpretation of this contract.

There is sufficient competent evidence in support of the finding that this defendant was an orthodox congregation, which observed the rule of the ancient Hebrew law as to separate seating during the services of the High Holiday Season; and also to the effect that the rule had been observed immemorially and invariably by the defendant in these services, without exception. As bearing on plaintiff's bona fide belief that such was the fact, at the time he contracted with the defendant, plaintiff was permitted to introduce in evidence the declarations of Rabbi Ebert, the rabbi of the defendant congregation, made to him prior to signing of the contract, in which the rabbi said: "There always was a separation between men and women" and "there is going to be strict separation between men and women", referring to the seating in the new synagogue. Rabbi Lipschitz, who was present, testified that Rabbi Ebert, in response to plaintiff's question "Will services be conducted as in the old Congregation" replied "Sure. There is no question about that" referring to the prior practice of separate seating. The relationship of rabbi to the congregation which he serves does not create the legal relationship of principal and agent. Cf. **Reifsnyder v. Dougherty, 301 Pa. 328, 152 A. 98.** And Rabbi Ebert in the absence of special authority to speak for the congregation could not legally bind the defendant by his declarations to the plaintiff prior to the execution of the contract. **Davidsville First Nat. Bank v. St. John's Church, 296 Pa. 467, 472, 146 A. 102.** But while the declarations of Rabbi Ebert, above referred to would have been inadmissible hearsay as proof of the truth of what was said, yet his declarations were properly admissible as bearing upon plaintiff's state of mind and his intent in entering into the contract. 1 Henry Pa. Evid., 4th Ed., §§ 22, 469. "Statements tending to show intent are admissible in evidence although self-serving. **Ickes v. Ickes, 237 Pa. 582, 591, 85 A. 885**", 44 L.R.A.,N.S., 1118. **Smith v. Smith, 364 Pa. 1, 9, 70 A.2d 630, 635.**

In determining the right of recovery in this case the question is to be determined under the rules of our civil law, and the ancient provision of the Hebrew law relating to separate seating is read into the contract only because implicit in the writing as to the basis—according to the evidence—upon which the parties dealt. Cf. **Canovaro v. Brothers of Order of H. of St. Aug., 326 Pa. 76, 86, 191 A. 140.** In our law the provision became a part of the written contract under a principle analogous to the rule applicable to the construction of contracts in the light of custom or immemorial and invariable usage. It has been said that: "When a custom or usage is once established, in absence of express provision to the contrary it is considered a part of a contract and binding on the parties though not mentioned therein, the presumption being that they knew of and contracted with reference to it". 1 Henry, Pa.Evid., 4th Ed., § 203. Cf. **Restatement, Contracts, § 248(2) and § 249.** In this case there was more than a presumption. From the findings of the trial judge supported by the evidence it is clear that the parties contracted on the common understanding that the defendant was an orthodox synagogue which observed the mandate of the Jewish law as to separate seating.

That intention was implicit in this contract though not referred to in the writing, and therefore must be read into it. It was on this ground that the court entered judgment for plaintiff in this case.

Judgment affirmed.

First National Bank of Lawrence v. Methodist Home for the Aged

FIRST NATIONAL BANK OF LAWRENCE, KANSAS, Plaintiff-Respondent

v.

METHODIST HOME FOR THE AGED, Defendant-Appellant

Kansas Supreme Court
309 P.2d 389 (Kan. 1957)

PARKER, Chief Justice.

Plaintiff is a banking corporation with its place of business at Lawrence, Kansas, and the duly appointed administrator, with the will annexed, of the will of Bertha C. Ellsworth, deceased. Defendant is the Methodist Home For the Aged, a corporation, with its principal place of business at Topeka, Kansas, where it operates a home for the aged.

The events leading up to the institution of this litigation are not in controversy and should be stated at the outset in order to insure a proper understanding of the appellate issues involved.

On September 13, 1953, Bertha C. Ellsworth, who desired to be admitted to the defendant's home and was then single and more than seventy-one years of age, made a written application for admission to such home. Thereafter, having been advised her application had been approved, she was admitted to the home on May 10, 1954, and on the same date entered into the written agreement with defendant which is actually the subject of this litigation. Pertinent portions of such agreement, which we pause to note had been prepared by defendant on one of its standard forms, used for admission of members, read:

> "This Agreement, made and entered into this 10th day of May, 1954, by and between The Methodist Home for the Aged, a Corporation, of Topeka, Kansas, Party of the First Part and Bertha C. Ellsworth, of Lawrence, Kansas, Party of the Second Part, Witnesseth:

"Party of the Second Part having this day given Party of the First Part, *without reservation*, the sum of $10,779.60 to be used and disposed of in the furtherance of its benevolence and charitable work as it may deem best, Party of the First Part *admits Party of the Second Part into its Home as a member thereof during the period of her natural life, and agrees to furnish*:

. . . .

"Fifth: *It is clearly understood that Party of the Second Part has been received in accordance with the new regulations on a probation period of two months in which time she has the opportunity of finding out whether she desires to remain in the Home; and also find out whether the Home is able to satisfy the requirements. If it should be found advisable to discontinue her stay in the Home, then her gift, with the exception of $80.00 per month shall be refunded.*

"*The rules and regulations and bylaws of the Home as they now are and as they from time to time may be adopted and promulgated by the Board of Directors of said Party of the First Part are hereby referred to and made a part hereof and the Party of the Second Part hereby agrees to be bound by same.* It is especially understood and agreed that in case of serious mental illness requiring hospital care and attention, that the First Party shall have the right to make proper arrangements for the treatment and care of the Second Party in a lawful manner in a proper State Institution, provided that if Second Party is discharged as completely cured to admit Second Party into the Home without further financial requirements." (Emphasis supplied.)

The parties concede that defendant's bylaw, article 12, was in full force and effect on the date of the execution of the agreement and therefore, according to the terms of that agreement, is a part of the contract. It reads:

"*Probationary membership means a short trial period while the member becomes adjusted to the life of the Home. The probationary membership shall not continue for a longer period than two consecutive months. If for any reason the trial member does not desire to remain in the Home he or she shall have the privilege of leaving. On the other hand, if the Home for any reason does not desire to continue the membership then the member shall be notified in writing and leave the Home within a week after such notice is given. Only members who do not have the money or securities to pay for their life Membership shall be granted the privilege of paying by the month.*" (Emphasis supplied.)

After execution of the May 10, 1954, agreement Bertha C. Ellsworth remained in the home until she died on June 10, 1954. At that time neither she nor the home had made an election as to whether she was to leave the home or remain therein after the expiration of the probationary period specified by its terms. However, it is conceded that during the interim, and on June 4, 1954, the plaintiff bank in its capacity as trustee had paid the defendant the sum of $10,799.60 by a check, which defendant had cashed, specifying that such check was "In Payment of Life Membership for Bertha C. Ellsworth in the Methodist Home for the Aged, as specified in Agreement dated May 10, 1954", and that defendant had acknowledged payment of that sum by a receipt of like import.

Upon the death of Bertha Ellsworth plaintiff was appointed by the probate court of Douglas County, Kansas, as Administrator CTA of such decedent. Thereafter it made written demand on defendant for performance under the agreement, including pertinent by-laws, and demanded that defendant refund the estate of its decedent the amount paid pursuant thereto, less any amounts due the Home under its terms, particularly the fifth clause thereof. When this demand was refused plaintiff procured authority from the probate court to institute the instant action to recover such amount as an asset of the estate of Bertha C. Ellsworth, deceased.

Following action as above indicated plaintiff commenced this lawsuit by filing a petition which . . . recites in a general way that . . . the defendant had never attained a life membership in the home by reason of her death prior to the expiration of the probationary membership period prescribed by the contract, hence the contract should be construed as contemplating her estate was entitled to a return of the money paid by her to defendant for such a membership. When a demurrer to this pleading, based on the ground it failed to state a cause of action, was overruled by the trial court defendant filed an answer alleging in substance that under the same facts, conditions and circumstances the contract between it and the decedent is to be construed as warranting its retention of the sum paid by such decedent for the life membership even though, prior to her death, such decedent neither indicated that she did not desire to remain in the Home nor that she desired the privilege of leaving it. It should perhaps be added that such answer contains an allegation that on May 10, 1954, decedent was permitted to enter the home without having paid her life membership; admits subsequent payment of such membership in the manner heretofore indicated; and makes decedent's application for admission to the home a part of such pleading.

. . . [T]he trial court, after holding that the salient question in the case was purely a question of law involving the interpretation of the contract, rendered judgment decreeing that plaintiff was entitled to recover the amount paid by Bertha C. Ellsworth to the Home, less $235 paid by the Home for her funeral expenses and less the sum of $80 provided for in the contract in the event she had elected not to remain in the Home. Thereupon defendant perfected this appeal wherein under proper specification of errors it charges the trial court erred in overruling the demurrer to the petition; in rendering judgment for plaintiff and against defendant, wholly contrary to the law and the terms of the agreement; and in overruling its motion for a new trial.

In a preliminary way it can be said a careful examination of the record leads to the inescapable conclusion the trial court was eminently correct in holding that the all decisive question involved in this case is purely a question of law involving the interpretation of the contract entered into between the appellant and Bertha C. Ellsworth, deceased. Indeed the parties make no serious contention to the contrary. For that reason, and others to be presently disclosed, we turn directly to appellant's claim the trial court's judgment was contrary to the terms of the agreement and to the law, mindful as we do so that where—as here—the terms of a contract are ambiguous, obscure or susceptible of more than one meaning there are certain well defined rules to which courts must adhere in construing its provisions. Four of such rules, which we believe have special application here, can be stated as follows:

> 1. That doubtful language in a contract is construed most strongly against the party preparing the instrument or employing the words concerning which doubt arises. [citations omitted]

> 2. That where a contract is susceptible of more than one construction its terms and provisions must, if possible, be construed in such manner as to give effect to the intention of the parties at the time of its execution. Braly v. Commercial Casualty Ins. Co., 170 Kan. 531, 227 P.2d 571.

> 3. That in determining intention of the parties where ambiguity exists in a contract the test is not what the party preparing the instrument intended its doubtful or ambiguous words to mean but what a reasonable person, in the position of the other party to the agreement, would have understood them to mean under the existing conditions and circumstances. Braly v. Commercial Casualty Ins. Co., supra.

> 4. That the intent and purpose of a contract is not to be determined by considering one isolated sentence or provision thereof but by considering and construing the instrument in its entirety. [citations omitted]

Stated, substantially in its own language, the principal contention advanced by appellant as grounds for reversal of the judgment is that the membership agreement between it and the involved decedent was fully executed inasmuch as decedent had been admitted to the Home as a life member on May 10, 1954, and thereafter caused her life membership to be paid; hence, since nothing further needed to be done by the parties to make the portion of the agreement relating to life membership binding, provisions of the contract with respect thereto had become fully executed and title to the fee paid for such membership had vested in appellant.

If we could limit our construction of the contract to its first two paragraphs, as heretofore quoted, we might well conclude that appellant's views respecting the status of the agreement and the gift therein mentioned could be upheld. However, as has been previously demonstrated, our obligation is not to consider isolated provisions of the contract but to consider and construe such instrument in its entirety. When succeeding paragraphs of the agreement, and the incorporated by-laws, particularly portions thereof which we have heretofore italicized for purposes of emphasis, are reviewed in the light of the rule to which we have just referred, as well as others heretofore mentioned, we have little difficulty in concurring in the views expressed by the trial court in rendering its judgment that the contract had never become executed and that title to the gift paid by the decedent for a life membership had not vested in the Home. In fact, and without repeating the emphasized portions of the agreement on which we base our conclusion, we go further and hold that, under the clear import and meaning of such emphasized provisions, Bertha C. Ellsworth, because of her untimely death during the probationary and/or trial period expressly required by their terms, never attained a life membership status in the Home. Indeed to hold otherwise would not only do violence to the language of the contract but read into it something that is not there.

One question remains in this lawsuit. Who, the Home or the decedent's estate, is entitled to the life membership fee paid by decedent to appellant? In this connection it is interesting to note that the money was paid by decedent by a check and receipted for by appellant in writing, each of which instruments contain a recital "In Payment of Life Membership for Bertha C. Ellsworth in the Methodist Home for the Aged, as specified in Agreement dated May 10, 1954." So, since it cannot be denied the contract contains no express provisions relating to where the money was to go if Bertha Ellsworth died during the probationary and/or trial period prescribed by its terms, it appears we are faced with the obligation of determining what was intended by the parties at the time of the execution of the agreement in the event of such a contingency.

Strange as it may seem, the question thus presented has been before the Courts on but few occasions. However, it has been decided under similar circumstances. An interesting discussion on the subject appears in 10 A.L.R.2d., Annotation, pp. 874, 875, § 12. It reads:

"Many entrance contracts provide for a probationary period during which the applicant for admission to the charitable home as well as the home itself can dissolve the agreement without cause. In case the applicant is refused permanent admission at the end of the trial period or withdraws during the period of his own volition, all payments made, less a fixed weekly charge for the time he stayed at the home, are refunded to him and his property rights are restored.

"An interesting situation arises if the applicant dies during the probationary period without having been either accepted or rejected as a permanent inmate. The legal question then is whether or not the charitable home may retain the applicant's property on the ground that the agreement had not been dissolved by either party.

"In a majority of cases this question has been answered in the negative and it has been held that the home may not claim or retain the applicant's property, on the ground that the death of the applicant has made it impossible to determine whether he would have become a permanent inmate at the end of the probationary period."

In connection with the foregoing quotation the author cites Evangelical Lutheran St. S. Cong. v. Bishop, 213 Ill.App. 137; Christenson v. Board of Charities, 253 Ill.App. 380; Kirkpatrick Home For Childless Women v. Kenyon, 119 Misc. 349, 196 N.Y.S. 250; Sup., 196 N.Y.S. 475; 206 App.Div. 728, 199 N.Y.S. 851, as supporting the conclusion reached by him in the concluding paragraph of his discussion and one case only, Dodge v. New Hampshire Centennial Home for the Aged, 95 N.H. 472, 67 A.2d 10, 10 A.L.R.2d 858, as holding to the contrary. We may add our somewhat extended research of the books, including our own reports, discloses no other cases which can be regarded as decisive of the question presented under similar facts, conditions and circumstances.

Again reviewing the contract in the light of the heretofore stated rules, and mindful that appellant, not the decedent, prepared the involved contract, we are impelled to the view that a reasonable person, in the position of the decedent at the time of the execution of the contract, would have understood the provisions of that instrument to mean that unless and until she attained the status of a life member in the appellant's home she, or her estate would be entitled to a return of the money paid by her for that right, less amounts specified in the agreement. Moreover we are convinced, that having prepared the contract, appellant's failure to make express provision therein for retaining the money paid by Bertha C. Ellsworth as a life membership fee, in the event of her death during the period of her probationary and/or trial membership status, precludes any construction of that agreement which would warrant its retention of such money upon the happening of that contingency.

After careful consideration of the decisions last above cited we have concluded those having the effect of holding, under similar circumstances, that the appellant cannot claim or retain Bertha Ellsworth's lifetime payment for the reason her death made it impossible for her to determine whether she was to become a permanent inmate of the Home at the end of the probation period, are more sound in principle and better reasoned than the one case holding to the contrary. Therefore, based on the conclusions heretofore announced and on what is said and held in such decisions, we hold that the trial court did not err in rendering the judgment from which the Home has appealed. . . .

The judgment is affirmed.

Wood v. Lucy, Lady Duff-Gordon

WOOD, Plaintiff-Appellant

v.

LUCY, LADY DUFF-GORDON, Defendant-Respondent

Court of Appeals of New York
118 N.E. 214 (N.Y. 1917)

CARDOZO, J.

Who's That?

Judge—later U.S. Supreme Court Justice—Benjamin Cardozo was one of the leading jurists in American history. Cardozo was born in 1870 in New York City, descended on his mother's side from the Seixas family, a prominent Jewish family whose members emigrated to the American colonies before the Revolutionary War. His father, a judge on the New York Supreme Court (the general trial court), resigned and

returned to private practice soon after Cardozo's birth in the midst of a judicial corruption scandal surrounding the Erie Railway takeover. Cardozo entered Columbia University as an undergraduate at age 15 and four years later enrolled in Columbia Law School. Some have suggested his choice of profession was in part to restore the reputation of his family after his father's resignation from the bench. After the Columbia law school faculty voted to add a third year to the standard two years of law school study, Cardozo and a number of other students chose instead to leave without their degrees (which were not required to take the bar or to practice law), and at the age of 21 he began his professional career. After 23 years as a trial and appellate lawyer, Cardozo was narrowly elected to the New York Supreme Court, taking office on January 1, 1914. Less than a month later, he was appointed to the New York Court of Appeals, at age 43 perhaps the youngest judge to serve on that court. He was later elected to a full term and then, in 1926, to be Chief Judge. He resigned in 1932 to accept appointment to the United States Supreme Court, where he served until his death in 1938. Cardozo is probably best known for the major opinions he wrote during his 18 years on the New York Court of Appeals, including three contracts cases included in this book (*Wood, Dougherty v. Salt*, page 30, and *Jacob & Youngs v. Kent*, page 895) and the prominent torts cases of *Macpherson v. Buick Motor Co.*, 111 N.E. 1050 (1916) (ruling that manufacturers could be held liable for injuries to consumers) and *Palsgraf v. Long Island Rail Road Co.*, 162 N.E. 99 (1929) (developing the concept of proximate cause). He gave a series of lectures at Yale University later published as *The Nature of the Judicial Process*, a book that is still used widely by judges and scholars and available at http://xroads.virginia.edu/~HYPER/CARDOZO/CarNat.html. Cardozo was a founding vice-president of the American Law Institute and the author of several books about the development of the law and about judicial decision-making. An insight into his jurisprudential philosophy may be gleaned from his comment that "justice is not to be taken by storm. She is to be wooed by slow advances." *See* Andrew Kaufman, *Cardozo and the Art of Biography* 20 Cardozo L. Rev. 1245 (1999); Andrew Kaufman, *Benjamin Cardozo on the Supreme Court*, 20 Cardozo L. Rev. 1259 (1999); Lawrence Cunningham, *Cardozo and Posner: A Study in Contracts*, 36 Wm. & Mary L. Rev. 1379 (1995).

The defendant styles herself "a creator of fashions." Her favor helps a sale. Manufacturers of dresses, millinery, and like articles are glad to pay for a certificate of her approval. The things which she designs, fabrics, parasols, and what not, have a new value in the public mind when issued in her name. She employed the plaintiff to help her to turn this vogue into money. He was to have the exclusive right, subject always to her approval, to place her indorsements on the designs of others. He was also to have the exclusive right to place her own designs on sale, or to license others to market them. In return she was to have one-half of "all profits and revenues" derived from any contracts he might make. The exclusive right was to last at least one year from April 1, 1915, and thereafter from year to year unless terminated by notice of 90 days. The plaintiff says that he kept the contract on his part, and that the defendant broke it. She placed her indorsement on fabrics, dresses, and millinery without his knowledge, and withheld the profits. He sues her for the damages, and the case comes here on demurrer.

The agreement of employment is signed by both parties. It has a wealth of recitals. The defendant insists, however, that it lacks the elements of a contract. She says that the plaintiff does not bind himself to anything. It is true that he does not promise in so many words that he will use reasonable efforts to place the defendant's indorsements and market her designs. We think, however, that such a promise is fairly to be implied. The law has outgrown its primitive stage of formalism when the precise word was the sovereign talisman, and every slip was fatal. It takes a broader view today. A promise may be lacking, and yet the whole writing may be "instinct with an obligation," imperfectly expressed (Scott, J., in **McCall Co. v. Wright**, 133 App. Div. 62, 117 N. Y. Supp. 775; **Moran v. Standard Oil Co.**, 211 N. Y. 187, 198, 105 N. E. 217). If that is so, there is a contract.

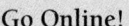

Go Online!

Recall that this case was discussed extensively in *B. Lewis Productions, Inc. v. Angelou,* in Chapter 4 (page 266). You can find much information online about Lucy, Lady Duff Gordon, including pictures of some of the dresses she designed and the story of her other claim to fame (or infamy) as a passenger on the Titanic.

The implication of a promise here finds support in many circumstances. The defendant gave an exclusive privilege. She was to have no right for at least a year to place her own indorsements or market her own designs except through the agency of the plaintiff. The acceptance of the exclusive agency was an assumption of its duties. **Phoenix Hermetic Co. v. Filtrine Mfg. Co.**, 164 App. Div. 424, 150 N. Y. Supp. 193; **W. G. Taylor Co. v. Bannerman**, 120 Wis. 189, 97 N. W. 918; **Mueller v. Mineral Spring Co.**, 88 Mich. 390, 50 N. W. 319. We are not to suppose that one party was to be placed at the mercy of the other. **Hearn v. Stevens & Bro.**, 111 App. Div. 101, 106, 97 N. Y. Supp. 566; **Russell v. Allerton**, 108 N. Y. 288, 15 N. E. 391. Many other terms of the agreement point the same way. We are told at the outset by way of recital that:

"The said Otis F. Wood possesses a business organization adapted to the placing of such indorsements as the said Lucy, Lady Duff-Gordon, has approved."

The implication is that the plaintiff's business organization will be used for the purpose for which it is adapted. But the terms of the defendant's compensation are even more significant. Her sole compensation for the grant of an exclusive agency is to be one-half of all the profits resulting from the plaintiff's efforts. Unless he gave his efforts, she could never get anything. Without an implied promise, the transaction cannot have such business "efficacy, as both parties must have intended that at all events it should have." . . . But the contract does not stop there. The plaintiff goes on to promise that he will account monthly for all moneys received by him, and that he will take out all such patents and copyrights and trade-marks as may in his judgment be necessary to protect the rights and articles affected by the agreement. It is true, of course, as the Appellate Division has said, that if he was under no duty to try to market designs or to place certificates of indorsement, his promise to account for profits or take out copyrights would be valueless. But in determining the intention of the parties the promise has a value. It helps to enforce the conclusion that the plaintiff had some duties. His promise to pay the defendant one-half of the profits and revenues resulting from the exclusive agency and to render accounts monthly was a promise to use reasonable efforts to bring profits and revenues into existence. For this conclusion, the authorities are ample. [citations omitted]

The judgment of the Appellate Division should be reversed, and the order of the Special Term affirmed, with costs in the Appellate Division and in this court.

CUDDEBACK, McLAUGHLIN, and ANDREWS, JJ., concur. HISCOCK, C. J., and CHASE and CRANE, JJ., dissent.

———————

§ 4.2. Duty of Good Faith

Parties may, in their contracts, explicitly create an obligation to perform in good faith, but even in the absence of such a clause, it is generally agreed that every contract carries with it an implied covenant of good faith that may not be disclaimed. The duty of good faith arises as part of the commitment each party makes to the other in the contract, so it generally applies to contract performance, enforcement, and modification, but not to contract formation. (Of course, problematic behavior in contract negotiation may result in tort liability for misrepresentation or fraud and could result in unenforceability of a contract or contract clause on the basis of misrepresentation, unconscionability, or some other defense. And, as discussed in Chapter 4 (page 257), an enforceable agreement to agree creates an obligation to negotiate in good faith in efforts to reach further agreement.)

Saying there *is* a covenant of good faith and fair dealing is only the starting point. What constitutes acting in good or bad faith? In an influential article in 1968, Professor Robert Summers suggested that good faith "is best understood as an 'excluder,'" a phrase with no general meaning of its own "but which serves to exclude many heterogeneous forms of bad faith" that may be found in the cases.* If a court finds a seller acted in bad faith because he concealed a defect in delivered goods, one can conclude that good faith includes fully disclosing material facts. If a court finds a contractor acted in bad faith because she abused her bargaining power to coerce an increase in contract price, one can conclude that good faith includes refraining from abusing bargaining power. Summers suggested that case law reveals a wide variety of forms of bad faith, including "evading the spirit of the transaction, lack of diligence, willfully rendering only substantial performance, and abusing the power to specify terms or to determine compliance[,] . . . interfering with or failing to cooperate in the other party's performance, pretending to dispute or arbitrarily disputing, adopting overreaching or 'weaseling' interpretations or constructions of contract language, taking advantage of the other party's weaknesses to get a favorable readjustment or settlement of a dispute, abusing the right to adequate assurances of performance, refusing for ulterior reasons to accept the other party's slightly defective performance, willfully failing to mitigate the other party's damages, and abusing a privilege to terminate contractual relations."**

The Restatement and the UCC offer their own attempts to articulate the application and meaning of the concept of good faith:

Restatement (Second) § 205. **Duty of Good Faith and Fair Dealing**

Every contract imposes upon each party a duty of good faith and fair dealing in its performance and its enforcement.

Comments:
a. Meanings of "good faith." . . . The phrase "good faith" is used in a variety of contexts, and its meaning varies somewhat with the context. Good

---

* Robert S. Summers, *"Good Faith" in General Contract Law and the Sales Provisions of the Uniform Commercial Code,* 54 Va. L. Rev. 195, 196 (1968).
** *Id.* at 216-17.

faith performance or enforcement of a contract emphasizes faithfulness to an agreed common purpose and consistency with the justified expectations of the other party; it excludes a variety of types of conduct characterized as involving "bad faith" because they violate community standards of decency, fairness or reasonableness. . . .

. . . .

d. Good faith performance. Subterfuges and evasions violate the obligation of good faith in performance even though the actor believes his conduct to be justified. But the obligation goes further: bad faith may be overt or may consist of inaction, and fair dealing may require more than honesty. A complete catalogue of types of bad faith is impossible, but the following types are among those which have been recognized in judicial decisions: evasion of the spirit of the bargain, lack of diligence and slacking off, willful rendering of imperfect performance, abuse of a power to specify terms, and interference with or failure to cooperate in the other party's performance.

e. Good faith in enforcement. The obligation of good faith and fair dealing extends to the assertion, settlement and litigation of contract claims and defenses. . . . The obligation is violated by dishonest conduct such as conjuring up a pretended dispute, asserting an interpretation contrary to one's own understanding, or falsification of facts. It also extends to dealing which is candid but unfair, such as taking advantage of the necessitous circumstances of the other party to extort a modification of a contract for the sale of goods without legitimate commercial reason. See Uniform Commercial Code § 2-209, Comment 2. Other types of violation have been recognized in judicial decisions: harassing demands for assurances of performance, rejection of performance for unstated reasons, willful failure to mitigate damages, and abuse of a power to determine compliance or to terminate the contract. . . .

————————

UCC § 1-304. **Obligation of Good Faith.**

Every contract or duty within [the Uniform Commercial Code] imposes an obligation of good faith in its performance and enforcement.

UCC § 1-201. **General Definitions.**

. . . .

UCC def.

> (b)(20). "Good faith," . . . means honesty in fact and the observance of reasonable commercial standards of fair dealing.*
>
> *Comment 20.* . . . . Although "fair dealing" is a broad term that must be defined in context, it is clear that it is concerned with the fairness of conduct rather than the care with which an act is performed. This is an entirely different concept than whether a party exercised ordinary care in conducting a transaction. Both concepts are to be determined in the light of reasonable commercial standards, but those standards in each case are directed to different aspects of commercial conduct. . . .

   In some circumstances, a court may imply (or parties may explicitly impose) an obligation that goes beyond the obligation to act in good faith. In both *Wood v. Lucy, Lady Duff-Gordon* (in the last section) and *B. Lewis Productions, Inc. v. Angelou* (in chapter 4), the court concluded that both parties had made implied promises to make "reasonable efforts" in furtherance of their agreement because of the exclusive dealings provision in each contract. Although the judge in *B. Lewis Productions* suggested the "reasonable efforts" obligation was a particular manifestation of the more general duty to act in good faith, the obligation to engage in "reasonable efforts" (sometimes also called "best efforts") is usually seen as requiring more than does the mere duty to act in good faith.   A similar requirement is articulated in the UCC:

> **UCC § 2-306. Output, Requirements and Exclusive Dealings.**
>
> (1)   . . . .
>
> (2)   A lawful agreement by either the seller or the buyer for exclusive dealing in the kind of goods concerned imposes unless otherwise agreed an obligation by the seller to use best efforts to supply the goods and by the buyer to use best efforts to promote their sale.

best efforts

---

* Authors' Note: The definition quoted in the text is used by most of the 45 jurisdictions that, as of February 1, 2013, had adopted the 2001 version of Article 1. Before the 2001 revision, good faith was defined differently for merchants ("honesty in fact and the observance of reasonable commercial standards of fair dealing in the trade") and non-merchants ("honesty in fact"). Jurisdictions operating under the older version of Article 1 continue to use this bifurcated definition, and some jurisdictions adopting revised Article 1 have retained that definition. Thus if "good faith" is to be invoked under the UCC, it will be important to identify which jurisdiction's law applies to the dispute and which definition of good faith has been adopted there.

Comment 5. Subsection (2), on exclusive dealing, makes explicit the commercial rule embodied in this Act under which the parties to such contracts are held to have impliedly, even when not expressly, bound themselves to use reasonable diligence as well as good faith in their performance of the contract. Under such contracts the exclusive agent is required, although no express commitment has been made, to use reasonable effort and due diligence in the expansion of the market or the promotion of the product, as the case may be. The principal is expected under such a contract to refrain from supplying any other dealer or agent within the exclusive territory. An exclusive dealing agreement brings into play all of the good faith aspects of the output and requirement problems of subsection (1).

Declaring that the parties must make reasonable or best efforts does not define what will satisfy that requirement, of course. In both *B. Lewis Productions* and *Wood,* the question addressed was whether sufficient commitment existed by both parties to find an enforceable contract, and the duty to make reasonable efforts supplied some of that commitment. If the question had instead been whether a party's performance satisfied the obligation to make "reasonable efforts" or "best efforts," the answer would inevitably be context-specific. Allan Farnsworth suggests the obligation is to "make such efforts as are reasonable in the light of that party's ability and the means at its disposal and of the other party's justifiable expectations." E. Allan Farnsworth, *Contracts* § 7.17 (4th ed. 2004). *See generally* Victor P. Goldberg, *Great Contract Cases: In Search of Best Efforts: Reinterpreting Bloor v. Falstaff,* 44 St. Louis L.J. 1465, 1465 (2000). As is true with respect to the obligation to act in good faith, it may be easier to define what constitutes *not* making reasonable or best efforts.

As should be clear from even this brief overview of the duty of good faith, breach of the implied obligation of good faith should be invoked as a last resort, only after identifying breaches of express terms of the contract and other implied terms. Good faith is notoriously hard to define specifically and apply successfully. Some courts refuse to recognize a separate obligation of good faith, believing that a claim of bad faith performance must be grounded in violation of express or implied contract terms. Even those that do recognize it are understandably reluctant to find a breach of so undefined an obligation. Any claim of bad faith must identify as precisely as possible the actions deemed troubling and why those actions should be considered to violate the other party's reasonable expectations regarding how the contract will be performed.

The first subsection below offers one approach to explaining the existence and nature of the general obligation of good faith. The rest of the subsections address the nature of the obligation of good faith in two particular circumstances in which it often arises: specifying quantity of goods in output and requirements contracts and exercising rights under termination clauses.

§ 4.2.1. Duty of Good Faith in Performance or Enforcement

Reading the Law Critically: *Market Street Associates*

1. How does the court identify or define the meaning of "good faith" both generally and in the specific context of this contract?

2. What evidence is relevant to establishing the existence of good or bad faith? What story will the plaintiffs and defendants each tell to the court on remand to establish that Market Street Associates acted in good or bad faith?

3. In his opinion for the court, Judge Posner says, "We could of course do without the term 'good faith,' and maybe even without the doctrine." Is he suggesting there are no obligations of good faith?

Market Street Associates Limited Partnership v. Frey

MARKET STREET ASSOCIATES LIMITED PARTNERSHIP
and WILLIAM ORENSTEIN, Plaintiffs-Appellants

v.

DALE FREY, et al., Defendants-Appellees

United States Court of Appeals, Seventh Circuit
941 F.2d 588 (7th Cir. 1991)

POSNER, Circuit Judge.

how far econ. analysis

Who's That?

Judge Richard Posner, the author of the *Market Street Associates* case (as well as *Morin Building Products Co.*, page 867, *Northern Indiana Public Service Co.*, page 1009, and the dissent in *Sally Beauty Co.*, page 1232), is a leading proponent of the law and economics school of legal theory (see the note on page 1173) and one of the country's most prominent, prolific, and most often-cited legal thinkers and scholars.   After clerking for Justice William Brennan, he served as Attorney-Advisor at the Federal Trade Commission, worked in the office of the U.S. Solicitor General, and served as general counsel of the President's Task Force on Communications Policy before becoming a member of the faculty at Stanford Law School and then, in 1969, at the University of Chicago Law School.   In 1981, he was appointed to the Seventh Circuit Court of Appeals, serving as Chief Judge from 1993 to 2000. He remains a senior lecturer at Chicago, co-authors a blog with Nobel-prize winning economist Gary Becker (see www.becker-posner-blog.com/), and has written more than 40 books on an extraordinary range of topics, including law and economics, law and literature, how judges think, moral philosophy, intellectual property, political theory, and legal history. Demonstrating the breadth of his expertise, he has taught administrative law, antitrust, economic analysis of law, history of legal thought, conflict of laws, regulated industries, law and literature, the legislative process, family law, primitive law, torts, civil procedure, evidence, health law and economics, law and science, and jurisprudence. He was the founding editor of the *Journal of Legal Studies* and the *American Law and Economics Review*. Generations of law students may sympathize with his advocacy of "Bluebook abolitionism," criticizing the citation system as "a monstrous growth, remote from the functional need for legal citation forms, that serves obscure needs of the legal culture and its student subculture." In his review of the then newly published 19th edition of the Bluebook, he noted that he had "dipped into it, much as one might dip one's toes in a pail of freezing water. I am put in mind of Mr. Kurtz's dying words in Heart of Darkness—"The horror! The horror!" . . . . "*

---

* Richard Posner, *The Bluebook Blues*, 120 Yale L.J. 850 (2011).

Market Street Associates Limited Partnership and its general partner appeal from a judgment for the defendants, General Electric Pension Trust and its trustees, entered upon cross-motions for summary judgment in a diversity suit that pivots on the doctrine of "good faith" performance of a contract. Cf. Robert Summers, "'Good Faith' in General Contract Law and the Sales Provisions of the Uniform Commercial Code," 54 *Va.L.Rev.* 195, 232-43 (1968). Wisconsin law applies common law rather than Uniform Commercial Code, because the contract is for land rather than for goods, UCC § 2-102; Wis.Stat. § 402.102, and because it is a lease rather than a sale and Wisconsin has not adopted UCC art. 2A, which governs leases. . . .

In 1968, J.C. Penney Company, the retail chain, entered into a sale and lease-back arrangement with General Electric Pension Trust in order to finance Penney's growth. Under the arrangement Penney sold properties to the pension trust which the trust then leased back to Penney for a term of 25 years. Paragraph 34 of the lease entitles the lessee to "request Lessor [the pension trust] to finance the costs and expenses of construction of additional Improvements upon the Premises," provided the amount of the costs and expenses is at least $250,000. Upon receiving the request, the pension trust "agrees to give reasonable consideration to providing the financing of such additional Improvements and Lessor and Lessee shall negotiate in good faith concerning the construction of such Improvements and the financing by Lessor of such costs and expenses." Paragraph 34 goes on to provide that, should the negotiations fail, the lessee shall be entitled to repurchase the property at a price roughly equal to the price at which Penney sold it to the pension trust in the first place, plus 6 percent a year for each year since the original purchase. So if the average annual appreciation in the property exceeded 6 percent, a breakdown in negotiations over the financing of improvements would entitle Penney to buy back the property for less than its market value (assuming it had sold the property to the pension trust in the first place at its then market value).

One of these leases was for a shopping center in Milwaukee. In 1987 Penney assigned this lease to Market Street Associates, which the following year received an inquiry from a drugstore chain that wanted to open a store

---

What's That?

In a "sale and leaseback," a financing company (like G.E. Pension Trust here) buys the property (realty or personalty), then leases it back to the seller. The seller retains possession and use of the property, but exchanges its capital interest in the property for a lump sum payment of cash and is able to claim the lease payments as business operating expenses. The buyer obtains title to the property purchased, a guaranteed income stream from the lease payments, and the right to the tax benefits from the property's depreciation. The buyer also benefits from a lower-than-market-value purchase price, and the lease payments may be enough to finance any loan the buyer obtained to finance the purchase.

in the shopping center, provided (as is customary) that Market Street Associates built the store for it. Whether Market Street Associates was pessimistic about obtaining financing from the pension trust, still the lessor of the shopping center, or for other reasons, it initially sought financing for the project from other sources. But they were unwilling to lend the necessary funds without a mortgage on the shopping center, which Market Street Associates could not give because it was not the owner but only the lessee. It decided therefore to try to buy the property back from the pension trust. Market Street Associates' general partner, Orenstein, tried to call David Erb of the pension trust, who was responsible for the property in question. Erb did not return his calls, so Orenstein wrote him, expressing an interest in buying the property and asking him to "review your file on this matter and call me so that we can discuss it further." At first, Erb did not reply. Eventually Orenstein did reach Erb, who promised to review the file and get back to him. A few days later an associate of Erb called Orenstein and indicated an interest in selling the property for $3 million, which Orenstein considered much too high.

That was in June of 1988. On July 28, Market Street Associates wrote a letter to the pension trust formally requesting funding for $2 million in improvements to the shopping center. The letter made no reference to paragraph 34 of the lease; indeed, it did not mention the lease. The letter asked Erb to call Orenstein to discuss the matter. Erb, in what was becoming a habit of unresponsiveness, did not call. On August 16, Orenstein sent a second letter—certified mail, return receipt requested—again requesting financing and this time referring to the lease, though not expressly to paragraph 34. The heart of the letter is the following two sentences: "The purpose of this letter is to ask again that you advise us immediately if you are willing to provide the financing pursuant to the lease. If you are willing, we propose to enter into negotiation to amend the ground lease appropriately." The very next day, Market Street Associates received from Erb a letter, dated August 10, turning down the original request for financing on the ground that it did not "meet our current investment criteria": the pension trust was not interested in making loans for less than $7 million. On August 22, Orenstein replied to Erb by letter, noting that his letter of August 10 and Erb's letter of August 16 had evidently crossed in the mails, expressing disappointment at the turn-down, and stating that Market Street Associates would seek financing elsewhere. That was the last contact between the parties until September 27, when Orenstein sent Erb a letter stating that Market Street Associates was exercising the option granted it by paragraph 34 to purchase the property upon the terms specified in that paragraph in the event that negotiations over financing broke down.

The pension trust refused to sell, and this suit to compel specific performance followed. Apparently the price computed by the formula in paragraph 34 is only $1 million. The market value must be higher, or Market Street Associates wouldn't be trying to coerce conveyance at the paragraph 34 price; whether it is as high as $3 million, however, the record does not reveal.

The district judge granted summary judgment for the pension trust on two grounds that he believed to be separate although closely related. The first was that, by failing in its correspondence with the pension trust to mention paragraph 34 of the lease, Market Street Associates had prevented the negotiations over financing that are a condition precedent to the lessee's exercise of the purchase option from taking place. Second, this same failure violated the duty of good faith, which the common law of Wisconsin, as of other states, reads into every contract. *In re Estate of Chayka,* 47 Wis.2d 102, 107, 176 N.W.2d 561, 564 (1970); *Super Valu Stores, Inc. v. D-Mart Food Stores, Inc.,* 146 Wis.2d 568, 577, 431 N.W.2d 721, 726 (App.1988); *Ford Motor Co. v. Lyons,* 137 Wis.2d 397, 442, 405 N.W.2d 354, 372 (App.1987); *Sunds Defibrator AB v. Beloit Corp.,* 930 F.2d 564, 566 (7th Cir.1991); *Restatement (Second) of Contracts* § 205 (1981); 2 E. Allan Farnsworth, *Farnsworth on Contracts* § 7.17a (1990). In support of both grounds the judge emphasized a statement by Orenstein in his deposition that it had occurred to him that Erb mightn't know about paragraph 34, though this was unlikely (Orenstein testified) because Erb or someone else at the pension trust would probably check the file and discover the paragraph and realize that if the trust refused to negotiate over the request for financing, Market Street Associates, as Penney's assignee, would be entitled to walk off with the property for (perhaps) a song. The judge inferred that Market Street Associates didn't want financing from the pension trust—that it just wanted an opportunity to buy the property at a bargain price and hoped that the pension trust wouldn't realize the implications of turning down the request for financing. Market Street Associates should, the judge opined, have advised the pension trust that it was requesting financing pursuant to paragraph 34, so that the trust would understand the penalty for refusing to negotiate.

We begin our analysis by setting to one side two extreme contentions by the parties. The pension trust argues that the option to purchase created by paragraph 34 cannot be exercised until negotiations over financing break down; there were no negotiations; therefore they did not break down; therefore Market Street Associates had no right to exercise the option. This argument misreads the contract. Although the option to purchase is indeed contingent, paragraph 34 requires the pension trust, upon demand by the lessee for the financing of improvements worth at least $250,000, "to give reasonable consideration to providing the financing." The lessor who fails to give reasonable consideration and thereby prevents the negotiations from taking place is breaking the contract; and a contracting party cannot be allowed to use his own breach to gain an advantage by impairing the rights that the contract confers on the other party. *Variance, Inc. v. Losinske,* 71 Wis.2d 31, 40, 237 N.W.2d 22, 26 (1976); *Ethyl Corp. v. United Steelwork-*

ers of America, 768 F.2d 180, 185 (7th Cir.1985); *Spanos v. Skouras Theatres Corp.*, 364 F.2d 161, 169 (2d Cir.1966) (en banc) (Friendly, J.); 3A *Corbin on Contracts* § 767, at p. 540 (1960). Often, it is true, if one party breaks the contract, the other can walk away from it without liability[—]can in other words exercise self-help. *First National Bank v. Continental Illinois National Bank*, 933 F.2d 466, 469 (7th Cir.1991). But he is not required to follow that course. He can stand on his contract rights.

But what exactly are those rights in this case? The contract entitles the lessee to reasonable consideration of its request for financing, and only if negotiations over the request fail is the lessee entitled to purchase the property at the price computed in accordance with paragraph 34. It might seem therefore that the proper legal remedy for a lessor's breach that consists of failure to give the lessee's request for financing reasonable consideration would not be an order that the lessor sell the property to the lessee at the paragraph 34 price, but an order that the lessor bargain with the lessee in good faith. But we do not understand the pension trust to be arguing that Market Street Associates is seeking the wrong remedy. We understand it to be arguing that Market Street Associates has no possible remedy. That is an untenable position.

Market Street Associates argues, with equal unreason as it seems to us, that it could not have broken the contract because paragraph 34 contains no express requirement that in requesting financing the lessee mention the lease or paragraph 34 or otherwise alert the lessor to the consequences of his failing to give reasonable consideration to granting the request. There is indeed no such requirement (all that the contract requires is a demand). But no one says there is. The pension trust's argument, which the district judge bought, is that either as a matter of simple contract interpretation or under the compulsion of the doctrine of good faith, a provision requiring Market Street Associates to remind the pension trust of paragraph 34 should be read into the lease.

It seems to us that these are one ground rather than two. A court has to have a reason to interpolate a clause into a contract. The only reason that has been suggested here is that it is necessary to prevent Market Street Associates from reaping a reward for what the pension trust believes to have been Market Street's bad faith. So we must consider the meaning of the contract duty of "good faith." The Wisconsin cases are cryptic as to its meaning though emphatic about its existence, so we must cast our net wider. We do so mindful of Learned Hand's warning, that "such words as 'fraud,' 'good faith,' 'whim,' 'caprice,' 'arbitrary action,' and 'legal fraud' . . . obscure the issue." *Thompson-Starrett Co. v. La Belle Iron Works*, 17 F.2d 536, 541 (2d Cir.1927). Indeed they do. Summers, *supra,* at 207-20; 2 *Farnsworth on Contracts*, supra, § 7.17a, at pp. 328-32. The particular confusion to which the vaguely moralistic overtones of "good faith" give rise is the belief that every contract establishes a fiduciary relationship. A fiduciary is required to treat his principal as if the principal were he, and therefore he may not take advantage of the principal's incapacity, ignorance, inexperience, or even naïveté. *Olympia Hotels Corp. v. Johnson Wax Development Corp.*, 908 F.2d 1363, 1373-74 (7th Cir.1990); *United States v. Dial*, 757 F.2d 163, 168 (7th Cir.1985); *Faultersack v. Clintonville Sales Corp.*, 253 Wis. 432, 435-37, 34 N.W.2d 682, 683-84 (1948); *Schweiger v. Loewi & Co.*, 65 Wis.2d 56, 64-65, 221 N.W.2d 882, 888 (1974); *Meinhard v. Salmon*, 249 N.Y. 458, 463-64, 164 N.E. 545, 546 (1928) (Cardozo, C.J.). If Market Street Associates were the fiduciary of General Electric Pension Trust, then (we may assume) it could not take advantage of Mr. Erb's apparent ignorance of paragraph 34, however exasperating Erb's failure to return Orenstein's phone calls was and however negligent Erb or his associates were in failing to read the lease before turning down Orenstein's request for financing.

But it is unlikely that Wisconsin wishes, in the name of good faith, to make every contract signatory his brother's keeper, especially when the brother is the immense and sophisticated General Electric Pension Trust, whose lofty indifference to small (= < $7 million) transactions is the signifier of its grandeur. In fact the law contemplates that people frequently will take advantage of the ignorance of those with whom they contract, without

What's That?

A "fiduciary" is a person required to act solely for the benefit of another person, not for his own benefit, usually on the basis of a special relationship of trust and confidence. For example, the executor of an estate is a fiduciary with respect to the estate of the person who wrote the will; a guardian is a fiduciary with respect to her ward. A fiduciary duty is the highest standard of care in law or equity. It requires undivided loyalty as well as reasonable care for the other person's assets. Although a contract may give rise to fiduciary obligations, contracting parties are not typically fiduciaries for one another, as the court opinion notes.

thereby incurring liability. *Restatement, supra*, § 161, comment d. The duty of honesty, of good faith even expansively conceived, is not a duty of candor. You can make a binding contract to purchase something you know your seller undervalues. *Laidlaw v. Organ*, 15 U.S. (2 Wheat.) 178, 181 n.2, 4 L.Ed. 214 (1817); *Teamsters Local 282 Pension Trust Fund v. Angelos*, 762 F.2d 522, 528 (7th Cir.1985); *United States v. Dial, supra*, 757 F.2d at 168; 1 *Farnsworth on Contracts, supra*, § 4.11, at pp. 406-10; Anthony T. Kronman, "Mistake, Disclosure, Information, and the Law of Contracts," 7 *J. Legal Stud.* 1 (1978). That of course is a question about formation, not performance, and the particular duty of good faith under examination here relates to the latter rather than to the former. But even after you have signed a contract, you are not obliged to become an altruist toward the other party and relax the terms if he gets into trouble in performing his side of the bargain. *Kham & Nate's Shoes No. 2, Inc. v. First Bank*, 908 F.2d

1351, 1357 (7th Cir.1990). Otherwise mere difficulty of performance would excuse a contracting party—which it does not. *Northern Indiana Public Service Co. v. Carbon County Coal Co.,* 799 F.2d 265, 276-78 (7th Cir.1986); *Jennie-O Foods, Inc. v. United States,* 217 Ct.Cl. 314, 580 F.2d 400, 409 (1978) (per curiam); 2 *Farnsworth on Contracts, supra,* § 7.17a, at p. 330.

But it is one thing to say that you can exploit your superior knowledge of the market—for, if you cannot, you will not be able to recoup the investment you made in obtaining that knowledge—or that you are not required to spend money bailing out a contract partner who has gotten into trouble. It is another thing to say that you can take deliberate advantage of an oversight by your contract partner concerning his rights under the contract. Such taking advantage is not the exploitation of superior knowledge or the avoidance of unbargained-for expense; it is sharp dealing. Like theft, it has no social product, and also like theft it induces costly defensive expenditures, in the form of overelaborate disclaimers or investigations into the trustworthiness of a prospective contract partner, just as the prospect of theft induces expenditures on locks. See generally Steven J. Burton, "Breach of Contract and the Common Law Duty to Perform in Good Faith," 94 *Harv.L.Rev.* 369, 393 (1980).

The form of sharp dealing that we are discussing might or might not be actionable as fraud or deceit. That is a question of tort law and there the rule is that if the information is readily available to both parties the failure of one to disclose it to the other, even if done in the knowledge that the other party is acting on mistaken premises, is not actionable. *Kamuchey v. Trzesniewski,* 8 Wis.2d 94, 98 N.W.2d 403 (1959); *Southard v. Occidental Life Ins. Co.,* 36 Wis.2d 708, 154 N.W.2d 326 (1967); *Lenzi v. Morkin,* 103 Ill.2d 290, 82 Ill. Dec. 644, 469 N.E.2d 178 (1984); *Guyer v. Cities Service Oil Co.,* 440 F.Supp. 630 (E.D.Wis.1977); W. Page Keeton *et al., Prosser and Keeton on the Law of Torts* § 106, at p. 737 (5th ed. 1984). All of these cases, however, with the debatable exception of *Guyer,* involve failure to disclose something in the negotiations leading up to the signing of the contract, rather than failure to disclose after the contract has been signed. (*Guyer* involved failure to disclose during the negotiations leading up to a renewal of the contract.) The distinction is important, as we explained in *Maksym v. Loesch,* 937 F.2d 1237, 1242 (7th Cir.1991). Before the contract is signed, the parties confront each other with a natural wariness. Neither expects the other to be particularly forthcoming, and therefore there is no deception when one is not. Afterwards the situation is different. The parties are now in a cooperative relationship the costs of which will be considerably reduced by a measure of trust. So each lowers his guard a bit, and now silence is more apt to be deceptive. Cf. *AMPAT/Midwest, Inc. v. Illinois Tool Works Inc.,* 896 F.2d 1035, 1040-41 (7th Cir.1990).

Moreover, this is a contract case rather than a tort case, and conduct that might not rise to the level of fraud may nonetheless violate the duty of good faith in dealing with one's contractual partners and thereby give rise to a remedy under contract law. Burton, *supra,* at 372 n. 17. This duty is, as it were, halfway between a fiduciary duty (the duty of *utmost* good faith) and the duty merely to refrain from active fraud. Despite its moralistic overtones it is no more the injection of moral principles into contract law than the fiduciary concept itself is. *Tymshare, Inc. v. Covell,* 727 F.2d 1145, 1152 (D.C.Cir.1984); Summers, *supra,* at 204-07, 265-66. It would be quixotic as well as presumptuous for judges to undertake through contract law to raise the ethical standards of the nation's business people. The concept of the duty of good faith like the concept of fiduciary duty is a stab at approximating the terms the parties would have negotiated had they foreseen the circumstances that have given rise to their dispute. The parties want to minimize the costs of performance. To the extent that a doctrine of good faith designed to do this by reducing defensive expenditures is a reasonable measure to this end, interpolating it into the contract advances the parties' joint goal.

It is true that an essential function of contracts is to allocate risk, and would be defeated if courts treated the materializing of a bargained-over, allocated risk as a misfortune the burden of which is required to be shared between the parties (as it might be within a family, for example) rather than borne entirely by the party to whom the risk had been allocated by mutual agreement. But contracts do not just allocate risk. They also (or some of them) set in motion a cooperative enterprise, which may to some extent place one party at the other's mercy. "The parties to a contract are embarked on a cooperative venture, and a minimum of cooperativeness in the event unforeseen problems arise at the performance stage is required even if not an explicit duty of the contract." *AMPAT/Midwest, Inc. v. Illinois Tool Works, Inc., supra,* 896 F.2d at 1041. The office of the doctrine of good faith is to forbid the kinds of opportunistic behavior that a mutually dependent, cooperative relationship might enable in the absence of rule. "'Good faith' is a compact reference to an implied undertaking not to take opportunistic advantage in a way that could not have been contemplated at the time of drafting, and which therefore was not resolved explicitly by the parties." *Kham & Nate's Shoes No. 2, Inc. v. First Bank, supra,* 908 F.2d at 1357. The contractual duty of good faith is thus not some newfangled bit of welfare-state paternalism or . . . the sediment of an altruistic strain in contract law, and we are therefore not surprised to find the essentials of the modern doctrine well established in nineteenth-century cases, a few examples being *Bush v. Marshall,* 47 U.S. (6 How.) 284, 291, 12 L.Ed. 440 (1848); *Chicago, Rock Island & Pac. R.R. v. Howard,* 74 U.S. (7 Wall.) 392, 413, 19 L.Ed. 117 (1868); *Marsh v. Masterson,* 101 N.Y. 401, 410-11, 5 N.E. 59, 63 (1886), and *Uhrig v. Williamsburg City Fire Ins. Co.,* 101 N.Y. 362, 4 N.E. 745 (1886).

. . . .

We could of course do without the term "good faith," and maybe even without the doctrine. We could, as just suggested, speak instead of implied conditions necessitated by the unpredictability of the future at the time the contract was made. Farnsworth, "Good Faith Performance and Commercial Reasonableness under the Uniform Commercial Code," 30 *U.Chi.L.Rev.* 666, 670 (1963). Suppose a party has promised work to the promisee's "satisfaction." As Learned Hand explained, "he may refuse to look at the work, or to exercise any real judgment on it, in which case he has prevented performance and excused the condition." *Thompson-Starrett Co. v. La Belle Iron Works, supra,* 17 F.2d at 541. See also *Morin Building Products Co. v. Baystone Construction, Inc.,* 717 F.2d 413, 415 (7th Cir.1983). That is, it was an implicit condition that the promisee examine the work to the extent necessary to determine whether it was satisfactory; otherwise the performing party would have been placing himself at the complete mercy of the promisee. The parties didn't write this condition into the contract either because they thought such behavior unlikely or failed to foresee it altogether. In just the same way—to switch to another familiar example of the operation of the duty of good faith—parties to a requirements contract surely do not intend that if the price of the product covered by the contract rises, the buyer shall be free to increase his "requirements" so that he can take advantage of the rise in the market price over the contract price to resell the product on the open market at a guaranteed profit. *Empire Gas Corp. v. American Bakeries Co.,* 840 F.2d 1333 (7th Cir.1988). If they fail to insert an express condition to this effect, the court will read it in, confident that the parties would have inserted the condition if they had known what the future held. Of similar character is the implied condition that an exclusive dealer will use his best efforts to promote the supplier's goods, since otherwise the exclusive feature of the dealership contract would place the supplier at the dealer's mercy. *Wood v. Duff-Gordon,* 222 N.Y. 88, 118 N.E. 214 (1917) (Cardozo, J.).

What's That?

In a "requirements contract," the seller promises to meet the buyer's needs (or requirements) in terms of quantity. The contract does not otherwise contain a quantity term. Requirements contracts are covered in greater detail starting on page 821.

But whether we say that a contract shall be deemed to contain such implied conditions as are necessary to make sense of the contract, or that a contract obligates the parties to cooperate in its performance in "good faith" to the extent necessary to carry out the purposes of the contract, comes to much the same thing. They are different ways of formulating the overriding purpose of contract law, which is to give the parties what they would have stipulated for expressly if at the time of making the contract they had had complete knowledge of the future and the costs of negotiating and adding provisions to the contract had been zero.

The two formulations would have different meanings only if "good faith" were thought limited to "honesty in fact," an interpretation perhaps permitted but certainly not compelled by the Uniform Commercial Code, see Summers, *supra*, at 207-20—and anyway this is not a case governed by the UCC. We need not pursue this issue. The dispositive question in the present case is simply whether Market Street Associates tried to trick the pension trust and succeeded in doing so. If it did, this would be the type of opportunistic behavior in an ongoing contractual relationship that would violate the duty of good faith performance however the duty is formulated. There is much common sense in Judge Reynolds' conclusion that Market Street Associates did just that. The situation as he saw it was as follows. Market Street Associates didn't want financing from the pension trust (initially it had looked elsewhere, remember), and when it learned it couldn't get the financing without owning the property, it decided to try to buy the property. But the pension trust set a stiff price, so Orenstein decided to trick the pension trust into selling at the bargain price fixed in paragraph 34 by requesting financing and hoping that the pension trust would turn the request down without noticing the paragraph. His preliminary dealings with the pension trust made this hope a realistic one by revealing a sluggish and hidebound bureaucracy unlikely to have retained in its brontosaurus's memory, or to be able at short notice to retrieve, the details of a small lease made twenty years earlier. So by requesting financing without mentioning the lease Market Street Associates might well precipitate a refusal before the pension trust woke up to paragraph 34. It is true that Orenstein's second letter requested financing "pursuant to the lease." But when the next day he received a reply to his first letter indicating that the pension trust was indeed oblivious to paragraph 34, his response was to send a lulling letter designed to convince the pension trust that the matter was closed and could be forgotten. The stage was set for his thunderbolt: the notification the next month that Market Street Associates was taking up the option in paragraph 34. Only then did the pension trust look up the lease and discover that it had been had.

The only problem with this recital is that it construes the facts as favorably to the pension trust as the record will permit, and that of course is not the right standard for summary judgment. The facts must be construed as favorably to the nonmoving party, to Market Street Associates, as the record permits (that Market Street Associates filed its own motion for summary judgment is irrelevant, as we have seen). When that is done, a different picture emerges. On Market Street Associates' construal of the record, $3 million was a grossly excessive price for the property, and while $1 million might be a bargain it would not confer so great a windfall as to warrant an inference that if the pension trust had known about paragraph 34 it never would have turned down Market Street Associates' request for financing cold. And in fact the pension trust may have known about paragraph 34, and either it didn't care or it believed that unless the request mentioned that paragraph the pension trust would incur no liability by turning it down. Market Street Associates may have assumed and have been entitled to assume that in reviewing a request for financing from one of its lessees the pension trust would take the time to read the lease to see whether it bore on the request. Market Street Associates did not desire financing from the pension trust initially—that is undeniable—yet when it discovered that it could not get financing elsewhere unless it had the title to the property it may have realized that it would have to negotiate with the pension trust over financing before it could hope to buy the property at the price specified in the lease.

On this interpretation of the facts there was no bad faith on the part of Market Street Associates. It acted honestly, reasonably, without ulterior motive, in the face of circumstances as they actually and reasonably appeared to it. The fault was the pension trust's incredible inattention, which misled Market Street Associates into believing that the pension trust had no interest in financing the improvements regardless of the purchase option. We do not usually excuse contracting parties from failing to read and understand the contents of their contract; and in the end what this case comes down to—or so at least it can be strongly argued—is that an immensely sophisticated enterprise simply failed to read the contract. On the other hand, such enterprises make mistakes just like the rest of us, and deliberately to take advantage of your contracting partner's mistake during the performance stage (for we are not talking about taking advantage of superior knowledge at the formation stage) is a breach of good faith. To be able to correct your contract partner's mistake at zero cost to yourself, and decide not to do so, is a species of opportunistic behavior that the parties would have expressly forbidden in the contract had they foreseen it. The immensely long term of the lease amplified the possibility of errors but did not license either party to take advantage of them.

The district judge jumped the gun in choosing between these alternative characterizations. The essential issue bearing on Market Street Associates' good faith was Orenstein's state of mind, a type of inquiry that ordinarily cannot be concluded on summary judgment, and could not be here. If Orenstein believed that Erb knew or would surely find out about paragraph 34, it was not dishonest or opportunistic to fail to flag that paragraph, or even to fail to mention the lease, in his correspondence and (rare) conversations with Erb, especially given the uninterest in dealing with Market Street Associates that Erb fairly radiated. To decide what Orenstein believed, a trial is necessary. As for the pension trust's intimation that a bench trial (for remember that this is an equity case, since the only relief sought by the plaintiff is specific performance) will add no illumination beyond what the summary judgment proceeding has done, this overlooks the fact that at trial the judge will for the first time have a chance to see the witnesses whose depositions he has read, to hear their testimony elaborated, and to assess their believability.

The judgment is reversed and the case is remanded for further proceedings consistent with this opinion.

---

§ 4.2.2. Duty of Good Faith in Requirements and Output Contracts

Most contracts for sale of goods contain express terms selecting the quantity of goods to be bought and sold. There is a breach of contract if the buyer refuses to take or pay for the full quantity in the contract or the seller refuses to deliver that amount. In contrast, a requirements or an output contract measures the quantity of goods by the needs of the buyer ("requirements") or by the production of the seller ("output"), thereby allowing buyers and sellers to have the quantities of goods bought and sold controlled by business operations and needs, which they may not be able or want to define with precision when the contract is created.

Older cases questioned whether the flexible quantity in requirements and output contracts meant those contracts would be unenforceable beacause of indefiniteness or because they lacked a quantity term to satisfy any applicable statutes of frauds. Later cases resolved those issues in favor of enforceability, but then had to determine if the buyer or seller had breached by demanding "too much" or supplying "too little" of the subject goods. UCC § 2-306 specifies the standard to be used, incorporating the notion of "good faith" and adding additional guiding principles.

Reading the Law Critically: *Feld* and UCC § 2-306

1. What behavior does the plaintiff claim constitutes a breach of the obligation of good faith?

2. What guidance do UCC § 2-306 and its Official Comment provide to help regulate the quantities that may reasonably be demanded and provided under requirements and output contracts?

3. UCC § 2-306 says a requirements or output contract means "such actual output or requirements as may occur in good faith . . . ." What purpose is served by adding good faith as a requirement in addition to the other specifictions in 2-306?

Feld v. Henry S. Levy & Sons, Inc.

FRED FELD, doing business as Crushed Toast Co., Appellant-Respondent

v.

HENRY S. LEVY & SONS, INC., Respondent-Appellant

Court of Appeals of New York
335 N.E.2d 320 (N.Y. 1975)

COOKE, Judge.

Plaintiff operates a business known as the Crushed Toast Company and defendant is engaged in the wholesale bread baking business. They entered into a written contract, as of June 19, 1968, in which defendant agreed to sell and plaintiff to purchase "all bread crumbs produced by the Seller in its factory at 115 Thames Street, Brooklyn, New York, during the period commencing June 19, 1968, and terminating June 18, 1969", the agreement to "be deemed automatically renewed thereafter for successive renewal periods of one year" with the right to either party to cancel by giving not less than six months notice to the other by certified mail. No notice of cancellation was served. . . .

Interestingly, the term "bread crumbs" does not refer to crumbs that may flake off bread; rather, they are a manufactured item, starting with stale or imperfectly appearing loaves and followed by removal of labels, processing through two grinders, the second of which effects a finer granulation, insertion into a drum in an oven for toasting and, finally, bagging of the finished product.

Subsequent to the making of the agreement, a substantial quantity of bread crumbs, said to be over 250 tons, were sold by defendant to plaintiff but defendant stopped crumb production on about May 15, 1969. There was proof by defendant's comptroller that the oven was too large to accommodate the drum, that it was stated that the operation was "very uneconomical", but after said date of cessation no steps were taken to obtain more economical equipment. The toasting oven was intentionally broken down, then partially rebuilt, then completely dismantled in the summer of 1969 and, thereafter, defendant used the space for a computer room. It appears, without dispute, that defendant indicated to plaintiff at different times that the former would resume bread crumb production if the contract price of 6 cents per pound be changed to 7 cents, and also that, after the crumb making machinery was dismantled, defendant sold the raw materials used in making crumbs to animal food manufacturers.

Special Term denied plaintiff's motion for summary judgment on the issue of liability and turned down defendant's counter-request for a summary judgment of dismissal. From the Appellate Division's order of affirmance, by a divided court, both parties appeal.

Defendant contends that the contract did not require defendant to manufacture bread crumbs, but merely to sell those it did, and, since none were produced after the demise of the oven, there was no duty to then deliver and, consequently from then on, no liability on its part. Agreements to sell all the goods or services a party may produce or perform to another party are commonly referred to as "output" contracts and they usually serve a useful commercial purpose in minimizing the burdens of product marketing (see 1 Williston, Contracts (3d ed.), § 104A). The Uniform Commercial Code rejects the ideas that an output contract is lacking in mutuality or that it is unenforceable because of indefiniteness in that a quantity for the term is not specified (6 Encyclopedia New York Law, Contracts, § 442, 1974-1975 Supp. by Professor Schwartz, p. 43). Official Comment 2 to section 2-306 (McKinney's Cons.Laws of N.Y., Book 62½ , Uniform Commercial Code, pp. 206-207) states in part: "Under this Article, a contract for output . . .is not too indefinite since it is held to mean the actual good faith output . . . of the particular party. Nor does such a contract lack mutuality of obligation since, under this section, the party who will determine quantity is required to operate his plant or conduct his business in good faith and according to commercial standards of fair dealing in the trade so that his output . . . will proximate a reasonably foreseeable figure." (See, also, Matter of United Cigar Stores Co. of Amer., D.C., 8 F.Supp. 243, 244, affd., 2 Cir., 72 F.2d 673, cert. den. Sub nom., Consolidated Dairy Prods. Co. v. Irving Trust Co., 293 U.S. 617, 55 S.Ct. 210, 79 L.Ed. 706; 9 N.Y.Jur., Contracts, § 10, p. 531.)

The real issue in this case is whether the agreement carries with it an implication that defendant was obligated to continue to manufacture bread crumbs for the full term. Section 2-306 of the Uniform Commercial Code, entitled "Output, Requirements and Exclusive Dealings" provides:

> (1) A term which measures the quantity by the output of the seller or the requirements of the buyer means such actual output or requirements as may occur in good faith, except that no quantity unreasonably disproportionate to any stated estimate or in the absence of a stated estimate to any normal or otherwise comparable prior output or requirements may be tendered or demanded. . . .

Section 2-306 is consistent with prior New York case law . . . . Every contract of this type imposes an obligation of good faith in its performance (Uniform Commercial Code, § 1-203; see Wigand v. Bachmann-Bechtel Brewing Co., 222 N.Y. 272, 277, 118 N.E. 618, 619; New York Cent. Iron Works Co. v. United States Radiator Co., 174 N.Y. 331, 335, 66 N.E. 967, 968). Under the Uniform Commercial Code, the commercial background and intent must be read into the language of any agreement and good faith is demanded in the performance of that agreement (Official Comment 1, McKinney's Cons.Laws of N.Y., Book 62½, Uniform Commercial Code, § 2-306), and, under the decisions relating to output contracts, it is clearly the general rule that good faith cessation of production terminates any further obligations thereunder and excuses further performance by the party discontinuing production . . . .

This is not a situation where defendant ceased its main operation of bread baking (see Neofotistos v. Harvard Brewing Co., supra). Rather, defendant contends in a conclusory fashion that it was "uneconomical" or "economically not feasible" for it to continue to make bread crumbs. Although plaintiff observed in his motion papers that defendant claimed it was not economically feasible to make the crumbs, plaintiff did not admit that as a fact. In any event, "economic feasibility", an expression subject to many interpretations, would not be a precise or reliable test.

There are present here intertwined questions of fact, whether defendant performed in good faith and whether it stopped its manufacture of bread crumbs in good faith, neither of which can be resolved properly on this record. The seller's duty to remain in crumb production is a matter calling for a close scrutiny of its motives (1 Hawkland, A Transactional Guide to the Uniform Commercial Code, p. 52, see, also, p. 48), confined here by the papers to financial reasons. It is

Take Note!

Although this court says that it is obvious that bankruptcy or a similar threat to the business "would warrant cessation of production," other courts have disagreed. In some contracts, the parties allocate the risk so that one or both parties take the risk of bankruptcy if their business strategy is not successful.

undisputed that defendant leveled its crumb making machinery only after plaintiff refused to agree to a price higher than that specified in the agreement and that it then sold the raw materials to manufacturers of animal food. There are before us no componential figures indicating the actual cost of the finished bread crumbs to defendant, statements as to the profits derived or the losses sustained, or data specifying the net or gross return realized from the animal food transactions.

The parties by their contract gave the right of cancellation to either by providing for a six months' notice to the other. The apparent purpose of such a stipulation was to provide an opportunity to either the seller or buyer to conclude their dealings in the event that the transactions were not as profitable or advantageous as desired or expected, or for any other reason. Correspondingly, such a notice would also furnish the receiver of it a chance to secure another outlet or source of supply, as the case might be. Short of such a cancellation, defendant was expected to continue to perform in good faith and could cease production of the bread crumbs, a single facet of its operation, only in good faith. Obviously, a bankruptcy or genuine imperiling of the very existence if its entire business caused by the production of the crumbs would warrant cessation of production of that item; the yield of less profit from its sale than expected would not. Since bread crumbs were but a part of defendant's enterprise and since there was a contractual right of cancellation, good faith required continued production until cancellation, even if there be no profit. In circumstances such as these and without more, defendant would be justified, in good faith, in ceasing production of the single item prior to cancellation only if its losses from continuance would be more than trivial, which, overall, is a question of fact.

The order of the Appellate Division should be affirmed, without costs.

BREITEL, C.J., and JASEN, GABRIELLI, JONES, WACHTLER and FUCHSBERG, JJ., concur.

Order affirmed, without costs. Question certified answered in the affirmative.

> UCC § 2-306. **Output, Requirements and Exclusive Dealings.**
>
> (1) A term which measures the quantity by the output of the seller or the requirements of the buyer means such actual output or requirements as may occur in good faith, except that no quantity unreasonably disproportionate to any stated estimate or in the absence of a stated estimate to any normal or otherwise comparable prior output or requirements may be tendered or demanded.
>
> (2) [reproduced on page 807]
>
> *Comments:*
> 1. Subsection (1) of this section, in regard to output and requirements, applies to this specific problem the general approach of this Act which requires the reading of commercial background and intent into the language of any agreement and demands good faith in the performance of that agreement. It applies to such contracts of nonproducing establishments such as dealers or distributors as well as to manufacturing concerns

2. Under this Article, a contract for output or requirements is not too indefinite since it is held to mean the actual good faith output or requirements of the particular party. Nor does such a contract lack mutuality of obligation since, under this section, the party who will determine quantity is required to operate his plant or conduct his business in good faith and according to commercial standards of fair dealing in the trade so that his output or requirements will approximate a reasonably foreseeable figure. Reasonable elasticity in the requirements is expressly envisaged by this section and good faith variations from prior requirements are permitted even when the variation may be such as to result in discontinuance.

A shut-down by a requirements buyer for lack of orders might be permissible when a shut-down merely to curtail losses would not. The essential test is whether the party is acting in good faith. Similarly, a sudden expansion of the plant by which requirements are to be measured would not be included within the scope of the contract as made but normal expansion undertaken in good faith would be within the scope of this section. One of the factors in an expansion situation would be whether the market price had risen greatly in a case in which the requirements contract contained a fixed price. Reasonable variation of an extreme sort is exemplified in **Southwest Natural Gas Co. v. Oklahoma Portland Cement Co., 102 F.2d 630 (C.C.A. 10 1939).** This Article takes no position as to whether a requirements contract is a provable claim in bankruptcy.

3. If an estimate of output or requirements is included in the agreement, no quantity unreasonably disproportionate to it may be tendered or demanded. Any minimum or maximum set by the agreement shows a clear limit on the intended elasticity. In similar fashion, the agreed estimate is to be regarded as a center around which the parties intend the variation to occur.

FYI

Good Faith and "Unreasonably Disproportionate" Quantities

You have seen that, in addition to imposing an obligation that the requirements or output quantity means "such actual output or requirements as may occur in good faith," UCC § 2-306(1) also specifies that "no quantity unreasonably disproportionate to any stated estimate or in the absence of a stated estimate to any normal or otherwise com-

parable prior output or requirements may be tendered or demanded." In *Orange and Rockland Utilities, Inc. v. Amerada Hess Corp.,* 397
N.Y.S.2d 814 (App. Div. 1977), the court explored the meaning of
both of those aspects of § 2-306. The contract in *Orange and Rockland
Utilities* was for supply of all the buyer's needs for fuel oil at a fixed price
for five years. When the price of oil skyrocketed, the buyer claimed to
need vastly increased amounts over the estimates stated in the contract,
but the buyer had begun to resell some of the oil to other utilities rather
than using it for power generation for its customers. The court ruled
that to the extent the buyer was reselling oil rather than using oil for
power generation, its "requirements" were not incurred in good faith.
The court also ruled that any demand for more than double the stated
estimates would be considered unreasonably disproportionate and thus
barred by § 2-306. The court did not "adopt the factor of more than
double the contract estimates as any sort of an inflexible yardstick."
Rather, it considered a number of factors "calculated to limit a party's
risk in accordance with the reasonable expectations of the parties":

> (1) the amount by which the requirements exceed the contract
> estimate; (2) whether the seller had any reasonable basis on
> which to forecast or anticipate the requested increase . . . ; (3)
> the amount, if any, by which the market price of the goods
> in question exceeded the contract price; (4) whether such
> an increase in market price was itself fortuitous; and (5) the
> reason for the increase in requirements.

397 N.Y.S.2d at 819, 821-22.

§ 4.2.3. Duty of Good Faith in Exercising Termination Rights

Agreements may contain express
clauses that permit one or both parties
to the contract to terminate it, either
for particular reasons ("termination for
cause") or for any reason ("termination
for convenience"). If a contract contains no specified end for performance
obligations and no provision for termination by the parties, a court may supply an implied term identifying when
the contract may be terminated. The

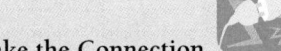

Make the Connection

Recall the Chapter 2 discussion
(page 103) regarding the possibility
that a termination clause might lead
to a determination that there is no
consideration and therefore no contract. Remember, too, that "termination" (the parties' agreed means of
ending performance obligations pursuant to the contract) is not the same
as "cancellation" (the legal right of an
aggrieved party to put an end to the
parties' performance obligations because of material breach of the contract performance obligations).

following cases consider what restrictions on exercise of such terms are imposed by the implied covenant of good faith and fair dealing.

Reading the Law Critically:
Questar Builders* and *Bak-A-Lum Corp.

1. Was the termination provision at issue in each case adopted expressly by the parties or was it implied? What restrictions, if any, did the provision place on one or both parties' rights to terminate?

2. Considering both cases together, how would you describe the obligation to act in good faith in termination of a contract?

3. On remand in *Questar Builders*, what version of the facts would lead to the conclusion that the termination was made in bad faith? What version of the facts would lead to the conclusion that it was not bad faith?

4. What led to the court's conclusion in *Bak-A-Lum* that the termination was made in bad faith?

Questar Builders, Inc. v. CB Flooring, LLC

QUESTAR BUILDERS, INC., Defendant-Appellant

v.

CB FLOORING, LLC., Plaintiff-Appellee

Maryland Court of Appeals
978 A.2d 651 (Md. Ct. App. 2009)

[The first part of this opinion appears in Chapter 2 (page 84). Recall that Questar and CB Flooring entered a contract for CB Flooring to install carpeting in a project being constructed by Questar. Questar exercised its option under the contract's termination clauses, claiming it was terminating for cause but that, even in the absence of breach, Questar had a right to terminate the contract "for convenience." The trial court concluded that CB Flooring had not breached the contract and that Questar did not appropriately exercise the termination-for-convenience clause. In the portion of the opinion you have already read, the Court of Appeals concluded that a termination-for-convenience clause is enforceable, "subject to an implied obligation to exercise the right to terminate in good faith and in accordance with fair dealing." Finding that the trial court had not adequately determined that issue, the Court of Appeals remanded to the trial court, offering in the following excerpt what it describes as "guidance on how the implied obligation of good faith and fair dealing may apply in this case." You may wish to review the more detailed statement of facts in the portion of the opinion in Chapter 2 to understand more precisely how the obligation to act in good faith operates here.]

II.

We now turn to whether the trial judge correctly found that Questar was not permitted to terminate the Subcontract for its convenience under the circumstances of this case. In reaching her conclusion, she rejected Questar's assertion that its subjective loss of faith in CB Flooring's ability to perform under the Subcontract provided sufficient justification for exercising its termination right. On appeal, Questar claims that the trial judge did not make a finding of bad faith, but, to the extent that she found facts that effectively are consistent with a finding of bad faith, those findings were clearly erroneous. We hold that the trial judge concluded properly that Questar's subjective belief (or "gut feeling") was sufficient to trigger application of the convenience termination clause; however, we agree with Questar that the trial judge did not render an express or implied finding on the ultimate fact of whether the general contractor acted in bad faith by terminating the Subcontract, although she made several findings of fact that could be viewed as contributory to reaching such a finding. Accordingly, we shall remand the matter to the Circuit Court to reach a conclusion as to the ultimate issue of whether Questar breached the Subcontract by not exercising in good faith its discretion to terminate the Subcontract for convenience. In doing so, we supply the following guidance on how the implied obligation of good faith and fair dealing may apply in this case.[25]

"'[U]nder the covenant of good faith and fair dealing, a party [exercising discretion must] refrain from doing anything that will have the effect of frustrating the right of the other party to receive the fruits of the contract between them.'" *Clancy*, 405 Md. at 571, 954 A.2d at 1109 (quoting *E. Shore Mkts., Inc.* v. *J.D. Assocs. Ltd. P'ship*, 213 F.3d 175, 184 (4th Cir.2000)). This means that each

---

[25] CB Flooring bears the initial burden of production to adduce a prima facie showing that Questar invoked the termination for convenience clause in bad faith, i.e., the absence of good faith. If it satisfies the trier of fact that this burden is met, the issue of "good faith" is in play and the burden of production shifts to Questar. Also, Questar, at this point has the burden of persuasion, on a preponderance of evidence standard, to prove the good faith exercise of its termination power. David A. Bramble, Inc. v. Thomas, 396 Md. 443, 467, 914 A.2d 136, 150 (2007); Port East Transfer, Inc. v. Liberty Mut. Ins. Co., 330 Md. 376, 386–88, 624 A.2d 520, 524–25 (1993); 23 Williston, Contracts, § 63:22 (4th ed. 2007).

party must "do nothing to destroy the rights of the other party to enjoy the fruits of the contract and [] do everything that the contract presupposes they will do to accomplish its purpose." *Photovest Corp. v. Fotomat Corp.*, 606 F.2d 704, 728 (7th Cir.1979). In addition, the obligation to act in good faith and deal fairly prohibits a party from terminating its contract (or otherwise exercising its discretion) to "recapture" an opportunity that it lost upon entering the contract. Greer Props., Inc. v. LaSalle Nat'l Bank, 874 F.2d 457, 461 (7th Cir.1989); Piantes v. Pepperidge Farm, Inc., 875 F.Supp. 929, 938 (D.Mass.1995). Upon entering a binding contract for a specified duration, the parties thereto "give up their opportunity to shop around for a better price." Greer Props., Inc., 874 F.2d at 461.

Where, as here, personal taste does not provide the basis for the exercise of discretion, an objective standard of what constitutes good faith and fair dealing applies. *See* Clancy, 405 Md. at 568–69, 954 A.2d at 1108 (noting difference between objective and subjective standards of good faith and applying subjective standard to author's decision on whether to withdraw his name from series of books published by partnership of which he was a partner). Stated otherwise, the obligation of good faith and fair dealing requires a party exercising discretion to do so in accordance with the "reasonable expectations" of the other party. Burton & Anderson, Contractual Good Faith § 2.3.3. What constitutes a "reasonable expectation," of course, depends on the language of the contract. *Id.* § 3.3.4. We agree with Professors Burton and Anderson, who explain:

> This accommodation requires meaningful review because a discretion-exercising party may be called upon to justify its actions by giving its reasons. A court or jury must decide whether those reasons reasonably deserved significant weight and were among the reasons allowed by the contract. If they satisfy these criteria, then the discretion-exercising party performed in good faith. At the same time, this standard requires deference to the discretion exercising party, not judge or jury. Accordingly, a reasonableness standard allows meaningful legal review of discretion without overreaching—a deferential standard that bites.

Id. § 3.3.4.

Here, the trial judge specifically found that Questar "schemed" to contract with CTI to install carpeting at Greenwich Place, after it contracted with CB Flooring. She based that finding on Maccherone's sending the ID Drawings to CTI's salesperson, despite having an agreement already with CB Flooring, as well as on the testimony of CTI's salesperson that she felt uncomfortable when Maccherone later asked her to send him a fax stating that New Stratford and Bigelow carpets were of comparable price. The trial judge found that CB Flooring did nothing to jeopardize timely performance of the Subcontract. Moreover, she resolved that Questar never communicated to CB Flooring its belief (asserted at trial) that the subcontractor was taking too long to respond to the changes advanced by the ID Drawings or that it was in any other way dissatisfied with the subcontractor. She also found that CB Flooring was not using the change order as leverage against the general contractor. These findings are relevant to the bad faith inquiry; however, we think it appropriate to remand the matter to the Circuit Court because it is not clear on what guiding legal principles the trial judge relied when she concluded that the right to terminate for convenience did not apply under the circumstances. To that end, it is not patent that the trial judge actually found bad faith.

As already explained, the right to terminate a contract for convenience is a risk-allocating tool, which allowed Questar to terminate the Subcontract if, in its discretion, it determined that continuing with the Subcontract would subject it potentially to a meaningful financial loss or some other difficulty in completing the project successfully. On remand, the trial judge must be persuaded that Questar breached the Subcontract by exercising its right to terminate for convenience in bad faith, or, stated otherwise, by not exercising its discretion to terminate in accordance with the implied obligation of good faith and fair dealing. As the party with the discretion to terminate for convenience, Questar was entitled to decide whether continuing with the contract would subject it to an unnecessary risk. It is not the court's role to make that decision for Questar; the court's role is to determine only whether Questar's determination was consistent with the reasonable expectations of CB Flooring, in light of the terms of the Subcontract.

CB Flooring may prevail if the trial court is convinced that Questar's asserted basis for the termination—a deterioration in its business relationship with CB Flooring—was not commercially reasonable under the circumstances, and therefore inconsistent with CB Flooring's reasonable expectations. Additionally, if the trial judge were to conclude that Questar sought to recapture a better bargain with CTI or that Questar did not make reasonable efforts to ensure that continuing its contractual relationship with CB Flooring remained convenient, CB Flooring may prevail. If the court resolves that Questar invoked its right to terminate for convenience in order to evade its obligation to perform under Paragraphs 13 or 16, as such an exercise would have been inconsistent with the subcontractor's reasonable expectations as well, CB Flooring may prevail.

Supplemental fact-finding may aid the Circuit Court in applying this Opinion on remand. Our review of the record revealed the following unresolved factual conflicts that potentially may be relevant to the ultimate conclusion whether Questar acted in bad faith. First, the trial judge did not discuss what significance, if any, should be attributed CB Flooring's attempt, in submitting its change order to Questar, to withhold from Questar 10% of the costs associated with the Shaw carpeting. This may have played a role in Questar's decision to terminate the Subcontract. Second, while the trial judge stated that she believed the price of CTI's original bid to be approximately $1,240,000 ($120,000 above what it agreed to in its 5 April 2006 subcontract with Questar), Questar asserts that that bid price did not reflect accurately the closeness of CTI's bid to that of CB Flooring. To that end, Questar claims that CTI's initial bid included items not included in its subcontract. The Circuit Court, on remand, may assess the merit of Questar's assertion, as the record indicates that the trial judge considered the disparity between the initial bids of CTI and CB Flooring relevant to her decision. Were the court to undertake this inquiry, it should consider reconciling the items included in the bid with those included in the subcontract.

Third, it also may be relevant whether Questar included, in its February 2006 draft subcontract with CTI, a provision allowing CTI to install Bigelow border carpeting at Greenwich Place. Maccherone claimed that it did not, that the provision was added later during negotiations with CTI, and that the document's February date was never changed. The trial judge's findings on this point are not clear on the current state of the record; however, if it turns out that Questar planned to permit CTI to install Bigelow carpeting before it terminated the Subcontract, that may shed significant light on Questar's motives. Fourth, the Circuit Court may wish to consider the reasonableness of Questar's assertions that CB Flooring was delaying its ordering of materials. Were it to do so, the court may want to determine whether Questar requested CB Flooring to order materials and, if so, how CB Flooring responded to such a request. Fifth, it may be relevant whether the length of time that passed before CB Flooring responded to either set of ID Drawings was commercially reasonable under the circumstances. Sixth, the Circuit Court also may wish to consider whether CB Flooring's error in not factoring border carpeting in its initial bid played a reasonable role in Questar's decision to terminate the Subcontract. It may be relevant whether CB Flooring attempted to shift the cost of its mistake to Questar. Finally, we note that Questar's subcontract with CTI was for the same price as the Subcontract at issue here. CB Flooring's allegation that Questar sought to obtain a better bargain from CTI may make this fact significant.

Judgment of the circuit court for Baltimore County vacated; case remanded for further proceedings consistent with this opinion; costs to abide the result.

—————————

Bak-A-Lum Corp. of America v. Alcoa Building Products, Inc.

BAK-A-LUM CORP. OF AMERICA, Plaintiff-Appellant and Cross-Respondent

v.

ALCOA BUILDING PRODUCTS, INC., Defendant-Respondent and Cross-Appellant

Supreme Court of New Jersey

351 A.2d 349 (N.J. 1976)

CONFORD, P.J.A.D., Temporarily Assigned.

Plaintiff corporation ("BAL" hereinafter) sued defendant ("ALCOA" hereinafter) for an injunction and damages for alleged breach of an exclusive distributorship of aluminum siding and related products manufactured by ALCOA. It was denied an injunction but awarded damages for breach of contract; at the same time the trial court granted defendant judgment on a counterclaim for merchandise sold to plaintiff, together with interest thereon. Plaintiff appealed on the ground the damages awarded were inadequate; the defendant cross-appealed, asserting its conduct was not actionable. The Appellate Division affirmed. We granted plaintiff's petition for certification and defendant's cross-petition. . . .

We find the record to support the trial court's finding of fact that in or about 1962 or 1963 BAL entered into a verbal agreement with ALCOA whereby BAL would be exclusive distributor in Northern New Jersey for ALCOA's aluminum siding and certain related products. Although the agreement did not preclude BAL handling other lines of siding, the understanding was that it would maintain an adequate organization and exert its best efforts to promote the sales of the ALCOA products, and the evidence and trial findings were that BAL produced to the satisfaction of ALCOA, even meeting fixed quotas of sales set by ALCOA during the latter phase of the relationship.

ALCOA terminated the "exclusive" in January 1970 by appointing four additional distributors to share the North Jersey territory with plaintiff, thereby precipitating the controversy that gave rise to this action. The trial court, although refusing a request for a preliminary injunction against the termination of the exclusive distributorship, held after trial that there was a binding agreement between the parties terminable only after a reasonable period of time and on reasonable notice. It found that a reasonable period of time had passed before termination but that a reasonable period of notice of termination would be seven months. It established plaintiff's damages at $5,000 per month and entered judgment in plaintiff's favor for $35,000 together with interest from September 1, 1970.

In addition to a complaint that it established losses in sales profits as a result of the termination of the exclusive at a rate of $10,000 per month rather than at the $5,000 rate determined by the court, plaintiff's major grievance is that in the Spring of 1969, at a time when defendant had already decided upon the termination of the distributorship but was secreting that plan from plaintiff, the latter undertook a major expansion of its warehouse facilities at substantial added operating expense. Plaintiff asserts that defendant knew of and encouraged this step, leading plaintiff to believe it was well warranted in view of the expected enlargement of the business of both of the contracting parties. On the basis of defendant's concealment of its intentions in the face of plaintiff's incurrence of a five year lease obligation for the new space, plaintiff asserts it is entitled to additional damages from defendant for the excess of its expense for the period of the lease over its operating expenses in its former headquarters—a loss allegedly attributable directly to defendant's breach of contract.

The trial court found that if ALCOA's decision, made in January or February of 1969, to enlarge the number of North Jersey distributors, had been promptly communicated to BAL's president, "it is unlikely that he would have signed the lease [for the new quarters] in April [1969] without first getting from [ALCOA] the assurance of continuance of the distributorship which he sought to get after the lease was signed". The court further found that all the circumstances surrounding the defendant's attitude to and treatment of plaintiff preceding and attending the disruption of the contractual arrangement "bespeak a certain hypocrisy as well as ruthlessness on the part of [ALCOA] toward its distributor of many years". The court further "surmised" that the reason defendant had concealed during the year 1969 its intention to terminate plaintiff's exclusive even though it had arrived at that intent before plaintiff entered into the new lease in 1969 was "that the men at [ALCOA] in charge of sales thought a period of secrecy ending with a sudden announcement to Mr. Diamond (plaintiff's president) of the accomplished fact of new distributors would avoid any risk of cooling plaintiff's interest in selling ALCOA products during the several months before the new distributors were named and made ready to go". Indeed, defendant's salesman induced plaintiff in January 1970, just before the announcement of the termination of the exclusive, to order $150,000 worth of merchandise—a very heavy order for that time of year.

In fixing seven months as a reasonable period of notice of termination of the exclusive agreement the trial court stated that the criterion for such a period of notice is the amount of time the notified party needs to make adjustments and to plan and arrange for business activities to replace those which are to be eliminated. However, the court apparently placed little if any weight on the circumstances of the new lease as an element going to the reasonableness of the period for notice of termination, although it stated that the lease was a "factor" for consideration. It pointed out that the decision to undertake the lease was plaintiff's and that plaintiff was able to use the space to store merchandise other than that purchased from defendant as well as defendant's lines.

Our review of the record leads us to concur in the trial court's holding that there was a valid distributorship agreement terminable only on reasonable notice. . . . Plaintiff's contention that the agreement was not terminable at all without "cause" based on the recent holding of this court in Shell Oil Co. v. Marinello, 63 N.J. 402, 307 A.2d 598 (1973), is without merit. The "franchise" agreement here is in no sense comparable with that which produced the holding of non-terminability in Shell.

However, we are constrained to differ with the trial court's assessment of seven months as an adequate period for notice of termination of this agreement. It may be true that defendant ordinarily would be under no strictly legal obligation to inform plaintiff that it was about to terminate its exclusive distributorship although it knew that in all probability plaintiff was enlarging its plant upon an assumption of the continuation of the business arrangement for the indefinite future. However, we have been at pains recently to point out that "[i]n every contract there is an implied covenant that 'neither party shall do anything which will have the effect of destroying or injuring the right of the other party to receive the fruits of the contract; in other words, in every contract there exists an implied covenant of good faith and fair dealing.'" Association Group Life, Inc. v. Catholic War Vets. of U.S., 61 N.J. 150, 153, 293 A.2d 382, 384 (1972). . . . [In that case,] we distinguished between an absence of literal violation of a contract and the breach of the implied covenant of good faith therein which could give rise to the sanction of damages. . . .

So, too, here. While the contractual relation of manufacturer and exclusive territorial distributor continued between the parties an obligation of reciprocal good-faith dealing similarly persisted between them. In such circumstances defendant's selfish withholding from plaintiff of its intention seriously to impair its distributorship although knowing plaintiff was embarking on an investment substantially predicated upon its continuation constituted a breach of the implied covenant of dealing in good faith of which we have spoken. As such it must be given substantial weight in determining the reasonableness of a period of notice of termination of the distributorship.

We cannot, however, agree with plaintiff that the period should encompass the remaining 4½ years of the lease as of the date of breach. The evidence justifies the conclusion that the prospects were fair for ultimate utilization to a substantial extent of the expanded warehouse space for new business plaintiff was able to obtain after defendant's breach or for other means of mitigating that phase of the damage attributable to defendant's conduct.

Exercising our original fact finding jurisdiction in order to bring this litigation to a close, it is our determination that a reasonable period of notice of termination of the distributorship, under all the circumstances, would have been 20 months.

Moreover, we find unwarranted the trial court's determination of plaintiff's monthly losses of profits of sales at $5,000 in the face of apparently unchallenged proofs by plaintiff, accepted by the court, that the damage figures were about $10,000 monthly. . . . [A]llowing for the trial court's feel for the credibility of the pertinent proofs, and taking into account what we have just said, we are led to fix the plaintiff's monthly losses at $7,500, or a total for the 20 months of $150,000, with interest from October 1, 1971 (20 months after breach).

. . . .

On defendant's appeal the judgment is affirmed, with costs. On plaintiff's appeal the judgment is modified in accordance with this opinion, with costs to plaintiff.

———

§ 5. Express Conditions

Contractual duties take the form of promises—commitments by each of the parties to do, or not do, something—and many contract terms consequently are in the form of promises. A contract provision may also contain a condition—specification of an event (a condition) that may or may not occur, and on which contractual duties may depend. Consider the following hypothetical examples:

- A construction company's duty to perform (begin building) is *subject to* a favorable ruling at an upcoming meeting of the metropolitan planning commission.
- Under a securities purchase agreement, the parties' transfer obligations are *contingent on* an expert's determination that the purchase will generate favorable tax consequences for both parties.
- A home buyer's duty to close on a purchase is *conditional on* the buyer being able to locate a 30-year mortgage at 6% with no points.
- An insurance company has a duty to pay the insured for a covered occurrence, *provided that* the insured files a claim within 60 days after the insured event.

In the examples above, a binding contract exists (the parties have committed themselves to the agreement) but the condition included in the contract terms means that some (or all) contractual duties may not be owed because the specified triggering circumstance may not occur.

> **Make the Connection**
>
> As noted earlier in this chapter (page 754), a condition for contract performance is distinct from a condition for contract formation. Only the former is a term of the contract.

Contracts may contain *express* conditions, through which the parties *explicitly* specify connections between promises and conditions. This section considers such express conditions—how to identify them, how they operate, and when they may be excused. Sets of promises within a contract are often also linked through the operation of "implied (or constructive) conditions," conditions that are not explicitly articulated by the parties but that are implicit in the expectations regarding the order of performance. For example, a construction contract contains promises by (1) a contractor to build a specified structure and (2) a home owner to pay for the construction work. In the absence of express language of condition, the contract will likely be interpreted to include an implied condition that the contractor must perform its obligations before the home owner is obligated to pay. Implied conditions reflect judgments about the implied order of performance (whether duties by one party must be performed before the other party is required to perform) and so will be treated in Chapter 8, when other issues related to contract performance are addressed.

A condition may be called a "condition precedent" or a "condition subsequent" depending upon whether it triggers a duty (that is, the duty does not exist unless the condition occurs) or instead terminates a duty (that is, the duty exists but is extinguished if the condition *does not* occur). The Restatement terminology differs: It does not use the term "condition subsequent" but instead refers to an "event that terminates a duty."*

The examples in the list above (the construction company's duty to build, the parties' duty to transfer securities, the home buyer's duty to close, and the insurance company's duty to pay) are all subject to conditions precedent because the associated duty is not owed unless the condition occurs. An insurer's obligation is often articulated, instead, as a condition subsequent: the insurance company has a duty to pay upon the happening of a contingency (e.g., a death) but the duty to pay is terminated if the insured individual does not file a claim within a specified number of days after the loss-causing event.

A condition may be a condition precedent or condition subsequent depending upon how it is articulated, as the last example suggests. The major consequence of identifying it as one or the other is evidentiary: the plaintiff has the duty of establishing the existence of a condition precedent to the defendant's contract duty while the defendant has the duty of establishing the existence of a condition subsequent that would extinguish its duty of performance.

---

* Restatement (Second) §§ 224, 230.

§ 5.1. Identifying and Enforcing Express Conditions

> **Reading the Law Critically:**
> *Morrison, Internatio-Rotterdam, Renovest,* **and** *Peacock*
>
> As you read each of the next three cases, consider these questions:
>
> 1. How does the court distinguish a "promise" from a "condition"? What happens if a contractual promise is not performed? How is this different from what happens if a condition is not satisfied? What effect, if any, does this distinction have on the resolution of the case?
>
> 2. Does the court conclude that the contract clause at issue established a condition? Why or why not? Is it a question of fact or of law?
>
> 3. A contract term can be both a condition *and* a promise. If the contract term at issue in the case is a condition, is it also a promise? Why or why not? If it is also a promise, what effect, if any, does this characteristic have on the resolution of the case?

Morrison v. Bare

JACK W. MORRISON, JR., Plaintiff-Appellant

v.

JONAS BARE, et al., Defendants-Appellees

Court of Appeals of Ohio
2007 WL 4415307 (Ohio Ct. App. Dec. 19, 2007)

DICKINSON, Judge.

INTRODUCTION

Jack W. Morrison Jr. is in the business of buying houses, refurbishing them, and renting them to college students. Tom Campensa, a real estate agent, showed Mr. Morrison a house owned by Jonas Bare. Mr. Morrison noticed a sticker on the furnace that indicated it had a cracked heat exchanger. After checking with Mr. Bare, Mr. Campensa told Mr. Morrison that the furnace had been repaired in 2004. Mr. Morrison executed a contract to purchase the house, but included a "special condition" in the contract that Mr. Bare would provide him a copy of the 2004 furnace repair bill within 14 days. Mr. Bare supplied a copy of a 2004 bill for repairs, but those repairs did not include replacing the heat exchanger. Instead of closing on the house, Mr. Morrison sued Mr. Bare for specific performance and breach of contract and sued Mr. Bare, Mr. Campensa, and Mr. Campensa's real estate agency for fraud. The trial court granted summary judgment to all three defendants, and Mr. Morrison appealed. His sole assignment of error is that the trial court incorrectly granted the defendants summary judgment. This court affirms the trial court's judgment because: (1) Mr. Morrison neither performed his part of the contract nor showed his "readiness and ability" to do so; (2) the requirement that Mr. Bare provide a bill showing that the heat exchanger was repaired was a condition for Mr. Morrison's performance, not a promise; and (3) Mr. Morrison did not justifiably rely upon Mr. Campensa's statement that the heat exchanger had been repaired.

BACKGROUND

Mr. Morrison noticed a for-sale sign on the house at issue in this case and told Mr. Campensa he would like to look at it. Mr. Campensa walked though the house with Mr. Morrison and Mr. Morrison's father. The house was in disrepair, and the utilities were disconnected. During the walkthrough, Mr. Morrison noticed a sticker on the furnace that indicated it had a cracked heat exchanger. When he was deposed, he said the sticker had caused him concern because he knew that a cracked heat exchanger meant the furnace would have to be replaced. He further testified that he questioned Mr. Campensa about the heat exchanger and Mr. Campensa said that he would check with the seller, Mr. Bare, to see whether it had been fixed.

At some point after the walkthrough, Mr. Campensa talked to Mr. Bare about the furnace. Mr. Campensa testified that he told Mr. Bare that the furnace had a sticker on it indicating that it had a cracked heat exchanger and that Mr. Bare told him the furnace had been repaired. Mr. Bare testified that he did not recall whether Mr. Campensa had specifically mentioned the cracked heat exchanger, but that he had told Mr. Campensa the furnace had been repaired. Either way, Mr. Morrison and Mr. Campensa agree that Mr. Campensa told Mr. Morrison that the heat exchanger had been repaired.

Mr. Morrison did a second walkthrough of the house, this time with an inspector. He testified that his purpose for having the inspector look at the house with him was to try to estimate the cost of needed repairs and to "generally just look [] around the property." The utilities were still off at the time of his second walkthrough. During the second walkthrough, Mr. Morrison concluded that the kitchen floor would have to be replaced. He and his inspector also noted some problems with windows and drywall. They looked at the sticker on the furnace, but did not attempt to independently determine whether the heat exchanger had been repaired.

Following his second walkthrough, Mr. Morrison made a written offer to purchase the house for $40,000, using a form real estate purchase agreement. The form included a provision permitting Mr. Morrison to have the house inspected and, if not satisfied, to notify Mr. Bare within fourteen days of the date of the agreement. If any unsatisfactory conditions could not be resolved, Mr. Morrison could void the agreement or accept the property in its "as is" condition. The form further provided that, if Mr. Morrison did not have the home inspected or did not notify Mr. Bare of any unsatisfactory conditions, he would take the property in its "as is" condition.

Under the heading "Special Conditions," Mr. Morrison wrote: "Seller to supply buyer with copy of furnace repair bill from 2004 within 14 days." Mr. Campensa acknowledged at his deposition that the purpose of the "special condition" was to allow Mr. Morrison to satisfy himself that the heat exchanger had been repaired. At the same time he signed the written offer, Mr. Morrison also signed a property disclosure form in which he acknowledged that he was purchasing the property "as is."

Four days after he made his written offer, Mr. Morrison signed an amendment to that offer, removing his right to inspect the property. The amendment further provided that Mr. Morrison recognized that neither Mr. Bare nor Mr. Campensa was warranting the property in any manner:

> In exercising or waiving their right to inspect, the Buyer(s) are not relying upon any representation about the property made by the Seller(s), Broker(s), Agent(s), other than those representations specified in the purchase agreement. The Buyer(s) understand that the Seller(s), Broker(s), Agent(s), and/or inspector(s) do not warrant or guarantee the condition of the property in any manner whatsoever.

Three days later, Mr. Bare signed both the form purchase agreement and the amendment, thereby accepting Mr. Morrison's offer to purchase the house.

Prior to the date set for closing, Mr. Campensa obtained a copy of the 2004 furnace repair bill. That bill indicated that repairs totaling $234 had been made to the furnace, but that the heat exchanger had not been repaired. In fact, it included a quote to replace the furnace for $1600 and a notation that, if a new furnace was installed within 30 days, the $234 for repairs would be deducted from the cost of the new furnace.

Mr. Campensa telephoned Mr. Morrison and told him that the heat exchanger had not been repaired. At that point, Mr. Morrison told Mr. Campensa that he would close on the house only if Mr. Bare either replaced the furnace or reduced

will only buy if none replaced w parts for furnace

the purchase price in an amount equal to what it would cost to replace the furnace. Mr. Bare was unwilling to do either.

Mr. Campensa sent Mr. Morrison a copy of the bill, along with a proposed addendum to the purchase agreement. The proposed addendum provided that Mr. Morrison agreed to accept the property with the furnace "in its as is condition and assume all responsibility for its repair and/or replacement." Mr. Morrison refused to execute the proposed addendum.

Prior to the date set for closing, Mr. Morrison filed his complaint in this case. Mr. Bare subsequently sold the house to another purchaser, who refurbished it and rented it to college students.

THIS COURT'S STANDARD OF REVIEW

Mr. Morrison's sole assignment of error is that the trial court incorrectly granted the defendants summary judgment. In reviewing an order granting summary judgment, this Court applies the same test a trial court is required to apply in the first instance: whether there are any genuine issues of material fact and whether the moving party is entitled to judgment as a matter of law. *Parenti v. Goodyear Tire & Rubber Co.*, 66 Ohio App.3d 826, 829 (1990).

MR. MORRISON'S CONTRACT CLAIMS

. . . .

By his second cause of action, Mr. Morrison sought damages for breach of contract. Mr. Bare has argued that the "special condition" was satisfied when he provided Mr. Morrison a copy of the 2004 bill for repairs to the furnace, even though, instead of showing that the heat exchanger had been repaired, it showed that it had not been repaired.

produced bill, but showed opposite of expected

There can be no doubt that, in order to satisfy the "special condition" that Mr. Morrison included in his offer, the repair bill had to show that the heat exchanger had been repaired. Mr. Campensa, who was Mr. Bare's agent, acknowledged that the purpose of the "special condition" was to allow Mr. Morrison to satisfy himself that the heat exchanger had been fixed:

Q. All right. On line 103 it says, "Seller to supply buyer with copy of furnace repair bill from 2004 within 14 days," correct?
A. Correct.
Q. Why was that provision put in the contract?
A. Because there was the potential that that was cracked in there was a cracked thing and Jack wanted to know if it was fixed or not.

Q. Okay. Because you believed it had been repaired based on your conversation with Jonas Bare, correct?

A. Yes.

Q. And you had told Jack that it had been repaired, did you not?

A. Yes.

Q. So Jack wanted to make sure as part of this deal that that furnace had already been repaired, correct?

A. Correct.

Mr. Bare's argument that he satisfied the condition by supplying a bill showing that the heat exchanger had not been repaired is, at best, disingenuous. Both parties knew at the time they entered the contract that the bill Mr. Bare needed to supply to satisfy the "special condition" was a bill showing that the heat exchanger had been repaired.

That, however, does not mean that Mr. Bare breached the purchase agreement by not delivering a bill that showed the heat exchanger had been repaired and by not replacing the furnace or lowering the purchase price. To begin with, the contract does not include a promise by Mr. Bare that, if the heat exchanger was not repaired in 2004, he would replace the furnace or reduce the purchase price. Further, the "special condition" that Mr. Morrison included in the contract was just that, a condition, not a promise:

> [P]romise and condition are very clearly different in character. One who makes a promise thereby expresses an intention that some future performance will be rendered and gives assurance of its rendition to the promisee. Whether the promise is express or implied, there must be either words or conduct by the promisor by the interpretation of which the court can discover promissory intention; a condition is a fact or an event and is not an expression of intention or an assurance. A promise in a contract creates a legal duty in the promisor and a right in the promisee; the fact or event constituting a condition creates no right or duty and is merely a limiting or modifying factor.

8 Catherine M.A. McCauliff, *Corbin On Contracts,* Section 30.12 (rev. ed.1999).

Mr. Campensa told Mr. Morrison that the heat exchanger had been repaired. Mr. Morrison made his offer to purchase the house contingent upon receiving proof that it had been:

> In contract law, "condition" is an event, other than the mere lapse of time, that is not certain to occur but must occur to *activate* an existing contractual duty, unless the condition is excused. The fact or event

properly called a condition occurs during the *performance* stage of a contract, i.e., after the contract is formed and prior to its discharge.

John Edward Murray Jr., *Murray on Contracts,* Section 99B (4th ed.2001) (emphasis in original); Restatement (Second) of Contracts, Section 224 (1981). While the failure to perform a promise is a breach of contract, the failure to satisfy a condition is not:

> A promise is always made by the act or acts of one of the parties, such acts being words or other conduct expressing intention. A fact can be made to operate as a condition only by the agreement of both parties or by the construction of the law. The purpose of a promise is to create a duty in the promisor. The purpose of constituting some fact as a condition is always the postponement or discharge of an instant duty (or other specified legal relation). The non-fulfillment of a promise is called a breach of contract, and creates in the other party a secondary right to damages. It is the failure to perform a legal duty. The non-occurrence of a condition will prevent the existence of a duty in the other party; but it may not create any remedial rights and duties at all, and it will not unless someone has promised that it shall occur.

Corbin on Contracts, at Section 30.12.

The fact that, to satisfy the "special condition," Mr. Bare would have had to do something (supply the bill showing that the heat exchanger had been repaired) did not mean that it was a promise rather than a condition. A condition can be an act to be done by one of the parties to the contract:

> Virtually any act or event may constitute a condition. The event may be an act to be performed or forborne by one of the parties to the contract, an act to be performed or forborne by a third party, or some fact or event over which neither party, or any other party, has any control.

Murray on Contracts, at Section 99C. In this case, Mr. Bare had partial control over the condition. Even if he had a bill showing that the heat exchanger had been repaired in 2004, he could have chosen not to deliver it to Mr. Morrison, in which case the condition would not have been satisfied. It also, however, was partially out of his control. Since the heat exchanger had not been repaired in 2004, he was unable to satisfy the condition. The material part of the condition was that Mr. Morrison had to be satisfied that the heat exchanger had been repaired.

Section 225 of the Restatement (Second) of Contracts (1981) describes the consequences of the non-occurrence of a condition:

> (1) Performance of a duty subject to a condition cannot become due unless the condition occurs or its non-occurrence is excused.

(2) Unless it has been excused, the non-occurrence of a condition discharges the duty when the condition can no longer occur.

(3) Non-occurrence of a condition is not a breach by a party unless he is under a duty that the condition occur.

In this case, Mr. Morrison's duty to pay the purchase price did not come due because Mr. Bare could not produce a 2004 bill showing that the heat exchanger had been repaired. Once it became clear that it was impossible for Mr. Bare to produce such a bill, Mr. Morrison could have excused the condition and closed on the property. Alternatively, he could have treated his duty to close as discharged and the contract terminated:

> [I]f a time comes when it is too late for the condition to occur, the obligor is entitled to treat its duty as discharged and the contract as terminated.

II E. Allan Farnsworth, *Farnsworth on Contracts,* Section 8.3 (3rd ed. 2004).

By informing Mr. Campensa that he was unwilling to close on the house unless Mr. Bare replaced the furnace or reduced the purchase price, Mr. Morrison chose to treat his duty to pay the original purchase price as discharged and the contract as terminated. His proposal to go forward under different conditions was, in effect, an offer to enter into a new contract; a new contract that Mr. Bare was free to reject, which he did.

Upon the failure of the "special condition" that he included in the real estate purchase agreement, Mr. Morrison treated the agreement as terminated, as he was entitled to do. The failure of the "special condition" was not a breach of contract.

There are no genuine issues of material fact, and Mr. Bare is entitled to judgment as a matter of law on Mr. Morrison's demand for specific performance and on his breach of contract claim. To the extent Mr. Morrison's assignment of error is addressed to the trial court's summary judgment on his contract claims, it is overruled.

. . . .

III.

Mr. Morrison's assignment of error is overruled. The judgment of the Summit County Common Pleas Court is affirmed.

Judgment affirmed.

———————

Internatio-Rotterdam, Inc. v. River Brand Rice Mills, Inc.

INTERNATIO-ROTTERDAM, INC., Plaintiff-Appellant

v.

RIVER BRAND RICE MILLS, INC., Defendant-Appellee

United States Court of Appeals Second Circuit
259 F.2d 137 (2d Cir. 1958)

HINCKS, Circuit Judge.

The defendant-appellee, a processor [and seller] of rice, in July 1952 entered into an agreement with the plaintiff-appellant, an exporter [and buyer of rice], for the sale of 95,600 pockets of rice. The terms of the agreement, evidenced by a purchase memorandum, indicated that the price per pocket was to be "$8.25 F.A.S. Lake Charles and/or Houston, Texas"; that shipment was to be "December, 1952, with two weeks call from buyer"; and that payment was to be by "irrevocable letter of credit to be opened immediately payable against" dock receipts and other specified documents.

In the fall, the appellant, which had already committed itself to supplying this rice to a Japanese buyer, was unexpectedly confronted with United States export restrictions upon its December shipments and was attempting to get an export license from the government. December is a peak month in the rice and cotton seasons in Louisiana and Texas, and the appellee became concerned about shipping instructions under the contract, since congested conditions prevailed at both the mills and the docks. The appellee seasonably elected to deliver 50,000 pockets at Lake Charles and on December 10 it received from the appellant instructions for the Lake Charles shipments. Thereupon it promptly began shipments to Lake Charles which continued until December 23, the last car at Lake Charles being unloaded on December 31.

What's That?

"F.A.S" stands for "Free Along Side" and "F.A.S. Lake Charles and/or Houston" means the seller is required to deliver the goods to a named port (in Lake Charles or Houston, Texas) alongside a vessel designated by the buyer. "Alongside" means that the goods are within reach of the ship's lifting tackle. "Dock receipts" are documents issued by an ocean carrier to acknowledge receipt of freight. The contract required Internatio-Rotterdam to obtain financing that guaranteed payment to River Brand once it presented the dock receipts evidencing its delivery of the goods

December 17 was the last date in December which would allow appellee the two week period provided in the contract for delivery of the rice to the ports and ships designated. Prior thereto, the appellant had been having difficulty obtaining either a ship or a dock in this busy season in Houston. On December 17, the appellee had still received no shipping instructions for the 45,600 pockets destined for Houston. On the morning of the 18th, the appellee rescinded the contract for the Houston shipments, although continuing to make the Lake Charles deliveries. It is clear that one of the reasons for the prompt cancellation of the contract was the rise in market price of rice from $8.25 per pocket, the contract price, to $9.75. The appellant brought this suit for refusal to deliver the Houston quota.

> **FYI**
> It appears that under the contract provisions, the seller had the option of specifying the port for delivery (Lake Charles or Houston) but the buyer had to issue the call for the goods to be delivered and had to identify the ship alongside which the goods would be delivered.

. . . .

The area of contest is also considerably reduced by the appellant's candid concession that the appellee's duty to ship, by virtue of the two-week notice provision, did not arise until two weeks after complete shipping instructions had been given by the appellant. Thus on brief the appellant says: "we concede (as we have done from the beginning) that on a fair interpretation of the contract appellant had a duty to instruct appellee by December 17, 1952 as to the place to which it desired appellee to ship . . . and that, being late with its instructions in this respect, appellant could not have demanded delivery (at either port) until sometime after December 31, 1952." This position was taken, of course, with a view to the contract provision for shipment "December, 1952": a two-week period ending December 31 would begin to run on December 17. But although appellant concedes that the two weeks' notice to which appellee was entitled could not be shortened by the failure to give shipping instructions on or before December 17, it stoutly insists that upon receipt of shipping instructions subsequent to December 17 the appellee thereupon became obligated to deliver within two weeks thereafter. We do not agree.

It is plain that a giving of the notice by the appellant was a condition precedent to the appellee's duty to ship. Corbin on Contracts, Vol. 3, § 640. Id. § 724. Obviously, the appellee could not deliver free alongside ship, as the contract required, until the appellant identified its ship and its location. Jacksboro Stone Co. v. Fairbanks Co., 48 Tex.Civ.App. 639, 107 S.W. 567; Fortson Grocery Co. v. Pritchard Rice Milling Co., Tex.Civ.App., 220 S.W. 1116. Thus the giving of shipping instructions was what Professor Corbin would classify as a "promissory condition": the appellant promised to give the notice and the appellee's duty to ship was conditioned on the receipt of the notice. Op. cit. § 633, p. 523, § 634, footnote 38. The crucial question is whether that condition was performed. And that depends on whether the appellee's duty of shipment was conditioned on notice on or before December 17, so that the appellee would have two weeks wholly within December within which to perform, or whether, as we understand the appellant to contend, the appellant could perform the condition by giving the notice later in December, in which case the appellee would be under a duty to ship within two weeks thereafter. The answer depends upon the proper interpretation of the contract: if the contract properly interpreted made shipment in December of the essence then the failure to give the notice on or before December 17 was nonperformance by the appellant of a condition upon which the appellee's duty to ship in December depended.

In the setting of this case, we hold that the provision for December delivery went to the essence of the contract. In support of the plainly stated provision of the contract there was evidence that the appellee's mills and the facilities appurtenant thereto were working at full capacity in December when the rice market was at peak activity and that appellee had numerous other contracts in January as well as in December to fill. It is reasonable to infer that in July, when the contract was made, each party wanted the protection of the specified delivery period; the appellee so that it could schedule its production without undue congestion of its storage facilities and the appellant so that it could surely meet commitments which it in turn should make to its customers. There was also evidence that prices on the rice market were fluctuating. In view of this factor it is not reasonable to infer that when the contract was made in July for December delivery, the parties intended that the appellant should have an option exercisable subsequent to December 17 to postpone delivery until January. **United Irr. Co. v. Carson Petroleum Co., Tex.Civ.App., 283 S.W. 692; Steiner v. United States, D.C., 36 F.Supp. 496.** That in effect would have given the appellant an option to postpone its breach of the contract, if one should then be in prospect, to a time when, so far as could have been foreseen when the contract was made, the price of rice might be falling. A postponement in such circumstances would inure to the disadvantage of the appellee who was given no reciprocal option. Further indication that December delivery was of the essence is found in the letter of credit which was provided for in the contract and established by the appellant. Under this letter, the bank was authorized to pay appellee only for deliveries "during December, 1952." It thus appears that the appellant's interpretation of the contract, under which the appellee would be obligated, upon receipt of shipping instructions subsequent to December 17, to deliver in January, would deprive the appellee of the security for payment of the purchase price for which it had contracted.

Since, as we hold, December delivery was of the essence, notice of shipping instructions on or before December 17 was not merely a "duty" of the appellant—

as it concedes: it was a condition precedent to the performance which might be required of the appellee. The nonoccurrence of that condition entitled the appellee . . . to treat its contractual obligations as discharged. Corbin on Contracts, §§ 640, 724 and 1252; Williston on Sales, §§ 452, 457; Restatement, Contracts, § 262; National Commodity Corp. v. American Fruit Growers, 6 Terry 169, 45 Del. 169, 70 A.2d 28; Alpena Portland Cement Co. v. Backus, 8 Cir., 156 F. 944; Jungmann & Co. v. Atterbury Bros., Inc., 249 N.Y. 119, 163 N.E. 123; Arnolt Corp. v. Stansen Corp., 7 Cir., 189 F.2d 5. On December 18th the appellant unequivocally exercised its right to rescind. Having done so, its obligations as to the Houston deliveries under the contract were at an end. And of course its obligations would not revive thereafter when the appellant finally succeeded in obtaining an export permit, a ship and a dock and then gave shipping instructions; when it expressed willingness to accept deliveries in January; or when it accomplished a "liberalization" of the outstanding letter of credit whereby payments might be made against simple forwarder's receipts instead of dock receipts.

. . . .

Affirmed.

Renovest Co. v. Hodges Development Corp.

RENOVEST CO., Plaintiff-Appellant

v.

HODGES DEVELOPMENT CORP., Defendant-Appellee

Supreme Court of New Hampshire
600 A.2d 448 (N.H. 1991)

HORTON, Justice.

The plaintiff has taken appeal from the Superior Court's order granting the defendant's motion to dismiss made at the close of the plaintiff's case during a jury-waived trial. . . . We find no errors and affirm.

The plaintiff, Renovest Company (Renovest), entered into a purchase and sale agreement with the defendant, Hodges Development Corporation (Hodges), on June 30, 1986, for a two-building apartment complex in Franklin. The agreed-upon purchase price was $1,476,000 and the initial deposit paid to Hodges at the signing of the contract was $65,000. The contract specified that the deposit would serve as liquidated damages if Renovest failed to close on or before September 3, 1986.

Three conditions precedent to the buyer's obligation to perform were contained in the contract. At issue here are paragraph 3(b), relating to physical inspection of the property, and paragraph 3(d) relating to the buyer's obtaining financing at certain rates and terms. No portion of the contract stated expressly that time was of the essence. The provision relating to inspection called for the inspection to be completed within fourteen working days, and specified that if the inspection was unsatisfactory, the "Buyer shall have three (3) days from the date of completion of such inspection in which to notify Seller of his disapproval, and this Agreement shall be null and void and all deposits hereunder shall be refunded in full." The outside date on this condition was July 24. The financing provision contained a forty-five-day limit, after inspection of the seller's business records, in which the buyer was required to notify the seller of an intention to invoke the financing condition clause. Paragraph 9 of the contract required that all notices be given in writing.

Renovest first inspected the buildings on July 10, 1986, sending a partner and a building inspector. It was during this inspection that Renovest discovered a crack in the exterior of one building, and it consulted with Hodges the next day. Whether Hodges agreed to extend the deadline in order to allow further inspection by Renovest is disputed. Further investigation was performed on July 17 and 23 by another engineer, and his report on August 6 contained his opinion that the building would require "underpinning" of the foundation in order to prevent further settling of the building. Underpinning involves stabilization of the building's foundation. Based on this report, Renovest wrote to Hodges on August 7, terminating the transaction and demanding return of the $65,000 deposit. Hodges undertook its own engineering study, which commenced with borings on August 12 and culminated in an evaluation report dated August 26. This report described the cracking as cosmetic, found the problem building structurally sound, and rejected the need for underpinning. Hodges shared this report with Renovest.

Renovest did initially undertake to secure the financing by approaching four banks. Two of these, the Bank of New England and the Shawmut Bank, were favorably disposed toward the financing application, up to the time that Renovest notified them of the results of the engineer's report about the building's structural problems. Upon receipt of this information, the banks indicated they would not continue to process the loan applications until the issue of the building's structural soundness was resolved. Although time still remained in which to meet the financing deadline, Renovest never pursued the applications further. A second letter sent by Renovest to Hodges on August 12 asserted the failure to obtain financing, as well as an unsatisfactory result of the inspection of Hodges's books and records, as additional grounds for the termination of the contract. Renovest no longer asserts the books and records contingency as a ground for the termination.

At trial on its suit to obtain return of its deposit, Renovest presented three witnesses and introduced the deposition of a fourth witness. After Renovest rested, Hodges moved to dismiss, both orally and in writing, and the judge granted the motion based on the court's findings of fact. Rather than making a determination of whether the plaintiff established a *prima facie* case, the judge specifically concluded that Renovest's objection to the building's structure was untimely, and that Renovest prematurely terminated its attempts to obtain financing. He therefore ruled that the plaintiff had failed to carry its burden of proof, and granted the defendant's motion to dismiss. Renovest appeals the findings of the court, and asserts that, viewing the evidence presented to the judge in the light most favorable to it, Renovest had met its initial burden of presenting a *prima facie* case.

. . . .

II. Time of the Essence

In his order dismissing the complaint, the trial judge found that time was of the essence for the exercise of the rights under the conditions precedent. The judge based his conclusion on the strict time provisions applicable to performance of the conditions, concluding that these provisions required strict compliance with the timetables established. The court therefore determined that the late notification precluded the plaintiff's invoking its right to terminate the agreement under the physical inspection condition. The court apparently also determined that no waiver of the deadline occurred during the relevant period.

Renovest correctly asserts that ordinarily time is not made of the essence in a contract, absent some indication that the parties intended otherwise. Moore v. Sterling Warner Indus. Inv. Corp., 114 N.H. 520, 522, 323 A.2d 581, 583 (1974). The mere fact that a date is stated in the contract is not sufficient, by itself, to alter this rule. *Id.* Renovest argues that the issue must be resolved based on the evidence adduced at trial up to the point of the judge's dismissal, and that none of this evidence established that time was of the essence. Citing Allard & Geary, Inc. v. Faro, 122 N.H. 573, 448 A.2d 377 (1982) (evidence that word "before" was inserted by closing date, as well as that defendant orally informed buyer that time was crucial), Renovest asserts that the trial judge incorrectly applied our precedents to find sufficient indicia of such intent.

Renovest's argument is inapplicable in the present case, because the terms involved are express conditions precedent. The plaintiff's duty to perform under the contract was made "subject to" performance of these conditions. Where "the occurrence of a condition is required by the agreement of the parties, rather than as a matter of law, a rule of strict compliance traditionally applies." E.A. Farnsworth, *Contracts* § 8.3, at 544 (8th ed. 1982); *see also* 5 S. Williston, *Contracts*

§ 669 (3d ed. 1961). The reasoning behind this rule is that when the parties expressly condition their performance upon the occurrence or non-occurrence of an event, rather than simply including the event as one of the general terms of the contract, the parties' bargained-for expectation of strict compliance should be given effect. Therefore, absent waiver or extension by the defendant, written notification of disapproval of the building inspection was required to be given by Renovest no later than July 24. Lemay v. Rouse, 122 N.H. 349, 351–52, 444 A.2d 553, 555 (1982). The trial court's finding of absence of timely compliance with the building inspection condition is correct.

III. *Waiver of Terms*

Renovest further argues that the express condition's deadline for notification was waived by Hodges in the July 11 phone conversation. During this conversation, Hodges's vice president, Barry Sanborn, agreed with Renovest's suggestion that Renovest hire a structural engineer to conduct further inspection. Renovest takes this approval to be a waiver of the notification time limit. We disagree.

Make the Connection

The court here discusses the possibility of denying enforcement of a condition because the party protected by the condition waived the operation of the term. We have seen waiver operate to excuse enforcement of contract provisions in other contexts as well (see pages 132 and 635). Conditions may also be excused based on forfeiture, a topic discussed later in this chapter (page 871).

A finding of waiver must be "based upon an intention expressed in explicit language to forego a right, or upon conduct under the circumstances justifying an inference of a relinquishment of it." *Kilgore v. Association*, 78 N.H. 498, 502, 102 A. 344, 346 (1917). A waiver may be express or implied. Renovest does not assert an express waiver.

Whether an implied waiver occurred is a question of fact, and we will not overturn the trial judge's determination that no waiver occurred, unless such finding is clearly erroneous. *See D.M. Holden, Inc. v. Contractor's Crane Serv., Inc.*, 121 N.H. 831, 834, 435 A.2d 529, 531 (1981). Thomas Sheedy, one of the partners in Renovest, testified at trial that Hodges's acquiescence in the follow-up inspection left him with the impression that he would get an extension of time. Although Renovest did introduce evidence that Hodges suggested the hiring of a structural engineer, Hodges responds that this suggestion does not show an intent to extend the time limit, because there were still ten days remaining in which the inspection could be accomplished.

All the evidence presented by Renovest does not compel the trier of fact to believe the assertion that a waiver occurred. *See 93 Clearing House, Inc. v. Khoury*, 120 N.H. 346, 350, 415 A.2d 671, 674 (1980). The trier of fact may simply choose to disbelieve a witness. See id. The judge could have based his conclusion on the cross-examination of Mr. Sheedy . . . .

As it was Renovest's duty to establish a waiver, the judge was not obligated to wait for credible evidence that no waiver occurred. Viewing this evidence, we cannot conclude that the trial judge's finding was clearly erroneous.

IV. *Financing Condition*

Renovest asserts that it was unable to obtain financing for the project and, therefore, was excused from performing by paragraph 3(d). That paragraph, under the heading "Conditions Precedent to Buyers [sic] Obligation to Perform," reads:

> "d. This Agreement is subject to Buyer obtaining a written commitment for First Mortgage financing from a lending institution with the following terms.... The commitment to be obtained within 45 days from the date of Buyers [sic] receipt of the books and records. Buyer shall notify Seller in writing within 45 days from review of the books and records of his intention to exercise the right to terminate this Offer under this mortgage contingency clause."

We also reject Renovest's reliance upon this provision.

Under New Hampshire law, every contract contains an implied covenant of good faith performance and fair dealing. *Seaward Constr. Co. v. City of Rochester*, 118 N.H. 128, 129, 383 A.2d 707, 708 (1978). Reasonable efforts must be undertaken to secure financing. *Lach v. Cahill*, 138 Conn. 418, 422, 85 A.2d 481, 482 (1951). While initially Renovest met this duty, by initiating the loan process, its later conduct supports the trial judge's finding that performance of the agreement was not excused by Renovest's inability to obtain financing. Renovest asserts that it sought the financing required under the contract, but after making the lending institutions aware of the purported construction deficiencies, it assumed that financing would be unavailable.

The question whether any structural defects were material to financing rested solely with the banks. Having undertaken to secure financing, Renovest was committed to affirmatively seeking such financing, with activity "reasonably calculated to obtain the approval by action or expenditure not disproportionate in the circumstances." *Stabile v. McCarthy*, 336 Mass. 399, 404, 145 N.E.2d 821, 824 (1957). Reasonable efforts by Renovest were required to determine and communicate the accurate status of the observed building flaws. The evidence showed that the engineering report reflecting absence of structural defects was not shared with the interested banks. The record lends ample support to the trial court's finding that Renovest's attempts to secure financing were terminated prematurely.

. . . .

Based on this evidence, the trial judge could have concluded that Renovest failed to make reasonable efforts to obtain the loan, and further concluded, as did the loan officer, that Renovest did not really wish to proceed with the loan process. Although Renovest concluded that the banks would not give financing, based on its own engineer's report, the fact that Renovest was aware of Hodges's engineering report stating that the building was structurally sound, and yet did not submit this in support of its application, could support a conclusion that Renovest did not use all reasonable efforts to obtain financing.

. . . .

Affirmed.

Peacock Construction Co. v. Modern Air Conditioning, Inc.

PEACOCK CONSTRUCTION CO., Defendant-Petitioner

v.

MODERN AIR CONDITIONING, INC. and OVERLY MANUFACTURING CO.,
Plaintiffs-Respondents

Supreme Court of Florida
353 So. 2d 840 (Fla. 1977)

BOYD, Acting Chief Justice.

We issued an order allowing certiorari in these two causes because the decisions in them of the District Court of Appeal, Second District, conflict with the decision in Edward J. Gerrits, Inc. v. Astor Electric Service, Inc., 328 So.2d 522 (Fla.3d DCA 1976). The two causes have been consolidated for all appellate purposes in this Court because they involve the same issue. That issue is whether the plaintiffs, Modern Air Conditioning and Overly Manufacturing, were entitled to summary judgments against Peacock Construction Company in actions for breaches of identical contractual provisions.

I promise to pay once I get paid

Peacock Construction was the builder of a condominium project. Modern Air Conditioning subcontracted with Peacock to do the heating and air conditioning work and Overly Manufacturing subcontracted with Peacock to do the "rooftop swimming pool" work. Both written subcontracts provided that Peacock would make final payment to the subcontractors,

> "within 30 days after the completion of the work included in this sub-contract, written acceptance by the Architect and full payment therefor by the Owner."

Modern Air Conditioning and Overly Manufacturing completed the work specified in their contracts and requested final payment. When Peacock refused to make the final payments the two subcontractors separately brought actions in the Lee County Circuit Court for breach of contract. In both actions it was established that no deficiencies had been found in the completed work. But Peacock established that it had not received from the owner full payment for the subcontractors' work. And it defended on the basis that such payment was a condition which, by express term of the final payment provision, had to be fulfilled before it was obligated to perform under the contract. On motions by the plaintiffs, the trial judges granted summary judgments in their favor. The orders of judgment implicitly interpreted the contract not to require payment by the owner as a condition precedent to Peacock's duty to perform.

The Second District Court of Appeal affirmed the lower court's judgment in the appeal brought by [Peacock]. In so doing it adopted the view of the majority of jurisdictions in this country that provisions of the kind disputed here do not set conditions precedent but rather constitute absolute promises to pay, fixing payment by the owner as a reasonable time for when payment to the subcontractor is to be made. When the judgment in the *Overly Manufacturing* case reached the Second District Court, *Modern Air Conditioning* had been decided and the judgment, therefore, was affirmed on the authority of the latter decision. These two decisions plainly conflict with *Gerrits*, supra.

In *Gerrits*, the Court had summarily ordered judgment for the plaintiff/sub-contractor against the defendant/general contractor on a contractual provision for payment to the subcontractor which read,

> "The money to be paid in current funds and at such times as the General Contractor receives it from the Owner."

Id. at 523.

In its review of the judgment, the Third District Court of Appeal referred to the fundamental rule of interpretation of contracts that it be done in accordance with the intention of the parties. Since the defendant had introduced below the issue of intention, a material issue, and since the issue was one that could be resolved through a factual determination by the jury, the Third District reversed the summary judgment and remanded for trial.

Peacock urges us to adopt *Gerrits* as the controlling law in this State. It concedes that the Second District's decisions are backed by the weight of authority. But it argues that they are incorrect because the issue of intention is a factual one which should be resolved after the parties have had an opportunity to present evidence on it. Peacock urges, therefore, that the causes be remanded for trial. If there is produced no evidence that the parties intended there be condition precedents, only then, says Peacock, should the judge, by way of a directed verdict for the subcontractors, be allowed to take the issue of intention from the jury.

The contractual provisions in dispute here are susceptible to two interpretations. They may be interpreted as setting a condition precedent or as fixing a reasonable time for payment. The provision disputed in *Gerrits* is susceptible to the same two interpretations. The questions presented by the conflict between these decisions, then, are whether ambiguous contractual provisions of the kind disputed here may be interpreted only by the factfinder, usually the jury, or if they should be interpreted as a matter of law by the court, and if so what interpretation they should be given.

Although it must be admitted that the meaning of language is a factual question, the general rule is that interpretation of a document is a question of law rather than of fact. 4 Williston on Contracts, 3rd Ed., § 616. If an issue of contract interpretation concerns the intention of parties, that intention may be determined from the written contract, as a matter of law, when the nature of the transaction lends itself to judicial interpretation. A number of courts, with whom we agree, have recognized that contracts between small subcontractors and general contractors on large construction projects are such transactions. Cf. **Thos. J. Dyer Co. v. Bishop International Engineering Co., 6 Cir., 303 F.2d 655 (1962).** The reason is that the relationship between the parties is a common one and usually their intent will not differ from transaction to transaction, although it may be differently expressed.

Think About It!

What policies support the competing rules being considered by the court? If you were the judge, which rule would you favor and why?

That intent in most cases is that payment by the owner to the general contractor is not a condition precedent to the general contractor's duty to pay the subcontractors. This is because small subcontractors, who must have payment for their work in order to remain in business, will not ordinarily assume the risk of the owner's failure to pay the general contractor. And this is the reason for the majority view in this country, which we now join.

Our decision to require judicial interpretation of ambiguous provisions for final payment in subcontracts in favor of subcontractors should not be regarded as anti-general contractor. It is simply a recognition that this is the fairest way to deal with the problem. There is nothing in this opinion, however, to prevent parties to these contracts from shifting the risk of payment failure by the owner to the subcontractor. But in order to make such a shift the contract must unambiguously express that intention. And the burden of clear expression is on the general contractor.

Think About It!

How could the contractual language here have been clearer? What would you advise future subcontractor clients, in light of this ruling?

The decisions of the Second District Court of Appeal to affirm the summary judgments were correct. We adopt, therefore, these two decisions as the controlling law in Florida and we overrule *Gerrits*, to the extent it is inconsistent with this opinion.

The orders allowing certiorari in these two causes are discharged. It is so ordered.

---

§ 5.2. Conditions of Satisfaction

One particular kind of express condition that may be included in a contract is a provision making one party's contractual duty conditional on that party's (or a third party's) "satisfaction" with the other party's performance. For example, a contract for a commissioned painting might make the recipient's duty to pay dependent on his satisfaction with the painting the artist produces. Or an owner's duty to pay for construction work may be conditioned on the approval of an architect or engineer. While we know that a conditioned event must occur precisely as articulated in the condition, an additional question is raised by such "conditions of satisfaction": How is satisfaction of this particular condition to be judged? The next two cases consider that question.

Reading the Law Critically:
Hutton and *Morin Building Products, Inc.*

1. What are the alternative interpretations of a satisfaction clause suggested by these cases? On what basis should a court decide between those interpretations?

2. Do you agree with the courts' applications of the articulated guidelines for deciding which interpretation to follow?

3. What role do the contract clauses themselves play in the courts' determinations?

4. Should it make a difference whether it is one of the contract parties or a third party (for example, an architect) whose satisfaction is required before performance is due? Does it make a difference in either of these cases?

Hutton v. Monograms Plus, Inc.

DAVID HUTTON, Plaintiff-Appellee

v.

MONOGRAMS PLUS, INC., Defendant-Appellant

Court of Appeals of Ohio
604 N.E.2d 200 (Ohio Ct. App. 1992)

WOLFF, Judge.

Monogram Plus, Inc. ("MPI") appeals from a summary judgment rendered in favor of David D. Hutton. In granting the summary judgment, the trial court determined that, as a matter of law, a satisfaction clause contained in a franchise agreement executed by MPI and Hutton called for Hutton's subjective satisfaction as to what qualified as "suitable financing."

The following facts are largely undisputed.

On August 4, 1989, Hutton and MPI executed a franchise agreement wherein MPI sold a monogramming franchise to Hutton. Hutton purchased the MPI franchise for $25,000. The terms of the agreement specified that MPI granted a nonexclusive ten-year license to Hutton to operate an MPI store. Pursuant to the agreement, Hutton was obligated to market and promote the retail sale of monogrammed items such as T-shirts, fleece wear, and jackets. On August 17, 1989, Hutton and MPI executed an addendum to the franchise agreement. The addendum supplemented the franchise agreement, providing in part that if Hutton were "unable . . . to obtain financing suitable to him" within ninety days of signing the franchise agreement, he would then be entitled to a refund of the $25,000 franchise fee. Hutton was responsible for the drafting of the addendum.

There were two primary areas of expenditure involved in the funding of the monogramming enterprise: the "start up" costs, and the purchase or lease of a Meistergram 800 XLC computerized monogramming machine. The purchase or lease of the monogramming machine represented a critical component of the required financing because the entire operation revolved around the application of monograms to imprintable items of clothing.

After executing the franchise agreement and addendum, Hutton obtained a $26,000 loan from Star Bank to cover the start-up costs of the business operation. The loan was secured by a mortgage executed by Hutton and his wife Pamela against their residence.

To facilitate the lease or purchase of the monogramming machine, MPI issued a franchise offering circular to Hutton. The circular, which MPI was required to provide under Ohio law, estimated that the total cost of an MPI franchise varied between $32,420 and $36,720, with an additional $9,150 to $31,150 cost for construction. The fee paid by Hutton accounted for $25,000 of the $36,720 total estimated franchise cost. The circular also estimated that the monogramming machine could be leased for $520, excluding taxes, per month for sixty months, or purchased at a cost of $21,000.

After receiving the circular, Hutton spoke with MPI representative Pam Totty, who functioned as a liaison between Dennis Hanley, MPI's financial director, and MPI franchisees. One of Totty's duties in this capacity was to assist MPI franchisees in securing leases for monogramming equipment. On November 20, 1989, Totty notified Hutton that she had secured a sixty-month lease through United Leasing Corporation. The monthly lease payments totalled $751.01, excluding taxes, with a total equipment cost of $45,060.60 over the life of the lease. The lease also required Hutton to make a ten percent down payment on the purchase price, which was listed at $24,751. Since Hutton considered these terms to be substantially less advantageous than the terms offered in the MPI circular, he rejected the financing. He then requested Totty to submit his application to Trinity Leasing despite the fact that she had told him that he did not meet Trinity's minimum leasing qualifications. At Hutton's insistence, Totty submitted his application to Trinity, which subsequently rejected it due to Hutton's inadequate financial position. When Totty notified Hutton that the application had been rejected, she recommended that he pursue other avenues of financing. In order to help Hutton obtain financing from other sources, Dennis Hanley prepared a financial statement for Hutton which Hutton then submitted with a loan application to Society Bank in December 1989. This application was rejected because of insufficient collateral.

On January 1, 1990, Hutton wrote to Larry Meyer, MPI's president, requesting a refund of the $25,000 franchise fee due to the difficulty he had experienced in securing financing. This request was denied. On March 5, 1990, Hutton filed a three-count complaint against MPI. In the first count, Hutton sought to recover the franchise fee. . . .

MPI counterclaimed on April 9, 1990, alleging, *inter alia*, that Hutton had breached the franchise agreement by failing to perform his obligations pursuant to the franchise agreement. According to MPI, Hutton's breach caused MPI to lose the opportunity to offer Hutton's franchise to others as well as the loss of a weekly royalty fee of six percent of Hutton's gross sales and one percent of the gross revenues payable to MPI as an advertising fee. MPI also sought attorney fees to which it alleged it was entitled under the terms of the franchise agreement.

Hutton moved for summary judgment on June 1, 1990, arguing that the language of the addendum clearly and unambiguously gave him the sole right to determine what financing was suitable to him. He claimed that since he failed to find financing which was in fact suitable to him, he was entitled as a matter of law to the return of the $25,000 franchise fee. In support of his motion, Hutton offered his sworn affidavit as well as the notice of the rejection of his loan application by Society Bank and excerpts from MPI's franchise circular. In rebuttal, MPI offered the affidavits of Pam Totty, Dennis Hanley, and Roger Guertin, the vice-president of Trinity Leasing. MPI also attached a copy of Hutton's response to MPI's interrogatories, which Hutton had filed on June 21, 1991.

There was a dispute over whether Hutton's father-in-law, Charles Allport, was a potential source of financing. Interrogatory No. 9 requested Hutton to:

> "Describe in detail the terms and conditions of any financing agreements and/or arrangements, and/or any support agreements and/or arrangements, between yourself and Charles Allport."

Hutton responded that there was no such arrangement between himself and Allport. However, in Paragraph 5 of Dennis Hanley's affidavit, Hanley averred that Hutton had represented to him that if the $26,000 loan was insufficient, he could obtain whatever additional funds were needed from his father-in-law. Hanley also averred in Paragraph 6 that he had had various conversations with Allport wherein Allport referred to himself as an investor in Hutton's franchise. Hanley swore that

Allport's conduct was consistent with Hutton's representations that Allport would supply additional funding for the franchise if necessary.

The trial court entered judgment on August 3, 1991, granting Hutton's motion. . . .

Key to the trial court's determination was its finding that the language of the addendum was clear and unambiguous. Based on this finding the court concluded that:

> "The $25,000 franchise fee was refundable if within 90 days Plaintiff was unable to obtain financing suitable *to him*. Defendant chose to live with the subjective language employed in the agreement and did not specify any steps Plaintiff would have to take in order to satisfy the condition. The language did not require the Plaintiff to accept any available financing, nor did it require the Plaintiff to exhaust all possible options in an effort to obtain financing. As a consequence Defendant must live with the agreement entered. This Court finds that the Plaintiff's efforts to obtain financing were adequate pursuant to the terms of the agreement in that the first available financing method was clearly out of line with the terms suggested by the Defendant company. The second attempt to obtain financing with a firm which often participates in leasing agreements with franchisees of the Defendant rejected Plaintiff's application without consideration because the Plaintiff did not meet the necessary requirements. The third attempt Plaintiff made to obtain financing through a local bank was rejected because Plaintiff did not have enough collateral. Plaintiff is not required to search endlessly when it seems further efforts will meet with similar results."

MPI has appealed . . . .

MPI advances two arguments . . . .

I. THE ADDENDUM LANGUAGE IS AMBIGUOUS

MPI first argues that the language of the addendum was ambiguous wherein it predicated Hutton's right to a refund upon his ability to secure financing which was "suitable to him." According to MPI, these words were susceptible to three interpretations. "Suitable to him" could mean that the financing had to be "suitable as determined by Hutton," "suitable *for* Hutton," or "suitable for Hutton's needs." We agree with the trial court's holding that the language of the addendum created no ambiguity. However, this does not dispose of the appeal because a question of interpretation remains.

Contract clauses which make the duty of performance of one of the parties conditional upon his satisfaction are generally referred to as "satisfaction clauses." These clauses have been divided by the courts into two categories, and have been interpreted in accordance with the category. *Mattei v. Hopper* (1958), 51 Cal.2d 119, 121, 330 P.2d 625, 626.

Where the satisfaction clause requires satisfaction as to such matters as commercial value or quality, operative fitness, or mechanical utility, dissatisfaction cannot be claimed unreasonably. In these contracts, an objective standard is applied to the satisfaction clause and the test is whether the performance would satisfy a reasonable person. *Id.; Cranetex, Inc. v. Precision Crane & Rigging of Houston, Inc.* (1988), 760 S.W.2d 298, 301-302.

If, on the other hand, the satisfaction clause relates to matters involving fancy, personal taste, or judgment, then a subjective standard is applied, and the test is whether the party is actually satisfied. *Id.* Although application of a subjective standard to a satisfaction clause would seem to give the obligor virtually unlimited latitude to avoid his duty of performance, such is not the case. In these situations, courts impose the limitation that the obligor act in good faith. *Mattei, supra,* 51 Cal.2d at 121, 330 P.2d at 626. Thus, under the subjective standard, the promisor can avoid the contract as long as he is genuinely, albeit unreasonably, dissatisfied. Which standard applies in a given transaction is a matter of the actual or constructive intent of the parties, which, in turn, is a function of the express language of the contract, or the subject matter of the contract. *Kadner v. Shields* (1971), 20 Cal.App.3d 251, 262-263, 97 Cal.Rptr. 742, 751-752.

. . . .

. . . [A] subjective standard governs when the language of the contract expressly calls for the application of such a standard. An example of such language is found in *Ard Dr. Pepper Bottling Co. v. Dr. Pepper Co.* (C.A.5, 1953), 202 F.2d 372.

Ard dealt with a satisfaction clause contained in a commercial licensing agreement which granted to Ard the exclusive license to bottle Dr. Pepper soda in a designated territory. The satisfaction clause at issue reserved Dr. Pepper Co.'s right to rescind Ard's license if Ard did not faithfully promote the sale of the Dr. Pepper product to Dr. Pepper Co.'s satisfaction. The satisfaction clause at issue was as follows:

> "'(e) To at all times loyally and faithfully promote the sale of and secure thorough distribution of Dr. Pepper throughout every part of said territory and to all dealers therein, and to develop an increase in volume

of sales of Dr. Pepper satisfactory to the Grantor. And in this connection, the Grantee agrees, represents and guarantees that the said territory included in this license, and every part thereof, and all dealers therein, ca-, [*sic*] and will be fully covered, solicited and worked by the Grantee in a systemkatic [*sic*] and business-like manner now, and at all times hereafter while this license agreement remains in effect.

"'The determination and judgment of Dr. Pepper Company as to whether or not this clause is being complied with when made in good faith, shall be sole, exclusive and final, and such determination by the Dr. Pepper Company that this clause is not being complied with shall . . . be grounds for forfeiture of this license. . . .

"' . . .

"'(k)5. That in case of the violation of any one or more of the terms or provisions of this license agreement by the Grantee or in the event Grantee fails, within the judgment of the Grantor, to faithfully comply with provisions as above set out, then Grantor shall be entitled to cancel or terminate this license upon giving written notice mailed to Grantee by registered mail and addressed to his last known place of business, and upon notice being given of such cancellation as herein provided, this license agreement and all rights hereunder shall be terminated and at an end, provided, however, that in the event of the termination of this license agreement as herein provided, or in any other manner, such termination shall not release the Grantee from the payment of any amount which may then be owing to Grantor. And upon any termination of this license agreement Grantee shall discontinue the use of the name of "Dr. Pepper" and the bottling of said product. The judgment and determination of Dr. Pepper Company when made in good faith, as to the failure of Grantee to comply with any of the terms of this license, shall be, and is hereby, made conclusive and final. . . .'" *Id.* at 374-375.

The decision in *Ard* to measure Dr. Pepper Co.'s satisfaction according to a subjective standard rested upon the construction of the contract terms which gave Dr. Pepper Co. the right to revoke Ard's license. The circuit court, agreeing with the district court's judgment, found that the contract expressly provided that absent bad faith, Dr. Pepper Co.'s judgment on the matter was conclusive. *Id.* at 376. The contract expressly made Dr. Pepper Co. the sole arbiter of satisfaction, circumscribed only by the exercise of its good faith judgment. Thus, the express language of the contract implicated a subjective standard of satisfaction.

In this case, we are not presented with an *Ard*-like situation where the contract language clearly mandated that Hutton's satisfaction be assessed subjectively.

Nowhere in the addendum does it state, as it did in the *Ard* contract, quoted *supra*, that Hutton's judgment as to the suitability of financing was to be "sole, exclusive or final." Nor did it impose a "good faith" limitation on his judgment. (Even if Hutton's satisfaction as to the financing were to be assessed subjectively, he was still required to present evidence that he was, in good faith, dissatisfied with the available financing. Since Hutton presented no evidence as to the genuineness of his dissatisfaction, the court should not have, for this additional reason, granted summary judgment in his favor.)

The addendum contained only a general satisfaction clause. The fact that a contract contains a general satisfaction clause, without more, does not mandate the application of a subjective standard. Absent express contract language, courts have looked to the nature of the contract as an indicator of which standard governs. In these cases, there still is no clear line of demarcation. Generally, the subjective standard applies to contracts involving matters of aesthetic taste, feasibility of operation, or management, regardless of financial impact. The objective standard of the reasonable person is generally applied where commercial or financial matters are involved. *Kadner, supra,* 20 Cal.App.3d at 263, 97 Cal.Rptr. at 752; *Cranetex, Inc. v. Precision Crane & Rigging of Houston, Inc., supra; Mattei v. Hopper, supra.* This is not to say that a subjective standard is always inapplicable to a contract involving commercial transactions. *Mattei v. Hopper, supra.*

Mattei involved an action for breach of contract by a purchaser against a vendor who failed to convey real estate in accordance with the terms of a deposit receipt executed by the parties. The real estate was to be developed into a commercial shopping center. The concluding paragraph of the deposit receipt contained a satisfaction clause which conditioned the purchaser's tender of the payment of the balance of the purchase price upon a bank's obtaining leases for the tenants of the shopping center which were satisfactory to the purchaser. The purchaser complied with the preliminary terms of the deposit receipt, but the vendor repudiated the contract while the purchaser was in the process of obtaining the leases. The purchaser secured satisfactory leases and offered payment of the balance due on the contract. The vendor refused to tender the deed. The precise issue in *Mattei* was whether the condition of the purchaser's "satisfaction," which satisfaction the court determined was to be scrutinized on a subjective basis, rendered the agreement illusory and unsupported by consideration, and thus unenforceable against the vendor.

While recognizing that an objective standard generally applied where the condition called for satisfaction as to commercial value or quality, as was the case therein, the California Supreme Court nevertheless applied a subjective standard. The court so concluded because application of an objective standard was impracticable under the facts presented:

". . . [I]t would seem that the factors involved in determining whether a lease is satisfactory to the lessor are too numerous and varied to permit the application of a reasonable man standard as envisioned by this line of cases. Illustrative of some of the factors which would have to be considered in this case are the duration of the leases, their provisions for renewal options, if any, their covenants and restrictions, the amounts of the rentals, the financial responsibility of the lessees, and the character of the lessees' businesses.

"This multiplicity of factors which must be considered in evaluating a lease shows that this case more appropriately falls within the second line of authorities dealing with 'satisfaction' clauses, being those involving fancy, taste, or judgment. Where the question is one of judgment, the promisor's determination that he is not satisfied, when made in good faith, has been held to be a defense to an action on the contract." (Citations omitted.) *Id.*, 51 Cal.2d at 123, 330 P.2d at 627.

Such a holding is consistent with the view taken by the Restatement of the Law 2d, Contracts (1981), Section 228, which states:

"When it is a condition of an obligor's duty that he be satisfied with respect to the obligee's performance . . . *and it is practicable to determine whether a reasonable person in the position of the obligor would be satisfied,* an interpretation is preferred under which the condition occurs if such a reasonable person in the position of the obligor would be satisfied." (Emphasis added.)

(The California Supreme Court rejected the vendor's contention that the subjective nature of the purchaser's satisfaction rendered the argument unenforceable.)

In this case, the evidence fails to establish that it would have been impracticable to apply an objective standard to the addendum. Hutton presented no evidence of impracticability. Indeed, he only presented evidence and argument as to the unambiguous nature of the addendum's language, resting his motion on the alleged inherently subjective nature of the language. Therefore, absent evidence of impracticability, we consider whether the nature of the contract indicated which standard controlled. . . .

In this case, the franchise agreement was clearly commercial in nature and pertained to matters of financial concern. Without express language to the contrary, or evidence of impracticability, the commercial nature of the contract, without more, dictated that Hutton's satisfaction had to be measured objectively.

There was nothing unique about this commercial contract that would implicate a subjective assessment of Hutton's satisfaction. Indeed, this contract presents a classic example of an arm's-length business transaction in which reasonable business concerns, relevant to the financing of equipment, dictated the terms of the contract.

Based on the foregoing analysis, we hold that, in the absence of express language to the contrary, or evidence of impracticability of application, an objective standard governs satisfaction clauses in contracts which involve commercial and financial matters. Accordingly, we conclude that the trial court improperly applied a subjective standard in assessing Hutton's satisfaction.

II. GENUINE ISSUES OF MATERIAL FACT EXIST AS TO WHETHER HUTTON WAS "UNABLE" TO LOCATE FINANCING SUITABLE TO HIM.

This argument requires us to determine whether the trial court correctly found that there was no genuine issue of material fact as to Hutton's *inability* to locate financing. This poses a discrete query separate from the issue of the *suitability* of available financing. In their briefs, the parties agree that even if the satisfaction clause were assessed according to a subjective standard, a separate "good faith" standard would govern the determination of whether Hutton was *able* to secure financing. The good faith inquiry focuses on whether Hutton exerted a reasonable effort to locate suitable financing. The following undisputed facts are relevant to this inquiry.

Hutton admitted that he could obtain financing from at least United Leasing. MPI had negotiated the lease terms with United Leasing on Hutton's behalf. Hutton refused to accept the United Leasing proposal in part because the monthly lease cost was almost $200 more than the monthly cost set forth in MPI's franchise circular. Aside from the United Leasing proposal, Hutton explored only two other avenues of financing. He first requested that MPI submit a lease application to Trinity Leasing despite his knowledge that he did not qualify for such financing under Trinity's leasing guidelines. Trinity denied his application. Hutton then submitted an application to Society Bank of Dayton which was prepared with Dennis Hanley's assistance. The application was rejected due to insufficient collateral.

The trial court apparently concluded that these efforts were sufficient to obviate any genuine issue of fact as to whether Hutton was able to locate financing. While we agree with the court's observation that Hutton "[was] not required to search endlessly when it seem[ed] further efforts [would] meet with similar results," we do not agree these efforts conclusively established that Hutton exerted a good faith effort to secure financing. Indeed, we identify two issues of material fact based on this uncontroverted evidence. The issues are whether contacting only one bank and only one other leasing institution constituted a reasonable effort to secure suitable financing, and whether Hutton could claim he made a reasonable attempt to secure suitable leasing with United Leasing and Trinity Leasing when MPI, not Hutton, arranged the United Leasing lease, and when Hutton knew before submitting an application to Trinity that he did not meet Trinity's leasing criteria.

Moreover, the record also contains critical, disputed evidence which precluded summary judgment. The affidavit of MPI's financial director, Dennis Hanley, contained evidence that Hutton told Hanley he could, in fact, have obtained the necessary financing from his father-in-law, Charles Allport. Hanley's affidavit also contained evidence that Allport had repeatedly represented himself to Hanley as one of Hutton's franchise investors. In his response to MPI's interrogatories, Hutton steadfastly denied any such arrangement existed. This conflicting evidence, without more, was sufficient to create a genuine issue of fact as to Hutton's ability to obtain satisfactory financing and to thus render summary judgment inappropriate. . . .

The judgment of the trial court will be reversed. The matter will be remanded for further proceedings consistent with this opinion.

Judgment accordingly.

FAIN, Presiding Judge, concurring in the judgment.

Although I concur in the judgment of the court, I would apply a subjective standard in determining whether reasonable minds could reach different conclusions as to whether Hutton was unable to obtain financing "suitable to him."

I find Judge Wolff's analysis of this issue to be excellent, but I would reach a different conclusion. There are many variables to consider in determining whether financing is "suitable." Besides the duration of the loan and the interest rate, there are (i) the scope and extent of the definitions of acts of default; (ii) the consequences of acts of default, which can range from modest to punitive; and (iii) the extent of personal collateral required for the loan. In my view, the many and diverse implications of the terms of possible financing packages makes this case similar to *Mattei v. Hopper* (1958), 51 Cal.2d 119, 330 P.2d 625, in which it was held to be impractical to apply an objective test for a contracting party's satisfaction.

Although I would employ a subjective test, I nevertheless agree that reasonable minds could reach different conclusions whether "suitable" financing was available to Hutton. There was some evidence that Hutton had refused MPI's help in seeking possible sources of financing, and there was some evidence, albeit controverted, that Hutton's father-in-law was a possible source of financing. In my view, reasonable minds could have reached different conclusions whether Hutton acted in good faith in declaring that no suitable financing was available to him. Therefore, I join in the judgment of this court reversing the summary judgment rendered in Hutton's favor, and remanding this cause to the trial court for further proceedings.

Morin Building Products Co. v. Baystone Construction, Inc.

MORIN BUILDING PRODUCTS CO., Plaintiff-Appellee

v.

BAYSTONE CONSTRUCTION, INC., Defendant-Appellant

United States Court of Appeals, Seventh Circuit

717 F.2d 413 (7th Cir. 1983)

POSNER, Circuit Judge.

This appeal from a judgment for the plaintiff in a diversity suit requires us to interpret Indiana's common law of contracts. General Motors, which is not a party to this case, hired Baystone Construction, Inc., the defendant, to build an addition to a Chevrolet plant in Muncie, Indiana. Baystone hired Morin Building Products Company, the plaintiff, to supply and erect the aluminum walls for the addition. The contract required that the exterior siding of the walls be of "aluminum type 3003, not less than 18 B & S gauge, with a mill finish and stucco embossed surface texture to match finish and texture of existing metal siding." The contract also provided "that all work shall be done subject to the final approval of the Architect or Owner's [General Motors'] authorized agent, and his decision in matters relating to artistic effect shall be final, if within the terms of the Contract Documents"; and that "should any dispute arise as to the quality or fitness of materials or workmanship, the decision as to acceptability shall rest strictly with the Owner, based on the requirement that all work done or materials furnished shall be first class in every respect. What is usual or customary in erecting other buildings shall in no wise enter into any consideration or decision."

Morin put up the walls. But viewed in bright sunlight from an acute angle the exterior siding did not give the impression of having a uniform finish, and General Motors' representative rejected it. Baystone removed Morin's siding and hired another subcontractor to replace it. General Motors approved the replacement siding. Baystone refused to pay Morin the balance of the contract price ($23,000) and Morin brought this suit for the balance, and won.

The only issue on appeal is the correctness of a jury instruction which, after quoting the contractual provisions requiring that the owner (General Motors) be satisfied with the contractor's (Morin's) work, states: "Notwithstanding the apparent finality of the foregoing language, however, the general rule applying to satisfaction in the case of contracts for the construction of commercial buildings is that the satisfaction clause must be determined by objective criteria. Under this standard, the question is not whether the owner was satisfied in fact, but whether the owner, as a reasonable person, should have been satisfied with the materials and workmanship in question." There was much evidence that General Motors' rejection of Morin's exterior siding had been totally unreasonable. Not only was the lack of absolute uniformity in the finish of the walls a seemingly trivial defect given the strictly utilitarian purpose of the building that they enclosed, but it may have been inevitable; "mill finish sheet" is defined in the trade as "sheet having a nonuniform finish which may vary from sheet to sheet and within a sheet, and may not be entirely free from stains or oil." If the instruction was correct, so was the judgment. But if the instruction was incorrect—if the proper standard is not whether a reasonable man would have been satisfied with Morin's exterior siding but whether General Motors' authorized representative in fact was—then there must be a new trial to determine whether he really was dissatisfied, or whether he was not and the rejection therefore was in bad faith.

Some cases hold that if the contract provides that the seller's performance must be to the buyer's satisfaction, his rejection—however unreasonable—of the seller's performance is not a breach of the contract unless the rejection is in bad faith. See, e.g., *Stone Mountain Properties, Ltd. v. Helmer*, 139 Ga.App. 865, 869, 229 S.E.2d 779, 783 (1976). But most cases conform to the position stated in **section 228 of the Restatement (Second) of Contracts (1979):** if "it is practicable to determine whether a reasonable person in the position of the obligor would be satisfied, an interpretation is preferred under which the condition [that the obligor be satisfied with the obligee's performance] occurs if such a reasonable person in the position of the obligor would be satisfied." See Farnsworth, Contracts 556-59 (1982); Annot., 44 A.L.R.2d 1114, 1117, 1119-20 (1955). *Indiana Tri-City Plaza Bowl, Inc. v. Estate of Glueck*, 422 N.E.2d 670, 675 (Ind.App.1981), consistently with hints in earlier Indiana cases, see *Andis v. Personett*, 108 Ind. 202, 206, 9 N.E. 101, 103 (1886); *Semon, Bache & Co. v. Coppes, Zook & Mutschler Co.*, 35 Ind.App. 351, 355, 74 N.E. 41, 43 (1905), adopts the majority position as the law of Indiana.

We do not understand the majority position to be paternalistic; and paternalism would be out of place in a case such as this, where the subcontractor is a substantial multistate enterprise. The requirement of reasonableness is read into a contract not to protect the weaker party but to approximate what the parties would have expressly provided with respect to a contingency that they did not foresee, if they had foreseen it. Therefore the requirement is not read into every contract, because it is not always a reliable guide to the parties' intentions. In particular, the presumption that the performing party would not have wanted to put himself at the mercy of the paying party's whim is overcome when the nature of the performance contracted for is such that there are no objective standards to guide the court. It cannot be assumed in such a case that the parties would have wanted a court to second-guess the buyer's rejection. So "the reasonable person standard is employed when the contract involves commercial quality, operative fitness, or mechanical utility which other knowledgeable persons can judge . . . . The standard of good faith is employed when the contract involves personal aesthetics or fancy." *Indiana Tri-City Plaza Bowl, Inc. v. Estate of Glueck, supra,* 422 N.E.2d at 675; see also *Action Engineering v. Martin Marietta Aluminum,* 670 F.2d 456, 460-61 (3d Cir.1982).

We have to decide which category the contract between Baystone and Morin belongs in. The particular in which Morin's aluminum siding was found wanting was its appearance, which may seem quintessentially a matter of "personal aesthetics," or as the contract put it, "artistic effect." But it is easy to imagine situations where this would not be so. Suppose the manager of a steel plant rejected a shipment of pig iron because he did not think the pigs had a pretty shape. The reasonable-man standard would be applied even if the contract had an "acceptability shall rest strictly with the Owner" clause, for it would be fantastic to think that the iron supplier would have subjected his contract rights to the whimsy of the buyer's agent. At the other extreme would be a contract to paint a portrait, the buyer having reserved the right to reject the portrait if it did not satisfy him. Such a buyer wants a portrait that will please him rather than a jury, even a jury of connoisseurs, so the only question would be his good faith in rejecting the portrait. *Gibson v. Cranage,* 39 Mich. 49 (1878).

This case is closer to the first example than to the second. The building for which the aluminum siding was intended was a factory—not usually intended to be a thing of beauty. That aesthetic considerations were decidedly secondary to considerations of function and cost is suggested by the fact that the contract specified mill-finish aluminum, which is unpainted. There is much debate in the record over whether it is even possible to ensure a uniform finish within and among sheets, but it is at least clear that mill finish usually is not uniform. If General Motors and Baystone had wanted a uniform finish they would in all likelihood have ordered a painted siding. Whether Morin's siding achieved a reasonable uniformity amounting to satisfactory commercial quality was susceptible of objective judgment; in the language of the Restatement, a reasonableness standard was "practicable."

But this means only that a requirement of reasonableness would be read into this contract if it contained a standard owner's satisfaction clause, which it did not;

and since the ultimate touchstone of decision must be the intent of the parties to the contract we must consider the actual language they used. The contract refers explicitly to "artistic effect," a choice of words that may seem deliberately designed to put the contract in the "personal aesthetics" category whatever an outside observer might think. But the reference appears as number 17 in a list of conditions in a general purpose form contract. And the words "artistic effect" are immediately followed by the qualifying phrase, "if within the terms of the Contract Documents," which suggests that the "artistic effect" clause is limited to contracts in which artistic effect is one of the things the buyer is aiming for; it is not clear that he was here. The other clause on which Baystone relies, relating to the quality or fitness of workmanship and materials, may seem all-encompassing, but it is qualified by the phrase, "based on the requirement that all work done or materials furnished shall be first class in every respect"—and it is not clear that Morin's were not. This clause also was not drafted for this contract; it was incorporated by reference to another form contract (the Chevrolet Division's "Contract General Conditions"), of which it is paragraph 35. We do not disparage form contracts, without which the commercial life of the nation would grind to a halt. But we are left with more than a suspicion that the artistic-effect and quality-fitness clauses in the form contract used here were not intended to cover the aesthetics of a mill-finish aluminum factory wall.

If we are right, Morin might prevail even under the minority position, which makes good faith the only standard but presupposes that the contract conditioned acceptance of performance on the buyer's satisfaction in the particular respect in which he was dissatisfied. Maybe this contract was not intended to allow General Motors to reject the aluminum siding on the basis of artistic effect. It would not follow that the contract put Morin under no obligations whatsoever with regard to uniformity of finish. The contract expressly required it to use aluminum having "a mill finish . . . to match finish . . . of existing metal siding." The jury was asked to decide whether a reasonable man would have found that Morin had used aluminum sufficiently uniform to satisfy the matching requirement. This was the right standard if, as we believe, the parties would have adopted it had they foreseen this dispute. It is unlikely that Morin intended to bind itself to a higher and perhaps unattainable standard of achieving whatever perfection of matching that General Motors' agent insisted on, or that General Motors would have required Baystone to submit to such a standard. Because it is difficult—maybe impossible—to achieve a uniform finish with mill-finish aluminum, Morin would have been running a considerable risk of rejection if it had agreed to such a condition, and it therefore could have been expected to demand a compensating increase in the contract price. This would have required General Motors to pay a premium to obtain a freedom of action that it could not have thought terribly important, since its objective was not aesthetic. If a uniform finish was important to it, it could have gotten such a finish by specifying painted siding.

All this is conjecture; we do not know how important the aesthetics were to General Motors when the contract was signed or how difficult it really would have been to obtain the uniformity of finish it desired. The fact that General Motors accepted the replacement siding proves little, for there is evidence that the replacement siding produced the same striped effect, when viewed from an acute angle in bright sunlight, that Morin's had. When in doubt on a difficult issue of state law it is only prudent to defer to the view of the district judge, *Murphy v. White Hen Pantry Co.*, 691 F.2d 350, 354 (7th Cir.1982), here an experienced Indiana lawyer who thought this the type of contract where the buyer cannot unreasonably withhold approval of the seller's performance.

Lest this conclusion be thought to strike at the foundations of freedom of contract, we repeat that if it appeared from the language or circumstances of the contract that the parties really intended General Motors to have the right to reject Morin's work for failure to satisfy the private aesthetic taste of General Motors' representative, the rejection would have been proper even if unreasonable. But the contract is ambiguous because of the qualifications with which the terms "artistic effect" and "decision as to acceptability" are hedged about, and the circumstances suggest that the parties probably did not intend to subject Morin's rights to aesthetic whim.

AFFIRMED.

---

§ 5.3. Waiver and Excuse of Conditions

As we have seen, if the occurrence of a condition is required by agreement of the parties—that is, if there is an express condition specified in the contract—strict compliance with the requirements of the condition is necessary, and any failure to meet its specifications will result in a conclusion that the condition has not been met. The requirement of strict compliance is based on the presumed intent of the parties who have created an express condition. Thus, if a condition requires filing of a claim by June 30 for the insurance company's duty to pay to arise, a filing on July 1 fails to comply with the condition, and the insurance company will not be required to pay.

Application of the requirement of strict compliance can sometimes result in harsh consequences. To avoid such outcomes, courts have several tools at their disposal, illustrated by the cases already considered in this section. They may:

- interpret contract language to avoid finding that it creates an express condition (as in *Peacock*);

- interpret the condition itself in a manner that reduces the risk of non-compliance (as in *Hutton* and *Morin*);
- find that the party whose performance duties would otherwise be affected waived the condition (as considered in *Renovest*).

The case below illustrates yet another tool available to avoid the harsh effects of a condition: excusing the condition based on a finding that the party who did not satisfy the condition would otherwise suffer a forfeiture.

Reading the Law Critically: *J.N.A Realty Corp.* and Restatement (Second) § 229

1. What is the condition identified in the contract? Why is it understood to be a condition rather than a promise?

2. What will happen if the condition is strictly enforced? Why is that consequence considered a forfeiture rather than simply the loss of an expectation under the contract?

3. According to the court, when should a condition be excused based on forfeiture? On remand, should the lower court enforce the condition or excuse it? Why?

4. Why would the dissenting judge deny relief, enforcing the strict requirements of the condition? Do you agree with the majority or with the dissent?

5. How does the Retatement standard below differ from the rule applied by the court in *J.N.A. Realty Corp.*? If the Restatement test were applied in *J.N.A. Realty Corp.*, would the outcome be the same as it is here?

6. Would the conditions in the other cases in this section (*Morrison, Internatio-Rotterdam, Renovest, Peacock Construction, Hutton,* and *Morin Building Products*) be appropriate cases in which to apply excuse on the basis of forfeiture?

> Restatement (Second) of Contracts § 229. **Excuse of a Condition to Avoid Forfeiture**
>
> To the extent that the non-occurrence of a condition would cause disproportionate forfeiture, a court may excuse the non-occurrence of that condition unless its occurrence was a material part of the agreed exchange.
>
> > *Comment b. Disproportionate forfeiture.* The rule stated in the present Section is, of necessity, a flexible one, and its application is within the sound discretion of the court. Here, as in § 227(1), "forfeiture" is used to refer to the denial of compensation that results when the obligee loses his right to the agreed exchange after he has relied substantially, as by preparation or performance on the expectation of that exchange. See Comment b to § 227. The extent of the forfeiture in any particular case will depend on the extent of that denial of compensation. In determining whether the forfeiture is "disproportionate," a court must weigh the extent of the forfeiture by the obligee against the importance to the obligor of the risk from which he sought to be protected and the degree to which that protection will be lost if the non-occurrence of the condition is excused to the extent required to prevent forfeiture. The character of the agreement may, as in the case of insurance agreements, affect the rigor with which the requirement is applied.

J.N.A. Realty Corp. v. Cross Bay Chelsea, Inc.

J. N. A. REALTY CORP., Petitioner-Appellee

CROSS BAY CHELSEA, INC. et al., Appellants- Respondents

[handwritten: Lease renewal a few months to late]

Court of Appeals of New York

366 N.E.2d 1313 (N.Y. 1977)

WACHTLER, Judge.

J. N. A. Realty Corp., the owner of a building in Howard Beach, commenced this proceeding to recover possession of the premises claiming that the lease has expired. The lease grants the tenant, Cross Bay Chelsea, Inc., an option to renew and although the notice was sent, through negligence or inadvertence, it was not sent within the time prescribed in the lease. The landlord seeks to enforce the letter of the agreement. The tenant asks for equity to relieve it from a forfeiture.

The Civil Court, after a trial, held that the tenant was entitled to equitable relief. The Appellate Term affirmed, without opinion, but the Appellate Division, after granting leave, reversed and granted the petition. The tenant has appealed to this court.

Two primary questions are raised on the appeal. First, will the tenant suffer a forfeiture if the landlord is permitted to enforce the letter of the agreement. Secondly, if there will be a forfeiture, may a court of equity grant the tenant relief when the forfeiture would result from the tenant's own neglect or inadvertence.

At the trial it was shown that J. N. A. Realty Corp. (hereafter JNA) originally leased the premises to Victor Palermo and Sylvester Vascellero for a 10-year term commencing on January 1, 1964. Paragraph 58 of the lease, which was attached as part of 12-page rider, granted the tenants an option to renew for a 10-year term provided "that Tenant shall notify the landlord in writing by registered or certified mail six (6) months prior to the last day of the term of the lease that tenant desires such renewal." The tenants opened a restaurant on the premises. In February, 1964 they formed the Foro Romano Corp. (Foro) and assigned the lease to the corporation.

By December of 1967 the restaurant was operating at a loss and Foro decided to close it down and offer it for sale or lease. In March, 1968 Foro entered into a contract with Cross Bay Chelsea, Inc. (hereafter Chelsea), to sell the restaurant and assign the lease. As a condition of the sale Foro was required to obtain a modification of the option to renew so that Chelsea would have the right to renew the lease for an additional term of 24 years.

The closing took place in June of 1968. First JNA modified the option and consented to the assignment. The modification, which consists of a separate document to be attached to the lease, states: "the Tenant shall have a right to renew this lease for a further period of Twenty-Four (24) years, instead of Ten (10) years, from the expiration of the original term of said lease . . . All other provisions of Paragraph # 58 in said lease, . . . shall remain in full force and effect, except as hereinabove modified." Foro then assigned the lease and sold its interest in the restaurant to Chelsea for $155,000. The bill of sale states that "the value of the fixtures and chattels included in this sale is the sum of $40,000 and that the remainder of the purchase price is the value of the leasehold and possession of the restaurant premises." At that point five and one-half years remained on the original term of the lease.

In the summer of 1968 Chelsea reopened the restaurant. JNA's president, Nicholas Arena, admitted on the stand that throughout the tenancy it regularly informed Chelsea in writing of its obligations under the lease, such as the need to pay taxes and insurance by certain dates. For instance on June 13, 1973 JNA sent a letter to Chelsea informing them that certain taxes were due to be paid. When that letter was sent the option to renew was due to expire in approximately two weeks but JNA made no mention of this. A similar letter was sent to Chelsea in September, 1973.

Arena also admitted that throughout the term of the tenancy he was "most assuredly" aware of the time limitation on the option. In fact there is some indication in the record that JNA had previously used this device in an attempt to evict another tenant. Nevertheless it was not until November 12, 1973 that JNA took any action to inform the tenant that the option had lapsed. Then it sent a letter noting that the date had passed and, the letter states, "not having heard from you as prescribed by paragraph # 58 in our lease we must assume you will vacate the premises" at the expiration of the original term, January 1, 1974. By letter dated November 16, 1973 Chelsea, through its attorney, sent written notice of intention to renew the option which, of course, JNA refused to honor.

At the trial Chelsea's principals claimed that they were not aware of the time limitation because they had never received a copy of paragraph 58 of the rider. They had received a copy of the modification but they had assumed that it gave them an absolute right to retain the tenancy for 24 years after the expiration of the original term. However, at the trial and later at the Appellate Division, it was found that Chelsea had knowledge of, or at least was "chargeable with notice" of, the time limitation in the rider and thus was negligent in failing to renew within the time prescribed.

Chelsea's principals also testified that they had spent an additional $15,000 on improvements, at least part of which had been expended after the option had expired. Toward the end of the trial JNA's attorney asked the court whether it would "take evidence from" Arena that he had negotiated with another tenant after the option to renew had lapsed. However, the court held that this testimony would be immaterial.

It is a settled principle of law that a notice exercising an option is ineffective if it is not given within the time specified (see, e. g., Restatement, Contracts 2d (Tent. Draft No. 1, 1964), § 64, subd. (b); 1A Corbin, Contracts (1963), § 264; 1 Williston, Contracts (3d ed. 1957), § 87; Sy Jack Realty Co. v. Pergament Syosset Corp., 27 N.Y.2d 449, 318 N.Y.S.2d 720, 267 N.E.2d 462). "At law, of course, time is always of the essence of the contract" (De Funiak, Modern Equity, § 80, p. 223). Thus the tenant had no legal right to exercise the option when it did, but to say that is simply to pose the issue; it does not resolve it. Of course the tenant would not be asking for equitable relief if it could establish its rights at law.

The major obstacle to obtaining equitable relief in these cases is that default on an option usually does not result in a forfeiture. The reason is that the option itself does not create any interest in the property, and no rights accrue until the condition precedent has been met by giving notice within the time specified. Thus equity will not intervene because the loss of the option does not ordinarily result in the forfeiture of any vested rights (see, e. g., *Fidelity & Columbia Trust Co. v. Levin*, 128 Misc. 838, 221 N.Y.S. 269, aff'd, 221 App.Div. 786, 223 N.Y.S.2d 866, aff'd, 248 N.Y. 551, 162 N.E. 521; *Doepfner v. Bowers*, 55 Misc. 561, 106 N.Y.S. 932; cf. *People's Bank of City of N. Y. v. Mitchell*, 73 N.Y. 406; but see *Noyes v. Anderson*, 124 N.Y. 175, 179-180, 26 N.E. 316, 317, where it is indicated that the "rule may not be without exception"). The general rule is customarily stated as follows: "There is a wide distinction between a condition precedent, where no title has vested and none is to vest until the condition is performed, and a condition subsequent, operating by way of a defeasance. In the former case equity can give no relief. The failure to perform is an inevitable bar. No right can ever vest. The result is very different where the condition is subsequent. There equity will interpose and relieve against the forfeiture". (*Davis v. Gray*, 16 Wall. (83 U.S.) 203, 229-230, 21 L.Ed. 447.) It has been suggested that even when the option has been paid for, nothing is forfeited when it expires, because the amount paid "is the exact agreed equivalent" of the power to exercise the right for the time allotted (see 1 Corbin, Contracts, § 35, p. 147).

But when a tenant in possession under an existing lease has neglected to exercise an option to renew, he might suffer a forfeiture if he has made valuable improvements on the property. This of course generally distinguishes the lease option, to renew or purchase, from the stock option or the option to buy goods. This was a distinction which some of the older cases failed to recognize (see, e.g., *Fidelity & Columbia Trust Co. v. Levin, supra; Doepfner v. Bowers, supra;* cf. *People's Bank of City of N. Y. v. Mitchell,* supra). More recently it has been noted that "although the tenant has no legal interest in the renewal period until the required notice is given, yet an equitable interest is recognized and protected against forfeiture in some cases where the tenant has in good faith made improvements of a substantial character, intending to renew the lease, if the landlord is not harmed by the delay in the giving of the notice and the lessee would sustain substantial loss in case the lease were not renewed" (2 Pomeroy, Equity Jurisprudence (5th ed.), § 453b, p. 296).

The leading case on this point is *Fountain Co. v. Stein*, 97 Conn. 619, 118 A. 47, 27 A.L.R. 976 and the rule has been accepted by noted commentators (see, e. g., 1 Corbin, op. cit., § 35, p. 146; 1 Williston, Contracts (3d ed.), § 76, p. 249, n. 4; 2 Pomeroy, op. cit., § 453b, p. 296). It has also been accepted and applied by this court. In *Jones v. Gianferante*, 305 N.Y. 135, 138, 111 N.E.2d 419, 420, citing the Fountain case we held that the tenant was entitled to "the benefit of the rule or practice in equity which relieves against such forfeitures of valuable lease terms when default in notice has not prejudiced the landlord, and has resulted from an honest mistake, or similar excusable fault." The rule was extended in *Sy Jack Realty Co. v. Pergament Syosset Corp.*, 27 N.Y.2d 449, 453, 318 N.Y.S.2d 720, 722, 267 N.E.2d 462, 464, supra, to preserve the tenant's interest in a "long-standing location for a retail business" because this is "an important part of the good will of that enterprise, [and thus] the tenant stands to lose a substantial and valuable asset."

In neither of those cases were we asked to consider whether the tenant would be entitled to equitable relief from the consequences of his own neglect or "mere forgetfulness" as the court had held in the Fountain case, supra. In Gianferante the default was due to an ambiguous lease, and in Sy Jack the notice was mailed but never delivered (but see *Roy's of North Syracuse v. P & C Food Markets*, 51 A.D.2d 641, 377 N.Y.S.2d 1019, mot. for lv. to app. den. 38 N.Y.2d 711, 384 N.Y.S.2d 1026, 348 N.E.2d 927; and the dissenting opn. in *Sy Jack, supra*, 27 N.Y.2d p. 456, n. 1, 318 N.Y.S.2d p. 725, 267 N.E.2d p. 466, where it is noted that the three cases cited in Williston the principle one being the Fountain case "obviously warranted equitable relief. For not only in those cases was there 'excusable fault', but also in each one the tenant had made substantial improvements"). But the principle involved is well established in this State. A tenant or mortgagor should not be denied equitable relief from the consequences of his own neglect or inadvertence if a forfeiture would result (*Giles v. Austin*, 62 N.Y. 486; *Noyes v. Anderson*, 124 N.Y. 175, 26 N.E. 316; *Roy's of North Syracuse v. P & C Food Markets*, supra; see, also, 2 Pomeroy, Equity Jurisprudence (5th ed.), § 452, p. 287). The rule applies even though the tenant or mortgagor, by his inadvertence, has neglected to perform an affirmative duty and thus breached a covenant in the agreement (*Giles v. Austin, supra*; *Noyes v. Anderson, supra*).

On occasion the court has cautioned that equitable relief would be denied where there has been a willful or gross neglect (*Noyes v. Anderson, supra*, 124 N.Y. p. 179, 26 N.E. p. 317), but it has been reluctant to employ the sanction when a forfeiture would result. In *Giles v. Austin, supra*, p. 491, for instance, the landlord sought to recover possession of the premises after the tenant had neglected to pay the taxes as required by a covenant in the lease. We held that although the tenant had not paid the taxes since the inception of the lease in 1859, and had only paid them after suit was commenced in 1868, the tenant's default was not "so willful, or his neglect so inexcusable, that a court of equity should have denied him any relief."

There are several cases in which this court has denied a tenant or mortgagor equitable relief because of his own neglect to perform within the time fixed in the lease or mortgage, but only when it has found that there was "no penalty, no forfeiture" (*Graf v. Hope Bldg. Corp.*, 254 N.Y. 1, 4, 171 N.E. 884, 885; *Fidelity & Columbia Trust Co. v. Levin*, 128 Misc. 838, 221 N.Y.S. 269, aff'd, 221 App. Div. 786, 223 N.Y.S.2d 866, aff'd, 248 N.Y. 551, 162 N.E. 521, supra; *People's Bank of City of N. Y. v. Mitchell*,73 N.Y. 406, supra). Cardozo took a different view. He felt that even though there may be no penalty or forfeiture "in a strict or proper sense" equity should "relieve against it if default has been due to mere venial inattention and if relief can be granted without damage to the lender". Even in those cases he would apply the general equitable principle that "the gravity of the fault must be compared with the gravity of the hardship" (*Graf v. Hope Bldg. Corp., supra,* 254 N.Y. pp. 9-10, 13, 171 N.E. p. 888 (Cardozo, Ch. J., dissenting); see, also, 2 Pomeroy, Equity Jurisprudence (5th ed.), § 439, p. 220).

Here, as noted, the tenant has made a considerable investment in improvements on the premises $40,000 at the time of purchase, and an additional $15,000 during the tenancy. In addition, if the location is lost, the restaurant would undoubtedly lose a considerable amount of its customer good will. The tenant was at fault, but not in a culpable sense. It was, as Cardozo says, "mere venial inattention." There would be a forfeiture and the gravity of the loss is certainly out of all proportion to the gravity of the fault. Thus, under the circumstances of this case, the tenant would be entitled to equitable relief if there is no prejudice to the landlord.

Make the Connection

Note Judge Cardozo's position in the cited case of *Graf v. Hope Bldg. Corp.* and compare his opinion in *Jacob & Youngs v. Kent* (page 895), in which he also contrasts the venial (that is, minor and easy to forgive) failure to follow contract terms with the grave hardship to be suffered if the contract were to be enforced as written.

However, it is not clear from the record whether JNA would be prejudiced if the tenant is relieved of its default. Because of the trial court's ruling, JNA was unable to submit proof that it might be prejudiced if the terms of the agreement were not enforced literally. Its proof of other negotiations was considered immaterial. It may be that after the tenant's default the landlord, relying on the agreement, in good faith, made other commitments for the premises. But if JNA did not rely on the letter of the agreement then, it should not be permitted to rely on it now to exact a substantial forfeiture for the tenant's unwitting default. This, however, must be resolved at a new trial.

Finally we would note, as the dissenters do, that it is possible to imagine a situation in which a tenant holding an option to renew might intentionally delay beyond the time prescribed in order to exploit a fluctuating market. However, as the dissenters also note, there is no evidence to suggest that that is what occurred here. On the contrary there has been an affirmed finding of fact that the tenant's late notice was due to negligence. Of course a tenant who has intentionally delayed should not be relieved of a forfeiture simply because this tenant, who was merely inadvertent, may be granted equitable relief. But, on the other hand, we do not believe that this tenant, or any tenant, guilty only of negligence should be denied equitable relief because some other tenant, in some other case, may be found to have acted in bad faith. By its nature equitable relief must always depend on the facts of the particular case and not on hypotheticals.

Accordingly, the order of the Appellate Division should be reversed and a new trial granted.

BREITEL, Chief Judge (dissenting).

Relieving the tenant of its negligent failure to exercise its option to renew a lease within the prescribed time upsets established precedent, introduces instability in business transactions, and disregards commercial realities. I therefore dissent.

This case involves an option to renew a lease, not a mortgage foreclosure or an acceleration clause in a lease or mortgage. The categories and applicable precedents are not to be confused.

. . . .

At issue is the availability of equitable relief to remedy a commercial tenant's failure, by the appointed date, to exercise its option to renew a lease when the only explanation is sheer negligence.

The order of the Appellate Division should be affirmed, and the landlord awarded possession. Mere negligence does not justify departing from the rule that notice of intention to exercise an option to renew must be given within the prescribed period. Equitable relief is never justified by the fact alone, always present, that the tenant will suffer some sort of economic detriment.

The record is unusually deficient in many respects. From it, however, may be culled what follows.

. . . .

. . . [In February 1968,] Peter and John Morfogen, principals of the present tenant Cross Bay Chelsea, responded to an advertisement in the New York Times and indicated their interest in purchasing the leasehold and the closed-down business.

The precise details of the initial conversations between the parties cannot be extracted from the record because they are included only in bits and pieces. Apparently, however, the prospective buyer, who at the time of trial was operating four other restaurants in Manhattan, Queens, and Nassau County, was ready to agree only if a 30-year lease could be arranged. To that effect, a meeting of the principals of landlord J. N. A., Foro, and Chelsea was held on March 16, 1968, and a "modification and extension of lease" agreement executed. While the modification agreement provided that the tenant have the "right to renew this lease for a further period of Twenty-Four (24) years, instead of Ten (10) years", it also continued in full force and effect "[a]ll other provisions of Paragraph # 58", which contained the requirement of six months' notice of election of the option to renew. The modified lease provided that a portion of the taxes and insurance premiums, and all of the interior repairs, be borne by the tenant. The starting rent reserved in the option was $1,000 per month.

J. N. A's principals attended this critical meeting without counsel, although the Chelsea principals, who now claim ignorance of the conditions to exercising the 24-year renewal option, were accompanied by their lawyer and an accountant. The transaction eventually involved a gross price of $155,000, much of it deferred, for the restaurant, fixtures, and the assignment of the leasehold. Of the $155,000, $40,000 was allocated to the chattels and fixtures, and the balance to the leasehold. Chelsea's lawyer also attended the June 8 closing of the transfer of the modified lease and the sale of the restaurant, following the March 16 lease modification meeting. Between the closing of the lease modification agreement in March, 1968 and the final closing in June, 1968, Chelsea arranged for a liquor license. Also before the June, 1968 closing, Chelsea had invested $15,000 in undescribed improvements in the premises. In short order the restaurant was reopened and was quite successful, or else this litigation would never have ensued.

On July 1, 1973, the date the renewal option was to be exercised, no notice or advice of any kind was sent or given to the landlord. It was not until November 16, 1973, some four and a-half months later, that Chelsea, in response to a letter from J. N. A., sent to the landlord a purported notice to exercise the option. J. N. A. refused to recognize the notice, and on March 4, 1974 instituted this holdover proceeding. The record is silent about the intervening period except to indicate that there were negotiations.

To excuse its failure to send a renewal notice by the July 1 deadline and to support a claim to equitable relief, Chelsea asserts that it never received a copy of the 12-page rider attached to the original lease. In addition to the 1968 modification agreement's reference to the 1963 rider, the entire lease, including that rider, was filed in April, 1968 with the Division of Alcoholic Beverage Control on Chelsea's preclosing application for a liquor license. While Chelsea contends that the 1963 rider found in the agency's file must have been taken from an earlier applica-

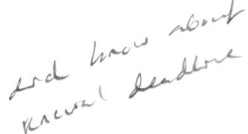

tion submission, the trial court resolved this issue of fact in favor of the landlord. The Appellate Division expressly found that Chelsea had knowledge, or at least should be chargeable with notice, of the provisions of paragraph 58 of the 1963 rider requiring six months' notice to renew.

What's That?

"Law day" is archaic terminology for the day appointed for a debtor to discharge a mortgage or else forfeit the property to the lender. The words are used here to refer to the day on which notice to renew the lease was due to be given.

Chelsea contends that J. N. A.'s representative was on the premises in the summer of 1973, after law day had passed, and failed to comment when he saw that additional improvements were still being made. There is no evidence of what these improvements were, how extensive they were, their value, or whether they were fixed or movable fixtures or equipment. J. N. A. never conceded that the visits had occurred or that such post law day improvements had been made.

Had an honest mistake or similar "excusable fault", as opposed to what is undoubtedly mere carelessness, occasioned the tenant's tardiness, absent prejudice to the landlord, equitable relief would be available (e. g., *Sy Jack Realty Co. v. Pergament Syosset Corp.*, 27 N.Y.2d 449, 453, 318 N.Y.S.2d 720, 722, 267 N.E.2d 462, 464; *Jones v. Gianferante*, 305 N.Y. 135, 138, 111 N.E.2d 419). At issue, instead, is the availability of equitable relief where the only excuse for the commercial tenant's dilatory failure to exercise its option to renew is sheer carelessness.

Enough has been said to uncover a common situation. Experienced and even hardened businessmen at cross-purposes over the renewal of a valuable lease term seek on the one hand to stand by the written agreement, and on the other, to loosen the applicable rules to receive ad hoc adjustment of equities and relief from economic detriment. The landlord wants a higher return. The tenant wants to keep the old bargain. Which of the profit-seeking parties in this particular case should prevail as a matter of morals is not within the province of the courts. The well-settled doctrine is that with respect to options, whether they be lease renewal options, options to purchase real or personal property, or stock options, time is of the essence. The exceptions, namely, estoppel, fraud, mistake, accident, or overreaching, are few. Commercial stability and certainty are paramount, and always the dangers of unsolvable issues of fact and speculative manipulation (as with stock options) are to be avoided.

The landlord should be awarded possession of the premises in accordance with the undisputed language and manifested intention of the written lease, its

for bad
for tenant

12-page rider, and modification. It does not suffice that the tenant may suffer an economic detriment in losing the renewal period. Nor does it suffice that the delay in giving notice may have caused the landlord no "prejudice", other than loss of the opportunity to relet the property or renegotiate the terms of a lease on a fresh basis. Once an option to renew a lease has been conditioned upon the tenant's giving timely notice, the commercial lessee should not be heard to complain that through carelessness a valued asset has been lost, anymore than one would allow the landlord to complain of the economic detriment to him in agreeing to an improvident option to renew.

The court unanimously accepts the general rule at law: an option to renew a commercial lease must be exercised within the appointed time period (e. g., *Sy Jack Realty Co. v. Pergament Syosset Corp.*, 27 N.Y.2d 449, 452, 318 N.Y.S.2d 720, 721, 267 N.E.2d 462, 463, supra, and authorities cited; see Restatement, Contracts 2d (Tent. Draft Nos. 1-7, 1973), § 64, Comment f ; 34 N.Y.Jur., Landlord and Tenant, §§ 418-419; 51C C.J.S. Landlord & Tenant § 59). Underlying the bar to equitable relief is the theory that until the condition precedent is fulfilled, that is, until the required timely notice is given, there is no "forfeiture" for which equity will extend protection (*Fidelity & Columbia Trust Co. v. Levin*, 128 Misc. 838, 844-845, 221 N.Y.S. 269, 275-276, aff'd, 221 App.Div. 786, 223 N.Y.S.2d 866, aff'd, 248 N.Y. 551, 162 N.E. 521; 2 Pomeroy, Equity Jurisprudence (5th ed.), § 453b, p. 296). While the rule has been bolstered by traditional concepts of estates in land, its basis has current commercial and economic validity.

neg not
enough; need
fraud, etc.

In this State, as in others, relief has been afforded tenants threatened with loss of an expected renewal period (see, generally, Effect of Lessee's Failure or Delay in Giving Notice Within Specified Time, of Intention to Renew Lease, Ann., 44 A.L.R.2d 1359, esp. 1362-1369). But in New York, as elsewhere, the circumstances conditioning such relief have been carefully limited. It is only where the tenant can show, not mere negligence, but an excuse such as fraud, mistake, or accident, that is, one or more of the categories common and integral to invocation of equity, that courts have, despite the literal agreement and intention of the parties, stepped in to prevent a loss (see, e. g., *Jones v. Gianferante*, 305 N.Y. 135, 138-139, 111 N.E.2d 419, 420, supra ; 1 McAdam, Landlord and Tenant (5th ed.), § 156, pp. 721-722).

Even in the case of excusable default by the tenant the court looks to the investment the tenant has made to bolster his right to equitable relief. But the fact of tenant investment alone is not enough to justify intervention. Thus, in the leading cases excusing the tenant's late notice, mention is perforce made of investments and improvements (e. g., *Sy Jack Realty Co. v. Pergament Syosset Corp.*, 27 N.Y.2d 449, 453, 318 N.Y.S.2d 720, 722, 267 N.E.2d 462, 464, supra; *Jones v. Gianferante*, 305 N.Y. 135, 138, 111 N.E.2d 419, supra). But the loss or "forfeiture" of these investments was not alone the trigger to granting relief. Indispensable is the existence of some mistake or excusable default. Thus, in *Jones v. Gianferante, supra*, p. 138, 111 N.E.2d p. 419, an ambiguous term in the lease excused the tenant's failure. And in *Sy Jack v. Pergament, supra*, 27 N.Y.2d p. 453, 318 N.Y.S.2d p. 722, 267 N.E.2d p. 464, it was reliance on the post office to deliver the notice, mailed three days before law day, that was forgiven. In no case of accepted or acceptable authority, however, were improvements alone enough to help the negligent tenant.

The majority facilely disposes of the tenant's delinquency in exercising its option by relying on cases in which a party, notwithstanding its negligence, was relieved from a forfeiture (e. g., *Giles v. Austin*, 62 N.Y. 486, 493-494, a conditional limitation in a lease; *Noyes v. Anderson*, 124 N.Y. 175, 182-183, 26 N.E. 316, 318, mortgagor's failure to pay an assessment). But indiscriminate application of principles evolved to deal with mortgage foreclosures or a lessor's right to re-enter upon a tenant's failure to pay taxes and assessments when due does not withstand analysis. Since ever so long, enforcement of a mortgage has rested in equity (see *Jamaica Sav. Bank v. M. S. Investing Co.*, 274 N.Y. 215, 219, 8 N.E.2d 493, 494; 38 N.Y.Jur., Mortgages and Deeds of Trust, § 317). It is also significant that as to foreclosure, time is not of the essence (see 10 N.Y.Jur., Contracts, s 270). Even where acceleration clauses are involved and a strong argument can be made for allowing relief, time has been of the essence and negligence has not been excused (see *Graf v. Hope Bldg. Corp.*, 254 N.Y. 1, 4, 7, 171 N.E. 884, 885, 886 (dissenting opn. per Cardozo, Ch. J.)). It is equally inappropriate to analogize to a lessee's failure to comply with a lease requirement that taxes and assessments be paid as they become due (see *Giles v. Austin, supra*, 62 N.Y. pp. 493-494). For the loss of an existing lease term subject to a condition subsequent distinguishes that situation from the loss of a possible option period subject to a condition precedent. An option is a right to purchase or acquire an interest in personal or real property in the future, and, if precise, it carries an invulnerable requirement to comply with all conditions, including that of time which is therefore of the essence in law and equity.

There are cases, not binding on this court, which express the principles discussed. For reasons that are not persuasive they would distinguish, however, between mere neglect or forgetfulness and gross or willful negligence, whatever that might be (see *Fountain Co. v. Stein*, 97 Conn. 619, 626-627, 118 A. 47; *Xanthakey v. Hayes*, 107 Conn. 459, 469, 140 A. 808; see, generally, 1 Williston, Contracts (3d ed.), § 76, p. 249, n. 4). This is not a distinction generally accepted and is hardly a pragmatic one to apply in an area where the opportunities for distortion and manipulation are so great. The instability and uncertainty would be dangerous and would allow for ad hoc dispensations in particular cases without reliable rule so essential to commercial enterprise.

To begin with, under the guise of sheer inadvertence, a tenant could gamble with a fluctuating market, at the expense of his landlord, by delaying his decision beyond the time fixed in the agreement. The market having resolved in favor of exercising the option, the landlord, even though the day appointed in the agreement has passed, could be held to the return set out in the option, although if the market had resolved otherwise, the tenant could not be held to the renewal period.

None of this is to say that the tenant in this case was guilty of any manipulation. Hardly so. But what the court is concerned with is a rule for this case which perforce must cover other cases of like kind, where there will be no assurance that the "forgetfulness" is no more than that. The worst of the matter is that the kind of paltry record made in this case is hardly one on which a new rule with potential for mischief should be based. When the option, especially one requiring notice well in advance of the expiration of the lease, permits of economic manipulation, in commercial fairness the parties, especially if represented by counsel, should be held to their bargain, if plainly expressed.

Considering investments in the premises or the renewal term a "forfeiture" as alone warranting equitable relief would undermine if not dissolve the general rule upon which there is agreement. For, it is difficult to imagine a dilatory commercial tenant, particularly one in litigation over a renewal, who would not or could not point, scrupulously or unscrupulously, to some threatened investment in the premises, be it a physical improvement or the fact of good will. As a practical matter, it is not unreasonable to expect the commercial tenant, as compared with his residential counterpart, to protect his business interests with meticulousness, a meticulousness to which he would hold his landlord. All he, or his lawyer, need do is red-flag the date on which he has to act.

Having established no excuse, other than its own carelessness, Chelsea's claim is unfounded. Even if Chelsea honestly thought it enjoyed a 30-year lease, it does not change the result. Nor is it helpful to argue that Chelsea, always represented by a lawyer, was unable to procure a copy of the entire lease agreement. Indeed, it borders on the utterly incredible that experienced, sophisticated businessmen and their lawyers would not have assembled and scrutinized every relevant document affecting a long-term lease covering, with a renewal, a 30-year period.

That adherence to well-settled principles, like a Statute of Limitations or a Statute of Frauds works a hardship on some does not, alone, permit a court to depart from sound doctrine and principles. Even if precedent did not control the same doctrines and principles discussed should be applied.

Accordingly, I dissent and vote that the order of the Appellate Division should be affirmed, and the landlord awarded possession of the premises.

————————

CHAPTER 8

Performance, Breach, and Excuse

What kind of promises will the law enforce?

How do parties demonstrate assent to a contract?

What defenses to enforcement exist?

Is a writing required for enforcement? If so, what kind?

How is the content of a contract ascertained?

What are parties' rights and duties after breach?

What situations lead to excusing contract performance?

What remedies are available for breach of contract?

What contractual rights and duties do non-parties to a contract have?

§ 1. Introduction

Once a contract is formed, the parties can begin to perform the contract according to the contract's terms, determined pursuant to the rules and policies described in Chapter 7. Performance may involve, for example, providing services, delivering goods, conveying of real estate, transfering a building, assigning contract rights, or payment for any of the above.

But with performance comes the possibility of breach. A "breach" is any performance that does not match the terms (express and implied) of the contract. Breaches come in many varieties:

- Repudiation (either party renounces the contract and refuses to perform)
- Nonperformance
- Late performance
- Incomplete or faulty performance (failing to finish performance, performing defectively)
- Wrongfully rejecting the other party's performance
- Failure to act in good faith in performance

Once a breach has occurred, the parties may be referred to as the "aggrieved party" and the "breaching party" with respect to any particular breach.

If a breach has caused injury, the aggrieved party will be entitled to a remedy, usually damages but sometimes an equitable form of relief such as specific performance (Chapter 9, page 1182). A breach may also entitle a party to suspend or cease performance. If both parties have breached at least some of their obligations, the court must analyze the sequence of breaches to determine which actions were justified and which were not—that is, who breached first, and when, if ever, the accumulated breaches justified a party in suspending or ceasing performance. Or a court may consider whether an unexpected event allows the breaching party to be excused from its performace. This chapter covers such questions of performance and breach.

§ 2. Categories of Implied Conditions

In the early common law of England, all contractual promises were considered independent of each other and not connected to any events external to the contract unless the parties attached an express condition to a promise (see Chapter 7, page 836). No conditions were implied. Thus, one party's breach of promise (for instance, the promise of a landlord to provide a house suitable for a residence) did not justify the other party in suspending or ceasing performance of its promise (for instance, the promise of a tenant to pay rent).

Slowly, though, the common law evolved rules recognizing that some promises were related to each other—one party's non-performance sometimes meant that the other party did not have to perform its promise, or could at least delay performance while waiting for the other party's performance to occur.

As recognized in current law, "constructive conditions of exchange" are implied conditions that connect contract performances together through conditional relationships implied from the agreement, thereby determining the order of the parties' performances within the contract. For example, in a contract for plumbing services, unless the agreement indicates otherwise, the plumber is ordinarily required to perform before the other party must pay, so performing the plumbing services is an implied condition of the customer's promise to pay. In other circumstances, performances are expected to be simultaneous (or nearly so), as in a real estate closing, where payment and title are expected to be transferred at the same time. In such cases, the tender of performance under each promise is an implied condition of the other promise. Note that all implied conditions of this sort are "promissory conditions" (see Chapter 7, page 838), because they are both promises and conditions. Courts may also find that a performance is implicitly dependent on the occurrence or nonoccurrence of an event rather than on the performance of the other party's promise. For instance, a landlord's promise to repair the rental premises may be implicitly conditional on the tenant giving notice of needed repairs. As we will see, the most significant difference between express and implied conditions (whether promissory conditions or not) is how completely the condition must be satisfied in order to trigger the need to perform the connected promise.

Courts may and often do imply conditions based on interpretation of contract language, extrinsic evidence, usage of trade, course of dealing, public policy considerations, or what reasonable persons would have intended in the circumstances. These implied conditions "play an essential role in assuring the parties to a bilateral contract that they will actually receive the performance that they have been promised. In the centuries since [*Kingston v. Preston,* the case below], courts have sensibly imposed such conditions whenever possible."*

 Reading the Law Critically: *Kingston*

In 1773, this well known English case divided contractual "covenants" (that is, promises and conditions) into three categories. Those categories will be useful in this chapter and in Chapter 9.

1. What are the three categories of covenants, and how does the court decide which kind of covenant was involved in this case?

---

* E. Allan Farnsworth, *Contracts* § 8.9, at 538 (4th ed. 2004).

2. How does the type of implied condition found to exist affect the determination of which party had to perfom first?

3. What interpretive guidelines does the court furnish to determine covenant categories in future cases?

Kingston v. Preston

KINGSTON, Plaintiff

v.

PRESTON, Defendant

Court of King's Bench

99 Eng. Rep. 437 (K.B. 1773)*

quoted from Jones v. Barkley, 99 Eng. Rep. 434 (K.B. 1781)

won't sell silk business

[Defendant, a "silk-mercer," and plaintiff entered into a contract in which

- Defendant "covenanted" to hire plaintiff for the next 15 months, to work in defendant's business at a rate of £200 per year. Plaintiff agreed to serve.
- Defendant "covenanted" to sell to the plaintiff and defendant's nephew ("or his** nominee")

>
> **What's That?**
>
> As used by Lord Mansfield in this opinion, "covenants" include promises, as well as events on which promises may be conditioned.

defendant's silk-mercer business and "his stock in trade, at a fair valuation," to be carried out at the end of the 15 months. Defendant promised to allow the buyers to conduct the business in defendant's house after the buyers executed 14-year deeds of partnership with defendant.

- Plaintiff "covenanted" to accept the business and stock in trade, to perform the other actions stated above, and to give defendant "good and sufficient security, . . . to be approved of by the defendant," to guarantee monthly payment by plaintiff to defendant of £250 in lieu of defendant receiving

---

* [Authors' Note: We have substantially edited the opinion to make it more readable and have summarized significant portions, while retaining as much of the opinion's language and general sense as possible.]

** [Authors' Note: The pronoun "his" is ambiguous here. The commentators differ on whether the nomination process was by plaintiff or defendant or defendant's nephew. This kind of pronoun confusion is reminiscent of Bugs Bunny's classic cartoon on "pronoun trouble." For the cartoon, go to YouTube and search for "Rabbit Seasoning," or read the cartoon's script at http://en.wikipedia.org/wiki/Rabbit_Seasoning.]

a share of the business's income each month after the sale, payments to continue "until the value of the stock should be reduced to £4000."

At the end of the 15 months, defendant refused to convey the business to plaintiff, even though plaintiff allegedly had performed and stood ready to perform his covenants. Plaintiff brought an action of debt for defendant's non-performance of covenants (the equivalent of an action for breach of contract). Defendant claimed that plaintiff did not offer or furnish sufficient security for his future monthly payments of £250 to defendant.]

[Plaintiff demurred to defendant's defenses and argued that the covenants were mutual and independent; even if plaintiff was in breach as to one of his obligations, plaintiff could still recover from defendant for his separate breach. One breach could not be a defense for the other breach.]

[Defendant countered that the covenants were impliedly dependent, so that the plaintiff must give the defendant adequate security before the defendant has any duty to convey the business to the plaintiff. Otherwise the defendant would have to give up a beneficial business and valuable stock in trade, based only on the plaintiff's promise, when the plaintiff's worth is admittedly zero.]

[Lord Mansfield wrote:] There are three kinds of covenants:

> **Make the Connection**
>
> Despite its age, *Kingston* remains a foundational opinion for the American law of conditions, as another measure of the influence of Lord Mansfield (recall his biography in Chapter 3, page 188).

1. Such as are called mutual and independent [promises], where either party may recover damages from the other, for the injury he may have received by a breach of the covenants in his favour, and where it is no excuse for the defendant, to allege a breach of the covenants [by] plaintiff.

2. There are covenants which are conditions and dependent, in which the performance of one depends on the prior performance of another, and, therefore, till this prior condition is performed, the other party is not liable to an action on his covenant.

3. There is also a third set of covenants, which are mutual conditions to be performed at the same time; and in these, if one party was ready, and offered, to perform his part, and the other neglected, or refused, to perform his part, he who was ready, and offered, has fulfilled his engagement, and may maintain an action for the default of the other[,] though it is not certain that either is obliged to do the first act."

. . . [D]ependence, or independence, of covenants [is] to be collected from the evident sense and meaning of the parties, and . . . however transposed they might be in the deed, their precedency must depend on the order of time in which the intent of the transaction requires their performance.

. . . [I]n the case before the Court, it would be the greatest injustice if the plaintiff should prevail[. T]he essence of the agreement was, that the defendant should not trust to the personal security of the plaintiff, but, before [defendant] delivered up his stock and business, [he] should have good security for the [plaintiff's] payment of the money. The giving such security, therefore, must necessarily be a condition precedent.*

Judgment was accordingly given for the defendant, because the part to be performed by the plaintiff was clearly a condition precedent.

Problems: The *Kingston* Covenants

8-1. Fill in the following chart to articulate the characteristics of the three categories of covenants.

Type of Covenant	Does either party's performance or readiness trigger other party's duty to perform or be ready?	If either party fails (or is not ready) to perform, is it a breach?	If either party fails (or is not ready) to perform, does it affect the other party's duty to perform?
Mutual and independent promises	No	yes	no

---

* [Authors' Notes: Another reporter of *Kingston v. Preston*, 98 Eng. Rep. 606 (K.B. 1773), recounted Lord Mansfield's reasoning as follows:

> It would be the most monstrous case in the world, if the argument [by plaintiff] was to prevail. It's of the very essence of the agreement, that the defendant will not trust the personal security of the plaintiff. . . . He is to let him into his house to squander everything there, without any thing to rely on but what he has absolutely refused to trust. This payment, therefore, was a precedent condition before the covenant of putting into possession was to be performed on the part of the defendant.

The "condition precedent" in the holding is synonymous with "dependent condition," the second kind of covenant described by Lord Mansfield. Commentators agree that plaintiff's covenant here was a promise and therefore a "promissory condition" to defendant's duty to sell.]

some performance
by A conditions
some duty by B

Dependent condition	yes	no, not if A doesn't perform - if A performs + B doesn't, B in breach	yes
Mutual and simultaneous conditions	yes	yes	yes

8-2. For the following set of contractual arrangements, identify to which *Kingston* category of covenants each belongs. If multiple categories are possible for a particular pair of promises, identify them and suggest which is the better result.

a. *ment + simul here* A hardware store enters into a contract with a local contractor, for 16 wheelbarrows, to be picked up next Friday, "cash on the barrelhead" (that is, money to be paid as the goods are delivered).

b. *Dep* *1. loan for note* A promises to make a loan to B, in return for B's signed promissory note, which says that B will repay the loan in 8 years with 8% interest compounded annually. *2. money for repayment*

c *ment + Ind* A business contracts with a technology firm to have work done on the business's premises. In the contract, the business promises to pay the firm's monthly invoices within 30 days; the firm promises to give its on-site employees training to avoid sexual harassment.

d. *Dep* A contracts to make alterations in B's home for $5,000. $500 is to be paid on the signing of the contract, $1,500 when work is started, $2,000 on the completion of rough carpentry and rough plumbing, and $1,000 on the completion of the job.*

§ 3. Performance and Breach under the Common Law

When one party to a contract breaches its performance obligations, a critical question for the aggrieved party is whether or when she is permitted to suspend

_____

* Restatement (Second) § 234 illus. 11.

performance or to cancel the contract in response. The answer to this question differs between the common law and Article 2. This section addresses the common law rules; **section 5 (page 962)** covers the rules in UCC Article 2. In either situation and regardless of whether the aggrieved party is permitted to suspend performance or cancel, she can obtain damages for the breach, covered in **Chapter 9**.

§ 3.1. Implied Conditions and Performance Responsibilities

Consider a construction contract in which the builder's performance must be completed in order to satisfy the dependent condition that triggers the owner's duty to pay.** At the end of the construction process, the architect and perhaps the owner will walk through the building to determine whether the general contractor is entitled to the remaining payment. The building will not be flawless. Some corners will not be perfect 90° angles, the plaster skim coat will have some blemishes, a few closets might be minus the requisite coathooks, and there no doubt will be other defects as well. The owner or architect will make a "punch list" of the remaining defects, and most of them will be remedied by the contractor, but some will not (perhaps the imperfect corners). If flawless construction (perfect performance) is a condition precedent that must be satisfied before the owner has a duty to pay, then the contractor will not receive payment.

But is that the fairest result? If not, how can the law protect both the performing party (the contractor, who deserves compensation for work done) and the aggrieved party (who did not get full performance)? In the next case, Judge Cardozo used two of the covenant categories set out in *Kingston v. Preston,* to fashion a solution to this dilemma.

> **Reading the Law Critically: *Jacob & Youngs***
>
> 1 Under the construction contract, Jacob & Youngs has promised to build and Kent has promised to pay. One would likely start with the assumption that Kent's promise to pay is conditional on the contractor's performance (just as the plumbing customer's promise to pay is presumed to be

---

** In such contracts, rather than expect all payment to depend on completion of the project, the parties are likely to establish a sequence of progress payments along the way, with each payment dependent upon completion of a portion of the total performance, and the final payment due upon completion of the whole project (as in the facts in Problem 2.d. (page 892)). Often, the contract reserves about 10% of the total payment for the final inspection and certification of the completed building by the architect. The principles discussed in this section apply to each performance and its progress payment, as well as to the final step in the sequence.

conditional on the plumber's performance), putting the covenants into the second of the *Kingston* categories (a dependent condition, see *Kingston, page 890*). But the court suggests that what starts as a dependent condition at some point becomes a different kind of covenant in the *Kingston* categories.

a.   What different category does the court use?

b.   Why does the court think the category should change? What policies underlie the decision to treat the relationship between the two promises as different?

c.   What effect does this change have on the parties' rights and obligations?

2.   After noting the shift from one *Kingston* category to another, the court suggests a variety of factors (as many as 8) that may be used to decide when the dependent condition between the parties' promises shifts into this new category. Identify as many of those factors as you can; you will have to look carefully at the court's discussion to see them. Why is each factor relevant? How do these factors apply to the facts in this case?

3.   What is the fundamental disagreement between the majority and the dissent? Does the dissenting judge disagree with the court's categorization of the promises or with the application of the category? What result would the dissent have supported? What policy underlies the dissent's reasoning?

4.   Recall *Wood v. Lucy Lady Duff Gordon* (discussed in B. *Lewis Productions* in Chapter 4, page 275, and included in Chapter 7, page 801), in which Judge Cardozo used reasonableness and common sense to imply a crucial term—a duty to use reasonable efforts in an exclusive dealings contract. How does his jurisprudential approach in *Wood* compare to his approach in *Jacob & Youngs*?

5.   Would it have helped the plaintiff here to have explained in the contract why he wanted Reading pipe?

Jacob & Youngs v. Kent

JACOB & YOUNGS, Plaintiff

v.

GEORGE KENT, Defendant

Court of Appeals of New York

129 N.E. 889 (N.Y. 1921)

CARDOZO, J.

The plaintiff built a country residence for the defendant at a cost of upwards of $77,000, and now sues to recover a balance of $3,483.46, remaining unpaid. The work of construction ceased in June, 1914, and the defendant then began to occupy the dwelling. There was no complaint of defective performance until March, 1915. One of the specifications for the plumbing work provides that—

"All wrought-iron pipe must be well galvanized, lap welded pipe of the grade known as 'standard pipe' of Reading manufacture."

The defendant learned in March, 1915, that some of the pipe, instead of being made in Reading, was the product of other factories. The plaintiff was accordingly directed by the architect to do the work anew. The plumbing was then encased within the walls except in a few places where it had to be exposed. Obedience to the order meant more than the substitution of other pipe. It meant the demolition at great expense of substantial parts of the completed structure. The plaintiff left the work untouched, and asked for a certificate that the final payment was due. Refusal of the certificate was followed by this suit.

What's That?

The "certificate" mentioned here is the architect's certification to the owner that the contractor has complied with the building plans. A contract of this type typically requires the architect's certification before the owner has a duty to make the final payment of the contract price.

The evidence sustains a finding that the omission of the prescribed brand of pipe was neither fraudulent nor willful. It was the result of the oversight and inattention of the plaintiff's subcontractor. Reading pipe is distinguished from Cohoes pipe and other brands only by the name of the manufacturer stamped upon it at intervals of between six and seven feet. Even the defendant's architect, though he inspected the pipe upon arrival, failed to notice the discrepancy. The plaintiff tried to show that the brands installed, though made by other manufacturers, were the same in quality, in appearance, in market value, and in cost as the brand stated in the contract—that they were, indeed, the same thing, though manufactured in another place. The evidence was excluded, and a verdict directed for the defendant. The Appellate Division reversed, and granted a new trial.

We think the evidence, if admitted, would have supplied some basis for the inference that the defect was insignificant in its relation to the project. The courts never say that one who makes a contract fills the measure of his duty by less than full performance. They do say, however, that an omission, both trivial and innocent, will sometimes be atoned for by allowance of the resulting damage, and will not always be the breach of a condition to be followed by a forfeiture. Spence v. Ham, 163 N.Y. 220, 57 N.E. 412, 51 L. R. A. 238. . . . The distinction is akin to that between dependent and independent promises, or between promises and conditions. Anson on Contracts (Corbin's Ed.) § 367; 2 Williston on Contracts, § 842. Some promises are so plainly independent that they can never by fair construction be conditions of one another. Rosenthal Paper Co. v. Nat. Folding Box & Paper Co., 226 N.Y. 313, 123 N.E. 766 . . . . Others are so plainly dependent that they must always be conditions. Others, though dependent and thus conditions when there is departure in point of substance, will be viewed as independent and collateral when the departure is insignificant. 2 Williston on Contracts, §§ 841, 842; Eastern Forge Co. v. Corbin, 182 Mass. 590, 592, 66 N.E. 419 . . . . Considerations partly of justice and partly of presumable intention are to tell us whether this or that promise shall be placed in one class or in another. The simple and the uniform will call for different remedies from the multifarious and the intricate. The margin of departure within the range of normal expectation upon a sale of common chattels will vary from the margin to be expected upon a contract for the construction of a mansion or a "skyscraper." There will be harshness sometimes and oppression in the implication of a condition when the thing upon which labor has been expended is incapable of surrender because united to the land, and equity and reason in the implication of a like condition when the subject-matter, if defective, is in shape to be returned. From the conclusion that promises may not be treated as dependent to the extent of their uttermost minutiae without a sacrifice of justice, the progress is a short one to the conclusion that they may not be so treated without a perversion of intention. Intention not otherwise revealed may be presumed to hold in contemplation the reasonable and probable. If something else is in view, it must not be left to implication. There will be no assumption of a purpose to visit venial [trivial or small] faults with oppressive retribution.

Those who think more of symmetry and logic in the development of legal rules than of practical adaptation to the attainment of a just result will be troubled by a classification where the lines of division are so wavering and blurred. Something, doubtless, may be said on the score of consistency and certainty in favor of a stricter standard. The courts have balanced such considerations against those of equity and fairness, and found the latter to be the weightier. The decisions in this state commit us to the liberal view, which is making its way, nowadays, in jurisdictions slow to welcome it. Dakin & Co. v. Lee, 1916, 1 K. B. 566, 579. Where the line is to be drawn between the important and the trivial cannot be settled by a formula. "In the nature of the case precise boundaries are impossible." 2 Williston on Contracts, § 841. The same omission may take on one aspect or another according to its setting. Substitution of equivalents may not have the same significance in fields of art on the one side and in those of mere utility on the other. Nowhere will change be tolerated, however, if it is so dominant or pervasive as in any real or substantial measure to frustrate the purpose of the contract. **Crouch v. Gutmann, 134 N.Y. 45, 51, 31 N.E. 271, 30 Am. St. Rep. 608.** There is no general license to install whatever, in the builder's judgment, may be regarded as "just as good." **Easthampton L. & C. Co., Ltd., v. Worthington, 186 N.Y. 407, 412, 79 N.E. 323.** The question is one of degree, to be answered, if there is doubt, by the triers of the facts (Crouch v. Gutmann; Woodward v. Fuller, supra), and, if the inferences are certain, by the judges of the law (Easthampton L. & C. Co., Ltd., v. Worthington, supra). We must weigh the purpose to be served, the desire to be gratified, the excuse for deviation from the letter, the cruelty of enforced adherence. Then only can we tell whether literal fulfillment is to be implied by law as a condition. This is not to say that the parties are not free by apt and certain words to effectuate a purpose that performance of every term shall be a condition of recovery. That question is not here. This is merely to say that the law will be slow to impute the purpose, in the silence of the parties, where the significance of the default is grievously out of proportion to the oppression of the forfeiture. The willful transgressor must accept the penalty of his transgression. **Schultze v. Goodstein, 180 N.Y. 248, 251, 73 N.E. 21** . . . . For him there is no occasion to mitigate the rigor of implied conditions. The transgressor whose default is unintentional and trivial may hope for mercy if he will offer atonement for his wrong. Spence v. Ham, supra.

[Damages discussion from this case appears in **Chapter 9, page 1059.**]

The order should be affirmed, and judgment absolute directed in favor of the plaintiff upon the stipulation, with costs in all courts.

Think About It!

If you had a client who wanted to be absolutely sure Reading pipe was used in constructing his home, how would you structure the contract between the contractor and your client in view of the majority opinion?

McLAUGHLIN, J.

I dissent. The plaintiff did not perform its contract. Its failure to do so was either intentional or due to gross neglect which, under the uncontradicted facts, amounted to the same thing, nor did it make any proof of the cost of compliance, where compliance was possible.

Under its contract it obligated itself to use in the plumbing only pipe (between 2,000 and 2,500 feet) made by the Reading Manufacturing Company. The first pipe delivered was about 1,000 feet and the plaintiff's superintendent then called the attention of the foreman of the subcontractor, who was doing the plumbing, to the fact that the specifications annexed to the contract required all pipe used in the plumbing to be of the Reading Manufacturing Company. They then examined it for the purpose of ascertaining whether this delivery was of that manufacture and found it was. Thereafter, as pipe was required in the progress of the work, the foreman of the subcontractor would leave word at its shop that he wanted a specified number of feet of pipe, without in any way indicating of what manufacture. Pipe would thereafter be delivered and installed in the building, without any examination whatever. Indeed, no examination, so far as appears, was made by the plaintiff, the subcontractor, defendant's architect, or any one else, of any of the pipe except the first delivery, until after the building had been completed. Plaintiff's architect then refused to give the certificate of completion, upon which the final payment depended, because all of the pipe used in the plumbing was not of the kind called for by the contract. After such refusal, the subcontractor removed the covering or insulation from about 900 feet of pipe which was exposed in the basement, cellar, and attic, and all but 70 feet was found to have been manufactured, not by the Reading Company, but by other manufacturers, some by the Cohoes Rolling Mill Company, some by the National Steel Works, some by the South Chester Tubing Company, and some which bore no manufacturer's mark at all. The balance of the pipe had been so installed in the building that an inspection of it could not be had without demolishing, in part at least, the building itself.

I am of the opinion the trial court was right in directing a verdict for the defendant. The plaintiff agreed that all the pipe used should be of the Reading Manufacturing Company. Only about two-fifths of it, so far as appears, was of that kind. If more were used, then the burden of proving that fact was upon the plaintiff, which it could easily have done, since it knew where the pipe was obtained. The question of substantial performance of a contract of the character of the one under consideration depends in no small degree upon the good faith of the contractor. If the plaintiff had intended to, and had, complied with the terms of the contract except as to minor omissions, due to inadvertence, then he might be allowed to recover the contract price, less the amount necessary to fully compensate the defendant for damages caused by such omissions. Woodward v. Fuller, 80 N. Y. 312 . . . . But that is not this case. It installed between 2,000 and 2,500 feet of pipe, of which only 1,000 feet at most complied with the contract. No explanation was given why pipe called for by the contract was not used, nor that any effort made to show what it would cost to remove the pipe of other manufacturers and install that of the Reading Manufacturing Company. The defendant had a right to contract for what he wanted. He had a right before making payment to get what the contract called for. It is no answer to this suggestion to say that the pipe put in was just as good as that made by the Reading Manufacturing Company, or that the difference in value between such pipe and the pipe made by the Reading Manufacturing Company would be either "nominal or nothing." Defendant contracted for pipe made by the Reading Manufacturing Company. What his reason was for requiring this kind of pipe is of no importance. He wanted that and was entitled to it. It may have been a mere whim on his part, but even so, he had a right to this kind of pipe, regardless of whether some other kind, according to the opinion of the contractor or experts, would have been "just as good, better, or done just as well." He agreed to pay only upon condition that the pipe installed were made by that company and he ought not to be compelled to pay unless that condition be performed. Schultze v. Goodstein, 180 N.Y. 248, 73 N.E. 21 . . . . The rule, therefore, of substantial performance . . . has no application. Crouch v. Gutmann, 134 N.Y. 45, 31 N.E. 271, 30 Am. St. Rep. 608 . . . . What was said by this court in Smith v. Brady, supra, is quite applicable here:

> "I suppose it will be conceded that every one has a right to build his house, his cottage or his store after such a model and in such style as shall best accord with his notions of utility or be most agreeable to his fancy. The specifications of the contract become the law between the parties until voluntarily changed. If the owner prefers a plain and simple Doric column, and has so provided in the agreement, the contractor has no right to put in its place the more costly and elegant Corinthian. If the owner, having regard to strength and durability, has contracted for walls of specified materials to be laid in a particular manner, or for a given number of joists and beams, the builder has no right to substitute his own judgment or that of others. Having departed from the agreement, if performance has not been waived by the other party, the law will not allow him to allege that he has made as good a building as the one he engaged to

Make the Connection

The dissent would not have required Kent to pay the contract price; it reasoned that the condition precedent to his duty to pay was not satisfied. The majority holds Kent liable for the contract price and holds Jacob & Youngs liable for damages caused by its failure to perform completely under the contract. The remainder of the majority opinion is in Chapter 9, page 1059.

erect. He can demand payment only upon and according to the terms of his contract, and if the conditions on which payment is due have not been performed, then the right to demand it does not exist. To hold a different doctrine would be simply to make another contract, and would be giving to parties an encouragement to violate their engagements, which the just policy of the law does not permit." (17 N.Y. 186, 72 Am. Dec. 422).

I am of the opinion the trial court did not err in ruling on the admission of evidence or in directing a verdict for the defendant.

For the foregoing reasons I think the judgment of the Appellate Division should be reversed and the judgment of the Trial Term affirmed.

HISCOCK, C. J., and HOGAN and CRANE, JJ., concur with CARDOZO, J.

POUND and ANDREWS, JJ., concur with McLAUGHLIN, J.

Order affirmed, etc.

Behind the Scenes

In the early 1900s, George Edward Kent was a lawyer in New York City. He and his wife, Lillias, arranged to have a country home built on Long Island (near the summer White House of Theodore Roosevelt). The lot's location on the Jericho Turnpike made it a convenient commute from the city. The town of Jericho was inhabited by fewer than 600 people, chiefly Quaker farmers. The cost of construction of the house was about $80,000 (at today's value, $1.5 million according to the consumer price index, or $24 million using the relative share of the GDP).*

Landscaped gardens were added to the house a few years later, designed by Olmsted Brothers & Company, the successor company to Frederick Law Olmstead (who was a collaborator on the plan for Central Park,

---

* *See* http://lawprofessors.typepad.com/contractsprof_blog/2005/12/today_in_histor_10.html (including two pictures in Jericho). For excerpts from the parties' contract, see Richard Danzig & Geoffrey R. Watson, *The Capability Problem in Contract Law* 96 (2d ed. 2004). Danzig and Watson were unable to uncover any business or family connections between Kent and the Reading Pipe Company. *Id.* at 109-10.

and later designed the U.S. Capitol Grounds, the park systems in Milwaukee and Rochester, New York, and, and the World's Columbian Exposition in Chicago). The Kent residence was later demolished.*

When the Kent home was built, wrought iron pipe was enjoying a surge in sales in New York City, where it was being used in construction of skyscrapers and upscale homes, apparently because of its claimed superiority to steel pipe. (Reading Pipe was used in the Chrysler Building and other famous buildings.) However, at trial, Kent was unable to prove that Reading's wrought iron pipe was superior to the competing wrought iron pipe that was substituted in Kent's house. It was common in that day for construction contracts to specify one of the four competing brands for wrought iron pipe as a standard, to avoid substitution of inferior steel pipe or other pretenders, so some have speculated that the clause was meant to require wrought iron pipe, but not a particular brand.**

The parties' correspondence and the pleadings show that, as their interactions became more contentious, the parties agreed to several contract modifications concerning time extensions and cost increases on the project. No particular dispute seemed to predominate. The Kent family moved into the house in June 1914; the contractor completed its work five months later, in November 1914, except for "minor details." Kent's architect discovered the non-Reading pipe in March 1915 and demanded its replacement, to no avail. (Commentators speculate that the architect probably was negligent in not discovering it before it was installed or covered over.) In January 1916, the architect used the non-conforming unreplaced pipe as the basis for exercising the owners' contractual right to terminate the contract with Jacob & Youngs, who waited until November 1916 to demand the architect's certificate and then filed suit in December.***

Even decades later, Reading Pipe's advertisements continued to focus on the claimed superiority of the company's wrought iron pipe, over steel and cheaper products:

---

* Further information about the house appears at http://www.philadelphiabuildings.org/pab/app/pj_display.cfm/126806, a website about Philadelphia architects and buildings.
** *See* Richard Danzig & Geoffrey R. Watson, *The Capability Problem in Contract Law* 110-12 (2d ed. 2004).
*** *Id.* at 114-15.

Unfailing supplies of clear, sparkling water, unclogged heating lines, and freedom from repairs at low cost are made possible by metal tested for 83 years.

For 83 years, Reading has been assuring clean water, unclogged pipe lines, and freedom from repairs for many, many years, by making pipe of genuine puddled wrought iron.

In modest home, in mansion, in factories and buildings, large and small, on locomotives, railroad cars and ships, under water, under ground, on the surface, between walls and floors, this pipe has been given all the terrible tests of service in every conceivable way for over four generations.

Only seven years ago, every inch of Reading Genuine Puddled Wrought Iron Pipe was marked with an indestructible indented spiral so that you can be sure of getting the pipe that has passed the tests of time.

It had to be marked because many people had become careless in using the word "iron". For many years "iron" had popularly meant puddled wrought iron as Reading made it then and still makes it. Quickly-rusting materials were developed that look like "iron", and often are sold as an "iron". But, of course, they failed to give the service which only genuine puddled wrought iron gives.

That's why, if you want permanence, freedom from repairs, and unfailing flow of water air, gas, oil, or other liquids, look for the honest spiral, mark of the pipe that has been tested for four generations.

Fortune Magazine, vol. 111, no. 2, p. 134 (Feb. 1931).

§ 3.2. Substantial Performance or Material Breach?

As reflected in *Jacob & Youngs*, a different level of performance is required to satisfy an implied condition than to satisfy an express condition. If party A fails to perform in some respect but achieves the level of performance necessary to satisfy the implied condition, it triggers party B's duty to perform the connected promise(s). Party A is then said to have committed a partial or non-material breach while rendering "substantial performance." Substantial performance does not mean full performance; if party A breaches in some respects while substantially performing, party B must perform (or pay) but is owed damages for any breach.

material breach: party doesn't complete enough

If party A does *not* achieve substantial performance, it is called a "material breach"—the opposite of substantial performance. Then party A has not satisfied the condition, so party B's duty to perform the connected promise(s) does not arise. In a construction contract, that would mean that party A cannot enforce the contract to make party B pay. Party A—who has done work benefiting party B, even while materially breaching—is not left without recourse, however. Chapter 9 (page 1148) examines the availability of restitution for party A if party B has no duty to pay under the contract.

substantial performance: yes, they did enough

As demonstrated in the next two cases, the line defining substantial performance and material breach is a fuzzy one, because it is decided by an aggregate standard—a standard that depends on the weighing of a number of factors arising from the particular circumstances in the case. Not all the factors need be present, and the articulations of the rule do not name every factor that may be taken into account. The outcome depends on an analysis of the strength or weakness of each factor that is present, making outcomes hard to compare from case to case. This level of uncertainty also creates a substantial potential for litigation on a critical issue.

standard weighs a lot of factors

Reading the Law Critically:
Roberts Contracting Co. and *Khiterer*

1. How does each court decide whether there was substantial performance or material breach? What factors are identified as important? How are they applied and weighed to determine the outcome?

2. Do the courts' rules match those in *Jacob & Youngs* (page 895)? Do these two courts use additional or different factors from those considered in *Jacobs & Youngs*? For instance, recall that the rule in *Jacob & Youngs* included consideration of whether the contractor's defective performance was "willful," as opposed to "innocent" and "unintentional." Is that factor considered by the *Roberts Contracting* court? If not, which factor seems to take its place?

Interestingly, the first Restatement follows the approach in *Jacob & Youngs*, while the court in *Roberts Contracting* uses the Restatement (Second) rule, so these two cases embody a major split in this area of law.

sewer contract
- completed 90%
before employees
quit
not done, won't pay

Roberts Contracting Co. v. Valentine-Wooten Road Public Facility Bd.

ROBERTS CONTRACTING COMPANY, INC., Plaintiff-Appellant

v.

VALENTINE-WOOTEN ROAD PUBLIC FACILITY BOARD, Defendant-Appellee

Court of Appeals of Arkansas

320 S.W.3d 1 (Ark. Ct. App. 2009)

RITA W. GRUBER, Judge.

Lots of
delays

This case involves a sewer system that was not fully completed. In June 2004, appellant Roberts Contracting Company, Inc. (Roberts), agreed to build and complete a sewer system for appellee Valentine-Wooten Road Public Facility Board (VWR) by April 12, 2005. Although VWR agreed to obtain all necessary easements, it did not resolve disputes with two landowners until very late in the project. Those issues, along with wet weather and a contract dispute between the project engineer, Bond Consulting Engineers, Inc., and Pulaski County, delayed construction. More than a year past the original completion date, with at least one extension granted, Roberts walked off the job and VWR refused to pay all of Roberts's last bill. The sewer system was not operational. Roberts sued VWR for breach of contract . . . . After a bench trial, the circuit court denied Roberts's claim on the ground that it had not substantially performed, and awarded liquidated damages for the delay to VWR. Roberts then filed this appeal, and VWR cross-appealed. The issues we must decide are whether Roberts substantially performed; whether Roberts may recover for the work it did complete; [and damages issues] . . . . We hold that . . . Roberts did not substantially perform . . . .

I. Facts and Procedural History

The contract provided that VWR would pay $2,088,166 for Roberts to build the sewer system, which was to be accepted by the City of Jacksonville . . . . Roberts received an extension from VWR until October 20, 2005, but did not finish the job by then. By fall 2005, Roberts had installed and tested the sewer lines, and had installed five pump stations and the force-main pipes and related equipment. The disputes over the easements across the Pickens and Harris properties, however, had frustrated completion. The pump station on the Pickens property still lacked power, and Mr. Harris had damaged a force main on his property that Roberts had, at VWR's direction, placed outside the easement. The Pickens easement was finally settled in January 2006, but the Harris dispute was not resolved until May 2006. Further, Bond Consulting Engineers stopped its on-site supervision of the job in December 2005 after a dispute with Pulaski County over payment. The parties disagree about whether VWR's failure to fulfill its obligations hindered Roberts's ability to perform and whether VWR agreed to another extension until May 1, 2006. Roberts left the job at this time.

On May 16, 2006, VWR refused to pay Roberts the entire amount of a bill on the ground that it had not completed all of the work. The pay estimate indicated that retainage (from work already performed and partially paid)[1] at that time was $104,408.30, and that Roberts had earned an additional $57,532.50, which had not yet been paid. Roberts refused to perform further and asserted that the pur-

What's That?

A "retainage" is the final payment due from the owner of the project, usually conditioned on full performance of the contract.

portedly incomplete work was not within the scope of the contract. It also claimed that its ability to perform had been hampered by VWR's failure to perform its obligations. A video inspection performed by Jacksonville Waste Water Utility in November 2006, more than a year after the lines had been successfully tested, revealed numerous defects and debris in the sewer system.

Roberts took the position that the problems in the lines had developed during the year-long interval between its completion of the lines and the taping.

Roberts sued VWR for breach of contract, alleging that it had substantially performed, and seeking $162,502.80. . . . VWR denied that Roberts had substantially performed . . . . According to VWR, Roberts failed to perform the following contractual obligations: installing a working SCADA system for each pump station;[2] adequately testing its work; completing the sewer system so that it could be accepted by the City of Jacksonville; and, after completing the system, submitting "as-built" drawings. . . .

. . . . At the conclusion of its case, Roberts moved to amend the pleadings to conform to its proof of damages in the sum of $177,390.80. The court granted this motion. . . .

II. The Circuit Court Ruling

The trial court issued a letter opinion finding that Roberts had not substantially completed[3] the project; that the sewer system was not operational; that VWR had not yet received any benefit from the project; and that Roberts would not suf-

---

[1] The contract provided that retainage would be released upon acceptance of the Certificate of Substantial Completion.

[2] The SCADA system electronically monitors a pump station. It does not operate it. Roberts bid $12,650 for each of the five SCADA units to be installed, for a total of $63,250.

[3] Though the trial court referred to Roberts's efforts under the contract as not having "substantially completed" the project, the precedent discusses similar efforts in terms of substantial performance.

fer forfeiture because it had been paid for the part of the job it had completed. The court noted that the pumping stations had not been tested or turned on because electricity was not provided to them, and that, by the "plain language" of the contract, Roberts had the responsibility for providing electricity. The court stated that Roberts was also required by the contract to provide the SCADA system. It further found that the contract required Roberts to provide the as-built drawings, although, if everything else had been accomplished, the court said that it would have found that Roberts had substantially complied. . . .

The court entered a judgment incorporating these findings and denying Roberts's request for damages because it had not substantially completed the project. In the judgment, the court directed Roberts to provide the SCADA system within 90 days, upon which it would be entitled to receive the contract price, and ordered it to provide VWR with as-built drawings. . . .

III. Standard of review

In civil bench trials, the standard of review on appeal is whether the trial court's findings were clearly erroneous or clearly against a preponderance of the evidence. *Rooke v. Spickelmier,* — Ark.App. —, [2009 WL 537546] (Mar. 4, 2009). A finding is clearly erroneous when, although there is evidence to support it, the reviewing court, on the entire evidence, is left with a firm conviction that a mistake has been committed. *Id.*

IV. Direct appeal

A. Substantial Performance - not done enough

Roberts first argues that the trial court's finding that it did not substantially perform its obligations under the contract was clearly erroneous, even though the system was not fully complete and operational. When a contractor is in default by having failed to complete the contract, he can recover in spite of his breach if his performance was sufficiently substantial. *Cox v. Bishop,* 28 Ark.App. 210, 772 S.W.2d 358 (1989). If omissions or deviations from the contract are inadvertent or unintentional; are not due to bad faith; do not impair the structure as a whole; and are remediable without doing material damage, substantial performance permits the contractor to be compensated, with deductions from the contract price. *Id.* "The doctrine of substantial performance is intended to protect the right to compensation of those who have performed in all material and substantive particulars, so that their right to compensation may not be forfeited by reason of mere technical, inadvertent, or unimportant omissions or defects." 15 Samuel Williston, *A Treatise on the Law of Contracts* § 44:52, at 220-21 (4th ed.2000). The *Restatement (Second) of Contracts* § 241 (1981) characterizes this question as whether a failure of performance was "material." A material breach is a failure

[handwritten margin note: does it defeat purpose?]

to perform an essential term or condition that substantially defeats the purpose of the contract for the other party. AMI Civ. 2427 (2005).

Substantial performance cannot be determined by a mathematical rule relating to the percentage of the cost of completion. *Cox, supra.* There is no precise formula to use, *Roberts & Co. v. Sergio,* 22 Ark.App. 58, 733 S.W.2d 420 (1987), and the issue of substantial performance is a question of fact. *Cox, supra.* In determining whether performance is substantial, the following considerations are significant: (1) the extent to which the injured party will be deprived of the benefit that he reasonably expected; (2) the extent to which the injured party can be adequately compensated for the part of that benefit of which he will be deprived; (3) the extent to which the party failing to perform or to offer to perform will suffer forfeiture; (4) the likelihood that the party failing to perform or offer to perform will cure his failure, taking account of all the circumstances, including any reasonable assurances; and (5) the extent to which the behavior of the party failing to perform or to offer to perform comports with standards of good faith and fair dealing. *Id.*; see also* 8 Arthur L. Corbin, *Corbin on Contracts* § 36.1 (rev. ed. 1999).

[handwritten margin note: how bad is nonperformance]

Roberts challenges the trial court's finding that VWR derived no benefit from the work that Roberts completed. It also argues that it was not required to arrange for permanent electrical power to the pump stations and asserts that VWR was obligated to make those arrangements, including the one on the Pickens property. As for the other unfinished work, Roberts asserts that its other failures—not installing the SCADA system; not repairing the cut

> **Think About It!**
>
> The court cites the *Cox* case for five enumerated factors, which were derived from the Restatement (Second) of Contracts § 241. That section appears on page 919.
>
> Why is each of these factors relevant to the issue of whether a breach is material? How are these factors applied by the court to the facts of this case? Are any factors not relevant to this case?

in the force main caused by Mr. Harris; not providing as-built drawings; and not repairing the problems disclosed by Jacksonville's video—did not render its performance less than substantial. It was undisputed that the gravity lines, manholes, and force mains (except for the one damaged by Mr. Harris) passed all tests required by the contract in the fall of 2005, a year before the video tape raised questions about the quality of Roberts's performance. It was undisputed that the specifications required a SCADA-system contractor to perform that installation; that Jacksonville wanted a SCADA system purchased and installed by the manufacturer with whom it had previously dealt; and that none of the SCADA-system funds held by VWR had been spent. It was also undisputed that the manufacturer

[handwritten margin note: we did good enough]

of the pump stations had already been paid and was obligated to perform the tests on them, once the stations got permanent electrical power.

Roberts also urges us to recognize that some major delays were caused by VWR's failure to settle the easement across the Harris property before May 2006 or to resolve the Pickens dispute before January 2006. We note that paragraph 5.1.2 of the contract expressly required VWR to obtain all land and rights-of-way necessary for the project before Roberts started work, but VWR failed to do so. . . .

B. Breach of Contract/Interpretation

Before addressing whether Roberts's purported breaches of the contract were material or sufficient to prevent its performance from being considered substantial, it is necessary to decide whether Roberts actually breached the contract. Roberts asserts that some of its purported omissions, especially arranging for permanent electrical power, were not even required by the contract.

An analysis of a breach-of-contract claim based upon the theory of substantial performance must begin with a determination of the contract's terms. 15 Samuel Williston, *A Treatise on the Law of Contracts* § 44:54, at 228. When performance of a duty under a contract is contemplated, any nonperformance of that duty is a breach. *Taylor v. George*, 92 Ark.App. 264, 212 S.W.3d 17 (2005). It is a well-settled rule that the intention of the parties to a contract is to be gathered, not from particular words and phrases, but from the whole context of the agreement. *Wal-Mart Stores, Inc. v. Coughlin*, 369 Ark. 365, 255 S.W.3d 424 (2007). The court is to give great weight to the construction of the contract given to it by the parties, *Synergy Gas Corp. v. H.M. Orsburn & Son, Inc.*, 15 Ark. App. 128, 689 S.W.2d 594 (1985), and it may look to the conduct of the parties to determine their intent. Taylor, supra. When a contract is free of ambiguity, its construction and legal effect are questions of law for the court to determine. *State Farm Fire & Cas. Co. v. Amos*, 32 Ark.App. 164, 798 S.W.2d 440 (1990). Language is ambiguous if there is doubt or uncertainty as to its meaning and it is fairly susceptible to more than one equally reasonable interpretation. *Nash v. Landmark Storage, LLC*, 102 Ark.App. 182, [283 S.W.3d 605] (2008). The determination of whether ambiguity exists is ordinarily a question of law for courts to resolve. *Magic Touch Corp. v. Hicks*, 99 Ark.App. 334, 260 S.W.3d 322 (2007).

The trial court concluded that the contract unambiguously required Roberts to provide the SCADA system and the electrical power, and that Roberts's failure to perform both of these obligations rendered its performance less than substantial. As for the permanent electrical power, we disagree. We conclude that this portion of the contract was ambiguous and the parties' course of performance demonstrated that they intended for VWR to be equally responsible with Roberts in arranging for permanent power. *Taylor, supra.*

Paragraph 3.1 of the contract, which set forth Roberts's responsibilities, provided in subparagraph 3.1.1:

> It is understood that unless otherwise specifically stated in the contract documents, the contractor shall provide and pay for all materials, labor, tools, equipment, water, light, power, transportation, superintendence, temporary construction of every kind, and all other services and facilities of every kind whatsoever necessary to execute, complete, and deliver the complete project within the specified time.

Brad Roberts testified that he interpreted the contract as simply requiring Roberts to provide temporary power to the pump stations. Roberts's expert witness, Michael Bolin, testified that "it's always the owner who provides the power . . . ." Although Josh Minton testified that the responsibility to provide power lay with Roberts, the parties' course of performance showed a joint effort to obtain power. Indeed, the parties acted as though the responsibility lay with both sides and required mutual cooperation. In the end, because of misunderstandings and miscommunication, electrical power to the remaining pump stations was not completed. We therefore hold that the trial court's finding that Roberts was solely required to provide the permanent electrical power was clearly erroneous.

VWR does not dispute that Roberts completed at least 90% of its work. By November 2005, Roberts had installed and tested the pipe and manholes required by Schedule I of the contract. It also installed the force-main pipe and related equipment, as well as five pump stations, set forth in Schedule II. We note that VWR approved the May 16, 2006 pay estimate reflecting that Schedule II of the contract was 100% complete, except for connecting to the Jacksonville pump stations, which (the evidence showed) Jacksonville was not yet ready to complete. The evidence demonstrated that Roberts's failure to complete the testing was, at least partially, excused by VWR's failure to timely acquire all of the necessary easements and to help get electrical power to the other pump stations. A property owner and VWR board member, Mr. Harris, dug up and with a chain saw damaged a force main that was installed where VWR and Bond had instructed Roberts to place it, outside the easement. Additionally, there also was no permanent power to the pump station on the Pickens property, where VWR failed to secure the easement until long after it was needed. As a result, neither the force main nor the pump station could be tested. In light of VWR's failure to fully perform its own obligations, we cannot say that Roberts materially breached the contract in regard to permanent electrical power.

Although the SCADA system was an "alternate bid," which Brad Roberts stated was something that Roberts would "help" VWR with, there was testimony that the parties understood that it was Roberts's responsibility to purchase the system for installation, and the total bid awarded included this purchase item. The trial court, therefore, did not clearly err in ruling that the SCADA system was Roberts's responsibility. But it was undisputed that the SCADA system was not essential to the sewer system's operation. The pump stations could be monitored manually. We therefore cannot agree that the SCADA system's omission was a material breach or rendered Roberts's performance less than substantial. . . .

Although Roberts was required to supply the as-built drawings, its only role in that process was to serve as a conduit. Bond Consulting Engineers was to prepare the drawings, and Roberts was to then deliver them to VWR. The trial court found as much in its final order. We therefore hold that no material breach occurred on the as-built drawing.

Nevertheless, we cannot say that the trial court's finding of fact that Roberts did not substantially perform is clearly erroneous. The court found that Roberts breached the contract because it did not complete the project. When Roberts walked off the job, VWR did not yet have the benefit it expected, a working sewer system. This is the first significant consideration in determining substantial performance. *Cox,* 28 Ark.App. at 213, 772 S.W.2d at 359. "[A] high degree of difference in form and usefulness may be decisive on the question of substantial performance . . . ." 8 Arthur L. Corbin, *Corbin on Contracts* § 36.7, at 347. We conclude that this consideration carries great weight in this case. A working sewer system was the essence of this contract. Unlike in the *City of Whitehall v. Southern Mechanical Contracting,* 269 Ark. 563, 599 S.W.2d 430 (1980), this case was not about which party was legally responsible for problems and costs incurred along the way to an operational sewer system. This sewer system was more like a building that—though much work had been done on it—could not be occupied and used when the contractor abandoned the job.

Roberts throwing its hands up and leaving the project is another significant consideration. *Cox,* 28 Ark.App. at 213, 772 S.W.2d at 360. While VWR fell short in cooperating on permanent power, Roberts walked out rather than continuing to push to resolve this important issue. There was no likelihood of Roberts curing, another factor that weighed against a finding of substantial performance. *Cox,* 28 Ark.App. at 213, 772 S.W.2d at 359. Next, because Roberts was paid for almost all of its work along the way—more than 1.8 million dollars—the scope of the contractor's potential forfeiture was relatively small. *Id.* The remaining factor pointed both ways: hypothetically, VWR could have been compensated for the lost benefit with cost-of-completion and cost-of-repair damages; in this case, however, VWR's proof on those issues failed. Without question, Roberts's work on the sewer system was considerable. Based upon the record as a whole, and the settled law about the significant considerations in determining substantial performance, however, we are not left with the definite and firm conviction that the circuit court erred in finding no substantial performance.

[The court then considered whether Roberts could be compensated in restitution for the work it did that had benefitted VWR, despite Roberts' failure to substantially perform, an issue discussed in Chapter 9. Further discussion of damages issues is omitted.]

VII. Conclusion

In the direct appeal, we affirm the trial court's finding that Roberts was required to provide the SCADA system . . . [and] affirm the trial court's finding that Roberts did not substantially perform . . . .

Khiterer v. Bell

INNA KHITERER, Claimant

v.

MINA BELL, Defendant

Civil Court, City of New York, Kings County
2005 WL 192354 (N.Y. City Civ. Ct. Jan. 28, 2005) (unreported opinion)

JACK M. BATTAGLIA, J.

A patient who proves breach of a contract for professional dental services, but does not also prove personal or economic harm, may recover only nominal damages for the breach.

Inna Khiterer began treating with Dr. Mina Bell in October 2001. The treatment included root canal therapy on two teeth and the fabrication and fitting of crowns for those teeth, as well as the fabrication and fitting of a replacement crown for a third tooth. The crowns were fitted in June 2002, and, after several broken appointments, Ms. Khiterer last saw Dr. Bell in December 2002. Ms. Khiterer treated with another dentist the following summer, and, according to her testimony at trial, learned that the crowns with which she was fitted by Dr. Bell were not fabricated in accordance with their agreement. Specifically, the crowns were made totally of porcelain, rather than of porcelain on gold as they, allegedly, should have been.

Ms. Khiterer's complaint in this Small Claims Part action alleges "defective services rendered and breach of contract". Advised prior to trial that any claim in the nature of dental malpractice required expert proof . . . , Ms. Khiterer elected to proceed on her breach of contract claim only.

"A breach of contract claim in relation to the rendition of medical or dental services by a physician or dentist will withstand a test of its legal sufficiency only when based upon an express special promise to effect a cure or accomplish some definite result." (*Clarke v. Mikail*, 238 A.D.2d 538, 538 (2d Dept 1997); *see also Robins v. Finestone*, 308 N.Y. 543, 546 (1955).) A contract cause of action might be based upon a "specific promise to deliver [a] baby without administration of blood" (*see Nicoleau v. Brookhaven Memorial Hospital Center*, 201 A.D.2d 544, 545 (2d Dept 1994); a "special contract" by a dentist "to remove every part of [extracted] teeth from every part of the [patient's] body" (*see Keating v. Perkins*, 250 AD 9, 10 (1st Dept 1937); a "promise" by a dentist to return the fee paid for "bridge and crown work" if the patient was "dissatisfied" (*see Aymar v. Bloomingdale*, 157 NYS 837, 837 (App Term, 1st Dept 1916)); and a "special agreement" by a plastic surgeon "to employ a different method than plastic surgeons use" (*see Paciocco v. Acker*, 121 Misc.2d 342, 342 (Sup Ct, Nassau County 1983)).

Make the Connection

Recall, from *Lawrence v. Ingham County Health Department Family Planning Clinic* on page 135 and from the Food for Thought box on page 142, how rarely physicians' services are held to include a promise of a particular result. The cases cited here are those exceptional instances.

The agreement alleged here, for dental services including root canal therapy and the fabrication and fitting of crowns made of porcelain on gold, had as its predominant purpose the furnishing of services, and is, therefore, governed by the general law of contracts and not by Article 2 of the Uniform Commercial Code. (*See Perlmutter v. Beth David Hospital*, 308 N.Y. 100, 106 (1954); *Betro v. GAC Intern., Inc.*, 158 A.D.2d 498, 499 (2d Dept 1990); *Goldfarb v. Teitelbaum*, 149 A.D.2d 566, 567 (2d Dept 1989).) . . .

Ms. Khiterer testified that, because she had previously been fitted with crowns made of porcelain on gold (actually an 86% gold alloy, as Dr. Bell explained), she requested that the three crowns that she would receive from Dr. Bell also be made of porcelain on gold. Ms. Khiterer also offered the testimony of a friend, Sergei Leontev, who said that he was present during a conversation between Ms. Khiterer and Dr. Bell, and heard Dr. Bell assure Ms. Khiterer that she would be receiving three "golden-based crowns". Mr. Leontev also testified that he made a similar agreement with Dr. Bell that was later changed to all-porcelain crowns.

Dr. Bell testified that she had no independent recollection of any conversation with Ms. Khiterer about the composite material for the crowns. She testified further that an all-porcelain crown was therapeutically superior to a crown containing any metal, including the gold alloy, because the presence of metal created a risk of patient reaction. The cost to her, she said, of an all-porcelain crown and a porcelain-on-metal crown is the same, but the cement that binds the all-porcelain crown is more expensive.

[handwritten margin note: pretty much the same cost]

Dr. Bell presented a copy of Ms. Khiterer's chart, showing an entry for the first visit on October 21, 2001 of "crowns metal-free". Impressions for the crowns, however, were apparently taken seven months later on May 30, 2002. Ms. Khiterer presented a summary of all treatment she received from Dr. Bell, handwritten by Dr. Bell, showing the notations for two teeth "rct / post / crown / pfm" and for one additional tooth "pfm". Dr. Bell explained that "rct" stood for "root canal therapy" and that "pfm" stood for "porcelain fused metal". She maintained that "pfm" was shorthand for any crown no matter the composition, but did not satisfactorily explain the then-redundant notation "crown/pfm".

The Court finds that the contract between Ms. Khiterer and Dr. Bell called for crowns made of porcelain on gold, but that the crowns with which Ms. Khiterer was fitted were made of all porcelain. There is no evidence that Dr. Bell intentionally substituted all porcelain for porcelain on gold. Intent is not required, of course, for a breach of contract, but, as will appear, it may affect the remedy for the breach. Dr. Bell pointed to an entry in Ms. Khiterer's chart for June 5, 2002, the date the crowns were fitted, that reads, "Patient satisfied w/ esthetic [*sic*] cementation", as evidence that Ms. Khiterer was satisfied with the all-porcelain crowns. But the entry cannot bear that weight, particularly in light of the evidence that Ms. Khiterer could not and did not know that the crowns were all porcelain until her teeth were x-rayed by her successor dentist.

[handwritten margin note: sued her for the breach of time]

. . . .

Developed in the context of construction contracts, the substantial performance doctrine allows the contractor to recover or retain the contract price for the work, with a deduction for the cost of completion or correction to contract requirements. (*See James E. McMurray Enterprises, Inc. v. Frohlich,* 309 A.D.2d 836, 837 (2d Dept 2003); *Teramo & Co., Inc. v. O'Brien-Sheipe Funeral Home, Inc.,* 283 A.D.2d 635, 637 (2d Dept 2001).) The doctrine is applicable to employment contracts (*see Hadden v. Consolidated Edison Co. of New York, Inc.,* 34 N.Y.2d 88, 96 (1974), real estate brokerage agreements (*see Kaye v. Greenspan,* 118 A.D.2d 831, 832 (2d Dept 1986)), and leases (*see Vanguard Diversified, Inc. v. Review Co.,* 35 A.D.2d 102, 105 (2d Dept 1970)), and no reason suggests itself for not applying the doctrine as well to contracts for medical or dental services.

[handwritten margin note: paid for what completed]

As articulated by Judge Cardozo in his seminal opinion in *Jacob & Youngs v. Kent* (230 N.Y. 239 (1921)), "The courts never say that one who makes a contract fills the measure of his duty by less than full performance. They do say, however, that an omission, both trivial and innocent, will sometimes be atoned for by allowance of the resulting damage, and will not always be the breach of a condition to be followed by a forfeiture" (*id.*, at 241). The doctrine is required by justice, so as not "to visit venial faults with oppressive retribution" (*see id.*, at 242), and "[t]he transgressor whose default is unintentional and trivial may hope for mercy if he will offer atonement for his wrong" (*id.*, at 244). But "[t]he willful transgressor must accept the penalty of his transgression." (*Id.*) "The interrupted work may have been better than called for in the plans. Even so, there can be no recovery if the contractor willfully and without excuse has substituted something else." (*Buccini v. Paterno Construction Co .*, 253 N.Y. 256, 258-59 (1930); *see also Hadden v. Consolidated Edison Co. of New York, Inc.*, 34 N.Y.2d at 98 n 9 ("treating willfulness ... as one of several factors to be considered in determining whether ... performance is substantial" when subject contract is "divisible").)

"[C]onveying a benefit upon a party does not ipso facto constitute substantial performance." (*Joson Iron Works, Inc. v. Staten Island Majors Realty Corp*, 1998 U.S. App LEXIS 22043, *7 (2d Cir) (applying New York law).) "A contractor is not entitled to compensation from an owner even for improvements which benefit the owner unless that is a benefit for which an owner agreed to pay." (*Nieman-Irving & Co. v. Lazenby*, 263 N.Y. 91, 94 (1933).)

"Substitution of equivalents may not have the same significance in fields of art on the one side and in those of mere utility on the other." (*Jacob & Youngs v. Kent*, 230 N.Y. at 243; *see also Lyon v. Belosky Construction Inc.*, 247 A.D.2d 730, 732 (3d Dept 1998) ("the aesthetic appearance of the home, both inside and out, was of utmost importance to the plaintiffs"); *Ferrari v. Barleo Homes, Inc.*, 112 A.D.2d 137, 138 (2d Dept 1985) ("the small difference in the thickness of the floors created by the substitution was not noticeable").) "Nowhere will change be tolerated, however, if it is so dominant or pervasive as in any real or substantial measure to frustrate the purpose of the contract . . . . There is no general license to install whatever, in the builder's judgment, may be regarded as 'just as good' . . . . We must weigh the purpose to be served, the desire to be gratified, the excuse for deviation from the letter, the cruelty of enforced adherence." (*Jacob & Youngs v. Kent*, 230 N.Y. at 243 (*quoting Easthampton Lumber & Coal Co. v. Worthington*, 186 N.Y. 407, 412 (1906).)

. . . .

Here, as already noted, there is no evidence that Dr. Bell intentionally substituted all porcelain for porcelain on gold as the material from which Ms. Khiterer's crowns were to be fabricated. The all-porcelain crowns were clearly suitable functionally for the intended purpose; indeed, there is no evidence to contradict Dr. Bell's opinion that they were better. Nor was there evidence to contradict her testimony of economic equivalence, and Ms. Khiterer testified that the fee she was charged by Dr. Bell was significantly less than the fee she had been quoted by other dentists. There is no evidence of physical harm to Ms. Khiterer from the all-porcelain crowns; although she testified that two of the crowns have been replaced by porcelain-on-gold crowns, there was no evidence that the replacement was necessitated by the composition of the all-porcelain crowns. And Ms. Khiterer was satisfied with the all-porcelain crowns from an aesthetic perspective.

still got quality crowns

If, therefore, there is to be a determination that Dr. Bell did not substantially perform her contract with Ms. Khiterer—or, to put it differently, that her performance was substantially defective it must rest on recognition of a patient's right to control, without qualification, any material that would become part of her body. The only decision of which this Court is aware that seems relevant to the issue suggests that the contract action against a doctor or dentist does not extend that far.

In *Semel v. Culliford* (120 A.D.2d 901), the patient alleged that the doctor "fail[ed] to accomplish what he specifically undertook and agreed to do, take out all of the wire sutures" that had been implanted in the patient during previous open-heart surgery (*see id., at 902*). The court held that, "[a]s drafted", the patient's contract cause of action could not withstand the doctor's motion for summary judgment. (*See id.*) Although the court saw "an issue of fact concerning the extent of the surgery [the doctor] actually contracted to perform", the only damage said to have been sustained is ... pain and suffering items of injury not obtainable in a contract action." (*See id.*)

. . . .

The Court concludes that Dr. Bell's breach of her contract with Ms. Khiterer, fitting her with all-porcelain crowns rather than porcelain-on-gold crowns, was not substantial . . . .

material

not B's problem, but still have to pay her

. . . .

Judgment is awarded to Ms. Khiterer . . . . [The court gave judgment to Ms. Khiterer for breach of contract, but awarded her only nominal damages. The damages portion of the opinion appears in **Chapter 9, page 1060**.]

$10

Problems: Substantial Performance or Material Breach?

8-3. Homeowners hired Rothco (a company selling and installing windows, doors, and millwork) to replace all fifteen windows and two external doors in their home with more energy-efficient ones. One of the doors was in a bedroom and led out to a second-story balcony. Rothco assured them that they would not have drafts or frost with their new doors and windows and that they would save considerably on energy costs. The entire job cost $12,000. As required, they paid half up front, with the remaining half due upon completion. Although most of the replacements fit well, Homeowners had numerous problems with the bedroom patio door, including cold drafts, moisture and frost, and the entry of bugs. They refused to pay the invoice for the remaining $6000 until the problems were fixed. Representatives from Rothco and the door manufacturer examined the patio door, said that there was no defect in the door or its installation, and recommended Homeowners buy and attach weather-stripping to the door to address the problems. Homeowners continued to refuse to pay the Rothco bill. Rothco sued Homeowners for the unpaid price. Did Rothco materially breach?

8-4. The multi-factor aggregate test for determining substantial performance is merely a default rule, so contractual parties can "contract out" of this test. What terms might a construction contractor favor? What terms might an owner/payor favor? How might parties draft terms to make the contract rights and duties more certain than the default rule does?

§ 3.3. Partial or Total Breach?

Upon any breach, the breaching party is responsible for paying damages for any injury caused by the breach. Whether an aggrieved party has the right to withhold performance from the breaching party depends on whether the breaching party has substantially performed or has materially breached. If the breaching party commits a material breach:

- The aggrieved party acquires the right to *suspend* or *withhold* her own performance until the breaching party substantially performs (e.g., the owner does not yet have to pay the construction contractor who has materially breached).

- The breaching party may be able to *cure* the breach within a reasonable time by furnishing the missing performance, by re-performing, or by repairing defective performance, in order to furnish at least substantial performance.
- If the cure is successful enough to alleviate the material breach, then the aggrieved party no longer has the right to suspend or withhold performance (often payment for the cured performance).

The breaching party may fail to cure, of course, and some breaches cannot be cured because the time or opportunity for performance has passed. If the breach is serious enough—for example, because the defects in performance are large, the need to find replacement performance is pressing, and the likelihood the breaching party will cure is remote—the material breach becomes a *total breach*. When a party commits a total breach:

- The aggrieved party retains both the right to damages for any injury and the right to suspend or withhold her own performance, because of the material breach;
- The aggrieved party acquires the right to cancel the contract, eliminating any further performance duties held by any parties to the contract; and
- After notifying the breaching party of cancellation, the aggrieved party can hire someone else to complete the performance once owed by the breaching party.

The following diagram shows the relationships among substantial performance, material breach, partial breach, and total breach:

Take Note!

"Cancelling" a contract differs from "terminating" a contract. Cancellation is the aggrieved party's right to put an end to any further performance by either party under the contract because of a total breach by the other party. Recall that termination (page 103) is a right granted in the parties' agreement, allowing one or both parties to declare contract performance to be at an end for a particular reason (termination for cause) or for no reason (termination for convenience). Courts are not consistent in their use of these terms, however, so you should always consider which concept is at issue, not simply which words a court uses. Whether a party terminates or cancels, it retains the right to remedies for any preceding breaches.

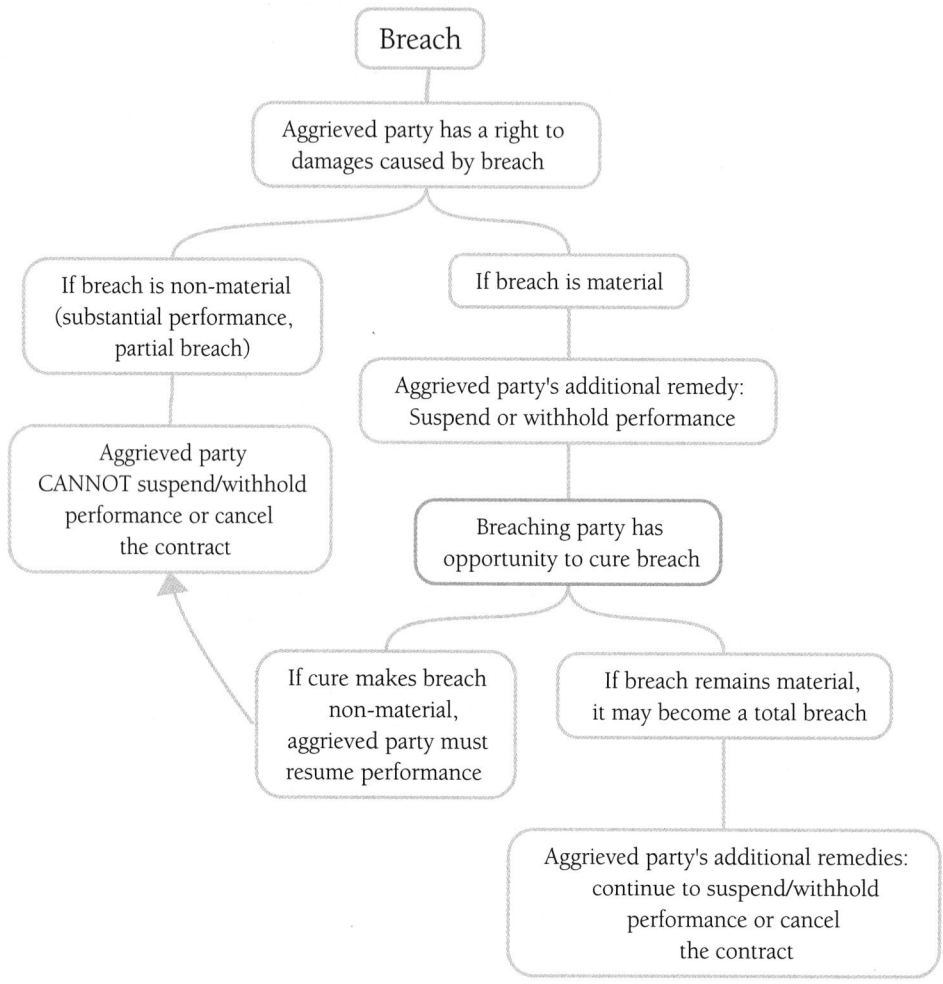

Courts have had difficulty articulating and defining exactly what constitutes total breach. Like the standard for finding material breach, it is an aggregate test, weighing a variety of factors and circumstances. In *San Carlos Irrigation & Drainage Dist. v. United States*,* the court said a total breach "may be by repudiation or by such a material failure of performance when due as to 'go to the essence' and frustrate substantially the purpose for which the contract was agreed to by the injured party." The Restatement (Second) provision contains some guidance about the factors to be considered in determining whether a total breach has occurred:

---

* 23 Cl. Ct. 276, 280 (1991).

Restatement (Second) § 241. **Circumstances Significant in Determining Whether a Failure Is Material***

In determining whether a failure to render or to offer performance is material, the following circumstances are significant:

(a) the extent to which the injured party will be deprived of the benefit which he reasonably expected;

(b) the extent to which the injured party can be adequately compensated for the part of that benefit of which he will be deprived;

(c) the extent to which the party failing to perform or to offer to perform will suffer forfeiture;

(d) the likelihood that the party failing to perform or to offer to perform will cure his failure, taking account of all the circumstances including any reasonable assurances;

(e) the extent to which the behavior of the party failing to perform or to offer to perform comports with standards of good faith and fair dealing.

Restatement (Second) § 242. **Circumstances Significant in Determining When Remaining Duties Are Discharged**

In determining the time after which a party's uncured material failure to render or to offer performance discharges the other party's remaining duties to render performance under the rules stated in §§ 237 and 238, the following circumstances are significant:

(a) those stated in § 241;

(b) the extent to which it reasonably appears to the injured party that delay may prevent or hinder him in making reasonable substitute arrangements;

(c) the extent to which the agreement provides for performance without delay, but a material failure to perform or to offer to perform on a stated day does not of itself discharge the other party's remaining duties unless the circumstances, including the language of the agreement, indicate that performance or an offer to perform by that day is important.

Comment a. Cure. Under §§ 237 and 238, a party's uncured material failure to perform or to offer to perform not only has the effect of suspending the other party's duties (§ 225(1)) but, when it is too late for the performance or the offer to perform to occur, the failure also has the

---

* Restatement (Second) § 241 is used in *Roberts Contracting Co. v. Valentine-Wooten Road Public Facility Board* (page 904).

effect of discharging those duties (§ 225(2)). Ordinarily there is some period of time between suspension and discharge, and during this period a party may cure his failure. Even then, since any breach gives rise to a claim, a party who has cured a material breach has still committed a breach, by his delay, for which he is liable in damages. Furthermore, in some instances timely performance is so essential that any delay immediately results in discharge and there is no period of time during which the injured party's duties are merely suspended and the other party can cure his failure.

Reading the Law Critically: *Sackett*

Sacket is divided into three parts in Chapters 8 and 9. The subsequent parts of the case address the issues of computing direct damages (page 1053) and mitigation of damages (page 1126).

1. The facts in *Sackett* present typical questions about when failure to perform constitutes material or total breach and therefore when the aggrieved party is entitled to suspend performance or cancel. At what point did Sackett's actions constitute material breach? At what point did they constitute total breach? (As is also somewhat typical, the court's terminology is not entirely consistent with the Restatement terminology, so be cautious as you consider the application of the categories of breach to the facts.)

2. What rights did Spindler have at each stage of the transaction? When was he entitled to cancel the transaction?

newspaper stock sale

Sackett v. Spindler

SHELDON SACKETT, Plaintiff, Cross-Defendant and Appellant

v.

PAUL R. SPINDLER, Defendant, Cross-Complainant and Respondent

California Court of Appeal
56 Cal. Rptr. 435 (Ct. App. 1967)

MOLINARI, Presiding Justice.

Plaintiff and cross-defendant, Sheldon Sackett, appeals from the judgment of the trial court determining that he take nothing on his complaint for money had and received and further awarding defendant and cross-complainant, Paul Spindler, $34,575.74 plus interest on his cross-complaint against Sackett for breach of contract. . . .

The Record

As of July 8, 1961 Spindler was the owner of a majority of the shares of S & S Newspapers, a corporation which, since April 1, 1959, had owned and operated a newspaper in Santa Clara known as the Santa Clara Journal. In addition, Spindler, as president of S & S Newspapers, served as publisher, editor, and general manager of the Journal. On July 8, 1961,[1] Spindler entered into a written agreement with Sackett whereby the latter agreed to purchase 6,316 shares of stock in S & S Newspapers, this number representing the total number of shares outstanding. The contract provided for a total purchase price of $85,000 payable as follows: $6,000 on or before July 10, $20,000 on or before July 14, and $59,000 on or before August 15. In addition the agreement obligated Sackett to pay interest at the rate of 6 percent on any unpaid balance. And finally, the contract provided for delivery of the full amount of stock to Sackett free of encumbrances when he made his final payment under the contract.

Sackett paid the initial $6,000 installment on time and made an additional $19,800 payment on July 21. On August 10 Sackett gave Spindler a check for the $59,200 balance due under the contract; however, due to the fact that the account on which this check was drawn contained insufficient funds to cover the check, the check was never paid. Meanwhile, however, Spindler had acquired the stock owned by the minority shareholders of S & S Newspapers, had endorsed the stock certificates, and had given all but 454 shares to Sackett's attorneys to hold in escrow until Sackett had paid Spindler the $59,200 balance due under the contract. However, on September 1, after the $59,200 check had not cleared, Spindler reclaimed the stock certificates held by Sackett's attorney.

Thereafter, on September 12 Spindler received a telegram from Sackett to the effect that the latter "had secured payments our transaction and was ready, willing and eager to transfer them" and that Sackett's new attorney would contact Spindler's attorney. In response to this telegram Spindler, by return telegram, gave Sackett the name of Spindler's attorney. Subsequently, Sackett's attorney contacted Spindler's attorney and arranged a meeting to discuss Sackett's performance of the contract. At this meeting, which was held on September 19 at the office of Sackett's attorney, in response to Sackett's representation that he would be able to pay Spindler the balance due under the contract by September 22, Spindler served Sackett with a notice to the effect that unless the latter paid the $59,200 balance due under the contract plus interest by that date, Spindler would not consider completing the sale and would assess damages for Sackett's breach of

---

[1] Unless otherwise indicated, all dates refer to the year 1961.

the agreement. Also discussed at this meeting was the newspaper's urgent need for working capital. Pursuant to this discussion Sackett on the same date paid Spindler $3,944.26 as an advance for working capital. However, Sackett failed to make any further payments or to communicate with Spindler by September 22, and on that date the latter, by letter addressed to Sackett, again extended the time for Sackett's performance until September 29. Again Sackett failed to tender the amount owing under the contract or to contact Spindler by that date, the next communication between the parties occurring on October 4 in the form of a telegram by which Sackett advised Spindler that Sackett's assets were now free as a result of the fact that his wife's petition to impress a receivership on his assets had been dismissed by the trial court in which divorce proceedings between Sackett and his wife were pending; that he was "ready, eager and willing to proceed to . . . consummate all details of our previously settled sale and purchase"; and that the decision of the trial court dismissing his wife's petition for receivership "will clear way shortly for full financing any unpaid balance." Accordingly, Sackett, in this telegram, urged Spindler to have his attorney contact Sackett's attorney "regarding any unfinished details." In response to this telegram Spindler's attorney, on October 5, wrote a letter to Sackett's attorney stating that as a result of Sackett's delay in performing the contract and his unwillingness to consummate the agreement, "there will be no sale and purchase of the stock . . . ." Following this letter Sackett's attorney, on October 6, telephoned Spindler's attorney and offered to pay the balance due under the contract over a period of time through a "liquidating trust." This proposal was rejected by Spindler's attorney, who, however, informed Sackett's attorney at that time that Spindler was still willing to consummate the sale of the stock provided Sackett would pay the balance in cash or its equivalent. No tender or offer of cash or its equivalent was made and Sackett thereafter failed to communicate with Spindler until shortly before the commencement of this action.

Beginning during the period scheduled for Sackett's performance of the contract Spindler found it increasingly difficult to operate the paper at a profit, particularly due to the lack of adequate working capital. In an attempt to remedy this situation Spindler obtained a loan of approximately $4,000 by mortgaging various items of personal property owned by him. In addition, in November, Spindler sold half of his stock in S & S Newspapers for $10,000. Thereafter, in December, in an effort to minimize the cost of operating the newspaper, Spindler converted the paper from a daily to a weekly. Finally, in July 1962 Spindler repurchased for $10,000 the stock which he had sold the previous November and sold the full 6,316 shares for $22,000, which sale netted Spindler $20,680 after payment of brokerage commission.

Breach of Contract

Sackett contends that the evidence reveals no "actionable breach" on his part. The basis of his argument is that despite his failure to tender over half of the purchase price for the stock of S & S Newspapers, his duty to consummate the contract was discharged by Spindler's conduct in two respects, namely, Spindler's "rescission" of the purchase agreement as a result of his reclamation of the stock certificates from Sackett's attorney on September 1 and Spindler's "repudiation" of the contract on October 5.

Think About It!

The court writes of "Spindler's 'rescission' of the purchase agreement" and "Spindler's 'repudiation' of the contract on October 5." How would you more accurately describe Spindler's actions?

To begin with, the undisputed evidence shows that of the $85,000 due from Sackett to Spindler under the purchase agreement the total amount which the former paid to the latter up to the time of trial was $29,744.26. Moreover, the purchase agreement reveals that Sackett's promise to pay Spindler $85,000 was an unconditional one once the respective dates on which the payments were due had arrived. Accordingly, since the trial court found that it was not impossible for Sackett to perform the subject contract either by virtue of his illness and hospitalization or his pending divorce litigation, it is clear that his failure to tender the balance due under the contract constituted a breach of the agreement, a breach being defined as an unjustified or unexcused failure to perform all or any part of what is promised in a contract. (Rest., Contracts, §§ 312, 314, pp. 462, 465.) The question remains, therefore, as to whether Sackett's duty to consummate the contract or to respond to Spindler in damages for the former's failure to perform the subject contract was in any way discharged by Spindler's conduct.

. . . . [W]ith regard to Sackett's claim that Spindler "repudiated" the contract on October 5, it is clear that the letter which Spindler's attorney wrote to Sackett's attorney on that date informing the latter that as a result of the "many delays" on the part of Sackett "there will be no sale and purchase of the [newspaper] stock" constituted notification to Sackett that Spindler considered his own duty of performance under the contract discharged as a result of Sackett's breach of the contract and that Spindler was thereby terminating the contract and substituting his legal remedies for his contractual rights. Such action was justifiable on Spindler's part if, but only if, Sackett's breach could properly be classified as a total, rather than a partial, breach of the contract. (Rest., Contracts, § 313, p. 464; 4 Corbin on Contracts, § 946, p. 809.) If, on the other hand, Sackett's breach at that time was not total so that Spindler was not entitled to consider himself discharged under the contract, then Spindler's action would constitute an unlawful repudiation of the contract, which would in turn be a total breach of the contract sufficient to discharge Sackett from any further duty to perform the contract. (6 Corbin on Contracts, § 1253, pp. 7, 13-16.)

wasn't total breach

Whether a breach of contract is total or partial depends upon its materiality. (Rest., Contracts, § 317, p. 471.) In determining the materiality of a failure to fully perform a promise the following factors are to be considered:

(1) The extent to which the injured party will obtain the substantial benefit which he could have reasonably anticipated;

(2) the extent to which the injured party may be adequately compensated in damages for lack of complete performance;

(3) the extent to which the party failing to perform has already partly performed or made preparations for performance;

(4) the greater or less hardship on the party failing to perform in terminating the contract;

(5) the wilful, negligent, or innocent behavior of the party failing to perform; and

(6) the greater or less uncertainty that the party failing to perform will perform the remainder of the contract.

> **Take Note!**
>
> This is the predecessor section to Restatement (Second) § 241, set out in *Roberts Contracting Co*, on page 907 and on page 919.

(Rest., Contracts, § 275, pp. 402-403.) In the instant case, although Sackett had paid part of the purchase price for the newspaper stock and although his delay in paying the balance due under the contract could probably be compensated for in damages, we are of the opinion that Spindler was justified in terminating the contract on October 5 on the basis that despite Sackett's "offers" to perform and his assurances to Spindler that he would perform, it was extremely uncertain as to whether in fact Sackett intended to complete the contract. In addition, in light of Spindlers' numerous requests of Sackett for the balance due under the contract, the latter's failure to perform could certainly not be characterized as innocent; rather it could be but ascribed to gross negligence or wilful conduct on his part.

The facts in the instant case are similar to those in **Coughlin v. Blair, 41 Cal.2d 587, 262 P.2d 305.** There the plaintiffs purchased a lot from the defendants, who, in the deposit receipt evidencing the sale, agreed to install utilities and to pave the road to the subject lot within one year from the date of the agreement. On May 30, 1949, the date that performance was due under the contract, the utilities had not been installed nor had the road been paved. During the following year the plaintiffs wrote several letters to the defendants demanding performance. The defendants, however, did not perform their obligations nor did they repudiate the contract. Ultimately, on May 24, 1950, the work still not having been done, the plaintiffs brought an action for general damages based on the difference in value of the property with and without the performance promised in the contract and for special damages. In affirming the judgment of the trial court insofar as it awarded the plaintiffs general damages, the Supreme Court considered whether, in view of the defendants' assertion that they intended to perform their obligations under the contract in the future, the trial court's award of damages to the plaintiffs allowed them a double recovery, that is, both the improvements and damages for failure to secure the improvements. In this context the Supreme Court pointed out that if the defendants' breach was total, the plaintiffs could recover all their damages, past and prospective, in one action and that a judgment for the plaintiffs in such an action would absolve the defendants from any duty to perform the contract. The Supreme Court then proceeded to consider whether the plaintiffs were entitled to treat the defendants' breach as total as of the date of the commencement of the action and concluded that "Although defendants had not expressly repudiated the contract, their conduct clearly justified plaintiffs' belief that performance was either unlikely or would be forthcoming only when it suited defendants' convenience." Under these circumstances it was held that the plaintiffs were not required to endure that uncertainty or to await the defendants' convenience but were justified in treating the defendants' nonperformance as a total breach of the contract. (Pp. 599-600, 262 P.2d p. 312; see also Gold Mining & Water Co. v. Swinerton, 23 Cal.2d 19, 29-30, 142 P.2d 22; Walker v. Harbor Business Blocks Co., 181 Cal. 773, 780-781, 186 P. 356.)

Similarly, in the instant case although Sackett at no time repudiated the contract and although he frequently expressed willingness to perform, the evidence was such as to warrant the inference that he did not intend to perform the subject contract. Certainly, the state of the record was such as to justify the conclusion either that it was unlikely that Sackett would tender the balance due or that he would do so at his own convenience. Spindler was not required to endure the uncertainty or to await Sackett's convenience and was therefore justified in treating the latter's nonperformance as a total breach of the contract. Accordingly, we conclude that the letter which Spindler's attorney wrote to Sackett's attorney on October 5 did not constitute an unlawful repudiation of the contract on Spindler's part, was therefore not a breach of the contract by him, and thus did not discharge Sackett's duty to perform the contract or, alternatively, to respond to Spindler in damages.

In any event, even if Spindler was not justified in treating Sackett's breach as total as of October 5, the latter's contention that his duty to perform was discharged by Spindler's repudiation of the contract as of that date is untenable. Since Spindler was not obligated to perform his promise at that time due to Sackett's failure to tender the balance due under the contract, Spindler's repudiation was, at best, anticipatory in nature. Its effect was nullified by Sackett's disregard of it and his treating the contract as still in force as evidenced by his attempt, through his attorney, to arrange an alternative method of financing the balance due under the agreement. (See Cook v. Nordstrand, 83 Cal.App.2d 188, 195, 188 P.2d 282; Rest., Contracts, § 319, p. 481.) Moreover, Spindler's repudiation was itself retracted by his attorney who, on Spindler's behalf, told Sackett's attorney in the same conversation at which the latter suggested an alternative method of financing that Spindler was still willing to consummate the sale provided Sackett would pay the balance due in cash or its equivalent. Such a retraction constitutes a nullification of the original effectiveness of the repudiation. (Rest., Contracts, § 319, p. 481.)

. . . .

The judgment is modified by deleting therefrom the award of interest from September 29, 1961 to the date of the entry of judgment. As so modified, the judgment is affirmed. Respondent Spindler to recover costs.

Sims and Bray, JJ., concur

———————

From the text and cases in the previous sections, you have seen the difficulty of determining whether a breach is material or total and therefore the difficulty for the aggrieved party in determining whether she has the right to suspend performance or cancel the contract. The picture becomes even more complex if the contract has a series of linked performances (so the aggrieved party must decide *which* performance may be suspended). And even in the face of total breach, an aggrieved party may wish to keep the contract operating and therefore encourage continued performance by the breaching party, rather than declare total breach.

The following case, *K & G Construction Co. v. Harris*, exemplifies the difficulties. The case involves a construction contract with progress payments due at various performance milestones, thereby creating a typical series of linked performances. In the cascading sequence of alleged breaches, each of the parties thought that it could justifiably suspend its performance, but (at least) one party was incorrect and therefore itself materially breached the contract. This kind of legal miscalculation is a surprisingly common cause of breach. The case is complicated further by the aggrieved party's willingness to try to keep the construction project going, in spite of a material and perhaps total breach by the contractor.

Reading the Law Critically: *K & G Construction Co.*

1. Make a list or timeline of the key events. What breaches occurred, and were they material breaches? If so, were they also total breaches? What remedies were available to the other party at each point?

2. What rules does the court use to determine whether there was a non-material or material breach? a partial or total breach?

K & G Construction Co. v. Harris

K & G CONSTRUCTION COMPANY, Plaintiff, Counter-Defendant, Appellant

v.

GLENDAL W. HARRIS and ARTHUR E. BROOKS, Defendants, Counter-Plaintiffs, Appellees

Court of Appeals of Maryland
164 A.2d 451 (Md. Ct. App. 1960)

PRESCOTT, Judge.

Feeling aggrieved by the action of the trial judge of the Circuit Court for Prince George's County, sitting without a jury, in finding a judgment against it in favor of a subcontractor,[1] the appellant, the general contractor on a construction project, appealed.

The principal question presented is: Does a contractor, damaged by a subcontractor's failure to perform a portion of his work in a workmanlike manner, have a right, under the circumstances of this case, to withhold, in partial satisfaction of said damages, an installment payment, which, under the terms of the contract, was due the subcontractor, unless the negligent performance of his work excused its payment? . . . .*

". . . . K & G Construction Company, Inc. (hereinafter called Contractor), plaintiff and counter-defendant in the Circuit Court and appellant herein, was owner and general contractor of a housing subdivision project being constructed (herein called Project). Harris and Brooks (hereinafter called Subcontractor), defendants and counter-plaintiffs in the Circuit Court

---

[1] There are two appellees; the statement of the case refers to them as "subcontractor." We shall do likewise.

* [Authors' Note: The quoted fact statement that follows this paragraph is the parties' stipulated statement of the case, as the court later notes.]

and appellees herein, entered into a contract with Contractor to do excavating and earth-moving work on the Project. Pertinent parts of the contract are set forth below:

"Section 3. The Subcontractor agrees to complete the several portions and the whole of the work herein sublet by the time or times following:

"(a) Without delay, as called for by the Contractor.

"(b) It is expressly agreed that time is of the essence of this contract, and that the Contractor will have the right to terminate this contract and employ a substitute to perform the work in the event of delay on the part of Subcontractor, and Subcontractor agrees to indemnify the Contractor for any loss sustained thereby, provided, however, that nothing in this paragraph shall be construed to deprive Contractor of any rights or remedies it would otherwise have as to damage for delay.

"Section 4.

. . . .

"(b) Progress payments will be made each month during the performance of the work. Subcontractor will submit to Contractor, by the 25th of each month, a requisition for work performed during the preceding month. Contractor will pay these requisitions, less a retainer equal to ten per cent (10%), by the 10th of the months in which such requisitions are received.[2]

"(c) No payments will be made under this contract until the insurance requirements of Sec. 9 hereof have been complied with.

"Section 5. The Contractor agrees—

"(1) That no claim for services rendered or materials furnished by the Contractor to the Subcontractor shall be valid unless written notice

Practice Pointer

The second clause of Section 3(b) ("Subcontractor agrees to indemnify the Contractor for any loss sustained thereby") is a "first-party" indemnification clause because one party is agreeing to indemnify (reimburse) the other party for that other party's losses. If instead (or in addition) the clause included indemnification of the other party for the damages that party had to pay injured third parties, then the clause would be a "third-party" indemnification clause. A close analogy of these clauses is first-party insurance (for instance, car insurance that insures the owner for damage to the car or owner's injuries) and third-party insurance (for instance, car insurance that insures the owner for damages paid to third parties injured by owner's car).

Recall that *Pacific Gas & Electric* (in Chapter 7, page 731) was about whether the contract's indemnification clause was a first-party or a third-party clause.

---

[2] This section is not a model for clarity.

thereof is given by the Contractor to the Subcontractor during the first ten days of the calendar month following that in which the claim originated.

. . . .

"Section 8. . . . All work shall be performed in a workmanlike manner, and in accordance with the best practices.

"Section 9. Subcontractor agrees to carry, during the progress of the work, . . . liability insurance against . . . property damage, in such amounts and with such companies as may be satisfactory to Contractor and shall provide Contractor with certificates showing the same to be in force."

"While in the course of his employment by the Subcontractor on the Project, a bulldozer operator drove his machine too close to Contractor's house while grading the yard, causing the immediate collapse of a wall and other damage to the house. The resulting damage to contractor's house was $3,400.00. Subcontractor had complied with the insurance provision (Sec. 9) of the aforesaid contract. Subcontractor reported said damages to their liability insurance carrier. The Subcontractor and its insurance carrier refused to repair damage or compensate Contractor for damage to the house, claiming that there was no liability on the part of the Subcontractor.

"Contractor gave no written notice to Subcontractor for any services rendered or materials furnished by the Contractor to the Subcontractor.

. . . .

"Contractor was generally satisfied with Subcontractor's work and progress as required under Sections 3 and 8 of the contract until September 12, 1958, with the exception of the bulldozer accident of August 9, 1958.

"Subcontractor performed work under the contract during July, 1958, for which it submitted a requisition by the 25th of July, as required by the contract, for work done prior to the 25th of July, payable under the terms of the contract by Contractor on or before August 10, 1958. Contractor was current as to payments due under all preceding monthly requisitions from Subcontractor. The aforesaid bulldozer accident damaging Contractor's house occurred on August 9, 1958. Contractor refused to pay Subcontractor's requisition due on August 10, 1958, because the bulldozer damage to Contractor's house had not been repaired or paid for. Subcontractor continued to work on the project until the 12th of September, 1958, at which time they discontinued working on the project because of Contractor's refusal to pay the said work requisition and notified Contractor by registered letters of their position and willingness to return to the job, but only upon payment. At that time, September 12, 1958, the value of the work completed by Subcontractor on the project for which they had not been paid was $1,484.50.

"Contractor later requested Subcontractor to return and complete work on the Project which Subcontractor refused to do because of nonpayment of work requisitions of July 25 and thereafter. Contractor's house was not repaired by Subcontractor nor compensation paid for the damage.

"It was stipulated that Subcontractor had completed work on the Project under the contract for which they had not been paid in the amount of $1,484.50 and that if they had completed the remaining work to be done under the contract, they would have made a profit of $1,340.00 on the remaining uncompleted portion of the contract. It was further stipulated that it cost the Contractor $450.00 above the contract price to have another excavating contractor complete the remaining work required under the contract. It was the opinion of the Court that if judgment were in favor of the Subcontractor, it should be for the total amount of $2,824.50.

". . . Contractor filed suit against the Subcontractor in two counts: (1) for the aforesaid bulldozer damage to Contractor's house, alleging negligence of the Subcontractor's bulldozer operator, and (2) for the $450.00 costs above the contract price in having another excavating subcontractor complete the uncompleted work in the contract. Subcontractor filed a counter-claim for recovery of work of the value of $1,484.50 for which they had not received payment and for loss of anticipated profits on uncompleted portion of work in the amount of $1,340.00. By agreement of the parties, the first count of Contractor's claim, i.e., for aforesaid bulldozer damage to Contractor's house, was submitted to jury who found in favor of Contractor in the amount of $3,400.00. Following the finding by the jury, the second count of the Contractor's claim and the counter-claims of the Subcontractor, by agreement of the parties, were submitted to the Court for determination, without jury. All of the facts recited herein above were stipulated to by the parties to the Court. Circuit Court Judge Fletcher found for counter-plaintiff Subcontractor in the amount of $2,824.50 from which Contractor has entered this appeal."

The $3,400 judgment has been paid.

It is immediately apparent that our decision turns upon the respective rights and liabilities of the parties under that portion of their contract whereby the subcontractor agreed to do the excavating and earth-moving work in "a workmanlike manner, and in accordance with the best practices," with time being of the essence of the contract, and the contractor agreed to make progress payments therefor on the 10th day of the months following the performance of the work by the subcontractor. The subcontractor contends, of course, that when the contractor failed to make the payment due on August 10, 1958, he breached his contract and thereby released him (the subcontractor) from any further obligation to perform. The contractor, on the other hand, argues that the failure of the subcontractor to perform his work in a workmanlike manner constituted a material breach of the contract, which justified his refusal to make the August 10 payment; and, as there was no breach on his part, the subcontractor had no right to cease performance on September 12, and his refusal to continue work on the project constituted another breach, which rendered him liable to the contractor for damages. The vital question, more tersely stated, remains: Did the contractor have a right, under the circumstances, to refuse to make the progress payment due on August 10, 1958?

Practice Pointer

A clause that says "time is of the essence" represents an attempt by one or both parties to indicate the importance of performance due dates. Such a clause may make it more likely that the performance deadline will be understood to be an express condition or that a failure to meet the deadline will be considered a material or total breach. But such declarations should not be taken at face value (as courts sometimes do). A "time-is-of-the-essence" clause should be read in context to determine the parties' manifested understanding of contract responsibilities.

The answer involves interesting and important principles of contract law. . . . In the early days, it was settled law that covenants and mutual promises in a contract were *prima facie* independent, and that they were to be so construed in the absence of language in the contract clearly showing that they were intended to be dependent. Williston, op. cit., ¶ 816 . . . . In the case of Kingston v. Preston, 2 Doug. 689, decided in 1774, Lord Mansfield, contrary to three centuries of opposing precedents, changed the rule, and decided that performance of one covenant might be dependent on prior performance of another, although the contract contained no express condition to that effect. . . . Williston, op. cit., ¶ 817. The modern rule, which seems to be of almost universal application, is that there is a presumption that mutual promises in a contract are dependent and are to be so regarded, whenever possible. . . . Restatement, Contracts, § 266. . . . [T]he intention of the parties, as shown by the entire contract as construed in the light of the circumstances of the case, the nature of the contract, the relation of the parties thereto, and the other evidence which is admissible to assist the court in determining the intention of the parties, is the controlling factor in deciding whether the promises and counter-promises are dependent or independent. . . . Williston, op. cit., ¶ 824. . . .

Considering the presumption that promises and counter-promises are dependent and the statement of the case, we have no hesitation in holding that the promise and counter-promise under consideration here were mutually dependent, that is to say, the parties intended performance by one to be conditioned on performance by the other; and the subcontractor's promise was, by the explicit wording of the contract, precedent to the promise of payment, monthly, by the contractor.

> ### Think About It
>
> The court initially adopts a presumption that mutual promises and counter-promises are dependent, based on Restatement § 266. What effect does the presumption have on the case? Does the presumption make sense? What kinds of evidence may rebut this presumption? Does this court need to use this presumption?

In **Shapiro Engineering Corp. v. Francis O. Day Co., 215 Md. 373, 380, 137 A.2d 695,** we stated that it is the general rule that where a total price for work is fixed by a contract, the work is not rendered divisible by progress payments. It would, indeed present an unusual situation if we were to hold that a building contractor, who has obtained someone to do work for him and has agreed to pay each month for the work performed in the previous month, has to continue the monthly payments, irrespective of the degree of skill and care displayed in the performance of work, and his only recourse is by way of suit for ill-performance. If this were the law, it is conceivable, in fact, probable, that many contractors would become insolvent before they were able to complete their contracts. As was stated by the Court in **Measures Brothers Ltd. v. Measures, 2 Ch. 248:** "Covenants are to be construed as dependent or independent according to the intention of the parties and the good sense of the case."

We hold that when the subcontractor's employee negligently damaged the contractor's wall, this constituted a breach of the subcontractor's promise to perform his work in a "workmanlike manner, and in accordance with the best practices." **Gaybis v. Palm, 201 Md. 78, 85, 93 A.2d 269** . . . . And there can be little doubt that the breach was material: the damage to the wall amounted to more than double the payment due on August 10. **Speed v. Bailey, 153 Md. 655, 661, 662, 139 A. 534.** 3A Corbin, Contracts, § 708, says: "The failure of a contractor's [in our case, the subcontractor's] performance to constitute "substantial" performance may justify the owner [in our case, the contractor] in refusing to make a progress payment . . . . If the refusal to pay an installment is justified on the owner's [contractor's] part, the contractor [subcontractor] is not justified in abandoning work by reason of that refusal. His abandonment of the work will itself be a wrongful repudiation that goes to the essence, even if the defects in performance did not." . . . Professor

Corbin, in § 954, states further: "The unexcused failure of a contractor to render a promised performance when it is due is always a breach of contract . . . . Such failure may be of such great importance as to constitute what has been called herein a 'total' breach. . . . For a failure of performance constituting such a 'total' breach, an action for remedies that are appropriate thereto is at once maintainable. Yet the injured party is not required to bring such action. He has the option of treating the non-performance as a 'partial' breach only . . . ." In permitting the subcontractor to proceed with work on the project after August 9, the contractor, obviously, treated the breach by the subcontractor as a partial one. As the promises were mutually dependent and the subcontractor had made a material breach in his performance, this justified the contractor in refusing to make the August 10 payment; hence, as the contractor was not in default, the subcontractor again breached the contract when he, on September 12, discontinued work on the project, which rendered him liable (by the express terms of the contract) to the contractor for his increased cost in having the excavating done—a stipulated amount of $450. . . .

Think About It!

Why might the contractor have elected to treat the subcontractor's total breach as a partial breach? What factors would a contractor need to weigh, in making such a decision?

In many jurisdictions, this kind of election by an aggrieved party is binding even without reliance by the other party. In discussing *K & G Construction*, Professor Farnsworth says that "the injured party cannot later reconsider, terminate, and recover damages for total breach unless the party in breach should commit a further breach, subsequent to the election, that would give the injured party a second chance to terminate." E. Allan Farnsworth, *Contracts* § 8.19, at 577 (4th ed. 2004).

just because breach is total doesn't mean you treat it as partial

breached twice

. . . .

Judgment against the appellant reversed; and judgment entered in favor of the appellant against the appellees for $450, the appellees to pay the costs.

Problem 8-5: Total or Partial Breach?

Pursuant to an Agreement for Sale for a condominium unit, Buyer deposited $118,643 into an escrow account as a down payment. The condominium was part of a planned development project converting an old warehouse into livingspace, and reconstruction work had not yet begun at the time the contract was signed. The Agreement stated that "the Premises shall include the standard features and other items described in Exhibit B." Exhibit B included a "Summary of Features," which listed, among other things, "high ceilings and expansive room arrangements." Exhibit B also included "Outline Specifications" for the condominiums, which stated:

> Ceilings will be painted drywall at approximately 9'-6" height in perimeter bedroom and living areas. Interior areas such as bathrooms, kitchens and closets will generally have slightly lower ceilings of approximately 9'-0". Some drywall soffits or ceiling height variation may result in these areas to conceal ductwork, sprinkler piping, electrical conduit and wiring, structural beams, drain piping, terrace insulation and to address other conditions as required by the construction documents and field conditions.

When built, the ceilings in the bedrooms and living areas of the condominium unit were approximately 8'-9". The contractor refused to correct the mistakes. Buyer sought to cancel the purchase agreement and demanded the return of the $118,643 deposit, claiming that the shorter ceilings were a total breach of the agreement. Is Buyer correct?

Practice Pointer: Divisible Contracts versus Severable Contracts

Contracts that are "divisible" are understood as being divided into two or more parts, each of which can stand on its own as a free-standing contract. If the court finds the contract to be divisible, then the court judges the performance of each part of the contract independently, so the question whether the performing party accomplished substantial performance or materially or totally breached is asked separately for each divisible part of the contract. Dividing the contract in this fashion means a performing party may more easily substantially perform, because the performance is compared only against what was promised for the divisible portion. That may disadvantage the paying party, who would have to pay for part of the contract without receiving the other part(s) of the performance. But dividing the contract also means a total breach will be easier to prove, because the question is whether there has been a total breach of the divisible part of the contract, not the whole. That may disadvantage the performing party. The courts' tests for divisibility often include the following factors:

- whether the parties intended that the agreement be divisible;
- whether the contract, "by its terms, nature, and purpose, is susceptible of division and apportionment"* (e.g., is it possible to determine the price of each separate performance?); and
- whether the division harms the value of performance reasonably expected by each party (e.g., can the injured party make full use of the incomplete performance? has the injured party received the full value for its payments to date?).

Divisibility may play a role in analyzing many other issues of contract law, in addition to substantial performance and total/partial breach.** A contract may be divisible for one purpose, but not for another. For instance, a contract may be divisible for statute of frauds purposes, allowing part of the contract to be enforced, rather than barring enforcement of the whole contract. But the same contract may not be divisible for purposes of substantial performance, because it would allow a payee to achieve substantial performance of a portion of the contract too easily, while the rest of the contract was materially breached.

Consider the following cases, in which the court determined the contract was divisible with respect to the issue of substantial performance:

- *Gill v. Johnstown Lumber Co*, 25 A. 120 (Pa. 1892): Plaintiff laborer agreed to drive four million feet of logs from various upstream points to the defendant's boom downstream. The promised compensation was $1 per 1000 feet of oak logs and 75¢ per 1000 feet of other logs. In addition, the laborer agreed to drive cross-ties downstream to another location, for another price per cross-tie. A flood carried away many of the logs, but plaintiff sued for partial payment. The court found that the contract was divisible so that plaintiff could recover compensation for each log and tie delivered to the promised location. However, the court refused to apportion the contract so as to allow compensation for logs and ties that plaintiff had driven part-way along the route. The court also refused compensation for logs transported or swept away by the flood.

---

* *In re American Home Mortgage, Inc.*, 379 Bankruptcy Reporter 503, 521 (D. Del. 2008).
** For a particularly astute discussion of the range of issues affected by divisibility, follow the index entries for divisibility in the three-volume treatise, E. Allan Farnsworth, *Farnsworth on Contracts* (3d ed. 2004).

- *Lowy v. United Pacific Insurance Co.*, 429 P.2d 577 (Cal. 1967): A real estate development company hired a contractor to do excavation and grading work, as well as street improvement work. The contract specified separate prices for each kind of work. The contractor completed 98% of the excavation and grading work, but ceased performance before doing the street improvement work. The court found that the contract was divisible for purposes of determining substantial performance. It allowed the contractor to recover the contract price for the excavation and grading work (minus the cost of finishing the remaining 2%), based on his substantial performance of that portion of the contract.

More often, though, the courts have rejected arguments claiming divisibility for purposes of determining substantial performance:

- *Menorah Chapels at Millburn v. Needle*, 899 A.2d 316 (N.J. Super. A.D. 2006): The son-in-law of the deceased contracted with a funeral home for services consistent with orthodox Jewish rituals, including the requirement that the body be attended by watchers ("shomers") who maintain their vigil in shifts. The funeral home's price list gave a separate price for this service. The funeral home failed to provide watchers for half of the time, and the son-in-law refused to pay. The funeral home sued for the contract price minus the price of the missing watchers. The court refused to find the contract to be divisible (in spite of the price list), because the contract's purpose was for a complete orthodox funeral. The court remanded the case on the issue of whether the breach was material and, if so, what the funeral home's recovery would be in quantum meruit.

- *Pittsburgh-Des Moines Steel Co. v. Brookhaven Manor Water Co.*, 532 F.2d 572 (7th Cir. 1976): The contract required the steel company to supply pieces of a water tank and to assemble it on site into a fixed water tank on a concrete base. Thus, the contract included goods (the water tank parts and the components of the concrete) as well as services (mixing and pouring the concrete into molds, and assembling the parts of the water tank). The court regarded the contract as non-divisible, applying UCC Article 2 to the entire contract because the goods predominated over the services.

- *K & G Construction Co. v. Harris,* 164 A.2d 451 (Md. Ct. App. 1960) (see page 927): The court said that "where a total price for work is fixed by a contract, the work is *not rendered divisible* by progress payments."

Some courts treat divisibility and "severability" as synonymous, but the latter term can have an entirely different meaning. Contract boilerplate often contains a "severability clause," which seeks to ensure that the contract remains valid and enforceable, even though part of the contract is struck down or ruled unenforceable. Some courts, in deciding divisibility, check the contract to see whether the parties included a severability clause. Here are some examples of severability clauses:

- If any provision or provisions of this Agreement is invalid, illegal, unenforceable, or in conflict with the law of any jurisdiction, the remaining provisions shall not in any way be affected or impaired thereby.
- Invalidity or unenforceability of one or more provisions of this Agreement shall not affect any other provision of this Agreement.

Of course, in some settings, no severability clause is needed. Recall from Chapter 5, page 512, that if part of a contract is unconscionable, the court can refuse to enforce just that part, rather than the whole contract. If a contract clause is invalid as against public policy, the court can choose to strike that clause, if that deletion does not materially alter the rest of the contract. Moreover, if a court has found one or more clauses to be unconscionable or void for public policy, the court does not have to honor the agreement's severability clause, because the rules of law governing these defenses are mandatory rules of law, not default rules of law that the parties can avoid by agreement.

§ 4. Repudiation — backing out of contract due t breach/non-performance

§ 4.1. Defining Repudiation (Renunciation)

Section 3 (page 892) dealt with breaches through defective performance or non-performance. A party may also breach by "renouncing" or "repudiating" the contract, indicating that she will not perform the contract or will not perform it further. If done in response to a total breach by the other party, a purported repudiation is really a justified cancellation of the contract, not a breach. But beware of accepting the labels the parties place on their actions, because a party might not use the technically correct term for its actions and might seek to camouflage its own breach by calling it a cancellation or termination. In each instance, you must evaluate the parties' actions based on the standards governing repudiation and breach, rather than accepting their self-characterizations.

Before analyzing the consequences of repudiation, it is first necessary to determine what words or actions constitute repudiation. As with other communications between parties, the meaning should be judged using the objective standard. As you might expect, establishing exactly what constitutes a repudiation often presents challenges.

Reading the Law Critically: *McCloskey & Co.*

1. What is the court's test for determining whether there was a "renunciation" of the contract (more commonly known as "repudiation")?

2. Why was the standard not met here?

McCloskey & Co. v. Minweld Steel Co.

McCLOSKEY & CO., Plaintiff-Appellant

v.

MINWELD STEEL CO., INC., and THE TRAVELERS INDEMNITY CO.,
Defendants-Appellees

United States Court of Appeals, Third Circuit
220 F.2d 101 (3d Cir. 1955)

McLAUGHLIN, Circuit Judge.

Plaintiff-appellant, a general contractor, sued on three contracts alleging an anticipatory breach as to each. At the close of the plaintiff's case the district judge granted the defense motions for judgment on the ground that plaintiff had not made out a cause of action.

By the contracts involved the principal defendant,[1] a fabricator and erector of steel, agreed to furnish and erect all of the structural steel required on two buildings to be built on the grounds of the Hollidaysburg State Hospital, Hollidaysburg,

---

[1] The Travelers Indemnity Company, which posted performance bonds on two of the contracts, is a co-defendant . . . .

Pa. and to furnish all of the long span steel joists required in the construction of one of the two buildings. Two of the contracts were dated May 1, 1950 and the third May 26, 1950. By Article V of each of the contracts[:]

> "Should the Sub-Contractor [the defendant herein] . . . at any time refuse or neglect to supply a sufficiency . . . of materials of the proper quality, . . . in and about the performance of the work required to be done pursuant to the provisions of this agreement . . . , or fail, in the performance of any of the agreements herein contained, the Contractor shall be at liberty, without prejudice to any other right or remedy, on two days' written notice to the Sub-Contractor, either to provide any such . . . materials and to deduct the cost thereof from any payments then or thereafter due the Sub-Contractor, or to terminate the employment of the Sub-Contractor for the said work and to enter upon the premises . . . ."

Food for Thought

Article V of the contract contains both an agreed remedy for breach (supplying the omitted performance and deducting appropriate amounts from payments made) and a termination clause. Is the termination clause really just an articulation of the right to cancel upon breach?

There was no stated date in the contracts for performance by the defendant subcontractor. Article VI provided for completion by the subcontractor of its contract work "by and at the time or times hereafter stated to-wit:

> "Samples, Shop Drawings and Schedules are to be submitted in the quantities and manner required by the Specifications, for the approval of the Architects, immediately upon receipt by the Sub-Contractor of the contract drawings, or as may be directed by the Contractor. All expense involved in the submission and approval of these Samples, Shop Drawings and Schedules shall be borne by the Sub-Contractor.

> "All labor, materials and equipment required under this contract are to be furnished at

What's That?

As indicated in footnote 1, Travelers Indemnity Co. furnished performance bonds on two of the contracts. Such bonds would have been required in the Minweld-McCloskey contracts so that, if Minweld failed to perform or did not finish performance, McCloskey could obtain damages or performance from the surety (Travelers), depending on the terms of the bond contract between Minweld and the surety. McCloskey was a third-party beneficiary to the bonding contract (a topic that is revisited in greater detail in Chapter 10 on page 1240) and therefore sued both Minweld and Travelers to obtain recovery.

such times as may be directed by the Contractor, and in such a manner so as to at no time delay the final completion of the building.

"It being mutually understood and agreed that prompt delivery and installation of all materials required to be furnished under this contract is to be the essence of this Agreement."

Appellee Minweld Steel Co., Inc., the subcontractor, received contract drawings and specifications for both buildings in May, 1950. On June 8, 1950, plaintiff McCloskey & Co. wrote appellee asking when it might "expect delivery of the structural steel" for the buildings and "also the time estimated to complete erection." Minweld replied on June 13, 1950, submitting a schedule estimate of expecting to begin delivery of the steel by September 1, and to complete erection approximately November 15. On July 20, 1950 plaintiff wrote Minweld threatening to terminate the contracts unless the latter gave unqualified assurances that it had effected definite arrangements for the procurement, fabrication and delivery within thirty days of the required materials. On July 24, 1950 Minweld wrote McCloskey & Co. explaining its difficulty in obtaining the necessary steel. It asked McCloskey's assistance in procuring it and stated that "We are as anxious as you are that there be no delay in the final completion of the buildings or in the performance of our contract, ..."

This letter in full is as follows:*

Minweld Steel Company Incorporated
Shaler and Wabash Streets Pittsburgh 20, Pa.

July 24, 1950.

McCloskey & Company
1620 Thompson Street
Philadelphia 21, Penna.

In re: New Hospital Buildings
Hollidaysburg State Hospital
Hollidaysburg, Pennsylvania

Attention of J. C. McCloskey, Vice President

---

* [Authors' Note: We moved the letter from the court's footnote into the text of the case opinion.]

Dear Sir:

This will acknowledge receipt of your letter of July 20th, 1950, which was received by us today.

Upon receipt of the architect's specifications, we completed the engineering and erection plans on the said specifications. Immediately after those details were available, we attempted to place orders for the steel with the Bethlehem Steel Company. Our order was held in the offices of the Bethlehem Steel Company for two weeks before we were notified that it could not be supplied. Since that time, we have tried the U.S. Steel Corporation and Carnegie-Illinois, both companies informing us that they were under contract for approximately one year and could not fulfill the order.

can't get steel

The recent directive by the President of the United States, with which we assume you are familiar, has further tightened up the steel market so that at the present writing we cannot give you any positive promise as to our ability to obtain the steel or delivery dates.

In view of the directive from Washington and the tightening up of the entire steel industry, we solicit your help and that of the General State Authority in aiding us to obtain the steel for these contracts.
We are as anxious as you are that there be no delay in the final completion of the buildings or in the performance of our contract, but we have nowhere else to turn at the present time for the supply of steel necessary under said contracts, unless through your aid and assistance, and that of the General State Authority, a supplier can be induced to give us the materials needed.

The U.S. Steel Corporation informs us that you have discussed this matter with them and are presently aware of our present difficulties.

If steel is to be supplied to these hospital buildings by governmental directive, we feel that the steel should be supplied to us for completion under our contract.

Very truly yours,

Minweld Steel Company, Inc. J. A. Roberts Sales Manager
JAR/fs

c/c Travelers Indemnity Co.,
Hartford, Conn.
General State Authority, Harrisburg, Penna.

Plaintiff-appellant claims that by this last letter, read against the relevant facts, defendant gave notice of its positive intention not to perform its contracts and thereby violated same.[3] Some reference has already been made to the background of the July 24th letter. It concerned Minweld's trouble in securing the steel essential for performance of its contract. Minweld had tried unsuccessfully to purchase this from Bethlehem Steel, U.S. Steel and Carnegie-Illinois. It is true as appellant urges that Minweld knew and was concerned about the tightening up of the steel market.[4] And as is evident from the letter it, being a fabricator and not a producer, realized that without the help of the general contractor on this hospital project particularly by it enlisting the assistance of the General State Authority,[5] Minweld was in a bad way for the needed steel. However, the letter conveys no idea of contract repudiation by Minweld. That company admittedly was in a desperate situation. Perhaps if it had moved earlier to seek the steel its effort might have been successful. But that is mere speculation for there is no showing that the mentioned producers had they been solicited sooner would have been willing to provide the material.

Minweld from its written statement did, we think, realistically face the problem confronting it. As a result it asked its general contractor for the aid which the latter, by the nature of the construction, should have been willing to give. Despite the circumstances there is no indication in the letter that Minweld had definitely abandoned all hope of otherwise receiving the steel and so finishing its undertaking. One of the mentioned producers might have relented. Some other supplier might have turned up. It was McCloskey & Co. who eliminated whatever chance there was. That concern instead of aiding Minweld by urging its plea for the hospital construction materials to the State Authority which represented the Commonwealth of Pennsylvania took the position that the subcontractor had repudiated its agreement and then moved quickly to have the work completed. Shortly thereafter, and without the slightest trouble as far as appears, McCloskey & Co. procured the steel from Bethlehem[6] and brought in new subcontractors to do the work contemplated by the agreement with Minweld.

Food for Thought

Could Minweld have profitably invoked the duty of good faith in its defense? Did McCloskey breach its implied duty of cooperation? How could each party have protected itself against the situation that arose here, either in the contract terms or through other action, to avoid the uncertainty that led to litigation?

---

[3] Plaintiff cancelled the contracts on July 26, 1950, on the ground that the July 24th letter constituted an admission of defendant's inability to perform the required work.

[4] The Korean War broke out on June 24, 1950.

[5] The Pennsylvania state agency which represented and owned the Hollidaysburg State Hospital.

[6] Bethlehem had originally submitted a bid in competition with Minweld. Its new proposals were dated July 28, 1950, and were finally accepted by McCloskey & Co. on August 7, 1950. The long span steel joists required by the third contract were procured from the Frederick Grundy Iron Works.

Under the applicable law Minweld's letter was not a breach of the agreement. The suit is in the federal court by reason of diversity of citizenship of the parties. Though there is no express statement to that effect the contracts between the parties would seem to have been executed in Pennsylvania with the law of that state applicable. In **McClelland v. New Amsterdam Casualty Co., 1936, 322 Pa. 429, 433, 185 A. 198, 200**, the Pennsylvania Supreme Court held in a case where the subcontractor had asked for assistance in obtaining credit, "In order to give rise to a renunciation amounting to a breach of contract, there must be an absolute and unequivocal refusal to perform or a distinct and positive statement of an inability to do so." Minweld's conduct is plainly not that of a contract breaker under that test. See also **Dingley v. Oler, 1886, 117 U.S. 490, 6 S.Ct. 850, 29 L.Ed. 984. Restatement of Contracts, Comment (i) to Sec. 318 (1932)** speaks clearly on the point saying:

> "Though where affirmative action is promised mere failure to act, at the time when action has been promised, is a breach, failure to take preparatory action before the time when any performance is promised is not an anticipatory breach, even though such failure makes it impossible that performance shall take place, and though the promisor at the time of the failure intends not to perform his promise."

See Williston on Contracts, Vol. 5, Sec. 1324 (1937), Corbin on Contracts, Vol. 4, Sec. 973 (1951).

Appellant contends that its letter of July 20, requiring assurances of arrangements which would enable appellee to complete delivery in thirty days, constituted a fixing of a date under Article VI of the contracts. The short answer to this is that the thirty day date, if fixed, was never repudiated. Appellee merely stated that it was unable to give assurances as to the preparatory arrangements. There is nothing in the contracts which authorized appellant to demand or receive such assurances.

The district court acted properly in dismissing the actions as a matter of law on the ground that plaintiff had not made out a prima facie case.

FYI

The court is correct that the common law did not give McCloskey a right to demand assurances of future performance—a right written into UCC § 2-609 (page 951) to provide more tools to parties dealing with circumstances like those presented here. Section 2-609, where applicable, allows a party who is reasonably concerned about another's performance to demand assurances of that performance and to consider the contract repudiated if adequate assurances are not received. Pennsylvania enacted the UCC as soon as it was adopted in 1952, the first state to do so, but the UCC did not apply to the Minweld-McCloskey contract, which was formed in 1950.

The order of the district court of July 14, 1954 denying the plaintiff's motions for findings of facts, to vacate the judgments and for new trials will be affirmed.

————————

§ 4.2. Anticipatory Repudiation

If a repudiation occurs before the date on which contract performance is due, it is called an "anticipatory repudiation." Such an act implicates the parties' interests in the stability and predictability of contracts and raises a number of questions about the appropriate consequences. When does the breach occur and from what point in time are damages measured—is it at the time of the repudiation (when performance is not yet due), or a reasonable time later, or on the performance due date? Is the other party allowed to claim total breach at the time of the repudiation and move on, or should she wait until performance is due? May the repudiating party change his mind and perform the original contract obligations? The following English case helped answer many of those questions, thereby establishing principles that provide a degree of security for an aggrieved party in the face of the uncertainty caused by anticipatory repudiation.

Reading the Law Critically: *Hochster*

1. How are the parties' promises connected to one another, using the *Kingston* categories of covenants (page 890)?

2. The court considers the verbal renunciation of a contract, as in *Hochster,* along with other situations in which a contracting party *acts* inconsistently with an intention to perform the contract. In none of those situations, the court suggests, is there a present breach of performance obligations because contract performance remains *possible.* What obligation does the court find *is* breached in all the cases? When does that breach occur—upon renunciation, when performance was to begin, or at some other time?

3. After a renunciation by one party to the contract, are the parties' contract duties necessarily ended? May the aggrieved party continue to insist on performance?

Hochster v. De la Tour

HOCHSTER, Plaintiff

v.

DE LA TOUR, Defendant

Court of Queen's Bench
118 Eng. Rep. 922 (Q.B. 1853)

. . . [P]laintiff was a courier, who, in April, 1852, was engaged by defendant to accompany him on a tour, to commence on 1st June 1852, on the terms mentioned in the declaration. On the 11th May 1852, defendant wrote to plaintiff that he had changed his mind, and declined [plaintiff's] services. He refused to make [plaintiff] any compensation. The action was commenced on 22d May. The plaintiff, between the commencement of the action and the 1st June, obtained an engagement with Lord Ashburton, on equally good terms, but not commencing till 4th July. The defendant's counsel objected that there could be no breach of the contract before the 1st of June. The learned Judge was of a contrary opinion, but reserved leave to enter a nonsuit on this objection. The other questions were left to the jury, who found for plaintiff.

. . . .

[On appeal,] Lord Campbell C.J. now delivered the judgment of the Court.

On this motion in arrest of judgment, the question arises, Whether, if there be an agreement between A. and B., whereby B. engages to employ A. on and from a future day for a given period of time, to travel with him into a foreign country as a courier, and to start with him in that capacity on that day, A. being to receive a monthly salary during the continuance of such service, B. may, before the day, refuse to perform the agreement and break and renounce it, so as to entitle A. before the day to commence an action against B. to recover damages for breach of the agreement; A. having been ready and willing to perform it, till it was broken and renounced by B.

The defendant's counsel very powerfully contended that, if the plaintiff was not contented to dissolve the contract, and to abandon all remedy upon it, he was bound to remain ready and willing to perform it till the day when the actual employment as courier in the service of the defendant was to begin; and that there could be no breach of the agreement, before that day, to give a right of action.

But it cannot be laid down as a universal rule that, where by agreement an act is to be done on a future day, no action can be brought for a breach of the agreement till the day for doing the act has arrived. If a man promises to marry a woman on a future day, and before that day marries another woman, he is instantly liable to an action for breach of promise of marriage; *Short v. Stone* (8 Q. B. 358). If a man contracts to execute a lease on and from a future day for a certain term, and, before that day, executes a lease to another for the same term, he may be immediately sued for breaking the contract; *Ford v. Tiley* (6 B. & C. 325). So, if a man contracts to sell and deliver specific goods on a future day, and before the day he sells and delivers them to another, he is immediately liable to an action at the suit of the person with whom he first contracted to sell and deliver them; *Bowdell v. Parsons* (10 East, 359).

One reason alleged in support of such an action is, that the defendant has, before the day, rendered it impossible for him to perform the contract at the day: but this does not necessarily follow; for, prior to the day fixed for doing the act, the first wife may have died, a surrender of the lease executed might be obtained, and the defendant might have repurchased the goods so as to be in a situation to sell and deliver them to the plaintiff. Another reason may be, that, where there is a contract to do an act on a future day, there is a relation constituted between the parties in the meantime by the contract, and that they impliedly promise that in the meantime neither will do anything to the prejudice of the other inconsistent with that relation. As an example, a man and woman engaged to marry are affianced to one another during the period between the time of the engagement and the celebration of the marriage. In this very case, of traveller and courier, from the day of the hiring till the day when the employment was to begin, they were engaged to each other; and it seems to be a breach of an implied contract if either of them renounces the engagement. This reasoning seems in accordance with the unanimous decision of the Exchequer Chamber in *Elderton v. Emmens* (6 C.B. 160), which we have followed in subsequent cases in this Court.

The declaration in the present case, in alleging a breach, states a great deal more than a passing intention on the part of the defendant which he may repent of, and could only be proved by evidence that he had utterly renounced the contract, or done some act which rendered it impossible for him to perform it. If the plaintiff has no remedy for breach of the contract unless he treats the contract as in force, and acts upon it down to the 1st June 1852, it follows that, till then, he must enter into no employment which will interfere with his promise "to start with the defendant on such travels on the day and year," and that he must then be properly equipped in all respects as a courier for a three months' tour on the continent of Europe.

But it is surely much more rational, and more for the benefit of both parties, that, after the renunciation of the agreement by the defendant, the plaintiff should be at liberty to consider himself absolved from any future performance of it, retaining his right to sue for any damage he has suffered from the breach of it. Thus, instead of remaining idle and laying out money in preparations which must be useless, he is at liberty to seek service under another employer, which would go in mitigation of the damages to which he would otherwise be entitled for a breach of the contract.

It seems strange that the defendant, after renouncing the contract, and absolutely declaring that he will never act under it, should be permitted to object that faith is given to his assertion, and that an opportunity is not left to him of changing his mind. If the plaintiff is barred of any remedy by entering into an engagement inconsistent with starting as a courier with the defendant on the 1st June, he is prejudiced by putting faith in the defendant's assertion . . . .

Suppose that the defendant, at the time of his renunciation, had embarked on a voyage for Australia, so as to render it physically impossible for him to employ the plaintiff as a courier on the continent of Europe in the months of June, July and August 1852: according to decided cases, the action might have been brought before the 1st June; but the renunciation may have been founded on other facts, to be given in evidence, which would equally have rendered the defendant's performance of the contract impossible. The man who wrongfully renounces a contract into which he has deliberately entered cannot justly complain if he is immediately sued for a compensation in damages by the man whom he has injured: and it seems reasonable to allow an option to the injured party, either to sue immediately, or to wait till the time when the act was to be done, still holding it as prospectively binding for the exercise of this option, which may be advantageous to the innocent party, and cannot be prejudicial to the wrongdoer.

An argument against the action before the 1st of June is urged from the difficulty of calculating the damages: but this argument is equally strong against an action before the 1st of September, when the three months would expire. In either case, the jury in assessing the damages would be justified in looking to all that had happened, or was likely to happen, to increase or mitigate the loss of the plaintiff down to the day of trial. . . .

If it should be held that, upon a contract to do an act on a future day, a renunciation of the contract by one party dispenses with a condition to be performed in the meantime by the other, there seems no reason for requiring that other to wait till the day arrives before seeking his remedy by action: and the only ground on which the condition can be dispensed with seems to be, that the renunciation may be treated as a breach of the contract.

Upon the whole, we think that the declaration in this case is sufficient. It gives us great satisfaction to reflect that, the question being on the record, our opinion may be reviewed in a Court of Error. In the meantime we must give judgment for the plaintiff. . . .

Reading the Law Critically:
Anticipatory Repudiation under the UCC

1. Under UCC § 2-610, what may an aggrieved party do after a repudiation? Does the UCC rule differ from the common law rule articulated in *Hochster*?

2. Under UCC § 2-611, in what circumstances may the repudiating party retract the repudiation? If retraction is permitted, what is the effect on the aggrieved party's rights and obligations? Is the rule in § 2-611 consistent with the reasoning in *Hochster*? At what point would the employer in *Hochster* have been unable to retract his repudiation?

UCC § 2-610. Anticipatory Repudiation

When either party repudiates the contract with respect to a performance not yet due the loss of which will substantially impair the value of the contract to the other, the aggrieved party may

(a) for a commercially reasonable time await performance by the repudiating party; or

(b) resort to any remedy for breach . . . , even though he has notified the repudiating party that he would await the latter's performance and has urged retraction; and

(c) in either case suspend his own performance or [take other measures to mitigate damages].

UCC § 2-611. Retraction of Anticipatory Repudiation

(1) Until the repudiating party's next performance is due he can retract his repudiation unless the aggrieved party has since the repudiation cancelled or materially changed his position or otherwise indicated that he considers the repudiation final.

(2) Retraction may be by any method which clearly indicates to the aggrieved party that the repudiating party intends to perform, but must include any assurance justifiably demanded under the provisions of this Article (Section 2-609).*

(3) Retraction reinstates the repudiating party's rights under the contract with due excuse and allowance to the aggrieved party for any delay occasioned by the repudiation.

[handwritten margin notes] Little bit of substantial performance

[handwritten margin notes] can say you will do it as long as other guy doesn't already have job — as her not required

§ 4.3. Reasonable Insecurity about Future Performance

Under *Hochster*, once an anticipatory repudiation occurred, the aggrieved party could consider the contract breached, could sue, and could enter into a substitute contract. If, however, one party merely had doubts about the other party's intention or ability to perform, but no repudiation had occurred, traditional common law offered the "insecure" party no recourse, as demonstrated in the *McCloskey* case. Although the party causing the sense of insecurity could be seen as breaching its implied promise not to impair the other party's expectation of receiving due performance, courts refused to extend the *Hochster* rule, continuing to require a showing of repudiation—an unequivocal refusal to perform or a statement of an inability to perform. Insecure parties were left to flounder, facing risk regardless of whether they continued under a contract that might not be performed or made substitute arrangements and became liable themselves for breaching the contract.

This gap in the law remained unaddressed until the early 1900s, when the courts slowly constructed a rule to protect insecure parties. In *Corn Products Refining Co. v. Fasola*, 109 A. 505 (N.J. 1920), Corn Products Refining contracted to furnish Fasola with 500 cases of No. 5 Mazola over a number of deliveries, on credit. In return, Fasola would repay the credit line within 30 days, or within 10 days for a 2% discount. Three days before the first delivery, Corn Products Refining learned from another source that Fasola's credit and ability to pay had diminished. Before shipment, Corn Products Refining informed Fasola that she would need to repay the line within 10 days. Fasola failed to pay within the 10-day requirement, even though she had paid within 10 days in previous transactions. Corn Products Refining refused to make further deliveries, relying on a clause within the contract that "[i]f at any time before shipment the financial responsibility of the buyer becomes impaired or unsatisfactory to the seller, cash payment or satisfactory security may be required by the seller before shipment." *Id.* at 505. Fasola claimed that Corn Products Refining had breached the contract and refused to pay the due amount. The lower court directed verdict for Corn Products Refining for the amount due. The appellate court affirmed, basing its judgment on a contract provision allowing the vendor to seek assurance. The court reasoned that "if for any reason not pretend or unreal, [the vendor] becomes dissatisfied with the financial responsibility of his debtor, he may invoke his contract and refuse to ship until secured according to the terms of the agreement." *Id.* at 505-06.

assurance clause

In *James B. Berry's Sons Co. of Illinois v. Monark Gasoline & Oil Co.*, 32 F.2d 74 (8th Cir. 1929), the court upheld a similar clause. Significantly, it stated in dictum:

---

* Section 2-609 is discussed on page 951.

reasonable assurance makes sense when finally arise [handwritten margin note]

> [I]f the clause in controversy had not been in this contract, the plaintiff would have had the right to demand cash or security and to refuse to deliver the goods on credit, even if the contract provided for credit, if the plaintiff had "become aware . . . that buyer was unable to pay debts as they became due in the ordinary course of business."

The court reasoned that reasonable assurance was both an express term and an implied term within the contract.

Finally, in *Jay Dreher Corp. v. Delco Appliance Corp.*, 93 F.2d 275 (2d Cir. 1937) the court based its holding on the implied term alone:

implied clause [handwritten margin note]

> Where a manufacturer gave a dealer an exclusive franchise for the sale of his product but on two or three occasions breached the exclusive dealing clause, although there was no default in orders, deliveries[,] or payments under the separate sales contract between the parties, the aggrieved dealer would be entitled to suspend his performance of the contract for sale . . . .

Id., as later described in U.C.C. § 2-609 cmt. 3. When UCC Art.2 was promulgated in the early 1950s, it included a similar rule, dealing specifically with contracts for the sale of goods.

The drafters of the Restatement followed with the promulgation of **Restatement (Second) § 251** in 1979. Some jurisdictions have adopted § 251, and some have applied UCC § 2-609 by analogy either generally or to particular types of contracts. Some gaps remain, however, so insecurity remains a concern in some jurisdictions for contracts outside Article 2.

Reading the Law Critically:

Demands for Adequate Assurance under the UCC,

Restatement (Second), and CISG

1. Under the UCC provision:

    a. Under what circumstances does a party have a right to demand adequate assurance of due performance?

    b. What happens if a party does not have a right to demand adequate assurance from the other party but does so anyway?

    c. What requirements exist regarding the form or content of the demand for adequate assurance?

> d. What makes a statement an adequate assurance of due performance?
>
> e. What happens if the insecure party does not receive adequate assurance?
>
> 2. How does the UCC provision compare to the Restatement provision?
>
> 3. In what ways do the CISG provisions differ from the UCC and Restatement standards?

UCC § 2-609. Right to Adequate Assurance

(1) A contract for sale imposes an obligation on each party that the other's expectation of receiving due performance will not be impaired. When reasonable grounds for insecurity arise with respect to the performance of either party the other may in writing demand adequate assurance of due performance and until he receives such assurance may if commercially reasonable suspend any performance for which he has not already received the agreed return.

(2) . . . .

(3) . . . .

(4) After receipt of a justified demand failure to provide within a reasonable time not exceeding thirty days such assurance of due performance as is adequate under the circumstances of the particular case is a repudiation of the contract.

Comment 3 [offering guidance on the meaning of "reasonable grounds for insecurity"]:*

- "[A] buyer who falls behind in 'his account' with the seller, even though the items involved have to do with separate and legally distinct contracts, impairs the seller's expectation of due performance.
- . . . [A] buyer who requires precision parts which he intends to use immediately upon delivery may have reasonable grounds for insecurity if he discovers that his seller is making defective deliveries of such parts to other buyers with similar needs.
- . . . [W]here a manufacturer gave a dealer an exclusive franchise for the sale of his product but on two or three occasions breached the exclusive dealing clause, although there was no default in orders, deliveries or payments under the separate sales contract between

---

* The examples in comments 3 and 4 have been displayed in a bulleted list for ease of reference, although they appear as straight narrative in the actual comments.

the parties, the aggrieved dealer would be entitled to suspend his performance of the contract for sale under the present section and to demand assurance that the exclusive dealing contract would be lived up to.

- . . . [A] report from an apparently trustworthy source that the seller had shipped defective goods or was planning to ship them would normally give the buyer reasonable grounds for insecurity [unless the buyer assumed the risk of such defects by promising payment in the contract without the right to inspect first.]"

Comment 4 [offering guidance on the meaning of "adequate assurance of due performance"]:

- "[W]here the buyer can make use of a defective delivery, a mere promise by a seller of good repute that he is giving the matter his attention and that the defect will not be repeated, is normally sufficient. Under the same circumstances, however, a similar statement by a known corner-cutter might well be considered insufficient without the posting of a guaranty or, if so demanded by the buyer, a speedy replacement of the delivery involved.
- . . . [W]here a delivery has defects, even though easily curable, which interfere with easy use by the buyer, no verbal assurance can be deemed adequate which is not accompanied by replacement, repair, money-allowance, or other commercially reasonable cure."

————

Restatement (Second) of Contracts § 251. When A Failure To Give Assurance May Be Treated As A Repudiation

(1) Where reasonable grounds arise to believe that the obligor will commit a breach by non-performance that would of itself give the obligee a claim for damages for total breach under § 243, the obligee may demand adequate assurance of due performance and may, if reasonable, suspend any performance for which he has not already received the agreed exchange until he receives such assurance.

(2) The obligee may treat as a repudiation the obligor's failure to provide within a reasonable time such assurance of due performance as is adequate in the circumstances of the particular case.

CISG Art. 71 (in **Ch. V Sec. I, Anticipatory Breach and Installment Contracts**)

(1) A party may suspend the performance of his obligations if, after the conclusion of the contract, it becomes apparent that the other party will not perform a substantial part of his obligations as a result of:

    (a) a serious deficiency in his ability to perform or in his creditworthiness; or

    (b) his conduct in preparing to perform or in performing the contract.

(2) . . . .

(3) A party suspending performance, whether before or after dispatch of the goods, must immediately give notice of the suspension to the other party and must continue with performance if the other party provides adequate assurance of his performance.

CISG Art. 72 (in **Ch. V Sec. I, Anticipatory Breach and Installment Contracts**)

(1) If prior to the date for performance of the contract it is clear that one of the parties will commit a fundamental breach of contract, the other party may declare the contract avoided.

(2) If time allows, the party intending to declare the contract avoided must give reasonable notice to the other party in order to permit him to provide adequate assurance of his performance.

(3) The requirements of the preceding paragraph do not apply if the other party has declared that he will not perform his obligations.

Reading the Law Critically: *Hornell Brewing Co.*

1. What created the reasonable grounds for insecurity for plaintiff?

2. Why didn't plaintiff need to make a written demand for adequate assurance?

3. Did defendants respond with an adequate assurance of due performance? Why or why not?

Hornell Brewing Co. v. Spry

HORNELL BREWING CO., Plaintiff

v.

STEPHEN A. SPRY and ARIZONA TEA PRODUCTS LTD., Defendants

Supreme Court, New York County, New York

664 N.Y.S.2d 698 (Sup. Ct. 1997)

LOUISE GRUNER GANS, Justice.

Plaintiff Hornell Brewing Co., Inc. ("Hornell"), a supplier and marketer of alcoholic and non-alcoholic beverages, including the popular iced tea drink "Arizona," commenced this action for a declaratory judgment that any rights of defendants Stephen A. Spry and Arizona Tea Products Ltd. to distribute Hornell's beverages in Canada have been duly terminated, that defendants have no further rights with respect to these products, including no right to market and distribute them, and that any such rights previously transferred to defendants have reverted to Hornell.

In late 1992, Spry approached Don Vultaggio, Hornell's Chairman of the Board, about becoming a distributor of Hornell's Arizona beverages. Vultaggio had heard about Spry as an extremely wealthy and successful beer distributor who had recently sold his business. In January 1993, Spry presented Vultaggio with an ambitious plan for distributing Arizona beverages in Canada. Based on the plan and on Spry's reputation, but without further investigation, Hornell in early 1993 granted Spry the exclusive right to purchase Arizona products for distribution in Canada, and Spry formed a Canadian corporation, Arizona Iced Tea Ltd., for that express purpose.

Initially, the arrangement was purely oral. In response to Spry's request for a letter he needed to secure financing, Hornell provided a letter in July 1993 confirming their exclusive distributorship arrangement, but without spelling out the details of the arrangement. Although Hornell usually had detailed written distributorship agreements and the parties discussed and exchanged drafts of such an agreement, none was ever executed. In the meantime, Spry, with Hornell's approval, proceeded to set himself up as Hornell's distributor in Canada. During 1993 and until May 1994, the Hornell line of beverages, including the Arizona beverages, was sold to defendants on 10-day credit terms. In May 1994, after an increasingly problematic course of business dealings, Hornell *de facto* terminated its relationship with defendants and permanently ceased selling its products to them.

The problem dominating the parties' relationship between July 1993 and early May 1994 was defendants' failure to remit timely payment for shipments of beverages received from plaintiff. Between November and December 1993, and February 1994, defendants' unpaid invoices grew from $20,000 to over $100,000, and their $31,000 check to Hornell was returned for insufficient funds. Moreover, defendants' 1993 sales in Canada were far below Spry's initial projections.

In March and April 1994, a series of meetings, telephone calls, and letter communications took place between plaintiff and defendants regarding Spry's constant arrearages and the need for him to obtain a line and/or letter of credit that would place their business relationship on a more secure footing. These contacts included a March 27, 1994 letter to Spry from Vanguard Financial Group, Inc. confirming "the approval of a $1,500,000 revolving credit facility" to Arizona Tea Products Ltd., which never materialized into an actual line of credit; Spry sent Hornell a copy of this letter in late March or early April 1994.

All these exchanges demonstrate that during this period plaintiff had two distinct goals: to collect the monies owed by Spry, and to stabilize their future business relationship based on proven, reliable credit assurances. These exchanges also establish that during March and April, 1994, Spry repeatedly broke his promises to pay by a specified deadline, causing Hornell to question whether Vanguard's $1.5 million revolving line of credit was genuine.

On April 15, 1994, during a meeting with Vultaggio, Spry arranged for Vultaggio to speak on the telephone with Richard Worthy of Metro Factors, Inc. The testimony as to the content of that brief telephone conversation is conflicting. Although Worthy testified that he identified himself and the name of his company, Metro Factors, Inc., Vultaggio testified that he believed Worthy was from an "unusual lending institution" or bank which was going to provide Spry with a line of credit, and that nothing was expressly said to make him aware that Worthy represented a factoring company. Worthy also testified that Vultaggio told him that once Spry cleared up the arrears, Hornell would provide Spry with a "$300,000 line of credit, so long as payments were made on a net 14 day basis." According to Vultaggio, he told Worthy that once he was paid in full, he was willing to resume shipments to Spry "so long as Steve fulfills his requirements with us."

Hornell's April 18, 1994 letter to Spry confirmed certain details of the April 15 conversations, including that payment of the arrears would be made by April 19, 1994. However, Hornell

What's That?

"Factoring" involves a business selling its accounts receivable to a third party (called a "factor") at a discount (less than the stated amount due in the accounts receivable). Traditionally, factoring is not a loan because the factor purchases the accounts receivable by paying the business a price. Can you tell whether Worthy represented a factoring company, as defined here?

received no payment on that date. Instead, on April 25, Hornell received from Spry a proposed letter for Hornell to address to a company named "Metro" at a post office box in Dallas, Texas. Worthy originally sent Spry a draft of this letter with "Metro Factors, Inc." named as the addressee, but in the copy Vultaggio received the words "Factors, Inc." were apparently obliterated. Hornell copied the draft letter on its own letterhead and sent it to Metro over Vultaggio's signature. In relevant part, the letter stated as follows:

> Gentlemen:
>
> Please be advised that Arizona Tea Products, Ltd. (ATP), of which Steve Spry is president, is presently indebted to us in the total amount of $79,316.24 as of the beginning of business Monday, April 25, 1994. We sell to them on "Net 14 days" terms. Such total amount is due according to the following schedule:
>
> . . . .
>
> Upon receipt of $79,316.24. (which shall be applied to the oldest balances first) by 5:00 P.M. (EST) Tuesday, May 2, 1994 by wire transfer(s) to the account described below, we shall recommence selling product to ATP on the following terms:
>
> 1) All invoices from us are due and payable by the 14th day following the release of the related product.
> 2) We shall allow the outstanding balance owed to us by ATP to go up to $300,000 so long as ATP remains "current" in its payment obligations to us. Wiring instructions are as follows: . . . .

Hornell received no payment on May 2, 1994. It did receive a wire transfer from Metro of the full amount on May 9, 1994. Upon immediate confirmation of that payment, Spry ordered 30 trailer loads of "product" from Hornell, at a total purchase price of $390,000 to $450,000. In the interim between April 25, 1994 and May 9, 1994, Hornell learned from several sources, including its regional sales manager Baumkel, that Spry's warehouse was empty, that he had no managerial, sales or office staff, that he had no trucks, and that in effect his operation was a sham.

On May 10, 1994, Hornell wrote to Spry, acknowledging receipt of payment and confirming that they would extend up to $300,000 of credit to him, net 14 days cash "based on your prior representation that you have secured a $1,500,000 US line of credit." The letter also stated,

Your current balance with us reflects a 0 balance due. As you know, however, we experienced considerable difficulty and time wasted over a five week time period as we tried to collect some $130,000 which was 90-120 days past due.

Accordingly, before we release any more product, we are asking you to provide us with a letter confirming the existence of your line of credit as well as a personal guarantee that is backed up with a personal financial statement that can be verified. Another option would be for you to provide us with an irrevocable letter of credit in the amount of $300,000.

Spry did not respond to this letter. Spry never even sent Hornell a copy of his agreement with Metro Factors, Inc., which Spry had signed on March 24, 1994 and which was fully executed on March 30, 1994. On May 26, 1994, Vultaggio met with Spry to discuss termination of their business relationship. Vultaggio presented Spry with a letter of agreement as to the termination, which Spry took with him but did not sign. After some months of futile negotiations by counsel this action by Hornell ensued.

At the outset, the court determines that an enforceable contract existed between plaintiff and defendants based on the uncontroverted facts of their conduct. Under Article 2 of the Uniform Commercial Code, parties can form a contract through their conduct rather than merely through the exchange of communications constituting an offer and acceptance. . . . Section 2–204(1) states: "A contract for sale of goods may be made in any manner sufficient to show agreement, including conduct by both parties which recognizes the existence of such a contract." Sections 2–206(1) and 2–207(3) expressly allow for the formation of a contract partly or wholly on the basis of such conduct. . . .

Here, the conduct of plaintiff and defendants which recognized the existence of a contract is sufficient to establish a contract for sale under [UCC] sections 2–204(1) and 2–207(3). Both parties' undisputed actions over a period of many months clearly manifested mutual recognition that a binding obligation was undertaken. Following plaintiff's agreement to grant defendant an exclusive distributorship for Canada, defendant Spry took certain steps to enable him to commence his distribution operation in Canada. These steps included hiring counsel in Canada to form Arizona Tea Products, Ltd., the vehicle through which defendant acted in Canada, obtaining regulatory approval for the labeling of Arizona Iced Tea in conformity with Canadian law, and obtaining importation approvals necessary to import Arizona Iced Tea into Canada. Defendants subsequently placed orders for the purchase of plaintiff's products, plaintiff shipped its products to defendants during 1993 and early 1994, and defendants remitted payments, albeit not timely nor in full. Under the [UCC], these uncontroverted business dealings constitute "conduct . . . sufficient to establish a contract for sale," even in the absence of a specific writing by the parties. UCC § 2–207(3) . . . .

Notwithstanding the parties' conflicting contentions concerning the duration and termination of defendants' distributorship, plaintiff has demonstrated a basis for lawfully terminating its contract with defendants in accordance with [UCC] section 2–609. Section 2–609(1) authorizes one party upon "reasonable grounds for insecurity" to "demand adequate assurance of due performance and until he receives such assurance . . . if commercially reasonable suspend any performance for which he has not already received the agreed return." The Official Comment to section 2–609 explains that this

> section rests on the recognition of the fact that the essential purpose of a contract between commercial men is actual performance and they do not bargain merely for a promise, or for a promise plus the right to win a lawsuit and that a continuing sense of reliance and security that the promised performance will be forthcoming when due, is an important feature of the bargain. If either the willingness or the ability of a party to perform declines materially between the time of contracting and the time for performance, the other party is threatened with the loss of a substantial part of what he has bargained for. A seller needs protection not merely against having to deliver on credit to a shaky buyer, but also against having to procure and manufacture the goods, perhaps turning down other customers. Once he has been given reason to believe that the buyer's performance has become uncertain, it is an undue hardship to force him to continue his own performance.

McKinney's Consolidated Laws of NY, Book 62½, UCC § 2–609 Official Comment 1, at 488.

Whether a seller, as the plaintiff in this case, has reasonable grounds for insecurity is an issue of fact that depends upon various factors, including the buyer's exact words or actions, the course of dealing or performance between the parties, and the nature of the sales contract and the industry. White & Summers, *Uniform Commercial Code, supra* § 6–2 at 286; *see also* Phibro Energy, Inc. v. Empresa De Polimeros De Sines Sarl, 720 F. Supp. 312, 322 (S.D.N.Y.1989); S & S Inc. v. Meyer, 478 N.W.2d 857, 863 (Iowa App.1991); AMF, Inc. v. McDonald's Corp., 536 F.2d 1167, 1170 (7th Cir.1976). Subdivision (2) defines both "reasonableness" and "adequacy" by commercial rather than legal standards, and the Official Comment notes the application of the good faith standard. White & Summers, *id.,* at 287; McKinney's Consolidated Laws of NY, Book 62½, UCC § 2–609 Official Comment at 488, 489; Turntables, Inc. v. Gestetner, 52 A.D.2d 776, 382 N.Y.S.2d 798 (1st Dep't 1976).

Once the seller correctly determines that it has reasonable grounds for insecurity, it must properly request assurances from the buyer. Although the Code requires that the request be made in writing, UCC § 2–609(1), courts have not strictly adhered to this formality as long as an unequivocal demand is made. White & Summers, *Uniform Commercial Code, supra* § 6–2 at 288; *see, e.g.,* **ARB, Inc. v. E–Systems, Inc.,** 663 F.2d 189 (D.C.Cir.1980); **Toppert v. Bunge Corp.,** 60 Ill. App.3d 607, 18 Ill. Dec. 171, 377 N.E.2d 324 (1978); **AMF, Inc. v. McDonald's Corp., supra.** After demanding assurance, the seller must determine the proper "adequate assurance." What constitutes "adequate" assurance of due performance is subject to the same test of commercial reasonableness and factual conditions. McKinney's Consolidated Laws of NY, Book 62½, UCC § 2–609 Official Comment at 489.

Applying these principles to the case at bar, the overwhelming weight of the evidence establishes that at the latest by the beginning of 1994, plaintiff had reasonable grounds to be insecure about defendants' ability to perform in the future. Defendants were substantially in arrears almost from the outset of their relationship with plaintiff, had no financing in place, bounced checks, and had failed to sell even a small fraction of the product defendant Spry originally projected.

Reasonable grounds for insecurity can arise from the sole fact that a buyer has fallen behind in his account with the seller, even where the items involved have to do with separate and legally distinct contracts, because this "impairs the seller's expectation of due performance." McKinney's Consolidated Laws of NY, Book 62½, UCC § 2–609 Official Comment 2, at 488; *see also* **Waldorf Steel Fabricators, Inc. v. Consolidated Systems, Inc.,** 1996 WL 480902 (S.D.N.Y.) (n.o.r.); **Turntables, Inc. v. Gestetner, supra.; American Bronze Corp. v. Streamway Products,** 8 Ohio App.3d 223, 456 N.E.2d 1295 (1982).

Here, defendants do not dispute their poor payment history, plaintiff's right to demand adequate assurances from them and that plaintiff made such demands. Rather, defendants claim that they satisfied those demands by the April 15, 1994 telephone conversation between Vultaggio and Richard Worthy of Metro Factors, Inc., followed by Vultaggio's April 18, 1994 letter to Metro, and Metro's payment of $79,316.24 to Hornell, and that thereafter plaintiff had no right to demand further assurance.

The court disagrees with both plaintiff and defendants in their insistence that only one demand for adequate assurance was made in this case to which there was and could be only a single response. Even accepting defendants' argument that payment by Metro was the sole condition Vultaggio required when he spoke and wrote to Metro, and that such condition was met by Metro's actual payment, the court is persuaded that on May 9, 1994, Hornell had further reasonable grounds for insecurity and a new basis for seeking further adequate assurances.

Defendants cite White & Summers, *Uniform Commercial Code*, § 6-2 at 289, for the proposition that "[i]f a party demands and receives specific assurances, then absent a further change of circumstances, the assurances demanded and received are adequate, and the party who has demanded the assurances is bound to proceed." Repeated demands for adequate assurances are within the contemplation of section 2–609. *See* McKinney's Consolidated Laws of NY, Book 62½, UCC § 2–609 Official Comment at 490.

Here, there was a further change of circumstances. Vultaggio's reported conversation with Worthy on April 15 and his April 25 letter to Metro both anticipate that once payment of defendants' arrears was made, Hornell would release *up to* $300,000 worth of product on the further condition that defendants met the 14 day payment terms. The arrangement, by its terms, clearly contemplated an opportunity for Hornell to test out defendants' ability to make payment within 14-day periods.

By placing a single order worth $390,000 to $450,000 immediately after receipt of Metro's payment, Spry not only demanded a shipment of product which exceeded the proposed limit, but placed Hornell in a position where it would have *no* opportunity learn whether Spry would meet the 14–day payment terms, before Spry again became indebted to Hornell for a very large sum of money.

At this point, neither Spry nor Worthy had fully informed Hornell what assurance of payment Metro would be able to provide. Leaving aside the question whether the factoring arrangement with Metro constituted adequate assurance, Hornell never received any documentation to substantiate Spry's purported agreement with Metro. Although Spry's agreement with Metro was fully executed by the end of March, Spry never gave Hornell a copy of it, not even in response to Hornell's May 10, 1994 demand. The March 27, 1994 letter from Vanguard coincided with the date Spry signed the Metro agreement, but contained only a vague reference to a $1.5 million "revolving credit facility," without mentioning Metro Factors, Inc. Moreover, based on the Vanguard letter, Hornell had expected that payment would be forthcoming, but Spry once again offered only excuses and empty promises.

These circumstances, coupled with information received in early May (on which it reasonably relied) that Spry had misled Hornell about the scope of his operation, created new and more acute grounds for Hornell's insecurity and entitled Hornell to seek further adequate assurance from defendants in the form of a documented line of credit or other guarantee. . . . Defendants' failure to respond constituted a repudiation of the distributorship agreement, which entitled plaintiff to suspend performance and terminate the agreement. UCC § 2–609(4); **Turntables, Inc. v. Gestetner, supra.; Creusot–Loire Int'l v. Coppus**

Engineering Corp., supra; AMF, Inc. v. McDonald's Corp., supra; ARB, Inc. v. E–Systems, Inc., supra; Toppert v. Bunge Corp., supra; *Waldorf Steel Fabricators, Inc. v. Consolidated Systems, Inc., supra.*

Even if Hornell had seen Spry's agreement with Metro, in the circumstances of this case, the agreement did not provide the adequate assurance to which plaintiff was entitled in relation to defendants' $390,000-$450,000 order. Spry admitted that much of the order was to be retained as inventory for the summer, for which there would be no receivables to factor within 14 days. Although the question of whether every aspect of Hornell's May 10 demand for credit documentation was reasonable is a close one, given the entire history of the relationship between the parties, the court determines that the demand was commercially reasonable. . . .

The court notes in conclusion that its evaluation of the evidence in this case was significantly influenced by Mr. Spry's regrettable lack of credibility. *See* Spanier v. New York City Transit Authority, 222 A.D.2d 219, 634 N.Y.S.2d 122 (1st Dep't 1995). The court agrees with plaintiff, that to an extent far greater than was known to Hornell in May 1994, Mr. Spry was not truthful, failed to pay countless other creditors almost as a matter of course, and otherwise engaged in improper and deceptive business practices.

For the foregoing reasons, it is hereby

ORDERED and ADJUDGED that plaintiff Hornell Brewing Co., Inc. have a declaratory judgment that defendants Stephen A. Spry and Arizona Tea Products, Ltd. were duly terminated and have no continuing rights with respect to plaintiff Hornell Brewing Co.'s beverage products in Canada or elsewhere.

. . . .

Problems: Demands for Adequate Assurance

8-6. Buyer and Seller entered a five-year contract for the sale of oil, with monthly deliveries of specified amounts, purchases to be made on 30 days' credit, 2% off for payment within 10 days of invoicing. From the beginning of the contract term, the buyer regularly paid invoices within 10 days, taking advantage of the discount. In the third year of the contract, the buyer failed for the first time to make payment within 10 days of invoicing shortly after the seller heard from others in the industry that the buyer had missed payment deadlines in other contracts.

a. At that point, was Seller entitled to demand an adequate assurance of performance? *no, still has time*

b. Assume Seller had a right to demand adequate assurance and did so. Buyer responded by letter declaring it was in solid financial condition, stating its intention to make payments when due on the 30-day terms, and insisting on further deliveries under the contract. What should Seller do? *accept it, but not very satisfied*

c. Would it make a difference in your previous answers if the contract called for payment on delivery and specified that "credit is to be extended to the buyer only if his financial responsibility is satisfactory to the seller"?

8-7. If **UCC § 2-609** or **Restatement (Second) § 251** had been available to the parties in *McCloskey & Co. v. Minweld Steel Co.*, **page TK**, would either party have been able to use the section to demand adequate assurances of future performance? How might that have affected the parties' dispute?

§ 5. Performance and Breach under UCC Article 2

As seen in § **3, on page 902**, under the common law only substantial performance, not complete performance, is required in order to trigger the other party's dependent duty to perform (unless the parties have agreed otherwise). For sales of goods under UCC Article 2, however, the rule is different. Consider § 2-601, which states what is generally known as the "perfect tender" rule:

UCC § 2-601. **Buyer's Rights on Improper Delivery**

Subject to the provisions of this Article on breach in installment contracts (**Section 2-612**) and unless otherwise agreed under the sections on contractual limitations of remedy (**Sections 2-718** and **2-719**), if the goods or the tender of delivery fail in any respect to conform to the contract, the buyer may

(a) reject the whole; or

(b) accept the whole; or

(c) accept any commercial unit or units and reject the rest.

Section 2-601 declares that, if the goods or tender fail "in any respect" to conform to the contract, the buyer may "reject" the goods. Although this appears to mean that the buyer's responsibility to take (and pay for) the goods is dependent on perfect conformity to the contract by the seller, in reality the perfect tender rule has some limitations:

- Section 2-601 says the rule does not apply to installment contracts or to contracts in which the parties agree the buyer will not have such a remedy.

- A buyer is not permitted to seize on a technical defect in order to reject (which would be operating in bad faith).

- If the contract involves a so-called "shipment contract," which means the seller's tender responsibilities involve delivering the goods to a carrier, only certain seller's breaches in transporting the goods give buyer the right to reject.

> ### What's That?
>
> Under UCC § 2-503, the "tender" of goods means seller's performance of its delivery responsibilities under the contract, which might require transporting the goods to a particular destination, or delivering them to a transport company, or making them available at a reasonable time and place for the buyer to pick up the goods.
>
> An "installment contract" is one in which the goods must or may be delivered in separate lots to be separately accepted. Under § 2-612, installment contracts are governed by a "substantial impairment" standard, similar to a substantial performance requirement for non-sale-of-goods contracts.

- Most importantly, if the buyer rejects the goods, the seller often has a right (but not a duty) to cure the non-conformity by repairing defective goods or replacing them with conforming goods.

If a buyer rejects a tender of goods that conformed to the contract specifications, the buyer breaches the contract by making a wrongful rejection. In order to make an effective rejection, the buyer must tell the seller it does not want to keep the goods, according to UCC § 2-602:

UCC § 2-602. Manner and Effect of Rightful Rejection.

(1) Rejection of goods must be within a reasonable time after their delivery or tender. It is ineffective unless the buyer seasonably notifies the seller.

(2) Subject to the provisions of the two following sections on rejected goods (Sections 2-603 and 2-604),

    (a) after rejection any exercise of ownership by the buyer with respect to any commercial unit is wrongful as against the seller; and

---

> (b) if the buyer has before rejection taken physical possession of goods in which he does not have a security interest under the provisions of this Article (subsection (3) of Section 2-711), he is under a duty after rejection to hold them with reasonable care at the seller's disposition for a time sufficient to permit the seller to remove them; but
> (c) the buyer has no further obligations with regard to goods rightfully rejected.
> (3) The seller's rights with respect to goods wrongfully rejected are governed by the provisions of this Article on Seller's remedies in general (Section 2-703).

If the buyer rejects the goods, the seller may, under § 2-508, have a right (not a duty) to "cure" the defect by repair or replacement:

 Reading the Law Critically: Cure under the UCC

1. What must a seller demonstrate in order to establish its right to cure a defective performance under each of the subsections?

2. Construct a scenario that would allow a seller to cure under § 2-508(2).

> **UCC § 2-508. Cure by Seller of Improper Tender or Delivery; Replacement**
>
> (1) Where any tender or delivery by the seller is rejected because non-conforming and the time for performance has not yet expired, the seller may seasonably notify the buyer of his intention to cure and may then within the contract time make a conforming delivery.
> (2) Where the buyer rejects a non-conforming tender which the seller had reasonable grounds to believe would be acceptable with or without money allowance the seller may if he seasonably notifies the buyer have a further reasonable time to substitute a conforming tender.

If the buyer does not reject the goods (perhaps because the buyer does not find the defect or can use the defective goods, or because the seller gives assurances of cure but does not cure), the buyer then "accepts" the goods, as defined in § 2-606. The consequences of acceptance are specified in § 2-607. Even if the buyer has a right to reject goods for any nonconformity, the buyer may instead (and often does) accept the goods (or some portion of the delivery) and seek damages for any defect.

Reading the Law Critically:
Acceptance of Goods under the UCC

1. What must be shown to prove acceptance of goods under each of the three scenarios in which acceptance of goods may occur?

2. What obligations does a buyer's acceptance of goods create? What can an accepting buyer not do?

UCC § 2-606. What Constitutes Acceptance of Goods

(1) Acceptance of goods occurs when the buyer
   (a) after a reasonable opportunity to inspect the goods signifies to the seller that the goods are conforming or that he will take or retain them in spite of their non-conformity; or
   (b) fails to make an effective rejection (**subsection (1) of Section 2-602**), but such acceptance does not occur until the buyer has had a reasonable opportunity to inspect them; or
   (c) does any act inconsistent with the seller's ownership; but if such act is wrongful as against the seller it is an acceptance only if ratified by him.
(2) Acceptance of a part of any commercial unit is acceptance of that entire unit.

UCC § 2-607. Effect of Acceptance; Notice of Breach; Burden of Establishing Breach After Acceptance; Notice of Claim or Litigation to Person Answerable Over

(1) The buyer must pay at the contract rate for any goods accepted.
(2) Acceptance of goods by the buyer precludes rejection of the goods accepted and if made with knowledge of a non-conformity cannot be revoked because of it unless the acceptance was on the reasonable assumption that the non-conformity would be seasonably cured but acceptance does not of itself impair any other remedy provided by this Article for non-conformity.
(3) Where a tender has been accepted
   (a) the buyer must within a reasonable time after he discovers or should have discovered any breach notify the seller of breach or be barred from any remedy; and

> (b) if the claim is one for [intellectual property] infringement or the like
> . . . and the buyer is sued as a result of such a breach he must so
> notify the seller within a reasonable time after he receives notice of
> the litigation or be barred from any remedy over for liability estab-
> lished by the litigation.
> (4) The burden is on the buyer to establish any breach with respect to the
> goods accepted.
>
> . . . .

An accepting buyer has a second but much more limited chance to return the goods by "revoking acceptance" of the goods:

Reading the Law Critically:
Revocation of Accptance under the UCC

1. What must the buyer prove in order to justify revoking acceptance (the substantive basis is revocation)?

2. What is the required form (the procedural requirements) for making an *effective* revocation of acceptance?

3. After revoking acceptance, what duties does the buyer have as to the goods? Which other UCC section lays out those duties?

4. What language in § 2-508 shows that sellers do not, by operation of the statute, have a right to cure after revocation of acceptance? Why might the drafters have chosen not to allow cure after revocation? What policies might support granting such a right anyway, as many courts have done?

UCC § 2-608. Revocation of Acceptance in Whole or in Part

(1) The buyer may revoke his acceptance of a lot or commercial unit whose non-conformity substantially impairs its value to him if he has accepted it
  (a) on the reasonable assumption that its non-conformity would be cured and it has not been seasonably cured; or
  (b) without discovery of such non-conformity if his acceptance was reasonably induced either by the difficulty of discovery before acceptance or by the seller's assurances.

(2) Revocation of acceptance must occur within a reasonable time after the buyer discovers or should have discovered the ground for it and before any substantial change in condition of the goods which is not caused by their own defects. It is not effective until the buyer notifies the seller of it.

(3) A buyer that so revokes has the same rights and duties with regard to the goods involved as if he had rejected them.

Regardless of whether the buyer ends up keeping defective goods or successfully rejects them or revokes acceptance, the buyer will be entitled to recover damages for injury caused by the breach, though the measure will be different under those different circumstances.

The following diagram illustrates the interconnection of the various aspects of performance under Article 2, if the seller tenders goods that don't conform to the contract:

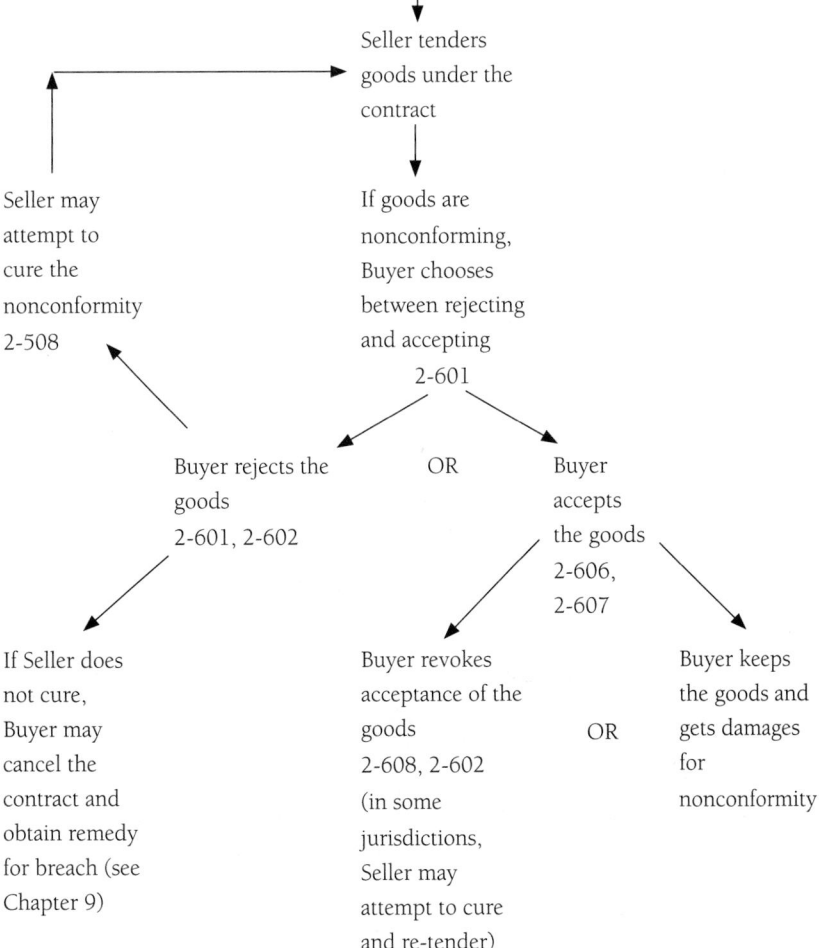

Seller tenders goods under the contract

Seller may attempt to cure the nonconformity 2-508

If goods are nonconforming, Buyer chooses between rejecting and accepting 2-601

Buyer rejects the goods 2-601, 2-602   OR   Buyer accepts the goods 2-606, 2-607

If Seller does not cure, Buyer may cancel the contract and obtain remedy for breach (see Chapter 9)

Buyer revokes acceptance of the goods 2-608, 2-602 (in some jurisdictions, Seller may attempt to cure and re-tender)   OR   Buyer keeps the goods and gets damages for nonconformity

A seller may also breach by repudiating the contract or otherwise failing to deliver. Under such circumstances, the buyer has no goods to reject but has other remedies available (damages or specific performance).

On the other side of the transaction, a buyer may breach by wrongfully rejecting or unjustifiably revoking acceptance, by failing to pay all or some of the contract price, by paying late, or by repudiating the contract in advance of delivery of the goods. The remedies for all of these breaches are covered in Chapter 9.

The following case demonstrates many of these concepts and their interrelationships.

Reading the Law Critically: *Ramirez*

1. Using the diagram and the UCC text in the preceding discussion, trace the transaction and the court's reasoning and holdings.

2. Did the buyer reject the goods or revoke acceptance of the goods? Does that choice make a difference in the court's reasoning or holding?

3. What policies underlie the UCC provisions related to rejection, cure, and revocation?

Ramirez v. Autosport

ERNEST RAMIREZ and ADELE RAMIREZ, Plaintiffs-Respondents

v.

AUTOSPORT, Defendant-Appellant

Supreme Court of New Jersey
440 A.2d 1345 (N.J. 1982)

POLLOCK, J.

This case raises several issues under the Uniform Commercial Code ("the Code" and "UCC") concerning whether a buyer may reject a tender of goods with minor defects and whether a seller may cure the defects. We consider also the remedies available to the buyer, including cancellation of the contract. The main issue is whether plaintiffs, Mr. and Mrs. Ramirez, could reject the tender by defendant, Autosport, of a camper van with minor defects and cancel the contract for the purchase of the van.

The trial court ruled that Mr. and Mrs. Ramirez rightfully rejected the van and awarded them the fair market value of their trade-in van. The Appellate Division affirmed in a brief per curiam decision which, like the trial court opinion, was unreported. We affirm the judgment of the Appellate Division.

I

Following a mobile home show at the Meadowlands Sports Complex, Mr. and Mrs. Ramirez visited Autosport's showroom in Somerville. On July 20, 1978 the Ramirezes and Donald Graff, a salesman for Autosport, agreed on the sale of a new camper and the trade-in of the van owned by Mr. and Mrs. Ramirez. Autosport and the Ramirezes signed a simple contract reflecting a $14,100 purchase price for the new van with a $4,700 trade-in allowance for the Ramirez van, which Mr. and Mrs. Ramirez left with Autosport. After further allowance for taxes, title and documentary fees, the net price was $9,902. Because Autosport needed two weeks to prepare the new van, the contract provided for delivery on or about August 3, 1978.

On that date, Mr. and Mrs. Ramirez returned with their checks to Autosport to pick up the new van. Graff was not there so Mr. White, another salesman, met them. Inspection disclosed several defects in the van. The paint was scratched, both the electric and sewer hookups were missing, and the hubcaps were not installed. White advised the Ramirezes not to accept the camper because it was not ready.

Mr. and Mrs. Ramirez wanted the van for a summer vacation and called Graff several times. Each time Graff told them it was not ready for delivery. Finally, Graff called to notify them that the camper was ready. On August 14 Mr. and Mrs. Ramirez went to Autosport to accept delivery, but workers were still touching up the outside paint. Also, the camper windows were open, and the dining area cushions were soaking wet. Mr. and Mrs. Ramirez could not use the camper in that condition, but Mr. Leis, Autosport's manager, suggested that they take the van and that Autosport would replace the cushions later. Mrs. Ramirez counteroffered to accept the van if they could withhold $2,000, but Leis agreed to no more than $250, which she refused. Leis then agreed to replace the cushions and to call them when the van was ready.

On August 15, 1978 Autosport transferred title to the van to Mr. and Mrs. Ramirez, a fact unknown to them until the summer of 1979. Between August 15 and September 1, 1978 Mrs. Ramirez called Graff several times urging him to complete the preparation of the van, but Graff constantly advised her that the van was not ready. He finally informed her that they could pick it up on September 1.

When Mr. and Mrs. Ramirez went to the showroom on September 1, Graff asked them to wait. And wait they did—for one and a half hours. No one from Autosport came forward to talk with them, and the Ramirezes left in disgust.

On October 5, 1978 Mr. and Mrs. Ramirez went to Autosport with an attorney friend. Although the parties disagreed on what occurred, the general topic was whether they should proceed with the deal or Autosport should return to the Ramirezes their trade-in van. Mrs. Ramirez claimed they rejected the new van and requested the return of their trade-in. Mr. Lustig, the owner of Autosport, thought, however, that the deal could be salvaged if the parties could agree on the dollar amount of a credit for the Ramirezes. Mr. and Mrs. Ramirez never took possession of the new van and repeated their request for the return of their trade-in. Later in October, however, Autosport sold the trade-in to an innocent third party for $4,995. Autosport claimed that the Ramirez' van had a book value of $3,200 and claimed further that it spent $1,159.62 to repair their van. By subtracting the total of those two figures, $4,359.62, from the $4,995.00 sale price, Autosport claimed a $600-700 profit on the sale.

On November 20, 1978 the Ramirezes sued Autosport seeking, among other things, rescission of the contract. Autosport counterclaimed for breach of contract.

II

Our initial inquiry is whether a consumer may reject defective goods that do not conform to the contract of sale. The basic issue is whether under the UCC, adopted in New Jersey as **N.J.S.A. 12A:1-101** et seq., a seller has the duty to deliver goods that conform precisely to the contract. We conclude that the seller is under such a duty to make a "perfect tender" and that a buyer has the right to reject goods that do not conform to the contract. That conclusion, however, does not resolve the entire dispute between buyer and seller. A more complete answer requires a brief statement of the history of the mutual obligations of buyers and sellers of commercial goods.

In the nineteenth century, sellers were required to deliver goods that complied exactly with the sales agreement. See **Filley v. Pope, 115 U.S. 213, 220, 6 S.Ct. 19, 21, 29 L.Ed. 372, 373 (1885)** (buyer not obliged to accept otherwise conforming scrap iron shipped to New Orleans from Leith, rather than Glasgow, Scotland, as required by contract); **Columbian Iron Works & Dry-Dock Co. v. Douglas, 84 Md. 44, 47, 34 A. 1118, 1120-1121 (1896)** (buyer who agreed to purchase steel scrap from United States cruisers not obliged to take any other kind of scrap). That rule, known as the "perfect tender" rule, remained part of the law of sales well into the twentieth century. . . .

. . . .

To the extent that a buyer can reject goods for any nonconformity, the UCC retains the perfect tender rule. **Section 2-106** states that goods conform to a contract "when they are in accordance with the obligations under the contract". N.J.S.A. 12A:2-106. **Section 2-601** authorizes a buyer to reject goods if they "or the tender of delivery fail in any respect to conform to the contract". N.J.S.A. 12A:2-601. . . .

Think About It!

The court writes of rejection occurring "before or after acceptance of the goods." Is rejection permitted after acceptance? Where in the Article 2 provisions do you find the answer to that question?

Initially, the rights of the parties vary depending on **whether the rejection occurs before or after acceptance of the goods**. Before acceptance, the buyer may reject goods for any nonconformity. N.J.S.A. 12A:2-601. Because of the seller's right to cure, however, the buyer's rejection does not necessarily discharge the contract. N.J.S.A. 12A:2-508. Within the time set for performance in the contract, the seller's right to cure is unconditional. Id., subsec. (1); see id., Official Comment 1. . . . Underlying the right to cure . . . is the recognition that parties should be encouraged to communicate with each other and to resolve their own problems. . . .

The rights of the parties also vary if rejection occurs after the time set for performance. After expiration of that time, the seller has a further reasonable time to cure if he believed reasonably that the goods would be acceptable with or without a money allowance. N.J.S.A. 12A:2-508(2). The determination of what constitutes a further reasonable time depends on the surrounding circumstances, which include the change of position by and the amount of inconvenience to the buyer. N.J.S.A. 12A:2-508, Official Comment 3. Those circumstances also include the length of time needed by the seller to correct the nonconformity and his ability to salvage the goods by resale to others. . . . Thus, the Code balances the buyer's right to reject nonconforming goods with a "second chance" for the seller to conform the goods to the contract under certain limited circumstances. N.J.S.A. 12A:2-508, New Jersey Study Comment 1.

After acceptance, the Code strikes a different balance: the buyer may revoke acceptance only if the nonconformity substantially impairs the value of the goods to him. N.J.S.A. 12A:2-608. . . . This provision protects the seller from revocation for trivial defects. . . . It also prevents the buyer from taking undue advantage of the seller by allowing goods to depreciate and then returning them because of asserted minor defects. See White & Summers, Uniform Commercial Code, § 8-3 at 391 (2 ed. 1980). Because this case involves rejection of goods, we need not decide whether a seller has a right to cure substantial defects that justify revocation of acceptance. . . .

. . . .

. . . . Because of the seller's right to cure, rejection does not terminate the contract. . . .

A further problem, however, is identifying the remedy available to a buyer who rejects goods with insubstantial defects that the seller fails to cure within a reasonable time. The Code provides expressly that when "the buyer rightfully rejects, then with respect to the goods involved, the buyer may cancel." N.J.S.A. 12A:2-711. "Cancellation" occurs when either party puts an end to the contract for breach by the other. N.J.S.A. 12A:2-106(4). . . .

. . . . Although neither "rejection" nor "revocation of acceptance" is defined in the Code, rejection includes both the buyer's refusal to accept or keep delivered goods and his notification to the seller that he will not keep them. White & Summers, supra, § 8-1 at 293. Revocation of acceptance is like rejection, but occurs after the buyer has accepted the goods. . . .

Although the complaint requested rescission of the contract, plaintiffs actually sought not only the end of their contractual obligations, but also restoration to their pre-contractual position. That request incorporated the equitable doctrine of restitution, the purpose of which is to restore plaintiff to as good a position as he occupied before the contract. Corbin, supra, § 1102 at 455. In UCC parlance, plaintiffs' request was for the cancellation of the contract and recovery of the price paid. N.J.S.A. 12A:2-106(4), 2-711.

. . . . Because a buyer may reject goods with insubstantial defects, he also may cancel the contract if those defects remain uncured. Otherwise, a seller's failure to cure minor defects would compel a buyer to accept imperfect goods and collect for any loss caused by the nonconformity. N.J.S.A. 12A:2-714.

. . . .

Underlying the Code provisions is the recognition of the revolutionary change in business practices in this century. The purchase of goods is no longer a simple transaction in which a buyer purchases individually-made goods from a seller in a face-to-face transaction. Our economy depends on

Think About It!

Under § 2-711, buyer can cancel for an uncured breach, regardless of whether the breach is material or not. That echoes the perfect tender rule. What is the common law rule about when the "buyer" of services may cancel the contract?

a complex system for the manufacture, distribution, and sale of goods, a system in which manufacturers and consumers rarely meet. Faceless manufacturers mass-produce goods for unknown consumers who purchase those goods from merchants exercising little or no control over the quality of their production. In an age of assembly lines, we are accustomed to cars with scratches, television sets without knobs and other products with all kinds of defects. . . . If a merchant sells defective goods, the reasonable expectation of the parties is that the buyer will return those goods and that the seller will repair or replace them.

Recognizing this commercial reality, the Code permits a seller to cure imperfect tenders. Should the seller fail to cure the defects, whether substantial or not, the balance shifts again in favor of the buyer, who has the right to cancel or seek damages. N.J.S.A. 12A:2-711. In general, economic considerations would induce sellers to cure minor defects. . . . Assuming the seller does not cure, however, the buyer should be permitted to exercise his remedies under N.J.S.A. 12A:2-711. The Code remedies for consumers are to be liberally construed, and the buyer should have the option of cancelling if the seller does not provide conforming goods. See N.J.S.A. 12A:1-106.

To summarize, the UCC preserves the perfect tender rule to the extent of permitting a buyer to reject goods for any nonconformity. Nonetheless, that rejection does not automatically terminate the contract. A seller may still effect a cure and preclude unfair rejection and cancellation by the buyer. N.J.S.A. 12A:2-508, Official Comment 2; N.J.S.A. 12A:2-711, Official Comment 1.

Think About It!

Define each of the following terms and indicate how they differ from each other: termination, cancellation, rescission, rejection, revocation, and repudiation.

III

The trial court found that Mr. and Mrs. Ramirez had rejected the van within a reasonable time under N.J.S.A. 12A:2-602. The court found that on August 3, 1978 Autosport's salesman advised the Ramirezes not to accept the van and that on August 14, they rejected delivery and Autosport agreed to replace the cushions. Those findings are supported by substantial credible evidence, and we sustain them. . . . Although the trial court did not find whether Autosport cured the defects within a reasonable time, we find that Autosport did not effect a cure. Clearly the van was not ready for delivery during August, 1978 when Mr. and Mrs. Ramirez rejected it, and Autosport had the burden of proving that it had corrected the defects. Although the Ramirezes gave Autosport ample time to correct the defects, Autosport did not demonstrate that the van conformed to the contract on September 1. In fact, on that date, when Mr. and Mrs. Ramirez returned at Autosport's invitation, all they received was discourtesy.

. . . .

Because Autosport had sold the trade-in to an innocent third party, the trial court determined that the Ramirezes were entitled not to the return of the trade-in, but to its fair market value, which the court set at the contract price of $4,700. A buyer who rightfully rejects goods and cancels the contract may, among other possible remedies, recover so much of the purchase price as has been paid. **N.J.S.A. 12A:2-711**. The Code, however, does not define "pay" and does not require payment to be made in cash.

A common method of partial payment for vans, cars, boats and other items of personal property is by a "trade-in". . . . . The ultimate issue is determining the fair market value of the trade-in. This Court has defined fair market value as "the price at which the property would change hands between a willing buyer and a willing seller when the former is not under any compulsion to buy and the latter is not under any compulsion to sell, both parties having reasonable knowledge of relevant facts." **In re Estate of Romnes, 79 N.J. 139, 144, 398 A.2d 543 (1978)**. Although the value of the trade-in van as set forth in the sales contract was not the only possible standard, it is an appropriate measure of fair market value.

For the preceding reasons, we affirm the judgment of the Appellate Division.

————————

Problem 8-7: Performance under UCC Article 2

In *Khiterer v. Bell (page 911)*, as you may recall, a dentist inserted porcelain crowns rather than the porcelain-on-gold crowns that were promised in the contract, but the court found substantial performance and therefore no liability. If instead the goods had been found to predominate over the dentist's services, what would the reasoning and result have been under Article 2?

§ 6. Excuse Defenses: Impossibility, Impracticability, and Frustration of Purpose

Parties enter contracts in order to plan future activity, knowing that circumstances may change after the contract is formed but their contractual obligations will remain the same. Because contracts are designed to hedge against the risk of change in this fashion, the early common law concluded that contractual duties were absolute and not excusable merely because of unanticipated circumstances. Over time, however, it was recognized that performance should be excused as the result of some kinds of unanticipated circumstances. The first recognized excuse defense was "impossibility." "Frustration of purpose" followed at the beginning of the twentieth century. Finally, impossibility was supplemented by "impracticability" another half century later. The materials below illustrate this evolution of the common law.

§ 6.1. Historical Background of the Excuse Defense

Originally, the common law did not allow any excuse for contract non-performance, even when a later event made performance impossible. If the promise was unqualified—if there was no express limitation to guard against events that might make performance impossible—then liability was absolute by the very terms of the contract, unless it contained a "force majeure" clause, an express term allocating particular risks between the parties. The first challenge to that understanding came in 1536, when an English court allowed the excuse of impossibility based on a supervening government action that prohibited contract performance, thereby making it legally impossible. In 1597, another court allowed excuse based on the promisor's death or disability when the contract required performance only by the promisor, not someone else in his or her stead. In 1628, a court excused a bailee from its bailment duty to return a horse to the owner at the end of the bailment, when the horse had died through no fault of the bailee.* The law remained in that posture for two centuries, recognizing a severely limited set of excuses, until the King's Bench decided *Taylor v. Caldwell* (see below) in 1863, pulling the precedents into a more cohesive (and expandable) framework.

> ### Make the Connection
>
> Note the similarity between the excuse of impracticability and the defense of mistake. Both are grounded in differences between the parties' expectations when they entered the contract and the realities of the situation they confront when they must perform the contract. Mistake (Chapter 5, page 431), as you remember, focuses on the unexpected facts in existence at the time of contract formation, while the excuse defense usually focuses on the unexpected facts that arise after contract formation. Mistake challenges contract formation, while excuse challenges contract performance.

---

* *See* *Paradine v. Jane*, 82 Eng. Rep. 897 (K.B. 1647); *Abbot of Westminster v. Clerke*, 73 Eng. Rep. 59, 63 (K.B. 1536); *Hyde v. Dean of Windsor*, 78 Eng. Rep. 798 (Q.B. 1597); *Williams v. Lloyd W. Jones*, 82 Eng. Rep. 95 (K.B. 1628).

§ 6.1.1. Impossibility

Reading the Law Critically: *Taylor* and *Unke*

1. Under what circumstances does each court conclude a party may be excused from performance?

2. What limitations on excuse do the courts articulate?

3. What rationale does the court offer for finding excuse?

4. Is just one party excused, or are both parties?

Taylor v. Caldwell

TAYLOR and another [Plaintiffs]

v.

CALDWELL and another [Defendants]

Court of King's Bench

122 Eng. Rep. 309 (K.B. 1863)

BLACKBURN J:

In this case the plaintiffs and the defendants, on 27 May 1861, entered into a contract by which the defendants agreed to let the plaintiffs have the use of the Surrey Gardens and music hall on four days then to come, namely, June 17, July 16, August 5 and August 17, for the purpose of giving a series of four concerts and day and night fetes at the gardens and hall on those days, and the plaintiffs agreed to take the gardens and hall on those days, and pay 100 pounds for each day.

The parties inaccurately call this a "letting," and the money to be paid a "rent;" but the whole agreement is such as to show that the defendants were to retain the possession of the hall and gardens, so that there was to be no demise of them, and that the contract was merely to give the plaintiffs the use of them on those days. Nothing, however, in our opinion depends on this. The agreement then [sets out what each was to supply for the concerts and the entertainments.]*

---

* [Authors' Note: The reporter's materials preceding the judge's opinion contain the contract language describing the elaborate events to occur during these "fêtes." The contract provided for an "organized military and quadrille band, the united bands to consist of from thirty-five to forty members; al fresco entertainments of various descriptions; . . . , fireworks and full illuminations; a ballet or divertissement, if permitted; a wizard and Grecian statues; tight rope performances; rifle galleries; air gun shooting; Chinese and Parisian games; boats on the lake, and (weather permitting) aquatic sports . . . ." *Taylor v. Caldwell*, 122 Eng. Rep. 309, 311 (K.B. 1863).]

The effect of this is to show that the existence of the music hall in the Surrey Gardens in a fit state for a concert was essential for the fulfillment of the contract; such entertainments as the parties contemplated in their agreement could not be given without it. After the making of the agreement, and before the first day on which a concert was to be given, the hall was destroyed by fire. This destruction, we must take it on the evidence, was without fault on either party, and was so complete that in consequence the concerts could not be given as intended; and the question we have to decide is whether, under these circumstances, the loss which the plaintiffs have sustained is to fall upon the defendants. The parties, when framing their agreement, evidently had not present to their minds the possibility of such a disaster, and they made no express stipulation with reference to it, so that the answer to the question must depend on the general rules of law applicable to such a contract.

There seems no doubt that, where there is a positive contract to do a thing not in itself unlawful, the contractor must perform it or pay damages for not doing it, although, in consequence of unforeseen accident, the performance of his contract has become unexpectedly burdensome, or even impossible. The law is so laid down in 1 Roll. Abr. 450, Condition (G), and in the note (2) to *Walton* v. *Waterhouse* (2 Wms. Saund. 421 a. 6th ed.), and is recognised as the general rule by all the Judges in the much discussed case of *Hall* v. *Wright* (E. B. & E. 746). But this rule is only applicable when the contract is positive and absolute and not subject to any condition either express or implied: and there are authorities which, as we think, establish the principle that where, from the nature of the contract, it appears that the parties must from the beginning have known that it could not be fulfilled unless, when the time for the fulfillment of the contract arrived, some particular specified thing continued to exist, so that when entering into the contract they must have contemplated such continued existence as the foundation of what was to be done, there, in the absence of any expressed or

See It!

Here is the music hall in Royal Surrey Gardens about three years before fire destroyed it:

For more information and pictures about the music hall, go to http://en.wikipedia.org/wiki/Royal_Surrey_Gardens.

[handwritten margin note: hall burned down]

[handwritten margin note: nothing in [unclear] about disasters]

implied warranty that the thing shall exist, the contract is not to be construed as a positive contract, but as subject to an implied condition that the parties shall be excused in case, before breach, performance becomes impossible from the perishing of the thing without default of the contractor.

. . . [T]his implication tends to further the great object of making the legal construction such as to fulfill the intention of those who enter into the contract, for, in the course of affairs, men, in making such contracts, in general, would, if it were brought to their minds, say that there should be such a condition.

. . . .

There is a class of contracts in which a person binds himself to do something which requires to be performed by him in person, and such promises—for example, promises to marry, or promises to serve for a certain time—are never in practice qualified by an express exception of the death of the party, and, therefore, in such cases, the contract is in terms broken if the promisor dies before fulfillment; yet it was very early determined that, if the performance is personal, the executors are not liable . . . . "Thus, if an author undertakes to compose a work and dies before completing it, his executors are discharged from the contract, for the undertaking is merely personal in its nature, and by the intervention of the contractor's death has become impossible to be performed." . . . "Where a contract depends upon personal skill, and the act of God renders it impossible, as, for instance, in the case of a painter employed to paint a picture, who is struck blind, it may be that the performance might be excused."

. . . .

These are instances where the implied condition is of the life of a human being, but there are others in which the same implication is made as to the continued existence of a thing. For example, where a contract of sale is made amounting to a bargain and sale, transferring presently the property in specific chattels, which are to be delivered by the vendor at a future day. There, if the chattels, without the fault of the vendor, perished in the interval, the vendor is excused from performing his contract to deliver, which has thus become impossible.

. . . .

. . . [I]n Williams v. Lloyd . . . the plaintiff had delivered a horse to the defendant who promised to re-deliver it on request. Breach, that they requested to redeliver the horse, he refused. Plea, that the horse was sick and died, and the plaintiff made the request after its death; and, on demurrer it was held a good plea, as the bailee was discharged from his promise by the death of the horse without default or negligence on the part of the defendant. "Let it be admitted," say the Court, "that he promised to deliver it on request, if the horse die before, that has become impossible by the act of God, so the party shall be discharged as much as if an obligation were made conditioned to deliver a horse on request, and he died before it." . . .

What's That?

The horse case involved a "bailment" under which a "bailee" (here, defendant) took temporary possession of goods. A bailee's duties are to take reasonable care of the goods and to return them to the owner/bailor at the end of the bailment period, unless the parties' contract says otherwise.

It may, I think, be safely asserted to be now English law that in all contracts of loan of chattels or bailment, if the performance of the promise of the borrower or bailee to return the thing lent or borrowed becomes impossible because it has perished, this impossibility, if not arising from the fault of the bailee, or from some risk which he has taken upon himself, excuses the borrower or bailee from the performance of his promise to redeliver the chattel.

. . . . The principle seems to us to be that in contracts in which the performance depends on the continued existence of a given person or thing, a condition is implied that the impossibility of performance arising from the perishing of the person or thing shall excuse the performance.

In none of these cases is the promise in words other than positive, nor is there any express stipulation that the destruction of the person or thing shall excuse the performance; that excuse is by law implied, because from the nature of the contract it is apparent that the parties contracted on the basis of the continued existence of the particular person or chattel. In the present case, looking at the whole contract, we find that the parties contracted on the basis of the continued existence of the music hall at the time when the concerts were to be given, that being essential to their performance.

We think, therefore, that, the music hall having ceased to exist without fault of either party, both parties are excused, the plaintiffs from taking the gardens and paying the money, the defendants from performing their promise to give the use of the hall and gardens, and other things. Consequently the rule must be made absolute to enter the verdict for the defendants.

DISPOSITION: Rule absolute.

Unke v. Thorpe

W. E. UNKE, Plaintiff-Appellant

v.

F. L. THORPE and C. W. WATERS, Defendants-Appellees

Supreme Court of South Dakota
59 N.W.2d 419 (S.D. 1953)

SMITH, Judge.

The complaint of the plaintiff, W. E. Unke, prays for damages because the defendants, F. L. Thorpe and C. W. Waters, who had agreed in writing to sell and deliver to him "600 to 800" bushels of alfalfa seed, delivered to him only about 301 bushels of such seed. The defense that the contract was induced by fraud was sustained by the trial court and judgment dismissing the action was entered. The principal assignments question the sufficiency of the evidence to support the findings, and whether the findings support the judgment. Because we have concluded the undisputed facts reveal that plaintiff does not have a cause of action, we affirm the judgment.

The trial was to the court without a jury. The evidence we are about to outline was received subject to the objection of the plaintiff that the contract in writing supersedes all of the oral negotiations or stipulations of the parties. Cf. SDC 10.0604.

Mr. Unke, the plaintiff, operates a seed and feed mill at Bridgewater, South Dakota. He deals in a considerable quantity of alfalfa seed, principally at wholesale to dealers. In the past he had purchased such seed through one O. Christopherson, who operates a seed and feed mill at Newell, South Dakota. In a telephone conversation on October 29, 1950, Christopherson advised Unke he "had two farmers that had considerable alfalfa seed" to sell. Unke arrived at Newell the next morning, examined a sample of the alfalfa seed which had been cleaned at a Newell elevator, and together with Christopherson drove into the country a few miles to the ranch of the defendants Thorpe and Waters. There they talked with Mr. Thorpe, examined some of the threshed seed in sacks and watched the threshing operation in process. Mr. Waters was not at the ranch

Think About It!

The court refers to "SDC" (South Dakota Code) 10.0604, to invoke a parol evidence rule that states, "The execution of a contract in writing, whether the law requires it to be written or not, supersedes all the oral negotiations or stipulations concerning its matter which preceded or accompanied the execution of the instrument." How does this parol evidence rule differ from the one we considered in Chapter 7 (page 749)?

and Mr. Thorpe did not care to deal without him. An arrangement was made for Thorpe and Waters to meet Unke at the Christopherson elevator in Newell at one o'clock that afternoon. After the parties met some talk was had about the amount of seed the defendants would have to sell, and about the price for which they would sell. After they had agreed on a price of 53 cents per pound if Mr. Unke would pay Christopherson's charges for cleaning the seed after it was threshed, and it appeared that they were going to reach a bargain, Unke prepared a written contract and tendered it to the defendants for their approval. In that writing he had inserted the figures "600 to 800 bushels". There is a conflict in the testimony with reference to the conversation that then followed about those figures. The defendants and two others present testified that they said they did not know how much seed they would have and they were selling only their 1950 crop. The plaintiff and his employee who was present deny that anything was said about the 1950 crop. The plaintiff, on the other hand, testified in substance that he said he must have a definite figure because he was intending to sell seed against this contract. Defendants deny that such a statement was made. According to other testimony plaintiff said he wanted a definite figure in there so in case the price went down the defendants could not buy up all of the seed in the area and load it on him at the contract price.

The contract was eventually signed and reads as follows:

"Purchase or Delivery Order
Bridgewater Milling Co.   No. 517
Bridgewater, S. D.

To Thorp & Waters	Date	Oct. 30, 1950
Address Box 427 Deadwood S D	Ordered by	W E Unke
Deliver to Bridgewater Milling Co.	Date wanted	When cleaned
Bridgewater S D	Via truck	next 30 days
	Terms Cash	
	F.O.B.	Christopherson Elev.

Quantity	Unit	Description of articles, including special instructions as to quality, size, and style of package, etc.	Unit Price
600 to 800	Bu.	S.D. Alfalfa-(like Sample taken) at to be recleaned at Christopherson Elev. Buyer to pay cleaning charge.—advance payment—$2500.00	53.00 cwt

Seller—
Seller—F. L. Thorpe (signed)

Issue only one copy of invoice and unless
otherwise instructed mail direct to   Bridgewater Milling Co.
    Bridgewater Milling Co.   By   W. E. Unke"
  at
Seller—C. W. Waters—Partner

Unke arranged with Christopherson to clean the seed. The threshing continued until about November 20th, and each day's threshing was delivered to Christopherson at Newell for cleaning. However, only 301 bushels of seed like the sample Unke had examined on October 30th were recovered by the threshing and cleaning process. That seed was delivered to Mr. Unke. In addition, about 30 sacks of third and fourth grade seed were recovered and sold to Mr. Christopherson. There is no indication in the evidence that a greater amount of seed like the sample could have been recovered by the Christopherson equipment.

It is axiomatic that the surrounding circumstances from which a contract stems are to be considered when interpreting its provisions. IX Wigmore, Evidence, 3d Ed., § 2471; 3 Williston, Contracts, Rev. Ed., § 618; **Janssen v. Tusha, 66 S.D. 604, 287 N.W. 501**; and **Eustis Mining Co. v. Beer, Sondheimer & Co., D.C., 239 F. 976**. Of controlling significance here are the facts that Unke appeared at Newell because some ranchers had alfalfa seed they desired to sell; there he examined some of the seed which had been cleaned, then he went to their ranch, watched the threshing process, and examined sacks of the threshed seed. The contract which he wrote provided that the seed he was purchasing was to be cleaned at his cost at the Christopherson elevator and provided also for delivery "when cleaned next 30 days". When the contract of these parties is read in the light of its setting and object, and the **oral expressions of intentions of the parties** are excluded from consideration, cf. IX Wigmore, 3d Ed., Evidence, § 2471, we think it is obvious that the contract is not subject to the interpretation placed upon it by plaintiff, viz., that it provides for the delivery by defendants to plaintiff

Think About It!

Is the court's interpretation of the written contract "obvious," as the court states? Was it appropriate to exclude from consideration "the oral expressions of intentions of the parties," as the court did? If the contract had been simply for 600 to 800 bushels of alfalfa seed, would the outcome have been different?

of not less than 600 nor more than 800 bushels of alfalfa seed in general of the quality exhibited at the time the contract was made. It is our opinion that the only interpretation which the undisputed surrounding circumstances and the words of the contract warrant is that the parties contracted for the delivery of 600 to 800 bushels of a specific crop of alfalfa, viz., the crop the defendants were threshing. Thus the question arises whether, having acted in good faith, and having delivered to plaintiff all of the seed of the described quality the mutually contemplated crop produced, are they under any further obligation to plaintiff? This court answered that question in **McCaull-Webster Elevator Company v. Steele Brothers, 43 S.D. 485, 180 N.W. 782**.

Make the Connection

When the court describes the sellers as "having acted in good faith, and having delivered to plaintiff all of the seed of the described quality the mutually contemplated crop produced . . . ," it is describing an output contract, even though this case was decided prior to the UCC. Recall Chapter 7's coverage of output contracts (page 821), which are governed by UCC § 2-306(1). Under that section, the measure of goods can be stated as the output of the seller (rather than a specific quantity), and the seller is obliged to produce the goods in good faith. In *Unke*, that rule would mean that the sellers were obligated to produce only as much alfalfa as they were capable of producing in good faith from that particular harvest.

In that case plaintiff and defendant entered into a written contract whereby defendants contracted to sell to plaintiff 5000 bushels of good sound, dry and merchantable corn to grade 3Y, "said grain being now in my possession". Both parties had in contemplation as the subject matter of this contract corn raised by defendant and standing in his fields. It turned out that they were in error in their mutual assumption; the corn would not grade 3Y. The defendant failed to deliver any corn and plaintiff sought damages. This court said, "In this case it is perfectly clear that both parties were so confident that the corn, then in the minds of the parties, would fulfill the conditions as to grade, that they made no provision whatsoever as to what should be done if this corn would not test No. 3. They contracted in the full belief that defendants had in their possession 5,000 bushels of yellow corn that would, at the time for delivery, grade No. 3. No corn that would, by mere lapse of time, become No. 3 corn, was in possession of defendants. Both parties assumed, as the very basis of the contract, that corn that would fulfill this contract did exist in the possession of defendants. Being mistaken as to this essential fact, there was no binding contract . . . ." And it was further written, "Let us suppose that No. 3 corn had not been worth the contract price and defendants had gone out and purchased No. 3 corn and tendered same to plaintiff, plaintiff knowing such fact would have had the right to, and would undoubtedly, have refused to accept such corn for the very simple reason that it never agreed to buy any corn other than the corn in possession of defendants when the contract was entered into."

In the foregoing case we grounded our holding on the mutual mistake of the parties. Restatement, Contracts, has formulated the applicable rule as a phase of the doctrine of impossibility in these words:

§ 460 "(1) Where the existence of a specific thing or person is, either by the terms of a bargain or in the contemplation of both parties, necessary for the performance of a promise in the bargain, a duty to perform the promise "(a) never arises if at the time the bargain is made the existence of the thing or person within the time for seasonable performance is impossible, and

"(b) is discharged if the thing or person subsequently is not in existence in time for seasonable performance, unless a contrary intention is manifested, or the contributing fault of the promisor causes the non-existence.

"(2) Material deterioration of such a specific thing or physical incapacity of such a specific person as is within the rule stated in Subsection (1) has the same effect as non-existence in preventing a promisor's duty from arising or in discharging it, except that if the other party remains ready and willing to render in full the agreed exchange for whatever performance remains possible, the promisor is under a duty to render such partial performance . . . ."

In dealing with this rule of impossibility, Williston, Contracts, § 1946, among others cites the case of **Barkemeyer Grain & Seed Co. v. Hannant,** 66 Mont. 120, 213 P. 208. The written contract in that case confirmed the purchase and sale of "about 6,000 pounds of alfalfa seed", but only 1800 pounds were delivered and the purchaser sued for damages. It was established by extrinsic evidence that the subject matter in contemplation of the parties was the 1919 crop of alfalfa seed of the defendant. Except for 200 pounds retained for reseeding defendant delivered all his crop. After approving the resort to extrinsic parol evidence to identify the object of the written contract, the court said,

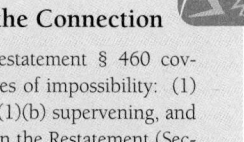

Make the Connection

Note that Restatement § 460 covers three types of impossibility: (1)(a) existing, (1)(b) supervening, and (2) partial. In the Restatement (Second), impossibility is widened to a broader topic—"impracticability"—which is split into seven sections:

- § 261 (supervening impracticability),
- § 262 (death or incapacity),
- § 264 (government regulation or order),
- § 263 (destruction or nonexistence),
- § 266 (existing impracticability),
- § 269 (temporary impracticability), and
- § 270 (partial impracticability). They appear starting on page 996.

"Since the parties in this case clearly contemplated delivery out of the crop of seed raised by the defendant, the plaintiff could not have been required to accept alfalfa seed bought upon the general market. For the same reason the plaintiff could not demand performance of the defendant in that manner. Had the defendant sold his crop elsewhere, or even through negligence allowed it to be destroyed, he would have been liable for failure to deliver all that was within his power to deliver. But he cannot be subjected to damages for failure to do that which, through no fault of his own, was impossible."

As indicated, we hold that plaintiff does not have a cause of action against defendants. It follows that the errors of the trial court, if any, were without prejudice to plaintiff. Dixson v. Ladd, 32 S.D. 163, 142 N.W. 259, 46 L.R.A.N.S. 206, Am.Ann.Cas. 1916A, 253; and Sejnoha v. Buchanan, 71 S.D. 220, 23 N.W.2d 142.

The judgment of the trial court is affirmed.

All the Judges concur.

———————————

Think About It!

The *Unke* court draws an analogy to a mutual mistake case (*McCall-Webster Elevator Co.*) that also could be analyzed as "existing impossibility," under Restatement § 460(1)(a). Both defenses—mutual mistake and existing impossibility—are premised on the absence of a crucial fact that both parties presumed to be true at the time of contract formation. The mistake defense makes the contract voidable (see page 431), while existing impossibility (under the first Restatement version) prevents a duty of performance from arising.

Strategically, a defendant in such a situation would be wise to raise both defenses, in the alternative. Can you articulate why? Which defense should the defendant argue first, and why? Why is this strategy limited to existing impossibility and not extended to supervening impossibility (§ 460(1)(b))?

§ 6.1.2. Frustration of Purpose

Reading the Law Critically:
Krell and *Adbar*

1. Although the court suggests that *Krell* is an application of *Taylor,* do the unanticipated circumstances here make performance impossible? What *is* the effect of the unanticipated circumstances? Whose performance is affected, and in what way?

2. *Krell* establishes an excuse called "frustration of purpose." According to the case, what is required to establish the excuse? How does it differ from impossibility?

3. What is the source of the alleged frustration of purpose in *Adbar*? Why is relief not granted? Is the result and analysis consistent with *Krell*?

4. Frustration of purpose is not adopted in all jurisdictions. Why do you think frustration of purpose is less compelling as an excuse than impossibility?

Krell v. Henry

PAUL KRELL, Plaintiff-Appellant

v.

C. S. HENRY, Defendant-Respondent

Court of King's Bench
2 K.B. 740 (1903)

The plaintiff, Paul Krell, sued the defendant, C. S. Henry, for 50£., being the balance of a sum of 75£., for which the defendant had agreed to hire a flat at 56A, Pall Mall on the days of June 26 and 27, for the purpose of viewing the processions to be held in connection with the coronation of His Majesty. The defendant denied his liability . . . .

The facts, which were not disputed, were as follows. The plaintiff on leaving the country in March, 1902, left instructions with his solicitor to let his suite of chambers at 56A, Pall Mall on such terms and for such period (not exceeding six months) as he thought proper. On June 17, 1902, the defendant noticed an announcement in the windows of the plaintiff's flat to the effect that windows to view the coronation processions were to be let. The defendant interviewed the housekeeper on the subject, when it was pointed out to him what a good view of the processions could be obtained from the premises, and he eventually agreed with the housekeeper to take the suite for the two days in question for a sum of 75£.

On June 20 the defendant wrote the following letter to the plaintiff's solicitor:—

I am in receipt of yours of the 18th instant, inclosing form of agreement for the suite of chambers on the third floor at 56A, Pall Mall, which I have agreed to take for the two days, the 26th and 27th instant, for the sum of 75£. For reasons given you I cannot enter into the agreement, but as arranged over the telephone I inclose herewith cheque for 25£. as deposit, and will thank you to confirm to me that I shall have the entire use of these rooms during the days (not the nights) of the 26th and 27th instant. You may rely that every care will be taken of the premises and their contents. On the 24th inst. I will pay the balance, viz., 50£., to complete the 75£. agreed upon.

On the same day the defendant received the following reply from the plaintiff's solicitor:—

I am in receipt of your letter of to-day's date inclosing cheque for 25£. deposit on your agreeing to take Mr. Krell's chambers on the third floor at 56A, Pall Mall for the two days, the 26th and 27th June, and I confirm the agreement that you are to have the entire use of these rooms during the days (but not the nights), the balance, 50£., to be paid to me on Tuesday next the 24th instant.

The processions not having taken place on the days originally appointed, namely, June 26 and 27, the defendant declined to pay the balance of 50£. alleged to be due from him under the contract in writing of June 20 constituted by the above two letters. Hence the present action.

Darling J., on August 11, 1902, held, upon the authority of Taylor v. Caldwell . . . , that there was an implied condition in the contract that the procession should take place, and gave judgment for the defendant on the claim . . . .

The plaintiff appealed.

. . . .

The real question in this case is the extent of the application in English law of the principle of the Roman law which has been adopted and acted on in many English decisions, and notably

Behind the Scenes

After having been the heir apparent for the longest period in English history, King Edward VII came to the throne at age 60 after the death of his mother, Queen Victoria. Two days before the coronation, Edward was diagnosed with appendicitis (a disease that was often fatal in that era), and he underwent life-saving surgery involving new surgical and anesthetic techniques.

The public announcement delaying the coronation and processions was made early on June 24. Under the contract, defendant Henry had all day on June 24 to pay the balance due on the room, and he learned of the delay soon enough to withhold that payment. The king made a very quick recovery, and the coronation took place later that summer, on August 9. For more information about the king for whom the Edwardian period was named, see http://en.wikipedia.org/wiki/Edward_VII_of_the_United_Kingdom#Accession.

in the case of Taylor v. Caldwell. That case at least makes it clear that "where, from the nature of the contract, it appears that the parties must from the beginning have known that it could not be fulfilled unless, when the time for the fulfillment of the contract arrived, some particular specified thing continued to exist, so that when entering into the contract they must have contemplated such continued existence as the foundation of what was to be done; there, in the absence of any express or implied warranty that the thing shall exist, the contract is not to be considered a positive contract, but as subject to an implied condition that the parties shall be excused in case, before breach, performance becomes impossible from the perishing of the thing without default of the contractor."

. . . . English law applies the principle not only to cases where the performance of the contract becomes impossible by the cessation of existence of the thing which is the subject-matter of the contract, but also to cases where the event which renders the contract incapable of performance is the cessation or non-existence of an express condition or state of things, going to the root of the contract, and essential to its performance. It is said, on the one side, that the specified thing, state of things, or condition the continued existence of which is necessary for the fulfillment of the contract, so that the parties entering into the contract must have contemplated the continued existence of that thing, condition, or state of things as the foundation of what was to be done under the contract, is limited to things which are either the subject-matter of the contract or a condition or state of things, present or anticipated, which is expressly mentioned in the contract. But, on the other side, it is said that the condition or state of things need not be expressly specified, but that it is sufficient if that condition or state of things clearly appears by extrinsic evidence to have been assumed by the parties to be the foundation or basis of the contract, and the event which causes the impossibility . . . cannot reasonably be supposed to have been in the contemplation of the contracting parties when the contract was made. . . .

I do not think that the principle . . . is limited to cases in which the event causing the impossibility of performance is the destruction or non-existence of some thing which is the subject-matter of the contract or of some condition or state of things expressly specified as a condition of it. I think that you first have to ascertain, not necessarily from the terms of the contract, but, if required, from necessary inferences, drawn from surrounding circumstances recognised by both contracting parties, what is the substance of the contract, and then to ask the question whether that substantial contract needs for its foundation the assumption of the existence of a particular state of things. If it does, this will limit the operation of the general words, and in such case, if the contract becomes impossible of performance by reason of the non-existence of the state of things assumed by both contracting parties as the foundation of the contract, there will be no breach of the contract thus limited.

Now what are the facts of the present case? . . . . In my judgment the use of the rooms was let and taken for the purpose of seeing the Royal procession. It was not a demise of the rooms, or even an agreement to let and take the rooms. It is a licence to use rooms for a particular purpose and none other. And in my judgment the taking place of those processions on the days proclaimed along the proclaimed route, which passed 56A, Pall Mall, was regarded by both contracting parties as the foundation of the contract; and I think that it cannot reasonably be supposed to have been in the contemplation of the contracting parties, when the contract was made, that the coronation would not be held on the proclaimed days, or the processions not take place on those days along the proclaimed route; and I think that the words imposing on the defendant the obligation to accept and pay for the use of the rooms for the named days, although general and unconditional, were not used with reference to the possibility of the particular contingency which afterwards occurred.

It was suggested in the course of the argument that if the occurrence, on the proclaimed days, of the coronation and the procession in this case were the foundation of the contract, and if the general words are thereby limited or qualified, so that in the event of the non-occurrence of the coronation and procession along the proclaimed route they would discharge both parties from further performance of the contract, it would follow that if a cabman was engaged to take some one to Epsom on Derby Day at a suitable enhanced price for such a journey, say 10£., both parties to the contract would be discharged in the contingency of the race at Epsom for some reason becoming impossible; but I do not think this follows, for I do not think that in the cab case the happening of the race would be the foundation of the contract. No doubt the purpose of the engager would be to go to see the Derby, and the price would be proportionately high; but the cab had no special qualifications for the purpose which led to the selection of the cab for this particular occasion. Any other cab would have done as well. Moreover, I think that, under the cab contract, the hirer, even if the race went off, could have said, "Drive me to Epsom; I will pay you the agreed sum; you have nothing to do with the purpose for which I hired the cab," and that if the cabman refused he would have been guilty of a breach of contract, there being nothing to qualify his promise to drive the hirer to Epsom on a particular day. Whereas in the case of the coronation, there is not merely the purpose of the hirer to see the coronation procession, but it is the coronation procession and the relative position of the rooms which is the basis of the contract as much for the lessor as the hirer; and I think that if the King, before the coronation day and after the contract, had died, the hirer could not have insisted on having the

> ### Think About It!
>
> Do you think the court correctly distinguishes the case of hiring a cab to see the Derby? Would a party booking a hotel and flight for a vacation trip be allowed to cancel on the basis of frustration of purpose if the weather was bad at the beach destination? If a hurricane or tsunami did substantial damage to the destination location, but the hotel remained in operation?

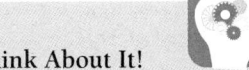

rooms on the days named. It could not in the cab case be reasonably said that seeing the Derby race was the foundation of the contract, as it was of the licence in this case. Whereas in the present case, where the rooms were offered and taken, by reason of their peculiar suitability from the position of the rooms for a view of the coronation procession, surely the view of the coronation procession was the foundation of the contract, which is a very different thing from the purpose of the man who engaged the cab—namely, to see the race—being held to be the foundation of the contract.

Each case must be judged by its own circumstances. In each case one must ask oneself, first, what, having regard to all the circumstances, was the foundation of the contract? Secondly, was the performance of the contract prevented? Thirdly, was the event which prevented the performance of the contract of such a character that it cannot reasonably be said to have been in the contemplation of the parties at the date of the contract? If all these questions are answered in the affirmative (as I think they should be in this case), I think both parties are discharged from further performance of the contract. I think that the coronation procession was the foundation of this contract, and that the non-happening of it prevented the performance of the contract; and, secondly, I think that the non-happening of the procession . . . was an event "of such a character that it cannot reasonably be supposed to have been in the contemplation of the contracting parties when the contract was made, and that they are not to be held bound by general words which, though large enough to include, were not used with reference to the possibility of the particular contingency which afterwards happened." The test seems to be whether the event which causes the impossibility was or might have been anticipated and guarded against. It seems difficult to say, in a case where both parties anticipate the happening of an event, which anticipation is the foundation of the contract, that either party must be taken to have anticipated, and ought to have guarded against, the event which prevented the performance of the contract.

. . . .

It is not essential to the application of the principle of Taylor v. Caldwell that the direct subject of the contract should perish or fail to be in existence at the date of performance of the contract. It is sufficient if a state of things or condition expressed in the contract and essential to its performance perishes or fails to be in existence at that time. In the present case the condition which fails and prevents the achievement of that which was, in the contemplation of both parties, the foundation of the contract, is not expressly mentioned

Think About It!

When the court states the rule from *Taylor,* what subtle wording change broadens the scope of the rule? How does that broader version of the *Taylor* rule assist the court in formulating its new excuse defense?

either as a condition of the contract or the purpose of it; but I think for the reasons which I have given that the principle of Taylor v. Caldwell ought to be applied. This disposes of the plaintiff's claim for 50£. unpaid balance of the price agreed to be paid for the use of the rooms.

doesn't have to pay balance

. . . .

See It

The distant building in the center, facing the viewer, contains the flat overlooking Pall Mall, where King Edward VII's coronation was scheduled to take place. The flat's ideal location on Pall Mall was one of Krell's primary advertising points for letting the flat and Henry's primary reason for renting the flat. Thanks to Jessica Zaiken for her permission to reproduce this photograph.

Adbar, L.C. v. New Beginnings C-Star

ADBAR, L.C., Plaintiff-Appellant

v.

NEW BEGINNINGS C-STAR, Defendant-Respondent

Missouri Court of Appeals

103 S.W.3d 799 (Mo. Ct. App. 2003)

GLENN A. NORTON, Judge.

Adbar, L.C. appeals the judgment in favor of New Beginnings C-Star on Adbar's claim for breach of lease. We reverse in part . . . .

I. BACKGROUND

New Beginnings provides rehabilitation services for alcohol and drug abuse to both adults and adolescents. In the fall of 1999, New Beginnings was searching for a new location and entered into negotiations with Adbar for lease of a building in the City of St. Louis. New Beginnings received a preliminary indication from the City's zoning administrator that its use of the property constituted a permitted use under the zoning regulations. New Beginnings and Adbar subsequently entered into a three-year lease. The total rent due for the three-year term was $273,000.

After the lease was executed, the City denied New Beginnings' application for an occupancy permit on the grounds that the operation constituted a nuisance use under the zoning regulations. At trial, Alderman Freeman Bosley, Sr. testified that due to his opposition to New Beginnings moving into his Ward, he had called the zoning administrator and asked him to reverse his preliminary indication that New Beginnings' operation constituted a permitted use.

New Beginnings appealed the denial of the occupancy permit to the board of adjustment. Alderman Bosley and other neighborhood residents testified in opposition to New Beginnings at the board's hearing. The board affirmed the denial of the permit. New Beginnings then sought a writ, which was granted by the circuit court, and New Beginnings was issued an occupancy permit. Alderman Bosley contacted the judge who issued the writ and asked him to reverse his decision. The judge declined. A few weeks later, at the City counselor's request, the City revoked New Beginnings' occupancy permit. New Beginnings filed a motion for contempt with the circuit court. The motion was granted, and the City re-issued the occupancy permit.

After the permit was reissued, New Beginnings began preparing to move in, including having some construction done on the building. At this same time, Alderman Bosley contacted then State Representative Paula Carter, chairwoman of the appropriations committee responsible for New Beginnings' state funding.

Alderman Bosley asked Representative Carter to "pull the funding" for New Beginnings. Alderman Bosley did not get a commitment from Representative Carter, but told her that "if you don't get their funding, you are going to have trouble running" for re-election.

New Beginnings alleges that it was then contacted by Michael Couty, director of the Missouri Division of Alcohol and Drug Abuse, who threatened to rescind all state contracts with New Beginnings if it moved into the new location. New Beginnings convened a meeting of its board of directors to conduct a conference call with Director Couty. New Beginnings alleges that during that conference call Director Couty repeated his threat to rescind funding if it moved into the new location. At the end of the meeting, New Beginnings' board decided not to occupy the building they had leased from Adbar. At trial Director Couty denied making any such threats to New Beginnings.

Adbar filed a petition for breach of the lease. New Beginnings asserted a defense of legal impossibility. On the first day of the trial, New Beginnings was granted leave to amend its answer to add the defense of commercial frustration. Following a bench trial, the trial court ruled that New Beginnings was excused from its performance under the lease because of commercial frustration. This appeal follows.

II. DISCUSSION

On review of this court-tried case, we will sustain the judgment of the trial court unless there is no substantial evidence to support it, it is against the weight of the evidence, it erroneously declares the law, or it erroneously applies the law. *Murphy v. Carron*, 536 S.W.2d 30, 32 (Mo. banc 1976). We accept the evidence and inferences favorable to the prevailing party and disregard all contrary evidence. *Kassebaum v. Kassebaum*, 42 S.W.3d 685, 692 (Mo.App. E.D.2001). We will defer to the factual findings of the trial judge, who is in a superior position to assess credibility; however, we independently evaluate the court's conclusions of law. *Id.*

A. Commercial Frustration

In its first point on appeal, Adbar asserts that the trial court erroneously applied the law when it excused New Beginnings' performance under the lease due to the doctrine of commercial frustration. We agree.

The doctrine of commercial frustration grew out of demands of the commercial world to excuse performance under contracts in cases of extreme hardship. *Kassebaum*, 42 S.W.3d at 699. Under the doctrine of commercial frustration, if the occurrence of an event, not foreseen by the parties and not caused by or under the control of either party, destroys or nearly destroys the value of the performance or the object or purpose of the contract, then the parties are excused from further

when foreseeable, no excuse [handwritten margin note]

performance. *Id.* If, on the other hand, the event was reasonably foreseeable, then the parties should have provided for its occurrence in the contract. *Werner v. Ashcraft Bloomquist, Inc.,* 10 S.W.3d 575, 577 (Mo.App. E.D.2000). The absence of a provision in the contract providing for such an occurrence indicates an assumption of the risk by the promisor. *Id.* In determining foreseeability, courts consider the terms of the contract and the circumstances surrounding the formation of the contract. *Id.* at 577-578. The doctrine of commercial frustration should be limited in its application so as to preserve the certainty of contracts. *Id.* at 578.

New Beginnings alleged that the troubles it faced obtaining its occupancy permit, along with the actions of Alderman Bosley and Director Couty, combined to rise to commercially frustrate the lease agreement with Adbar. Ultimately, New Beginnings' funding was never rescinded. In this case the intervening event was merely the *possibility* that the funding may be rescinded. For an organization that receives funding from the State, the possibility that their funding may be reduced or even completely rescinded is foreseeable. Furthermore, while the zeal with which Alderman Bosley attempted to keep New Beginnings out of his ward may have been surprising to the parties, it is certainly foreseeable that a drug and alcohol abuse treatment facility might encounter neighborhood resistance when attempting to move into a new location. At trial, the CEO of New Beginnings admitted that both the elimination of New Beginnings' funding and opposition from neighborhood groups were foreseeable.

foreseeable [handwritten margin note]

This court has addressed similar intervening events before. In *Conlon Group, Inc. v. City of St. Louis,* this Court found that structural defects in a 100 year-old building were foreseeable and, despite increased development costs, the agreement with the City's redevelopment authority remained intact. 980 S.W.2d 37, 40-41 (Mo.App. E.D.1998). In *Shop 'N Save Warehouse Foods, Inc. v. Soffer,* this Court found that a lessor could foresee that its supermarket tenant might bring an action to enforce a radius restriction in the lease to keep him from leasing property to another supermarket chain. 918 S.W.2d 851, 863 (Mo.App. E.D.1996). The Court noted that, while neither party wanted the eventual result, the doctrine of commercial frustration did not provide a means to avoid a bad result. *Id.* The possibility that New Beginnings' funding may be threatened was foreseeable. Yet, New Beginnings did not provide for that possibility in the lease. Therefore, New Beginnings assumed the risk that their funding may be threatened and that it might frustrate the purpose of the lease.

In addition to this event being foreseeable, neither the value of the performance nor the purpose of the lease was destroyed. The purpose of the lease was to allow New Beginnings to operate a rehabilitation center at the location of the property. New Beginnings' funding was never rescinded or even restricted. Alderman Bosley's continued interference with New Beginnings efforts to provide rehabilitation treatment to addicts of drugs and alcohol certainly made, and would have continued to make, business difficult for New Beginnings. However, neither the value of the performance nor the object or purpose of the lease was destroyed or nearly destroyed.

Therefore, the doctrine of commercial frustration does not excuse New Beginnings performance under the lease. . . .

        . . . .

III. CONCLUSION

The judgment that New Beginnings is excused from the lease under the defense of commercial frustration is reversed and the cause is remanded for a new trial in accordance with this opinion. The judgment in all other respects is affirmed.

not excused for lease

WILLIAM H. CRANDALL, P.J., and SHERRI B. SULLIVAN, J., concurring.

Food for Thought

In Nicholas R. Weiskop, *Frustration of Contractual Purpose—Doctrine or Myth*, 70 St. John's L. Rev. 239 (1996), Professor Weiskop methodically analyzes some of the prominent cases utilizing the defense of frustration of purpose and concludes that the defense is built on a thin foundation and perhaps doesn't even exist. He argues that *Krell v. Henry* was only superficially decided on the doctrine of frustration, because the King's Bench essentially cancelled the contract for lack of performance as specified in the terms of the agreement.

Moreover, Weiskop argues that courts have been reluctant to allow frustration of purpose as a defense because (1) by using frustration of purpose, courts are implying terms into a contract, which could obscure the actual intentions of the parties; (2) the aggrieved party is often left with uncompensated damages, because its ability to perform is unimpeded; (3) courts are disinclined to grant relief for parties' misassumptions about the future; (4) courts cannot easily determine at what point payment should be excused based on the lost value of performance; and (5) freedom of contract and other policies driving contract law encourage performance and therefore weigh against a court's decision to excuse performable contract duties. Do you agree?

cts reluctant to use frustration of purpose as defense

§ 6.2. Impossibility Broadens into Impracticability

During the 20th century, impossibility was broadened to include claims of "impracticability," codified first in UCC §§ 2-615 and 2-616 and later in the Restatement (Second). Impracticability expands the category of cases in which relief may be granted based on unanticipated circumstances, but as the cases below demonstrate, the excuse is rarely successful.

Reading the Law Critically: The Excuse Defense in the Restatement (Second)

1. How do the Restatement tests for existing and supervening impracticability differ?

2. Several sections require the party seeking excuse to establish "the occurrence of an event the non-occurrence of which was a basic assumption on which the contract was made". Which three sections specify how to prove that element? Why do those three sections "plug into" the rules on supervening impracticability and frustration in §§ 261 and 265, but not into the rules on existing impracticability or frustration in § 266?

3. Why do you suppose § 270 covers only partial impracticability, not partial frustration?

4. Which section(s) would have governed each of the preceding cases (*Taylor*, *Unke*, *Krell*, and *Adbar*)? Would the result or reasoning have been different if the Restatement (Second) had applied?

Restatement (Second) § 261. **Discharge by Supervening Impracticability**

Where, after a contract is made, a party's performance is made impracticable without his fault by the occurrence of an event the non-occurrence of which was a basic assumption on which the contract was made, his duty to render that performance is discharged, unless the language or the circumstances indicate the contrary.

Comment d. Impracticability. Events that come within the rule stated in this Section are generally due either to "acts of God" or to acts of third parties. . . . Although the rule stated in this Section is sometimes phrased in terms of "impossibility," it has long been recognized that it may operate to discharge a party's duty even though the event has not made performance absolutely impossible. This Section, therefore, uses "impracticable," the term employed by Uniform Commercial Code § 2-615(a), to describe the required extent of the impediment to performance. Performance may be impracticable because extreme and unreasonable difficulty, expense, injury, or loss to one of the parties will be involved. A severe shortage of raw materials or of supplies due to war, embargo, local crop failure, unforeseen shutdown of major sources of supply, or the like, which either causes a marked increase in cost or prevents performance altogether may bring the case within the rule stated in this Section. Performance may also be impracticable because it will involve a risk of injury to person or to property, of one of the parties or of others, that is disproportionate to the ends to be attained by performance. However, "impracticability" means more than "impracticality." A mere change in the degree of difficulty or expense due to such causes as increased wages, prices of raw materials, or costs of construction, unless well beyond the normal range, does not amount to impracticability since it is this sort of risk that a fixed-price contract is intended to cover. Furthermore, a party is expected to use reasonable efforts to surmount obstacles to performance (see § 205), and a performance is impracticable only if it is so in spite of such efforts.

Restatement (Second) § 262. **Death or Incapacity of Person Necessary for Performance**

If the existence of a particular person is necessary for the performance of a duty, his death or such incapacity as makes performance impracticable is an event the non-occurrence of which was a basic assumption on which the contract was made.

[handwritten margin notes: "impracticable = not impossible, but very hard"; "can't just be harder"; "still need to try to overcome"]

Restatement (Second) § 263. Destruction, Deterioration or Failure to Come Into Existence of Thing Necessary for Performance

If the existence of a specific thing is necessary for the performance of a duty, its failure to come into existence, destruction, or such deterioration as makes performance impracticable is an event the non-occurrence of which was a basic assumption on which the contract was made.

Restatement (Second) § 264. Prevention by Governmental Regulation or Order

If the performance of a duty is made impracticable by having to comply with a-domestic or foreign governmental regulation or order, that regulation or order is an event the non-occurrence of which was a basic assumption on which the contract was made.

Restatement (Second) § 265. Discharge by Supervening Frustration

Where, after a contract is made, a party's principal purpose is substantially frustrated without his fault by the occurrence of an event the non-occurrence of which was a basic assumption on which the contract was made, his remaining duties to render performance are discharged, unless the language or the circumstances indicate the contrary.

Restatement (Second) § 266. Existing Impracticability or Frustration

(1) Where, at the time a contract is made, a party's performance under it is impracticable without his fault because of a fact of which he has no reason to know and the non-existence of which is a basic assumption on which the contract is made, no duty to render that performance arises, unless the language or circumstances indicate the contrary.

(2) Where, at the time a contract is made, a party's principal purpose is substantially frustrated without his fault by a fact of which he has no reason to know and the non-existence of which is a basic assumption on which the contract is made, no duty of that party to render performance arises, unless the language or circumstances indicate the contrary.

Restatement (Second) § 269. Temporary Impracticability or Frustration

Impracticability of performance or frustration of purpose that is only temporary suspends the obligor's duty to perform while the impracticability or frustration exists but does not discharge his duty or prevent it from arising unless his performance after the cessation of the impracticability or frustration would be materially more burdensome than had there been no impracticability or frustration.

Restatement (Second) § 270. **Partial Impracticability**

Where only part of an obligor's performance is impracticable, his duty to render the remaining part is unaffected if
(a) it is still practicable for him to render performance that is substantial, taking account of any reasonable substitute performance that he is under a duty to render; or
(b) the obligee, within a reasonable time, agrees to render any remaining performance in full and to allow the obligor to retain any performance that has already been rendered.

Note that the Restatement (Second) sections cover the following (sometimes overlapping) topics:

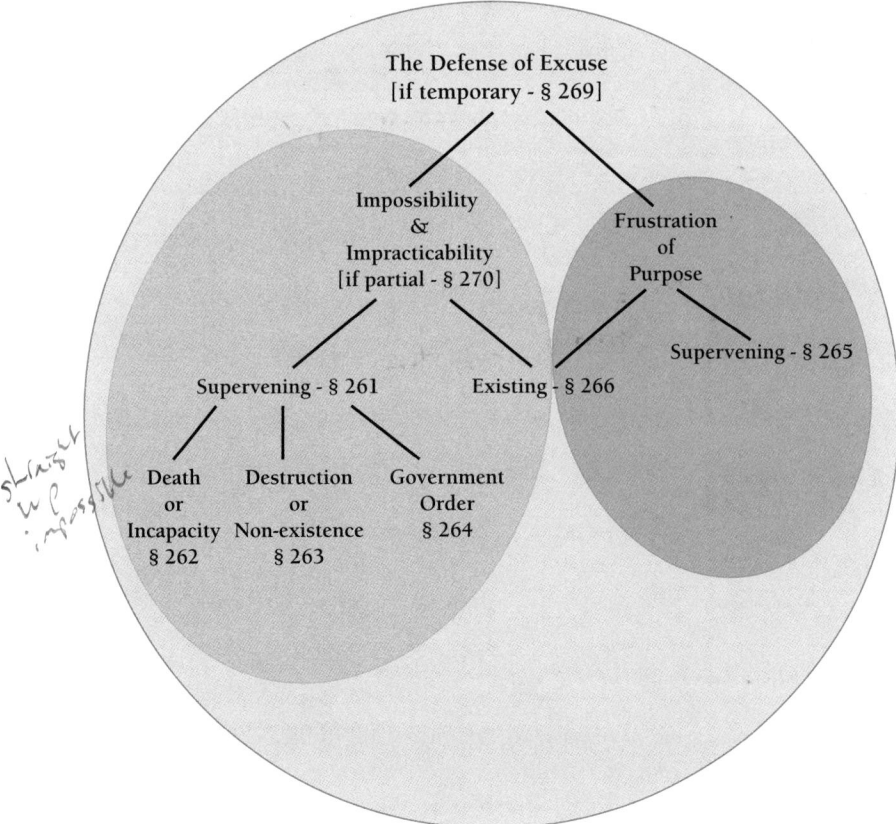

Reading the Law Critically:

Transatlantic Financing Corp

1. What is required to establish an excuse based on impracticability as articulated in *Transatlantic*? Do you agree with the court's application of the legal standard to the facts?

2. As already noted, the excuse of impracticability bears some resemblance to the defense of mistake. How are the standards alike? How are they different?

3. What role does the concept of quantum meruit play in this case?

Behind the Scenes

The *Transatlantic* case involves a controversy stemming from the Suez Crisis in 1956. The Suez Canal is an artificial waterway that cuts through the Sinai Peninsula to connect the Mediterranean Sea with the Red Sea, allowing for shorter and quicker shipments of goods between Europe and Asia. Without the canal, ships would have to sail around the southern-most point of the African continent, the Cape of Good Hope.

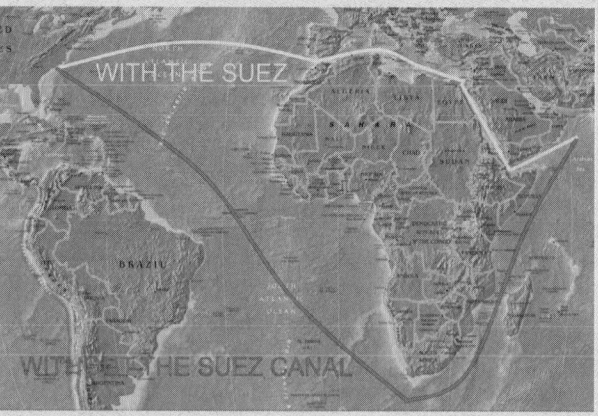

Transatlantic involved a shipment from the Gulf of Mexico port in the United States to Iran, and the route around the Cape of Good Hope was a 30% longer distance than the route through the Suez Canal.

In ancient times, several canals connected the Nile River with the Red Sea, but the annual spring floods of the Nile caused silt to fill the canals, eventually making them unusable.

Replacing those failed waterways, the Suez Canal was built in 1859-1869 by the Suez Canal Co, which was founded by a French diplomat with the permission of the Ottoman Empire's "khedive" (similar to a governor or viceroy) of Egypt and Sudan.

Britain opposed the project, fearing that it would interfere with British trade with India. However, in 1882, Britain invaded Egypt and Sudan, to suppress an uprising, and in 1888, Britain gained control over the

canal, when the Convention of Constantinople declared the canal to be a neutral zone under the protection of Britain, even though the Ottoman Empire maintained nominal sovereignty over the region until 1914.

During the British-backed monarchy, there were intermittent riots in Cairo by groups seeking to overthrow the monarchy. In 1948, the creation of the state of Israel generated regional instability. In 1951, Egypt repudiated the canal treaty (the Convention of Constantinople). In 1952, the military and civilian forces within Egypt finally toppled the UK-backed monarchy and brought General Gamal Nasser to power.

Nasser was a strong proponent of Pan-Arab nationalism, arguing that Middle Eastern countries should govern themselves in a manner excluding Western influences and interests. One of Nasser's goals during the 1950s was to build the Aswan High Dam on the Nile River to produce hydroelectric power for industrialization in Egypt. Nasser sought funding from Western nations and was initially able to secure a loan from the World Bank that was contingent upon US financial support for the project. Meanwhile, Nasser attempted to purchase military supplies to protect Egypt from the continuing regional instability surrounding the state of Israel. When he was unable to secure military supplies from Western nations, he turned to the Soviet Union, igniting Cold War tensions between the US and the Soviet Union. When Nasser recognized the People's Republic of China, the US pulled its support from the Aswan High Dam Program, and the World Bank followed suit.

Nasser then nationalized the Suez Canal during a speech in Alexandra on July 26, 1956. Nasser hoped that he could use fees from the Canal to pay for the Aswan High Dam. The *Transatlantic* case picks up the historical account at that point.

Transatlantic Financing Corp. v. United States

TRANSATLANTIC FINANCING CORPORATION, Libellant-Appellant

v.

UNITED STATES OF AMERICA, Defendant-Appellee

United States Court of Appeals, District of Columbia Circuit
363 F.2d 312 (D.C. Cir. 1966)

J. SKELLY WRIGHT, Circuit Judge:

This appeal involves a voyage charter between Transatlantic Financing Corporation, operator of the SS CHRISTOS, and the United States covering carriage of a full cargo of wheat from a United States Gulf port to a safe port in Iran. The

District Court dismissed a libel filed by Transatlantic against the United States for costs attributable to the ship's diversion from the normal sea route caused by the closing of the Suez Canal. We affirm.

US doesn't have to pay for ship having to go around

On July 26, 1956, the Government of Egypt nationalized the Suez Canal Company and took over operation of the Canal. On October 2, 1956, during the international crisis which resulted from the seizure, the voyage charter in suit was executed between representatives of Transatlantic and the

> **What's That?**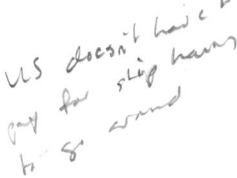
>
> In a suit brought under federal admiralty jurisdiction, the suit is known as the "libel," and the plaintiff is known as the "libellant."

United States. The charter indicated the termini of the voyage but not the route. On October 27, 1956, the SS Christos sailed from Galveston for Bandar Shapur, Iran, on a course which would have taken her through Gibraltar and the Suez Canal. On October 29, 1956, Israel invaded Egypt. On October 31, 1956, Great Britain and France invaded the Suez Canal Zone. On November 2, 1956, the Egyptian Government obstructed the Suez Canal with sunken vessels and closed it to traffic.

On or about November 7, 1956, Beckmann, representing Transatlantic, contacted Potosky, an employee of the United States Department of Agriculture, who appellant concedes was unauthorized to bind the Government, requesting instructions concerning disposition of the cargo and seeking an agreement for payment of additional compensation for a voyage around the Cape of Good Hope. Potosky advised Beckmann that Transatlantic was expected to perform the charter according to its terms, that he did not believe Transatlantic was entitled to additional compensation for a voyage around the Cape, but that Transatlantic was free to file such a claim. Following this discussion, the Christos changed course for the Cape of Good Hope and eventually arrived in Bandar Shapur on December 30, 1956.

want more money for longer route

Transatlantic's claim is based on the following train of argument. The charter was a contract for a voyage from a Gulf port to Iran. Admiralty principles and practices, especially stemming from the doctrine of deviation, require us to imply into the contract the term that the voyage was to be performed by the "usual and customary" route. The usual and customary route from Texas to Iran was, at the time of contract, via Suez, so the contract was for a voyage from Texas to Iran via Suez. When Suez was closed this contract became impossible to perform. Consequently, appellant's argument continues, when Transatlantic delivered the cargo by going around the Cape of Good Hope, in compliance with the Government's demand under claim of right, it conferred a benefit upon the United States for which it should be paid in quantum meruit.

credit take usual route

The doctrine of impossibility of performance has gradually been freed from the earlier fictional and unrealistic strictures of such tests as the "implied term"

Think About It!

What makes the tests for impossibility "fictional and unrealistic" as the court suggests? Does the more modern test for impracticability avoid that problem?

and the parties' "contemplation." Page, The Development of the Doctrine of Impossibility of Performance, 18 Mich.L.Rev. 589, 596 (1920). . . . . "A thing is impossible in legal contemplation when it is not practicable; and a thing is impracticable when it can only be done at an excessive and unreasonable cost." **Mineral Park Land Co. v. Howard, 172 Cal. 289, 293, 156 P.**

458, 460, L.R.A. 1916F, 1 (1916). Accord . . . . Uniform Commercial Code (U.L.A.) § 2-615, comment 3. The doctrine ultimately represents the ever-shifting line, drawn by courts hopefully responsive to commercial practices and mores, at which the community's interest in having contracts enforced according to their terms is outweighed by the commercial senselessness of requiring performance. When the issue is raised, the court is asked to construct a condition of performance based on the changed circumstances, a process which involves at least three reasonably definable steps. First, a contingency—something unexpected—must have occurred. Second, the risk of the unexpected occurrence must not have been allocated either by agreement or by custom. Finally, occurrence of the contingency must have rendered performance commercially impracticable. Unless the court finds these three requirements satisfied, the plea of impossibility must fail.

The first requirement was met here. It seems reasonable, where no route is mentioned in a contract, to assume the parties expected performance by the usual and customary route at the time of contract. Since the usual and customary route from Texas to Iran at the time of contract was through Suez, closure of the Canal made impossible the expected method of performance. But this unexpected development raises rather than resolves the impossibility issue, which turns additionally on whether the risk of the contingency's occurrence had been allocated and, if not, whether performance by alternative routes was rendered impracticable.

Proof that the risk of a contingency's occurrence has been allocated may be expressed in or implied from the agreement. Such proof may also be found in the surrounding circumstances, including custom and usages of the trade. . . . The contract in this case does not expressly condition performance upon availability of the Suez route. Nor does it specify "via Suez" or, on the other hand, "via Suez or Cape of Good Hope." Nor are there provisions in the contract from which we may properly imply that the continued availability of Suez was a condition of performance.[8] Nor is there anything in custom or trade usage, or in the surrounding circumstances generally, which would support our constructing a condition of performance. The numerous cases requiring performance around the Cape when Suez was closed, see e.g., Ocean Tramp Tankers Corp. v. V/O Sovfracht (The Eugenia), (1964) 2 Q.B. 226, and cases cited therein, indicate that the Cape route is generally regarded as an alternative means of performance. So the implied expectation that the route would be via Suez is hardly adequate proof of an allocation to the promisee of the risk of closure. In some cases, even an express expectation may not amount to a condition of performance. The doctrine of deviation supports our assumption that parties normally expect performance by the usual and customary route, but it adds nothing beyond this that is probative of an allocation of the risk.[10]

If anything, the circumstances surrounding this contract indicate that the risk of the Canal's closure may be deemed to have been allocated to Transatlantic. We know or may safely assume that the parties were aware, as were most commercial men with interests affected by the Suez situation, see The Eugenia, supra, that the Canal might become a dangerous area. No doubt the tension affected freight rates, and it is arguable that the risk of closure became part of the dickered terms. Uniform Commercial Code § 2-615, comment 8. We do not deem the risk of closure so allocated, however. Foreseeability or even recognition of a risk does not neces-

---

[8] The charter provides that the vessel is "in every way fitted for the voyage", and the "P. & I. Bunker Deviation Clause" refers to "the contract voyage" and the "direct and/or customary route." Appellant argues that these provisions require implication of a voyage by the direct and customary route. Actually they prove only what we are willing to accept—that the parties expected the usual and customary route would be used. The provisions in no way condition performance upon nonoccurrence of this contingency. There are two clauses which allegedly demonstrate that time is of importance in this contract. One clause computes the remuneration "in steaming time" for diversions to other countries ordered by the charterer in emergencies. This proves only that the United States wished to reserve power to send the goods to another country. It does not imply in any way that there was a rush about the matter. The other clause concerns demurrage and despatch. The charterer agreed to pay Transatlantic demurrage of $1,200 per day for all time in excess of the period agreed upon for loading and unloading, and Transatlantic was to pay despatch of $600 per day for any saving in time. Of course this provision shows the parties were concerned about time, see Gilmore & Black, The Law of Admiralty § 4-8 (1957), but the fact that they arranged so minutely the consequences of any delay or speedup of loading and unloading operates against the argument that they were similarly allocating the risk of delay or speed-up of the voyage.

[10] The deviation doctrine, drawn principally from admiralty insurance practice, implies into all relevant commercial instruments naming the termini of voyages the usual and customary route between those points. 1 Arnould, Marine Insurance and Average § 376, at 522 (10th ed. 1921). Insurance is cancelled when a ship unreasonably "deviates" from this course, for example by extending a voyage or by putting in at an irregular port, and the shipowner forfeits the protection of clauses of exception which might otherwise have protected him from his common law insurer's liability to cargo. See Gilmore & Black, supra Note 8, § 2-6, at 59-60. This practice, properly qualified, see id. § 3-41, makes good sense, since insurance rates are computed on the basis of the implied course, and deviations in the course increasing the anticipated risk make the insurer's calculations meaningless. Arnould, supra, § 14, at 26. Thus the route, so far as insurance contracts are concerned, is crucial, whether express or implied. But even here, the implied term is not inflexible. Reasonable deviations do not result in loss of insurance, at least so long as established practice is followed. See Carriage of Goods by Sea Act § 4(4) . . . . The doctrine provides no evidence of an allocation of the risk of the route's unavailability.

sarily prove its allocation. Compare Uniform Commercial Code § 2-615, Comment 1; Restatement, Contracts § 457 (1932). Parties to a contract are not always able to provide for all the possibilities of which they are aware, sometimes because they cannot agree, often simply because they are too busy. Moreover, that some abnormal risk was contemplated is probative but does not necessarily establish an allocation of the risk of the contingency which actually occurs. In this case, for example, nationalization by Egypt of the Canal Corporation and formation of the Suez Users Group did not necessarily indicate that the Canal would be blocked even if a confrontation resulted. The surrounding cir-

Think About It!

Why is insurance relevant to the analysis of impracticability?

cumstances do indicate, however, a willingness by Transatlantic to assume abnormal risks, and this fact should legitimately cause us to judge the impracticability of performance by an alternative route in stricter terms than we would were the contingency unforeseen.

We turn then to the question whether occurrence of the contingency rendered performance commercially impracticable under the circumstances of this case. The goods shipped were not subject to harm from the longer, less temperate Southern route. The vessel and crew were fit to proceed around the Cape. Transatlantic was no less able than the United States to purchase insurance to cover the contingency's occurrence. If anything, it is more reasonable to expect owner-operators of vessels to insure against the hazards of war. They are in the best position to calculate the cost of performance by alternative routes (and therefore to estimate the amount of insurance required), and are undoubtedly sensitive to international troubles which uniquely affect the demand for and cost of their services. The only factor operating here in appellant's favor is the added expense, allegedly $43,972.00 above and beyond the contract price of $305,842.92, of extending a 10,000 mile voyage by approximately 3,000 miles. While it may be an overstatement to say that increased cost and difficulty of performance never constitute impracticability, to justify relief there must be more of a variation between expected cost and the cost of performing by an available alternative than is present in this case, where the promisor can legitimately be presumed to have accepted some degree of abnormal risk, and where impracticability is urged on the basis of added expense alone.[15]

We conclude, therefore, as have most other courts considering related issues arising out of the Suez closure, that performance of this contract was not rendered

---

[15] See Uniform Commercial Code § 2-615, comment 4: "Increased cost alone does not excuse performance unless the rise in cost is due to some unforeseen contingency which alters the essential nature of the performance." See also 6 Corbin, supra, § 1333; 6 Williston, supra, § 1952, at 5468.

legally impossible. Even if we agreed with appellant, its theory of relief seems untenable. When performance of a contract is deemed impossible it is a nullity. In the case of a charter party involving carriage of goods, the carrier may return to an appropriate port and unload its cargo, The Malcolm Baxter, Jr., 277 U.S. 323, 48 S.Ct. 516, 72 L.Ed. 901 (1928), subject of course to required steps to minimize damages. If the performance rendered has value, recovery in quantum meruit for the entire performance is proper. But here Transatlantic has collected its contract price, and now seeks quantum meruit relief for the additional expense of the trip around the Cape. If the contract is a nullity, Transatlantic's theory of relief should have been quantum meruit for the entire trip, rather than only for the extra expense. Transatlantic attempts to take its profit on the contract, and then force the Government to absorb the cost of the additional voyage. When impracticability without fault occurs, the law seeks an equitable solution, see 6 Corbin, supra, § 1321, and quantum meruit is one of its potent devices to achieve this end. There is no interest in casting the entire burden of commercial disaster on one party in order to preserve the other's profit. Apparently the contract price in this case was advantageous enough to deter appellant from taking a stance on damages consistent with its theory of liability. In any event, there is no basis for relief.

Affirmed.

Think About It!

The case law on excuse tends to cluster around unexpected events. *Krell v. Henry* was not the only case brought by a disappointed party when Edward VII's coronation was delayed. *Transatlantic Financing Corp. v. U.S.* was one of many cases involving excuse that were brought after the Suez Canal was closed in 1956. Another collection of cases were filed after the Hunt brothers cornered the silver market in 1979 and caused worldwide silver prices to more than quadruple (several wikis cover this incident). So it should come as no surprise that some post-9/11 cases involve the defense of excuse:

- *U.S. Bancorp Equipment Finance, Inc. v. Ameriquest Holdings LLC*, 55 UCC Rep. Serv. 2d 423 (D. Minn. 2004) (immense losses to airline industry following Sept. 11 attacks and consequent extreme devaluation of purchased airplane did not excuse buyer from paying the contract price to purchase the plane).

- *Sub-Zero Freezer Co. v. Cunard Line Ltd.*, 2002 WL 32357103 (D. Wisc. Mar. 12, 2002) (plaintiff was not excused or entitled to a refund of its prepayment of the contract price for 7-night cruise for its employees on defendant's vessel in early October 2001; the cruise could still occur in the immediate aftermath of Sept. 11 attacks even though it might not be "the safe and relaxing cruise" plaintiff alleged that defendant had agreed to provide).

- *Bush v. Protravel International, Inc.*, 746 N.Y.S.2d 790 (Civil Ct. 2002) (defendant's summary judgment motion denied; plaintiff was permitted to proceed to trial to demonstrate excuse on basis of impossibility for her failure to cancel her safari reservation before the cancellation deadline of Sept. 15, 2001, in view of extreme circumstances in New York in the days following the Sept. 11 attack on the World Trade Center).

From your knowledge of the Sept. 11, 2001, attacks on the World Trade Center, were the attacks or the resulting disruptions or losses sufficiently unforeseeable to the contracting parties to merit the excuse defense? Was the absence of such attacks, disruptions, or losses a basic assumption on which the contracts were premised? Were any of these risks implicitly allocated in the contract? What kinds of facts might indicate an implicit allocation of risk?

Reading the Law Critically:
Northern Indiana Public Service Co.

This opinion by Judge Richard Posner illustrates his law-and-economics approach to the subject of excuse. (Recall his earlier case, *Market Street Associates*, on page 809.)

1. The court discusses a variety of rationales and mechanisms for determining who bears the risk of unanticipated circumstances in a contract. How is the risk allocated in this case? Why?

2. Does the court's description of the history of the impossibility, impracticability, and frustration defenses match the progression you have seen in the other cases in this section?

3. What is the function of a *force majeure* clause? What effect does the *force majeure* clause have in the case?

4. How does the court's articulation and application of the excuse of impracticability compare with that in *Transatlantic*?

5. Is this an impracticability or a frustration-of-purpose case?

Northern Indiana Public Service Co. v. Carbon County Coal Co.

NORTHERN INDIANA PUBLIC SERVICE CO., Plaintiff-Appellant

v.

CARBON COUNTY COAL CO., Defendant-Appellee

United States Court of Appeals, Seventh Circuit
799 F.2d 265 (7th Cir. 1986)

POSNER, Circuit Judge.

These appeals bring before us various facets of a dispute between Northern Indiana Public Service Company (NIPSCO), an electric utility in Indiana, and Carbon County Coal Company, a partnership that until recently owned and operated a coal mine in Wyoming. In 1978 NIPSCO and Carbon County signed a contract whereby Carbon County agreed to sell and NIPSCO to buy approximately 1.5 million tons of coal every year for 20 years, at a price of $24 a ton subject to various provisions for escalation which by 1985 had driven the price up to $44 a ton.

NIPSCO's rates are regulated by the Indiana Public Service Commission. In 1983 NIPSCO requested permission to raise its rates to reflect increased fuel charges. Some customers of NIPSCO opposed the increase on the ground that NIPSCO could reduce its overall costs by buying more electrical power from neighboring utilities for resale to its customers and producing less of its own power. Although the Commission granted the requested increase, it directed NIPSCO, in orders issued in December 1983 and February 1984 (the "economy purchase orders"), to make a good faith effort to find, and wherever possible buy from, utilities that would sell electricity to it at prices lower than its costs of internal generation. The Commission added ominously that "the adverse effects of entering into long-term coal supply contracts which do not allow for renegotiation and are not requirement contracts, is a burden which must rest squarely on the shoulders of NIPSCO management." Actually the contract with Carbon County did provide for renegotiation of the contract price—but one-way renegotiation in favor of Carbon County; the price fixed in the contract (as adjusted from time to time in accordance with the escalator provisions) was a floor. And the contract was indeed not a requirements contract: it specified the exact amount of coal that NIPSCO must take over the 20 years during which the contract was to remain in effect. NIPSCO was eager to have an assured supply of low-sulphur coal and was therefore willing to guarantee both price and quantity.

Unfortunately for NIPSCO, as things turned out it was indeed able to buy electricity at prices below the costs of generating electricity from coal bought under the contract with Carbon County; and because of the "economy purchase orders," of which it had not sought judicial review, NIPSCO could not expect to be allowed by the Public Service Commission to recover in its electrical rates the costs of buying coal from Carbon County. NIPSCO therefore decided to stop accepting coal deliveries from Carbon County, at least for the time being; and on April 24, 1985, it brought this diversity suit against Carbon County in a federal district court in Indiana, seeking a declaration that it was excused from its obligations under the contract either permanently or at least until the economy purchase orders ceased preventing it from passing on the costs of the contract to its ratepayers. In support of this position it argued that . . . NIPSCO's performance was excused or suspended—either under the contract's *force majeure* clause or under the doctrines of frustration or impossibility—by reason of the economy purchase orders.

On May 17, 1985, Carbon County counterclaimed for breach of contract and moved for a preliminary injunction requiring NIPSCO to continue taking delivery under the contract. On June 19, 1985, the district judge granted the preliminary injunction, from which NIPSCO has appealed. Also on June 19, rejecting NIPSCO's argument that it needed more time for pretrial discovery and other trial preparations, the judge scheduled the trial to begin on August 26, 1985. Trial did begin then, lasted for six weeks, and resulted in a jury verdict for Carbon County of $181 million. The judge entered judgment in accordance with the verdict, rejecting Carbon County's argument that in lieu of damages it should get an order of specific performance requiring NIPSCO to comply with the contract. Upon entering the final judgment the district judge dissolved the preliminary injunction, and shortly afterward the mine—whose only customer was NIPSCO—shut down. NIPSCO has appealed from the damage judgment, and Carbon County from the denial of specific performance . . . .

. . . .

The contract permits NIPSCO to stop taking delivery of coal "for any cause beyond [its] reasonable control . . . including but not limited to . . . orders or acts of civil . . . authority . . . which wholly or partly prevent . . . the utilizing . . . of the coal." This is what is known as a *force majeure* clause. See, e.g., *Northern Illinois Gas Co. v. Energy Co-op., Inc.,* 122 Ill.App.3d 940, 949-52, 78 Ill.Dec. 215, 223-24, 461 N.E.2d 1049, 1057-58 (1984). NIPSCO argues that the Indiana Public Service Commission's "economy purchase orders" prevented it, in whole or part, from using the coal that it had agreed to buy, and it complains that the district judge instructed the jury incorrectly on the meaning and application of the clause. The complaint about the instructions is immaterial. The judge should not have put the issue of *force majeure* to the jury. It is evident that the clause was not triggered by the orders.

All that those orders do is tell NIPSCO it will not be allowed to pass on fuel costs to its ratepayers in the form of higher rates if it can buy electricity cheaper than it can generate electricity internally using Carbon County's coal. Such an order does not "prevent," whether wholly or in part, NIPSCO from using the coal; it just prevents NIPSCO from shifting the burden of its improvidence or bad luck in having incorrectly forecasted its fuel needs to the backs of the hapless ratepayers. The purpose of public utility regulation is to provide a substitute for competition in markets (such as the market for electricity) that are naturally monopolistic. Suppose the market for electricity were fully competitive, and unregulated. Then if NIPSCO signed a long-term fixed-price fixed-quantity contract to buy coal, and during the life of the contract competing electrical companies were able to produce and sell electricity at prices below the cost to NIPSCO of producing electricity from that coal, NIPSCO would have to swallow the excess cost of the coal. It could not raise its electricity prices in order to pass on the excess cost to its consumers, because if it did they would buy electricity at lower prices from NIPSCO's competitors. By signing the kind of contract it did, NIPSCO gambled that fuel costs would rise rather than fall over the life of the contract; for if they rose, the contract price would give it an advantage over its (hypothetical) competitors who would have to buy fuel at the current market price. If such a gamble fails, the result is not *force majeure*.

This is all the clearer when we consider that the contract price was actually fixed just on the downside; it put a floor under the price NIPSCO had to pay, but the escalator provisions allowed the actual contract prices to rise above the floor, and they did. This underscores the gamble NIPSCO took in signing the contract. It committed itself to paying a price at or above a fixed minimum and to taking a fixed quantity at that price. It was willing to make this commitment to secure an assured supply of low-sulphur coal, but the risk it took was that the market price of coal or substitute fuels would fall. A *force majeure* clause is not intended to buffer a party against the normal risks of a contract. The normal risk of a fixed-price contract is that the market price will change. If it rises, the buyer gains at the expense of the seller (except insofar as escalator provisions give the seller some protection); if it falls, as here, the seller gains at the expense of the buyer.

The whole purpose of a fixed-price contract is to allocate risk in this way. A *force majeure* clause interpreted to excuse the buyer from the consequences of the risk he expressly assumed would nullify a central term of the contract.

The Indiana Public Service Commission is a surrogate for the forces of competition, and the economy fuel orders are a device for simulating the effects in a competitive market of a drop in input prices. The orders say to NIPSCO, in effect: "With fuel costs dropping, and thus reducing the costs of electricity to utilities not burdened by long-term fixed-price contracts, you had better substitute those utilities' electricity for your own when their prices are lower than your cost of internal generation. In a freely competitive market consumers would make that substitution; if you do not do so, don't expect to be allowed to pass on your inflated fuel costs to those consumers." Admittedly the comparison between competition and regulation is not exact. In an unregulated market, if fuel costs skyrocketed NIPSCO would have a capital gain from its contract (assuming the escalator provisions did not operate to raise the contract price by the full amount of the increase in fuel costs, a matter that would depend on the cause of the increase). This is because its competitors, facing higher fuel costs, would try to raise their prices for electricity, thus enabling NIPSCO to raise its price, or expand its output, or both, and thereby increase its profits. The chance of this "windfall" gain offsets, on an ex ante (before the fact) basis, the chance of a windfall loss if fuel costs drop, though NIPSCO it appears was seeking a secure source of low-sulphur coal rather than a chance for windfall gains. If as is likely the Public Service Commission would require NIPSCO to pass on any capital gain from an advantageous contract to the ratepayers (which is another reason for thinking NIPSCO wasn't after windfall gains—it would not, in all likelihood, have been allowed to keep them), then it ought to allow NIPSCO to pass on to them some of the capital loss from a disadvantageous contract—provided that the contract, when made, was prudent. Maybe it was not; maybe the risk that NIPSCO took was excessive. But all this was a matter between NIPSCO and the Public Service Commission, and NIPSCO did not seek judicial review of the economy purchase orders.

If the Commission had ordered NIPSCO to close a plant because of a safety or pollution hazard, we would have a true case of *force majeure*. As a regulated firm NIPSCO is subject to more extensive controls than unregulated firms and it therefore wanted and got a broadly worded *force majeure* clause that would protect it fully (hence the reference to partial effects) against government actions that impeded its using the coal. But as the only thing the Commission did was prevent NIPSCO from using its monopoly position to make consumers bear the risk that NIPSCO assumed when it signed a long-term fixed-price fuel contract, NIPSCO cannot complain of *force majeure;* the risk that has come to pass was one that NIPSCO voluntarily assumed when it signed the contract.

The district judge refused to submit NIPSCO's defenses of impracticability and frustration to the jury, ruling that Indiana law does not allow a buyer to claim impracticability and does not recognize the defense of frustration. Some background (on which see Farnsworth, Contracts §§ 9.5-9.7 (1982)) may help make these rulings intelligible. In the early common law a contractual undertaking unconditional in terms was not excused merely because something had happened (such as an invasion, the passage of a law, or a natural disaster) that prevented the undertaking. See *Paradine v. Jane*, Aleyn 26, 82 Eng.Rep. 897 (K.B.1647). Excuses had to be written into the contract; this is the origin of *force majeure* clauses. Later it came to be recognized that negotiating parties cannot anticipate all the contingencies that may arise in the performance of the contract; a legitimate judicial function in contract cases is to interpolate terms to govern remote contingencies—terms the parties would have agreed on explicitly if they had had the time and foresight to make advance provision for every possible contingency in performance. Later still, it was recognized that physical impossibility was irrelevant, or at least inconclusive; a promisor might want his promise to be unconditional, not because he thought he had superhuman powers but because he could insure against the risk of nonperformance better than the promisee, or obtain a substitute performance more easily than the promisee. See *Field Container Corp. v. ICC*, 712 F.2d 250, 257 (7th Cir.1983); Holmes, The Common Law 300 (1881). Thus the proper question in an "impossibility" case is not whether the promisor could not have performed his undertaking but whether his nonperformance should be excused because the parties, if they had thought about the matter, would have wanted to assign the risk of the contingency that made performance impossible or uneconomical to the promisor or to the promisee; if to the latter, the promisor is excused.

would they have excused it if they had known

Section 2-615 of the Uniform Commercial Code takes this approach. It provides that "delay in delivery . . . by a seller . . . is not a breach of his duty under a contract for sale if performance as agreed has been made impracticable by the occurrence of a contingency the non-occurrence of which was a basic assumption on which the contract was made . . . ." Performance on schedule need not be impossible, only infeasible—provided that the event which made it infeasible was not a risk that the promisor had assumed. Notice, however, that the only type of promisor referred to is a seller; there is no suggestion that a buyer's performance might be excused by reason of impracticability. The reason is largely semantic. Ordinarily all the buyer has to do in order to perform his side of the bargain is pay, and while one can think of all sorts of reasons why, when the time came to pay, the buyer might not have the money, rarely would the seller have intended to assume the risk that the buyer might, whether through improvidence or bad luck, be unable to pay for the seller's goods or services. To deal with the rare case where the buyer or (more broadly) the paying party might have a good excuse based on some unforeseen change in circumstances, a new rubric was thought necessary, different from "impossibility" (the common law term) or "impracticability" (the Code term, picked up in R**ESTATEMENT** (S**ECOND**) **OF** C**ONTRACTS** § 261 (1979)), and it received the name "frustration." Rarely is it impracticable or impossible for the payor to pay; but if something has happened to make the performance for which he would be paying worthless to him, an excuse for not paying, analogous to impracticability or impossibility, may be proper. See R**ESTATEMENT**, *supra*, § 265, comment a.

The leading case on frustration remains *Krell v. Henry*, [1903] 2 K.B. 740 (C.A.). Krell rented Henry a suite of rooms for watching the coronation of Edward VII, but Edward came down with appendicitis and the coronation had to be postponed. Henry refused to pay the balance of the rent and the court held that he was excused from doing so because his purpose in renting had been frustrated by the postponement, a contingency outside the knowledge, or power to influence, of either party. The question was, to which party did the contract (implicitly) allocate the risk? Surely Henry had not intended to insure Krell against the possibility of the coronation's being postponed, since Krell could always relet the room, at the premium rental, for the coronation's new date. So Henry was excused.

NIPSCO is the buyer in the present case, and its defense is more properly frustration than impracticability; but the judge held that frustration is not a contract defense under the law of Indiana. He relied on an Indiana Appellate Court decision which indeed so states, *Ross Clinic, Inc. v. Tabion*, 419 N.E.2d 219, 223 (Ind.App.1981), but solely on the basis of an old decision of the Indiana Supreme Court, *Krause v. Board of Trustees*, 162 Ind. 278, 283-84, 70 N.E. 264, 265 (1904), that doesn't even discuss the defense of frustration and anyway precedes by years the recognition of the defense by American courts. At all events, the facts of the present case do not bring it within the scope of the frustration doctrine, so we need not decide whether the Indiana Supreme Court would embrace the doctrine in a suitable case.*

> **Think About It!**
>
> What does the court mean when it says the facts "do not bring [the case] within the scope of the frustration doctrine"?

. . . .

Whether or not Indiana recognizes the doctrine of frustration, and whether or not a buyer can ever assert the defense of impracticability under **section 2-615 of the Uniform Commercial Code**, these doctrines, so closely related to each other and to *force majeure* as well, see *International Minerals & Chemical Corp.*

---

* [Authors' Note: Indiana continues to reject the defense of frustration of purpose. *See, e.g., In re Rezendes*, 318 B.R. 436 (Bankr. N.D. Ind. 2004) (citing Ind. cases); *Justus v. Justus*, 581 N.E.2d 1265 (Ind. Ct. App. 1991).]

v. Llano, Inc., 770 F.2d 879, 885-87 (10th Cir.1985), cannot help NIPSCO. All are doctrines for shifting risk to the party better able to bear it, either because he is in a better position to prevent the risk from materializing or because he can better reduce the disutility of the risk (as by insuring) if the risk does occur. Suppose a grower agrees before the growing season to sell his crop to a grain elevator, and the crop is destroyed by blight and the grain elevator sues. Discharge is ordinarily allowed in such cases. See, e.g., *Matousek v. Galligan,* 104 Neb. 731, 178 N.W. 510 (1920) . . . . The grower has every incentive to avoid the blight; so if it occurs, it probably could not have been prevented; and the grain elevator, which buys from a variety of growers not all of whom will be hit by blight in the same growing season, is in a better position to buffer the risk of blight than the grower is.

Since impossibility and related doctrines are devices for shifting risk in accordance with the parties' presumed intentions, which are to minimize the costs of contract performance, one of which is the disutility created by risk, they have no place when the contract explicitly assigns a particular risk to one party or the other. As we have already noted, a fixed-price contract is an explicit assignment of the risk of market price increases to the seller and the risk of market price decreases to the buyer, and the assignment of the latter risk to the buyer is even clearer where, as in this case, the contract places a floor under price but allows for escalation. If, as is also the case here, the buyer forecasts the market incorrectly and therefore finds himself locked into a disadvantageous contract, he has only himself to blame and so cannot shift the risk back to the seller by invoking impossibility or related doctrines. See Farnsworth, *supra,* at 680 and n. 18; White & Summers, Handbook of the Law under the Uniform Commercial Code 133 (2d ed. 1980). It does not matter that it is an act of government that may have made the contract less advantageous to one party. See, e.g., *Connick v. Teachers Ins. & Annuity Ass'n,* 784 F.2d 1018, 1022 (9th Cir.1986) . . . . Government these days is a pervasive factor in the economy and among the risks that a fixed-price contract allocates between the parties is that of a price change induced by one of government's manifold interventions in the economy. Since "the very purpose of a fixed price agreement is to place the risk of increased costs on the promisor (and the risk of decreased costs on the promisee)," the fact that costs decrease steeply (which is in effect what happened here—the cost of generating electricity turned out to be lower than NIPSCO thought when it signed the fixed-price contract with Carbon County) cannot allow the buyer to walk away from the contract. . . .

. . . .

Reading the Law Critically: The Excuse Defense in the UCC and UNIDROIT

1. Recall that the UCC was approved by NCCUSL and the ALI in the early 1950s, while the Restatement (Second) was approved by the ALI in 1979. Which Restatement (Second) sections on pages 996-998 seem to have drawn their influence from UCC § 2-615? How similar are the Restatement (Second) and UCC provisions?

2. What additional rules does § 2-616 furnish?

3. How does the UNIDROIT provision compare with the Restatement (Second) and UCC provisions?

UCC § 2-615. Excuse by Failure of Presupposed Conditions.

Except so far as a seller may have assumed a greater obligation and subject to the preceding section on substituted performance:

(a) Delay in delivery or non-delivery in whole or in part by a seller who complies with paragraphs (b) and (c) is not a breach of his duty under a contract for sale if performance as a greed has been made impracticable by the occurrence of a contingency the non-occurrence of which was a basic assumption on which the contract was made or by compliance in good faith with any applicable foreign or domestic governmental regulation or order whether or not it later proves to be invalid.

(b) Where the causes mentioned in paragraph (a) affect only a part of the seller's capacity to perform, he must allocate production and deliveries among his customers but may at his option include regular customers not then under contract as well as his own requirements for further manufacture. He may so allocate in any manner which is fair and reasonable.

(c) The seller must notify the buyer seasonably that there will be delay or non-delivery and, when allocation is required under paragraph (b), of the estimated quota thus made available for the buyer.

Comments:

4. Increased cost alone does not excuse performance unless the rise in cost is due to some unforeseen contingency which alters the essential nature of the performance. Neither is a rise or a collapse in the market in itself a justification, for that is exactly the type of business risk which

business contracts made to fixed prices are intended to cover. But a severe shortage of raw materials or of supplies due to a contingency such as war, embargo, local crop failure, unforeseen shutdown of major sources of supply or the like, which either causes a marked increase in cost or altogether prevents the seller from securing supplies necessary to his performance is within the contemplation of this section. (See Ford & Sons, Ltd., v. Henry Leetham & Sons, Ltd., 21 Com.Cas.55 (1915, K.B.D.).)

8. The provisions of this section are made subject to assumption of greater liability by agreement and such agreement is to be found not only in the expressed terms of the contract but in the circumstances surrounding the contracting, in trade usage and the like. Thus the exemptions of this section do not apply when the contingency in question is sufficiently foreshadowed at the time of contracting to be included among the business risks which are fairly to be regarded as part of the dickered terms, either consciously or as a matter of reasonable, commercial interpretation from the circumstances. (See Madeirense Do Brasil, S.A. v. Stulman-Emrick Lumber Co., 147 F.2d 399 (C.C.A., 2 Cir., 1945).) The exemption otherwise present through usageof trade under the present section may also be expressly negated by the language of the agreement. Generally, express agreements as to exemptions designed to enlarge upon or supplant the provisions of this section are to be read in the light of mercantile sense and reason, for this section itself sets up the commercial standard for normal and reasonable interpretation and provides a minimum beyond which agreement may not go.

Agreement can also be made in regard to the consequences of exemption as laid down in paragraphs (b) and (c) and the next section on procedure on notice claiming excuse.

UCC § 2-616. Procedure on Notice Claiming Excuse.

(1) Where the buyer receives notification of a material or indefinite delay or an allocation justified under the preceding section he may by written notification to the seller as to any delivery concerned, and where the prospective deficiency substantially impairs the value of the whole contract under the provisions of this Article relating to breach of installment contracts (Section 2-612), then also as to the whole,

    (a) terminate and thereby discharge any unexecuted portion of the contract; or

    (b) modify the contract by agreeing to take his available quota in substitution.

(2) If after receipt of such notification from the seller the buyer fails so to modify the contract within reasonable time not exceeding thirty days the contract lapses with respect to any deliveries affected.

(3) The provisions of this section may not be negated by agreement except in so far as the seller has assumed a greater obligation under the preceding section.

———————————

UNIDROIT Art. 7.1.7. Force Majeure

(1) Non-performance by a party is excused if that party proves that the non-performance was due to an impediment beyond its control and that it could not reasonably be expected to have taken the impediment into account at the time of the conclusion of the contract or to have avoided or overcome it or its consequences.

(2) When the impediment is only temporary, the excuse shall have effect for such period as is reasonable having regard to the effect of the impediment on the performance of the contract.

(3) The party who fails to perform must give notice to the other party of the impediment and its effect on its ability to perform. If the notice is not received by the other party within a reasonable time after the party who fails to perform knew or ought to have known of the impediment, it is liable for damages resulting from such non-receipt.

(4) . . . .

Reading the Law Critically: *City of Vernon*

1. What is the court's legal basis for determining that defendant should be excused because of impossibility or impracticability? Do you agree with the court's assessment?

2. What are the key differences between the majority and dissenting opinions? Which opinion do you think is better reasoned?

3. Compare how the excuse doctrine is used in *Transatlantic* and *NIPSCO* with its use in the *City of Vernon* case. Is the excuse doctrine applied differently in cases where a party's performance is hindered by government abatement action? How might this case be decided under the Restatement (Second) provisions?

City of Vernon v. City of Los Angeles

CITY OF VERNON, Plaintiff-Appellant

v.

CITY OF LOS ANGELES, Defendant-Respondent

Supreme Court of California, In Bank
290 P.2d 841 (Cal. 1955)

SCHAUER, Justice.

The City of Vernon by its complaint for declaratory relief and injunction seeks a determination that under contracts entered into between it and defendant City of Los Angeles in 1909, 1925, 1931, and 1938 it is entitled to discharge a certain amount of its sewage through the sewer system of Los Angeles without payment to Los Angeles; Vernon also seeks injunctive enforcement of the contracts and damages in the amount which Vernon is required to pay by the judgment in People v. City of Los Angeles (1948), 83 Cal.App.2d 627, 189 P.2d 489 (an action in which the State obtained judgment against the parties to this action and others to abate the nuisance caused by their discharge of sewage into Santa Monica Bay). By its answer Los Angeles seeks determinations that the contracts are without effect; that Vernon be required to finance its share of the cost of new sewage disposal facilities built by Los Angeles in accordance with the decision for the State in People v. City of Los Angeles (1948), supra, 83 Cal.App.2d 627, 189 P.2d 489, and that Vernon has no right to use the sewage system of Los Angeles except on payment of its share of the cost of the facilities used.

After trial the superior court decreed that Vernon is not entitled to the relief sought; that the contracts between Vernon and Los Angeles (except for certain salvageable elements) are terminated and "have been invalid and unenforceable since a time not later than the entry of . . . judgment in the State Abatement Action"; and that Vernon is entitled to use the new facilities only on payment of its share of their cost. Vernon has appealed. . . . We have concluded that [the trial court] judgment can and should be upheld on the basis of its . . . determination that the performance of the contracts was excused and the contracts were discharged because performance became impossible except at impractical, excessive, unreasonable expense not contemplated by the parties when the contracts were made.

. . . .

The factual background of this litigation and the abatement action is as follows: Years ago cities (including Vernon) other than Los Angeles and sanitation districts in the Los Angeles area which subsequently became defendants in the abatement action found themselves financially unable to construct adequate sewage disposal facilities. The City of Los Angeles had constructed an outfall sewer system with a capacity which exceeded its then expected needs. Beginning in 1909 with Vernon, the cities other than Los Angeles and the sanitation districts made contracts with Los Angeles by which Los Angeles agreed to dispose of their sewage. "[T]he contracts between the city of Los Angeles and the other municipalities and sanitation districts under discussion were for an indefinite period, or, in some instances, for the life of the outfall sewer system itself, and in no instance carried any provision permitting the contracts to be cancelled when or if the city of Los Angeles required the use of that portion of the capacity of its outfall sewer system covered by the above-mentioned contracts" . . . .

Sewage was originally disposed of by Los Angeles under its 1909 contract with Vernon by transporting it through an outfall sewer to Hyperion and discharging it raw into Santa Monica Bay about 900 feet offshore. In 1922, pursuant to requirements of the State Department of Public Health, Los Angeles commenced construction of new facilities, including a screening plant and a submarine tube extending about a mile offshore at Hyperion. These facilities were operated under a permit issued to Los Angeles in 1923.

In 1940, because Los Angeles had violated the terms of the 1923 permit and created a nuisance, the State suspended the permit; however, it granted a temporary permit on condition that Los Angeles at once prepare plans for the construction and financing of adequate sewage disposal works. Los Angeles did not comply with the terms of the temporary permit and the State revoked such permit. It also revoked permits of other defendants, including Vernon. Thus all rights of the contracting parties to dispose of sewage through the existing facilities were terminated.

In 1943 the State brought the abatement action. Judgment for the State was entered on February 1, 1946, and affirmed in People v. City of Los Angeles (1948), supra, 83 Cal.App.2d 627, 189 P.2d 489. This court denied a hearing, and the United States Supreme Court denied certiorari (335 U.S. 852, 69 S.Ct. 80, 93 L.Ed. 400).

Both before and after the institution of the abatement action Los Angeles attempted to work out means, alone or in cooperation with the other cities, whereby the sewage could be adequately disposed of by methods conforming with health and safety laws. Vernon did not make similar efforts; it sat by, resting on its claim that all its responsibility for disposition of its sewage, including its responsibility to the People of the State of California, had been assumed by Los Angeles. Through the years the pressing need for continued and improved disposition of sewage increased with the increase of the volume of sewage originating in the cities which used the Los Angeles facilities, including, as found by the trial court, "the enormous increase in volume of sewage originating in the City of Vernon as a result of the greatly increased industrial activity within its boundaries."

. . . .

In the abatement action the trial court . . . . ordered that Los Angeles build a new plant of sufficient capacity to abate the nuisance; that each other defendant either provide its own facilities for disposing of its sewage in a safe and sanitary manner or arrange to finance its share of the cost of the new plant proportionate to gallonage allotted to it; that such other defendants notify the court of the manner in which they elected to comply with the abatement injunction. The decree provided for continuing supervision by the court. . . .

. . . .

After the affirmance of the abatement injunction and the denial of a hearing and of certiorari, Vernon instituted the present action. It did not take steps, by levy of taxes or issuance of bonds or imposition of charges, to raise funds for payment of its share of the cost of the new sewage plant, and it was found guilty of contempt for failing to comply with the abatement injunction. It sought review of the contempt judgment, contending, among other things, that bringing the present action was compliance with the injunction. This court rejected that contention and affirmed the contempt judgment. (City of Vernon v. Superior Court (1952), supra, 38 Cal.2d 509, 518, 241 P.2d 243.) We said, "The obvious purpose of the injunction was to get the nuisance promptly abated and to that end to get the new plant built and paid for without the delay attendant on independent or later ensuing litigation to determine the validity and effect of the old contracts of Vernon and other corporate defendants. . . . This ruling preserves to petitioners all contractual rights they may possess under the mentioned contracts but likewise it requires them to settle or litigate those rights independently of compliance with the injunction decree."

. . . .

Legal Impossibility

. . . [T]he trial court determined that there was available to Los Angeles the defense of impossibility—not literal impossibility, but impracticability due to excessive and unreasonable expense. . . . For the reasons hereinafter stated, we conclude that this determination of the trial court is tenable.

Pursuant to the 1909 agreement, Los Angeles built within Vernon and connected to the Los Angeles disposal system a main sewer and a lateral sewer for the joint use of the two cities. By that contract Los Angeles agrees to operate and maintain the joint sewers and Vernon agrees to pay five per cent of the cost of operation and maintenance. Each city agrees to operate and maintain its own sewer system at its own expense, "other than those portions which are constructed and used by them jointly. . . . [I]n consideration of the construction of the [joint] sewers above named, by the City of Los Angeles at its own cost and expense, and of the connection of said sewers with the outfall sewer also constructed by the said City of Los Angeles (for discharge of sewage into the bay) and of the privilege of connecting the sewer system to be constructed hereafter by the said City of Vernon with said sewers, and of discharging the sewage of said City of Vernon with said sewers," Vernon shall pay Los Angeles fifty per cent of the cost of the main sewer, not to exceed $12,000, and twenty per cent of the cost of the lateral sewer, not to exceed $1,300. The agreement contains no provision as to its termination.

As previously stated, pursuant to a state permit issued in 1923, Los Angeles built a screening plant and submarine tube at Hyperion. These facilities were used in performance of the 1909 contract.

By the 1925 contract Vernon agrees in its use of sewers to abide by the rules which Los Angeles prescribes for the use of its sewers.

The 1931 agreement (which was never carried out but rather became the subject of much controversy between the parties) provides that Vernon shall be permitted to discharge not more than 11.7 cubic feet of sewage per second[1] into the Los Angeles sewer system pursuant to the 1909 contract; for this right Vernon is not required to pay anything; [the agreement provides for substantial payments by Vernon "for the right to discharge additional amounts of sewage" and to pay its share of the cost of construction of a relief sewer in Vernon and operation and maintenance of sewage lines used by Los Angeles for sewage discharged by Vernon in excess of 11.7 cubic feet per second.]

Vernon did not perform its promises to pay [the sums specified] under the 1931 agreement. In 1937 Los Angeles filed two actions against Vernon, one for payments under the 1931 agreement and one for an injunction against discharging sewage into the Los Angeles system.

The 1938 agreement states that Los Angeles and Vernon desire to settle all controversies as to the prior agreements and to provide for future operation and maintenance of sewage disposal facilities. The right of Vernon to dispose of 11.7 cubic feet of sewage per second through the Los Angeles outfall sewers is acknowledged. Los Angeles agrees to sell and Vernon agrees to buy the right

---

[1] The amount of sewage discharged by Vernon has always been and now is less than 11.7 cubic feet per second.

to dispose of an additional 4.3 cubic feet per second; for this right to dispose of additional sewage Vernon agrees to pay $112,885.45 by April 1, 1939, together with specified annual payments, until 1965, totaling $135,356.60; "in lieu of such annual payments, Vernon may . . . pay the then current worth of unpaid future annual payments, discounted at the rate of 3% per annum compounded annually." Vernon further agrees that if it exercises its right to dispose of sewage in excess of 11.7 cubic feet per second, it will pay its proportionate share, measured by the ratio of its sewage in excess of 11.7 cubic feet per second to the total flow of sewage through the Los Angeles outfall sewers and treatment plant, of the cost to Los Angeles of operation, repair, replacement, construction and reconstruction of the Los Angeles outfall sewers and treatment plant. The contract provides for dismissal of the 1937 actions instituted by Los Angeles. There are additional provisions as to gauging stations, a relief sewer, and other matters which need not be set out. The agreement contains no provision as to its termination.

Vernon made the $112,885.45 payment provided for by the 1938 contract after it was due, with interest to compensate for the delay; it prepaid the annual payments as the contract provided it might do; Los Angeles accepted the payments in discharge of the obligations for which they were tendered.

The trial court in the present action determined that pursuant to the [injunction in the state abatement action] the lawful existence of the screening plant and the tube built pursuant to the 1923 permit has expired; that Los Angeles is required to build a new plant and tube at a cost of approximately $41,000,000; that the cost of operating and maintaining the new plant and tube will be approximately $500,000 per annum; that Los Angeles cannot continue performance under its contracts with Vernon "except at an excessive and unreasonable cost; that it is not practicable for the City of Los Angeles to continue the performance under the terms of the contracts . . . with the use of the new . . . plant and . . . tube."

The trial court in the present action further determined "That it was not intended by the plaintiff and defendant herein that the City of Los Angeles was obligating itself, under the terms . . . of the contracts heretofore entered into between said parties, to build . . . and operate large and extensive facilities or treatment works for the purification of sewage . . . ; that neither nor all (sic) of said contracts provide for, nor was it contemplated by either of the parties hereto in entering into said contracts, that the City of Los Angeles was or would be required under said contracts to erect . . . and operate a . . . treatment plant costing approximately $41,000,000 for the treatment of sewage arising within the boundaries of the City of Vernon."

The foregoing determinations of the trial court support the position of Los Angeles, succinctly stated in its brief, that "since further use of the facilities contemplated by the parties would be unlawful and the use of new facilities (ordered by the Court [in the abatement action] would be unreasonably excessive in cost, further performance under said contracts by Los Angeles is excused."

The controlling principles as to legal impossibility excusing performance . . . are stated in Mineral Park Land Co. v. Howard (1916), supra, 172 Cal. 289, 293, 156 P. 458, L.R.A.1916F, 1, where defendants contracted to take gravel from plaintiff's land at a certain price, and it was subsequently found that the gravel, although present, could be taken only at prohibitive cost: "'A thing is impossible in legal contemplation when it is not practicable; and a thing is impracticable when it can only be done at an excessive and unreasonable cost.' (1 Beach on Contracts, sec. 216.) We do not mean to intimate that the defendants could excuse themselves by showing the existence of conditions which would make the performance of their obligation more expensive than they had anticipated, or which would entail a loss upon them. But where the difference in cost is so great as here, and has the effect, as found, of making performance impracticable, the situation is not different from that of a total absence of earth and gravel."

As we understand the composite contracts of the parties, and as is implicit in the trial court's findings, the parties contemplated that there would be available for legal use disposal facilities, whether those in existence or to be constructed, the cost of which would not be completely disproportionate to the costs expressly referred to in those contracts. Therefore, the case is not like the cases relied upon by Vernon where it was held that unforeseen hardship or unexpected expense did not excuse performance. (Western Industries Co. v. Mason M. etc. Co. (1922), 56 Cal.App. 355, 360, 205 P. 466; Orr v. Forde (1929), 101 Cal.App. 694, 702, 282 P. 429; see also Lloyd v. Murphy (1944), 25 Cal.2d 48, 55, 153 P.2d 47 ("laws or other governmental acts that make performance unprofitable or more difficult or expensive do not excuse the duty to perform a contractual obligation").)

Vernon points out undisputed evidence that both before and after the parties entered into the 1938 contract officials of Los Angeles were concerned with and attempting to arrange for financing and construction of new sewage disposal facilities; such evidence, it says, shows that Los Angeles at the time of the making of the contract recognized and assumed that risk of the possibility that it would have to build expensive new facilities. Such a conclusional finding is not impelled as a matter of law. It is reasonable to believe that what was in the contemplation of the parties when they negotiated the 1938 contract was not the radical development of the 1943 abatement action but the working out of past and then existing difficulties without expense running into many millions.

. . . . The findings, conclusions, and judgment herein . . . [determine] that conditions were such, by the time the [state abatement action] judgment was entered, that performance of the contracts had become impracticable.

. . . [T]he effect of the judgment herein is not to determine that when performance by one party became impracticable the contracts were altogether abrogated, regardless of what performances had already been rendered by either party. Such a determination would be incorrect. (See Ogren v. Inner Harbor Land Co. (1927), 83 Cal.App. 197, 199, 256 P. 607.) More accurately, the judgment determines that certain described "facilities and rights" created under the contracts (such as the gauging stations and relief sewer provided for by the 1938 contract) can and should be salvaged, and although the case was not tried in such a way that all obligations between the parties could be precisely adjusted by the judgment herein, such judgment expressly contemplates an adjustment of those obligations; it decrees that Vernon is liable to Los Angeles for any monetary obligations accrued under the contracts prior to the entry of judgment in the abatement action, "provided, however, that if all the benefits received by her from the City of Los Angeles under all said agreements prior to the entry of said judgment in said State Abatement Action have had a fair value less than the total payments made by her and those now owing to the City of Los Angeles, she, Vernon, shall be credited with such excess of payments over such value of benefits received."[3]

[The court rejected Vernon's remaining arguments.]

For the reasons above stated, the judgment is affirmed.

GIBSON, C. J., SPENCE, J., and BRAY, J. pro tem., concur.

CARTER, Justice (dissenting).

I dissent.

. . . I am [convinced] that the trial court erred . . . in concluding that Los Angeles is excused from performing its contractual obligations by reason of impossibility.

. . . [T]he mere fact that performance of a promise is made more difficult and expensive than the parties anticipated when the contract was made, will not excuse the promisor from his obligation to perform his part of the contract. Metzler v. Thye, 163 Cal. 95, 124 P. 721; Coulter v. Sausalito Bay Water Co., 122 Cal.App. 480, 10 P.2d 780; Williston on Contracts (Rev.Ed.), Vol. 6, § 1963;

---

[3] Concerning the subject of this declaration the court made the following statement in a memorandum opinion:

The case (for declaratory relief) was not tried by either side on a theory that required presentation of evidence which would have enabled the court to make a financial adjustment between the parties. Hence, the court presently can only suggest a program that seems to be just, doing so with the understanding that the parties are free to work out an amicable adjustment at variance with the court's suggestions. In any such adjustment Vernon, it seems, should be charged with all payments accrued under the composite agreement up to the entry of judgment in the State Abatement Action, and, if up to that time the benefits received by her under the agreements had a fair value less than the total cost to her, she should be credited with the difference.

Rest., Contracts, § 467. "Parties should be careful about making contracts, for once made the courts will not relieve them for light or trivial reasons. Public policy is subserved by leaving the parties and their rights to be measured by the terms of their engagements. California Cured Fruit Ass'n v. Stelling, 141 Cal. 713 (75 P. 320). They may have made an unfortunate arrangement, but when they have entered into it voluntarily, they are bound by it in the absence of equitable grounds for avoidance. Cook v. Snyder, 16 Cal.App.2d 587 (61 P.2d 53). They must be presumed to have contracted with reference to existing conditions known to them. Dore v. Southern Pac. Co., 163 Cal. 182 (124 P. 817). A person contracting with eyes open and aware of the facts is presumed to undertake performance at the risk of interference from agencies not expressly provided against. McCulloch v. Liguori, 88 Cal.App.2d 366 (199 P.2d 25). Moreover, contracting parties cannot escape performance of their undertakings because of unforeseen hardship. Metzler v. Thye, 163 Cal. 95 (124 P. 721)." (12 Cal.Jur.2d Contracts, §226.) . . . [L]aws or other governmental acts that make performance unprofitable or more difficult or expensive do not excuse the duty to perform a contractual obligation. . . . Lloyd v. Murphy, 25 Cal.2d 48, 153 P.2d 47; Sample v. Fresno Flume etc. Co., 129 Cal. 222, 61 P. 1085; Klauber v. San Diego St. Car Co., 95 Cal. 353, 30 P. 555.

Looking at the present factual situation, we note that a governmental act—the abatement action—has caused Los Angeles to make certain expenditures, and has made performance by Los Angeles of its contractual obligations more expensive. Applying the general rule to this factual situation, we would conclude that Los Angeles is not excused from performing its contractual obligations, and that Los Angeles therefore has no right to retain all of the payment made by Vernon under court order to help finance the construction of a facility whereby Los Angeles may legally perform its contractual obligation.

. . . .

The following characteristics should be particularly noted in regard to this defense of legal impossibility: First, it operates to excuse a non-performing obligor from liability for his failure to perform. Second, it operates only when performance of the obligor's part of the contract is impracticable. Third, the unanticipated expense which will render performance impracticable must be very much greater (in the Mineral Park case it was 10 or 12 times greater) than the expected or usual cost of performance. With these characteristics in mind, it is evident that the majority opinion has erred in supporting the trial court's judgment on the basis of legal impossibility.

Among the contractual obligations of Los Angeles, which the majority opinion says are excused, is a duty to accept at designated places, and to dispose of a specified quantity (up to 16 cubic feet per second) of sewage from Vernon. It should be noted that this duty was performed by Los Angeles up until the time of commencement of this action; it is presumably being performed by Los Angeles while this case is pending in the courts; and it will assuredly be performed in the future, after a decision is rendered in this case. It is obvious, then, that the doctrine of legal impossibility as here applied by the majority does not excuse an obligor from liability for failure to perform a contractual duty; instead that doctrine is employed by the majority to rewrite the contract between these parties. Los Angeles will continue to perform the services which it undertook to perform by this contract; Vernon will continue to dispose of its sewage at designated points on the Los Angeles outfall sewer; but Vernon, the obligee, will be required to pay more money, now and in the future, for this continuation of performance of the contractual obligations of Los Angeles.

I am aware of no prior decision of this or any other court in which the doctrine of legal impossibility has been applied to increase the consideration to be paid by the promisee while recognizing that the promisor will continue to perform as before. By the same token, I can find neither law nor logic to support a decision which terms "impracticable" or "impossible" of performance, a contract which both parties and this court recognize as having been performed and is expected to be performed for an indefinite period in the future. This situation comes as near approaching a legal paradox as any which has come under my observation.

As an additional matter, careful examination of the record in this case raises a question as to whether the cost of performing the contract, using the new facilities, is substantially disproportionate to the anticipated cost of performance. . . . The total sum which Vernon had paid up to the time of trial for the use of the facilities of the Los Angeles sewer system was $296,801.50, in addition to the granting of flowage rights through Vernon. . . . Los Angeles is required to build a new treatment plant and tube at a cost of about $41,000,000, and . . . operation and maintenance of these facilities will cost about $500,000 per year. . . .

. . . . Los Angeles is building a sewage disposal plant with capacity for 260 million gallons per day; . . . 10 million gallons per day of this capacity is allotted to Vernon. If the plant were designed and constructed without allotment of gallonage to Vernon, it would still have capacity for 250 million gallons per day. The increased cost of performing the contract is the difference in cost of construction between a 260 million gallon per day plant and a 250 million gallon per day plant. What this difference would be is impossible to determine from the record before us. . . . [H]owever, . . . the cost of construction would not increase in direct proportion to the increase in capacity; the structural differences between a 250 million gallon per day plant and a 260 million gallon per day plant would presumably be slight. It is clear, at any rate, that the increase in cost attributable to making the plant large enough to take care of Vernon's sewage, and thus the increased cost of performing the Vernon sewage contract, would not be 10 or 12 times as great as the approximately $300,000 which it would have cost to perform the contract if the abatement action had not intervened.

. . . .

In my opinion Los Angeles should be held to the terms of the contract which it made with Vernon. Vernon's contractual right to flow 11.7 cubic feet per second of sewage into the Los Angeles sewer system without further payment should be upheld. Vernon should have the further right to flow an additional 4.3 cubic feet per second of sewage into the Los Angeles sewer system, subject to payment of a proportionate share of the sewage disposal cost as provided in the contract. Los Angeles should be ordered to return to Vernon so much of the payment made by Vernon pursuant to the decree in the abatement action as is attributable to the 16 cubic feet per second flow which Los Angeles is contractually bound to accept.

For the reasons above stated I would reverse the judgment.

TRAYNOR, J., concurs.

Behind the Scenes

The City of Vernon is an industrial city of 5.2 square miles located several miles to the southeast of downtown Los Angeles in southern California. It has the smallest population of any incorporated city in California, with only 28 households; its 2010 population was 112. Vernon's website states that Vernon has more than 1,800 businesses that employ approximately 50,000 people. According to the Southern California Association of Governments, in 2011, Vernon had 39,412 jobs, including manufacturing (51%), wholesale (20%), retail (11%), and transportation-warehousing-utilities (7%). Its industrial sectors include food, agriculture, apparel, steel, plastics, logistics, and home furnishings.

Vernon was founded and incorporated in 1905 by ranchers James J. and Thomas J. Furlong and John B. Leonis. Recognizing the significance of the three major railroads running through the area, Leonis, a merchant, convinced railroad executives to run spur tracks off the main lines and incorporated the adjacent three miles as the first "exclusively industrial" city in the southwestern United States. After 1919, with the opening of two giant stockyards, meat packing quickly became the city's signature industry, with 27 slaughterhouses. In the 1920s and 30s, heavy industries such as steel (U.S. and Bethlehem), aluminum (ALCOA), glass (Owens), can-making (American Can), and automobile production (Studebaker) grew in Vernon. The 1940s and 1950s added aerospace contractors (Norris Industries); box and paper manufacturers; drug companies (Brunswig); and food processors (General Mills and Kal Kan). Giant meat packers (Farmer John and Swift) continued to grow. In 1932, after a dispute with Southern California Edison over industrial rates for electricity, Leonis orchestrated a Vernon bond measure to authorize the construction of the city's own light and power plant, which is still operational today. The city's businesses receive very low rates for water, electricity, gas, and fiber optics as a result of Vernon's independent utilities. In 2008, L.A. County Economic Development Corporation named Vernon as Los Angeles County's "Most Business Friendly City" for cities with fewer than 50,000 residents.

Vernon also has a history of corruption and public malfeasance. In 2006, after twenty-five years without a contested city council election, a bitter fight erupted in which the city contested the eligibility of three challengers, then refused to count ballots for six months. The incumbents won. Vernon's longtime mayor, Leonis Malburg, the grandson of Vernon's founder John Leonis, was convicted of voter fraud in 2009 after he and his wife falsely claimed a small apartment in Vernon as their legal residence, when in fact they were living in Hancock Park, an affluent Los Angeles neighborhood.

Two of Vernon's city administrators have also been involved in scandal. Bruce V. Malkenhorst pleaded guilty in May 2011 to misappropriating $60,000 in public funds and using the money for political contributions and various personal expenses such as golf, massages, a personal trainer, and a home security system. As part of his plea, Malkenhorst received three years of probation and was ordered to pay $35,000 in fines and penalties and $60,000 back to the City of Vernon in restitution. Malkenhorst, however, will still receive his annual pension of more than $500,000, because the California law states that only elected officials convicted of public corruption can have their pensions reduced or revoked; Malkenhorst was not an elected official.

Ironically, Malkenhorst's guilty plea came the same day the Vernon City Council approved a reform plan including pay cuts, term limits for council members, and salary caps for other officials. The council members, however, delayed the effective date of the pay cuts until the end of their terms. Until then, they will be paid about $70,000 a year for part-time work, through terms that last up to five years. At that point, future council members' pay will drop to $25,000. Additionally, Donal O'Callaghan, Vernon's former city administrator, faces public corruption charges for allegedly hiring his wife as a city contractor.

In response to Vernon's alleged public corruption, California State Assembly Speaker, John A. Perez, drafted a bill that would disband all cities with a population under 150; Vernon was the only city that would have been affected by the bill. In April 2011, the state Assembly overwhelmingly approved that bill. However, it was ultimately defeated in the Senate in August 2011.*

Do any of these facts influence your understanding of the *City of Vernon* case? How so? Should they?

§ 6.3. Force Majeure Clauses

The contract in *NIPSCO v. Carbon County Coal Co.* (page 1009) contained a force majeure clause: "The contract permits NIPSCO to stop taking delivery of coal 'for any cause beyond [its] reasonable control . . . including but not limited to . . . orders or acts of civil . . . authority . . . which wholly or partly prevent . . . the utilizing . . . of the coal.'"

Force majeure clauses specify how particular risks are allocated between the parties and may also help define how the excuse defense will be applied. Here are examples of two force majeure clauses:

This contract is subject to force majeure, and is contingent on strikes, accidents, acts of God, weather conditions, inability to secure labor, fire regulations or restrictions imposed by any government or governmental agency, or other delays beyond the control of the parties. If performance

---

* *Pérez Reveals New Details about Vernon Disincorporation Plan*, Los Angeles Times, June 17, 2011, available at http://latimesblogs.latimes.com/lanow/2011/06/perez-reveals-new-details-about-vernon-disincorportion-plan.html; Hector Becerra & Sam Allen, *Former Vernon Official Pleads Guilty to Illegally Using Public Money*, Los Angeles Times, May 27, 2011, available at http://articles.latimes.com/2011/may/27/local/la-me-05-26-vernon-20110527; *Bill to Dissolve Vernon Overwhelmingly Approved by State Assembly*, Los Angeles Times, Apr. 28, 2011; Adam Nagourney, *Plan Would Erase All Business Town*, New York Times, Mar. 2, 2011, at A12; www.cityofvernon.org/; www.scag.ca.gov/resources/pdfs/2011LP/LosAngeles/Vernon.pdf; http://en.wikipedia.org/wiki/Vernon,_California.

within the contract time is prevented by any cause of force majeure, then this contract shall be void without penalty to either party for any such portion not delivered.*

Lesser shall not be required to perform any covenant or obligation in this Lease, or be liable in damages to Lessee, so long as the performance or nonperformance of the covenant or obligation is delayed, caused or prevented by an act of God or force majeure. . . . An "act of God" or "force majeure" is defined for purposes of this Lease as strikes, lockouts, sit-downs, material or labor restrictions by any governmental authority, unusual transportation delays, riots, floods, washouts, explosions, earthquakes, fire, storms, weather (including wet grounds or inclement weather which prevents construction), acts of the public enemy, wars, insurrections and any other cause not reasonably within the control of Lessor and which by the exercise of due diligence Lessor is unable, wholly or in part, to prevent or overcome.**

A well drafted clause may serve one or more of the following functions:

- Specifying and clarifying aspects of the excuse doctrine:
  - which events the parties assume will not occur and why those non-occurrences are basic assumptions on which the contract is made,
  - payor's principal purpose (relevant for frustration of purpose),
  - which risks are allocated to one of the parties, and
  - how much difficulty of performance is necessary to find impracticability.
- Adding events that can serve as excuses (for instance, strikes, economic downturns, technology failures, etc.).
- "Contracting out" of the default rules on excuse.

Unfortunately many force majeure clauses are dropped into contracts without much thought, often as boilerplate. These clauses often purport to excuse both parties for nonperformance due to acts of God, war, earthquake, hurricane, pestilence, and other events beyond the control of the parties, but only the performing party (the payee) is often excused because the listed events will not impede the payor's ability to pay. It is important for the payor, who is often unexcused under such a clause, to consider carefully the risks and burdens being shouldered before agreeing to any broadly worded force majeure clause.

For More Information

For analysis of force majeure clauses, a drafting checklist, and a template clause, see P.J.M Declercq, *Modern Analysis of the Legal Effect of Force Majeure Clauses in Situations of Commercial Impracticability* 15 J.L. & Comm. 213 (1995).

---

* 5 *Williston on Contracts 4th Forms* § 77F:3 (4th ed. 2012).
** 4A *Florida Jur. Forms Legal & Bus.* § 16A:320 (2012).

§ 6.4. When *Do* Courts Grant Excuse?

Adbar, *Transatlantic* (and the other Suez cases), and *NIPSCO* are typical in denying relief based on impracticability or impossibility. *Taylor*, *Krell*, *Unke*, and *City of Vernon* illustrate the occasional but rare ruling in favor of relief. Analyzing why certain cases have been successful may help parties draft contracts and litigate disputes when the unexpected happens. One cluster of successful cases involved health and safety concerns:

- *Northern Corp. v. Chugach Elec. Assn.*, 518 P.2d 76 (Alaska 1974) (duty to supply rock across lake discharged when unsafe ice conditions made it dangerous to haul rock across lake and this was the means of delivery "contemplated" by the parties).
- *Lakeman v. Pollard*, 43 Me. 463 (1857) (mill employee "was under no obligation to imperil his life by remaining at work in the vicinity of a [cholera] epidemic . . . nor does it make any difference that the men who remained there at work after [he] left were healthy, and continued to be so").
- *Hanford v. Connecticut Fair Assn.*, 103 A. 838 (1918) (party excused from putting on baby show by apprehension of danger to babies from epidemic of infantile paralysis).
- *The Kronprinzessin Cecilie*, 244 U.S. 12 (1917) (owner of German steamship excused from completing voyage from US to England by apprehension on eve of WWI that she would be seized as prize).

An unusual pair of successful cases involved huge increases in the cost of performance, even though usually a large cost increase alone will not be grounds for excuse:

- *Florida Power & Light Co. v. Westinghouse Elec. Corp.* 826 F.2d 239 (4th Cir. 1987) (difference in cost of disposing of spent fuel is "percentages in the hundreds range" and use of alternative method would not only "wipe out the expected profit but [result] in a loss some four or five times the expected profit").
- *Mineral Park Land Co. v. Howard*, 156 P. 458 (1916) (excavator could take no further earth and gravel by "ordinary means" and "any greater amount could have been taken only at a prohibitive cost, that is, at an expense of ten or twelve times as much as the usual cost per yard").

In yet another pair of successful cases, the subject matter or purpose of the contract ceased to exist:

- *Alabama Football, Inc. v. Wright,* 452 F. Supp. 182 (N.D. Tex. 1977) (the unexpected and unplanned-for financial failure of the World Football League and Alabama Football rendered it impossible for Alabama Football to provide a team position for Wright, excusing both parties from their remaining duties under the contract).
- *Aluminum Company of America v. Essex Group, Inc.,* 499 F. Supp. 53 (W.D. Pa. 1980) (ALCOA's unexpected and huge increase in production costs excused its non-performance in conversion of alumina to molten aluminum, because performance became impracticable and because ALCOA's purpose ("an expected profit") was frustrated by the resulting extraordinary losses.

Aluminum Company of America is an oddity in the application of the excuse doctrine and has remained a controversial case among legal scholars. Some even view the court's reasoning as a misuse of the mistake doctrine because it allowed relief for mistake related to future occurrences. *See, e.g.,* E. Allan Farnsworth, *Farnsworth on Contracts* § 9.7 n.14 (3d ed. 2004).

Frustration of purpose has been an even more difficult excuse to obtain. Not all jurisdictions recognize the defense. In the jurisdictions that do, courts have required the party's "principal purpose" (viewed broadly) to be frustrated nearly completely. If the subject of the contract can be used in some other way, albeit not as profitably or even at a loss, the excuse is often denied. Probably the most commonly discussed case is *Lloyd v. Murphy,* 153 P.2d 47 (Cal. 1944), which was cited in *City of Vernon* by both the majority and the dissent, in which a car dealer sought to be released from his payment obligations under a five-year commercial lease created shortly before the United States entered World War II. The lease limited use of the property to selling new cars and operating a gas station and forbade subletting except with lessor's permission. The government subsequently severely restricted sales of new cars, and the lessee vacated the property, even though lessor offered to waive the use restrictions, lower the rent, and allow subletting. The court noted that "the applicability of the doctrine of frustration depends on the total or nearly total destruction of the purpose for which, in the contemplation of both parties, the transaction was entered into," *id.* at 50, and found no such destruction where the leased property was on a main traffic route in Los Angeles (Wilshire Bldv. in Beverly Hills), making it usable for other purposes. Moreover, the court found that the lessee had assumed the risk of the wartime restrictions on new car sales, because the regulations were widely foreseen:

At the time the lease in the present case was executed the National Defense Act, . . . authorizing the President to allocate materials and mobilize industry for national defense, had been law for more than a year. The automotive industry was in the process of conversion to supply the needs of our growing mechanized army and to meet lend-lease commitments. Iceland and Greenland had been occupied by the army. Automobile sales were soaring because the public anticipated that production would soon be restricted. These facts were commonly known and it cannot be said that the risk of war and its consequences necessitating restriction of the production and sale of automobiles was so remote a contingency that its risk could not be foreseen by defendant, an experienced automobile dealer. Indeed, the conditions prevailing at the time the lease was executed, and the absence of any provision in the lease contracting against the effect of war, gives rise to the inference that the risk was assumed.

Id. at 51.

––––––––––––

Problems: Impracticability

8-9. Ben is a freelance delivery driver who contracts with Callie, a horticulturist, to ship a load of tropical plants from Florida to the upper peninsula of Michigan, in January. The trailer is well insulated but poorly heated, so Ben must make the trip as quickly as possible. The written contract states that Ben "shall make the absolute minimum of stops en route to the delivery site." However, as Ben reaches southern Michigan, he encounters a severe blizzard, which reduces visibility to less than 100 feet. Snow begins to accumulate faster than plows can remove it from the highway, and crosswinds gust at 20 to 30 miles per hour.

Ben typically drives routes in the South, but he has encountered blizzards before. He debates whether or not he is capable of completing his route without stopping and waiting for the blizzard to pass. If Ben stops, the plants are likely to freeze and die. Ben finally decides that the trip may be possible, but the safety risk that he would incur by continuing is too great. Ben stops, and as expected, all of the plants die.

If Callie brings a claim for breach of contract, can Ben successfully raise the defense of impracticability? Consider arguments for both sides.

8-10. In 1979, the Vikings professional football team signed a lease with the Commission that administered the Metrodome, a domed sports stadium, to play in the Metrodome through the 2011-12 football season. Included in the lease was the following clause:

> In the event of total or partial destruction rendering the Stadium not suitable for playing home games or of a valid governmental order prohibiting use of the Stadium for home games, this Agreement will be suspended immediately as to playing home games until the governmental order ceases to prohibit use for home games or the Stadium is repaired.
>
> The Commission shall notify the Team within ninety days from the date the Stadium is no longer suitable for playing home games, whether the Commission will rebuild or repair the Stadium. If the Commission decides to rebuild or repair the Stadium, this Agreement will continue to be suspended until the Stadium is suitable for playing home games; and the Commission shall notify the Team of the Commission's best estimate of when the Stadium will be suitable for playing home games again.
>
> For each football season, or part of football season, while this Agreement is suspended, the term of this Agreement as provided in section 3 shall be extended by one football season.

Before the roof collapse, the Vikings had been lobbying to get a new stadium built, while considering whether to move to a different city. The Commission argued that, under the above clause, the Vikings were bound to an additional year's lease on the stadium, even though only two of ten games had been affected by the torn roof. The Commission replaced the original roof with a stronger, more expensive roof (with some unknown amount of reimbursement from its insurance), even though the stadium might be used for only another 2-3 years, depending on the shifting politics of state funding and the worst economy since the Great Depression of the 1930s.

Now fast forward and put yourself in the shoes of counsel for the Vikings and the Commission, as they negotiate a 30-year lease for a new stadium, to be built on the Metrodome site in 2013-14. Assume that the previous lease language is the starting point for their negotiations, and construct arguments *for each side* as to how to edit or redraft the above clause. Be sure you look for counter-arguments to your arguments from the other side. Limit your efforts to the scope of the 1979 clause.

8-11. In July 1972, Exoshale Corporation and ChemX Industries (both companies are based in the U.S.) entered into a contract for Exoshale to supply ChemX with "Spirits Grade Ethanol" for three years. The price would be adjusted at the beginning of each year of the contract to reflect changes in Exoshale's production cost, as specified in the following formula:

> The contract price of $.2450 per gallon shall be adjusted by four-tenths of one cent ($.004) per gallon for each one-tenth of one cent ($.001) per pound increase or decrease from the "base value" in the average of Seller's Standard Cost for Ethylene [a major ingredient] used in the manufacture of Ethanol at its Texas City, Texas plant during the calendar year immediately preceding the then current calendar year.

> - The "base value" referred to above shall be the average of Seller's Standard Cost for Ethylene used in the production of Ethanol at its Texas City, Texas plant during the calendar year 1972.
> - "Seller's Standard Cost for Ethylene" shall mean the charge Exoshale makes to all of its Gulf Coast internal consumers for Gulf-Coast-produced Ethylene.

> In no event, however, shall the amount of said increase in the contract price . . . cause the price . . . to exceed the price listed below:

> During the calendar year 1974 .... $.2550 per gallon
> During the calendar year 1975 .... $.2650 per gallon
> During the calendar year 1976 .... $.2750 per gallon
> During the calendar year 1977 .... $.2850 per gallon

The contract also contained the following clause:

> Neither party shall be liable for its failure to perform hereunder if said performance is made impracticable due to any occurrence beyond its reasonable control, including

acts of God, fires, floods, wars, sabotage, accidents, labor disputes or shortages, governmental laws, ordinances, rules and regulations, inability to obtain material, equipment or transportation, and any other similar or different occurrence. The party whose performance is made impracticable by any such occurrence shall have the right to omit during the period of such occurrence all or any portion of the quantity deliverable during such period.

War broke out in the Middle East in 1973, and the Arab Oil Embargo* forced gasoline prices to record levels. In July 1974, Exoshale asked ChemX to agree to amend the contract to remove the price ceilings from the Ethylene price escalator provision quoted above. When ChemX refused, Exoshale said it would cease supplying Ethanol unless ChemX agreed to the proposed changes. ChemX brought an action for specific performance to compel Exoshale to perform the contract. Exoshale claimed excuse on the basis of impracticability.

Among the evidence produced by the parties:

- Exoshale's experts testified that the price ceiling for 1974 was based upon their forecast that the ethylene price for 1974 would be $.0375 a pound, but by July 1974 the price had risen to $.07 a pound. As a result, defendant's cost per gallon of ethanol rose from $.212 a gallon in 1973 to $.372 a gallon by the middle of 1974. Confronted with a price fixed at $.255 per gallon for 1974, defendant was losing over $.10 a gallon when it refused to continue performance. If forced to complete performance under the present contract, Exoshale would suffer an aggregate loss of over $5.8 million.
- ChemX introduced evidence that in 1971, the oil-producing nations joined together to effect a 25% price increase and that another Arab Oil Embargo had occurred in 1968, although the earlier embargo had little effect on oil prices in the United States because of lack of solidarity among the oil producers.

---

* The Arab Oil Embargo led many disadvantaged parties to raise the excuse of impracticability. For additional information about the Arab Oil Embargo, go to http://en.wikipedia.org/wiki/Arab_Oil_Embargo.

Which impracticability rule(s) from this unit govern this dispute? What kind of alleged impracticability is involved here? What arguments should Exoshale raise to establish the elements of its claimed defense of impracticability? What arguments should ChemX make to defeat or limit the defense? Can Exoshale meet ChemX's arguments? Consider how your reasoning is affected by the details of how the parties jointly drafted the contract, the pricing structure and "caps," and the force majeure clause. How would a court rule on this issue?

CHAPTER 9

Remedies

What kind of promises will the law enforce?

How do parties demonstrate assent to a contract?

What defenses to enforcement exist?

Is a writing required for enforcement? If so, what kind?

How is the content of a contract ascertained?

What are parties' rights and duties after breach?

What situations lead to excusing contract performance?

What remedies are available for breach of contract?

What contractual rights and duties do non-parties to a contract have?

§ 1. Overview

After a breach, the aggrieved party is entitled to seek remedies against the breaching party. These remedies may be "at law" (money damages) or "in equity" (court orders to perform, or to act or refrain from acting in specific ways). Historically, courts have preferred to award damages rather than to order equitable (often called "extraordinary") relief. As noted in Chapter 3 (page 162) parties had access to the old English courts of chancery only if they could not be made whole by an award of damages from a court of law (King's Bench or Queen's Bench). Most U.S. courts now combine the courts of law and equity, while retaining the limitation that equitable relief is unavailable. The aggrieved party has "no adequate remedy at law." Some jurisdictions also require the aggrieved party to prove that it would suffer "irreparable harm" if the equitable remedy were not granted. Courts' preference for damage awards is also grounded in hesitation to have the court become involved in administering or supervising a remedy, often necessary with equitable forms of relief.

This chapter begins with the preferred remedies at law, followed by equitable remedies. The chart below shows the organization of the chapter and its coverage of the kinds of remedies:

[handwritten margin note: monetary damages are prefered]

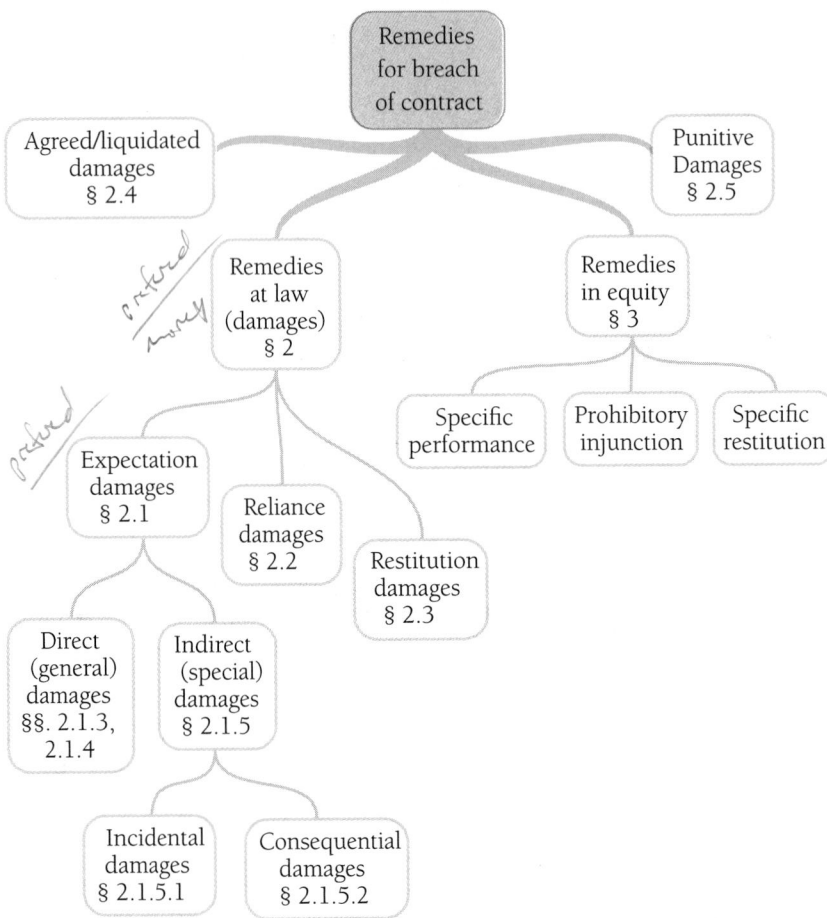

§ 2. Remedies at Law (Damages)

Students often expect that damages will be computed from a collection of formulas, but determining the appropriate damages is more dependent on understanding the purposes and policies served by damage awards and their limitations than it is on any mathematical construct.

Policy	Corollary/competing policy
Award only those damages caused by the breach.	Do not award damages for injuries that the aggrieved party could have avoided/prevented/mitigated (because they were not caused by the breaching party).
Avoid over-compensation, windfalls, and double recovery.	Avoid under-compensation, forfeitures, and penalties.
Avoid speculative damages.	Avoid letting the breaching party profit from the uncertainty caused by the breach, even if the measure of damages is somewhat uncertain, and resolve uncertainties in favor of the aggrieved party to ensure adequate compensation.
Award consequential damages for injury foreseeable to breaching party at time of contract formation	Avoid burdening the breaching party with damages the risk of which was not reasonably contemplated when deciding whether to enter into the agreement.

Sometimes all of these policies can be satisfied when determining a damage award. Other times—particularly when the contract performances are complicated and the interrelationships complex—it will be necessary to balance policy goals to select the appropriate damage award. As you read the cases on damages in this chapter, note when the courts invoke (or could invoke) these policies in supporting their damage determinations.

Recall from the introduction to damages in Chapter 3 (page 148) that there are three kinds of recovery, and hence three ways of computing damages for breach of contract:

- "Expectation damages" are designed to put the aggrieved party into the position that it would have been in if it had received the full performance promised (and had fully performed its own part of the bargain). Expectation damages make the plaintiff whole by paying the amount necessary to approximate the value of full performance.
- "Reliance damages" are designed to put the aggrieved party back in the position that it would have been in *today* if the parties had not entered the contract. Reliance damages compensate the out-of-pocket expenses incurred by the aggrieved party in reliance on the existence of the contract, as well as opportunities the aggrieved party let pass in reliance on the contract ("lost opportunity costs").
- "Restitution damages" are designed to avoid unjust enrichment of a party by forcing that party to restore ("disgorge") to the other party any as-yet-unpaid-for benefits it retained.

Expectation damages are the preferred form of damages, on the theory that full compensation should mean giving the aggrieved party the "benefit of the bargain." To do anything else does not seem to be truly enforcing the contract. But if expectation damages are inadequate or too speculative or do not otherwise fulfill the policies noted on page 1043, courts will consider reliance or restitution damages. Most often, reliance damages provide a higher damage award and are more compensatory than restitution damages, so reliance damages will be preferred over restitutionary relief, but the critical inquiry is to ask which measure best fulfills the policies underlying damage awards.

You will recall that, for claims based on promissory estoppel, Restatement (Second) § 90 (page 154) invites courts to limit the remedy for breach of promise "as justice requires." That standard suggests that in such cases courts might award reliance damages instead of expectation because the claim itself is grounded in acts of reliance. In fact, many courts operating under Restatement (Second) § 90 nevertheless elect to award expectation damages, concluding that the recipient of such promises are entitled to the benefit of what was promised, even though there is often no "bargain" to be enforced. Courts operating under the first Restatement provision also typically award expectation damages, when that is possible.

If liability is based on restitution (recall the cases in Chapter 3, pages 181 and 202), the courts will award restitution damages.

§ 2.1. Expectation Damages

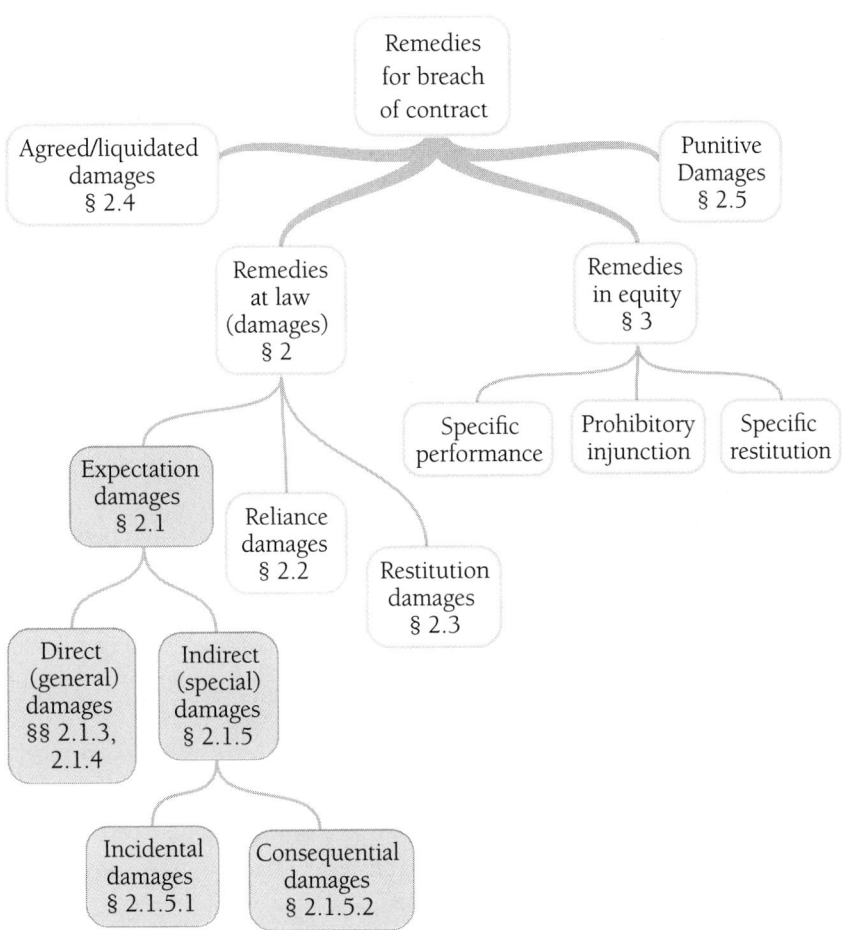

§ 2.1.1. Categories of Expectation Damages

Expectation damages include "direct" (also known as "general") damages and "indirect" (also known as "specific") damages:

- Direct damages are the amounts awarded for injury to or loss of the value of the performance promised in the contract. It measures the difference between the value of full performance and the value of performance actually received. For example, direct damages would compensate for the value of services not performed, purchased real estate or rental property not conveyed, payments not made, or a defect in the goods or services.

- Indirect damages are the amounts awarded for other secondary losses resulting from the breach. They are classified as "incidental damages" or "consequential damages."
  - ◊ Incidental damages are extra costs incurred by the aggrieved party in dealing with the breach or mitigating losses from the breach, for example, by handling a defective delivery or arranging for purchase of substitute goods. Incidental damages might include costs incurred in storing or reshipping or reselling defective or repudiated goods, paying a broker to find a substitute buyer, boarding up and paying extra insurance on a building left unfinished by a vendor, or spending employee time negotiating a replacement contract with a new party.
  - ◊ Consequential damages are other losses arising as a consequence of the breach. They may include such items as lost profits, lost customers, lost business volume, and downstream breaches caused by the original breach.

[handwritten margin note: not always recoverable]

Consider a simple dispute: Suppose that a professional freelance photographer purchases a digital camera for $1500 and spends $5000 to travel to Thailand to take pictures for a magazine spread on which she would earn $8000 profit. The camera malfunctions on the trip (unbeknownst to her until she returns), and all of the pictures are lost. Even the photo files on the back-up flash drive are corrupted and cannot be recovered. Repairs to the camera will cost $600, plus $20 in shipping the insured camera back to the manufacturer. How will the photographer's damages be characterized?

[handwritten margin note: repair or new]

- Direct damages: The cost of repairing ($600) or replacing ($1500) the defective camera (she was promised a working camera, so the direct damages are the cost of making sure she gets one)
- Incidental damages: The cost of investigating the options for repairing or repurchasing (unknown cost), and the cost of driving to the repair shop (de minimis cost) or shipping the camera to the manufacturer ($20)
- Consequential damages: The lost profit on the magazine spread ($8000) and the reputational injury (perhaps speculative); or the cost of returning to Thailand to re-take the pictures ($5,000)

This example demonstrates how various damage amounts are characterized and therefore under which set of damages rules they are evaluated. Categorizing the damage awards does not mean they are all recoverable. As you will see in the material that follows, direct and incidental damages (if proved with sufficient certainty) are generally recoverable, but there are additional limits placed on the award of consequential damages. Moreover, the contract terms may limit recovery (e.g., the seller of the camera is likely to have barred or limited consequential damages, to limit its exposure to what is likely to be the most expensive injury that might be caused by a breach).

§ 2.1.2. Thinking Sensibly About Expectation Damages

The goal of expectation damages is to put the aggrieved party in the position it would have been in if both parties had fully performed. That means ensuring the aggrieved party receives the value of the performance promised, reduced by the costs and expenses the aggrieved party would have "spent" in performing its own promises. Courts awarding expectation damages seek to "make whole" the aggrieved party, without giving a windfall or awarding speculative damages. Professor Farnsworth suggests a helpful formulation for categorizing and computing expectation damages,* used with slight modifications and additional explanations in the chart below:

Traditional Formula	Explanation
+ Direct Loss	Difference in value between what was promised and what was received ("direct" or "general" damages)
+ Extra loss	Additional costs and losses caused by the breach and mitigating the breach ("indirect" or "special" damages: incidental and consequential damages)
- Cost avoided	Expenses that the aggrieved party did not incur because performance stopped early
- Loss avoided	Losses that the aggrieved party would have suffered but was able to prevent/avoid because of its own mitigation efforts or other circumstances

The UNIDROIT Principles use a similar formulation:

UNIDROIT Art. 7.4.2. **Full Compensation**

(1) The aggrieved party is entitled to full compensation for harm sustained as a result of the non-performance. Such harm includes both any loss which it suffered and any gain of which it was deprived, taking into account any gain to the aggrieved party resulting from its avoidance of cost or harm.

(2) . . . .

This formulation is helpful as you begin to think about identifying and categorizing damages for breach of contract, making clear that you must account for the lost expectation from the other party's failure to perform and other losses that may be caused by the breach, while not compensating for costs and losses that were or could havee been avoided. But the identification and computation of damages is not formulaic, and courts and advocates approach damage calculation

---

* E. Allan Farnsworth, *Contracts* § 12.9 (4th ed. 2004).

in whatever way best measures the injury suffered in a particular case, using the policies described in the chart on page 1043. What is important is to think clearly and methodically about the circumstances following a breach, comparing the economic circumstances of the aggrieved party after breach with the economic circumstances it would have been in if the contract had been performed, and attempting to categorize and quantify each injury.

Problems: Determining Expectation Damages

In the following problems,* identify the damages that should be awarded to compensate the aggrieved party fully for the injury caused, attempting to put that party in the position it would have been in if the contract had been fully performed. Use the general formula above if you find it helpful, but do not feel constrained by it. If you can find an alternative way of computing damages that accommodates the policies described above, feel free to break away from the traditional formula and use your own common sense to fashion a measure. Some of the issues you are likely to identify in these problems are explored in subsequent sections.

9-1.   Case #1: What damages for the aggrieved Employee?

Handwritten margin note:
$100,000 - 25,000 = 75,000$
$+ 1,000$
$- 45,000$
$\overline{31,000}$

- Employer and Employee enter into two-year contract for $50,000/year
- *Employer wrongfully discharges Employee after six months*
- Employee unsuccessfully looks for work for three months
- Employee hires employment agency for $1000
- After three more months (six months total out of work), Employee finds new job at $45,000/year

9-2.   Should the result in Case #1 change if the Employee stopped looking for work? If she had declined to take the $45,000 job, should she be able to collect her whole salary as damages? If the only job she could find was temporary work at a fast food *[handwritten: no]* restaurant for minimum wage and she refused, should she collect her whole lost salary as damages?

9-3.   Case #2: What damages for the aggrieved Employer?

- Employer and Employee enter into two-year contract for $50,000/year

———————————————————————
* These problems are based, with some variation, on examples used by Farnsworth to illustrate his fomula for computing expectation damages. *See id.*

- *Employee wrongfully quits after six months*
- For three months, the position remains vacant while Employer advertises the position.
- Having had no success in finding a suitable new hire, Employer pays employment agency $2000 to conduct search
- Employer pays $30,000 for temporary worker for three months
- After three more months (six months total after Employee quit), Employer hires permanent employee at $55,000/year

9-4. Case #3: What damages for the aggrieved Builder?

- Builder and Owner contract for new house to be built for $200,000
- Total cost of construction estimated to be $180,000
- Value of house if completed: $225,000
- *Owner breaches by repudiating contract when construction half-completed*
- Owner has paid Builder $70,000
- Builder has spent $95,000 on labor and materials
- Builder resells materials for $10,000

9-5. Case #4: What damages for the aggrieved Owner?

- Builder and Owner contract for new house to be built for $200,000
- Total cost of construction estimated to be $180,000
- Value of house if completed: $225,000
- *Builder breaches by walking off job when construction half-completed*
- Value of house as partially constructed: $50,000
- Owner has paid Builder $70,000
- Builder has spent $95,000 on labor and materials
- Builder resells materials for $10,000
- Owner hires another contractor to finish the job for $150,000 (what if it was $300,000?)

9-6. Consider again Case #4 but assume that the Owner had so far paid the Builder nothing. Should the breaching Builder be entitled to damages? How might they be measured?

> ### Think About It!
>
> In the preceding problems, Case #4 posits a value for the house as completed and for the structure as partially built. How would each of those values be measured? What kinds of evidence might a party submit to establish them?

§ 2.1.3. Measuring Typical Direct Damages

If a case involves a *breach by a buyer/recipient* of goods or services, the seller/supplier who is left with the goods or with excess service capacity often sells the item or service to another party.

- If the replacement contract price is *lower* than the original (breached) contract price, then the seller/supplier's direct damages are typically measured by the difference between those two contract prices, as long as the resale is made reasonably (e.g., at a reasonable price under the circumstances, in a reasonable setting, and within a reasonable time after the default).

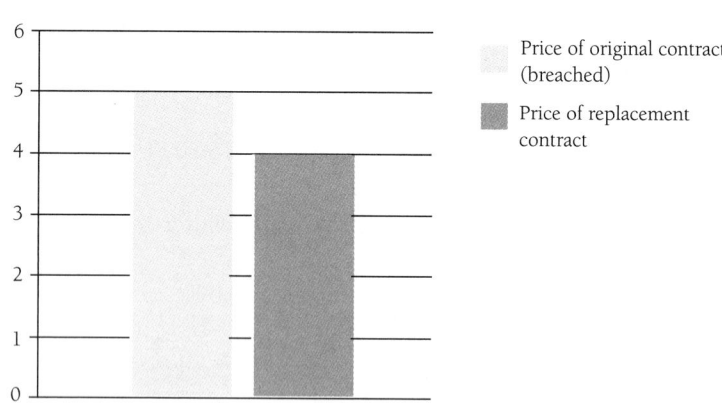

Price of original contract (breached)

Price of replacement contract

- If the replacement contract price is *higher* than the original (breached) contract price, the seller/supplier has no direct damages, but might still be able to recover indirect damages, if any.
- If the seller/supplier does not enter into a replacement contract, the market price for the promised goods or services (if a market exists) can fulfill the same function as the replacement contract price. The direct damages measure will be how much the market price is below the contract price, if at all.

To ascertain the market price, you need to know the time and place at which the market should be measured, and there might even be a dispute about which market provides an appropriate measure. UCC Article 2 and other rules govern the choice of the appropriate time and place. For goods, UCC § 2-708(1) specifies using the market price at the time and place at which the seller was to tender the goods to the buyer under the contract. The common law has similar rules.*

If a case involves *breach by a seller/supplier*, the buyer/recipient often enters a replacement contract to obtain the goods or services not supplied, or supplied defectively, by the breaching party. The re-purchase is often called a "cover" purchase.

- If the replacement contract price is *higher* than the original (breached) contract price, then the buyer/recipient's direct damages are typically measured by the difference between those two contract prices, as long as the cover is made reasonably (e.g., at a reasonable price under the circumstances, within a reasonable time after the default, for comparable goods or services).

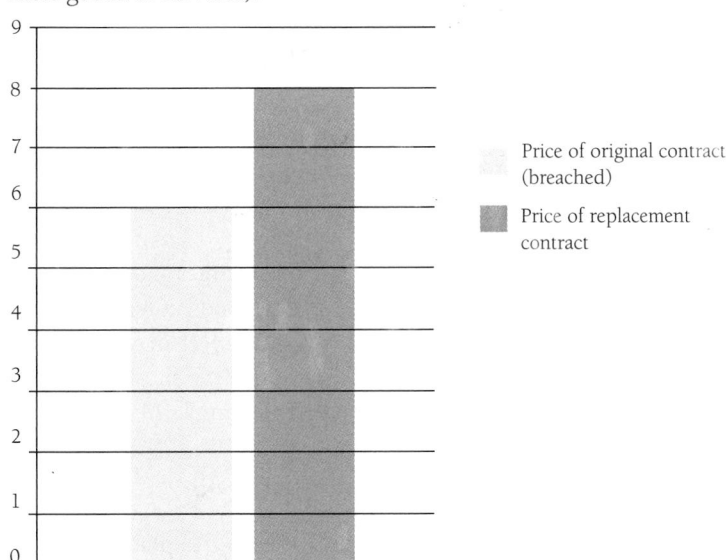

Price of original contract (breached)

Price of replacement contract

- If the price of the replacement contract is *lower* than the price of the original (breached) contract, then the buyer/recipient has no direct damages, but might still be able to recover indirect damages, if any.

---

* E. Allan Farnsworth, *Contracts* § 12.12 (4th ed. 2004).

- If the buyer/recipient does not obtain cover, the market price for the promised goods or services (if a market exists) can fulfill the same function as the replacement contract price. The direct damages measure will be how much the market price exceeds the contract price, if at all.

For goods, UCC § 2-713(1) specifies using the market price at the time when the buyer learned of the breach. If the seller has repudiated or failed to perform, the market price is at the place where the seller was supposed to have tendered the goods (often to a carrier, for delivery). If the seller has tendered defective goods or otherwise breached, the market price is at the place where the goods arrive. The common law has similar rules.*

Think About It!

Notice that the contract price is subtracted from the buyer/recipient's cover or market price, while the seller/supplier's resale or market price is subtracted from the contract price. Why does that reciprocal relationship make sense?

The international provisions cover buyer's and seller's replacement contracts together:

CISG Art. 75 **(in Ch. V. Provisions Common to the Obligations of the Seller and of the Buyer, Sec. II. Damages)**

If the contract is avoided and if, in a reasonable manner and within a reasonable time after avoidance, the buyer has bought goods in replacement or the seller has resold the goods, the party claiming damages may recover the difference between the contract price and the price in the substitute transaction as well as any further damages recoverable under article 74.

———————

UNIDROIT Art. 7.4.5. **Proof of Harm in Case of Replacement Transaction**

Where the aggrieved party has terminated the contract and has made a replacement transaction within a reasonable time and in a reasonable manner it may recover the difference between the contract price and the price of the replacement transaction as well as damages for any further harm.

---

* E. Allan Farnsworth, *Contracts* § 12.12 (4th ed. 2004).

Reading the Law Critically: *Sackett*

The first part of this case, establishing the buyer's total breach, appears in Chapter 8 (page 916). The third part, on mitigation of damages appears later in this chapter, on page 1126.

1. What alternative measures of damages does the court suggest? What alternative does it adopt, and why?

2. The court says that the usual measure of damages is the difference between market price and contract price. Other courts use the difference between contract price and resale (or cover) price as the default. In some jurisdictions, the aggrieved party has a choice between the two. Which do you think is the better rule?

Sackett v. Spindler

SHELDON SACKETT, Plaintiff, Cross-Defendant and Appellant

v.

PAUL R. SPINDLER, Defendant, Cross-Complainant and Respondent

California Court of Appeal

56 Cal. Rptr. 435 (Ct. App. 1967)

[The parties entered into an $85,000 purchase agreement for a majority of the shares of S & S Newspapers. The buyer (plaintiff) made the first payment for $6000 on time, the second payment for $20,000 a week late and $200 short, and the third payment of $59,000 with a check that bounced. Despite several offers to cure, the buyer never paid the remaining balance. The seller eventually canceled the contract and sought another buyer. He finally sold the stock nearly a year later for a net payment of $20,680. The parties sued each other for breach. The court found that buyer/plaintiff had committed a total material breach, after which seller/defendant was entitled to cancel the contract and was therefore not in breach for doing so.]

Measure of Damages

As revealed in the findings of fact in the instant case, the $34,575.74 award of damages to Spindler was calculated by subtracting from the $85,000 contract price all sums of money received by him from Sackett ($29,744.26) and Spindler's net proceeds from his subsequent sale of the stock in July 1962 ($20,680). Sackett contends that the trial court erred in measuring damages by the difference between the contract price for the stock and the price at which Spindler ultimately resold the stock to a third party and that the proper measure of damages in the instant case should instead have been the difference between the price which Sackett agreed to pay for the stock and its value at the date of the breach. In addition, Sackett argues that even assuming the trial court used the correct measure of damages it erred in its computation of damages under this measure. In this regard he contends that since, under his contract with Spindler, he not only agreed to pay Spindler $85,000 but also agreed to assume the liabilities of the newspaper, which at the time of the agreement amounted to $201,849.33, and since under Spindler's sale of the stock in 1962 the buyer was also to assume the newspaper's liabilities, which at that time were approximately $219,844.63, the increase in liabilities during this interval, i.e., $17,995.30, constituted "gross income" to Spindler and "should have been deducted from the judgment as money which had been received by the seller." We concern ourselves initially with the question of what measure of damages was appropriate in the instant case.

. . . .

[**Cuthill v. Peabody** (1912), 125 P. 926] . . . was an action by the vendor of shares of stock against the vendee to recover the purchase price of the stock, which the vendee had contracted to purchase. In considering whether such a remedy was available to the vendee, the appellate court applied to sales of corporate stock the provisions of the Civil Code and rules of law in cases dealing with personal property, as those rules existed before the adoption of the Sales Act. Based upon those principles, the court in Cuthill concluded that since the title to the stock had passed, the vendor could sue for the purchase price. However, in its opinion, the court, articulated the rule that where title to corporate stock has not passed, the vendor, upon the refusal of the vendee to accept the stock and pay the agreed price therefor, cannot sue for the purchase price but is compelled to recoup his loss, if any, solely by an action for damages founded upon a breach of the vendee's contract to accept and pay for the property. (125 P. 926.) In this regard, Cuthill noted that the applicable remedy, under the general rule, is that "[T]he vendor may treat and keep the property as his own, and recover from the vendee the difference between the contract price and the market price at the time and place of delivery." (125 P. 928.)

. . . .

It is the general rule, both under the Uniform Sales Act and apart from it, that where the title to goods has not passed to the buyer and the seller has the property in his possession or under his control, the measure of damages upon the buyer's refusal to accept and pay for goods for which there is an available market is, in the absence of special circumstances, the difference between the contract price and the market or current price or value at the time and the place where the goods ought to have been delivered and accepted, or, if no time is fixed for acceptance, then at the time of the refusal to accept. (78 C.J.S. Sales § 478, p. 137; see Southern Pacific Milling Co. v. Billiwhack etc. Farm (1942) 50 Cal.App.2d 79, 87, 122 P.2d 650.) As used in this measure, the words "market price" and "market value" mean the same thing, that is, the price or value of the article as established or shown by sales in the way of ordinary business; the price at which goods are freely offered in the market to all the world. (Southern Pacific Milling Co. v. Billiwhack, etc. Farm, supra, p. 88, 122 P.2d 650; Kings County Packing Co. v. Sunland Sales etc. Assn. (1929) 100 Cal.App. 126, 133, 279 P. 1036 . . . .)

The above-stated measure of damages, however, does not ordinarily apply when there is no market available at the time and place of performance. In such cases resort may be had to the market value of the goods at the nearest available market; and in the absence of an available market, it has been held that the measure of damages may be the difference between the contract price and the value of the goods as best as can be ascertained, or the difference between the contract price and the best offer that can be obtained for the goods, or the difference between the contract price and the price obtained on a resale, or the actual damages naturally and directly resulting from the buyer's

Think About It!

Notice the wide range of sources from which the court is drawing rules of law for this damages measure, including the repealed Uniform Sales Act and its successor, UCC Article 2 (here cited as "Comm. Code § 2708"). Which body of law governs this dispute? Which other bodies of law provide useful analogies and policies?

breach. (78 C.J.S., supra, § 478(c) and cases cited; and see Los Angeles Coin-O-Matic Laundries v. Harow, 195 Cal.App.2d 324, 331-335, 15 Cal.Rptr. 693; and see subd. 2 of former § 1784 and Comm.Code § 2708). Moreover, even where there is an available market, "The general rule that the measure of damages is the difference between the contract price and the market value is not a hard-and-fast rule, but may be varied if circumstances require it; and it will not be followed where a better method of measuring loss or damages is available under the circumstances." (78 C.J.S., supra, p. 138; see subd. 3 of former § 1784; Comm. Code § 2708; and see Los Angeles Coin-O-Matic Laundries, supra.)

It is apparent from the foregoing principles that the measure of damages applied by the trial court in the instant case, namely, the difference between the contract price and the net amount of $20,680 received by Spindler from the resale in July 1962, was proper under the circumstances of this case since the record contains evidence from which the trial court could properly conclude

Think About It!

How did the court calculate damages? Why did it reject the argument to use the market price of the newspaper? If the seller had breached by failing to turn over the stock, would the same measure of damages be appropriate for the buyer, with or without adjustments?

that there was no available market for the stock at the time of Sackett's breach. We refer to the testimony of Joseph Snyder, a newspaper broker, to the effect that because the prospective sale of the newspaper by Spindler to Sackett had been publicized in the local newspaper, the former would have great difficulty making a resale of the newspaper after the latter's failure to consummate the purchase agreement, and that Spindler was in fact extremely fortunate to sell his stock in July 1962. In view of this evidence which tends to show the unavailability of a market for the stock at the time of the breach, we conclude that the trial court was entitled to use the resale price in determining Spindler's damages. . . .

Having concluded that the trial court applied the correct measure of damages in the instant case, we consider Sackett's argument that in computing damages under this measure the trial court should have taken into consideration the fact that the liabilities of the newspaper increased some $17,995.30 during the one-year period between the time he agreed to purchase Spindler's stock and the sale of the stock which the latter ultimately effected. This contention is without merit for the reason that both agreements of sale involved an exchange of the stock of S & S Newspapers for a fixed amount of money, in the one case $85,000 and in the other $22,000. The newspaper's liabilities at each of these times, or more properly the relationship of its liabilities to its assets, was obviously a primary factor in determining the amount which each buyer was willing to pay for the stock and was thus reflected in the contract price of the stock at each date. To this extent the increase in the newspaper's liabilities was necessarily and properly considered by the trial court in awarding damages to Spindler. Any separate or additional consideration by the trial court of the increase in liabilities would have been improper. . . .

> At the end of the opinion, when the court says that Spindler is to recover "costs," it is not referring to the costs that may be part of computing general or specific damages, but rather to court costs such as fees to file the lawsuit, charges for serving subpoenas to compel the appearance of witnesses at trial, and the cost of ordering trial transcripts and of making copies of trial exhibits.

. . . .

The . . . judgment is affirmed. Respondent Spindler to recover costs.

SIMS and BRAY, JJ., concur.

§ 2.1.4. Special Problems in Measuring Direct Damages

Expectation damages can sometimes be measured in more than one way, and choosing among the alternatives requires balancing and selecting among competing policies. Some situations present special challenges in measuring direct damages. The cases in this section deal with such special challenges and demonstrate how courts have made choices between alternative measures in typical cases. The issues presented include deciding when to measure damages after anticipatory repudiation, measuring loss from incomplete or defective performance of a construction contract, and measuring lost profits.

§ 2.1.4.1. Damages Resulting from Anticipatory Repudiation

Recall from Chapter 8 (page 943) that a repudiation (also called a renunciation) is "an absolute and unequivocal refusal to perform or a distinct and positive statement of an inability to do so."* An *anticipatory* repudiation is a repudiation that occurs *before* the date on which performance is due. As noted earlier, if a repudiation occurs *at the time or after* performance is due and market price is used to determine damages, UCC § 2-713 uses the market price when the aggrieved party "learned of the breach"—when she could have acted to replace the performance lost through breach. But when should the market be measured if the repudiation occurs before the time for performance?

Courts and commentators have identified three possible interpretations of the phrase "learned of the breach." If seller anticipatorily repudiates, buyer learns of the breach:

(1) When he learns of the repudiation,
(2) When he learns of the repudiation plus a commercially reasonable time, or
(3) When performance is due under the contract.

A majority of courts (in both UCC and common law cases) have chosen the middle solution—a commercially reasonable time after the aggrieved buyer learns of the seller's repudiation. That time period gives the buyer a chance to size up the market, locate alternative suppliers, and decide whether to merely seek market damages or to obtain substitute goods ("cover") and seek cover damages. It also encourages the buyer to mitigate before the contract date for performance arrives; recall that this was a strong consideration by the court in *Hochster,* page 945 (the courier case where the buyer anticipatorily repudiated). For a thorough discussion of the rationale for choosing among the three solutions for timing the measure of damages, see *Cosden Oil & Chemical Co. v. Karl O. Helm Aktiengesellschaft,* 736 F.2d 1054 (5th Cir. 1984).

---

* *McCloskey & Co. v. Minweld Steel Co.,* 220 F.2d 101, 104 (3d Cir. 1955).

As reflected in the majority approach, the direct market damages for a seller's anticipatory repudiation are measured by this formula:

Market price (at a commercially reasonable time after aggrieved party learned of the repudiation)
− Contract price
———————————————
Damages

The aggrieved buyer can also recover indirect damages, such as consequential and incidental damages (see page 1084). The law governing common law contracts has evolved in similar directions.*

§ 2.1.4.2. Owner's Cost to Complete versus Diminution in Value

While it is clear that an aggrieved party is entitled to direct damages for breach, it is sometimes less clear how to measure those damages. Is the non-breaching party entitled to the amount necessary to purchase from someone else the performance that was promised in the original contract (the "cost to complete")? Or should the non-breaching party be compensated, instead, by awarding the amount representing the difference between the value that would have accrued to the aggrieved party with full performance and the value held as the result of the defective performance (the "diminution in value")? The issue comes up regularly (though not exclusively) in construction contracts, where the choice is between using the cost to hire another contractor to complete the work and using the difference in the value of the property with full versus defective performance. As the next several cases demonstrate, standards have been developed to regulate the choice between the two measures of damage, but application of the standards raises questions that go to the heart of the policies underlying award of damages.

Reading the Law Critically:
*Jacob & Youngs, *Khiterer*, and *Lyon**

1. What standards or rules does each court select to govern the choice between cost to complete and diminution in value as the measure of damages? Can you reconcile the standards and outcomes in all the cases?

2. Why does each court choose the damages measure that it selects?

3. Do you agree with each court's choice of damages? Why or why not? Are there circumstances under which you think the breach that occurred in each contract should be compensated by the alternative measure?

---

* *See* E. Allan Farnsworth, *Contracts* § 12.12, at 782-83 (4th ed. 2004).

Jacob & Youngs v. Kent

JACOB & YOUNGS, Plaintiff

v.

GEORGE KENT, Defendant

Court of Appeals of New York

129 N.E. 889 (N.Y. 1921)

CARDOZO, J.

[The facts and decision with respect to whether there was substantial performance appear in Chapter 8 on page 895 and are summarized here: The contractor deviated from the contract specification that Reading pipe be used, using another pipe in most of the construction, but the owner and his architect did not discover the substitution until the house was nearly completed and was already occupied by owner. Contractor sued for its final payment under the contract. The district court held for the defendant, concluding that the plaintiff had breached the contract. The Appellate Division reversed and granted a new trial. The Court of Appeals held that the contractor had substantially performed the contract and therefore had earned the contract price. The court then turned to the question of measuring the damages owed by the contractor for its failure to use Reading pipe as promised; the district court and appellate division had not addressed this issue.]

In the circumstances of this case, we think the measure of the allowance is not the cost of replacement, which would be great, but the difference in value, which would be either nominal or nothing. Some of the exposed sections might perhaps have been replaced at moderate expense. The defendant did not limit his demand to them, but treated the plumbing as a unit to be corrected from cellar to roof. In point of fact, the plaintiff never reached the stage at which evidence of the extent of the allowance became necessary. The trial court had excluded evidence that the defect was unsubstantial, and in view of that ruling there was no occasion for the plaintiff to go farther with an offer of proof. We think, however, that the offer, if it had been made, would not of necessity have been defective because directed to difference in value. It is true that in most cases the cost of replacement is the measure. Spence v. Ham, supra. The owner is entitled to the money which will permit him to complete, unless the cost of completion is grossly and unfairly out of proportion to the good to be attained. When that is true, the measure is the difference in value. Specifications call, let us say, for a foundation built of granite quarried in Vermont. On the completion of the building, the owner learns that through the blunder of a subcontractor part of the foundation has been built of granite of the same quality quarried in New Hampshire. The measure of allowance is not the cost of reconstruction. "There may be omissions of that which could not afterwards be supplied exactly as called for by the contract without taking down the building to its foundations, and at the same time the omission may not affect the value of the building for use or otherwise, except so slightly as to be hardly appreciable." Handy v. Bliss, 204 Mass. 513, 519, 90 N. E. 864, 134 Am. St. Rep. 673. Cf. Foeller v. Heintz, 137 Wis. 169, 178, 118 N. W. 543, 24 L. R. A. (N. S.) 321 . . . . The rule that gives a remedy in cases of substantial performance with compensation for defects of trivial or inappreciable importance has been developed by the courts as an instrument of justice. The measure of the allowance must be shaped to the same end.

The order should be affirmed, and judgment absolute directed in favor of the plaintiff upon the stipulation, with costs in all courts.

———————

Khiterer v. Bell

INNA KHITERER, Claimant

v.

MINA BELL, Defendant

Civil Court, City of New York, Kings County
2005 WL 192354 (N.Y. City Civ. Ct. Jan. 28, 2005) (unreported opinion)

[The facts and decision with respect to whether there was substantial performance appear in Chapter 8 on page 911 and are summarized here: Patient sued dentist for damages because her dental treatment, for which she had already paid, was allegedly to have included a porcelain-on-gold crown, rather than the porcelain crown that she discovered a half year later. The court held that the dental contract was predominantly for services and thus not governed by UCC Article 2. It found that the contract had called for porcelain-on-gold crowns, but that the substitution was not intentional. The dentist's uncontradicted testimony showed that the porcelain crown was "therapeutically superior" and that the cost was the same, except that more expensive cement was required for the porcelain crown. The court held that the dentist's breach was not substantial.]

. . . .

Where substantial performance has been rendered, the remedy is the cost of completion or correction, unless that cost "is grossly and unfairly out of proportion to the good to be attained. When that is true, the measure is the difference in value." ([*Jacob & Youngs v. Kent*, 129 N.E. 889]); *see also Ferrari v. Barleo Homes, Inc.*, 112 A.D.2d at 137-38 (awarding "difference in value between the contract materials and the substituted materials actually utilized").) The "difference in value rule" is applied to avoid "economic waste". (*See Bellizzi v. Huntley Estates, Inc.*, 3 N.Y.2d 112, 115 (1957); *Lyon v. Belosky Construction Inc.*, 247 A.D.2d at 731.) But where the defect in performance is substantial,* the cost of completion or correction will be awarded "notwithstanding the relatively small fee . . . charged for services rendered." (*See id.*, at 732.)

. . . .

"[T]he inquiry must always be, what is an adequate remedy to the party injured"; "the law awards to the party injured a just indemnity for the wrong which has been done him, and no more." (*Baker v. Drake*, 53 N.Y. 211, 220 (1873); *see also Campagnola v. Mulholland, Minion & Roe*, 76 N.Y.2d 38, 42 (1990).) The tort cases for lack of consent to medical treatment support a conclusion that an invasion of the interest to control one's body is not compensable beyond an award of nominal damages, in the absence of proof of other harm, presumably including, in an appropriate case, emotional harm. (*See Hawkins v. Brooklyn-Caledonian Hospital*, 239 A.D.2d 549, 553 (2d Dept 1997).)

The Court concludes that Dr. Bell's breach of her contract with Ms. Khiterer, fitting her with all-porcelain crowns rather than porcelain-on-gold crowns, was not substantial,** so as to warrant a return of her total fee. An award based upon the cost of replacement (which, in any event, has not been established by competent evidence) would be "grossly and unfairly out of proportion to the good to be obtained." (*See Jacob & Youngs v. Kent*, 230 N.Y. at 244.) And, under the circumstances here, the "difference in value rule" yields an award of only nominal damages, to which Ms. Khiterer is entitled upon proof of breach of contract. (*See Manhattan Savings Institution v. Gottfried Baking Co.*, 286 N.Y. 398, 400 (1941); *Magu Realty Company v. Spartan Concrete Corp.*, 239 A.D.2d 469, 470 (2d Dept 1997).)

[handwritten note: full replacement cost, too much]

. . . .

Judgment is awarded to Ms. Khiterer for $10.00, plus disbursements.

———————————

* See footnote on page 1063.

** [Authors' Note: It appears that a defect may be considered "substantial" even though the breaching party has provided "substantial" performance and therefore has not materially breached. Although the terminology is similar, the meaning of "substantial" in the two inquiries is not identical.]

Lyon v. Belosky Construction, Inc.

MARY C. LYON et al., Plaintiffs-Respondents

v.

BELOSKY CONSTRUCTION, INC., et al., Defendants-Appellants

Supreme Court, Appellate Division, New York
669 N.Y.S.2d 400 (App. Div. 1998)

CARDONA, P. J.

Appeal from a judgment of the Supreme Court (Ellison, J.), entered November 11, 1996 in Chemung County, upon a decision of the court in favor of plaintiffs.

In October 1993, plaintiff Mary C. Lyon and her sister, plaintiff Martha Clute, entered into a contract with defendant Belosky Construction, Inc. for the construction of a custom home in the City of Elmira, Chemung County, at a base cost of $247,000 with approximately $42,000 in additional features. Lyon, who is a resident of South Carolina, retained an architectural firm in South Carolina to prepare the design drawings. Upon Belosky's advice, plaintiffs retained defendant Kirk Vieselmeyer, a professional engineer, to, *inter alia,* prepare construction documents and conduct periodic inspections to insure that the home was constructed in conformity with the drawings.

Construction commenced in November 1993. In April 1994, plaintiffs became aware of a problem with a dormer over the main entrance of the home. The dormer was removed and rebuilt. Plaintiffs, however, found the rebuilt dormer unsatisfactory and directed Belosky to remove it. The home was subsequently completed with the exception of the interior and exterior of the main entrance. After moving into the home, plaintiffs learned that the roof had been centered over the library rather than the living room as represented in the drawings resulting in a change in the roof proportions and enlargement of the overhang over the main entrance. In addition, the entrance pillars could not be used in the manner depicted in the drawings.

Plaintiffs subsequently commenced this action against defendants for breach of contract. In their respective answers, defendants raised, *inter alia,* the affirmative defense of economic waste claiming that damages, if any, should be based upon the diminution in value of the structure rather than the value of replacement. Following a nonjury trial, Supreme Court found that defendants had breached their respective contracts and plaintiffs were entitled to damages in an amount necessary to replace the roof so as to bring it in conformity with the drawings. Supreme Court awarded plaintiffs judgment in the sum of $73,182.66, the agreed-upon cost of replacement including costs and interest. Defendants appeal.

We affirm. As a general rule, the proper measure of damages in cases involving the breach of a construction contract is "the difference between the amount due on the contract and the amount necessary to properly complete the job or to replace the defective construction, whichever is appropriate" (*Sherman v. Hanu*, 195 A.D.2d 810. . . . Where, however, "the contractor's breach was unintentional and constituted substantial performance in good faith" (*Roudis v. Hubbard*, 176 A.D.2d 388, 389), and remedying the defective performance would result in unreasonable economic waste (*see, City School Dist. v. McLane Constr. Co.*, 85 A.D.2d 749, 750, *lv denied* 56 NY2d 504), damages should be based upon "the difference between the value of the property as constructed and the value if performance had been properly completed" (*American Std. v. Schectman*, 80 A.D.2d 318, 321, *lv denied* 54 NY2d 604. . . .

It is undisputed that the defect in the main entrance, including the overhead dormer, was due to the misalignment of the roof which was constructed under the supervision and control of Belosky and purportedly overseen by Vieselmeyer. Belosky hired a framer to frame the roof but testified that he did not personally inspect the roof to insure that it and the dormer complied with the drawings. In fact, Belosky admitted that he had little experience reading drawings and relied upon the framer to whom he had subcontracted the work to make sure the home was constructed properly. Vieselmeyer, who was specifically hired to inspect the construction to make sure that it complied with the drawings, did not discover the problem with the roof until after he took certain field measurements at the request of plaintiffs' architect. By this time, however, the dormer had already been rebuilt and removed, and the entire roof had been shingled. Inasmuch as plaintiffs' expert testified that the misalignment of the roof should have been discovered when problems with the dormer became apparent, the evidence supports Supreme Court's finding that defendants, at the very least, acted negligently in failing to detect the problem.

In addition, there is evidence that, under the circumstances presented here, the defect was substantial.* Plaintiffs contracted to build a custom home at significant expense which, in fact, exceeded the fair market value of the home as completed per the drawings. Because they were away from the work site during most of the construction, plaintiffs retained and relied upon various professionals to assist them in successfully completing the project. It is clear from the record that the aesthetic appearance of the home, both inside and out, was of utmost importance to plaintiffs. Our review of the photographs of the home as constructed compared with the design drawings convinces us that plaintiffs did not get

---

* [Authors' Note: As in *Khiterer*, the court finds a "substantial" defect even though the court apparently believes there was substantial performance, as it does not question the contractor's entitlement to the contract price, offest by the damages for its breach.]

the benefit of their bargain and that requiring defendants to remedy the problem would not, under these particular circumstances, result in unreasonable economic waste. Accordingly, we find that Supreme Court applied the appropriate measure of damages (*see, City School Dist. v. McLane Constr. Co.*, 85 A.D.2d 749, 750-751, *supra; cf., Jacob & Youngs v. Kent*, 230 N.Y. 239). Lastly, inasmuch as the evidence establishes that Vieselmeyer's breach of contract was a proximate cause of the damages sustained by plaintiffs, Supreme Court properly awarded judgment against him notwithstanding the relatively small fee he charged for services rendered to plaintiffs.

Mercure, White, Spain and Carpinello, JJ., concur.

Ordered that the judgment is affirmed, with costs.

———————————————

Problem 9-7: Damages for Incomplete Performance

Contractor agreed to build a house for Owners based on a stock floor plan and specifications on standard printed forms. When Contractor completed construction, Owners did a final walk-through inspection during which they documented that Contractor had furnished kitchen cabinets with a much darker finish than specified (so that the countertops and woodwork in the room did not match). The Contractor also had failed to furnish gutters and downspouts, clothes closet poles, an entrance seat, and the outside sidewalks, each of which was promised in the contract. The plaster on the ceiling was cracked in the living room and kitchen. The patio floor and patio wall were defectively constructed and needed to be repaired by mud jacking and reconstruction.

In addition, Owners noted (and the stock floor plan shows) that Contractor misplaced a wall between the living room and the kitchen by more than a foot. The record at trial was not clear why and when this wall was misplaced, but there was no evidence that, during construction, Owners had requested or demanded the repositioning of the wall called for by the specifications. Expert real estate witnesses for both parties, testifying as to the value of the house, agreed that the misplacement of the wall (resulting in a smaller living room) had no effect on the market price. A home remodeling expert witness testified that tearing down and rebuilding the wall in its proper place would cause some additional damage to other parts of the house and would require replastering and redecorating the walls and ceilings of at least two rooms. The cost of tearing down this wall and rebuilding it would be approximately $40,000.

Contractor sued Owners for breach of contract, because Owners refused to pay the contract price of $200,000. Owners claimed that Contractor had not substantially performed and therefore was not entitled to any payment. The court held that Contractor had substantially performed the contract, so it had earned the contract price, but that Owners were entitled to reduce payment by the amount of their damages. How should the court compute Owners' damages? If dollar amounts are not specified for certain injuries, identify the items for which recovery should be awarded and how the amount of recovery might be proven or ascertained.

Reading the Law Critically: *Peevyhouse*

1. The previous cases might all be characterized as contracts for services that were performed badly, with a consequent need to measure the value of the performance defects. Is the contract in *Peevyhouse* the same kind of contract? If not, does or should the difference matter in determining the appropriate measure of damages?

2. Do you agree with the majority opinion or with the dissent? Why? What additional information does the Supplemental Opinion on Rehearing provide, and how, if at all, should it change the analysis presented in the original opinions?

3. How could a landowner protect itself against this ruling in drafting future coal mining leases?

Peevyhouse v. Garland Coal & Mining Co.

WILLIE PEEVYHOUSE and LUCILLE PEEVYHOUSE, Plaintiffs-Appellants

v.

GARLAND COAL & MINING COMPANY, Defendant-Respondent

Supreme Court of Oklahoma
382 P.2d 109 (Okla. 1962), *modified* (1963)

JACKSON, Justice.

In the trial court, plaintiffs Willie and Lucille Peevyhouse sued the defendant, Garland Coal and Mining Company, for damages for breach of contract. Judgment was for plaintiffs in an amount considerably less than was sued for. Plaintiffs appeal and defendant cross-appeals.

[The parties' arguments all revolve around] the basic question of whether the trial court properly instructed the jury on the measure of damages.

. . . [P]laintiffs owned a farm containing coal deposits, and in November, 1954, leased the premises to defendant for a period of five years for coal mining purposes. A "stripmining" operation was contemplated in which the coal would be taken from pits on the surface of the ground, instead of from underground mine shafts. In addition to the usual covenants found in a coal mining lease, defendant specifically agreed to perform certain restorative and remedial work at the end of the lease period. It is unnecessary to set out the details of the work to be done, other than to say that it would involve the moving of many thousands of cubic yards of dirt, at a cost estimated by expert witnesses at about $29,000.00. However, plaintiffs sued for only $25,000.00.

During the trial, it was stipulated that all covenants and agreements in the lease contract had been fully carried out by both parties, except the remedial work mentioned above; defendant conceded that this work had not been done.

Plaintiffs introduced expert testimony as to the amount and nature of the work to be done, and its estimated cost. Over plaintiffs' objections, defendant thereafter introduced expert testimony as to the "diminution in value" of plaintiffs' farm resulting from the failure of defendant to render performance as agreed in the contract—that is, the difference between the present value of the farm, and what its value would have been if defendant had done what it agreed to do.

At the conclusion of the trial, the court instructed the jury that it must return a verdict for plaintiffs, and left the amount of damages for jury determination. On the measure of damages, the court instructed the jury that it might consider the cost of performance of the work defendant agreed to do, "together with all of the evidence offered on behalf of either party".

Think About It!

Why should the plaintiffs have objected to the jury instruction language? Why didn't they?

It thus appears that the jury was at liberty to consider the "diminution in value" of plaintiffs' farm as well as the cost of "repair work" in determining the amount of damages.

It returned a verdict for plaintiffs for $5000.00—only a fraction of the "cost of performance", *but more than the total value of the farm even after the remedial work is done.*

On appeal, . . . [p]laintiffs contend that the true measure of damages . . . is what it will cost plaintiffs to obtain performance of the work that was not done because of defendant's default. Defendant argues that the measure of damages is the cost of performance "limited, however, to the total difference in the market value before and after the work was performed".

. . . [T]his precise question has not . . . been presented to this court. . . . In the case before us, it is argued by defendant with some force that the performance of the remedial work defendant agreed to do will add at the most only a few hundred dollars to the value of plaintiffs' farm, and that the damages should be limited to that amount because that is all plaintiffs have lost.

Plaintiffs rely on Groves v. John Wunder Co., 205 Minn. 163, 286 N.W. 235, 123 A.L.R. 502. In that case, the Minnesota court, in a substantially similar situation, adopted the "cost of performance" rule—as opposed to the "value" rule. The result was to authorize a jury to give plaintiff damages in the amount of $60,000, where the real estate concerned would have been worth only $12,160, even if the work contracted for had been done.

. . . Groves v. John Wunder Co., supra, is the only case which has come to our attention in which the cost of performance rule has been followed under circumstances where the cost of performance greatly exceeded the diminution in value resulting from the breach of contract. Incidentally, it appears that this case was decided by a plurality rather than a majority of the members of the court.

Defendant relies principally upon Sandy Valley & E. R. Co., v. Hughes, 175 Ky. 320, 194 S.W. 344; Bigham v. Wabash-Pittsburg Terminal Ry. Co., 223 Pa. 106, 72 A. 318; and Sweeney v. Lewis Const. Co., 66 Wash. 490, 119 P. 1108. These were all cases in which, under similar circumstances, the appellate courts followed the "value" rule instead of the "cost of performance" rule. Plaintiff points out that in the earliest of these cases (Bigham) the court cites as authority on the measure of damages an earlier Pennsylvania *tort* case, and that the other two cases follow the first, with no explanation as to why a measure of damages ordinarily followed in cases sounding in tort should be used in contract cases. Nevertheless, it is of some significance that three out of four appellate courts have followed the diminution in value rule under circumstances where, as here, the cost of performance greatly exceeds the diminution in value.

The explanation may be found in the fact that the situations presented are artificial ones. It is highly unlikely that the ordinary property owner would agree to pay $29,000 (or its equivalent) for the construction of "improvements" upon his property that would increase its value only about ($300) three hundred dollars. The result is that we are called upon to apply principles of law theoretically based upon reason and reality to a situation which is basically unreasonable and unrealistic.

In Groves v. John Wunder Co., supra, in arriving at its conclusions, the Minnesota court apparently considered the contract involved to be analogous to a building and construction contract, and cited authority for the proposition that the cost of performance or completion of the building as contracted is ordinarily the measure of damages in actions for damages for the breach of such a contract.

In an annotation following the Minnesota case beginning at 123 A.L.R. 515, the annotator places the three cases relied on by defendant (Sandy Valley, Bigham and Sweeney) under the classification of cases involving "grading and excavation contracts."

We do not think either analogy is strictly applicable to the case now before us. The primary purpose of the lease contract between plaintiffs and defendant was neither "building and construction" nor "grading and excavation". It was merely to accomplish the economical recovery and marketing of coal from the premises, to the profit of all parties. The special provisions of the lease contract pertaining to remedial work were incidental to the main object involved.

Even in the case of contracts that are unquestionably building and construction contracts, the authorities are not in agreement as to the factors to be considered in determining whether the cost of performance rule or the value rule should be applied. The . . . Restatement of the Law, Contracts, [§] 346(1)(a) (i) and (ii) [states] that the cost of performance is the proper measure of damages "if this is possible and does not involve *unreasonable economic waste*"; and that the diminution in value caused by the breach is the proper measure "if construction and completion in accordance with the contract would involve *unreasonable economic waste*". (Emphasis supplied.) In a . . . comment . . . , the Restatement makes it clear that the "economic waste" referred to consists of the destruction of a substantially completed building or other structure. Of course no such destruction is involved in the case now before us.

On the other hand, in McCormick, Damages, Section 168, it is said with regard to building and construction contracts that ". . . in cases where the defect is one that can be repaired or cured without *undue expense*" the cost of performance is the proper measure of damages, but where ". . . the defect in material or construction is one that cannot be remedied without *an expenditure for reconstruction disproportionate to the end to be attained*" (emphasis supplied) the value rule should be followed. The same idea was expressed in Jacob & Youngs, Inc. v. Kent, 230 N.Y. 239, 129 N.E. 889, 23 A.L.R. 1429, as follows:

"The owner is entitled to the money which will permit him to complete, unless the cost of completion is grossly and unfairly out of proportion to the good to be attained. When that is true, the measure is the difference in value."

It thus appears that the prime consideration in the Restatement was "economic waste"; and that the prime consideration in McCormick, Damages, and in Jacob & Youngs, Inc. v. Kent, supra, was the relationship between the expense involved and the "end to be attained"—in other words, the "relative economic benefit".

In view of the unrealistic fact situation in the instant case . . . , we are of the opinion that the "relative economic benefit" is a proper consideration here. . . .

We therefore hold that where, in a coal mining lease, lessee agrees to perform certain remedial work on the premises concerned at the end of the lease period, and thereafter the contract is fully performed by both parties except that the remedial work is not done, the measure of damages in an action by lessor against lessee for damages for breach of contract is ordinarily the reasonable cost of performance of the work; however, where the contract provision breached was merely incidental to the main purpose in view, and where the economic benefit which would result to lessor by full performance of the work is grossly disproportionate to the cost of performance, the damages which lessor may recover are limited to the diminution in value resulting to the premises because of the non-performance.

> **Food for Thought**
>
> Why might the court state its holding in such narrow, fact-specific terms? Is the holding really limited in that fashion?

We believe the above holding is in . . . harmony with the better-reasoned cases from the other jurisdictions where analogous fact situations have been considered. . . . [T]he rule as stated does not interfere with the property owner's right to "do what he will with his own" Chamberlain v. Parker, 45 N.Y. 569), or his right, if he chooses, to contract for "improvements" which will actually have the effect of reducing his property's value. Where such result is in fact contemplated by the parties, and is a main or principal purpose of those contracting, it would seem that the measure of damages for breach would ordinarily be the cost of performance.

The above holding disposes of all of the arguments raised by the parties on appeal.

Under the most liberal view of the evidence herein, the diminution in value resulting to the premises because of non-performance of the remedial work was $300.00. After a careful search of the record, we have found no evidence of a higher figure, and plaintiffs do not argue in their briefs that a greater diminution in value was sustained. It thus appears that the judgment was clearly excessive, and that the amount for which judgment should have been rendered is definitely and satisfactorily shown by the record.

. . . .

We are of the opinion that the judgment of the trial court for plaintiffs should be, and it is hereby, modified and reduced to the sum of $300.00, and as so modified it is affirmed.

WELCH, DAVISON, HALLEY, and JOHNSON, JJ., concur.

WILLIAMS, C. J., BLACKBIRD, V. C. J., and IRWIN and BERRY, JJ., dissent.

IRWIN, Justice (dissenting).

By the specific provisions in the coal mining lease under consideration, the defendant agreed as follows:

> "7b. Lessee agrees to make fills in the pits dug on said premises on the property line in such manner that fences can be placed thereon and access had to opposite sides of the pits.
> "7c. Lessee agrees to smooth off the top of the spoil banks on the above premises.
> "7d. Lessee agrees to leave the creek crossing the above premises in such a condition that it will not interfere with the crossings to be made in pits as set out in 7b.
> . . . .
> "7f. Lessee further agrees to leave no shale or dirt on the high wall of said pits. . . ."

Following the expiration of the lease, plaintiffs made demand upon defendant that it carry out the provisions of the contract and to perform those covenants contained therein.

Defendant admits that it failed to perform its obligations that it agreed and contracted to perform under the lease contract and there is nothing in the record which indicates that defendant could not perform its obligations. Therefore, in my opinion defendant's breach of the contract was wilful and not in good faith.

Although the contract speaks for itself, there were several negotiations between the plaintiffs and defendant before the contract was executed. Defendant admitted . . . that plaintiffs insisted that the above provisions be included in the contract and that they would not agree to the coal mining lease unless the above provisions were included.

In consideration for the lease contract, plaintiffs were to receive a certain amount as royalty for the coal produced and marketed and in addition thereto their land was to be restored as provided in the contract.

Defendant received as consideration for the contract, its proportionate share of the coal produced and marketed and in addition thereto, the *right to use* plaintiffs' land in the furtherance of its mining operations.

The cost for performing the contract in question could have been reasonably approximated when the contract was negotiated and executed and there are no conditions now existing which could not have been reasonably anticipated by the parties. Therefore, defendant had knowledge, when it prevailed upon the plaintiffs to execute the lease, that the cost of performance might be disproportionate to the value or benefits received by plaintiff for the performance.

Defendant has received its benefits under the contract and now urges, in substance, that plaintiffs' measure of damages for its failure to perform should be the economic value of performance to the plaintiffs and not the cost of performance.

If a peculiar set of facts should exist where the above rule should be applied as the proper measure of damages (and in my judgment those facts do not exist in the instant case), before such rule should be applied, consideration should be given to the benefits received or contracted for by the party who asserts the application of the rule.

Defendant did not have the right to mine plaintiffs' coal or to use plaintiffs' property for its mining operations without the consent of plaintiffs. Defendant had knowledge of the benefits that it would receive under the contract and the approximate cost of performing the contract. With this knowledge, it must be presumed that defendant thought that it would be to its economic advantage to enter into the contract with plaintiffs and that it would reap benefits from the contract, or it would have not entered into the contract.

Therefore, if the value of the performance of a contract should be considered in determining the measure of damages for breach of a contract, the value of the benefits received under the contract by a party who breaches a contract should also be considered. . . .

. . . .

Food for Thought

If the Peevyhouses had instead sought relief under real property law, rather than contract law, they could have argued that they had given the mining company a "profit a prendre," a non-possessory interest in land that "consists of a right of access to land for the limited purpose of removing some naturally occurring substance from the land," such as fossil fuels, minerals, timber, sand, gravel, and confined standing water. Most commentators believe that such rights should be governed by the same rules as easements. Upon unlawful use of an easement, the owners can obtain damages or (if damages are inadequate) injunctive relief. 8 *Thompson on Real Property, Second Thomas Edition* §§ 60.03(a)(7), 60.06(a), 65.01, 65.03(b), 65.04(a) (David A. Thomas, ed., 2005) (citing Restatement of Property (Servitudes) § 1.2 (2000)). Does this affect your analysis of the case?

In my judgment, we should follow the case of Groves v. John Wunder Company, 205 Minn. 163, 286 N.W. 235, 123 A.L.R. 502, ...

. . . .

. . . [T]he proper measure of damages should be the cost of performance. Any other measure of damage would be holding for naught the express provisions of the contract; would be taking from the plaintiffs the benefits of the contract and placing those benefits in defendant which has failed to perform its obligations; would be granting benefits to defendant without a resulting obligation; and would be completely rescinding the solemn obligation of the contract for the benefit of the defendant to the detriment of the plaintiffs by making an entirely new contract for the parties.

I therefore respectfully dissent to the opinion promulgated by a majority of my associates.

SUPPLEMENTAL OPINION ON REHEARING

JACKSON, Justice.

In a Petition for Rehearing, plaintiffs Peevyhouse have raised certain questions not presented in the original briefs on appeal.

They insist that the trial court excluded evidence as to the total value of the premises concerned, and, in effect, that they have not had their "day in court". . . .

The defendant offered the testimony of five witnesses in the trial court; four of them testified as to "diminution in value". They were not cross examined by plaintiffs. . . .

[The court reviewed references in the defendant's briefs to the evidence it presented about the value of the property, including the following:]

"Defendant offered evidence that the total value of the property involved before the mining operation would be $60.00 per acre, and $11.00 per acre after the mining operation (60 acres at $49.00 per acre is $2940.00). Other evidence was that the property was worth $5.00 to $15.00 per acre after the mining, but before the repairs; and would be worth an increase of $2.00 to $5.00 per acre after the repairs had been made (60 acres at $5.00 per acre is $300.00)

[Plaintiffs' reply brief included the following:]

". . . Plaintiffs in error pointed out in their initial brief that this evidence concerning land values was objectionable as being incompetent and refused to cross-examine or offer rebuttal for the reason that they did not choose to waive their objections to the competency of the evidence by disproving defendant in error's allegations as to land values. We strongly urged at the trial below, and still do, that market value of the land has no application . . . ."

> **Think About It!**
>
> Note which party presented evidence of cost to complete and which party presented evidence of diminution in value. What effect did that have on the outcome? Should the Peevyhouses' lawyer have approached this issue differently?

. . . .

The whole record in this case justifies the conclusion that plaintiffs tried their case upon the theory that the "cost of performance" would be the sole measure of damages and that they would recognize no other. . . . [W]e conclude that they so tried it *with notice* that defendant would contend for the "diminution in value" rule. [Plaintiffs claim the trial court improperly excluded testimony about the rest of their property, which adjoined the 60 acres at issue in the stripmining contract, but the court concludes that] such evidence was *not within the scope of the pleadings*. At no time did plaintiffs ask permission to amend their petition, either with or without prejudice to trial, so as to describe *all* of the lands they own or lease, and no evidence was admitted which could broaden the scope of the petition.

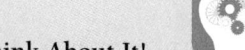

. . . .

We think plaintiffs' present position is that of a plaintiff in any damage suit who has failed to prove his damages—opposed by a defendant who has proved plaintiff's damages; and that plaintiffs' complaint that the record does not show the total "diminution in value" to their lands comes too late. It is well settled that a party will not be permitted to change his theory of the case upon appeal. Knox v. Eason Oil Co., 190 Okl. 627, 126 P.2d 247.

Also, plaintiffs' expressed fear that by introducing evidence on the question of "diminution in value" they would have waived their objection to similar evidence by defendant was not justified. . . .

. . . .

The petition for rehearing is denied.

HALLEY, V. C. J., and WELCH, DAVISON and JOHNSON, JJ., concur.

BLACKBIRD, C. J., and WILLIAMS, IRWIN and BERRY, JJ., dissent.

———————————

Food for Thought

Cases like *Peevyhouse, Jacob & Youngs,* and *Lyon* illustrate the importance of the advocate framing the narrative of the case in a compelling story line. Is *Jacob & Youngs* more about an owner who made an irrational choice in the contract, a careless contractor who didn't check the pipe order or delivery, a contractor who chose a cheaper pipe, or an architect who didn't inspect the premises carefully enough when the pipe was first installed? Is *Lyon* more about two owners whose dream house was drastically altered by a careless or even negligent contractor, or is it instead about a perfectly good house that's rejected by two finicky owners? What alternative narratives can be constructed for *Peevyhouse?* Are some of these narratives more compelling than others? Why? The political climate may also be part of the narrative. Consider the political culture created in a region where strip mining is profitable and common. How do those pressures affect the decisions of landowners and the resulting contracts? For a similar situation, consider the present-day controversy surrounding the natural gas industry's use of fracking methods. *See generally* www.nytimes.com/interactive/us/DRILLING_DOWN_SERIES.html. In light of *Peevyhouse,* what advice would you give to a landowner who has been approached by a representative of a natural gas extraction company to negotiate extraction rights on that property?

For additional background on the *Peevyhouse* case, *see* Judith L. Maute, *Peevyhouse v. Garland Coal & Mining Co. Revisited: The Ballad of Willie and Lucille,* 89 Nw. U. L. Rev. 1341 (1995); Douglas Baird, Robert Gertner, & Randal Picker, *Game Theory and the Law* 150-53, 224-32 (1994) (concluding that an award of specific performance would have been a mistake); Judith Maute, *The Unearthed Facts of Peevyhouse v. Garland Coal & Mining Co,* in *Contracts Stories* 265 (Douglas G. Baird ed. 2007). The video by Judith Maute, *The Ballad of Willie and Lucille: Disappointed Expectations of Contract Law and the Legal System,* contains interviews with Willie Peevyhouse, footage of the farm, and interviews with leading law professors discussing the outcome of the case, its rationale, and its shortcomings. You can see a Google Earth picture of the Peevyhouse Farm here. Despite much criticism of the *Peevyhouse* outcome, the judgment was affirmed in Oklahoma in 1994. *See Schneberger v. Apache Corp.,* 890 P.2d 847 (Okla. 1994).

§ 2.1.4.3. Damages for "Lost Profits" and "Lost Volume"

The following two cases consider when it is appropriate for a seller to receive lost profits from a sale (rather than the difference between contract and resale price) as direct damages for a buyer's repudiation. They also discuss how to measure a seller's lost profits.

Reading the Law Critically: *Neri*

1. When a buyer breaches a purchase contract by repudiating the sale, the seller can usually be compensated fully by being awarded the amount by which the contract price exceeds the resale or market price. Under what circumstances does *Neri* say that is not sufficient, so that a seller is entitled, instead, to receive the profit lost when the original sale did not go through?

Neri v. Retail Marine Corp.

ANTHONY NERI et al., Plantiffs-Respondents

v.

RETAIL MARINE CORP., doing business as
Emmette Marine Corporation, Defendant-Appellant

Court of Appeals of New York
334 N.Y.S.2d 165 (1972)

GIBSON, Judge.

The appeal concerns the right of a retail dealer to recover loss of profits and incidental damages upon the buyer's repudiation of a contract governed by the Uniform Commercial Code. This is, indeed, the correct measure of damage in an appropriate case and to this extent the code (§ 2-708, subsection (2)) effected a substantial change from prior law, whereby damages were ordinarily limited to "the difference between the contract price and the market or current price". Upon the record before us, the courts below erred in declining to give effect to the new statute and so the order appealed from must be reversed.

The plaintiffs contracted to purchase from defendant a new boat of a specified model for the price of $12,587.40, against which they made a deposit of $40. They shortly increased the deposit to $4,250 in consideration of the defendant dealer's agreement to arrange with the manufacturer for immediate delivery on the basis of "a firm sale", instead of the delivery within approximately four to six weeks originally specified. Some six days after the date of the contract plaintiffs' lawyer sent to defendant a letter rescinding the sales contract for the reason that plaintiff Neri was about to undergo hospitalization and surgery, in consequence of which, according to the letter, it would be "impossible for Mr. Neri to make any payments". The boat had already been ordered from the manufacturer and was delivered to defendant at or before the time the attorney's letter was received. Defendant declined to refund plaintiffs' deposit and this action to recover it was commenced. Defendant counter-claimed, alleging plaintiffs' breach of the contract and defendant's resultant damage in the amount of $4,250, for which sum defendant demanded judg-ment. Upon motion, defendant had summary judgment on the issue of lia-bility tendered by its counterclaim; and Special Term directed an assessment of damages, upon which it would be

Think About It!

Although the buyer's letter "rescinds" the contract and says it is "impossi-ble" for him to pay, the buyer is not claiming the legal defense of impos-sibility. What is the accurate legal term for buyer's action?

determined whether plaintiffs were entitled to the return of any portion of their down payment.

Upon the trial so directed, it was shown that the boat ordered and received by defendant in accordance with plaintiffs' contract of purchase was sold some four months later to another buyer for the same price as that negotiated with plaintiffs. From this proof the plaintiffs argue that defendant's loss on its contract was recouped, while defendant argues that but for plaintiffs' default, it would have sold two boats and have earned two profits instead of one. Defendant proved, without contradiction, that its profit on the sale under the contract in suit would have been $2,579 and that during the period the boat remained unsold incidental expenses aggregating $674 for storage, upkeep, finance charges and insurance were incurred. . . .

. . . .

[Section 2-708 (1)] provides that "the measure of damages for non-acceptance or repudiation by the buyer is the difference between the market price at the time and place for tender and the unpaid contract price together with any incidental damages provided in this Article (Section 2-710), but less expenses saved in consequence of the buyer's breach." However, this provision is made expressly subject to subsection (2), providing: "(2) If the measure of damages provided in subsection (1) is inadequate to put the seller in as good a position as performance would have done then the measure of damages is the profit (including reasonable overhead) which the seller would have made from full performance by the buyer, together with any incidental damages provided in this Article (Section 2-710), due allowance for costs reasonably incurred and due credit for payments or proceeds of resale."

. . . .

. . . . The conclusion is clear from the record—indeed with mathematical certainty—that "the measure of damages provided in subsection (1) is inadequate to put the seller in as good a position as performance would have done" (Uniform Commercial Code, § 2-708, subsection (2)) and hence—again under subsection (2)—that the seller is entitled to its "profit (including reasonable overhead) . . . together with any incidental damages . . . , due allowance for costs reasonably incurred and due credit for payments or proceeds of resale."

It is evident, first, that this retail seller is entitled to its profit and, second, that the last sentence of subsection (2), as hereinbefore quoted, referring to "due credit for payments or proceeds of resale" is inapplicable to this retail sales contract. Closely parallel to the factual situation now before us is that hypothesized by Dean Hawkland as illustrative of the operation of the rules: "Thus, if a private party agrees to sell his automobile to a buyer for $2,000, a breach by the buyer would cause the seller no loss (except incidental damages, i.e., expense of a new sale) if the seller was able to sell the automobile to another buyer for $2000. But the situation is different with dealers having an unlimited supply of standard-priced goods. Thus, if an automobile dealer agrees to sell a car to a buyer at the standard price of $2000, a breach by the buyer injures the dealer, even though he is able to sell the automobile to another for $2000. If the dealer has an inexhaustible supply of cars, the resale to replace the breaching buyer costs the dealer a sale, because, had the breaching buyer performed, the dealer would have made two sales instead of one. The buyer's breach, in such a case, depletes the dealer's sales to the extent of one, and the measure of damages should be the dealer's profit on one sale. Section 2-708 recognizes this, and it rejects the rules developed under the Uniform Sales Act by many courts that the profit cannot be recovered in this case." (Hawkland, Sales and Bulk Sales (1958 ed.), pp. 153-154; and see Comment, 31 Fordham L.Rev. 749, 755-756.)

The record which in this case establishes defendant's entitlement to damages in the amount of its prospective profit, at the same time confirms defendant's cognate right to "any incidental damages provided in this Article (Section 2-710)" (Uniform Commercial Code, § 2-708, subsection (2)). From the language employed it is too clear to require discussion that the seller's right to recover loss of profits is not exclusive and that he may recoup his "incidental" expenses as well (Procter & Gamble Distr. Co. v. Lawrence Amer. Field Warehousing Corp., 16 N.Y.2d 344, 354, 266 N.Y.S.2d 785, 792, 213 N.E.2d 873, 878). . . . [The trial court found] "that defendant completely failed to show that it suffered any incidental damages." We find no basis for the court's conclusion with respect to a deficiency of proof inasmuch as the proper items of the $674 expenses (being for storage, upkeep, finance charges and insurance for the period between the date performance was due and the time of the resale) were proven without objection and were in no way controverted, impeached or otherwise challenged, at the trial or on appeal. Thus the court's finding of a failure of proof cannot be supported upon the record and, therefore, and contrary to plaintiffs' contention, the affirmance at the Appellate Division was ineffective to save it.

Make the Connection

Article 2, like the common law, allows recovery of both direct damages (here, the lost profit) and indirect (incidental) damages. For more detail on incidental damages, see page 1084.

. . . .

It follows that plaintiffs are entitled to restitution of the sum of $4,250 paid by them on account of the contract price less an offset to defendant in the amount of $3,253 on account of its lost profit of $2,579 and its incidental damages of $674.*

The order of the Appellate Division should be modified, with costs in all courts, in accordance with this opinion, and, as so modified, affirmed.

FULD, C.J., and BURKE, SCILEPPI, BERGAN, BREITEL and JASEN, JJ., concur.

 **Reading the Law Critically:** *Vitex Mfg. Corp.*

The question raised in *Vitex* is whether fixed costs ("overhead" in this opinion) may be included along with variable costs (the materials and labor actually expended on the job) in determining the service-provider's lost profit and therefore its direct damages. Many cases address this issue, most of them agreeing with the outcome in *Vitex*.

1. How does the court calculate plaintiff's damages in this services contract? What rationale and policies support the court's result?

2. What calculation does the losing party advocate? Why does the court reject it?

Vitex Mfg. Corp. v. Caribtex Corp.

VITEX MANUFACTURING CORPORATION, Ltd., Plaintiff-Appellee

v.

CARIBTEX CORPORATION, Defendant-Appellant

United States Court of Appeals, Third Circuit
377 F.2d 795 (3d Cir. 1967)

STALEY, Chief Judge.

This is an appeal by Caribtex Corporation from a judgment of the District Court of the Virgin Islands finding Caribtex in breach of a contract entered into with Vitex Manufacturing Company, Ltd., and awarding $21,114 plus interest to Vitex for loss of profits. The only substantial question raised by Caribtex is whether it was error for the district court, sitting without a jury, not to consider

---

* [Authors' Note: We omitted the court's discussion of UCC § 2-718 (2), (3), which allows a breaching buyer to recover any prepaid amount, minus seller's damages from the breach. The other complexities of this section are beyond the scope of this course.]

overhead as part of Vitex's costs in determining the amount of profits lost. We conclude that under the facts presented, the district court was not compelled to consider Vitex's overhead costs, and we will affirm the judgment.

Before discussing the details of the controversy between the parties, it will be helpful to briefly describe the peculiar legal setting in which this suit arose. At the time of the events in question, there were high tariff barriers to the importation of foreign wool products. However, under § 301 of the Tariff Act of 1930, 19 U.S.C.A. § 1301a, repealed but the provision continued under Revised Tariff Schedules, 19 U.S.C.A. § 1202, note 3(a)(i)(ii) (1965), if such goods were imported into the Virgin Islands and were processed in some manner so that their finished value exceeded their importation value by at least 50%, then the high tariffs to importation into the continental United States would be avoided. Even after the processing, the foreign wool enjoyed a price advantage over domestic products so that the business flourished. However, to keep the volume of this business at such levels that Congress would not be stirred to change the law, the Virgin Islands Legislature imposed "quotas" on persons engaging in processing, limiting their output. 33 V.I.C. § 504 (Supp.1966).

Vitex was engaged in the business of chemically shower-proofing imported cloth so that it could be imported duty-free into the United States. For this purpose, Vitex maintained a plant in the Virgin Islands and was entitled to process a specific quantity of material under the Virgin Islands quota system. Caribtex was in the business of importing cloth into the islands, securing its processing, and exporting it to the United States.

In the fall of 1963, Vitex found itself with an unused portion of its quota but no customers, and Vitex closed its plant. Caribtex acquired some Italian wool and subsequently negotiations for a processing contract were conducted between the principals of the respective companies in New York City. Though the record below is clouded with differing versions of the negotiations and the alleged final terms, the trial court found upon substantial evidence in the record that the parties did enter into a contract in which Vitex agreed to process 125,000 yards of Caribtex's woolen material at a price of 26 cents per yard.

Vitex proceeded to re-open its Virgin Islands plant, ordered the necessary chemicals, recalled its work force and made all the necessary preparations to perform its end of the bargain. However, no goods were forthcoming from Caribtex, despite repeated demands by Vitex, apparently because Caribtex was unsure that the processed wool would be entitled to duty-free treatment by the customs officials. Vitex subsequently brought this suit to recover the profits lost through Caribtex's breach.

Vitex alleged, and the trial court found, that its gross profits for processing said material under the contract would have been $31,250 and that its costs would have been $10,136, leaving Vitex's damages for loss of profits at $21,114. On appeal, Caribtex asserted numerous objections to the detailed computation of lost profits. While the record below is sometimes confusing, we conclude that the trial court had substantial evidence to support its findings on damages. It must be remembered that the difficulty in exactly ascertaining Vitex's costs is due to Caribtex's wrongful conduct in repudiating the contract before performance by Vitex. Caribtex will not be permitted to benefit by the uncertainty it has caused. Thus, since there was a sufficient basis in the record to support the trial court's determination of substantial damages, we will not set aside its judgment. Stentor Elec. Mfg. Co. v. Klaxon Co., 115 F.2d 268 (C.A.3, 1940) . . . .

Caribtex first raised the issue at the oral argument of this appeal that the trial court erred by disregarding Vitex's overhead expenses in determining lost profits. In general, overhead ". . . may be said to include broadly the continuous expenses of the business, irrespective of the outlay on a particular contract." Grand Trunk W.R.R. Co. v. H.W. Nelson Co., 116 F.2d 823, 839 (C.A.6, 1941). Such expenses would include executive and clerical salaries, property taxes, general administration expenses, etc. Although Vitex did not expressly seek recovery for overhead, if a portion of these fixed expenses should be allocated as costs to the Caribtex contract, then under the judgment of the district court Vitex tacitly recovered these expenses as part of its damages for lost profits, and the damages should be reduced accordingly. Presumably, the portion to be allocated to costs would be a pro rata share of Vitex's annual overhead according to the volume of business Vitex would have done over the year if Caribtex had not breached the contract.

> **FYI**
> When the appellate court says that the trial court "disregarded" the overhead expenses, it really means that the trial court did not subtract them from the company's gross profits, thereby increasing Vitex's lost profit damages.

> **FYI**
> Students are sometimes puzzled that Vitex continued to owe executive and clerical salaries, pay property taxes, and incur general administration expenses, even when its manufacturing plant was closed or inoperative. But closing down a manufacturing plant does not mean the business itself is shut down. The business may continue to employ people who look for additional work for the business, maintain and secure the manufacturing plant, and continue to run the financial infrastructure of the business (e.g., paying taxes and other ongoing expenses of the business).

Although there is authority to the contrary, we feel that the better view is that normally, in a claim for lost profits, overhead should be treated as a part of gross profits and recoverable as damages, and should not be considered as part of the seller's costs. A number of cases hold that since overhead expenses are not affected by the performance of the particular contract, there should be no need to deduct them in computing lost profits. E.g., Oakland California Towel Co. v. Sivils, 52 Cal.App.2d

517, 520, 126 P.2d 651, 652 (1942) . . . . The theory of these cases is that the seller is entitled to recover losses incurred and gains prevented in excess of savings made possible, Restatement, Contracts § 329 (made part of the law of the Virgin Islands, 1 V.I.C. § 4); since overhead is fixed and nonperformance of the contract produced no overhead cost savings, no deduction from profits should result.

The soundness of the rule is exemplified by this case. Before negotiations began between Vitex and Caribtex, Vitex had reached a lull in business activity and had closed its plant. If Vitex had entered into no other contracts for the rest of the year, the profitability of its operations would have been determined by deducting its production costs and overhead from gross receipts yielded in previous transactions. When this opportunity arose to process Caribtex's wool, the only additional expenses Vitex would incur would be those of re-opening its plant and the direct costs of processing, such as labor, chemicals and fuel oil. Overhead would have remained the same whether or not Vitex and Caribtex entered their contract and whether or not Vitex actually processed Caribtex's goods. Since this overhead remained constant, in no way attributable-to or affected-by the Caribtex contract, it would be improper to consider it as a cost of Vitex's performance to be deducted from the gross proceeds of the Caribtex contract.

However, Caribtex may argue that this view ignores modern accounting principles, and that overhead is as much a cost of production as other expenses. It is true that successful businessmen must set their prices at sufficient levels to recoup all their expenses, including overhead, and to gain profits. Thus, the price the businessman should charge on each transaction could be thought of as that price necessary to yield a pro rata portion of the company's fixed overhead, the direct costs associated with production, and a "clear" profit. Doubtless this type of calculation is used by businessmen and their accountants. Pacific Portland Cement Co. v. Food Mach. & Chem. Corp., 178 F.2d 541 (C.A.9, 1949). However, because it is useful for planning purposes to allocate a portion of overhead to each transaction, it does not follow that this allocate[d] share of fixed overhead should be considered a cost factor in the computation of lost profits on individual transactions.

First, it must be recognized that the pro rata allocation of overhead costs is only an analytical construct. In a similar manner one could allocate a pro rata share of the company's advertising cost, taxes and/or charitable gifts. The point is that while these items all are paid from the proceeds of the business, they do not normally bear such a direct relationship to any individual transaction to be considered a cost in ascertaining lost profits.

Secondly, even were we to recognize the allocation of overhead as proper in this case, we should uphold the tacit award of overhead expense to Vitex as a "loss incurred." Conditioned Air Corp. v. Rock Island Motor Transit Co., 114 N.W.2d 304, cert. denied, 371 U.S. 825, 83 S.Ct. 46, 9 L.Ed.2d 64 (1962). By the very nature of this allocation process, as the number of transaction[s] over which overhead can be spread becomes smaller, each transaction must bear a greater portion or allocate share of the fixed overhead cost. Suppose a company has fixed overhead of $10,000 and engages in five similar transactions; then the receipts of each transaction would bear $2000 of overhead expense. If the company is now forced to spread this $10,000 over only four transactions, then the overhead expense per transaction will rise to $2500, significantly reducing the profitability of the four remaining transactions. Thus, where the contract is between businessmen familiar with commercial practices, as here, the breaching party should reasonably foresee that his breach will not only cause a loss of "clear" profit, but also a loss in that the profitability of other transactions will be reduced. Resolute Ins. Co. v. Percy Jones, Inc., 198 F.2d 309 (C.A.10, 1952).... Therefore, this loss is within the contemplation of "losses caused and gains prevented," and overhead should be considered to be a compensable item of damage.

Significantly, the Uniform Commercial Code, adopted in the Virgin Islands, 11A V.I.C. §§ 1-101 et seq., and in virtually every state today, provides for the recovery of overhead in circumstances similar to those presented here. Under 11A V.I.C. § 2-708, the seller's measure of damage for non-acceptance or repudiation is the difference between the contract price and the market price, but if this relief is inadequate to put the seller in as good position as if the contract had been fully performed, ". . . then the measure of damages is the profit (including reasonable overhead) which the seller would have made from full performance by the buyer . . . ." 11A V.I.C. § 2-708(2). While this contract is not controlled by the Code, the Code is persuasive here because it embodies the foremost modern legal thought concerning commercial transactions. Indeed, it may overrule some of the cases denying recovery for overhead. E.g., Wilhelm Lubrication Co. v. Brattrud, 197 Minn. 626, 632, 268 N.W. 634, 636, 106 A.L.R. 1279 (1936).

Make the Connection

Recall the defense of unconscionability in Chapter 5 (page 512). Note that the court does not categorically reject business-to-business unconscionability. In response to Caribtex's unconscionability argument, what facts does the court find to be persuasive?

Caribtex also argued that the contract should not be enforced because it was unconscionable. While Vitex was to make a large profit on the processing and Caribtex did bear the risk of failure to meet customs standards, the contract was freely entered-into, after much negotiation, between parties of apparently equal bargaining strength. This was not a contract of adhesion— Vitex was not the only processor in the Virgin Islands and Caribtex's bargaining strength was evidenced by the successive and substantial price reductions it wrested from Vitex during the negotiations.

Compare, Campbell Soup Co. v. Wentz, 172 F.2d 80 (C.A.3, 1948); Henningsen v. Bloomfield Motors, Inc., 161 A.2d 69 (N.J. 1960).

The judgment of the district court will be affirmed.

————————————

§ 2.1.5. Indirect Expectation Damages

We turn now to a consideration of indirect (special) damages, which are comprised of incidental and consequential damages:

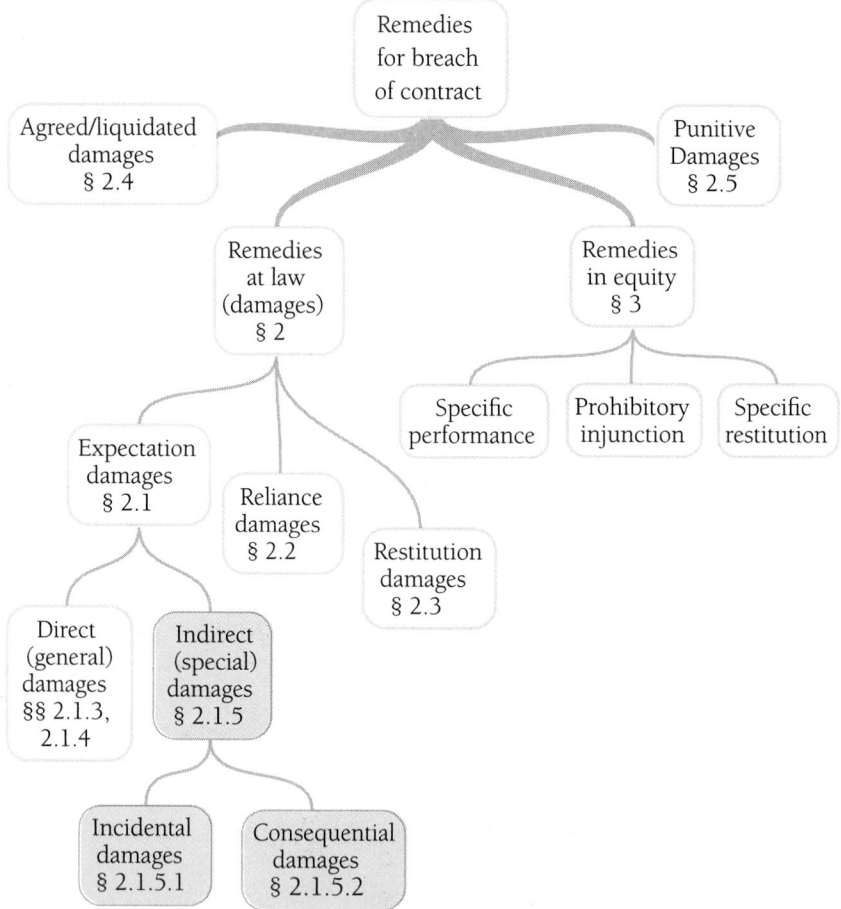

§ 2.1.5.1. Incidental Damages

As indicated on page 1046, incidental damages are extra costs incurred by the aggrieved party in dealing with the breach or trying to prevent (mitigate) further losses. They may include the costs of storing or reshipping or reselling defective or repudiated goods, boarding up and paying extra insurance on a building left unfinished by a vendor, handling a defective delivery, arranging the purchase of substitute goods, paying a broker to find a substitute buyer, or spending employee time negotiating a replacement contract with a new party. In *Neri v. Retail Marine Corp.* (page 1076) the court awarded incidental damages to the seller for storage, upkeep, finance charges, and insurance for the boat during the time the seller held the boat for resale.

The UCC provisions below identify common items of incidental damages in sale-of-goods contracts:

UCC § 2-710. **Seller's Incidental Damages.**

Incidental damages to an aggrieved seller include any commercially reasonable charges, expenses or commissions incurred in stopping delivery, in the transportation, care and custody of goods after the buyer's breach, in connection with return or resale of the goods or otherwise resulting from the breach.

UCC § 2-715. **Buyer's Incidental . . . Damages.**

(1) Incidental damages resulting from the seller's breach include expenses reasonably incurred in inspection, receipt, transportation and care and custody of goods rightfully rejected, any commercially reasonable charges, expenses or commissions in connection with effecting cover and any other reasonable expense incident to the delay or other breach.

. . . .

Although attorneys fees fit conceptually into the category of incidental damages, under U.S. law they are not recoverable as incidental damages unless (1) they are specified as recoverable in the parties' agreement, (2) they are granted by statute, or (3) the lawsuit is frivolous or in bad faith.

attys fees not generally recoverable as incid. dam.

Problem 9-8: Incidental Damages

Big Company, Inc. and Papers R Us, Inc. sign a written agreement in which Big Company agrees to buy 5000 reams of photocopy paper from Papers R Us at a stated price, deliverable as called for by the buyer. Half-way through the year, Big Company demands that Papers R Us reduce the price for the remaining deliveries because the market price has decreased. Papers R Us refuses to do so, and Big Company does not take or pay for any more deliveries. Assume that Big Company is in breach. Papers R Us sues Big Company for breach of contract.

Which **two** of the following items are clearly recoverable incidental damages under the UCC, and which additional item is arguably recoverable as incidental damages?

a. Paper R Us's costs to store the paper after Big Company refuses to order according to the contract, until Papers R Us can find another buyer for it

b. Paper R Us's taxes paid on <u>all</u> of its paper held in inventory

c. The cost of hiring an attorney to figure out how to induce Big Company to honor the contract

d. Paper R Us's loss of profit on the Big Company contract

e. Paper R Us's costs to hire a broker to find another buyer for the paper that Big Company was supposed to take.

f. Paper R Us's interest paid on a loan to cover the missing cash flow that was supposed to result from the Big Company contract

§ 2.1.5.2. Consequential Damages

As noted on page 1046, consequential damages are the downstream *losses* caused by the breach. They are often where the "real money" is in the dispute, because these ripple effects of the breach can cause lost profits, lost customers, lost business volume, and downstream breaches caused by the original breach. As with other damages, the aggrieved party must prove the consequential injury was caused by the breach. Causation alone is not enough, however. The cases that follow illustrate additional standards that govern the award of consequential damages.

Reading the Law Critically:
Hadley, Redgrave, and *Kenford* (I) and (II)

1. What limitation(s) does the court identify for the award of consequential damages in each case?

2. What justification is or might be offered for the limitation(s)? Are there competing policies that should be taken into account?

3. Does each court apply the limitation(s) appropriately to the facts of the case?

Hadley v. Baxendale

JOSEPH HADLEY and JONAH HADLEY, Plaintiffs

v.

BAXENDALE, Defendant

Court of Exchequer

156 Eng. Rep. 145 (Ct. Exch. 1854)

mill w/ broken crank shaft

At the trial before Crompton, J., at the last Gloucester Assizes, it appeared that the plaintiffs carried on an extensive business as millers at Gloucester; and that on the 11th on May, their mill was stopped by a breakage of the crank shaft by which the mill was worked. The steam-engine was manufactured by Messrs. Joyce & Co., the engineers, at Greenwich, and it became necessary to send the shaft as a pattern for a new one to Greenwich. The fracture was discovered on the 12th, and on the 13th the plaintiffs sent one of their servants to the office of the defendants, who are the well-known carriers trading under the name of Pickford & Co., for the purpose of having the shaft carried to Greenwich. The plaintiffs' servant told the clerk that the mill was stopped, and that the shaft must be sent immediately; and in answer to the inquiry when the shaft would be taken, the answer was, that if it was sent up by twelve o'clock any day, it would be delivered at Greenwich on the following day. On the following day the shaft was taken by the defendants, before noon, for the purpose of being conveyed to Greenwich, and the sum of 2£. 4s. was paid for its carriage for the whole distance; at the same time the defendants' clerk was told that a special entry, if required, should be made to hasten its delivery. The delivery of the shaft at Greenwich was delayed by some neglect; and the consequence was, that the plaintiffs did not receive the new shaft for several days after they would otherwise have done, and the working of their mill was thereby delayed, and they thereby lost the profits they would otherwise have received.

broken shaft sent to repairs

neglectful delay = lost profits

On the part of the defendants, it was objected that these damages were too remote, and that the defendants were not liable with respect to them. The learned Judge left the case generally to the jury, who found a verdict with damages beyond the amount paid into Court.

Whateley, in last Michaelmas Term, obtained a rule nisi for a new trial, on the ground of misdirection.

What's That?

A "rule nisi" is an order to show cause. The "rule" will take effect unless the affected party shows the court why it should be set aside. At the end of the opinion, the court makes the rule effective with a "rule absolute."

Alderson, B. We think that there ought to be a new trial in this case; but, in so doing, we deem it to be expedient and necessary to state explicitly the rule which the Judge, at the next trial, ought, in our opinion, to direct the jury to be governed by when they estimate the damages.

. . . .

. . . . Where two parties have made a contract which one of them has broken, the damages which the other party ought to receive in respect of such breach of contract should be such as may fairly and reasonably be considered either arising naturally, i.e., according to the usual course of things, from such breach of contract itself, or such as may reasonably be supposed to have been in the contemplation of both parties, at the time they made the contract, as the probable result of the breach of it. Now, if the special circumstances under which the contract was actually made were communicated by the plaintiffs to the defendants, and thus known to both parties, the damages resulting from the breach of such a contract, which they would reasonably contemplate, would be the amount of injury which would ordinarily follow from a breach of contract under these special circumstances so known and communicated. But, on the other hand, if these special circumstances were wholly unknown to the party breaking the contract, he, at the most, could only be supposed to have had in his contemplation the amount of injury which would arise generally, and in the great multitude of cases not affected by any special circumstances, from such a breach of contract. For, had the special circumstances been known, the parties might have specially provided for the breach of contract by special terms as to the damages in that case; and of this advantage it would be very unjust to deprive them. . . . Now, in the present case, if we are to apply the principles above laid down, we find that the only circumstances here communicated by the plaintiffs to the defendants at the time of the contract was made, were, that the article to be carried was the broken shaft of a mill, and that the plaintiffs were the millers of the mill.

> ### Take Note!
>
> Just what was communicated to the defendants is not clear. Compare what Baron Alderson says in the opinion to what is said in the summary of the facts that begins the case report, which was likely prepared by someone else. Whatever was actually communicated, the ruling in the case is based on the facts stated in the opinion itself.

But how do these circumstances show reasonably that the profits of the mill must be stopped by an unreasonable delay in the delivery of the broken shaft by the carrier to the third person? Suppose the plaintiffs had another shaft in their possession put up or putting up at the time, and that they only wished to send back the broken shaft to the engineer who made it; it is clear that this would be quite consistent with the above circumstances, and yet the unreasonable delay in the delivery would have no effect upon the intermediate profits of the mill. Or, again, suppose that, at the time of the delivery to the carrier, the machinery of the mill had been in other respects defective, then, also, the same results would follow. Here it is true that the shaft was actually sent back to serve as a model for the new one, and that the want of a new one was the only cause of the stoppage of the mill, and that the loss of profits really arose from not sending down the new shaft in proper time, and that this arose from the delay in delivering the broken one to serve as a model. But it is obvious that, in the great multitude of cases of millers sending off broken shafts to third persons by a carrier under ordinary circumstances, such consequences would not, in all probability, have occurred; and these special circumstances were here never communicated by the plaintiffs to the defendants. It follows therefore, that the loss of profits here cannot reasonably be considered such a consequence of the breach of contract as could have been fairly and reasonably contemplated by both the parties when they made this contract. For such loss would neither have flowed naturally from the breach of this contract in the great multitude of such cases occurring under ordinary circumstances, nor were the special circumstances, which, perhaps, would have made it a reasonable and natural consequence of such breach of contract, communicated to or known by the defendants. The Judge ought, therefore, to have told the jury that upon the facts then before them they ought not to take the loss of profits into consideration at all in estimating the damages. There must therefore be a new trial in this case.

See It!

This print shows a steam engine of the type that was commonly used in flour mills in England in the mid-1800s. The crankshaft is the lengthwise shaft in the right half of the picture. Its function is to transmit the power of the steam pistons in order to power the rest of the machine. A treatise described a steam engine crankshaft as follows: "Let the crank of an engine be 2 1/2 feet radius, and the piston will make a stroke of 5 feet long; let the connecting rod be 15 feet long, and the great lever 15 feet long, or 7 1/2 feet radius." John Farey, A Treatise on the Steam Engine: Historical, Practical and Descriptive 415 (1827). From this description, we surmise that the crankshaft in Hadley was fairly large and long. If true, how does this affect your view of the court's decision?

Rule absolute.

Behind the Scenes

Above is Joseph and Jonah Hadley's City Flour Mills in June 2005. "This photograph shows the Mill after renovation was completed. The upper floors are now residential, and the ground floor will be occupied by a restaurant-pub. The view is looking from the Docks toward Gloucester Cathedral (seen in the background). Grain, much of it from the Ukraine and Canada, was carried by wagon from the barges to the Mill. It is believed that the steam engine was on the ground floor of the central building. The building to the left, of typical Gloucestershire stone, was the Mill's office. The one on the right is a warehouse."*

Prior to *Hadley,* courts had given juries unfettered discretion to set the amount of damages for breach of contract. In the mid-nineteenth century, judicial policy had begun to favor the growth of industry. In *Hadley,* on this appeal from a jury trial that had awarded the plaintiff full damages, Baron Alderson introduced a new rule—the rule later (and now) accepted as authoritative in limiting juries' freedom to award consequential damages. Richard Danzig, Hadley v. Baxendale: *A Study in the Industrialization of the Law*, in *Contracts Stories* 1 (Douglas G. Baird ed. 2007).

Equally interesting is the two different fact versions articulated in *Hadley.* Baron Alderson's opinion stated that plaintiff had not given proper

---

* The photograph is courtesy Michael Thorpe, Gloucester City Council, which has granted permission for its use in all educational or nonprofit contexts. http://lawprofessors.typepad.com/contractsprof_blog/2005/06/hadleys_mill.html .

notice to the defendant and suggested that a mill might have another shaft in possession or that other defects might have stopped the mill's operation. However, the reporter's statement of the facts says that "the plaintiffs' servant told the clerk that the mill was stopped, and that the shaft must be sent immediately; . . . that a special entry, if required, should be made to hasten its delivery." Richard Danzig & Geoffrey R. Watson, *Hadley & Another v. Baxendale & Another,* in *The Capability Problem in Contract Law* 48, at 61-64, 66-67 (2d ed. 2004).

There is debate as to how these facts were overlooked—or simply discarded—by the court. One argument is that Baron Alderman applied his rule to the wrong set of facts. However, in *Victoria Laundry Ltd. v. Newman Indus.*, 2 K.B. 528, 537 (1949), the court opined that Baron Alderman's statement of the facts was accurate and that the reporter's version was not, insofar as they conflicted. Joseph M. Perillo, *Calamari and Perillo on Contracts* 493 n.4 (6th ed. 2009). Whatever the facts, we are left with a holding based on the court's version.

Redgrave v. Boston Symphony Orchestra, Inc.

VANESSA REDGRAVE and VANESSA REDGRAVE ENTERPRISES, LTD.,
Plaintiffs-Appellants

v.

BOSTON SYMPHONY ORCHESTRA, INC., Defendant-Appellee

United States Court of Appeals, First Circuit
855 F.2d 888 (1st Cir. 1988)

OPINION EN BANC

COFFIN, Circuit Judge.

. . . .

The plaintiffs, actress Vanessa Redgrave and Vanessa Redgrave Enterprises, Ltd. (hereinafter Redgrave), brought suit against the Boston Symphony Orchestra (hereinafter the BSO) for cancelling a contract for Redgrave's appearance as narrator in a performance of Stravinsky's "Oedipus Rex." The cancellation occurred in

s-ll-ts CLD

the wake of protests over Redgrave's participation because of her support of the Palestine Liberation Organization. She sought recovery . . . for breach of contract. [Redgrave's civil rights claim is omitted here.]

A jury awarded Redgrave $100,000 in consequential damages caused by the BSO's breach of contract . . . . On the BSO's motion for judgment notwithstanding the verdict on the consequential damages issue, the district court held that the evidence of consequential damages was sufficient but that Redgrave could not recover these damages because of First Amendment limitations. . . . Redgrave appealed from these rulings, and the BSO cross-appealed, arguing that the evidence of consequential damages was insufficient.

Who's That?

A member of a prestigious acting family, Vanessa Redgrave is an acclaimed dramatic actress who has been hailed by playwrights Arthur Miller and Tennessee Williams as "the greatest living actress of our times." Her films include *Camelot* (1967), *Morgan: A Suitable Case for Treatment* (1966), *Isadora* (1966), *Mary, Queen of Scots* (1971), and *Julia* (1978), for which she won an Academy Award. For more information, see http://en.wikipedia.org/wiki/Vanessa_redgrave.

We conclude, in Part II, that the district court erred in reversing the jury's award of consequential damages, but that Redgrave has presented sufficient evidence to prove only $12,000 in consequential damages, minus certain expenses. . . . We therefore . . . remand for entry of a reduced judgment for consequential damages on the contract claim.

I. Procedural History

In March 1982, the Boston Symphony Orchestra (BSO) engaged Vanessa Redgrave to narrate Stravinsky's "Oedipus Rex" in a series of concerts in Boston and New York. Following announcement of the engagement, the BSO received calls from its subscribers and from community members protesting the engagement because of Redgrave's political support for the Palestine Liberation Organization and because of her views regarding the state of Israel. On or about April 1, 1982, the BSO cancelled its contract with Redgrave and its performances of "Oedipus Rex."

Redgrave sued the BSO for breach of contract . . . . The BSO argued at trial that the contract rightfully was cancelled because the cancellation was the result of "a cause or causes beyond the reasonable control" of the BSO. In response to the civil rights claim, BSO agents testified that they had not cancelled the performances in order to punish Redgrave for her past speech or repress her future speech, but because it was felt that potential disruptions, given the community reaction, would implicate the physical safety of the audience and players and would detract from the artistic qualities of the production.

Following a sixteen-day trial, the jury found that the BSO wrongfully had breached its contract with Redgrave. On that basis, the district court awarded Redgrave her stipulated performance fee of $27,500. The jury also found that the BSO's cancellation had damaged Redgrave's career by causing loss of future professional opportunities, and awarded Redgrave $100,000 in consequential damages. The district court found that the question whether there was sufficient evidence to support a finding of $100,000 in consequential damages was a "close and debatable" one, but concluded that there was sufficient evidence to support the award. Nevertheless, the district court overturned the grant of consequential damages,[2] finding that a First Amendment right of freedom of speech was implicated by the theory of consequential damages advanced by Redgrave and that Redgrave had not met the strict standards required by the First Amendment for recovery of damages. *Redgrave v. Boston Symphony Orchestra, Inc.*, 602 F.Supp. 1189, 1193-1203 (D.Mass.1985).

. . . .

Redgrave appealed from the district court's entry of judgment notwithstanding the verdict on the consequential damages claim . . . . The BSO cross-appealed, arguing that even if the First Amendment should be found inapplicable to the consequential damages claim, the evidence of those damages was insufficient to support the verdict.

II. The Consequential Damages Claim
A. *Consequential Damages for Loss of Professional Opportunities*

In response to special interrogatories, the jury found that the BSO's cancellation of the "Oedipus Rex" concerts caused consequential harm to Redgrave's professional career and that this harm was a foreseeable consequence within the contemplation of the parties at the time they entered the contract. 602 F.Supp. at 1204. A threshold question is whether Massachusetts contract law allows the award of such consequential damages for harm to a claimant's professional career.

Redgrave's consequential damages claim is based on the proposition that a significant number of movie and theater offers that she would ordinarily have received in the years 1982 and following were in fact not offered to her as a result of the BSO's cancellation in April 1982. The BSO characterizes this claim as one

---

[2] The court apparently submitted the factual question to the jury either before it decided the legal issue or to protect against the need for a retrial in the event of reversal on appeal.

for damage to Redgrave's reputation,[3] and argues that the recent Massachusetts state court decisions in *McCone v. New England Telephone & Telegraph Co.*, 393 Mass. 231, 471 N.E.2d 47 (1984), and *Daley v. Town of West Brookfield*, 19 Mass.App.Ct. 1019, 476 N.E.2d 980 (1985), establish that Massachusetts law does not permit plaintiffs in breach of contract actions to recover consequential damages for harm to reputation.

In *McCone v. New England Telephone & Telegraph Co.*, plaintiffs alleged that their employer's breach of an implied covenant of good faith had caused them loss of salary increases, loss of pension benefits, and "damage to their professional reputations, disruption of their personal lives, and great pain of body and mind." 393 Mass. at 234 n.8. The Massachusetts Supreme Judicial Court held that the claims for damages to reputation and other emotional injury could not be sustained in the suit because "these additional damages are not contract damages." *Id.* In *Daley v. Town of West Brookfield*, a Massachusetts appellate court observed that "[d]amages for injury to reputation are usually not available in contract actions," noting that the rationale most often given is that "such damages are remote and not within the contemplation of the parties." 19 Mass.App.Ct. at 1019 n.1, 476 N.E.2d at 980 n.1.

The BSO notes that Massachusetts is in agreement with virtually all other jurisdictions in holding that damages for reputation are not available in contract actions. *See, e.g., Volkswagen Interamericana, S.A. v. Rohlsen*, 360 F.2d 437, 446 (1st Cir.1966) (applying federal law); *Stancil v. Mergenthaler Linotype Co.*, 589 F.Supp. 78, 84-85 (D.Haw.1984); *O'Leary v. Sterling Extruder Corp.*, 533 F.Supp. 1205, 1209 (E.D.Wis.1982); *Skagway City School Board v. Davis*, 543 P.2d 218, 225-27 (Ala.1975); *Tousley v. Atlantic City Ambassador Hotel Corp.*, 25 N.J.Misc. 88, 50 A.2d 472, 474-75 (N.J.Sup.Ct.1947). This impressive line of cases, however, becomes less impressive for our purposes when the reasoning in these cases is analyzed with reference to the particular claim put forth by Redgrave.

In cases that have analyzed the reasons for disallowing a contract claim for reputation damages, courts have identified two determinative factors. First, courts have observed that attempting to calculate damages for injury to reputation is "unduly speculative." *Skagway City School Board*, 543 P.2d at 225. *See O'Leary*, 533 F.Supp. at 1209; *Tousley*, 50 A.2d at 474-75. In many cases, the courts have viewed the claims for damages to reputation as analogous to claims for physical or emotional distress and have noted the difficulty in ascertaining such damages for contract purposes. *See, e.g., Westwater v. Rector, Warden and Vestry of Grace Church*, 140 Cal. 339, 342, 73 P. 1055 (1903) ("Damages to health, reputa-

---

[3] The BSO notes that Redgrave contended that "the cancellation, as communicated to other employers through the news media, harmed Vanessa Redgrave because it carried with it the message 'that Vanessa Redgrave was unemployable,' a claim for damage to Redgrave's reputation."

tion, or feelings are not clearly ascertainable either in their nature or origin."). As the court in *Skagway* noted, an estimate of injury to reputation "must rest upon a number of imprecise variables," including the causal connection between the breach of contract and the injury to reputation and the amount by which any future earnings would be decreased by causes other than the breach. *Skagway City School Board,* 543 P.2d at 225.

The second factor that courts identify is that damages for injury to reputation "cannot reasonably be presumed to have been within the contemplation of the parties when they entered into the contract." *Skagway City School Board,* 543 P.2d at 225. These courts state that the basic rule of *Hadley v. Baxendale,* 9 Ex. 341, 156 Eng.Rep. 145 (1854), which requires that contract damages be of the kind that arise naturally from the breach of a contract or be of a kind that reasonably may have been in the contemplation of the parties when they entered the contract, cannot possibly be met in a claim for general damages to reputation occurring as the result of a breach of contract. *See Skagway City School Board,* 543 P.2d at 225; *O'Leary,* 533 F.Supp. at 1209-10; *Tousley,* 50 A.2d at 474-75; *Mastoras v. Chicago, M. & St. P.R.R.,* 217 F. 153, 154 (W.D.Wash.1914). The Massachusetts Supreme Judicial Court seems to have accepted this rationale as a legitimate one for disallowing claims for injury to reputation as a contract damage. *See Daley v. Town of West Brookfield,* 476 N.E.2d at 980 n. 1 ("The rationale often given [for disallowing damages for injury to reputation in contract actions] is that such damages are remote and not within the contemplation of the parties."). *See also* 5 *Corbin on Contracts,* § 1007-11 at 70-87 (1964); 11 Williston, *Contracts,* § 1344 at 226-29 (1968) (discussing *Hadley v. Baxendale* general rule of consequential damages).

The claim advanced by Redgrave is significantly different, however, from a general claim of damage to reputation. Redgrave is not claiming that her general reputation as a professional actress has been tarnished by the BSO's cancellation. Rather, she claims that a number of specific movie and theater performances that would have been offered to her in the usual course of events were not offered to her as a result of the BSO's cancellation. This is the type of specific claim that, with appropriate evidence, can meet the *Hadley v. Baxendale* rule, as adopted by the Massachusetts Supreme Judicial Court in *John Hetherington & Sons, Ltd. v. William Firth Co.,* 210 Mass. 8, 21; 95 N.E. 961, 964 (1911) (in breach of contract action, injured party receives compensation for any loss that follows as a natural consequence from the breach, was within the contemplation of reasonable parties as a probable result of breach, and may be computed by "rational methods upon a firm basis of facts"). As the district court correctly noted in a preliminary memorandum:

[I]f plaintiffs proved other employers refused to hire Redgrave after termination of the BSO contract because of that termination (that loss of the other employment "followed as a natural consequence" from the termination of the contract), that this loss of other employment would reasonably have been foreseen by the parties at the time of contracting and at the time of termination, and that damages are rationally calculable, then plaintiffs may be entitled to damages that include monies for loss of the other employment. Although plaintiffs have a heavy burden to carry here, it cannot be said with certainty at this time that they will not be able to meet this burden.

Redgrave v. BSO, 557 F.Supp. 230, 234 (D.Mass.1983).

The jury was given appropriate instructions to help it determine whether Redgrave had suffered consequential damages through loss of future professional opportunities. They were told to find that the BSO's cancellation was a proximate cause of harm to Redgrave's professional career only if they determined that "harm would not have occurred but for the cancellation and that the harm was a natural and probable consequence of the cancellation." *Redgrave v. BSO*, 602 F.Supp. at 1211. In addition, they were told that damages should be allowed for consequential harm "only if the harm was a foreseeable consequence within the contemplation of the parties to the contract when it was made." *Id.* at 1212. In response to special interrogatories, the jury found that the BSO's cancellation caused consequential harm to Redgrave's career and that the harm was a foreseeable consequence within the contemplation of the parties. 602 F.Supp. at 1204.

Although we find that Redgrave did not present sufficient evidence to establish that the BSO's cancellation caused consequential harm to her professional career in the amount of $100,000, *see infra* at 896-900, we hold that, as a matter of Massachusetts contract law, a plaintiff may receive consequential damages if the plaintiff proves with sufficient evidence that a breach of contract proximately caused the loss of identifiable professional opportunities. This type of claim is sufficiently different from a nonspecific allegation of damage to reputation that it appropriately falls outside the general rule that reputation damages are not an acceptable form of contract damage.

. . . .

III. First Amendment Restrictions

. . . [The court concludes that awarding relief to Redgrave does not raise First Amendment issues because Redgrave's claim was that damages flowed from the BSO's cancellation, rather than any protected communication about Redgrave.]

. . . .

C. *Sufficiency of the Evidence*

The requirements for awarding consequential damages for breach of contract are designed to ensure that a breaching party pays only those damages that have resulted from its breach. Thus, to receive consequential damages, the plaintiff must establish a "basis for an inference of fact" that the plaintiff has actually been damaged, Williston, *Contracts,* § 1345 at 231, and the factfinder must be able to compute the compensation "by rational methods upon a firm basis of facts." *John Hetherington & Sons,* 210 Mass. at 21, 95 N.E. at 964.

In analyzing the evidence presented by Redgrave on her claim for consequential damages, we are guided by the basic principle that on a motion for judgment notwithstanding the verdict the evidence must be viewed in the light most favorable to the party for whom the jury found, and that that party must be given "the benefit of every favorable inference that may be fairly drawn." *Borras v. Sea-Land Service, Inc.,* 586 F.2d 881, 885 (1st Cir.1978) (quoting *Dumas v. MacLean,* 404 F.2d 1062, 1064 (1st Cir.1968)). In examining the evidence, however, we must not neglect uncontradicted evidence offered by the other party. *Layne v. Vinzant,* 657 F.2d 468, 472 (1st Cir.1981); *Allen Pen Co. v. Springfield Photo Mount Co.,* 653 F.2d 17, 19 (1st Cir.1981). Further, the party for whom the jury found is not entitled to "unreasonable inferences which rest on conjecture and speculation." *Carlson v. American Safety Equipment Corp.,* 528 F.2d 384, 386 (1st Cir.1976); *see also Goldstein v. Kelleher,* 728 F.2d 32, 39 (1st Cir.1984).

In order for Redgrave to prove that the BSO's cancellation resulted in the loss of other professional opportunities, she must present sufficient facts for a jury reasonably to infer that Redgrave lost wages and professional opportunities subsequent to April 1982, that such losses were the result of the BSO's cancellation rather than the result of other, independent factors, and that damages for such losses are capable of being ascertained "by reference to some definite standard, either market value, established experience or direct inference from known circumstances." *John Hetherington & Sons,* 210 Mass. at 21, 95 N.E. at 964. During trial, evidence was presented regarding losses Redgrave allegedly suffered in film offers and American theater offers. Based on this testimony, the jury found that the BSO's cancellation of its contract with Redgrave caused Redgrave $100,000 in consequential damages. We find that the evidence presented by Redgrave was not sufficient to support a finding of damages greater than $12,000, less expenses.

Most of Redgrave's annual earnings prior to April 1982 were derived from appearances in films and the English theater.[6] Redgrave presented evidence at trial that she earned more than $200,000 on the average since her company's fiscal year 1976, and she testified that she had a constant stream of offers from which she could choose films that had secure financial backing. After the BSO's

---

[6] Although Redgrave received a number of offers to appear in Broadway plays between 1975 and 1980, the only offer she accepted and received payment for was a 1976 play, *Lady From the Sea,* performed in off-Broadway's Circle in the Square theater, for which Redgrave received $9,000.

work hard up

cancellation in April 1982, Redgrave contended, her career underwent a "startling turnabout." Redgrave testified that she did not work at all for the fourteen months following the cancellation and that the only offers she received during that time were for films with insufficient financial backing.

The evidence demonstrates that Redgrave accepted three firm film offers in the fourteen months following the BSO cancellation. If these three films had been produced, Redgrave would have earned $850,000 during that period. The first offer, for a film entitled *Annie's Coming Out,* was for a role in which Redgrave had expressed interest in February 1982, two months prior to the BSO cancellation. The offer for the role was made in July 1982, a short time after the BSO's cancellation, and was finalized in August 1982. The film was to be financed by Film Australia, a government production company, and no evidence was presented that Redgrave believed the film might experience financial difficulties. Redgrave's fee for the film was to be $250,000.

From July 1982 until approximately the end of October 1982, Redgrave believed that she would be filming *Annie's Coming Out* sometime during the fall.[7] Because of that commitment, Redgrave turned down other firm offers that had secure financial backing. These included an offer received in July 1982 to do a cameo appearance in a Monty Python film entitled *Yellowbeard* for $10,000 and an offer received in September 1982 to star in the television film *Who Will Love My Children?* for $150,000. In late October or early November 1982, Redgrave was informed that *Annie's Coming Out* would not be produced because of financial difficulties. No evidence was presented that the film's financial failure was related to the BSO cancellation.

films keep falling through

In February 1983, Redgrave accepted an offer to appear in the film *No Alternatives,* for a fee of $350,000. Until June or July of 1983, Redgrave assumed that she would be filming *No Alternatives.* During that period, Redgrave turned down other offers, including an offer to appear in a film about Andre Sakharov for a fee of $70,000.[8] In June or July of 1983, Redgrave was informed that *No Alternatives* would not be filmed because of financial difficulties. Redgrave received $25,000 as a forfeiture on the contract.

In June 1983, Redgrave accepted an offer to appear in a film entitled *Track 39,* for a fee of $250,000. This film fell through in late July 1983. There was no allegation that the financial failures of either *No Alternatives* or *Track 39* were directly related to the BSO cancellation.

---

[7] Redgrave testified that the original departure date for Australia had been postponed from October 11th to November 2d, and that she could not recall whether it was in late October or early November that she found out that the film had fallen through.

[8] Redgrave testified that she turned down the offer for the Sakharov film because she obtained "alternative work" and because she was afraid the film might be used as anti-communist propaganda. There was no evidence that this film did not have secure financial backing.

Although there is no doubt that Redgrave did not have a successful financial year following the BSO cancellation, we cannot say that she presented sufficient evidence to prove that her financial difficulties were caused by the BSO cancellation. . . . If *Annie's Coming Out* had been produced, Redgrave would have earned $250,000 in the year following the BSO cancellation—an amount equal to Redgrave's average earnings before April 1982. . . .

We have some doubt as to whether Redgrave presented sufficient evidence to prove that the type of film offers she received in the year following the BSO cancellation were radically different from the film offers received before the cancellation . . . . [T]he evidence does not present an effective comparison between the type of film offers received before and after the BSO cancellation and we are left primarily with Redgrave's allegation that the film offers received in the two time periods were significantly different.

Even if we accept, however, that Redgrave proved she had experienced a drop in the quality of film offers following the BSO cancellation, Redgrave must also prove that the drop was proximately caused by the BSO cancellation and not by other, independent factors. Redgrave failed to carry her burden of presenting evidence sufficient to allow a jury reasonably to infer this causal connection.

. . . .

To the extent that Redgrave may have experienced a decline in the quality of film offers received subsequent to April 1982, that decline could have been the result of Redgrave's political views and not the result of the BSO's cancellation.[11] Even if the cancellation highlighted for producers the potential problems in hiring Redgrave, it was Redgrave's burden to establish that, in some way, the cancellation itself caused the difference in film offers rather than the problems as highlighted by the cancellation. Redgrave produced no direct evidence from film producers who were influenced by the cancellation. Thus, the jury's inference that the BSO cancellation had caused Redgrave consequential damages was one based more on "conjecture and speculation," *Carlson v. American Safety Equipment Corp.,* **528 F.2d at 386,** than on a sufficient factual basis.

Redgrave also claims that the BSO's cancellation caused a drop in her offers to perform on Broadway. Bruce Savan, Redgrave's agent, testified regarding all offers to perform in American theater that had been made to Redgrave prior to April 1982. The offers averaged from two to four plays in the years 1976-1980. There was no evidence of any offers to perform on Broadway made to Redgrave in 1981, the year immediately preceding the BSO cancellation. . . .

---

[11] In addition, immediately following the BSO cancellation, Redgrave stopped using the services of her long-term agent, Bruce Savan, and engaged the services of the William Morris agency. After one year, Redgrave re-engaged Savan. The BSO contends that the change in agencies could have been an additional factor causing any decline in offers.

Redgrave contends that, as a result of the BSO cancellation, she no longer received offers to appear on Broadway. She testified that in April 1983 she was appearing in a successful English theater production of *The Aspern Papers* and was led to believe by the producers that the show would move to New York. Although it was Redgrave's opinion that the reason the play did not move to Broadway was because of the "situation" caused by the BSO cancellation, there was no testimony from the producers or others as to why the production did not go to Broadway. Redgrave also testified that in August 1983 she was asked by the Jujamson producers to appear in *The Abdication,* but that the play was never produced. Again, there was no testimony from the producers or others as to why the production did not materialize. In addition, Redgrave testified that Lillian Hellman had wished Redgrave to portray Hellman in a theater production on Broadway, but that Hellman was concerned about the BSO incident. Finally, Redgrave testified that Theodore Mann had considered offering her a role in *Heartbreak House* at Circle in the Square, but decided not to extend the offer because of the ramifications of the BSO cancellation.

Theodore Mann was the one producer who testified regarding his decision not to employ Redgrave in a Broadway production. He explained that

> the Boston Symphony Orchestra had cancelled, terminated Ms. Redgrave's contract. This had a—this is the premier or one of the premier arts organizations in America who, like ourselves, seeks support from foundations, corporations, individuals; have subscribers; sell individual tickets. I was afraid . . . and those in my organization were afraid that this termination would have a negative effect on us if we hired her. And so we had conferences about this. We were also concerned about if there would be any physical disturbances to the performance . . . . And it was finally decided . . . that we would not hire [Redgrave] because of all the events that had happened, the cancellation by the Boston Symphony and the effects that we felt it would have on us by hiring her.

The evidence presented by Redgrave concerning her drop in Broadway offers after April 1982, apart from Mann's testimony, is not sufficient to support a finding of consequential damages.[12] We do not, of course, question Redgrave's credibility in any way. Our concern is with the meager factual evidence. Redgrave had to introduce enough facts for a jury reasonably to infer that any drop in Broadway offers was proximately caused by the BSO cancellation and not by the fact that producers independently were concerned with the same factors that had motivated the BSO. Mann's testimony itself reflects the fact that many producers in

---

[12] We note that Redgrave's claim regarding American theater offers is both stronger and weaker than her claim regarding film offers. On the one hand, Redgrave indeed did not receive any Broadway offers in 1982, in contrast to various film offers and inquiries that she did receive throughout 1982. On the other hand, Redgrave failed to present evidence of any Broadway offers made to her in 1981, weakening her assertion that a dramatic decline in such offers occurred subsequent to April 1982.

New York may have been hesitant about hiring Redgrave because of a feared drop in subscription support or problems of physical disturbances. Apart from Mann's testimony, Redgrave presented nothing other than the fact that three expected offers or productions did not materialize. This type of circumstantial evidence is not sufficient to support a finding of consequential damages.

only circumstantial evidence

In addition, we note that it would be difficult for any assessment of damages resulting from the lack of Broadway theater offers to meet the standard that damages must be "capable of ascertainment by reference to some definite standard, either market value, established experience or direct inference from known circumstances." *John Hetherington & Sons*, 210 Mass. at 21, 95 N.E. at 964. *See Lowrie v. Castle*, 225 Mass. 37, 51-52, 113 N.E. 206 (1916); Williston, *Contracts*, § 1346 at 239-40. The three specific performances to which Redgrave referred, other than Mann's, were never performed on Broadway and there is no indication of the compensation Redgrave would have received. In addition, Redgrave had accepted only one Broadway offer among the many she had received over the years because, according to Redgrave, the scripts were not good enough for her first Broadway appearance. There was no evidence that Redgrave would necessarily have accepted any Broadway offer made in 1982.

no ev. of her lost salary

Mann's testimony regarding the production of *Heartbreak House* is the one piece of evidence from which reasonable factfinders could draw conflicting inferences and upon which a reasonably ascertainable damage award could be granted. We therefore defer to the inferences drawn by the jury from that testimony and grant Redgrave damages on that basis.

Mann's ev is enough for the one play

Mann's testimony reveals that, in considering whether to hire Redgrave, he and his partners were concerned about losing support from foundations and subscribers, having difficulty selling tickets, and dealing with possible physical disruptions. These are factors that result from the community response to Redgrave's political views. They are the same factors that apparently motivated the BSO to cancel its contract with Redgrave and are not the result of that cancellation. Thus, one possibly could infer from Mann's testimony that the BSO cancellation was not a proximate cause of the damage suffered by Redgrave in being denied the part in *Heartbreak House*.

Mann also testified, however, that he and his partners were affected by the BSO cancellation because the BSO was a premier arts organization and was dependent on the same type of support as Circle in the Square. A jury reasonably could infer that the BSO's cancellation did more than just highlight for Mann the potential problems that hiring Redgrave would cause but was actually a cause of Mann's decision, perhaps because Mann's theater support was similar to that of the BSO or because Mann felt influenced to follow the example of a "premier arts organization." Because this is a possible inference that a jury could draw from

BSO was apt opener

Mann's testimony, we defer to that inference. We therefore find that Redgrave presented sufficient evidence to prove consequential damages of $12,000, the fee arrangement contemplated by Mann for Redgrave's appearance in *Heartbreak House,* minus expenses she personally would have incurred had she appeared in the play.

———————————

Behind the Scenes: The Houston Astrodome

In the next case, *Kenford Co. v. County of Erie,* the court considers the claims of disappointed investors in a domed stadium project near Buffalo, New York, that never got built. One of the project developers was Roy Hofheinz, who had been the moving force behind the construction and management of the Houston Astrodome—the only existing stadium of that kind at the time of the case.

Built in the early 1960s to house the Houston Astros (professional baseball) and the Houston Oilers (professional football), the Houston Astrodome, in its heyday, was often referred to as the Eighth Wonder of the World. The Astrodome was the first enclosed stadium to house baseball and football in air-conditioned comfort with cushioned seats and multiple sit-down restaurants. Largely from Hofheinz's vision, it also was the first stadium built with luxury Skyboxes (53 of them), which were designed to appeal to corporate fans; they sold out before the first season. The Astrodome's innovative scoreboard stood over four stories high, with more than 50,000 lights and 1200 miles of wiring, so that it could show game statistics, serve as a cheerleader, and run promotional spots. The roof was covered with translucent Lucite panels, but the resulting glare made a white baseball nearly impossible to see, so—after unsuccessful experiments with sun-

glasses for the players and baseballs dyed orange, yellow, and cerise—Hofheinz had the panels painted over and the grass on the field replaced with a new artificial surface never used before—Astroturf.

As a young man, Hofheinz graduated from law school at age 19, was elected to the Texas legislature at age 22, and became a judge at age 24. After two terms on the bench, he lost an election and turned to pioneering FM radio stations and building a network of radio and television stations in the late 1940s. In the 1950s, he served two terms as mayor of Houston and acted as campaign manager for Lyndon B. Johnson's campaigns for Congress and the Senate. Meanwhile, Hofheinz and three others formed the Houston Sports Association (HSA), which joined with other cities to form the short-lived Continental League to pressure the American and National Leagues to expand major-league baseball into more cities. The pressure succeeded—the National League awarded the HSA a franchise for a new team, which was initially called the Colt .45s. The HSA quickly built a temporary outdoor stadium, then broke ground on the Astrodome project (with six-shooters!).

The HSA built the stadium with the help of county bonding and eventually got a long-term lease on the building. Two years later, when the team moved into the Astrodome, Hofheinz renamed the team the Astros, in honor of Houston-based NASA. The Astrodome remained the home of the teams until 2000, when Houston built Enron Field (now Minute Maid Park) with a dome, air-conditioning, and a retractable roof.

In 1967, Hofheinz and two others purchased the Ringling Bros. and Barnum & Bailey Circus. He developed Astroworld, the first major theme park in coastal Texas, and later sold it to Six Flags. He also joined Edward Cottrell (the president and sole shareholder of Kenford Company) to form Dome Stadium, Inc. (DSI) to lease or manage a proposed domed stadium near Buffalo, New York. When Erie County finally accepted the offer from DSI and Kenford Company in 1969, the contract terms dictated that Kenford Co. would donate 178 acres of land for the project and that the county would negotiate a 40-year lease with DSI for the operation of the stadium. When the county terminated the contract in 1971, it prevented the project from moving forward and set the stage for this case. For more information, *see* www.historicamerica.net/baseballhouston.html; Mike Acosta, *Rain or Shine: How Houston Developed Space City Baseball,* Sports (vol. 6, no. 3).

Kenford Co. v. County of Erie (I)

KENFORD COMPANY and DOME STADIUM, INC., Plaintiffs-Appellants

v.

COUNTY OF ERIE, et al., Defendants-Respondents

Supreme Court, Appellate Division, Fourth Department, New York
489 N.Y.S.2d 939 (App. Div. 1985)

DOERR, Justice.

This appeal presents for our review the extent to which plaintiffs may recover damages following defendant's breach of contract.

In the late 1960s the County of Erie obtained enabling legislation permitting it to finance and construct a sports stadium. Edward Cottrell, a local businessman, put together an assemblage of properties in the Town of Lancaster. Cottrell eventually obtained options to purchase in excess of 700 acres of land, some of which he tried to interest the County in purchasing for the purpose of building a domed stadium facility. Cottrell, who formed plaintiff Kenford Co., Inc. in 1968 [hereinafter Kenford] planned to develop the land surrounding the stadium and he also hoped to acquire a major league baseball franchise to play in the stadium. When Cottrell's efforts to interest the County in buying his land were unsuccessful, he consulted Judge Roy Hofheinz, who had developed the Houston Astrodome. Hofheinz suggested donating the Lancaster property to the County in exchange for the County permitting Hofheinz and Cottrell to lease or manage the stadium, which was to be built by the County. In May of 1969 Cottrell and Hofheinz formed plaintiff Dome Stadium, Inc. [DSI], which was owned two-thirds by Hofheinz and one-third by Cottrell. The two also agreed to share the peripheral land development scheme.

In June 1969 the Erie County Legislature passed a resolution authorizing the plan suggested by Hofheinz. Cottrell, as agent for Kenford, thereafter exercised his options on the Lancaster property, paying some $2.6 million for the total assemblage. On August 8, 1969 the County, Kenford, and DSI signed a contract by which Kenford agreed to convey 178 acres of land in exchange for the County's promise to construct a domed stadium facility. The contract further provided that the County would either lease the stadium to DSI for 40 years, or permit DSI to manage the stadium for 20 years in accordance with an attached management agreement, if no acceptable lease could be arranged within three months. Title to the property was duly conveyed, but the parties thereafter failed to agree to lease terms, and the management contract came into being automatically.

The County sought bids on the stadium, but they were $20 million over budget. On August 8, 1970 the County Legislature voted to abandon the project. Cottrell unsuccessfully sought to obtain substitute funding. Plaintiffs commenced the instant action [in June 1971] alleging breach of contract and seeking specific performance or, alternatively, $90 million in damages. Plaintiffs were granted summary judgment on the issue of liability (*Kenford Co. v. County of Erie*, 88 A.D.2d 758, 451 N.Y.S.2d 1021) and a trial was ordered on the issue of damages.

The damage trial lasted nine months, consuming over 25,000 pages of transcript. Plaintiffs attempted to prove that the breach caused them to suffer $495 million in damages, including lost profits on a baseball franchise, a theme park, three hotels, an office park, a golf course, and a specialty retail center. Plaintiffs also sought to recover lost profit on the management contract, loss of appreciation in the value of the land surrounding the stadium site, and out-of-pocket expenses incurred in reliance on the contract. The trial court dismissed Kenford's claims of lost profits on the peripheral land development and the baseball franchise as being too speculative, but the court submitted the other items of damage to the jury, which awarded DSI lost profits of $25.6 million on the management contract. The jury also awarded Kenford $18 million for its lost appreciation in land value and it granted Kenford over $6 million in out-of-pocket expenses. On appeal, the recoverability of all elements is challenged.

I. Lost Profits on the Peripheral Development

In a breach of contract case, the goal of a damage award is to place plaintiff in the position he would have been in absent the breach, no worse but no better

(*Western Geophysical Co. of Am. v. Bolt Assocs.*, 584 F.2d 1164, 1172 . . .). Only such damages as are the natural and probable result of the breach may be recovered. Ordinarily, plaintiff may not recover for a collateral enterprise upon which he might have embarked, had defendant not breached the contract (. . . *Czarnikow-Rionda Co. v. Federal Sugar Refining Co.*, 255 N.Y. 33, 41, 173 N.E. 913; *Chapman v. Fargo*, 223 N.Y. 32, 119 N.E. 76). This rule is derived from the doctrine enunciated in *Hadley v. Baxendale* (156 Eng.Rep. 145, 151). Under this rule, recovery is limited to such damages as may fairly and reasonably have been in the contemplation of the parties when the contract was made (*Kerr S.S. Co. v. Radio Corp. of Am.*, 245 N.Y. 284, 157 N.E. 140). Thus, damages may not be recovered where the consequences of the breach are remote and indirect. "No one is answerable in law for all the remote consequences of his own acts" (. . . *Hoffman v. King*, 160 N.Y. 618, 55 N.E. 401 . . .).

In addition to the foreseeability requirement, to be recoverable "'damages must be not merely speculative, possible and imaginary, but they must be reasonably certain . . . . They may be so uncertain, contingent and imaginary as to be incapable of adequate proof, and then they cannot be recovered because they cannot be proved'" (. . . *Wakeman v. Wheeler & Wilson Mfg. Co.*, 101 N.Y. 205, 209, 4 N.E. 264). Damages may not be awarded on the basis of conjecture and guesswork (*Schanbarger v. Edward Dott's Garage*, 72 A.D.2d 882, 883, 421 N.Y.S.2d 937 . . .). Damages that are uncertain contingent, or speculative may not be recovered (*Broadway Photoplay Co. v. World Film Corp.*, 225 N.Y. 104, 121 N.E. 756 . . .). It is for the court to determine, in the first instance, whether as a matter of law the damages claimed are too remote to permit recovery (*Fifty States Mgt. Corp. v. Niagara Permanent Sav. & Loan Assn.*, 58 A.D.2d 177, 396 N.Y.S.2d 925 . . .).

Application of these rules to the instant case leads to the inescapable conclusion that the trial court properly refused to submit to the jury Kenford's claims pertaining to the peripheral land development and the baseball franchise. Although it was known that Kenford would try to buy a baseball franchise and would try to develop the land surrounding the stadium, it was by no means certain that Kenford would have been successful in doing so or that these enterprises would have thrived. Not all business ventures prove to be profitmaking. Moreover, although Cottrell had ideas for developing the peripheral land, these plans were by no means certain as of August 8, 1969. We know of no precedent for holding a defendant liable for profits lost on collateral matters that are as remote and undeveloped as the plans involved herein (*cf. Contemporary Mission v. Famous Music Corp.*, 557 F.2d 918 (permitting plaintiff to recover for lost sales on a record following defendant's breach of contract to promote the record, but denying lost profits on a proposed concert tour, etc.)). The office buildings, golf course, and theme park for which plaintiff now seeks lost profits were nothing more than visions at the time the parties entered into the contract. No specific plans had been drawn for any of these ventures. The proposed baseball franchise was equally speculative. It was by no means certain that Cottrell would have been able to purchase a baseball franchise since such a purchase would have required approval of a percentage of league owners. Moreover, it is completely speculative to say that the franchise would have been a profitable one.

II. Loss of Appreciation in Peripheral Land Values

There is no dispute that Kenford suffered a monetary loss in land appreciation as a result of defendant's breach of contract. Defendant's own expert admitted that construction of the Dome would have caused the peripheral land to appreciate in value fourfold. Nor can it be doubted that both parties contemplated this appreciation, since the contract itself states that the County expected to receive increased property taxes from the peripheral lands purchased by Cottrell and/or Kenford. Unlike Kenford's specific development plans, which were remote and uncertain at the time of contracting, the purchase of the land was a completed fact of which the County had full notice. Also, while it was uncertain whether any particular development scheme would prove profitable, there was no possibility of the land depreciating in value. Thus damage was certain. It is well settled in New York that in a breach of contract case a plaintiff may recover not only losses sustained, but also gains prevented (*Lieberman v. Templar Motor Co.*, 236 N.Y. 139, 140 N.E. 222; *Witherbee v. Meyer*, 155 N.Y. 446, 50 N.E. 58; *Wakeman v. Wheeler & Wilson Mfg. Co.*, 101 N.Y. 205, 4 N.E. 264, *supra*), and where damage is certain, recovery will not be denied because the amount is uncertain; the breaching party bears the risk of the uncertainty created by his breach (*Bigelow v. PKO Radio Pictures*, 327 U.S. 251, 264-265; *Story Parchment Co. v. Paterson Parchment Paper Co.*, 282 U.S. 555; *Lee v. Joseph E. Seagram & Sons*, 552 F.2d 447, 455-456; *Berley Inds. v. City of New York*, 45 N.Y.2d 683, 687, 412 N.Y.S.2d 589, 385 N.E.2d 281 . . .). In our view, Kenford's loss was both foreseeable and certain, and plaintiff is entitled to recover for its loss.[5]

---

[5] We disagree with the view espoused in the dissenting opinion suggesting that the court take this opportunity to adopt the disproportionate recovery test suggested by the Restatement (Second) of Contracts. Were we to agree that the rule should be adopted, we would not apply it so as to deny plaintiff a recovery of its loss of appreciation in land value in the instant case. The Restatement, itself, notes that a court should limit damages that are otherwise recoverable only if there is "an extreme disproportion" between the loss and the benefit to be derived by defendant under the contract (Restatement (Second) of Contracts § 351 comment f). Thus, for example, one breaching a contract to deliver machinery should not be responsible for plaintiff's subsequent lost profits, which are greatly in excess

Nevertheless, we conclude that the award of damages on this issue must be reversed because it was based on improper appraisal evidence. Plaintiff's appraiser valued the land as of projected completion dates ranging from 1973 to 1979 and based his estimates on the assumption that the property was improved with the specific items that we now find speculative as a matter of law, i.e., theme park, office buildings, and golf course. Plaintiff should have produced appraisal testimony indicating what the land would have been worth as raw acreage immediately following construction of the stadium. Any further appreciation to the land resulting from theme parks and the like makes the evidence of value too speculative to permit recovery. We conclude that a new trial is warranted on this issue because the experts were in agreement that plaintiff suffered some loss, and because the motion to strike plaintiff's evidence was made after both sides had rested. Moreover, had the trial court correctly granted the motion, plaintiff could have moved to reopen the case to present proper proof. On this view of the record, we find a new trial appropriate (*see Borne Chem. Co. v. Dictrow*, 85 A.D.2d 646, 650–651, 445 N.Y.S.2d 406 (granting a new trial where the parties and the court misunderstood the law)).

Upon retrial, the proper measure of damages will be the value of the land as raw acreage following construction of the Dome less the value of the land when purchased. The parties' experts may develop a pre-construction estimate of value using familiar principles of valuation, notably the market data approach. The sales price of the subject property may be the best evidence of value (*W.T. Grant Co. v. Srogi*, 52 N.Y.2d 496, 511, 438 N.Y.S.2d 761, 420 N.E.2d 953), particularly the early sales before it was widely known that Cottrell was acquiring an assemblage. A post-construction estimate of value may similarly be derived by using the

---

of the consideration defendant would have derived from full performance (Restatement (Second) of Contracts § 351 illustration 17). This analysis has no application to the facts at hand, since a recovery of a few million dollars is not out of proportion to the benefit defendant would have derived from performance of the contract. Defendant was given title to 178 acres of land and would have had the opportunity to realize substantial income from both stadium operations and increased tax revenues. Defendant has not obtained these benefits only because defendant chose to breach the contract. The proper test is not what defendant actually derived from the contract, but what benefit it would have derived from performance (Fuller & Perdue, The Reliance Interest in Contract Damages: 1, 46 Yale L.J. 52, 88 n. 58 (1936)).

We also find unpersuasive the dissenters' reasoning that County officials did not "contemplate" the liability now at issue because, had they done so, they would have inserted a standard clause limiting their liability (*see infra* dissenting opinion, note 7). It is speculative to say that such a clause would have been proposed and more speculative to assume that plaintiffs would have agreed to it. For example, on the summary judgment motion, Special Term noted that the County desired to insert a cost limitation in the contract, but plaintiffs refused to agree to that term.

We also reject the argument that there is no reason to treat lost appreciation in land value differently from lost profits on the theme park, etc. The principal reason for denying lost profits on the latter is that there is no way of knowing whether these proposed ventures would have been profitable, and thus plaintiffs' proof cannot meet the certainty requirement of the lost profits test (*Wakeman v. Wheeler & Wilson Mfg. Co.*, 101 N.Y. 205, 217, 4 N.E. 264, *supra; see infra* note 8). Loss of appreciation in land value, by contrast, was conceded by defendant.

market data approach. The experts may rely on the appreciation experienced by lands surrounding other major developments in Western New York as well as in other similar metropolitan areas. We stress, however, that as nearly as possible, the comparables to be relied upon should be large parcels of raw acreage.[6] The objective, after all, is simply to ascertain fair market value, i.e., what a willing buyer would pay a willing seller for the property (*W.T. Grant Co. v. Srogi, supra*, p. 510, 438 N.Y.S.2d 761, 420 N.E.2d 953), viewing the property exactly as it was in the early 1970s, except assuming that it was located on the periphery of a domed stadium.[7]

III. Lost Profits on the Management Contract

The issue of DSI's lost profits on the management contract involves two questions: whether an unestablished business may recover lost profits in New York and, if so, whether plaintiff's proof was adequate.

a. Per Se Rule v. Rule of Evidence

We begin our analysis by noting that we found no case from a New York State court permitting a recovery of lost profits to a new business. The seminal case on the subject is *Cramer v. Grand Rapids Show Case Co.*, 223 N.Y. 63, 119 N.E. 227. The defendant in *Cramer* breached its contract to deliver furniture to plaintiffs thereby preventing the latter from opening their ladies clothing store in a timely fashion. In reversing an award of lost profits, the court noted that evidence of plaintiffs' subsequent profit, earned after they were able to open their store, was insufficient proof of what their lost profits would have been had defendant not breached the contract. The court did not establish a per se rule of nonrecovery of lost profits; the court merely stated that, as an evidentiary matter, a new business would almost never be able to establish sufficient proof to recover lost profits. New York has thus been characterized as having a per se rule of nonrecoverability of lost profits to a new business (*Manniello v. Dea*, 92 A.D.2d 426, 429, 461 N.Y.S.2d 582 . . . .

In juxtaposition to the New York State cases, there are several Federal cases in New York permitting new businesses to recover lost profits. The key case was *Perma Research & Devel. Co. v. Singer Co.* 402 F.Supp. 881, *affd.* 542 F.2d 111,

---

[6] For example, plaintiff's expert relied on small parcels and valued the land on a square foot basis rather than an acreage basis, resulting in an inflated estimate of value.

[7] We note that the County's expert used proper methodology by developing a pre-construction value based on comparable sales in the area during the late 1960s. He also developed a post-construction value by examining the experience of other local properties that surrounded major Western New York developments such as Rich Stadium and the SUNY campus. Using this data he arrived at a pre-construction value of $1,100 per acre and a post-construction value of $4,400, indicating lost appreciation of some $3,300 per acre (a total of approximately $1,815,000 for the 550 acre parcel).

cert. den. 429 U.S. 987, 97 S.Ct. 507, 50 L.Ed.2d 598. In *Perma Research,* the court cited *Cramer v. Grand Rapids Show Case Co. (supra)* for the proposition that lost profits in a new venture are not ordinarily recoverable, but then went on to hold that lost profits may be awarded if plaintiff establishes three elements: that the lost profits are the direct and proximate result of the breach; that profits were contemplated by the parties; and that there is a rational basis on which to calculate the lost profits (*Perma Research & Devel. Co. v. Singer Co., supra,* p. 898). The first two criteria reflect the lost profits test applicable to established businesses as enunciated in *Witherbee v. Meyer,* 155 N.Y. 446, 449–450, 50 N.E. 58, supra). What the court did in *Perma Research,* in essence, was to add a third requirement for new businesses by requiring them to establish some rational basis on which to calculate the lost profits. The *Perma Research* test has been subsequently employed in the Second Circuit (*Lexington Prods. Ltd. v. B.D. Communications,* 677 F.2d 251, 253; *Western Geophysical Co. of Am. v. Bolt Assocs.,* 584 F.2d 1164, 1172, *supra; Contemporary Mission v. Famous Music Corp.,* 557 F.2d 918, 926, *supra; see also, For Children, Inc. v. Graphics Intl.,* 352 F.Supp. 1280, 1284 (upon which the *Perma Research* case relied)).

. . . . [W]e now hold that there is no per se rule precluding a new business from recovering lost profits and we adopt the test employed by the Second Circuit Court of Appeals in *Perma Research & Devel. Co. v. Singer Co. (supra).*

b. Application of the Perma Test

The first two *Perma Research* criteria are clearly met. The County's failure to build the stadium was clearly the proximate cause of any loss of profits stemming from the management contract and it is unquestionable that profits by DSI from the management contract were contemplated by the parties. We conclude, however, that plaintiff has failed to establish a rational basis upon which lost profits may be calculated.

Profit, of course, involves two variables—income less expenses. The management contract provided that DSI would receive 11% of gross revenues from major events (i.e., professional baseball and football) and 89% of gross revenues on "open time" events. The contract further provided that DSI would do the negotiating for all contracts, but that major event contracts would be between the performer and the County while open time events would be between the performer and DSI. To establish its lost profits, plaintiff called an expert who prepared a series of projections based on the experience of other domed facilities as well as an analysis of the market in the Buffalo area. The expert opined that the facility would hold 10 professional football games a year, as well as 42 open time events including three consumer shows, six high school football games, five circuses and seven musical or entertainment events. The expert then developed an average ticket price per event, which was multiplied by his estimate of anticipated attendance. The expert also developed an approximation of what each person would spend on parking and concessions. These figures were then computed to arrive at an anticipated revenue stream. The expert also gave his opinion of what the expenses of running the operation would be. He used a flat figure for salaries and then estimated that other expenses, such as advertising and legal fees, would be a percentage of gross revenue. His projected expenses were then subtracted from his projected revenue to arrive at a before-tax net income figure. One sheet summarizing the foregoing information was prepared for each of the 20 years of the management contract. The expert's opinion of net profit for each year ranged from just under $1 million for the first year to over $4 million in the twentieth year. Based upon these projections of net income, the jury found lost profits totalling over $28 million, which the court reduced to $25.6 million after applying a formula to arrive at present value.

The issue is whether the figures supplied by the expert are sufficient, as a matter of law, upon which to base an award of lost profits. Once again, we find a decided split between the New York State cases and the Federal cases. Several Federal cases have permitted statistical analyses to support an award of lost profits to a new business. Significantly, however, all of those cases involved only a royalty payment or the sale of a single product.

The common thread running through those cases is that only one variable was involved, i.e., how many of the product would have been sold. Thus it was certain that plaintiff would have made money and the only uncertainty was the amount. The instant case, by contrast, is filled with conjecture. The expert had to estimate, first, how many, if any, events would be held at the sta-

What's That?

A royalty payment is paid by a licensee for the use of the licensor's intellectual property (patent, copyright, trademark, or trade secret)— here, by the sale of products containing that intellectual property.

dium; how many people would attend each event; and how much each person would spend on parking and concessions. Additionally, and even more compelling, the expert also had to estimate all expense items. Highly significant in our view is that the expert assumed that various expenses would be a percentage of gross revenue, such as advertising. In short, the expert was assuming the fact to be proved, to wit, that revenues would exceed expenses. It is not inconceivable that DSI could have ended up spending more promoting events than it took in as receipts (*Broadway Photoplay Co. v. World Film Corp.*, 225 N.Y. 104, 107–108, 121 N.E. 756, *supra; Bernstein v. Meech*, 130 N.Y. 354, 29 N.E. 255; *Moss v. Tompkins*, 69 Hun 288, *affd.* 144 N.Y. 659, 39 N.E. 858).

The cases from New York State courts are even more restrictive than the Federal cases, since they have precluded projections even in the context of a royalty case (*see,* e.g., *Freund v. Washington Sq. Press*, 34 N.Y.2d 379, 357 N.Y.S.2d 857, 314 N.E.2d 419 (royalties on a book are too speculative); *Spitz v. Lesser*, 302 N.Y. 490, 99 N.E.2d 540, *supra* (loss of royalties is limited to the minimum amount stated in the contract); *see also Wakeman v. Wheeler & Wilson Mfg. Co.*, 101 N.Y. 205, 4 N.E. 264, *supra* (opinion testimony as to how many sewing machines could have been sold is inadmissible)). Moreover, not only have the New York State cases excluded evidence of projections to justify lost profits, but New York cases have even excluded proof of plaintiff's own subsequent profits (*Cramer v. Grand Rapids Show Case Co., supra*).[10] Although we agree with the view expressed in a recent law review article that lost profits are too often denied because of "an arbitrary disregard of possibly relevant evidence other than a history of past profits" (Comment, Remedies—Lost Profits as Contract Damages for an Unestablished Business: The New Business Rule Becomes Outdated, 56 N.C. L. Rev. 693, 695 (1978)), and while we recognize the increasing acceptance of expert opinion in statistical projections (*see,* e.g., *Espana v. United States*, 616 F.2d 41, 44 (mortality tables); *De Long v. County of Erie*, 89 A.D.2d 376, 455 N.Y.S.2d 887, *aff'd*, 60 N.Y.2d 296, 469 N.Y.S.2d 611, 457 N.E.2d 717 (expert opinion of a homemaker's services)), the projections used in the instant case simply involve too many variables to permit them to support an award of lost profits. Although a breaching party bears the risk of any uncertainty as to the amount of damage . . . , plaintiff

---

[10] The treatise on lost profits suggests several ways in which a plaintiff might establish lost profits. These methods include: plaintiff's prior experience; plaintiff's subsequent experience; plaintiff's experience at other locations; the comparable experience of others; defendant's subsequent profits; and industry averages (R. Dunn, *supra*, §§ 5.5–5.10). Not all methods would be available in all cases. In the instant case, the Dome was never built, and the plaintiff did not before or after engage in the management business. Nor is this type of contract narrow enough to permit of an industry average. Plaintiff's only recourse, therefore, is to rely on the comparable experience of others. Unfortunately, this method is not particularly reliable under the facts herein because of the wide divergence of variables between stadium facilities in different cities. We agree with the view expressed by the Seventh Circuit approving of the comparable business approach (also known as the yardstick measure), but noting that "'the business used as a standard must be as nearly identical to the plaintiffs as possible'" (*Cates v. Morgan Portable Bldg. Corp.*, 591 F.2d 17, 21 n.7, quoting *Lehrman v. Gulf Oil*, 500 F.2d 659, 667).

must first establish that he has, in fact, suffered lost profits . . . . We find plaintiff's projections insufficient as a matter of law to support an award of lost profits.[11]

IV. Out-of-Pocket Expenses

Lastly, defendant seeks reversal of the $6 million awarded Kenford as reliance and mitigation damages. It is well settled, of course, that a party may not recover both the expense of performing his side of the contract and the profit to be received under it, since "an award of lost profits ... will make plaintiff whole" (R & I Electronics v. Neuman, 66 A.D.2d 836, 837, 411 N.Y.S.2d 401; *see also,* Schultz & Son v. Nelson, 256 N.Y. 473, 177 N.E. 9; Oswego Falls Pulp & Paper Co. v. Stecher Lithographic Co., 215 N.Y. 98, 109 N.E. 92; Borden v. Chesterfield Farms, 27 A.D.2d 165, 277 N.Y.S.2d 494). By contrast, a party may recover mitigation expenses in addition to lost profit, because mitigation expenses would not have been incurred had defendant not breached the contract, and hence there is no double recovery. We view all damages awarded after the date of breach (August 8, 1970) as mitigation damages properly submitted to the jury, and accordingly we affirm the jury's finding of mitigation damages of $6,160,030.46. The jury's finding of expenses prior to that date ($6,218.17 and $636,502.34), however, is reversed and the matter remitted for a new trial. Upon retrial, plaintiff's proof should not include any sums expended for land acquisition expenses (i.e., brokerage commissions, recording fees, etc.) or for interest paid on the mortgages, since these sums would have been paid even without the breach and since plaintiff will be compensated for these sums by being awarded loss of appreciation of land value. Only expenses incurred as preparatory to the aborted management agreement, for which no lost profits are recoverable, may be awarded.[12]

---

[11] We have considered the cases cited to us from other jurisdictions but find that, even under the holdings of those cases, the instant award of lost profits could not be sustained (*see* S. Jon Kreedman & Co. v. Meyers Bros. Parking-Western Corp., 58 Cal.App.3d 173, 130 Cal.Rptr. 41 (parking garage operator was permitted lost profits after developer failed to construct garage, but court noted that lessee was experienced in the business and the operation of a parking garage is a relatively simple operation with sufficiently few decisions to make the prediction of profits reasonably possible); Smith Dev. Corp. v. Bilow Enterprises, 112 R.I. 203, 308 A.2d 477 (allowing a McDonald's Restaurant lost profits based on the experience of other McDonald's restaurants in the area; the court noted the high degree of similarity among restaurants in this franchise); *see also* Riley v. General Mills, 226 F.Supp. 780 (permitting recovery of loss of commissions on insurance policies); Sandler v. Lawn-A-Mat Chem. & Equip. Corp., 141 N.J.Super 437, 358 A.2d 805 (breach of a distributorship agreement)). Of these cases, only two involved projections of expenses, and in these cases (involving the McDonald's restaurant and the parking garage) there was a high degree of similarity between the business not constructed and the businesses from which data was derived.

The instant case is more analogous to those cases denying recovery to a new business (China Doll Rest. v. Schweiger, 119 Ariz. 315, 580 P.2d 776 (a restaurant); Evergreen Amusement Corp. v. Milstead, 206 Md. 610, 112 A.2d 901 (drive-in theater); Albin Elevator Co. v. Pavlica, 649 P.2d 187 (Wyo.) (wheat farm)).

[12] We feel compelled to note that the Court is unanimous in its determination of all major issues raised on this appeal, save one—loss of appreciation of peripheral land values . . . .

Accordingly, the judgment should be modified and the matter remitted for further proceedings in accordance with this opinion.

Judgment modified, on the law, and as modified, affirmed, without costs, and matter remitted to Supreme Court, Erie County, for a new trial, in accordance with this opinion.

O'DONNELL and SCHNEPP, JJ., concur.

HANCOCK, J.P., and BOOMER, J., dissent in part in the following opinion by HANCOCK, J.P.

HANCOCK, Justice Presiding (dissenting).

The appeal, as we see it, turns on this overriding question: whether the County of Erie, in addition to repaying plaintiffs for mitigation damages and for their out-of-pocket losses incurred in reliance on the county's promise to build the Dome, should also pay a sum equal to the financial benefits plaintiffs would supposedly have achieved if the Dome had been built and had proved to be a success.

. . . .

In our opinion, for reasons set forth in Part I, *infra,* plaintiffs, under the circumstances here, may not, as a matter of law—and irrespective of the speculative nature of the proof—recover *any part* of their claimed expectancy losses including the land appreciation claim. For this reason alone, there should be no retrial on that issue. Additionally, aside from the legal objections to any expectancy recovery discussed in Part I, we are of the view, as explained in Part II, *infra,* that whatever proof plaintiffs may offer in support of their land appreciation claim on a retrial would necessarily be too speculative to constitute a valid legal basis for the claim. Thus, we differ with the majority on two points: (1) whether, regardless of the proof offered, there can be a recovery for any expectancy losses, and (2) assuming, arguendo, that there can be such a recovery, whether the proof on the loss of expected land appreciation would, in any event, be too speculative.

We must, therefore, dissent from so much of the judgment as grants a new trial on this issue. We agree that the judgment for the recovery of mitigation damages should be affirmed but would grant a new trial to permit plaintiff Kenford to recover whatever additional reliance damages it may establish including the cost of acquiring the properties it assembled for the Dome development.

I

. . . . In applying the general *Hadley v. Baxendale* foreseeability test to the expectancy damages claimed here, it is not enough to ask whether the defendant, when it agreed to the contract, could reasonably have foreseen that plaintiffs' hoped-for benefits from the Dome's construction would not be realized if the Dome were not built. . . . What must have been reasonably foreseeable is that if the county did not build the Dome, it would not be built at all; for it is clear that the Dome's ultimate nonexistence results as much from plaintiffs' inability to arrange other means of funding the project as from defendant's decision not to go ahead with it. The proper question then is whether the county should have foreseen that plaintiffs would be unsuccessful in making other arrangements and would eventually look to the county as the sole means for making their hopes a reality . . . . The record supports the conclusion, applying the general *Hadley v. Baxendale* rule, that it was not reasonably foreseeable that plaintiffs would ultimately fail and would look to the county as their sole source of available financing. There is no evidence that plaintiffs discussed the point with the county and, indeed, no claim that this special circumstance was ever brought to the county's attention. And plaintiffs' persistent and prolonged attempts to find other sources of private and public financing after the county decided not to proceed must be taken as proof that *they* certainly did not believe that the county was the only possibility.

Think About It!

Is the dissent's point about foreseeability consistent with your understanding of *Hadley*? Why should it matter whether it was foreseeable that Kenford and DSI would be unsuccessful in obtaining other financing?

It is not the general *Hadley v. Baxendale* foreseeability rule (*see* Restatement (Second) of Contracts § 351(1), (2) (1979)) which, however, affords the county its chief legal basis for objecting to plaintiffs' expectancy claims—but rather a refinement of the general rule which has evolved from the efforts of courts to find a workable way of limiting recoveries of expectancy claims when they result in unfairly disproportionate damages. Under this special application of the general rule we conclude that the expectancy losses here should be disallowed for reasons of justice as excessive and disproportionate damages (*see* Restatement (Second) of Contracts § 351(3) (1979)) or as damages resulting from an unfair allocation of the risks which defendant could not have contemplated . . . .

. . . .

Put simply, plaintiffs' version of what was contemplated comes to this. The county not only promised to build the Dome but to back up its promise with what amounts to a guarantee that if for any reason it could not build it, plaintiffs would receive whatever benefits the Dome could have produced. Plaintiffs were to win with or without the Dome and to win more without it than with it because they would then not have to perform their contracts and there would be no risks of the operation's failure. On the other hand, the county, if, for example the construction bids proved to be too high, would have to choose the lesser of two evils: either build a stadium that it did not want because it was too costly or not build it and pay for plaintiffs' huge expectancy losses on the "guarantee". In blunt terms, it was "heads or tails" plaintiffs win. It is inconceivable that such an unfair and disproportionate allocation of the risks could have been contemplated by the county as part of the bargain, and it would be highly unjust to impose the result of that allocation as a foreseeable consequence of the breach.

Courts have devised various solutions to the problem of loss of expectancy claims which result in damages that are disproportionate and unfair. . . . The approach taken by the American Law Institute in the Restatement (Second) of Contracts is that the "court may limit damages for foreseeable loss by excluding recovery for loss of profits, by allowing recovery only for loss incurred in reliance, or otherwise if it concludes that *in the circumstances justice so requires in order to avoid disproportionate compensation*" (Restatement (Second) of Contracts § 351(3) (1979); (emphasis added); *see* Harvey, *Discretionary Justice under the Restatement (Second) of Contracts*, 67 Cornell L. Rev. 666, 677–679 (1982)).

. . . . [W]e recently held that under *Hadley v. Baxendale* the parties could not reasonably have contemplated that for the breach of a first refusal option for additional billboards in a lease for advertising space (providing an annual rental to defendant in the amount of $600 per year) defendant would be held responsible for loss of profits in the amount of $227,000 based on what plaintiff would have earned from the billboards in its advertising business if it had been permitted to exercise the option (see *Whitmier & Ferris Co. v. Buffalo Structural Steel Corp., supra,* 104 A.D.2d p. 279, 482 N.Y.S.2d 927). And in *Cayuga Harvester v. Allis-Chalmers Corp.,* 95 A.D.2d 5, supra, 465 N.Y.S.2d 606, we rejected plaintiff's contention as an unreasonable allocation of the risks that defendant's failure to repair and replace defective parts in a harvesting machine should "despite its good-faith efforts to fulfill its obligations, subject it to a lawsuit for consequential damages and loss of profits which, in view of the size of plaintiff's operation, could result in a recovery many times the value of the N–7 combine" (*Cayuga Harvester v. Allis-Chalmers Corp., supra,* p. 14, 465 N.Y.S.2d 606).

Moreover, in cases not involving expectancy losses but claims for reliance damages only, the courts in applying *Hadley v. Baxendale* have yielded to the "impulse to preserve some proportion between liability imposed on the defendant and the compensation which was paid to him under the contract" (Fuller & Perdue, *The Reliance Interest in Contract Damages: 1,* 46 Yale L.J. 52, 88 (1936)).

For example, in *Rochester Lantern Co. v. Stiles & Parker Press Co.,* 135 N.Y. 209, 31 N.E. 1018, *supra*), the court rejected plaintiff's claims for expenditures for room rent, for rental of business premises and for salaries paid to employees all wasted by defendant's failure to supply steel dies. In holding under the *Hadley v. Baxendale* rule that such losses "could not have been contemplated", it commented (135 N.Y., at p. 218, 31 N.E. 1018): "If we should adopt the rule of damages contended for by the plaintiff, what would be the limits of its application? Suppose instead of employing two men the plaintiff had projected an extensive business in which the dies were to be used, and had employed one hundred men . . . and had kept the men and the building unemployed for months and, perhaps, years, could the whole expense of the men and building be visited on the defendant as a consequence of its breach of contract? If it could we should have a rule of damages which might cause ruin to parties unable from unforeseen events to perform their contracts."

. . . .

Factors other than the illogic of the notion that the county could have agreed to bear such an unfair allocation of the risks compel the conclusion that the possibility of paying for plaintiffs' expectancy losses could not have been in the county's contemplation at the time it made the contract. For one thing, the remarkably informal and almost casual nature of the dealings between the parties and of the contract documents (*see particularly*, Exhibit 82–A, the county's contract with Kenford and *see infra*, n. 7) indicates that little, if any, thought could have been given to what risks the county was undertaking. We must assume that the county, if there had been the slightest hint of the allocation of risks which plaintiffs now seek to impose, would either never have signed the Kenford contract or would, through its attorneys, have insisted on a contract appropriate for a governmental entity with proper clauses excluding claims for consequential damages and loss of profits.[7] And the nature of the contract must be considered—that, from the standpoint of the officials who dealt with the proposal's sponsors, it was not a commercial contract at all but one to be made in the public interest on behalf of a municipal government.

. . . .

---

[7] The county's agreement with Kenford for the construction of the multi-million dollar domed stadium is in a five-page agreement (Exhibit 82–A) consisting of six paragraphs, almost all of which concern the terms of a lease agreement to be agreed upon in the future. The single clause pertaining to the County's undertaking to construct the domed stadium is as follows: "The County shall construct domed facilities comparable to the Houston Astrodome on the stadium site area, and shall construct access roadways as generally depicted on the attached map, Schedule B. Such construction of the domed stadium facilities shall be commenced by the County within twelve (12) months after execution of this Agreement." There are no limits on costs or other safeguards. The promise is unconditional and absolute. . . .

. . . . In applying the section 351(3) justice standard, it makes no difference whether we compare what plaintiffs would receive (if permitted to recover for the full extent of their expectancies) with what defendant has actually received (no benefit at all since the Dome was not built) or, as the majority contend we should (*see supra,* majority opn., n.5), with what defendant supposedly would have received from its own performance, assuming there had been no breach. For, very simply, the county has determined that the potential benefits to be derived from performance were outweighed by the cost of obtaining those benefits. The result of going forward with the Dome project, the county has found, would be a detriment, not a benefit—a net loss, not a gain. But even without considering the prohibitive cost, it seems apparent that in any application of the section 351(3) justice standard plaintiffs' recovery for their full expectancies would outweigh the value of whatever

Think About It!

Do you agree with the dissent's argument against disproportionately large damage awards?

benefits defendant might have received from performance. The expected tax revenues from increased assessments cannot reasonably be counted in the equation as a benefit to the county since they are not part of the consideration flowing from plaintiffs and would, in any event, be only what the owners of the peripheral land would have to pay in taxes for the additional municipal services required by their completed improvements. It seems equally inappropriate to count as a benefit to the county the dubious expectancy of profits to be derived from the Dome operation both because such profits are at best conjectural and uncertain (*see* majority opn., Point III, *supra*) and because the profits, if any, would be nothing more than what the county would be entitled to earn as a return on its own multi million dollar investment and for the millions of dollars it would be obligated to pay in interest on the bond issue. Thus, whether or not defendant's completed performance is assumed for the purpose of the analysis under the section 351(3) justice standard, permitting the recovery of plaintiffs' expectancy losses presupposes a decidedly unfair allocation of the risks and results in disproportionate damages.

In sum, it would be unjust to compensate plaintiffs with an award of damages which would put them in the same position they would have been in if the Dome had been built. It is one thing to keep plaintiffs from being made worse off than they were before their reliance on the contract and before defendant's breach; it is quite another to put them in a far better position and to do it at vast expense to defendant. Therefore, under the rules discussed above, Kenford's claim for loss of enhanced land value as well as the claims of DSI and Kenford for lost profits should be rejected: either as damages that could not have been within defendant's contemplation under *Hadley v. Baxendale* (*see Whitmier & Ferris Co. v. Buffalo Structural Steel Corp.,* 104 A.D.2d 277, 482 N.Y.S.2d 927, *supra*) or in the interest of justice "in order to avoid disproportionate compensation" (Restatement (Second) of Contracts § 351(3) (1979), comment f).

II

The additional question presented by plaintiffs' claim for loss in enhancement of value in its peripheral lands is whether, considering the extraordinary nature of the Kenford domed stadium proposal, such claimed damages can ever be anything but too speculative to permit recovery. No case has been cited where a plaintiff in a suit for defendant's failure to build a promised improvement has recovered damages based on what his adjoining land would have been worth if the defendant had performed. We have found no helpful precedent. Arguably, such damages are always too speculative since the values on which they are based must necessarily depend on hypothesizing a construction which did not take place and its consequent effect on market values. . . .

. . . .

. . . . [T]he proof, we believe, must be incurably speculative and for that reason we find a retrial on the land enhancement issue unwarranted.

For these reasons, we believe that the judgment for the recovery of mitigation damages should be affirmed and that a new trial should be granted only on the issue of Kenford's reliance damages. Plaintiffs' other claims should be dismissed and the judgment appealed from insofar as it dismisses plaintiff Kenford's claim for loss of profits on the projected improvements on the peripheral lands should be affirmed.

BOOMER, J., concurs.

Kenford Co. v. County of Erie (II)

KENFORD COMPANY and DOME STADIUM, INC., Plaintiffs-Appellants

v.

COUNTY OF ERIE et al., Defendants-Respondents

Court of Appeals of New York
493 N.E.2d 234, 502 N.Y.S.2d 131 (1986)

PER CURIAM.

The issue in this appeal is whether a plaintiff, in an action for breach of contract, may recover loss of prospective profits for its contemplated 20-year operation of a domed stadium which was to be constructed by defendant County of Erie (County).

. . . .

. . . . On appeal to this court, we are concerned only with that portion of the verdict which awarded DSI money damages for loss of prospective profits during the 20-year period of the proposed management contract, as appended to the basic contract. That portion of the verdict was set aside by the Appellate Division and the cause of action dismissed. The court concluded that the use of expert opinion to present statistical projections of future business operations involved the use of too many variables to provide a rational basis upon which lost profits could be calculated and, therefore, such projections were insufficient as a matter of law to support an award of lost profits. We agree with this ultimate conclusion, but upon different grounds.

Loss of future profits as damages for breach of contract have been permitted in New York under long-established and precise rules of law. First, it must be demonstrated with certainty that such damages have been caused by the breach and, second, the alleged loss must be capable of proof with reasonable certainty. In other words, the damages may not be merely speculative, possible or imaginary, but must be reasonably certain and directly traceable to the breach, not remote or the result of other intervening causes (*Wakeman v. Wheeler & Wilson Mfg. Co.*, 101 N.Y. 205, 4 N.E. 264). In addition, there must be a showing that the particular damages were fairly within the contemplation of the parties to the contract at the time it was made (*Witherbee v. Meyer*, 155 N.Y. 446, 50 N.E. 58). If it is a new business seeking to recover for loss of future profits, a stricter standard is imposed for the obvious reason that there does not exist a reasonable basis of experience upon which to estimate lost profits with the requisite degree of reasonable certainty (*Cramer v. Grand Rapids Show Case Co.*, 223 N.Y. 63, 119 N.E. 227; 25 C.J.S. Damages, § 42[b]).

Think About It!

Note that a buyer's lost profits are indirect damages (consequential damages) because a buyer's direct damages pertain to bargained-for exchange—the purchased item (real estate, services, goods, or intangibles). Any profit that the buyer could have made on that item is compensated with indirect damages. On the other hand, a seller's lost profits are direct damages, because a seller's bargained-for exchange in a contract is usually the price. The profits are part of that price. Recall *Neri* (page 1076) and *Vitex* (page 1079).

These rules must be applied to the proof presented by DSI in this case. We note the procedure for computing damages selected by DSI was in accord with contemporary economic theory and was presented through the testimony of recognized experts. Such a procedure has been accepted in this State and many other jurisdictions (*see, De Long v. County of Erie*, 60 N.Y.2d 296, 469 N.Y.S.2d 611,

457 N.E.2d 177). DSI's economic analysis employed historical data, obtained from the operation of other domed stadiums and related facilities throughout the country, which was then applied to the results of a comprehensive study of the marketing prospects for the proposed facility in the Buffalo area. The quantity of proof is massive and, unquestionably, represents business and industry's most advanced and sophisticated method for predicting the probable results of contemplated projects. Indeed, it is difficult to conclude what additional relevant proof could have been submitted by DSI in support of its attempt to establish, with reasonable certainty, loss of prospective profits. Nevertheless, DSI's proof is insufficient to meet the required standard.

The reason for this conclusion is twofold. Initially, the proof does not satisfy the requirement that liability for loss of profits over a 20-year period was in the contemplation of the parties at the time of the execution of the basic contract or at the time of its breach (*see, Chapman v. Fargo, 223 N.Y. 32, 119 N.E. 76 . . .*). Indeed, the provisions in the contract providing remedy for a default do not suggest or provide for such a heavy responsibility on the part of the County. In the absence of any provision for such an eventuality, the commonsense rule to apply is to consider what the parties would have concluded had they considered the subject. The evidence here fails to demonstrate that liability for loss of profits over the length of the contract would have been in the contemplation of the parties at the relevant times.

Next, we note that despite the massive quantity of expert proof submitted by DSI, the ultimate conclusions are still projections, and as employed in the present day commercial world, subject to adjustment and modification. We of course recognize that any projection cannot be absolute, nor is there any such requirement, but it is axiomatic that the degree of certainty is dependent upon known or unknown factors which form the basis of the ultimate conclusion. Here, the foundations upon which the economic model was created undermine the certainty of the projections. DSI assumed that the facility was completed, available for use and successfully operated by it for 20 years, providing professional sporting events and other forms of entertainment, as well as hosting meetings, conventions and related commercial gatherings. At the time of the breach, there was only one other facility in this country to use as a basis of comparison, the Astrodome in Houston. Quite simply, the multitude of assumptions required to establish projections of profitability over the life of this contract require speculation and conjecture, making it beyond the capability of even the most sophisticated procedures to satisfy the legal requirements of proof with reasonable certainty.

Think About It!

Which approach is more correct– *Kenford Co. (I)* (majority or dissent) or *Kenford Co. (II)*?

The economic facts of life, the whim of the general public and the fickle nature of popular support for professional athletic endeavors must be given great weight in attempting to ascertain damages 20 years in the future. New York has long recognized the inherent uncertainties of predicting profits in the entertainment field in general (*see, Broadway Photoplay Co. v. World Film Corp.,* 225 N.Y. 104, 121 N.E. 756) and, in this case, we are dealing, in large part, with a new facility furnishing entertainment for the public. It is our view that the record in this case demonstrates the efficacy of the principles set forth by this court in *Cramer v. Grand Rapids Show Case Co.* (223 N.Y. 63, 119 N.E. 227, *supra*), principles to which we continue to adhere. . . .

Accordingly, that portion of the order of the Appellate Division being appealed from should be affirmed.

WACHTLER, C.J., and MEYER, ALEXANDER, TITONE and KANE, JJ., concur in Per Curiam opinion.

SIMONS, KAYE and HANCOCK, JJ., taking no part.

———————

Reading the Law Critically: Consequential Damages in the UCC, CISG and UNIDROIT

1. UCC § 2-715(2) defines *buyers'* consequential damages and establishes a foreseeability limitation similar to the standard in *Hadley v. Baxendale.* What similarities and differences are there between the two rules? How do they compare with the two international provisions?

2. Although common law cases allow consequential damages for sellers if the damages can be proved (see *Redgrave* and *Kenford*), UCC Article 2 does not. Why would seller's consequential damages be excluded? To answer this question, consider what kind of consequential damages a seller might suffer if a buyer fails to take the goods or pay for them.

3. Do the international provisions allow consequential damages for sellers?

UCC § 2-715. **Buyer's Incidental and Consequential Damages.**

(1) [Incidental damages provision appears on page 1084]
(2) Consequential damages resulting from the seller's breach include
    (a) any loss resulting from general or particular requirements and needs of which the seller at the time of contracting had reason to know and which could not reasonably be prevented by cover or otherwise; and
    (b) injury to person or property proximately resulting from any breach of warranty.

CISG Art. 74 (in Ch. V. Provisions Common to the Obligations of the Seller and of the Buyer, Sec. II. Damages)

Damages for breach of contract by one party consist of a sum equal to the loss, including loss of profit, suffered by the other party as a consequence of the breach. Such damages may not exceed the loss which the party in breach foresaw or ought to have foreseen at the time of the conclusion of the contract, in the light of the facts and matters of which he then knew or ought to have known, as a possible consequence of the breach of contract.

UNIDROIT Art. 7.4.4. Foreseeability of Harm

The non-performing party is liable only for harm which it foresaw or could reasonably have foreseen at the time of the conclusion of the contract as being likely to result from its non-performance.

---

§ 2.1.6. Mitigation of Damages (Avoidable Damages)

As noted on page 1043, one of the policies underlying damages is avoiding the award of damages that the aggrieved party could reasonably have prevented or avoided, either by stopping performance or by taking affirmative steps to avoid further loss. The aggrieved party thus cannot exact revenge on the breaching party by "running up the ante," piling up damages that would punish the breaching party through actions not necessary to protect the interests of the non-breaching party. Such damages are considered to have been caused in some sense by the aggrieved party's failure to take reasonable steps to avoid further injury, rather than by the breaching party. Promoting acts in mitigation also encourages the aggrieved party to engage in productive economic behavior, rather than sit idle and rely upon being compensated for the lost expectancy or continue performing a clearly broken contract and compel the other party to pay for that performance. This is sometimes said to represent the aggrieved party's "duty to mitigate damages," though it is not a duty such that the failure to perform it makes the aggrieved party affirmatively liable.

UCC § 2-715 limits consequential damages for buyers to those "which could not be reasonably prevented by cover or otherwise." The CISG and UNIDROIT articulate the mitigation concept in slightly different ways:

CISG Art. 77 **(in Ch. V. Provisions Common to the Obligations of the Seller and of the Buyer, Sec. II. Damages)**

A party who relies on a breach of contract must take such measures as are reasonable in the circumstances to mitigate the loss, including loss of profit, resulting from the breach. If he fails to take such measures, the party in breach may claim a reduction in the damages in the amount by which the loss should have been mitigated.

UNIDROIT Art 7.4.8. **Mitigation of Harm**

(1) The non-performing party is not liable for harm suffered by the aggrieved party to the extent that the harm could have been reduced by the latter party's taking reasonable steps.
(2) The aggrieved party is entitled to recover any expenses reasonably incurred in attempting to reduce the harm.

Declaring that the aggrieved party must take reasonable steps to avoid or mitigate damages is easier than defining just what actions are required to satisfy that responsibility. Most straightforward is the requirement that, after one party repudiates the contract, the other party should cease performing unless there is a reasonable chance that the additional work will decrease rather than increase damages. For example, in *Rockingham County v. Luten Bridge Co.*, 35 F.2d 301 (M.D. N.C. 1929), the County Board withdrew approval of a bridge-building project and then repudiated its contract with Luten. Despite the repudiation, the company built the bridge—"in the midst of the forest" because the county had also decided not to build the road of which the bridge was to be a part—and then sought recovery of the contract price. The court refused to award the company damages for any work done after receiving notice of the cancellation.

Behind the Scenes

There is more to the *Rockingham* County case than a foolish contractor continuing work in the face of a clear repudiation. "A closer look at the case reveals that the underlying dispute was more about the legitimacy of local government. The dispute emerged when angry taxpayers charged the county commissioners with pursuing a corrupt agenda on behalf of the industrialist who sponsored their political campaigns.

But the conflict also revealed traditional tensions between the county's farmers and its mercantile mill owners and constituted a microcosm of the larger political conflict—endemic throughout North Carolina and the South—over investing in public improvements to promote industrialization. Judge Parker's opinion was an effort to arm county governments with the powers necessary to facilitate industrialization and secure good governance. The duty to mitigate damages was merely an afterthought." Barak Richman, Jordi Weinstock, & Jason Mehta, *A Bridge, a Tax Revolt, and the Struggle to Industrialize: The Story and Legacy of Rockingham County v. Luten Bridge Co.*, 84 N.C. L. Rev. 1841 (2006).

But even the "duty" to stop working is qualified. Under some circumstances, the aggrieved party may reasonably conclude that continuing to perform will reduce, not increase, damages. For instance, a seller manufacturimg custom goods for a buyer who repudiates may well decide that it should stop manufacture because the completed goods won't be saleable to other buyers. The UCC takes this into account in § 2-704:

UCC § 2-704. **Seller's Right to Identify Goods to the Contract Notwithstanding Breach or to Salvage Unfinished Goods.**

(1) An aggrieved seller under the preceding section may
    (a) identify to the contract conforming goods not already identified if at the time he learned of the breach they are in his possession or control;
    (b) treat as the subject of resale goods which have demonstrably been intended for the particular contract even though those goods are unfinished.

(2) Where the goods are unfinished an aggrieved seller may in the exercise of reasonable commercial judgment for the purposes of avoiding loss and of effective realization either complete the manufacture and wholly identify the goods to the contract or cease manufacture and resell for scrap or salvage value or proceed in any other reasonable manner.

The second, and often more difficult, mitigation question is determining what affirmative steps a party should take to avoid further losses. The following cases examine that question.

Reading the Law Critically: *Sackett* and *Parker*

This is the third part of *Sackett;* the first and second parts appeared on pages 920 and 1053.

1. According to each court, what responsibility does an aggrieved party have to mitigate damages? Are the rules articulated by the two courts consistent?

2. Does the dissenting judge in *Parker* disagree with the *Parker* majority as to the standard to be used, or as to its application to the facts of the case?

3. How does the particular type of contract (e.g., an employment contract or a sale of business) affect the application of the mitigation principles?

Sackett v. Spindler

SHELDON SACKETT, Plaintiff, Cross-Defendant and Appellant

v.

PAUL R. SPINDLER, Defendant, Cross-Complainant and Respondent

California Court of Appeal

56 Cal. Rptr. 435 (Ct. App. 1967)

The parties entered into an $85,000 purchase agreement for a majority of the shares of S & S Newspapers. The buyer (plaintiff) made the first payment for $6000 on time, the second payment for $20,000 a week late and $200 short, and the third payment of $59,000 with a check that bounced. Despite several offers to cure, the buyer never paid the remaining balance. The seller eventually canceled the contract and sought another buyer. He finally sold the stock nearly a year later for a net payment of $20,680. The parties sued each other for breach. The court held that buyer/plaintiff had committed a total material breach, after which seller/defendant was entitled to cancel the contract and was therefore not in breach for doing so. The trial court awarded—and the appellate court affirmed—$34,575.74 in damages to Spindler, calculated by subtracting from the $85,000 contract price all sums of money received by him from Sackett ($29,744.26) and Spindler's net proceeds from his subsequent sale of the stock in July 1962 ($20,680). The court rejected the market price as a measure, holding that the stock had no market at the time of the breach.]

. . . .

Mitigation of Damages

The trial court specifically found that Spindler "spent all reasonable efforts in minimizing damages to plaintiff . . ." and that "[t]he diminution in value of the 'S & S Newspapers' business after September 9, 1961 and the consequent diminution in value of the corporate stock in 'S & S Newspapers' after September 9, 1961 was directly caused by the conduct of plaintiff . . . in breaching the aforesaid contract of July 8, 1961 and plaintiff['s] . . . failure to pay to defendant . . . the entire purchase price on or before October 5, 1961." Sackett contends that these findings are not supported by the evidence.

It is well established in California that a party injured by a breach of contract is required to do everything reasonably possible to minimize his own loss and thus reduce the damages for which the other party has become liable. (Valencia v. Shell Oil Co., 23 Cal.2d 840, 844, 147 P.2d 558; Johnson v. Comptoir etc. D'Exportation, 135 Cal.App.2d 683, 689, 288 P.2d 151; Hunter v. Croysdill, 169 Cal.App.2d 307, 318, 337 P.2d 174.) From this rule it follows that a person who has been injured by a breach of contract cannot recover damages for detriment which he could have avoided by reasonable effort and without undue expense. (Hunter v. Croysdill, supra; Murphy v. Kelly, 137 Cal.App.2d 21, 31, 289 P.2d 565; Valencia v. Shell Oil Co., supra.) The question of whether the injured party has acted reasonably in mitigating damages is one of fact. (Jegen v. Berger, 77 Cal.App.2d 1, 11, 174 P.2d 489.) Accordingly, where, as in the instant case, the trial court has made findings of fact to the effect that the injured party has acted reasonably in minimizing his damages, this finding must be upheld on appeal if the record contains any substantial evidence in support of such finding.

In the instant case it is clear that the record contains ample evidence tending to show that Spindler acted reasonably in minimizing damages. Firstly, in order to improve the financial condition of the newspaper he made several efforts to raise working capital for the business. This he did by personally borrowing money for additional capital and by selling one-half of his stock. In addition, he cut costs by changing the newspaper from a daily to a weekly paper. Sackett argues that after Spindler had determined that Sackett had breached the contract, Spindler did not list the newspaper for sale with a broker nor did he take any other steps to sell the newspaper. However, according to Snyder's testimony, such action on the part of Spindler would have been futile since it would be almost impossible for him to sell the newspaper after the publicized sale to Sackett had fallen through. In addition, since the record reveals that the financial condition of the newspaper immediately after Sackett's breach was worse than its financial condition approximately one year later, it is apparent that Spindler's damages would have been greater if he had been able to sell the stock at an earlier date. Finally, Sackett contends that Spindler was required to accept Sackett's so-called "offer" of October 4 in order to minimize damages. However, Sackett's telegram of October 4 contained no tender of performance, but only an expression of willingness to proceed to consummate the sale as soon as the release of his assets from threatened receivership in his divorce action would permit "full financing" of the unpaid balance.

[The court awarded the full amount of damages to Spindler, unreduced by any failure to mitigate.]

Parker v. Twentieth Century-Fox Film Corp.

SHIRLEY MACLAINE PARKER, Plaintiff-Respondent

v.

TWENTIETH CENTURY-FOX FILM CORP., Defendant-Appellant

Supreme Court of California, In Bank
474 P.2d 689 (Cal. 1970)

BURKE, Justice.

Defendant Twentieth Century-Fox Film Corporation appeals from a summary judgment granting to plaintiff the recovery of agreed compensation under a written contract for her services as an actress in a motion picture. As will appear, we have concluded that the trial court correctly ruled in plaintiff's favor and that the judgment should be affirmed.

Plaintiff is well known as an actress, and in the contract between plaintiff and defendant is sometimes referred to as the "Artist." Under the contract, dated August 6, 1965, plaintiff was to play the female lead in defendant's contemplated production of a motion picture entitled "Bloomer Girl." The contract provided that defendant would pay plaintiff a minimum "guaranteed compensation" of "53,571.42 per week for 14 weeks commencing May 23, 1966, for a total

Who's That?

The older sister of actor Warren Beatty, Shirley MacLaine is a Hollywood film actress whose career spans from the 1950s to the present day. Discovered by Hollywood while performing on Broadway in *The Pajama Game*, she was initially famous for her singing and dancing talents. After moving the Hollywood, she demonstrated exceptional skills as a dramatic and comedic actress. Today, she is perhaps best known for her Academy-Award-winning role in *Terms of Endearment* (1983) along with other roles in *The Apartment* (1960), *Sweet Charity* (1968), *Guarding Tess* (1994), and *Rumor Has It* (2005). For more information, see http://en.wikipedia.org/wiki/Shirley_maclaine.

of $750,000." Prior to May 1966 defendant decided not to produce the picture and by a letter dated April 4, 1966, it notified plaintiff of that decision and that it would not "comply with our obligations to you under" the written contract.

By the same letter and with the professed purpose "to avoid any damage to you," defendant instead offered to employ plaintiff as the leading actress in another film tentatively entitled "Big Country, Big Man" (hereinafter, "Big Country"). The compensation offered was identical, as were 31 of the 34 numbered provisions or articles of the original contract.[1] Unlike "Bloomer Girl," however, which was to have been a musical production, "Big Country" was a dramatic "western type" movie. "Bloomer Girl" was to have been filmed in California; "Big Country" was to be produced in Australia. Also, certain terms in the proffered contract varied from those of the original.[2] Plaintiff was given one week within which to accept; she did not and the offer lapsed. Plaintiff then commenced this action seeking recovery of the agreed guaranteed compensation.

The complaint sets forth two causes of action. The first is for money due under the contract; the second, based upon the same allegations as the first, is for damages resulting from defendant's breach of contract. Defendant in its answer admits the existence and validity of the contract, that plaintiff complied with all the conditions, covenants and promises and stood ready to complete the performance, and that defendant breached and "anticipatorily repudiated" the contract.

---

[1] Among the identical provisions was the following found in the last paragraph of Article 2 of the original contract: "We [defendant] shall not be obligated to utilize your [plaintiff's] services in or in connection with the Photoplay hereunder, our sole obligation, subject to the terms and conditions of this Agreement, being to pay you the guaranteed compensation herein provided for."

[2] Article 29 of the original contract specified that plaintiff approved the director already chosen for "Bloomer Girl" and that in case he failed to act as director plaintiff was to have the right of approval of any substitute director. Article 31 provided that plaintiff was to have the right of approval of the "Bloomer Girl" dance director, and Article 32 gave her the right of approval of the screenplay.

Defendant's letter of April 4 to plaintiff, which contained both defendant's notice of breach of the "Bloomer Girl" contract and offer of the lead in "Big Country," eliminated or impaired each of those rights. It read in part as follows: "The terms and conditions of our offer of employment are identical to those set forth in the 'BLOOMER GIRL' Agreement, Articles 1 through 34 and Exhibit A to the Agreement, except as follows:

1. Article 31 of said Agreement will not be included in any contract of employment regarding 'BIG COUNTRY, BIG MAN' as it is not a musical and it thus will not need a dance director.

2. In the 'BLOOMER GIRL' agreement, in Articles 29 and 32, you were given certain director and screenplay approvals and you had preapproved certain matters. Since there simply is insufficient time to negotiate with you regarding your choice of director and regarding the screenplay and since you already expressed an interest in performing the role in 'BIG COUNTRY, BIG MAN,' we must exclude from our offer of employment in 'BIG COUNTRY, BIG MAN' any approval rights as are contained in said Articles 29 and 32; however, we shall consult with you respecting the director to be selected to direct the photoplay and will further consult with you with respect to the screenplay and any revisions or changes therein, provided, however, that if we fail to agree . . . the decision of . . . [defendant] with respect to the selection of a director and to revisions and changes in the said screenplay shall be binding upon the parties to said agreement."

new role must be particular mitigated

It denies, however, that any money is due to plaintiff either under the contract or as a result of its breach, and pleads as an affirmative defense to both causes of action plaintiff's allegedly deliberate failure to mitigate damages, asserting that she unreasonably refused to accept its offer of the leading role in "Big Country."

B won

Plaintiff moved for summary judgment under Code of Civil Procedure section 437c, the motion was granted, and summary judgment for $750,000 plus interest was entered in plaintiff's favor. This appeal by defendant followed.

The familiar rules are that the matter to be determined by the trial court on a motion for summary judgment is whether facts have been presented which give rise to a triable factual issue. The court may not pass upon the issue itself. Summary judgment is proper only if the affidavits or declarations in support of the moving party would be sufficient to sustain a judgment in his favor and his opponent does not by affidavit show facts sufficient to present a triable issue of fact. . . .

other employment must be similar

The general rule is that the measure of recovery by a wrongfully discharged employee is the amount of salary agreed upon for the period of service, less the amount which the employer affirmatively proves the employee has earned or with reasonable effort might have earned from other employment. . . . However, before projected earnings from other employment opportunities not sought or accepted by the discharged employee can be applied in mitigation, the employer must show that the other employment was comparable, or substantially similar, to that of which the employee has been deprived; the employee's rejection of or failure to seek other available employment of a different or inferior kind may not be resorted to in order to mitigate damages. (Gonzales v. Internat. Assn. of Machinists (1963) 213 Cal.App.2d 817, 822-824, 29 Cal.Rptr. 190 . . . .

In the present case defendant has raised no issue of *reasonableness of efforts* by plaintiff to obtain other employment; the sole issue is whether plaintiff's refusal of defendant's substitute offer of "Big Country" may be used in mitigation. Nor, if the "Big Country" offer was of employment different or inferior when compared with the original "Bloomer Girl" employment, is there an issue as to whether or not plaintiff acted reasonably in refusing the substitute offer. Despite defendant's arguments to the contrary, no case cited or which our research has discovered holds or suggests that reasonableness is an element of a wrongfully discharged employee's option to reject, or fail to seek, different or inferior employment lest the possible earnings therefrom be charged against him in mitigation of damages.[5]

Applying the foregoing rules to the record in the present case, with all intendments in favor of the party opposing the summary judgment motion—here, defendant—it is clear that the trial court correctly ruled that plaintiff's failure to accept defendant's tendered substitute employment could not be applied in mitigation of damages because the offer of the "Big Country" lead was of employment both different and inferior, and that no factual dispute was presented on that issue. The mere circumstance that "Bloomer Girl" was to be a musical review calling upon plaintiff's talents as a dancer as well as an actress, and was to be produced in the City of Los Angeles, whereas "Big Country" was a straight dramatic role in a "Western Type" story taking place in an opal mine in Australia, demonstrates the difference in kind between the two employments; the female lead as a dramatic actress in a western style motion picture can by no stretch of imagination be considered the equivalent of or substantially similar to the lead in a song-and-dance production.

Additionally, the substitute "Big Country" offer proposed to eliminate or impair the director and screenplay approvals accorded to plaintiff under the original "Bloomer Girl" contract (see fn. 2, Ante), and thus constituted an offer of inferior employment. No expertise or judicial notice is required in order to hold that the deprivation or infringement of an employee's rights held under an original employment contract converts the available "other employment" relied upon by the employer to mitigate damages, into inferior employment which the employee need not seek or accept. (See Gonzales v. Internat. Asst. of Machinists, *supra*, 213 Cal.App.2d 817, 823-824, 29 Cal.Rptr. 190 . . . .)

Statements found in affidavits submitted by defendant in opposition to plaintiff's summary judgment motion, to the effect that the "Big Country" offer was

---

[5] Instead, in each case the reasonableness referred to was that of the *efforts* of the employee to obtain other employment that was not different or inferior; his right to reject the latter was declared as an unqualified rule of law. Thus, Gonzales v. Internat. Assn. of Machinists, *supra*, 213 Cal.App.2d 817, 823-824, 29 Cal.Rptr. 190, 194, holds that the trial court correctly instructed the jury that plaintiff union member, a machinist, was required to make "such *efforts* as the average [member of his union] desiring employment would make at that particular time and place" (italics added); but, further, that the court *properly rejected* defendant's *offer of proof of the availability of other kinds of employment* at the same or higher pay than plaintiff usually received and all outside the jurisdiction of his union, as plaintiff could not be required to accept different employment or a nonunion job.

In Harris v. Nat. Union, etc., Cooks and Stewards, *supra*, 116 Cal.App.2d 759, 761, 254 P.2d 673, 676, the issues were stated to be, inter alia, whether comparable employment was open to each plaintiff employee, and if so whether each plaintiff made a *reasonable effort* to secure such employment. It was held that the trial court *properly sustained an objection to an offer to prove a custom of accepting a job in a lower rank* when work in the higher rank was not available, as "The duty of mitigation of damages . . . does not require the plaintiff 'to seek or to accept other employment of a different or inferior kind.' . . . Damages may be mitigated 'by a showing that the employee, by the exercise of reasonable diligence and effort, could have procured comparable employment. . . .'."

not of employment different from or inferior to that under the "Bloomer Girl" contract, merely repeat the allegations of defendant's answer to the complaint in this action, constitute only conclusionary assertions with respect to undisputed facts, and do not give rise to a triable factual issue so as to defeat the motion for summary judgment. . . .

In view of the determination that defendant failed to present any facts showing the existence of a factual issue with respect to its sole defense—plaintiff's rejection of its substitute employment offer in mitigation of damages—we need not consider plaintiff's further contention that for various reasons, ... plaintiff was excused from attempting to mitigate damages.

The judgment is affirmed.

SULLIVAN, Acting Chief Justice (dissenting).

The basic question in this case is whether or not plaintiff acted reasonably in rejecting defendant's offer of alternate employment. The answer depends upon whether that offer (starring in "Big Country, Big Man") was an offer of work that was substantially similar to her former employment (starring in "Bloomer Girl") or of work that was of a different or inferior kind. To my mind this is a factual issue which the trial court should not have determined on a motion for summary judgment. The majority have not only repeated this error but have compounded it by applying the rules governing mitigation of damages in the employer-employee context in a misleading fashion. Accordingly, I respectfully dissent.

The familiar rule requiring a plaintiff in a tort or contract action to mitigate damages embodies notions of fairness and socially responsible behavior which are fundamental to our jurisprudence. Most broadly stated, it precludes the recovery of damages which, through the exercise of due diligence, could have been avoided. Thus, in essence, it is a rule requiring reasonable conduct in commercial affairs. This general principle governs the obligations of an employee after his employer has wrongfully repudiated or terminated the employment contract. Rather than permitting the employee simply to remain idle during the balance of the contract period, the law requires him to make a reasonable effort to secure other employment.[1] He is not obliged, however, to seek or accept any and all

---

[1] The issue is generally discussed in terms of a duty on the part of the employee to minimize loss. The practice is long-established and there is little reason to change despite Judge Cardozo's observation of its subtle inaccuracy. "The servant is free to accept employment or reject it according to his uncensored pleasure. What is meant by the supposed duty is merely this: That if he unreasonably reject, he will not be heard to say that the loss of wages from then on shall be deemed the jural consequence of the earlier discharge. He has broken the chain of causation, and loss resulting to him thereafter is suffered through his own act." (McClelland v. Climax Hosiery Mills (1930) 252 N.Y. 347, 359, 169 N.E. 605, 609, concurring opinion.)

types of work which may be available. Only work which is in the same field and which is of the same quality need be accepted.[2]

Over the years the courts have employed various phrases to define the type of employment which the employee, upon his wrongful discharge, is under an obligation to accept. Thus in California alone it has been held that he must accept employment which is "substantially similar"; "comparable employment"; employment "in the same general line of the first employment"; "equivalent to his prior position"; "employment in a similar capacity"; employment which is "not . . . of a different or inferior kind. . . ." [cites omitted throughout paragraph].

For reasons which are unexplained, the majority cite several of these cases yet select from among the various judicial formulations which contain one particular phrase, "Not of a different or inferior kind," with which to analyze this case. I have discovered no historical or theoretical reason to adopt this phrase, which is simply a negative restatement of the affirmative standards set out in the above cases, as the exclusive standard. Indeed, its emergence is an example of the dubious phenomenon of the law responding not to rational judicial choice or changing social conditions, but to unrecognized changes in the language of opinions or legal treatises. However, the phrase is a serviceable one and my concern is not with its use as the standard but rather with what I consider its distortion.

The relevant language excuses acceptance only of employment which is of a *different kind.* (Gonzales v. Internat. Assn. of Machinists, *supra,* 213 Cal. App.2d 817, 822, 29 Cal.Rptr. 190 . . .). It has never been the law that the mere existence of *differences between two jobs in the same field* is sufficient, as a matter of law, to excuse an employee wrongfully discharged from one from accepting the other in order to mitigate damages. Such an approach would effectively eliminate any obligation of an employee to attempt to minimize damage arising from a wrongful discharge. The only alternative job offer an employee would be required to accept would be an offer of his former job by his former employer.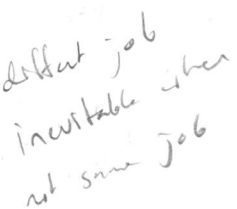

Although the majority appear to hold that there was a difference "in kind" between the employment offered plaintiff in "Bloomer Girl" and that offered in "Big Country", an examination of the opinion makes crystal clear that the majority merely point out differences between the two *films* (an obvious circumstance)

---

[2] This qualification of the rule seems to reflect the simple and humane attitude that it is too severe to demand of a person that he attempt to find and perform work for which he has no training or experience. Many of the older cases hold that one need not accept work in an inferior rank or position nor work which is more menial or arduous. This suggests that the rule may have had its origin in the bourgeois fear of resubmergence in lower economic classes.

and then apodically assert that these constitute a difference in the *kind of employment*. The entire rationale of the majority boils down to this: that the "*mere circumstances*" that "Bloomer Girl" was to be a musical review while "Big Country" was a straight drama "demonstrates the difference in kind" since a female lead in a western is not "the equivalent of or substantially similar to" a lead in a musical. This is merely attempting to prove the proposition by repeating it. It shows that the vehicles for the display of the star's talents are different but it does not prove that her employment as a star in such vehicles is of necessity different *in kind* and either inferior or superior.

What's That?

The dissent may have meant that the majority "apodictically" (rather than "apodically") asserted that the differences between the two jobs meant there was a difference "in kind" between the two. "Apodictic" means "demonstrably or indisputably true"; the dissent believes the majority declared a truth about the difference between the jobs without demonstrating it.

I believe that the approach taken by the majority (a superficial listing of differences with no attempt to assess their significance) may subvert a valuable legal doctrine.[5] The inquiry in cases such as this should not be whether differences between the two jobs exist (there will always be differences) but whether the differences which are present are substantial enough to constitute differences in the *kind* of employment or, alternatively, whether they render the substitute work employment of an *inferior kind*.

It seems to me that *this* inquiry involves, in the instant case at least, factual determinations which are improper on a motion for summary judgment. Resolving whether or not one job is substantially similar to another or whether, on the other hand, it is of a different or inferior kind, will often (as here) require a critical appraisal of the similarities and differences between them in light of the importance of these differences to the employee. This necessitates a weighing of the evidence, and it is precisely this undertaking which is forbidden on summary judgment. (Garlock v. Cole (1962) 199 Cal.App.2d 11, 14, 18 Cal. Rptr. 393.)

This is not to say that summary judgment would never be available in an action by an employee in which the employer raises the defense of failure to mitigate damages. No case has come to my attention, however, in which summary judgment has been granted on the issue of whether an employee was obliged to accept available alternate employment. Nevertheless, there may well

---

[5] The values of the doctrine of mitigation of damages in this context are that it minimizes the unnecessary personal and social (e.g., nonproductive use of labor, litigation) costs of contractual failure. If a wrongfully discharged employee can, through his own action and without suffering financial or psychological loss in the process, reduce the damages accruing from the breach of contract, the most sensible policy is to require him to do so. I fear the majority opinion will encourage precisely opposite conduct.

be cases in which the substitute employment is so manifestly of a dissimilar or inferior sort, the declarations of the plaintiff so complete and those of the defendant so conclusionary and inadequate that no factual issues exist for which a trial is required. This, however, is not such a case.

It is not intuitively obvious, to me at least, that the leading female role in a dramatic motion picture is a radically different endeavor from the leading female role in a musical comedy film. Nor is it plain to me that the rather qualified rights of director and screenplay approval contained in the first contract are highly significant matters either in the entertainment industry in general or to this plaintiff in particular. Certainly, none of the declarations introduced by plaintiff in support of her motion shed any light on these issues.

Nor do they attempt to explain why she declined the offer of starring in "Big Country, Big Man." Nevertheless, the trial court granted the motion, declaring that these approval rights were "critical" and that their elimination altered "the essential nature of the employment."

. . . .

I believe that the judgment should be reversed so that the issue of whether or not the offer of the lead role in "Big Country, Big Man" was of employment comparable to that of the lead role in "Bloomer Girl" may be determined at trial.

. . . .

Behind the Scenes:
The Hollywood Studio System and "Bloomer Girl"

The Hollywood studio system functioned differently in the past than it does today. In the early years of Hollywood, the studios exerted tight contractual control over actors, who spent their entire careers working for one studio, which made decisions about an actor's physical appearance, scrutinized the actor's behavior "off the lot," and dictated which roles and movies the actor appeared in. A noncompliant actor would be placed on suspension without pay. Some studio doctors furnished drugs to actors, to help them work longer hours and sleep "on command." Judy Garland later recalled that MGM "had us working day and nights on end… they'd give us pep pills to keep us on our feet long after we were exhausted, then they'd knock us cold with sleeping pills, then after four hours they'd give us the pep pills again."

Some actors rebelled against this system, initially unsuccessfully. James Cagney and Myrna Loy brought unsuccessful suits in the 1930s. Bette Davis famously became involved in a lawsuit with Warner Bros. when she walked out on her studio contract in protest for better roles. The first successful suit by a Hollywood star against a studio was mounted by Olivia de Haviland, famous for playing Melanie in *Gone with the Wind*. Her case, *De Haviland v. Warner Bros. Pictures, Inc.*, 67 Cal. App. 2d 225 (1944), limited the length of studio contracts to seven years and held that time under suspension counted as part of this time. For a fascinating account of the "De Haviland Law," see http://en.wikipedia.org/wiki/De_Havilland_Law.

During the 1950s, Hollywood stars continued to separate themselves from studios through litigation and by creating their own production companies, following the examples of Lucille Ball and husband Desi Arnaz in 1950 (Desilu Productions) and Marilyn Monroe in 1955. Many historians consider *Parker v. Twentieth Century Fox Film Corp.*, to be the official end of the Hollywood studio system. After this case, movie actors were free to pick their own roles, negotiate their own contract terms, and work for a variety of studios.

In this case, Parker entered in a contract to make a movie of a Broadway musical that had already succeeded on Broadway and that featured compelling characters and plot. "Bloomer Girl" debuted in 1944 as a Broadway musical, with lyricist E.Y. Harburg and composer Harold Arlen (who had composed "Somewhere Over the Rainbow" in 1938). In the story, "Horatio Applegate . . . [is] an upstate New York manufacturer of hoop skirts who has married off five of his daughters to his regional salesmen. He is, as the show begins, playing Cupid with the sixth, Evelina . . . , and his new employee, Jeff Calhoun . . . , a slave owner from Kentucky. Evelina, however, is devoted to her aunt, Dolly Bloomer, a stubborn women's activist and abolitionist. . . . The battles of the sexes and North and South are played out in the courtship of Evelina and Jeff until finally love and liberalism win."* The character of Dolly, who gave the movie its name, is based on Amelia Jenks Bloomer, a suffrage pioneer and temperance advocate. Because of her promotion of changing dress standards for women to free them from activity-restricting clothing, her name became associated with the development

---

* http://theater.nytimes.com/mem/theater/treview.html?html_title=&tols_title=BLOOMER%20GIRL%20(PLAY)&pdate=20010324&byline=By%20BRUCE%20WEBER&id=1077011429344

of "bloomers," loose trousers gathered at the ankles and topped by a short dress or skirt. "Bloomer Girl" ran for 654 performances and was recorded in a cast album. In the mid-1950s, "Bloomer Girl" was resurrected in an abridged version on TV.* The 1965 film of "Bloomer Girl" that was scrapped in this case was to have starred Shirley MacLaine (Parker) and Katharine Hepburn.

"Big Country, Big Man," which was also never made, was based on the novel "Call Me When the Cross Turns Over," a reference to a comment often made by sheep shearers in the Australian outback as they went to sleep (the "Cross" is the Southern Cross in the night sky). The scriptwriter of "Big Country" was Bill Strutton, who "worked on some of the best-remembered 1960s television shows including Ivanhoe, The Saint, The Avengers, and Doctor Who."**

Do these facts affect your analysis of the *Parker* case? If so, how?

§ 2.2. Reliance Damages — *put ptp back into pre-k condition, reimburse for reliance*

As discussed on page 1043, reliance damages are designed to put the aggrieved party into the position that it would have been in *today* if the parties had not entered the contract. Reliance damages compensate for out-of-pocket expenses incurred by the aggrieved party in reliance on the existence of the contract, as well as lost opportunity costs, if provable. While expectation damages are the preferred remedy for enforcing contractual promises, reliance damages may be appropriate if there are no identifiable expectation damages, if such damages are too speculative in amount, or if for other reasons expectation damages do not seem appropriate. Reliance damages also may be awarded when a promise is enforced under Restatement (Second) § 90; recall that the remedy for promissory estoppel "may be limited as justice requires," though few courts have chosen that route.

---

*www.answers.com/topic/bloomer-girl; http://en.wikipedia.org/wiki/Bloomer_Girl; http://www.ibdb.com/production.php?id=1583.
**http://en.wikipedia.org/wiki/Bill_Strutton.

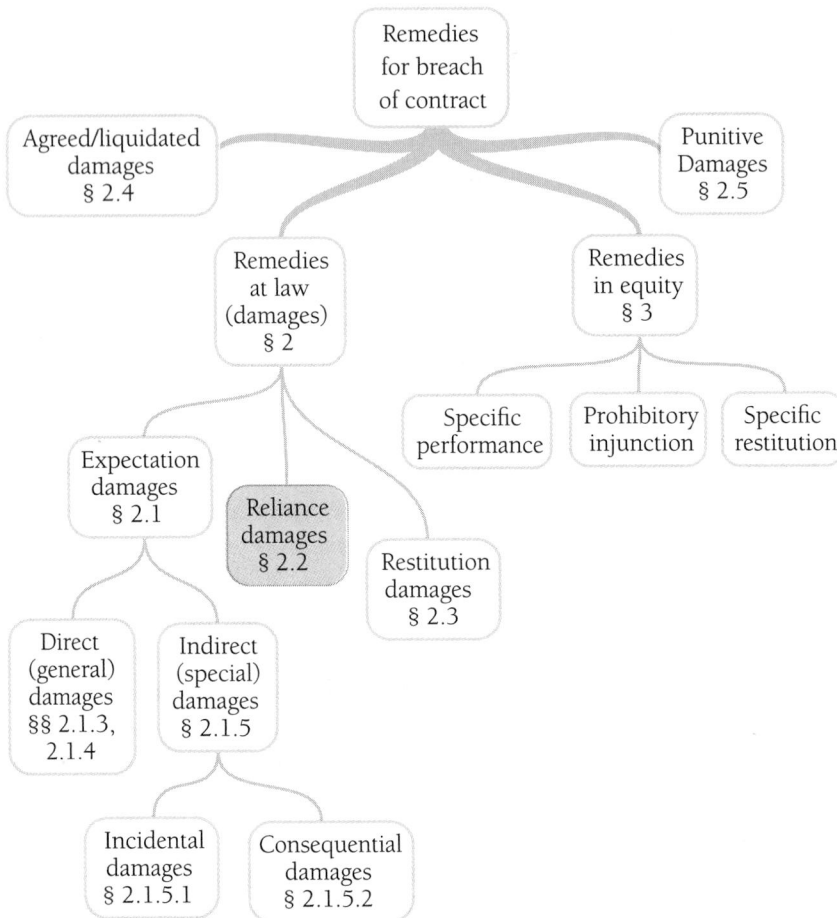

Recall the policies governing damages as listed in the chart on page 1043. Reliance damages are available only for *reasonable* expenses incurred *in reliance* on the existence of the promise, and the aggrieved party may not recover for expenses that could have been avoided through reasonable actions to mitigate or avoid losses. In a promissory estoppel case, the reliance must be the kind that "the promisor should reasonably expect" to have been induced by the promise. Because the promisor would not expect a promisee to spend more than it would have made on the contract, the promisee cannot recover more in reliance damages than it could have gotten in expectation damages.

Reading the Law Critically:
Security Stove and *Goodman*

1. Why are reliance damages rather than expectation damages considered appropriate in each of these cases?

2. How does each court compute reliance damages?

3. Are reliance damages "capped" so that they do not exceed the contract price or the expected profit on the contract? Should they be capped? Can the aggrieved party be put in a better position with reliance damages than it would have been in with expectation damages?

Security Stove & Mfg. Co. v. American Ry. Express Co.

SECURITY STOVE & MANUFACTURING CO., Plaintiff-Appellee

v.

AMERICAN RAILWAY EXPRESS CO., Defendant-Appellant

Kansas City Court of Appeals, Missouri

51 S.W.2d 572 (Mo. Ct. App. 1932)

BLAND, J.

This is an action for damages for the failure of defendant to transport, from Kansas City to Atlantic City, New Jersey, within a reasonable time, a furnace equipped with a combination oil and gas burner. The cause was tried before the court without the aid of a jury, resulting in a judgment in favor of plaintiff in the sum of $801.50 and interest, or in a total sum of $1,000.00. Defendant has appealed.

The facts show that plaintiff manufactured a furnace equipped with a special combination oil and gas burner it desired to exhibit at the American Gas Association Convention held in Atlantic City in October, 1926. The president of plaintiff testified that plaintiff engaged space for the exhibit for the reason "that the Henry L. Dougherty Company was very much interested in putting out a combination oil and gas burner; we had just developed one, after we got through, better than anything on the market and we thought this show would be the psychological time to get in contact with the Dougherty Company"; that "the thing wasn't sent there for sale but primarily to show"; that at the time the space was engaged it was too late to ship the furnace by freight so plaintiff decided to ship it by express, and, on September 18th, 1926, wrote the office of the defendant in Kansas City, stating that it had engaged a booth for exhibition purposes at Atlantic City, New Jersey, from the American Gas Association, for the week beginning October 11th; that its exhibit consisted of an oil burning furnace, together with two oil burners which weighed at least 1,500 pounds; that, "In order to get this exhibit in place on time it should be in Atlantic City not later than October the 8th. What we want you to do is to tell us how much time you will require to assure the delivery of the exhibit on time."

Mr. Bangs, chief clerk in charge of the local office of the defendant, upon receipt of the letter, sent Mr. Johnson, a commercial representative of the defendant, to see plaintiff. Johnson called upon plaintiff taking its letter with him. Johnson made a notation on the bottom of the letter giving October 4th, as the day that defendant was required to have the exhibit in order for it to reach Atlantic City on October 8th.

On October 1st, plaintiff wrote the defendant at Kansas City, referring to its letter of September 18th, concerning the fact that the furnace must be in Atlantic City not later than October 8th, and stating what Johnson had told it, saying: "Now Mr. Bangs, we want to make doubly sure that this shipment is in Atlantic City not later than October 8th and the purpose of this letter is to tell you that you can *have your truck call for the shipment between 12 and 1 o'clock on Saturday, October 2nd for this.*" (Italics plaintiff's.) On October 2d, plaintiff called the office of the express company in Kansas City and told it that the shipment was ready. Defendant came for the shipment on the last mentioned day, received it and delivered the express receipt to plaintiff. The shipment contained 21 packages. Each package was marked with stickers backed with glue and covered with silica of soda, to prevent the stickers being torn off in shipping. Each package was given a number. They ran from 1 to 21.

Plaintiff's president made arrangements to go to Atlantic City to attend the convention and install the exhibit, arriving there about October 11th. When he reached Atlantic City he found the shipment had been placed in the booth that had been assigned to plaintiff. The exhibit was set up, but it was found that one of the packages shipped was not there. This missing package contained the gas manifold, or that part of the oil and gas burner that controlled the flow of gas in the burner. This was the most important part of the exhibit and a like burner could not be obtained in Atlantic City.

Wires were sent and it was found that the stray package was at the "over and short bureau" of defendant in St. Louis. Defendant reported that the package would be forwarded to Atlantic City and would be there by Wednesday, the 13th. Plaintiff's president waited until Thursday, the day the convention closed, but the package had not arrived at the time, so he closed up the exhibit and left. About a week after he arrived in Kansas City, the package was returned by the defendant.

Bangs testified that the reasonable time for a shipment of this kind to reach Atlantic City from Kansas City would be four days; that if the shipment was received on October 4th, it would reach Atlantic City by October 8th; that plaintiff did not ask defendant for any special rate; that the rate charged was the regular one; that plaintiff asked no special advantage in the shipment; that all defendant, under its agreement with plaintiff was required to do was to deliver the shipment at Atlantic City in the ordinary course of events; that the shipment was found in St. Louis about Monday afternoon or Tuesday morning; that it was delivered at Atlantic City at the Ritz Carlton Hotel, on the 16th of the month. There was evidence on plaintiff's part that the reasonable time for a shipment of this character to reach Atlantic City from Kansas City was not more than three or four days.

. . . .

Plaintiff asked damages, which the court in its judgment allowed as follows: $147.00 express charges (on the exhibit); $45.12 freight on the exhibit from Atlantic City to Kansas City; $101.39 railroad and pullman fares to and from Atlantic City, expended by plaintiff's president and a workman taken by him to Atlantic City; $48.00 hotel room for the two; $150.00 for the time of the president; $40.00 for wages of plaintiff's other employee and $270.00 for rental of the booth, making a total of $801.51.

Defendant contends . . . . that the court erred in allowing plaintiff's expenses as damages; that the only damages, if any, that can be recovered in cases of this kind, are for loss of profits and that plaintiff's evidence is not sufficient to base any recovery on this ground.

. . . .

We think, under the circumstances in this case, that it was proper to allow plaintiff's expenses as its damages. Ordinarily the measure of damages where the carrier fails to deliver a shipment at destination within a reasonable time is the difference between the market value of the goods at the time of the delivery and the time when they should have been delivered. But where the carrier has notice of peculiar circumstances under which the shipment is made, which will result in an unusual loss by the shipper in case of delay in delivery, the carrier is responsible for the real damage sustained from such delay if the notice given is of such character, and goes to such extent, in informing

Think About It!

This case, like *Hadley*, involves a contract directly with a carrier. Carriers are often third parties in contracts between buyers and sellers, hired to transport the goods. Why would the ordinary measure of damages for carrier's failure to timely deliver goods be as the court describes it here? Does that measure make sense in a contract like the one in this case?

the carrier of the shipper's situation, that the carrier will be presumed to have contracted with reference thereto. Central Trust Co. of New York v. Savannah & W. R. Co. (C. C.) 69 F. 683, 685.

In the case at bar defendant was advised of the necessity of prompt delivery of the shipment. Plaintiff explained to Johnson the "importance of getting the exhibit there on time." Defendant knew the purpose of the exhibit and ought to respond for its negligence in failing to get it there. As we view the record this negligence is practically conceded. The undisputed testimony shows that the shipment was sent to the over and short department of the defendant in St. Louis. As the packages were plainly numbered this, prima facie, shows mistake or negligence on the part of the defendant. No effort was made by it to show that it was not negligent in sending it there, or not negligent in not forwarding it within a reasonable time after it was found.

There is no evidence of claim in this case that plaintiff suffered any loss of profits by reason of the delay in the shipment. . . .

Defendant contends that plaintiff "is endeavoring to achieve a return of the status quo in a suit based on a breach of contract. Instead of seeking to recover what he would have had, had the contract not been broken, plaintiff is trying to recover what he would have had, had there never been any contract of shipment"; that the expenses sued for would have been incurred in any event. It is no doubt, the general rule that where there is a breach of contract the party suffering the loss can recover only that which he would have had, had the contract not been broken . . . . But this is merely a general statement of the rule and is not inconsistent with the holdings that, in some instances, the injured party may recover expenses incurred in relying upon the contract, although such expenses would have been incurred had the contract not been breached. See Morrow v. Railroad, 140 Mo. App. 200, 212, 213, 123 S. W. 1034; Bryant v. Barton, 32 Neb. 613, 616, 49 N. W. 331; Woodbury v. Jones, 44 N. H. 206; Driggs v. Dwight, 17 Wend. (N. Y.) 71, 31 Am. Dec. 283.

In Sperry et al. v. O'Neill-Adams Co. (C.C.A.) 185 F. 231, the court held that the advantages resulting from the use of trading stamps as a means of increasing trade are so contingent that they cannot form a basis on which to rest a recovery for a breach of contract to supply them. In lieu of compensation based thereon the court directed a recovery in the sum expended in preparation for carrying on business in connection with the use of the stamps. The court said, loc. cit. 239:

> "Plaintiff in its complaint had made a claim for lost profits, but, finding it impossible to marshal any evidence which would support a finding of exact figures, abandoned that claim. Any attempt to reach a precise sum would be mere blind guesswork. Nevertheless a contract, which

both sides conceded would prove a valuable one, had been broken and the party who broke it was responsible for resultant damage. In order to carry out this contract, the plaintiff made expenditures which otherwise it would not have made. * * * The trial judge held, as we think rightly, that plaintiff was entitled at least to recover these expenses to which it had been put in order to secure the benefits of a contract of which defendant's conduct deprived it."

In the case of Gilbert v. Kennedy, 22 Mich. 117, involved the question of the measure of plaintiff's damages, caused by the conduct of defendant in wrongfully feeding his cattle with plaintiff's in the latter's pasture, resulting in plaintiff's cattle suffering by the overfeeding of the pasture. The court said loc. cit. 135, 136:

"There being practically no market value for pasturage when there was none in the market, that element of certainty is wanting, even as to those cattle which were removed from the Pitcher farm to the home farm of the plaintiff for pasturage; and, as it could not apply to the others at all, and there being no other element of certainty by which the damages can be *accurately* measured, resort must be had to such principle or basis of calculation applicable to the circumstances of the case (if any be discoverable) as will be most likely to *approximate* certainty, and which may serve as a guide in making the most probable estimate of which the nature of the case will admit; and, though it may be less certain as a scale of measurement, yet if the principle be just in itself, and more likely to approximate the *actual damages*, it is better than any rule, however certain, which must certainly produce injustice, by excluding a large portion of the damages actually sustained."

. . . .

The case at bar was to recover damages for loss of profits by reason of the failure of the defendant to transport the shipment within a reasonable time, so that it would arrive in Atlantic City for the exhibit. There were no profits contemplated. The furnace was to be shown and shipped back to Kansas City. There was no money loss, except the expenses, that was of such a nature as any court would allow as being sufficiently definite or lacking in pure speculation. Therefore, unless plaintiff is permitted to recover the expenses that it went to, which were a total loss to it by reason of its inability to exhibit the furnace and equipment, it will be deprived of any substantial compensation for its loss. The law does not contemplate any such injustice. It ought to allow plaintiff, as damages, the loss in the way of expenses that it sustained, and which it would not have been put to if it had not been for its reliance upon the defendant to perform its contract. There is no contention that the exhibit would have been entirely valueless and whatever it might have accomplished defendant knew of the circumstances and ought to respond for whatever damages plaintiff suffered. In cases of this kind the method of estimating the damages should be adopted which is the most definite and certain and which best achieves the fundamental purpose of compensation. . . . Miller v. Robertson, 266 U. S. 243, 257, 45 S.Ct. 73, 78, 69 L. Ed. 265. Had the exhibit been shipped in order to realize a profit on sales and such profits could have been realized, or to be entered in competition for a prize, and plaintiff failed to show loss of profits with sufficient definiteness, or that he would have won the prize, defendant's cases might be in point. But as before stated, no such situation exists here.

Think About It!

If the exhibit had been shipped "in order to realize a profit on sales . . . and plaintiff failed to show loss of profits with sufficient definiteness," what would or should the result have been?

While, it is true that plaintiff already had incurred some of these expenses, in that it had rented space at the exhibit before entering into the contract with defendant for the shipment of the exhibit and this part of plaintiff's damages, in a sense, arose out of a circumstance which transpired before the contract was even entered into, yet, plaintiff arranged for the exhibit knowing that it could call upon defendant to perform its common law duty to accept and transport the shipment with reasonable dispatch. The whole damage, therefore, was suffered in contemplation of defendant performing its contract, which it failed to do, and would not have been sustained except for the reliance by plaintiff upon defendant to perform it. It can, therefore, be fairly said that the damages or loss suffered by plaintiff grew out of the breach of the contract, for had the shipment arrived on time, plaintiff would have had the benefit of the contract, which was contemplated by all parties, defendant being advised of the purpose of the shipment.

The judgment is affirmed. All concur.

————————————

Goodman v. Dicker

HERMAN E. GOODMAN et al., Defendants-Appellants

v.

ALBERT P. DICKER et al., Plaintiffs-Appellees

United States Court of Appeals, District of Columbia
169 F.2d 684 (D.C. Cir. 1948)

PROCTOR, Associate Justice.

This appeal is from a judgment of the District Court in a suit by appellees for breach of contract.

Appellants are local distributors for Emerson Radio and Phonograph Corporation in the District of Columbia. Appellees, with the knowledge and encouragement of appellants, applied for a "dealer franchise" to sell Emerson's products. The trial court found that appellants by their representations and conduct induced appellees to incur expenses in preparing to do business under the franchise, including employment of salesmen and solicitation of orders for radios. Among other things, appellants represented that the application had been accepted; that the franchise would be granted, and that appellees would receive an initial delivery of thirty to forty radios. Yet, no radios were delivered, and notice was finally given that the franchise would not be granted.

The case was tried without a jury. The court held that a contract had not been proven but that appellants were estopped from denying the same by reason of their statements and conduct upon which appellees relied to their detriment. Judgment was entered for $1500, covering cash outlays of $1150 and loss of $350, anticipated profits on sale of thirty radios.

The main contention of appellants is that no liability would have arisen under the dealer franchise had it been granted because, as understood by appellees, it would have been terminable at will and would have imposed no duty upon the manufacturer to sell or appellees to buy any fixed number of radios. From this it is argued that the franchise agreement would not have been enforceable (except as to acts performed thereunder) and cancellation by the manufacturer would have created no liability for expenses incurred by the dealer in preparing to do business. Further, it is argued that as the dealer franchise would have been unenforceable for failure of the manufacturer to supply radios appellants would not be liable to fulfill their assurance that radios would be supplied.

We think these contentions miss the real point of this case. We are not concerned directly with the terms of the franchise. We are dealing with a promise

Make the Connection

When the *Goodman* court says that "the appellants were estopped from denying" the contract, even though the plaintiffs failed to prove a contract, it is using promissory estoppel to bar the defendants from raising the argument that no contract was formed. In *Ricketts v. Scothorn* (Chapter 3, page 152), the court used promissory estoppel in a similar fashion—to bar the defendant from raising the defense of lack of consideration. In some jurisdictions promissory estoppel may bar the defendant from raising the defense of the statute of frauds (Chapter 6, page 645). Thus, it can be either a cause of action or a defense for a plaintiff.

Equitable estoppel, on the other hand, can be used only as a defense, not a cause of action. Equitable estoppel is based on a factual misrepresentation by the defendant, on which the plaintiff relies in a way that is foreseeable and reasonable. Plaintiff's cause of action for a factual misrepresentation is in tort, not contract.

As reflected in these materials, promissory estoppel can be "both a sword and a shield," while equitable estoppel can be "only a shield."

by appellants that a franchise would be granted and radios supplied, on the faith of which appellees with the knowledge and encouragement of appellants incurred expenses in making preparations to do business. Under these circumstances we think that appellants cannot now advance any defense inconsistent with their assurance that the franchise would be granted. Justice and fair dealing require that one who acts to his detriment on the faith of conduct of the kind revealed here should be protected by estopping the party who has brought about the situation from alleging anything in opposition to the natural consequences of his own course of conduct. Dair v. United States, 1872, 16 Wall. 4, 4, 21 L.Ed. 491. In Dickerson v. Colgrove, 100 U.S. 578, 580, the Supreme Court, in speaking of equitable estoppel, said: "The law upon the subject is well settled. The vital principle is that he who by his language or conduct leads another to do what he would not otherwise have done, shall not subject such person to loss or injury by disappointing the expectations upon which he acted. Such a change of position is sternly forbidden. * * * This remedy is always so applied as to promote the ends of justice." See also Casey v. Galli, 94 U.S. 673, 680; Arizona v. Copper Queen Mining Co., 233 U.S. 87, 95.

In our opinion the trial court was correct in holding defendants liable for moneys which appellees expended in preparation to do business under the promised dealer franchise. These items aggregated $1150. We think, though, that the court erred in adding the item of $350 for loss of profits on radios promised under an initial order. The true measure of damage is the loss sustained by expenditures made in reliance upon the assurance of a dealer franchise. As thus modified, the judgment is [a]ffirmed.

§ 2.3. Restitution Damages

Restitution is relief that seeks to return the parties to their pre-contract positions—the "status quo ante"—by requiring each party to restore ("disgorge") to the other party any benefits conferred by that other party that it would be unjust to retain. Restitutionary relief comes in two forms—damages (paying the value of benefits conferred) and "specific restitution" (an order in equity to restore a particular object to the rightful person). Damages are preferred, as are all remedies at law. This section addresses restitution damages.

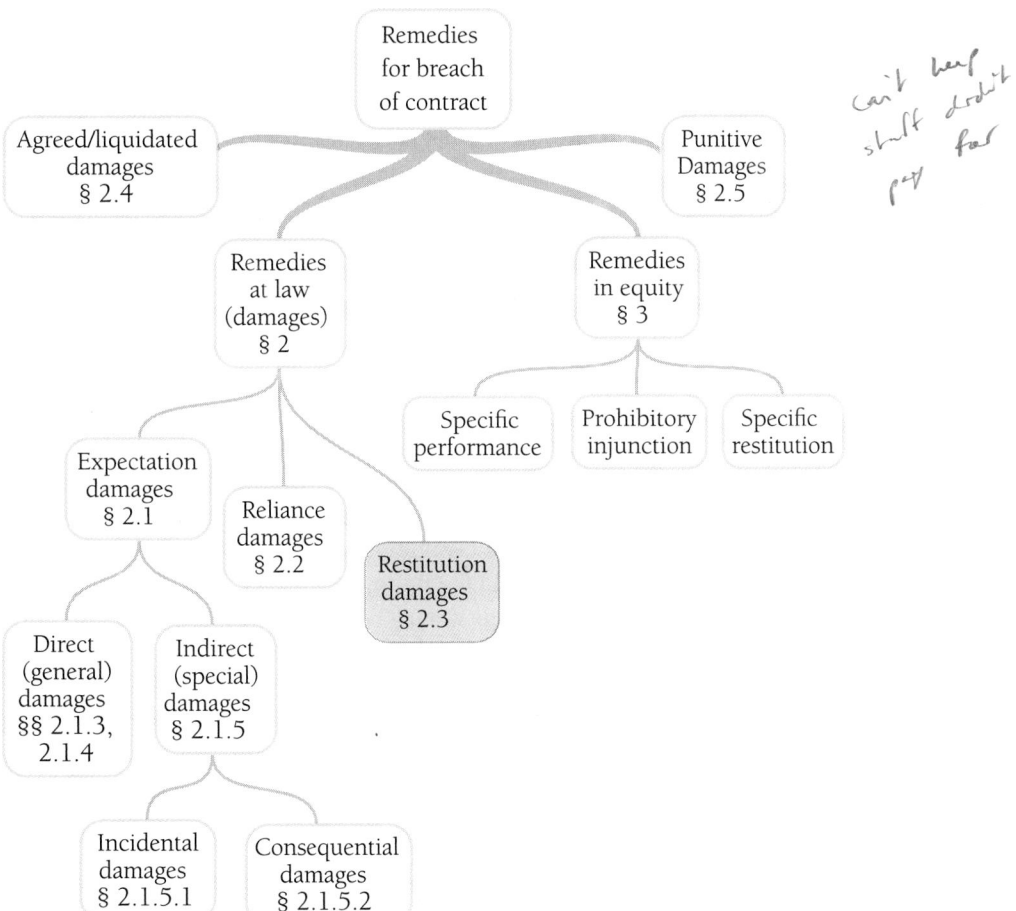

Determining the value of a benefit conferred on a party presents challenges, because multiple measures may be possible. For example, if a construction contractor or other service provider has breached after doing some work for the other party, the following measures may be considered:

- Net enrichment: How much the aggrieved party's wealth has been increased measured by
  - ◊ the appraised value of the construction or other material retained by the aggrieved party,
  - ◊ the amount by which the value of the aggrieved party's property has been increased, or
  - ◊ the value of the retained services to the aggrieved party.
- Cost of the services provided: What it would cost the aggrieved party to purchase the retained services on the open market (quantum meruit).
- Pro rata portion of the contract price.

In practice, "net enrichment" often furnishes a lesser amount than "cost of the services" or "pro rata contract price" since the market and contract prices almost always include profit for the performing party, but that profit is often not included in measuring the value obtained or retained by the aggrieved party.*

Chapter 3 (page 202) covered the concept of restitution as a basis for liability when benefits are conferred on another individual but no promise was made to pay for those benefits. In such cases, restitution is the only remedy available. (The concept of restitution plays a role in promissory restitution as well, but the remedy for promissory restitution is enforcement of the promise made, perhaps limited "as justice requires.") Chapter 5 (page 430) noted that restitution is an appropriate remedy when a contract is voided on the basis of mistake, misrepresentation, or other defenses. Chapter 8 covered restitution as an aspect of another form of recovery: If a seller fails to deliver goods, the buyer is entitled to a return of the purchase price paid (restitution of the benefit conferred (*Ramirez, page* 968, applying UCC § 2-711). And in this chapter, *Neri v. Retail Marine Corp.* (page 1076) dealt with a repudiating buyer who was entitled to restitution of its deposit, while remaining liable for paying damages for the breach. The damages measure used will vary according to the above circumstances. Faced with multiple measures, a court will likely favor an aggrieved party over a breaching party, but will be more neutral if restitution follows excuse.

The cases below address two additional uses of restitution damages and suggest how restitution damages may be measured or computed. As you read them, consider how the policies listed on page 1043 apply to help fashion the relief in those cases.

§ 2.3.1. Damages for the Party Who Materially Breaches

A party who substantially performs is entitled to enforce the contract and therefore obtain the contract price, albeit reduced by the damages owed the non-breaching party for the uncompleted performance. But what happens when

---

* *See generally* E. Allan Farnsworth, *Contracts* §§ 2.20, 8.14, 12.20 (4th ed. 2004).

the payee does not achieve substantial performance and therefore is in material breach? Because the condition precedent to payment has not been satisfied, the payee is not entitled to sue under the contract to receive any portion of the contract price. Under older common law rulings, that was the end of the inquiry and the breaching party was left without further recourse.

In 1834, however, the first crack in the common law rule appeared. In *Britton v. Turner,** the New Hampshire Superior Court of Judicature allowed restitutionary recovery to the breaching party, upending the common law rule to the contrary. In *Britton*, a laborer contracted to perform services for an employer for a year, in return for $120. The laborer worked for nine and a half months, then left voluntarily. The employer refused to pay the laborer, based on the common law reasoning that his promise to pay $120 was a conditional promise. If the condition to the promise (one year of service) was not satisfied, then no payment was due under the contract. The court agreed that the employer owed no contract liability, but raised the concern that the aggrieved party was unjustly enriched by receiving the labor without having to pay for it. The closer the laborer came to satisfying the condition, the more the employer was unjustly enriched. The court turned to quasi-contract and used quantum meruit to compensate the laborer. The laborer's recovery was the *value* received and pocketed by the employer (not necessarily the same as, but no more than, the contract price), minus any damages to the employer caused by non-completion. If the employer could and did reject and return any of the value (for instance, any goods furnished by the laborer), then that amount would also be subtracted from the recovery. This result was a default rule that applied only if the parties had not agreed otherwise.

> **FYI**
>
> You might wonder what Britton lived on during the year-long contract, with payment postponed until he completed his fixed-term contract. Such employment contracts were common in the nineteenth century for seamen (who might otherwise abandon ship in Tahiti) and farmworkers (who were easy to hire in the winter but might leave in search of higher wages during the harvest). In each case, the employer provided room and board during the term of the employment. For more background information on the case, *see* Robert W. Gordon, *Britton v. Turner: A Signpost on the Crooked Road to "Freedom" in the Employment Contract,* in *Contract Stories* 186 (Douglas G. Baird ed. 2007).

The following case picks up that story a century and a half later.

---

* 26 Am. Dec. 713, 1834 WL 1176 (N.H. 1834).

Reading the Law Critically: *Lancellotti*

1. What rule does the court adopt with respect to recovery of damages by a breaching party? What rationale does the court offer for adopting that rule? Why does the dissenting judge disagree, and what rule would he apply? Which is the better rule, and why?

2. On remand, how do you think the trial court will decide this case?

3. Articulate the measure of restitutionary recovery under Restatement (Second) § 374. Under what circumstances is recovery not available? In what ways is the first Restatement rule similar? In what ways is it different?

Lancellotti v. Thomas

JOHN LANCELLOTTI, Plaintiff-Appellant

v.

ALBERT THOMAS and LILLIAN THOMAS, Defendants-Appellees

Superior Court of Pennsylvania
491 A.2d 117 (Pa. Super. 1985)

SPAETH, President Judge.

This appeal raises the question of whether a defaulting purchaser of a business who has also entered into a related lease for the property can recover any part of his payments made prior to default. The common law rule precluded a breaching buyer from recovering these payments. Today, we reject this rule, which created a forfeiture of the breaching buyer's payments and unjustly enriched the nonbreaching seller, and adopt § 374 of the Restatement (Second) Contracts (1979), which permits limited restitution. This case is remanded for further proceedings so that the trial court may apply the Restatement rule.

-1-

On July 25, 1973, the parties entered into an agreement in which appellant agreed to purchase appellees' luncheonette business and to rent from appellees the premises on which the business was located. Appellant agreed to buy the name of the business, the goodwill, and equipment; the inventory and real estate were not included in the agreement for the sale of the business. Appellees agreed to sell the business for the following consideration: $25,000 payable on signing of the agreement; appellant's promise that only he would own and operate the business; and appellant's promise to build an addition to the existing building, which would measure 16 feet by 16 feet, cost at least $15,000, and be 75 percent complete by May 1, 1973.[1]

It was also agreed that appellees would lease appellant the property on which the business was operated for a period of five years, with appellant having the option of an additional five-year term. The rent was $8,000 per year for a term from September 1, 1973, to August 31, 1978. A separate lease providing for this rental was executed by the parties on the same date that the agreement was executed. This lease specified that the agreement to build the existing building was a condition of the lease. In exchange for appellant's promise to build the addition, there was to be no rental charge for the property until August 31, 1973. Further, if the addition was not constructed as agreed, the lease would terminate automatically. An addendum, executed by the parties on August 14, 1973, modi-fied this agreement, providing that "if the addition to the building as described in the Agreement is not constructed in accordance with the Agreement, the Buyer shall owe the Sellers $6,665 as rental for the property . . ." for the period from July 25, 1973, to the end of that summer season. The addendum also provided that all the equipment would revert to appellees upon the appellant's default in regard to the addition.

Appellant paid appellees the $25,000 as agreed, and began to operate the business. However, at the end of the 1973 season, problems arose regarding the construction of the addition. Appellant claims that the building permit neces-sary to construct the addition was denied. Appellees claim that they obtained the building permit and presented it to appellant, who refused to begin construction. Additionally appellees claim that appellant agreed to reimburse them if they built the addition. At a cost of approximately $11,000, appellees did build a 20 feet by 40 feet addition. In the spring of 1974 appellees discovered that appellant was no longer interested in operating the business. There is no evidence in the record that appellant paid any rent from September 1, 1973, as the first rental payment was not due until May 15, 1974. Appellees resumed possession of the business and, upon opening the business for the 1974 summer season, found some of their equipment missing.

Appellant's complaint in assumpsit demanded that appellees return the $25,000 plus interest. Appellees denied that appellant was entitled to recovery of this sum and counterclaimed for damages totalling $52,000: $6,665 as rental for the property for the 1973 summer season and the remainder as compensation

---

[1] The parties agree that this date was incorrect, and that the date the parties intended was May 1, 1974.

for "grievous damage to [appellees'] business, its goodwill and its physical operation . . ." and appellee Lillian Thomas suffering "nervous illness, pain and suffering inclusive of serious bodily injury and necessitating bed rest and physicians" supervision for one year after [appellant's] default." . . . In his answer, Appellant only conceded liability for the $6,665 rent under the terms of the addendum. . . . The trial court, sitting without a jury, found against appellant on the original claim, allowing appellees to retain the $25,000 paid by appellant, and for appellees on the counterclaim, allowing them to recover the $6,665 rent.

-2-

At one time the common law rule prohibiting a defaulting party on a contract from recovering was the majority rule. J. Calamari and J. Perillo, The Law of Contracts § 11-26, at 427 (2d ed. 1977). However, a line of cases, apparently beginning with *Britton v. Turner,* 6 N.H. 481 (1834), departed from the common law rule. The merit of the common law rule was its recognition that the party who breaches should not be allowed "to have advantage from his own wrong." Corbin, The Right of a Defaulting Vendee to the Restitution of Instalments Paid, 40 Yale L.J. 1013, 1014 (1931). As Professor Perillo states, allowing recovery "invites contract-breaking and rewards morally unworthy conduct." Restitution in the Second *Restatement of Contracts,* 81 Colum.L.Rev. 37, 50 (1981). Its weakness, however, was its failure to recognize that the nonbreaching party should not obtain a windfall from the breach. The party who breaches after almost completely performing should not be more severely penalized than the party who breaches by not acting at all or after only beginning to act. Under the common law rule the injured party retains more benefit the more completely the breaching party has performed prior to the default. Thus it has been said that "to allow the injured party to retain the benefit of the part performance . . . , without making restitution of any part of such value, is the enforcement of a penalty or forfeiture against the contract-breaker." Corbin, *supra,* at 1013.

Critics of the common law rule have been arguing for its demise for over fifty years. *See* Corbin, *supra. See also* Calamari and Perillo, *supra,* at § 11-26; 5A Corbin on Contracts §§ 1122-1135 (1964); 12 S. Williston, A Treatise on the Law of Contracts §§ 1473-78 (3d ed. 1970). In response to this criticism an alternative rule [was] adopted in the Restatement of Contracts. [Text of Restatement § 357 omitted here.]

In 1979, this rule was liberalized. Restatement (Second) of Contracts § 374 (1979) provides:

§ 374. Restitution in Favor of Party in Breach

(1) Subject to the rule stated in Subsection (2), if a party justifiably refuses to perform on the ground that his remaining duties of perfor-

mance have been discharged by the other party's breach, the ~~party in breach is entitled to restitution for any benefit that he has conferred by way of part performance or reliance in excess of the loss that he has caused by his own breach.~~

(2) To the extent that, under the manifested assent of the parties, a party's performance is to be retained in the case of breach, that party is not entitled to restitution if the value of the performance as liquidated damages is reasonable in the light of the anticipated or actual loss caused by the breach and the difficulties of proof of loss.

. . . .

Many jurisdictions have rejected the common law rule and permit recovery by the defaulting party. [The court cites to cases from Alaska, California, Florida, Idaho, Kansas, Nevada, New Hampshire, New Jersey, North Dakota, Oregon, Texas, Washington, and Wisconsin, many following or noting with approval either Restatement § 357 or Restatement (Second) Restatement (Second) of Contracts § 374).]

> **FYI**
>
> "Liquidated damages" (referred to in Restatement (Second) § 374(2)) are damages agreed to by the parties in their original agreement, before any dispute arose. Because the more powerful party might overreach and obtain the other party's agreement to liquidated damages that are unreasonably high, the law refuses to enforce liquidated damages that are unreasonable in amount. The phrasing of the rule here ("reasonable in the light of the anticipated or actual loss caused by the breach and the difficulties of proof of loss") matches the rule in UCC § 2-718(1) and Restatement (Second) § 356(1). Liquidated damages are covered later, on page 1162.

This development has been called the modern trend. *See Quillen v. Kelley,* 216 Md. 396, 140 A.2d 517 (1958). *See also* 12 S. Williston, *supra,* § 1473, at 222 (cases permitting recovery are now the weight of the authority); 5A Corbin on Contracts, *supra,* § 1122, at 3 (common law rule is broad statement not supported by the actual decisions). *But see* 1 G. Palmer, *The Law of Restitution* 568 (1978) (no valid generalization may be made regarding when a defaulting vendee can recover). It may be that the growing number of jurisdictions permitting recovery have been influenced by the widespread adoption of the Uniform Commercial Code § 2-718. *See, e.g., Maxey v. Glindmeyer,* 379 So.2d 297 (Miss.1980) (allowing recovery of excess of seller's actual damages in land sale contract by following the logic of the state statute equivalent to § 2-718 of the Uniform Commercial Code). Indeed, the common law rule is no longer intact even with respect to land sales contracts. *See, e.g., Honey v. Henry's Franchise Leasing Corp.,* 64 Cal.2d 801, 415 P.2d 833, 52 Cal.Rptr. 18 (1966); *McLendon v. Safe Realty Corp.,* 401 N.E.2d 80 (Ind.App.1980); *Newcomb v. Ray, supra; De Leon v. Aldrete, supra; and see* 1 G. Palmer, *supra,* at 596 n. 15 (citing cases).

In Pennsylvania, the common law rule has been applied to contracts for the sale of real property. *Kaufman Hotel & Restaurant Co. v. Thomas,* 411 Pa. 87, 190 A.2d 434 (1963); *Luria v. Robbins,* 223 Pa.Super. 456, 302 A.2d 361 (1973). In such cases, however, the seller has several remedies against a breaching buyer, including, in appropriate cases, an action for specific performance or for the purchase price. *See Trachtenburg v. Sibarco Stations, Inc.,* 477 Pa. 517, 384 A.2d 1209 (1978). *See also* 5A Corbin on Contracts, *supra,* § 1145. As long as the seller remains ready, able, and willing to perform a contract for the sale of real property, the breaching buyer has no right to restitution of payments made prior to default. *See* 5A Corbin on Contracts, *supra,* at § 1130.

The common law rule has also been applied in Pennsylvania to contracts for the sale of goods. *Atlantic City Tire and Rubber Corp. v. Southwark Foundry & Machine Co.,* 289 Pa. 569, 137 A. 807 (1927). However, Pennsylvania has since adopted the Uniform Commercial Code, which, as to contracts for the sale of goods, has modified the common law rule by 13 Pa.C.S. § 2718(b), which permits a breaching party to recover restitution. *See* note 2, *supra.*

The viability of the common law rule permitting forfeiture has also been undermined in other areas of Pennsylvania law. In *Estate of Cahen,* 483 Pa. 157, 168 n. 10, 394 A.2d 958, 964 n. 10 (1978), the Supreme Court held that assuming that a breaching fiduciary could recover in unjust enrichment, the basis would be Restatement of Contracts § 357 (1932), which allows recovery by a breaching party to the extent that the benefits exceed the losses sustained by the other party.

-3-

In regard to the present case, § 374 of the Restatement (Second) of Contracts represents a more enlightened approach than the common law rule. "Rules of contract law are not rules of punishment; the contract breaker is not an outlaw." Perillo, *supra,* at 50. The party who committed a breach should be entitled to recover "any benefit . . . in excess of the loss that he has caused by his own breach." Restatement (Second) of Contracts § 374(1).

This conclusion leads to the further conclusion that we should remand this case to the trial court. The trial court rested its decision on the common law rule. Slip op. of trial court at 7-8. Thus it never considered whether appellant is entitled to restitution, Restatement (Second) of Contracts § 374(1), nor, if appellant is not entitled

Think About It!

If the *Lancellotti* court, on remand, had decided to award restitution damages, what measure of recovery would best have met the goals of restitution and why?

to restitution, whether retention of the $25,000 was "reasonable in the light of the anticipated or actual loss caused by the breach and the difficulties of proof of loss," *id.,* § 374(2).[5]

Remanded for further proceedings consistent with this opinion. Jurisdiction relinquished.

TAMILIA, Judge, dissenting:

I strongly dissent. In the first instance, the majority does not and cannot cite *any* Pennsylvania authority adopting the rule cited in § 374 of the Second Restatement of Contracts. Although the ostensible basis for remand is the trial court's reliance on outmoded law, the majority relies on law so new as to be virtually unknown in this jurisdiction. The law in Pennsylvania has been and continues to be that where a binding contract exists, and there is no allegation that the contract itself is void or voidable, a breaching party is not entitled to recovery. *Luria v. Robbins,* 223 Pa.Super. 456, 302 A.2d 361 (1978). While our Supreme Court may yet abrogate the forfeiture principle in this Commonwealth, it has not yet seen fit to do so, and we may not usurp its prerogatives, particularly when the result would be unjust.

Secondly, the Uniform Commercial Code § 2718, cited by the majority in (partial) support, is applicable only to the sale of goods, and, while it and some of the equally inapplicable cases referred to by the majority may be part of a trend, the mainstream of contract law in Pennsylvania has not yet been diverted by it. Indeed the identification of the jurisdictions cited as the vanguard of change is for the most part questionable, as of those states relied upon to confer legitimacy on the majority's somewhat arbitrary conclusion, only one may be termed authoritative.

Lastly, and given the current state of the law, the most important determinant of the proper result in this case is the trial judge's assessment of the witness' credibility, here resolved in appellee's favor. The majority, far from according these findings their due, ignores them, contrary to law and our mandate. *Knepp v. Nationwide Insurance Co.,* 324 Pa.Super. 479, 471 A.2d 1257 (1984).

The trial court correctly points out that the understanding of the parties is clearly evidenced by the agreements they signed. In breaching those agreements, appellant has engaged in what might charitably be termed sharp practice. The facts reasonably support the inference that appellant learned the hoagie business,

---

[5] . . . . We are remanding so that the trial court may consider whether appellant is entitled to restitution. If the trial court again finds that it was the intention of the parties that the $25,000 be retained in the event of a breach . . . then the court must determine whether this sum is reasonable. If the sum is unreasonable, appellant is entitled to restitution. *See* Restatement (Second) of Contracts § 374 comment c.

played them—learned secret recipe in own restaurant

full restitution to owed for behavior?

benefited from the acquired trade and good will at appellees' place of business, then conducted the hoagie business at its previously owned pizza shop in the following season. Restitution in this instance constitutes a wholly unmerited reward for bad faith. We do not feel that such a result is consistent with the intent of law or the expectations of equity.

————————

§ 2.3.2. Damages for the Party Who Is Prevented from Performing

Reading the Law Critically: *Blanton*

1. Why does the plaintiff have a choice between recovering under the contract and quantum meruit? What facts trigger plaintiff's right to this choice?

2. Why was plaintiff's evidence insufficient to prove the amount of restitution damages? What kinds of evidence will the plaintiff need to furnish on remand?

Blanton v. Friedberg

EUGENE W. BLANTON; LANDMARK ENTERPRISES, INC., Plaintiffs-Appellees
v.
RICHARD H. FRIEDBERG, Defendant-Appellant
United States Court of Appeals, Fourth Circuit
819 F.2d 489 (4th Cir. 1987)

K.K. HALL, Circuit Judge:

Defendant, Richard H. Friedberg, appeals a judgment entered on a jury verdict in favor of plaintiffs, Eugene W. Blanton and Landmark Enterprises, Inc. ("Landmark") in this diversity action, alleging breach of contract and *quantum meruit* claims. We affirm in part and reverse in part.

I.

This case involves a dispute between the parties concerning the development of several tracts of real estate in South Carolina. Blanton, a South Carolina real estate broker, claims that he entered into an oral agreement with Friedberg during 1978 and 1979 to develop a parcel of land, known as the Liberty Hall Tract,

oral property judgment k

1st property

situated in Berkeley County, South Carolina. According to plaintiffs' evidence, the contract provided that Blanton would represent Friedberg, who owned the tract, in connection with all activities necessary for the development and marketing of the land. Blanton testified that under the agreement he and Landmark, a company which he had organized, would receive either a 10% commission on all sales of property from the development, or the reasonable value of their services, plus expenses. Blanton also maintained that defendant agreed to pay him a 5% commission on the sale of any timber from the Liberty Hall property.

According to Blanton, from 1978 to 1981, he invested considerable time and money in the development of Liberty Hall, seeking to enhance the property's marketability. Blanton stated that although he had arranged for the sale of timber from the land in the amount of $417,905, he was not paid the 5% commission of $20,895.25. Blanton also stated that the Liberty Hall property was ultimately not developed due to a problem with the reservation of mineral rights.

Blanton further testified that in November, 1979, he had contacted Friedberg about another tract of land for sale in Mt. Pleasant, South Carolina, and that on June 1, 1980, Friedberg agreed to purchase the property, orally contracting with Blanton and Landmark to manage its development. According to Blanton, he and his company were to act as the property's sales agent and were also to obtain all zoning approvals, sell portions of the land, manage and coordinate the design and construction of the roads, water, drainage, and sewage facilities, construct buildings on the tract for rental purposes, and arrange for the lease of developed commercial space to tenants who would ultimately occupy a shopping center located on the tract.

The shopping center was eventually developed into Patriots Plaza. Blanton and Landmark claimed that they had performed their part of the contractual agreement regarding this property, including obtaining a lease from the Kroger Company ("Kroger") and referring other prospective tenants to Friedberg. At one point in his testimony, Blanton conceded that he had received partial payment for his services in connection with the Mt. Pleasant property, which included one payment of $100,000 and a monthly payment of $5,000 for a ten-month period between September, 1980, and June, 1981.

In August 1981, Friedberg terminated his relationship with Landmark and Blanton. Plaintiffs maintained that they were discharged without reason or cause, and without being fully compensated for their services and expenses. Friedberg claimed that Blanton had been his employee from June, 1980, until August, 1981, at which time he was terminated for unsatisfactory performance. According to Friedberg, beginning in June, 1980, he had paid Blanton a monthly salary of $5,000, which was later increased to $6,000, for all services which Blanton per-

proof of employment

formed on defendant's behalf up to the time of his termination. Defendant introduced into evidence Blanton's 1981 tax return and W-2 form, which listed him as an employee of Friedberg's company. Defendant's evidence further demonstrated that Blanton was given a leased automobile and that his car and other expenses, including office overhead, were fully paid. Friedberg denied the existence of any contract for commissions in connection with the real estate at issue, except for commissions on actual sales of property, contending that when Blanton was terminated in August, 1981, he and Landmark claimed a balance due of only $21,937.67 and made no request for commissions or development fees.

Defendant maintained that he never agreed to pay plaintiffs any commission on any lease in the developed shopping center or at any other developed facility. It is uncontested that Blanton's services were terminated before Kroger ever occupied the Mt. Pleasant property. Furthermore, according to defendant, most of the development of that property was planned and took place after Blanton's termination in August, 1981, and the contractor who built much of the shopping center did not even know Blanton. Moreover, defendant maintained that at the time of Blanton's termination, improvements of only $600,000 had been completed on the property, no tenant had occupied it, and no acceptable leases had ever been produced by plaintiffs. Finally, according to evidence presented by Friedberg, subsequent to Blanton's termination, he had paid substantial commissions to another realtor each time a lease was consummated and plaintiffs did not notify this realtor, pursuant to industry custom, that they were entitled to or were claiming any of these commissions.

In July, 1983, Blanton and Landmark filed an action in state court for breach of contract, as well as fraud and deceit. This action was subsequently removed by defendant to federal court on the ground of diversity. Defendant denied the existence of a contract with plaintiffs and, following removal, plaintiffs were permitted to amend their complaint to assert an additional cause of action in *quantum meruit*.

Following a trial on the merits, the district court directed a verdict for defendant on plaintiffs' fraud claim and submitted the alternative contract and *quantum meruit* claims to the jury, which returned a verdict on behalf of Blanton and Landmark in the total amount of $438,580. The form of the verdict discloses that the jury awarded Blanton $20,895 and Landmark $21,000 on their breach of contract action and that it awarded Blanton $394,525 and Landmark $2,160 on the action in *quantum meruit*.[1] Friedberg's post-trial motions for judgment notwithstanding the verdict ("JNOV"), an amended judgment, and a new trial, were denied and this appeal followed.

---

[1] Normally, damages for breach of contract and recovery for *quantum meruit* are mutually exclusive remedies. In this instance, however, the jury found that Friedberg's promises to pay commissions on the sale of timber and real estate were enforceable as separate contracts while Blanton's service as a development manager could only be addressed under *quantum meruit*.

II.

On appeal, Friedberg raises a number of issues. . . .

We agree with appellant insofar as he argues that plaintiffs failed to produce sufficient evidence of services which they claim to have performed or of the reasonable value of those services to sustain the jury's verdict on their *quantum meruit* claim. We, therefore, conclude that the jury's *quantum meruit* verdict must be reversed and the case remanded for a new trial on that claim. . . .

In previous cases, this Court has enunciated the principles of *quantum meruit* relief available to South Carolina litigants. In *United States v. Algernon Blair, Incorporated,* 479 F.2d 638, 641 (4th Cir.1973), we held that:

> The impact of quantum meruit is to allow a promisee to recover the value of services he gave to the defendant irrespective of whether he would have lost money on the contract and been unable to recover in a suit on the contract.

(citations omitted). Moreover, as we later pointed out in *W.F. Magann Corporation v. Diamond Manufacturing Company, Inc.,* 775 F.2d 1202, 1208 (4th Cir.1985):

> One who has rendered a service or supplied work, labor and materials under a contract with another, but who has been wrongfully discharged or otherwise prevented from so fully performing as to earn the agreed compensation, may regard the contract as terminated and get judgment for the reasonable value of all that the defendant has received in performance of the contract . . . .
>
> The underlying purpose of allowing *quantum meruit* recovery is two-fold, i.e. to prevent the breaching party from being unjustly enriched and to restore the aggrieved party in the contract to the position he occupied prior to entry into the contract. *Quantum meruit* merely seeks to return to the plaintiff the reasonable value of the services and goods provided to the defendant.

(citations omitted). In *Blair,* a prime contractor had breached a contract but continued to receive the benefit of his subcontractor's services. *Magann* involved a breach of a subcontract by a prime contractor which justified a rescission of the subcontract. In both cases we held that the subcontractors were entitled to *quantum meruit* damages. In the instant case, plaintiffs sought to recover initially on the contract but then, after Friedberg denied the contract's existence, asserted an alternative cause of action in *quantum meruit.* Under these circumstances, we have no hesitation in finding that *quantum meruit* relief is likewise available. The question in this appeal is not whether the remedy is available but whether the amount of the *quantum meruit* recovery is supported by the evidence. We conclude that it is not.

In order to prove his claim against Friedberg, Blanton offered into evidence records purporting to show 1,800 hours of time which he and others who worked for him expended in attempting to develop Liberty Hall. Blanton claimed that he was entitled to an agreed-upon consulting fee of $40.00 per hour for these services, amounting to a total of $72,000.

As for his services in connection with the Mt. Pleasant property, Blanton claimed $91,195.50. He arrived at this figure by subtracting a credit of $64,000 for consulting fees, which he claimed to have received, from $155,195.50, the latter figure representing 5% of the total development costs of $3,103,910. In addition, Blanton claimed entitlement to $267,525.48 for his services in connection with the Kroger lease. Blanton points out that, pursuant to his agreement with Friedberg, he was to have been paid 5% of the gross rent for the entire 20-year lease term and that his expert testimony indicated that this type of lease commission was generally paid up front or, at least, within the first year. Blanton submits that he obtained the lease with Kroger and that Kroger occupied the shopping center based upon his efforts. Therefore, according to Blanton, the full leasing commission was due even though the lease had not been signed prior to the termination of his services. Moreover, Blanton claimed payment at the rate of 75% of projected gross rents for contacting several other tenants, arranging for leases, and laying the groundwork for tenant occupancy.

Finally, Blanton relies upon the testimony of two expert witnesses, realtors Robert L. Selman and Emerson B. Read, as confirmation of the reasonable value of his services. Selman testified that a reasonable fee for the Mt. Pleasant property development, "may be anywhere from 3 to 5 per cent of the cost," the customary fee charged in the industry, and in line with what Blanton and Landmark were to have been paid under their alleged agreement. Concerning the salary issue, Selman also testified on cross-examination that he knew of "situations where a monthly or a periodic . . . fee would be paid to a developer for his ongoing expertise and activity, and then upon completion some additional fee" would be paid. Read testified that in his opinion a reasonable leasing commission would be 6% of gross rents and a reasonable development fee would be between 5% and 10% of the project cost or gross rents.

Our review of the record convinces us that the evidence presented is insufficient to prove either the exact services performed by plaintiffs or the reasonable value of such services. *Blair* makes clear that:

> The measure of recovery for *quantum meruit* is the reasonable value of the performance . . . and recovery is undiminished by any loss which would have been incurred by complete performance . . . While the contract price may be evidence of reasonable value of the services, it does not measure the value of the performance or limit recovery. Rather, the standard for measuring the reasonable value of the services rendered is the amount for which such services could have been purchased from one in the plaintiff's position at the time and place the services were rendered.

479 F.2d at 641 (citations and footnotes omitted). Finding that a mere approximation of *quantum meruit* damages was insufficient, we remanded *Blair* to require the factfinder to accurately determine the reasonable value of labor and equipment use furnished to the contractor. Similarly, in *Magann,* holding that "profits per se have no place in a *quantum meruit* recovery," 775 F.2d at 1208, we remanded the matter to the district court for a precise finding of the reasonable value of services rendered to the contractor at the time those services were provided. We noted, however, that lost profits "may be considered to the extent that they may have a bearing upon assessing the reasonable value of the aggrieved party's performance." *Id.*

Think About It!

Does this court "cap" restitution damages so that they don't exceed the expectation measure? The courts are split on this issue, and this court uses the majority rule. Why might the courts be split on this issue? (This case doesn't discuss the split.)

Does this court subtract plaintiffs' anticipated losses from the restitution damages?

Applying these tenets to the case before us, we hold that plaintiff's anticipated consulting and leasing fees, based upon percentages of development costs and gross rents, cannot provide the sole or exclusive basis for proving their *quantum meruit* damages. In this case, Blanton and his company stopped far short of completing the two projects at issue. The mere fact that they would have received a certain fee, which might have been customary in the industry had they completed their work, does not control the measure of recovery for such services as they actually performed. If factors such as consulting and leasing fees, or percentages of development costs and gross rents, are to be considered at all, they may only be considered in the remanded proceedings after plaintiffs have demonstrated *with accuracy and precision* the number of hours devoted *actually* to rendering services to Friedberg. Moreover, plaintiffs must establish on remand that any compensation which they have already received, as evidenced by the $5,000-$6,000 monthly payments to Blanton during 1980 and 1981, was inadequate to cover the services for which they are now claiming reimbursement.

III.

For the foregoing reasons, we affirm the judgment in favor of plaintiffs' contract claims, in the amounts of $20,895 for Blanton and $21,000 for Landmark; we reverse the judgment in favor of plaintiffs' *quantum meruit* claims; and we remand the *quantum meruit* claims for a new trial consistent with this opinion.

Affirmed in Part, Reversed in Part, and Remanded.

————————

Problem 9-9: Restitution Damages

In *Roberts Contracting Company v. Valentine-Wooten Road Public Facility Board*, 320 S.W.3d 1 (Ark. Ct. App. 2009) (page 904), the court ruled that the contractor who voluntarily walked off the sewer job had not substantially performed the contract. In a portion of the opinion omitted from this text book, the court awarded restitutionary damages based on the pricing in the contract, because the opposing party did not present any valuation evidence. If supporting evidence were available, what measure of recovery would best have met the goals of restitution, and why?

Pro Rata

§ 2.4. Agreed and Liquidated Damages

Given the uncertainties surrounding the measurement of damages, parties may agree upon particular remedies, including damages, that will be owed upon any breach or a specific kind of breach. They can agree to allow categories of damages not generally allowed in contract actions (e.g., attorneys fees). In a liquidated damages provision, they can agree on the dollar amount of (or formula for computing) damages for a particular type of breach. To prevent unconscionability and results contrary to public policy, the law places some limits on agreed and liquidated damages, reviewed in the case below and reflected in the excerpted Restatement and UCC provisions.

write in breach amount

Reading the Law Critically: *Wassenaar*

1. What is the content of the liquidated damage provision in the contract?

2. What rule does the court establish for when a liquidated damage clause will, and will not, be enforceable? What is the nomenclature for an unenforceable clause?

3. What policies support the court's rulings on burden of proof and mitigation? How do those rulings affect the court's ultimate holding?

4. Compare the court's rule to the rules appearing in UCC § 2-718(1) and in Restatement (Second) § 356(1). Under which rule(s) is a liquidated damages clause more likely to be upheld?

UCC § 2-718. **Liquidation or Limitation of Damages**

(1) Damages for breach by either party may be liquidated in the agreement but only at an amount which is reasonable in the light of the anticipated or actual harm caused by the breach, the difficulties of proof of loss, and the inconvenience or nonfeasibility of otherwise obtaining an adequate remedy. A term fixing unreasonably large liquidated damages is void as a penalty.

. . . .

Restatement (Second) § 356. **Liquidated Damages And Penalties**

(1) Damages for breach by either party may be liquidated in the agreement but only at an amount that is reasonable in the light of the anticipated or actual loss caused by the breach and the difficulties of proof of loss. A term fixing unreasonably large liquidated damages is unenforceable on grounds of public policy as a penalty.

. . . .

---

amount must be reasonable for harm

unreasonable = unenforceable

employment contract terminated early

Wassenaar v. Panos

DONALD WASSENAAR, Plaintiff-Respondent-Petitioner

v.

THEANNE PANOS, d/b/a The Towne Hotel, Defendant-Appellant

Supreme Court of Wisconsin
331 N.W.2d 357 (Wis. 1983)

ABRAHAMSON, Justice.

This is a review of an unpublished decision of the court of appeals filed May 6, 1982, reversing a judgment of the circuit court for Milwaukee County, Louis J.

Ceci, Circuit Judge. The circuit court entered a judgment in favor of an employee, Donald Wassenaar, against his former employer, Theanne Panos, d/b/a The Towne Hotel, enforcing the stipulated damages clause in the employment contract and confirming a $24,640 jury award. The circuit court interpreted the stipulated damage clause in the contract as providing that in the event of wrongful discharge the employee was to be paid a sum equal to his salary for the unexpired term of the contract. The court of appeals reversed, holding the stipulated damages clause unenforceable as a penalty and remanding the cause to the circuit court for a new trial on the issue of damages only.

This court granted the employee's petition for review limiting the issue on review to whether the clause in the employment contract stipulating damages is a valid and enforceable liquidated damages provision or is, as a matter of public policy, an unenforceable penalty. We use the term "stipulated damages" herein to refer to the contract and the term "liquidated damages" to refer to stipulated damages which a court holds to be reasonable and will enforce. This court also asked the parties to address the sub-issue of whether a liquidated damages clause in an employment contract may serve to eliminate the employee's duty to mitigate damages, a question the court of appeals did not address. We conclude that where the stipulated damages clause is a valid provision for liquidated damages, the doctrine of mitigation of damages is not applicable to determine the damages awarded the nonbreaching party. In this case we hold that the stipulated damages clause is a valid provision for liquidated damages, not a penalty, and that the employee's earnings after the breach do not reduce the damages award. Accordingly, we reverse the decision, 107 Wis.2d 747, 322 N.W.2d 700 of the court of appeals and affirm the judgment of the circuit court.

The dispute centers on the stipulated damages clause of a written employment contract by which the employee-plaintiff, Donald Wassenaar, was hired as general manager of the employer-defendant, Towne Hotel. The employment contract is

Who's That?

Justice Shirley S. Abrahamson was appointed to the Wisconsin Supreme Court in 1976—the first woman to serve on Wisconsin's highest court and, until 1993, the only woman member. She has served as the court's chief justice since 1996 and later served as president of the National Conference of Chief Justices and as chair of the board of the National Center for State Courts. www.wicourts. gov/about/judges/supreme/abrahamson.htm. You can find out more about her judicial philosophy at http://judgepedia.org/index.php/Shirley_Abrahamson.

brief. It sets forth the employee's duties, his beginning salary, and his periodic pay increases. The contract further provides for a three-year term of employment beginning on January 1, 1977, renewable at the employee's option, and stipulates damages in case the employer terminates the employee's employment before the expiration of the contract. The stipulated damages clause in issue here reads as follows:

> IT IS FURTHER UNDERSTOOD, that should this contract be terminated by the Towne Hotel prior to its expiration date, the Towne Hotel will be responsible for fulfilling the entire financial obligation as set forth within this agreement for the full period of three (3) years.[1]

The employer terminated Wassenaar's employment as of March 31, 1978, 21 months prior to the contract's expiration date. Wassenaar was unemployed from April 1, 1978, until June 14, 1978, when he obtained employment in a Milwaukee area hotel where he remained employed at least until the time of trial in May, 1981.

The employee sued for damages. The employer answered the complaint and as an affirmative defense asserted that the employee had failed to mitigate damages. In a pretrial motion to strike the employer's affirmative defense that the employee had failed to mitigate damages, the employee argued that mitigation was irrelevant because the contract contained a valid stipulated damages clause. The circuit court struck the employer's affirmative defense, ruling that the employee had no duty to mitigate damages, apparently inferentially ruling that the stipulated damages clause was valid.

After a trial on the remaining issues and in response to special verdict questions, the jury found that the person negotiating the contract on behalf of the employer was authorized as the employer's agent to enter into the employment contract and that the employer terminated the employment without just cause. The circuit court, over the employee's objection, submitted to the jury the question of what sum of money would compensate the employee for his losses resulting from the breach of the employment agreement. The jury answered $24,640, which is the sum the employee had calculated as his damages on the basis of the stipulated damages clause of the contract, that is, his salary for 21 months, the unexpired term of the contract.

On review, the court of appeals characterized the question of whether a stipulated damages clause should be held void as a penalty because it fixes unreason-

---

[1] The clause can be interpreted to provide that the employee will receive the entire salary for three years regardless of when the employment was terminated. We reject this interpretation of the clause, as did the employee and the circuit court.

ably large damages as a question of law to be determined independently by the reviewing court. It then scrutinized the stipulated damages clause and decided that the clause was void as a penalty. The court of appeals reached that conclusion, reasoning that the amount of damages for breach of an employment contract could easily be measured and proved at trial and that the contractual formula fixing damages at full salary without considering how long the employee would need to find a new job or the probable earnings from substitute employment was unreasonable on its face. In its analysis, the court of appeals did not consider any facts other than the actual contract language and the black-letter law relating to the measure of damages for breach of employment contracts.

. . . . [T]he validity of a stipulated damages clause is a question of law for the trial judge rather than a mixed question of fact and law for the jury. The validity of a stipulated damages clause is a matter of public policy, and as in other contract cases the question of contractual validity as a matter of public policy is an issue the trial judge initially decides. . . .

. . . . The reviewing court will uphold the factual determinations underlying its legal conclusion unless they are contrary to the great weight and clear preponderance of the evidence. . . . Whether the facts fulfill the legal standard, here reasonableness, is a determination of law, . . . and ordinarily the appellate court need not defer to the trial court's determination of a question of law. . . . Nevertheless, because the trial court's legal conclusion, that is, whether the clause is reasonable, is so intertwined with the factual findings supporting that conclusion, the appellate court should give weight to the trial court's decision, although the trial court's decision is not controlling. *See* Wright, *The Doubtful Omniscence of Appellate Courts,* 41 Minn.L.Rev. 751, 778-82 (1956); Morris, *Law and Fact,* 55 Harv.L.Rev. 1303, 1304 (1942).

. . . .

Because the employer sought to set aside the bargained-for contractual provision stipulating damages, it had the burden of proving facts which would justify the trial court's concluding that the clause should not be enforced. *Northwestern Motor Car, Inc. v. Pope,* 51 Wis.2d 292, 295, 187 N.W.2d 200 (1971). Placing the burden of proof on the challenger is consistent with giving the nonbreaching party the advantage inherent in stipulated damages clauses of eliminating the need to prove damages, and with the general principle that the law assumes that bargains are enforceable and that the party asking the court to intervene to invalidate a bargain should demonstrate the justice of his or her position. As we discuss below, we conclude that the employer failed to carry its burden, and we affirm the circuit court's conclusion that the stipulated damages clause is valid.

We turn now to the test that the trial court (and the appellate court) should apply in deciding whether a stipulated damages clause is valid. The overall single test of validity is whether the clause is reasonable under the totality of circumstances.[7] *See* sec. 356(1), Restatement (Second) of Contracts (1979),[8] and sec. 402.718(1), Stats.1979-80.[9]

The reasonableness test is a compromise the courts have struck between two competing viewpoints toward stipulated damages clauses, one favoring enforcement of stipulated damages clauses and the other disfavoring such clauses.

Enforcement of stipulated damages clauses is urged because the clauses serve several purposes. The clauses allow the parties to control their exposure to risk by setting the payment for breach in advance. They avoid the uncertainty, delay, and expense of using the judicial process to determine actual damages. They allow the parties to fashion a remedy consistent with economic efficiency in a competitive market, and they enable the parties to correct what the parties perceive to be inadequate judicial remedies by agreeing upon a formula which may include damage elements too uncertain or remote to be recovered under rules of damages applied by the courts. In addition to these policies specifically relating to stipulated damages clauses, considerations of judicial economy and freedom of contract favor enforcement of stipulated damages clauses.

A competing set of policies disfavors stipulated damages clauses, and thus courts have not been willing to enforce stipulated damages clauses blindly without carefully scrutinizing them. Public law, not private law, ordinarily defines the remedies of the parties. Stipulated damages are an exception to this rule. Stipulated damages allow private parties to perform the judicial function of providing the remedy in breach of contract cases, namely, compensation of the nonbreaching

---

[7] . . .*Dick v. Heisler,* 184 Wis. 77, 82, 198 N.W. 734 (1924); *Fields Foundation, Ltd. v. Christensen,* 103 Wis.2d 465, 475, 309 N.W.2d 125 (Ct.App.1981).

. . . .

See also Clarkson, Miller, and Muris, *Liquidated Damages v. Penalties: Sense or Nonsense?,* 1978 Wis.L.Rev. 351, 356; Goetz and Scott, *Liquidated Damages, Penalties and the Just Compensation Principle: Some Notes on an Enforcement Model and a Theory of Efficient Breach,* 77 Colum.L.Rev. 554 (1977); Macneil, *Power of Contract and Agreed Remedies,* 47 Cornell L.Q. 495, 503 (1962) . . . .

[8] Sec. 356(1), Restatement (Second) of Contracts (1979), sets forth the test as follows:

"Damages for breach by either party may be liquidated in the agreement but only at an amount that is reasonable in the light of the anticipated or actual loss caused by the breach and the difficulties of proof of loss. A term fixing unreasonably large liquidated damages is unenforceable on grounds of public policy as a penalty."

[9] Sec. 402.718(1), Stats. 1979-80, which is U.C.C. sec. 2-718(1), provides that liquidated damages may be agreed upon, "but only at an amount which is reasonable in the light of the anticipated or actual harm caused by the breach, the difficulties of proof of loss, and the inconvenience or nonfeasibility of otherwise obtaining an adequate remedy. A term fixing unreasonably large liquidated damages is void as a penalty." . . .

party, and courts must ensure that the private remedy does not stray too far from the legal principle of allowing compensatory damages. Stipulated damages substantially in excess of injury may justify an inference of unfairness in bargaining or an objectionable *in terrorem* agreement to deter a party from breaching the contract, to secure performance, and to punish the breaching party if the deterrent is ineffective.

The reasonableness test strikes a balance between the two competing sets of policies by ensuring that the court respects the parties' bargain but prevents abuse. . . .

Over time, the cases and commentators have established several factors to help determine whether a particular clause is reasonable: (1) Did the parties intend to provide for damages or for a penalty?[11] (2) Is the injury caused by the breach one that is difficult or incapable of accurate estimation at the time of contract?[12] and (3) Are the stipulated damages a reasonable forecast of the harm caused by the breach?[13]

Recent discussions of the test of reasonableness have generally discarded the first factor, subjective intent of the parties, because subjective intent has little bearing on whether the clause is objectively reasonable.[14] The label the parties apply to the clause, which might indicate their intent, has some evidentiary value, but it is not conclusive. *Seeman v. Biemann,* 108 Wis. 365, 374, 84 N.W. 490 (1900).

The second factor, sometimes referred to as the "difficulty of ascertainment" test, is generally viewed as helpful in assessing the reasonableness of the clause. The greater the difficulty of estimating or proving damages, the more likely the stipulated damages will appear reasonable. *Sheffield-King Milling Co. v. Jacobs,* 170 Wis. 389, 402-403, 175 N.W. 796 (1920). If damages are readily ascertainable, a significant deviation between the stipulated amount and the ascertainable amount will appear unreasonable. *City of Madison v. American Sanitary Engineering Co.,* 118 Wis. 480, 503-504, 95 N.W. 1097 (1903). The "difficulty of ascertainment" test has several facets, depending on whether the stipulated damages clause is viewed from the perspective of the time of contracting or the time of breach (or trial). These facets include the difficulty of producing proof of damages at trial; the difficulty of determining what damages the breach caused;

---

11 . . . *McConnell v. L.C.L. Transit Co.,* 42 Wis.2d 429, 438, 167 N.W.2d 226 (1969).

12 . . . Sheffield-King Milling Co. v. Jacobs, 170 Wis. 389, 399, 175 N.W. 796 (1920). . . .

13 Davis v. La Crosse Hospital Association, 121 Wis. 579, 589, 99 N.W. 351 (1904); United Leasing & Financial Services, Inc. v. R.F. Optical, 103 Wis.2d 488, 492, 309 N.W.2d 23 (Ct. App.1981). . . .

14 5 Williston, *Contracts,* sec. 778, p. 687, 693 (Jaeger 3d ed. 1961); 5 Corbin, *Contracts,* sec. 1058, p. 337 (1964); Calamari and Perillo, *Law of Contracts,* sec. 14-31, p. 565 (2d ed. 1977); Restatement (Second) of Contracts, sec. 356(1), comment *c* (1979).

the difficulty of ascertaining what damages the parties contemplated when they contracted; the absence of a standardized measure of damages for the breach; and the difficulty of forecasting, when the contract is made, all the possible damages which may be caused or occasioned by the various possible breaches.

The third factor concerns whether the stipulated damages provision is a reasonable forecast of compensatory damages. Courts test the reasonableness of the parties' forecast, as they test the "difficulty of ascertainment" by looking at the stipulated damages clause from the perspective of both the time of contracting and the time of the breach (or trial).

The second and third factors are intertwined, and both use a combined prospective-retrospective approach. Although courts have frequently said that the reasonableness of the stipulated damages clause must be judged as of the time of contract formation (the prospective approach) and that the amount or existence of actual loss at the time of breach or trial is irrelevant, except as evidence helpful in determining what was reasonable at the time of contracting (the retrospective approach), the cases demonstrate that the facts available at trial significantly affect the courts' determination of the reasonableness of the stipulated damages clause. If the damages provided for in the contract are grossly disproportionate to the actual harm sustained, the courts usually conclude that the parties' original expectations were unreasonable.[16] Our prior decisions indicate that this court has employed the prospective-retrospective approach in determining the reasonableness of the stipulated damages clauses and has looked at the harm anticipated at the time of contract formation and the actual harm at the time of breach (or trial). *See, e.g., Fields Foundation, Ltd. v. Christensen*, 103 Wis.2d 465, 475-76, 309 N.W.2d 125 (Ct.App.1981); *Seeman v. Biemann*, 108 Wis. 365, 374-75, 84 N.W. 490 (1900).

As the above discussion demonstrates, the various factors and approaches to determine reasonableness are not separate tests, each of which must be satisfied for a stipulated damages clause to stand. Reasonableness of the stipulated damages clause cannot be determined by a mechanical application of the three factors cited above. 3 Hawkland, *Uniform Commercial Code Series*, sec. 2-718:01, p. 426 (1982). Courts may give different interpretations to or importance to the various factors in particular cases. . . .

---

[16] 5 Corbin, Contracts, sec. 1063, pp. 362-64 (1964), states:

"The probable injury that the parties had reason to foresee is a fact that largely determines the question whether they made a genuine pre-estimate of that injury; but the justice and equity of enforcement depend also upon the amount of injury that has actually occurred. It is to be observed that hindsight is frequently better than foresight, and that, in passing judgment upon the honesty and genuineness of the pre-estimate made by the parties, the court cannot help but be influenced by its knowledge of subsequent events." . . . .

. . . .

With the reasonableness test and the policies underlying the test in mind, we now consider the circuit court's conclusion that the stipulated damages clause is reasonable. The employer argues that the stipulated damages clause is void as a penalty because the harm to the employee was capable of estimation at the formation of the contract and was relatively easy to prove at trial. The employer further contends that calculating damages based on the entire wage for the unexpired term of the employment contract does not reasonably forecast the loss caused by the breach because such a calculation gives the employee a windfall recovery. The employer's arguments are not without merit. . . .

When the parties to an employment contract estimate the harm which might result from the employer's breach, they do not know when a breach might occur, whether the employee will find a comparable job, and if he or she does, where the job will be or what hardship the employee will suffer. Nevertheless, the standard measure of damages provides, as the court of appeals noted in its opinion, a simple formula which is generally fairly easy to apply. According to black-letter law, when an employee is wrongfully discharged, damages are the salary the employee would have received during the unexpired term of the contract plus the expenses of securing other employment reduced by the income which he or she has earned, will earn, or could with reasonable diligence earn, during the unexpired term. These damages are usually easily ascertainable at the time of trial.

The standard calculation of damages after breach, however, may not reflect the actual harm suffered because of the breach. In addition to the damages reflected in the black-letter formulation, an employee may suffer consequential damages, including permanent injury to professional reputation, loss of career development opportunities, and emotional stress. When calculating damages for wrongful discharge courts strictly apply the rules of foreseeability, mitigation, and certainty and rarely award consequential damages. Damages for injury to the employee's reputation, for example, are generally considered too remote and not in the parties' contemplation.[19] Thus, actual harm suffered and damages that would be awarded in a legal action for breach of contract may not be the same. Nevertheless, in providing for stipulated damages, the parties to the contract

---

[19] *Smith v. Beloit Corp.*, 40 Wis.2d 550, 559, 162 N.W.2d 585 (1968) . . . .

Apparently some jurisdictions do allow recovery of consequential damages for breach of certain employment contracts. *See* cases in Annot., *Recovery by Writer, Artist, or Entertainer for Loss of Publicity or Reputation Resulting from Breach of Contract*, 96 ALR 3d 437 (1979).

Dean McCormick, in his 1935 treatise on damages, foreshadowed the inadequacy of the measure of damages for wrongful discharge: "[T]he courts might expand their measure of compensation for breach of the employment *contract* by recognizing that deprivation of a job, if more than a casual one, not only affects usually a man's reputation and prestige, but ordinarily may so shake his sense of security as to inspire, even in men of firmness, deep fear and distress. . . ." McCormick, *Damages*, sec. 163, p. 639.

could anticipate the types of damages not usually awarded by law. The usual arguments against allowing recovery for consequential damages—that they are not foreseeable and that no dollar value can be set by a court— fail when the parties foresee the possibility of such harm and agree on an estimated amount.

We do not know in the case at bar how the parties calculated the stipulated amount, but we do know that both the employee and employer were concerned about job security. The employee desired a steady, long-term job and the employer wanted the employee, who was experienced in managing the Towne Hotel, to remain on the job. The parties did not suggest that the stipulated damages clause resulted from unequal bargaining power. The contract drafted by the employer provided for a fixed term of employment with a provision for stipulated damages in the amount of unpaid wages if the employer breached. Under these circumstances it is not unreasonable to assume that the parties might have anticipated elements of consequential damages and drafted the stipulated damages clause to include salary lost while out of work, expenses of finding a new job, lower salary on the new job, and consequential damages.

In examining the instant stipulated damages clause and the record, we conclude that the parties' estimate at the time of contract formation of anticipated damages was reasonable when consequential damages are taken into account. Consequential damages may be difficult to ascertain at the time of contracting or breach and are difficult to prove at trial. The contract formula of full salary for the period after breach seems to be a simple and fair way of calculating all damages.

The employer argues that even if the stipulated amount is a reasonable forecast at the time of contract formation of anticipated loss, the amount is unreasonable from the perspective of the time of trial because the employee suffered no loss whatsoever, or if he suffered any loss it is disproportionate to (that is, significantly less than) the stipulated damages.

. . . .

In this case . . . there is evidence in the record that the employee did suffer harm in being unemployed for approximately two and a half months after his discharge. At the end of this time, the employee obtained employment at another hotel, but there is no evidence that the jobs he held were comparable in terms of salary, opportunity for advancement, etc., to the job he held as manager of the Towne Hotel. There is no evidence that the employee's total compensation from the new job was equal to or exceeded the salary under the breached contract, and the record does not reveal whether the employee suffered consequential damages. All we know is that the employee appears to have suffered some harm. . . .

Since the record in this case can be read to show that the employee suffered some harm, the question remains whether the stipulated damages are so much greater than the loss suffered by the employee that the stipulated damages constitute a penalty.

. . . . The employer argues that allowing the employee to recover the stipulated damages in this case gives the employee a windfall because he receives both the agreed upon salary and the ability to sell his services to another employer during the unexpired term of the contract: the employee will receive 21 months salary from the defendant employer and 18 months salary from the new employer. Ordinarily the circuit court would, in this type of stipulated damages case, use evidence of the employee's actual or potential earnings in assessing the overall reasonableness of the clause, since subsequent earnings would be relevant to the issue of the employee's actual loss resulting from the breach. In this case, as we discuss further below, there is no evidence in the record showing the employee's subsequent earnings, so there is no evidence supporting the employer's position that the employee would get a windfall from enforcement of the stipulated damages clause.

As we said previously, the employer, the party challenging the contract, carries the burden of proving that the stipulated amount of damages is grossly disproportionate to the actual harm and thus unreasonable. *Northwestern Motor Car, Inc. v. Pope*, 51 Wis.2d 292, 295, 187 N.W.2d 200 (1971). The employer has failed to carry the burden of production and persuasion in this case. . . . The employer insisted that the employee had a duty to mitigate despite the stipulated damages clause. The circuit court granted the employee's motion to strike the defense on the basis of pretrial briefs, ruling that the employee had no duty to mitigate damages because the parties had stipulated their damages as part of their bargain. The circuit court thus inferentially upheld the validity of the clause.

At trial the employer attempted to put in evidence regarding the employee's salary at his new job. The circuit court refused to admit this evidence indicating that it had already ruled on the mitigation issue.

. . . . At trial the employer took the erroneous position that the burden was on the employee to prove the reasonableness of the stipulated damages clause, not on the employer to prove the unreasonableness of the clause. . . .

The employer failed to get facts into the record showing that the employee suffered no damages or that his damages were significantly less than the stipulated amount. In short, the employer did not meet his burden of proof on the unreasonableness of the stipulated damages clause. Since we conclude that the record shows that the employee suffered some actual injury and that the record does not show that actual damages are disproportionate to the stipulated damages, we affirm the circuit court's ruling that the stipulated damages provision is reasonable and enforceable.

This court asked the parties to brief what it characterized as a sub-issue, namely, the employee's duty to mitigate damages. In breach of contract cases not involving liquidated damages clauses, this court has consistently held that a discharged employee has a duty to use ordinary care and reasonable efforts to seek other comparable employment and that in calculating damages the employer should be credited to the extent that the employee obtains work and earns wages or might have done so. *Klug v. Flambeau Plastics Corp.*, 62 Wis.2d 141, 155, 214 N.W.2d 281 (1974) . . . .

. . . .

While evidence of the employee's earnings after the employer's breach may be relevant in meeting the employer's burden of proving that the stipulated damages clause is unreasonable, once the court determines that the clause is reasonable, proof of the employee's actual loss (including what he earned or might have earned on another job) is no longer relevant. *See* 5 Corbin, *Contracts* sec. 1062, p. 355 (1964). . . . [O]nce a stipulated damages clause is found reasonable, the liquidated damages should not be reduced at trial by an amount the employee did earn or could have earned. *See Tollefson v. Green Bay Packers, Inc.*, 256 Wis. 318, 41 N.W.2d 201 (1950). Recalculating liquidated damages to credit the breaching party with the amount the employee earned or could have earned is antithetical to the policies favoring liquidated damages clauses. Our holding comports with the rule in other jurisdictions . . . .

For the reasons set forth, we conclude that the judgment of the circuit court should be affirmed. The decision of the court of appeals is reversed; the judgment of the circuit court is affirmed.

CECI, J., not participating.

Food for Thought: The Theory of Efficient Breach

Either party to a contract may have an incentive to breach if that party will reap a benefit from the breach, even after paying damages to the aggrieved party. Adherents of the "law and economics" movement support breach under such circumstances, arguing that this allows societal resources to be utilized in their most productive manner and therefore is socially desirable in the sense that it results in a gain in efficiency by moving the assets that are exchanged to higher valued uses. To assist in maximizing economic efficiency, the law should be structured to encourage such "efficient breaches" while deterring inefficient breaches. Although courts only occasionally explicitly acknowledge "efficiency" as a goal in determining damages, to some extent the law on contract remedies is structured to encourage efficient breaches. For example, courts prefer to award damages, rather than specific performance, so the party contemplating a breach can roughly quantify the cost of the breach (what it will owe in damages) and weigh it against the potential gain from the breach. In addition, willfulness of a breach does not affect damage calculations, so a party may purposely breach without increasing damage exposure, except in the rare circumstances that give rise to liability for punitive damages (page 1176).

Judge Posner is a leading proponent of efficient breach. In *Lake River Corp. v. Carborundum Co.*, 769 F.2d 1284, 1288-89 (7th Cir. 1985), he included consideration of the efficient breach theory in a long disquisition about whether penalties (excessive agreed remedies) should never be enforceable:

> The hardest issue in the case is whether the formula in the minimum-guarantee clause imposes a penalty for breach of contract or is merely an effort to liquidate damages. Deep as the hostility to penalty clauses runs in the common law, . . . we still might be inclined to question, if we thought ourselves free to do so, whether a modern court should refuse to enforce a penalty clause where the signator is a substantial corporation, well able to avoid improvident commitments. Penalty clauses provide an earnest of performance. The clause here enhanced Carborundum's credibility in promising to ship the minimum amount guaranteed by showing that it was willing to pay the full contract price even if it failed to ship anything. On the other side it can be pointed out that by raising the cost of a breach of contract to the contract breaker, a penalty clause increases the risk to his other creditors; increases (what is the same thing and more, because bankruptcy imposes "deadweight" social costs) the risk of bankruptcy; and could amplify the business cycle by increasing the number of bankruptcies in bad times, which is when contracts are most likely to be broken. But since little effort is made to prevent businessmen from assuming risks, these reasons are no better than makeweights.
>
> A better argument is that a penalty clause may discourage efficient as well as inefficient breaches of contract. Suppose a breach would cost the promisee $12,000 in actual damages but would yield the promisor $20,000 in additional profits. Then there would be a net social gain from breach. After being fully

compensated for his loss the promisee would be no worse off than if the contract had been performed, while the promisor would be better off by $8,000.　But now suppose the contract contains a penalty clause under which the promisor if he breaks his promise must pay the promisee $25,000. The promisor will be discouraged from breaking the contract, since $25,000, the penalty, is greater than $20,000, the profits of the breach; and a transaction that would have increased value will be forgone.

On this view, since compensatory damages should be sufficient to deter inefficient breaches (that is, breaches that cost the victim more than the gain to the contract breaker), penal damages could have no effect other than to deter some efficient breaches. But this overlooks the earlier point that the willingness to agree to a penalty clause is a way of making the promisor and his promise credible and may therefore be essential to inducing some value-maximizing contracts to be made. It also overlooks the more important point that the parties (always assuming they are fully competent) will, in deciding whether to include a penalty clause in their contract, weigh the gains against the costs— costs that include the possibility of discouraging an efficient-breach somewhere down the road—and will include the clause only if the benefits exceed those costs as well as all other costs.

On this view the refusal to enforce penalty clauses is (at best) paternalistic—and it seems odd that courts should display parental solicitude for large corporations. But however this may be, we must be on guard to avoid importing our own ideas of sound public policy into an area where our proper judicial role is more than usually deferential. The responsibility for making innovations in the common law of Illinois rests with the courts of Illinois, and not with the federal courts in Illinois. And like every other state, Illinois, untroubled by academic skepticism of the wisdom of refusing to enforce penalty clauses against sophisticated promisors, . . . continues steadfastly to insist on the distinction between penalties and liquidated damages. See, e.g., *Bauer v. Sawyer*, 8 Ill.2d 351, 359-61, 134 N.E.2d 329, 333-34 (1956) . . . . [The court then applies existing Illinois precedent.]

so controversy

State ctr should decide new damages rules

If you were an Illinois judge or legislator, would you be receptive to Judge Posner's arguments? What are the counter-arguments to Posner's position and to the efficient breach theory in general?

§ 2.5. Punitive Damages

Courts rarely award punitive damages in a contract case. Breaking a contract is not considered "bad" behavior, and even a willful breach should simply result in compensation for the injury to the non-breaching party, not in punishment for the contract breacher. In a few special kinds of cases, however, courts have discretion to award punitive damages against a defendant, to deter that defendant and others from engaging in similar conduct in the future. The majority rule is that punitive damages may be awarded when the breach of contract is also an independent tort.

Restatement (Second) § 355. **Punitive Damages**

Punitive damages are not recoverable for a breach of contract unless the conduct constituting the breach is also a tort for which punitive damages are recoverable.

The case below provides examples of cases in which punitive damages are allowed under various common law rules.

Reading the Law Critically: *Romero*

1. What is the court's rule regarding when punitive damages may be awarded?

2. What policies are furthered by awarding punitive damages?

3. What guidelines are furnished as to the amount?

Romero v. Mervyn's

LUCY ROMERO, Plaintiff-Appellee

v.

MERVYN'S and DENNIS WOLF, Defendants-Appellants

Supreme Court of New Mexico
784 P.2d 992 (N.M. 1989)

RANSOM, Justice.

This is an appeal by defendant Mervyn's from a verdict in favor of plaintiff Lucy Romero for $2,041 in compensatory and $25,000 in punitive damages on a breach of contract claim. . . . We affirm.

On November 23, 1984, Romero and two of her adult daughters were shopping in Mervyn's Department Store in Albuquerque. It was the day after Thanksgiving and the store was crowded with Christmas shoppers. As Romero and her daughters were descending on an escalator, another customer either intentionally or accidentally pushed her. She fell to her hands and knees, hitting her jaw as she fell. One of her daughters testified that a commotion ensued. When Romero reached the bottom of the escalator, a salesperson at a temporary station helped her to her feet and out of the path of other shoppers. Either this employee or a security guard watching from a two-way mirror summoned the store manager to the scene.

Dennis Wolf, the acting store manager, came in response to this call. His usual job as operations manager of the store entailed responsibility for directing and training employees. It was also his duty to investigate and gather information on incidents involving customer injuries on the premises. Wolf testified that he could tell Romero was in pain and asked her whether she needed a wheelchair or ambulance. Romero replied that she did not. Wolf also testified that Romero's daughters were "very upset, a little bit hysterical," and kept asking who would pay for their mother's medical expenses. Wolf himself, according to Romero's testimony, "seemed to be kind of nervous and in a hurry since the store was busy." According to testimony by Romero and her daughters, Wolf told them that Mervyn's would pay any medical expenses. Wolf testified that, pursuant to company policy, he only told Romero that Mervyn's would submit the claim to its insurer, who would make the decision whether to pay any claims arising from the incident.

Immediately following this conversation, Romero's daughters helped their mother out of the store, brought the car around, and returned to their home in Santa Fe. The following Monday, Romero still was in pain and decided she should seek medical attention. She had another of her daughters, who lived in Albuquerque, call Mervyn's and confirm with Wolf his promise that Mervyn's would pay the expenses. She also asked him if any forms needed to be completed when her mother went to the doctor. He told her to come down to the store and pick up the necessary forms. When she did so, however, Wolf told her that he was out of the forms and then, according to her testimony, told her to go ahead and have her mother go to the doctor, and Mervyn's would pay the expenses. Wolf testified the "forms" in question were insurance claim forms. Romero's daughter confirmed that Wolf told her the forms were for the insurance company but insisted that Wolf reiterated the promise that Mervyn's would pay the bill.

Thereafter, Romero consulted a physician and underwent physical therapy. The cost of her treatment came to $2,041. Mervyn's, however, refused to pay the bills. Romero filed suit in Santa Fe District Court, alleging liability under theories of negligence and contract. She did not rely on a theory of promissory estoppel. [Facts of first trial and appeal omitted] On remand, the jury found in favor of Romero on her contract claim, and awarded punitive damages. Mervyn's appeals, arguing the court erred: . . . . (5) in submitting the issue of punitive damages to the jury when there was no evidence of malice on the part of Mervyn's in refusing to pay Romero's medical bills, or in refusing to grant Mervyn's motions for judgment n.o.v. or for a new trial because the award of punitive damages was based on sympathy, passion, and prejudice . . . .

. . . .

(5) *Trial court acted correctly in instructing the jury on the issue of punitive damages and in denying j.n.o.v. or new trial.* Over Mervyn's objection, the trial court submitted an instruction that the jury could find Mervyn's liable for punitive damages if it determined the acts of Mervyn's were "maliciously intentional, fraudulent, oppressive, or committed recklessly or with a wanton disregard of the Plaintiff's rights." *See* SCRA 1986, 13-1827.

. . . .

After objecting to the absence of proof of any malicious or wanton conduct, . . . Mervyn's also stated it did not believe *any* punitive damage instruction would be proper in such a situation. Thus, . . . Mervyn's objection may be construed as an argument that malicious or wanton conduct is a prerequisite to punitive damages. We feel this argument raises important questions concerning the meaning and purpose of New Mexico's punitive damage rule when applied to contract cases. In the following two sections, therefore, we discuss these issues. We conclude our discussion on punitive damages with an examination of the evidence supporting an instruction of malice.

—*Malice, wantonness and punitive damages.* Our previous cases clearly establish that, in contract cases not involving insurance, punitive damages may be recovered for breach of contract when the defendant's conduct was malicious, fraudulent, oppressive, or committed recklessly with a wanton disregard for the plaintiff's rights. *Green Tree Acceptance, Inc. v. Layton,* 108 N.M. 171, 769 P.2d 84 (1989) . . . .

Each of the terms listed, standing alone, will support an award of punitive damages. *See Green Tree Acceptance,* 108 N.M. at 174, 769 P.2d at 87. In a literal sense, therefore, it is incorrect to argue that "malice" or "wantonness" are essential terms to the exclusion of, e.g., fraud or oppression. However, in the sense that malice and wantonness, interpreted broadly, suggest an absence either of a good faith reason or of an innocent mistake, they describe the conduct targeted by our punitive damages rule.

"Malice" as used in our punitive damages instruction does not imply "actual malice" or "malice in fact" in the sense of an intent to harm. *Galindo v. Western States Collection Co.*, 82 N.M. 149, 154, 477 P.2d 325, 330 (Ct.App.1970). Instead, malice, as defined in *Loucks,* means

> the intentional doing of a wrongful act without just cause or excuse. This means that the defendant not only intended to do the act which is ascertained to be wrongful, but that he knew it was wrong when he did it.

76 N.M. at 747, 418 P.2d at 199. This definition is a broad one and undoubtedly encompasses situations that also connote "fraudulent" or "oppressive" conduct. The term "wanton," as used in our punitive damages instruction, suggests a similar quality of wrongfulness when the evidence demonstrates conduct committed without concern for the consequences, rather than intentionally, and connotes an "utter indifference to or conscious disregard for the rights of others." *See Curtiss v. Aetna Life Ins. Co.*, 90 N.M. 105, 108, 560 P.2d 169, 172 (Ct.App.), *cert. denied,* 90 N.M. 7, 558 P.2d 619 (1976).

Thus, these words broadly distinguish "wrongful" breaches of contract from those committed intentionally for legitimate business reasons or those that are the result of inadvertence. In this sense, it may be argued that "malice" or "wantonness" are prerequisites to punitive damages. Nonetheless, we remain convinced that the nuances distinguishing the terms "malice," "fraud," and "oppression" make it useful to retain these words as distinct standards to guide the jury's exercise of discretion in particular cases.

—*Purpose of punitive damages in contract cases.* Mervyn's argues, even taking the evidence in the light most favorable to Romero, "the only thing shown was that Mr. Wolf said Mervyn's would pay the bill and then refused to do so." Mervyn's argues this conduct does not demonstrate malice or wantonness and, unless we reverse the award of punitive damages, "every breach of contract, even if justified, will result in a claim for punitive damages."

. . . .

The general rule limiting recovery in contract case to compensatory damages . . . seems in part calculated to leave undisturbed the allocation of risks and benefits to which both parties have agreed. Such a policy readily is accommodated by awarding money damages, if the measure of damages is based on the justified expectations of the injured party under the contract. Moreover, in most commercial settings,

> [t]he fact that [compensatory] damages must be paid tends directly to the prevention of breaches of contract. It makes, therefore, for the security of business transactions and helps to make possible the vast structure of credit, upon which so large a part of our modern prosperity depends.

5 A. Corbin, *Corbin on Contracts* § 1002, at 34 (1964).

Notwithstanding the general exclusion of punitive damages from contract cases, however, exceptions long have been recognized. *See, e.g., Welborn v. Dixon,* 70 S.C. 108, 49 S.E. 232 (1904) (punitive damages allowed for fraudulent breach of contract); *Stewart v. Potter,* 44 N.M. 460, 104 P.2d 736 (1940) (same). Many courts have conceptualized the conduct necessary to afford recovery of punitive damages as consisting of an independent tort. *See, e.g., Bituminous Fire & Marine Ins. Co. v. Culligan Fyrprotexion, Inc.,* 437 N.E.2d 1360 (Ind.Ct. App.1982) (breach of contract may support an award of punitive damages when elements of fraud, malice, gross negligence, or oppression mingle in the controversy); *Consolidated Am. Life Ins. Co. v. Toche,* 410 So.2d 1303 (Miss.1982) (punitive damages available when breach attended by intentional wrong, insult, abuse, or such gross negligence as to consist of an independent tort); *see generally,* 1 J. Ghiardi and J. Kircher, *Punitive Damages Law and Practice* § 5.16 (1985); Sullivan, *Punitive Damages in the Law of Contract: The Reality and the Illusion of Legal Change,* 61 Minn.L.Rev. 207, 236-40 (1977). Similarly, the text of Section 355 of the *Restatement (Second) of Contracts* recognizes an exception when "the conduct constituting the breach is also a tort for which punitive damages are recoverable."

Other jurisdictions, including California, have justified the award of punitive damages in terms of breach of the implied covenant of good faith and fair dealing, particularly in cases involving insurance contracts. *See Gruenberg v. Aetna Ins. Co.,* 9 Cal.3d 566, 510 P.2d 1032, 108 Cal.Rptr. 480 (1973). "Broadly stated, that covenant requires that neither party do anything which will deprive the other of the benefits of the agreement." *Seaman's Direct Buying Serv.,* 36 Cal.3d at 768, 686 P.2d at 1166, 206 Cal.Rptr. at 362.

For More Information

For a survey of jurisdictional differences as to punitive damages, as well as a wide-ranging evaluation of various policy grounds for punitive damages, see William S. Dodge, *The Case for Punitive Damages in Contracts,* 48 Duke L.J. 629 (1999).

We believe, regardless of whether conceptualized in terms of an independent tort, breach of the implied covenant of good faith, or, as in New Mexico, in terms of the quality of the conduct constituting the breach itself, the award of punitive damages in some cases serves important social ends. . . .

Overreaching, malicious, or wanton conduct such as targeted by our rule is inconsistent with legitimate business interests, violates community standards of decency, and tends to undermine the stability of expectations essential to contractual relationships. When this is the case, it is appropriate to allow the jury to determine whether "the public interest will be served by the deterrent effect punitive damages will have upon future conduct." *Jones v. Abriani,* 169 Ind.App. 556, 578, 350 N.E.2d 635, 649 (1976) (quoting, *Vernon Fire & Cas. Ins. Co. v. Sharp,* 264 Ind. 599, 608, 349 N.E.2d 173, 180 (1976)).

—*Substantial evidence supported instructions on malice and wanton conduct, denial of j.n.o.v. or new trial not error.* Contrary to Mervyn's argument, we do not believe the evidence demonstrated only that Wolf made a promise which subsequently he did not keep. Consistent with the definition of malice under *Loucks,* the trial court instructed the jury that malice denoted "the intentional doing of a wrongful act without just cause or excuse. This means * * * [Mervyn's] not only intended to do the act which is ascertained to be wrongful, but that it knew it was wrong when it did it." We note that, in closing argument to the jury, Romero's attorney contended Mervyn's made the promise to pay her client's medical bills in order to get her out of the store without causing a disturbance, but had its "fingers crossed" and never intended to keep that promise.

"promises you don't intend to keep" [handwritten margin note]

The evidence reasonably could be viewed as indicating the promise was made because, on one of the busiest shopping days of the year, Wolf wanted to get the Romeros out of the store as quickly as reasonably possible without causing a scene. Mervyn's also presented evidence that Wolf's promise was inconsistent with the store's policy regarding customer injuries, and that Wolf subsequently took no action other than to submit the claim to Mervyn's insurer. This evidence reasonably supports the inference that Wolf entered into the contract simply to end his encounter with Romero and her daughters, without intending to follow through on the promise, and with knowledge that his employer thereafter would not perform.

> FYI
>
> "The amount of actual damages sustained by a plaintiff is one indication of the culpability of the defendant's acts, but it cannot be the sole criterion for the assessment of punitive damages. Also relevant is the prospective deterrent effect of such an award upon persons situated similarly to the defendant, the motives actuating the defendant's conduct, the degree of calculation involved in the defendant's conduct, and the extent of the defendant's disregard of the rights of others. These are legitimate concerns of the law, and the application of any fixed arithmetic ratio to all cases in which punitive damages are assessed would be arbitrary. It therefore must be recognized that the requirement of a "reasonable relation" between actual and punitive damages serves as a rough device available to trial and appellate courts for the purpose of paring down plainly extreme awards of punitive damages." *Boise Dodge, Inc. v. Clark,* 453 P. 2d 551 (Idaho 1969).

bad for business norms [handwritten margin note]

We thus conclude the jury could have inferred knowledge on Wolf's part that his employer would not honor the contract with Romero, and thus that he acted with malice. This determination leads to the conclusion that the jury also could infer Wolf made the promise with a conscious disregard for whether his employer subsequently would perform, and thus that he acted recklessly with a wanton disregard for Romero's rights. We conclude substantial evidence supported the instructions on malicious or wanton conduct. Consequently, the denial of j.n.o.v. and of a new trial was well within the discretion of the trial court. *See Cienfuegos v. Pacheco*, 56 N.M. 667, 248 P.2d 664 (1952). Furthermore, the amount of the award of punitive damages is not so plainly unrelated to the injury or actual damages, such as to raise a question of sympathy, passion and prejudice as a matter of law. *See Faubion v. Tucker*, 58 N.M. 303, 270 P.2d 713 (1954).

. . . .

For the foregoing reasons, the judgment of the trial court is affirmed in its entirety.

IT IS SO ORDERED.

————————————

§ 3. Equitable Remedies: The "Extraordinary Remedies"

As noted on page 1041, equitable remedies are reserved for instances in which there is no adequate remedy at law (meaning that damages are inadequate) and plaintiff would suffer irreparable harm in the absence of equitable relief. This rule is an historical vestige from the separate English courts of law and equity (long since merged in nearly every U.S. court). The English jurisdictional separation of these courts still plays out in American rules about when equitable remedies can be awarded.

This section considers three equitable remedies: specific performances, prohibitory injunction, and specific restitution.

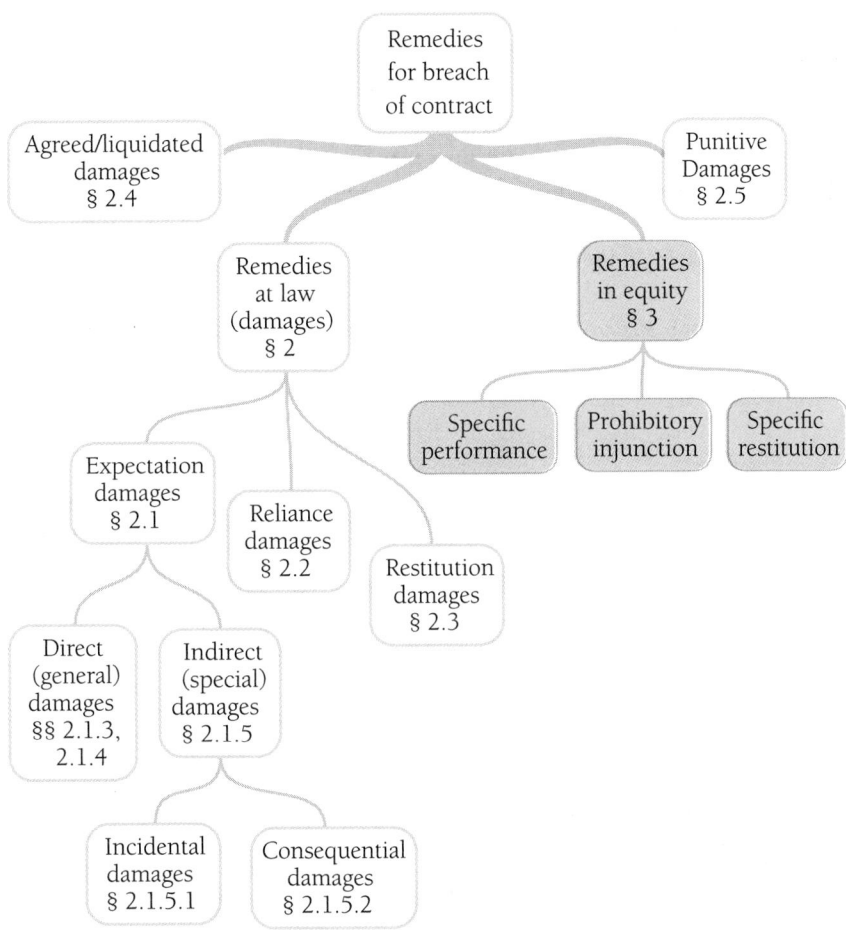

In addition, reformation (see Chapter 5. page 430) is an equitable remedy.

§ 3.1. Specific Performance

Specific performance is a remedy by which the court orders a party to perform the unfulfilled promises in the contract, rather than ordering payment of the value of those performances; the other party receives actual performance rather than damages representing the value of performance. For instance, in *Lucy v. Zehmer* (in Chapter 4, page 237), the court ordered "entry of a proper decree requiring the defendants to perform the contract"* and the plaintiffs received the actual land promised in the contract. Specific performance is most common as a remedy in real estate contracts, because real estate is understood to be unique in most cases; receiving money in lieu of the land is not considered adequate. Simi-

---

* 84 S.E.2d at 523.

larly, specific performance may be ordered in a contract for the purchase of rare or sentimental items, which are unique and irreplaceable. UCC § 2-716(1) expands the class of goods for which specific performance may be ordered, allowing the remedy in "other proper circumstances," especially when the aggrieved buyer is unable to locate substitute goods ("cover") for those involved in the breach or knows that a substitute is unlikely to be available.

Grants of specific performance and other injunctive relief are within the discretion of the court, guided by a collection of factors (often in a loose aggregate test) and general policies of equity and fairness. For instance, the court may decide that the consideration supporting the promise at issue was so disproportionate that the consideration is deemed "inadequate" to support equitable enforcement. Recall from Chapter 2 that the amount of the consideration is not relevant, as long as it was bargained for. However, a court in its equitable role may consider the balance between the value of the promise and the return consideration to determine whether principles of justice and fairness support the use of an extraordinary remedy.

 Reading the Law Critically: *Ammerman* **and** *Laclede*

1. Why are damages inadequate for the plaintiffs in these cases?

2. What arguments do the defendants raise against the use of specific performance?

3. What factors are important to each court in deciding whether to grant specific performance? Which factors seem specific to particular fact situations, and which seem more generally applicable?

Ammerman v. City Stores Co.

H. MAX AMMERMAN et al., Defendants-Appellants

v.

CITY STORES COMPANY, Plaintiff-Appellee

United States Court of Appeals, District of Columbia Circuit
394 F.2d 950 (D.C. Cir. 1968)

Before DANAHER, TAMM and ROBINSON, Circuit Judges.

PER CURIAM:

Appellants, builders and developers of Tyson's Corner Shopping Center in Fairfax County, Virginia, challenge the District Court's decision (1) that the builders had given City Stores Company, owners of Lansburgh's Department Store, a binding option to lease one of the major buildings to be constructed at the contemplated shopping center and (2) that the option-lease agreement is sufficiently definite and certain in terms of design, type of construction, and price to be specifically enforced.

What's That?

The defendants raise the issue of "laches." This equitable defense precludes a claimant from bringing a claim—typically an equitable claim—after waiting for an unreasonable time and prejudicing the other party. The precluded party is said to have "slept on his or her rights," or have been "estopped by laches." In that way, laches operates as a rough equivalent to a statute of limitations in equity.

The appellants in their statement of points have here contended that the District Court erred: in ordering specific performance in that the existence and terms of the contract had not been established by clear and convincing evidence; in granting equitable relief despite the appellants' claim that the appellee had been guilty of "laches and unclean hands"; and in ordering specific performance of the contract since some substantial details will require future negotiations and yet others are said to be unclear or can not be performed.

At the core of the dispute is an undated letter (text, infra), from the appellants to one Jagels, then President of Lansburgh's, given at a time when the builders were attempting to obtain a ruling from the Fairfax Board of County Supervisors which would permit the rezoning of their tract of land for use as a shopping center. Prospects for a favorable outcome at a May 31, 1962, hearing, then yet in the future, were in doubt. The county planning commission and the planning staff had already recommended against the appellants' application, and another group of developers, Rouse-Reynolds, had a similar petition before the Board for a different center but in the same general area.

In early 1962, during the course of negotiations with Messrs. Gudelsky and Lerner for a lease at one of their developments in Maryland, Lansburgh's president, Jagels, had expressed an interest in the Tyson's Corner project. Thereafter Lerner requested a letter from Jagels, expressing Lansburgh's preference for appellants' site over the Rouse-Reynolds tract, which the builders could use in the Fairfax zoning hearing. Although Lansburgh's would ordinarily have been unwilling to risk offending the Rouse-Reynolds group by committing itself to the Gudelsky-Lerner project, it was eager to improve its declining economic position in the Washington area by expanding into the suburbs. Jagels provided the requested letter[4] which the appellants subsequently presented at the rezoning hearing to support their application.

Judge Gasch agreed with the appellee that the Jagels letter was given in exchange for a promise that Lansburgh's be given an opportunity to become a major tenant at Tyson's Corner on terms equal to those given other major tenants. The trial judge further found that this promise had been memorialized in the following undated letter given to Mr. Jagels on or about May 29, 1962:[6]

Dear Mr. Jagels:

We very much appreciate the efforts which you have expended in endeavoring to assist Mr. Gudelsky and me in our application for zoning at Tyson's Corner for a Regional Shopping Center.

You have our assurance that in the event we are successful with our application, that we will give you the opportunity to become one of our contemplated center's major tenants with rental and terms at least equal to that of any other major department store in the center.

Sincerely yours, (s) Isadore M. Gudelsky (s) Theodore N. Lerner

---

[4] The text of the Jagels letter is reprinted in full:

May 29, 1962

Dear Mr. Gudelsky and Mr. Lerner: In view of our several discussions on the Tyson's Corner area as a place for a Regional Shopping Center, I am pleased to say that we have now completed our rather exhaustive surveys and are in a position to give you our firm position on the subject. We are convinced that the Gudelsky-Lerner tract, to which you refer as the Tyson's Triangle, is superior to any other. Being located on the Beltway, it has an unexcelled advertising value. Its location on both Route 7 and Route 123 gives it access to all local traffic. Since the Tyson's Triangle site will be developed almost exclusively to commercial uses, it also assures a live center with no dead spots. It is also readily available to automobile traffic without other competing uses within the Triangle. If you and your associates gain approval to build a Regional Shopping Center on this property, Lansburgh's would be very interested in becoming a major tenant with a full line department store. This interest is, however, restricted to this particular location only and is further conditional upon their being only one regional center in the Tyson's Corner area.

[6] The statute of frauds for the District of Columbia reads in pertinent part:

An action may not be brought . . . to charge a person upon . . . a contract or sale of real estate (or) of any interest in or concerning it . . . unless the agreement upon which the action is brought, or a memorandum or note thereof, is in writing, which need not state the consideration and signed by the party to be charged therewith. . . .

D.C.Code § 28-3502 (1967).

The letter signed by these builders, together with appellee's full performance of the requested services, is sufficient evidence of a unilateral contract to satisfy this statute. . . . The appellee's change of position induced by the appellants' parol promise would estop the latter from setting up the statute of frauds. Brewood v. Cook, 92 U.S.App.D.C. 386, 389, 207 F.2d 439, 441 (1953). . . .

I.

Deeming the assistance afforded by the appellee to the appellants, particularly the May 29, 1962 letter, to be adequate consideration for a valid unilateral contract binding on the appellants, Judge Gasch considered whether the contract, so found, was an option. . . .

II.

Judge Gasch found that Lansburgh's had exercised its option and was entitled to an order compelling the builders to grant it a lease equal in terms to that of the Hecht lease. The appellants argue that the option-lease agreement is too indefinite and uncertain to be specifically enforced because substantial terms have been left to future negotiation. We approve the trial judge's recognition as a rule of law that the mere fact that a contract, definite in material respects, contains some terms which are subject to further negotiation between plaintiff and defendant will not bar a decree for specific performance, if in the court's discretion specific performance should be granted.

The rule so stated violates no precedent in this jurisdiction, but rather is in accord with such of our cases as have considered not dissimilar situations.

Treating the enforcement of construction contracts as a question novel to the District of Columbia,[17] Judge Gasch emphasized that the essential basis for interposition by the court is the inadequacy or impracticability of the plaintiff's legal remedy rather than the generic subject matter of the contract.

Here it is apparent that Lansburgh's could have had no adequate remedy in damages for any attempt in that respect would have been impractical because of the impossibility of an appropriate measurement. Moreover, damages could hardly compensate for the loss of the sought for opportunity to raise Lansburgh's image and economic position in the Metropolitan Washington area by its antici-

---

[17] Despite a paucity of cases in this jurisdiction, we may properly look to the decisions of other courts, recognizing that the "principles and maxims of equity as they existed in England and the colonies in 1776" are part of the law of the District of Columbia . . . . The English Chancery long ago enforced a building contract. Holt v. Holt, 2 Vern. 322, 23 Eng.Rep. 808 (Ch. 1694). There the plaintiff's father had "articled" to have a house built on part of his land but died intestate before it was constructed. The court ruled that the son, on whose inheritance the house was to be built, could compel the builder to build it and his father's administratrix to pay for it. . . . Although the Chancellor would not specifically enforce rebuilding contracts in two cases decided shortly after 1776, . . . the conflict was resolved in Mosely v. Virgin, 3 Ves.Jr. 184, 30 Eng.Rep. 959 (1796), in a rule with a remarkably modern ring: "If the transaction and agreement is in its nature defined, perhaps there would not be much difficulty to decree specific performance; but if it is loose and undefined, and it is not expressed distinctly, what the building is, so that the Court could describe it as a subject for the report of the Master, the jurisdiction could not apply.". . .

pated expansion into the suburbs, and for that reason alone could have been deemed inadequate.

Thus, where the contractual obligation being enforced involves more than the mere construction of a building and the building is to be built on land controlled by its owner (making it impossible for the enforcing party to have the job done by another and charged to the defaulting owner), specific enforcement becomes entirely appropriate. Nor should relief be withheld merely because it would order construction unless the difficulties of supervision by the court outweigh the importance of enforcement to the plaintiff. In this case, as the District Judge found, the construction criteria set forth in the Hecht and Woodward & Lothrop leases are sufficiently detailed to allow the court, applying the standard of equality required by the option, to enforce the lease contract with little difficulty of supervision. The District Court here has retained jurisdiction and can appoint a special master to settle such details as the parties may not agree upon or which can not be resolved through arbitration.

Affirmed.

———————————

Behind the Scenes

Lansburgh's, a large department chain like Macy's or Nieman Marcus, opened its flagship store in Washington, D.C., in 1860 and shortly thereafter supplied the black crepe for Abraham Lincoln's funeral. In the mid-twentieth century, the store's economic standing began to decline, so it sought to expand into suburban branches. In 1959, Lansburgh's opened a branch in Langley Park, Maryland, followed quickly by a branch in Arlington, Virginia. This set the context for Lansburgh's interest in expanding into Tyson's Corner International Shopping Center, in Fairfax, Virginia. However, because of the conflict discussed in *Ammerman*, the branch opening was postponed by approximately seven years, until 1969. By the time the branch opened, Lansburgh's had suffered high legal fees, and its growth had slowed. The department store opened two more branches in Rockville, Maryland and Springfield, Virginia, but eventually liquidated in 1973. At that time, Lansburgh's ranked eighth in the Washington, D.C., retail market.

Although the *Ammerman* court found that there were no remedies at law adequate to compensate Lansburgh's and its owner, City Stores Co., it turned out that even an equitable remedy was inadequate to make City Stores Co. whole after a seven-year battle.

Laclede Gas Co. v. Amoco Oil Co.

LACLEDE GAS COMPANY, doing business as Midwest Missouri Gas Company,
Plaintiff-Appellant

v.

AMOCO OIL COMPANY, Defendant-Appellee

United States Court of Appeals, Eighth Circuit
522 F.2d 33 (1975)

ROSS, Circuit Judge.

The Laclede Gas Company (Laclede), a Missouri corporation, brought this diversity action alleging breach of contract against the Amoco Oil Company (Amoco), a Delaware corporation. It sought relief in the form of a mandatory injunction prohibiting the continuing breach or, in the alternative, damages. The district court held a bench trial on the issues of whether there was a valid, binding contract between the parties and whether, if there was such a contract, Amoco should be enjoined from breaching it. It then ruled that the "contract is invalid due to lack of mutuality" and denied the prayer for injunctive relief. The court made no decision regarding the requested damages. Laclede Gas Co. v. Amoco Oil Co., 385 F. Supp. 1332, 1336 (E.D.Mo.1974). This appeal followed, and we reverse the district court's judgment.

On September 21, 1970, Midwest Missouri Gas Company (now Laclede), and American Oil Company (now Amoco), the predecessors of the parties to this litigation, entered into a written agreement which was designed to provide central propane gas distribution systems to various residential developments in Jefferson County, Missouri, until such time as natural gas mains were extended into these areas. The agreement contemplated that as individual developments were planned the owners or developers would apply to Laclede for central propane gas systems. If Laclede determined that such a system was appropriate in any given development, it could request Amoco to supply the propane to that specific development. This request was made in the form of a supplemental form letter, as provided in the September 21 agreement; and if Amoco decided to supply the propane, it bound itself to do so by signing this supplemental form.

Once this supplemental form was signed the agreement placed certain duties on both Laclede and Amoco. Basically, Amoco was to "[i]nstall, own, maintain and operate . . . storage and vaporization facilities and any other facilities necessary to provide [it] with the capability of delivering to [Laclede] commercial propane gas suitable . . . for delivery by [Laclede] to its customers' facilities." Amoco's facilities were to be "adequate to provide a continuous supply of commercial propane gas at such times and in such volumes commensurate with [Laclede's] requirements for meeting the demands reasonably to be anticipated in each Development while this Agreement is in force." Amoco was deemed to be "the supplier," while Laclede was "the distributing utility."

For its part Laclede agreed to "[i]nstall, own, maintain and operate all distribution facilities" from a "point of delivery" which was defined to be "the outlet of [Amoco] header piping." Laclede also promised to pay Amoco "the Wood River Area Posted Price for propane plus four cents per gallon for all amounts of commercial propane gas delivered" to it under the agreement.

Since it was contemplated that the individual propane systems would eventually be converted to natural gas, one paragraph of the agreement provided that Laclede should give Amoco 30 days written notice of this event, after which the agreement would no longer be binding for the converted development.

Another paragraph gave Laclede the right to cancel the agreement. However, this right was expressed in the following language:

> This Agreement shall remain in effect for one (1) year following the first delivery of gas by [Amoco] to [Laclede] hereunder. Subject to termination as provided in Paragraph 11 hereof (dealing with conversions to natural gas), this Agreement shall automatically continue in effect for additional periods of one (1) year each unless [Laclede] shall, not less than 30 days prior to the expiration of the initial one (1) year period or any subsequent one (1) year period, give [Amoco] written notice of termination.

There was no provision under which Amoco could cancel the agreement.

For a time the parties operated satisfactorily under this agreement, and some 17 residential subdivisions were brought within it by supplemental letters. However, for various reasons, including conversion to natural gas, the number of developments under the agreement had shrunk to eight by the time of trial. These were all mobile home parks.

During the winter of 1972-73 Amoco experienced a shortage of propane and voluntarily placed all of its customers, including Laclede, on an 80% allocation basis, meaning that Laclede would receive only up to 80% of its previous requirements. Laclede objected to this and pushed Amoco to give it 100% of what the

Take Note

These facts suggest that Amoco followed procedures provided in UCC § 2-615 (page 1016). Amoco likely provided notification that it would allocate only 80% of Laclede's demand, claiming excuse under § 2-615. Upon receipt of notice, Laclede would typically have the right to terminate or modify the contract, as provided in § 2-616 (page 1016).

developments needed. Some conflict arose over this before the temporary shortage was alleviated.

Then, on April 3, 1973, Amoco notified Laclede that its Wood River Area Posted Price of propane had been increased by three cents per gallon. Laclede objected to this increase also and demanded a full explanation. None was forthcoming. Instead Amoco merely sent a letter dated May 14, 1973, informing Laclede that it was "terminating" the September 21, 1970, agreement effective May 31, 1973. It claimed it had the right to do this because "the Agreement lacks 'mutuality.'"[1]

Think About It!

Amoco claims to have "terminated" the contract. Was it terminating, cancelling, or repudiating the contract?

The district court felt that the entire controversy turned on whether or not Laclede's right to "arbitrarily cancel the Agreement" without Amoco having a similar right rendered the contract void "for lack of mutuality" and it resolved this question in the affirmative. We disagree with this conclusion and hold that settled principles of contract law require a reversal.

I.

A bilateral contract is not rendered invalid and unenforceable merely because one party has the right to cancellation while the other does not. There is no necessity "that for each stipulation in a contract binding the one party there must be a corresponding stipulation binding the other." James B. Berry's Sons Co. v. Monark Gasoline & Oil Co., 32 F.2d 74, 75 (8th Cir. 1929). . . .

The important question in the instant case is whether Laclede's right of cancellation rendered all its other promises in the agreement illusory so that there was a complete failure of consideration. This would be the result had Laclede retained the right of immediate cancellation at any time for any reason. . . .

Here Laclede's right to terminate was neither arbitrary nor unrestricted. It was limited by the agreement in at least three ways. First, Laclede could not cancel until one year had passed after the first delivery of propane by Amoco. Second, any cancellation could be effective only on the anniversary date of the first delivery under the agreement. Third, Laclede had to give Amoco 30 days written notice of termination. These restrictions on Laclede's power to cancel clearly bring this case within the rule [that the contract is not illusory].

---

[1] While Amoco sought to repudiate the agreement, it resumed supplying propane to the subdivisions on February 1, 1974, under the mandatory allocation guidelines promulgated by the Federal Energy Administration under the Federal Mandatory Allocation Program for propane. It is agreed that this is now being done under the contract.

. . . .

II.

Since he found that there was no binding contract, the district judge did not have to deal with the question of whether or not to grant the injunction prayed for by Laclede. He simply denied this relief because there was no contract. Laclede Gas Co. v. Amoco Oil Co., supra, 385 F.Supp. at 1336.

Generally the determination of whether or not to order specific performance of a contract lies within the sound discretion of the trial court. Landau v. St. Louis Public Service Co., 364 Mo. 1134, 273 S.W.2d 255, 259 (1954). However, this discretion is, in fact, quite limited; and it is said that when certain equitable rules have been met and the contract is fair and plain "specific performance goes as a matter of right." Miller v. Coffeen, 365 Mo. 204, 280 S.W.2d 100, 102 (1955)
. . . .

With this in mind we have carefully reviewed the very complete record on appeal and conclude that the trial court should grant the injunctive relief prayed.
. . .

Amoco contends that four of the requirements for specific performance have not been met. Its claims are: (1) [omitted]; (2) the remedy of specific performance would be difficult for the court to administer without constant and long-continued supervision; (3) the contract is indefinite and uncertain; and (4) the remedy at law available to Laclede is adequate. The first three contentions have little or no merit and do not detain us for long.

. . . .

While a court may refuse to grant specific performance where such a decree would require constant and long-continued court supervision, this is merely a discretionary rule of decision which is frequently ignored when the public interest is involved. See, e. g., Joy v. St. Louis, 138 U.S. 1, 47, 11 S.Ct. 243, 34 L.Ed. 843 (1891) . . . .

Here the public interest in providing propane to the retail customers is manifest, while any supervision required will be far from onerous. Section 370 of the Restatement of Contracts (1932) provides:

> Specific enforcement will not be decreed unless the terms of the contract are so expressed that the court can determine with reasonable certainty what is the duty of each party and the conditions under which performance is due.

We believe these criteria have been satisfied here. As discussed in part I of this opinion, as to all developments for which a supplemental agreement has been signed, Amoco is to supply all the propane which is reasonably foreseeably required, while Laclede is to purchase the required propane from Amoco and pay the contract price therefor. The parties have disagreed over what is meant by "Wood River Area Posted Price" in the agreement, but the district court can and should determine with reasonable certainty what the parties intended by this term and should mold its decree, if necessary accordingly. Likewise, the fact that the agreement does not have a definite time of duration is not fatal since the evidence established that the last subdivision should be converted to natural gas in 10 to 15 years. This sets a reasonable time limit on performance and the district court can and should mold the final decree to reflect this testimony.

It is axiomatic that specific performance will not be ordered when the party claiming breach of contract has an adequate remedy at law. Jamison Coal & Coke Co. v. Goltra, 143 F.2d 889, 894 (8th Cir.), cert. denied, 323 U.S. 769, 65 S.Ct. 122, 89 L.Ed. 615 (1944). This is especially true when the contract involves personal property as distinguished from real estate.

However, in Missouri, as elsewhere, specific performance may be ordered even though personalty is involved in the "proper circumstances." Mo.Rev.Stat. § 400.2-716(1); Restatement of Contracts, supra, § 361. And a remedy at law adequate to defeat the grant of specific performance "must be as certain, prompt, complete, and efficient to attain the ends of justice as a decree of specific performance." National Marking Mach. Co. v. Triumph Mfg. Co., 13 F.2d 6, 9 (8th Cir. 1926). Accord, Snip v. City of Lamar, 239 Mo.App. 824, 201 S.W.2d 790, 798 (1947).

One of the leading Missouri cases allowing specific performance of a contract relating to personalty because the remedy at law was inadequate is Boeving v. Vandover, 240 Mo.App. 117, 218 S.W.2d 175, 178 (1949). In that case the plaintiff sought specific performance of a contract in which the defendant had promised to sell him an automobile. At that time (near the end of and shortly after World War II) new cars were hard to come by, and the court held that specific performance was a proper remedy since a new car "could not be obtained elsewhere except at considerable expense, trouble or loss, which cannot be estimated in advance."

We are satisfied that Laclede has brought itself within this practical approach taken by the Missouri courts. As Amoco points out, Laclede has propane immediately available to it under other contracts with other suppliers. And the evidence indicates that at the present time propane is readily available on the open market. However, this analysis ignores the fact that the contract involved in this lawsuit is for a long-term supply of propane to these subdivisions. The other two contracts under which Laclede obtains the gas will remain in force only until March 31, 1977, and April 1, 1981, respectively; and there is no assurance that Laclede will be able to receive any propane under them after that time. Also it is unclear as to whether or not Laclede can use the propane obtained under these contracts to supply the Jefferson County subdivisions, since they were originally entered into to provide Laclede with propane with which to "shave" its natural gas supply during peak demand periods.[4] Additionally, there was uncontradicted expert testimony that Laclede probably could not find another supplier of propane willing to enter into a long-term contract such as the Amoco agreement, given the uncertain future of worldwide energy supplies. And, even if Laclede could obtain supplies of propane for the affected developments through its present contracts or newly negotiated ones, it would still face considerable expense and trouble which cannot be estimated in advance in making arrangements for its distribution to the subdivisions.

Specific performance is the proper remedy in this situation, and it should be granted by the district court.

CONCLUSION

For the foregoing reasons the judgment of the district court is reversed and the cause is remanded for the fashioning of appropriate injunctive relief in the form of a decree of specific performance as to those developments for which a supplemental agreement form has been signed by the parties.

———————————

Think About It:
CISG Provisions on Specific Performance

The CISG makes specific performance more available to the aggrieved party than does the common law or the UCC. Also note that these rules allow both buyers and sellers to obtain specific performance. In large part, these differences are due to the more widespread availability of specific performance in the civil law, which had a strong influence in the drafting process.

---

[4] During periods of cold weather, when demand is high, Laclede does not receive enough natural gas to meet all this demand. It, therefore, adds propane to the natural gas it places in its distribution system. This practice is called "peak shaving."

Some commentators have advocated a similar broadening of U.S. law. *See, e.g.*, Schwartz, *The Case for Specific Performance*, 89 Yale L.J. 271 (1979). What arguments favor the broadening of the availability of specific performance? What policies favor or disfavor such a broadening?

CISG Art. 46 (in Ch. II. Obligations of the Seller, Sec. III. Remedies for Breach of Contract by the Seller)

(1) The buyer may require performance by the seller of his obligations unless the buyer has resorted to a remedy which is inconsistent with this requirement.

(2) If the goods do not conform with the contract, the buyer may require delivery of substitute goods only if the lack of conformity constitutes a fundamental breach of contract and a request for substitute goods is made either in conjunction with notice given under article 39 or within a reasonable time thereafter.

(3) If the goods do not conform with the contract, the buyer may require the seller to remedy the lack of conformity by repair, unless this is unreasonable having regard to all the circumstances. A request for repair must be made either in conjunction with notice given under article 39 or within a reasonable time thereafter.

CISG Art. 62 (in Ch. III. Obligations of the Seller, Sec. III. Remedies for Breach of Contract by the Buyer)

The seller may require the buyer to pay the price, take delivery or perform his other obligations, unless the seller has resorted to a remedy which is inconsistent with this requirement.

---

§ 3.2. Prohibitory Injunction

An order of specific performance is a "positive injunction," instructing the parties what to do to complete the contract. A court instead may issue a negative (prohibitory) injunction, forbidding a party from taking particular action in violation of the contract. As with other forms of equitable relief, an injunction cannot be granted unless the plaintiff will suffer irreparable harm without the injunction and there is no adequate remedy at law.

Reading the Law Critically:
American Broadcasting Companies

1. What standard does the court establish for evaluating whether negative injunctive relief should be available during the term of the employment contract? How does that differ from the standard for granting injunctive relief after the end of the employment contract?

2. What competing policies are relevant to determining whether injunctive relief should be available?

3 Why is injunctive relief not granted in this case? Why does the dissent disagree with that result?

American Broadcasting Companies v. Wolf

AMERICAN BROADCASTING COMPANIES, INC., Plaintiff-Appellant

v.

WARNER WOLF et al., Defendants-Respondents

Court of Appeals of New York
420 N.E.2d 363, 438 N.Y.S.2d 482 (1981)

COOKE, Chief Judge. This case provides an interesting insight into the fierce competition in the television industry for popular performers and favorable ratings. It requires legal resolution of a rather novel employment imbroglio.

The issue is whether plaintiff American Broadcasting Companies, Incorporated (ABC), is entitled to equitable relief against defendant Warner Wolf, a New York City sportscaster, because of Wolf's breach of a good faith negotiation provision of a now expired broadcasting contract with ABC. In the present circumstances, it is concluded that the equitable relief sought by plaintiff—which would have the effect of forcing Wolf off the air—may not be granted.

I.

Warner Wolf, a sportscaster who has developed a rather colorful and unique on-the-air personality, had been employed by ABC since 1976. In February, 1978, ABC and Wolf entered into an employment agreement which, following exercise of renewal option, was to terminate on March 5, 1980. The contract contained a clause, known as a good-faith negotiation and first-refusal provision, that is at the crux of this litigation: "You agree, if we so elect, during the last ninety (90) days prior to the expiration of the extended term of this agreement, to enter into good faith negotiations with us for the extension of this agreement on mutually agreeable terms. You further agree that for the first forty-five (45) days of this renegotiation period, you will not negotiate for your services with any other person or company other than WABC-TV or ABC. In the event we are unable to reach an agreement for an extension by the expiration of the extended term hereof, you agree that you will not accept, in any market for a period of three (3) months following expiration of the extended term of this agreement, any offer of employment as a sportscaster, sports news reporter, commentator, program host, or analyst in broadcasting (including television, cable television, pay television and radio) without first giving us, in writing, an opportunity to employ you on substantially similar terms and you agree to enter into an agreement with us on such terms." Under this provision, Wolf was bound to negotiate in good faith with ABC for the 90-day period from December 6, 1979 through March 4, 1980. For the first 45 days, December 6 through January 19, the negotiation with ABC was to be exclusive. Following expiration of the 90-day negotiating period and the contract on March 5, 1980, Wolf was required, before *accepting* any other offer, to afford ABC a right of first refusal; he could comply with this provision either by refraining from accepting another offer or by first tendering the offer to ABC. The first-refusal period expired on June 3, 1980 and on June 4 Wolf was free to accept any job opportunity, without obligation to ABC.

Wolf first met with ABC executives in September, 1979 to discuss the terms of a renewal contract. Counterproposals were exchanged, and the parties agreed to finalize the matter by October 15. Meanwhile, unbeknownst to ABC, Wolf met with representatives of CBS in early October. Wolf related his employment requirements and also discussed the first refusal-good faith negotiation clause of his ABC contract. Wolf furnished CBS a copy of that portion of the ABC agreement. On October 12, ABC officials and Wolf met, but were unable to reach agreement on a renewal contract. A few days later, on October 16 Wolf again discussed employment possibilities with CBS.

Not until January 2, 1980 did ABC again contact Wolf. At that time, ABC expressed its willingness to meet substantially all of his demands. Wolf rejected the offer, however, citing ABC's delay in communicating with him and his desire to explore his options in light of the impending expiration of the 45-day exclusive negotiation period.

On February 1, 1980, after termination of that exclusive period, Wolf and CBS orally agreed on the terms of Wolf's employment as sportscaster for WCBS-TV, a CBS-owned affiliate in New York. During the next two days, CBS informed Wolf that it had prepared two agreements and divided his annual compensation between the two: one covered his services as an on-the-air sportscaster, and the other was an off-the-air production agreement for sports specials Wolf was to produce. The production agreement contained an exclusivity clause which barred Wolf from performing "services of any nature for" or permitting the use of his "name, likeness, voice or endorsement by, any person, firm or corporation" during the term of the agreement, unless CBS consented. The contract had an effective date of March 6, 1980.

Wolf signed the CBS production agreement on February 4, 1980. At the same time, CBS agreed in writing, in consideration of $100 received from Wolf, to hold open an offer of employment to Wolf as sportscaster until June 4, 1980, the date on which Wolf became free from ABC's right of first refusal. The next day, February 5, Wolf submitted a letter of resignation to ABC.

Representatives of ABC met with Wolf on February 6 and made various offers and promises that Wolf rejected. Wolf informed ABC that they had delayed negotiations with him and downgraded his worth. He stated he had no future with the company. He told the officials he had made a "gentlemen's agreement" and would leave ABC on March 5. Later in February, Wolf and ABC agreed that Wolf would continue to appear on the air during a portion of the first-refusal period, from March 6 until May 28.[1]

Make the Connection

Notice that the agreement included the exchange of $100 for a promise "to hold open an offer of employment to Wolf as a sportscaster until June 4, 1980 . . . ." This agreement was an option contract supported by consideration, discussed on page 332.

ABC commenced this action on May 6, 1980, by which time Wolf's move to CBS had become public knowledge. The complaint alleged that Wolf, induced by CBS breached both the good-faith negotiation and first-refusal provisions of his contract with ABC. ABC sought specific enforcement of its right of first refusal and an injunction against Wolf's employment as a sportscaster with CBS.

After a trial, Supreme Court found no breach of the contract, and went on to note that, in any event, equitable relief would be inappropriate. A divided Appellate Division, while concluding that Wolf had breached both the good-faith negotiation and first-refusal provisions, nonetheless affirmed on the ground that equitable intervention was unwarranted. There should be an affirmance.

---

[1] The agreement also provided that on or after June 4, 1980 Wolf was free to "accept an offer of employment with anyone of [his] choosing and immediately begin performing on-air services." The parties agreed that their rights and obligations under the original employment contract were in no way affected by the extension of employment.

II.

Initially, we agree with the Appellate Division that defendant Wolf breached his obligation to negotiate in good faith with ABC from December, 1979 through March [4], 1980. When Wolf signed the production agreement with CBS on February 4, 1980, he obligated himself not to render services "of any nature" to any person, firm or corporation on and after March 6, 1980. Quite simply, then, beginning on February 4 Wolf was unable to extend his contract with ABC; his contract with CBS precluded him from legally serving ABC in any capacity after March 5. Given Wolf's existing obligation to CBS, any negotiations he engaged in with ABC, without the consent of CBS, after February 4 were meaningless and could not have been in good faith.

At the same time, there is no basis in the record for the Appellate Division's conclusion that Wolf violated the first-refusal provision by entering into an oral sportscasting contract with CBS on February 4. The first-refusal provision required Wolf, for a period of 90 days after termination of the ABC agreement, either to refrain from accepting an offer of employment or to first submit the offer to ABC for its consideration. By its own terms, the right of first refusal did not apply to offers accepted by Wolf prior to the March 5 termination of the ABC employment contract. It is apparent, therefore, that Wolf could not have breached the right of first refusal by accepting an offer during the term of his employment with ABC.[2] Rather, his conduct violates only the good-faith negotiation clause of the contract. The question is whether this breach entitled ABC to injunctive relief that would bar Wolf from continued employment at CBS.[3] To resolve this issue, it is necessary to trace the principles of specific performance applicable to personal service contracts.

III.

-A-

Courts of equity historically have refused to order an individual to perform a contract for personal services (e.g., 4 Pomeroy, Equity Jurisprudence [5th ed.], § 1343, at pp. 943-944; 5A Corbin, Contracts, § 1204; see *Haight v. Badgeley,* 15 Barb. 499; Willard, Equity Jurisprudence, at pp. 276-279). Originally this rule

---

[2] In any event, the carefully tailored written agreement between Wolf and CBS consisted only of an option prior to June 4, 1979. Acceptance of CBS's offer of employment as a sportscaster did not occur until after the expiration of the first-refusal period on June 4, 1979.

[3] In its complaint, ABC originally sought specific enforcement of the right of first refusal. ABC now suggests that Wolf be enjoined from performing services for CBS for a two-year period. Alternatively, ABC requests this court to "turn the clock back to February 1, 1980" by: (1) setting aside Wolf's agreement with CBS and enjoining CBS from enforcing the agreement; (2) ordering Wolf to enter into good-faith negotiations with ABC for at least the period remaining under the negotiation clause when Wolf breached it; (3) ordering Wolf to honor the 90-day first-refusal period should the parties fail to reach agreement; and (4) enjoining CBS from negotiating with Wolf "for a period sufficient to render meaningful the above-described relief".

evolved because of the inherent difficulties courts would encounter in supervising the performance of uniquely personal efforts[4] (e. g., 4 Pomeroy, Equity Jurisprudence, § 1343; 5A Corbin, Contracts, § 1204; see, also, *De Rivafinoli v. Corsetti*, 4 Paige Ch. 264, 270). During the Civil War era, there emerged a more compelling reason for not directing the performance of personal services: the Thirteenth Amendment's prohibition of involuntary servitude. It has been strongly suggested that judicial compulsion of services would violate the express command of that amendment (*Arthur v. Oakes*, 63 F. 310, 317; Stevens, Involuntary Servitude by Injunction, 6 Corn.L.Q. 235; Calamari & Perillo, The Law of Contracts [2d ed.], § 16-5). For practical, policy and constitutional reasons, therefore, courts continue to decline to affirmatively enforce employment contracts.

Over the years, however, in certain narrowly tailored situations, the law fashioned other remedies for failure to perform an employment agreement. Thus, where an employee refuses to render services to an employer in violation of an existing contract, and the services are unique or extraordinary, an injunction may issue to prevent the employee from furnishing those services to another person for the duration of the contract (see, e.g., *Shubert Theatrical Co. v. Gallagher*, 206 App.Div. 514, 201 N.Y.S. 577). Such "negative enforcement" was initially available only when the employee had expressly stipulated not to compete with the employer for the term of the engagement (see, e.g., *Lumley v. Wagner*, 1 De G.M.&G. 604, 42 Eng.Rep. 687 . . . . Later cases permitted injunctive relief where the circumstances justified implication of a negative covenant (see, e.g., *Montague v. Flockton*, L.R. 16 Eq. 189 [1873] . . . . In these situations, an injunction is warranted because the employee either expressly or by clear implication agreed not to work elsewhere for the period of his contract. And, since the services must be unique before negative enforcement will be granted, irreparable harm will befall the employer should the employee be permitted to labor for a competitor (see 5A Corbin, Contracts, § 1206, at p. 412).

-B-

After a personal service contract terminates, the availability of equitable relief against the former employee diminishes appreciably. Since the period of service

---

[4] The New York Court of Chancery in *De Rivafinoli v. Corsetti* (4 Paige Chs. 264, 270) eloquently articulated the traditional rationale for refusing affirmative enforcement of personal service contracts: "I am not aware that any officer of this court has that perfect knowledge of the Italian language, or possesses that exquisite sensibility in the auricular nerve which is necessary to understand, and to enjoy with a proper zest, the peculiar beauties of the Italian opera, so fascinating to the fashionable world. There might be some difficulty, therefore, even if the defendant was compelled to sing under the direction and in the presence of a master in chancery, in ascertaining whether he performed his engagement according to its spirit and intent. It would also be very difficult for the master to determine what effect coercion might produce upon the defendant's singing, especially in the livelier airs; although the fear of imprisonment would unquestionably deepen his seriousness in the graver parts of the drama. But one thing at least is certain; his songs will be neither comic, [n]or even semi-serious, while he remains confined in that dismal cage, the debtor's prison of New York."

has expired, it is impossible to decree affirmative or negative specific performance. Only if the employee has expressly agreed not to compete with the employer following the term of the contract, or is threatening to disclose trade secrets or commit another tortious act, is injunctive relief generally available at the behest of the employer . . . . Even where there is an express anticompetitive covenant, however, it will be rigorously examined and specifically enforced only if it satisfies certain established requirements . . . . Indeed, a court normally will not decree specific enforcement of an employee's anticompetitive covenant unless necessary to protect the trade secrets, customer lists or good will of the employer's business, or perhaps when the employer is exposed to special harm because of the unique nature of the employee's services. . . . And, an otherwise valid covenant will not be enforced if it is unreasonable in time, space or scope or would operate in a harsh or oppressive manner . . . . There is, in short, general judicial disfavor of anticompetitive covenants contained in employment contracts (e.g., *Reed, Roberts Assoc. v. Strauman, supra,* 40 N.Y.2d at p. 307, 386 N.Y.S.2d 677, 353 N.E.2d 590).

Underlying the strict approach to enforcement of these covenants is the notion that, once the term of an employment agreement has expired, the general public policy favoring robust and uninhibited competition should not give way merely because a particular employer wishes to insulate himself from competition (e. g., *Clark Paper & Mfg. Co. v. Stenacher,* 236 N.Y. 312, 319-320, 140 N.E. 708, supra; . . .). Important, too, are the "powerful considerations of public policy which militate against sanctioning the loss of a man's livelihood" (*Purchasing Assoc. v. Weitz,* 13 N.Y.2d at p. 272, 246 N.Y.S.2d 600, 196 N.E.2d 245, *supra*). At the same time, the employer is entitled to protection from unfair or illegal conduct that causes economic injury. The rules governing enforcement of anticompetitive covenants and the availability of equitable relief after termination of employment are designed to foster these interests of the employer without impairing the employee's ability to earn a living or the general competitive mold of society.

-C-

Specific enforcement of personal service contracts thus turns initially upon whether the term of employment has expired. If the employee refuses to perform during the period of employment, was furnishing unique services, has expressly or by clear implication agreed not to compete for the duration of the contract and the employer is exposed to irreparable injury, it may be appropriate to restrain the employee from competing until the agreement expires. Once the employment contract has terminated, by contrast, equitable relief is potentially available only to prevent injury from unfair competition or similar tortious behavior or to enforce an express and valid anticompetitive covenant. In the absence of such circumstances, the general policy of unfettered competition should prevail.

IV.

Applying these principles, it is apparent that ABC's request for injunctive relief must fail. There is no existing employment agreement between the parties; the original contract terminated in March, 1980. Thus, the negative enforcement that might be appropriate during the term of employment is unwarranted here. Nor is there an express anticompetitive covenant that defendant Wolf is violating, or any claim of special injury from tortious conduct such as exploitation of trade secrets. In short, ABC seeks to premise equitable relief after termination of the employment upon a simple, albeit serious, breach of a general contract negotiation clause.[7] To grant an injunction in that situation would be to unduly interfere with an individual's livelihood and to inhibit free competition where there is no corresponding injury to the employer other than the loss of a competitive edge. Indeed, if relief were granted here, any breach of an employment contract provision relating to renewal negotiations logically would serve as the basis for an open-ended restraint upon the employee's ability to earn a living should he ultimately choose not to extend his employment.[8] Our public policy, which favors the free exchange of goods and services through established market mechanisms, dictates otherwise.

Equally unavailing is ABC's request that the court create a noncompetitive covenant by implication. Although in a proper case an implied-in-fact covenant not to compete for the term of employment may be found to exist, anticompetitive covenants covering the postemployment period will not be implied. Indeed, even an express covenant will be scrutinized and enforced only in accordance with established principles.

This is not to say that ABC has not been damaged in some fashion or that Wolf should escape responsibility for the breach of his good-faith negotiation obligation. Rather, we merely conclude that ABC is not entitled to equitable relief. Because of the unique circumstances presented, however, this decision is without prejudice to ABC's right to pursue relief in the form of monetary damages, if it be so advised.

---

[7] Even if Wolf had breached the first-refusal provision, it does not necessarily follow that injunctive relief would be available. Outside the personal service area, the usual equitable remedy for breach of a first-refusal clause is to order the breaching party to perform the contract with the person possessing the first-refusal right (e.g., 5A Corbin, Contracts, § 1197, at pp. 377-378). When personal services are involved, this would result in an affirmative injunction ordering the employee to perform services for plaintiff. Such relief, as discussed, cannot be granted.

[8] Interestingly, the negative enforcement ABC seeks—an injunction barring Wolf from broadcasting for CBS—is for a two-year period. ABC's request is premised upon the fact that Wolf and CBS entered into a two-year agreement. Had the agreement been for 10 years, presumably ABC would have requested a 10-year restraint. In short, since it lacks an express anticompetitive clause to enforce, plaintiff seeks to measure its relief in a manner unrelated to the breach or the injury. This well illustrates one of the reasons why the law requires an express anticompetitive clause before it will restrain an employee from competing after termination of the employment.

Accordingly, the order of the Appellate Division should be affirmed.

FUCHSBERG, Judge (dissenting).

I agree with all the members of this court, as had all the Justices at the Appellate Division, that the defendant Wolf breached his undisputed obligation to negotiate in good faith for renewal of his contract with ABC. Where we part company is in the majority's unwillingness to mold an equitable decree, even one more limited than the harsh one the plaintiff proposed, to right the wrong.

Central to the disposition of this case is the first-refusal provision. Its terms are worth recounting. They plainly provide that, in the 90-day period immediately succeeding the termination of his ABC contract, before Wolf could accept a position as sportscaster with another company, he first had to afford ABC the opportunity to engage him on like terms. True, he was not required to entertain offers, whether from ABC or anyone else, during that period. In that event he, of course, would be off the air for that 90 days, during which ABC could attempt to orient its listeners from Wolf to his successor. On the other hand, if Wolf wished to continue to broadcast actively during the 90 days, ABC's right of first refusal put it in a position to make sure that Wolf was not doing so for a competitor. One way or the other, however labeled, the total effect of the first refusal agreement was that of an express conditional covenant under which Wolf could be restricted from appearing on the air other than for ABC for the 90-day post-termination period.

One need not be in the broadcasting business to understand that the restriction ABC bargained for, and Wolf granted, when they entered into the original employment contract was not inconsequential. The earnings of broadcasting companies are directly related to the "ratings" they receive. This, in turn, is at least in part dependent on the popularity of personalities like Wolf. It therefore was to ABC's advantage, once Wolf came into its employ, especially since he was new to the New York market, that it enhance his popularity by featuring, advertising and otherwise promoting him. This meant that the loyalty of at least part of the station's listening audience would become identified with Wolf, thus enhancing his potential value to competitors, as witness the fact that, in place of the $250,000 he was receiving during his last year with ABC, he was able to command $400,000 to $450,000 per annum in his CBS "deal". A reasonable opportunity during which ABC could cope with such an assault on its good will had to be behind the clause in question.

Moreover, it is undisputed that, when in late February Wolf executed the contract for an extension of employment during the 90-day hiatus for which the parties had bargained, ABC had every right to expect that Wolf had not already committed himself to an exclusivity provision in a producer's contract with CBS in violation of the good-faith negotiation clause. Surely, had ABC been aware of this gross breach, had it not been duped into giving an uninformed consent, it would not have agreed to serve as a self-destructive vehicle for the further enhancement of Wolf's potential for taking his ABC-earned following with him.

In the face of these considerations, the majority rationalizes its position of powerlessness to grant equitable relief by choosing to interpret the contract as though there were no restrictive covenant, express or implied. However, as demonstrated, there is, in fact, an express three-month negative covenant which, because of Wolf's misconduct, ABC was effectively denied the opportunity to exercise. Enforcement of this covenant, by enjoining Wolf from broadcasting for a three-month period, would depart from no entrenched legal precedent. Rather, it would accord with equity's boasted flexibility (see 11 Williston, Contracts [3d ed.], § 1450, at pp. 1043-1044; 6A Corbin, Contracts, § 1394, at p. 100; see, generally, 20 N.Y.Jur. [rev.], Equity, §§ 79, 83, 84).

That said, a few words are in order regarding the majority's insistence that Wolf did not breach the first-refusal clause. It is remarkable that, to this end, it has to ignore its own crediting of the Appellate Division's express finding that, as far back as February 1, 1980, fully a month before the ABC contract was to terminate, "Wolf and CBS orally agreed on the terms of Wolf's employment as sportscaster for WCBS-TV" (majority opn.). It follows that the overt written CBS-Wolf option contract, which permitted Wolf to formally accept the CBS sportscasting offer at the end of the first-refusal period, was nothing but a charade.

Further, on this score, the majority's premise that Wolf could not have breached the first-refusal clause when he accepted the producer's agreement, exclusivity provision and all, *during* the term of his ABC contract, does not withstand analysis. So precious a reading of the arrangement with ABC frustrates the very purpose for which it had to have been made. Such a classical exaltation of form over substance is hardly to be countenanced by equity (see *Washer v. Seager*, 272 App.Div. 297, 71 N.Y.S.2d 46, affd. 297 N.Y. 918, 79 N.E.2d 745).

For all these reasons, in my view, literal as well as proverbial justice should have brought a modification of the order of the Appellate Division to include a 90-day injunction—no more and no less than the relatively short and certainly not unreasonable transitional period for which ABC and Wolf struck their bargain.

JASEN, GABRIELLI, JONES, WACHTLER and MEYER, JJ., concur with COOKE, C. J.

FUCHSBERG, J., dissents in part and votes to modify in a separate opinion.

Order affirmed, with costs.

———————

Practice Pointer: Non-compete Clauses

Non-compete clauses are also known as non-competition clauses and covenants not to compete. They may or may not be enforceable, at least in their entirety. On one hand, the policy of freedom of contract supports parties' agreed-upon terms. On the other hand, personal freedom and social welfare are undermined by clauses that restrict a person's ability to earn a living. A balancing of these policies dictates that an employer's non-compete clause

- must be contained within a valid contract (with consideration)
- cannot be harmful to the public:
  - ◊ For instance, in an area with a shortage of physicians, most courts would not prevent a doctor from practicing medicine, because the compelling public need for the doctor's service would outweigh the interest of the employer.
  - ◊ Non-compete clauses are rarely effective to restrict lawyers' employment by other law firms because the ethics rules governing law practice give a client the right to choose its own lawyer (and to follow her to another firm).
- must be written as narrowly as possible while protecting the legitimate business interests of the employer:
  - ◊ The employer's legitimate interests might include protecting its trade secrets and other confidential information, customer lists and customer relationships (the longer term, the better), goodwill, and unique or extraordinary skills.
  - ◊ If a non-disclosure agreement would protect trade secrets and other confidential information just as well or better, then the employer cannot use a non-compete clause for that purpose, because a non-disclosure agreement has less impact on a person's ability to earn a living.
  - ◊ Likewise, if a non-solicitation agreement would protect the employer's legitimate interests, then a non-compete clause is unlikely to be upheld.
- and therefore must be reasonable in restricting the time, place, and manner of the employee's future employment
  - ◊ The clause should restrict employment for as short a time period and for as small a geographical area as possible while protecting the employer's legitimate business interests.

◊ In addition, the employee's scope of restricted activities should be drafted to cover as few activities as possible, so that the employee has the fullest possible range of ways to learn a living.

◊ The question of reasonableness is generally for the court.

In some jurisdictions, a covenant not to compete must be ancillary to some other agreement, because a contract cannot restrain competition as its sole or primary purpose. Thus, parties often include the non-compete clause in an employment agreement or the sale of a business.

Using the so-called "blue-pencil test," a court can "reform" (rewrite) the unreasonable aspects of a non-compete clause to prevent the clause from being invalidated. For instance, if the duration of the restraint is longer than needed to protect the employer's legitimate business interests, the court can reduce, say, a three-year period to a nine-month period, if that is the extent of a reasonable time in the circumstances. Similarly, an otherwise reasonable clause with a nationwide scope can be rewritten to encompass a narrower, more reasonable geographical area. Some courts, though, refuse to use the "blue pencil" and will strike the entire clause rather than reforming it.

§ 3.3. Specific Restitution

Specific performance is a remedy focused on granting expectation relief, because it seeks to place the non-breaching party in the position it would have been in if the contract had been fully performed voluntarily. Specific restitution is a restitutionary remedy, because it seeks to place the parties in the position they would have been in if the contract had never existed, by forcing disgorgement of unjust enrichment gained pursuant to the contract. Specific restitution is available if the court determines that restitution relief should be awarded, but restitutionary damages are not an adequate remedy. Specific restitution involves a court order that a particular item (usually something rare or of sentimental value) be restored to the plaintiff.

CHAPTER 10

Third-Party Rights and Duties

What kind of promises will the law enforce?

How do parties demonstrate assent to a contract?

What defenses to enforcement exist?

Is a writing required for enforcement? If so, what kind?

How is the content of a contract ascertained?

What are parties' rights and duties after breach?

What situations lead to excusing contract performance?

What remedies are available for breach of contract?

What contractual rights and duties do non-parties to a contract have?

§ 1. Introduction

This final chapter considers the rights and duties of persons who are not in "privity" (that is, not parties) to the original contract, but who acquire rights or duties by assignment (of contract rights), by delegation (of contract duties), or by being third-party beneficiaries of contracts made by other parties. You have seen examples of assignment, delegation, and third-party beneficiaries in cases in earlier chapters, although the focus then was on the rights of the direct parties to the contract. In the complex commercial environment in which contracting individuals and businesses operate, however, the rights and obligations of non-parties are of significant concern. Although the complete canvassing of third party rights and duties is beyond the scope of this book and most contracts courses, the material in this chapter provides an introduction to the issues and concepts involved.

§ 2. Assignment of Rights and Delegation of Duties

You may recall that Hamer v. Sidway (Chapter 2, page 19) involved a plaintiff who had "acquired [her claim] through several mesne assignments from William E. Story, 2d," the nephew who allegedly had a right of recovery from his deceased uncle's estate. Hamer was not a party to the original contract, but had acquired her right to recover because William Story had "assigned" whatever contract rights he had to his wife, who then "assigned" them to Louisa Hamer.

In most contracts, as in *Hamer*, a third party can gain rights under a contract by obtaining an "assignment of rights" from the contract. The assigning party is the "assignor," and the receiving party is the "assignee." The party whose payments are assigned (Uncle William or his estate, in *Hamer*) is the "obligor" (the person who is obligated to perform). The assignor is an "obligee" (the person who will receive the performance) until that right is transferred to the assignee, who becomes the obligee. Contract performance is then owed to the assignee, not to the original obligee. A common example of assignment is the transfer by a creditor of payment rights under a contract for sale of goods, services, or property; the creditor (e.g., the seller of goods) assigns to another the right to payment from the purchasers, usually in exchange for immediate cash for a discounted sum.

It is also possible for a party to "delegate duties" from the contract to a third party. Recall Baehr v. Penn-O-Tex (Chapter 2, page 34), in which Baehr claimed (unsuccessfully) that Penn-O-Tex had assumed responsibility for Kemp's duties under the service-station lease. The delegating party (allegedly Kemp) is the "delegator," and the newly responsible party (Penn-O-Tex) is the "delegatee" or "delegate." The delegate is now the "primary obligor," and the original "obligor" is now the "secondary obligor."

In drafting practice, many attorneys use the term "assignment" or "assign-ability" to refer to transfer of both rights and duties under the contract. Indeed, the court in *Baehr* phrased the issue as whether Kemp had "assigned" his lease to Penn-O-Tex. However, because assignment and delegation are subject to different rules and policies, it is better to use "assignment" more narrowly, to refer only to the assignment of rights, and to use "delegation" for the transfer of performance duties. This book will use the more precise terminology.

To better understand the textual discussion and the cases, you may find it helpful to diagram the relationships among the individuals involved in the assign-ments and delegations. The template below is an example of such a diagram. On it you can note the promises made by promisor and promisee, the intent of the assignor or delegator toward the third party, and the parties involved in the lawsuit seeking performance:

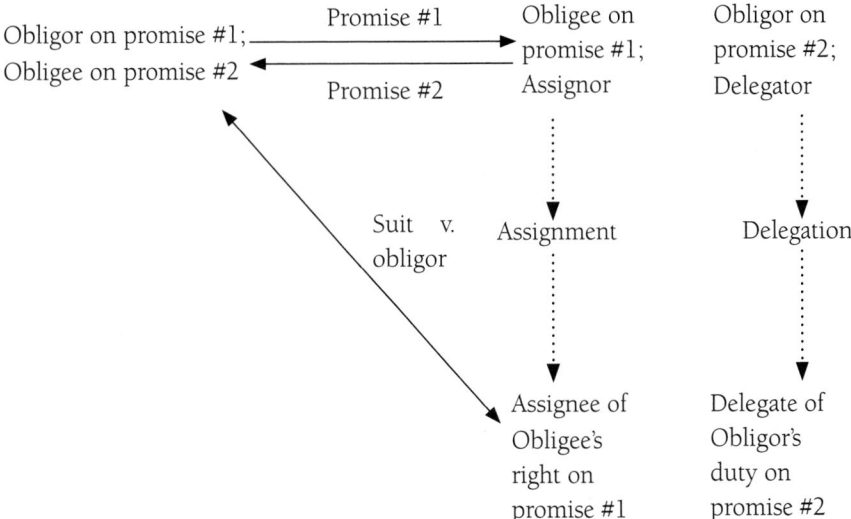

Using the template, the initial *Hamer* situation would appear as drawn below, including both assignments apparently made:

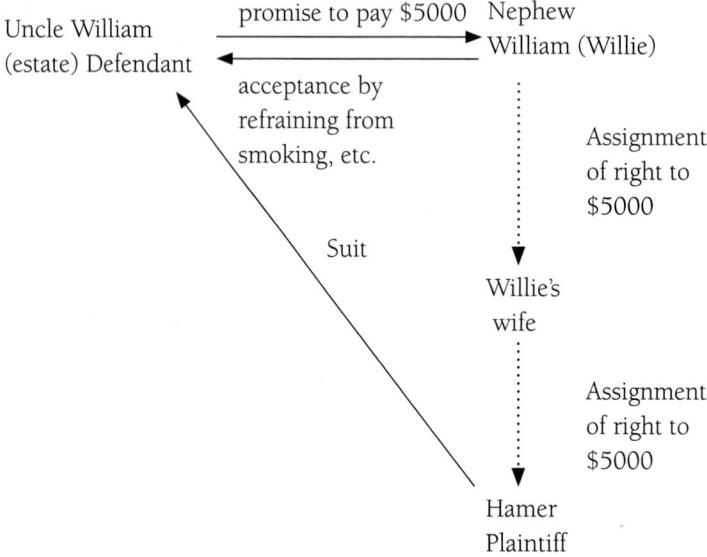

The alleged delegation of duties in *Baehr* would be drawn this way:

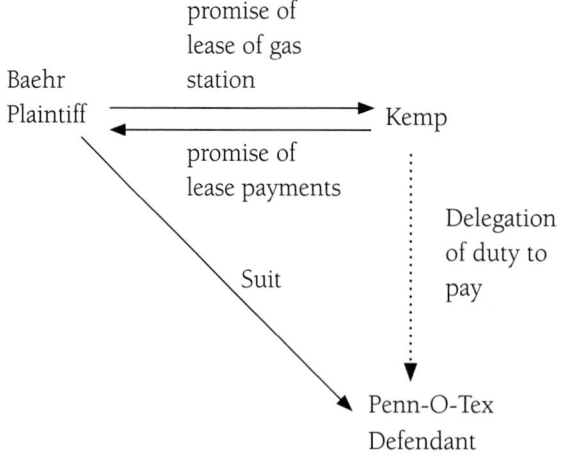

right to stability

right to flexibility

Competing policy concerns underlie common law and statutory responses to assignment and delegation. On the one hand, the original contract parties have an interest in the stability of their contract rights and duties. If a right to receive performance is assigned, the obligor may be faced with somewhat different performance responsibilities. Likewise, if a responsibility to perform duties is delegated, the obligee may receive different performance than originally promised. On the other hand, contracting parties and others have a strong interest in the "free alienability" of contract rights and duties—the ability to transfer those rights and duties to others, which makes them more valuable and provides more flexibility to contracting parties. The law in this area seeks to balance those competing policies.

As will be seen in the materials that follow, small additional burdens for obligors and obligees are tolerated to accommodate alienability, but if substantial burdens are likely, the right to assign or delegate will be restricted. As also will be seen, delegation of duties is more restricted than assignment of rights, because assignment typically produces more economic value while creating fewer additional burdens.

§ 2.1. Common Law Approach

In the nineteenth century, British common law furnished many of the rules and principles for the developing law in the United States. The following case shows the British struggle to define which contracts are delegable and which are not. The resulting rule is still a mainstay of U.S. law.

 Reading the Law Critically: *British Waggon Co.*

1. Who were the parties to the contract and what rights/duties were assigned/delegated? Creating a diagram may help (see page 1209 for a model).

2. Under what circumstances does the court allow a supplier/seller to transfer its duties to another? In what situations does a supplier/seller not have that right? What policies support these rules?

3. Why might the court be concerned about whether Parkgate is completely dissolved or continues to exist in some form, however "wound down"? Can you surmise what the case holding might have been if Parkgate had ceased to exist after the transfer?

British Waggon Co. v. Lea & Co.

THE BRITISH WAGGON CO. and THE PARKGATE WAGGON CO., Plaintiffs

v.

LEA & CO., Defendant

Court of Queen's Bench

5 Q.B.D. 149 (1880)

COCKBURN, C.J.

This was an action brought by the plaintiffs to recover rent for the hire of certain railway waggons, alleged to be payable by the defendants to the plaintiffs, or one of them, under the following circumstances:

By an agreement in writing of the 10th of February, 1874, the Parkgate Waggon Company let to the defendants, who are coal merchants, fifty railway waggons for a term of seven years, at a yearly rent of 600£. a year, payable by equal quarterly payments. By a second agreement of the 13th of June, 1874, the company in like manner let to the defendants fifty other waggons, at a yearly rent of 625£., payable quarterly like the former. Each of these agreements contained the following clause:

"The owners, their executors, or administrators, will at all times during the said term, except as herein provided, keep the said waggons in good and substantial repair and working order, and, on receiving notice from the tenant of any want of repairs, and the number or numbers of the waggons requiring to be repaired, and the place or places where it or they then is or are, will, with all reasonable despatch, cause the same to be repaired and put into good working order."

On the 24th of October, 1874, the Parkgate Company passed a resolution, under the 129th section of the Companies Act, 1862, for the voluntary winding up of the company. Liquidators were appointed, and by an order of the Chancery Division of the High Court of Justice, it was ordered that the winding-up of the company should be continued under the supervision of the Court.

By an indenture of the 1st of April, 1878, the Parkgate Company assigned and transferred, and the liquidators confirmed to the British Company and their assigns, among other things, all sums of money, whether payable by way of rent, hire, interest, penalty, or damage, then due, or thereafter to become due, to the Parkgate Company, by virtue of the two contracts with the defendants, together with the benefit of the two contracts, and all the interest of the Parkgate Company and the said liquidators therein; the British Company, on the other hand covenanting with the Parkgate Company "to observe and perform such of the stipulations, conditions, provisions, and agreements contained in the said contracts as, according to the terms thereof were stipulated to be observed and performed by the Parkgate Company." On the execution of this assignment the British Company took over from the Parkgate Company the repairing stations, which had previously been used by the Parkgate Company for the repair of the waggons let to the defendants, and also the staff of workmen employed by the latter company in executing such repairs. It is expressly found that the British Company have ever since been ready and willing to execute, and have, with all due diligence, executed all necessary repairs to the said waggons. This, however, they have done under a special agreement come to between the parties since the present dispute has arisen, without prejudice to their respective rights.

In this state of things the defendants asserted their right to treat the contract as at an end, on the ground that the Parkgate Company had incapacitated themselves from performing the contract, first, by going into voluntary liquidation, secondly, by assigning the contracts, and giving up the repairing stations to the British Company, between whom and the defendants there was no privity of contract, and whose services, in substitution for those to be performed by the Parkgate Company under the contract, they the defendants were not bound to accept. The Parkgate Company not acquiescing in this view, it was agreed that the facts should be stated in a special case for the opinion of this Court, the use of the waggons by the defendants being in the meanwhile continued at a rate agreed on between the parties, without prejudice to either, with reference to their respective rights.

The first ground taken by the defendants is in our opinion altogether untenable in the present state of things, whatever it may be when the affairs of the company shall have been wound up, and the company itself shall have been dissolved under the 111th section of the Act. Pending the winding-up, the company is by the effect of §§ 95 and 131 kept alive, the liquidator having power to carry on the business, "so far as may be necessary for the beneficial winding-up of the company," which the continued letting of these waggons, and the receipt of the rent payable in respect of them, would, we presume, be.

What would be the position of the parties on the dissolution of the company it is unnecessary for the present purpose to consider.

The main contention on the part of the defendants, however, was that, as the Parkgate Company had, by assigning the contracts, and by making over their repairing stations to the British Company, incapacitated themselves to fulfil their obligation to keep the waggons in repair, that company had no right, as between themselves and the defendants, to substitute a third party to do the work they had engaged to perform, nor were the defendants bound to accept the party so substituted as the one to whom they were to look for performance of the contract; the contract was therefore at an end.

The authority principally relied on in support of this contention was the case of Robson v. Drummond, approved of by this Court in Humble v. Hunter. In Robson v. Drummond a carriage [was] hired by the defendant of one Sharp, a coachmaker, for five years, at a yearly rent, payable in advance each year, the carriage to be kept in repair and painted once a year by the maker—Robson being then a partner in the business, but unknown to the defendant[. Sharp retired] from the business after three years had expired, and making over all interest in the business and property in the goods to Robson[. It] was held, that the defendant could not be sued on the contract: by Lord Tenterden on the ground that "the defendant might have been induced to enter into the contract by reason of the personal confidence which he reposed in Sharp, and therefore might have agreed to pay money in advance, for which reason the defendant had a right to object to its being performed by any other person;" and by Littledale and Parke, JJ., on the additional ground that the defendant had a right to the personal services of Sharp, and to the benefit of his judgment and taste, to the end of the contract.

In like manner, where goods are ordered of a particular manufacturer, another, who has succeeded to his business, cannot execute the order, so as to bind the customer, who has not been made aware of the transfer of the business, to accept the goods. The latter is entitled to refuse to deal with any other than the manufacturer whose goods he intended to buy. . . . We entirely concur in the principle on which the decision in Robson v. Drummond rests, namely, that where a person contracts with another to do work or perform service, and it can be inferred that the person employed has been selected with reference to his individual skill, competency, or other personal qualification, the inability or unwillingness of the party so employed to execute the work or perform the service is a sufficient answer to any demand by a stranger to the original contract of the performance of it by the other party, and entitles the latter to treat the contract as at an end, notwithstanding that the person tendered to take the place of the contracting party may be equally well qualified to do the service. Personal performance is in such a case of the essence of the contract, which, consequently, cannot in its absence be enforced against an unwilling party. But this principle appears to us inapplicable in the present instance, inasmuch as we cannot suppose that in stipulating for the repair of these waggons by the company—a rough description of work which ordinary workmen conversant with the business would be perfectly able to execute—the defendants attached any importance to whether the repairs were done by the company, or by any one with whom the company might enter into a subsidiary contract to do the work. All that the hirers, the defendants, cared for in this stipulation was that the waggons should be kept in repair; it was indifferent to them by whom the repairs should be done. Thus if, without going into liquidation, or assigning these contracts, the company had entered into a contract with any competent party to do the repairs, and so had procured them to be done, we cannot think that this would have been a departure from the terms of the contract to keep the waggons in repair. While fully acquiescing in the general principle just referred to, we must take care not to push it beyond reasonable limits. And we cannot but think that, in applying the principle, the Court of Queen's Bench in Robson v. Drummond went to the utmost length to which it can be carried, as it is difficult to see how in repairing a carriage when necessary, or painting it once a year, preference would be given to one coachmaker over another. Much work is contracted for, which it is known can only be executed by means of subcontracts; much is contracted for as to which it is indifferent to the party for whom it is to be done, whether it is done by the immediate party to the contract, or by someone on his behalf. In all these cases the maxim qui facit per alium facit per se applies.

Think About It!

What facts allow the court to infer that the defendants were "indifferent . . . by whom the repairs should be done"? How do these facts differ from the coach maintenance case discussed by the court, where the opposite inference was drawn?

It's Latin to Me

"Qui facit per alium facit per se" means "he who acts through another acts himself." In this setting, the acts of the subcontractor are the acts of the contractor.

In the view we take of the case, therefore, the repair of the waggons, undertaken and done by the British Company under their contract with the Parkgate Company, is a sufficient performance by the latter of their engagement to repair under their contract with the defendants. Consequently, so long as the Parkgate Company continues to exist, and, through the British Company, continues to fulfill its obligation to keep the waggons in repair, the defendants cannot, in our opinion, be heard to say that the former company is not entitled to the performance of the contract by them, on the ground that the company have incapacitated themselves from performing their obligations under it, or that, by transferring the performance thereof to others, they have absolved the defendants from further performance on their part. . . .

We are therefore of opinion that our judgment must be for the plaintiffs for the amount claimed.

Reading the Law Critically: *Crane Ice Cream Co.*

1. Who were the parties to the contract and what rights/duties were assigned/delegated? Creating a diagram may help (see page 1209 for a template).

2. What limitations does the court place on assignment or delegation? What policies underlie those rules?

3. Who had the greater risk in the original contract, the buyer or the seller? Why did that party take on that risk? How does that risk affect the court's reasoning?

4. This case reaches a different result than does *British Waggon*. Is that because it applies a different rule or because the facts of the cases are distinguishable?

Crane Ice Cream Co. v. Terminal Freezing & Heating Co.

CRANE ICE CREAM CO., Plaintiff-Appellant

v.

TERMINAL FREEZING & HEATING CO., Defendant-Appellee

Court of Appeals of Maryland
128 A. 280 (Md. Ct. App. 1925)

PARKE, J.

The appellee and one W. C. Frederick entered into a contract for the delivery of ice by the appellee to Frederick, and, before the expiration of the contract, Frederick executed an assignment of the contract to the appellant; and on the refusal of the appellee to deliver ice to the assignee it brought an action on the contract against the appellee to recover damages for the alleged breach. . . .

At the execution of the contract the Terminal Freezing & Heating Company, appellee, was a corporation engaged in the manufacture and sale of ice at wholesale within the state of Maryland, and William C. Frederick made and sold ice cream in Baltimore, where his plant was located. The original contract between these two parties was made on April 2, 1917, and ran until April 2, 1920. The contract was modified on June 3, 1918, by the increase of the original contract price of ice from $2.75 a ton to $3.25, and before its expiration the contract was renewed by the parties for another three years so that the contract was continued until April 2, 1923, without change, save as to the higher agreed cost of the ice delivered.

The contract imposed upon the appellee the liability to sell and deliver to Frederick such quantities of ice as he might use in his business as an ice cream manufacturer to the extent of 250 tons per week, at and for the price of $3.25 a ton of 2,000 pounds on the loading platform of Frederick. The contractual rights of the appellee

Think About It!

What kind of supply contract did the appellee have with Frederick? What difference does this fact ultimately make in the court's decision?

were (a) to be paid on every Tuesday during the continuation of the contract, for all ice purchased by Frederick during the week ending at midnight upon the next preceding Saturday; (b) to require Frederick not to buy or accept any ice from any other source than the appellee, except in excess of the weekly maximum of 250 tons; (c) to annul the contract upon any violation of the agreement by Frederick; and (d) to sustain no liability for any breach of contract growing out of causes beyond its control. The converse of these rights and liabilities of the appellee were the correlative liabilities and rights of Frederick under the contract.

There was a further provision that the contract in its entirety should continue in force from term to term, unless either party thereto gave to the other party at least 60 days' notice in writing before the expiration of the term of the intention to end the contract. The contract did not expressly permit or inhibit an assignment, but neither did it contain any word, such as assigns, to indicate that the parties contemplated an assignment by either.

Before the first year of the second term of the contract had expired Frederick, without the consent or knowledge of the appellee, executed and delivered to the appellant, for a valuable consideration, a written assignment dated February 15, 1921, of the modified agreement between him and the appellee. The attempted transfer of the contract was a part of the transaction between Frederick and the appellant whereby the appellant acquired by purchase the plant, equipment, rights, and credits, choses in action, "good will, trade, custom, patronage, rights, contracts," and other assets of Frederick's ice cream business, which had been established and conducted by him in Baltimore. The purchaser took full possession and continued the former business carried on by Frederick. It was then and is now a corporation "engaged in the ice cream business upon a large and extensive scale in the city of Philadelphia, as well as in the city of Baltimore, and state of Maryland," and had a large capitalization, ample resources, and credit to meet any of its obligations "and all and singular the terms and provisions" of the contract; and it was prepared to pay cash for all ice deliverable under the contract.

As soon as the appellee learned of this purported assignment and the absorption of the business of Frederick by the appellant, it notified Frederick that the contract was at an end, and declined to deliver any ice to the appellant. Until the day of the assignment the obligations of both original parties had been fully performed and discharged.

. . . [A] contract cannot be enforced by or against a person who is not a party to it, but there are circumstances under which either of the contracting parties may substitute another for himself in the rights and duties of the contract without obtaining the consent of the other party to the contract. The inquiry here is if the facts bring the case within the scope of the general rule, and the answer must be found from a consideration in detail of the relation of the parties concerned, the subject-matter of the contract, its terms, and the circumstances of its formation.

The basic facts upon which the question for solution depends must be sought in the effect of the attempted assignment of this executory bilateral contract on both the rights and the liabilities of the contracting parties, as every bilateral contract includes both rights and duties on each side while both sides remain executory. I Williston on Contracts, § 407. If the assignment of rights and the assignment of duties by Frederick are separated, they fall into these two divisions: (1) The rights of the assignor were (a) to take no ice, if the assignor used none in his business, but, if he did (b) to require the appellee to deliver, on the loading platform of the assignor, all the ice he might need in his business to the extent of 250 tons a week, and (c) to buy any ice he might need in excess of the weekly 250 tons from any other person; and (2) the liabilities of the assignor were (a) to pay to the appellee on every Tuesday during the continuance of the contract the stipulated price for all ice purchased and weighed by the assignor during the week ending at midnight upon the next preceding Saturday, and (b) not directly or indirectly, during the existence of this agreement, to buy or accept any ice from any other person, firm, or corporation than the said the Terminal Freezing & Heating Company, except such amounts as might be in excess of the weekly limit of 250 tons.

Whether the attempted assignment of these rights, or the attempted delegation of these duties must fail because the rights or duties are of too personal a character, is a question of construction to be resolved from the nature of the contract and the express or presumed intention of the parties. . . . The contract was made by a corporation with an individual, William C. Frederick, an ice cream manufacturer, with whom the corporation had dealt for 3 years, before it executed a renewal contract for a second like period. The character, credit, and resources of Frederick had been tried and tested by the appellee before it renewed the contract. Not only had his ability to pay as agreed been established, but his fidelity to his obligation not to buy or accept any ice from any other source up to 250 tons a week had been ascertained. In addition, the appellee had not asked in the beginning, nor on entering into the second period of the contract, for Frederick to undertake to buy a specific quantity of ice or even to take any. Frederick simply engaged himself during a definite term to accept and pay for such quantities of ice as he might use in his business to the extent of 250 tons a week. If he used no ice in his business, he was under no obligation to pay for a pound. In any week, the quantity could vary from zero to 250 tons, and its weekly fluctuation, throughout the life of the contract, could irregularly range between these limits. The weekly payment might be nothing or as much as $812.50; and for every week a credit was extended to the eighth day from the beginning of every week's delivery. From the time of the beginning of every weekly delivery of the ice to the date of the payment therefor the title to the ice was in the purchaser, and the seller had no security for its payment except in the integrity and solvency of Frederick. The performances, therefore, were not concurrent, but the performance of the nonassigning party to the contract was to precede the payments by the assignor.

When it is also considered that the ice was to be supplied and paid for, according to its weight on the loading platform of Frederick, at an unvarying price without any reference either to the quantity used, or to the fluctuations in the cost of production or to market changes in the selling price, throughout 3 years, the conclusion is inevitable that the inducement for the appellee to enter into the original contract and into the renewal lay outside the bare terms of the contract, but was implicit in them, and was the appellee's reliance upon its knowledge of an average quantity of ice consumed, and probably to be needed, in the usual course of Frederick's business, at all times throughout the year, and its confidence in the stability of his enterprise, in his competency in commercial affairs, in his probity, personal judgment, and in his continuing financial responsibility. The contract itself emphasized the personal equation by specifying that the ice was to be bought for "use in his business as an ice cream manufacturer," and was to be paid for according to its weight "on the loading platform of the said W. C. Frederick."

When Frederick went out of business as an ice cream manufacturer, and turned over his plant and everything constituting his business to the appellant, it was no longer his business, or his loading platform, or subject to his care, control, or maintenance, but it was the business of a stranger, whose skill, competency, and requirements of ice were altogether different from those of Frederick. The assignor had his simple plant in Baltimore. The assignee, in its purchase, simply added another unit to its ice cream business which it had been, and is now, carrying on "upon a large and extensive scale in the city of Philadelphia and state of Pennsylvania, as well as in the city of Baltimore and state of Maryland." The appellee knew that Frederick could not carry on his business without ice wherewith to manufacture ice cream at his plant for his trade. It also was familiar with the quantities of ice he would require, from time to time, in his business at his plant in Baltimore, and it consequently could make its other commitments for ice with this knowledge as a basis.

The appellant, on the other hand, might wholly supply its increased trade acquired in the purchase of Frederick's business with its ice cream produced upon a large and extensive scale by its manufactory in Philadelphia, which would result in no ice being bought by the assignee of the appellee, and so the appellee would be deprived of the benefit of its contract by the introduction of a different personal relation or element which was never contemplated by the original contracting parties. Again, should the price of ice be relatively high in Philadelphia in comparison with the stipulated price, the assignee could run its business in Baltimore and furnish its patrons, or a portion of them, in Philadelphia with its product from the weekly maximum consumption of 250 tons of ice throughout the year. There can be no denial that the uniform delivery of the maximum quantity of 250 tons a week would be a consequence not within the normal scope of the contract, and would impose a greater liability on the appellee than was anticipated. . . .

Moreover, the contract here to supply ice was undefined except as indicated from time to time by the personal requirements of Frederick in his specified business. The quantities of ice to be supplied to Frederick to answer his weekly requirements must be very different from, and would not be the measure of the quantities needed by his assignee, and, manifestly, to impose on the seller the obligation to obey the demands of the substituted assignee is to set up a new measure of ice to be supplied, and so a new term in the agreement that the appellee never bound itself to perform. Up to 250 tons of ice a week Frederick engaged not to buy or accept any ice from any other party than the appellee. After Frederick had sold away his business, this covenant could not bind the assignee of his business, and, even if it continued to bind Frederick, his refraining from not buying ice elsewhere was not a contemplated consideration for selling ice to any one except Frederick himself. . . . It was argued that Frederick was entitled to the weekly maximum of 250 tons, and that he might have expanded his business so as to require this weekly limit of ice, and that therefore the burdens of the contract might have been as onerous to the appellee, if Frederick had continued in business, as they could become under the purporting assignment by reason of the increased requirements of the larger business of the assignee. The unsoundness of this argument is that the law accords to every man freedom of choice in the party with whom he deals and the terms of his dealing. He cannot be forced to do a thing which he did not agree to do because it is like and no more burdensome than something which he did contract to do.

Under all the circumstances of the case, . . . the rights and duties of the contract under consideration were of so personal a character that the rights of Frederick cannot be assigned nor his duties be delegated without defeating the intention of the parties to the original contract. When Frederick went out of the business of making ice cream, he made it impossible for him to complete his performance of the contract, and his personal action and qualifications upon which the appellee relied were eliminated from a contract which presupposed their continuance. Frederick not only attempted an assignment, but his course is a repudiation of the obligations of the contract. He is not even alleged to be ready to pay for any ice which might be delivered after the date of the purporting assignment, but the allegations of the declaration simply aver that the assignee alone had undertaken to perform the further contractual obligations of the assignor. Frederick, however, cannot be heard to say that he has not repudiated a contract, whose contemplated performance his own act has made it impossible for him to fulfill. . . .

While a party to a contract may as a general rule assign all his beneficial rights, except where a personal relation is involved, his liability under the contract is not assignable inter vivos, because any one who is bound to any performance whatever or who owes money cannot by any act of his own, or by any act in agreement with any other person than his creditor or the one to whom his performance is due, cast off his own liability and substitute another's liability. If this were not true, obligors could free themselves of their obligations by the simple expedient of assigning them. A further ground for the rule is that, not only is a party entitled to know to whom he must look for the satisfaction of his rights under the contract, but in the familiar words of Lord Denman in Humble v. Hunter, 12 Q. B. 317, "you have a right to the benefit you contemplate from the character, credit, and substance of the person with whom you contract." For these reasons it has been uniformly held that a man cannot assign his liabilities under a contract, but one who is bound so as to bear an unescapable liability may delegate the performance of his obligation to another, if the liability be of such a nature that its performance by another will be substantially the same thing as performance by the promisor himself. In such circumstances the performance of the third party is the act of the promisor, who remains liable under the contract and answerable in damages if the performance be not in strict fulfillment of the contract. British Waggon Co. v. Lea, 5 Q. B. D. 149; Robson & Sharpe v. Drummond, 2 B. & Ad. 303 . . . .

[handwritten margin note: personal relationship can't be reassigned]

However, the analysis of the facts on this appeal leaves no room for doubt that the case at bar falls into the category of those assignments where an attempt is made both to transfer the rights and to delegate the duties of the assignor under an executory bilateral contract whose terms and the circumstances make plain that the personal qualification and action of the assignor, with respect to both his benefits and burdens under the contract, were essential inducements in the formation of the contract, and, further, that the assignment was a repudiation of any future liability of the assignor. The attempted assignment before us altered the conditions and obligations of the undertaking. The appellee would here be obliged not only to perform the subsequent stipulations of the contract for the benefit of a stranger and in conformity with his will, but also to accept the performance of the stranger in place of that of the assignor with whom it contracted, and upon whose personal integrity, capacity, and management in the course of a particular business he must be assumed to have relied by reason of the very nature of the provisions of the contract and of the circumstances of the contracting parties. The nature and stipulations of the contract prevent it being implied that the nonassigning party had assented to such an assignment of rights and delegation of liabilities. The authorities are clear, on the facts at bar, that the appellant could not enforce the contract against the appellee.

. . . . "The rule was thus stated in Delaware County v. Diebold Safe Co., 133 U. S. 488, and in Burck v. Taylor, 152 U. S. 651: 'A contract to pay money may doubtless be assigned by the person to whom the money is payable, if there is nothing in the terms of the contract which manifests the intention of the parties to it that it shall not be assignable. But when rights arising out of contract are coupled with obligations to be performed by the contractor, and involve such a relation of personal confidence that it must have been intended that the rights should be exercised, and the obligations performed by him alone, the contract, including both his rights and his obligations, cannot be assigned without the consent of the other party to the original contract.'" Kemp v. Baerselman, [1906] 2 K.B. 604 . . . .

. . . .

. . . [T]he judgment . . . will be affirmed without comment on the ability of an assignee of an executory contract for the sale of goods to bring an action in his own name. . . .

———————

Think About It!

Would the result in *Crane Ice Cream* have been different today under the UCC? More specifically, would the seller/obligor have been adequately protected by the good faith duties under § 2-306(1)? See Chapter 7, page 807. If the seller/obligor had felt insecure, would its rights have been adequately protected by the right to demand adequate assurance under 2-609? See Chapter 8, page 951.

———————

Reading the Law Critically: *Sally Beauty Co.*

1. Who were the parties to the contract, and what rights/duties were assigned/delegated? Creating a diagram may help (see page 1209 for a template).

2. The district court and the appellate court disagree on whether UCC Article 2 applies to this transaction. What factors matter in the Seventh Circuit's decision on this issue? What effect does this choice have on the reasoning and the result in this case? Do you agree?

3. Under the rules and policies governing delegation, should Nexxus take the risk that the delegation will take a "bad turn," or should Best be barred from delegating because it might cause the "bad turn"?

4. Why is Judge Posner opposed to the majority position? What are the crucial points of disagreement between majority and dissent? How would Judge Posner have decided this case if he had been in the majority? Which result do you think is better?

Sally Beauty Co. v. Nexxus Products Co.

SALLY BEAUTY COMPANY, Plaintiff-Appellant

v.

NEXXUS PRODUCTS COMPANY, Defendant-Appellee

United States Court of Appeals, Seventh Circuit
801 F.2d 1001 (7th Cir. 1986)

CUDAHY, Circuit Judge.

Nexxus Products Company ("Nexxus") entered into a contract with Best Barber & Beauty Supply Company, Inc. ("Best"), under which Best would be the exclusive distributor of Nexxus hair care products to barbers and hair stylists throughout most of Texas. When Best was acquired by and merged into Sally Beauty Company, Inc. ("Sally Beauty"), Nexxus cancelled the agreement. Sally Beauty is a wholly-owned subsidiary of Alberto-Culver Company ("Alberto-Culver"), a major manufacturer of hair care products and a competitor of Nexxus'. Sally Beauty claims that Nexxus breached the contract by cancelling; Nexxus asserts by way of defense that the contract was not assignable or, in the alternative, not assignable to Sally Beauty. The district court granted Nexxus' motion for summary judgment, ruling that the contract was one for personal services and therefore not assignable. We affirm on a different theory—that this contract could not be assigned to the wholly-owned subsidiary of a direct competitor under section 2-210 of the Uniform Commercial Code.

I.

Only the basic facts are undisputed and they are as follows. Prior to its merger with Sally Beauty, Best was a Texas corporation in the business of distributing beauty and hair care products to retail stores, barber shops and beauty salons throughout Texas. Between March and July 1979, Mark Reichek, Best's president, negotiated with Stephen Redding, Nexxus' vice-president, over a possible distribution agreement between Best and Nexxus. Nexxus, founded in 1979, is a California corporation that formulates and markets hair care products. Nexxus does not market its products to retail stores, preferring to sell them to independent distributors for resale to barbers and beauticians. On August 2, 1979, Nexxus executed a distributorship agreement with Best, in the form of a July 24, 1979 letter from Reichek, for Best, to Redding, for Nexxus:

Dear Steve:

It was a pleasure meeting with you and discussing the distribution of Nexus Products. The line is very exciting and we feel we can do a substantial job with it—especially as the exclusive distributor in Texas (except El Paso).

If I understand the pricing structure correctly, we would pay $1.50 for an item that retails for $5.00 (less 50%, less 40% off retail), and Nexus will pay the freight charges regardless of order size. This approach to pricing will enable us to price the items in the line in such a way that they will be attractive and profitable to the salons.

Your offer of assistance in promoting the line seems to be designed to simplify the introduction of Nexus Products into the Texas market. It indicates a sincere desire on your part to assist your distributors. By your agreeing to underwrite the cost of training and maintaining a qualified technician in our territory, we should be able to introduce the line from a position of strength. I am sure you will let us know at least 90 days in advance should you want to change this arrangement.

By offering to provide us with the support necessary to conduct an annual seminar (i.e., mailers, guest artist) at your expense, we should be able to reinforce our position with Nexus users and introduce the product line to new customers in a professional manner.

To satisfy your requirement of assured payment for merchandise received, each of our purchase orders will be accompanied by a Letter of Credit that will become negotiable when we receive the merchandise. I am sure you will agree that this arrangement is fairest for everybody concerned.

While we feel confident that we can do an outstanding job with the Nexus line and that the volume we generate will adequately compensate you for your continued support, it is usually best to have an understanding should we no longer be distributing Nexus Products—either by our desire or your request. Based on our discussions, cancellation or termination of Best Barber & Beauty Supply Co., Inc. as a distributor can only take place on the anniversary date of our original appointment as a distributor—and then only with 120 days prior notice. If Nexus terminates us, Nexus will buy back all of our inventory at cost and will pay the freight charges on the returned merchandise.

Steve, we feel that the Nexus line is exciting and very promotable. With the program outlined in this letter, we feel it can be mutually profitable and look forward to a long and successful business relationship. If you agree that this letter contains the details of our understanding regarding the distribution of Nexus Products, please sign the acknowledgment below and return one copy of this letter to me.

Very truly yours,

/s/ Mark E. Reichek
President
Acknowledged /s/ Stephen Redding Date 8/2/79.

In July 1981 Sally Beauty acquired Best in a stock purchase transaction and Best was merged into Sally Beauty, which succeeded to Best's rights and interests in all of Best's contracts. Sally Beauty, a Delaware corporation with its principal place of business in Texas, is a wholly-owned subsidiary of Alberto-Culver. Sally Beauty, like Best, is a distributor of hair care and beauty products to retail stores and hair styling salons. Alberto-Culver is a major manufacturer of hair care products and, thus, is a direct competitor of Nexxus in the hair care market.

Shortly after the merger, Redding met with Michael Renzulli, president of Sally Beauty, to discuss the Nexxus distribution agreement. After the meeting, Redding wrote Renzulli a letter stating that Nexxus would not allow Sally Beauty, a wholly-owned subsidiary of a direct competitor, to distribute Nexxus products:

As we discussed in New Orleans, we have great reservations about allowing our NEXXUS Products to be distributed by a company which is, in essence, a direct competitor. We appreciate your argument of autonomy for your business, but the fact remains that you are totally owned by Alberto-Culver.

Since we see no way of justifying this conflict, we cannot allow our products to be distributed by Sally Beauty Company.

In August 1983 Sally Beauty commenced this action by filing a complaint in the Northern District of Illinois, claiming that Nexxus had violated the federal antitrust laws and breached the distribution agreement. In August 1984 Nexxus filed a counterclaim alleging violations of the Lanham Act, the Racketeer Influenced and Corrupt Organizations Act ("RICO") and the unfair competition laws of North Carolina, Tennessee and unidentified "other states." On October 22, 1984 Sally Beauty filed a motion to dismiss the counterclaims arising under RICO and "other states' law." Nexxus filed a motion for summary judgment on the breach of contract claim the next day.

The district court . . . granted Sally's motion to dismiss the two counterclaims and also granted Nexxus' motion for summary judgment. In May 1985 it dismissed the remaining claims and counterclaims (pursuant to stipulation by the parties) and directed the entry of an appealable final judgment on the breach of contract claim.

II.

Sally Beauty's breach of contract claim alleges that by acquiring Best, Sally Beauty succeeded to all of Best's rights and obligations under the distribution agreement. It further alleges that Nexxus breached the agreement by failing to give Sally Beauty 120 days notice prior to terminating the agreement and by terminating it on other than an anniversary date of its formation. Nexxus, in its motion for summary judgment, argued that the distribution agreement it entered into with Best was a contract for personal services, based upon a relationship of personal trust and confidence between Reichek and the Redding family. As such, the contract could not be assigned to Sally without Nexxus' consent.

In opposing this motion Sally Beauty argued that the contract was freely assignable because (1) it was between two corporations, not two individuals and (2) the character of the performance would not be altered by the substitution of Sally Beauty for Best. It also argued that "the Distribution Agreement is nothing more than a simple, non-exclusive contract for the distribution of goods, the successful performance of which is in no way dependent upon any particular personality, individual skill or confidential relationship."

In ruling on this motion, the district court framed the issue before it as "whether the contract at issue here between Best and Nexxus was of a personal nature such that it was not assignable without Nexxus' consent." It ruled:

> The court is convinced, based upon the nature of the contract and the circumstances surrounding its formation, that the contract at issue here was of such a nature that it was not assignable without Nexxus's consent. First, the very nature of the contract itself suggests its personal character. A distribution agreement is a contract whereby a manufacturer gives another party the right to distribute its products. It is clearly a contract for the performance of a service. In the court's view, the mere selection by a manufacturer of a party to distribute its goods presupposes a reliance and confidence by the manufacturer on the integrity and abilities of the other party . . . . In addition, in this case the circumstances surrounding the contract's formation support the conclusion that the agreement was not simply an ordinary commercial contract but was one which was based upon a relationship of personal trust and confidence between the parties. Specifically, Stephen Redding, Nexxus's vice-president, travelled to Texas and met with Best's president personally for several days before making the decision to award the Texas distributorship to Best. Best itself had been in the hair care business for 40 years and its president Mark Reichek had extensive experience in the industry. It is reasonable to conclude that Stephen Redding and Nexxus would want its distributor to be experienced and knowledgeable in the hair care field and that the selection of Best was based upon personal factors such as these.

The district court also rejected the contention that the character of performance would not be altered by a substitution of Sally Beauty for Best: "Unlike Best, Sally Beauty is a subsidiary of one of Nexxus' direct competitors. This is a significant distinction and in the court's view, it raises serious questions regarding Sally Beauty's ability to perform the distribution agreement in the same manner as Best."

We cannot affirm this summary judgment on the grounds relied on by the district court. . . . The burden on the movant is stringent: "all doubts as to the existence of material fact must be resolved against the movant." Moore v. Marketplace Restaurant, Inc., 754 F.2d 1336, 1339 (7th Cir.1985) . . . . Nexxus did not meet its burden on the question of the parties' reasons for entering into this agreement. Although it might be "reasonable to conclude" that Best and Nexxus had based their agreement on "a relationship of personal trust and confidence," and that Reichek's participation was considered essential to Best's performance, this is a finding of fact. . . . Since the parties submitted conflicting affidavits on this question, the district court erred in relying on Nexxus' view as representing undisputed fact in ruling on this summary judgment motion. *See* Cedillo v. Local 1, International Association of Bridge & Structural Iron Workers, 603 F.2d 7, 11 (7th Cir.1979) ("questions of motive and intent are particularly inappropriate for summary adjudication").

We may affirm this summary judgment, however, on a different ground if it finds support in the record. United States v. Winthrop Towers, 628 F.2d 1028, 1037 (7th Cir.1980). Sally Beauty contends that the distribution agreement is freely assignable because it is governed by the provisions of the Uniform Commercial Code (the "UCC" or the "Code"), as adopted in Texas. We agree with Sally that the provisions of the UCC govern this contract and for that reason hold that the assignment of the contract by Best to Sally Beauty was barred by the UCC rules on delegation of performance, UCC § 2-210(1), Tex.Bus & Com.Code Ann. § 2-210(a) (Vernon 1968).

III.

The UCC [Article 2] codifies the law of contracts applicable to "transactions in goods." UCC § 2-102, Tex.Bus. & Com.Code Ann. § 2-102 (Vernon 1968). Texas applies the "dominant factor" test to determine whether the UCC applies to a given contract or transaction: was the essence of or dominant factor in the formation of the contract the provision of goods or services? Montgomery Ward & Co., Inc. v. Dalton, 665 S.W.2d 507, 511 (Tex.App.1983) (contract for repair of roof predominantly involves services); Garcia v. Rutledge, 649 S.W.2d 307, 310 (Tex.App.1982) (contract for repair of truck predominantly a contract for services); Potts v. W.Q. Richards Memorial Hospital, 558 S.W.2d 939, 946 (Tex.Civ.App.1977) (essence of hospital stay is the furnishing of services); Freeman v. Shannon Construction, Inc., 560 S.W.2d 732, 738 (Tex.Civ.App.1977) (sale of bulk cement in construction contract outweighed by predominant service of building structure). No Texas case addresses whether a distribution agreement is a contract for the sale of goods, but the rule in the majority of jurisdictions is that distributorships (both exclusive and non-exclusive) are to be treated as sale of goods contracts under the UCC. *See* Kirby v. Chrysler Corp., 554 F.Supp. 743 (D.Md.1982) (automobile dealership) (applying Maryland law); Quality Performance Lines v. Yoho Automotive, Inc., 609 P.2d 1340 (Utah 1980) (automotive parts distribution contract); Meuse-Rhine-Ijssel Cattle Breeders of Canada, Ltd. v. Y-Tex Corp., 590 P.2d 1306 (Wyo.1979) (cattle semen exclusive dealing contract); Corenswet v. Amana Refrigeration, Inc., 594 F.2d 129 (5th Cir.), *cert. denied*, 444 U.S. 938, 100 S.Ct. 288, 62 L.Ed.2d 198 (1979) (exclusive refrigerator distributorship) (applying Iowa law); Leibel v. Raynor Manufacturing Co., 571 S.W.2d 640 (Ky.App.1978) (exclusive garage door distributorship); Warrick Beverage Corp. v. Miller Brewing Co., 170 Ind.App. 114, 352 N.E.2d 496 (1976) (exclusive beer distribution contract); Ashland Oil, Inc. v. Donahue, 159 W.Va. 463, 223 S.E.2d 433 (1976) (gas station dealership); Aaron E. Levine & Co. v. Calkraft Paper Co., 429 F.Supp. 1039 (E.D.Mich.1976) (paper products distributorship) (applying Michigan law); Artman v. International Harvester Co., 355 F.Supp. 482 (W.D.Pa.1973) (truck distribution franchise) (Pennsylvania law). *See also* Zapatha v. Dairy-Mart, Inc., 381 Mass. 284, 408 N.E.2d 1370 (1980) (dicta); Brattleboro Auto Sales, Inc. v. Subaru of New England, Inc., 633 F.2d 649 (2nd Cir.1980) (assuming without deciding that Vermont UCC applies to automobile dealership); Jacob Aronowicz v. Nalley's, Inc., 30 Cal.App.3d 27, 106 Cal.Rptr. 424 (2d Dist.1972) (applying UCC to food distributorship without discussion); Division of Triple T Service, Inc. v. Mobil Oil Corp., 60 Misc.2d 720, 304 N.Y.S.2d 191 (S.Ct.1969), aff'd, 34 A.D.2d 618, 311 N.Y.S.2d 961 (1970) (same). *But see* Vigano v. Wylain, Inc., 633 F.2d 522 (8th Cir.1980) (federal court bound to apply Missouri rule that UCC does not cover distribution agreements).

Several of these courts note that "a distributorship agreement is more involved than a typical sales contract," Quality Performance Lines, 609 P.2d at 1342, but apply the UCC nonetheless because the sales aspect in such a contract is predominant. *See* Corenswet, 594 F.2d at 134 ("Although most distributorship agreements, like franchise agreements, are more than sales contracts, the courts have not hesitated to apply the Uniform Commercial Code to cases involving such agreements."); Zapatha, 408 N.E.2d at 1374-75 n. 8 (courts have applied UCC to distribution agreements because the sales aspect is predominant). This is true of the contract at issue here (as embodied in the July 24, 1979 letter from Reichek to Redding). Most of the agreed-to terms deal with Nexxus' sale of its hair care products to Best. We are confident that a Texas court would find the sales aspect of this contract dominant and apply the majority rule that such a distributorship is a contract for "goods" under the UCC.

IV.

The fact that this contract is considered a contract for the sale of goods and not for the provision of a service does not, as Sally Beauty suggests, mean that it is freely assignable in all circumstances. The delegation of performance under a sales contract (whether in conjunction with an assignment of rights, as here, or not) is governed by UCC section 2-210(1) . . . . The UCC recognizes that in many cases an obligor will find it convenient or even necessary to relieve himself of the duty of performance under a contract, *see* Official Comment 1, UCC § 2-210 ("[T]his section recognizes both delegation of performance and assignability as normal and permissible incidents of a contract for the sale of goods."). The Code therefore sanctions delegation except where the delegated performance would be unsatisfactory to the obligee: "A party may perform his duty through a delegate unless otherwise agreed to or unless the other party has a substantial interest in having his original promisor perform or control the acts required by the contract." UCC § 2-210(1) .... Consideration is given to balancing the policies of free alienability of commercial contracts and protecting the obligee from having to accept a bargain he did not contract for.

We are concerned here with the delegation of Best's duty of performance under the distribution agreement, as Nexxus terminated the agreement because it did not wish to accept Sally Beauty's substituted performance.[6] Only one Texas case has construed section 2-210 in the context of a party's delegation of performance under an executory contract. In McKinnie v. Milford, 597 S.W.2d 953 (Tex.Civ.App.1980, writ ref'd, n.r.e.), the court held that nothing in the Texas Business and Commercial Code prevented the seller of a horse from delegating to the buyer a pre-existing contractual duty to make the horse available to a third party for breeding. "[I]t is clear that Milford [the third party] had no particular interest in not allowing Stewart [the seller] to delegate the duties required by the contract. Milford was only interested in getting his two breedings per year, and such performance could only be obtained from McKinnie [the buyer] after he bought the horse from Stewart." Id. at 957. In *McKinnie,* the Texas court recognized and applied the UCC rule that bars delegation of duties if there is some reason why the non-assigning party would find performance by a delegate a substantially different thing than what he had bargained for.

In the exclusive distribution agreement before us, Nexxus had contracted for Best's "best efforts" in promoting the sale of Nexxus products in Texas. UCC § 2-306(2) ... states that "[a] lawful agreement by either buyer or seller for exclusive dealing in the kind of goods concerned imposes unless otherwise agreed an obligation by the seller to use best efforts to supply the goods and by the buyer to use best efforts to promote their sale." This implied promise on Best's part was the consideration for Nexxus' promise to refrain from supplying any other distributors within Best's exclusive area. . . . It was this contractual undertaking which Nexxus refused to see performed by Sally.

In ruling on Nexxus' motion for summary judgment, the district court noted: "Unlike Best, Sally Beauty is a subsidiary of one of Nexxus' direct competitors. This is a significant distinction and in the court's view, it raises serious questions regarding Sally Beauty's ability to perform the distribution agreement in the same manner as Best." Memorandum Opinion and Order at 7. In Berliner Foods

---

[6] If this contract is assignable, Sally Beauty would also, of course, succeed to Best's rights under the distribution agreement. But the fact situation before us must be distinguished from the assignment of contract rights that are no longer executory (e.g., the right to damages for breach or the right to payment of an account), which is considered in UCC section 2-210(2) .... The policies underlying these two situations are different and, generally, the UCC favors assignment more strongly in the latter. See UCC § 2-210(2) (non-executory rights assignable even if agreement states otherwise).

Corp. v. Pillsbury Co., 633 F.Supp. 557 (D.Md.1986), the court stated the same reservation more strongly on similar facts. Berliner was an exclusive distributor of Haagen-Dazs ice cream when it was sold to Breyer's, manufacturer of a competing ice cream line. Pillsbury Co., manufacturer of Haagen-Dazs, terminated the distributorship and Berliner sued. The court noted, while weighing the factors for and against a preliminary injunction, that "it defies common sense to require a manufacturer to leave the distribution of its products to a distributor under the control of a competitor or potential competitor." Id. at 559-60. We agree with these assessments and hold that Sally Beauty's position as a wholly-owned subsidiary of Alberto-Culver is sufficient to bar the delegation of Best's duties under the agreement.

We do not believe that our holding will work the mischief with our national economy that the appellants predict. We hold merely that the duty of performance under an exclusive distributorship may not be delegated to a competitor in the market place—or the wholly-owned subsidiary of a competitor—without the obligee's consent. We believe that such a rule is consonant with the policies behind section 2-210, which is concerned with preserving the bargain the obligee has struck. Nexxus should not be required to accept the "best efforts" of Sally Beauty when those efforts are subject to the control of Alberto-Culver. It is entirely reasonable that Nexxus should conclude that this performance would be a different thing than what it had bargained for. At oral argument, Sally Beauty argued that the case should go to trial to allow it to demonstrate that it could and would perform the contract as impartially as Best. It stressed that Sally Beauty is a "multi-line" distributor, which means that it distributes many brands and is not just a conduit for Alberto-Culver products. But we do not think that this creates a material question of fact in this case.[8] . . . [I]t is undisputed that Sally Beauty is wholly owned by Alberto-Culver, which means that Sally Beauty's "impartial" sales policy is at least acquiesced in by Alberto-Culver—but could change whenever Alberto-Culver's needs changed. Sally Beauty may be totally sincere in its belief that it can operate "impartially" as a distributor, but who can guarantee the outcome when there is a clear choice between the demands of the parent-manufacturer, Alberto-Culver, and the competing needs of Nexxus? The risk of an unfavorable outcome is not one which the law can force Nexxus to take. Nexxus has a substantial interest in not seeing this contract performed by Sally Beauty, which is sufficient to bar the delegation under section 2-210, Tex. Bus. Com. Code Ann. § 2-210 (Vernon 1968). Because Nexxus should not be forced to accept performance of the distributorship agreement by Sally, we hold that the contract was not assignable without Nexxus' consent.

---

[8] We do not address here the situation in which the assignee is not completely under the control of a competitor. If the assignee were only a partially-owned subsidiary, there presumably would have to be fact-finding about the degree of control the competitor-parent had over the subsidiary's business decisions.

The judgment of the district court is AFFIRMED.

POSNER, Circuit Judge, dissenting.

My brethren have decided, with no better foundation than judicial intuition about what businessmen consider reasonable, that the Uniform Commercial Code gives a supplier an absolute right to cancel an exclusive-dealing contract if the dealer is acquired, directly or indirectly, by a competitor of the supplier. I interpret the Code differently.

Nexxus makes products for the hair and sells them through distributors to hair salons and barbershops. It gave a contract to Best, cancellable on any anniversary of the contract with 120 days' notice, to be its exclusive distributor in Texas. Two years later Best was acquired by and merged into Sally Beauty, a distributor of beauty supplies and wholly owned subsidiary of Alberto-Culver. Alberto-Culver makes "hair care" products, too, though they mostly are cheaper than Nexxus's, and are sold to the public primarily through grocery stores and drugstores. My brethren conclude that because there is at least a loose competitive relationship between Nexxus and Alberto-Culver, Sally Beauty cannot—as a matter of law, cannot, for there has been no trial on the issue—provide its "best efforts" in the distribution of Nexxus products. Since a commitment to provide best efforts is read into every exclusive-dealing contract by section 2-306(2) of the Uniform Commercial Code, the contract has been broken and Nexxus can repudiate it. Alternatively, Nexxus had "a substantial interest in having his original promisor perform or control the acts required by the contract," and therefore the delegation of the promisor's (Best's) duties to Sally Beauty was improper under section 2-210(1).

My brethren's conclusion that these provisions of the Uniform Commercial Code entitled Nexxus to cancel the contract does not leap out from the language of the provisions or of the contract; so one would expect, but does not find, a canvass of the relevant case law. My brethren cite only one case in support of their conclusion: a district court case from Maryland, Berliner Foods Corp. v. Pillsbury Co., 633 F.Supp. 557 (D.Md.1986), which, since it treated the contract at issue there as one for personal services, id. at 559 (a characterization my brethren properly reject for the contract between Nexxus and Best), is not helpful. *Berliner* is the latest in a long line of cases that make the propriety of delegating the performance of a distribution contract depend on whether or not the contract calls for the distributor's personal (unique, irreplaceable, distinctive, and therefore nondelegable) services. See, e.g., Bancroft v. Scribner, 72 Fed. 988 (9th Cir.1896); Detroit Postage Stamp Service Co. v. Schermack, 179 Mich. 266, 146 N.W. 144 (1914); W.H. Barber Agency Co. v. Co-Op. Barrel Co., 133 Minn. 207, 158 N.W. 38 (1916); Paige v. Faure, 229 N.Y. 114, 127 N.E. 898

(1920). By rejecting that characterization here, my brethren have sawn off the only limb on which they might have sat comfortably.

A slightly better case for them (though not cited by them) is Wetherell Bros. Co. v. United States Steel Co., 200 F.2d 761, 763 (1st Cir.1952), which held that an exclusive sales agent's duties were nondelegable. The agent, a Massachusetts corporation, had agreed to use its "best endeavors" to promote the sale of the defendant's steel in the New England area. The corporation was liquidated and its assets sold to a Pennsylvania corporation that was not shown to be qualified to conduct business in Massachusetts, the largest state in New England. On these facts the defendant was entitled to treat the liquidation and sale as a termination of the contract. The *Wetherell* decision has been understood to depend on its facts. See Jennings v. Foremost Dairies, Inc., 37 Misc.2d 328, 235 N.Y.S.2d 566, 574 (1962); 4 Corbin on Contracts, 1971 Pocket Part § 865, at p. 128. The facts of the present case are critically different. So far as appears, the same people who distributed Nexxus's products for Best (except for Best's president) continued to do so for Sally Beauty. Best was acquired, and continues, as a going concern; the corporation was dissolved, but the business wasn't. Whether there was a delegation of performance in any sense may be doubted. Cf Rossetti v. City of New Britain, 163 Conn. 283, 303 A.2d 714, 718-19 (1972). The general rule is that a change of corporate form—including a merger—does not in and of itself affect contractual rights and obligations. United States Shoe Corp. v. Hackett, 793 F.2d 161, 163-64 (7th Cir.1986).

The fact that Best's president has quit cannot be decisive on the issue whether the merger resulted in a delegation of performance. The contract between Nexxus and Best was not a personal-services contract conditioned on a particular individual's remaining with Best. Compare Jennings v. Foremost Dairies, Inc., supra, 235 N.Y.S.2d at 574. If Best had not been acquired, but its president had left anyway, as of course he might have done, Nexxus could not have repudiated the contract.

No case adopts the per se rule that my brethren announce. The cases ask whether, as a matter of fact, a change in business form is likely to impair performance of the contract. *Wetherell* asked this. So did Arnold Productions, Inc. v. Favorite Films Corp., 298 F.2d 540, 543-44 (2d Cir.1962), and Des Moines Blue Ribbon Distributors, Inc. v. Drewrys Ltd., 256 Iowa 899, 129 N.W.2d 731, 738-39 (1964). Green v. Camlin, 229 S.C. 129, 92 S.E.2d 125, 127 (1956), has some broad language which my brethren might have cited; but since the contract in that case forbade assignment it is not an apt precedent.

My brethren find this a simple case—as simple (it seems) as if a lawyer had undertaken to represent the party opposing his client. But notions of conflict of interest are not the same in law and in business, and judges can go astray by assuming that the legal-services industry is the pattern for the entire economy. The lawyerization of America has not reached that point. Sally Beauty, though a wholly owned subsidiary of Alberto-Culver, distributes "hair care" supplies made by many different companies, which so far as appears compete with Alberto-Culver as vigorously as Nexxus does. Steel companies both make fabricated steel and sell raw steel to competing fabricators. General Motors sells cars manufactured by a competitor, Isuzu. What in law would be considered a fatal conflict of interest is in business a commonplace and legitimate practice. The lawyer is a fiduciary of his client; Best was not a fiduciary of Nexxus.

Selling your competitor's products, or supplying inputs to your competitor, sometimes creates problems under antitrust or regulatory law—but only when the supplier or distributor has monopoly or market power and uses it to restrict a competitor's access to an essential input or to the market for the competitor's output, as in Otter Tail Power Co. v. United States, 410 U.S. 366, 93 S.Ct. 1022, 35 L.Ed.2d 359 (1973) . . . . There is no suggestion that Alberto-Culver has a monopoly of "hair care" products or Sally Beauty a monopoly of distributing such products, or that Alberto-Culver would ever have ordered Sally Beauty to stop carrying Nexxus products. Far from complaining about being squeezed out of the market by the acquisition, Nexxus is complaining in effect about Sally Beauty's refusal to boycott it!

How likely is it that the acquisition of Best could hurt Nexxus? Not very. Suppose Alberto-Culver had ordered Sally Beauty to go slow in pushing Nexxus products, in the hope that sales of Alberto-Culver "hair care" products would rise. Even if they did, since the market is competitive Alberto-Culver would not reap monopoly profits. Moreover, what guarantee has Alberto-Culver that consumers would be diverted from Nexxus to it, rather than to products closer in price and quality to Nexxus products? In any event, any trivial gain in profits to Alberto-Culver would be offset by the loss of goodwill to Sally Beauty; and a cost to Sally Beauty is a cost to Alberto-Culver, its parent. Remember that Sally Beauty carries beauty supplies made by other competitors of Alberto-Culver; Best alone carries "hair care" products manufactured by Revlon, Clairol, Bristol-Myers, and L'Oreal, as well as Alberto-Culver. Will these powerful competitors continue to distribute their products through Sally Beauty if Sally Beauty displays favoritism for Alberto-Culver products? Would not such a display be a commercial disaster for Sally Beauty, and hence for its parent, Alberto-Culver? Is it really credible that Alberto-Culver would sacrifice Sally Beauty in a vain effort to monopolize the "hair care" market, in violation of section 2 of the Sherman Act? Is not the ratio of the profits that Alberto-Culver obtains from Sally Beauty to the profits it obtains from the manufacture of "hair care" products at least a relevant consideration?

Another relevant consideration is that the contract between Nexxus and Best was for a short term. Could Alberto-Culver destroy Nexxus by failing to push its products with maximum vigor in Texas for a year? In the unlikely event that it could and did, it would be liable in damages to Nexxus for breach of the implied best-efforts term of the distribution contract. Finally, it is obvious that Sally Beauty does not have a bottleneck position in the distribution of "hair care" products, such that by refusing to promote Nexxus products vigorously it could stifle the distribution of those products in Texas; for Nexxus has found alternative distribution that it prefers—otherwise it wouldn't have repudiated the contract with Best when Best was acquired by Sally Beauty.

Not all businessmen are consistent and successful profit maximizers, so the probability that Alberto-Culver would instruct Sally Beauty to cease to push Nexxus products vigorously in Texas cannot be reckoned at zero. On this record, however, it is slight. And there is no principle of law that if something happens that trivially reduces the probability that a dealer will use his best efforts, the supplier can cancel the contract. Suppose there had been no merger, but the only child of Best's president had gone to work for Alberto-Culver as a chemist. Could Nexxus have canceled the contract, fearing that Best (perhaps unconsciously) would favor Alberto-Culver products over Nexxus products? That would be an absurd ground for cancellation, and so is Nexxus's actual ground. At most, so far as the record shows, Nexxus may have had grounds for "insecurity" regarding the performance by Sally Beauty of its obligation to use its best efforts to promote Nexxus products, but if so its remedy was not to cancel the contract but to demand assurances of due performance. See UCC § 2-609; Official Comment 5 to § 2-306.

No such demand was made. An antici-patory repudiation by conduct requires conduct that makes the repu-diating party unable to perform. Farn-sworth, Contracts 636 (1982). The merger did not do this. At least there is no evidence it did. The judgment should be reversed and the case remanded for a trial on whether the merger so altered the conditions of performance that Nexxus is entitled to declare the contract broken.

Think About It!

Do you agree with the dissent that UCC § 2-609 (see Chapter 8, page 951) would give Nexxus a sufficient remedy, by allowing it to demand adequate assurances from Sally Beauty, upon reasonable grounds for insecurity, and by allowing it to regard the contract as repudiated if adequate assurances are not given?

---

§ 2.2. UCC and Restatement Provisions

Many jurisdictions still retain their common law rules, but some jurisdictions have adopted the Restatement's approach, which tracks some of the rules in UCC § 2-210:

Reading the Law Critically: Assignment and Delegation under the UCC and Restatement (Second)

Compare the UCC and Restatement (Second) rules pertaining to these questions:

1. Upon an assignment, what happens to the assignor's right under the contract?

2. In what situations would an assignment be invalid?

3. Upon a delegation, what happens to the delegator's obligation under the contract? Are there any exceptions to that rule?

4. In what situations would a delegation be invalid?

5. How, if at all, do these rules reshape the common law rules in *British Waggon* and in *Crane Ice Cream*?

6. What is the legal effect of each of the following contract terms under the UCC and the Restatement (Second)? Note any exceptions to or limitations imposed by the provisions. Analyze each term separately from the others.

    a. "Neither party may assign the contract."

    b. "Neither party may assign its rights under the contract."

    c. "Neither party may delegate its duties under the contract."

    d. "Neither party may assign its rights or delegate its duties under the contract. Any attempted assignment or delegation is void."

    e. "Party A hereby assigns the contract to Party B."

    f. "Party A hereby assigns her rights under the contract to Party B."

    g. "Party A hereby assigns her rights under the contract to Party B. Party B hereby accepts that assignment."

    h. "Party A hereby delegates his duties under the contract to Party B."

UCC § 2-210. **Delegation of Performance; Assignment of Rights**

(1) A party may perform his duty through a delegate unless otherwise agreed or unless the other party has a substantial interest in having his original promisor perform or control the acts required by the contract. No delegation of performance relieves the party delegating of any duty to perform or any liability for breach.

(2) Except as otherwise provided in Section 9-406, unless otherwise agreed, all rights of either seller or buyer can be assigned except where the assignment would materially change the duty of the other party, or increase materially the burden or risk imposed on him by his contract, or impair materially his chance of obtaining return performance. A right to damages for breach of the whole contract or a right arising out of the assignor's due performance of his entire obligation can be assigned despite agreement otherwise.

(3) . . . .

(4) Unless the circumstances indicate the contrary a prohibition of assignment of "the contract" is to be construed as barring only the delegation to the assignee of the assignor's performance.

(5) An assignment of "the contract" or of "all my rights under the contract" or an assignment in similar general terms is an assignment of rights and unless the language or the circumstances (as in an assignment for security) indicate the contrary, it is a delegation of performance of the duties of the assignor and its acceptance by the assignee constitutes a promise by him to perform those duties. This promise is enforceable by either the assignor or the other party to the original contract.

(6) The other party may treat any assignment which delegates performance as creating reasonable grounds for insecurity and may without prejudice to his rights against the assignor demand assurances from the assignee (Section 2-609).

––––––––––

Restatement (Second) § 317. **Assignment of a Right**

(1) An assignment of a right is a manifestation of the assignor's intention to transfer it by virtue of which the assignor's right to performance by the obligor is extinguished in whole or in part and the assignee acquires a right to such performance.

(2) A contractual right can be assigned unless

  (a) the substitution of a right of the assignee for the right of the assignor would materially change the duty of the obligor, or materially increase the burden or risk imposed on him by his contract, or materially impair his chance of obtaining return performance, or materially reduce its value to him, or

(b) the assignment is forbidden by statute or is otherwise inoperative on grounds of public policy, or

(c) assignment is validly precluded by contract.

Restatement (Second) § 318. **Delegation of Performance of Duty**

(1) An obligor can properly delegate the performance of his duty to another unless the delegation is contrary to public policy or the terms of his promise.

(2) Unless otherwise agreed, a promise requires performance by a particular person only to the extent that the obligee has a substantial interest in having that person perform or control the acts promised.

(3) Unless the obligee agrees otherwise, neither delegation of performance nor a contract to assume the duty made with the obligor by the person delegated discharges any duty or liability of the delegating obligor.

Restatement (Second) § 322. **Contractual Prohibition Of Assignment**

(1) Unless the circumstances indicate the contrary, a contract term prohibiting assignment of "the contract" bars only the delegation to an assignee of the performance by the assignor of a duty or condition.

(2) A contract term prohibiting assignment of rights under the contract, unless a different intention is manifested,

(a) does not forbid assignment of a right to damages for breach of the whole contract or a right arising out of the assignor's due performance of his entire obligation;

(b) gives the obligor a right to damages for breach of the terms forbidding assignment but does not render the assignment ineffective;

(c) is for the benefit of the obligor, and does not prevent the assignee from acquiring rights against the assignor or the obligor from discharging his duty as if there were no such prohibition.

§ 2.3. Additional Issues

A variety of additional issues may arise with respect to assignment and delegation, including

1. whether the owner of a contract right or the obligor has manifested the intent to assign contract rights or delegate contract duties;
2. whether an assignment or delegation can be revoked by the party making it;
3. what defenses are available to the assignee or delegate based on the original contract; and
4. what rights and liabilities remain for the original contracting parties after the transfer.

The detailed rules on assignment and delegation—especially assignments governed by UCC Article 9—are beyond the scope of an introductory contracts course, but the basic contours of these additional issues are summarized here. First, the intent of the contracting party to make an assignment or delegation (issue #1) is judged as are other questions of intent, from all the circumstances, including words and conduct. To make an effective assignment of rights, the party must manifest the intent to make an assignment, that is, to make a present transfer of rights to contract performance. A promise to pay another later, when contract performance occurs, is not an assignment because it does not immediately transfer the right to collect. An order from the obligee to the obligor to pay someone else is not an assignment because it does not transfer the right to receive payment; it merely directs the obligor to pay another and gives the third party no right to demand payment (unless the third party thereby obtains rights as a third party beneficiary—see page 1240). A purported delegation is judged similarly, to determine whether delegator and delegate manifested the intent to make a delegation.

Under what circumstances may an assignment or delegation be revoked by the party making it (issue #2)? An assignment or delegation is usually made as part of a contract agreement (e.g., a seller that is owed money from purchasers might assign the right to collect from the purchasers to a bank in exchange for a lump sum cash payment of some amount less than the total of all the accounts receivable). In such cases, the assignment is a term in a contract supported by consideration and the assignment cannot be revoked. If an assignment is made as a gift (for example, if nephew Willie Story had assigned his contract right to his wife as an anniversary gift), then it is governed by the rules regarding gifts, which makes it revocable until "delivered." How a gift of this kind might be delivered is complicated because an assignment is an intangible right, but it may be manifested in a deliverable instrument such as a promissory note or other written form. The details are beyond the scope of these materials; it is enough at this stage to understand that delivery is the issue to be addressed.

If the obligor could have asserted a defense against paying the original obligee (the other party to the contract), can the obligor assert that defense against payment to the assignee (issue #3)? For example, if services are performed unsatisfactorily but the right to receive payment for the services was assigned to a bank, can the buyer of those services defend against the bank's suit for payment by pointing to the defects in performance? The simple answer is yes; the assignee stands in the shoes of the assignor. But this picture is complicated by the existence of contract clauses that purport to waive the assertion of defenses if the right to collect is assigned (so-called "waiver-of-defense" clauses) and by the use of accompanying promissory notes, which are usually freely negotiable, that is, they can pass to purchasers without being encumbered by the defenses that could otherwise be asserted. Courts, statutes, and regulations have intervened to protect consumers in such situations, so that no simple answer can be given to the question whether the obligor can assert a defense against an assignee. Again, it is enough at this stage to understand the nature of the issue raised.

Finally, what rights and liabilities remain for the original contracting parties after the transfer (issue #4)? If an assignment is made, the assignor no longer has the right to receive the performance owed under the original contract. By definition, that right now belongs to the assignee. The picture is complicated further if the obligor performs for the wrong person after an assignment is made or revoked. Whether the obligor remains liable after such performance depends on whether proper notice of assignment (or revocation) was received by the obligor. Again, the details are beyond the scope of this book.

If a delegation of duties is made, the original obligor remains responsible to the obligee, unless the obligee consents to a substitution. "While an obligee can rid itself of a right merely by making an effective assignment, an obligor cannot rid itself of a duty merely by making an effective delegation. If obligors could do so, they could discharge their duties simply by finding obliging insolvents to whom performance could be delegated."*

§ 3. Third-Party Beneficiaries

In several of the cases covered in earlier chapters, you encountered third-party beneficiaries, although you might not have recognized them as such. For instance, some construction contracts require that the general contractor purchase a performance bond for the protection of the project owner, to compensate the project owner for deficient or incomplete construction work. The obligated party (the general contractor in the example) obtains a bond by entering into a contract with the bonding company. The benefited party (the project owner) is named as the beneficiary of the bond but is not a party to the bonding contract, so it is a "third-party beneficiary" to the bonding contract. A third-party beneficiary to a contract may be expressly identified, as in the example, or may be implied from

---

* E. Allen Farnsworth, *Contracts*, § 11.10 (4th ed. 2004).

the nature of the contract. Identifying a third-party beneficiary is only the first step, as not all third-party beneficiaries of a contract have a right to enforce that contract. The cases below, as well as the Restatement rules that follow, establish the standards determining if a third-party beneficiary may enforce a contract to which it is not a party.

As with assignment and delegation, diagramming the relationships of the parties and third-party beneficiary may be helpful. The template below provides a model for that purpose:

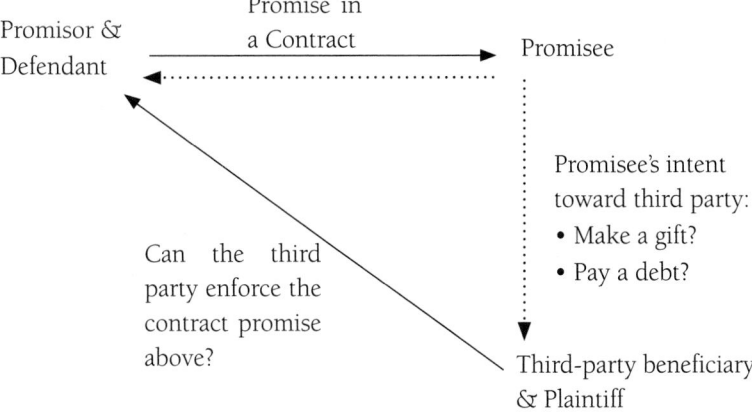

Here is how to draw the diagram:

1. Start by figuring out which contract promise the third party would like to enforce. Place that promise on the top horizontal line. Place the person who made that promise in the "promisor" position on the left side and the recipient in the "promisee" position on the right side.

2. Place the third party at the bottom of the diagram, beneath the promisee. On the vertical arrow between the two, note what the promisee intended to do for the third party (make a gift? pay a debt?).

3. Now draw a diagonal arrow from the third party to promisor, and ask the crucial question: Can the third party enforce the contract promise made by the promisor? That is the focus of ths portion of Chapter 10.

For instance, if a construction contract requires the contractor to obtain a performance bond to benefit the owner of the project, the relationship may be diagrammed this way:

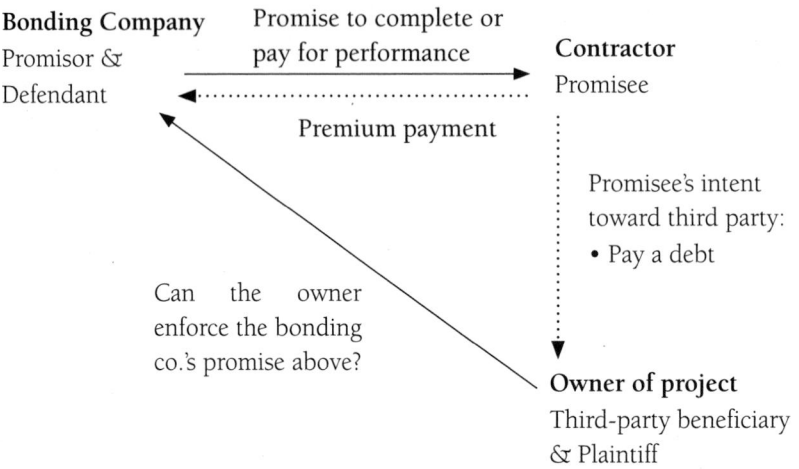

If the contract between the contractor and the owner requires the owner to obtain a "payment bond" to benefit the contractor, the relationship may be diagrammed this way:

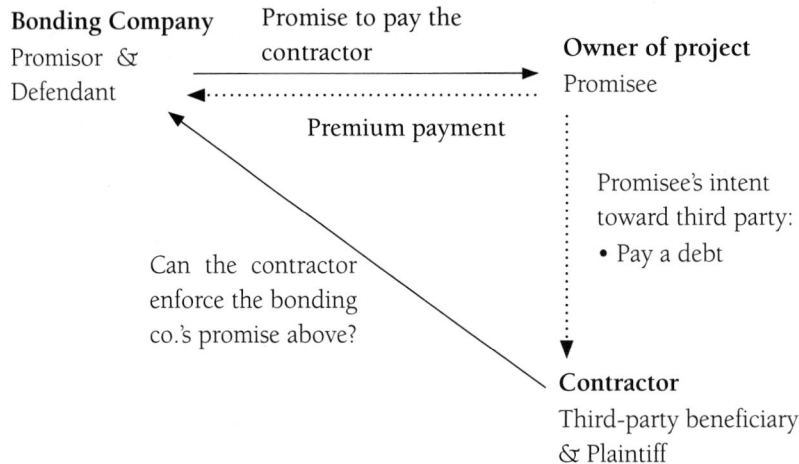

Make the Connection

Recall that in *Quake Construction, Inc. v. American Airlines, Inc.* (page 249), the contract required the subcontractor to obtain a "100% performance and payment bond" for the benefit of the general contractor, who would be the third-party beneficiary of the bond.

Likewise in *McCloskey & Co. v. Minweld Steel Co.* (page TK), the contract required the subcontractor to obtain a performance bond for the benefit of the contractor.

For practice, try diagramming the third-party beneficiary relationships described in the above cases.

§ 3.1. Common Law Roots of the Doctrine

Third-party beneficiary doctrine developed from the two early New York cases below. Despite the age of the cases, they are still delineate the categories of third-party beneficiaries and determine which beneficiaries can enforce a contract.

Reading the Law Critically: *Lawrence*

1. On what factual basis did Lawrence claim that Fox owed him money? Be sure to sort out the actions and relationships among the parties, which can be confusing in a third-party beneficiary case. A diagram may help (see the template on page 1241). The reported facts are sparse; additional background follows the case.

2. The court discusses the case of *Farley v. Cleaveland*. Diagram the transaction in that case as well. What does that case help to establish?

3. Why does the court permit Lawrence to enforce the contract? What rationale does the court offer? What arguments against that outcome does the court outline, and how does the court respond to those arguments?

4. Based on the court's reasoning, how would you describe the category of third-party beneficiaries who have the right to recover on a promise made by another?

Lawrence v. Fox

DON R. LAWRENCE, Plaintiff-Appellee

v.

ARTHUR W. FOX, Defendant-Appellant

Court of Appeals of New York
1859 WL 8352 (N.Y. 1859)

APPEAL from the Superior Court of the city of Buffalo. On the trial before Mr. Justice MASTEN, it appeared by the evidence of a bystander, that one Holly, in November, 1857, at the request of the defendant, loaned and advanced to him $300, stating at the time that he owed that sum to the plaintiff for money borrowed of him, and had agreed to pay it to him the then next day; that the defendant in consideration thereof, at the time of receiving the money, promised to pay it to the plaintiff the then next day. Upon this state of facts the defendant moved for a nonsuit, upon three several grounds, viz.: That there was no proof tending to show that Holly was indebted to the plaintiff; that the agreement by the defendant with Holly to pay the plaintiff was void for want of consideration, and that there was no privity between the plaintiff and defendant. The court overruled the motion, and the counsel for the defendant excepted. The cause was then submitted to the jury, and they found a verdict for the plaintiff for the amount of the loan and interest, $344.66, upon which judgment was entered; from which the defendant appealed to the Superior Court, at general term, where the judgment was affirmed, and the defendant appealed to this court. The cause was submitted on printed arguments.

H. GRAY, J. . . . [I]t is claimed that . . . this promise . . . was void for the want of consideration. It is now more than a quarter of a century since it was settled by the Supreme Court of this State . . . that a promise in all material respects like the one under consideration was valid; and the judgment of that court was unanimously affirmed by the Court for the Correction of Errors. (Farley v. Cleveland, 4 Cow., 432; same case in error, 9 id., 639.) In that case one Moon owed Farley and sold to Cleveland a quantity of hay, in consideration of which Cleveland promised to pay Moon's debt to Farley; and the decision in favor of Farley's right to recover was placed upon the ground that the hay received by Cleveland from Moon was a valid consideration for Cleveland's promise to pay Farley, and that the subsisting liability of Moon to pay Farley was no objection to the recovery. The fact that the money advanced by Holly to the defendant was a loan to him for a day, and that it thereby became the property of the defendant, seemed to impress the defendant's counsel with the idea that because the defendant's promise was not a trust fund placed by the plaintiff in the defendant's hands, out of which he was to realize money as from the sale of a chattel or the collection of a debt, the promise although made for the benefit of the plaintiff could not enure to his benefit. The hay which [Moon delivered to Cleveland] was not to be paid to Farley, but the debt incurred by Cleaveland for the purchase of the hay, like the debt incurred by the defendant for money borrowed, was what was to be paid. That case . . . puts to rest the objection that the defendant's promise was void for want of consideration.

>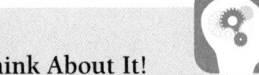
>
> **Think About It!**
>
> The court declares that *Farley* establishes there was consideration for Fox's promise to pay Lawrence on Holly's behalf. What *was* the consideration for that promise?

The report of [*Farley v. Cleveland*] shows that the promise was not only made to Moon but to the plaintiff Farley. In this case the promise was made to Holly and not expressly to the plaintiff; and this difference between the two cases presents the question, raised by the defendant's objection, as to the want of privity between the plaintiff and defendant. As early as 1806 it was announced by the Supreme Court of this State, upon what was then regarded as the settled law of England, "That where one person makes a promise to another for the benefit of a third person, that third person may maintain an action upon it." **Schermerhorn v. Vanderheyden** (1 John. R., 140), has often been re-asserted by our courts and never departed from. . . .

But it is urged that because the defendant was not in any sense a trustee of the property of Holly for the benefit of the plaintiff, the law will not imply a promise. I agree that many of the cases where a promise was implied were cases of trusts, created for the benefit of the promiser. . . . In this case the defendant, upon ample consideration received from Holly, promised Holly to pay his debt to the plaintiff; the consideration received and the promise to Holly made it as plainly his duty to pay the plaintiff as if the money had been remitted to him for that purpose, and as well implied a promise to do so as if he had been made a trustee of property to be converted into cash with which to pay. . . . The principle illustrated by the example so frequently quoted (which concisely states the case in hand) "that a promise made to one for the benefit of another, he for whose benefit it is made may bring an action for its breach," has been applied to trust cases, not because it was exclusively applicable to those cases, but because it was a principle of law, and as such applicable to those cases.

It was also insisted that Holly could have discharged the defendant from his promise, though it was intended by both parties for the benefit of the plaintiff, and therefore the plaintiff was not entitled to maintain this suit for the recovery of a demand over which he had no control. It is enough that the plaintiff did not release the defendant from his promise, and whether he could or not is a question not now necessarily involved; but if it was, I think it would be found difficult to maintain the right of Holly to discharge a judgment recovered by the plaintiff upon confession or otherwise, for the breach of the defendant's promise; and if he could not, how could he discharge the suit before judgment, or the promise before suit, made as it was for the plaintiff's benefit and in accordance with legal presumption accepted by him (Berly v. Taylor, 5 Hill, 577-584, et seq.), until his dissent was shown. . . . Suppose the defendant had given his note in which, for value received of Holly, he had promised to pay the plaintiff and the plaintiff had accepted the promise, retaining Holly's liability. Very clearly Holly could not have discharged that promise, be the right to release the defendant as it may.

No one can doubt that he owes the sum of money demanded of him, or that in accordance with his promise it was his duty to have paid it to the plaintiff; nor can it be doubted that whatever may be the diversity of opinion elsewhere, the adjudications in this State, from a very early period, approved by experience, have established the defendant's liability; if, therefore, it could be shown that a more strict and technically accurate application of the rules applied, would lead to a different result (which I by no means concede), the effort should not be made in the face of manifest justice.

The judgment should be affirmed. . . .

COMSTOCK, J. (Dissenting.)

The plaintiff had nothing to do with the promise on which he brought this action. It was not made to him, nor did the consideration proceed from him. If he can maintain the suit, it is because an anomaly has found its way into the law on this subject. In general, there must be privity of contract. The party who sues upon a promise must be the promisee, or he must have some legal interest in the undertaking. In this case, it is plain that Holly, who loaned the money to the defendant, and to whom the promise in question was made, could at any time have claimed that it should be performed to himself personally. He had lent the money to the defendant, and at the same time directed the latter to pay the sum to the plaintiff. This direction he could countermand, and if he had done so, manifestly the defendant's promise to pay according to the direction would have ceased to exist. The plaintiff would receive a benefit by a complete execution of the arrangement, but the arrangement itself was between other parties, and was under their exclusive control. If the defendant had paid the money to Holly, his debt would have been discharged thereby. So Holly might have released the demand or assigned it to another person, or the parties might have annulled the promise now in question, and designated some other creditor of Holly as the party to whom the money should be paid. It has never been claimed, that in a case thus situated, the right of a third person to sue upon the promise rested on any sound principle of law. . . .

. . . . In the case before us there was nothing in the nature of a trust or agency. The defendant borrowed the money of Holly and received it as his own. The plaintiff had no right in the fund, legal or equitable. The promise to repay the money created an obligation in favor of the lender to whom it was made and not in favor of any one else.

. . . .

The judgment of the court below should therefore be reversed, and a new trial granted.

GROVER, J., also dissented.

Judgment affirmed.

_____

Behind the Scenes

In *The Property in the Promise: A Study of the Third Party Beneficiary Rule,** Professor Anthony Waters provides additional background on the circumstances of *Lawrence v. Fox.* "Holly" was named as "Samuel Hawley" in the complaint. Historical research of census documents by Professor Waters did not reveal any such person in Buffalo at that time, but there were several Hawleys, only one of whom (Merwin Spencer Hawley) had the financial wherewithal to make a cash loan of $300, a very substantial sum in those days, even for a one-day loan. Hawley was a prominent merchant who became president of the Buffalo Board of Trade in 1856, and Fox was involved in that organization as well, at least at some point.

New York adopted the Field Code in 1856, so pleading the wrong "form" of action was no longer fatal, as it had been under the older rules. Now the complaint had to include allegations of facts sufficient to prove the elements of the claim, regardless of the label attached to

_____

* 98 Harv. L. Rev. 1109 (1985).

the claim. At trial, the plaintiff had to prove each fact alleged in the complaint. Lawrence's complaint was an action for money had and received. This action had evolved over the centuries to apply when a person received money that in equity and good conscience he should refund to the true owner.

The only witness at trial—the "bystander" mentioned at the beginning of the opinion—was William Riley, who testified for Lawrence to establish the elements of the claim. On cross-examination, Fox's attorney elicited from Riley that "Lawrence was not present when Hawley made the loan to Fox; that the deal took place at Mr. Purdy Merritt's on Washington Street; that there were 'two or three persons present . . . doing nothing but standing near them'; and that Hawley counted out the money as he handed it to Fox."*

Both William Riley and Purdy Merritt were horse traders. Nearby was Canal Street, with over a hundred saloons and dives. From these facts, Professor Waters surmised that Hawley loaned the money to Fox for gambling, and that Fox gave a return promise to repay the loan to Lawrence the next day, possibly satisfying Hawley's gambling debt to Lawrence from the day before. Fox's cross-examination questions were meant to signal to the judge that this was a transaction involving gambling, because some New York precedents had refused to enforce contracts tainted by gambling, an unlawful purpose. However, the trial judge disallowed any direct testimony on the link to gambling. Professor Waters concluded,

> Lawrence chose to sue not his debtor, Hawley, but his debtor's debtor, Fox. If, as seems to be the fact, Hawley was a person of considerable wealth in Buffalo, and if, as alleged, he owed three hundred dollars to Lawrence, then Lawrence must have had compelling reason to neglect the obvious action—suing Hawley—in favor of the much more difficult task of seeking recovery from Fox. A gambling debt would have presented just such a reason. If Hawley's debt to Lawrence from the day before, in the round sum of three hundred dollars, was itself the outcome of gambling and thus unenforceable at law, Lawrence was well advised to look for someone other than Hawley to sue.*

If Professor Waters is correct, *Lawrence* is at least the second case you have seen (recall *Kirksey v. Kirksey* in Chapter 2, page 150) in which a plaintiff manipulated a claim to avoid a defense of illegality.

---

* *Id.* at 1125.
** Id..at 1127.

Reading the Law Critically: *Seaver*

1. On what factual basis did Seaver claim that she was owed money by the defendants? A diagram may help (see the template on page 1241).

2. In the course of its analysis, the court reviews and categorizes previous cases in which relief was granted to third-party beneficiaries. In what kinds of cases was such relief allowed? How does the court here synthesize those cases and create a single category of third-party beneficiary with a right to recover?

3. How does the category of third-party beneficiary described in *Seaver* differ from the category articulated in *Lawrence*?

4. You will see within *Seaver* recognition of varying rules regarding the degree to which privity should be required in order to claim breach of contract. Based on the discussion in both *Lawrence* and *Seaver*, what policies support retaining the requirement of privity? What policies support weakening it?

Seaver v. Ransom

SEAVER, Plaintiff-Appellee

v.

RANSOM et al., Defendants-Appellants

promised bequest not in will

Court of Appeals of New York
120 N.E. 639 (N.Y. 1918)

POUND, J.

Judge Beman and his wife were advanced in years. Mrs. Beman was about to die. She had a small estate, consisting of a house and lot in Malone and little else. Judge Beman drew his wife's will according to her instructions. It gave $1,000 to plaintiff, $500 to one sister, plaintiff's mother, and $100 each to another sister and her son, the use of the house to her husband for life, and remainder to the American Society for the Prevention of Cruelty to Animals. She named her husband as residuary legatee and executor. Plaintiff was her niece, 34 years old, in ill health [and] sometimes a member of the Beman household. When the will was read to Mrs. Beman, she said that it was not as she wanted it. She wanted to leave

will not quite right, but not enough energy to write new one

didn't fix it

the house to plaintiff. She had no other objection to the will, but her strength was waning, and, although the judge offered to write another will for her, she said she was afraid she would not hold out long enough to enable her to sign it. So the judge said, if she would sign the will, he would leave plaintiff enough in his will to make up the difference. He avouched the promise by his uplifted hand with all solemnity and his wife then executed the will. When he came to die, it was found that his will made no provision for the plaintiff.

This action was brought, and plaintiff recovered judgment in the trial court, on the theory that Beman had obtained property from his wife and induced her to execute the will in the form prepared by him by his promise to give plaintiff $6,000, the value of the house, and that thereby equity impressed his property with a trust in favor of plaintiff. [The court concludes that no trust existed because Beman received only the right to use the house during his lifetime, not a property interest that could be the basis of a trust.]

An action on the contract for damages . . . stands on different ground. Farmers' Loan & Trust Co. v. Mortimer, 219 N. Y. 290, 294, 295, 114 N. E. 389. The Appellate Division properly passed to the consideration of the question whether the judgment could stand upon the promise made to the wife, upon a valid consideration, for the sole benefit of plaintiff. The judgment of the trial court was affirmed by a return to the general doctrine laid down in the great case of Lawrence v. Fox, 20 N. Y. 268, which has since been limited as herein indicated.

. . . . The general rule, both in law and equity . . . was that privity between a plaintiff and a defendant is necessary to the maintenance of an action on the contract. The consideration must be furnished by the party to whom the promise was made. The contract cannot be enforced against the third party, and therefore it cannot be enforced by him. On the other hand, the right of the beneficiary to sue on a contract made expressly for his benefit has

Take Note!

As early as 1677, the English courts recognized the right of a third-party beneficiary to enforce a contract created by other parties. That rule was reaffirmed a century later but was repudiated in 1861. Meanwhile, in 1857, the New York high court recognized third-party beneficiary rights and expanded those rights in 1918, in *Seaver.* The English common law rule remained opposed to third-party beneficiary rights.* However, UK statutory law slowly expanded third-party beneficiary rights in the late twentieth century, culminating in a 1999 statute that "conferred rights on contract beneficiaries generally."**

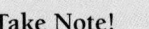

---

* *See* Gary Monserud, *Blending the Law of Sales with the Common Law of Third Party Beneficiaries,* 39 Duq. L. Rev. 111, 114-115 (2000).

** E. Allen Farnsworth, *Farnsworth on Contracts* § 10.2 (3rd ed. 2004).

been fully recognized in many American jurisdictions, either by judicial decision or by legislation, and is said to be "the prevailing rule in this country." Hendrick v. Lindsay, 93 U. S. 143, 23 L. Ed. 855; Lehow v. Simonton, 3 Colo. 346. . . . The reasons for this view are that it is just and practical to permit the person for whose benefit the contract is made to enforce it against one whose duty it is to pay. Other jurisdictions still adhere to the present English rule (7 Halsbury's Laws of England, 342, 343 . . .) that a contract cannot be enforced by or against a person who is not a party . . . .

In New York the right of the beneficiary to sue on contracts made for his benefit is not clearly or simply defined. It is at present confined: First. To cases where there is a pecuniary obligation running from the promisee to the beneficiary, "a legal right founded upon some obligation of the promisee in the third party to adopt and claim the promise as made for his benefit." Farley v. Cleveland, 4 Cow. 432, 15 Am. Dec. 387; Lawrence v. Fox, supra; . . . . Secondly. To cases where the contract is made for the benefit of the wife (Buchanan v. Tilden, 158 N. Y. 109, 52 N. E. 724, 44 L. R. A. 170, 70 Am. St. Rep. 454; Bouton v. Welch, 170 N. Y. 554, 63 N. E. 539), affianced wife (De Cicco v. Schweizer, 221 N. Y. 431, 117 N. E. 807, Ann. Cas. 1918C, 816), or child (Todd v. Weber, 95 N. Y. 181, 193, 47 Am. Rep. 20; Matter of Kidd, 188 N. Y. 274, 80 N. E. 924) of a party to the contract. The close relationship cases go back to the early King's Bench case (1677), long since repudiated in England, of Dutton v. Poole, 2 Lev. 211 (s. c., 1 Ventris, 318, 332). See Schemerhorn v. Vanderheyden, 1 Johns. 139, 3 Am. Dec. 304. The natural and moral duty of the husband or parent to provide for the future of wife or child sustains the action on the contract made for their benefit. "This is the farthest the cases in this state have gone," says Cullen, J., in the marriage settlement case of Borland v. Welch, 162 N. Y. 104, 110, 56 N. E. 556.

The right of the third party is also upheld in, thirdly, the public contract cases (Little v. Banks, 85 N. Y. 258; . . . where the municipality seeks to protect its inhabitants by covenants for their benefit; and, fourthly, the cases where, at the request of a party to the contract, the promise runs directly to the beneficiary although he does not furnish the consideration (Rector, etc., v. Teed, 120 N. Y. 583, 24 N. E. 1014. . . . It may be safely said that a general rule sustaining recovery at the suit of the third party would include but few classes of cases not included in these groups, either categorically or in principle.

The desire of the childless aunt to make provision for a beloved and favorite niece differs imperceptibly in law or in equity from the moral duty of the parent to make testamentary provision for a child. The contract was made for the plaintiff's benefit. She alone is substantially damaged by its breach. The representatives of the wife's estate have no interest in enforcing it specifically. It is said in Buchanan

v. Tilden that the common law imposes moral and legal obligations upon the husband and the parent not measured by the necessaries of life. It was, however, the love and affection or the moral sense of the husband and the parent that imposed such obligations in the cases cited, rather than any common-law duty of husband and parent to wife and child. If plaintiff had been a child of Mrs. Beman, legal obligation would have required no testamentary provision for her, yet the child could have enforced a covenant in her favor identical with the covenant of Judge Beman in this case. . . . The dependent or faithful niece may have a stronger claim than the affluent or unworthy son. . . .

The court in [*Lawrence v. Fox*] attempted to adopt the general doctrine that any third person, for whose direct benefit a contract was intended, could sue on it. . . . but Vrooman v. Turner, supra, confined its application to the facts on which it was decided. "In every case in which an action has been sustained," says Allen, J., "there has been a debt or duty owing by the promisee to the party claiming to sue upon the promise." 69 N. Y. 285, 25 Am. Rep. 195. As late as Townsend v. Rackham, 143 N. Y. 516, 523, 38 N. E. 731, 733, we find Peckham, J., saying that, "to maintain the action by the third person, there must be this liability to him on the part of the promisee." Buchanan v. Tilden went further than any case since Lawrence v. Fox in a desire to do justice rather than to apply with technical accuracy strict rules calling for a legal or equitable obligation. . . .

In Wright v. Glen Telephone Co., 48 Misc. Rep. 192, 195, 95 N. Y. Supp. 101, the learned presiding justice who wrote the opinion in this case said at Trial Term:

> "The right of a third person to recover upon a contract made by other parties for his benefit must rest upon the peculiar circumstances of each case rather than upon the law of some other case."

. . . .

But, on principle, a sound conclusion may be reached. If Mrs. Beman had left her husband the house on condition that he pay the plaintiff $6,000, and he had accepted the devise, he would have become personally liable to pay the legacy, and plaintiff could have recovered in an action at law against him, whatever the value of the house. Gridley v. Gridley, 24 N. Y. 130; Brown v. Knapp, 79 N. Y. 136, 143 . . . . That would be because the testatrix had in substance bequeathed the promise to plaintiff, and not because close relationship or moral obligation sustained the contract. The distinction between an implied promise to a testator for the benefit of a third party to pay a legacy and an unqualified promise on a valuable consideration to make provision for the third party by will is discernible, but not obvious. The tendency of American authority is to sustain the gift in all such cases and to permit the donee beneficiary to recover on the contract. Matter of Edmundson's Estate (1918, Pa.) 103 Atl. 277, 259 Pa. 429. The equities are with the plaintiff, and they may be enforced in this action, whether it be regarded as an action for damages or an action for specific performance to convert the defendants into trustees for plaintiff's benefit under the agreement.

The judgment should be affirmed, with costs.

HOGAN, CARDOZO, and CRANE, JJ., concur. HISCOCK, C. J., and COLLIN and ANDREWS, JJ., dissent.

---

§ 3.2. Third-Party Beneficiaries in the Restatements

In the early twentieth century, American jurisdictions struggled with defining the rights of third-party beneficiaries, and the rules varied among jurisdictions. Professor Gary Monserud argues persuasively that "[t]he development of twentieth century law pertaining to third party beneficiaries seems, in hindsight, very improbable had it not been for the labors of the two great scholars, Professors Samuel Williston and Arthur Corbin," who wrote influential articles assessing the state of third-party beneficiary law and urging the recognition of third party rights.* The two then worked together to add recognition of third-party beneficiary rights to the first Restatement of Contracts.

The Restatement (Second) reconfigured the categories in 1979, but each Restatement is in effect in some jurisdictions, as is the approach reflected in the two New York cases that began this portion of the chapter. The courts continue to struggle with articulating the most appropriate rule regarding the rights of third-party beneficiaries to contracts, as reflected in the contemporary cases below.

Reading the Law Critically:
Third-Party Beneficiaries in the [First] Restatement

Restatement § 133 defines three categories of third-party beneficiaries. Other sections of the Restatement establish that donee and creditor beneficiaries have the right to enforce a contract, but incidental beneficiaries do not.

---

* Gary Monserud, *Blending the Law of Sales with the Common Law of Third Party Beneficiaries*, 39 Duq. L. Rev. 111, 118-19 (2000).

1.   How do the categories in § 133 compare to the types of third-party beneficiaries described in *Lawrence* and *Seaver*? How do the duties in §§ 135 and 136 compare to the duties in the two cases?

2.   Would the third-party beneficiaries in *Lawrence* and *Seaver* have a right to recover under the first Restatement?

Restatement § 133. **Definition Of Donee Beneficiary, Creditor Beneficiary, Incidental Beneficiary**

(1) Where performance of a promise in a contract will benefit a person other than the promisee, that person is, except as stated in Subsection (3):

(a) a donee beneficiary if it appears from the terms of the promise in view of the accompanying circumstances that the purpose of the promisee in obtaining the promise of all or part of the performance thereof is to make a gift to the beneficiary or to confer upon him a right against the promisor to some performance neither due nor supposed or asserted to be due from the promisee to the beneficiary;

(b) a creditor beneficiary if no purpose to make a gift appears from the terms of the promise in view of the accompanying circumstances and performance of the promise will satisfy an actual or supposed or asserted duty of the promisee to the beneficiary, or a right of the beneficiary against the promisee which has been barred by the Statute of Limitations or by a discharge in bankruptcy, or which is unenforceable because of the Statute of Frauds;

(c) an incidental beneficiary if neither the facts stated in Clause (a) nor those stated in Clause (b) exist.

(2) Such a promise as is described in Subsection (1a) is a gift promise [see § 135]. Such a promise as is described in Subsection (1b) is a promise to discharge the promisee's duty [see § 136].

. . . .

Restatement § 135. **Duties Created By A Gift Promise**

Except as stated in § 140,

(a) a gift promise in a contract creates a duty of the promisor to the donee beneficiary to perform the promise; and the duty can be enforced by the donee beneficiary for his own benefit;

(b) a gift promise also creates a duty of the promisor to the promisee to render the promised performance to the donee beneficiary.

Restatement § 136. **Duties Created By A Promise To Discharge A Duty**

(1) Except as stated in §§ 140, 143,
  (a) a promise to discharge the promisee's duty creates a duty of the promisor to the creditor beneficiary to perform the promise;
  (b) a promise to discharge the promisee's duty creates also a duty to the promisee;
  (c) whole or partial satisfaction of the promisor's duty to the creditor beneficiary satisfies to that extent the promisor's duty to the promisee;
  (d) whole or partial satisfaction of the promisor's duty to the promisee in any other way than by rendering the promised performance in whole or in part does not limit the promisor's duty to the creditor beneficiary.

(2) . . . .

can't fulfil debt some other way

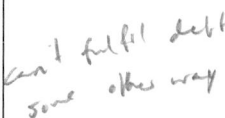

Reading the Law Critically: Third-Party Beneficiaries in the Restatement (Second) and UNIDROIT

1. Under the Restatement (Second) rules, what is the legal consequence of being an intended beneficiary? An incidental beneficiary?

2. Compare the categories of third-party beneficiaries articulated in the Restatement (Second) and those articulated in the first Restatement. What effect might those differences have on the availability of relief for third parties?

3. Would the third-party beneficiaries in *Lawrence* and *Seaver* have a right to recover under the Restatement (Second)?

4. How do the UNIDROIT provisions compare to the Restatement (Second)?

Restatement (Second) § 302. **Intended And Incidental Beneficiaries**

(1) Unless otherwise agreed between promisor and promisee, a beneficiary of a promise is an intended beneficiary if recognition of a right to performance in the beneficiary is appropriate to effectuate the intention of the parties and either
  (a) the performance of the promise will satisfy an obligation of the promisee to pay money to the beneficiary; or
  (b) the circumstances indicate that the promisee intends to give the beneficiary the benefit of the promised performance.

> (2) An incidental beneficiary is a beneficiary who is not an intended beneficiary.
>
> Restatement (Second) § 304. **Creation Of Duty To Beneficiary**
>
> A promise in a contract creates a duty in the promisor to any intended beneficiary to perform the promise, and the intended beneficiary may enforce the duty.
>
> Restatement (Second) § 315. **Effect Of A Promise Of Incidental Benefit**
>
> An incidental beneficiary acquires by virtue of the promise no right against the promisor or the promisee.
>
> ——————
>
> UNIDROIT, Art. 5.2.1. **Contracts in Favour of Third Parties**
>
> (1) The parties (the "promisor" and the "promisee") may confer by express or implied agreement a right on a third party (the "beneficiary").
> (2) The existence and content of the beneficiary's right against the promisor are determined by the agreement of the parties and are subject to any conditions or other limitations under the agreement.
>
> UNIDROIT, Art. 5.2.2. **Third Party Identifiable**
>
> The beneficiary must be identifiable with adequate certainty by the contract but need not be in existence at the time the contract is made.

§ 3.3. Contemporary Cases

The cases below provide an opportunity to see the application of third-party beneficiary doctrine in complex but common circumstances. The first case considers the relationships among persons performing construction work when only some of the actors are identified explicitly in bonds mandated in the construction contract. The second case raises important questions about beneficiaries' rights to enforce contracts entered by the government to obtain goods or services for a portion of the public.

 Reading the Law Critically: *Cretex Companies*

1. Who were the parties to the various contracts, and which third-party beneficiary(ies) could recover under the contract? A diagram may help (see page 1241 for a template).

2. Immediately prior to this case, what was Minnesota's test for determining which third-party beneficiaries can enforce a contract? Does this court's adoption of the Restatement (Second) scheme of classifying third-party beneficiaries pre-empt Minnesota's existing common law test? If not, what is the existing Minnesota rule?

3. What is the dissent's core disagreement with the majority? Is it the pertinent facts, the interpretations of those facts, the application of the law, or a policy disagreement?

Cretex Companies v. Construction Leaders, Inc.

THE CRETEX COMPANIES, INC., and ESS BROTHERS & SONS, INC.,
Plaintiffs-Respondents

v.

CONSTRUCTION LEADERS, INC., Defendant

and

TRAVELERS INDEMNITY COMPANY, Defendant-Appellant

Supreme Court of Minnesota
342 N.W.2d 135 (Minn. 1984)

SIMONETT, Justice.

We conclude that unpaid materialmen, plaintiff-respondents on this appeal, are not intended third-party beneficiaries under the defaulting general contractor's performance bond and, therefore, are not entitled to recover from the defendant-appellant surety. We reverse the trial court.

Northland Mortgage Company owns property in Maple Grove and Plymouth, Minnesota. It engaged defendant Construction Leaders, Inc., as its general contractor, to do the utilities construction for the development projects on the two properties. Defendant-appellant Travelers Indemnity Company wrote the performance bonds for the construction projects. There were two construction contracts and, since the work was to be done in five phases, five performance bonds. For each performance bond Travelers was the surety, Construction Leaders, Inc., as general contractor, was the principal, and Northland Mortgage Company, as owner of the projects, was the obligee.

Thereafter, during the course of its work, Construction Leaders defaulted and is now apparently insolvent. Travelers stepped in and hired another contractor, who completed the work. Some of Construction Leader's suppliers and subcontractors, however, were left unpaid, including plaintiff-respondents, The Cretex Companies, Inc., and Ess Brothers & Sons, Inc. Although Cretex and Ess Brothers could have filed mechanic's liens against Northland's property, they failed to do so; apparently they assumed their materials were to be used by the general contractor on public projects and they did not discover otherwise until it was too late to file liens. Having lost their lien rights, Cretex and Ess Brothers brought this action against Travelers in an attempt to collect on the performance bonds. In addition, plaintiffs sued the general contractor, Construction Leaders, for breach of their subcontracts.

Make the Connection

Recall the earlier discussion of mechanic's liens in *Drake v. Bell* (Chapter 3, page 187).

On cross-motions for summary judgment, the trial court granted summary judgment in favor of the plaintiff suppliers against both the surety and the general contractor on the issue of liability. The parties then stipulated to the amount of damages. Travelers alone appeals, raising only the issue whether plaintiffs are entitled to recover their unpaid claims under the performance bonds.

The issue is whether unpaid materialmen are third-party intended beneficiaries under Travelers' bonds. First of all, it should be noted that the two construction contracts between Northland (the owner) and Construction Leaders (the general contractor) plainly call for a performance rather than a payment bond. The contracts require:

> A good and sufficient *performance bond* in the sum of not less than the full amount of the Contract, payable to the Owner, as provided by law, shall be made and delivered . . . .

> The *Performance Bond* shall guarantee the Contractors: [sic] performance as required by these Contract Documents, satisfaction of all lien rights of Sub-contractors and materials suppliers, ...

(Emphasis added.) Pursuant to this contract requirement, Travelers, as surety, issued its "Contract Bond" with Construction Leaders as principal and Northland as obligee, providing:

> NOW, THEREFORE, the condition of this obligation is such, that if the Principal shall faithfully perform the contract on his part, free and clear of all liens arising out of claims for labor and materials entering into the construction, and indemnify and save harmless the Obligee from all loss,

cost or damage which he may suffer by reason of the failure so to do, then this obligation shall be void; otherwise to remain in full force and effect.

It seems clear enough, at least so far, that the contracting parties intended to have only a performance bond. The purpose of a performance bond is to ensure that the principal or his surety will perform the contract for an agreed price. Because performance of the work alone is not sufficient to protect the owner-obligee, the surety also agrees to indemnify the owner-obligee for any loss from liens filed against the property by reason of the contractor-principal's default in payment of his materialmen. Thus Travelers claims here that its bonds were intended for the exclusive use and benefit of its obligee, Northland, and afford no contractual rights to third-party subcontractors or suppliers.

Travelers points out that if the owner and general contractor had wished to protect third-party materialmen they could have purchased, for a separate premium, a "labor and material payment bond," a bond which Travelers also sells and which is usually issued simultaneously with the performance bond. A "payment" bond expressly provides for the surety to pay the claims of third-party subcontractors and materialmen if the general contractor fails to do so.[1] The distinction between performance bonds and payment bonds is well recognized in the construction industry; the two bonds cover different risks and premiums are set accordingly. *See, e.g.,* Scales-Douwes Corp. v. Paulaura Realty Corp., 24 N.Y.2d 724, 301 N.Y.S.2d 980, 249 N.E.2d 760 (1969) . . . .

Plaintiff-respondents argue, however, that though Travelers' bond may be in form a "performance" bond, intended for the protection of the owner-obligee, it is also in fact a "payment" bond, intended for the benefit of third persons who are not parties to the surety's contract. To reach this conclusion, respondents rely on the third-party contract beneficiary doctrine.

The trial court found, and Travelers does not dispute, that the provisions of the underlying construction contracts are incorporated by reference into the bonds, and apparently not just for identification purposes. Each bond identifies the construction contract between Northland and Construction Leaders and adds "a copy of which is by reference made a part hereof." Among other things, section 9 of the construction contract reads that "the Contractor shall provide and pay for all materials, labor, water, tools, equipment, light, power, transportation and other facilities necessary for the execution and completion of the work." Other sections provide that if the contractor fails to pay subcontractors or materialmen, the owner may terminate the contract or withhold payments. From this respon-

---

[1] Thus Travelers' form of "labor and material payment bond" reads that the surety is bound to the owner-obligee "for the use and benefit of claimants as hereinbelow defined," and the bond then defines claimants as those having a contract with the principal to provide materials and services.

dents argue as follows: the bond is conditioned on full and faithful performance of the construction contract by the principal-general contractor; performance of the contract by the contractor includes payment by the contractor of the claims of his subcontractors and materialmen; therefore, the surety has agreed that if the contractor does not pay his suppliers, the surety will do it for him, thus making the suppliers third-party intended beneficiaries of the bond. . . .

The parties all cite Buchman Plumbing Co. v. Regents of the University of Minnesota, 298 Minn. 328, 215 N.W.2d 479 (1974), as setting out the controlling test or tests for a third-party contract beneficiary. There we described two tests: first, an "intent to benefit" test, *i.e.,* the contract must express some intent by the parties to benefit the third party through contractual performance; and, second, a "duty owed" test, *i.e.,* that the promisor's performance under the contract must discharge a duty otherwise owed the third party by the promisee. Respondents contend that the "duty owed" requirement is satisfied in this case where payment of their claims by the surety would discharge a duty owed them by Northland, as owner of the project improved at their expense. We disagree. Clearly, Northland has no legal responsibility to pay the subcontractors and materialmen who made their own separate contracts with the general contractor. Duluth Lumber & Plywood Co. v. Delta Development, Inc., 281 N.W.2d 377, 384 (Minn.1979). Indeed, plaintiffs seem to concede as much because they have not sued Northland. Consequently, if plaintiffs are to recover on the bonds, they must do so under the "intent to benefit" test. Travelers, however, reads Buchman to require that *both* the "duty owed" and the "intent to benefit" tests must be met before a third party obtains rights in the contract. Although the language in Buchman is somewhat opaque, we do not think this is what *Buchman* requires or says.

At this point, it may be helpful to review briefly the status of our third-party contract beneficiary law. By 1940 this court, relying on Restatement of Contracts § 133 (1932), was recognizing three kinds of third-party contract beneficiaries: creditor, donee, and incidental. In Northern National Bank v. Northern Minnesota National Bank, 244 Minn. 202, 209, 70 N.W.2d 118, 124 (1955), we defined, in dictum, a donee beneficiary as "one to whom the promisee intends to make a gift." In Buchman, supra , we observed in a footnote that the then tentative draft of the second edition of the Restatement of Contracts proposed to substitute the term "intended" beneficiary for both "creditor" and "donee" beneficiary. Id., 298 Minn. at 333-34 n. 2, 215 N.W.2d at 483 n. 2. This proposed change was, indeed, incorporated into Restatement (Second) of Contracts in 1979 and appears at section 302. The Reporter's note explains that the new classification between "intended" and "incidental" beneficiaries eliminates the subclass of "donee beneficiary" which has proved confusing in the many instances where the promisee's purpose is not "to make a gift" but "to confer a right." In Duluth Lumber & Plywood Co. v. Delta Development, Inc., 281 N.W.2d 377 (1979), we used the new "intended-incidental" analysis. There a materialman sued as a third-party beneficiary under a Housing and Urban Development contract made with the Housing Authority of the Indian reservation for construction work to be performed on the Indian reservation. Because the property was public, no liens could be filed. We found no duty owed by the owner to pay the materialman but nevertheless found that the materialman was an "intended beneficiary" under the HUD contract. . . .

We hereby adopt the intended beneficiary approach outlined in Restatement (Second) of Contracts § 302 (1979). Under this approach, if recognition of third-party beneficiary rights is "appropriate" and *either* the duty owed *or* the intent to benefit test is met, the third party can recover as an "intended beneficiary." For the third party to recover, there is no need to satisfy *both* the duty owed and the intent to benefit tests, and, contrary to Travelers' contention, the language in Buchman does not so require. Consequently, even though respondent materialmen have failed to meet the "duty owed" test here, they may still recover if they can show an intent by the contracting parties to confer on them a benefit. We conclude, however, that the requisite intent to make subcontractors and material-men third-party intended beneficiaries of Travelers' bonds is not shown here and that plaintiff-respondents are, at best, incidental third-party beneficiaries.

Travelers' performance bond, read alone, evidences an intent to protect and benefit only the owner-obligee. Plaintiff-respondent argues, however, that if the underlying construction contract is read as part of the bond, a further intent to confer a benefit on materialmen appears, notwithstanding that the construction contract itself expressly states that the general contractor need furnish only a performance bond. Because the contractor promises in the construction con-tract to "pay for all materials [and] labor," respondents contend that the surety's "guaranty" of this promise shows an intent by the parties to the bond to confer a benefit on those who have furnished the materials and labor. We do not think this conclusion necessarily follows, for while in fact the materialmen receive a benefit when paid by the surety, the issue is whether that benefit was intended by the contracting parties.

Other courts have reached differing results on whether materialmen can recover on a performance bond, the result often depending on the particular facts of the case, particularly the wording of the bond. . . .

The contract must be read in the light of all the circumstances and it is per-tinent, in ascertaining intent, to inquire to whom performance is to be rendered. Buchman, 298 Minn. at 334, 215 N.W.2d at 483. Here we are dealing with a contract of suretyship and, it seems to us, the fair import of this contract is that the contracting parties intended the surety's performance to be rendered to

Northland, the owner-obligee, not to the materialmen. The language of the bond, quite clearly, intends to make certain (1) that the contract will be performed; (2) that the property will be "free and clear of all liens arising out of claims for labor and materials entering into the construction"; and (3) that the owner-obligee will be indemnified and saved harmless from all loss "which he may suffer by reason of the failure so to do." In other words, if the contractor-principal defaults, the surety is obligated to complete the project. If there are any liens filed, the surety is obligated to satisfy them—and the lienholders, quite plainly, would be third-party intended beneficiaries of the bond. If, finally, there are any materialmen left unpaid by the defaulting contractor who have failed to file liens, the surety need only pay these claims to the extent necessary to save the owner-obligee harmless from loss by reason of the contractor-principal's failure "so to do." These obligations the surety must perform to the amount of the bond. If unpaid, non-lienholding subcontractors can collect under the bond, the fund provided by the bond might be so depleted as to jeopardize completion of the project, which would surely be contrary to the intent of the contracting parties.

Another circumstance to be considered in ascertaining the intent of the parties is whether the suretyship contract is for a private or public construction project. There would seem to be no reason for the contracting parties to intend to confer a benefit on materialmen who can protect their own interests by filing liens against the property. In Hedberg & Sons Co. v. Galvin, 274 Minn. 422, 144 N.W.2d 263 (1966), the surety issued a bond to a cement contractor, guaranteeing, as required by a city ordinance licensing contractors, that the contractor would pay for any materials used by him in his construction projects "for the benefit of and to protect any person for whom such cement work shall be done." It was held that the bond was not intended for the protection of the unpaid materialmen but for the owner, for whom the "work shall be done." We stated that if unpaid materialmen wanted to be protected their recourse was to file a lien on the owner's property, whereupon the owner would have the surety bond for protection. We think these same considerations are relevant here. In Duluth Lumber & Plywood Co. v. Delta Development, Inc., 281 N.W.2d 377, 385 (Minn.1979), by way of significant contrast, we held unpaid materialmen to be third-party intended beneficiaries of a contract for the disbursement of federal funds for payment of housing on an Indian reservation because "if construction work is performed on public property that is exempt from a mechanics lien, then promises in the contract concerning payment of materialmen will be deemed to be for the benefit of the materialmen because the public owner does not need protection against a mechanics lien and because of the injustice which would otherwise be suffered by the materialmen who have no lien rights."

While we acknowledge that third-party recovery is warranted in cases where the surety bond explicitly or by reasonable implication expresses an intent to benefit third-party subcontractors and materialmen, we do not believe an "intent to benefit" third parties should be imputed to a surety on the basis of a private construction contract to which that surety was not a party, when the language of the surety's bond, though incorporating the construction contract by reference, evinces no more than an incidental intent to benefit those third parties. We hold that plaintiff-respondents, as unpaid subcontractors and material-men, are not third-party intended beneficiaries of Travelers' surety bonds covering performance of this private construction project.

Think About It!

Would the result have been different if there had been a payment bond? Would the result have been different if the materialmen had filed liens?

Reversed.

YETKA, Justice (dissenting).

Travelers' bond obligates it "faithfully [to] perform the contract." The majority unnecessarily restricts this language when it holds that the surety is only obligated to "complete the project." Here, the Travelers' bond incorporated portions of the general contract between Northland and Construction Leaders. Section 9 of that contract contained language, as the majority acknowledges, which read as follows: "The Contractor shall provide and pay for all materials, labor, water, tools, equipment, light, power, transportation and other facilities necessary for the execution and completion of the work." Under this language, the contract is not "performed" until all materials provided thereunder are paid for.

Construction jobs are not negotiated in a vacuum. Almost all of the parties, including subcontractors, are experienced people and are aware of the conditions of the general contract. If Travelers wanted to limit their obligation under the bond to completion of the project only, it should have clearly stated so. It did not; therefore, in my opinion, the subcontractors had a right to rely on the conditions of the general contract as guaranteed by the bond.

I would affirm the trial court.

Food for Thought

The Restatement (Second) provisions on third-party beneficiaries were drafted in response to criticism of the two-pronged definition of donee beneficiaries in Restatement § 133, but the modern categories have continued to raise problems. Among the concerns is the fact that Restatement (Second) § 302 first says that whether a beneficiary is "intended" or not depends on "the intentions of *the parties*" but then adds a requirement, in one branch, that "the *promisee* intends" to give the beneficiary the benefit of the performance. "This double use of intent, coupled with the inherent ambiguity of the term 'intent,' has perplexed courts and stimulated commentators since the Restatement Second's adoption."* Suggestions for reconfiguring the categories to bring more coherence to the doctrine can be found in Harry G. Prince, *Perfecting the Third Party Beneficiary Standing Rule Under Section 302 of the Restatement (Second) Contracts*, 25 B.C. L. Rev. 919 (1984); Jean F. Powers, *Expanded Liability and Intent Requirement in Third Party Beneficiary Contracts*, 1993 Utah L. Rev. 67; Melvin A. Eisenberg, *Third Party Beneficiaries*, 92 Colum. L. Rev. 1358 (1992); Orma S. Paglin, *Criteria for the Recognition of Third Party Beneficiaries' Rights*, 24 New Eng. L. Rev. 63 (1989).

Reading the Law Critically: *Martinez*

1. Who were the parties to the various contracts? Which third-party beneficiary(ies) could recover under each contract? A diagram may help (see page 1241 for a template).

2. Why did these plaintiffs fail to get relief? Do you agree with the majority or the dissent in *Martinez*?

3. Is the standard defining intended beneficiaries applied correctly in *Martinez*? If you think so but also think the plaintiffs should have been allowed to enforce the contract entered into by the United States, what line would you draw between intended and incidental beneficiaries? What line would the dissent draw?

---

* Gary Monserud, *Blending the Law of Sales with the Common Law of Third Party Beneficiaries*, 39 Duq. L. Rev. 111, 124 (2000).

Martinez v. Socoma Companies, Inc.

IGNACIO MARTINEZ et al., Plaintiffs-Appellants

v.

SOCOMA COMPANIES, INC., et al., Defendants-Respondents

Supreme Court of California

521 P.2d 841 (Cal. 1974)

WRIGHT, Chief Justice.

Plaintiffs brought this class action on behalf of themselves and other disadvantaged unemployed persons, alleging that defendants failed to perform contracts with the United States government under which defendants agreed to provide job training and at least one year of employment to certain numbers of such persons. Plaintiffs claim that they and the other such persons are third party beneficiaries of the contracts and as such are entitled to damages for defendants' nonperformance. General demurrers to the complaint were sustained without leave to amend, apparently on the ground that plaintiffs lacked standing to sue as third party beneficiaries. Dismissals were entered as to the demurring defendants, and plaintiffs appeal.

We affirm the judgments of dismissal. As will appear, the contracts nowhere state that either the government or defendants are to be liable to persons such as plaintiffs for damages resulting from the defendants' nonperformance. The benefits to be derived from defendants' performance were clearly intended not as gifts from the government to such persons but as a means of executing the public purposes stated in the contracts and in the underlying legislation. Accordingly, plaintiffs were only incidental beneficiaries and as such have no right of recovery.

The complaint names as defendants Socoma Companies, Inc. ("Socoma"), Lady Fair Kitchens, Incorporated ("Lady Fair"), Monarch Electronics International, Inc. ("Monarch"), and eleven individuals of whom three are alleged officers or directors of Socoma, four of Lady Fair, and four of Monarch. Lady Fair and the individual defendants associated with it, a Utah corporation and Utah residents respectively, did not appear in the trial court and are not parties to this appeal.

The complaint alleges that under 1967 amendments to the Economic Opportunity Act of 1964 (81 Stat. 688-690, 42 U.S.C.§§ 2763-2768, repealed by 86 Stat. 703 (1972)) "the United States Congress instituted Special Impact Programs with the intent to benefit the residents of certain neighborhoods having especially large concentrations of low income persons and suffering from dependency, chronic unemployment and rising tensions." Funds to administer these programs were appropriated to the United States Department of Labor. The department subsequently designated the East Los Angeles neighborhood as a "Special Impact area" and made federal funds available for contracts with local private industry for the benefit of the "hard-core unemployed residents" of East Los Angeles.

On January 17, 1969, the corporate defendants allegedly entered into contracts with the Secretary of Labor, acting on behalf of the Manpower Administration, United States Department of Labor (hereinafter referred to as the "Government"). Each such defendant entered into a separate contract and all three contracts are made a part of the complaint as exhibits. Under each contract the contracting defendant agreed to lease space in the then vacant Lincoln Heights jail building owned by the City of Los Angeles, to invest at least $5,000,000 in renovating the leasehold and establishing a facility for the manufacture of certain articles, to train and employ in such facility for at least 12 months, at minimum wage rates, a specified number of East Los Angeles residents certified as disadvantaged by the Government, and to provide such employees with opportunities for promotion into available supervisorial-managerial positions and with options to purchase stock in their employer corporation. Each contract provided for the lease of different space in the building and for the manufacture of a different kind of product. As consideration, the Government agreed to pay each defendant a stated amount in installments. Socoma was to hire 650 persons and receive $950,000; Lady Fair was to hire 550 persons and receive $999,000; and Monarch was to hire 400 persons and receive $800,000. The hiring of these persons was to be completed by January 17, 1970.

Plaintiffs were allegedly members of a class of no more than 2,017 East Los Angeles residents who were certified as disadvantaged and were qualified for employment under the contracts. Although the Government paid $712,500 of the contractual consideration to Socoma, $299,700 to Lady Fair, and $240,000 to Monarch, all of these defendants failed to perform under their respective contracts, except that Socoma provided 186 jobs of which 139 were wrongfully terminated, and Lady Fair provided 90 jobs, of which all were wrongfully terminated.

The complaint contains 11 causes of action. The second, fourth, and sixth causes of action seek damages of $3,607,500 against Socoma, $3,052,500 against Lady Fair, and $2,220,000 against Monarch, calculated on the basis of 12 months' wages at minimum rates and $1,000 for loss of training for each of the jobs the defendant contracted to provide. [The remaining causes of action are omitted.]

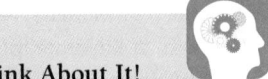

Think About It!

Do the plaintiffs seek expectation, reliance, or restitution damages from Socoma, Lady Fair, and Monarch? Would a claim for a different measure of damages have fared better?

. . . [W]e must determine whether the pleaded written contracts support plaintiffs' claim either on their face or under any interpretation to which the contracts are reasonably susceptible and which is pleaded in the complaint or could be pleaded by proper amendment. . . .

Plaintiffs contend they are third party beneficiaries under Civil Code section 1559, which provides: "A contract, made expressly for the benefit of a third person, may be enforced by him at any time before the parties thereto rescind it." This section excludes enforcement of a contract by persons who are only incidentally or remotely benefited by it. (Lucas v. Hamm (1961) 56 Cal.2d 583, 590, 15 Cal.Rptr. 821, 824, 364 P.2d 685, 688.) American law generally classifies persons having enforceable rights under contracts to which they are not parties as either creditor beneficiaries or donee beneficiaries. (Rest., Contracts, §§ 133, subds. (1), (2) . . . see Rest.2d Contracts (Tentative Drafts 1973) § 133, coms. b, c.) California decisions follow this classification. . . .

A person cannot be a creditor beneficiary unless the promisor's performance of the contract will discharge some form of legal duty owed to the beneficiary by the promisee. (. . . Rest., Contracts, § 133, subd. (1)(b).) Clearly the Government (the promisee) at no time bore any legal duty toward plaintiffs to provide the benefits set forth in the contracts and plaintiffs do not claim to be creditor beneficiaries.

A person is a donee beneficiary only if the promisee's contractual intent is either to make a gift to him or to confer on him a right against the promisor. (Rest., Contracts, § 133, subd. (1)(a).) If the promisee intends to make a gift, the donee beneficiary can recover if such donative intent must have been understood by the promisor from the nature of the contract and the circumstances accompanying its execution. (Lucas v. Hamm, supra, 56 Cal.2d at pp. 590-591, 15 Cal.Rptr. 821, 364 P.2d 685.) This rule does not aid plaintiffs, however, because, as will be seen, no intention to make a gift can be imputed to the Government as promisee.

Unquestionably plaintiffs were among those whom the Government intended to benefit through defendants' performance of the contracts which recite that they are executed pursuant to a statute and a presidential directive calling for programs to furnish disadvantaged persons with training and employment opportunities. However, the fact that a Government program for social betterment confers benefits upon individuals who are not required to render contractual consideration in return does not necessarily imply that the benefits are intended as gifts. Congress' power to spend money in aid of the general welfare (U.S.Const., art. I, § 8) authorizes federal programs to alleviate national unemployment. (Helvering v. Davis (1937) 301 U.S. 619, 640-645, 57 S.Ct. 904, 81 L.Ed. 1307.) The benefits of such programs are provided not simply as gifts to the recipients but as a means of accomplishing a larger public purpose. The furtherance of the public purpose is in the nature of consideration to the Government, displacing any governmental intent to furnish the benefits as gifts. (See County of Alameda v. Janssen (1940) 16 Cal.2d 276, 281, 106 P.2d 11 . . .).

Even though a person is not the intended recipient of a gift, he may nevertheless be "a donee beneficiary if it appears from the terms of the promise in view of the accompanying circumstances that the purpose of the promisee in obtaining the promise . . . is . . . to confer upon him a right against the promisor to some performance neither due nor supposed or asserted to be due from the promisee to the beneficiary." (Rest., Contracts, § 133, subd. (1)(a) . . .). The Government may, of course, deliberately implement a public purpose by including provisions in its contracts which expressly confer on a specified class of third persons a direct right to benefits, or damages in lieu of benefits, against the private contractor. But a governmental intent to confer such a direct right cannot be inferred simply from the fact that the third persons were intended to enjoy the benefits. The Restatement of Contracts makes this clear in dealing specifically with contractual promises to the Government to render services to members of the public: "A promisor bound to the United States or to a State or municipality by contract to do an act or render a service to some or all of the members of the public, is subject to no duty under the contract to such members to give compensation for the injurious consequences of performing or attempting to perform it, or of failing to do so, unless, . . . an intention is manifested in the contract, as interpreted in the light of the circumstances surrounding its formation, that the promisor shall compensate members of the public for such injurious consequences. . . ." (Rest., Contracts, § 145 . . .)

The present contracts manifest no intent that the defendants pay damages to compensate plaintiffs or other members of the public for their nonperformance. To the contrary, the contracts' provisions for retaining the Government's control over determination of contractual disputes and for limiting defendants' financial risks indicate a governmental purpose to exclude the direct rights against defendants claimed here.

Each contract provides that any dispute of fact arising thereunder is to be determined by written decision of the Government's contracting officer, subject to an appeal to the Secretary of Labor, whose decision shall be final unless determined by a competent court to have been fraudulent, capricious, arbitrary, in bad faith, or not supported by substantial evidence. These administrative decisions may include determinations of related questions of law although such determinations are not made final. The efficiency and uniformity of interpretation fostered by these administrative procedures would tend to be undermined if litigation such as the present action, to which the Government is a stranger, were permitted to proceed on the merits.

In addition to the provisions on resolving disputes each contract contains a "liquidated damages" provision obligating the contractor to refund all amounts received from the Government, with interest, in the event of failure to acquire and equip the specified manufacturing facility, and, for each employment opportunity it fails to provide, to refund a stated dollar amount equivalent to the total contract compensation divided by the number of jobs agreed to be provided. This liquidated damages provision limits liability for the breaches alleged by plaintiffs to the refunding of amounts received and indicates an absence of any contractual intent to impose liability directly in favor of plaintiffs, or, as claimed in the complaint, to impose liability for the value of the promised performance. To allow plaintiffs' claim would nullify the limited liability for which defendants bargained and which the Government may well have held out as an inducement in negotiating the contracts.

It is this absence of any manifestation of intent that defendants should pay compensation for breach to persons in the position of plaintiffs that distinguishes this case from Shell v. Schmidt (1954) 126 Cal.App.2d 279, 272 P.2d 82, relied on by plaintiffs. The defendant in Shell was a building contractor who had entered into an agreement with the federal government under which he received priorities for building materials and agreed in return to use the materials to build homes with required specifications for sale to war veterans at or below ceiling prices. Plaintiffs were 12 veterans, each of whom had purchased a home that failed to comply with the agreed specifications. They were held entitled to recover directly from the defendant contractor as third party beneficiaries of his agreement with the government. The legislation under which the agreement was made included a provision empowering the government to obtain payment of monetary compensation by the contractor to the veteran purchasers for deficiencies resulting from failure to comply with specifications. Thus, there was "an intention . . . manifested in the contract . . . that the promisor shall compensate members of the public for such injurious consequences (of nonperformance)." . . .

. . . . The congressional declaration of purpose of the Economic Opportunity Act as a whole points up the public nature of its benefits on a national scale. Congress declared that the purpose of the act was to "strengthen, supplement, and coordinate efforts in furtherance of (the) policy" of "opening to everyone the opportunity for education and training, the opportunity to work, and the opportunity to live in decency and dignity" so that the "United States can achieve its full economic and social potential as a nation." (42 U.S.C. § 2701.)

In providing for special impact programs, Congress declared that such programs were directed to the solution of critical problems existing in particular neighborhoods having especially large concentration of low-income persons, and that the programs were intended to be of sufficient size and scope to have an appreciable impact in such neighborhoods in arresting tendencies toward dependency, chronic unemployment, and rising community tensions. (42 U.S.C. former § 2763.) Thus the contracts here were designed not to benefit individuals as such but to utilize the training and employment of disadvantaged persons as a means of improving the East Los Angeles neighborhood. Moreover, the means by which the contracts were intended to accomplish this community improvement were not confined to provision of the particular benefits on which plaintiffs base their claim to damages—one year's employment at minimum wages plus $1,000 worth of training to be provided to each of 650 persons by one defendant, 400 by another, and 550 by another. Rather the objective was to be achieved by establishing permanent industries in which local residents would be permanently employed and would have opportunities to become supervisors, managers and part owners. . . .

The fact that plaintiffs were in a position to benefit more directly than certain other members of the public from performance of the contract does not alter their status as incidental beneficiaries. . . . For example, in City & County of San Francisco v. Western Air Lines, Inc., supra, 204 Cal.App.2d 105, 22 Cal.Rptr. 216, the agreement between the federal government and the city for improvement of the airport could be considered to be of greater benefit to air carriers using the airport than to many other members of the public. Nevertheless, Western, as an air carrier, was but an incidental, not an express, beneficiary of the agreement and therefore had no standing to enforce the contractual prohibition against discrimination in the airport's availability for public use. The court explains the distinction as follows: "None of the documents under consideration confers on Western the rights of a third-party beneficiary. The various contracts and assurances created benefits and detriments as between only two parties—the United States and the City. Nothing in them shows any intent of the contracting parties to confer any benefit directly and expressly upon air carriers such as the defendant. It is true that air carriers, including Western, may be incidentally benefited by City's assurances in respect to nondiscriminatory treatment at the airport. They may also be incidentally benefited by the fact that, through federal aid, a public airport is improved with longer runways, brighter beacons, or larger loading ramps, or by the fact a new public airport is provided for a community without one. . . ."

For the reasons above stated we hold that plaintiffs and the class they represent have no standing as third party beneficiaries to recover the damages sought in the complaint under either California law or the general contract principles which federal law applies to government contracts.[10]

The judgments of dismissal are affirmed.

---

[10] In the absence of controlling provisions in the federal Constitution, statutes or regulations, the United States government's rights and obligations under its contracts are ordinarily construed according to general contract law rather than the law of any particular state. . . .

McCOMB, SULLIVAN, and CLARK, JJ., concur.

BURKE, Justice (dissenting).

I dissent. The certified hard-core unemployed of East Los Angeles were the express, not incidental, beneficiaries of the contracts in question and, therefore, have standing to enforce those contracts. . . .

. . . I conclude that plaintiffs are express beneficiaries of the contracts between defendants and the government and are therefore entitled to enforce the contracts.

The majority contend that the congressional purpose in enacting the Economic Opportunity Act of 1964 . . . was to benefit only the general public and particularly the local neighborhoods where these programs were to be implemented. . . .

The majority err in the above conclusion because the congressional purpose was to benefit both the communities in which the impact programs are established and the individual impoverished persons in such communities. The benefits from the instant contracts were to accrue directly to the members of plaintiffs' class, as a reading of the contracts clearly demonstrates. These direct benefits to members of plaintiffs' class were not merely the "means of executing the public purposes," as the majority contend . . . , but were the ends in themselves and one of the public purposes to which the legislation and subsequent contracts were addressed. Accordingly, I cannot agree with the majority that "the contracts here were designed not to benefit individuals as such but to utilize the training and employment of disadvantaged persons as a means of improving the East Los Angeles neighborhood."

The intent of the contracts themselves is expressed in their preambles: "WHEREAS, the Secretary of Labor is authorized . . . to enter into contracts to provide for Special Impact Programs . . . directed to the solution of the critical problems existing in particular communities and neighborhoods within urban areas of the Nation having especially large concentrations of low-income persons and [] WHEREAS, the President of the United States on October 2, 1967, launched a major test program to mobilize the resources of private industry and the Federal Government *to help find jobs and provide training for thousands of the Nation's hardcore unemployed, or underemployed,* by inviting private industry throughout the country to join with the agencies and departments of the Federal Government in assuming responsibility *for providing training and work opportunities for such seriously disadvantaged persons.* [] NOW THEREFORE, pursuant to the aforesaid statutory authority, and the directive of the President, the parties hereto, in consideration of the mutual promises herein expressed, agree as follows: . . . ."

[handwritten margin note: these are exactly people who are supposed to benefit]

(Italics added.) By these provisions, the contracting parties clearly state as one of their purposes their intent to find jobs for the hard-core unemployed.

In accord with this expressed intent, the substantive provisions of the contracts confer a direct benefit upon the class seeking to enforce them. The contracts call for the hiring of stated numbers of hard-core unemployed from the East Los Angeles Special Impact Area for a period of at least one year at a starting minimum wage of $2.00 per hour for the first 90 days and a minimum wage of $2.25 per hour thereafter, or for the prevailing wage for the area, whichever is higher. In addition to requiring appropriate job training for such employees, the contracts also require "That the Contractor will arrange for the orderly promotion of persons so employed into available supervisory-managerial and other positions, and will arrange for all contract employees to obtain a total ownership interest not exceeding thirty (30) percent in the Contractor through an appropriate stock purchase plan . . . ." The scope of the stock purchase plans is detailed in each of the contracts.

. . . .

The language of section 133, standing alone, could reasonably suggest that members of the general public are "donee beneficiaries" under any contract whose purpose is to confer a "gift" upon them. . . .

It is my conclusion, therefore, that the trial court erred in sustaining the demurrer without leave to amend. I would order the trial court to determine the propriety of plaintiffs' class action prior to proceeding upon the merits of the complaint.

TOBRINER and MOSK, JJ., concur.

————

Food for Thought

Is Restatement (Second) § 313, included below, consistent with the result in *Martinez*? If not, which do you think is the better approach?

Restatement (Second) § 313. **Government Contracts**

(1) . . . .

(2) In particular, a promisor who contracts with a government or governmental agency to do an act for or render a service to the public is not subject to contractual liability to a member of the public for consequential damages resulting from performance or failure to perform unless

    (a) the terms of the promise provide for such liability; or

    (b) the promisee is subject to liability to the member of the public for the damages and a direct action against the promisor is consistent with the terms of the contract and with the policy of the law authorizing the contract and prescribing remedies for its breach.

Index

Because the electronic version of this book is searchable, only a brief index is included here. In most instances, only references in authors' text (not in cases) are included. If a discussion continues over multiple pages, only the first reference is noted in the index. The tables of contents (at the beginning of the book and the beginning of each chapter) provide an additional tool for navigating through the contents.

†